Encyclopedia of World Literature
in the 20th Century

Encyclopedia of
in the

REVISED EDITION

BASED ON THE FIRST EDITION EDITED BY

IN FOUR VOLUMES

World Literature 20th Century

LEONARD S. KLEIN, General Editor

Wolfgang Bernard Fleischmann

VOLUME 2: E to K

FREDERICK UNGAR PUBLISHING CO., NEW YORK

Copyright © 1967, 1969, 1975, 1982
Frederick Ungar Publishing Co., Inc.

Printed in the United States of America
Designed by Patrick Vitacco

Library of Congress Cataloging in Publication Data

Main entry under title:
Encyclopedia of world literature in the 20th century.

    Includes bibliographies.
    1.   Literature, Modern—20th century—Bio-bibli-
ography.   2.   Literature, Modern—20th century—
Dictionaries.   I.   Klein, Leonard S.
PN771.E5   1982   803   81–3357
ISBN 0–8044–3136–1 (v. 2)   AACR2

Board of Advisers

v

vi

Contributors to Volume 2

Hazard Adams
Frye

Roger M. A. Allen
Egyptian Literature
Idrīs

Edward Allworth
Fitrat
Kazakh Literature

John B. Alphonso-Karkala
Indian Literature

James J. Alstrum
Huidobro

Salih J. Altoma
Iraqi Literature

Gorka Aulestia
French Literature: Basque Literature

Evelyn Avery
Hansberry

Ayumongol Sonakul
Kukrit

David Bakish
Himes

Maria Němcová Banerjee
Kundera

Lowell A. Bangerter
Hacks
Hermlin
Hesse
Hofmannsthal
Kästner
Krolow

David F. Beer
Ethiopian Literature
Farah

Carl D. Bennett
Hardy
Jhabvala

Bernard Benstock
Joyce

Robert L. Berner
Fugard

Jo Brantley Berryman
Imagism

Gian-Paolo Biasin
Gadda

Konrad Bieber
Goes
Guilloux

Philip Binham
Haavikko

CONTRIBUTORS TO VOLUME 2

Thomas E. Bird
Ehrenburg
Grade
Honchar

Vera Blackwell
Halas

Anthony Boxill
Harris

B. R. Bradbrook
Hašek

Edgar M. Branch
Farrell

Germaine Brée
French Literature

Dalma H. Brunauer
József
Kaffka
Kosztolányi

Peter Bruning
Heijermans

Barbara J. Bucknall
Hébert

Lee A. Burress
Jones, J.

Robert L. Busch
Gladkov

Vicente Cabrera
Goytisolo

Matei Calinescu
Eliade

Harry G. Carlson
Forssell

Boyd G. Carter
Guzmán

Leonard Casper
Gonzalez
Joaquim

David Castronovo
Howe
Irish Literature

Peter J. Chelkowski
Farrokhzad
Hedayat
Iranian Literature

Samuel C. Coale
Kosinski

Arthur B. Coffin
Jarrell
Jeffers

Henry R. Cooper, Jr.
Gałczyński

Carlo Coppola
Faiz
Ghose
Iqbal

Jane E. Cottrell
Ginzburg

Andonis Decavalles
Elytis

Ann Demaitre
Hungarian Literature

D. J. Dooley
Golding
Green, H.
Hinde
Hughes, R.

Peter W. Dowell
Frost

Evelio Echevarría
Gallegos
Güiraldes

Martin Esslin
Hochwälder

Marion Faber
Hildesheimer

CONTRIBUTORS TO VOLUME 2

John H. Ferres
English-Caribbean Literature

Kjetil A. Flatin
Falkberget
Holt

Martha Fodaski-Black
Kavanagh

Albert M. Forcadas
Foix

Marianne Forssblad
Hansen, T.
Kampmann
Kirk

Leonard Fox
Gamsakhurdia
Georgian Literature

Eberhard Frey
Koeppen

Alan Warren Friedman
Faulkner updating

Rose Adrienne Gallo
Fitzgerald
Hughes, T.

Xenia Gasiorowska
Goetel
Kruczkowski

Janet Powers Gemmill
Jones, D.

Frances Devlin Glass
Furphy

Jerry Glenn
German Literature
Heissenbüttel
Höllerer
Huchel
Kunze

Howard Goldblatt
Ho

Ilona Gražytė-Maziliauskas
Grušas

Geoffrey Green
Empson

Frederic J. Grover
Jouhandeau

Igor Hájek
Havel
Hrabal
Jilemnický

Talat Sait Halman
Eskimo Literature
Hikmet
Karaosmanoğlu
Kemal

Russell G. Hamilton
Guinea-Bissau Literature

Thomas Svend Hansen
Kolb

Harold P. Hanson
Grieg
Hamsun

Charles B. Harris
Kerouac

Adnan Haydar
Hāwī

Nicholas Hern
Handke

Charles G. Hill
Existentialism
Gide

Edward Hirsch
Fuller
Heaney
Hill

Keith Hitchins
Kurdish Literature

CONTRIBUTORS TO VOLUME 2

Charles G. Hoffmann
Huxley

Sona Stephan Hoisington
Ilf and Petrov
Kaverin

Marlon K. Hom
Hu
Kuo

Andrew Horton
Film and Literature
Kambanellis

Sveinn Skorri Höskuldsson
Guðmundsson
Gunnarsson
Hjartarson

Renée Riese Hubert
Éluard

Frank Hugus
Jæger

Paul Ilie
Jarnés

A. Illiano
Gozzano

Niels Ingwersen
Kristensen

Ivar Ivask
Guillén, J.
Gütersloh

Blyden Jackson
Hughes, L.

Nadja Jernakoff
Fadeev
Fedin
Kataev

Manly Johnson
English Literature
Gass

Edward T. Jones
Hartley

Lothar Kahn
Feuchtwanger

Alexander Karanikas
Haris

Louis Kibler
Futurism: Italian Futurism

Robert F. Kiernan
Eliot
Gaddis

Joseph M. Kirschbaum
Karvaš
Krasko
Kukučin

Alexis Klimoff
Ivanov

Gerhard P. Knapp
Expressionism

Wulf Koepke
Huch

Stephen W. Kohl
Izumi

Imre Kovács
Illyés

Egbert Krispyn
Eeden

Magnus Jan Kryński
Hłasko

Serge Kryzytski
Kuprin

Jerzy R. Krzyżanowski
Hłasko
Konwicki

Robert Lafont
French Literature: Occitan Literature

Rosette C. Lamont
Ionesco

Amanda Langemo
Hoel

Charles Larson
Kesey

Richard H. Lawson
Grass
Kafka

Peter H. Lee
Korean Literature

Judith Leibowitz
Heppenstall

Sara Lennox
Johnson, U.

Morton P. Levitt
Kazantzakis

Robert W. Lewis
Hemingway

Anthony V. Liman
Ibuse

Bernth Lindfors
Kenyan Literature

Irving Yucheng Lo
Hsü

Gerhard Loose
Jünger

Torborg Lundell
Jersild

Sverre Lyngstad
Fangen

Jerzy J. Maciuszko
Herbert

Albert N. Mancini
Jovine

Tom Marshall
Klein

Yoko McClain
Enchi

George R. McMurray
Elizondo
García Márquez

Judica I. H. Mendels
Elsschot
Gijsen

Erika A. Metzger
George

Michael M. Metzger
George

Priscilla Meyer
Kazakov

Fredric Michelman
Ivory Coast Literature

Mario B. Mignone
Fo

Charles Molesworth
Kinnell

Robert K. Morris
Fowles

Walter D. Morris
Eidem

Mildred Mortimer
Guinean Literature

Edward Możejko
Kaden-Bandrowski

Edward Mullen
González Martínez

Antonino Musumeci
Hermeticism

Kostas Myrsiades
Karyotakis

xiii

CONTRIBUTORS TO VOLUME 2

Paul Nadanyi
Juhász

Kim Nilsson
Huldén

Njörður P. Njarðvík
Grímsson
Icelandic Literature
Jóhannes úr Kötlum

William Van O'Connor
Faulkner

Kurt Opitz
Jahnn

Eugene Orenstein
Glatstein
Halpern

Kostas Ostrauskas
Krėvė

H. F. Pfanner
Graf

M. Pierssens
Faye

Sanford Pinsker
Fiedler

Vivian Pinto
Elin Pelin

Gerald Pirog
Gumilyov
Khlebnikov
Klyuev

Debra Popkin
France
Giraudoux

Michael Popkin
Feydeau
Genet
Jarry

Edward M. Potoker
Firbank

Joy M. Potter
Gatto

John Povey
Gambian Literature
Ghanaian Literature

Malgorzata Pruska-Carroll
Iwaszkiewicz
Jastrun
Kossak

George Quinn
Indonesian Literature

Judith Radke
Gascar

Philippe Radley
Khodasevich

John R. Ranck
Kuzmin

Aleksis Rannit
Estonian Literature

K. Bhaskara Rao
Hanley
Karanth

Alo Raun
*Finno-Ugric Literatures of the
Soviet Union*

Richard M. Reeve
Fuentes

Robert M. Rehder
Jennings

Walter A. Reichart
Hauptmann

John E. Rexine
Greek Literature

M. Ricciardelli
Italian Literature

CONTRIBUTORS TO VOLUME 2

Blandine M. Rickert
Emmanuel
Giono
Gracq
Jammes

Friedhelm Rickert
Fleisser
Frank
Hauptmann updating
Kaiser

J. Thomas Rimer
Kishida

Daniel E. Rivas
Jouve

James E. Rocks
Gordon

Wilbert J. Roget
French-Caribbean Literature

Marilyn Gaddis Rose
Green, J.

Sven H. Rossel
Jensen

Jay Rubin
Kunikida

Judith Ruderman
Forster

Leo D. Rudnytzky
Franko

Stephen Rudy
Futurism: Russian Futurism

Anna Rutherford
Frame

Marleigh Grayer Ryan
Futabatei

Mariolina Salvatori
Fenoglio

Peter Sander
Kroetz

Ivan Sanders
Karinthy
Kassák
Krúdy

Yvonne L. Sandstroem
Ekelund
Gustafsson
Gyllensten

Vilas Sarang
Khandekar

George D. Schade
Herrera y Reissig

Helene Scher
Frisch
Hochhuth
Kunert

Marshall J. Schneider
García Lorca
Jiménez

George C. Schoolfield
Enckell
Finnish Literature
Jansson

H. Wayne Schow
Ford
Hansen, M.

Louise Rypko Schub
Fargue

Peter Z. Schubert
Hora

Max F. Schulz
Hawkes

Kessel Schwartz
Ecuadorian Literature
Gómez de la Serna
Guillén, N.
Hernández
Icaza

CONTRIBUTORS TO VOLUME 2

Murray M. Schwartz
Freud

Ronald Schwartz
Gironella

Steven Schwartz
Ginsberg

Jules Seigel
Housman

Eric Sellin
Feraoun
Kateb

David Semah
al-Hakīm
Husayn

Monica Setterwall
Johnson, E.

V. A. Shahane
Kipling

Ross P. Shideler
Ekelöf
Enquist

Viktoria Skrupskelis
Jacob

Biljana Šljivić-Šimšić
Krleža

Mary Carroll Smith
Hippius

Rowland Smith
Gordimer

Katherine Snipes
Graves

Svat Soucek
Kirgiz Literature

Murray A. Sperber
Koestler

Martin S. Stabb
González Prada

Rita Stein
Hellman

Earl E. Stevens
Galsworthy

Philip Stratford
Greene

Rudolf Sturm
Hostovský
Jirásek

Claude J. Summers
Isherwood

Elizabeth R. Suter
Freyre

Alan Swanson
Ferlin

Carolyn Wedin Sylvander
Johnson, J. W.

Larry ten Harmsel
Ellison
Enright

Ewa Thompson
Gombrowicz

Frank Trommler
Eich

Reiko Tsukimura
Kawabata

Kinya Tsuruta
Hayashi

Martin Tucker
Ekwensi

Makoto Ueda
Hagiwara

CONTRIBUTORS TO VOLUME 2

Frederick Ungar
Kraus

K. Börje Vähämäki
Haanpää

Jack A. Vaughn
Fry
Johnston

Reino Virtanen
Kilpi

Rosmarie Waldrop
Enzensberger
Jabès

Lars G. Warme
Gullberg

Philip M. Weinstein
James

Anni Whissen
Kaschnitz

Kenneth S. White
Ghelderode

James Wieland
Hope

William Willeford
Jung

Rita Williams
French Literature: Breton Literature

Thomas G. Winner
Fuks

Krishna Winston
Horváth

Donald A. Yates
Gálvez

T. Yedlin
Gorky

Melanie Young
Heller

Leon I. Yudkin
Greenberg
Israeli Literature

Harry Zohn
Friedell
Kolmar
Kramer

Leon M. Zolbrod
Ishikawa
Japanese Literature

Virpi Zuck
Kallas

Abbreviations for Periodicals, Volume 2

AAS	Asian and African Studies	*CentR*	Centennial Review
AGR	American-German Review	*ChiR*	Chicago Review
AJFS	Australian Journal of French Studies	*CL*	Comparative Literature
ALS	Australian Literary Studies	*CLAJ*	College Language Association Journal
AR	Antioch Review	*CollG*	Colloquia Germanica
ArielE	Ariel: A Review of International English Literature	*CompD*	Comparative Drama
		ConL	Contemporary Literature
ASR	American Scandinavian Review	*CP*	Concerning Poetry
AWR	Anglo-Welsh Review	*Crit*	Critique: Studies in Modern Fiction
BA	Books Abroad		
BB	Bulletin of Bibliography	*CritI*	Critical Inquiry
BF	Books from Finland	*Critique*	Critique: Revue générale des publications françaises et étrangères
BHS	Bulletin of Hispanic Studies		
BMMLA	Bulletin of the Midwest Modern Language Association	*CritQ*	Critical Quarterly
		CSP	Canadian Slavonic Papers
BSpS	Bulletin of Spanish Studies	*DQR*	Dutch Quarterly ·Review of Anglo-American Letters
BUJ	Boston University Journal		
BuR	Bucknell Review	*DR*	Dalhousie Review
CanL	Canadian Literature	*DU*	Der Deutschunterricht
CARHS	Canadian-American Review of Hungarian Studies	*EA*	Études anglaises
		ECr	L'esprit créateur
CAsJ	Central Asiatic Journal	*Éire*	Éire-Ireland
CCrit	Comparative Criticism	*ELT*	English Literature in Transition
CE	College English	*ETJ*	Educational Theatre Journal

Evergreen	Evergreen Review	*JPC*	Journal of Popular Culture
FI	Forum Italicum	*JSoAL*	Journal of South Asian Literature
FMLS	Forum for Modern Language Studies	*JSSTC*	Journal of Spanish Studies: Twentieth Century
FR	French Review	*KFLQ*	Kentucky Foreign Language Quarterly
GaR	Georgia Review		
GL&L	German Life and Letters	*KR*	Kenyon Review
GN	Germanic Notes	*KRQ*	Kentucky Romance Quarterly
GQ	German Quarterly	*LAAW*	Lotus: Afro-Asian Writings
GR	Germanic Review	*LE&W*	Literature East and West
HAHR	Hispanic American Historical Review	*LitR*	Literary Review
HC	Hollins Critic	*London*	London Magazine
HR	Hispanic Review	*LuK*	Literatur und Kritik
HudR	Hudson Review	*MAL*	Modern Austrian Literature
I&FR	Indian & Foreign Review	*MEF*	Middle East Forum
IndL	Indian Literature	*MES*	Middle Eastern Studies
IowaR	Iowa Review	*MFS*	Modern Fiction Studies
IQ	Italian Quarterly	*MHL*	Modern Hebrew Literature
IranS	Iranian Studies	*MissQ*	Mississippi Quarterly
IRLI	Italianistica: Rivista di letteratura italiana	*ML*	Modern Languages
		MLN	Modern Language Notes
IS	Italian Studies	*MLQ*	Modern Language Quarterly
JArabL	Journal of Arabic Literature	*MLR*	Modern Language Review
JATJ	Journal of the Association of Teachers of Japanese	*MN*	Monumenta Nipponica
		MR	Massachusetts Review
JBalS	Journal of Baltic Studies	*MW*	The Muslim World
JBlS	Journal of Black Studies	*NAR*	North American Review
JCL	Journal of Commonwealth Literature	*NDH*	Neue deutsche Hefte
JCS	Journal of Croatian Studies	*Neophil*	Neophilologus
JEGP	Journal of English and Germanic Philology	*NGS*	New German Studies
		NHQ	New Hungarian Quarterly
JIL	Journal of Irish Literature	*NL*	Les nouvelles littéraires
JNALA	Journal of the New African Literature and the Arts	*NLH*	New Literary History
JOL	Journal of Oriental Literature	*NR*	New Republic

NRF	Nouvelle revue française	*RusL*	Russian Literature
NS	New Statesman	*RusR*	Russian Review
NYRB	New York Review of Books	*SatR*	Saturday Review
NYT	New York Times	*SBL*	Studies in Black Literature
NYTBR	New York Times Book Review	*Scan*	Scandinavica
OSP	Oxford Slavonic Papers	*SCR*	South Carolina Review
PakR	Pakistan Review	*SEEJ*	Slavic and East European Journal
PCLS	Proceedings of the Comparative Literature Symposium	*SEER*	Slavonic and East European Review
PFr	Présence francophone	*SHR*	Southern Humanities Review
PMLA	Publications of the Modern Language Association of America	*SlavonicR*	Slavonic Review
PolP	Polish Perspectives	*SlavR*	Slavic Review
PolR	Polish Review	*SoR*	Southern Review
PPNCFL	Proceedings of the Pacific Northwest Conference on Foreign Languages	*SR*	Sewanee Review
		SS	Scandinavian Studies
PR	Partisan Review	*SSF*	Studies in Short Fiction
PSM	Philippine Studies	*StIsl*	Studia Islamica
QRFS	Quarterly Review of Film Studies	*SWR*	Southwest Review
		TA	Theatre Annual
RAL	Research in African Literatures	*TAH*	The American Hispanist
RALS	Resources for American Literary Study	*TCL*	Twentieth Century Literature
REH	Revista de estudios hispánicos	*TDR*	Tulane Drama Review/ The Drama Review
RevI	Revista/Review interamericana	*TheatreQ*	Theatre Quarterly
RH	Revue hebdomaire	*TLS*	[London] Times Literary Supplement
RHM	Revista hispánica moderna		
RI	Revista iberoamericana	*TM*	Les temps modernes
RLT	Russian Literature Triquarterly	*Transatlantic*	Transatlantic Review
RNL	Review of National Literatures	*TriQ*	TriQuarterly
ROMM	Revue de l'Occident musulman et de la Méditerranée	*TuK*	Text + Kritik
RomN	Romance Notes	*UDR*	University of Dayton Review
RR	Romanic Review	*UQ*	Ukrainian Quarterly
RS	Research Studies	*VQR*	Virginia Quarterly Review
RSI	Revista storica italiana	*WascanaR*	Wascana Review

WCR	West Coast Review	*WZUG*	Wissenschaftliche Zeitschrift der Ernst Moritz Arndt-Universität Greifswald
WLT	World Literature Today		
WLWE	World Literature Written in English	*YFS*	Yale French Studies
WSCL	Wisconsin Studies in Contemporary Literature	*YItS*	Yale Italian Studies
		YR	Yale Review
WSJ	Wiener slavistisches Jahrbuch	*Y/T*	Yale/Theatre

Illustrations

Acknowledgments

For permission to reproduce the illustrations in this volume,
the publisher is indebted to the following:

T. S. ELIOT	Süddeutscher Verlag, Munich
PAUL ÉLUARD	Wilfrid Göpel, Berlin
ODYSSEUS ELYTIS	C. Megaloconomou, Greek Photo News
WILLIAM FAULKNER	USIS
F. SCOTT FITZGERALD	Charles Scribner's Sons
FORD MADOX FORD	The Bettman Archive
E. M. FORSTER	John McCallum
ANATOLE FRANCE	The Bettman Archive (drawing from life by Pierre Calmettas)
SIGMUND FREUD	Austrian Information Service, New York, N.Y.
MAX FRISCH	Ullstein/Kröner, Berlin
ROBERT FROST	David H. Rhinelander and Holt, Rinehart & Winston, Inc., N.Y.
CARLOS FUENTES	Lola Alvarez Bravo and Farrar, Straus & Giroux, Inc., N.Y.
FEDERICO GARCÍA LORCA	Bildarchiv Herder, Freiburg im Breisgau
GABRIEL GARCÍA MÁRQUEZ	Rodrigo Moya and Harper & Row, Publishers, N.Y.
JEAN GENET	Jerry Bauer and Grove Press, Inc., N.Y.
STEFAN GEORGE	Bildarchiv Herder, Freiburg im Breisgau
MICHEL DE GHELDERODE	Institut Belge d'Information et de Documentation
ANDRÉ GIDE	Süddeutscher Verlag, Munich
MARNIX GIJSEN	Bildarchiv Herder, Freiburg im Breisgau
JEAN GIRAUDOUX	Verlag Ullstein, Berlin
JACOB GLATSTEIN	Yivo Institute for Jewish Research, New York
WILLIAM GOLDING	Conway Studios Corp. and Harcourt Brace Jovanovich, Inc., N.Y.
WITOLD GOMBROWICZ	Bogdan Paczowski and Grove Press, Inc., N.Y.
MAXIM GORKY	Historia-Foto, Berlin
JUAN GOYTISOLO	Jerry Bauer and The Viking Press, Inc., N.Y.
GÜNTER GRASS	German Information Center, N.Y.
ROBERT GRAVES	Doubleday & Company, Inc., N.Y.
GRAHAM GREENE	Islay Lyons and The Viking Press, Inc., N.Y.
JORGE GUILLÉN	Dr. Ivar Ivask
KNUT HAMSUN	Süddeutscher Verlag, Munich
PETER HANDKE	Jürgen Seuss and Farrar, Straus & Giroux, Inc., N.Y.
THOMAS HARDY	The Bettman Archive
JAROSLAV HAŠEK	Line drawing by Francis Reisz, from a photograph
GERHART HAUPTMANN	Verlag Ullstein, Berlin
ERNEST HEMINGWAY	Süddeutscher Verlag, Munich
HERMANN HESSE	Martin Hesse SWB, Bern
ROLF HOCHHUTH	German Information Center, N.Y.
HUGO VON HOFMANNSTHAL	Bildarchiv Herder, Freibug im Breisgau
ÖDÖN VON HORVÁTH	Austrian Information Service, New York, N.Y.
RICARDA HUCH	Fritz Eschen, Berlin
TED HUGHES	Harper & Row, Publishers, N.Y.
ALDOUS HUXLEY	Bildarchiv Herder, Freiburg im Breisgau
EUGÈNE IONESCO	Jerry Bauer and Grove Press, Inc., N.Y.
HENRY JAMES	USIS

ACKNOWLEDGMENTS

JUAN RAMÓN JIMÉNEZ	Verlag Ullstein, Berlin
UWE JOHNSON	Presse- und Informationsamt der Bundesregierung, Bonn, and German Information Center, N.Y.
JAMES JOYCE	Ulrike Friedrich-Schreiber, Starnberg
CARL GUSTAV JUNG	Princeton University Press, Princeton, N.J.
ERNST JÜNGER	Neske-Verlag, Pfullingen
FRANZ KAFKA	Bildarchiv Herder, Freiburg im Breisgau
GEORG KAISER	Line drawing by Francis Reisz, from a photograph
KAWABATA YASUNARI	Harold Strauss and Alfred A. Knopf, Inc.
NIKOS KAZANTZAKIS	Simon and Schuster
YAŞAR KEMAL	Günes Karabuda and William Morrow & Company
KARL KRAUS	Verlag Otto Müller, Salzburg
MIROSLAV KRLEŽA	Mile Rupcic, New York

Encyclopedia of World Literature
in the 20th Century

ECUADORIAN LITERATURE

In the 19th c. Ecuador produced two major literary figures: Juan León Mera (1832–1894), whose *Cumandá* (1879; Cumandá) may be the best Indianist novel of Spanish America, and Juan Montalvo (1832–1889), an essayist reputed to be one of the two or three great stylists of the continent.

Ecuadorian literature of the 20th c., largely social, was conditioned by the Russian Revolution and a series of disasters to the cacao crop, Ecuador's principal source of revenue. From 1922 on, revolts, strikes, and Indian massacres were commonplace. In 1925 army officers led a successful socialist revolution, which the young writers of the time, equating literature and revolutionary struggle, saw as a cure for their country's ills.

Fiction

Among 20th-c. novels devoted to Ecuadorian sociological problems, *A la costa* (1904; to the coast) by Luis A. Martínez (1869–1909) is the outstanding early example. But it was a tradition-shattering book of short stories, *Los que se van* (1930; those who go off), a brutal documentation of social ills, that set the style and themes for Ecuadorian fiction for the next forty years. The authors of the collection were Joaquín Gallegos Lara (1911–1947), Enrique Gil Gilbert (b. 1912), and Demetrio Aguilera Malta (b. 1909). Gallegos Lara, the most revolutionary, also wrote *Cruces sobre el agua* (1946; crosses on the water). Gil Gilbert, in *Nuestro pan* (1942; *Our Daily Bread*, 1943), created the definitive work about the workers in the rice fields.

Aguilera Malta, the best known of the group, in *Don Goyo* (1933; *Don Goyo,* 1942) depicts mythic aspects of the telluric—it is about a 140-year-old patriarch who chooses union with nature over the white man's civilization—and he continued the theme of man against nature in *La isla virgen* (1942; the virgin island). In addition to his portrayal of the sordid, he has also excelled at historical fiction. *La caballeresa del sol: El gran amor de Bolívar* (1964; *Manuela, la Caballeresa del Sol,* 1967) typifies this aspect of his literary creation. An outstanding exponent of the fantastic and of magic realism (q.v.), he also wrote *Siete lunas y siete serpientes* (1970; seven moons and seven serpents), about a mythical town and African-Christian mythology.

José de la Cuadra (1903–1941), Ecuador's leading short-story writer, and a member of the so-called Group of Guayaquil, concentrated on sexual aberrations, deep, primitive passions, superstitions, and corrupt government in a number of collections, such as *Horno* (1932; oven). Another member of the Group of Guayaquil, Alfredo Pareja Diezcanseco (b. 1908), produced powerful novels about social and political problems and the proletariat. Among these are *El muelle* (1933; the dock), about the tragedy of an Ecuadorian worker; *Las tres ratas* (1944; the three rats), which mixes smugglers, sex, and fighting with social realism; and *Las pequeñas estaturas* (1970; small statures), part of a series about his era and generation.

Ecuador's most notorious novel, *Huasipungo* (1934; *The Villagers,* 1964), by the country's most famous novelist, Jorge Icaza (q.v.), is about the torture, degradation, and brutalization of Indians. In other novels Icaza examined race relations and urban and rural social ills.

Adalberto Ortiz (b. 1914), primarily a poet and short-story writer, in *Juyungo* (1943; Juyungo), an exotic fictional epic, created one of the outstanding novelistic treatments of Blacks. *Juyungo* combines magic realism, barbaric rhythms, and sensuality with a passion for justice and a desire for human dignity.

Poetry

The modernist (q.v.) poets Humberto Fierro (1890–1929) and Medardo Angel Silva (1898–1919) combined formal perfection with the morbid, melancholy, and metaphysical. In the following generation, Gonzalo Escudero (b. 1903) wrote about the transcendent and cosmic in works like *Hélices de huracán y de sol* (1934; helixes of hurricane and sun). Jorge Carrera Andrade (q.v.), Ecuador's greatest poet, exhibited brilliant visual imagery while giving primitive and sensual force to a variety of themes, from solitude to universal brotherhood.

Later poets include Alejandro Carrión (b. 1915), who wrote revolutionary works of social despair like *Agonía del árbol y la sangre* (1948; agony of tree and blood); César Dávila Andrade (1918–1967), a leading member of the Madrugada group, which experimented and brought new vigor to Ecuadorian poetry; and Rafael Díaz Icaza (b. 1925), author of tormented, transcendent, and hermetic poems.

Drama and the Essay

Ecuador's best dramatist, Francisco Tobar García (b. 1928), also a poet, produced many plays about existential themes and inevitable death. His most popular work was *La llave del abismo* (1961; the key to the abyss). Icaza and Aguilera Malta also wrote for the theater. The latter's *Lázaro* (1941; Lázaro) examines the illusory nature of reality; his *Infierno negro* (1967; black hell) attacks racial discrimination.

Benjamín Carrión (1898–1979), an internationally known representative of Ecuadorian culture, was the author of the important essay *Los creadores de la nueva América* (1928; creators of the new America) and several biographies and collections of literary criticism through the 1970s.

Ecuadorian writers have essentially used their art as an instrument for reform. In this pursuit they have continually stressed commitment to their fellow men as they opposed the dehumanizing forces dominating their country.

BIBLIOGRAPHY: Carrera Andrade, J., *Guía de la joven poesía ecuatoriana* (1939); Arias, A., *Panorama de la literatura ecuatoriana* (1948); Schwartz, K., *The Contemporary Ecuadorian Novel* (1953); Barrera, I., *Historia de la literatura ecuatoriana* (4 vols., 1955); Ribadeneira, E., *La moderna novela ecuatoriana* (1958); Sacoto, A., *The Indian in the Ecuadorian Novel* (1967); Descalzi, R., *Historia crítica del teatro ecuatoriano* (1968); Pérez, G. R., *Pensamiento y literatura del Ecuador* (1972)

KESSEL SCHWARTZ

EEDEN, Frederik Willem van

Dutch novelist, dramatist, and poet, b. 3 May, 1860, Haarlem; d. 16 June, 1932, Bussum

In his parents' home and at school E. was steeped in the positivistic, materialistic atmosphere prevalent in the second half of the 19th c. But as he reached adulthood, he developed a mystical outlook, which in 1922 culminated in his conversion to Roman Catholicism. He also took a strong interest in social issues, which induced him to establish a short-lived communal living project named Walden, in honor of Thoreau. In 1908–9 E., who was on friendly terms with Upton Sinclair (q.v.), made a trip to the U.S., in the course of which he founded another commune in North Carolina.

A psychiatrist by profession, E. nonetheless vigorously pursued his literary career. He belonged to the generation of the "Movement of '80," and was involved in its journal, but his religious and political preoccupations were irreconcilable with the movement's predominantly aesthetic orientation. He had a greater affinity with such foreign authors as Tolstoy and the German romantics, whose favorite motifs—the mysterious, hypnosis, dreams, the Orient, death, spiritism, demons, lunacy—he incorporated into his own books. The novel which established him as a writer and which remains his best-known work, *De kleine Johannes* (3 vols., 1887, 1905, 1906; *The Quest*, 1907), is based on a narrative by E. T. A. Hoffmann (1776–1822). It relates the evolution of a child's ineradicable idealism, which in defiance of the rationalistic pressures of the modern world matures into faith in man's eternal soul.

Van de koele meren des doods (1900; *The Deeps of Deliverance*, 1902) is E.'s most significant novel, the one he himself considered to be a synthesis of all his main themes. The plot, dealing with a woman's erotic misadventures, decline into drug addiction and prostitution, and eventual religious salvation, was derived from an actual case history. The outspoken treatment of female sexuality was sufficiently daring to create a stir, but formally the novel lacks sophistication.

E.'s literary output was by no means limited to novels. Besides prodigious translating activity, which included nine volumes of Rabindranath Tagore's (q.v.) work, E. wrote copious amounts of poetry. Many of his contemporaries considered his writing for the theater to be particularly important. He had, in fact, started his literary career with some comedies, and he went on to write historical plays, as well as social satires for the stage. E.'s work in the drama—a relative rarity in modern Dutch literature—was in great demand, especially in German theaters. Although his work lacks enduring aesthetic value, E. was a major figure in the literary renewal in the Netherlands, which began in the late 19th c.

FURTHER WORKS. *Het rijk der wijzen* (1882); *Het poortje of de duivel in Kruimelburg* (1884); *Het sonnet* (1884); *Panopticum* (1884); *Frans Hals* (1884); *Grassprietjes* (1885, under pseud. Cornelis Paradijs); *De student thuis* (1885); *Kunstmatige voeding bij tuberculose* (1886); *De psychische geneeswijze* (1888); *Don Torribio* (1890); *Aan den keizer aller Russen* (1890); *Ellen* (1890); *Studies* (6 vols., 1890, 1894, 1897, 1904, 1908, 1918); *Johannes Viator* (1892); *Het beginsel der psychotherapie* (1892); *De broeders* (1894; also known as *De broederveete*); *Het lied van schijn en wezen* (3 vols., 1895, 1910, 1922); *Lioba* (1897); *Enkele verzen* (1898); *Twaalf sonnetten* (1898); *Waarvoor werkt gij?* (1899); *Waarvan leven wij?* (1899); *Van de passielooze lelie* (1901); *De blijde wereld* (3 vols., 1903, 1905, 1906; *Happy Humanity*, 1908); *In kenterend getij* (1906); *De vrije arbeid op Walden* (1906); *Brieven* (1907); *Minnestral* (1907); *IJsbrand* (1908; *Ysbrand*, 1910); *Dante en Beatrice* (1908); *De nachtbruid* (1909; *The Bride of Dreams*, 1913); *De idealisten* (1909); *Het paleis van Circe* (1910); *Welt-Eroberung durch Heldenliebe* (1911); *Open brief aan de padvinders* (1911); *Sirius en Siderius* (3 vols., 1912, 1914, 1924); *Nieuwe nederlandsche dichtkunst* (1913); *Paul's ontwaken* (1913); *Aan de vrije jeugd* (1914); *Bij 't licht van de oorlogsvlam* (1915); *De heks van Haarlem* (1915); *De bokkenrijder* (1918); *Jezus' leer en verborgen leeven* (1919); *Literatuur en leeven* (1920); *Kerk en communisme* (1921); *Het roode lampje* (1921); *Het godshuis in de lichtstad* (1921); *Uit Jezus' oopenbaar leeven* (1922); *Aan mijn engelbewaarder, en andere gedichten* (1922); *Isméa of de stervende vlinder* (1923); *De geest der waarheid* (1923); *Deutsch-Chinesische Liebes-Mosaik* (1923); *Eucharistie* (1924); *Langs de weg* (1925); *De legende van Sancta Sura* (1926); *Jeugdverzen* (1926); *Mijn dagboek* (9 vols., 1931–45); *Over dromen* (1956); *De briefwisseling tussen F. v. E. en Lod. van Deyssel* (1964).

BIBLIOGRAPHY: Macdonald, M. I., "Poet, Novelist, and Practical Communist," *Craftsman*, 14 (1908), 126–36; Meijer, R. P., *Literature of the Low Countries* (1978), pp. 248–50 and passim

EGBERT KRISPYN

EGYPTIAN LITERATURE

As with other literary traditions within the Arab world, modern Egyptian literature is the product of two major forces: the revival of the great Arabic heritage of the past and the influence of modernization through contact with Europe and America. The force of the impact between these two phenomena varied considerably according to time and place. In the case of Egypt, the process was abrupt, resulting from Napoleon's invasion in 1798. This military incursion served both to rid Egypt of its Mamlūk rulers and to expose its intellectual leaders to European thought. The process was further stimulated after 1860 by the arrival of numerous writers from Syria, where civil war had forced many Christian families to flee to Europe and the Americas as well as to Egypt. Many members of those families had already been involved in the revival of interest in the Arabic language and its literature. These and other Syrians were now to join Egyptian writers in making major contributions to the emergence of an indigenous modern Arabic literature in Egypt and of the press (which has always been and remains the principal means of propagating literature in Egypt).

At the turn of the century, the prevalence of the "traditional" or the "modern" varied according to genre. It is hardly surprising that poetry, by far the most prevalent medium of literary expression in the "classical" period, should have produced a modern neoclassical revival, the more conservative proponents of which carefully watched and often vigorously resisted attempts at change well into the 1950s. Pride of place as pioneer in this movement must go to Mahmūd Sāmī al-Bārūdī (1839–1904), while the patriotic fervor and violent attacks on the British occupying forces guaranteed Hāfiz Ibrāhīm (1871–1932) a warm place in Egyptian hearts. However, it is Ahmad Shawqī (1868–1932) who is undoubtedly the greatest poet of the period. While some commentators have rightly drawn attention to glimmerings of a more individual vision that can occasionally be seen in poems of these and other poets like them, it remains true that the vast bulk of their writings are occasional verse (*shi'r al-munāsabāt*), a fact that elicited the wrath of later critics.

While both fiction and drama may have had precedents of one kind or another in the earlier tradition of Arabic literature, the beginnings of both genres in the modern period point to their derivative origins in the West. While poets were imitating the stentorian tones of earlier exemplars, pioneers in fiction and drama translated and imitated European models, before attempting their own creative offerings. 'Uthmān Jalāl (1828–1898) translated some of Molière's plays into colloquial Egyptian. An Egyptian Jew, Ya'qūb Sanū' (1839–1912), began to write a series of satirical playlets poking fun at the aristocracy and the Khedive Ismā'īl (ruled 1863–79). Drama at this time was very much a "popular" phenomenon, with much melodrama, and singing and dancing almost as a *sine qua non*. The tradition was carried on into this century by Najīb al-Rīhānī (1891–1949), who followed Sanū''s example by writing comedies that poked fun at the foibles of various segments of society.

The rise of fiction is closely associated with the rapid expansion of the press in the 1880s and 1890s. Newspapers would regularly publish stories and novels in serial form. It was in this way that Jurjī Zaydān (1861–1914) published a whole series of historical novels dealing with Islamic history; these had a plainly educational purpose, but were "spiced" with local interest and romance so as to make them at least somewhat similar to the love, murder, and intrigue narratives that characterized other fictional writings of the era. Equally educational but more topical was Muhammad al-Muwaylihī's (1868–1930) *Hadīth 'Īsā ibn Hishām* (1898–1902; *Hadīth 'Īsā ibn Hishām*, 1974), which provided a marvelous exposé of the many faults of Egyptian society and its institutions under British administration. More straightforward in both style and sentiment were the series of essays on a variety of topics by Mustafā Lutfī al-Manfalūtī (1876–1924), which have remained popular among adolescents for many decades.

These writers and others were to carry out the vital tasks of adapting the older tradition to the needs of modern times, of experimenting with new genres, and of applying new language to the older genres. All this was an essential preliminary to the emergence of an indigenous tradition of modern Egyptian literature.

Poetry

In 1908 Khalīl Mutrān (1872–1949), known as the "poet of the two countries" (Leb-

anon and Egypt), published a collection of poetry, *Dīwān al-Khalīl* (the diwan of al-Khalīl) with an important introduction, in which he stated that the poet should be able to express his own feelings and urged poets to devote more attention to the unity of their compositions. While some of his poems show signs of such precepts of romanticism, the bulk of Mutrān's poetry was as occasional as that of Ahmad Shawqī and Hāfiz Ibrāhīm. The real motivating force toward romanticism was the émigré school in the Americas, where a group of poets experimented with form, language, and mood in surroundings essentially detached from the forces of conservatism that were so strong in the Middle East. In Egypt the advocacy of romanticism fell to the so-called "Diwan" school of poets, 'Abbās Mahmūd al-'Aqqād (1889–1964), Ibrāhīm al-Māzinī (1890–1949), and 'Abd al-Rahmān Shukrī (1886–1958), all of whom were strongly influenced by the English romantic poets and critics such as William Hazlitt (1778–1830). Of the three, Shukrī was the greatest poet, while the other two had more influence at the time through their critical writings, which appeared in a volume called *Al-Dīwān* (1921; the diwan). This work contained iconoclastic attacks on Shawqī for his occasional versifying and on al-Manfalūtī for his morbid sentimentality, but more vicious and destructive was al-Māzinī's attack on Shukrī himself, something that had a profound effect on the poet.

In the 1930s a new school of romantic poets emerged who took their name from the magazine *Apollo*, published under the aegis of Ahmad Zakī Abū Shādī (1892–1955). He and other poets like Ibrāhīm Nājī (1893–1953) and 'Alī Mahmūd Tāhā (1902–1949) introduced poetry of a new sensibility to Egypt, particularly during the 1930s. While Abū Shādī wrote a vast amount of poetry and Nājī also wrote a great deal, mainly about unrequited love, Tāhā is probably the most enduring poet of the group.

In a collection called *Plutoland* (1947; Plutoland) the litterateur and critic Lewis 'Awad (b. 1915), who terms the poetry of the romantics "*mal de siècle* poetry," made what some critics consider to be the first attempts at writing free verse; the earliest poem dates from the late 1930s. If this is so, he predates by almost a decade the efforts of Nāzik al-Malā'ika (b. 1923) and Badr Shākir al-Sayyāb (q.v.) in Iraq. At any rate, Egyptian poets have, since the end of World War II, joined their colleagues in other Arab countries in writing poetry outside the dictates of the classical metrical system, ranging from poems using some of the traditional feet in different combinations, to free verse and the prose poem.

The most famous of these poets is Salāh 'Abd al-Sabūr (1931–1981); his first collection, *Al-Nāsu fī bilādī* (1957; the people in my country), displays considerable commitment to the ideals of the emerging revolutionary society, with its realistic descriptions of life (as in the title poem). During the 1960s this vigorous posture changed to a more personal, melancholy vision. One of 'Abd al-Sabūr's most successful works is the verse play *Ma'sāt al-Hallāj* (1966; *Murder in Baghdad*, 1972), which recounts the story of the crucifixion of a medieval Islamic mystic with considerable skill and impact and with a not too covert contemporary import. Other poets have also made contributions to this genre: the yet more committed 'Abd al-Rahmān al-Sharqāwī (b. 1920), with such plays as *Ma'sāt Jamīla* (1962; the tragedy of Jamīla) and *Tha'r Allāh* (1969; God's revenge); and the very Brechtian contributions of Najīb Surūr (?–197?) in the form of elongated poetic tableaux drawing their inspiration from popular tales of Egypt, such as *Yāsīn wa Bahiyya* (1963; Yāsīn and Bahiyya). Another Egyptian poet whose writings continue to capture the imagination of readers throughout the Arab world is Ahmad 'Abd al-Mu'tī Hijāzī (b. 1935), who, having come to the modern metropolis after a village childhood, depicted the depersonalization and crushing anonymity of the big city, as, for example, in *Madīna bilā qalb* (1959; heartless city). Thereafter, his poetry became more concerned with the cause of commitment to the Egyptian revolution and its leader, Jamāl 'Abd al-Nāsir (Gamal Abdel Nasser).

While Egyptian poetry has tended to stand apart from the more conspicuous attempts at innovation, such as those of Adūnīs (q.v.) in Lebanon, in recent times a small group of younger poets in Egypt has been experimenting with new forms and new language; among these we should mention Amal Dunqul (b. 1940) and Muhammad Abū Sinna (b. 1937). It remains generally true, however, that, in the Egypt of the early 1980s, poetry no longer commands the public attention it has traditionally held since the beginnings of Arabic literature. Its position as the preeminent genre has been taken over by fiction, particularly short fiction.

Fiction

The first work of fiction in Egypt that had any pretensions of depicting contemporary reality was the novel *Zaynab* (1913; Zaynab) by Muhammad Husayn Haykal (1888–1956), written in France and published under a pseudonym. By the time of the second edition of this work (1929), a whole school of Egyptian writers had begun producing short stories. It was between 1910 and 1920 that attempts had first been made to emulate the European short story, and especially those of France and Russia. The early efforts of Muhammad Taymūr (1892–1921) were followed by stories by his brother Mahmūd Taymūr (b. 1894), by one of Egypt's major contributors to this genre, Mahmūd Tāhir Lāshīn (1894–1954), by Yahyā Haqqī (b. 1905), and by others. The efforts of this "new school" during the 1920s, as well as the great impact of the first volume of Tāhā Husayn's (q.v.) *Al-Ayyām* (3 vols., 1925, 1939, 1967; *An Egyptian Childhood*, 1932; *The Stream of Days*, 1948; *A Passage to France*, 1976), fostered an increasing interest in fiction.

The 1930s saw tremendous activity in this genre. It began with a competition in novel writing, which was won by Ibrāhīm al-Māzinī with *Ibrāhīm al-kātib* (1931; *Ibrahim the Author*, 1976), which, in spite of the author's denials, seems to be an autobiographical piece. A major advance in the use of dialogue in the novel was achieved by Tawfīq al-Hakīm (q.v.) is his *'Awdat al-rūh* (1933; the return of the spirit), the first part of which gives a lively portrayal of a group of Egyptian characters within a limited environment. The psychological dimension is investigated by 'Abbās Mahmūd al-'Aqqād in his *Sāra* (1938; *Sara*, 1978) to a degree which robs it of some of its artistic appeal but which was to serve as a model for later novelists. These and other experiments served to develop the different facets of this complex genre; the writers of the next generation were able to proceed on the basis of the successes and failures of their predecessors.

At the end of the 1930s there emerged the figure who has dominated Egyptian fiction for the last two decades, Najīb Mahfūz (q.v.). With his series of novels set in the old quarters of Cairo, written in the 1940s and early 1950s, the Egyptian novel may be said to have achieved its full maturity. To a tremendous skill in construction is added great attention to detail, a clear, straightforward style typical of a well-read civil servant (his career until his retirement in 1971), and an underlying social-realist purpose of showing the gradual breakdown of the societal fabric in Egypt as mirrored in the antagonisms and violence preceding the revolution of 1952. By April of that year, he had completed his monumental *Al-Thulāthiyya* (1956–57; the trilogy), a trilogy tracing an

Egyptian family through three generations, with a sweep worthy of a Galsworthy (q.v.). During the 1960s, Mahfūz produced a further set of novels of which *Al-Liss wa al-kilāb* (1961; the thief and the dogs) and *Tharthara fawq al-Nīl* (1966; chatter on the Nile) are probably the best. These concentrate more than his earlier works on the individual within society and his sense of alienation. After the debacle of the Six Day War in June 1967, he expressed his views in lengthy short stories and even a few plays, before returning to the novel during the 1970s.

In the realm of the short story, Yūsuf Idrīs (q.v.) has shown a particular talent. His works not only display a clear development in technique and themes, but also an adventurous attitude toward the use of language. Mahfūz's language tends to be relatively uncomplicated, even to the point of being occasionally colorless. Idrīs, on the other hand, sprinkles his style with colloquialisms and unorthodox syntax, which lend to his stories an attractive element of liveliness and innovation.

While Mahfūz and Idrīs have dominated Egyptian fiction, there are a number of other excellent writers of their generation. The novels of al-Sharqāwī, especially *Al-Ard* (1954; *Egyptian Earth*, 1962), present a realistic and obviously committed view of the Egyptian peasant. Fathī Ghānim (b. 1924) has written several fine novels such as *Al-Rajul alladhī faqada zillahu* (1960; *The Man Who Lost His Shadow*, 1962) and *Al-Jabal* (1957; the mountain). In the realm of the short story, Edward al-Kharrāt (b. 1926) and Yūsuf al-Shārūnī (b. 1924) both write with intense meticulousness.

Egyptian writers reacted with varying degrees of fury, sorrow, and contemplation to the events of June 1967. A younger generation of writers, who emerged in the 1960s, expressed these feelings with particular clarity. These younger writers have in many ways found their path blocked, not only by the tremendous popularity of the writers of older generations, who, with a few exceptions, have kept a hold on most of the positions of influence within the cultural sector, but also as a result of the cultural policies of the Sādāt government, which tended to offer publication opportunities in Egypt only to writers who were prepared to tolerate—or, at least, not express opposition to—the political and social status quo. Writing fiction has never been a full-time occupation in Egypt, and that is certainly more true today than ever before. Many of the younger authors do their writing in their spare time, and, with

this in mind, the quality of work produced by such short-story writers as Majīd Tūbiyā (b. 1938) and Yahyā al-Tāhir 'Abdallāh (1942–1980) and novelists like 'Abd al-Hakīm Qāsim (b. 1935) and Jamāl al-Ghītānī (b. 1945?) is remarkable. The late 1970s offered signs of the revival of a vigorous fictional tradition.

Drama

The dramatic tradition in Egypt traces its origins back to the 19th c., although some critics find precedents of one kind or another in still earlier works of belles lettres or folk literature. The popular theater began with the works of Ya'qūb Sanū' and was carried on into this century by Najīb al-Rīhānī. This tradition has continued with undiminished vigor to the present day, and its success can be attributed not only to the popular predilection for farce but also to its unabashed use of the colloquial language, which appeals to the broadest spectrum of society.

The development of "literary" or "serious" drama has been dogged by two issues. The first is the initial association of the genre with music and singing; the historical verse dramas of Ahmad Shawqī, which contain much fine poetry, have been preserved and even revived on the basis of certain songs that were made extremely popular by famous singers. The second issue is the much discussed question of language: particularly to conservative critics, anything not composed in the written language was not literature, whereas to practitioners of the drama, plays not in the spoken language were restricted in their possible themes and extremely difficult to act. It has been the great contribution of Tawfīq al-Hakīm to raise the status of the genre and provide it with plays of more stimulating intellectual content. To critics like Tāhā Husayn, al-Hakīm's first lengthy play, *Ahl al-kahf* (1933; *The People of the Cave*, 1971) is a major monument in the history of Arabic literature. Al-Hakīm has followed it with a whole series of similar intellectual plays, the latest of which is *Al-Sultān al-hā'ir* (1960; *The Sultan's Dilemma*, 1973). All these plays have proved difficult, if not impossible, to stage effectively, a fact that has led several commentators, al-Hakīm included, to retreat to a position that claims them as "plays to be read." Al-Hakīm has also produced a huge number of short plays, on social and political issues.

The revolution of 1952 saw the beginning of

the two most productive decades in the history of Egyptian drama. A new generation of playwrights emerged who made significant innovations in both language and form. In a whole series of works, Nuʿmān ʿĀshūr (dates n.a.) brilliantly captured the combination of dynamism and uncertainty following the revolution at all levels of society within the new political structure and exposed many of the inherent problems by showing the clash of generations. In the 1960s Saʿd al-dīn Wahba (dates n.a.) began by describing society in realistic terms, although he concentrated initially on the countryside. Later, in plays such as *Kubrī al-nāmūs* (1964; mosquito bridge) and *Sikkat al-salāma* (1965; road to safety), a more symbolic trend can be seen. In two of his most recent works, *Al-Masāmīr* (1967; the nails) and *Sabʿ sawāqī* (1969; seven waterwheels), he discusses the implications of 1967 with a bitter frankness that led to the banning of the latter play.

Alfred Faraj (dates n.a.) drew the inspiration for his comments on the present from history and the folktale; his plays on historical subjects include *Sulaymān al-Halabī* (1965; Sulaymān from Aleppo) and *Al-Zīr Sālim* (1967; Prince Salim). From the famous *1001 Nights* Faraj took themes for two of his best and most popular works, *Hallāq Baghdād* (1964; the barber of Baghdad) and *ʿAlī Janāh al-Tibrīzi wa tābiʿuhu Qufa* (1969; ʿAlī Janāh from Tabriz and Qufa his henchman). Among the most important of Faraj's contributions is the use of the literary language in a way that permitted effective stage productions.

A number of other plays were performed with great success in the 1960s: Mahmūd Diyāb's (b. 1932) *Al-Zawbaʿa* (1964; *The Storm,* 1967); Rashād Rushdī's (b. 1915) *Rihla khārij al-sūr* (1963; *Journey outside the Wall,* 1974), with its heavy symbolism; Yūsuf Idrīs's *Al-Farāfīr* (1964; *The Farfoors,* 1974; also tr. as *Flipflap and His Master,* 1977), with its combination of folklore, slapstick, and the absurd.

The drama being the most public of all literary genres, has in recent years been particularly subject to the vicissitudes of politics and cultural policy. The term "theater crisis" has become a stock phrase of the majority of commentators on the drama, and the forced or unforced absence from the country of a number of critics and directors, and the reticence of several prominent dramatists mentioned above suggests that the present cultural milieu will need to change before we may see a revival of the dynamic tradition of earlier decades.

Criticism

As is the case with the literature itself, the early criticism of the modern period harks back to the classical ideals, as is clearly seen in the writing of Husayn al-Marsafī (?–1889) and the celebrated criticism on the poet Ahmad Shawqī written by Muhammad al-Muwaylihī in 1898. The first signs of change can be seen in the writings of the Dīwān school. Al-ʿAqqād, the most prominent critic in the group, was one of a select number of writers who contributed to the development of literary sensibilities and critical taste in Egypt during the first half of this century. Particular mention should be made of Tāhā Husayn, whose iconoclastic work *Fī al-shiʿr al-jāhilī* (1926; on pre-Islamic poetry) was among the first to apply the objective principles of literary criticism to the earliest examples of Arabic literature; Muhammad Husayn Haykal, whose advocacy of objectivity in criticism and of the concept of national literature did much to foster a particularly Egyptian identity during the 1920s and 1930s; and Muhammad Mandūr (1907–1965), a disciple of Tāhā Husayn, whose brilliant studies of both literature and literary criticism were to lay the foundation for the emergence of a number of critics still writing today.

In the aftermath of World War II, ʿAbd al-ʿAzīm Anīs (dates n.a.) and Mahmūd Amīn al-ʿĀlim (dates n.a.) produced a famous work of criticism, *Fī al-thaqāfa al-Misriyya* (1955; on Egyptian culture), in which they advocated the need for commitment in literature. This book started a fierce debate among literary scholars, including Tāhā Husayn, who vigorously opposed this notion. During the 1950s and into the 1960s al-ʿĀlim remained a very prominent figure in Egyptian criticism along with Lewis ʿAwad, the cultural editor of *Al-Ahrām.* Other writers tended to concentrate on one particular aspect of literature: ʿAlī al–Rāʿī (dates n.a.), Rajāʾ al-Naqqāsh (dates n.a.), and Bahāʾ Tāhir (dates n.a.), for example, tended to deal with the theater, ʿAbd al-Muhsin Tāhā Badr (dates n.a.) and Sabrī Hāfiz (b. 1941?) concentrated more on fiction, and ʿIzz al-dīn Ismāʿīl (dates n.a.) turned his attention to a number of studies on literary theory from a variety of viewpoints.

It is an apt reflection on the current milieu in Egypt that the majority of its more famous and productive literary critics, such as Mahmūd Amīn al-ʿĀlim, Ghālī Shukrī (dates n.a.), ʿAlī al-Rāʿī, and Lewis ʿAwad (dismissed from his post at *Al-Ahrām*), no longer publish in their homeland. A number of younger writers have made themselves known to a wide audience, but they suffer, along with their colleagues, from a lack of sponsorship and a dearth of criticism. It is to be hoped that their talents will not be stunted by the present difficult circumstances but that they will prove to be the vanguard of a new generation.

BIBLIOGRAPHY: Sakkut, H., *The Egyptian Novel and Its Main Trends 1913–1952* (1971); Kilpatrick, H., *The Modern Egyptian Novel* (1974); Semah, D., *Four Egyptian Literary Critics* (1974); Badawi, M., *A Critical Introduction to Modern Arabic Poetry* (1975), passim; Hafiz, S., "Innovation in the Egyptian Short Story," in Ostle, R. C., ed., *Studies in Modern Arabic Literature* (1975), pp. 99–113; Hafiz, S., "The Egyptian Novel in the Sixties," *JArabL*, 7 (1976), 68–84; Allen, R., "Egyptian Drama and Fiction in the 1970s," *Edebiyat*, 1 (1976), 219–33; al-Jayyusi, S., *Trends and Movements in Modern Arabic Poetry* (1977), passim; Allen, R., "Egyptian Drama after the Revolution," *Edebiyat*, 4 (1979), 97–134

ROGER M. A. ALLEN

EHRENBURG, Ilya Grigorevich

Russian novelist, memoirist, journalist, and poet, b. 27 Jan. 1891, Kiev, Ukraine; d. 1 Sept. 1967, Moscow

E. was born in Kiev, but when he was five his parents moved to Moscow, where he grew up and received his secondary education. He was active in the 1905 revolution, was imprisoned, and then from 1909 to 1917 lived abroad, writing poetry. In 1914 he became war correspondent for a major St. Petersburg newspaper and, in the wake of the February 1917 revolution, returned to Russia. Four years later he left the U.S.S.R. once more, spending much of the 1920s and 1930s in Belgium, France, and Germany. He covered the Spanish Civil War, and in 1941 settled for good in Russia, traveling abroad after that only for visits or on official assignments. During World War II he reported from the eastern front. Having survived the "black years" of the Stalinist period, he heralded the new, more open mood of Soviet society with a novel, *Ottepel* (1956; *A Change of Season*, 1962).

E.'s writing during the 1920s reflected the approach then in vogue, of ridiculing the rhetoric and pretensions of both the capitalist and the communist systems. *Neobyknovennye pokhozh-*

denia Khulio Khurenito (1922; *The Extraordinary Adventures of Julio Jurenito and His Disciples*, 1930; later tr. under same title, 1963), a remarkable grotesquerie and probably E.'s best work of fiction, dates from this period. *Burnaya zhizn Lazika Roytshvantsa* (1928; *The Stormy Life of Lasik Roitschwantz*, 1960), describing the "magnificent absurdity" of the revolution, is a Soviet version of Jaroslav Hašek's (q.v.) *The Good Soldier Švejk*. Of his work of the mid-1930s two novels stand out: *Den vtoroy* (1933; *Out of Chaos*, 1934) and *Ne perevodya dykhania* (1935; without pausing for a breath). *Den vtoroy* is a vulgar apologia for Socialist Realism (q.v.); *Ne perevodya dykhania* shows E.'s acceptance of official governmental policy in economic and political matters.

E. was one of the most popular and widely read writers of World War II, his searing, indignant reportage serving as a catalytic inspiration to the Red Army, then beleaguered by the invasion of Nazi forces. His *Padenie Parizha* (1941; *The Fall of Paris*, 1943), a crushing indictment of Nazism, earned him his first Stalin Prize; *Burya* (1949; *The Storm*, 1949), his second. These two books, together with *Devyaty val* (2 vols., 1952; *The Ninth Wave*, 1955), make up an engrossing if manipulative historical series, set in France and Russia.

During the more repressive early postwar years E. was, predictably, attacked for his "cosmopolitanism," his Jewish parentage, and his positive assessment of the cultural and intellectual give-and-take of the 1920s in Russia. (E. described himself as a "Soviet citizen of Jewish nationality," and in another place wrote, "I belong to those whom it is proper to persecute.") Having survived against considerable odds the treacherous zigzags of the Stalinist era—among other ways, by discreet reticence, by aiding in the purge of Soviet Jewish intellectuals and writers, and by ridiculing the newly established State of Israel—E. was, after Stalin's death in March 1953, among those who championed intellectual liberation, freer artistic expression, and the dismantling of the reigning political mythology. While not an enduring work of art, his *Ottepel* was a harbinger of the fundamental shifts to come and was emblematic of the transition from Stalinist terrorism to the next stages of Soviet history.

The last years of E.'s life were given over to promoting "rehabilitated" writers and to writing six books of valuable memoirs, an occupation which he shared with other Soviet literati of the 1960s such as Valentin Kataev, Konstantin Paustovsky (qq.v.), Korney Chukovsky

(1882–1969), Samuil Marshak (1887–1964), and Viktor Shklovsky (b. 1893). These volumes—*Lyudi, gody, zhizn* (1961–66; *People and Life, 1891–1921,* 1962; *Memoirs: 1921–1941,* 1964; *The War, 1941–1945,* 1964; *Post-War Years, 1945–1954,* 1966)—constitute a historical panorama, describing from a sophisticated and refined perspective the writers and artists E. had known and the political movements, gatherings of the intelligentsia, and artistic schools he had observed or participated in.

History will record that E.'s prolific output enjoyed wide popularity during his lifetime. Finally, however, his political adaptability, mordant cynicism, and cautious ideological aggressiveness—punctuated by recantations—had the impact of trivializing his talent, too often pushing him in the direction of opportunism and compromise and raising serious questions about how enduring his place in literature will be. The recipient of two Stalin Prizes for literature, the Lenin Peace Prize, and the Order of Lenin, E. was a paradigm of survival in the Soviet context: negotiating the shoals of Party-line shifts, retreating, advancing, retracting, and then adopting an apparently bold public stand. His silence about the destruction of Soviet Jewish intellectuals in August 1952 was the moral nadir of his career. He seems to have attempted to atone for this during the last years of his life by a concerted campaign to have published works by writers who had earlier been politically condemned by the regime; and by advocating the value of artistic innovation, individual creativity, and personal integrity.

FURTHER WORKS: *Stikhi* (1910); *Ya zhivu* (1911); *Oduvanchiki* (1912); *Budni* (1913); *Poety Frantsii, 1870–1913: Perevody* (1914); *Detskoe* (1914); *Povest o zhizni nekoy Nadenki i o veshchikh znameniyakh, yavlennykh ey* (1916); *O zhilete Semyona Drozda* (1917); *Molitva o Rossii* (1918); *Ogon* (1919); *V zvezdakh* (1919); *Lik voyny: Vo Frantsii* (1920); *Razdumya* (1921); *Kanuny: Stikhi 1915–1921* (1921); *Portrety russkikh poetov* (1922); *Zarubezhnye razdumya* (1922); *Zolotoe serdtse, misteria* (1922); *Veter, tragedia* (1922); *Moskovskie razdumya* (1922); *Opustoshayushchaya lyubov* (1922); *A vsyo-taki ona vertitsya* (1922); *Chetyre povesti o lyogkikh kontsakh* (1923); *Otrechennye* (1923); *Zverinoe teplo* (1923); *Trinadtsat trubok* (1923); *Trest D. E.* (1923); *Zhizn i gibel Nikolaya Kurbova* (1923); *Lyubov Zhanny Ney* (1924; *The Love of Jeanne Ney,* 1930); *Trubka* (1924); *Rvach* (1925); *Ne-*

pravdopodcbnye istorii (1925); *Leto 1925 goda* (1926); *Uslovnye stradania zavsegdataya kafe* (1926); *V Protochnom pereulke* (1927; *A Street in Moscow,* 1932); *Bely ugol; ili, Slyozy Vertera* (1928); *Zagovor ravnykh* (1928); *Viza vremeni* (1929); *10 l. s.: Khronika nashego vremeni* (1929; *The Life of the Automobile,* 1976); *Ediny front* (1930); *My i oni* (1931); *Fabrika snov: Khronika nashego vremeni* (1931); *Ispania* (1933); *Moskva slyozam ne verit* (1933); *Moy Parizh* (1933); *Zatyanuvshayasya razvyazka* (1934); *Khronika nashikh dney* (1935); *Kniga dlya vzroslykh* (1936); *Chetyre trubki* (1936); *Granitsy nochi* (1936); *Chto cheloveku nado* (1937); *No parasan* (1937); *Vne peremiria: Sbornik rasskazov* (1937); *Ispanski zakal: Fevral–iyul 1937* (1938); *Beshenye volki* (1941); *Fashistskie mrakobesy* (1941); *Vernost, stikhi* (1941); *Za zhizn* (1942); *Ozhestochenie* (1942); *Solntsevorot* (1942); *Svoboda, poemy* (1943); *Stikhi o voyne* (1943); *Padenie duche* (1943); *Voyna, iyul 1941–aprel 1942* (1943; *Russia at War,* 1943); *Rasskazy etikh let* (1944); *Derevo, stikhi, 1938–1945 gg.* (1946); *Dorogi Evropy* (1946; *European Crossroad,* 1947); *Lev na ploshchadi, komedia* (1947); *Za mir* (1950); *Nadezhda mira* (1950); *Sochinenia* (5 vols., 1952–54); *Lyudi khotyat zhit* (1953); *Volya narodov* (1953); *O rabote pisatelya* (1954; *The Writer and His Craft,* 1954); *Sovest narodov* (1956); *Frederik Zholio-Kyuri* (1958); *Frantsuzskie tetradi* (1958); *Indiyskie vpechatlenia, yaponskie zametki, razmyshlenia v Gretsii* (1958); *Stikhi, 1938–1958* (1959); *Karel Purkine* (1960); *Perechityvaya Chekhova* (1960; *Chekhov, Stendhal, and Other Essays,* 1962); *Sobranie sochineny* (9 vols., 1962–67); *Ya zhivu, stikhi* (1971); *Stikhotvorenia* (1972); *Letopis muzhestva: Publitsisticheskie stati voennykh let* (1974)

BIBLIOGRAPHY: Slonim, M., *Modern Russian Literature: From Chekhov to the Present* (1953), pp. 375–79; Ehrlich, V., "The Metamorphoses of I. E.," *Problems of Communism,* 12, 4 (1963), 12–24; Alexandrova, V., *A History of Soviet Literature* (1964), pp. 127–42; Slonim, M., *Soviet Russian Literature: Writers and Problems* (1964), pp. 208–17; Friedberg, M., "I. G. E.," in Simmonds, G. W., ed., *Soviet Leaders* (1967), pp. 272–81; Brown, E., *Russian Literature since the Revolution,* 2nd ed. (1969), pp. 247–57; Hingley, R., *Russian Writers and Soviet Society 1917–1978* (1979), pp. 110, 116, 223–24, 233–34

THOMAS E. BIRD

EICH, Günter

German poet and radio dramatist, b. 1 Feb. 1907, Lebus an der Oder; d. 20 Dec. 1972, Gross-Gmain, Austria

E. studied law and sinology in Leipzig, Berlin, and Paris, but in 1932 he began devoting himself exclusively to writing. During World War II he served in the German army, was captured by the Americans, and held as a prisoner of war until 1946. After the war he became one of the founding members of Group 47. In 1953 he married the Austrian writer Ilse Aichinger (q.v.). Until 1963 he lived in Lenggries, Bavaria, and afterward in Gross-Gmain, Austria, where he died.

It was not until after World War II, when he published the poetry collections *Abgelegene Gehöfte* (1948; remote farmsteads) and *Untergrundbahn* (1949; subway), in which he gave a sober lyrical assessment of life in troubled times, that E. won fame and recognition as one of the foremost contemporary German poets. His matter-of-fact poem "Inventur" (1948; "Inventory," 1976), which takes stock of the possessions of a prisoner of war, became the most frequently quoted poem in postwar German literature.

The collection of poems *Botschaften des Regens* (1955; messages of the rain) marks the high point of his lyrical achievement. E.'s poems derive their substance directly from nature or everyday experience and thereby open up a feeling for the mystery of life in a seemingly inconspicuous way. Truth may be found in a feather that a bird lost in front of the house, or in the sound of falling rain, or in an unexpected instance where the ultimate inadequacy of "normal" perception becomes shockingly clear. E.'s images tend to turn this shock into a warning against complacency, in keeping with his often quoted statement that the writer should be gravel rather than grease in the workings of the world.

The enormous success of E.'s radio play *Träume* (1950; dreams) contributed to establishing the genre as a dominant one in Germany. In extending the radio play's poetic expression, E. offered glimpses into the mystery of reality, a technique that also forms the basis of his poems. One of his principal contributions was to oppose, in his quiet but effective way, the forgetfulness of the German people after World War II. His best radio play, *Die Mädchen aus Viterbo* (1953; the girls from Viterbo) presents the fate of two Jews awaiting arrest by the Gestapo in a Berlin hiding place.

In later years, E.'s works showed an increasing impatience with "poetic" messages, and evidenced an abbreviation, almost a fragmentation of lyrical forms and a pattern of rebellion against the established order that corresponded to the protests of the younger generation in the late 1960s.

FURTHER WORKS: *Gedichte* (1930); *Katharina* (1936); *Zu den Akten* (1964); *Fünfzehn Hörspiele* (1966); *Anlässe und Steingärten* (1966); *Kulka, Hilpert, Elefanten* (1968); *Maulwürfe* (1968); *Ein Tibeter in meinem Büro* (1970); *Nach Seumes Papieren* (1972); *Gesammelte Werke* (1973). FURTHER VOLUMES IN ENGLISH: *Journeys* (1968); *Selected Poems* (1971)

BIBLIOGRAPHY: Enzensberger, H. M., "In Search of the Lost Language," *Encounter*, 30, 3 (1963), 44–51; Fowler, F. M., "G. E.," in Keith-Smith, B., ed., *German Men of Letters* (1966), Vol. IV, pp. 89–107; Müller-Hanpft, S., ed., *Über G. E.* (1970); Krispyn, E., *G. E.* (1971); Unseld, E., ed., *G. E. zum Gedächtnis* (1973); Schafroth, H. F., *G. E.* (1976)

FRANK TROMMLER

EIDEM, Odd

Norwegian essayist, dramatist, and theater critic, b. 23 Oct. 1913, Oslo

E. has been the most distinctive critic in Norway in modern times, not only of the theater, but also of nations, politics, religion, manners, and individual personalities. He took a master's degree in literary history in 1938, and since then has been a critic for *Tidens tegn*, *Verdens gang*, and *Aftenposten*.

E.'s distinctive qualities are his clear, highly readable style, his light touch, his satirical yet loving attitude toward life, and, above all, his close, seemingly naïve relationship to the reader. He can and does talk about himself a great deal without revealing too much, obtruding himself on the subject at hand, or seeming to be arrogant or sentimental. Thus, he woos the reader, draws him in, and shares experiences with him. The result has been great success and popularity.

As a theater critic, E. is both feared and respected. He has a wide knowledge of all phases of the theater, including actors, acting, rehearsals, staging, and audiences. His great desire for excellence in Norwegian theater has led him to reject everything mediocre and to call for a concentration of talent in the National Theater in Oslo.

Although he dismisses his own dramas modestly, the comedy *MIN kvinne!* (1956; MY wife!), was quite a success, as was one he wrote together with André Bjerke (q.v.), *Videnskap og lidenskap* (1951; science and passion).

An active socialist when he was young, E. later adopted a more aesthetic, detached view of life. This attitude comes to the fore in his highly popular, clever, subtle, and mischievous *flanerier* ("strolls"), as he calls them, or books that contain leisurely observations of life in the form of essays or short stories, always told from a personal viewpoint. Whether he is describing the way Norwegians eat, drink, and make love, Disneyland's complete lack of exhibits using live animals, Sonny Liston's attitude toward boxing, or a cremation in India, E. is always lively and interesting, and he always has a point to make that is both witty and revealing. In the fall of 1978, four of these sketches were dramatized, filmed, and broadcast on Norwegian television.

In a recent semiautobiographical novel, *Pieter og jeg* (1979; Pieter and I), E. revisits Holland, where he had lived when he was twenty, meets a young socialist, Pieter, relives his own socialist past, and compares his experiences to Pieter's—a well-done, serious, fast-moving, absorbing story.

FURTHER WORKS: *Diktere i landflyktighet* (1937); *Uten fane* (1939); *Segerstedt* (1946); *Varm aske* (1947); *Spillet om Bly-Petter* (1947); *Vinden blåser fra nord* (1948); *Fuglen som aldri sang* (1949); *Det norske språk fra uke til uke* (1949); *Fire glass konjakk* (1950); *Frank visitt i Sovjet* (1952); *Den bakvendte familieboken* (1955, with André Bjerke); *Kefir og chiante* (1958); *Guds gjøglere* (1960); *Sett fra Sirius* (1963); *Sett fra min plass* (1965); *Zikzak* (1967); *Jeppe Jansens giraff* (1969); *Det fjerde øye* (1971); *Kala* (1971); *Flaskepost* (1973); *Karjol* (1975); *Tilskueren* (1976); *Goddag og adjø til nitten herrer* (1977); *Fløyten og orgelet* (1978); *Cruise* (1978)

WALTER D. MORRIS

EKELÖF, Gunnar

Swedish poet and essayist, b. 15 Sept. 1907, Stockholm; d. 16 March 1968, Sigtuna

Born into a wealthy family, E. had a disturbed childhood because of his father's mental illness. Considering himself an "outsider," as a college student he studied music and Oriental culture in London, Uppsala, and Paris. He returned from Paris with his first collection of poems, *Sent på jorden* (1923; late on the earth), influenced by Stravinsky's music and reflecting E.'s own suicidal crisis. At the time of its publication, no one realized that *Sent på jorden* would eventually be considered one of the first truly modernist (q.v.) collections of poetry to appear in Sweden. With his free-form poetry, apparent spontaneity, and dreamlike intensity, E. was hailed in the journal *Spektrum* as Sweden's first "surrealist" (q.v.). He accepted the title unwillingly, since he admired the symbolists (q.v.) Rimbaud and Mallarmé, and only one surrealist, Robert Desnos (q.v.).

E.'s next two volumes continued his musical, neoromantic exploration of dreams, but in *Köp den blindes sång* (1938; buy the blind man's song), E. refers to Hitler's rise to power in Germany and ponders man's paradoxical nature. *Non serviam* (1945; Latin: I will not serve) contrasts the intellectual and the mystical, and concludes with one of the finest Swedish poems of this century: "Absentia animi" (Latin: absence of mind) literally turns words into music, yet manages to pose the relation between absence and presence, nearness and farness in vivid, resonating imagery.

Om hösten (1951; in the autumn) reaffirmed E.'s searchingly sad brilliance as a poet of the world around him and the subconscious life within him. In this volume the poem "Röster under jorden" (voices under the ground) portrays E.'s sense of the closeness of the past to the present, the voices of the dead, the bodies and lives of the past that live within us as we, too, blend into the single liquid substance of time. In 1955 he published *Strountes* (nonsense), a volume that plays with the ambiguous and trivial in order to approach ironically the meaninglessness of the universe. This "antipoetic" volume served as a major influence on the next generation of Swedish poets. In *Opus incertum* (1959; Latin: uncertain work) and in *En natt i Otočac* (1961; a night in Otočac) E. continued to employ the antithetical and antipoetic to pursue, occasionally in burlesque fashion, the problems of death and meaninglessness. During these years he also wrote the long allusive and autobiographical poem *En Mölna-elegi* (1960; *A Mölna Elegy*, 1979).

Throughout his career E. wrote several collections of critical and autobiographical essays. These prose works provided additional insight into the sources of E.'s inspiration. Although already established as the major Swedish poet of the 20th c., E. reached the peak of his career with a trilogy of poems based upon a personal mystical experience: *Dīwān över Fursten av Emgión* (1965; divan of the Prince of Emgion), *Sagan om Fatumeh* (1966; the saga of Fatumeh), and *Vägvisare till underjorden* (1967; *Guide to the Underworld*, 1980). In the trilogy, E. identifies himself with an exiled and tortured Byzantine prince. A young prostitute, Fatumeh, who serves as guide, mistress, and archetypal woman to the blinded prince, functions as the second narrator of the trilogy. As a whole, the three volumes explore the range of human experience from the agonies of a torturous physical life to the ecstasies of the mystical, the archetypal life which usually lies hidden within man but which can appear in moments of brilliant illumination.

E. is one of the truly original Swedish poets of the 20th c. Diverse, personal, intimate, obscure, profound, mystical, he dominated the craft of poetry and throughout his life played with his craft like a master weaving new tapestries. For a poet of such depth and complexity, perhaps the finest tribute to be paid to him is the Swedish people's acceptance of him as their own national *skald,* or bard. The recipient of every major literary prize awarded in Scandinavia, E. received an honorary doctorate from the University of Uppsala and became a member of the Swedish Royal Academy in 1958. His writings, from his earliest to his last works, continue to be translated and admired throughout the world.

FURTHER WORKS: *Dedikation* (1934); *Sorgen och stjärnan* (1936); *Promenader* (1941); *Utflykter* (1947); *Dikter* (1949); *Dikter 1932–1951* (1956); *Blandade kort* (1957); *Verklighetsfykt* (1958); *Valfrändskaper* (1960); *Sent på jorden, med Appendix 1962, och En natt vid horisonten* (1962); *Lägga patience* (1969); *Partitur* (1969); *G. E.: En självbiografi* (1970); *En röst* (1973). FURTHER VOLUMES IN ENGLISH: *Selected Poems* (1967); *I Do Best Alone at Night* (1968); *Selected Poems* (1971); *Friends, You Drank Some Darkness* (1975)

BIBLIOGRAPHY: Sjöberg, L., *A. Reader's Guide to G. E.'s "A Mölna Elegy"* (1973); Shideler, R., *Voices under the Ground: Themes and Images in the Poetry of G. E.* (1973); Perner, C., *G. E.'s "Nacht am Horizont" und seine Begegnung mit Stéphane Mallarmé* (1974); Sjöberg, L., "Translating with W. H. Auden: G. E.'s Last Poems," *CCrit,* 1 (1979), 185–97; Sjöberg, L., "G. E.'s *A Mölna Elegy:* The At-

tempted Reconstruction of a Moment," *CCrit,* 1 (1979), 199–214

ROSS P. SHIDELER

EKELUND, Vilhelm

Swedish poet and essayist, b. 14 Oct. 1880, Stehag; d. 3 Sept. 1949, Saltsjöbaden

When E. was fourteen, his family moved from the country village of Stehag to the university town of Lund (both in the southern Swedish district of Skåne). Later E. attended Lund University, without, however, taking a degree (in 1937 he received an honorary doctorate from Lund University). He spent the years 1908–12 in Germany and the following nine years in Denmark, returning to live in Sweden in 1921.

E.'s first seven books were volumes of poetry, including *Melodier i skymning* (1902; melodies at dusk) and *Dityramber i aftonglans* (1906; dithyrambs in evening light). Most of the poems in the early collections, including *Melodier i skymning,* are in rhymed verse; later collections are written in masterful, highly sophisticated free verse. Many of the early lyric poems (examples are the much admired "Kastanjeträden trötta luta" [tired the chestnuts lean] and "Då voro bokarna ljusa" [then the beeches were light], both from *Melodier i skymning*) use the southern Swedish settings of E.'s childhood to explore subjective moods. There is, in E.'s poetry, a continuous struggle between the lyric and romantic on the one hand, and the severe and classical on the other. The latter predominates in *Dityramber i aftonglans;* E.'s next work, *Grekisk bukett* (1906; Greek bouquet), is a collection of translations from Greek poetry in classical meters.

Beginning with *Antikt ideal* (1909; antique ideal), E. abandoned poetry in favor of essays, and, more frequently, aphorisms. Later books, especially *Metron* (1918; Greek: measure) and *Attiskt i fågelperspektiv* (1919; Attic thoughts from a bird's-eye view), are reflections on the works of great writers and thinkers. The classical influence reached E. both directly from Greek writers, especially Plato and Pindar, and by way of German writers who had themselves been influenced by the classics: Goethe, Nietzsche, and August von Platen (1796–1835). E.'s admiration for Nietzsche contributed to both the form and the content of *Dityramber i aftonglans;* Goethe and Nietzsche are the informing spirits of *Antikt ideal.*

Later, E. had some reservations about Nietzsche's prophetic stance. E. himself moved further toward the classical ideal of balance and the golden mean, as exemplified in *Metron* and *Nordiskt and klassiskt* (1914; Nordic and classical). Emerson, whose idealism and humility E. admired, was also an important later influence. *Tyska utsikter* (1913; German views) has the subtitle *Nytt och gammalt om Emerson m.m.* (new and old on Emerson, etc.). Emerson, like Plato and Goethe, remained a literary hero to E. for the rest of his life. *Veri similia* (2 vols., 1915–16; verisimilitudes) includes a short essay on Carlyle and Emerson; more importantly, Emerson's thought pervades the two books.

E.'s prose, like his poetry, evinces a search for beauty in the Platonic sense and for greatness of soul. This search is connected with the necessity, as E. sees it, for the individual to define his own values and to live his life according to the insights he has garnered. In *Plus salis* (1945; Latin: salt added) E. stresses the desirability of a confluence of theory and practice, thought and life. While E. will never be a popular writer—he did not wish to be—his highly wrought and deeply considered poetry and prose continue to win the admiration of discerning readers.

FURTHER WORKS: *Våbris* (1900); *Syner* (1901); *Elegier* (1903); *In Candidum* (1905); *Havets stjärna* (1906); *Böcker och vandringar* (1910); *Båge och lyra* (1912); *Valda dikter* (1913); *Sak och sken* (1922); *På hafsstranden* (1922); *Levnadsstämning* (1925); *Väst-Östligt* (1925); *Passioner emellan* (1927); *Lyra och Hades* (1930); *Spår och tecken* (1930); *Det andra ljuset* (1935); *Elpidi* (1939); *Concordia animi* (1942); *Atticism-humanism* (1943); *Dikter* (1951); *Prosa* (2 vols., 1952); *Nya vakten* (1953); *Ars magna* (1955); *Saltet och Helichrysus* (1956); *In Silvis cum libro* (1957); *Skoltal* (1961); *Själens tillflykt* (1962); *Campus et dies* (1963); *Brev* (2 vols., 1968, 1970); *Hjärtats vaggvisor* (1970); *Hemkomst och flykt* (1972). FURTHER VOLUME IN ENGLISH: *Agenda* (1976)

BIBLIOGRAPHY: Gustafson, A., "Two Early Fröding Imitations: V. E.'s 'Skördefest' and 'I pilhäcken,' (1901)," *JEGP*, 35 (1936), 566–80; Shideler, R., " 'The Glassclear Eye of Dreams' in Twentieth-Century Swedish Poetry," *WLT*, 51 (1977), 530–34; Gustafsson, L., *Forays into Swedish Poetry* (1978), pp. 65–71

YVONNE L. SANDSTROEM

EKWENSI, Cyprian

Nigerian novelist and short-story writer (writing in English), b. 26 Sept. 1921, Minna

E. studied at Achimota College, near Accra, Ghana, and obtained a degree in pharmacy at the University of London. On his return to Nigeria, he taught science at colleges in Lagos and in Yaba. He joined the staff of the Nigerian Broadcasting Corporation in Lagos in 1951, later serving as director of information in the federal ministry of information in Lagos. In 1966 E., an Ibo, resigned his position to move to Biafra. When the Nigerian-Biafran conflict (1967–70) ended, he proclaimed that he was "happy to be a Nigerian again." E. is now a practicing pharmacist.

E.'s first two novels show his ambivalence to the city. The first, *People of the City* (1954; rev. ed., 1963), is an episodic work in which a newspaperman, Amusa Sango, serves as commentator on life in Lagos. E.'s view of Lagos is both grim and fascinating. Several of his characters are overwhelmed by the city, turning to prostitution and thievery or committing suicide. Amusa, the protagonist, must work through the "hell" of Lagos (E. uses Dantesque imagery) in order to gain a mastery of life. The destructiveness of the city is strongly presented in E.'s portrait of a beautiful woman, Beatrice the First, who comes to the city, has several lovers (in a descending order of wealth and status), dies unattended and loveless, and is buried in a pauper's grave. Amusa's salvation comes through another Beatrice—Beatrice the Second —who, in her quiet, simple way, provides stability for him.

E.'s second novel, probably his best-known and most influential work, *Jagua Nana* (1961), shows E.'s continuing fascination with the city and its women. A series of events, particularly a romance with a young political idealist, leads Jagua Nana, a sleek, beautiful prostitute, to a new awareness. Her road to understanding, however, is strewn with twists of fate. Unable to bear children for many years, the one thing Jagua wants desperately is a child. Finally, at forty-five, she does give birth, but the child dies two days later. Jagua overcomes her sense of loss and sets off for a new life in a small country town.

E.'s first two novels have been criticized for sentimentality, romanticism, and journalistic exploitation of sensational events. Yet, even his detractors admit the vitality of his characterizations and his broad canvas of urban events. Some critics see in his work a Dickensian sense of comedy and a talent for reportage and the picaresque similar to that of Defoe. E. himself has said that he is less interested in literary style than in getting to the "heart of the truth which the man in the street can recognize." E. calls himself a "writer for the masses," and he prefers to "go down to the people." His stated allegiance to the masses and his fear of literary pretentiousness provide some of the reasons he regards Georges Simenon (q.v.) and Edgar Wallace (1875–1932) as two great influences on his work. Both Simenon and Wallace wrote their novels quickly, disdaining any pretensions of precious writing.

E.'s third novel, *Burning Grass* (1962), was written before his two earlier published novels. It reveals his deep commitment to the countryside as a source of respite for the battered soul. In *Burning Grass,* the action of which takes place in the northern Fulani countryside, the sense of an older way of life that is passing is conveyed against the ominous undertones of an encroaching city life. In *Beautiful Feathers* (1963), E. shifted the setting to the city again and explored the life of a young, earnest, respected politician, Wilson Iyari, cuckolded by his wife.

E.'s later work shows an increasing concern with style and less reliance on the episodic and sensational. *Iska* (1966)—the title is the name given to the wind that blows through the countryside—is the story of a young girl tragically blown about by the inevitable raging winds of tribal conflicts.

E. is also a prolific writer of short stories and juvenile literature. His best-known collection of stories is *Lokotown* (1966). In a recent collection, *Restless City and Christmas Gold* (1975), E. utilizes sketches of modern conflict—the sophisticated "been-to" bored with his white wife; the innocent girl corrupted by jaded pleasure seekers; the pettiness of industrial society. Much of his children's literature utilizes the motif of a young wanderer through strange lands and forests, settings inspired by his own experience in the forestry service.

E.'s work, various in its moods, style, and genres, centers on the individual act of choice. Far from bearing only simple messages and moralisms, E.'s work suggests unending ambiguities in man. His conclusions are pat, but his people are real and complex.

FURTHER WORKS: *When Love Whispers* (1947); *The Leopard's Claw* (1947); *The Dummer Boy* (1960); *Passport of Mallam Ilia* (1960); *An African Night's Entertainment*

(1962); *Rainmaker* (1965); *Juju Rock* (1966)

BIBLIOGRAPHY: Mphahlele, E., *The African Image* (1962), pp. 276–78; Gleason, J., *This Africa* (1965), pp. 118–30; Tucker, M., *Africa in Modern Literature* (1967), pp. 73–82; Laurence, M., *Long Drums and Cannons* (1968), pp. 148–69; Cartey, W., *Whispers from a Continent* (1969), pp. 147–73, 193–95; Pieterse, C., and Deurden, D., eds., "Interview with E.," *African Writers Talking* (1972), pp. 77–83; Emenyou, E., *C. E.* (1974)

MARTIN TUCKER

EL SALVADOR LITERATURE
See Central American Literature

ELIADE, Mircea
Romanian novelist, essayist, historian of religions, and Orientalist (writing also in French and English), b. 9 March 1907, Bucharest

E. studied philosophy in Bucharest and, between 1928 and 1931, in Calcutta, India, under Surendranath Dasgupta (1885–1952). He taught at the University of Bucharest between 1933 and 1939 and during the next several years served as his country's cultural attaché in London, and after 1941, in Lisbon. An émigré after World War II, he lived in Paris from 1945 to 1956, taught for a while at the École des Hautes Études, and established himself as one of the foremost contemporary scholars of myth and religion. Since 1956 he has taught at the University of Chicago.

The unifying element of E.'s early fiction is a strong, immediately recognizable autobiographical bent. Some of his most characteristic works of this period are actually direct outgrowths of his journal, conceived (as he later reveals) as a "storehouse" of reflections, recollections, intimate experiences, intellectual discoveries, and even imaginative experiments. From the existential-sexual obsessions straightforwardly presented in *Isabel și apele diavolului* (1930; Isabel and the devil's waters) to the thinly disguised love affair between a European man and an Indian girl, poetically recounted in *Maitreyi* (1933; Maitreyi), to the unconcealed use of his Indian diary in *Șantier* (1935; work in progress), E.'s early novels are clearly derived from the personal experiences of a young intellectual torn between his Western urge for "modernity" and his fascination with the Eastern negation of time. Even E.'s fiction on Romanian themes, as exemplified by *Intoarcerea din rai* (1934; the return from paradise) and *Huliganii* (1935; the hooligans), shares in the general autobiographical quality of his early writing, although here the author goes beyond his personal self and tries to embrace the "collective self" of his generation of metaphysical "hooligans" (20th-c. reincarnations of the older "nihilists"), intent on rejecting their society and culture in the name of a feverishly expected revolutionary apocalypse.

The most forward-looking of E.'s early works is, curiously, the one that was received least favorably, *Lumina ce se stinge* (1934; the light that fails), an experimental novel using a Joycean stream-of-consciousness technique, which represents E.'s first encounter with the "fantastic" and anticipates his growing interest in tracing the ways in which the "supernatural" both hides and reveals itself in the world of everyday "reality." This trend is increasingly visible in the works published during the second half of the 1930s, in the "tale of terror" *Domnişoara Christina* (1936; Mademoiselle Christina); in *Şarpele* (1937; the snake), a short novel that starts realistically, and ends "mythically" with a vision of sexuality as a cosmologic force and a manifestation of the sacred; and, most explicitly, in the two tales of the occult included in *Secretul Doctorului Honigberger* (1940; *Two Tales of the Occult*, 1972).

With the exception of the great symbolic novel of initiatory quest, *La forêt interdite* (1955; *The Forbidden Forest*, 1978)—written in Romanian but first published in French translation; published in Romanian in Paris as *Noaptea de Sânziene* (2 vols., 1971; midsummer night)—a synthesis of all the major tendencies of E.'s creative activity, in the postwar years E.'s literary production has consisted of novellas and stories of the fantastic, in which the finest narrative qualities of his writing are most effectively realized. *Pe Strada Mântuleasa* (1968; *The Old Man and the Bureaucrats*, 1979), *La ţigănci, şi alte povestiri* (1969; with the gypsy girls, and other stories), *Die Pelerine* (1976; the cloak; written in Romanian but published only in German translation), or *In curte la Dionis* (1977; at Dionysus's court) are independent fictional explorations of the problems and paradoxes involved in the dialectic of the sacred and the profane, and are an original literary complement to E.'s

theoretical and scholarly works, from *Le mythe de l'éternel retour* (1949; *The Myth of the Eternal Return*, 1954) and *Traité d'histoire des religions* (1949; *Patterns in Comparative Religion*, 1958) to his projected four-volume *History of Religious Ideas*, of which two volumes have appeared (1976, 1978).

The more recent literary productions of E. stand, in many respects, in stark contrast to his early personal-fictional works. They display a more objective fantasy (and a richer one, for that matter); their deep themes are more authentically philosophical; and they are, unlike the rather loosely structured early works, artful and powerful narratives. Between *Isabel şi apele diavolului* and the postwar novellas, E. has gone all the way from the modernist obsession with self and existential immediacy to the timeless and serenely impersonal art of storytelling.

FURTHER WORKS: *Soliloquii* (1932); *Intr-o mănăstire din Himalaya* (1932); *Oceanografie* (1934); *India* (1934); *Alchimia asiatică* (1934); *Yoga: Essai sur les origines de la mystique indienne* (1936); *Cosmologie şi alchimie babiloniană* (1937); *Nunta în cer* (1938); *Fragmentarium* (1939); *Mitul reintegrării* (1942); *Salazar şi revoluţia în Portugalia* (1942); *Comentarii la legenda Meşterului Manole* (1943); *Insula lui Euthanasius* (1943); *Techniques du yoga* (1948); *Le chamanisme* (1951; *Shamanism*, 1964); *Iphigenia* (1951); *Images et symboles* (1952; *Images and Symbols*, 1961); *Le yoga: Immortalité et liberté* (1952; *Yoga, Immortality and Freedom*, 1958); *Forgerons et alchimistes* (1956; *The Forge and the Crucible*, 1962); *Mythes, rêves et mystères* (1957; *Myths, Dreams, and Mysteries*, 1960); *The Sacred and the Profane* (1959); *Naissances mystiques* (1959; *Birth and Rebirth*, 1958); *Méphistophélès et l'androgyne* (1962; *The Two and the One*, 1965); *Patanjali et le yoga* (1962; *Patanjali and Yoga*, 1969); *Nuvele* (1963); *Aspects du mythe* (1963; *Myth and Reality*, 1964); *Amintiri: I, Mansarda* (1966); *From Primitives to Zen* (1967); *The Quest: History and Meaning in Religion* (1969); *De Zalmoxis à Gengis-Khan* (1970; *Zalmoxis, the Vanishing God*, 1972); *Australian Religions* (1973); *Fragments d'un journal* (1973; *No Souvenirs*, 1977); *Occultism, Witchcraft, and Cultural Fashions* (1976); *Histoire des croyances et des idées religieuses*, Vol. I (1976; *A History of Religious Ideas*, 1978); *Histoire des croyances et des idées religieuses,* Vol. II (1978); *Mémoires (1907–1937)* (1980; *Autobiography: Volume I, 1907–1937,* 1981)

BIBLIOGRAPHY: Altizer, T. J. J., *M. E. and the Dialectic of the Sacred* (1963); Kitagawa, J. K., and Long, C., eds., *Myths & Symbols: Studies in Honor of M. E.* (1969); Allen, D., *Structure and Creativity in Religion: M. E.'s Phenomenology and New Directions* (1977); Calinescu, M., "Imagination and Meaning: Aesthetic Attitudes and Ideas in M. E.'s Thought," *Journal of Religion,* 57, 1 (1977), 1–15; Calinescu, M., "The Disguises of Miracle: Notes on M. E.'s Fiction," *WLT,* 52 (1978), 558–64; Tacou, C., ed., *L'Herne: Cahier M. E.* (1978); Marino, A., *L'herméneutique de M. E.* (1981)

MATEI CALINESCU

ELIN PELIN

(pseud. of Dimitur Ivanov Stoyanov) Bulgarian short-story and novella writer, b. 18 July 1877, Baylovo; d. 3 Dec. 1949, Sofia

Brought up in the *shopp* (that is, western Bulgarian) countryside, where he taught school for a brief time, E. resided in Sofia from 1899 on. Originally he wanted to be a painter, but he turned instead to writing and published his *narodnik* (populist) magazine *Selska razgovorka* (1902–3). He was employed by the University Library in 1903, and in 1906 was sent for a year to Paris at state expense to broaden his literary horizons. He was appointed to a position at the National Library in 1908, and in 1926 he became the Ivan Vazov Museum's first curator (he retired in 1944). E. worked on various periodicals, notably *Bulgaran* and *Razvigor.*

Chronically impecunious himself, E. began by depicting the hardships of early 20th-c. Bulgarian village life and *narodnik* teachers' efforts to ameliorate these conditions. But local resilience is the theme of his still famous "Andreshko" (1903; Andreshko), in which a magistrate-bailiff is left stranded in the mud by his not so dumb *shopp* driver. E.'s popularity rests solidly in his gallery of *shopp* portraits in *Razkazi* (2 vols., 1904, 1911; stories). His village tragedies, *Geratsite* (1911; the Gerak family), *Zemya* (1922; land), and *Nechista sila* (1909; unclean power), are novellas; the longer form was less congenial to him.

The Orthodox clergy of village church and monastery also figure in E.'s stories: he considered his best work to be his cycle of such tales about the clergy entitled *Pod manastirskata loza* (1936; under the monastery vine). On the other hand, he considered to be of slight literary value his feuilletons, collected in *Az, ti, toy* (1936; I, thou, he). The latter epitomize E.'s *bêtes noires,* such as the bureaucracy, the former his warm antipuritanical morality, pungently put in the proverb "Too saintly can be too much, even for God."

E. has been represented variously as a dialect and genre writer, a *narodnik,* a "critical realist," an anticlerical writer, and a pessimist. Yet, his dialect sketches *Pizho i Pendo* (1917; Pizho and Pendo) excepted, standard Bulgarian is his language even for dialogue. As with his lyrical landscapes, local color is the setting for his microcosm of humanity, not an end in itself. E. was concerned with his former fellow-villagers' suffering, but also with their joys and dreams. As early as "Kosachi" (1903; mowers) everyday "reality" is rejected; it is no match for E.'s *istina,* the reality of the creative imagination. His clergymen are not so much evil as inevitably human. So it is more as an idealist, even a romantic, that E. emerged in, for example, "Mechtateli" (1910; dreamers) and "Imyanari" (1921; treasure hunters), which stresses the beneficent power of illusion and poetic imagination. The latter is a prose-poem that later appeared in *Cherni rozi* (1928; black roses). These miniatures, along with E.'s many verse fantasies for children, fill four of the ten volumes of his collected works.

Lionized after World War II as a "living classic," E. wrote a final story, "Vrabchetata na strina Doyna" (1948; Auntie Doyna's wee sparrows), which views the new youth movement through a peasant woman's eyes as "bustling little sparrows." In "Kak pisha" (1949; how I write) he urged colleagues to transfer their attention from tractors to the men upon them, that is, to the inner world of the inhabitant of Bulgaria's rural regions, which was E.'s own consuming interest.

FURTHER WORKS: *Pepel ot tsigarite mi* (1905); *Ot prozoretsa* (1906); *Kitka za yunaka* (1907); *Gori tilileyski* (1919); *Tsar Shishko* (1925); *Yan Bibiyan* (1934); *Yan Bibiyan na lunata* (1934); *Subrani suchineniya* (10 vols., 1958–59)

BIBLIOGRAPHY: Pinto, V., "E. P. (1877–1949): Humanist of Shopsko," *SEER,* 41 (1962), 158–81; Moser, C. A., *A History of Bulgarian Literature, 865–1944* (1972), 185–93

VIVIAN PINTO

ELIOT, T(homas) S(tearns)

Anglo-American poet, b. 26 Sept. 1888, St. Louis, Mo.; d. 4 Jan. 1965, London, England

A descendant of Sir Thomas Elyot, the 16th-c. author of *The Boke Named the Governour*, and the grandson of William Greenleaf Eliot, the founder of Washington University in St. Louis, E. grew up in a family that prided itself upon its ancestors and took seriously its Unitarian faith. E.'s mother was especially influential upon him: his moral passion can be traced to her, as well as his intellectual energy, his obsession with the loss and restoration of grace, his industry, and even his interest in poetry. E. had difficulty in reconciling his poetic interest with the Eliot family tradition, however, and as a student at Harvard he fretted about the kind of practical career that his family would approve. Because his bachelor's degree in English and his master's degree in philosophy seemed to point toward an academic career, he completed his Ph.D. dissertation, *Experience and Objects of Knowledge in the Philosophy of F. H. Bradley* (published 1964), in 1916 while in residence at Oxford University. But E. chose not to return to Harvard to defend his dissertation: in response to the encouragements of Ezra Pound (q.v.), he decided to put academic ambitions aside and to concentrate on his poetry.

The family tradition, however, did not admit of E. starving in a garret. Thus, after one unhappy year teaching schoolboys, E. took a clerk's position in Lloyds Bank, a position which he found comfortable but which scandalized the literary world. In 1925 he left the bank and entered the London publishing firm of Faber & Gwyer (later Faber & Faber), where he remained happily until his death, very much the responsible man of business that his family would have respected, and decorous to a degree that approached self-caricature. Indeed, the Nobel Prize awarded E. in 1948 was probably testament not only to his literary achievement but also to his gentlemanly stance vis-à-vis the literary establishment.

But dramatic rebellions punctured the conformist surface of E.'s life and hint at ferments that the surface concealed. He affected religious skepticism as a young man, a rebellious posture in itself, yet in 1927 he capped years of scrupulosity and religious anguish by requesting baptism into the Anglican communion. Six months later, in an echoic gesture, he exchanged American for British citizenship. The most radical of his rebellions, however, was his sudden marriage in 1914 to the unstable Vivienne Haigh-Wood, a woman his family (and E. himself)

thought déclassé. The marriage turned out to be E.'s personal wasteland, and, as such, it was the emotional foundation of his major poetry. He separated from Vivienne in 1933 after nineteen grim years, and she died in a mental institution in 1947.

There were many literary influences on E. Preeminently, there was Ezra Pound, E.'s first sponsor and his poetic tutor. There was also Arthur Symons (1865–1945), whose *The Symbolist Movement in Literature* (1899) E. read in 1918. There was the French poet Jules Laforgue (1860–1887), whose verse showed E. how to play one voice against another with wit and self-mockery. There was Dante, a touchstone of personal success for E., and there were the late-Elizabethan and Jacobean dramatists, from whom he learned how to energize a poetic line. There was the British philosopher F. H. Bradley (1846–1924), whom E. admired for his ability to accept the disjunction between absolute truth and everyday experience, and there were the Christian mystics—Theresa of Ávila (1515–1582), Julian of Norwich (fl. 1416), Mme. Guyon (1648–1717), John of the Cross (1542–1591), Jakob Böhme (1575–1624), and Bernard of Clairvaux (1091–1153)—who revivified in him his mother's injunctions to spiritual transcendence. And there was the English prelate and scholar Lancelot Andrewes (1555–1626), whose gentle sermons moved him to religious assent.

Implicit in the conjunction of the decorous E. and these heroic influences is the hesitant stance that almost invariably characterizes E.'s poetry, for, in the language of his undergraduate poem "Spleen" (1910), E. tended to see "Life . . . Punctilious of tie and suit . . . On the doorstep of the Absolute." Certainly this stance is at the heart of E.'s first major poem, "The Love Song of J. Alfred Prufrock" (1917), in which the title character is paralyzed by self-consciousness and unable to step off the doorstep to "disturb the universe." Prufrock is not the pale personification of life that we find in "Spleen," however, but a vividly realized consciousness, tormented by the difficulty of articulating his complex feelings, harrowed by juxtapositions of himself with heroic figures, and cognizant that the you/I polarity of the traditional love song has become the ego/id polarity of himself. "Prufrock" is the single masterpiece of *Prufrock, and Other Observations* (1917), although many of the other poems in that first volume are admirable. "Portrait of a Lady" should be remarked for its masterful control of tone and inflection, and "Preludes" for its imagistic rendering of four units of urban experience, the four brought together at the end in a Bradleyan interpenetration of subject and object. "Preludes" should also be noted as an early example of an assemblage—an ingenious combination of fragments into a single poem. E.'s Yankee parsimony found this method of composition congenial, for it enabled him to make use of "found" quotations as well as previously discarded material, and the success he had with this approach in "Preludes" is an important step toward the construction of complex assemblages in his major poems.

The poems of E.'s second volume, *Ara Vos Prec* (1920; published in the U.S. as *Poems*), develop the dry and cynical strain of the *Prufrock* poems rather to excess, for the Sweeney poems and the religious satires in the volume bespeak not only the young poet's cleverness but also his inability to handle emotion in a substantive way. As a result the poems tend to be brittle and affected, and "Gerontion" is the only poem among them that is impressive. "Gerontion" is also the only poem in this collection that is in the mainstream of E.'s development: it anticipates *The Waste Land* (1922) in abandoning the vivid characterizations of the early dramatic monologues in favor of a generalized, abstract persona who functions as a cultural seismograph, and it tends to use allusions with the same density and complexity as the mature poetry.

The Waste Land is E.'s masterpiece; it is also the most celebrated poem of the 20th c., and it is probably the most famous assemblage in literary history as well. Divided into five sections, it is a series of fragmentary dramatic monologues that fade one into another, sometimes abruptly and sometimes imperceptibly. The effect suggests a dense chorus of voices, a kind of atonal polyphony, and that effect is underscored by numerous quotations and allusions. The unity of the poem is in its pervasive themes of sterility and disordered sexuality; the most powerful aspect of the poem, however, is its rendering of a collective consciousness, nominally belonging to Tiresias, that embraces all of the voices and holds them, meditatively, at its anguished core. E. had always an acute sense of the temper of his age and an instinctive knowledge of its proper symbols: he disclaimed any intention to do so, but the poem gave definitive expression to the doubts and uncertainties of the period, and it haunted its age as no other literary text.

In 1971 Valerie Fletcher, E.'s second wife and his former secretary, published a facsimile edition of the first version of *The Waste Land*, making clear the exact role that Ezra Pound had played in the poem's editing. Pound cut the manuscript poem almost in half, canceling great chunks of material (some anti-Semitic and misogynistic lines among them), and criticizing the rhythms and indecisiveness of some passages he retained. E. was unsure of the quality of his poem, and he accepted most of Pound's editing readily, much to the poem's improvement. It should not be assumed, however, that E. thought of the poem as final in the manuscript form he gave to Pound and that he would not himself have improved the poem substantially before publication. Indeed, it has been argued that Pound's greatest contribution to *The Waste Land* may have been his assurance, first to E., and then to the world, that the poem was a masterpiece.

Some overtly religious poems, reflective of E.'s conversion, followed *The Waste Land;* they are written in a less idiosyncratic style than the earlier poems and in a newly personal, almost confessional, tone. Foremost among these poems is "Ash-Wednesday" (1930), which depicts the doorstep stage of religious conversion as filled with difficulties and indecisions. Dantean and liturgical imagery give resonance to the crabbed twistings of the narrator's feelings, and lyrical interjections from the King James Bible and the *Book of Common Prayer* are juxtaposed with passages of tortured analysis in the chiaroscuric manner that is always E.'s best effect. "Journey of the Magi" (1927) and "A Song for Simeon" (1928) are straightforward dramatic monologues on the same theme of the convert's agony, both moving from realistic details and sentiments to inexplicable visions on the doorstep of the Absolute, and both are distinguished examples of their genre, although they do not rank with "Ash-Wednesday," which is at a point just below the achievement of *The Waste Land*.

The sequence of poems entitled *Four Quartets* (1943) is the great output of E.'s maturity. The sequence is composed of four, quite separate poems, each occasioned by a different landscape, and each poem is a prolonged meditation, alternating abstract, philosophical reflections with moments of lyricism, expressing thereby the hesitant, doorstep mentality that was E.'s essential subject. Uncharacteristically, however, the four meditations of the sequence end with a vision of total synthesis, as if the lifetime that E.'s characters had spent hesitating on the doorstep of the Absolute were finally over. Indeed, *Four Quartets* is in every sense the culmination of E.'s lifetime of work. The interwoven subjects of the meditations are his familiar ones—redemption, time, and history

—but they are approached now with a climactic intensity of thought. Finding its architecture in Beethoven's late quartets, the sequence also brings to culmination E.'s long-standing interest in the possibilities of musical form in poetry. The confessional strain that had been in the ascendancy in E.'s poetry since 1930 emerges with unprecedented clarity, and E. seems even to have echoed images and passages from his earlier work, as if through allusion to establish *Four Quartets* as the capstone of his poetic edifice. This deliberate effort to shape and crown the body of his poetry is not surprising on E.'s part, since he had long argued in terms of Dante and Shakespeare that an artist's greatness is measured by the unity of his lifetime's work. The artistic success of *Four Quartets* is very much disputed, however. For some readers, it is the greatest of E.'s works and one of the great poetic sequences of the 20th c.; for others, it is marred by strain and pretentiousness.

E.'s religious conversion resulted not only in his writing a newly public poetry, but in his writing poetic drama as well. Indeed, he wrote *The Rock* (1934 [the choruses only]) and *Murder in the Cathedral* (1935) at the suggestion of churchmen and for church performance. *The Family Reunion* (1939), *The Cocktail Party* (1950), *The Confidential Clerk* (1954), and *The Elder Statesman* (1959) were written for the commercial theater, but they are concerned, like their churchly predecessors, with the struggle for spiritual fulfillment in a world divided between the natural and the supernatural orders. E.'s theatrical notions were always more sophisticated than his theatrical instincts, however: his dramatic verse became increasingly indistinguishable from prose, and his attempt in his commercial plays to overlay drawing-room comedy with Greek tragedy is generally thought unsuccessful. His one play of genuine merit is the early *Murder in the Cathedral*. Its central situation is compelling; its chorus is used effectively to amplify the spiritual dimensions of the action; and both its poetry and its prose suit the dramatic medium very well. It overshadows all other attempts to write verse drama in English in the 20th c., and it compares favorably with most such attempts since the 17th c.

E. also enjoyed a notable career as a literary critic. As an assistant to the editor of *The Egoist*, as a reviewer for the *Times Literary Supplement*, and as editor of *The Criterion* from 1922 to 1939, he established a critical dictatorship, in fact, equal to that of Matthew Arnold in the 19th c. He employed no systematic critical method, but his magisterial tone, the intensity of his intelligence, the breadth of his standards for comparison and analysis, and his considerable gift for quotation gave weight to his judgments. His revaluations of such writers as Shakespeare, Milton, and Donne affected the mainstream of literary thought, even when his remarks were merely incidental, and his manner of linking cultural survival to literary distinctions gave a considerable urgency and a propagandist edge not only to his own criticism but to critical activity in general. His critical formulae—most notably the "objective correlative" and the "dissociation of sensibility"—have largely disappeared from the critical vocabulary, but his insistence that tradition is a living force in literature is still influential.

E. had a complex career, then, and he made an enduring mark for himself as a poet, as a dramatist, and as a critic. If his influence in the last categories now belongs to literary history, his major poetry remains vital, continuing to speak with eloquence of man hesitating on the doorstep of the Absolute, caught between his will to act and his terror of the abyss, fully knowing his dilemma and fully recognizing his neurosis, and yet unable to take the step that promises life.

FURTHER WORKS: *Poems* (1920); *The Sacred Wood* (1920); *Homage to John Dryden* (1924); *Poems 1909–1925* (1925); *Selected Essays 1917–1932* (1932); *The Use of Poetry and the Use of Criticism* (1933); *After Strange Gods* (1934); *Elizabethan Essays* (1934); *Collected Poems 1909–1935* (1936); *The Idea of a Christian Society* (1939); *Old Possum's Book of Practical Cats* (1939); *Notes towards the Definition of Culture* (1948); *Selected Essays* (1950); *Poetry and Drama* (1951); *The Complete Poems and Plays* (1952; enl. ed., 1962); *On Poetry and Poets* (1957); *Essays on Poetry and Criticism* (1959); *Collected Plays* (1962); *Collected Poems 1909–1962* (1963); *To Criticize the Critic, and Other Writings* (1965); *Poems Written in Early Youth* (1967)

BIBLIOGRAPHY: Matthiessen, F. O., *The Achievement of T. S. E.* (1935); Drew, E., *T. S. E.: The Design of His Poetry* (1949); Gardner, H., *The Art of T. S. E.* (1950); Maxwell, D. E. S., *The Poetry of T. S. E.* (1952); Smith, G., *T. S. E.'s Poetry and Plays* (1957); Kenner, H., *The Invisible Poet: T. S. E.* (1959); Smith, C. H., *T. S. E.'s Dramatic Theory and Practice* (1963); Howarth, H., *Notes on Some Figures Behind T. S. E.*

(1964); Unger, L., *T. S. E.: Moments and Patterns* (1966); Tate, A., ed., *T. S. E.: The Man and His Work* (1967); Martin, G., ed., *E. in Perspective* (1970); Kirk, R., *E. and His Age* (1971); Patterson, G., *T. S. E.: Poems in the Making* (1971); Bergonzi, B., *T. S. E.* (1972); Litz, A. W., ed., *E. in His Time* (1973); Schneider, E., *T. S. E.: The Pattern in the Carpet* (1975); Traversi, D., *T. S. E.: The Longer Poems* (1976); Gordon, L., *E.'s Early Years* (1977); Gardner, H., *The Composition of "Four Quartets"* (1978); Freed, L., *T. S. E.: The Critic as Philosopher* (1979)

ROBERT F. KIERNAN

More than one critic has remarked that in E. the over-all organization of the poem as a whole is not lyrical in any recognizable and traditional way; nor is the poem organized in terms of narrative; nor is it dramatic in the literal theatrical sense; and it is certainly not logical, argumentative, or expository. . . . Where poets in the past would have used a logical, emotional, dramatic, or narrative basis for the transition from part to part, E. uses some one of these kinds of transition freely and alternatively and without committing himself to any one of them or to any systematic succession of them; or he omits the connection between one passage and the next, one part and the part which succeeds it. . . . The characteristic over-all organization of the poem—of which "The Waste Land" is the vividest example—can be called, for the lack of a better phrase, that of sibylline (or subliminal) listening.

Delmore Schwartz, "T. S. E.'s Voice and His Voices," *Poetry*, 85 (1955), 236–37

The image of structural unity pervades E.'s social and literary criticism. What of his own poetry? Is he able to reach his goal of organic unity and write poems which live because they share the life of the European mind?

Most of E.'s poems depend on the assumption that the poet can enlarge his private consciousness to coincide with a collective consciousness. This assumption is so easily and persuasively sustained that it is easy to forget what an extraordinary arrogation of power it is. Only a few early poems, such as "Prufrock" or "Portrait of a Lady," are limited to the perspective of a single ego. In most poems the reader is placed within everybody's mind at once. An act of self-surrender has expanded the private mind of the poet into the universal sphere of the mind of Europe. It may take long years of hard work to assimilate the riches of that mind, but this is now the exploration of an inner space, not the effort to comprehend something other than the self.

J. Hillis Miller, *Poets of Reality* (1965), p. 172

. . . It seems to me that the more we see of the hidden side of E. the more he seems to resemble Milton, though he thought of Milton as a polar opposite. As we look at all the contraries reconciled in E.—his schismatic traditionalism, his romantic classicism, his highly personal impersonality—we are prepared for the surprise (which E. himself seems in some measure to have experienced) of finding in the dissenting Whig regicide a hazy mirror-image of the Anglo-Catholic royalist. Each, having prepared himself carefully for poetry, saw that he must also, living in such times, explore prose, the cooler element. From a consciously archaic standpoint each must characterize the activities of the sons of Belial. Each saw that fidelity to tradition is ensured by revolutionary action. . . . Each knew the difficulty of finding "answerable style" in an age too late. With the Commonwealth an evident failure, Milton wrote one last book to restore it, and as the élites crumbled and reformed E. wrote his *Notes [towards the Definition of Culture]*. If Milton killed a king, E. attacked vulgar democracy and shared with the "men of 1914" and with Yeats some extreme authoritarian opinions.

Frank Kermode, "A Babylonish Dialect," *SR*, 74 (1966), 228–29

It won't be easy to reclaim his work from the conceptual and scholarly currency already invested in it. It will mean forcing ourselves to forget most of what exegesis has burdened us with, and it will mean returning for help to those very few difficult critics I've mentioned [Leavis, Blackmur, Kenner], all of whom have insisted, to almost no effect, on E.'s deliberate irrationality. In trying to release E. from schematizations contrived mostly for the clarification and boredom of undergraduates, these, and a few others, direct us away from the seductions of neatness and into the wonderful mystery at the center of E.'s poetry and criticism. What we find there, if we stay long enough, is that for E. ideas have no more organizational power than do literary allusions and that neither is as preoccupying as are the furtive memories and hallucinations, the sensuous images that stimulate a poem like "Preludes" but which remain at the end as unassimilated to any design as they were at the beginning.

Richard Poirier, "T. S. E. and the Literature of Waste," *NR*, 20 May 1967, 19–20

. . . What set [E.] apart from the hesitant desiccated figure that he drew of [Henry] Adams was precisely the quality of his sensuous perceptions, his awareness of the abyss and the deepest terrors and desires, and his familiarity with the lonely, painful act of creation. As a poet E. was solitary and unaffected by being culturally institutionalized. If he is less significant now as a force for literary orthodoxy, this is irrelevant to his true

T. S. ELIOT

PAUL ÉLUARD

ODYSSEUS ELYTIS

stature as a poet; when the cultural idol has been displaced the voice of the poet may be heard more clearly. If that voice is to go on being listened to, as I believe it will, the present decline in E.'s reputation may be both inevitable and salutary. Future readers will acknowledge E.'s genius, but they will see different things in him from his first readers, and from ourselves. All of which, we may be sure, he would have calmly understood and welcomed.

Bernard Bergonzi, *T. S. E.* (1972), p. 192

Prufrock was solitary, knew that he was, accepted essential character as fate, and looked forward in resignation to an unchanging life. The rather more vital man behind Prufrock, instead, ventured out into the world of human beings, of sex, of external insecurity; found it bitter; said so by projections of disgust bordering on horrors, getting back at the human race through the Burbanks and Bleisteins and pimpled adolescents, taking refuge in the exercise of technical skill and ingenuities of mosaic constructions; found refuge and a function for himself in concern with theories of "tradition" and "unity of culture," and satisfaction in the role (even in youth) of society's elder critic; found the darkened spirit could still create by looking outward upon a waste land of moral and emotional distortions, a world of the heartless and the irresponsible, which might—just might—be saved by the cultivation of human decency ("give, sympathize, control"). But this proves after all no solution. . . . A renewed Christianity becomes the one hope: for the world at large a discipline and perhaps a way of devotion; for the solitary self these, and also a human relationship, acceptable perhaps because less individual than institutional, relieving solitude without invading it.

Elisabeth Schneider, *T. S. E.: The Pattern in the Carpet* (1975), pp. 210–211

At each stage of his career E. defined his identity and measured his distance from enlightenment. There was, in his poetry, a persistent self-portraiture—from the languid, well-dressed gentleman in "Spleen," who waited impatiently on the doorstep of the Absolute, to Prufrock, whose impulse to assault the universe with a prophetic truth beat beneath his anxiously correct façade; and from the phantom pilgrim searching the city for a miraculous cure for depression to the anxious penitent patiently climbing the purgatorial stair. One developing personality redefined, in each poem, the position won in the previous poem. From the start, E. was preoccupied with his own special fate, but he was uncertain how to characterize himself. He sensed his identity as a "shadow of its own shadows, spectre in its own gloom." E. haunted his poems like an irresolute ghost seeking shape and form and visible role. When at length he was sure of his best self, he suddenly revealed a preacher,

his outlines distinct, his feet firmly planted on an Anglican platform.

Lyndall Gordon, *E.'s Early Years* (1977), p. 138

ELIZONDO, Salvador

Mexican novelist, short-story writer, and essayist, b. 19 Dec. 1932, Mexico City

After having completed his secondary education in Mexico City, E. studied philosophy and literature in France, Germany, Italy, England, Canada, and the U.S. He has produced experimental films and contributed to numerous Mexican journals. He is now professor of literature at the National University in Mexico City.

E. first attracted the attention of a sophisticated reading public with *Farabeuf; o, La crónica de un instante* (1965; Farabeuf; or, the account of one moment). An experiment in narrative technique with virtually no antecedent in Mexican literature, this disconcerting antinovel attempts to capture a climactic moment of orgasm and death. The characters are Dr. Farabeuf (a fictionalized version of a 19th-c. French anatomist) and his mistress, a woman of shifting identities whom we suspect he is preparing to dissect alive. The themes of eroticism and sadism are intensified by a style reminiscent of the French New Novel (q.v.), which presents reality not in terms of logical cause-and-effect relationships but rather as fleeting sensations produced by the perception of opaque objects. Repeated in kaleidoscopic patterns, these sharply defined images give the impression of a haunting, surrealistic dream.

El hipogeo secreto (1968; the secret hypogeum) is based on the philosophy of Ludwig Wittgenstein (1889–1951), who states that the limits of language coincide with the limits of the world and, consequently, that language has no meaning when applied to metaphysics. Like *Farabeuf*, this novel relies on the juxtaposition of poetic images to convey a semblance of plot, the essence of which in this case is the psychic tension experienced by an author as he attempts to create his work of art. His failure to reach the ideal city he is seeking implies that both esthetic perfection and absolute truth are unattainable.

Narda; o, El verano (1966; Narda; or, summertime) is a collection of deftly structured tales conveying a wide range of themes and moods. The erotic adventures of amoral youths vacationing on the Italian Riviera are described in the title story, which can be read as a pastiche of "new wave" European films. In "En la playa" (on the beach) the absurd human experience is dramatized by a terrified fat man's flight from an implacable enemy, a symbol of the senseless but inevitable fate threatening all mortals. Philosophical idealism emerges as the basic ingredient of "La historia según Pao Cheng" (history according to Pao Cheng) when the protagonist discovers that his existence depends on being perceived by another.

E. is one of Latin America's talented young writers who have taken their cue from Jorge Luis Borges (q.v.). But although E. shares many of Borges's literary and philosophical preoccupations, he has developed his own distinctive mode of expression.

FURTHER WORKS: *Poemas* (1960); *Luchino Visconti* (1963); *Nuevos escritores mexicanos del siglo XX presentados por sí mismos: S. E.* (1966); *El retrato de Zoe, y otras mentiras* (1969); *El grafógrafo* (1972); *Contextos* (1973); *Antología personal* (1974)

BIBLIOGRAPHY: Carballo, E., "Prólogo," *Nuevos escritores mexicanos del siglo XX presentados por sí mismos: S. E.* (1966), pp. 5–12; McMurray, G. R., "S. E.'s *Farabeuf*," *Hispania*, 50 (1967), 596–600; McMurray, G. R., "S. E.'s *El hipogeo secreto*," *Hispania*, 53 (1970), 330–34; Langford, W. M., *The Mexican Novel Comes of Age* (1971), pp. 192–94; Durán, M., *Tríptico mexicano: Juan Rulfo, Carlos Fuentes, S. E.* (1973), pp. 134–73; Foster, D. W., and Foster, V. R., eds., "S. E.," *Modern Latin American Literature* (1975), Vol. I, pp. 320–23; Larson, R., *Fantasy and Imagination in the Mexican Narrative* (1977), pp. 45–49, 70–71, 87–88

GEORGE R. MCMURRAY

ELLISON, Ralph

American novelist and critic, b. 1 March 1914, Oklahoma, City, Okla.

Three years after E.'s birth his father died, and thereafter his mother supported herself and her child by working as a domestic. While growing up, E. met and became friendly with a number of jazz musicians playing in Oklahoma City and began to perform on the trumpet while in high school. He studied music at Tuskegee Institute in Alabama from 1933 to 1936, when he dropped out to pursue a career in the visual arts. From Alabama he moved to New York City; there chance meetings with Langston Hughes (q.v.), and later with Richard Wright

(q.v.), led to his first attempts at fiction. E. participated in the Federal Writers' Project, and his stories and essays appeared in *New Masses* and other periodicals. After service in the Merchant Marine (1943–45) he won a Rosenwald Fellowship (1945). After the publication of *Invisible Man* (1952) E. received many honors, including a National Book Award (1953), the National Newspaper Publishers' Award (1954), a fellowship at the American Academy in Rome (1955–57), and the Medal of Freedom (1969). He was appointed to the American Institute of Arts and Letters in 1964, and has been a Consultant in American Letters to the Library of Congress. Since 1970 E. has been Albert Schweitzer Professor in the Humanities at New York University.

E.'s only novel published to date, *Invisible Man*, has become a classic. A *Book Week* poll of artists and critics cited it as "the most significant work of fiction written by an American" between 1945 and 1965. *Invisible Man* tells the story of the adolescent and adult search for identity of a young black man who remains, throughout the novel, nameless. Enduring a series of picaresque adventures—by turns comic, satirical, agonizing, absurd, and deadly—the protagonist discovers emphatically who he is not; he undertakes a progress *away* from all the seductive and false identities offered to him and finds himself ultimately moving away from identity itself. The dramatic episodes that illuminate this unique character development have been chosen with brilliant care: they are a compendium of nearly all the inept, humiliating stereotypes with which American society has saddled black men.

Best known of the scenes from *Invisible Man* is the widely anthologized "Battle Royal," which begins the novel. It shows the young protagonist as one of a dozen half-naked, blindfolded young black men boxing in a ring for the entertainment of a white men's club. Battered, terrified, and degraded at the end of the match, the invisible man is singled out for special attention and rewards, and is asked to give his high school commencement speech about Negro social responsibility. When he slips, substituting the word "equality" for "responsibility," he is momentarily threatened, but avoids punishment by apologizing, with the excuse that he was "swallowing blood." Similarly ironic vignettes and exchanges appear throughout the novel, showing the invisible man as a master of the sly macabre.

At the novel's end its hero makes an absurd, surrealistic, and telling choice for his life: he takes up residence in a cavern beneath the city's surface, a secret hole, which he furnishes with 1,369 light bulbs powered by an illegal tap into the nearby lines of the Monopolated Light and Power Company, and waits to see how he might be reborn.

Shadow and Act (1964) is a work of criticism and an intellectual autobiography; it has been acclaimed almost as universally as *Invisible Man*. Its critical eye ranges over a wide spectrum of literary experience, focusing on what is central to the artistic vision of, among many others, Melville, Mark Twain, Conrad (q.v.), Faulkner (q.v.), and Eliot (q.v.). E. invariably sees in the works of masters a profound social and human concern that may be located in, but is never limited to, the metaphor and fact of race. In his criticism, as in his fiction, E. uses racial issues to express something more than social awareness: the particular dilemma of race is an external manifestation of a universal dilemma which is inward, or spiritual, and which is the source of the external problem.

Irving Howe (q.v.) and other critics have expressed disappointment at E.'s refusal to write works of overt social consciousness and radical protest. He has frequently been called an "Uncle Tom" because of this propensity, and has responded by insisting that the task of becoming fully human—the artist's central task —requires "a discipline far more demanding than loyalty to a racial group."

E. is at work on a second novel, from which many selections have been published as short stories. Although his short stories and criticism are superbly vivid and intelligent, it is finally on *Invisible Man* that E.'s reputation rests. As both artist and critic, E. has successfully avoided the pigeonhole of black writer, a term he sees as laden with condescension far more damaging than the limited aesthetic boundaries it implies. An ironic idealist, able to describe powerfully what should be and what is, and to hold the two in balance, E. has been compared to writers such as Melville and Hawthorne more often than to black American writers. He has identified in the plight of American blacks a universal predicament, a universal alienation transcending petty categories.

FURTHER WORKS: *The Writer's Experience* (1964, with Karl Shapiro)

BIBLIOGRAPHY: Littlejohn, D., *Black on White: A Critical Survey of Writing by American Negroes* (1966), pp. 109–16; Bluestein, G., "The Blues as a Literary Theme," *MR*, 8 (1967), 593–617; special E. issue, *CLAJ*, 13, 3 (1970); Gottesman, R., ed., *Studies in "Invisible Man"* (1971); Covo, J., *The Blinking Eye: R. W. E. and His American, French, German, and Italian Critics, 1952–1971* (1974); Gray, V., *"Invisible Man"'s Literary Heritage: "Benito Cereno" and "Moby-Dick"* (1978); O'Meally, R. G., *The Craft of R. E.* (1980)

LARRY TEN HARMSEL

ELSSCHOT, Willem

(pseud. of Alphonsus Josephus de Ridder) Belgian novelist (writing in Flemish), b. 7 May 1882, Antwerp; d. 31 May 1960, Antwerp

E. grew up in a middle-class urban environment. After having been expelled from school at the age of sixteen, he worked as an errand boy, but afterward he made up for his lost years and obtained a certificate in business, consular, and colonial science from the Higher Institute of Business Science. He went to Paris, where he was employed by a South American businessman. He subsequently worked in various businesses in the Netherlands, but in 1911 he returned to Belgium, settling in Brussels, where he was a bookkeeper. At the outbreak of World War I E. fled with his family to Antwerp, where he remained for the rest of his life, earning his living as the owner of a publicity agency.

E. began his literary career in 1900 by writing romantic, idealistic poems. However, his poems were not published in book form until 1934, in *Verzen van vroeger* (poems of long ago). Most probably because of his experiences in Paris and his business involvements in the Netherlands, E. became cynical. He wrote several novels, which were practically ignored by the critics as well as by the public. The first one, *Villa des roses* (written 1910, pub. 1913; villa of the roses), depicts E.'s Paris years. The main subject, the relation between the cynical boarder Grünewald and the naïve chambermaid Louise is drawn against the background of the bleak boardinghouse in which each person feels lonely and depressed.

Een ontgoocheling (written 1914, pub. 1921; a deception) tells the story of a proud father who wants his son to become a lawyer. The boy, however, is not the studious type and must drop out of school. He holds different jobs but is never quite accepted by his colleagues. Still, although the son is not unhappy, the father becomes increasingly depressed. He loses faith not only in his son but also in himself when he is not reelected president of his card club. The story contains many reminiscences of the author's youth.

Lijmen (1924; *Soft Soap*, 1965) presents the characters Boorman and Laarmans, who reappear in several of E.'s later novels. Boorman is the shrewd businessman, hard as nails and seemingly the personification of the crass world of the publicity business. Laarmans is the sensitive type, forced into business in order to make a living. His pity for deceived customers is a business liability. Boorman and Laarmans most likely express the two sides of the author's personality. E. was a tough businessman, but also a sensitive, dreamy poet, who warmly sympathized with those suffering from illness, old age, loneliness, or poverty; he pointed with sarcasm to the weak spots in a capitalistic society, represented by Boorman, for whom money is more important than happiness.

For ten years after *Lijmen* E. did not publish anything. Then he was "discovered" by two young Dutch writers, Jan Greshoff (1888–1971) and Menno ter Braak (q.v.), who published ten of his early poems in their literary journal *Forum*. Their favorable reception encouraged E. to write again, and in hardly a month's time he finished his novel *Kaas* (1933; cheese). In this book Laarmans is talked into entering a wholesale business in cheese, but the enterprise fails. Laarmans is too honest and scrupulous. He ends by returning to the routine of his office job, feeling secure and protected in the midst of his family.

Tsjip (1934; Tsjip), one of his best works, is based on members of his own family. Adèle, the oldest daughter, marries a Polish student and follows him to his native country. Shortly after her baby is born, she leaves her husband and returns home with her son. When the child is in Poland for a visit, his father does not seem inclined to send him back. But Adèle fetches the boy and takes him home. Here the principal part of the novel begins: the description of the relation between grandfather and grandson and the influence they have on one another.

E.'s last novel, *Het dwaallicht* (1946; *Will-o'-the-Wisp*, 1956), is his masterpiece. This time Laarmans appears without his counterpart Boorman. With three Afghan sailors he looks for a girl, Maria, wandering through Antwerp on a drizzly November night. It is an adventure for him, and for a moment he feels free from all conventional ties. But then he returns to the routine of his family life.

E. is one of the best novelists Flanders has produced. He pictures the average middle-class citizen with his sorrows and his small joys, and pays especial attention to the distress people cause each other. He looks at human life and loneliness with a melancholy smile and expresses himself in extremely clear and matter-of-fact language. His works have been reprinted many times and remain popular today.

FURTHER WORKS: *De verlossing* (1921); *Pensioen* (1937); *Het been* (1938; *The Leg*, 1965); *Het tankschip* (1941); *De leeuwentemmer* (1943); *Verzameld werk*, 2nd ed. (1976); *Zwijgen kan niet verbeterd worden* (1979)

BIBLIOGRAPHY: on *Three Novels: Soft Soap; The Leg; Will-o'-the-Wisp*, TLS, 3 March 1966, 157; Clements, R. J., on *Three Novels*, SatR, 2 July 1966, 23; Meijer, R. P., *Literature of the Low Countries*, new ed. (1978), pp. 334–36

JUDICA I. H. MENDELS

ÉLUARD, Paul

(pseud. of Eugène Grindel) French poet, b. 13 Dec. 1895, Saint-Denis; d. 18 Nov. 1952, Charenton-le-Pont

É. came from a lower-middle-class background: his father was a bookkeeper, his mother a dressmaker. In 1908 É. had to interrupt his studies in Paris and spend two years in a Swiss sanitarium for treatment of tuberculosis. During World War I he served in the infantry. Soon after his discharge he met three major Dadaists (q.v.): Tristan Tzara, Louis Aragon, and André Breton (qq.v.). A founding member of the surrealist (q.v.) movement, É. became politically involved in the 1930s, when he joined the Communist Party. During World War II he actively participated in the Resistance. After the war his political activity took on an international flavor, for he participated in several peace conferences, particularly in Communist-bloc countries.

É., considered one of the most eminent of 20th-c. poets, favored the short lyric. In his verse and prose poems, he eschewed grandiloquence, the artifices of rhetoric, traditional prosody, and syntactical complexity. Unlike the other surrealists, he did not break with the lyricism of the past, as evidenced by the title of one of his major volumes, *Poésie ininterrompue* (1946; uninterrupted poetry), where he proclaims his faith in the continuous presence of poetry and in its power to unite what time and space have torn asunder. When the poet, whether by personal recollection or through other texts, rediscovers a state of consciousness belonging to the past, he endeavors to make it present, to rejuvenate it. He aims at a state of Edenic purity capable of shaping a future devoid of oppression. Nonetheless, É. continued to share the surrealist belief in the need for revolution, and identified with their struggle for political, social, and sexual liberation.

According to É., the mission of poetry was to renew language in order to effect radical changes in all areas of existence. He envisioned the writing of poetry as an action capable of arousing awareness in his readers and of leading them to more purposeful activities.

Several chronological phases can be distinguished in E.'s creative activity: (1) a Dadaist phase, characterized by the enigmatic and subversive texts of *Répétitions* (1922; repetitions); (2) a surrealist period, rich in paradoxical imagery and dream exploration, as exemplified in *Capitale de la douleur* (1926; *Capital of Pain*, 1973); (3) an interlude marked by overt political advocacy, as expressed in *Cours naturel* (1936; natural course), about the Spanish Civil War, and *Poésie et vérité 1942* (1942; *Poetry and Truth, 1942*, 1944), about the Resistance; (4) a final development showing a greater awareness of the mysteries of poetic creation, exemplified in *Le phénix* (1952; the phoenix). But these chronological divisions, however convenient, do not go very far, because the fundamental unity and continuity of E.'s poetic output is undeniable.

Indeed, a dominant theme resounds through all his poetry: love in all its universality. Although he may have addressed his poems to specific women—Gala, Nusch, and Dominique —he unhesitantly transcends the particular. This tendency to universalize individual experience or to use it as a bridge to knowledge appears in its most intense form in *La vie immédiate* (1932; immediate existence), where, however idealized, woman becomes a physical presence whose sexuality is fully acknowledged. Her eyes, her lips, her breasts metonymically stand for her mysterious powers where the poet can discover his own true identity. Woman performs as a liberating force, capable of detaching the poet from the false bonds of the everyday world and the irrelevant chains of memory. Thanks to her mediation, he can transgress boundaries, overcome distances, experience communion. Love for É. was indissociably linked to hope and affirmation. Contemplation and gestures become simultaneous, just

as the object of love and the lover ultimately become fused. The woman provides the focal point of new, unlimited images, capable of regenerating the world by transcending both time and space. In this new realm, expressed by images of growth and fertility, contradictions become impossible, and innocence is regained. As dream becomes reality, the intense poetic web spreads ever wider. Like other surrealists, É. transforms the world of objects, which by becoming more nebulous and undefinable lend themselves to unexpected associations.

É.'s love lyrics do not separate the lover and his beloved from the rest of the world, for their love provides the best way to reach universal solidarity and to assure humanity's significance in the universe. Similarily, the political poems reiterate a message of peace and hope for all mankind, by calling for brotherhood and relief of suffering.

In É.'s poetry, the ever-present eye encompasses the outer world while giving physical presence to an even more intense inner vision. Not surprisingly, painting, which is both vision and spectacle, stands out as a source of inspiration second only to love. *Donner à voir* (1939; offering to sight) and *Voir* (1948; to see) consist of poetic texts devoted to contemporary painters, particularly Picasso and Max Ernst. By adding word to line and color, by recuperating their vibrations, É. creates a new experience for his readers. At the same time, he affirms his solidarity with other artists. In his monumental *Anthologie des écrits sur l'art* (1952–54; anthology of writings on art) he shows the same uninterrupted continuity in the visual arts that he had found in poetry. É. strove to abolish the barrier between the "seeing" subject and the "perceived" object. In his universe, "to see," "to know," "to be" ultimately become synonymous when the poet tries to reduce to transparency even the most tenacious opaqueness. Painting, like poetry, according to É., was destined to disseminate truth belonging to both the real and the imaginary. É., especially in his later years, saw a political destiny for art, which should be made available and relevant to all.

Throughout his career he had frequently collaborated with painters in the creation of illustrated books. With Man Ray he produced *Facile* (1935; easy), consisting of love poems where text and image combine in the celebration of woman, where the contours of the printed word and the photographs harmonize. With Ernst he created *Les malheurs des immortels* (1922; *Misfortunes of the Immortals*, 1943). There, the satirical verbal collages, in which both the poet and the painter collaborated, constantly interfere with their plastic collages so as to produce simultaneous movements of attraction and repulsion.

É., eager to suppress the barriers between individual consciousnesses, collaborated with André Breton in writing *L'Immaculée Conception* (1930; the Immaculate Conception) and in composing with René Char (q.v.) and Breton *Ralentir travaux* (1930; slow down work).

É.'s most remarkable achievement would seem to consist in his repeated efforts to eliminate the barriers between intimacy and the problems of the community, between the outside world and inner visions, between verbal and plastic art, efforts that have resulted in an eternal poetry whose appeal will never be lost.

FURTHER WORKS: *Premiers poèmes* (1913); *Dialogues des inutiles* (1914); *Le devoir* (1916); *Le devoir et l'inquiétude* (1917); *Poèmes pour la paix* (1918); *Les animaux et leurs hommes, les hommes et leurs animaux* (1920); *Les nécessités de la vie et les conséquences des rêves* (1921); *Mourir de ne pas mourir* (1924); *152 proverbes mis au goût du jour* (1925); *Au défaut du silence* (1925); *Les dessous d'une vie ou la pyramide humaine* (1926); *Défense du savoir* (1928); *L'amour la poésie* (1929); *A toute épreuve* (1930); *Dors* (1931); *Certificat* (1932); *Comme deux gouttes d'eau* (1933); *La rose publique* (1934); *Nuits partagées* (1935); *Le front couvert* (1936); *Notes sur la poésie* (1936, with André Breton); *La barre d'appui* (1936); *Les yeux fertiles* (1936); *L'evidence poétique* (1937); *Avenir de la poésie* (1937); *Premiéres vues anciennes* (1937); *Les mains libres* (1937); *Appliquée* (1937); *Quelques-uns des mots qui jusqu'ici m'étaient mystérieusement interdits* (1937); *Dictionnaire abrégé du surréalisme* (1938, with André Breton); *Solidarité* (1938); *Facile proie* (1938); *Ode à Salvador Dali* (1938); *Chanson complète* (1939); *Médieuses* (1939); *Charles Baudelaire* (1939); *Jeux vagues la poupée* (1939); *Le livre ouvert I* (1940); *Blason des fleurs et des fruits* (1940); *Divers poèmes du livre ouvert* (1941); *Moralité du sommeil* (1941); *Choix de poèmes* (1941); *Sur les pentes inférieures* (1941); *Le livre ouvert II* (1942); *La dernière nuit* (1942); *Poésie involontaire et poésie intentionnelle* (1942); *Les sept poèmes d'amour en guerre* (1943); *Pour vivre ici* (1944); *Le lit la table* (1944); *Les armes de la douleur* (1944); *Dignes de vivre* (1944); *Quelques mots rassemblés pour Monsieur Dubuffet* (1944); *Liberté* (1944); *Au rendez-vous*

allemand (1944); *À Pablo Picasso* (1944; *Pablo Picasso*, 1947); *En avril 1944: Paris respirait encore!* (1945); *Doubles d'ombre* (1945); *Lingères légères* (1945); *Une longue réflexion amoureuse* (1945); *Le vœu* (1945); *Souvenirs de la maison des fous* (1946); *Le dur désir de durer* (1946); *Figure humaine* (1946); *Objet des mots et des images* (1947); *Elle se fit élever un palais* (1947); *Le temps déborde* (1947); *Marc Chagall* (1947); *Corps mémorable* (1947); *Deux poètes d'aujourd'hui* (1947); *Le meilleur choix de poèmes est celui que l'on fait pour soi* (1947); *À l'intérieur de la vue* (1948); *Gabriel Péri* (1948); *Premiers poèmes* (1948); *Poèmes politiques* (1948); *Le bestiaire* (1948); *Perspectives* (1949); *Léda* (1949); *La saison des amours* (1949); *Grèce ma rose de raison* (1949); *Je l'aime, elle m'aimait* (1949); *Une leçon de morale* (1949); *Hommage aux martyrs et aux combattants du ghetto de Varsovie* (1950); *Pouvoir tout dire* (1951); *Un poème* (1951); *Première anthologie vivante de la poésie du passé* (1951); *La jarre peut-elle être plus belle que l'eau?* (1951); *Le visage de la paix* (1951); *Grain-d'aile* (1951); *Picasso, dessins* (1952); *Marines* (1952); *Les sentiers et les routes de la poésie* (1952); *Poèmes pour tous* (1952); *Œuvres complètes* (2 vols. plus *Album É.*, 1968). FURTHER VOLUMES IN ENGLISH: *Thorns of Thunder* (1936); *Selected Writings* (1951); *Last Love Poems of P. É.* (1980; bilingual ed.)

BIBLIOGRAPHY: Balakian, A. "The Post-Surrealism of Aragon and É.," *YFS*, 2 (1948), 93–102; Poulet, G., *Études sur le temps humain* (1964), Vol. 3, pp. 126–60; Richard J.-P., *Onze études sur la poésie moderne* (1964), pp. 105–39; Jean, R., *P. É. par lui-même* (1968); Wake, C. H., "É.: 'L'extase,'" in Nurse, P., ed., *The Art of Criticism* (1969), pp. 287–99; Vernier, R., *"Poésie ininterrompue" et la poétique de P. É.* (1971); Greet, A. H., "P. É.'s Early Poems for Painters," *FMLS*, 9 (1973), 86–102; Hubert, R. R., "Ernst and É., a Model of Surrealist Collaboration," *KRQ*, 21 (1974), 113–21; Nugent, R., *P. É.* (1974); Bowie, M., "P. É.," in Cardinal, R., ed., *Sensibility and Creation* (1977), pp. 149–67

RENÉE RIESE HUBERT

ELYTIS, Odysseus

(pseud. of Odysseus Alepoudhelis) Greek poet and art critic, b. 2 Nov. 1911, Heraklion, Crete

Although E. was born on Crete, his parents and ancestors came from the island of Lesbos, with which he feels close emotional and cultural ties. His family settled in Athens in 1914; in his youth E. studied law at the University of Athens, but never graduated. In 1929 his reading of the poetry of Paul Éluard (q.v.) initiated his decisive commitment to surrealism (q.v.), which was further stimulated by his friendship with the Greek poet Andreas Embirikos (1901–1975), who introduced surrealism to Greek poetry. E. made his first appearance in the periodical *Nea grammata,* the harbinger of the Greek poetic renascence, in 1936. To the tragic conscience of modern Greece as then projected by the poetry of George Seferis (q.v.), E.'s extraordinary lyrical gifts were to counterpose that country's eternal youthfulness and natural and spiritual beauty, and would exert a salutary and liberating influence upon a literature that had long stagnated in postsymbolist decadence and despair.

In 1940–41, to defend his country from the attack of Italian Fascism, he served as second lieutenant on the Albanian front. In 1945–46 and again in 1953–54 he was director of broadcasting and programming for the National Broadcasting Institute in Athens. From 1948 to 1952 he studied literature at the Sorbonne in Paris, traveled in Europe, and became friends with André Breton, Tristan Tzara, René Char, Pierre Jean Jouve, Henri Michaux, Giuseppe Ungaretti (qq.v.), Éluard, Matisse, Picasso, and other outstanding modernists in literature and art. An art critic and a painter himself, he has produced illustrations of his poetic world in gouaches and collages. From 1953 to 1958 he served as member of the Greek critical and prize-awarding Group of the Twelve, and as president and governing-board member of Karolos Koun's Art Theater and of the Greek Ballet. In 1960 he was awarded the First National Prize for Poetry, and from 1965 to 1968 he served as a member of the administrative board of the Greek National Theater. In 1962 the Greek Government made him Commander of the Order of the Phoenix. During the regime of the military junta in his country he settled once again in France, from 1969 to 1971. He won the Nobel Prize for literature in 1979, and has been awarded a number of honorary degrees.

Widely known and popular since his early verse as the "poet of the Aegean," E. has been the dominant lyrical voice of that sunlit realm —with its sea and islands under a pure blue sky —where he was born, grew up, and still spends most of his summers. "Adapting surrealism to Greek reality" (E.'s own words) through sub-

mitting the liberating force in that movement to the high discipline of a constantly experimenting, exploring, and developing art, he has mostly created in his verse a world of lucidity, purity, balance, beauty, newness, youth, and love as inspired and inspirited by, as E. has said, the "sanctity of the perceiving senses" and that of the natural world itself. His primary concern for the Greek language as it has developed since Homer's time led to his expressive richness, while the scintillating freshness of his imagery is drawn from the ancient birthplace of the Ionian-Greek culture, where the sun, as life-giving sovereign, reigns supreme, penetrating and revealing with its light the physical yet mystical essence of life: man is inseparable from nature, since in both of them the eternal processes of Eros as inspired by beauty are carried on. A feast of the senses, his early poetry as gathered in his first collection, *Prosanatolizmi* (1939; *Orientations,* 1974), has careless young boys and girls initiated into and communing with the power of love in nature's eternal elements and processes.

The war brought a cloud of painful awareness, of maturity, into his sunlit realm, as seen in his collection *Ilios of Protos, mazi me tis parallayies se mian ahtidha* (1943; *Sun the First, together with Variations of a Sunbeam,* 1974). But the war experience found its outstanding expression in *Azma iroiko ke penthimo yia ton hameno anthipolohagho tis Alvanias* (1945; *Heroic and Elegiac Song for the Lost Second Lieutenant of the Albanian Campaign,* 1965), in which the youthful hero killed on the battlefield, the embodiment of the perennial youthful victim of the world's evils, is miraculously resurrected through his youth and heroism to become a symbol and promise of life itself in its eternity.

Fourteen years of apparent silence, devoted by the poet to other intellectual and artistic activities, including his four years of study in Paris, were in fact years of gestation that resulted in the publication of his masterpiece, *To Axion Esti* (1959; *The Axion Esti,* 1974). (The title means "worthy it is," a quotation from the Byzantine laudations to Christ and the Virgin Mary.) It was soon followed by *Exi ke mia tipsis yia ton ourano* (1960; *Six and One Remorses for the Sky,* 1974), considered its contemplative companion piece.

To Axion Esti is a large unity wonderfully constructed out of an immense variety of language, meter, manner, and tone, built with mathematical accuracy and ranging from epic to song, and intended to be the "Aegean" equivalent of a Byzantine mass. In its three sections, "I Ghenesis" ("The Genesis"), "Ta Pathi" ("The Passion"), and "To Dhoxastikon" ("The Gloria"), the poet identifies himself in his life experience with the sun, with his race, and with his country since its physical and spiritual creation from the initial light, then passes through the sufferings of the war decade, which he equates with Christ's Passion, and eventually emerges into the glory of a resurrection in the rebuilding of an earthly yet spiritual paradise of justice, freedom, love, and beauty. To the grimness of our postwar reality E. thus counterposed a bright promise for the future of humankind.

The historical and moral awareness that characterizes *To Axion Esti* was to yield, in the "third stage" of his development as inaugurated by *Exi ke mia tipsis yia ton ourano*, to what he has called his "solar metaphysics," best expressed in *To fotodhentro ke i dhekati tetarti omorfia* (1971; *The Light Tree and the Fourteenth Beauty*, 1974), in which a series of "instantaneous," "ascending," "meteoric," and deeply revealing solar and lunar epiphanies unfold the mystery of the Greek light in its search for and creation of a paradise as incorporated in our own world.

His most recent collection, *Maria Nefeli* (1978; *Maria Nephele,* 1981), received with great enthusiasm, in parallel monologues by a "hippie" girl and by the poet as the "counterspeaker" gives an account of the discrepancies, the alienation, the confusing and disheartening absurdity of our modern times, and shows the poet's effort to discover and appreciate in that reality the positive and eternal elements that would support his convictions and beliefs about the meaning and worth of poetry and life.

FURTHER WORKS: *O ilios o iliatoras* (1971); *To monoghramma* (1971; *The Monogram,* 1974); *Ta ro tou erota* (1972); *Ta eterothali* (1974); *Anihta hartia* (1974); *I mayiia tou Papadhiamandi* (1974). FURTHER VOLUMES IN ENGLISH: *The Sovereign Sun: Selected Poems of E.* (1974); *O. E.: Analogies of Light* (1981); *O. E.: Selected Poems* (1981)

BIBLIOGRAPHY: Friar, K., ed., "A Critical Mosaic," *The Charioteer,* 1, 2 (1960), 20–24; Friar, K., *Modern Greek Poetry: From Cavafis to E.* (1973), pp. 82–88, 695–700; Friar, K., Introduction, notes, and bibliography to *The Sovereign Sun: Selected Poems of E.* (1974), pp. 3–44, 179–95; Keeley, E., and Savidis, G., Preface and notes to *The Axion Esti* (1974), pp. xiii–xv, 151–58; Ivask, I., ed., *O. E.: Analogies of Light* (1981)

ANDONIS DECAVALLES

EMMANUEL, Pierre

(pseud. of Noël Mathieu) French poet and essayist, b. 3 May 1916, Gan

E. spent his early years in the U.S., where his parents had emigrated, before he was sent to Lyon to study in a Catholic school. There he lived with an uncle who wanted him to become an engineer. But E. was far more interested in philosophy. He became a teacher and started writing poems closely modeled on those of Paul Éluard (q.v.). The decisive influence on his poetic career proved to be the poetry of Pierre Jean Jouve (q.v.), whom he met in 1936. E. has been awarded the Legion of Honor and several honorary doctorates, and was elected to the French Academy in 1968.

Three powerful images of mythic proportions dominate the work of E.: Christ, Orpheus, and, to a lesser degree, the German poet-seer Hölderlin, to whom E. devoted an entire collection of poems, *Le poète fou* (1944; *The Mad Poet,* 1956). E.'s poetic creations are firmly rooted in Christian thought. The figure of Christ, the exemplary innocent victim and implacable witness of human frailty and cruelty, is present throughout his work. E.'s Christ, however, is not the "King of Glory," but the "Man of Sorrow." With *Le poète et son Christ* (1942; the poet and his Christ), he established the image of the suffering Christ between death (Good Friday) and new life (Easter), thus creating a powerful symbol of human anguish that inevitably evokes the gruesome reality of Nazi atrocities. This image of the anguished Christ also permeates his "Resistance" poetry.

The other archetypal figure, Orpheus, appeared for the first time in *Le tombeau d'Orphée* (1941; Orpheus' tomb), the work that brought E. sudden fame. Orpheus here appears as the poet's double who, in search of his lost love, descends into hell, from which he emerges on the third day as "the pure poet born of Christ and his beloved."

With *Jour de colère* (1942; day of wrath), *Combats avec tes défenseurs* (1942; fight with your defenders), and *La liberté guide nos pas* (1945; liberty guides our steps), E. turned away from his own metaphysical quest, taking his inspiration from the immediate historical situation: the German occupation of France and the French Resistance movement. The poems, homages to a tortured nation and its victims, are a horrified indictment of a human race that forsakes the divine image in which it was created.

In spite of his very successful beginnings, E. soon became somewhat disillusioned and turned to himself and his past life. The resulting autobiographical works in prose, *Qui est cet homme?; ou, Le singulier universel* (1948; *The Universal Singular*, 1951) and *L'ouvrier de la onzième heure* (1954; the worker of the eleventh hour), deal with the torments, errors, and deceptions—but also with the joys and pleasures—of the writer. During this period of critical self-evaluation, there also appeared his perhaps most ambitious poetic creation, *Babel* (1952; Babel), which reflects the poet's war experience and can be called a meditation on the pernicious hubris of man's boundless desires and misguided ambition. The principal theme deals with the rejection of God and the subsequent rise of a man, readily accepted as a substitute for God by his fellow men, who becomes an ugly tyrant of immense power, only to collapse in the end into nothingness. In *Babel* the demise of God is accompanied by the individuals' loss of their truly human qualities.

Babel did not become a great success, and perhaps did not fulfill the poet's ambition. So, after a rather long unproductive phase, E. tried his hand at a new kind of poetry, that of *Evangéliaire* (1961; evangeliary), a series of short, somewhat naïve poems, whose simplicity is in marked contrast with the difficulty of previous creations. During the 1960s, E. wrote little poetry, but a number of essays, which are very personal meditations on the act of writing itself—*Le goût de l'un* (1963; the taste for unity)—and the fundamental meaning of faith—*La face humaine* (1965; the face of man). But with the poem *Jacob* (1970; Jacob) he returned to the inspiration and style characteristic of *Babel*, which he considers his main work.

A poet of the Resistance and a passionate Christian, E. tried to express the anxiety and frustrations of his generation in poems abounding in Christian symbols and pagan myths. His poems gain in significance from the fact that they are parts of a vast ensemble conceived as the spiritual epic of an era.

In an age in which the distrust of the communicative and evocative aspects of language has become commonplace, E. firmly believes in the creative power of the biblical *logos* to capture the essence of modern man's spiritual crisis. In his poetry realistic and mystical elements are fused into powerful, suggestive images and intricate metaphors. His versification shows him to be a master of poetic form: free verse, prose poems, alexandrines.

FURTHER WORKS: *Élégies* (1940); *XX Cantos* (1942); *Orphiques* (1942); *La colombe* (1943); *Le je universel dans l'œuvre d'Éluard* (1943); *Prière d'Abraham* (1943); *Cantos* (1944); *Hymne à la France* (1944); *Sodome* (1945); *Tristesse, ô ma patrie* (1946); *Memento des vivants* (1946); *Chansons du dé à coudre* (1947); *Poésie, raison ardente* (1948); *Car enfin je vous aime* (1950); *Visage nuage* (1955); *Versant de l'âge* (1958); *Les jours de la nativité* (1960); *Les jours de la passion* (1962); *La nouvelle naissance* (1963); *Ligne de faîte* (1966); *Baudelaire devant Dieu* (1967); *Le monde est intérieur* (1967); *Notre Père* (1969); *Autobiographies* (1970); *Choses dites* (1970); *Pour une politique de la culture* (1971); *Sophia* (1973); *La révolution parallèle* (1975); *La vie terrestre* (1976); *Tu* (1977)

BIBLIOGRAPHY: Chiari, J., *Contemporary French Poetry* (1952), pp. 95–114; Brereton, G., *An Introduction to the French Poets* (1956), pp. 293–95; Bosquet, A., *P. E.* (1959); Siegrist, S. E., *Pour ou contre Dieu: P. E.; ou, La poésie de l'approche* (1971); Picon, G., *Contemporary French Literature: 1945 and After* (1974), pp. 143–44

                                    BLANDINE M. RICKERT

EMPSON, William
English literary critic and poet, b. 27 Sept. 1906, Howden

E. received a double degree in English and mathematics from Magdalene College, Cambridge, where he studied with I. A. Richards (q.v.) and absorbed the generalized influence of an intellectual climate fostering the integration of science, literature, and philosophy. He occupied the chair of English literature at Bunrika Daigaku University, Tokyo, from 1931 to 1934, and was professor of English literature at the Peking National University from 1937 to 1939. During World War II he lived in London, serving as BBC Chinese editor. In 1947 he became professor of the Western languages department in Peking and served there for six years, until he was appointed to the chair of English literature at the University of Sheffield, where he remained until he retired in 1971.

E.'s *Seven Types of Ambiguity* (1930; rev. ed., 1953), one of the most influential works of modern criticism, grew out of his tutorial with I. A. Richards. Responding to the influence of T. S. Eliot (q.v.) and the enlightened rationalistic sensibility of the day, E. wished to extend the possibilities of the method of "close reading" invented by Robert Graves (q.v.) and Laura Riding (b. 1901) in *A Survey of Modernist Poetry* (1927). Ambiguity, a "phenomenon of compression," was, for E., "any verbal nuance, however slight, which gives room for alternative reactions to the same piece of language." These multiple meanings act to enrich our sense of poetic meaning. The reader often balances several contradictory senses of a word while pondering his own reaction; a reader sorting out the multiple ambiguities has "moving in him . . . the traces of a great part of his past experience and of the structure of his past judgments." The seven particular types are arbitrary, as well: "which class any particular poem belongs to depends in part on your own mental habits and critical opinions." Thus, each individual's interpretation of ambiguous meanings will differ, depending upon the relative circumstances of previous experience and thought. An ambiguous aspect of the work is evident: between its objective appearance as a series of close readings that, when taken together, lead to a heightened understanding of the whole; and its subjective essence as a series of idiosyncratic literary explorations that seeks to establish a communicative situation for "maintaining oneself between contradictions that can't be solved by analysis."

Some Versions of Pastoral (1935) is E.'s most ambitious critical work. In it his sprightly, discursive prose style illuminates his ideas within a historical and generic framework. "Pastoral," for E., recalling his earlier idea of "compression," puts "the complex into the simple." E.'s method is to explore a wide variety of works as they relate to the social implications of pastoral forms. The resulting discussions remain eccentric and personal, yet stylistically compelling as they grapple with moral and philosophical questions from alternatively objective and subjective perspectives. For instance, his statement that "the human creature is essentially out of place in the world and needed no fall in time to make him so" represents his detached, cosmic vantage point; but his suggestion that we, like Alice in Wonderland, should "keep from crying by considering things" underscores his individual tendency toward dexterous, epicurean intellectual investigations. Benevolent rationalistic ideas are held in ephemeral suspension with essentially irreconcilable signals from Einstein's relativistic universe: when E. is successful, we perceive particular truths in a new way; when he is off, we experience a profound tedium.

E.'s later critical work falls short of his earlier achievements. *The Structure of Complex Words* (1951), E.'s most demanding work, presents a machinery of interpretation that never manages to engage the literary examples with the same acuity as his glibly entertaining

encompassing discussion. *Milton's God* (1961; rev. ed., 1965) is really a diatribe against religion: the Christian God "is the wickedest thing yet invented by the black heart of man." Milton's accomplishment is the creation of a fictional deity, one considerably more pleasant than E.'s conception of God. E., who once proposed that "the object of life, after all, is not to understand things, but to maintain one's defenses and equilibrium," here sheds his detachment for an accessible (but unpersuasive) literary tirade.

Early in his career, E. produced several volumes of poetry, all assembled in *Collected Poems* (1949; rev. ed., 1961). These recall the work of Eliot and evidence the renewed interest in the metaphysical poets: E.'s conceits are derived from philosophy, physics, and mathematics. At their best, E.'s poems emit a cautious radiance; at their worst, they are cluttered and obscure. Nevertheless, they are important for influencing later poets such as John Wain, Kingsley Amis, Philip Larkin (qq.v.), and Donald Davie (b. 1922).

E.'s critical output, brilliant and flawed, is of inestimable significance for its pervasive effect upon the American New Critics, and for his cultivated attempt at questioning the ambiguities of our modern age.

FURTHER WORKS: *Letter IV* (1929); *Poems* (1935); *Shakespeare Survey* (1937, with George Garrett); *The Gathering Storm* (1940)

BIBLIOGRAPHY: Kenner, H., "Alice in Empsonland," *Gnomon: Essays in Contemporary Literature* (1958), pp. 249–62; Willis, J. H., Jr., *W. E.* (1969); Sale, R., "The Achievement of W. E.," *Modern Heroism* (1973), pp. 107–92; Gill, R., ed., *W. E.: The Man and His Work* (1974); Alpers, P., "E. on Pastoral," *NLH*, 10 (1978), 101–22; Gardner, P., and Gardner, A., *The God Approached: A Commentary on the Poems of W. E.* (1978); Norris, C., *W. E. and the Philosophy of Literary Criticism* (1978)

GEOFFREY GREEN

ENCHI Fumiko
Japanese novelist and short-story writer, b. 2 Oct. 1905, Tokyo

E. was the second daughter of the well-known Japanese linguist Ueda Kazutoshi (1867–1937). Sickly and precocious as a child,

E. often stayed home from school, and instead read voraciously, thereby familiarizing herself with both modern and classic literary works. This early exposure to literature, plus frequent trips to the Kabuki theater and many hours of listening to tales told by her grandmother, helped forge E.'s own views on love. In her early teens E. was fascinated by the aesthetically sensuous descriptions prevalent in the works of Tanizaki Jun'ichirō and Nagai Kafū (qq.v.). She also enjoyed reading such Western writers as Oscar Wilde and Edgar Allan Poe. Frustrated and unchallenged, she quit high school after the tenth grade and studied English, French, and classical Chinese at home under tutors.

E. began her literary career by publishing a short drama at the age of twenty-one. At twenty-three another of her plays was produced on the stage. After her marriage two years later and the subsequent birth of her only child, E. found that writing plays did not provide her enough freedom to express what was in her mind. Turning to fiction, she attempted to bring out the complexities of human psychology. Her career as a novelist, however, did not have an easy start. Not until twenty years later, at the age of forty-eight, with the publication of her short story "Himojii tsukihi (1953; the starving years), did E. finally gain recognition. She was awarded the sixth Women's Literary Award for this work in the following year. Her literary activities have been vigorous since then.

Onnazaka (1957; *The Waiting Years*, 1971) is probably the best known of E.'s works. It is also her only novel translated into English so far. Unlike many of her stories, which are admixtures of reality and fantasy, *Onnazaka* is strictly realistic, and has none of E.'s usual "amoral" topics (adultery and seduction). Neither does it deal with eroticism of middle-aged woman, E.'s recurrent theme. Instead, Tomo, the stoic heroine, endures long years of humiliation by her lustful husband, who keeps two mistresses—all three women under the same roof. She vents her spite in curt, strikingly revengeful words spoken on her deathbed, which makes a powerfully effective conclusion. The Noma Literary Prize was awarded this work in 1957.

E.'s autobiographical trilogy, *Ake o ubau mono* (1957; one who steals red), *Kizu aru tsubasa* (1962; the injured wing), and *Niji to shura* (1968; rainbow and carnage), is probably more representative of her work. In these novels she depicts a woman's loveless, acrimonious marriage and her relationships with other

men. The heroine's intense frustration as a novelist undoubtedly parallels E.'s own experience before she established herself as a writer. She received the fifth Tanizaki Jun'ichirō Award for the trilogy in 1969.

It is in many of her short stories that E. often exhibits her profound knowledge of classical Japanese literature by weaving elements from it into contemporary settings, which become fascinating combinations of reality and fantasy, actuality and apparition. For example, in "Nise no enishi: shūi" (1957; the conjugal ties: gleanings), she borrows the theme of a mysterious tale with the same title by Ueda Akinari (1734–1809), in which a man long dead returns to life, to create a bizarre story about a woman who gives herself over to wild fantasies.

One of E.'s latest accomplishments is the translation into modern Japanese of *The Tale of Genji*, the long 11th-c. tale by the court lady Murasaki Shikibu; E. succeeds well in reproducing the sensitivity of the original.

Now in her mid-seventies, E. is highly respected by critics for her profound knowledge of classical Japanese literature, her careful choice of words, and her literary versatility. Yet her work is also loved by the general public for being neither overintellectual nor too theoretical.

FURTHER WORKS: *Aki no mezame* (1958); *Onnamen* (1958); *Watashi mo moete iru* (1960); *Aijō no keifu* (1961); *Hanachirusato* (1961); *Minami no hada* (1961); *Onna no mayu* (1962); *Onna obi* (1962); *Tsui no sumika* (1962); *Shishijima kidan* (1963); *Yukimoe* (1964); *Komachi hensō* (1965); *Namamiko Monogatari* (1965); *Azayaka na onna* (1965); *Kakeru mono* (1965); *Senhime shunjūki* (1966); *Saimu* (1976); *Shokutaku no nai ie* (1979)

YOKO MCCLAIN

ENCKELL, Rabbe

Finnish poet, dramatist, essayist, and critic (writing in Swedish), b. 3 March 1903, Tammela; d. 17 June 1974, Helsinki

E. was a member of a distinguished Finland-Swedish intellectual family: his father was a well-known agronomist, and of his brothers, one, Olof E. (b. 1900) has been a prolific critic and literary scholar, while another, Torger E. (b. 1901), is a painter and etcher with an international reputation. On the surface, E.'s career was notably serene and successful; among the Finland-Swedish modernists (q.v.), his verse in particular won early acclaim because of its clarity and precision, and his career was capped, in 1960, by his selection as the resident in the Poet's House at Porvoo, that is, as poet laureate of Swedish Finland. The last decade of his life was darkened, however, by attacks from the political left, which considered him to be an elitist—as he was—in both life and letters.

Even E.'s debut revealed the master; the brief but intense love lyrics of *Dikter* (1923; poems), as free from sentimentality as they were from traditional rhymes and meters, were followed by the epithalamiums of *Flöjtblåsarlycka* (1925; flutist's happiness), directed both to the beloved and to nature. *Vårens cistern* (1931; the spring's cistern) was distinguished by E.'s "matchstick poems," equivalents of the Japanese haiku, in which he apprehended specifically Finnish pastoral scenes.

As a result of a crisis in his personal life, the poetry of the later 1930s changed tone; yet *Tonbrädet* (1935; the sounding board) and *Valvet* (1937; the vault) are not patently confessional, but speak through allusions to classical myth; simultaneously, E.'s sense of form became more conservative, and he sometimes employed regular strophes suggesting those of the Horatian ode. The fascination with antiquity continued into *Lutad över brunnen* (1942; bent over the well), in which the careful reader can find references to the perils then besetting Finland. However, E. was neither an academic poet (although in some ways he resembled his Finland-Swedish predecessor in quasiclassical verse, Emil Zilliacus [1878–1961]) nor a political one; his main poetic concerns now lay with specific literary questions, and in *Andedräkt av koppar* (1947; breath of copper) he analyzed modern poetry itself. It was this collection, and its main poem, "O spång av mellanord" (oh bridge of words between), that firmly established him on the Parnassus of Sweden proper; the major Swedish modernist poet Erik Lindegren (q.v.) wrote the introduction to the retrospective selection from E.'s lyrics, *Nike flyr i vindens klädnad* (1947; Nike flees in the wind's raiment), which marks the closing off of the middle phase of E.'s career.

The seven collections of poems that subsequently appeared, from *Sett och återbördat* (1950; seen and restored) to the posthumous *Flyende spegel* (1974; fleeting mirror), might be compared to a long poetic diary, sketches by a skilled hand that had wholly mastered the arts of compression and concision. Of these books, *Det är dags* (1965; it is time), with its

sense of leave-taking, its tributes to the towns of E.'s beloved Italy, its self-confessed misanthropy, and its deep-seated cultural pessimism, is the most impressive.

Previously, Greek myth had also informed a series of brief plays on classical themes: *Orpheus och Eurydike* (1938; Orpheus and Eurydice), inspired by the personal crisis and intimate loss that had also given rise to E.'s verse collections of the time; *Iokasta* (1939; Jocasta); the several playlets included in *Lutad över brunnen*; and then *Agamemnon* (1949; Agamemnon); *Hekuba* (1952; Hecuba); *Mordet på Kiron* (1954; the murder of Chiron); and the relatively lighthearted *Alkman* (1959; Alcman). These plays had some success when performed on radio; in the introduction to *Dikt* (1966; poem), where E. reprinted *Iokasta*, together with two new plays (*Laios* [Laius] and *Latona* [Latona]), he conceded that the language of the earlier dramas had been excessively lofty—a fact that may contribute to their neglect in the future. Nonetheless, they are an integral part of E.'s oblique self-revelations.

The prose of E., like his lyrics, shows a mixture of passion and coolness, expressed in a language of quiet elegance. E. analyzed his own personality in *Tillblivelse* (1929; becoming) and *Ljusdunkel* (1930; chiaroscuro), turning then to his first wife in *Ett porträtt* (1931; a portrait); all three of these works could be described as half-narrative, half-essayistic. The reflective novellas *Landskapet med den dubbla skuggan* (1933; the landscape with the double shadow) and *Herrar till natt och dag* (1937; lords of night and day) were artistically less convincing, and he did not try the narrative again. Even in the 1920s, though, he had proved himself to be one of the North's leading critics, and his essays were collected in *Relation i det personliga* (1950; personal report), followed by *Essay om livets framfart* (1961; essay on life's sweep), which contained personal analysis, still more diaristic fragments, poetry, and E.'s portrait of his father. The four later volumes of aphoristic prose (often interlarded with pieces of verse) likewise have the air of being entries in a meditative notebook.

E. is a central figure in Swedish-language poetry of the 20th c. The stamp of a lucid and varied intelligence—one is tempted to use the word "Goethean"—is borne by everything he wrote.

FURTHER WORKS: *Traktat* (1953); *Skuggors lysen* (1953); *Strån över backen* (1957); *Dikter i urval* (1957); *Landskapet med den dub-*

bla skuggan: Ungdomsprosa 1928–1937 (1958); *Kärnor av ögonblick* (1959); *Kalender i fragment* (1962); *Och sanning?* (1966); *Tapetdörren* (1968); *Resonören med fågelfoten* (1971); *Dikter 1923–1937* (1971)

BIBLIOGRAPHY: Schoolfield, G. C., "Canals on Mars: The Recent Scandinavian Lyric, I," *BA,* 36 (1962), 9–19; Schoolfield, G. C., "R. E., *Mot Itaka,*" *GN,* 7 (1976), 17–22, 36–39; Petherick, K., "Four Finland-Swedish Prose Modernists: Aspects of the Work of Hagar Olsson, Henry Parland, Elmer Diktonius, and R. E.," *Scan,* 15 (1976), 45–62

GEORGE C. SCHOOLFIELD

ENGLISH LITERATURE

Poetry

In tracing the movements within a poetry so rich and varied as that of England in this century, a cautionary word is in order. Poetic movements are not monolithic. The imagists (q.v.), the Georgians, the Auden (q.v.) group, the Movement, are motley crews when closely examined—nor do they maintain orderly ranks through time. That they sometimes appear more of a piece than they really are, originates in misconceptions promoted by critics (who may also be writers of poetry) more zealous to establish a pantheon of poets than to examine the variable substance of poetry itself.

English poetry of this century rightly begins with Thomas Hardy (q.v.). After the adverse critical reception of his last novel, *Jude the Obscure* (1895), Hardy kept to poetry, where he could say, without public censure, what he wanted to about the moral vagaries of human existence and what he took to be cosmic indifference to man's fate. The emphasis in his fiction on dignity, courage, and love is even more evident in the shorter compass and compression of imagery and rhythm in verse.

The integrity with which he maintained his belief that the world could be improved (his "meliorism") in a language of both surface and depth made him attractive to the Georgians, who wanted to anchor their own revulsion against easy moralizing and ornate language in a poetry of nature and an unsentimental view of life. Hardy's influence on individual writers was considerable, appearing in such major poets as Auden and Robert Graves (q.v.).

W. B. Yeats (q.v.), although Irish of Protestant heritage, lived for some time in England and had close professional relationships with English writers. He, probably more than any other, exemplifies that cultural cross-fertilization within the British Empire and Commonwealth nations, which developed and grew strong even as the Empire was disintegrating. There is a sense in which Yeats's poetry projects a similar inner pressure for renewal. His early poems are vaguely melancholy, as if muted like Ireland itself by North Atlantic mists.

But the maxims of folklore, observation of rural hardships, the struggle for Irish national expression, and most importantly his own profound commitment to the discipline of poetry, toughened the fiber of his verse and brought him to reject "impersonal beauty." These are considerations that in a century of disillusionments made Yeats attractive to the poets who followed.

The association of Yeats with Lady Gregory (1852–1932) in the Irish National Theatre enlarged his outlook and style to accommodate in his poems the frustrations, responsibilities, and bitterness of public affairs. Adjusting to the lead of T. S. Eliot and Ezra Pound (qq.v.) in seeking a more rigorous poetic language, Yeats began to write direct, epigrammatic verse, which incorporated, paradoxically, a symbolic system, described in *A Vision* (1925), based on occultist concepts and automatic writing.

Yeats's poetry illustrates that a poet's world view does not have to be credible to be impressive, even profound. His strength lies in the cadence of day-to-day English enriched by Irish rhythms and subtle echoes of English verse, in the selection of images that induce the intended sensory experience, and in the creation of a poetic world imbued with vitality.

Imagism, reacting against Victorian poeticism, originated in casual meetings of the "Poets Club" at Oxford in 1908, called together by T. E. Hulme (1883–1917). Though of limited achievement, it left a mark on subsequent poetry in rhythm, economy, and in treatment of the subject. Hulme, originally a mathematician and biologist, was one of the first scientific minds in the 20th c. to turn to literature as a way of thought as inevitable as that of science. By early 1909 he had drawn F. S. Flint (1885–1966) into discussions of French, Japanese, and Hebrew poetic practices. The object was to rescue English poetry from the lockstep of iambic meter and to reinvigorate it with fresh images. Hulme's "society" was soon after joined by Ezra Pound, who introduced his own similar ideas into their discussions.

Another American, Hilda Doolittle (q.v.), along with Richard Aldington (1892–1962), joined the Pound group in 1911. Their practice was formulated in three rules: direct treatment of the thing, economy and precision of language, and composition in the sequence of the musical phrase instead of regular beat. Four annual anthologies followed; the first, *Des Imagistes* (1914), contains poems by the self-styled imagists—Pound, Doolittle, Aldington, and Flint—as well as verse by James Joyce, Ford Madox Ford, William Carlos Williams, Amy Lowell (qq.v.) and others. Before the appearance of *Some Imagist Poets* in 1915, Pound had joined Wyndham Lewis's (q.v.) Vorticism movement.

The Georgians also reacted against the meretricious moralizing, orotundity, and metaphysical pretentiousness of Victorian poetry at its worst, and against the Decadent aestheticism of the 1890s. Their poetry is distinguished by subject matter (English pastoral life and the worlds of children, animals, and dreams) and style (a spare Wordsworthian plainness).

But the Georgian poets could not withstand the trauma of World War I nor compete with the more rigorous theories and practices of imagism and Vorticism. Although the solidarity of the Georgians could not be maintained, the major principles of their verse and many of their objectives are evident in subsequent writing.

World War I hastened the change in attitude toward subject matter and treatment begun by the Georgians and imagists. Edward Thomas (q.v.), the most accomplished of the Georgians, was killed in 1917. He had earned a living by writing stories for children and travel books, and produced in the last few years of his life a small but distinguished corpus of poetry.

Wilfred Owen (q.v.), killed at the war's end, had worked back from his subject to discover the materials and to forge the techniques for expressing in fresh and powerful ways the "pity" of war. The poetry of Isaac Rosenberg (q.v.) remains the most enigmatic of all those who died in the conflict, leaving unanswered the question of whether his striking although unfulfilled originality would have been possible without the pressures of combat and imminent death. The poetic talent of Siegfried Sassoon (q.v.), one of the survivors, did not last beyond the war. He will be remembered for his help to Robert Graves and Owen, for his bitter, denunciatory poems about combat, and for the single lyric that best expresses the feeling at the armistice: "Suddenly everyone burst out singing" (1918).

The eclecticism that had set in during the last decades of the 19th c. proliferated after the shattering impact of World War I. T. S. Eliot, reacting against the disintegration of standards, worked out an aesthetic based on conservative social, political, and religious principles. His poetry was both admired and condemned for defending the establishment. His program for poetry succeeded in part because it advanced what appeared to be new and exciting solutions to formal problems: the elimination of transitions, and telescoping of images for presenting archetypal ideas.

Beyond new techniques, however, Eliot also proposed several basic principles, which had been prepared for in the work of the 17th-c. metaphysical poets, of Gerard Manley Hopkins, and of the French writer Jules Laforgue (1860–1887). One was the concept of cultural synchronicity, which unified past and present in shared values. The idea that the past had not irrevocably disappeared was welcome in an age when time sped ever faster and when the war had seemed to cut a chasm between this age and what went before.

Another idea ready for its time was the appeal for a "unified sensibility" that would bring together intellect and feeling, sundered, as Eliot theorized, by the first great impact of science in the 17th c. The 20th-c. secular version of the 19th-c. warfare between science and religion was sustained by the ever more startling revelations of science. Humanistic thought, on all fronts vulnerable as a result of its comparative inactivity, aspired to adopt science and technology as its own. Reconciling thought and feeling was, on this level of insecurity, a consummation to be desired. It was often overlooked that consummation really amounted to capitulation, in which intellect was defined as thinking, and thinking the province of science.

It was Owen who wrote, "true poets must be truthful," a principle that sums up the intent of the imagists and the Vorticists, and establishes for poets of the two decades between the wars the objective of recalling or discovering what that could mean. Such poets as Pound attempted to catch the truth of translation and the truth of satire; Eliot and Graves would recall it from its classical origins, Yeats would look for it in the rag-and-bone shop of the heart, and Auden and Stephen Spender (q.v.) would seek to discover it blossoming out of the dustbins of urban life and industrial ruins, and in the new verities of psychology and communism.

Pound, although American-born, lived in

England (1908-20) during the crucial years of change in English poetry. His self-confidence, energy, and commitment to world poetry made his influence irresistible and indelible. In *Hugh Selwyn Mauberly* (1920) Pound satirizes Western culture, that "bitch gone in the teeth." His translations, from Provençal, Italian Renaissance, and Chinese poetry are often small miracles of re-creation. Pound was generous with his help (to Joyce, Wyndham Lewis, and Eliot). His personality and critical theories influenced many others. His own work lacks the amplitude he tried to achieve in the *Cantos* (1917–68) and, except for *Hugh Selwyn Mauberly,* coherence.

The aberrations of his own mind—the discontinuity of both intellectual and imaginative faculties, the intermittently virulent anti-Semitism—are reflected in the *Cantos*, many of the later ones in fragments. Critical opinion remains divided about these "magnificent conversations," unfinished at his death. All that can be said with certainty is that like Joyce's *Finnegans Wake* (1939) and David Jones's (q.v.) *Anathemata* (1952), they represent the attempt to bring literature into a comparable complexity and universality with science and philosophy.

The long perspective distorts. To describe the 1920s and 1930s as dominated by Eliot, the 1940s and 1950s by Auden, largely reflects a predilection for critical theory over the poetry itself, and fails to take into account the richness and variety of poetry written during those decades.

Edwin Muir (q.v.) was born in the Orkneys and for many years lived in Glasgow. His poetry reflects both these environmental influences —the island's amplitude of nature and the city's feeling of confinement. Rhythmic variety, exciting imagery, music, are not prominent in his poetry. They reflect, nevertheless, the power of his own sweetness of temperament, a mystical insight into the relations of nature and human nature, and an ability to represent the relationship in myths of his own making.

The early poetry of Edith Sitwell (q.v.) continues to be heard in the music of *Façade* by William Walton, and read in those anthologies careful to include the truly experimental. Sitwell's childhood was miserable, dominated by eccentric, rich, and ambitious parents. Attributable to her unhappy early life are the radical syncopation of rhythm, rich color, and surrealistic images, all expressions of a powerful emotional reaction.

Arthur Waley (1889–1966) exercised a strong influence on 20th-c. poetic practice and theory through his translation from the Chinese: *170 Chinese Poems* (1919), *The Book of Songs* (1937), *Chinese Poems* (1946). His own descriptive translations of Chinese ideograms, admired by Pound and Yeats, encouraged a dense imagery and, in subsequent decades, a proliferation of imitators of Chinese and Japanese style and forms.

John Masefield (q.v.) produced several fine narrative poems, the best known being *The Everlasting Mercy* (1911). His attempts at a genuine realism were inhibited by a gentility that he could not shake off.

W. H. Davies (q.v.), tramp-poet of the open road, had little formal education. He wrote a number of fine, simple lyrics among a good many that appear too calculated to impress with their simplicity. Harold Munro (1879–1940), after writing much Georgian verse, expressed a true poetic talent in a few late poems. Herbert Read (1893–1968), distinguished as a critic of art and literature, published several volumes of poetry. He influenced the resurgent romanticism of the "New Apocalyptics" in the 1940s.

Another of the war survivors, Wilfred Gibson (1878–1962) left behind his early poetry, Victorian in style and manner, and went on to contribute to the early move in the century toward realistic treatment. His studies of everyday life are brought together in *Collected Poems* (1926). He continued to publish poetry until 1947 (*Cold Knuckles*), including a number of verse dramas.

The best work of Edmund Blunden (1896–1974) is contained in *Poems 1914–1930* (1930). He turned from citing the horrors of war to write a kind of nature poetry that at its best has something of Walter de la Mare's (q.v.) magical overtones.

The poetry of Robert Graves is fascinating in part for what lies behind it—vast reading in anthropology and mythology and the poetic schema based on these sources. All mythology, in his view, retains evidence of a matriarchal order found in allegiance to the Triple Goddess, destroyed by invading northern patriarchal forces and replaced by a male sun god. Graves's poetry also retains evidence of its origins in Georgian principles. It is a poetry of nature with correspondences to the muse world elaborated in *The White Goddess* (1945).

The 1920s was a decade of innovative poetry, beginning with the publication of Pound's *Hugh Selwyn Mauberley*. This attempt "to condense the James novel" exhibited the polyglot texture and abrupt transitions that characterize T. S. Eliot's *The Waste Land* (1922). Pound was already at work on the *Cantos*, in which these qualities were dominant.

After World War I journals of small circulation carried writers' work and critical positions to a small, elite readership. This development promoted a sectarian spirit in poetry that polemicists like Pound and Wyndham Lewis were able to exploit in advancing and consolidating their own literary program. Such journals as *Blast* (1914–19) edited by Wyndham Lewis, and *The Criterion* (1922–39), edited by Eliot, encouraged innovative writing and internationalist art. Special forums of this kind advanced the obscurity and elitism so often characteristic of experimental writing from the 1920s through the 1950s. In the 1950s small presses (such as Fulcrum, Migrant, Anvil, and Trigram) performed a signal service in bringing relatively obscure poets into print.

A number of poets were outside the stream of experimentation in the early decades. For example, Ruth Pitter (q.v.) bears some resemblance to Muir in the contemplative intensity of her vision. Her poems, often about nature and domesticity, are Christian in thought and feeling. Although neglected through most of her early and middle life, she received more attention in the 1970s, in part because of the publication of *Collected Poems* in 1969.

There were other poets writing formally traditional verse. Sylvia Townsend Warner (q.v.) with a well-established following as a novelist, has been underestimated as a poet. Her poems are carefully wrought, succinct, and regular, qualities that may help to explain her neglect by many contemporary readers, who prefer a more robust enthusiasm. The poems of Charlotte Mew (1896–1928) reveal a cool, precise observation, something like that of Hardy (who recognized her talent and encouraged her), but her somber, stoic tone, which matched her way of life, is all her own. Anna Wickham (1884–1947), like Mew, committed suicide. Her poems record a wry disenchantment with the urban scene and its inhabitants.

Apart from the public figures of the 1920s and 1930s was Stevie Smith (q.v.); her *Collected Poems* (1976), illustrated by drawings by the poet, reveals a mind of high seriousness that perceives that the comic and the bitter in life are often associated. Also apart from the public involvement of the 1930s generation was Eliot, who, having expressed his sense of the world's fragmentation and emptiness in *The Waste Land* and "The Hollow Men," (1925), joined the Church of England and worked dur-

ing the 1930s on *The Four Quartets* (1943) in his search for the "still center."

Poetry in the first three decades of the century exhibited the usual opposed tendencies: a "return" to tradition (however identified) and a search for innovation. The Georgians are an example of the first tendency, the imagists of the second.

Those poets in each movement who had something compelling to say—Graves and Pound, chiefly—went on to other means of poetic formulation. The emphasis of Pound on precision of images and rhythms derived from the subject rather than imposed on it, and Eliot's similar views, especially the importance of finding the just right objects or persons or sensation to represent an emotion (the "objective correlative" for that emotion), had much to do with the kind of poetry written between 1917 ("The Love Song of J. Alfred Prufrock") and 1930 ("Ash-Wednesday")—but not everything.

During these years Graves was staking out his own territory by traditional means in classical form—helped by the example and companionship of Laura Riding (b. 1901)—and beginning to defend it (*A Survey of Modernist Poetry*, 1927, with Riding). Muir was molding the timeless experiences of childhood into poems with archetypal themes of persistent attractiveness.

The personal influence of Pound lessened after he took up residence in Italy, and Eliot, after his public affirmation of royalism and Anglo-Catholicism, was too high above the fray despite the continued respect in which he was held, to make a significant impression on the practice of a new generation of poets. These—the "thirties generation"—found a new leader, a congenial style, and new subject matter, in the person and poetry of W. H. Auden.

Most of the poets of the thirties generation were born too late to participate in the 1914–18 baptism by fire and mud. A sense of guilt and displacement in their time was compounded by the general strike, economic depression, and antiwar movements during the period of their maturation, all of which marked their poetry in subtle ways. Among the representative poets of this generation—Louis MacNeice, C. Day Lewis (qq.v.), Spender—Auden was clearly the dominant figure. The special Auden issue of *New Verse*, brought out in his thirtieth year, 1937, viewed him as possibly a genius, and his poetry likely to develop and endure despite its occasional pedantry and fixation on adolescent gamesmanship. He was, wrote Dylan Thomas (q.v.), whose approach to poetry was quite different, "a wide and deep poet."

War and the notion of war spread over the decade. Its vocabulary permeates much of the 1930s poetry. At first the tone was pacifistic, in reaction to the horrors of the past war. But when the Spanish Civil War began to develop as a symbolic struggle between privilege and socialism, many of the thirties generation felt the need to make a personal commitment.

What they wrote from Spain exhibits the usual complexity of war poetry in its obsession with the senseless acts of brutality and betrayal, and in its meditations on sacrifice, heroism, and loneliness of the spirit. This war, like World War I, took its toll of poets: Julian Bell (1908–1937), Christopher Caudwell (1907–1937), and John Cornford (1915–1936).

Auden appropriated the vocabulary of social struggle and class war (the enemy, armies, frontiers, leaders) and combined it with the concept of "moralized landscape" to construct a poetry of topopsychography, in which the times' guilt, masochism, struggle, and hedonism are displayed in symbolic landscapes.

Poems of the 1930s often preached the doctrines of social solidarity, envisioning an ultimate ideal independence for the individual. Spender's flirtation with communism is characteristic in its search for alleviation of loneliness through the comradeship of those joined in a common enterprise. Spender's life and his writing are characterized by painful self-scrutiny, disarming honesty, and persistent involvement with rebellious youth movements from generation to generation. Following Auden's lead, he attempted to incorporate the imagery of modern technology into his poetry, with only moderate success.

The idealism and reformist zeal of the early 1930s darkened under the events of the middle years. Faith in social action gave way to savage attacks on the system and to a symbolism expressing a more subjective accomodation to an intractable public scene. Poets of this "new generation," George Barker (q.v.), Dylan Thomas, Kenneth Allott (b. 1912), David Gascoyne (b. 1916), Roy Fuller (q.v.), Bernard Spencer (1910–1963), and others, found expressionism, surrealism (qq.v.), and romanticism suitable for describing their disintegrating world. It was a poetry suited to an apocalyptic time of genocide, air raids, and the lives of deprivation and restrictions imposed on the population of England.

World War II had a different effect on the imagination from that of the first war with its nightmare of intermittent mass slaughter and persistent misery of the trenches. Sometimes the intervals between military engagements or bombings were more stimulating to the deeper regions of the mind than the trauma of combat. A number of writers developed their talents during time in the Fire Service including Spender and John Lehmann (b. 1907).

In long periods of inactivity during his duty in Kenya, Roy Fuller found himself observing nature intently, and produced poems about animals with profound implications for the meaning of human life (*The Middle of a War*, 1942). For Fuller, as for others, the war had a catastrophic impact on the spirit. Some, broken by the impact, were unable to bring their creative faculties through to a time of relative calm. Others were stimulated by the dangers to which they were exposed to write what they might not otherwise have been able to write. Others scarcely into their careers were killed, notably Alun Lewis (1915–1944) and Keith Douglas (q.v.). Among the war poets were Henry Reed (b. 1914) and Frank Prince (b. 1912), whose "Naming of Parts" (1948) and "Soldiers Bathing" (1953) capture perfectly two characteristic moments of military service. David Gascoyne survived to continue writing his delicately surrealistic poems.

As the equally freighted rhetoric of Winston Churchill was no longer so moving when the events that provoked it were no more, so the new romantics suffered reaction, the more rapid after Dylan Thomas's death in 1953. The language and rhythms of Thomas's poems at their best, as in the villanelle "Do Not Go Gentle..." (1946) and the meticulous syllabic verse of "Fern Hill" (1946), convey an exciting vitality, especially when read aloud in his own sonorous voice. At their worst, they are turgid, emotionally overstated, and pretentiously cryptic. The successors of the new romantics, the primary reaction, were those poets anthologized in Robert Conquest's (b. 1917) *New Lines* (1955), such as Philip Larkin, Elizabeth Jennings, and D. J. Enright (qq.v.). They were reacting, in general, to overstatement and lushness, and turning to British ways and scenes in preference to the modernism that was dissolving national cultural boundaries. It was perhaps a return to secure insularity after so much outreach during the war and its drain on feelings and affection.

Larkin's models were Hardy and Edward Thomas, and to the degree that Thomas was one of the Georgian poets and Hardy had been a strong influence, the "New Lines" poets have made a somewhat similar progress, some of them, such as Jennings and Larkin, continuing to write without strong propulsion to say much beyond what they had been saying so well, while others, such as Donald Davie (b. 1922) and Thom Gunn (b. 1929), gravitated toward the international scene under the modernist impulse of Pound.

Basil Bunting (q.v.) was one of those strongly influenced by Pound who developed a voice of his own—sensuous, musical, and dramatic. His long poem *Briggflatts* (1966) draws on his imprisonment for pacifism during World War I, his years with Pound at Rapallo, and his service with the diplomatic corps in Iran after 1945.

English poetry in the two decades after the war began to show the effects of outside influences, particularly from the Russians Pasternak and Mayakovsky (qq.v.) and the German Trakl (q.v.). The impact on poets of the Surrealist Exhibition (London, 1935), with its collection of works illustrating what was believed to be an ultimately beneficial "derangement" of the senses, was neutralized by the hypersurrealism of World War II, with its spectacular means of destruction and daily atrocities. Surrealism's absurd collocations began to exercise an appeal once more as the gray postwar years of rationing and pedestrian politics wore on, although David Gascoyne, for one, was writing in this mode before, during, and after the war.

Philip Larkin, in his fourth volume of poetry, *High Windows* (1974), expresses the condition of the people with few hopes and attempts to discover in unheroic present a consolation, like the "regenerative union" of the crowd at a fair. His approach to writing poetry has changed little from the beginning. His language is direct, highly wrought, and restrained in feeling. Although aware that his poems have readers, he is, like so many other postwar poets, writing for himself.

Auden's last volume was *Thank You, Fog* (1974), published after his death. His own analysis of his progress over fifty years is given in a poem from this volume, "A Thanksgiving," interesting for the history of poetry, because it represents in a general way its progress during this period. In the late 1920s he "sat at the feet of Hardy, Thomas, and Frost" in a fascination with nature. Then, falling in love, he transferred his poetic admiration to Yeats and Graves. With the economic disasters of the 1930s, he looked to Marxism. At the end of that decade, disillusioned by his experience in Spain during the civil war, and the gathering enormities of Franco, Stalin, and Hitler, his thoughts turned to religion, his guides now

Kierkegaard, Charles Williams (1886–1945), and C. S. Lewis (q.v.). Toward the end of his life he found his imagination turning more to nature again, this time under the tutelage of Horace and Goethe.

No greater contrast could be made with Auden's poetry than that of Ted Hughes (q.v.). "Explosive" is the term often applied to his work. The poetry establishes an elemental relationship between himself and the natural world of animals and weather, especially impressive in his first two volumes, *Hawk in the Rain* (1957) and *Lupercal* (1960). In his later work, from *Crow* (1971) on, the language becomes more expressionistic and the tone more forceful and sometimes forced to the point of stridency.

A somewhat older poet still productive is D. J. Enright, who expresses a distrust of the uses to which language is put. In his long poem *Paradise Illustrated* (1978) he argues, not altogether facetiously, that simile and rhetoric are instruments of Satan: language destroys, but "silences speak for survival."

Clearly, the poetry of the fourth quarter of the century presents a continuing vitality, oscillating as it had throughout the century between the two poles of convention and innovation.

Drama

English drama, which had been in decline for two and half centuries, received new inspiration in the 20th from four external sources. The plays of the Norwegian Ibsen were made available to English readers in William Archer's translations (1906–12). They were publicized by George Bernard Shaw (q.v.) and followed in his practice. Yeats, in Ireland, was experimenting with poetic drama. His plays in verse —from *The Countless Cathleen* (1892) to *Purgatory* (1939)—helped to reestablish poetic drama as a practical option in the English theater. The epic drama of the German Bertolt Brecht (q.v.) aimed at distancing the incidents and characters of the play from the audience in the interests of intellectual involvement instead of emotional identification, provided an incentive for such writers as Auden, Christopher Isherwood (q.v.), Eliot, and Christopher Fry (q.v.) to write plays in verse with popular appeal. The contribution to English drama of Samuel Beckett (q.v.), Irish-French writer, belongs to the consideration of the Theater of the Absurd (q.v.) after World War II.

Shaw remains the major figure in 20th-c. English theater. As a Fabian socialist, Shaw was committed to the practicability of social reform. He found Ibesen's drama of social criticism attractive to his beliefs and compelling as dramaturgy. His wit, scandalous subjects (for example, *Mrs. Warren's Profession*, 1898), and provocative ideas helped to generate a new respectability for plays and playgoing. His long prefaces to the printed versions of his plays broadened public knowledge of drama and theatrical technique, and promoted an interest in the theater where it had never existed before.

Despite their unconventional subjects and provocative treatment, Shaw's plays flourished in the context of an established social order. Shaw and other successful playwrights before World War I—John Galsworthy (q.v.), Arthur Wing Pinero (1855–1934), Henry Arthur Jones (1851–1929), W. Somerset Maugham (q.v.)— dramatized themes that belonged properly to a structured society and depended on a public understanding of that structure for their meaning—themes such as ambition, social responsibility, leadership, marriage. Along with these, there were the complementary themes dealing with threats to the established order, like pride, greed, and sensuality.

Yeats wrote in 1904 that "the modern theatre has died away to what it is because the writers have thought of their audiences instead of their subjects." His comment has meaning for the drama of the first two decades. The "problem plays," for instance, of Pinero were strong for their time but compromised with public taste and intellectual expectations. Shaw's estimate of Pinero's drama is fair, commending his craftsmanship while faulting his weak Ibsenism.

Much the same is true of Henry Arthur Jones, whose social comedies were eclipsed first by Oscar Wilde's and then Somerset Maugham's. Maugham wrote twenty-nine plays during the first three decades of the century, many highly successful, such as *The Circle* (1921) and *The Constant Wife* (1926). The latter, despite its polished wit and high comedy situations (adultery recognized but overlooked in the interests of preserving appearances), has serious implications about the sexual parity of men and women, which might have come straight out of Ibsen.

The episodic, expressionist (q.v.) plays of W. H. Auden in collaboration with Christopher Isherwood reflect pervasive aspects of the 1930s, such as pacifism, political heterodoxy, and anticapitalism. Of their three collaborative efforts, *The Dog beneath the Skin* (1935) evidences the eclecticism of their style and temper, with signs of Gilbert and Sullivan, Brecht, and surrealism.

T. S. Eliot's first verse drama, for which he had made some preparation in the scenic and episodic elements and dramatic monologues of his poetry, was *Murder in the Cathedral* (1935), a religious play for a religious audience. His succeeding plays, from *The Family Reunion* (1939) to *The Elder Statesman* (1959), were religious plays for secular audiences. Thus, Eliot moved from an overt expression of religious themes to a drama of manners in which the moral imperatives of *The Waste Land* (give, be compassionate, control) are only partly concealed by drawing-room comedy, contemporary idiom, and speech rhythms. These changes reduce the elevated tone of his drama. But here, too, Eliot was practicing Old Possum's characteristically sly deception. For in writing his plays for the London theaters, he created a loose, four-stress line which sounds much like prose but which provides the emotional tension and inner rhythmic discipline of poetry.

Christopher Fry, like Eliot, first wrote a religious play, *The Boy with a Cart* (1939), a mode to which he returned at the end of his career. But his reputation as a neo-Elizabethan came with *A Phoenix Too Frequent* (1946) and *The Lady's Not for Burning* (1949). These are scintillating verse dramas, in which highly comic situations and exchanges of wit nearly conceal underlying serious themes, which are not, however, directed toward discernible resolutions.

Drama after World War II developed in several directions, expressing the boredom of a war-weary public, the continuing deprivations, the long-deferred expectations, the accumulated bitterness. Playwrights turned their attention to themes provided by a deteriorating social structure—pointlessness, deformity, ignorance, the fascination with scatology, the failure of belief.

The reaction against traditional ways and values is well reflected in plays of the 1950s and 1960s. Playwrights experimented with the stage, lighting, costumes, dramatic structure, language, and the audience itself. They took their cues from the surrealists, the expressionist film directors, composers such as Schoenberg, Stravinsky, and Bartók, and partly from the existentialist (q.v.) writers who were formulating the pervasive sense of alienation, futility, and anger left over from the preceding decades, exacerbated by postwar dislocations and the psychological impact of the new apocalyptic threat, the atomic bomb.

The most accomplished literary technician of the innovators was Samuel Beckett. The rising internationalism in the arts generally and his English-speaking Irish origin made his *Waiting for Godot* (French 1952; English 1954), although originally written in French, a power in shaping the concern for basic human predicaments that characterizes the new drama. The dramaturgy of *Waiting for Godot*, with its "Nothing happens, nobody comes, nobody goes," epitomizes the Theater of the Absurd. Beckett's unsequential dialogue and pointless action expose the universal despair afflicting individuals who can then, conscious of their plight, face it without illusion, with courage, and possible the grace of humor.

There is no doubt a certain fashionable chic in such movements as the absurd, promoted in self-interest by critics and producers. John Whiting's (1917–1963) *Saint's Day* (1951), which savages the pretensions and self-destructive tendencies of artists and intellectuals, fared badly at the hands of critics, in part because of its animus directed against the intellectual establishment.

It took John Osborne's (q.v.) *Look Back in Anger* (1956), with its broader base in society, to create an explosive mixture out of antiestablishment slogans, invective, and uncompromising misanthropy. It set the tone for the "angry young men" to follow.

Arnold Wesker (q.v.) and Bernard Kops (b. 1926) modified the "angry" mode of Osborne with plays reminiscent of those of Israel Zangwill (1864–1926) from the early years of the century, in their attacks on religious hypocrisy, war, and social evils. Wesker's trilogy, *Chicken Soup with Barley* (1958), *Roots* (1959), and *I'm Talking about Jerusalem* (1960), exhibit the postwar mood of "anger" with conditions in a Jewish working-class neighborhood in London's East End. *The Friends* (1972) continues the theme of working-class aspiration and defeat.

Kops, like Wesker, exploits the symbolic weight of a Jewish milieu and characters, with more comedy and Brechtian music-hall routines, thereby encountering less audience resistance to his underlying attacks on the human wastefulness of a technological culture.

Harold Pinter's (q.v.) "comedy of menace" derives its impact from several sources: Kafka's (q.v.) timeless and mysterious situations, Pirandello's (q.v.) disillusionment, Beckett's cosmic despair, and Hollywood gangster films. In *The Dumbwaiter* (1959) the two hired killers waiting in a basement kitchen for orders gradually realize how little knowledge they

have on which to act. The dumbwaiter signifies the forces beyond their understanding that govern them. The outraged attempts of the two men to relate cause and effect on the basis of their insufficient knowledge points to the similar state in large of human affairs and suggests the importance we attach to those means of search for understanding, one of which is literature. *No Man's Land* (1975) emphasizes the constriction that ignorance imposes on the human situation. Its "inaction" is clearly related to Beckett's *Endgame* and Eliot's "Prufrock," in their depiction of a moribund world. Pinter's play is, in effect, *about* stasis. The characters are fearful of change, of the unknown. They cherish an immobility that negates the need for decisions or action. The static, centripetal form of the play suggests that its meaning is solely contained in what is seen and heard in the play itself, without reference to a contemporary external society. Pinter's comic situations, saturated with an atmosphere of threat, humiliation, and disorientation, are conveyed by "Pinteresque" effects—broken speech, incoherencies, and expressive silences.

John Arden (q.v.) brought a different quality into the new drama—an analytical intelligence like Shaw's in exploring ideas, but without Shaw's certainty of solution. His ambiguities are projected through fascinating plots, situations, and music-hall lyrics that owe something to Brecht.

Edward Bond's (q.v.) plays, from *Saved* (1966) through *Lear* (1972), reveal a controlling thesis that interprets our present society of cruelty and injustice as being the result of humans (and animals) having to live unnaturally in masses in technological, urban environments. In this state, the older generation imposes its neuroses on the younger. Thus "the fall," Bond's symbolic term for this process, recurs periodically.

Robert Bolt (q.v.), more traditional, has chosen historical subjects for his two best-known dramas, the life (and death) of Thomas More in *A Man for All Seasons* (1960), and the relationship of Elizabeth I and Mary, Queen of Scots in *Vivat, Vivat Regina!* (1970). The steady but impassioned rhetoric of his best scenes demonstrates that "anger" is not the only weapon serviceable in combating the Establishment.

Tom Stoppard's (q.v.) plays show several points of origin: Shaw, in his enthusiasm for the life of the mind and passion for scintillating dialogue; Wilde and Fry in the play of verbal wit (puns, misnomers, word games); Sophocles, for the play of detection; and the dramatists of the absurd in their collocation of disharmonies and disjunctures. In Stoppard's reflexive drama there is something of Pinter's concern with the theater as a means to explore our understanding of the world. A Stoppard play takes into itself fragments of other plays and investigates the consequences of juxtaposing these fragments.

David Storey's (q.v.) plays have received unusually diverse critical analysis. They are regarded as naturalism lightened with the poetry of life, or as documentaries thinly disguised as plays, or as celebrations of life. Like Bond, Storey views modern neurosis in long perspective. Western society suffers from the Platonic dualism of body and spirit. A false spirituality revolts against the body. And in the larger context of the city, society does not permit the individual (soul) to rise above the mass (body). The insanity that marks modern society is a consequence of "puritanism" and its associated fear, shame, and loneliness.

Simon Gray's (b. 1936) *Butley,* produced in 1971, was prophetic of what the decade was to be. It is set in a university, where the academic standards are decaying under the guardianship of moral and professional delinquents. Yet through all its painful psychic lacerations (visibly present in the razor cut on Butley's chin) and the quotidian analgesics to ease them (Butley's nursery rhymes and bottle of whiskey) there is a sense of humanity struggling to humanize itself.

Peter Shaffer (q.v.), if his subjects were less contemporary, would bear comparison with Robert Bolt in his preference for the conventional well-made plot set in the theater of spectacle. Also like Bolt, he has something large and coherent to say about the quality of modern life. In *The Royal Hunt of the Sun* (1964), *Equus* (1973), and *Shrivings* (reworked in 1974), he uses the middle-aged man linked in various ways to an ancient culture (for example, Dysart's preoccupation in *Equus* with Greece) to point up the inability of religion in Western society to satisfy the human need for ritual worship and faith.

The pattern that emerges from recent English drama is composed of playwrights' response to the contemporary world as artists and as critics of that world. Recurrent armed conflicts, extermination camps, nuclear weapons, and the politics of starvation are dramatized in the observable results on individuals (as in Beckett, Gray, Bolt, Pinter) and indictments made (as Storey, Shaffer, Bond).

Such distinctions of theatrical intent can be drawn too closely, but the vectors are definite enough to indicate that contemporary drama has taken over from the novel part of the function of serving as the conscience of society, without as yet in the 1980s forgoing its aesthetic function to delight and excite in favor of didacticism and propaganda.

The Novel

A survey of the English novel in this century begins with the Irishman George Moore (q.v.), an important and often undervalued transitional figure. Although not English, he represents two powerful germinal influences on English writing. His kind of fiction, produced between 1883 and 1930, had one tributary from the Continent and one from Ireland. He modeled his writing on the French naturalistic novel, and in *Esther Waters* (1894) produced a remarkable English version. Esther is an ordinary, credible human being, treated sympathetically but without sentimentality. Viewing the world and people "with the eye of God," Moore's idea of the creative process, can lead in quite the opposite direction—into mysticism, as it does later with L. H. Myers (q.v.). But Moore keeps his eye metaphysically impartial and his intentions purely artistic. His work in the 20th c., with its fluent oral tradition derived from Irish folktales, exemplifies his theory of art as rhythmic sequence.

The work of Joseph Conrad (q.v.), the transplanted French-speaking Pole, shows influence from within the English tradition. Although the exotic qualities of his fiction owe much to the particularities of his adventurous life—the gun-running and sea duty—he was conscious of Henry James's (q.v.) style and narrative technique and of lasting impressions gained from his early reading in Shakespeare and Dickens. The high seriousness of his themes is implied by such titles as *An Outcast of the Islands* (1896) and "Heart of Darkness" (1902).

Lord Jim (1900) is an example of Conrad's narrative layering. Jim's cowardice, shame, and redemption are recounted from numerous points of view, all controlled by Conrad's master narrator, Marlow. *The Secret Agent* (1907) and *Under Western Eyes* (1911) are the forerunners of innumerable novels of spies and international terrorism, among the best of which are those of Graham Greene (q.v.). Conrad's sense of the world's mystery is profound. He was fascinated by moral dilemmas and the struggles of individuals in conflict with the forces of nature.

The contrast between Conrad and his contemporaries, John Galsworthy and Arnold Bennett (q.v.), is stark. Galsworthy is best known for his "saga" of the Forsyte family. It has historical interest and certain psychological attraction in the passage of Soames Forsyte, "the man of property," from the Victorian milieu, which is "his," to the modern world, which is not. Two trilogies, published between 1906 and 1922, and later additions, established the Forsyte series as the earliest of many novel sequences to appear during the first three quarters of the century.

The increasing frequency of multivolume panoramic novels indicates a fascination with rapid social and technological changes: the impulse to record the details of a rapidly shifting daily existence, to fix in a pattern of images whatever currents could be discerned in the confusing stream of contemporary life, and to discover a meaning. Thus, Ford Madox Ford called his tetralogy *Parade's End* (1924–28), Anthony Powell (q.v.) titled his multivolume sequence *A Dance to the Music of Time* (1951–75), and C. P. Snow (q.v.) his sequence *Strangers and Brothers* (1940–70). These reflect preoccupations in the modern world with the menace of armed conflict, with the permutations of time, and with the syndrome of power, alienation, and betrayal.

Ford Madox Ford had a powerful influence on other writers both as a personality and as an artist. His early historical novels, the Tudor Trilogy—*Fifth Queen* (1906), *Privy Seal* (1907), *The Fifth Queen Crowned* (1908)—fascinating and circumstantially persuasive as they are, do not measure up to his novels on contemporary subjects. The first of these, *The Good Soldier* (1915), influenced by the French realistic novel, anticipates by a decade the stylistically level rendering of moral inertia in postwar fiction. It exemplifies the narrative technique (worked out in association with Joseph Conrad) of "progression d'effet," the selection of event and word to carry a story forward with gathering "rendering" instead of narrating, had a marked effect on the work of such diverse writers as Pound, Joyce, and Hemingway (q.v.). Ford's masterpiece, and one of the great novels of the century, is the Tietjens Tetralogy, published in America as *Parade's End*: *Some Do Not* (1924), *No More Parades* (1925), *A Man Could Stand Up* (1926), *The Last Post* (1928). Through Christopher Tietjens, Ford reiterates the value of loyalty to a personal creed rooted in established codes of conduct.

Arnold Bennett, like Moore, worked in the French tradition, which enabled him to treat the unlovely setting of Staffordshire pottery towns in such a way as to establish the appeal of life lovingly described. He records, in cumulative detail, provincial places and people undergoing slow change. But even his first novel, *Anna of the Five Towns* (1902), reveals more than a concern for surfaces in its sympathetic rendering of Anna. Caught in the conflicts generated by religious zeal and commercial greed, she remains true to self even through the consequences of her own bad judgment.

In later novels of the century fidelity to self and principles becomes more and more problematical. The tension between social or political necessity and a personal ideal creates ironic changes in self-evaluation (much as in *Gulliver's Travels*) for many midcentury fictional characters such as these delineated in Angus Wilson's (q.v.) *The Old Men at the Zoo* (1961).

Bennett's representational mode at its best was consolidated in *Clayhanger* (1910), an autobiographical novel, and *The Old Wives' Tale* (1908). Bennett's quotidian view of time and the amassing of external details were to draw the ire of Virginia Woolf (q.v.), who used Bennett, along with Galsworthy and H. G. Wells (q.v.), as examples of old-fashioned novel-writing. The conventional novel, which had been tested by generations of novelists, survived the theories and experimentation of the decades between the wars by assimilating the experiments. It showed new strength in work by diverse writers like Elizabeth Bowen, William Golding, Olivia Manning, Margaret Drabble (qq.v.), C. P. Snow, and Pamela Hansford Johnson (b. 1912).

Rudyard Kipling (q.v.) brought the meaning of Empire back to the homeland at a time just before that meaning was to be gradually eroded by rising nationalism in the colonies. Although he attempted several novels, one of which is the memorable *Kim* (1901), Kipling worked more easily in shorter fiction.

H. G. Wells was a complex figure, interesting enough to attract the attention of Henry James, with whom he argued the relative merits of art and journalism. James was right: Wells worked too exclusively with ideas, with social reform achieved through scientific advance, and with types instead of individuals. The argument between James and Wells opened a debate that continued in various modified forms into the 1980s. Prominent among them was the "two cultures" controversy initiated by C. P. Snow.

Virginia Woolf's case against Galsworthy, Bennett, and Wells, "Mr. Bennett and Mrs. Brown" (1924), captures the difference between the old novel and the new. Her analysis of the difference is striking, if oversimplified. Wells, she conjectures, looking at the elderly, threadbare Mrs. Brown seated across from him in a railway compartment, would imagine a utopian world in which no Mrs. Browns existed. Galsworthy, looking at her, would seethe with indignation at social injustice. Bennett would really look at Mrs. Brown, then neglect her in noting all the details of dress and the furnishings of the compartment. All three writers, she insists, laid too much stress on "the fabric of things," losing sight of Mrs. Brown's personality and uniqueness.

Woolf was one of several writers with a new approach to narration and characterization. The psychological novel developed in a variety of directions with Joyce, Dorothy Richardson (1872–1957), Woolf, and D. H. Lawrence (q.v.), but all in reaction against a descriptive representational realism. In place of the surface complexity of the realistic novel they offered the psychological complexities of the mind.

Richardson's contributions to the stream-of-consciousness technique, although substantial (*Pilgrimage* came out between 1914 and 1938 in twelve volumes), are far less engaging than Woolf's multiplicity of techniques and Joyce's more rigorous formal and linguistic exploitation of the mode.

The contributions of Virginia Woolf to the novel emerged from her upbringing in a literary family, from her association with the Bloomsbury group, and from her lifelong illness. Her novels have a rarefied atmosphere that from the beginning made them suspect in some quarters as not being in contact with "real life." They have few scenes of passion, little brutality, and a limited social perspective. But they do have power to convince the reader of their beauty, seriousness, and integrity as art.

In "Mr. Bennett and Mrs. Brown" Woolf had contrasted Bennett's preoccupation with representing the literal surface of character and event and her own concern for the ambiguities of the inner life. Such novels as *Jacob's Room* (1922), *Mrs. Dalloway* (1925), and *To the Lighthouse* (1927) utilize the interiors of dwellings as surrogates for the externalized mind, substantive locales in which psychological dramas are acted out. These dramas are depicted, in *The Waves* (1931), *The Years* (1937), and *Between the Acts* (1941), as tragicomedies, in which the dramatis personae are overshadowed by the ceaseless, implacable actions of external nature.

James Joyce's *A Portrait of the Artist as a Young Man* (1916) is one of many novels relating the story of a young man's growth to maturity and self-realization that are descended from Samuel Butler's (1835–1902) *The Way of All Flesh* (written in the 1870s but published in 1903). It depicts the protagonist's growing resistance to being netted and immobilized by family, church, and country. This classic *Künstlerroman* takes the mythological Daedalus, the namesake of its hero, Stephen, as the cue for creating wings of language to fly over the triple nets into the larger domain of art.

Joyce's masterwork, *Ulysses* (1922), is a monumental product of linguistic art that creates the effect of a mind captured in its entirety through the course of a day. *Finnegans Wake* (1939), his intended masterwork, ransacks the resources of myriad languages to give the impression of nonlogical patterns underlying conscious levels of thought. Such a work stands in a reciprocal relationship to several schools of psychology that emerged in the early decades, with critical systems based on them—for example, those influenced by Freud and Jung (qq.v.) —and with other critical modes such as linguistic, structural, and semiotic. Subsequent writers have found *Ulysses* an almost endless source of formal and linguistic innovation. *Finnegans Wake* has been a more recalcitrant model, and may prove to be either a century ahead of its time or one of literature's dead ends.

D. H. Lawrence's kind of psychological novel could more accurately be called a psychosomatic novel by reason of his insistence on knowledge by intuition as represented by the primacy of blood and the "solar plexus" over the brain and intellect. His ability to uncover and delineate the depths of primitive experience operating at the social level is at its best in *Sons and Lovers* (1913), classic rendition of mother fixation and its consequences for early heterosexual relationships.

Lawrence's influence—through his theory of blood knowledge, and on style in occasional expressionistic passages of great power and beauty about nature—is limited but observable in several subsequent writers, even in some who have established their own kind of novel, such as William Golding, David Storey, and the Australian Patrick White (q.v.).

In the 1920s and 1930s the novel as satire began to reflect the change in values after 1914. Better than most of the topical satires is

Richard Hughes's (q.v.) exposure of the fragile basis of conventional morality in *The Innocent Voyage* (1928), which returns to a Blakean concept of innocence and experience as belonging not to youth and age but to contrary states of the soul. This novel, with its skillfully objective depiction of children living in their precariously naïve and dogmatic world, anticipates the more pessimistic *Lord of the Flies* (1954) by Golding.

Aldous Huxley's (q.v.) social comedies both described and to an extent promoted the fashion of brittle gaiety in the 1920s especially *Crome Yellow* (1921) and *Antic Hay* (1923). Toward the end of the decade, *Point Counter Point* (1928) presented some of Huxley's contemporaries, including Lawrence (and Huxley himself) in a substantial roman à clef. *Brave New World* (1932), more dystopian social satire than novel, has, like Anthony Burgess's (q.v.) *A Clockwork Orange* (1962), added to the English language terms for new kinds of experience.

Like Huxley, Evelyn Waugh (q.v.) in his early novels—*Decline and Fall* (1928), *Vile Bodies* (1930), and *A Handful of Dust* (1934)—satirized the upper-class society of the 1920s and 1930s, but with such brittleness that the satire rings hollow, leaving only the meticulously crafted shell of his hatred. It is, however, a fascinating shell, owing something to Ronald Firbank (q.v.). His dehumanizing approach works in *The Loved One* (1948), which displays the California world of morticians who exploit the living through the dead, and in the novel many consider to be his best, *The Ordeal of Gilbert Pinfold* (1957), essentially autobiographical, centered around bouts of hallucination similar to those he suffered himself.

Among the more popular satires, with literary merit of its own kind (althought at last it deteriorates into coy sentimentality), is *Cold Comfort Farm* (1932) by Stella Gibbons (b. 1902). Unlike the customary satire of high society in town and country, this is a parody of the popular novel of farm and cottage and of much Georgian poetry such as Lawrence's "Love on the Farm" (1913). Gibbons has something of the flair for names and the light touch of P. G. Wodehouse (q.v.)

Distaste for the constrictions of a class society and ossified institutions, and fear of the trauma of daily aggressions, motivated a variety of escapist literature, most of it transitory. The exceptions, however, are noteworthy. Influenced by Jules Verne and H. G. Wells, David Lindsay (1878–1945) created a serious metaphysical fable in *Voyage to Arcturus* (1920) in which Schopenhauer's "nothing" is identified with the real world. In a more literary tradition, with medieval and classical antecedents, are David Garnett's (b. 1892) *Lady into Fox* (1922) and *A Man in the Zoo* (1924), whose titles convey the singularity of their themes. A favorite, often reissued, is *Mr. Weston's Good Wine* (1927) by T. F. Powys (q.v.). Weston's name derives from the World War I expression for dying, "going west." Mr. Weston is thus the "West One," that is, God, and death itself his good wine.

Somewhat later is J. R. R. Tolkien's (q.v.) *Lord of the Rings* (3 vols., 1954–55), derived from folklore, legend, fairy tale, and anthropology. A critical industry burgeoned in the wake of the popular fascination with Tolkien's Middle Earth, with its hobbits and elves and other creaturely constructs.

The breakup of the British Empire was a psychological factor that even while predictable, was at work shaping certain aspects of English writing after World War I, when the winds of nationalism began to blow following the territorial realignments of the Versailles Treaty. Social relations between colonials and English were perceived by novelists as symbolic, expressing racial and religious divergencies and political conflicts.

These ruler/ruled relationships had been displayed in Conrad's "Heart of Darkness" suitably modified to fit the political conditions of the Belgian Congo. The classic novel of colonial relations, however, is E. M. Forster's (q.v.) *A Passage to India* (1924), in which a careful balance of character, episode, and setting reveals the essential contrasts between the English and the Indian ways. Forster depicts the "muddle" that is India and the orderly dogmatism of English administration. But he also contrasts the Indian sense of cosmic order with the confusion of the English mind confronting an incomprehensible universe.

A decade later George Orwell (q.v.), who had served with the Indian Imperial Police in Burma, wrote his novel of the meeting of East and West, *Burmese Days* (1934). Orwell's style, with its debt to the naturalism of Zola, could report with clarity and force situations similar to those in *A Passage to India*, but the novel's characters, in their two-dimensional conflicts, are not Forster's, who have the personal and moral resonance of living people.

On the home front, however, a different kind of opposition was developing within the novel genre itself. Ronald Firbank and Wyndham

Lewis represent two poles of creativity developing in England in the 1920s—the aesthetic and the philosophical, although both labels are misleading.

The work of Firbank, underneath a surface exquisiteness, contends with desperations encountered in the more shadowy purlieus of the spirit. Such slight, stylistically elegant novels as *Caprice* (1917) and *Prancing Nigger* (1925) influenced writers such as Waugh, Huxley, Angus Wilson, Iris Murdoch (q.v.), and Anthony Powell in the uses of silence, significant ommissions, the emphasis on dialogue, and what Anthony Burgess calls the achievement of "weight through lightness."

Wyndham Lewis is to Firbank as an eagle is to a butterfly. A prolific writer of great power, Lewis was an externalist, as befitted an accomplished painter. His approach to characterization tends to deprive his humans of ordinary motivation, guilt and other psychological qualities, leaving them vulnerable to interpretation as "hallucinated automata" (Eliot's view). But his unfinished tetralogy, *The Human Age*, presents two characters who are specifically and unforgettably ordinary people. This work— *The Childermass* (1928), *Monstre Gai* (1956), *Malign Fiesta* (1956), and *The Trial of Man* (unpublished)—depicts landscapes representing psychological states with stunning visual impact.

Markedly different from either Firbank or Lewis was Henry Green (q.v.). He was unobtrusively symbolist, working in a realist tradition. The Midlands speech of *Living* (1929) is freshly attractive. The Anglo-Saxon overtones and rhythms introduce vitality and strangeness into the drab monotony of the industrial life it depicts. *Party Going* (1939) captures the prewar spiritual stasis, and *Loving* (1945) objectifies the early wartime atmosphere from the distance of its Irish locale.

The novels of L. H. Myers, emphasizing man's essential goodness, attacked the corrupt morals and temper of modern commercial values. He persisted in an extraordinary singleness of purpose—the search for moral sensitivity in human experience. To this end he attempted to minimize the "machinery of a life that is familiar" to his readers. In his tetralogy *The Near and the Far* (1943) he achieved this objective by setting his story in 16th-c. India.

Myers's novels illustrate philosophical and religious themes in the context of Eastern mysticism, an orientation seen also in Aldous Huxley and Christopher Isherwood, and taken up obliquely into science fiction.

A near contemporary of Myers, Joyce Cary (q.v.), took a more pragmatic approach to the basic questions of existence. Cary wrote first, in *Aissa Saved* (1932), about the effect on a young African woman of being converted to Christianity. Of the three African novels, dealing with now dated situations, *Mister Johnson* (1939) is probably the best. His two trilogies, both major works, brought his classic English protestantism to bear on art.

When we encounter life itself as the subject of satire, instead of institutions or individuals, we are confronting the novels of Ivy Compton-Burnett (q.v.). Her dislike for the random quality of existence led to intricate plots, witty, urbane dialogue, and balanced titles. *Pastors and Masters* (1925) was the first of seventeen mordant questionings of end-of-the-century life in upper-middle-class families; the last was *A God and His Gifts* (1963).

Two other markedly skeptical views of life appear in the works of Rose Macaulay and Nigel Dennis (qq.v.). Rose Macaulay brought out twenty-three novels between 1906 and 1956. Her reservations about the future of civilization after World War I resulted in *Orphan Island* (1924). It is a forerunner of William Golding's *Lord of the Flies* in situation (children marooned on an island), but the tone, as in all her fiction, is comic, an almost absurdly lighthearted coruscation of language and imagery veiling serious themes. Macaulay's last novel, *The Towers of Trebizond* (1956), embodies her personal reactions to adultery and agnosticism. These matters were treated in an earlier novel, *And No Man's Wit* (1940), set in Spain after the war of 1937.

Witty surface and sophistication mark the novels of Nigel Dennis. His second novel, *A Sea Change* (1949), established his reputation for wit and a kind of black comedy. *Cards of Identity* (1955) displays ironically the search for self in a world of psychiatrists, priests, and politicians, all scheming to provide a ready-made identity. What Dennis wrote about the images of Beckett and Ionesco (q.v.), "We are to watch them move in parallel to reality," points to the quality of parable in his fourth novel, *A House in Order* (1966).

The novels of Rebecca West (q.v.), although not skeptical in the metaphysical way of Macaulay or Dennis, manifest a searching quality of their own. Her early feminism obscured for a time the multiplicity of her concerns, especially her preoccupation with the persistence of evil. Her writing has tended to reduce the differences between fiction and nonfiction. The concerns of her early work, *The Judge* (1922) and *The Thinking Reed* (1936) open out into the "nonfiction" of *Black Lamb and Grey Falcon* (1941), the report of a journey through Yugoslavia, and expand into the psychological complexity and historical breadth of *The Birds Fall Down* (1966).

A similarly exploring mind is that of Doris Lessing (q.v.), whose writing, in her words, examines "individual conscience in its relation with the collective." Her novel sequence *The Children of Violence* (1952–69) treats that relationship first in a social and political context (*Martha Quest, 1952*), then in a psychological context in *The Four-Gated City* (1969). *The Golden Notebook* (1962) places the relationship in an aesthetic context, and *The Memoirs of a Survivor* (1974) in a context derived from Sufi mysticism. Lessing's later fiction, to *The Marriages between Zones Three, Four, and Five* (1980), exploits the paraphernalia and cosmic settings of science fiction in the examination of self and other.

Quite different from Lessing in his concern for artistic expression is Lawrence Durrell (q.v.), who, in *The Alexandria Quartet* (1957–60) extended to new limits the self-conscious investigation of the storyteller into his own art, and established the "reality of the artificial" (Robert Scholes) in characterization. His later work, from *Tunc* (1968) through *Livia* (1978), has continued to attract the descriptive term "sensuous."

A large body of work, from before the beginning of the century on, describes quite another kind of English life. One of the chief practitioners of the novel of country life was Henry Williamson (1895–1977). Writing for over half a century, he has so far received little critical attention for a sustained chronicle of that time in more than eighteen novels. His subject matter, like that of Hardy and the Georgians, and his traditional novelistic style, have worked against him.

The appearance of Melvyn Bragg (b.1939), almost two generations younger than Williamson but much in the same tradition, suggests the persistent attraction of the novel of country life. Novels about life on the land have a basic appeal to English experience, perhaps especially in the middle of the 20th c., when that way of living, its manner and conditions, is rapidly disappearing or being reshaped. It is a literature not often of the highest quality but frequently moving and, with the most capable writers, persuading readers that they are in touch with elemental aspects of life.

H. E. Bates (1905–1974), one of the most prolific of writers about the country scene and people, made the distinction between "the earth" and "the land" that is implicitly recognized in this kind of novel: the earth is "vague, primitive, poetic," the land a composite force of living things, fields, and weather, an "opponent" or "master." This distinction applies in an almost pure state to L. A. G. Strong's (1896–1958) tale of the Dartmoor country of southern England, *Dewer Rides* (1929). His novel *The Garden* (1931), set in Ireland, is less rigorously elemental.

Hardy and Lawrence, although going beyond it, were masters of this mode. Another was John Cowper Powys (q.v.), whose early novels set in Norfolk, Dorset, and Somerset, relate landscape and human inscape so completely as to make the country and its people a microcosm of the universal human condition. The best-known of these are *Wolf Solent* (1929), *A Glastonbury Romance* (1932), and *Weymouth Sands* (1934).

Graham Greene has been one of the most durable writers of the middle half of the century. Like the poet W. H. Auden, his contemporary, Greene had an uncanny knack for perceiving what were the pressing concerns of each generation—espionage, revolution, finance, evangelism, civil war, gambling, international warfare. These are the subjects in which he displays the conflicts in his characters. Greene's view of life after the mid-1920s, when he became a convert to Roman Catholicism, is tenaciously Christian. But it is a special kind of Christianity which, as Walter Allen points out, gives his work a special quality derived from his fascination with "sanctified sinners." There is a dogmatism that is open only to grace, one that rejects everything else as unworthy.

A gift like that of Henry Green for combining fancy and the matter-of-fact characterizes the writing of Elizabeth Bowen. One of the important literary Anglo-Irish, she brings wartime London and an Irish country house into a symbiotic relationship in *The Heat of the Day* (1949). Setting is important in her work, but no more so than the psychological states that it often clarifies, as in her best novel, *The Death of the Heart* (1938).

One of the most impressive novel sequences for its coverage of both time and events in Anthony Powell's *A Dance to the Music of Time*. Powell has described in great detail upper-class English social life in twelve volumes that begin in the pre-war 1914 years with *A Question of Upbringing* (1951) and delivers its narrator

Nicholas Jenkins into the seventh decade of the century in *Hearing Secret Harmonies* (1975). Powell's characters are credible as representative types, and a few are memorable. The sequence, like Snow's *Strangers and Brothers,* with which it can be compared for two quite different kinds of writing, the one aesthetic, the other pragmatic, is instructive as social history and entertaining in its episodes and gallery of reappearing characters. Powell's style verges on the mandarin, but avoids settling there.

C. P. Snow, for so sound a traditional novelist, has been a controversial figure, partly for his criticism, in which he takes a firm stand against modernism, and partly for the kind of fiction he writes, which has been faulted for developing characters who in some essential way do not correspond to the nature of 20th-c. man. Snow's involvement in the scientific bureaucracy before and during World War II gave his novels an air of authenticity, as his university novels have an authority deriving from his experience as a don. But there remains in Snow's fiction a sense that the modern world is being less written about than rewritten.

In the mid-1950s, a writer quite different from Snow appeared, much under the influence of Joyce in the use of language, but uniquely exuberant. Anthony Burgess is highly talented and productive, having published a dozen novels just during his first decade of professional writing. He is not, however, superficial. Burgess writes persuasively about many subjects. His *The Malayan Trilogy* (1956–59; Am., *The Long Day Wanes,* 1965) is an inside look at the declining British power in southeast Asia. In this respect it deserves comparison with *The Raj Quartet* (1966–78) of Paul Scott (1920–1979). The work of Burgess exhibits a broad range of interests and represents a complex reaction to the postwar malaise of spirit. *A Clockwork Orange* (1962) portrays a society degenerating under foreign influences, and his Enderby novels are speculations about the fundamental nature of poetic inspiration and about the poet as an emblem for the individual struggling with meretricious contemporary values.

The "Angry Young Men" of the 1950s brought the accumulated resentment of the between-the-wars generations to a boil, a combined reaction against hypocrisy, deception and phoniness. Something of Virginia Woolf's hatred for "old men in clubs and cabinets," the war mongers, waste makers, destroyers of the young, and the institutions they dominated appears in the novels of John Wain, Kingsley Amis, John Braine, and Alan Sillitoe (qq.v.). But their attitude is tougher, more surly and rebellious than hers—in part because they sensed that part of the problem was their own inertia. Braine's *Life at the Top* (1962), sequel to *Room at the Top* (1957), displays this form of self-betrayal. In *Lucky Jim* (1954), Amis makes his serious observations of society through comic situations and dialogue. He chose to exploit more oblique forms of satire in the 1960s and 1970s by using the modes of the mystery story—*The Riverside Villas Murder* (1973)—and the spy thriller—*The Anti-Death League* (1966). This tendency in Amis's work characterizes the movement of the Angry Young Men away from protest in novels of class conflict toward subtler approaches to analysis of a disturbed, complex, and wayward society.

Similar to Murdoch in his preoccupation with love as a mark of social value, and to Burgess in his reaction to the midcentury decline of values, Malcolm Lowry (q.v.) wrote one impressive novel incorporating these themes: *Under the Volcano* (1947) reveals that Lowry's mentors were Joyce in language, and Conrad Aiken (q.v.), the American novelist and poet, in the psychology of isolation and the death wish. Much in the tone ond outlook of this novel is typical of the decade; the volcano itself is an always present reminder of the bomb.

As wide-ranging as Burgess, William Golding claims a large field for his fiction: Neanderthal man (*The Inheritors,* 1955), medieval clergy (*The Spire,* 1964), a variety of modern subjects, leading to *Darkness Visible* (1979), whose protagonist is a burn victim of the fire bombings of London possessed with extraordinary powers.

Muriel Spark (q.v.) employs a mannered writing that is reminiscent of Sylvia Townsend Warner without Warner's compassion. A convert to Roman Catholicism, she writes, under the aspect of eternity, with an almost medieval clarity and also callousness, as it were. She also writes economically, as if time were of the essence—except in her elaborate and lengthy *The Mandelbaum Gate* (1965), in which both the moment and eternity fail her. While profundity is not her forte, wit and psychological analysis are, as in *The Prime of Miss Jean Brodie* (1961).

Even more astringent than Spark is Angus Wilson, a novelist of powerful satiric effects. They are of a kind usually associated with expressionism, but in Wilson's writings are achieved via a realistic accumulation of details and characterizations. Representing this mode at its most intense is *The Old Men at the Zoo*, with a range of brutal, sanguinary incidents that provide a disturbing significance for elemental human relationships, professional and domestic.

A novelist emergent in the 1950s, whose constant struggles with her own formidable talents gives the appearance of uncertain progress, is Iris Murdoch. Her strength from the beginning (*Under the Net,* 1954) has been her ability to tell an interesting story. But the novels also engage the reader's mind with philosophical ideas and moral concepts. They illustrate her belief that each person represents a uniqueness that is partly defined by social relationships, that uniqueness warrants acceptance, and that love is the relationship which exemplifies acceptance in its most binding form.

By the time of her sixth novel, *The Needle's Eye* (1972), Margaret Drabble had an established critical reputation. But her next novel, *The Realms of Gold* (1975), was received with mixed reviews. Rather than consistently using a first- or third-person narrator, she was now employing a variety of points of view in individual characters, although authorial oversight remains overt in commentary and occasional direct address to the reader. This unexpectedly old-fashioned effect is less a technique than a habit. From her Quaker background Drabble has inherited the practice of self-examination, the results of which are passed on to the reader as admonitions, advice, and moral commentary.

The working-class novels of the 1960s and 1970s are not remarkable for their spirit of rebellion or political doctrine. The novels of Alan Sillitoe, Wain, and others, view the conditions of labor and poverty from a safe distance. They are more nostalgic than revolutionary.

David Storey offers both theory and detailed descriptions of laboring families and their children, who find nonlaboring positions for themselves. His theory, however, is more psychological than sociological (about the spirit-body relationship), and the second generation is apt to discover that intellectual work is less "real" than the physical labor of their parents. A concept that Storey labels "puritan" refers to the disinclination of society to allow an individual to rise above the mass, and to an accompanying revulsion against things of the body. From his first novel, *This Sporting Life* (1960), still among his best work, to *Saville* (1976), about Yorkshire working-class life, his style has remained much the same: spare, taut, barren of ornament, and unremittingly serious.

Among many novelists establishing reputa-

tions in the 1960s and 1970s is Simon Raven (b. 1927), who in 1976 published *The Survivors*, tenth and last volume in the sequence *Alms for Oblivion*. Beryl Bainbridge's (q.v.) skilled evocations of middle-class behavior and misbehavior have appeared at the rate of almost one a year. Her singular view of life imparts to her descriptions a dreamlike resonance. So idiosyncratic is her style that *Injury Time* (1977) has been taken by some to be a self-parody.

The first novel of John Fowles (q.v.), *The Collector* (1963), he has called a parable about the struggle based on inequality between the Few (the prisoner) and the Many (the kidnapper). His favorite book, *The Magus* (1965; rev. ed., 1977), he describes as a "young Man's book for young people." The concerns of subsequent works—the evolution of a moral and intellectual elite, the "defense and illustration of humanism," and the realistic representation of the dilemmas of the middle class in a disintegrating society, as in *The French Lieutenant's Woman* (1969) and *Daniel Martin* (1977)—suggest the reasons for his popularity among readers who look to serious fiction for illumination of historical as well as psychological processes.

Edna O'Brien (q.v.) is a novelist of impulse and sensuous delight. In such novels as *A Pagan Place* (1970), eroticism becomes in its variations and variable intensity the true measure of human experience.

A long-established writer, Olivia Manning evoked in a distinguished line of fiction a tragic view of life and suggested the moral courage needed for confronting it.

The psychic scar of colonial status, like the blue birthmark on the face of Flory, the hero of Orwell's *Burmese Days*, persists in the English literary imagination. It is there in the disparaging treatment that is received by Louis in Virginia Woolf's *The Waves* for being Australian, and in the humiliation that Kumar is subjected to in Paul Scott's *The Jewel in the Crown* (1966). The waves of immigration after 1950 from India, the Caribbean, and Africa, caused changes in social relationships marked by various kinds of ostracism and calculated reactions ranging from rudeness to brutality.

In the work of V. S. Naipaul (q.v.), a Trinidad-born writer, many of whose novels have London settings, the birthmark is the dark skin of immigrants. Naipaul's is the substantial beginning for a literature dealing with the racial adjustments of the Passage to England that has yet to find full expression.

A less specific cultural disorientation already

had been reflected in the self-conscious treatment of language in a remarkable range of novels, poems, and plays. The best-known is probably Orwell's "Newspeak" in *1984* (1949), a basic English shorn of connotations by Big Brother and aimed at suppressing all deviant or emotional responses. The origin of this lobotomized language was Orwell's response to institutionalized propaganda, the verbiage of "public relations," and advertising, which were clearly subverting the honest use of linguistic resources.

If the English novel is indeed dying, as is periodically diagnosed, it is curiously lacking symptoms of serious disease. A certain preoccupation with style may indicate the onset of a silver age, but leaves uncertain whether the golden age has been or is yet to come.

The Short Story

To look at the modern short story is to look at the developing edge of a narrative form thousands of years old. As a literary form, however, it dates from the middle of the 19th c.

In England in the 1890s writers like James and Conrad were producing short fiction of a kind that could not be profitably imitated, as being too long or too special. Others, like Kipling, Robert Louis Stevenson (1850–1894), and George Moore, were writing true short stories in a memorable style or manner. These and others (Wilde, Bennett, Galsworthy, Maugham) were writing well-plotted short stories at a level of aesthetic achievement that would have to be surpassed if the form were to develop and be established alongside the novel and poetry.

Inspiration for the development of a new style in the English story came from abroad and was provided in the main by Maupassant and Chekhov (q.v.). George Moore early introduced Maupassant's naturalism in *The Untilled Field* (1903), which established a pattern of brevity, economy of structure, and simplicity of subject. Moore also learned from his Irish sources how to display the racy idiom and the marvels that make up the attractions of all his short stories from the 1903 volume through *A Storyteller's Holiday* (1918).

One of the English followers of Chekhov (and also of Turgenev) was A. E. Coppard (q.v.), who subordinated action to feeling and established mood through a skillful use of setting. His language—precise, allusive, fanciful —has something of the rich ambiguity of the early 17th-c. masters. His best work appears in *Adam and Eve and Pinch Me* (1921) and the other collections through *Silver Circus* (1928) before the influence of Henry James on his style began to outweigh that of Chekhov.

Moore and Coppard had continued the work of James and Conrad in cultivating an audience capable of appreciating effects beyond those of suspense and resolution. Another 20th-c. master educating a readership was H. G. Wells. Trained in science, he was particularly aware of discoveries and innovations of his time.

Rudyard Kipling also aspired to educate as well as entertain his readers. The first of his story collections in this century, *Puck of Pook's Hill* (1906) and *Rewards and Fairies* (1910), have their settings in Anglo-Saxon and Roman Britain. The burden of these stories, as in the many to follow, is the obligation of Englishmen to practice the prime virtues: courage, discipline, obedience. They retain the edifying impulse characteristic of Victorianism.

D. H. Lawrence, in some ways Victorian, most nearly approaches modernism in his short fiction. In the stories of *The Prussian Officer* (1914) the focus is limited to a spare delineation of persons displayed in vividly realized places. The beautiful and the ugly receive equally careful treatment by a highly sensitized imagination that seemed to miss nothing but had the discipline (in the short story) to include only the essential.

Katherine Mansfield (q.v.), who came to England from New Zealand, wrote for only a decade before she died. In that time she extended the influence of Chekhov into a style unmistakably her own. From Chekhov she learned oblique ways of narration, to tell the story through implication rather than statement and by what is left out. She published three volumes in quick succession until the last and best known, *The Garden Party* (1922). The reasons for Mansfield's influence are difficult to assess. Her work did not have time to mature, nor did she create a variety of characters either in depth or range. But the women and children who populate her stories ring true to the parts of her they express.

Mansfield and Virginia Woolf gained from the competition between them. Not satisfied with her first two novels, Woolf had begun to write short, plotless sketches of an intense meditative quality published between 1917 and 1921. Especially notable among these are "Kew Gardens" (1919) and "An Unwritten Novel" (1921). Woolf explored in these sketches approaches to dealing with time as it is experienced by the mind and with the intensity of experience as time's true measure. They are "short stories" of a special kind in that the narrative line is almost nonexistent. They generate an interest as experimental short fictions quite apart from their role in turning conventional fiction toward the state of poetry.

Following after Lawrence in commitment to the integrity of place and persons through the 1930s were such talents as L. A. G. Strong, W. H. Hudson (1841–1922), V. S. Pritchett (q.v.), Elizabeth Bowen, James Hanley (q.v.), and L. P. Hartley (q.v.). They brought to the short story lyric intensity together with descriptive and psychological realism.

These qualities dominated, even when the intention was to create fable or allegory, as in Sylvia Townsend Warner, David Garnett, and T. F. Powys. Among these belongs E. M. Forster, whose stories of suppressed sexual ambivalence and of a delicate, Bloomsbury-related idealism began to appear in the second decade. The titles of his story collections—*The Celestial Omnibus* (1911), *The Eternal Moment* (1928)—imply their inclination toward fantasy.

Another external source of lyricism in the English short story was Ireland. In 1914 James Joyce published *Dubliners*. These were highly original in avoiding contrived plots, two-dimensional characters, and a reliance on action. In *Dubliners* Joyce created a realistic narrative style the surface of which is inconspicuous. But throughout there is a skillful use of language in evoking musical effects that induce emotional responses.

From the Aran Islands, Liam O'Flaherty (b. 1896) went to London in the 1920s. He was encouraged by Edward Garnett to return to Ireland to write about what he knew best. When he got in touch with his native materials the result was a vivid reflection of the elemental passions and scenes that he recorded in *Spring Sowing* (1924), *The Tent* (1926), and *The Mountain Tavern* (1929). His "sensuous poetic energy" (H. E. Bates) was different from Joyce's quieter effects, but equally revolutionary in its impact.

Sean O'Faoláin (b. 1900) brought the transparency and evocativeness of Turgenev and the early Moore to his account (in *Midsummer Night Madness,* 1932) of revolutionary ardors displayed against the background of hauntingly beautiful landscapes. Frank O'Connor (q.v.), O'Faoláin's associate in the Irish Rebellion, is less evocative and overtly poetic, more the detached, judicious observer in *Guests of the Nation* (1954) than O'Flaherty and O'Faoláin.

The Irish contribution to English short fiction was to transmit, in rhythms of English as spoken in Ireland, the Russian explorations of life by Turgenev and Chekhov in subtle renditions of the poetry of place and the bittersweet quality of ordinary lives under duress.

At the end of the first decade the 20th-c. the English short story had appeared to be falling into decay as the result of popular magazines vulgarizing the genre. Three decades later, the rise in the popular appeal of articles in magazines again appeared to be responsible for a decline in "worthwhile" short stories. The short story had failed to develop new techniques and fresh attractions while the article had. But these appearances were deceptive, the perspective distorted by proximity to the events observed. The short story could hardly have been more changed than by the innovations of Joyce, Woolf, Mansfield, and others.

In addition, by this time in the 1930s there were changes in the English story resulting from innovations of American writers. Sherwood Anderson (q.v.) was proving the value of looking at ordinary people in diverse local settings and describing their situations pictorially without drawing moral conclusions. In the wake of Anderson appeared Hemingway (q.v.), who had put the language on a diet, reducing its previous bulk (as in James) to the minimal skeleton, nerves, and muscle. He provided the snapshots of scenes with no retouching of metaphor, and a tight-lipped dialogue that is left to speak for itself. These American developments served English writers not as models but as inspiration for making changes in the technique of the story suitable to English scenes and society.

One development, largely unnoticed, was occurring in the fiction of Jean Rhys (q.v.). Not until 1968 were the stories from *The Left Bank* (1927) brought together with work published in the 1960s to make the volume *Tigers Are Looking Better*. Rhys is concerned to describe mainly the lives of women trying to cope in a man's world. The "respectable" women of the stories (wives, mistresses, and mothers) are even greater threats than the men. Rhys's use of direct narration and compressed imagery suggest an influence from the French, a linguistic adaptation to be observed later also in the prose of Samuel Beckett.

The well-established and popular story of country life, exemplified in the diverse manners of Coppard, De la Mare, and Lawrence, was carried on into midcentury by H. E. Bates. His stories about rural people in *Country Life* (1938) are effective through direct narration of the beauty of the land and of the hard practical life of those who live on it. No morals are pointed, no conclusions imposed on the reader.

A Welsh contribution to the developing English short story was Dylan Thomas's *A Portrait of the Artist as a Young Dog* (1940). His lush and rhythmic prose was an exotic intrusion into the understated narratives of the 1930s. His unfinished novel, *Adventures in the Skin Trade* (1955), did not appear until the postwar reaction against romanticism was well advanced.

Graham Greene's *Collected Stories* (1973), from three previous collections published in the 1960s, often reveal a kind of severe religious orientation that permeates his longer fiction with an emphasis on the centrality of grace and the subordination of other considerations. Greene makes no innovation in the short story form but, as in the novels, maintains the integrity of his subjects through a disciplined style and economical characterization.

World War II was not the great divide that World War I was between one kind of literature and another. The first generated a new consciousness and approach to aesthetics, the second did not. The decay of values and social conventions during and after the war has benefited the short story because, unlike the novel, it can deal successfully with fragments of life.

During the war, William Sansom (q.v.) was one writer who worked with fragments of an exploding world in his experiments with language and style. After the war his collections *South* (1948) and *The Passionate North* (1950) suggest mosaics constructed out of a shattered Europe.

The intensity of Angus Wilson's satire of contemporary ways, which cannot maintain its bite over the long run of the novel, is particularly suited to the range of short fiction. From his first work, *The Wrong Set* (1949), through his uncollected stories of the 1970s, Wilson has maintained a high level of wry, sometimes wicked revelations of human insufficiency.

One of the more durable writers of short fiction is V. S. Pritchett. His work is uncomplicated and enjoyable at a level that has reduced his professional value among academic critics. He employs a deliberately colorful prose style, full of closely observed detail. The early work, from the 1930s, was marred by exuberant metaphors, which in the later stories have been disciplined. Pritchett can, however, in a more sober fashion, still convey persuasively the subjective character of people through a certain distortion of the external world that is more Dickensian than expressionistic.

Edna O'Brien represents a later stream of the Irish tributary to English short-story writing in subject and style. Rebel from a Catholic background in the West of Ireland, where, as she puts it, there were no books and a lot of barbarity and a certain innocence, she can describe nonintellectual people convincingly. Through her, too, the concern of Tolstoy and Chekhov for ordinary people and the Russian understanding of the restrictions of country life and the longing for adventure come back into the English short story.

Alan Sillitoe, like O'Brien and Pritchett, attempts to describe the feelings of people who are not themselves disposed to do so and, if they were, not capable of doing so. In *Men, Women and Children* (1973), about working-class people in Nottingham, the characters are unsophisticated, have difficulty coping with life, and have little time or energy for anything except work. Their situations, however, in Sillitoe's imagination become those of any human being anywhere. It is this sense of a common, shared humanity that makes his stories attractive. Sillitoe sees the problems of short-story writing as "essentially poetic problems." The result confirms Bowen's view that the story is as much like poetry as the novel. Sillitoe's stories depend on short, quick revelations of consequence or motive and, like the music of some contemporary composers, does not end on the tonic but hangs unresolved, suggesting continuation.

William Trevor (pseud. of William Trevor Cox, b. 1928), by diminishing authorial presence to objective perception through a style of simplicity and plainness, is able to illustrate ordinary lives in their drabness and stubborn pride without bitterness, irony, or sentimentality. The people in the collection *Lovers of Their Time* (1979) simply are what they are, trapped by the conditions of history and the circumstances of their immediate lives, often driven to the point of madness, yet clinging to a center of integrity.

John Fowles, better known as a novelist, has written in *The Ebony Tower* (1974) stories that are variations on some of the themes of his novels. They embody an ordeal or quest and are reminiscent of medieval romances in the persistent thread of love or eroticism that runs through them. Still, their reference is the modern world, and their central concern is for the spiritual condition of man.

The main body of short fiction in the century exhibits similar themes and concerns. With stimulating innovations from South America

(Borges, Cortázar [qq.v.]) to reinforce those from France, Russia, and the U.S. already at work in the native tradition, the short story continues to flourish.

Literary Criticism and the Essay

English criticism in the 20th c. has moved through many phases, answering in a variety of ways to Matthew Arnold's hope for the "right tone and temper of mind" and to his supposition that English critics would have to look abroad in the endeavor "to learn and propagate the best that is known and thought in the world."

Looking abroad, as it turned out, meant looking beyond literature to psychology, anthropology, political economy, the sciences, and arts, although it was also abroad in the national sense, considering the origins of such scientific innovators and theorists as Max Planck, Einstein, and Wittgenstein, political economists such as Marx and Engels, musicians such as Schoenberg and Stravinsky, and painters such as Kandinsky and Klee. These—as well as natives Alfred North Whitehead (1861–1947), Bertrand Russell (1872–1970), and John Maynard Keynes (1883–1946)—provided challenges to the primacy of literary studies as a civilizing force and to its pretensions to being an intellectual discipline.

English criticism did not, however, develop entirely as a response to forces outside literature. The asthetic movement of the *fin de siècle* continued in the work of Arthur Symons (1865–1945), historical criticism in the monumental work of such writers as William Courthope (1842–1917), George Saintsbury (1845–1933), and W. P. Ker (1855–1923), and the mediation between literature and public by such men of letters as Edmund Gosse (1849–1928), Walter Raleigh (1861–1922), Arthur Quiller-Couch (1863–1944), and H. W. Garrod (1878–1960).

But criticism tended to become more theoretical and rigorous. T. E. Hulme's *Speculations* (1924) was an attempt to foster strictness and precision in poetry. His early death in World War I interrupted his critical thinking in a still eclectic phase.

From the U.S. came Ezra Pound and T. S. Eliot to announce and develop an even more rigorous kind of criticism. Eliot's *Selected Essays* (1932) reveal the derivations of his theories: from the English metaphysical poets that intellect and passion must be joined, from the

French symbolists (q.v.) that images could be both specific and allusive, both theories anchored in the tradition of western Europe that was classical and Christian. He advanced his views as founder and editor of the influential quarterly *Criterion*.

I. A. Richards (q.v.) invoked the aid of psychology and utilitarian theory in *Principles of Literary Criticism* (1924) and *Practical Criticism* (1929) to promote an empirical approach to literary criticism.

Richards influenced a number of critics, some of whom had been his students. Notable among these, William Empson (q.v.), in *Seven Types of Ambiguity* (1930; rev. ed., 1953) analyzes the effects of multiple meanings inherent in words and images on our awareness of pleasure in aesthetic experience. The purpose of art, in his view, is utilitarian, facilitating our power to deal with our problems. Although a Marxist, Christopher Caudwell, who died in 1937 in the Spanish Civil War, had views similar to Empson's in this respect: that criticism evaluates the suitability of art's "mock world" for translation into action, as well as the work's degree of success in achieving the relationship between a work and its time.

F. R. Leavis (q.v.) proposed, following I. A. Richards, that the arts are "our storehouse of recorded values." In the periodical *Scrutiny* (1932–53) he advanced the proposition that great artists are important to a culture because they promote awareness of our human place in the world. Q. D. Leavis (b. 1906), Leavis's wife and associate, argues in parallel fashion that civilization depends to a high degree on the arts. This emphasis on the importance of art to civilization brought Leavis into conflict with C. P. Snow, who defended (in "The Two Cultures," 1956) what he considered the equal importance of the sciences.

Among those critics attempting to establish for literature a unifying function in a disintegrating world was Owen Barfield (b. 1898); in *Poetic Diction* (1928) he sees the language of poetry working to restore the original perception of unity between people and nature, of which humanity is the last stage. Barfield's basic optimism is qualified by awareness that humanity may choose instead abstraction and conceptualization "until it withers altogether."

Cyril Connolly (1903–1974), editor of the monthly *Horizon*, in *Enemies of Promise* (1938; rev. ed., 1948) and *The Condemned Playground* (1946) picked up on Barfield's idea that humanity through language and literature is capable of achieving a higher level of awareness.

David Daiches (b. 1912) renews the position of earlier critics such as E. M. Forster, who thought the critic's job is to "civilize the community," Percy Lubbock (1879–1965), whose *Craft of Fiction* (1921) deals with the literary representation of life in an "ideal shape," and Virginia Woolf, whose essays in *The Common Reader* (1925) took up the problems of the ordinary reader. Daiches, in *The Novel and the Modern World* (1939; rev. ed., 1960), developed the view that because literature manifests several kinds of discourse, criticism is obliged to be pluralistic, and the critic's job that of promoting "appreciation."

An influential eclectic critic is Herbert Read, who modernized romantic theory via Jung's psychology. *Selected Writings* (1964) represents his view that education through art is essential for satisfying the "symbolic needs of the unconscious."

Another critic whose personal influence has been extensive is Stephen Spender. The title of *The Struggle of the Modern* (1963) signifies both his sense of the literary scene in the middle decades and of his own commitment to breaking through social and political strictures on literary art. He worked for a time with Cyril Connolly on *Horizon*.

V. S. Pritchett is an autonomous and reliable critic whose observations reflect the clarity and unpretentiousness of his own fictions. In this respect, the novelist Walter Allen (b. 1911) has produced similarly cogent and enlightening commentary in *The English Novel* (1954) and *Tradition and Dream* (1964; Am., *The Modern Novel in Britain and the United States*, 1965).

From *Purity of Diction in English Verse* (1953) to *The Poet in the Imaginary Museum: Essays of Two Decades* (1976), Donald Davie has advocated a new classicism in language and an antiauthoritarian attitude in the poet.

The essay in England, aside from the critical essay, is not amenable to being surveyed. Its character is to be detached, personal, idiosyncratic, especially so in this eclectic, experimental century. The early decades produced the whimsical, charming, and always adroit pieces of Hilaire Belloc, G. K. Chesterton (qq.v.), and Max Beerbohm (1872–1956).

Writing into midcentury were E. M. Forster, George Orwell, Aldous Huxley, and Bertrand Russell, liberal commentators on the social and moral as well as cultural issues. Three collections characterize the midcentury: *Delight* (1949) by J. B. Priestley (q.v.), which describes ways of coping with various pressures; *Reflections in a Mirror* (1945), various forays

in search of values, by Charles Morgan (1894–1958); and *The Seven Deadly Sins* (1962), Angus Wilson and others, in which notable literary figures write on their "favorite sin."

The apocalyptic mood of the 1960s and 1970s is sounded in *Beyond All This Fiddle* (1968) and *The Savage God* (1971) by A. Alvarez (b. 1929), while W. H. Auden sounded the eclectic international note in *The Dyer's Hand* (1962) and *Forewords and Afterwords* (1973). In his eclecticism, Auden represents the trend in both literary criticism and the essay to assimilate the massive accretions to knowledge and understanding contributed by midcentury scientists and humanists.

BIBLIOGRAPHY: Graves, R., and Hodge, A., *The Long Week-end: A Social History of Great Britain 1918–1939* (1940); Leavis, F. R., *New Bearings in English Poetry* (1950); Tindall, W. Y., *Forces in Modern British Literature* (rev. ed., 1956); Allsop, K., *The Angry Decade* (1958); Alvarez, A., *Stewards of Excellence: Studies in Modern English and American Poets* (1958); Daiches, D., *The Present Age in British Literature* (1958); Gindin, J., *Postwar British Fiction* (1962); Karl, F., *A Reader's Guide to the Contemporary English Novel* (1962); Hall, J., *The Tragic Comedians: Seven Modern British Novelists* (1963); Johnstone, J. K., *The Bloomsbury Group* (1963); O'Connor, F., *The Lonely Voice: A Study of the Short Story* (1963); Stewart, J. I. M., *Eight Modern Writers*, *The Oxford History of English Literature*, Vol. XII (1963); Ford, B., ed., *The Pelican Guide to English Literature*, Vol. VII: *The Modern Age* (1964); Stead, C. K., *The New Poetic* (1964); Allen, W., *The Modern Novel in Britain and the United States* (1965); Ross, R., *The Georgian Revolt* (1965); Shapiro, C., ed., *Contemporary British Novelists* (1965); Enright, D. J., *Conspirators and Poets* (1966); Rosenthal, M. L., *The New Poets* (1967); Press, J., *Map of Modern English Verse* (1969); Bradbury, M., *The Social Context of Modern English Literature* (1971); Burgess, A., *The Novel Now* (1971); Sisson, C. H., *English Poetry, 1900–1950: An Assessment* (1971); Taylor, J. R., *The Second Wave: British Drama for the Seventies* (1971); Roy, E., *British Drama since Shaw* (1972); Stade, G., ed., *Six Modern British Novelists* (1974); Fussell, P., *The Great War and Modern Memory* (1975); Gillie, C., *Movements in English Literature, 1900–1940* (1975); Kenner, H., *The*

Pound Era (1975); Elsom, J., *Post-war British Theatre* (1976); Morris, R. K., ed., *Old Lines, New Forces: Essays on the Contemporary British Novel* (1976); Cavaliero, G., *The Rural Tradition in the English Novel 1900–1939* (1977); Homberger, E., *The Art of the Real: Poetry in England and America since 1939* (1977); Hynes, S., *The Auden Generation* (1977); Kerensky, O., *The New British Drama: Fourteen Playwrights since Osborne and Pinter* (1977); Hayman, R., *British Theatre since 1955: A Reassessment* (1979)

MANLY JOHNSON

ENGLISH-CARIBBEAN LITERATURE

Widespread illiteracy, the difficulty of publishing, and an isolated working environment prevented the emergence of English-Caribbean literature until the 20th c., despite the long colonial history of the region. Because publication abroad is harder to achieve for poets and dramatists than for fiction writers, there is still only one English-Caribbean poet of recognized distinction: Derek Walcott (q.v.), born in St. Lucia. Walcott is also the only dramatist of note.

The numerous "English" islands of the Caribbean (plus mainland Guyana) have an extremely diverse social and cultural heritage, but they share with other present and former British Commonwealth countries a common reaction to the restlessness and disaffiliation accompanying the struggle to discover traditions and establish a new society. It is not surprising, then, that the following themes recur in English-Caribbean literature: a sense of dislocation and dispossession among the black majority, and a consequent feeling that there is little history to be proud of in the region; the absence of a set of values acceptable to the majority; the social and economic discrimination suffered by the majority; and an overriding awareness of the role of race and color in the search for an authentic Caribbean identity. This last theme is now moving the literature away from social issues and toward cultural revolution, both on a group and individual level.

In his *The Pleasures of Exile* (1960), the Barbadian George Lamming (q.v.) argues that the third most important event in British-Caribbean history, after the actual discovery of the West Indies by Europeans and the abolition of slavery, was the "discovery of the novel by the West Indians as a way of projecting and investigating the inner experience of the West Indian

community." Lamming's own fiction, especially the classic *In the Castle of My Skin* (1953), does much to substantiate this claim. Where Lamming's fiction is concerned with the legacy of black slavery, the Trinidadian V. S. Naipaul (q.v.), in *The Mimic Men* (1967) and *A House for Mr. Biswas* (1961), investigates the restless alienation of the descendants of indentured servants from India in the New World. Transcending Naipaul's sense of desolation, the visionary Wilson Harris (q.v.) takes a simultaneous rather than a chronological or linear view of history in his novels in order to seek the hidden essences of the Caribbean experience. A Guyanese writer with a strong claim to universal significance, Harris offers, in the face of micro- and macrocosmic disruption brought on by economic, social, and ideological disorder, not a revolution of outward forms, but a more radical restructuring of modes of self-perception.

Other English-Caribbean fiction writers of note include the Jamaicans Claude McKay (q.v.), an early voice of protest against racism in the West Indies and the U.S.; Victor S. Reid (b. 1913), whose *New Day* (1949) is a revelation of the linguistic resources of West Indian English; and Andrew Salkey (b. 1928), whose *The Adventures of Catullus Kelly* (1969) treats the familiar expatriate theme of deracination; the Trinidadians Samuel Selvon (b. 1924), the chaotic lives of whose West Indians in London contrast oddly with the orderly form and language of his novels, and Michael Anthony (b. 1932), an explorer of sensibility and developing consciousness in the young; the Guyanese Edgar Mittelholzer (q.v.), a skillful exponent of Gothic melodrama, a favorite West Indian genre; and Jean Rhys (q.v.), whose *Voyage in the Dark* (1934) and *Wide Sargasso Sea* (1966) use the physical and mental conflicts and congruencies between England and her native Dominica to transcend the inherent melodrama of her subject matter.

Although still unemancipated from Victorian moralizing and Edwardian mannerisms at the turn of the century, English-Caribbean poetry went on to finer things in the work of A. L. Hendriks (b. 1923) of Jamaica, Edward Brathwaite (b. 1930) of Barbados, and Derek Walcott. Where Hendriks offers subdued meditations on the journey of the individual soul, Brathwaite's trilogy—*Rights of Passage* (1967), *Masks* (1968), *Islands* (1969)—dramatizes the destruction of the soul of the black race in his native Barbados. Walcott uses the idioms and rhythms of Caribbean dialects in the poetry of *In a Green Night* (1962) and *The Gulf, and Other Poems* (1969) and in plays such as *Dream on Monkey Mountain* (1970), but he achieves a universal resonance in his connection of the Caribbean situation with those of exploited peoples everywhere.

BIBLIOGRAPHY: Coulthard, G. R., *Race and Color in Caribbean Literature* (1962); Van Sertima, I., *Caribbean Writers* (1968); Moore, G., *The Chosen Tongue: English Writing in the Tropical World* (1969), pp. 3–131; Ramchand, K., *The West Indian Novel and Its Background* (1970); New, W. H., *Among Worlds: An Introduction to Modern Commonwealth and South African Fiction* (1975), pp. 7–37; New, W. H., ed., *Critical Writings on Commonwealth Literature* (1975), pp. 270–81, 311–12; Ramchand, K., *An Introduction to the Study of West Indian Literature* (1976); Griffiths, G., *A Double Exile: African and West Indian Writing between Two Cultures* (1978), pp. 79–139, 171–93; King, B., ed., *West Indian Literature* (1979); Gilkes, M., *The Development of the West Indian Novel* (1981)

JOHN H. FERRES

ENQUIST, Per Olov

Swedish novelist, dramatist, critic, and columnist, b. 23 Sept. 1934, Hjoggböle

Born and raised in northern Sweden, E. left the religious, provincial forest region to study at the University of Uppsala. A highly successful high-jumper as well as an academic, E. completed two degrees while working on his first novel, *Kristallögat* (1961; the crystal eye). With his third novel, *Magnetisörens femte vinter* (1964; the magnetizer's fifth winter), E. received widespread public and critical acclaim. A semidocumentary work, the novel narrates the story of a man resembling the famous experimenter in magnetism F. A. Mesmer. Even in this early work, the relationship between past and present appears as one of E.'s major themes. In *Hess* (1966; Hess) E. experimented with the novel form, developing techniques from the French New Novel (q.v.) to explore the unanswered questions about Rudolf Hess, who parachuted into England, supposedly on a peace mission, during World War II.

Legionärerna (1968; *The Legionnaires,* 1973) established E. as one of Sweden's most important young writers. In this novel E. attempted to retell the entire story of Sweden's deportation of a number of Baltic soldiers who fled from the German army at the end of World War II. The novel caused extensive debate, and E. was awarded Scandinavia's most important literary prize for it. *Sekonden* (1971; the second) builds on an actual sports event while it weaves together the puzzle of a dishonest athlete and his emotionally paralyzed son. This novel once again takes up E.'s preoccupation with the fraudulent man. As in *Magnetisörens femte vinter* and *Hess*, E. presents and analyzes the motives within those who deceive, as well as the need for deception in the general public. In *Magnetisörens femte vinter* this need derived from people's desire for faith in something, even if it is an illuison. In *Hess* the deception remains unresolved, while in *Sekonden,* the deceiver himself is revealed as a victim of society's need for progress, for new records and accomplishments, whether honestly or dishonestly attained. E.'s strong socialist orientation and human compassion pervade *Sekonden.*

A collection of essays, *Katedralen i München* (1972; the cathedral in Munich), resulted from newspaper articles he wrote at the Olympic Games in 1972, and a collection of stories, *Berättelser från de inställda upprorens tid* (1974; stories from the age of suspended revolutions), reflects his six months of lecturing at the University of California, Los Angeles, in 1973. *Tribadernas natt* (1975; *The Night of the Tribades,* 1977), E.'s first play, portrays August Strindberg's (q.v.) marital life in 1889. It attained international success.

E.'s most recent works continue his political concerns while employing documentary or historical techniques to probe the psychological and philosophical problems of modern man. The novel *Musikanternas uttåg* (1978; the exodus of the musicians) vividly describes the lives and working conditions of nonunion laborers in the early 1900s in northern Sweden. A central theme of this book, similar to that of *Tribadernas natt,* is the tragedy of those people who never find a way to make their lives meaningful, who seem to rot from the inside and destroy their own lives because they have no purpose in life. Hailed as a brilliant work and perhaps his finest novel, *Musikanternas uttåg* solidified E.'s position as a leading, albeit controversial, author.

FURTHER WORKS: *Färdvägen* (1963); *Chez nous* (1976, with Anders Ehnmark); *Mannen på trottoaren* (1979, with Anders Ehnmark); *Till Fedra* (1980); *En triptyk* (1981)

BIBLIOGRAPHY: Shideler, R., "The Swedish Short Story: P.O.E.," *SS*, 49 (1977), 241–62; Shideler, R., "Putting Together the Puzzle in P. O. E.'s *Sekonden*," *SS*, 49 (1977), 311–29; Shideler, R., Introduction to *The Night of the Tribades* (1977), pp. vii–xiv; Gill, B., "Fear of Women," *New Yorker*, 24 Oct. 1977, 143–44; Simon, J., "Strindberg Agonistes," *New York*, 31 Oct. 1977, 59; Björksten, I., "The Monumental Seventies," *Sweden Now*, 13, 1 (1979), 48–54

ROSS P. SHIDELER

ENRIGHT, D(ennis) J(oseph)
English poet, critic, and novelist, b. 11 March 1920, Leamington

E. received his B.A. (with honors) from Downing College, Cambridge, in 1944, and D. Litt. from the University of Alexandria (Egypt) in 1950. An international lecturer for the British Council, he taught at the Free University of West Berlin, the University of Alexandria, Chulalongkorn University in Bangkok, Thailand, and the University of Malaya at Singapore. A series of absurd clashes with regional authorities, beginning with an arrest in 1948 as a Jewish spy in Egypt (occasioned by a description of his religion as "lapsed Wesleyan Methodist," a persuasion that struck the secret police as seditious), early marked E. as "difficult"; his appointments with the British Foreign Service were frequently short-lived. As an independent scholar and lecturer, E. has also resided in Japan, Hong Kong, and London. In 1961 he was elected a Fellow of the Royal Society of Literature; he was coeditor (1972–74) of *Encounter* magazine; he is a director of the London publishing house Chatto and Windus.

E.'s critical interests range widely: he has written about Shakespeare, Goethe, Japanese poetry, travel literature, Third World academia, and Thomas Mann (q.v.). Although his criticism is not considered the most important aspect of his work, it is persistently learned and humane, "mixing," according to William Walsh, "moral sanity and sensitive charitableness in its judgments." E. dismisses the novels he has written as inconsequential, as "really travel books, I am afraid." *Heaven Knows Where* (1957), a gently satirical utopia, describes the happiness of an English teacher on the mythical Far Eastern island of Velo, where peace reigns supreme, love conquers all, and travel-poster clichés come to life.

E.'s poetry harbors far less coziness than his criticism or fiction, and it is for his poetry that he has achieved literary standing. His brittle, edgy descriptions of the excolonial Third World mock the few remaining nightmares of British Empire and wonder fearfully about the new tyrannies erupting in its place. Despite a preoccupation with formal prosody, the dominant mood of E.'s writing is anything but mannered; it is jagged, tormented, uncomfortably modern. In *The Old Adam* (1965) E.'s most common persona, the unregenerate observer, describes himself: "all my articulations flapping freely,/ Free from every prejudice, shaking all over." An instinct for naked nerve endings pervades E.'s small poems and intimate tragedies. He catalogues items of Third World existence that governments tend to ignore (legless beggars, starving prostitutes, blind suicides) and insists on their reality, their need for attention and love. He can be merciless in depicting the idiocy of officialdom while noting parenthetically that poetry, too, lives in a kind of "rotting ivory tower."

E.'s control of the complex tasks he sets for himself is admirable but not always perfect. His penchant for wordplay at times deflates the serious attention his work otherwise seems to demand. A jarring and sometimes unforgiveable cleverness ("Should one enter a caveat/Or a monastery?") drives out false profundity but it also, unfortunately, makes genuine concern difficult.

At his best, however, E. controls his tone carefully and speaks a compelling language. The condition of expatriate suits his subjects well. A perennial outsider, he captures the sense of transience, displacement, and loss that accompanies being foreign; he creates brilliant portraits of people who are homeless in their own land. While disclaiming any political bent, E. nonetheless writes almost exclusively about the wars—cultural, military, economic, and always intensely human—that dominate the political life of our times. The poet he sees as a minor but necessary combatant. His assessment of the role of poetry is modest: it should show the agony of the poor and voiceless in "words blurred by sweat," and work "some mild magic." And finally it should resurrect, from the exotic and extraordinary, a faith in the ordinary life of humankind.

FURTHER WORKS: *A Commentary on Goethe's "Faust"* (1949); *The Laughing Hyena, and Other Poems* (1953); *Academic Year* (1955); *The World of Dew: Aspects of Living Japan* (1955); *Literature for Man's Sake*

(1955); *Bread Rather than Blossoms* (1956); *The Apothecary Shop* (1957); *Some Men are Brothers* (1960); *Insufficient Poppy* (1960); *Addictions* (1962); *Figures of Speech* (1965); *Conspirators and Poets* (1966); *Unlawful Assembly* (1968); *Selected Poems* (1969); *Memoirs of a Mendicant Professor* (1969); *Shakespeare and the Students* (1970); *The Typewriter Revolution, and Other Poems* (1971); *In the Basilica of the Annunication* (1971); *Daughters of Earth* (1972); *Man Is an Onion: Essays and Reviews* (1972); *Foreign Devils* (1972); *The Terrible Shears: Scenes from a Twenties Childhood* (1973); *Rhymes Times Rhyme* (1974); *The Joke Shop* (1977); *Paradise Illustrated* (1978); *A Faust Book* (1980); *Collected Poems* (1981)

BIBLIOGRAPHY: Rosenthal, M. L., *The New Poets*, rev. ed. (1967), pp. 222–23; Gardner, P., "D. J. E. under the Cherry Tree," *ConL,* 9 (1968), 100–111; Dunn, D., "Underwriter," *NS,* 28 June 1974, 927–28; Walsh, W., *D. J. E.: Poet of Humanism* (1974); Bayley, J., "Word of an Englishman," *Listener,* 20 Nov. 1975, 681–83

LARRY TEN HARMSEL

ENZENSBERGER, Hans Magnus

West German poet and critic, b. 11 Nov. 1929, Kaufbeuren

E. grew up in Nuremberg, was drafted into the Volkssturm in 1944, and spent the early postwar years interpreting for the Americans and, like many Germans, dealing on the black market. He studied philosophy and literature in Erlangen, Freiburg, Hamburg, and at the Sorbonne in Paris. He later worked as an editor for the radio and for Suhrkamp publishers. After stays in the U.S., Mexico, Cuba, Italy, and Norway, he settled in Munich. He received the Büchner Prize in 1963 and was a member of Group 47.

E.'s first book of poems, *verteidigung der wölfe* (1957; defense of the wolves), immediately established him as Germany's angry young poet—angry not only at the "wolves" but also at the "lambs" who remain passive in the face of the wolves, that is, the establishment, the bureaucracy, advocates of rearmament, and so forth. His poetry draws on the whole breadth of literary tradition, myth, and folk poetry, as well as on contemporary science, politics, and advertising slogans. He de- and

re-forms these materials through montage, pun, and parody, and fuses the heterogeneous elements into a brilliant new diction that gives his satires their richness and bite. But it is their structural clarity that fixes their intellectual impact. Although E. does not use traditional forms, his poems are highly formal, with carefully worked out correspondences and parallels. Within this frame, syntactical ambiguities add surprise and a texture of multiple possibilities.

In *landessprache* (1960; language of the country), he continued in the vein of the first book, while in *blindenschrift* (1964; braille) the virtuosity gives way to a simpler, sparer mode that can be compared with Brecht's (q.v.) late poems. In *blindenschrift* E. wrote what he himself calls the best kind of political poem: where politics "creeps in, as it were, through cracks between the words." *Mausoleum* (1975; *Mausoleum,* 1976) shows E. at the height of maturity and skill, handling incisively, yet with ease, the ironies and contradictions of progress. He does it in a series of ballads, a portrait gallery of culture heroes, their achievements and disasters, their public and private nightmares.

E.'s literary activity includes editing many anthologies, in particular, *Museum der modernen Poesie* (1960; museum of modern poetry), and translating poets like William Carlos Williams, César Vallejo, and Pablo Neruda (qq.v.). He has from the beginning also written cultural and social criticism.

Einzelheiten (1962; *The Consciousness Industry,* 1974) contains pieces on contemporary writers and an essay on the poetics of commitment, but it is mostly noted for its sharp and witty analyses of the media—the "consciousness industry"—from newsreel to tourism, from the paperback book industry to the *Frankfurter Allgemeine Zeitung.* As the title (literally "details") announces, these essays criticize details, assumptions underlying common practices, rather than elaborating political theories. They plead for a life in accordance with reason while giving a good demonstration of it.

Politik und Verbrechen (1964; *Politics and Crime,* 1974) tries, more ambitiously, to reveal the criminal nature of politics by presenting well-documented parallels between the actions and methods of famous gangsters, businessmen, and statesmen. More recently, *Das Verhör von Habana* (1970; the Havana hearings), a dramatic condensation of the Cuban trials after the Bay of Pigs invasion, and *Der kurze Sommer der Anarchie* (1972; the short summer of anarchy), on the life of Buenaventura Durruti, a key figure of the Spanish revolution of 1936, fuse documentation with literary method to hold up a mirror in which we see ourselves and our society with truly double vision. Since 1965 E. has also edited *Kursbuch*, Germany's most important and original progressive journal. Its contributors represent as wide an international scale as the topics, which range from literature to Third World problems.

While E.'s political position took on a pro-revolutionary sharpness in the late 1960s, his refusal to subscribe to any ideology has been attacked by the left as well as the right. In his social criticism he remains eager to find the "right way," but doubtful that *the* right way exists. His particular importance lies in the fusion of high critical intelligence and extraordinary literary gifts. It is likely that his poems will indeed be poltical by his own definition, that is, by affecting our consciousness.

FURTHER WORKS: *Zupp* (1958); *Gedichte* (1962); *Einzelheiten*, Vol. II (1964); *Deutschland, Deutschland unter anderm* (1967); *Freisprüche* (1973); *Der Untergang der Titanic* (1978); *Die Furie des Verschwindens* (1980). FURTHER VOLUMES IN ENGLISH: *Poems* (1966); *Poems for People Who Don't Read Poems* (1968)

BIBLIOGRAPHY: Bridgwater, P., "H. M. E.," in Keith-Smith, B., ed., *Essays on Contemporary German Literature* (1966), pp. 239–58; Bridgwater, P., "The Making of a Poet: H. M. E.," *GL&L*, 21 (1967), 27–44; Gutmann, H., "Die Utopie der reinen Negation: Zur Lyrik H. M. E.s," *GQ*, 43 (1970), 435–52; Schickel, J., ed., *Über H. M. E.* (1970); Grimm, R., "The Commitment and Contradiction of H. M. E.," *BA,* 47 (1972), 285–98; Lohner, E., "H. M. E.," in Wiese, B. von, ed., *Deutsche Dichter der Gegenwart* (1972), pp. 531–44; Zimmermann, A., *H. M. E.: Die Gedichte und ihre literaturkritische Rezeption* (1976)
                                    ROSMARIE WALDROP

ESENIN, Sergey
See Yesenin, Sergey

ESKIMO LITERATURE

Among Eskimo communities, with a combined population of less than eighty thousand spread over a vast geographic area from Siberia to Scandinavia and from Greenland to Canada and Alaska, literature has traditionally been oral and unwritten. It consists mainly of poems and tales; fiction and drama are virtually nonexistent except for a few works by some Greenland authors.

One may consider as part of written literature the collecting, writing down, and translating of the oral heritage in the 20th c. Important recent anthologies in English include: *Beyond the High Hills: A Book of Eskimo Poems* (1961), *I Breathe a New Song: Poems of the Eskimo* (1971), *Songs of a Dream People* (1972), and *Eskimo Poems from Greenland and Canada* (1973).

The Eskimo language, which has numerous dialects, is part of the Eskimo-Aleut family, and may be related morphologically to the Turkic and Monogolian languages. Aside from some primitive picture-writing, Eskimo never had its own orthography. Under the influence of Scandinavian and North American missionaries and scholars who have circulated among them, most Eskimo communities, particularly in the 20th c., have adopted the Latin alphabet. But written literature and publication activity remain scarce.

In the latter part of the 20th c. the anonymous oral tradition is still dominant. Although many poets are identified by their names, it is not always certain if the poems attributed to them are their own individual compositions or merely recitations, with perhaps some modifications, of the received tradition as transcribed by Scandinavian and North American researchers. This uncertainty between originality versus restatement of patrimony is compounded by longstanding Eskimo custom whereby when a poet dies, his or her poems or versions become common property with scarcely a reference to the poet's name. It is fair to assume that, although the vast majority of Eskimo poems and tales seem to have been created spontaneously, they conform to rather rigid conventions handed down from generation to generation.

Eskimo history or life has yet to express itself in the form of an encompassing epic, although various communities have engendered many myths, legends, and tales. There have been no novels or short stories in the tradition of European or American fiction, except for a few tentative beginnings among some contemporary Greenland authors raised in the Christian tradition. Perhaps the most important Greenland Eskimo writer employing the Eskimo language was Henrik Lund (?–1948), who composed Christian hymns and published some nonreligious poems. Jonatan Petersen (dates n.a.) is also well known for many refined poems, which exhibit distinct Danish influences.

Autochthonous Eskimo poetry is the direct outcome of an arduous existence in a spare environment. Its aesthetic concerns are related to work, seasonal change, ritual, and daily life. Despite many fine lyrics expressing love of nature, human sentiments, lament, and the simple joys of life, Eskimo creativity is more utilitarian than artistic per se. The Eskimo language, which is rich in vocabulary relating to concrete objects but deficient in abstract terms, has no word meaning "art." Poetic as well as narrative style is spare, with no apparent concern for systematic form. Eskimo works convey images without embellishment, and make their statements in a straightforward manner with few emotive and affective terms.

Eskimo poetics include no set stanzaic forms, no prosody or rhyme patterns. From the outset, the entire poetic output seems to have been in free verse utilizing the natural built-in rhythmic patterns of the agglutinative language and the occasional, probably accidental, rhyming that results from identical or similar suffixes. It is, however, rich in formulaic and vocative expressions, alliterative devices, and frequent refrains, particularly in work songs that require a functional beat.

The typology of Eskimo poetry could be put into five distinct, occasionally overlapping categories, which share the above-mentioned aesthetic and linguistic features:

1. *Lyrics.* Chanted, usually with some musical accompaniment, these poems express human joy or suffering, scenes from nature, simple observations about life and fauna and flora; they include elegies and love poems.

2. *Work poems and functional verses.* These are recited rhythmically by one person or by a group engaged in rowing or hunting. Women's songs while doing the daily chores and lullabies may be included in this category, since they serve specific functions.

3. *Religious verse.* Much of Eskimo poetry is shamanic: the *angakok* (shamanistic priest), often to the accompaniment of drumbeat, presents stereotyped or improvisational poems for the purpose of sorcery, intercession with the spirits on behalf of his community, and thaumaturgy and cure. These magic prayers, incantations and songs probably have the most resourceful verbal imagination and the most compelling dramatic effect of any type of Eskimo poetic experience.

4. *Festive poetry.* In nonritualistic festivities, joyous songs are presented, with musical accompaniment and dances, mimic acts, various simple dramatic representations, etc., purely for entertainment. Children's songs, which exude joy and are usually accompanied by games, are also in this category.

5. *Satirical verse.* Eskimo communities have a long tradition of poetic satire, which ranges from short verses criticizing human foibles to vitriolic insults. Particularly interesting are the contests that pit two men or two women against one another in an exchange of accusations and contempt. In some Eskimo communities, such encounters take place for juridical purposes, whereby disputes may be settled as a result of poetic superiority.

Most of the myths and tales have interspersed in them a variety of verses, some of which are integral to the storyline and some of which provide lyric interludes.

The evolution of written literature by individual authors and poets will probably gain momentum by the end of the 20th c., and collective creativity will gradually diminish among Eskimo communities. The challenge facing the new generation of Eskimo writers will be to adapt various borrowed genres to their long tradition of oral poetry and narrative.

BIBLIOGRAPHY: Frederiksen, S., *Stylistic Forms in Greenland Eskimo Literature* (1954); Thalbitzer, W., "Eskimo Poetry," in *Encyclopedia of Poetry and Poetics* (1965), pp. 253–55; Carpenter, E., *Eskimo Realities* (1973), pp. 50–57; Rasmussen, K., ed., Introduction to *Eskimo Poems from Canada and Greenland* (1973), pp. xv–xxii

TALAT SAIT HALMAN

ESTONIAN LITERATURE

The Estonian language belongs to the western branch of the Finno-Ugric tongues, and its closest lexical affinities are with Finnish. There has been no illiteracy in Estonia since the beginning of the 19th c., a fact that helped to develop a rich body of literature. In proportion to the size of its population, Estonia has published more titles, and printed them in larger editions, than any other nation in Europe except Iceland.

The principal monuments of Estonian literature before the 20th c. are the great number of of folksongs (400,000 for a population of 1,300,000), and the *Kalevipoeg* (Kalev's son), a folk epic that fused into an organic whole the ancient Estonian myths and legends. It was conceived from the 10th to 13th cs., but was written down in the 19th c. and somewhat awkwardly edited by the poet Friedrich Reinhold Kreutzwald (1803–1882)—an English version was published under the title *The Hero of Estonia* (1895). Unfortunately, the first translations of the Bible (1688, 1715, 1739), all made by German theologians, lacked literary quality and thus could not help to create a national literary language. Estonian literary writing started to develop in the 17th c. but it achieved its first maturity in the spontaneous lyrics of Kristjan Jaak Peterson (1801–1822), Lydia Koidula (1843–1886), Anna Haava (1864–1957), and Juhan Liiv (q.v.). Although deeply immersed in 19th-c. romantic traditions, Haava and Liiv belong in the greater part of their work to the 20th c., and Liiv, as highly original, passionate inventor of symbols, was the first Estonian poet to achieve true visionary significance.

Compared with Finnish and Scandinavian literatures, the literature of the Estonian people presents a strangely broken and interrupted course. The explanation of this irregularity of development is to be found in Estonia's checkered political history and in the provocative character of the national mind as expressed in literature. The real significance of its 20th-c. intellectual history is outside literature, namely in five forces that changed it: the abortive revolution of 1905 against Russian government and German landlords; the successful war of independence against Russia in 1918–20; the period of modern national sovereignty between 1918 and 1940; the Soviet annexation of Estonia in 1940; and the mass exodus in 1943–44 of writers who sought abroad the freedom and intellectual springs of action that Estonia under German and Soviet occupation withheld from them.

Poetry

The first artistically perfect work of the 20th c. was Villem Ridala's (1885–1942) *Laulud* (1908; songs). It had flowing meter, a breadth of genuine poetic enthusiasm as well as a melancholy not before touched, and a softness of language in the manner of Verlaine that has not been surpassed in Estonian. At the same time, Ridala was the first to establish in literary poetry what has been the austere rhythmical rule of Estonian folk poetry: the exact union of the phonetic duration of a given syllable with the metrical accent, an acoustic method used by

Greek and Latin poets. Ridala's ballads lack the needed epic strength, but in his shorter pieces he remains a poet of indubitable mastery. He contributed to the widening of the Estonian imagination by introducing to Estonians remote literary settings, largely under Italian inspiration. He translated Giosuè Carducci (1835–1907) and Benedetto Croce (q.v.) earlier than anybody else in Europe, believing that the Italian example was needed for the renascence of Estonian culture.

The great stimulus and activity of the period came, however, from Gustav Suits (1883–1956), a poet, critic, journalist, and literary historian. A volume of lyrical, patriotic, and political poems, *Elutuli* (1905; fire of life), written in part in the vein of the Finnish poet Eino Leino (q.v.), established his fame, and four collections published in 1913, 1920, 1922, and 1950 contain a number of neosymbolist poems that still hold the Estonian reader. Suits's tragedy is that his influence as a public figure and inspiring intellectual leader, who fought successfully against the provincialism of Estonian culture as the leader of the Young Estonia group, is greater than his importance as a poet. Like the German poet Stefan George (q.v.), his mentor (although Suits seldom achieved the latter's monumentality and finished elegance), he, too, wanted to be a modern Dante, an idea that led him to the autocratic dreams of the cult of self, cramping and almost destroying his considerable creative faculties.

The opposite of Suits, the humble poet Liiv, who lived a tragedy-filled life, did not ask for any recognition or esteem, but he is, nonetheless, the only talent of the period who stands above his time. He was followed by the expressionist (q.v.) Jaan Oks (1884–1918), a prose writer and poet of striking intensity, whose stylistic, philosophical, and mystico-pathological originality has not been fully recognized, and yet may in its power be compared to Strindberg's (q.v.).

Other strongly instinctive poetic talents of the period are the very musical, mystically and theosophically inclined symbolist (q.v.) Ernst Enno (1875–1934); the symbolist-expressionist August Alle (1890–1952), one of the most gifted Estonian poets, whose work sharply declined in quality after he became an offical spokesman for the Soviet regime in 1940; Henrik Visnapuu (1890–1951) and Marie Under (q.v.), the two most important figures of the Siuru group; Hendrik Adamson (1891–1946), a nature poet who used the south-central Estonian dialect called *mulgi* for his poems resembling folk songs; and the master of quantitative Estonian verse, who successfully used both the meter of old Estonian folk songs and the meter of the *Iliad* and the *Odyssey*, August Annist (1899–1972).

Marie Under's greatness lies in a mind remarkable for its intelligent sincerity and independent temper, as well as in the rhythmical urgency, vivid language, and intense fluency of her line. She started as an impressionist of flaming youth. Her book *Sonetid* (1917; sonnets) contained poems of erotic sensibility that shocked and delighted Estonian's Protestant readers. Under the influence of German expressionism she changed drastically in the early 1920s and ventured into verse full of somber and vehement moral and social pronouncements. By 1930, having matured emotionally, she introduced a philosophical tone into her poetry; her whole being now strained toward the hidden mystery of existence. Without losing her poetic power, she continued to produce books of symbolic and metaphysical insight, her acclaimed and also representative titles being *Kivi südamelt* (1935; the stone off the heart) and *Ääremail* (1963; in the borderlands). Under is today recognized both by the discriminating few and by the mass of readers as Estonia's national poet.

The work of Henrik Visnapuu is somewhat similar to that of the early Under. His first books were masterpieces of mannerist experiment and showed great promise. Mixing the elements of Estonian folksong with the musical devices of the Russian poets Konstantin Balmont (q.v.) and Igor Severyanin (1887–1941), Visnapuu achieved sensuous splendor rarely exhibited in the Protestant culture of Estonia. The lyrical impulse, exquisite in local color and fidelity to national characteristics, was present in his work until the middle 1930s (when he became an official poet), and was then replaced by a militantly nationalistic, didactic, and even journalistic weariness foreign to his innermost fire of genius.

There are younger poets whose styles are likewise chiefly lyrical, among them Arno Vihalemm (b. 1911), who started in the tradition of the Arbujad, or Soothsayers, movement of the 1930s, and later followed the styles of Liiv and of the Swede Nils Ferlin (q.v.), incorporating into them elements of "pop" poetry; the intimate pantheist Bernard Kangro (b. 1910); the modernist stylizer of folk song and patriotic poet Kalju Lepik (b. 1920); the surreal visionary Artur Alliksaar (1923–1966); the uneven

but authentic lyricist of emotional rhapsodic style Paul-Eerik Rummo (b. 1942); and a refined mannerist, poet and prose writer, as well as geologist and hunter, Nikolai Baturin (b. 1936), whose fine, linguistically and metaphorically innovative work is an impressive artistic achievement.

In contrast to the practitioners of emotional verse that had themes relating to the soil, and to the current of arrogant "titanism" that was developing, Estonia also produced several modernist poets. After Suits there was first Valmar Adams (b. 1899), who excelled in melodious, cerebral poems and *vers de société*, being the only master of Estonian light verse. He matured formally and philosophically up until *Tunnetuse tund* (1939; hour of cognition), his finest book, and then, after having spent several years in Soviet prisons, he went into almost total decline.

Poet-thinkers and metrists of the first order, the married couple Heiti Talvik and Betti Alver (qq.v.), leaders of the Arbujad group, started as distant disciples of Suits but surpassed him in technique and formal elegance, having molded the language into perfect elasticity. They venerated especially the work of Ants Oras (b. 1900), poet-translator and critic-stylist who combined a cosmopolitan polish with a profound insight. Oras, Alver, and Talvik together created a school of intellectual poetry that is still flourishing. Among their important followers are the "unautomatic" surrealist (q.v.) Ilmar Laaban (b. 1921), whose every word and image is aesthetically premeditated; the lyrical classicist Harri Asi (b. 1922); a surreal poet of strong psychic tension, who is at the same time a craftsman of closed form, Ivar Grünthal (b. 1924); and two intellectual poets of surgical grace, Ain Kaalep (b. 1926) and Jaan Kaplinski (b. 1941). Uku Masing (q.v.), who was a member of the original Arbujad group, is an outsider of metaphysical vigor, originality of form, and extraordinary command in the poetical appeal in sound, imagery, and suggestion filled with mysticism and spiritual significance; he has been compared to Gerard Manley Hopkins and T. S. Eliot (q.v.).

Criticism

A collection of Ants Oras's selected essays and studies, published under the title *Laiemasse ringi* (1961; into a wider circle), showed him as an adversary of criticism that emphasized sociological, ethnological, and political factors in literary creation. For him, literature was an expression of spirituality and form, and he elevated aesthetic appreciation to the primary position. Oras's studies manifest the highest scholarly and stylistic values reached in Estonian thought and show him as a man of almost universal attainment, but it is mainly in his verse that he has left his mark on the literature of Estonia. He also brought to Estonia the influence of English and American belles lettres and criticism. With him Estonian thought and literature arrived in the 1930s at that stability in form and ideas essential to a great literary period.

Next to Oras stands Aleksander Aspel (1908–1975), his friend and codefender of the "spirit of lightness" directed against the "spirit of heaviness" of the naturalists. He, too, turned criticism into an expression of learning, intelligence, and refinement, but guided writers and readers toward French literary art. He introduced French modernist writers to Estonian readers; a romanticist and a pupil-associate of the French philosopher and critic Gaston Bachelard (1884–1962), he insisted that vision should not be dominated by reason alone.

In addition to the studies by Oras and Aspel, much research of scholarly value has been done by Johannes Aavik (1880–1973), August Annist, Oskar Urgart (1900–1953), Viktor Terras (b. 1921), Viktor Kõressaar (b. 1916), Paul Saagpakk (b. 1910), Endel Nirk (b. 1925), Ivar Ivask (b. 1927)—a noted poet as well, who was praised by Boris Pasternak (q.v.)—Jaak Põldmäe (1942–1980), Helmi Eller (dates n.a.), Jaan Puhvel (b. 1931), and Heino Puhvel (b. 1926). Among the intuitive critics, Friedebert Tuglas (1886–1971), Bernard Kangro, Karl Ristikivi (1912–1977), Asta Willmann (b. 1916), and Ilmar Laaban must be mentioned.

Fiction

Like Estonian poetry, Estonian fiction, which has not matched the accomplishments of the poetry, is a braid of alien roots. Its development shows Scandinavian, German, French, and Russian influences. In symbolist prose Friedebert Tuglas and especially Aleksander Tassa (1882–1955) manifested skill in short stories. Tuglas's most mature book, *Väike Illimar* (1937; little Illimar), demonstrates, however, the subtle use of descriptive realism. Before Oras, Tuglas was considered the leading Estonian literary critic; he came to the fore under the influence of impressionism and left behind him a vast legacy of novellas, essays, and reviews.

Two of the most esteemed authors of the 1920s and 1930s were August Gailit (1891–1960) and Karl Rumor (pseud. of Karl Ast, 1886–1971). Gailit began as a writer of great promise—his novel *Toomas Nipernaadi* (1928; Toomas Nipernaadi), written in an impressionistic style, is one of the books most beloved by Estonian readers—but his artisitic powers later declined. Rumor was an intellectual journalist whose work belongs more to the history of Estonian thought than to literature, although in his old age he produced a powerful novel, *Krutsifiks* (1960; the crucifix), characterized by Ants Oras as a work of "exciting unity of vision and style."

The leading realists were Eduard Vilde (1865–1933) and A. H. Tammsaare (q.v.). Tammsaare is generally acclaimed for his monumental five-volume novel (or, more accurately, lengthy prose drama) *Tõde ja õigus* (1926–33; truth and righteousness). Strong in its first volumes, it becomes very uneven in the later ones and accentuates that tendency toward the formlessness and length that always have been weaknesses of the Estonian novel. Tammsaare's truly consummate craftsmanship is displayed in the grotesque philosophical novel *Põrgupõhja uus vanapagan* (1939; *The Misadventures of the New Satan*, 1978).

Perhaps the purest single example of critical realism is Karl Ristikivi's (q.v.) concentrated socioethical novel *Tuli ja raud* (1938; fire and iron). But this remarkable book, which was praised by Tammsaare, stands alone in Ristikivi's work, since he later changed his style to deeply felt philosophical and poetical realism. Among Tammsaare's and Ristikivi's contemporaries were Karl August Hindrey (1875–1947), who used expertly stylized settings and poetic dialogue, and Peet Vallak (1893–1959), in whose colorful work a thematic collision between idealism and naturalism takes place.

Other writers of fiction of distinction have moved into the spotlight in recent decades. They are Katrin Jakobi (b. 1909), whose sole collection of short stories *Suvekodumaa* (1975; summer's homeland) is probably the most refined work of Estonian prose; Bernard Kangro, a lyric fictionalist whose rhapsodic style may be partly compared with Lawrence Durrell's (q.v.) and who claims surreal room for the play of creative imagination; Asta Willmann, who in her experimental expressionistic masterpiece *Hundisõidul* (1975; tracking down the wolves) unites theater and novel; the subtly ironic and stirring intellectual Enn Vetemaa (b.

1936); and Asta Põldmäe (b. 1944), distinguished by her ability to produce in a laconic style the complex structures of natural symbolism, a fact that gives her works the force of parables. The historical novelist Jaan Kross (b. 1920) has put aside the idealizing glasses of his predecessors and is trying to destroy the myths of the heroes of the National Awakening of the 19th c. Markedly tendentious but showing talent and taste, his work reveals the incompatibility of political conformity and artistic achievement.

Of writers translated into English and other languages, the most noted is the novelist Arved Viirlaid (b. 1922). He began as a poet, and in both poetry and prose is a politically engaged writer. His novels *Sadu jõkke* (pub. 1965; *Rain for the River*, 1964) and *Ristideta hauad* (1952; *Graves without Crosses*, 1972), both about Estonia during World War II, are examples of a fundamentally 19th-c. realist tradition.

Drama

Drama has not been a preeminent form in Estonian literature. The popular dramatists at the beginning of the century were Eduard Vilde and August Kitzberg (1855–1927), who had no lasting significance. The only play of the early part of the 20th c. that relied on implication and suggestion rather than mere bald statement was Tammsaare's masterful symbolist and expressionist poetic drama *Juudit* (1921; Judith). His later play, *Kuningal on külm* (1936; the king feels cold), is a pamphleteering allegory striving for effect but not reaching the depth of *Juudit*. Among the successful political dramatists were Oskar Luts (1887–1953) and Hugo Raudsepp (1883–1952), who provoked controversy by their insistence on painful social themes. New talents emerged after World War II, both in exile and, after Stalin's death, in Soviet-occupied Estonia. Of these, the most important are Paul-Eerik Rummo, Ain Kaalep, and Artur Alliksaar, all three poets as well, and Bernard Kangro, Asta Willmann, Ilmar Külvet (b. 1920), and Mati Unt (b. 1944). The various experiments with new techniques—primarily Theater of the Absurd (q.v.)—as a reaction to Socialist Realism (q.v.) in Estonia proper, and the wish to convey significant symbolic commentaries in plays written abroad, have made Estonian drama more alive and artistic in the last two decades than for many years before.

Estonian literature in Soviet-occupied Estonia, literature as belles lettres, has been emerging slowly and with great difficulty from its subservience to Soviet utilitarian didacticism and the dogma of Socialist Realism. A number of important writers living in Estonia have aimed at continuing the work of the period of Estonian independence under the new conditions, expressing a restricted, private, and passive spirit of compromise between frustrated idealism and possible accomplishment and fulfillment. Estonian literature in exile, on the other hand, has lost through death many of its best writers and is today, although still representative, in a state of crisis. Both in Estonia and abroad there is undoubtedly a considerable breadth of literary dexterity, and not perhaps a small one of creative spirit, but it requires the settling, clarifying, and distinguishing effects of time to separate the artist from the minor writer.

BIBLIOGRAPHY: Harris, E. H., *Literature in Estonia*, 2nd ed. (1947); Kõressaar, V., and Rannit, A., eds., *Estonian Poetry and Language: Studies in Honor of Ants Oras* (1965); Jänes, H., *Geschichte der estnischen Literatur* (1965); Oras, A., *Estonian Literature in Exile: An Essay*, with a bio-bibliographical appendix by B. Kangro (1967); Aspel, A., et al., *The Yale Lectures on Estonian Poetry* (1968); Mägi, A., *Estonian Literature: An Outline* (1968); Valgemäe, M., "Recent Developments in Soviet Estonian Drama," *Bulletin of the Institute for the Study of the USSR* (Munich), 16, 9 (1969), 16–24; Rubulis, A., *Baltic Literature: A Survey of Finnish, Estonian, Latvian, and Lithuanian Literatures* (1970), pp. 55–104; Nirk, E., *Estonian Literature: Historical Survey with Bio-bibliographical Appendix* (1970); Ziedonis, A., ed., *Baltic Literature and Linguistics* (1973); Ivask, I., "Estonian Literature," in Ivask, I., and Wilpert, G. von, eds., *World Literature since 1945* (1973), pp. 168–77; special Estonian section, *BA*, 47, 4 (1973), 636–63; Mallene, E., *Estonian Literature in the Early 1970s* (1978); Terras, V., "American-Estonian Poets," *PCLS*, 9 (1978), 175–92; Valgemäe, M., "Estonian Drama," in Straumanis, A., ed., *Baltic Drama* (1981), pp. 1–112; Leitch, B., ed., *The Poetry of Estonia* (1982)

ALEKSIS RANNIT

For the contributions of the author of this article to Estonian literature, please see separate entry.—Ed.

ETHIOPIAN LITERATURE

Ethiopia possesses a rich and ancient literary tradition, yet only in recent decades has a truly modern Ethiopian literature begun to evolve. This literature, unlike that of most African countries, has emerged under noncolonial conditions, and thus is not a literature of protest against foreign domination. Instead it has drawn heavily upon centuries of religious and moral writings in Ge'ez, the old Ethiopic literary language which still survives as a liturgical language in the Ethiopian Orthodox Church but which is now meaningless to all but a small number of Church-educated Ethiopians.

Ethiopia's official language, Amharic, existed for centuries as a vernacular before finally becoming in the 20th c. an accepted literary language. The early 1900s saw the beginnings of Amharic literature, even though it had to compete initially with Ge'ez. Earliest Amharic writing tended to be infused with stock moral didacticism, and often still is, influenced as it has been by the traditional association of Ge'ez literature with ethical instruction.

The first Amharic novel, *Lebb wallad tarik* (1908; *Tobbya,* 1964), by Afawarq Gabre Yesus (1868–1947), clearly presented its moral purpose with the introductory comment that "much is due to him who is kind to others, much is lost to him who does evil to others." Other early writers, such as Makonnen Endalkachew (1892–1963) and Kebebe Mikael (b. 1915), concentrated on moral edification and glorification of Ethiopia's past in their short fiction and plays.

More recent Amharic writing has frequently remained in line with tradition or else risked government suppression, and as yet consists largely of short pamphlet-novels, some didactic poetry, and short patriotic plays.

Unfortunately, only a handful of non-Ethiopians can read Amharic, with its unique syllabic script, and Ethiopians have felt the same artistic and economic impulses to write in a language of wider currency that have motivated other African authors. After World War II English became the accepted second language of Ethiopia, and English translations of Amharic and Ge'ez works soon became popular. Such translations directly preceded significant creative work in English. In 1964 the *Ethiopia Observer* published in translation *Marriage by Abduction,* a short play, first published in Amharic in 1955, by Menghistu Lemma (b. 1925), and thus brought this notable author to the attention of the English-speaking world.

This play breaks with traditional Ethiopian sermonizing drama by being a comedy of manners based on reconciling tribal marriage customs with modern ones. It sets the tone for a longer and more important play by the same author, first published in Amharic in 1957 and in English as *The Marriage of Unequals* (1970), whose satire focuses on social and economic inequality, highlighted by the main character, Baharu, an Ethiopian version of the "been-to" who instead of using his foreign education to get the usual cushy administrative job in Addis Ababa, goes to live in a remote village, where he starts a school and a number of self-help programs.

Abbe Gubegna (b. 1934) is well known in Ethiopia for his popular moralistic Amharic writing. Unfortunately his *The Savage Girl* (1964), the first Ethiopian play written in English, does not possess the technical qualities of Menghistu Lemma's drama. An allegory based on history, the play teaches the virtues of isolationism and hatred of change; a forest girl living an idyllic natural life—she has a Bible, however, symbolizing Ethiopia's sixteen centuries of Christianity—finds the impact of the outside world to be fatal.

The weaknesses of *The Savage Girl* are not to be found in the drama of Tsegaye Gabre-Medhin (b. 1936), Ethiopia's leading playwright. He has written and directed over twenty Amharic plays dealing with social and historic themes, and has also written some internationally noted English poetry and drama. His short historical play *Tewodros*, first performed in 1963, led to the opening of the Creative Arts Center in Addis Ababa. Emperor Tewodros (fl. 1855–68), a popular figure in Ethiopian literature and art, is here portrayed as a heroic visionary dreaming of a homeland free of factionalism who is prepared to sacrifice all to this end, beset as he is on all sides by foreign intrigue and local warring chieftains.

Tsegaye Gabre-Medhin's more recent play, *Collision of Your Altars* (1977), turns to a more ancient historical period, that of the disintegration of Emperor Kaleb's Auxmite Ethiopia (A.D. 587–629), but this author's best-known English work, *Oda-Oak Oracle* (1965), has found its popularity at least partly because of its more universal and archetypal plot, which includes an ancestoral command, an obligatory sacrifice, and a tribal "strong son" who has been blessed with a strength that is also a great curse.

In 1961 the *Ethiopia Observer* published "Truth," an English translation of an Amharic short story (1958) by Alamayyawh Mogas (dates n.a.). Although strictly in the moralistic tradition, relating how a successful man rejects true friendship for a false lover, this story was the harbinger of a series of stories soon to be written in English. Unfortunately, few are available outside of Ethiopia, mostly appearing in *Something*, a transitory journal of the English department of what was then Haile Sellassie I University. Most are concerned with moral instruction, although some venture into social criticism—as does Tesfaye Gessesse's (dates n.a.) "Ayee My Luck," which attained wider recognition through its publication in *African Arts* (1971).

Amharic poetry has as yet shown only limited development, in the work of Menghistu Lemma and Solomon Deressa (b. 1937). Deressa's "Legennaat" (1968; childhood) might be considered the beginnings of modern Amharic poetry. Poetry in English ranges from weak, amateurish attempts published locally by their authors to the inspired work of Tsegaye Gabre-Medhin and Solomon Deressa. A weighty awareness of their country's ancient heritage permeates the work in both English and Amharic of Ethiopia's poets; this heritage is frequently judged an albatross to be rid of, as, by implication, are the traditional ideas of Ge'ez and Amharic literature. Fiercely contrasting images depict Ethiopia; it is a nation with a rich and ancient heritage perhaps, yet also a land of hideous poverty, feudal exploitation, and numbing lethargy. Modernism might be shunned, yet like it or not, after centuries of slumber the nation must awaken, no matter how uncertain the world it awakens to might be.

The artistic limitations of didacticism often found in Ge'ez and Amharic writing are also evident in *Confession* (1962), the first English-language novel by an Ethiopian. Yet its author, Ashenafi Kebede (b. 1937), effectively presents a picture of the problems of an Ethiopian student abroad in race-conscious America—a new theme for Ethiopian literature. Another writer, Sahle Sellassie (b. 1936), places his novels only in indigenous settings. After his successful translation (from his Chaha-language original) of *Shinega's Village* (1964), dealing with village life and the inevitable conflicts with modern influences, Sahle Sellassie wrote his next novel, *The Afersata* (1968), in English.

The Afersata suffers from a thin plot resting on the burning of a villager's hut and an ensuing investigation carried out by a local committee, or *afersata*, yet the author achieves an effective feeling for the highly communal and self-sufficient nature of peasant society. In his next novel, *Warrior King* (1974), he turned to the ever-popular Emperor Tewodros and the sense of patriotism and pride evoked by this historical figure.

Any technical shortcomings in these novels are more than compensated for in *The Thirteenth Sun* (1973), written in English by Daniachew Worku (b. 1936), an author who has also written some Amharic plays, short stories, and poems. Taking its title from the Ethiopian calendar, which consists of a thirteen-month year, the novel is set in the present yet is full of an awareness of the past—a past seen with the critical eye of recent poets rather than traditional or patriotic authors. The past is the pollutant of contemporary life. Goytom's pilgrimage up Mount Zekwala to Abbo Shrine with his half-sister and dying father allows to unfold a broad panorama of the brutal realities of present-day Ethiopia, rooted as they are in the medieval nature of that society. Violence and exploitation overwhelm the reader; the Church is the great profiteer of the poor, the sick, and the superstitious. The land, long ravished by an unenlightened peasantry, now enslaves them; their ignorance, poverty, and the feudal system that victimizes them all work to transform them into callous, sullen, and brutish creatures.

It is not yet evident that *The Thirteenth Sun* is the precursor of a new, sophisticated Ethiopian novel aimed at an international audience. Time may prove it to be, but so far it has been succeeded only by Sahle Sellassie's *Warrior King* and by Abbe Gubegna's *Defiance* (1975), two novels primarily concerned with extolling Ethiopia's past. Set in Addis Ababa in 1937 during the Italian occupation, *Defiance* focuses on an old patriot, Fitawrari Abesha, and his family's resistance to their Italian persecutors. It is clear from the handling of his material that the author has matured considerably since the publication of his drama *The Savage Girl* a decade earlier. Some effective description brings to life a Fascist dungeon for Ethiopians, atrocities, and a hillside battle. If *Defiance* is a timely reminder to Ethiopians of hardships suffered once before under an oppressive rule, it is also an indication, along with the best of Sahle Sellassie, Daniachew Worku, Tsegaye Gabre-Medhin, and others, that Ethiopian writers possess the resources and potential for significant literary contributions to African literature.

BIBLIOGRAPHY: Harden, J. M., *An Introduction to Ethiopic Christian Literature* (1926); Gérard, A. S., *Four African Literatures: Xhosa, Sotho, Zulu, Amharic* (1971), pp. 271–376; Huntsberger, P. E., comp., *Highland*

Mosaic: A Critical Anthology of Ethiopian Literature in English (1973), pp. 1–13, 28–47, 72–82, 106–15; Beer, D. F., "Ethiopian Literature and Literary Criticism in English: An Annotated Bibliography," *RAL*, 6 (1975), 44–57; Kane, T. L., *Ethiopian Literature in Amharic* (1975); Beer, D. F., "The Sources and Content of Ethiopian Creative Writing in English," *RAL*, 8 (1977), 99–124; Molvaer, R. K., *Tradition and Change in Ethiopia: Social and Cultural Life as Reflected in Amharic Fictional Literature, ca. 1930–1974* (1980)

DAVID F. BEER

EVTUSHENKO, Evgeny

See Yevtushenko, Yevgeny

EXISTENTIALISM

Existentialism became important as a philosophical position in Germany following World War I, and it dominated the philosophical and literary scene in France for twenty years or so beginning in the late 1930s, particularly during the decade following World War II. Existentialist thinkers can hardly be said to have formed a school or even a coherent group, however; rather than being a systematic philosophy, existentialism is a form of the individualistic, antirationalist current that can be traced back to the very beginnings of Western civilization.

Modern existentialism has its origins in the antirationalism of the late 18th and early 19th cs. The romantics' emphasis on individual experience as opposed to the general human values stressed by neoclassicists; their upholding of emotion and instinct over reason; their revolt against and alienation from the dominant bourgeois society; and their anguish in their alienation can be seen in retrospect as an expression of the existentialist point of view. We find these tendencies in varying degrees in Blake, the early Goethe, Hölderlin, and Musset, to mention only a few major writers, as well as in many minor figures less gifted in formulating their anguish in literary terms. These characteristics are even stronger in poets like Baudelaire and Rimbaud, and are present in many early 20th-c. writers.

None of these 19th-c. antecedents could be said to be a conscious source for modern existentialism, however. The one figure to whom all existentialists acknowledge their indebtedness is Søren Kierkegaard (1813–1855), the Danish thinker who was as much a poet as a philosopher. He reacted sharply against established Christianity and the systematic philosophy of Hegel (1770–1831), who defended a rational Christianity and saw human history as God's intelligible plan for mankind. Kierkegaard insisted rather that the individual make an irrational choice between Christ and the world, a "leap of faith," and that he live, that is, take the responsibility for that choice, not merely reason about it. The primacy of existential reality, the necessity of choice, and the anguish in the face of the responsibility the choice imposes are all found in modern existentialist philosophy and literature.

Friedrich Nietzsche (1844–1900), like Kierkegaard a colorful, nonacademic philosopher, is a second major source for modern existentialist thought. He attacked the basic foundations of Christianity and of the decadent rational world he encountered. He insisted that the superior individual strive toward the creation of new values through his power of self-perfection, eventually emerging as a "superman." Whereas Kierkegaard's point of view was theistic (the religious experience was on a higher level than the aesthetic or the ethical), for Nietzsche the historical God was dead, as were all absolutes in which man had traditionally found his values. They were replaced by the power of the new superman, who had to create himself by transcending the nihilism around him.

Along with Kierkegaard, the poet of theological anguish, and Nietzsche, the dramatizer of philosophical nihilism, a third major 19th-c. source for modern existentialism is Fyodor Dostoevsky. Neither a theologian nor a philosopher, he was nonetheless strongly attached to Russian Orthodox Christianity, and his characters suffer the agony of the struggle between the forces of evil and weakness in themselves and the miracle and mystery of redemption. His exploration of the irrational and the depths of human despair has been a major influence on 20th c. thought and fiction, and particularly on existentialism.

The two most important philosophical descendents of Kierkegaard and Nietzsche writing in 20th-c. Germany were Karl Jaspers (1883–1969) and Martin Heidegger (1889–1976). Jaspers's *Die geistige Situation der Zeit* (1931; *Man in the Modern Age*, 1933) responded to the crumbling of the German middle class following World War I; he maintained that the historical meaning of existential philosophy is its attempt to awaken in the individual the possibilities for an authentic and genuine life in our highly organized, technological, depersonalizing society. He joined Kierkegaard in rejecting rationalistic systems like Hegel's, but Kierkegaard's Christian perspective became merely a sense that human limitations imply only some source of being beyond man. Gabriel Marcel (q.v.) in France was also a part of this theistic orientation, but the influence of Henri Bergson (q.v.) on him was just as important as Kierkegaard's. Existentialist elements are also present in the work of Martin Buber (q.v.) and of many other modern theologians and philosophers.

Heidegger was a more formal philosopher and a more direct descendent of Nietzsche, in that God is absent from his world. In *Sein und Zeit* (1927; *Being and Time,* 1962) he attempted to revise and complete the history of ontology, the study of Being. Heidegger went beyond his teacher, the phenomenologist Edmund Husserl (1859–1938), for whom philosophy was a description of what is, of things themselves, and maintained that the phenomena of existence would reveal themselves if we did not impose our preconceptions on them. Man is not defined by his thought and its relationship to the physical world, as Descartes (1596–1650), with his *Cogito ergo sum* (I think, therefore I am), and traditional Western thought claimed, but by his being-in-the-world (*Dasein,* being-there), as distinguished from the abstract *Sein* (being) and the concrete *Seiendes* (beings). And only by an existential awareness of our own death (nonbeing or nothingness) as an integral element of our being can we find the authentic existence sought in various ways by Kierkegaard, Nietzsche, Dostoevsky, and Jaspers.

Marcel's *Journal métaphysique* (1927; *Metaphysical Journal,* 1952) was the first specifically existentialist work in France, and he tried later to popularize his search for Christian being in his plays. But Jean-Paul Sartre (q.v.), who studied in Germany and knew Husserl's and Heidegger's work well, was by far the most influential existentialist figure in Paris. In his major early philosophical work, *L'être et le néant* (1943; *Being and Nothingness,* 1956), he carried further Heidegger's concept of nonbeing. He divided being into the *en-soi* (being-in-itself), the static being of things, and the *pour-soi* (being-for-itself), the dynamic being of living persons. The *pour-soi* is aware of the nothingness of human existence, the total lack of established principles, and therefore the total freedom and concomitant responsibility to create itself and its own values. But this free

pour-soi often insists on denying its freedom by becoming an *en-soi*, on adopting set values for its own. By exploring the conflicts between this bad faith and the authentic action of the *pour-soi*, Sartre developed and gave new meaning to the existential modes of thought characteristic of his predecessors: the primacy of experience or existence over values or essence; the importance of nothingness or nonbeing as an integral part of existence; the sense of anguish and of man's contingency and mortality resulting from this ontological nihilism; the burden of choice and the responsibility imposed on the individual for the creation of new values.

All the existentialist thinkers discussed here were literary stylists as well as philosophers, but Sartre stands out from the others in his ability to convey his philosophy in literary forms that captured the imagination of the general public. He burst on the Paris literary scene in the final year of the German occupation (1943–44) with the production of two plays, *Les mouches* (1943; *The Flies,* 1947) and *Huis clos* (1944; *No Exit,* 1947). Here, and later in *Les mains sales* (1948; *Dirty Hands,* 1949), he presented graphically various aspects of the conflict between *en-soi* and *pour-soi*. The themes of solitude, freedom, alienation, and commitment, seen by audiences needing to take action against the authority of the occupying forces, and after the war wanting to create a new and better society, gave immediate practical meaning to Sartre's philosophy of existence. His plays had a much greater impact than Marcel's, whose characters and situations tended to express too abstractly a philosophical or theological position.

But in his early novel *La nausée* (1938; *Nausea,* 1949), Sartre had already recorded his protagonist's growing consciousness of the gratuitous contingency of his existence, that is, his freedom, producing the anguish of nausea. This reality is contrasted with the inauthenticity of his banal bourgeois surroundings, mercilessly satirized as *en-soi*. And in his trilogy *Les chemins de la liberté* (1945–49; *The Roads to Freedom,* 1947–51) Sartre analyzed the various forms of bad faith that prevent, among a host of characters, a young philosopher from assuming the burden of his freedom until just before his death at the hands of invading Germans in 1940. The most original of these novels is *Le sursis* (1945; *The Reprieve,* 1947), in which, by moving without transition among groups of characters in different parts of the world, Sartre shows that everyone was equally responsible for the appeasement of Hitler by England and

France in the 1938 Munich pact. For example, a private citizen in Paris may complete a sentence begun by a public figure negotiating the pact.

Sartre's early literary criticism is also existentialist. In *Baudelaire* (1947; *Baudelaire*, 1949) and *Qu'est-ce que la littérature?* (in *Situations II*, 1948; *What Is Literature?*, 1949), he insisted on the artist's responsibility to be "committed to his time." But this gave way to a recognition of the social and historical conditioning that formed writers like Jean Genet (q.v.) and Flaubert, on whom he wrote exhaustive studies.

This evolution reflects the gradual shift in Sartre's philosophical position away from his early concern with existence and being toward the historical and sociological perspectives of Marxism. *Critique de la raison dialectique, I: Théorie des ensembles pratiques* (1960; *Critique of Dialectical Reason, I: Theory of Practical Ensembles*, 1976) is an attempt to reconcile existentialism and Marxism.

Just as Sartre's literary works made his philosophy accessible to the general public, many modern writers who have had little or no formal training in philosophy have used existentialist themes and situations in their quest for meaning in a world devoid of values. For example, in *Der Prozeß* (1925; *The Trial*, 1937) and *Das Schloß* (1926; *The Castle*, 1930), Franz Kafka (q.v.) shows the anguish of man in his search for meaning in an incomprehensibly absurd world and universe. Yet his style is so vivid and harmonious, so savagely satirical, that his importance remains literary rather than philosophical.

The same can be said of the importance of André Malraux (q.v.) in *La condition humaine* (1933; *Man's Fate*, 1934), for example, his novel of violence and heroism in the face of tragic death, and even of Albert Camus (q.v.), who was often linked with the existentialists. Both were atheistic humanists upholding the need for action in the face of the absurd, but for Camus action was less violent, as in his early essay *Le mythe de Sisyphe* (1942; *The Myth of Sisyphus*, 1955) and novel *L'étranger* (1942; *The Stranger*, 1946). *La peste* (1947; *The Plague*, 1948) turns a quarantined city into a Pascalian prison, where death and resistance are again, however, less violent than in Malraux. And as the latter turned to art as an expression of revolt against the absurd, Camus's *L'homme révolté* (1951; *The Rebel*, 1954) traced the history of individual revolt and extolled it against collective revolution.

Camus was then not only in direct opposition to Sartre's growing insistence that individual action was always conditioned by history, but both Malraux and Camus rejected the existentialist notion that man, in creating his life, also creates new values.

Of the writers who came into prominence in the 1950s, Samuel Beckett (q.v.) is perhaps the most obviously indebted to existentialism and the intellectual climate of the 1940s. His play *En attendant Godot* (1952; *Waiting for Godot*, 1954) and his novel *Molloy* (1951; *Molloy*, 1955) explore the depths of man's alienation and despair, as the existentialists did, but they do not allow for the existentialists' creative action and commitment. This is true as well of the Theater of the Absurd (q.v.) of Jean Genet and Eugène Ionesco (qq.v.), among others. And the New Novel (q.v.) writers Alain Robbe-Grillet, Michel Butor, and Nathalie Sarraute (qq.v.), for example, also reflect the absence of established principles depicted by the existentialists, but neither do they permit the creation of new values.

Although an existentialist current will probably always be present in Western thought and literature, its importance as a philosophical and literary movement is confined to a relatively short historical period in Germany and France, when the philosophical preoccupations of Jaspers, Heidegger, Marcel, and Sartre in particular, and a host of literary figures, coincided with social, political, and psychological conditions to produce a sense of solitude, anguish, and despair, a void to be filled by individual creative action. But Sartre's position evolved in response to changing political, social, and intellectual conditions, and with his death, following those of his elders, we must conclude that existentialism as a formal philosophical position can no longer be considered a vital force.

BIBLIOGRAPHY: Blackham, H. J., *Six Existentialist Thinkers* (1952); Hubben, W., *Four Prophets of Our Destiny* (1952); Barrett, W., *Irrational Man: A Study of Existential Philosophy* (1958); Heinemann, P. H., *Existentialism and the Modern Predicament* (1958); Schrag, C., *Existence and Freedom* (1961); Breisach, E., *Introduction to Modern Existentialism* (1962); Hanna, T., *The Lyrical Existentialists* (1962); McElroy, D., *Existentialism and Modern Literature* (1963); Borowitz, E., *A Layman's Introduction to Religious Existentialism* (1965); Sanborn, P., *Existentialism* (1968); Luijpen, W., *Existential Phenomenology* (1969); Harper, R., *The Existential Expe-*

rience (1972); Macquarrie, J., *Existentialism* (1972); Poster, M., *Existential Marxism in Postwar France: From Sartre to Althusser* (1975); Barnes, H., *Existentialist Ethics* (1978)

CHARLES G. HILL

EXPRESSIONISM

Expressionism was a cultural revolution that centered around the verbal arts but extended into most areas of artistic, social, and political life. It originated in Germany around 1910 and remained dominant there until 1925. Deriving its name and its emphatic subjectivism from the preceding revolt of the visual arts—pictorial expressionism was initiated by J. A. Hervé in Paris in 1901 and gave rise in Germany to the leagues called The Bridge (1905) and The Blue Rider (1912)—it was the first major trend within the greater framework of international modernism (q.v.). Based on disparate intellectual impulses ranging from Nietzsche, Dostoevsky, and Strindberg (q.v.) to Walt Whitman and Marinetti's (q.v.) futurism (q.v.), as well as, more indirectly, French symbolism (q.v.), expressionism did not emerge as a unified aesthetic program. The often used term "movement" thus misleadingly suggests a homogeneity that never existed. In its initial phase (1910–14), expressionism erupted as a cry of protest against obsolete artistic and societal norms from a highly diverse generation of authors. All, however, had in common their revolt against an oppressive, moribund caste system, their resultant radically antibourgeois stance, and their denunciation of naturalism as a mere extension of reality. German expressionism, unlike related phenomena abroad, directly mirrored the feeling of impending doom prior to 1914 and remained closely linked to the subsequent historical developments.

In 1911 Kurt Hiller (1885–1972) proclaimed the goals of this new generation: "We are expressionists. Once more, we are concerned about content, willpower, and ethos." From its beginnings, expressionist art was radically antimimetic. Thus, Kasimir Edschmid (1890–1966) postulated: "The world is already here. There is no sense in duplicating it." Expressionism was idea-oriented to the point of abstraction and visionary declamation: "For the expressionist artist, all space becomes vision. . . . There is no longer a chain of facts: factories, houses, illness, whores, shouting, hunger. Now there is only the vision of these" (Ed-schmid). Its driving force was the artistic rendering of an ethical imperative, shared by hundreds of authors in their plea for mankind's spiritual and societal renewal.

German expressionism gained additional importance as a mainstay of pacifism during World War I. Although defying all attempts at canonization, it nevertheless produced a flood of manifestos, including inane affronts to the bourgeoisie, essays on poetics and language, and political statements. Fluctuating literary circles were formed through the efforts of various periodicals and their editors. Most influential among these were *Der Sturm* (1910–32), edited by Herwarth Walden (1878–1941); *Die Aktion* (1911–32), edited by Franz Pfemfert (1879–1954); and *Die weißen Blätter* (1913–20), edited by Franz Blei (1871–1942) and René Schickele (1883–1940). These publications were primarily responsible for the dissemination of expressionism abroad, especially after 1918. At the apex of the epoch (1916–20), many expressionists turned toward political activism, propagating socialist and revolutionary thought. After the unsuccessful German revolution of 1918–19, the drive for revolt and renewal gradually gave way to the more resigned tone typical for years of decline (1920–25). By this time expressionism had already reached out to England, the U.S., and to eastern and northern Europe. In Germany it was banned by the Nazis in 1933.

The stylistic and formal innovations of expressionism are as manifold as its authors. Expressionist style does away with traditional logic and grammar. It strives toward the essential, the global and visionary statement, often by means of compression and unorthodox imagery. Its most lasting achievement is the creation of a contemporary poetic language fit to juxtapose the most disparate phenomena: the ugly and the beautiful, death and rebirth, the rhythm of the teeming metropolis and religious ecstasy. Most of the early poetry heralding this stylistic revolution portrays disaster and, at the same time, prophesies the dawn of a new age: the flamboyant eschatological imagery of Georg Heym (1887–1912), evoking the specter of big-city life, poverty and disease, and the more subdued premonitions of doom poured into Georg Trakl's (q.v.) darkly allusive poems. Jakob van Hoddis (1887–1942) and Alfred Lichtenstein (1889–1914) created the techniques of image collage and poetic simultaneity—devices that linked some of the early expressionists to cubism (q.v.), despite the cubists' different artistic goals. August Stramm (q.v.), one of the most innovative talents of the epoch, worked with total syntactic fragmentation. (A similar, highly condensed language was later utilized by the Dadaists [q.v.], who aimed to evict all "meaning" from poetry and thus initiated a counterrevolt against idea-laden expressionism.) Yvan Goll (1891–1950), Else Lasker-Schüler (1869–1945), and Oskar Loerke (1884–1941) were among the most talented poets; their poetry centered around the intense feelings of the "I" and often carried overtones of religious or erotic ecstasy.

Gottfried Benn's (q.v.) collections *Morgue* (1912; morgue) and *Söhne* (1913; sons) contributed to a new aesthetic concept based on grotesque disillusionment, whereas Ernst Wilhelm Lotz (1890–1914) and Ernst Stadler (1883–1914) sounded the dithyrambic call for awakening and departure to a new millennium. Both the pacifistic poems in Franz Werfel's (q.v.) *Der Weltfreund* (1911; friend of the world) and the later activist and revolutionary poetry by Johannes R. Becher (1891–1958), Karl Otten (1889–1963), Rudolf Leonhard (1889–1953), and many others share the appeal for the revitalization of humanity characteristic of the epoch.

Of the many anthologies, *Menschheitsdämmerung* (1919; the dawn of mankind), edited by Kurt Pinthus (1886–1975), remains the most impressive document of expressionist poetry. On the international scene, English vorticism and its proponents Wyndham Lewis and Ezra Pound (qq.v.) were stylistically influenced by expressionist poetry, as well as, to a certain extent, the earlier poems of Stephen Spender and T. S. Eliot (qq.v.). The Belgian expressionist Paul van Ostaijen (q.v.) virtually shaped the development of modern Flemish literature, whereas in the Netherlands Hendrik Marsman (q.v.) and others founded an influential expressionist circle. In America, E. E. Cummings and William Carlos Williams (qq.v.) utilized grammatical fragmentation and rapidly changing, contrasting images—devices they owed to expressionism. Some of the expressionist innovations were also absorbed by surrealism (q.v.).

Expressionist drama is considered the most important pioneer movement of the 20th-c. stage. Among its precursors were the 19th-c. dramatists Georg Büchner (1813–1837) and Christian Dietrich Grabbe (1801–1836), and the plays of Frank Wedekind, Alfred Jarry (qq.v.), and Paul Scheerbart (1863–1915).

After the first violently antimimetic experiments, mostly in the form of a single scene—for example, *Sphinx und Strohmann* (1907; sphinx and strawman) and *Mörder, Hoffnung der Frauen* (1907; *Murderer the Women's Hope*, 1963) by Oskar Kokoschka (1886–1980) and *Der gelbe Klang* (1910; the yellow sound) by Wassily Kandinsky (1866–1944)—it focused on the motif of spiritual renewal. The stage, having disposed of most naturalistic devices, became a battleground for conflicting ideas represented by typical or symbolical rather than individualized figures. Characteristic of this drama of ideas are an episodic, acausal structure juxtaposing realistic and visionary, dreamlike scenes; the abolition of coherent plot lines in favor of the inner development of the characters; and a highly abstract, declamatory language that might occasionally strike the modern reader as ludicrous. Such plays as Reinhard Johannes Sorge's (1892–1916) *Der Bettler* (1912; *The Beggar*, 1963) and Walter Hasenclever's (1890–1940) *Der Sohn* (1914; the son) and *Die Menschen* (1918; *Humanity*, 1963) are prototypical of the plea for collective rebirth, also present in many of Georg Kaiser's (q.v.) plays. Among the outstanding talents of the epoch are Ernst Toller, Ernst Barlach, and Carl Sternheim (qq.v.). The early Bertolt Brecht (q.v.), with his plays *Baal* (1918; *Baal*, 1963), *Trommeln in der Nacht* (1918; *Drums in the Night*, 1961), and *Im Dickicht der Städte* (1923; *In the Jungle of Cities*, 1961) was definitely under the spell of expressionism, even though he conceived *Baal* as an antiexpressionist provocation.

Expressionist drama's immediate offshoot was the early cinema, a medium ripe to absorb many of its techniques (see Film and Literature). Its classics include Robert Wiene's *Das Kabinett des Dr. Caligari* (1919; the cabinet of Dr. Caligari), Paul Wegener's two versions of *Der Golem* (1914, 1920; the golem); and Fritz Lang's *Metropolis* (1926). Both expressionist theater and film had a tremendous impact on European and American drama. In the U.S. many structural and dramaturgic devices were adopted by Eugene O'Neill, Elmer Rice, Thornton Wilder, Archibald MacLeish (qq.v.), Paul Green (1894–1981), and many others.

In both drama and poetry expressionism had other ramifications. In Scandinavia, it was embraced and modified by Pär Lagerkvist (q.v.) in Sweden, Sigurd Hoel (q.v.) in Norway, and Emil Bønnelycke (1893–1953) in Denmark. Sean O'Casey (q.v.) used expressionist devices in a number of his plays. Russian expressionism emerged in 1919 and particularly influenced the dramatic works of Vladimir Mayakovsky (q.v.).

Expressionist fiction, while less important than poetry and drama, produced highly subjective experimental novels—such as *Bebuquin; oder, Die Dilettanten des Wunders* (1909; Bebuquin; or, miracle's dilettantes) by Carl Einstein (1885–1940) and a multitude of emotionally charged sketches and short stories by Benn, Alfred Döblin (q.v.), Edschmid, Albert Ehrenstein (1886–1950), and others. Later expressionist prose was often influenced by James Joyce (q.v.)

In the 1920s expressionism lost the creative energy once generated by its revolutionary fervor and its attack on reality. Although its emotional intensity and bombast were spent forever, its formal and stylistic innovations had been absorbed internationally. Through its proclamation of man's freedom to revolt against a stifling reality, it not only unleashed a deep cultural shock on the threshold of the 20th c. but also irrevocably established subjectivism as a driving force in modern art and literature.

Thus, directly or indirectly, it inspired the revival of the subjective in the poetry of the 1940s—particularly in the visionary imagery of Dylan Thomas (q.v.)—and in various postwar literary trends, especially in German and Swiss drama. Most notably under the influence of expressionism have been the playwrights Wolfgang Borchert, Friedrich Dürrenmatt, Max Frisch, and Fritz Hochwälder (qq.v.). In the poetry of Nelly Sachs and Paul Celan (qq.v.) expressionist and symbolist techniques merged to form a contemporary lyrical language. Günter Eich (q.v.) used the nonlinear plot development derived from expressionism in numerous radio plays, whereas Hans Erich Nossack (q.v.) and other novelists modified expressionist structural devices. Even the documentary theater of the 1960s and 1970s—represented by Rolf Hochhuth, Peter Weiss (qq.v.), and Heinar Kipphardt (b. 1922)—makes frequent use of a declamatory language and other elements of stage technique that derive in part from the expressionist heritage.

BIBLIOGRAPHY: Samuel, R., and Thomas, R., *Expressionism in German Life, Literature and the Theater 1910–1924* (1939); Sokel, W., *The Writer in Extremis: Expressionism in Twentieth-Century Literature* (1959); Krispyn, E., *Style and Society in German Literary Expressionism* (1964); Arnold, A., *Die Literatur des Expressionismus: Sprachliche und thematische Quellen* (1966); Rothe, W., ed., *Expressionismus als Literatur: Gesammelte Studien* (1969); Willet, J., *Expressionism* (1970); Furness, R., *Expressionism* (1973); Weisstein, U., ed., *Expressionism as an International Literary Phenomenon* (1973); Hamann, R., and Hermand, J., *Expressionismus* (1977); Knapp, G., *Die Literatur des deutschen Expressionismus: Einführung, Bestandsaufnahme, Kritik* (1979); Pickar, G., and Webb, E., eds., *Expressionism Reconsidered* (1979); Paulsen, W., "Form and Content in German Expressionist Literature," *MR*, 21 (1980), 137–56

GERHARD P. KNAPP

FADEEV, Alexandr Alexandrovich

Russian novelist and short-story writer, b. 24
Dec. 1901, Kimry; d. 13 May 1956, Moscow

Of peasant origin, F. spent his childhood and
was educated in eastern Siberia. He became a
member of the Communist Party in 1918, took
part in the civil war, and was active as a Party
organizer in Siberia and in the Ukraine. He
began his literary career as a "proletarian" novelist in the 1920s at the time of the NEP (New
Economic Policy). His novels are inspired by
Communist ideology and express his faith in
and support of the regime.

F.'s first story, "Protiv techenia" (1923;
against the current) and his short novel *Razliv*
(1924; the flood) were of no special importance, but his next work, *Razgrom* (1927; *The
Nineteen,* 1929; also tr. as *The Rout,* 1955),
secured for its author a niche in the pantheon
of Soviet writers.

During the 1920s, while still displaying a diversity of points of view and varied artistic
methods, writers of the Soviet Union all wrote
about the revolution. F.'s *Razgrom* became a
classic novel on that subject, for it was the
story of a small detachment of Red guerrillas
fighting in Siberia against the Whites and the
Japanese. Its chief protagonist, Commander
Levinson, may be taken to represent the perfect
Bolshevik, an early "positive hero" of Soviet literature. A minimum of stylization and the psychological verisimilitude of most of the characters in this well-made, distinctly realistic novel
show F. to be a follower of Tolstoy's "psychological realism." F.'s Tolstoyan views on
"truth-in-art" are contained in a famous 1928
manifesto in which he challenges the doctrine
of "factography"—tendentious naturalism and
social behaviorism—put forth by adherents of

the antipsychological school of Soviet literature
in the years 1927–32.

The year 1932 witnessed the creation of the
Union of Soviet Writers, with the result that literature became incorporated in the fabric of the
state and was subjected to far more thorough
controls than before. The literary doctrine
known as Socialist Realism (q.v.) became the
only block on which all subsequent Soviet literature was to be built. The early works of F.,
the supporter of realism in literature and a convinced Communist, predate the actual formulation of Socialist Realism as a doctrine and
paved the way for its adoption.

F.'s unfinished novel *Posledny iz Udege* (4
vols., 1929–40; the last of the Udeges) was
conceived as a large-scale work dealing with a
multitude of characters and a complex idea.
The ideal revolutionary, Langovoy, emerges in
the novel as the ubiquitous "positive hero" of
Socialist Realism, while one of the book's
themes deals with the "rehabilitation" of the
Udeges—a primitive Siberian tribe—and their
incorporation into the collective farm system.
F. knew that his capabilities as a writer did not
measure up to the complexity of the task, and
although it was heralded by the critics as a true
work of Socialist Realism, he realized that the
novel was not a successful one.

When first published, F.'s *Molodaya gvardia*
(1945; *The Young Guard,* 1959) won great
critical praise. But two years later, during a period of political and literary reaction, it was denounced for "serious ideological and artistic errors of the writer." In order to conform to the
official doctrine, F. was forced to revise his
highly popular novel of anti-German resistance
fighting among teenagers in Krasnodon. The
"corrected" version was published in 1951.

For many years F. had been a high Party
functionary—a member of the Central Committee of the Communist Party as well as the powerful and power-hungry secretary general of
the Union of Soviet Writers, but the beginning
of the de-Stalinization period brought about his
downfall. The dictatorial power held by F. the
bureaucrat over Soviet letters was denounced
in 1956 by Mikhail Sholokhov (q.v.) in a
strongly worded speech to the Twentieth Congress of the Communist Party at the height of
the "thaw." By then a victim of alcoholism,
unable to write a good story, and suspected of
having taken part in Stalin's political purges,
F. ended his life by suicide.

FURTHER WORKS: *Stolbovaya doroga proletar-
skoy literatury* (1929); *Partizanskie povesti*

(1938); *Literatura i zhizn* (1939); *Leningrad v dni blokady* (1944; *Leningrad in the Days of the Blockade*, 1945); *Chyornaya metallurgia* [chapters from unfinished novel] (1954); *Za tridtsat let* (1957); *Sobranie sochineny* (7 vols., 1969–71)

BIBLIOGRAPHY Reavey, G., *Soviet Literature Today* (1947), pp. 82–84; Swayze, H., *Political Control of Literature in the USSR, 1946–1959* (1962), passim; Brown, E. J., *Russian Literature since the Revolution* (1963), pp. 163, 172–79, 216; Brown, E. J., *The Proleterian Episode in Russian Literature, 1928–1932* (1971), passim; Struve, G., *Russian Literature under Lenin and Stalin, 1917–1953* (1971), pp. 134–37, 217–18, 319–20, 332, 354–55; Slonim, M., *Soviet Russian Literature: Writers and Problems, 1917–1967* (1973), pp. 174–79, 287, 299–300; Mathewson, R. W., Jr., *The Positive Hero in Russian Literature* (1975), pp. 191–200, 213–15

NADJA JERNAKOFF

FAIZ, Faiz Ahmed

(pseud. of Faiz Ahmed) Pakistani poet (writing in Urdu), b. 1912?, Sialkot (then in India)

F.'s family were well-to-do landowners, his father a prominent English-educated lawyer. F. received his education at mission schools in Sialkot in the English language and later earned M.A. degrees in both English and Arabic literatures from Punjab University, Lahore. He came under the influence of the Marxist-oriented Progressive Movement in the late 1930s.

When the Islamic Republic of Pakistan was established in 1947, F. was serving as editor of the leftist English-language daily, the *Pakistan Times*, and as managing editor of the Urdu daily *Imroz*. He was also actively involved in organizing trade unions. In 1951 he and a number of army officers were implicated in the so-called Rawalpindi Conspiracy Case in which the government of Pakistan alleged that the accused were planning a coup d'état. Under sentence of death for several years, F. was quietly released from prison in 1955. In 1962 he received the Soviet Lenin Peace Prize and since then has been active in various Pakistani arts and literary organizations. In recent years he has lent his considerable support to a movement among some of the regional languages of Pakistan, notably Punjabi, Sindhi, Balochi, and Pashto, to gain recognition as legitimate vehi-

cles for public instruction, government, the media, and literary expression. In this connection F. has composed some poems in Punjabi, his first language.

F.'s reputation as the foremost Urdu poet since Muhammad Iqbal (q.v.) rests on four slender volumes: *Naqsh-e faryadi* (1943; image of complaint), which drew considerable critical attention because of the author's blend of traditional meters and imagery with nationalist and leftist sentiments; *Dast-e saba* (1952; hand of the wind), and *Zindan namah* (1956; prison narrative), in which he meticulously chronicles his prison experiences in some of his most famous poems; and *Dast-e tah-e sang* (1965; hand beneath the stone), where he reflects upon his extensive travels abroad and his aspirations for a better world.

F.'s poetry is highly introspective and symbolic, yet markedly positive in outlook. He has infused traditional romantic imagery with new meaning, usually tinged with political overtones. For example, in premodern love poetry the poet (lover) and his rival vie for the affection of the cruel and indifferent beloved. In his famous poem "Raqib se" (1943; "To the Rival," 1971) F. asks the rival to join him in putting aside their differences and to work together to overcome the country's enemies. Similarly, in "Mujh se pahli si mahabbat, meri mahbub na mang" (1943; "Do Not Ask Me, My Beloved, Love Like That Former One," 1971) F. indicates to the beloved that he can no longer offer her the kind of love she has enjoyed in the past; he is now preoccupied with the more important issues of human exploitation and suffering.

F. is perhaps the only contemporary Urdu poet to write both political verse and love poetry of a consistently high quality. He is regarded in Pakistan as that country's unofficial poet laureate and is held in equal esteem by Urdu speakers of India.

FURTHER WORKS: *Mizan* (1964); *Harf harf* (1965); *Sar-e vadi-ye sina* (1971); *Rat di rat* (1975); *Sham-e shahri-yaran* (1978); *Mere dil, mere musafir* (1980). FURTHER VOLUME IN ENGLISH: *Poems of F.* (1971)

BIBLIOGRAPHY: Ali, M., "The Poetry of F.," *PakR*, 12 (1964), 5–8; Faiz, A., "F.: A Personality Sketch," *JSoAL*, 10, 1 (1974), 123–30; [Jones, A., and Coppola, C.], "Interview with F.," *JSoAL*, 10, 1 (1974), 141–44; Malik, M., "The Pakistan Poet: F.," *LAAW*, 22 (1974) 36–41; Narang, G., "Tradition and

Innovation in Urdu Poetry," in *Poetry and Renaissance: Kumaran Asan Birth Centenary Volume* (1974), pp. 415–34; Lall, I. J., "F.: Poet with Vitality," *IndL*, 18, 4 (1975), 58–62

CARLO COPPOLA

FALKBERGET, Johan

Norwegian novelist and short-story writer, b. 30 Sept. 1879, Rugeldalen; d. 5 April 1967, Rugeldalen

F. grew up in a copper-mining community near Røros and worked in the mines from age eight to twenty-seven. From 1907 on he made his living as journalist, editor, and writer, mainly in the Oslo region, before settling on the family farm in Rugeldalen (1922), where he lived until his death. From 1930 to 1933 he was member of the Norwegian parliament representing the Labor Party.

F.'s first novels were cast in the semiromantic mold of Bjørnstjerne Bjørnson's (1832–1910) peasant tales, but with *Svarte Fjelde* (1907; black mountains) he introduced the mining community, a setting he used in almost all his later novels, into Norwegian literature. The notable exceptions are *Lisbeth på Jarnfjeld* (1915; *Lisbeth of Jarnfjeld*, 1930), a grim psychological study of a marriage, set in a mountain community in 19th-c. Norway, and *Brændoffer* (1917; burnt offering), an equally grim study of human degradation with the advance of urbanization. Set in the early part of the 20th c., this novel depicts how the protagonist and his family move from rural Norway into Christiania (now Oslo) and succumb to boundless physical and spiritual poverty.

In his early years F. was strongly influenced by utopian socialist thought, and his lifelong commitment to the labor movement was marked by his Christian humanistic ethics. He never accepted the dogmas of Marxism, but the despair depicted in *Brændoffer* could not be overcome within his traditional ethical framework, a fact that undoubtedly contributed to his exclusive interest in historical fiction from 1920 on. F.'s concern with new themes is evident in his first great novel, *Den fjerde nattevakt* (1923; *The Fourth Night Watch*, 1968), in which the power of erotic love—a motif in several earlier novels as well—is put within a Christian ethical framework. The newly arrived parish minister falls madly in love with a young married woman of his congregation, and the ensuing struggle between the laws of Christian ethics and the conscience, on the one hand, and the power of *eros*, on the other, is portrayed with great narrative and psychological force. The novel is set in Røros in the early part of the 19th c., and is faithful to the historical setting, but it is in essence a modern psychological novel in which the historical setting serves as background only.

His next work, the trilogy *Christianus Sextus* (1927–35; Christian VI [the title refers to the name of a copper mine]), is considered his best novel by many critics. It portrays the Røros community in the 1720s and combines intimate knowledge of historical details with epic force and psychological and historical insight. *Christianus Sextus* has been referred to as a collective novel: the entire copper-mining community, in a sense, is the center of the narrative. Not one, but many, persons arise from the shadows of history and give life to the novel. It contains one of the most moving portrayals of a child in Norwegian literature—the story of the little Gølin—but also portrayals of the grim fight for survival, against starvation, mining accidents, and madness.

F.'s last great novel is the tetralogy *Nattens brød* (1940–59; bread of night), which depicts life in the community surrounding one of the smelters thirty miles north of the Røros mines during the latter half of the 17th c. Again F. has made every effort to depict accurately the historical setting: the harsh poverty and brutality of a society being devastated by the uncontrolled advance of industrialization and market economics. But more clearly than before the reader sees F.'s defense of humanistic values—of love, tolerance, and compassion—and of the Protestant ethic: honesty, hard work, and the fear of God. An-Magritt, the young woman protagonist, represents the quintessence of F.'s view of life. She is physically strong and conquers all in her relentless struggle to improve the living conditions of herself and her fellow human beings. She is filled with an unyielding belief in the goodness of man, and borders on being an allegorical figure in her almost supernatural achievements.

Although espousing a strongly traditional view of life, F.'s main works are imbued with a poetic force and a mythic quality that continue to fascinate new readers. He remains one of the pivotal figures in 20th-c. Norwegian literature.

FURTHER WORKS: *Mineskud* (1908); *Ved den evige sne* (1908); *Fakkelbrand* (1909); *Urtidsnat* (1909); *Vargfjeldet* (1910); *Nord i haugene: Eventyr* (1910); *Fimbulvinter*

(1911); *En finnejentes kjærlighetshistorie*
(1912); *Eli Sjursdotter* (1913); *Jutul-historier*
(1913); *Av jarleætt* (1914); *Eventyrfjeld:
Historier for barn* (1916); *Helleristninger*
(1916); *Sol* (1918); *Barkebrødstider* (1919);
Bjørne-Skyttern (1919); *Vidden* (1919); *Bør
Børson jr.* (1920); *Byd lykken hånden; eller,
Da Johannes Mo løste rebusen* (1920); *Nag-
lerne; eller, Jernet fra Norden* (1921); *I nor-
denvindens land* (1924); *Vers fra Rugelsjøen*
(1925); *Den nye Bør Børson* (1927); *Det
høie fjell* (1928); *Solfrid i Bjørnstu og de syv
svende* (1928); *Runer på fjeldveggen: Sagn og
fortellinger* (1944); *Jeg så dem*–(1963)

BIBLIOGRAPHY: Falkberget, J., "Røros: The
Copper Town of Norway," *ASR,* 13 (1925),
412–21; Freding, T., "J. F.," *ASR,* 21 (1933),
401–6; Beck, R., "J. F.," *SS,* 16 (1941),
304–16; Beck, R., "J. F.: A Great Social
Novelist," *ASR,* 38 (1950), 248–51; Kojen,
J., "Grand Old Man of Literature: J. F.,"
Norseman, No. 6 (1962), 10–13; Popperwell,
R. G., Introduction to *The Fourth Night Watch*
(1968), pp. vii–xviii; Raastad, O., "J. F.: An
Appreciation," *ASR,* 58 (1970), 154–56
KJETIL A. FLATIN

FANGEN, Ronald

Norwegian novelist, dramatist, and essayist, b.
29 April 1895, Kragerø; d. 22 May 1946, For-
nebu

F. was the son of a Norwegian mining engineer
and his English wife. Raised in Bergen by two
aunts after his parents' early divorce, he compensated for his loneliness as a sickly child
prodigy who was rather bored with school by
voracious solitary reading. At thirteen he published his first critical essay, at fifteen his first
poem, both in a Bergen daily. From 1913 on F.
engaged in prolific journalistic activities as a
reviewer for various newspapers and as editor of
literary magazines.

F. was a key figure in Norwegian cultural life
during the interwar period. With his intellectual
depth, moral fervor, and religious disposition,
he became a tireless champion of Christian humanism not only in *Vor verden,* the journal he
founded and edited from 1923 to 1930, but
also in most of his belletristic writings.

F.'s early plays, *Syndefald* (1920; the fall),
Fienden (1922; the enemy), and *Den forjættede
dag* (1926; the promised day), generated hopes
that he would renew the Norwegian drama. The

form of his first two plays was influenced by the
late works of Strindberg (q.v.) and by German expressionism (q.v.), their themes by
Nietzsche; the third is more realistic, and its
theme of illusion is Ibsenesque. But in the late
1920s F. returned to fiction, which he had earlier, but not especially successfully, essayed.

Several of F.'s later novels are remarkably
good. With Nietzsche yielding to Freud (q.v.)
and Alfred Adler (1870–1937), and German
expressionism to the discussion technique of
Aldous Huxley (q.v.), F. develops an effective
instrument for probing beneath the surfaces of
bourgeois culture and personality. At his best,
in *Duel* (1932; *Duel,* 1934), *En kvinnes vei*
(1933; a woman's way), and *Mannen som elsket rettferdigheten* (1934; the man who loved
justice), discussion is less important than reflection and retrospective rumination. Their
routine existences shattered by some untoward
event, F.'s characters undertake a ruthless self-
scrutiny, the result of which is either Christian
conversion or disaster, often in the form of suicide. The action occurring chiefly in the characters' minds, the plot consists of the progressive
unveiling of the layers of deception that sustain
their functional personalities—self-deceptions
ingrained by habit, vanity, the power drive, and
false philosophy. *Duel,* widely translated, has
been F.'s most popular book, but *Mannen
som elsket rettferdigheten,* a Norwegian *Michael Kohlhaas* (by Heinrich von Kleist,
1777–1811) or Book of Job, is artistically superior. In this work, theme, setting, characterization, and style are perfectly blended—a rare
occurrence in F.'s novels.

After his conversion to Frank Buchman's
(1878–1961) Oxford Group movement in
1934, F.'s social consciousness increased, but
the quality of his writing deteriorated. In *På
bar bunn* (1936; on rock bottom) and *Al-
lerede nu* (1937; already now), the form
changed from individual to group novel, better
suited to F.'s Christian message. Here plot is
superseded by a largely spatial structure of juxtaposed "case histories" presenting representative intellectuals whose painful life experiences
lead them inexorably to religious conversion.
Møllen som maler langsomt (the mill that
grinds slowly), a planned trilogy of which only
one volume, *Borgerfesten* (1939; civic festival), was finished, is set in the 1880s and
1890's; yet F.'s concern is still with *Weltanschauung,* specifically the characters' religious
development.

En lysets engel (1945; *Both Are My Cousins,* 1949), F.'s last novel before his death in

an airplane crash, investigates the roots of Nazism by counterpointing the divergent spiritual evolution of two cousins before and during the German occupation of Norway. Nazism and other subjects are also illuminatingly analyzed in F.'s many collections of essays.

F.'s literary affinities range from Dostoevskian psychology to the balanced humanism of Thomas Mann (q.v.); his religious-philosophical thought is polarized between Nietzschean moral nihilism and Christian personalism. While some of his contemporaries showed greater narrative talent and stylistic flair, F. surpassed most of them by the spiritual passion with which he pursued themes similar to theirs: the disguises and perversions of love, the dark labyrinth of power, the elusiveness of personal identity. A true European by his broad literary and intellectual culture, F. brought to these themes the new knowledge of psychoanalysis as well as the accumulated wisdom of the Christian tradition. This combination invests his novels with an abiding interest.

FURTHER WORKS: *De svake* (1915); *Slægt føder slægt* (1916); *En roman* (1918); *Krise* (1919); *Streiftog i digtning og tænkning* (1919); *Tegn og gjærninger* (1927); *Nogen unge mennesker* (1929); *Erik* (1931); *Dagen og veien* (1934); *Det nye liv* (1934); *En kristen verdensrevolusjon* (1935); *Som det kunde ha gått* (1935); *Paulus og vår egen tid* (1936); *Kristen enhet* (1937); *Kristendommen og vår tid* (1938); *Krig og kristen tro* (1940); *Presten* (1946); *Nåderiket* (1947); *Om frihet, og andre essays* (1947); *Samlede verker* (9 vols., 1948–49); *Essays* (1965); *I nazistenes fengsel* (1975)

BIBLIOGRAPHY: Strauss, H., on *Duel, NYTBR*, 17 June 1934, 8; Plomer, W., on *Duel, Spectator*, 22 June 1934, 978; Quennell, P., on *Duel, TLS*, 28 June 1934, 458; Beyer, H., *A History of Norwegian Literature* (1956), pp. 321–22; Govig, S. D., "R. F.: A Christian Humanist," *ASR*, 49 (1961), 152–59; Friese, W., *Nordische Literaturen im 20. Jahrhundert* (1971), pp. 171–73

SVERRE LYNGSTAD

FARAH, Nuruddin

Somali novelist (writing in English and Somali), b. 24 Nov. 1945, Baidoa

Although F. came to English as a fourth language, his reputation as a writer rests on the novels he has written in English. After studying literature in India at the University of Chandigarh, F. returned to Somalia and taught in Mogadisho, then lived in England for a time; he now resides in Rome. Besides his English-language work, he has also written a novel, plays, and short stories in Somali, and has translated children's stories from Arabic, Italian, French, and English into Somali.

F.'s novels are set in 20th-c. Somalia, with most of the action occurring in the capital, Mogadisho. In *From a Crooked Rib* (1970) Mogadisho becomes the home of Ebla, a nomad girl who flees her family's camp because she has been promised in marriage to an old man. Her pilgrimage from desert to small town and eventually on to the capital teaches her to exploit men as they exploit her. Ebla is inquiring and analytical; in rejecting the traditional role of the Somali woman, she becomes her own person, with a thoroughly existential attitude. The book is a sociological novel and a novel of character, and realistically portrays some grim realities of Somali life.

A Naked Needle (1976) possesses more breadth and depth, is more cosmopolitan, and is also technically more complex. Written in the present tense, its tone is reminiscent of Wole Soyinka's (q.v.) *The Interpreters*, the favorite novel of F.'s protagonist, Koschin. Koschin, a Mogadisho teacher, while studying overseas had promised to marry an English girl who now, two years later, arrives in Somalia expecting him to keep his promise. A potential situation comedy becomes in F.'s hands an unsettling novel on the sordidness of mid-1970s Somalia. Koschin, like Ebla, is a complex character who reveals himself as he filters his experiences through his consciousness and internally expresses his attitudes toward them.

F.'s most recent novel, *Sweet and Sour Milk* (1979), received the English-Speaking Union Literary Award. The book explores even further the almost unrelieved grimness of Somali life. This time the all-powerful state's license to arrest, imprison without trial, and torture are sharply focused upon. Loyaan's search for the facts behind the sudden death of his twin brother Soyaan, an economic adviser to Somalia's president, is undertaken in an aura of sheer political terror mitigated only by F.'s constraint and his skillful use of interior monologue (q.v.)—a skill already developed in *A Naked Needle*.

F. has a keen eye for physical and psychological details. His use of English is mature, possessing a colloquial flavor that happily blends with an increasingly cosmopolitan stance that retains its authentically Somali subject matter. He is not a self-consciously African writer, but makes the novel form his own, creating an effective bond between mythic and local references and those aspects of his message that have far-reaching human significance.

BIBLIOGRAPHY: Beer, D., "Somali Literature in European Languages," *Horn of Africa*, 2, 4 (1979), 27–35; Cochrane, J., "The Theme of Sacrifice in the Novels of N. F.," *WLWE*, 18 (1979), 69–77; Okomilo, I., on *Sweet and Sour Milk, Africa*, No. 101 (1980), 72–73; Imfeld, A., and Meuer, G., "N. F.: A Modern Nomad," *Afrika* (Munich), 21, 9 (1980), 23–25
DAVID F. BEER

FARGUE, Léon-Paul

French poet and columnist, b. 4 March 1876, Paris; d. 24 Nov. 1947, Paris

As an adolescent, F. made friends in the arts, then dominated by symbolism (q.v.) and impressionism. Later, in spite of his modest middle-class background and his idiosyncrasies, such as chronic lateness to appointments and absent-mindedness, his intimates included leading French and foreign writers, painters and musicians. His company was sought after in the most elegant salons for his conversation, which was fantastically rich in word and image. His brilliant success in oral improvisation meant that he was not very interested in publishing. All his life F. lived in Paris; he knew the city intimately enough to earn the sobriquet the "Paris stroller," a name he himself used as the title of one of his collections of prose poems, *Le piéton de Paris* (1939).

In spite of F.'s many friends, one of his leitmotifs is loneliness—a mood suggested in his first poems, which were published in the journal *L'art littéraire* (1893). This theme becomes obvious in *Tancrède* (Tancred), published in the review *Pan* (Berlin, 1895); this was the first text he later acknowledged by allowing his friend Valery Larbaud (q.v.) to publish it privately (1911; republished commercially in 1943). It is a group of overrefined and affected —in a word, *précieux*—poems, in prose or verse, somewhat inspired by Rimbaud.

Ten other prose poems printed privately as *Poème, premier cahier* (1907; poem, first notebook) were to become the nucleus of his first important work, *Poèmes* (1912, 1919, 1931, 1944, 1947 [painstakingly revised each time];

poems). Some of these prose poems, rich in music, imagery, and emotion, are highly lyrical: outstanding and universal are those expressing his despair at the death of his father (1909), who was disappointed by his son's apparent failure. Other themes include separation, nostalgia, absence of loved ones, and unrequited love.

Most of his long prose poems of the 1920s appearing in *Commerce* (of which he was coeditor from 1924 to 1930 with Paul Valéry [q.v.] and Larbaud), *Mesures, Mercure de France, Nouvelle revue française*, and *transition* were published in four books with significant titles: *Banalité* (1928; banality), which takes daily life as its inspiration; *Vulturne* (1928; title, an invented word, untranslatable), which contains fantastic visions comparable to those of the painters Hieronymus Bosch and Odilon Redon; *Épaisseurs* (1928; densities), through which his images rise to the surface; and *Suite familière* (1929; familiar suite), which contains his poetic theory. Later collections, *Haute solitude* (1941; high solitude) and *Refuges* (1942; refuges), show his sensitivity to his surroundings in language filled with unusual metaphors and inventive Rabelaisian vocabulary. A stroke he suffered in 1943 gave him illness as an added theme in *Méandres* (1946; meanders).

Financial need forced F. to become a columnist (1930–47); in hundreds of articles, sometimes reprinted in various publications, he re-created his ramblings throughout Paris and wrote about other memories. Lacking the quality of his poetry, these pieces were nevertheless published in a dozen books.

His poems, continually revised in his endless search for perfection, are the true basis of his fame, for they reveal the dazzling inventiveness in word and image of the lyrical creative artist.

FURTHER WORKS: *Pour la musique* (1914); *Ludions* (1930); *D'après Paris* (1931); *Déjeuners de Soleil* (1942); *Lanterne magique* (1944; *The Magic Lantern*, 1946); *Contes fantastiques* (1944); *Composite* (1944, with André Beucler); *Une saison en astrologie* (1945); *Les quat' saisons* (1947); *Portraits de famille* (1947); *Les grandes heures du Louvre* (1948); *Etc.* (1949); *Les XX arrondissements de Paris* (1952); *Pour la peinture* (1955); *Au temps de Paris* (1964); *Correspondance L.-P. F.—Valery Larbaud* (1971)

BIBLIOGRAPHY: special F. issue, *Les feuilles libres*, Nos. 45–46 (1927); Chonez, C., *L.-P.*

F. (1950); Beucler, A., *The Last of the Bo-hemians: Twenty Years with L.-P. F.* (1954); La Rochefoucauld, E. de F. de, *L.-P. F.* (1959); Schub, L. R., *L.-P.F.* (1973)

LOUISE RYPKO SCHUB

FAROESE LITERATURE
See section under Danish Literature

FARRELL, James T.
American novelist and critic, b. 27 Feb. 1904, Chicago, Ill.; d. 22 Aug. 1979, New York, N.Y.

A second-generation American, F. came from a working-class, Irish-Catholic family of limited means, but when he was three years old he was taken to live with his more prosperous maternal grandparents and their unmarried children. For most of his first twenty-seven years he remained in Chicago, where he went to parochial schools and later worked as a clerk in an express company. He attended the University of Chicago from 1925 to 1929, for him a period of rapid intellectual growth that culminated in his first publication of short stories and criticism. After his marriage and a year in Paris, where he completed and sold his first two novels, in 1932 he took up permanent residence in New York City. There he plunged directly into the city's literary and intellectual life and quickly emerged, during the early Depression years, as a leading spokesman of the anti-Stalinist Left and a champion of oppressed groups. Over the next four decades he remained politically active in a long odyssey that took him from membership in the Trotskyite Socialist Workers Party in the 1930s to vigorous support of liberal Democrats in the 1960s and 1970s. An omnivorous reader with broad international interests, F. occasionally taught in universities; for many years he lectured throughout America and, in 1956, on a world tour.

Most of F.'s energies, however, went into the writing of fiction. His work was significantly influenced by Chekhov, Dreiser, Sherwood Anderson, Joyce, Hemingway (qq.v.), and the pragmatists George H. Mead (1863–1931) and John Dewey (1859–1952). Firmly rooted in the realistic tradition, but intensely personal in its reflection of his spiritual growth, his fiction explores the realities of lower-class and middle-class American urban culture, especially of the 1920s and 1930s, by following the interweaving careers of hundreds of characters. F.'s most famous work is the Chicago trilogy consisting of *Young Lonigan* (1932), *The Young Manhood of Studs Lonigan* (1934), and *Judgment Day* (1935), subsequently published in one volume as *Studs Lonigan* (1935), which should be considered as a complete and unified whole. This first of three major series he completed, powerfully portrays its hero's degradation and death through a fatal susceptibility to inferior values. The Danny O'Neill pentalogy (*A World I Never Made,* 1936; *No Star Is Lost,* 1938; *Father and Son,* 1940; *My Days of Anger,* 1943; *The Face of Time,* 1953), closely following F.'s Chicago experience, is rich in family characterizations and traces the growth of the child Danny into the incipient artist and the social rebel. The Bernard Carr trilogy, consisting of *Bernard Clare* (1946; repub. as *Bernard Carr*), *The Road Between* (1949), and *Yet Other Waters* (1952), completes the story of the artist's emergence, and his fight to maintain his integrity in the face of economic hardship and the pressures of American communists and literary fellow travelers in New York City from 1927 to 1936. In this connection, F.'s *A Note on Literary Criticism* (1936) is a forceful attack on the methods of Marxist literary critics.

F.'s many collections of short stories and other of his novels, especially *Gas-House McGinty* (1933), *Ellen Rogers* (1941), *Boarding House Blues* (1961), and *New Year's Eve/1929* (1967), interlace with his major series and fill out his story of the education of Americans—for life or death. The result is a unified body of work notable for its singleness of vision and the objective validity with which it re-creates an authentic American past.

In 1958 F. began a new fictional cycle collectively titled "A Universe of Time." This work was planned to include at least twenty-five volumes that would interlock with his earlier fiction but would yield a view of experience more panoramic than that of his three earlier series. Its integrating theme, F. wrote, was "man's creativity and his courageous acceptance of impermanence." At his death he had completed ten books in the cycle (most notably *The Silence of History,* 1963; *What Time Collects,* 1964; *Invisible Swords,* 1971; *Judith, and Other Stories,* 1973; *The Dunne Family,* 1976; and *The Death of Nora Ryan,* 1978) and was working on several others. Central to "A Universe of Time" is the autobiographical character Eddie Ryan. Employing F.'s rigorous realism, the incomplete cycle mainly portrays segments of Eddie's personal, family, and professional past, while reaching out to the broader picture of 20th-c. America that F. had planned.

During his lifetime F. published fifty-two books (fifty-three if *Studs Lonigan* is considered a separate work, as it should be), including twenty-five novels and seventeen short-story collections. These establish him as a major figure in American realism. Philosophically F. is a naturalist whose values are strongly humanistic. The constant assumption of his critical realism is man's capacity for reason and dignity. Although in his writing he often dwells upon man's impressionability and pettiness in the face of debasing conditions, more basically he asserts the possibility of progress toward a humane and democratic society, and the individual's power to attain a degree of freedom and self-fulfillment by means of knowledge and a tenacious will. These same values inform F.'s essays of social and literary criticism in *The League of Frightened Philistines* (1945), *Literature and Morality* (1947); *Reflections at Fifty, and Other Essays* (1954), and *Literary Essays 1954–1974* (1976).

FURTHER WORKS: *Calico Shoes, and Other Stories* (1934); *Guillotine Party, and Other Stories* (1935); *Can All This Grandeur Perish?, and Other Stories* (1937); *The Short Stories of J. T. F.* (1937); *Tommy Gallagher's Crusade* (1939); *$1,000 a Week, and Other Stories* (1942); *To Whom It May Concern, and Other Stories* (1944); *When Boyhood Dreams Come True* (1946); *The Life Adventurous, and Other Stories* (1947); *An American Dream Girl* (1950); *The Name Is Fogarty: Private Papers on Public Matters* (1950); *This Man and This Woman* (1951); *French Girls Are Vicious, and Other Stories* (1955); *An Omnibus of Short Stories* (1956); *My Baseball Diary* (1957); *It Has Come to Pass* (1958); *Side Street, and Other Stories* (1961); *Sound of a City* (1967); *Selected Essays* (1964); *The Collected Poems of J. T. F.* (1965); *When Time Was Born* (1966); *Lonely for the Future* (1966); *A Brand New Life* (1968); *Judith* (1969); *Childhood Is Not Forever* (1969); *Olive and Mary Anne* (1977)

BIBLIOGRAPHY: Beach, J. W., *American Fiction, 1920–1940* (1941), pp. 271–305; Gelfant, B. H., *The American City Novel* (1954), pp. 175–227; Grattan, C. H., "J. T. F.: Moralist," *Harper's*, Oct. 1954, 93–94, 96, 98; Gregory, H., "J. T. F.: Beyond the Provinces of Art," *New World Writing*, 5 (1954), 52–65; Branch, E. M., *A Bibliography of J. T. F.'s Writings, 1921–1957* (1959); Branch, E. M., *J. T. F.* (1971); Salzman, J., "J. T. F.: An Essay in Bibliography," *RALS*, 6 (1976), 131–63; Wald, A. M., *J. T. F.: The Revolutionary Socialist Years* (1978)

EDGAR M. BRANCH

FARROKHZAD, Forugh
Iranian poet, b. Jan. 1935, Tehran; d. 14 Feb. 1967, Tehran

F. went to school in Tehran but did not receive a high-school diploma. At fourteen she began composing poetry in the classical mode. Married unhappily at sixteen, she was soon divorced after giving birth to a son, who was given into the custody of her husband. F.'s trips to Europe in the late 1950s (she learned Italian, German, and English quite well) had a great impact on her poetry. In 1960, after studying in England, she became very active and successful in documentary film making. In 1965 UNESCO produced a half-hour film about her. She was killed in an automobile accident.

F.'s first collection of verse, *Asir* (the captive), was published in 1952. In 1955 a different collection with the same title appeared. This second volume made her the subject of scandal: for the first time in Persian poetry a writer spoke about her love for a man with all the sensuality and frankness of a personal confession. For perceptive critics, however, this volume signaled the appearance of a shining star among the poets of the so-called "new wave."

The four volumes of her poetry provide us with a guide by which to analyze F.'s development until just before her fatal accident. In her simple and clear poetic style, these poems reflect a transition, both personal and artistic; her art was inextricably bound to her personal growth. She gradually moves away from the bonds of tradition to a yearning for an attainment of freedom and ultimately to a new self and a pure art.

The titles of the collections indicate this progression: *Asir*; *Divar* (1956; the wall); *'Osyan* (1958; the rebellion), and *Tavvalod-e degar* (1964; another birth) reflect a move away from the restrictions of traditional poetry; in this, she was a close follower of the doctrines of Nima Yushij (1895?–1959), the pioneer of Persian free verse. The first two titles represent the poet's understanding and assessment of those bonds; the second two, the struggle against them and the emergence, from their destruction, of a new poetic form.

She did not, however, cut herself off from the literary past. She took many of her best images from the classical mystical repertoire, particularly her use of light versus dark and her concentration on shadows. Her most consistent appeal is to love, love that ranges from the contentment felt among friends to the devotion of religious activity or the passion of human sensuality. On a deeper plane, F.'s poetry represents the struggle of the individual against the power of evil and ugliness, alienation, fear, and frustration. She is rightly acclaimed a master of modern Persian poetry and the second female poet of greatness in the language, after Parvin E'tesami (1906–1941).

BIBLIOGRAPHY: Tikku, G., "F. F.: A New Direction in Persian Poetry," *StIsl*, 26 (1967), 149–73; Hillmann, M. C., "F. F.: Modern Iranian Poet," in Fernea, E. W., and Bezirgan, B. Q., eds., *Middle Eastern Muslim Women Speak* (1977), pp. 291–317; Hillmann, M. C., "Sexuality in the Poetry of F. F. and the Structuralist View," *Edebiyat*, 3 (1978), 191–211

PETER J. CHELKOWSKI

FAULKNER, William

American novelist and short-story writer, b. 25 Sept. 1897, New Albany, Miss.; d. 6 July 1962, Oxford, Miss.

In 1902 F.'s father moved the family to Oxford, where, except for a period in the Canadian air force (F. did not serve in France, despite occasional stories to the contrary), a few months in New York City, a half-year stay in New Orleans, stints of script writing in Hollywood, etc., F. spent the major part of his life. His ancestors were hard-working professional men, his great-grandfather having been a popular novelist and an outstanding (even legendary) figure in his region. Most of F.'s short stories and novels are set in the South and owe much of their character to their local color. His Southern origin is also responsible for the historical element in F.'s work, as well as for his preoccupation with racial problems and with points of honor. Likewise his aptitude for spinning a yarn and the highly rhetorical element in his writings derive from this Southern association. The South, more than the North, lives with a sense of the past, and this fact probably accounts for much of F.'s awareness of the past living on into the present.

However, F. did not begin his career with a schematic plan for portraying the history of the South. Sometimes, as in *Light in August* (1932), he is harshly critical of his region, and sometimes, as in *Intruder in the Dust* (1948), he is almost polemical in his defense of it. In an early novel, *Sartoris* (1929), he describes in a rather uncritical manner the hero's preoccupation with the gallant gesture, but in *The Unvanquished* (1938) he depicts Southern bravery as headlong heroics and the region's concern with honor as an easy rationalization for thoughtless and sometimes even vicious conduct. There is in F.'s work a tremendous admiration for selflessness, love, endurance, and human dignity. These are seen by him as human virtues which transcend race and class and which are found in different places and at different times. In other words, he does not present, as has sometimes been maintained, a specific class as the representatives of noble conduct and of a way of life above criticism.

F.'s work may without difficulty be divided into three major periods, with certain themes, techniques, and mannerisms being common to all of them. Among his writings of the first period, *Soldiers' Pay* (1926), *Mosquitoes* (1927), and some of the stories in the short-story collection *These Thirteen* (1931) possess many characteristics in common. All of them bear witness to F.'s early reading of Keats, Tennyson, Swinburne, and the literature of the 1890s. There is a Victorian air about them, but one that by comparison with Victorian literature is at once more pallid and more flamboyant. F., incidentally, has never belonged to the school of "a pure American prose," insofar as that means a strong tendency toward understatement and sentences built on frequent use of the conjunction.

To the second period, when F. really found himself as an artist, belong *The Sound and the Fury* (1929), *As I Lay Dying* (1930), *Sanctuary* (1931), *Light in August*, *Doctor Martino, and Other Stories* (1934), *Pylon* (1935), *Absalom, Absalom!* (1936), *The Unvanquished*, and *The Wild Palms* (1939). Most of these are stories of terrifying violence, exacerbated humor, and grim dignity. The horrors are steadily kept in the foreground, and sometimes a thin margin of victory is allowed a protagonist. In many, but not all of these volumes, F. is mainly concerned with his own region, and in almost all of them he experiments endlessly with methods of narration, drawing the reader into and through the involutions of page-long sentences and forcing him to hold in mind details and phrases that are meaningful only at the end, when the story, in all of its contexts, evolves brilliantly, with fact illuminating fact. No two stories are told in quite the same way. In *The Sound and the Fury* the consciousness of three characters is revealed as though the reader lived successively in each mind, and then the range of consciousness broadens, enlarging in focus, until a history begins to be clear. In *As I Lay Dying* each character develops in terms of his own awareness (each is a narrator) and through the way he is seen by the other characters; and all of them are seen in terms of the way they react to their part in the symbolic, yet highly painful, funeral journey. Most of the remaining stories are episodic, but each has devices peculiar to itself: the Gothic framework of *Absalom, Absalom!*, the double plot and analogous actions of *Light in August* (this is probably closest of all of his novels to the typical Elizabethan double plot), the foreshortened action of *Pylon* (similar in narrative technique to F. Scott Fitzgerald's [q.v.] *The Great Gatsby*), the sequence of related short stories in *The Unvanquished*, and the merely thematic (if that) relationship between the alternating stories of *The Wild Palms*. *Sanctuary* is not nearly so experimental in structure, but, through its careful imagery (there are alternate patterns of overripeness and of the mechanical) and symbolism it suggests the conventions of a highly stylized play.

These novels make it clear that F. is not a realistic writer in any of the senses that bear upon verisimilitude or upon the novel as documenting a region. In fact, it is extremely misleading to read him as a strict realist. They also make it clear that F. is at the same time indebted to the tradition of the modern novel and a contributor to that tradition. Not the least of these contributions is the way in which his language (like that of Joyce [q.v.]) seems to be of a piece with his character or subject, evoking each in the appropriate way, then rising on itself as a choral voice, richly rhetorical and hypnotic.

In the third period, beginning with *The Hamlet* (1940), F. offers some hope for the human condition, a promise of release. The hope is explored in *Go Down, Moses* (1942), most significantly in "The Bear" and "Delta Autumn." In *Intruder in the Dust, Knight's Gambit* (1949), and *Requiem for a Nun* (1951) there are various attempts to elevate political programs and sermons into the self-sufficient isolated entities of art forms. *Go Down, Moses* contains some of F.'s most brilliant and sustained rhetoric. A mythical wilderness is evoked with great power, but unfortun-

ately the dialectic side of the novel is unsatisfactory. In *Intruder in the Dust* and in *Knight's Gambit* there is a merging of detective-story solutions and regional sociological themes. The former, although it is sectional in the thesis it argues regarding the place of the Negro, is much the more serious novel. *Requiem for a Nun* combines a play and historical documentation, interlarding acts and chapters from the history of Jefferson (F.'s fictional town), and suggesting thereby the judgments the past makes on the actions of Temple Drake, the "heroine." *A Fable* (1954), certainly the most highly stylized and rhetorical of F.'s books, and perhaps so stylized and rhetorical that most readers feel the reality behind it only as an extended blur, seems to invite the reader to reconcile himself to the conflicting impulses in human beings.

In the later years of his life, F. returned to the Snopes saga, with *The Town* (1947) and *The Mansion* (1959). Neither book has the imaginative force of the first book of the trilogy, *The Hamlet*, in which the Snopeses take on mythical proportions. All of the characters are reduced in scale, and only Mink Snopes, in *The Mansion*, continues the lemminglike drive of the Snopeses as may be observed in *The Hamlet*. For about two-thirds of the novel, F. is back in his old form.

With *The Reivers* (1962) F. nostalgically revisits his childhood, and also revisits and extends the world of *Sanctuary*. Set early in the 20th c., the novel is both a paean to the preindustrial world, the small-town and agrarian world of F.'s parents, and the newer world of the automobile and the city. As a novel, it is not equal in stature to the books of the middle period, but it has its own quiet comedy and dignity. It also enlarges the Yoknapatawpha world (his mythical county).

F. died a few months after the publication of *The Reivers*, almost exactly one year after Hemingway (q.v.). The careers of these two writers illuminate each other, and thus invite critical comparison. F. was almost two years older than Hemingway, but his success came more slowly, except that he was awarded the Nobel Prize before Hemingway. F. was sometimes critical of Hemingway, saying he learned at an early stage what he could do, and was satisfied to repeat himself. One book in particular shows the nature of F.'s "quarrel" with Hemingway—*The Wild Palms*. Read carefully, it can be seen as a "dialogue," as a critique of *A Farewell to Arms* and a questioning of the "Hemingway world." There are many parallels in the actions of the two novels, and clearly the character McCord, in *The Wild Palms*, is based on Hemingway himself. "The Wild Palms" story, the love story, is largely a parallel to *A Farewell to Arms*, but "Old Man," the story of the Tall Convict, the chapters of which are interlarded with "The Wild Palms," is a fundamental criticism of the characters in "The Wild Palms" and therefore of the "Hemingway world."

Hemingway divides society into the "initiates," and the "messy ones," who believe all the slogans about patriotism and accept easy middle-class affirmations. He admires the initiates, who reject the world, except on their own terms. The universe is meaningless, and the sensitive man meets it on his terms—as a good athlete, a courageous soldier, a skilled physician, or a skilled writer. He lives the physical life to the full, with sex, drinking, and hunting or fishing. The initiate wrests his narrow victory.

The F. "hero" is very different. He learns to accept the world. The Tall Convict, like Byron Bunch in *Light in August*, knows, although he would not know how to say it, that "love no more exists just at one spot and in one moment and in one body out of all the earth and all time . . . than sunlight does." The Hemingway world, with the sleepless man, tricked by the universe, emphasizes defeat and rejection. After his early "lost generation" stance, F. moved toward acceptance.

This contrast between the "F. world" and the "Hemingway world" is of considerable importance. It has something to do with the way both men lived their lives, and a great deal to do with their literary legacies.

The three periods in F.'s career suggest the varieties of attitudes and of themes to be found in his work. Through several of the books, either as major or minor themes, runs his intense dislike of the repressions caused by the rigid mind. *Light in August* presents outrages done and violences caused by literal-minded pietists. *Absalom, Absalom!* may be interpreted as a story of the violence caused by the literal adherence to a code. And several of the short stories may be read in similar terms. *The Hamlet* is folk comedy, making ample use of the tall tale and farcical situations. Several of the earlier novels present a vision of things not unlike that presented in Eliot's (q.v.) *The Waste Land;* perhaps the most successful of these is *The Sound and the Fury*.

In reply to a question once put to him by an interviewer, F. said he had read very little about the history of the Civil War and of the South generally. What he knew, he knew by word of mouth, by having assimilated some beliefs and prejudices and rejecting others. Considering that he is commonly looked upon as the "historian" of Yoknapatawpha County, his stories of the 19th c. are relatively not numerous. Perhaps it is safest to regard him as a fiction writer whose mind and imagination are best engaged by certain themes; on the other hand, he has written about his region, and it is a compliment to him that he has written in so luminous a fashion that he seems to be telling the actual, historical truth about it. He is an apologist for the virtues of his region, and a ruthless critic of its vices.

That F. was an original writer probably made it inevitable that his fellow Americans would be a little slow in recognizing his abilities, but he has now been widely recognized, to which his winning of the Nobel Prize (1950) and numerous other awards bears witness. Undoubtedly he belongs to the small group of novelists who transcend region or country.

FURTHER WORKS: *New Orleans Sketches* (1953); *F. at Nagano* (1956); *F. in the University* (1959); *W. F.: Early Prose and Poetry* (1962); *F. at West Point* (1964); *Essays, Speeches and Public Letters* (1966); *The F.–Cowley File: Letters and Memories 1944–1962* (1968); *Flags in the Dust* (1973); *The Marionettes* (1975); *Mayday* (1977); *Selected Letters of W. F.* (1977); *Uncollected Stories of W. F.* (1979); *Sanctuary: The Original Text* (1981)

BIBLIOGRAPHY: Warren, R. P., *W. F.: His South* (1951); Howe, I., *W. F.: A Critical Study* (1952; 2nd rev. ed., 1962); O'Connor, W. V., *The Tangled Fire of W. F.* (1954); Stein, J., "The Art of Fiction XII: W. F." [interview], *Paris Review*, No. 12 (1956), 28–52; Vickery, O., *The Novels of W. F.* (1959; rev. ed., 1964); Woodworth, S. D., *W. F. en France* (1959); Slatoff, W. J., *Quest for Failure: A Study of W. F.* (1960); Hoffman, F. J., *W. F.* (1961); Meriwether, J. B., *The Literary Career of W. F.* (1961); Beck, W., *Man in Motion: F.'s Trilogy* (1961); Swiggart, P., *The Art of F.'s Novels* (1962); Brooks, C., *W. F.* (1963); Faulkner, J., *My Brother Bill* (1963); Thompson, L. R., *W. F.: An Introduction and Interpretation* (1963); Dain, M. J., *F.'s Country* (1964); Volpe, E. L., *A Reader's Guide to W. F.* (1964); Nilon, C. H., *F. and the Negro* (1965); Blackman, M., *F.:*

The Major Years (1966); Millgate, M., *The Achievement of W. F.* (1966); Blotner, J. L., *F.: A Biography* (1974); Bassett, J., ed., *W. F.: The Critical Heritage* (1975); Guerard, A. J., *The Triumph of the Novel: Dickens, Dostoevsky, F.* (1976); Brooks, C., *W. F.: Toward Yoknapatawpha and Beyond* (1978); Minter, D., *W. F.: His Life and Work* (1980)

WILLIAM VAN O'CONNOR
UPDATED BY ALAN W. FRIEDMAN

In addition to being a fatalist, F. is also an idealist, more strongly so than any other American writer of our time. The idealist disguises itself as its own opposite, but that is because he is deeply impressed by and tends to exaggerate the contrast between the life around him and the ideal picture in his mind . . . of how the land and the people should be—a picture of painted, many-windowed houses, fenced fields, overflowing barns, eyes lighting up with recognition. . . . And both pictures are not only physical but moral; for always in the background of his novels is a sense of moral standards and a feeling of outrage at their being violated or simply brushed aside. Seeing little hope in the future, he turns to the past, where he hopes to discover a legendary and recurrent pattern that will illuminate and lend dignity to the world about him.

Malcolm Cowley, "W. F.'s Legend of the South," in Allen Tate, ed., *A Southern Vanguard* (1947), pp. 26–27

To speak of greatness with regard to one's contemporaries is dangerous. But if there are any American novels of the present century which may be called great, which bear comparison—serious if not favorable—with the achievements of twentieth-century European literature, then surely *The Sound and the Fury* is among them. It is one of the three or four American works of prose fiction written since the turn of the century in which the impact of tragedy is felt and sustained. Seized by his materials, F. keeps, for once, within his esthetic means, rarely trying to say more than he can or needs to. *The Sound and the Fury* is the one novel in which his vision and technique are almost in complete harmony, and the vision itself whole and major. Whether taken as a study of the potential for human self-destruction, or as a rendering of the social disorder particular to our time, the novel projects a radical image of man against the wall. Embodied and justified, this is an image of great writing.

Irving Howe, *W. F.* (1952), pp. 126–27

The European reader finds something uniquely American in F., and obviously no European could have written his books; the few European commentators that I have read seem to me to glorify W. F. in a provincial American (or Southern) vacuum. I believe that as his personality fades from view he will be recognized as one of the great craftsmen of the art of fiction which Ford Madox Ford called the Impressionistic Novel. From Stendhal through Flaubert and Joyce there is a direct line to F., and it is not a mere question of influence. F.'s great subject, as it was Flaubert's and Proust's, is passive suffering, the victim being destroyed either by society or by dark forces within himself. F. is one of the great exemplars of the international school of fiction which for more than a century has reversed the Aristotelian doctrine that tragedy is an action, not a quality.

Allen Tate, "W. F., 1897–1962," *SR*, 71 (1963), 162

To the neophyte F. reader, the prose may seem a continual flow of words that obscures the story action rather than developing it. The difficulties should not be minimized. The diction, the syntax, seem designed to obfuscate, not communicate. F. sometimes deliberately withholds important details, and the narrators frequently refer to people or events that the reader will not learn about until much later, making the style seem even more opaque than it actually is. And the long sentences are difficult to follow, with clauses that proliferate, developing not from the main subject or verb of the sentence, but growing out of preceding clauses. As a result, the main thought is often lost in the mass of amplifying or qualifying ideas. Antecedents of personal pronouns are frequently not clear. F.'s style does not provide relaxing reading, but forces the reader to participate in the search for understanding and truth. . . . Had F. been a U.S. senator, his speeches would have been squarely in the tradition of Southern oratory. Some of his sentences sound almost like selected passages from a filibuster. Rather than run the risk of interruption and lose the floor, he does not pause; he rolls on, using all the rhetorical devices of the speechmaker: colorful, grandiloquent and emotive words, repetition, parallel structure, a series of negative clauses preceding a positive, delayed climax.

Edmund L. Volpe, *A Reader's Guide to W. F.* (1963), pp. 38–39

Out of F.'s sharply realized portraits of individual men and women, there gradually emerges a view of man which involves making a crucial distinction between the social and moral definitions of his nature. The former simply places the individual in certain exclusive categories, the latter restores to him his identity with all humanity. The one provides a formula for morality and enforces it with law, the other leaves moral action undefined and therefore unfettered. In short, the social definition of man predetermines the individual's response to experience by creating an expectation of conformity to certain codes which govern the behavior of each social unit. The moral definition forces man to assume responsibility for recognizing and enacting his own moral nature. At the very heart of the Yoknapatawpha novels and *A Fable* is the problem created by the conflict between the inflexible morality of society and the ethics of the individual based on experience, grounded in specific situations, and usually incapable of formulation beyond the simplest of maxims and platitudes. . . .

Since any social system or moral code tends to replace internal morality with external controls, the only healthy relationship between men and their society is one of mutual suspicion and unrelaxed vigilance. Only such an attitude can ensure the continued existence of a critical revaluation of the former's behavior and the latter's conventions. If this balance is destroyed, the result is either anarchy or social and governmental dictatorship. Because it completely obliterates freedom, because it reduces the individual to an unquestioning automaton, the second is more dangerous. F. levels some of his bitterest and most forthright criticism at this accelerating process of regimentation which he describes in almost all of his novels, though it becomes increasingly prominent in the later works, beginning with *Go Down, Moses.*

Olga Vickery, *The Novels of W. F.,* rev. ed. (1964), pp. 282–83

F.'s achievement can be adequately estimated only by our seeing him as a great novelist in the context not merely of the South, or even of the United States, but of the whole western tradition. His deep identification with his own region is one of his greatest strengths, especially as it emerges in the marvellous sense of place, whether it be the heart of the wilderness or the interior of Miss Reba's brothel, and in the rich evocation of the world of Yoknapatawpha County; and certainly the intensity of his tragic power in novels such as *The Sound and the Fury, Light in August,* and *Absalom, Absalom!* derives both from this profoundly localised sense of social reality and from a poignant awareness of the proud and shameful history of the courageous, careless, gallant and oppressive South. At the same time, to concentrate too exclusively on this aspect of his work is to be in danger of mistaking means for ends and of seeing F. as a lesser figure than he really is. The solidity of F.'s provinciality provides the unshakable foundation for his immensely ambitious exploration of the fundamental human themes with which he is always primarily concerned, and the examples of Hardy and Emily Brontë may suggest that F. is not alone among novelists in pursuing the universal in terms of the intensely local. But it is Dickens whom F. most resembles, in the passionate humanity of his tragi-comic vision, in the range and vitality of his characterisation and the

profusion of his social notation, in the structural complexity of his novels and their broad symbolic patterns. It is also Dickens whom F. most resembles in the sheer quantity and sustained quality of his achievement, and it is alongside Dickens, the greatest of the English novelists, that F. must ultimately be ranked.

Michael Millgate, *The Achievement of W. F.* (1966), p. 292

The issue of millennialism is . . . one that sets F. off from a great many other American writers. He does not, of course, stand alone; yet his more old-fashioned notion of history has disquieted and confused many a twentieth-century literary critic, and it sets him off sharply from such writers as Hart Crane or, to mention one whose talents he greatly admired, Thomas Wolfe. F. is far less visionary than Wolfe, less optimistic, less intoxicated with the greatness of America. By contrast, F.'s view is more "Southern," and though one should not claim him for Christian orthodoxy, much closer to St. Augustine's view of history. . . .

F. did not scorn the American Dream. Rather, he mourned the fact that it had not been fulfilled. He grieved at having to conclude in 1955 that "the American air, which was once the living breath of liberty [has] now become one vast down-crowding pressure to abolish [freedom], by destroying man's individuality. . . ." F., however, was skeptical about the full realization of *any* utopian dream, even the noblest. That is to say, he was evidently seriously concerned that his country might be undone by her sometimes overweening faith in the future, by her belief that progress was inevitable, by her confidence that man's happiness would result from sociological know-how and the right set of plans, by her reliance on her technological might, by her incautious trust in her own virtues and good intentions, and, most dangerous of all, by her unprecedented record of military victories. (F. died before Americans went into Vietnam.) Americans could easily get the impression that they, unlike the other nations of the earth, were immune to defeat, loss, and evil. Such innocence might in the end prove disastrous.

Cleanth Brooks, *W. F.: Toward Yoknapatawpha and Beyond* (1978), pp. 281–82

Early in his life as an artist F. had begun to dread the moment "when not only the ecstasy of writing would be gone, but the unreluctance and the something worth saying too." In part because the division within him ran deep, in part because work was what he did best, and in part because his relation to his art was so intense and satisfying, he came to that moment slowly. Gradually, however, as his confidence in what he had done increased and his confidence in what he was doing slipped away, he began identifying himself with

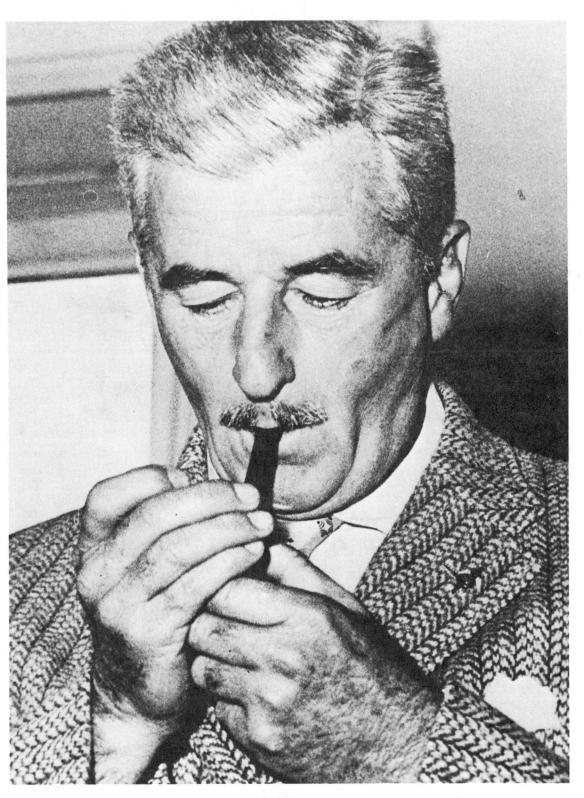

WILLIAM FAULKNER

F. SCOTT FITZGERALD

FORD MADOX FORD

the work he had finished, the selves he had become, as though he knew that what was valuable was what he had already created and so had lost not shabbily. Repeatedly testing the self that remained, he went on waiting for "the moment, instant, night: dark: sleep: when I would put it all away forever that I anguished and sweated over, and it would never trouble me anymore." Having looked at that moment many times, with mixed fear and desire but with defiance, too, he came to it, as he thought Albert Camus had, knowing that he had done all things in his life that he could.

David Minter, *W. F.: His Life and Work* (1980), pp. 250–51

FAYE, Jean-Pierre

French novelist, poet, and literary theoretician, b. 19 July 1925, Paris

After studying law and economics at the Sorbonne and anthropology at the Museum of Man under Claude Lévi-Strauss (q.v.), F. went to live in the U.S. in 1954–55. Back in France, he started publishing fiction in 1958 and was on the staff of the journal *Tel quel* from 1963 until 1967. From 1959 to 1972 he was a frequent visitor to Germany, collecting documents for his *Les langages totalitaires* (1972; totalitarian languages).

From the start of his career as a writer and a literary theoretician, F. denied any validity to the established categories. He focused instead on experimentation in order to explore how literary forms, historical discourses, and philosophical constructs combine in the very act of narration. F.'s driving idea throughout his work, whether fictional, historical, or political, is that of a universal process of "change" affecting all symbolic forms, languages as well as societies as a whole. Fictions are but the means through which such a process assumes a form significant for the imagination. More recently, F. has found in the linguistic theories of Noam Chomsky (b. 1928) a conceptual basis for his own theory of "transformatism," the generic name he uses to describe his overall vision of things human, a vision shared by a group of writers whose work appears in the journal and the book series *Change*, edited by F. since 1968, after he left *Tel quel*.

The unity of F.'s endeavor appears most clearly in the way he wants his first six novelistic works to be read as a series, retrospectively titled *Hexagramme* (hexagram) by the author. In those works, characters are variables in complex narrative functions that put into play the very structures of narrative: linguistic events, space, time, point of view. All these elements take part in a polyphony designed to create a well-controlled network of meanings against the backdrop of historically and geographically significant settings. In this fashion, F. uses to a considerable extent the characteristics of some almost mythic cities, between which he creates complex fictional resonances: Berlin in *L'écluse* (1964; the lock), Troyes in France and Troy in *Les Troyens* (1970; the Trojans), his two most successful works. Paris, Munich, and Chicago appear in his earlier novels also.

Two more books have been added to this series. *Inferno, versions* (1975; inferno, versions) and *L'ovale, detail* (1975; the oval, detail), both set in Jerusalem, while complementary to each other, can also be read as a single work belonging to the set of all potential narratives made possible by the "hexagram" structure. The superimposition of the various narratives and their multiplication, and the overlapping of plots and points of view thus appear more and more as F.'s central concerns in his attempt to create new fictional worlds and techniques.

Better known for his important historical essays—such as *Les langages totalitaires*—and his political involvements and writings—such as *Le Portugal d'Otelo* (1976; *Portugal: The Revolution in the Labyrinth*, 1976)—than for his more ambitious fictions, F. nevertheless should appear in the course of time as a gifted creator of intricate, intriguing stories, as an elegant writer, and as the possessor of a complex mind. His qualities as a writer are sometimes obscured, however, by his somewhat excessive penchant for allusions, hyperbole, and all-encompassing generalizations.

FURTHER WORKS: *Entre les rues* (1958); *Fleuve renversé* (1959); *La cassure* (1961); *Battement* (1962); *Analogues* (1965); *Théâtre* (1964); *Couleurs pliées* (1965); *Hypothèses* (1972); *Iskra; Cirque* (1972); *Luttes de classes à Dunkerque* (1972); *Théorie du récit* (1972); *La critique du langage et son économie* (1973); *Migrations du récit sur le peuple juif* (1974); *Langue: Théorie générative étendue* (1977); *Les portes des villes du monde* (1977); *Verres* (1978); *Les minorités dans la pensée* (1979); *Commencement d'une figure en mouvement* (1980); *Syeeda* (1980); *Les grandes journées du Père Duchesne* (1981)

BIBLIOGRAPHY: Boyer, P., "Le grand écart," *Critique*, 27 (1971), 770–82; Pierssens, M.,

"L'entreprise de *Change*," *Sub-stance*, 4 (1972), 107–16; Teysseire, D., "Mort des mots: Mots de mort," *Critique*, 29 (1973), 1038–45; Pierssens, M., "J.-P. F.: Vers une sémantique de l'Histoire," *ECr*, 14 (1974), 369–75; Ronat, M., *F.* (1980); Partouche, M., *J.-P. F.* (1981)

M. PIERSSENS

FEDIN, Konstantin Alexandrovich

Russian novelist, short-story writer, and essayist, b. 24 Feb. 1892, Saratov; d. 15 July 1977, Moscow

F. belonged to the group of Russian writers who bridged the events of October 1917 and personified the link between traditional 19th-c. and Soviet literature. Born in the Volga region, F. spent his formative years in the midst of a family belonging to the radical intelligentsia, and he sharpened his literary tastes by reading the great Russian classics. His first literary piece appeared in a St. Petersburg magazine as early as 1913. The outbreak of World War I found him in Germany, where he was interned for the duration of the war. The autobiographical events of those years served as the backdrop for his first full-length novel, *Goroda i gody* (1924; *Cities and Years*, 1962).

Returning to Russia after the revolution, F. joined the Communist Party; while working in Petrograd (formerly St. Petersburg) he met Maxim Gorky (q.v.) and through him made the acquaintance of other Petrograd writers who formed the literary group known as the Serapion Brothers. Under their influence, F.'s muse flourished, and in 1921 he withdrew from the Party.

Clearly influenced by Gogol, Dostoevsky, Chekhov (q.v.), and Bunin (q.v.), F. published a collection of seven stories, *Pustyr* (1923; the wasteland), in which he described the world of the past populated by lonely little people.

The main thrust of F.'s first novel, *Goroda i gody*, may be viewed as the tragedy of individualism in the new world created by the Russian Revolution. It is an ambitious attempt to portray within a mixed chronology the lives of its Russian and German protagonists against the background of social and political events in the cities. The protagonist of the novel, Andrey Startsov, is a utopian idealist, repelled by the bloody struggle, who comes face to face with the revolutionary zeal of his German friend, the painter Kurt Wahn. Andrey's incapacity for action and his own sense of futility earmark him

for the category of "superfluous men" so prominent in 19th-c. Russian novels.

In his second important novel, *Bratya* (1928; the brothers), F. again drew on his own life and past to create the hero of the story, Nikita Karev, a composer who is almost crushed in his efforts to adjust to the revolutionary present. Despite Nikita's ultimate acceptance of Soviet reality at the conclusion of the novel, F. had posed in it the problem of the artist having to reconcile his vocation with the revolution.

Throughout his life F.'s creative output was strongly influenced by his knowledge of the West and its people. Nowhere was it more apparent than in his novel *Pokhishchenie Evropy* (2 vols., 1933–35; the rape of Europe), which deals with a Dutch family of timber merchants with business ties in Russia during the time of the first Five-Year Plan. The "Russian question," as it was apprehended in Europe in the early 1930s, is at the center of the story. The tone of the novel is decidedly pro-Soviet, and the realism of its scenes is often striking, but the lack of unity of design is its main weakness. With this novel, F. clearly chose the role of a "fellow-traveling" Soviet writer.

F.'s next published work was a short novel, *Sanatory Arktur* (1940; *Sanatorium Arktur*, 1957), which, departing from an autobiographical experience, is a psychological study of an illness containing several excellent characterizations.

In the early 1940s F. became drawn more and more to the socialist present as a political and artistic concept. Yet F. was not spared public condemnation and an official rebuttal in *Pravda* in connection with the second volume of his literary reminiscences, *Gorky sredi nas* (2 vols., 1943–44; Gorky among us), an honest, wise, and objective book in which F.'s own artistic and social views appear to be out of step with the Party line.

F.'s most ambitious and mature work is a trilogy embracing a vast period of Russian life. It was begun during World War II and was prompted, in F.'s own words, by his search "for a great contemporary hero . . . a Communist whose active will was synonymous with victory." Kirill Izvekov is such a hero in *Pervye radosti* (1945; *Early Joys*, 1948), *Neobyknovennoe leto* (1947–48; *No Ordinary Summer*, 1950), and *Koster* (1961–65; *The Conflagration*, 1968).

F. left his mark on Soviet literature as the writer who, after the political and cultural upheaval brought on by the 1917 revolution, initiated a return to the realistic narrative of the 19th-c. Russian novel and began probing the psychological problems of the revolution, rather than merely describing or exalting it. In F.'s works, the characteristic themes are the individual in relationship to his times, the sensitive intellectual faced with the hard choice between the old and the new, and the question of art and its place in contemporary Soviet life. Despite the orthodox Soviet tenor of F.'s fiction, it is colored by sympathetic understanding of the Russian past and, artistically, his doubting intellectuals are consistently more successful than his idealistic Bolsheviks.

FURTHER WORKS: *Bakunin v Drezdene* (1922); *Transvaal* (1927); *Ya byl akterom* (1937); *Ispytanie chuvstv* (1942); *Neskolko naselennykh punktov* (1943); *Svidanie s Leningradom* (1944); *Pisatel, iskusstvo i vremya* (1957); *Sobranie sochineny* (10 vols., 1969–73)

BIBLIOGRAPHY: Reavey, G., *Soviet Literature Today* (1947), pp. 93–94, 120–23; Simmons, E. J., *Russian Fiction and Soviet Ideology: Introduction to F., Leonov, and Sholokhov* (1958), pp. 9–87; Simmons, E. J., Introduction to *Early Joys* (1960), pp. vii–xvi; Brown, E. J., *Russian Literature since the Revolution* (1963), pp. 124–31; Blum, J. M., *K. F.: A Descriptive and Analytic Study* (1967); Struve, G., *Russian Literature under Lenin and Stalin, 1917–1953* (1971), pp. 94–98, 289–91, 342–43, 378–80; Holthusen, J., *Twentieth-Century Russian Literature: A Critical Study* (1972), pp. 102–3, 197–200; Slonim, M., *Soviet Russian Literature: Writers and Problems, 1917–1967* (1973), pp. 130–39, 319–20

NADJA JERNAKOFF

FENOGLIO, Beppe

Italian novelist and short-story writer, b. 1 March 1922, Alba; d. 18 Feb. 1963, Turin

A reserved and introverted person, F. spent most of his life in his native town, where he pursued his major cultural interest—the study and the translation of English literature. As a writer he found the two basic sources of inspiration in his attachment to his native province (Langhe, in Piedmont), and in his experience as a partisan in the Italian Resistance during World War II. The themes of war and peasant life constantly alternate in his literary production, and at times they fuse with one another against the omnipresent and precisely drawn background of Langhe. F.'s love for English literature and the English language was to become an integral part of his fiction. He attributed this interest to several of his characters, and he used his knowledge of the English language for his own linguistic experimentation.

In his first published work, *I ventitrè giorni della città di Alba* (1952; the twenty-three days of the town of Alba), a collection of short stories, F. ordered his own experience as a partisan. Far from posing as the impersonal chronicler of events, F. alternates between a corrosive tragiccomic representation of the historical material—thus distancing and diffusing the horrors of war—and the painful and more realistic description of how war irremediably upsets human relationships even among the partisans, the harbingers of a new message of freedom.

In *Primavera di bellezza* (1959; spring of beauty), another work based on his own wartime experiences, F. vividly portrays the climate of civil and moral disorder in Italy in 1943. His resentment toward Mussolini for not having set up an adequate Italian army, and toward Marshal Badoglio for handing the army over to the Germans, shapes the vitriolic strength of his language, which deforms and caricatures those characters who represent and still defend the collapsed regime. Although F.'s style in this novel has received almost unanimous praise for its artistic and formal maturity, his characterization of Johnny, the young Anglophile who joins the partisans after Mussolini's fall and dies in a German ambush, has been judged in contradictory ways. Some critics view Johnny's enigmatic detachment from military life and from Fascist rhetoric as the ideal means to document the historical and political events leading to the inevitable conclusion of collective tragedy; other critics, however, view Johnny's detachment as the author's inability or unwillingness to express, through his protagonist, his own interpretation of such events.

La malora (1954; ruin), a short novel set in Langhe, represents one view of the savage and unmerciful world of the agricultural fields and the peasants, where neither political ideology nor unionization can help the protagonist escape his enslaving condition and regain human dignity. On the other hand, the posthumously published short stories in *Un giorno di fuoco* (1963; a day of fire), also set in Langhe, document F.'s attachment to life in the fields and his hope of finding traces there of archaic religiosity, which might function as a substitute for the moral and civil values destroyed by the war. Occasionally, however, F.'s ironic detachment from the barbaric and primitive actions of the protagonists reveals his awareness of the dangers intrinsic in the blind and promordial world of the peasantry.

The publication of *Il partigiano Johnny* (1968; Johnny the partisan), five years after F.'s death, generated considerable critical interest, which has resulted in an overwhelming positive reevaluation of F.'s writings. This unfinished novel, also set in the time of the Resistance, bears witness to the author's relentless attempt to penetrate and to understand the human condition as it is dominated by the tragic necessity for violence, and his exhausting search for artistic and formal maturity.

Early death, so ominously lying in wait for many of F.'s young protagonists, did not rob this remarkable writer of the opportunity to enrich the literature of the Resistance with what Italo Calvino (q.v.) defined as the "book our generation wanted to write." On the basis of what he did produce, F. is to be ranked among the most perceptive writers on the phenomenon of violence and among the most sensitive observers of a tragic period of Italian history.

FURTHER WORKS: *Frammenti di romanzo* (1963); *La storia di Aloysius Butor* (1964); *Epigrammi* (1974)

BIBLIOGRAPHY: Merry, B., "More on F.: An Unpublished Novel in English and an English Source," *Italica*, 49 (1971), 3–17; Merry, B., "Thomas Hardy and T. E. Lawrence: Two English Sources for B. F.?" *RomN*, 14 (1971), 230–35; Merry, B., "The Thaumaturgy of Violence," *Books*, 12 (Summer, 1973), 11–16

MARIOLINA SALVATORI

FERAOUN, Mouloud

Algerian novelist (writing in French), b. 8 March 1913, Tizi-Hibel; d. 15 March 1962, El Biar, Algiers

F., whose parents were poor peasants, was born and raised in the rugged mountains of Kabylia, east of Algiers. After secondary school he attended the teachers' college at Bouzaréah, outside Algiers. He then held a series of teaching and administrative positions in Kabylia and Algiers. In March 1962, three days before the signing of the cease-fire at the Évian negotiations, F. and five colleagues were assassinated in a suburb of Algiers by a terrorist squad of the illegal Secret Army Organization, which was bent on subverting the impending peace between France and Algeria.

From the mid-1930s on F. associated with Albert Camus, Emmanuel Roblès (qq.v.), and other writers of the so-called Algiers School. Roblès urged F. to tell the untold story of his own people. Indeed, F.'s major works all focus on himself, the territorial identity so important in Berber tradition, and the alienation of the emigrant worker.

F.'s first novel, *Le fils du pauvre* (1950; the poor man's son), was published at F.'s own expense and republished in 1954 by Éditions du Seuil. It has the distinction of being the first novel in the new wave of Algerian literature in French, which would become more readily identifiable when the first novels by Mohammed Dib and Mouloud Mammeri (qq.v.) appeared in 1952. *Le fils du pauvre*, whose protagonist bears the anagrammatic name Fouroulou Menrad, is an autobiographical novel about F.'s childhood and youth.

F.'s second novel, *La terre et le sang* (1953; earth and blood), explores the social consequences when an émigré returns with a French wife to his village in Kabylia and then falls in love with another woman. The passions, honor code, and sense of the immediacy of the earth are impenetrable to the outsider but have a firm hold on the Berbers of the area.

Les chemins qui montent (1957; the climbing roads) is ostensibly a fateful love story involving a man named Amer, a young orphan girl named Dehbia, and Amer's rival Mokrane; but it, again, examines Kabylian social constraints and the terrain that holds its inhabitants even as it repels them.

The three novels F. completed fall—as do the early novels of Dib, Mammeri, Malek Ouary (b. 1916), and others—into the category of the "ethnographic novel," written largely to explain to European readers the hidden, true side of Algeria. Because of their simple, naturalistic, accessible style, F.'s novels are more widely read in Algeria than are works by some of his more talented compatriots.

F.'s masterpiece, however, is his posthumously published *Journal 1955–1962* (1962; journal 1955–1962), which chronicles the physical horrors and cultural uncertainties of the Algerian war years (1954–62) and displays in its authentic humanity, quiet courage, and tragic dénouement qualities and a tone all too seldom achieved in fiction.

FURTHER WORKS: *Jours de Kabylie* (1954; new ed., 1968); *Les poèmes de Si Mohand*

(1960); *Lettres à ses amis* (1969); *L'anniversaire* (1972)

BIBLIOGRAPHY: Khatibi, A., *Le roman maghrébin* (1968), pp. 49–52; Ortzen, L., *North African Writing* (1970), pp. 3–5, 100–111; Déjeux, J., *Littérature maghrébine de langue française* (1973), pp. 114–42; Déjeux, J., *La littérature algérienne contemporaine* (1975), pp. 62–66

ERIC SELLIN

FERLIN, Nils

Swedish poet, b. 11 Dec. 1898, Karlstad; d. 21 Oct. 1961, Uppsala

F.'s early years were filled with diverse occupations, but centered chiefly around journalism and songwriting. In the 1920s he toured Sweden as an actor, and this experience left clear traces in his poetry. By the 1930s he was living in Stockholm with his mother, whose death in 1936 affected him deeply. For most of the next ten years he led a wandering life in Sweden.

F.'s early poetry largely took the form of popular songs for revues and gramophone recordings, and his ability to deal inventively with strict forms carried over into his first book, *En döddansares visor* (1930; songs of a death-dancer). Generally speaking, the poems in this collection are suffused with a soft melancholy, rather than, as might be expected, showing anger at the hard times. These are in a sense transitional poems; many are ballads very much in the tradition of Gustaf Fröding (1860–1911), but without his bitterness. F.'s poetry is always pervaded by a certain geniality and tolerance of mankind, especially the poor and the suffering.

In *Barfotabarn* (1933; barefoot children) the tone is considerably sharper: there is a satiric bite here not present earlier. There is also further experimentation with form and a new level of abstraction. Here, he also begins to play with larger structures, linking several poems by a word, a character, or an idea. These new techniques were brought to fruition in his third collection, *Goggles* (1938; title in English), in which all his talent seems to come into focus. The tone, so superficially laconic, and the language, so apparently loose, are carefully wed to his always strong sense of rhythm, and the reader/listener is propelled along. F. is one of the most aural of Swedish poets, sitting well in the mainstream of the Swedish troubadour tradition of Lucidor (1638–1674), Carl

Michael Bellman (1740–1795), and Birger Sjöberg (1885–1929).

F.'s fourth collection, *Med många kulörta lyktor* (1944; with many Chinese lanterns), does not reveal any technical advances over his earlier work, although the opening "Monolog i månsken" (monologue by moonlight) is an engaging discourse on the poet's view of the world around him. If there is less intensity in his later poetry, there is a reliability to it that is not to be despised. And, as always, there is the musicality that helped make him the most popular poet of his day.

Throughout F.'s poetry there are several recurring images and themes. From his theater days comes the image of the circus and its clowns. From those restless days, too, come the images of impermanence and transitoriness that course through so many of his poems. From his early interest in theosophy come returning considerations of the divine, although F. had no interest in organized religion. Priests were as vulnerable to attack as politicians. In fact, authority of any kind is lampooned. F. called himself a hobo, and in so doing, clearly aligned himself with others, such as Harry Martinson (q.v.), who championed the underdog.

FURTHER WORKS: *Tio stycken splitter nya visor* (1941); *Kanonfotografen* (1943); *Yrkesvisor* (1944); *Får jag lämna några blommor* (1948); *Kejsarens papegoja* (1951); *Auktion: En lantlig komedi* (1954); *Från mitt ekorrhjul* (1957); *En gammal cylinderhatt* (1962)

BIBLIOGRAPHY: Vowles, R., "N. F.: The Poet as Clown and Scapegoat," *The Norseman*, 12 (1954), 424–29; Gustafson, A., *A History of Swedish Literature* (1961), pp. 480–85

ALAN SWANSON

FERREIRA DE CASTRO, José Maria

See Castro, José Maria Ferreira de

FEUCHTWANGER, Lion

German novelist and dramatist, b. 7 July 1884, Munich; d. 21 Dec. 1958, Los Angeles, Cal., U.S.A.

F. rebelled early against his wealthy and Orthodox Jewish background. He studied philology and literature in Munich and Berlin. A honeymoon trip that lasted for two years ended with an adventurous escape from French North Africa at the outbreak of war in 1914. F. started publishing as early as 1903, but his first serious writing came during World War I, and he achieved international fame in the mid-1920s. Between 1933 and 1940 he lived in exile in Sanary-sur-Mer in France; in 1936–37 he visited the Soviet Union, had a controversial interview with Stalin, and thereafter was often tagged with the communist label. In 1939 and again in 1940 he was interned by the French as an enemy alien. After another harrowing escape he came to the U.S., where, after 1941, he lived in California.

His wartime dramas—such as *Die Perser des Aischylos* (1914; the Persians of Aeschylus), *Friede* (1917; peace)—both adaptations, the second of the play by Aristophanes—and *Die Kriegsgefangenen* (1918; *Prisoners of War*, 1934)—represented an attack on nationalism and war and also addressed the philosophical polarities represented by Nietzsche and Buddha, that is, of activism versus resignation. His drama *Thomas Wendt* (1918–19; Thomas Wendt; later retitled *1918; 1918,* 1934), may have influenced his friend and protégé Bertolt Brecht (q.v.). *Die häßliche Herzogin Margarete Maultasch* (1923; *The Ugly Duchess*, 1928) was his first successful novel, but it was *Jud Süss* (1925; *Power,* 1927) that quickly established him as a writer of international stature. F. had intended the novel (as well as an earlier play by that title) to serve as a further elaboration of the activism-resignation theme, but against the background of mounting anti-Semitism the story of the 18th-c. court Jew was seen in a different light, more specifically as a statement against anti-Semitism.

While F. continued to write plays, his principal contribution lay in the social and political historical novel. His trilogy *Der Wartesaal* (the waiting room)—*Erfolg* (1930; *Success,* 1930); *Die Geschwister Oppenheim* (1933; *The Oppermanns,* 1934), and *Exil* (1939; *Paris Gazette,* 1940)—dealt with different phases of the Nazis' rise to power and their exercise of it. Nazism and various political and economic issues of the 20th c. also form the basis of the Josephus trilogy—*Der jüdische Krieg* (1932; *Josephus,* 1932); *Die Söhne* (1935; *The Jew of Rome,* 1936), and *Der Tag wird kommen* (1945; repub. as *Das gelobte Land,* 1952; *Josephus and the Emperor,* 1942)—the gripping story of the Jewish-Roman historian and perhaps F.'s best work. *Der falsche Nero* (1936; *The Pretender,* 1937) and *Die Brüder Lautensack* (1945; *Double, Double, Toil and Trouble,* 1943), which in historical guise are attacks on the Nazi leadership, are of lesser literary quality.

After 1945 F. delved into the theme of revolution. *Waffen für Amerika* (1946; *Proud Destiny,* 1947) focuses on the efforts of Beaumarchais and Benjamin Franklin to secure weapons for the American revolutionaries; *Goya* (1950; *This Is the Hour,* 1951) follows Goya's career from uninspired court painter to a socially committed artist; and *Narrenweisheit* (1952; *'Tis Folly to Be Wise,* 1952) dealt with the impact of Rousseau's writings on the French revolutionaries. *Spanische Ballade* (1955; *Raquel: The Jewess of Toledo,* 1956) seems a reworking of the Jew Süss novel in a medieval Spanish setting. His final novel, *Jefta und seine Tochter* (1957; *Jephta and His Daughter,* 1957) was set in biblical times.

F. used the historical novel less to vivify the past than to present a contemporary issue in a historical setting, thereby gaining distance and detachment. He experimented little with style, but was a compelling storyteller whose leftist sympathies were barely discernible in his work. F. was immensely skilled in portraying politicians, industrialists, upper-class women, and intellectuals; he was less adept in depicting workers or the common man.

FURTHER WORKS: *Die Einsamen* (1903); *Kleine Dramen* (1905–6); *Der Fetisch* (1907); *Heinrich Heines Fragment "Der Rabbi von Bacharach"* (1907); *Der tönerne Gott* (1910); *Warren Hastings* (1916; reworked in part with Bertolt Brecht and retitled *Kalkutta, 4. Mai,* 1925; *Warren Hastings,* 1928); *Vasantasena* (1916); *Der König und die Tänzerin* (1916–17); *Der Amerikaner; oder, Die entzauberte Stadt* (1921); *Der Frauenverkäufer* (1923); *Der holländische Kaufmann* (1923; *The Dutch Merchant,* 1934); *Leben Eduards II von England* (1924, with Brecht; *Edward II,* 1966); *Drei angelsächsische Stücke* (1927; contains *Die Petroleuminseln* [*The Oil Islands,* 1928]; *Kalkutta, 4. Mai; Wird Hill amnestiert?*); *Pep: J. L. Wetcheeks amerikanisches Liederbuch* (1928; *Pep: J. L. Wetcheek's American Song Book,* 1929); *Marianne in Indien* (n.d.; *Marianne in India,* 1935); *Stücke in Prosa* (1936; *Little Tales,* 1935); *Moskau 1937* (1937; *Moscow 1937,* 1937); *Unholdes Frankreich* (1942; *The Devil in France,* 1941); *Venedig/Texas, und vierzehn andere Erzählungen* (1946); *Wahn; oder, Der Teufel in Boston* (1946; *The Devil in Boston,* 1948); *Centum Opuscula* (1956); *Odysseus und die Schweine* (1960; *Odysseus and the Swine,* 1949); *Stücke in Versen* (1954); *Die Witwe Capet* (1956; *The Widow Capet,* 1956); *Das*

Haus der Desdemona (1961; *The House of Desdemona*, 1963)

BIBLIOGRAPHY: Yuill, W. E., "L. F.," in Natan, A., ed., *German Men of Letters* (1964), Vol. III, pp. 179–206; Spalek, J., ed., *L. F.: The Man, His Ideas, His Work* (1964); Kahn, L., *Insight and Action: The Life and Work of L. F.* (1975); Pischel, J., *L. F.: Versuch über Leben und Werk* (1976); Fischer, L. M., *Vernunft und Fortschritt: Geschichte und Fictionalität im historischen Roman L. F.s* (1979)

LOTHAR KAHN

FEYDEAU, Georges

French dramatist, b. 8 Oct. 1862, Paris; d. 5 June 1921, Paris

The son of Ernest Feydeau (1821–1873), a writer who was best known for realistic fiction, F. began writing monologues and humorous sketches. Until 1886, when his first full-length play was performed, F. was unsure whether to concentrate on writing or acting. The success of *Tailleur pour dames* (perf. 1886, pub. 1888; ladies' tailor), however, determined his vocation. F.'s next few efforts were failures, but the double success in 1892 of *Monsieur chasse* (pub. 1892; the master goes hunting) and *Champignol malgré lui* (pub. 1925; Champignol in spite of himself) established him as the foremost writer of *vaudevilles* in France.

The *vaudeville*, a vastly popular form of theater, combined the rapid movement and minimal psychological development of farce with the elaborate construction of the "well-made play" (a concept of mechanically efficient drama originated by Eugène Scribe, 1791–1861). F. is usually compared to a clockmaker or a mathematician because of the precision with which the elements in his plays fit together and the inevitability of the "equations" that result. Directors have always agreed that it is impossible to cut even a few lines from a play by F. without destroying large sections of the play as a whole. As the critic Francisque Sarcey (1827–1899) once noted, even a minor prop such as a hat placed on a chair will eventually have an importance in the larger scheme of the play. Stage directions are lengthy and elaborate—the famous second act of *La puce à l'oreille* (perf. 1907; pub. 1909; *A Flea in Her Ear*, 1968) begins with three pages of detailed instructions, meticulously explaining such matters as a revolving bed and a reversible costume for an actor who has to play a double role. It is probably physically impossible to stage the act on any set but the one described by F.

F.'s plays begin slowly, partly because so many props have to be planted and so much exposition is necessary, but every play inevitably builds into a crescendo of mistaken identities, rapid entrances at precisely the worst moments, incomprehensible explanations, and hopeless attempts at concealment. The second act of *Occupe-toi d'Amélie* (perf. 1908; pub. 1911; *Keep an Eye on Amélie!*, 1958), for example, begins with two characters in bed together; they never discover how they got there or what (if anything) happened between them the night before. Yet by the time the girl's father, the man's mistress, the girl's lover, a visiting prince, and assorted servants have successively burst into the room, it is as idle to seek a precise explanation as to seek the precise point at which a hurricane begins to spin. Usually when F.'s comedies end, therefore, the characters have hardly had a moment to take a deep breath, much less indulge in sin. Thus, the once notorious "immortality" of F.'s comedies is by current standards mild indeed, a matter of married women out for a fling and cocottes who would not be averse to a wealthy husband.

Attempts have been made recently to discover serious significance in F. His plays certainly show the absurdity of man's condition, and Ionesco (q.v.) has seen a resemblance between the rhythm and structure of his own plays and those of F. Nevertheless, it is primarily as the master creator of mechanisms for producing laughter that F. is noted. In his final plays, one-act comedies that savagely satirize marriage, and in individual scenes such as the wedding in the town hall in *Occupe-toi d'Amélie*, F. shows great zest in mocking the bourgeois institutions of his day. To the contemporary playgoer, however, F. himself seems to be the great bourgeois institution of his day. In 1900 it was said that visitors to Paris had two essential items on their agenda: the International Exposition and *La dame de chez Maxim* (perf. 1899; pub. 1914; *The Lady from Maxim's*, 1971). Today, F.'s great three-act farces seem the incarnation of the spirit of Paris at the turn of the century.

F.'s plays fell into almost total oblivion in the period between the two world wars. A revival began in the 1940s, gaining impetus with a production of *Occupe-toi d'Amélie* by Jean-Louis Barrault in 1948, and the publication of F.'s complete dramatic works (thirty-nine farces have survived) that began the same year. In his preface to that collection, Marcel Achard (1899–1974) called F. "the greatest French comic dramatist after Molière," and although Achard's statement is sweeping, there is no question that F. is now the most frequently performed French comic dramatist after Molière. England and America, as well as France, have seen many productions of F. in recent years.

FURTHER WORKS: *Un fil à la patte* (perf. 1894, pub. 1899; *Not by Bed Alone*, 1970); *L'hôtel du libre échange* (perf. 1894, pub. 1928; *Hotel Paradiso,* 1959); *Le dindon* (perf. 1896, pub. 1949); *Théâtre complet* (9 vols., 1948–56). FURTHER VOLUME IN ENGLISH: *Four Farces by G. F.* (1970)

BIBLIOGRAPHY: Achard, M., "G. F.," in Bentley, E., ed., *Let's Get a Divorce!, and Other Plays* (1958), pp. 350–64; Shapiro, N. R., Introduction to *Four Farces by G. F.* (1970); Lorcey, J., *G. F.* (1972); Shenkan, A., *G. F.* (1972); Pronko, L. C., *G. F.* (1975)

MICHAEL POPKIN

FIEDLER, Leslie A.
American critic, novelist, and short-story writer, b. 8 March 1917, Newark, N.J.

Being Busted (1970), F.'s autobiographical meditation on the unending battle between the forces of societal repression and the individual rebel, suggests something of the spirit that has been at the center of F.'s work as a writer and cultural critic. *Being Busted* begins as an account of F.'s arrest on a marijuana charge and ends as a Kafkaesque allegory about the rights of an individual versus the bureaucratic state. It is a saga that begins with his adolescence in Newark—where he was almost arrested for participating in a political rally—and continues through his conventional education at the University of Wisconsin and New York University. With a Ph.D. in hand F. moved west, to a teaching post at the University of Montana, in 1940. In 1963 he joined the faculty of the English Department at the State University of New York at Buffalo, where he now teaches.

In *An End to Innocence* (1955) F. introduced the hard-hitting prose and wide-ranging concerns that were to become his trademarks. The collection is subtitled *Essays on Culture and Politics*. Topics ranged from the cold war and the Rosenberg trial to a discussion of Mark Twain's classic, *Huckleberry Finn*, the well-known "Come Back to the Raft Ag'in, Huck Honey!"

For F., the mythic patterns found in literature can tell us much about the culture that produced the literature. Although his method is psychologically oriented—drawing on the work of Freud and Jung (qq.v.)—the result has been a vision uniquely his own. F.'s major works, *Love and Death in the American Novel* (1960) and *No! In Thunder: Essays on Myth and Literature* (1960), portray the American psyche as a continuing fantasy of boyhood innocence, blissful immaturity, and self-styled rebellion. According to F., "the mythic America is boyhood" and the quintessential American hero is the adolescent male in desperate flight from the threats of marriage, domesticity, and eventual fatherhood.

F.'s critical technique is to weave the scattered threads of separate literary works into a tapestry of meaning. In such representative figures as Washington Irving's Rip Van Winkle, James Fenimore Cooper's Natty Bumppo, and Huck Finn, F. sees ingrained fears about heterosexual love and a yearning for less threatening, homoerotic relationships. Thus, the true love of Natty Bumppo is directed toward the Indian Chingachgook; that of Ishmael, in Melville's *Moby Dick*, for a savage Queequeg; that of Huck Finn for Nigger Jim. F. sees this recurring pattern as distinctly American: "The quest which has distinguished our fiction from Brockden Brown and Cooper, through Poe and Melville and Twain, to Faulkner and Hemingway is the search for an innocent substitute for adulterous passion and marriage alike."

For F., it is but a short step from American literature to American life. He moves easily—too easily, his detractors say—from observations on literature to conclusions about American culture. He has been the tireless champion of the youth culture and the editor of an anthology of science fiction entitled *In Dreams Awake* (1976), the defender of the comic book and the soap opera, as well as the author of *Freaks: Myths & Images of the Secret Self* (1978). In this unusual book F. wears a variety of hats—cultural historian, literary critic, psychoanalyst, guru—to investigate our secret-sharing with those who expand, and thereby define, the human possibility: "The true Freak stirs both supernatural terror and natural sympathy [and] . . . challenges the conventional boundaries between male and female, sexed and sexless, animal and human, large and small, self and other, and consequently, between reality and illusion, experience and fantasy, fact and myth."

F.'s fiction has always seemed an extension of his critical vision. In novels such as *The Second Stone* (1963) and *The Last Jew in America* (1966), F.'s cherished theories intrude upon the fictional fabric. When the mode is comic (as it is in *The Last Jew in America*), the result is wryly amusing, if something less than profound. His collection of short stories, *Pull Down Vanity* (1962), contains, however, some finely wrought satirical, roman-à-clef portrayals of the world of academe.

Collected Essays (1971) established F.'s stature as a major critic. These essays range over wide horizons, both literary and cultural. *A F. Reader* (1977) made F.'s work available in an attractively packaged one-volume sampler. It was a sure-fire indicator that the name alone could attract readers.

It is likely that F.'s work will survive the controversy his ideas have generated. His method of applying literary motifs to cultural phenomena looks deceptively easy, and many an imitator has tried to adopt it. F., the unrepentant "bad boy" of American letters, is, however, always his own man, always lighting out for new territories when the threat of civilization seems too near. His energetic prose style and incisive vision have made a distinctive mark on the way we think about American culture.

FURTHER WORKS: *The Art of the Essay* (1958); *Back to China* (1965); *The Return of the Vanishing American* (1968); *Nude Croquet* (1969); *The Stranger in Shakespeare* (1972); *The Messenger Will Come No More* (1974); *The Inadvertent Epic* (1980)

BIBLIOGRAPHY: Chase, R., "L. F. and American Culture," *ChiR*, 14 (1960), 8–18; Bellman, S., "The Frontiers of L. F.," *SWR*, 48 (1963), 86–89; Davis, R., "L. F.'s Fictions," *Commentary*, Jan. 1967, 73–77; Alter, R., "Jewish Dreams and Nightmares," *Commentary*, Jan. 1968, 48–54; Bluefarb, S., "Pictures of the Anti-Stereotype: L. F.'s Triptych, *The Last Jew in America*," *CLAJ*, 18 (1975), 412–21; Walden, D., "L. F.," *JPC*, 12 (1978), 208–9; Masilamoni, E. H. L., "Fiction of Jewish Americans: An Interview with L. F.," *SWR*, 64 (1979), 44–59

SANFORD PINSKER

FIJI LITERATURE
See Pacific Islands Literature

FILM AND LITERATURE

"I'm sure there's a sort of talking-film cinema in our heads," says the Greek peasant Zorba in Nikos Kazantzakis's (q.v.) novel *Zorba the Greek* (1946). In his simple way, Zorba expresses the truth that film is the medium most like the human imagination: the flow of photographically captured images mechanically reproduced can blend dream and reality much as the human mind can. Furthermore Zorba's remark suggests the degree to which cinema has become a part of individual and international social consciousness in the 20th c. The relationship between film and literature is thus one of cross influences in technique and content based on an ever-increasing awareness of the distinct capabilities and limitations of each medium.

In the beginning was the human perception of images. This consciousness found artistic visual expression in work such as the cave paintings of animals "in motion." Language and thus literature evolved as a symbolic and metaphorical representation of images and emotions. The growth of film, which began with the silent flow of images, has seen the incorporation and juxtaposition of the spoken word with the visual image. It is possible to consider film as a further development of a visual and literary process that stretches back to prehistoric times.

Film is a hybrid art form that has borrowed freely and adapted from literature for its effects and subjects. Like poetry it is able to juxtapose and join images to create moods and illustrate ideas; like drama, film employs actors, dialogue, lighting, *mise-en-scène* in general; and as in prose fiction, film is effective as a narrative art that may manipulate time and space at will.

But for all of these similarities, film differs distinctly from literature. The French critic André Bazin (1918–1958) once stated that "cinema has not yet been invented." He was alluding to the ability of film because of its photographic base to mechanically reproduce reality. As the technology of cinema improves, so does film more closely re-create the world "in its own image, an image unburdened by the freedom of interpretation of the artist or the irreversibility of time." Film is thus a reproduction of reality *in time*, a fact that differentiates it from pure photography. Literature, on the other hand, is language-based and is a symbolic representation of reality. Thus, the means of perceiving literature and film are opposites. Whereas a reader must transform language into an internal visualization of a character, scene, or emotion, the film viewer must internalize the cinematic images to "read" their meaning.

The acceptance of film as an art form was slow in coming. Thomas Edison, for instance, considered his early experiments with film as a kind of toy until he understood the commercial possibilities of film as a form of mass entertainment. From the first films in the 1890s of Louis Lumière (1864–1948) and Georges Méliès (1861–1938) in France, R. W. Paul (1869–1943) in England, and Edison, the technology and popularity of film rapidly developed. In the U.S. film became cheap entertainment for the millions of immigrant workers with a poor command of English, who could not afford or understand books, poetry, or drama. Until the end of World War II film could claim to have been the major form of popular entertainment in America in the 20th c.

But while film was accepted by the masses, it was often rejected or ignored by those in the literary world. Particularly in America, the gap between the development of art and literature on the one hand and film on the other was great. Hollywood, which was for the most part founded by immigrants such as Adolph Zukor, William Fox, and Marcus Loew, began and has largely remained dedicated to 19th-c. approaches to plot and character development. Literature, in contrast, experimented with style and content in the "modernist" phase and with social commitment during the 1930s. While Ernest Hemingway (q.v.) was publishing *The Sun Also Rises* in 1926, William S. Hart was still a major box-office star with his simple Western tales about good and evil on the range.

Others were quick to grasp the potential of film. Vachel Lindsay (q.v.) wrote in *The Art of the Moving Picture* (1922) before the advent of sound that the invention of film was as great a step "as was the beginning of picture writing in the stone age." His judgment was based in large part on the works of D. W. Griffith (1874–1948), that pioneer who not only developed (but did not invent) the basic language of film but who also helped to make film "respectable" with the quality and scale of *The Birth of a Nation* (1915), itself an adaptation of Thomas Dixon's (1864–1946) novel *The Clansman* (1905). Griffith, an indifferent playwright and actor, used poetry, fiction, and drama as source material for his films, adapting works of such diverse writers as Robert Browning (*Pippa Passes*, 1909), Alfred Lord Tennyson (*Enoch Arden*, 1911), Edgar Allan Poe,

George Eliot, Frank Norris (*A Corner in Wheat,* 1909), Jack London, Shakespeare, Dickens, Mark Twain, Montaigne, Victor Hugo, Guy de Maupassant, and Tolstoy (*Resurrection,* 1909).

In Russia, Lenin seized on film as the official art form for the revolution and the Russian masses. Sergey Eisenstein (1898–1948) emerged not only as one of the Soviet Union's first important filmmakers, but also as one of the significant film theoreticians yet to appear. Eisenstein was concerned with film as a "language" and with montage (editing) as the most effective tool of cinematic language. But he was perceptive enough to understand that the basis of film language developed by Griffith may actually be found in literature and, more specifically, in the works of Charles Dickens. Crosscutting between scenes and story lines, the characterization of protagonists with objects and animals (kittens with young women, bulldogs with strong men, for instance), close-ups, dissolves, and double-exposure effects are all prefigured in Dickens's fiction. Since Dickens was Griffith's favorite author, the influence of literature on the structure and style of film is plain to see.

Eisenstein also noted the similarity between poetry and film. In its most basic form, montage is the combination of two different images or shots to create an "explosion" or third image in one's mind. The Japanese haiku, he points out in *Film Form* (1949), is constructed the same way for the same effect. Eisenstein, who began his career in theater, discussed such examples as a means to point out the *plastic* ability of film in the hands of the filmmaker to create a poetic quality to his art. And in fact, early critics felt that the silent film was the highest development of film art, which was ruined by the coming of the talkies in the late 1920s. Films such as F. W. Murnau's (1889–1931) *Sunrise* (1927), Carl Dreyer's (1889–1968) *La passion de Jeanne d'Arc* (1928; the passion of Joan of Arc), and the comic surrealism of Charles Chaplin's (1889–1977) *The Gold Rush* (1925) achieved what Susan Sontag (q.v.) has called " . . . a new language, a way of talking about emotion through the direct experience of the language of faces and gestures." The absence of sound, and the use of black and white, both of which run counter to everyday reality, helped to free early cinema from a literal representation of reality, as the critic Rudolf Arnheim (b. 1904), in *Film as Art* (1957) has made clear. Filmmakers were thus able to make films in the tradition of Méliès and of Luis Buñuel's (b. 1900) *Un chien andalou* (1928; an Andalusian dog) that suggested dreams and fantasy, or more poetically realistic films such as Dziga Vertov's (1896–1954) *Chelovek s kinoapparatom* (1928; the man with a movie camera).

The similarity and closeness of poetry and cinema is best represented in film by the avant-garde movement. Because of the much greater expenses involved, the division between commercial and "experimental" film is much more strictly drawn in film than in literature. "Avant-garde" is a loose term that has come to be applied to noncommercial filmmakers who work on their own or in small groups on limited budgets to pursue personal interests in producing "new" approaches to film. Growing out of the convergence of literary, art, and film interests in European movements such as Dadaism, expressionism, surrealism, and cubism (qq.v.) in the 1920s that resulted in films by such filmmakers as Buñuel, Man Ray (1890–1976), Marcel Duchamp (1887–1968), Fernand Léger (1881–1955), and Jean Epstein (1897–1953), the avant-garde has most recently come to mean the wide variety of experimental filmmaking primarily in the U.S. Maya Deren (1908–1961), for instance, was one of the first American filmmakers to explore the poetic combination of images to create a form of surrealistic dream in *Meshes of the Afternoon* (1943). In the 1950s and 1960s the avant-garde film came also to be known as the "underground" film. Gregory Markopoulos (b. 1928) with *Psyche* (1948), Kenneth Anger (b. 1932) with *Scorpio Rising* (1962–64), and Jonas Mekas (b. 1922) with his impressionistic "diary" films represent filmmakers who create on film worlds as personal and as intense as those in poetry. Even Andy Warhol (b. 1926), with his extreme documentary approach in a film such as *Sleep* (1963), could be argued to have created a "poetry of the commonplace" by freeing the viewer from all expectation of plot, character, and action and thus involving the viewer in his own fantasies, memories, and images.

If there was a clear split between those in the forefront of film and literature in the U.S., the opposite has quite often been true in Europe. From the beginning of cinema, many European filmmakers were also writers, artists, or intellectuals in touch with the trends and movements in the literature, art, and ideas of their time. The result has been that the cross-influences

and parallel development of film, literature, and the arts in Europe have tended to be much closer than in the U.S. Jean Renoir (1894–1979) was certainly influenced by his father's paintings in the composition of his films and in his general vision of humanity as expressed through his acting, writing, directing, and producing of his films. Jean Cocteau (q.v.) moved easily between poetry, drama, fiction, and film, drawing from all of them as well as from the music and art of the times to produce such poetic myths as *Le sang d'un poète* (1930; script pub. 1948; *The Blood of a Poet*, 1949), *La Belle et la Bête* (1946; script pub. in Eng. as *Beauty and the Beast: Diary of a Film*, 1950), and *Orphée* (1950; screenplay pub. 1951; *Orphée*, 1972).

European filmmakers have learned from their literary traditions to think of themselves as "auteurs" who often work from original filmscripts to write (*écriture*, as Roland Barthes [q.v.] would call it) their own films in their own style. Although film is a cooperative venture, Europeans have stressed the desirability of the director's being the guiding force in creating and controlling a film. Hollywood, with its emphasis on the studio production line during the 1930s through the 1950s, would seem to be in direct contrast. Yet the New Wave French critics and filmmakers of the late 1950s helped us to see that the security of the studio allowed American directors such as John Ford (1895–1973), Howard Hawks (1896–1977), and Alfred Hitchcock (1899–1980) to develop as *auteurs*, making films that reflect their personal style and vision as clearly as any work of literature expresses its author.

The relationship between film and literature has depended in part on technology. Once sound was introduced there was a mad rush by Hollywood for Broadway. Plays and playwrights were shipped west, but in those early days of sound, seldom were there results that amounted to more than filmed drama captured with a static camera. The development of lightweight "silent" cameras, of new lenses, of color and faster-stock film, of improved sound quality, and of more sophisticated editing techniques has meant that the plasticity of film has increased. Whereas in the early 1930s film was often no more than a cinematic version of a stage production with the "fourth wall" removed, movies now may be as free-wheeling in form and content as experimental prose.

Although film makes use of many forms of literature, it is prose fiction that it has come most closely to resemble. The commercial feature film represents a narrative art form, as does fiction, and both may manipulate time and space at will to present characters in a narration. For this reason popular novels have always been a fertile source for popular films. *Gone with the Wind* (1939) is a prime example of the Hollywood formula: films that Pauline Kael (b. 1919) says are made up of " . . . love and rape and incest and childbirth and storms at sea and battles and fires and epidemics." Such adaptations occasionally improve upon the original, as in the case of Francis Ford Coppola's (b. 1939) *The Godfather,* Parts I and II (1971, 1974) from Mario Puzo's (b. 1920) 1970 novel and George Roy Hill's (b. 1922) *Slaughterhouse Five* (1973) from the novel by Kurt Vonnegut (q.v.). In general, however, Hollywood productions tend to make unimaginative use of the film medium to bring popular fiction to the screen, as if films were no more than lifelike picture books. The commercialization of film and literature has more recently been carried to another extreme with the phenomenon of novelizations. This type of book is contracted to an author to be written based on the screenplay (*Saturday Night Fever* [1977], for instance) *before* the film is made, and it is published simultaneously with the release of the film.

But the differences between film and the novel are also significant. Above all else, film is an *immediate* experience: photography directly reproduces images of people and objects as we know them. Literature is language-bound, however, and is limited to expressing only what can be represented in words. This distinction has further implications: while a writer or artist may impose his control and vision over every aspect of his art, the filmmaker, no matter how carefully he controls the *mise-en-scène*, editing, and camera work, can never control every element within the movie frame. Because cinema is based on photography, the filmmaker shares his creation with the reality of the objects that appear *immediately* and *all at once* as soon as the camera lens opens upon them.

More critical attention has been given recently to the creative possibilities of adaptation from literature to film. In the Hollywood tradition, a film such as John Ford's *The Grapes of Wrath* (1939) with a screenplay by Nunnally Johnson (1897–1977) and cinematography by Gregg Toland (1904–1948)—who also shot *Citizen Kane*—was so effective in transferring the novel to the screen that the author, John Steinbeck (q.v.), claimed the film was more powerful than his book. Not all of the novel

could be represented on the screen, however. Steinbeck's juxtaposition of prose *styles* ranging from the omniscient-epic to an impressionistic flow of first-person speeches is lost (although Steinbeck's style could have been approximated on the screen had the producer, Darryl F. Zanuck, chosen to). Furthermore, because a film is commercially limited to a time span of a few hours, adaptation is by necessity an exercise in condensation. But what Ford's film does well is to capture the documentary directness of the migrant workers' experiences combined with an almost expressionistic use of light and shadow to suggest the conflicts and themes of the drama. Critics often point out that we cannot necessarily speak of the film as "better" or "worse" than the novel: they are two different experiences presented by two different media.

Many European directors have tended to adapt lesser-known literary works so that they may feel freer to transform the original material for their own purposes. Directors such as François Truffaut (b. 1932), Jean-Luc Godard (b. 1930), Claude Chabrol (b. 1930), Wim Wenders (b. 1943), and others have, for instance, used American detective fiction as a basis for films set in their own countries reflecting their own times and concerns. Less literal adaptations may take a variety of forms. A filmmaker may simply alter one significant detail: Thomas Mann's (q.v.) *Death in Venice* (1911) is written as the internal monologue of a famous writer, but because it is difficult to suggest internal states of being on film, Luchino Visconti (1906–1978) transformed the central protagonist into a famous composer so that we can hear his music represent the emotions he experiences in the 1971 film. Similarly, time and place may be switched: Michelangelo Antonioni's (b. 1912) *Blow-Up* (1967) is set in trendy London during the 1960s, although it is based on a short story by Julio Cortázar (q.v.) set in Paris at an undesignated time. And finally, the literary text may be used in such a freewheeling manner that only marginal resemblances remain between the film and the source. Godard's *Masculin-féminin* (1966; masculine-feminine), is "suggested" by two Guy de Maupassant short stories, yet the similarities are more thematic than dramatic and literal.

Since World War II in many countries and since the 1960s with the "new American cinema" in the U.S., the direction and concern of those in the forefront of literature and film have become remarkably similar. Like much of experimental fiction, film has come to reflect ever more complex and challenging states of consciousness. Early examples of such "modern" films would include Orson Welles's (b. 1915) masterpiece *Citizen Kane* (1941) and Akira Kurosawa's (b. 1910) *Rashomon* (1950), both of which experiment with multiple points of view and multiple story lines to suggest the relativity of truth and reality.

Modernist literature and film often suggest a fusion of style and content. There are works such as those mentioned above that employ the fragmentation of narrative to destroy the psychological neatness of Aristotelian character and plot. Godard, influenced by Bertolt Brecht (q.v.) and his concept of the "alienation effect," has said that he believes in a story having a beginning, a middle, and an end, but not necessarily in that order. Such destruction of traditional modes of style and narration means that there is a much greater level of self-consciousness about writing and filmmaking. The manipulation of language-as-language and convention-as-convention in fiction (as in the fiction of Jorge Luis Borges [q.v.], for instance), has its correspondence in the contemporary filmmakers' manipulation, often in a playful spirit, of film-as-film. Ingmar Bergman (b. 1918) "frames" *Persona* (1966) with shots of a movie projector and film running through it, while François Truffaut in *La nuit américaine* (1973; script pub. in Eng. as *Day for Night*, 1975) devotes the entire film to an inside story of filming a film.

Contemporary film, like contemporary literature, has simultaneously become more subjective as it enters the private world of "self" and more socially conscious and *engagé* as it relates that subjectivity to a social realm. South American fiction and film is a prime example. The "magic realism" (q.v.) of a novel such as Gabriel García Márquez's (q.v.) *One Hundred Years of Solitude* (1967) consists of the blending of a fertile imagination and fantasy with a strong sense of the social injustice. Similarly, the Brazilian Bruno Barreto's (b. 1946) film *Dona Flor e seus dois maridos* (1976; Dona Flor and her two husbands), based on the novel by Jorge Amado (q.v.), seamlessly fuses dream and reality, fantasy and fact in one work that both delineates the limitations of reality and celebrates the triumphant power of the imagination.

It is much easier to document the influence of literature on film than vice versa. Yet clearly, film has had a pervasive influence on literature and the other arts. In drama, for instance, Brecht acknowledged the influence of silent film, and in particular the comic genius of Chaplin, on his development of "epic theater."

Even the breaking up of the silent films with title cards became a technique adopted by Brecht to help distance the audience from events on the stage. Critics have pointed to the similarity between poetry and montage and especially to poets such as Walt Whitman, whose flow of disparate images of the American scene suggests a film montage. While Whitman wrote before the development of film, other poets around the world have used film for subject matter (Hart Crane's [q.v.] "Chaplinesque"), and technique, consciously attempting to catch in language a *sense* of montage, even though such imitation is always only an approximation.

In a general sense, the influence of film on literature is simply the influence of a lifetime of moviegoing that each writer has experienced. Such an influence is, as critics such as Stanley Cavell (b. 1926) in *The World Viewed* (1971) suggest, tied to our deepest childhood memories and fantasies. But there are specific influences that have been felt in literature, most clearly in fiction. The French novelist, screenwriter, and director Alain Robbe-Grillet (q.v.) reflects this influence when he speaks of the New Novel (q.v.) as depending on the recording of what is visible rather than the creation of internal projections: "the sense of sight remains, in spite of everything, our best weapon, especially if it keeps exclusively to outlines" (*Pour un nouveau roman,* 1963; *For a New Novel,* 1965). Film has, therefore, helped novelists sharpen their ability to capture the visual aspect of their narratives as well as to convey much of their story through dialogue rather than through the lengthy descriptive passages typical of 18th and 19th c. novels. The lean story line and crisp dialogue of Hemingway's work would be an example of fiction that developed at a time, the 1930s, when story and dialogue were at their best in Hollywood.

As has been suggested, film and prose fiction are different media that can never merge totally. But on numerous occasions the two forms have come as close as they can with interesting results. Partially this is so because writers may write with the screen in mind. Arthur Miller (q.v.) transformed his short story "The Misfits" into what he named a "cine-novel" and then wrote the screenplay for John Huston's (b. 1906) film based on that story. At other times, film technique approximated in prose is an effort to speed up the action while drawing upon the reader's ability to visualize events. Alexandr Solzhenitsyn (q.v.) wrote the battle scenes in his documentary novel *August 1914* (1971) in screenplay format, complete with camera directions, while John Dos Passos (q.v.) interspersed "camera-eye" montages throughout his trilogy *U.S.A.* (1937–38) to add a sense both of documentary and of a larger objective reality to the personal stories related in between. More recently, the Austrian novelist Peter Handke (q.v.) lived with film-maker Wim Wenders while writing his novel *The Goalie's Anxiety at the Penalty Kick* (1970), knowing that it would be made into a film by Wenders. Finally, James Joyce (q.v.), who once ran one of the first movie theaters in Dublin for a few years, was strongly influenced by what he termed the "sixty-miles-an-hour pathos of cinematographs" in the writing of *Ulysses* (1922), especially in the surrealistic scenes in the Nighttown sequence, and of *Finnegans Wake* (1939), which becomes a nightmare of images and language as experimental as any avant-garde film.

In less than a century, film has appeared, caught on, and begun to come of age. The sophistication of many contemporary feature films by directors around the world, of experimental avant-garde cinema, and even of the documentary tradition of film is equal to that of literature. Especially since the eclipse of film as the mass-entertainment form by television, such a development of sophistication has meant that much of film has become an elite art form like experimental literature, reaching a relatively small audience. But popular film, like popular literature, remains a medium for expressing the joys and sorrows of the human condition in human terms. The future for both literature and film is uncertain. In many countries the general level of literacy has declined, and the beginning of the video revolution has meant that movies are now on tape and that therefore the living room is fast replacing the cinema. Yet no matter how much television and video have cornered the image market, there seems to be a social and psychological need to share the experience of the large screen in a dark room with other people. Pauline Kael addresses this point when she notes that ". . . unlike books, but like rock music, movies could be experienced tribally, yet they also provide aesthetic experiences of a sensual complexity that it's merely priggish to deny" (*Reeling*, 1976).

The relationship between film and literature is also seen in criticism and theory. In many ways, a film can be discussed and analyzed like a poem, play, novel. Yet film criticism and theory requires in addition an understanding of the technical aspects of cinema as they apply to the aesthetic experiences they create. Because of the complexity of the film medium and because of its relative youth as an art form, film theory and criticism are still very much in their adolescent period. To date there is no consistent and complete theory of film.

Eisenstein represents the single most important attempt to establish a systematic understanding of film aesthetics to date. His concern with montage led him to discuss the "language" of film, often citing examples from literature. The writings of André Bazin and Siegfried Kracauer (1889–1966) opposed Eisenstein's emphasis on editing as a form of manipulating reality. Both critics championed films that were in their view closer to a sense of uninterrupted "reality" as we know it, represented through *mise-en-scène*. The French New Wave critic-filmmakers, along with Andrew Sarris (b. 1928) in the U.S., have put forth the *auteur* theory mentioned earlier, a theory that at its best helps us focus on the organic development of a director's style and themes. By extension, the study of the entire oeuvre of an actor, cinematographer, screenwriter, or even editor can help us better understand his or her individual contributions and the nature of film.

More recently, film criticism has been influenced by anthropological and literary interest in structuralism (q.v.) and semiology. The French critic Christian Metz (b. 1931) in *Essais sur la signification au cinéma* (2 vols., 1971–72; *Film Language: A Semiotics of the Cinema,* 1974) and *Langage et cinéma* (1971; *Language and Cinema,* 1974), and the Italian critic Emilio Garroni (b. 1925) in *Semiotica ed estetica* (1968; semiotics and aesthetics) go further than Eisenstein in analyzing film and its relationship to language. Pointing out that film duplicates reality while language transforms it into symbol, they suggest that the difficulty in analyzing the "codes" of film is that it is often impossible to distinguish between the "signified" and the "signifier." Metz in particular thus argues against the possibility of speaking of film as a "language" with a grammar similar to written language. Metz's own analysis of films becomes so detailed about a few codes in a film that his approach offers no clear means of grasping the significance and structure of the whole work. A more fruitful approach has been the influence of Roland Barthes's (q.v.) pluralistic vision of literature expressed in *S/Z* (1970; *S/Z*, 1974) and later writings. His feeling that "to interpret a text is not to give it a . . . meaning, but on the contrary to appreciate what *plural* constitutes it," can easily be applied to film as well as literature and the other arts. While much remains to be done in the history and theory of film, it seems certain that such a broad pluralistic approach will be of use in seeing films as individual "texts" and as parts of a medium used around the world.

BIBLIOGRAPHY: Eisenstein, S., *The Film Sense* (1947); Eisenstein, S., *Film Form* (1949); Arnheim, R., *Film as Art* (1957); Bluestone, G., *Novels into Film*, rev. ed. (1966); Bazin, A., *What Is Cinema?* (2 vols., 1967, 1971); Richardson, R., *Literature and Film* (1969); Kawin, B., *Telling It Again and Again: Repetition in Literature and Film* (1972); Maddux, R., et al., *Fiction into Film* (1972); Magny, C.-E., *The Age of the American Novel: The Film Aesthetic of Fiction between the Two Wars* (1972); Murray, E., *The Cinematic Imagination* (1972); Barthes, R., *S/Z* (1974); Fell, J., *Film and the Narrative Tradition* (1974); Metz, C., *Film Language: A Semiotics of the Cinema* (1974); Enser, A. G. S., *Filmed Books and Plays 1928–74*, rev. ed. (1975); Wagner, G., *The Novel and the Cinema* (1975); Armes, R., *The Ambiguous Image* (1976); Spiegel, A., *Fiction and the Camera Eye: Visual Consciousness in Film and the Modern Novel* (1976); Peary, G., and Shatzkin, R., eds., *The Classic American Novel and the Movies* (1977); Kawin, B., *Mindscreen: Bergman, Godard, and First-Person Film* (1978); Peary, G., and Shatzkin, R., eds., *The Modern American Novel and the Movies* (1978); Beja, M., *Film and Literature* (1979); Goodwin, J., "Literature and Film: A Review of Criticism," *QRFS*, 4 (1979), 227–46; Kittredge, W., and Krauzer, S. M., *Stories into Film* (1979); McConnell, F., *Storytelling and Mythmaking: Images from Film and Literature* (1979); Berger, J., *About Looking* (1980); Henderson, B., *A Critique of Film Theory* (1980); Horton, A. S., and Margretta, J., eds., *Modern European Filmmakers and the Art of Adaptation* (1981)

ANDREW HORTON

FINNISH LITERATURE

Several external factors helped to shape the development of Finland's literature as the 20th c. began. The country's Swedish-speaking minority, which then stood at about fourteen percent, had realized that its days of cultural hegemony were numbered, while the Finnish majority felt that it had come into its own at last. However, its triumphant sense of youth and of mission was accompanied by an awareness of the brevity and paucity of a genuinely Finnish tradition; after all, modern Finnish-language literature had begun with the dramas (from the 1860s) and the great novel *Seitsemän veljestä* (1870; *Seven Brothers*, 1923) of Aleksis Kivi (1834–1872). At the same time, both Finland-Swedes and Finns had to confront the sharp Slavophile swerve of tsarist policy; what had generally been a benevolent rule, ever since the country had passed from Swedish to Russian hands in the War of 1808–9, had suddenly turned oppressive. Finland-Swedish authors began to regard themselves, somewhat melodramatically, as doubly lonely sentinels of the West, threatened both by Finnicization and Russification. The Swedish-language lyric of that time is full of symbols of isolation and exhaustion; the tired trees of Mikael Lybeck (1864–1925), the bleak skerries of Arvid Mörne (1876–1946), the "last Germanics" of Bertel Gripenberg (1878–1947), dying at their posts; Richard Malmberg (1877–1944), calling himself "Gustav Alm," talked about dark autumn days and Finnish aggressiveness, and Ture Janson (1886–1954) used the term "the lonely Swedes" as a title, while Runar Schildt (1888–1925), in novellas that have become classics, looked with sad eyes at Finland-Swedish enervation and self-protective arrogance. (Another writer of the period met the predicted onslaught of barbarism in quite a different way, with exceptional wit: Guss Mattsson [1873–1914], the virtuoso of the *causerie*.)

Some Finnish-language authors, anxious to demonstrate that their own literature was capable of taking a part in the European concert, used similar themes of overripeness and decay; nonetheless, such elegant academic poets as Otto Manninen (1872–1950) and V. A. Koskenniemi (1885–1962) were a great deal more positive toward life than were their Finland-Swedish contemporaries. The often cynical eroticism of Maria Jotuni (1880–1943), in her novellas and plays, resembles that of Schildt; L. Onerva (Hilja Onerva Lehtinen-Madetoja, 1882–1972), in her rather bookish affection for the bizarre and the perverse, drew on the same Continental sources as Gripenberg. The greatest lyricist of the time, Eino Leino (q.v.), could not resist the temptation to weave some motifs of European decadence (the *femme fatale*, the cursed knight, the superman) into the first part of his masterpiece, *Helkavirsiä* (1903; *Whitsongs*, 1978), while in the second part (1916), he wrote about an end of the world. Yet Leino's poem was born, in fact, out of the Finnish national epic, the *Kalevala* (1849), reconstructed by Elias Lönnrot (1802–1884). Yearning for Europe, Finnish literature still wanted to pay homage to the pristine Finnish landscape, the honest Finnish rustic (often seen as a more or less noble savage), the distinctive Finnish past. The national romanticism that informed Sibelius's tone poems on *Kalevala* themes also captured literary men: Leino himself, the poet and dramatist J. H. Erkko (1849–1906) in his *Kalevala* plays, and the lyric poet Larin-Kyösti (pseud. of Karl Gustaf Larson, 1873–1948), who repeatedly used the folklore and landscape of the semi-exotic eastern province of Karelia (traditionally regarded as the *Kalevala*'s place of origin) and of his native Häme. Even such a proponent of realism and clarity as Juhani Aho (1861–1921) was caught up in this ethnocentric patriotism, writing his later novels about Finnish heathendom —*Panu* (1897; Panu); about the zealous efforts of Lönnrot and others to conjure up medieval Finland—*Kevät ja takatalvi* (1906; spring and late winter); about a backwoods erotic triangle—*Juha* (1911; Juha). The novelists and playwrights Teuvo Pakkala (1862–1925) and Johannes Linnankoski (pseud. of Juho Vihtori Peltonen, 1869–1913) celebrated a folk hero and free spirit, the Finnish lumberjack, even as Santeri Alkio (1862–1930) and Artturi Järviluoma (1879–1942) gave a literary gloss to the so-called "knife fighters" of their home region of Ostrobothnia. These stalwarts were turned by Järviluoma, in his play-with-music, *Pohjalaisia* (1914; Ostrobothnians), into freedom fighters against the Russians.

It is quite possible to detect a split in Finnish attitudes of the early 20th c., a split already evident in Lönnrot's *Kalevala* and Kivi's *Seitsemän veljestä*. The literature loves the freedom of the wilderness but feels impelled to teach moral and behavioral standards; indeed, two novelists taken very seriously in their time are not readily swallowed today, because of their urge to edification—the Tolstoyan Arvid Järnefelt (1861–1932) and the schematist of georgic purity and urban rottenness, Maila Talvio (1871–1951). Probably, the rise during the 1960s and 1970s of the critical fortunes of "Maiju Lassila" (the best-known of the several pseudonyms of Algoth Untola, 1868–1918) resulted not only from his having been the leading leftist polemicist in Finland's civil war, but from the zany and quite unedifying humor of some of his novels, particularly *Tulitikkuja lainaamassa* (1910; the match-borrowing expedition), which builds upon still another strain in Kivi, the love for amusing confabulation.

Finland's sudden independence from Russia (December 1917), the White victory over the Reds in a brief but bloody civil war (January–May 1918), and the establishment of the Republic of Finland in 1919 brought about an optimistic (but not unreflective) atmosphere. Shedding much of its negativism, Finland-Swedish literature entered a period of unexpected brilliance; the modernist (q.v.) poets —Edith Södergran, Gunnar Björling, Elmer Diktonius, and Rabbe Enckell (qq.v.)—supported and supplemented by the critic, novelist, and playwright Hagar Olsson (1893–1978), created a body of lyrics quite unlike anything the North had seen before; closely attentive to developments from abroad, hoping to reach an international public, Finland-Swedish modernism succeeded at least in changing the character of poetry in the rest of Scandinavia. The linguistic minority, which had played a leading role in the formation of the new country, subsequently met renewed hostility from certain Finnish quarters; but its literature acquired a reputation outside Finland that it had never had before, and not only because of the modernists: the lushly romantic verse of Jarl Hemmer (1893–1944), and Runar Schildt's play *Den stora rollen* (1923; the great role), a Finland-Swedish counterpart to O'Casey's (q.v.) *Juno and the Paycock*, set in Helsinki during the civil war, also got extensive attention in Sweden and elsewhere.

It has often been argued, incorrectly, that the civil war remained a taboo subject until the middle of the century, or that its portrayal in literature consisted mostly of propaganda for the winning side; yet, just as Finland's government, after initial excesses, adopted an intelligent policy of reconciliation toward the vanquished, in literature there was a repeated effort to get at the causes for the conflict. Both Schildt and Hemmer, although members of the Finland-Swedish patrician class, dealt with the matter frankly, as in Hemmer's novel, *En man och hans samvete* (1931; *A Fool of Faith*, 1935), where he makes no bones about the brutality of the White prison camps. And still another Finland-Swedish novelist, Sigrid Backman (1886–1938), to be sure, from less privileged circumstances, was not afraid to discuss the war from the standpoint of common humanity. Artistically, however, their investigations stand far below the works of three major Finnish-language novelists. Frans Eemil Sillanpää, Joel Lehtonen (qq.v.), and Ilmari Kianto (1874–1970)—the last-named with his novel about Finnish backwoods poverty, *Ryysyrannan Jooseppi* (1924; Joseph of Ryysyranta)—looked either at the conflict or its immediate antecedents, giving their attention in particular to the landless countrymen from whom the Reds had recruited many of their followers.

(That the trio was indifferent to the lot of the industrial worker is significant; the literature's tradition, as it had developed out of Kivi, found the "child of nature," for all his wretchedness, more fascinating—and more authentically "Finnish"—than the factory laborer; besides, to their minds, the latter had been tainted by the theories of socialism.)

Thus, some authors tried valiantly to deal with Finland's most recent past, and with the gap between what Lehtonen termed Finland's "aborigines" and its civilized (and perhaps more superficial) citizens; others looked farther back in time. The dramatist Lauri Haarla (1890–1944) examined the civil war in his *Kaksiteräinen miekka* (1932; the two-edged sword), but the best of his work for the stage lay in his expressionistic plays of the 1920s on themes taken from the *Kalevala* and from Finland's 18th-c. history. Aino Kallas (q.v.) stylized the history and mythology of a related country, likewise recently become independent, in her short and balladlike novels about Estonia. One might propose that the mixture of intense emotionalism and equally intense self-discipline among the poets of the Flame Bearers group sprang from somewhat the same source as Haarla's and Kallas's application of extreme literary artifice to elemental passion. There is a desire to reconcile the irreconcilable, the primitive world and ordered culture, a desire that, in the case of the poets, led to a mystical thanatophilia. Katri Vala (1901–1944), Uuno Kailas (1901–1933), and Kaarlo Sarkia (1902–1945) rejoiced, in fact, in presentiments of early death; their immediate predecessor in the Finnish lyric, Juhani Siljo (1888–1918), had been killed in the civil war, on the White side, and their comrade Yrjö Jylhä (1903–1956) would write the most important book of verse to come out of Finland's 1939–40 Winter War with the U.S.S.R., with duty and death side by side.

At the start of the 1930s, Finland had witnessed an attempt at a fascist coup by Vihtori Kosola (1884–1936), "Finland's Mussolini"; the Winter War came at the decade's end. The temper of literature grew anxious, with a flaring-up of various literary and emotional fads, many of them escapist—the idyll flourished in the last novels of Sillanpää and the poems of the sometime revolutionary, Diktonius; the endangered reaches of Karelia, which the Finns were forced to cede to the U.S.S.R. in 1940, were written about again and again, in the Finnish-language novels of Unto Seppänen (1904–1955) and the Swedish-language novels of Olof Enckell (b. 1900) and Hagar Olsson;

a cult of the flesh appeared in the Finnish narratives of Iris Uurto (b. 1905); and the Russian-born Finland-Swede Tito Colliander (b. 1904), fascinated by sex, was still more fascinated by Dostoevskian repentance. (Although overt frictions between Finland's two language groups continued throughout the 1930s, their literatures show a remarkable number of resemblances and parallels.) It was a febrile time, and even an essentially cool-headed observer, the young Mika Waltari (1908–1979), writing in Finnish, found life-ecstasy at work in Helsinki, while a character in Hagar Olsson's *Chitambo* (1933; Chitambo) beholds the angel of death in one of the capital's parks. Direct political statements were made only occasionally, although both Colliander and the brilliant Finnish-language essayist Olavi Paavolainen (1903–1964) visited Hitler's Germany as neutral observers. The Finland-Swede poet Örnulf Tigerstedt (1900–1962) espoused a rhetorical fascism; the Marxist-Leninist left organized itself into the Wedge group, of which Arvo Turtiainen (1904–1980) and Viljo Kajava (b. 1909), both writing in Finnish, were the first lyric stars, producing poetry about the working man reminiscent of that Diktonius, and, in Turtiainen's case, of Edgar Lee Masters (q.v.). However, a potentially vigorous voice of the left, the Estonian-born Finnish-language writer Hella Wuolijoki (1886–1954), made a place for herself in the literature of the 1930s—writing under the pseudonym of Juhani Tervapää —with plays about the family of the "Niskavuori estate" that seemed quite unrelated to their author's political convictions. As for Toivo Pekkanen (1902–1957) and his novels in Finnish about the new factory town of Kotka, he was an unimpeachable member of the proletariat, but refused to align himself with any political faction. Pekkanen's presentation of the worker in literature, by the way, was something of a pioneering deed, even in the 1930s. It is noteworthy that the two most advanced structural and stylistic experiments of the decade still deal with characters who, as it were, have not been incorporated in an industrial society. The main figure of Elmer Diktonius's "woodcut in words," *Janne Kubik* (1932; Janne Kubik), is a drifter, the voices in the Finnish-language novelist Volter Kilpi's (q.v.) giant *Alastalon salissa* (1933; in the hall of Alastalo) belong to the sailors and farmers of the skerries.

The Winter War has been accepted as a heroic episode in Finland's history; the so-called "Continuation War" of 1941–44, in which the nation was a "cobelligerent" of Nazi Germany, ended with a sense of relief, of exhaustion, and (in the case of the political left) of vindication. Finland lost about an eighth of its area to the Soviet Union, and heavy reparations had to be paid to the victor; no wonder that literary vitality dwindled. Swedish-language literature seemed ready to vanish (the abrupt failure of Diktonius's talent, the early death of the poet Christer Lind [1912–1942], the suicide of diarist Kerstin Söderholm [1897–1943], and the departure for Sweden of the essayist Hans Ruin [1891–1980], are but a few cases in point); and Finnish-language literature was but little better off—Sillanpää shared Diktonius's fate, such distinct lyric poets as Vala and Sarkia died too soon, Mika Waltari entered upon his new career of composing international best sellers. The sort of "end of Finland" at which Paavolainen hinted in his great war journal, *Synkkä yksinpuhelu* (1946; gloomy monologue), seemed to be at hand. Yet the return to poetry of Aaro Hellaakoski (1893–1952), once the Finnish disciple of Apollinaire (q.v.), was a sign that Finnish lyric was once again about to try to catch up with that of the rest of Europe, and the novelist Pentti Haanpää (q.v.) showed new life, first with an ironic treatment of the late war, and then with a comical depiction of an earlier catastrophe, the great famine of 1867–68. Patriotic fervor and patriotic pathos were swept away: for the nonce, wry humor took their place.

The 1950s were years of promises fulfilled. Rather abruptly, after the political crisis of 1948 (when it was feared that Finland might go the way of Czechoslovakia), the nation appeared capable of survival. Promising debutants from the late 1930s and 1940s now flowered again; Finland-Swedish literature got attention around the world by means of the children's books of Tove Jansson (q.v.), while the warm-hearted and observant lyrics and stories of Solveig von Schoultz (b. 1907), the carefully made elegiac verse of Bo Carpelan (q.v.), and the emotionally perceptive dramas of Walentin Chorell (q.v.) were readily exported to the rest of Scandinavia. It was, to be sure, a literature that traveled easily, having little that was identifiably "Finnish" about it, concerned with the human lot taken large, and excelling at close psychological analysis, a trait that was shared, to a good extent, by some new Finnish-language authors, Juha Mannerkorpi (b. 1915) Eila Pennanen (b. 1916), and Marja-Liisa Vartio (1924–1966). The experiences of the 1930s and 1940s may have fostered such inwardness, or such concern with the problems of everyday life; the complications of Finland's recent reality were too painfully near, and too ambiguous, to contemplate. The sensitivity to emotional states was coupled, in many cases, with the desire (encouraged by Hellaakoski's example) to give the Finnish-language lyric what Finland-Swedish poetry had long had, as a result of the modernists, a full liberation from the worn-out imagery, rhyme, and rhetoric of the past. In the 1950s, the victory was finally won, by Eeva-Liisa Manner (q.v.), Aili Meriluoto (b. 1924), Tuomas Anhava (b. 1927), and, above all, Paavo Haavikko (q.v.), writers of poetry that is rich in allusion (but not specifically Finnish allusion) and filled with personal rather than national myth—as a myth-maker, Helvi Juvonen (1919–1959) is of particular interest and value.

Nonetheless, the most notable productions of the 1950s may well be those where, again, Finnish problems and the Finnish past are directly addressed. Haavikko himself, early on, thought about the political and geographical situation of Finland in his parabolic plays; a less intellectual and more gripping address to Finland's abiding difficulties—its fateful location, its social extremes—came, as usual, in the Finnish-language novel. Lauri Viita's (q.v.) broad and tragicomic chronicle of an industrial community, *Moreeni* (1950; the moraine), opened the decade; Väinö Linna's (q.v.) vastly popular war novel *Tuntematon sotilas* (1954; *Unknown Soldier*, 1957) marked its middle; and the first two volumes of Linna's trilogy about a tenant farmer's family closed it. Viita and Linna are clearly spokesmen for the Finnish masses, putting themselves inside their characters in a way that, for example, would have been quite impossible for Lehtonen and Kianto in their time. The question of the Finnish "savage" is no longer of the essence; he still appears, but only as a subsidiary figure to, say, Linna's responsible and clear-thinking common soldier and common man. Similarly, Veijo Meri (q.v.), is on the side of simple folk, in his accounts of the recent war against Russia and the civil war; but his attitude toward his material and his craft is different from Linna's. An heir to Haanpää, he turns national catastrophes into Black Humor (q.v.), and, instead of practicing sequential narration, as Linna does—and other such widely read novelists as Veikko Huovinen (b. 1927) and Paavo Rintala (b. 1930)—he constantly toys with narrative forms, although taking care always to entertain his readers. Other prose writers were less careful of their audience, i.e., less aware of their old-fashioned Finnish function as storytellers (and both Haanpää and Meri construct novels that are, in effect, fabrics made up of short stories). Pentti Holappa (b. 1927) with his maze-like novels and Antti Hyry (b. 1931) with his detailed and compressed tales, in their studied objectivity and their concern with the apparently trivial, found themselves regarded as leaders in the "Europeanization" of their literature —Finnish equivalents, say, of Michel Butor (q.v.). It is not difficult, though, to perceive another of Finnish literature's favorite themes in their texts: that of the man quite outside society, without family or friends, the man for whom neither the wilderness nor civilization provides a refuge.

Irony and double-edged humor lost ground to social and political consciousness during the 1960s and the 1970s, in Finland as in the rest of the North, while the nation enjoyed a prosperity it had never known before: there was a nostalgia, almost, for the unhappy past, a bad conscience about the affluent present. A kind of preaching of the benefits of iron social planning (or a dogmatic harping on the faults that result from its absence) entered the work of one author after another. For example, Christer Kihlman (b. 1930) began as an explorer of what he found to be the rottenness of his own group, the Finland-Swedish upper class, and slid slowly—seducing readers with his graceful style—toward suggestions of armed revolution. Hannu Salama (q.v.), writing in Finnish, started with a look at several kinds of Finnish *malaise* (residual Lutheranism, moral hypocrisy, isolation), to move along to a eulogy of Finnish Communists in the Continuation War. Claes Andersson (b. 1937), in his unadorned Swedish poetry, complained at first about obvious ills (for example, the treatment of the emotionally disturbed), then laid the blame at the feet of an "undirected" society; in his lively Finnish lyric poetry Pentti Saarikoski (q.v.) tried to show his nation its own absurdities by shocking it with linguistic and personal absurdities of his own. Legitimate complaints became, all too easily, tirades against the establishment. The common man was forever good and forever the victim—as in the novels in Finnish of Alpo Ruuth (b. 1943) and Antti Tuuri (b. 1944). Finland's literature has always been keenly interested in the nation's past; now, particularly in Finnish-language writing, a ransacking of that past took place, a march through the battlefields and prison camps of the civil war in search of heroes of the defeated side, a reexamination of the fascistic episode of the early 1930s, which became the subject of the great stage success of the 1960s, the *Lapualaisoopera* (1967; the Lappo opera) of Arvo Salo (b.

1932) and the composer Kaj Chydenius (b. 1939). In short, the process of "democratization" of Finland's society that had begun in 1944, in many respects a laudable effort, had given birth to a literary spirit that came close to a monotonous intolerance, and which, in rightly praising the efforts of the Finnish masses to achieve a measure of dignity and freedom, went in the direction of freedom's denial. Authors could find themselves in situations fraught with irony; in his novels, Timo K. Mukka (1944–1973) described and apparently approved of an undisciplined north Finnish society of reindeer herders quite free of any sexual taboos, yet—like so many of his contemporaries—he entertained an admiration for his nation's thoroughly disciplined eastern neighbor, the Soviet Union; the Finland-Swedish autobiographer Henrik Tikkanen (b. 1924) revelled in telling about his blue-blooded family and *its* sexual excesses, as well as his own, meanwhile interjecting appropriate moralizings about capitalist and elitist corruption along the way.

The word "Finlandization," that is, the transformation of an ostensibly neutral country into what is, in effect, a part of Europe's Eastern bloc, has become popular in discussions of international politics. It cannot be denied that a creeping dogmatism—with a goal not unlike that of "Finlandization"—has entered much of Finland's recent literature. And Kivi's ambiguity of stance, his dialogue between the pull of the wilderness and the requirements of civilization, is by no means the only tradition, or habit, to have come down from the 19th c. Among Kivi's contemporaries were men of a much more rigid and self-righteous stripe, for example, Johan Ludvig Runeberg (1804–1877), with his call for stoic patriotism, and Johan Vilhelm Snellman (1806–1881), with his demand that Finland become monolingual in Finnish. Yet the country's culture appears to have gained most from its balancing acts—between disorder and discipline, between languages, between East and West. Happily, in its contemporary literature, Finland possesses central figures who reflect or smile, rather than accuse or denigrate. The Finn Paavikko has spoken more and more directly about the lot of the nation caught in the middle, and the ways it must take to survive; the Finland-Swede Lars Huldén (q.v.) has joked about much that was once sacred in Finland, including Runeberg himself: his jokes are penetrating, even serious, but never hateful.

BIBLIOGRAPHY: Hein, M. P., Introduction to *Moderne finnische Lyrik* (1962), pp. 3–16;

Laitinen, K., *Finlands moderne Literatur* (1969); Schoolfield, G. C., "The Spirit of Finland's Literature," *BF*, 5, 3 (1972), 7–14; Ahokas, J. A., *A History of Finnish Literature* (1973); Laitinen, K., Introduction to *Modern Nordic Plays: Finland* (1973), pp. 7–16; Ahokas, J. A., Introduction to *Prose finlandaise* (1973), pp. 13–73; Schoolfield, G. C., Introduction to *Swedo-Finnish Short Stories* (1974), pp. 1–17; Hein, M. P., Introduction to *Finnland: Moderne Erzähler der Welt* (1974), pp. 9–42; Dauenhauer, R., and Binham, P., Introductions to *Snow in May: An Anthology of Finnish Writing 1945–1972* (1978), pp. 21–101; Plöger, A., ed., Afterword to *Neue finnische Prosa* (1979), pp. 255–60; Tiusanen, T., "Introduction to 20th Century Drama in Finland"; Zilliacus, C., "Group Theatre in Finland during the Seventies"; and Niemi, I., "The Lapua Opera," in Wrede, J., et al., eds., *20th Century Drama in Scandinavia* (1979), pp. 19–25, 79–89, 177–86; special Finland issue, "The Two Literatures of Finland Today," *WLT*, 54, 1 (1980); Lomas, H., Introduction to *Territorial Song: New Writing in Finland* (1981), pp. vii–xx

GEORGE C. SCHOOLFIELD

FINNO-UGRIC LITERATURES OF THE SOVIET UNION

The Finno-Ugric peoples of the Soviet Union, arranged in descending order by the numbers of their native speakers, are Estonians, Mordvins, Udmurts (or Votyaks), Maris (or Cheremis), Komis (both Komi-Zyrians and Komi-Permyaks, Hungarians, Karelians (including Olonetsians and Ludes), Finns, Khantys (or Ostyaks), Vepsians, Mansis (or Voguls), Saams (or Lapps), Ingrians, Livonians, Votes. Linguistically related to the Finno-Ugrians are the Samoyeds: Nenets (or Yuraks), Selkups (or Ostyak-Samoyeds), Nganasans (or Tavgis), and Enets (or Yenisei-Samoyeds). The Finno-Ugric and Samoyed languages make up the Uralic language family.

The national groups who number only a few hundred or thousand do not have a literature, although the Mansi Yuvan Shestalov (b. 1937) has published more than ten volumes of poetry and lyrical prose. Khanty literature has developed mainly since the 1960s; one Khanty poet, Mikul (officially Ivan Ivanovich) Shulgin (b. 1940) is a member of the Writers' Union of the U.S.S.R. Karelian has been very little

used as a literary language, Finnish being the official language of the Karelian A.S.S.R. (which was temporarily called the Karelo-Finnish S.S.R.). Among those writing in Finnish, Antti Timonen (b. 1915) is best known, especially for his novel *Me karjalaiset* (1971; we, the Karelians). The Hungarians in the Transcarpathian Ukraine have not yet produced an independent literature. (Estonian literature is treated in a separate article.) Thus, the focus here is on the central Finno-Ugric group, consisting of Permic (Komi and Udmurt) and Volga-Finnic (Mari and Mordvin). These are essentially rural peoples, all of them exposed to similar cultural influences, throughout their histories, with Russian now the overwhelming one.

Until the Russian Revolution hardly anything could be published in local minority languages, except translations of religious brochures, some calendars, and other occasional publications. Since the tsarist authories did not want native secular literatures, the outstanding Komi poet Ivan Kuratov (1839–1875), for instance, could publish only five of his poems, disguised as folk poetry. When the native literatures began to take shape after 1917, there was much enthusiasm. Since there was no agreement about a fixed literary language, more than one dialect was used. To this day only the Udmurts have a unified literary language.

Many of the early writers were elementary-school teachers active in the Communist Party. Nevertheless, they were not spared the persecutions of the 1930s. The writers were accused of "bourgeois nationalism," that is, of giving too much attention to the past and present of their national cultures. Numerous writers were arrested, and some were executed. After the Twentieth Communist Party Congress (in 1956, under Khrushchev) the doomed could be posthumously rehabilitated, but irreparable damage had been done.

Soviet literary historians often distinguish the following periods in the development of young native literatures: one or two periods from 1917 to 1941, one from 1941 to 1945, one from 1945 to 1956 (the year of the Twentieth Party Congress), and one thereafter. It seems simpler to allow for a preparatory period (before 1917) and to count only three periods after that: (1) unfolding and crisis (from 1917 to 1938 or 1941); (2) transition (until 1956); (3) improved continuation (since 1956).

These literatures usually began with relatively short works, expecially poems. If there were enough talented writers, the development of multiple genres was achieved quite early. This was the case with modern Komi literature, whose four founders complemented each other. There was a dramatist, poet, and prose writer, Viktor Savin (pseud.: Ńobdinsa Vittor, 1888–1943); a "romantic" lyric poet and prose writer, Venyamin Chistalev (pseud.: Tima Veń, 1890–1939); an "epic" poet, prose writer, and dramatist, Mikhail Lebedev (1877–1951); and a lyric poet and linguist, Vasily Lytkin (pseud.: Iĺĺa Vaś, b. 1895). The leader of the second generation of Komi Soviet writers is Gennady Fedorov (b. 1909), whose principal work is the historical novel *Kya petigön* (1959–62; it is daybreak). Among those of the third generation, Gennady Yushkov (b. 1932) has written lyric poems, prose works, and dramas.

Udmurt writers displayed high artistry as early as the 1920s. Their leader was Kuźma Chaynikov (pseud.: Gerd Kuzebai, 1898–1937 or 1941), who was an excellent lyric poet, prose writer, folklorist, and author of textbooks. In 1932 he was accused of bourgeois nationalism, arrested, and later executed, and only in 1958 was he posthumously rehabilitated. Another Udmurt writer, the novelist Dmitry Korepanov (pseud.: Kedra Mitrei, 1892–1949) was exiled to Siberia, and was posthumously rehabilitated in 1956. A highly talented woman poet is the Udmurt Lina Vekshina (pseud.: Ashaĺtsi Oki, b. 1898). She, too, was accused of nationalism and was forced to give up her literary career. Mikhail Petrov (1905–1955) wrote the best Udmurt historical novel of the postwar period, *Vuzh Multan* (1954; old Multan). Important among the younger generation was the prose writer Gennady Krasiĺnikov (1928–1975). The Udmurts have also produced a genuinely modern poet, Flor Vasilev (b. 1934).

In Mari literature, Sergey Grigoŕev (pseud.: Chavain, 1888–1942) was a leading writer even before 1917, but he, too, became a victim of the "personality cult." The first Mari novelist was Yakov Mayorov (pseud.: M. Shketan, 1898–1937), who also wrote plays. Nikolay (Miklai) Kazakov (b. 1918) is representative of the older generation of poets, and Valentin Kolumb (b. 1937) of the younger ones. The best-known Mari dramatist is Sergey Nikolaev (b. 1908). Kim Vasin (b. 1924) is very active as a literary historian and as a prose writer.

Modern Mordvin literature started with poetry. To this day there are a great number of poets, among whom two older writers, Nikolay Irkaev (pseud.: Nikul Erkai, b. 1906) and Artur Moro (b. 1909) are predominant. The Mordvin novel was established by Timofey Raptanov (1906–1936). Among modern novelists, Kuźma Abramov (b. 1914) stands out. Mordvin drama started with the ill-fated Fyodor Chesnokov (1896-1938), who was a victim of the purges and only posthumously rehabilitated. Later, Pyotr Kirillov (1910–1955) was the main contributor to the development of this genre.

Among the Samoyeds, only the Nenets have been able to produce some literature, initiated by Tyko Vylka (1886–1960). There are even a few Nenets writers who are members of the Soviet Writers' Union.

The future of these literatures will depend on the competence of the writers, the reactions of the public, and, most importantly on the regulations of the Communist Party.

BIBLIOGRAPHY: Domokos, P., "Literaturen finnisch-ugrischer und samojedischer Völker in der Sowjetunion," *Nachrichten der Akademie der Wissenschaften in Göttingen*, 1, 2 (1977), 37–64

ALO RAUN

FIRBANK, Ronald

English novelist, dramatist, and short-story writer, b. 17 Jan. 1886, London; d. 21 May 1926, Rome, Italy

F. came from a conventional, modish, and socially ambitious family whose large fortune had been made by his paternal grandfather, an energetic collier who rose from the Durham pits to become one of England's wealthiest railway contractors. Ineffectually urged by his parents to enter the British Diplomatic Service, F. went to France in 1903, where he studied those French and Belgian writers—Baudelaire, Flaubert, Gautier, Huysmans, and Maeterlinck (q.v.)—who were to influence profoundly his literary career. His first publication, *La princesse aux soleils* (1904; *La Princesse aux Soleils,* 1974 [bilingual]), written in French, was a prose poem that illustrated his enduring interest in *fin-de-siècle* literature.

Entering Trinity Hall, Cambridge, in 1906, F. led a leisurely existence. He took no examinations, entertained lavishly, and made frequent excursions to the London theater, opera, and ballet. In 1908, following the examples of Oscar Wilde, Ernest Dowson (1867–1900), Aubrey Beardsley (1872–1898), and Frederick Rolfe (Baron Corvo, 1860–1913), F. was

received into the Roman Catholic Church. He
left Cambridge in 1909 without a degree and
planned to enter the Vatican Service. Unable,
however, to secure a Vatican post, F. felt the
Church had rejected him, an attitude that imbued his fiction.

Though F.'s professional career as a novelist
began with the publication of *Vainglory*
(1915), he had already written numerous
poems, plays, and short stories, many of them
still unpublished. He was a superstitious, dis-
trustful aesthete whose dominating ambition
was to realize himself as an artist and achieve
fame. Between 1915 and 1926 F. published,
largely at his own expense and to slight critical
acclaim, seven richly comic novels, the best of
which are *Valmouth* (1919) and *The Flower
beneath the Foot* (1923). Usually exotic, the
settings of these books reflect F.'s varied so-
journs in Italy, Spain, North Africa, and Cuba,
where his eccentricities were less conspicuous
perhaps than in England. His central theme is
the dilemma of the hypersensitive individual,
often a female, who is somehow isolated and
destroyed by the futility and depravity of the
surrounding world. Creating sympathy for his
alienated victims, F. bitterly satirizes the characters and values opposed to them. If his fictional world is one of frivolity, perversion, and
decay, he continually redeems it by gaiety, wit,
and elegance. The elaborate flippancy of his
tone is the flippancy of honest desperation.

While F.'s humor was too idiosyncratic to
become a literary force, his technical innovations were employed by Aldous Huxley, Evelyn
Waugh, and Anthony Powell (qq.v.), among
others. F.'s best novels, teeming with brilliant
dialogue and meticulously patterned prose,
offer no explicit messages but much sardonic
artistry and a unique vision of the absurd. He
used a baroque humor verging upon the freak-
ish to define the fragmented society around
him. Distantly related to the Dadaists (q.v.), F.
anticipates, through his demoralizing comedy,
outrageous fantasy, and grotesque pathos, the
work of Beckett, Ionesco, and Genet (qq.v.).

FURTHER WORKS: *Odette d'Antrevernes, and A
Study in Temperament* (1905); *The Wavering
Disciple* (1906); *A Study in Opal* (1907);
Odette (1916); *Inclinations* (1916); *Caprice*
(1917); *The Princess Zoubaroff* (1920); *San-
tal* (1921); *Sorrow in Sunlight* (1924; pub. as
Prancing Nigger, 1925); *Concerning the Ec-
centricities of Cardinal Pirelli* (1926); *Works*
(1928); *The Artificial Princess* (1934); *The
Complete R. F.* (1961); *The New Rhythm, and
Other Pieces* (1962); "The Wind the Roses"

(1966); *Far Away* (1966); *An Early Flemish
Painter* (1969); *La Princesse aux Soleils, &
Harmonie* (1974); *When Widows Love, & A
Tragedy in Green: Two Stories* (1980)

BIBLIOGRAPHY: Waugh, E., "R. F.," *Life and
Letters, II* (1929), pp. 191–96; Brooke, J., *R.
F.* (1951); Benkovitz, M., *R. F.: A Bibliography* (1963); Benkovitz, M., *R. F.: A Biography* (1969); Merritt, J. D., *R. F.* (1969); Potoker, E. M., *R. F.* (1970); Fletcher, I. K.,
ed., *R. F.: Memoirs and Critiques* (1977);
Benkovitz, M., *Supplement to a Bibliography of
R. F.* (1980)

EDWARD M. POTOKER

FITRAT, Abdalrauf (Abdurauf)

Bukharan dramatist, poet, short-story writer,
and literary scholar (writing in Turki and Persian), b. 1886, Bukhara; d. 1937, Tashkent,
Uzbekistan

F. was regarded as the most promising student
sent by the Bukharan Cultural Society to get
advanced education in Istanbul seminaries. He
was a leading social thinker in the "Young
Bukharan" movement between 1908 and 1920
and wrote for the Jadid (reformist) press. He
served in the Afghan consulate in Tashkent in
1918 and held high posts in the government
of the Bukhara People's Conciliar Republic
between 1921 and 1923. Additionally, he
founded the influential Tashkent literary circle
called the Chaghatay Conference in 1918 and
headed it until it vanished under Communist
pressure in 1922. After the Soviet partition of
central Asia in 1924–25, F. lived and worked
in Samarkand and Tashkent, where he taught
literary history in higher educational institutions. In the 1930s he was imprisoned for alleged "nationalism" and met his death at the
hands of Soviet secret police.

Three of F.'s most widely known works were
first issued in Turkey in the Persian language:
Munazara (1909; the dispute), mainly in
prose; *Sayha* (1910; the cry), in verse; and
Bayyanat-e sayyah-e hindi (1912; tales of a
Hindu traveler), in prose. The prose pieces
were soon translated into Russian or Turki and
republished within central Asia. Like most of
his extensive imaginative writing now known,
these three were didactic but entertaining, even
stirring in their open appeal to the survival instincts of central Asians. Aware of a pressing
need to reach the largely uneducated society of
the region, F. poured out a series of plays like
Chin sewish (1919; real love) and *Timurning*

saghanäsi (1919; Tamerlane's tomb), both in Turki, mainly historical dramas with patriotic themes.

His most important creative writings of the 1920s were his powerful poems of personal and group identity printed in the anthology *Ozbek yash shairläri* (1922; young Uzbek poets), and his plays *Hind ikhtilalchilari* (1920; pub. 1923; Hindu insurrectionists), written in Turki, and *'Isyan Vose* (1927; Vose's uprising), written in Persian. These dramas achieved their aim of gaining audiences and stirring feeling throughout central Asia with implicit calls for resistance to Russian domination; for the same reasons they attracted unfavorable official attention.

Two of F.'s principal literary studies appeared in the 1920s: *Ädäbiyat qa'adaläri* (1926; theory of literature) and *Persidsky poet Omar Khayyam* (1929; title in Russian: the Persian poet Omar Khayyam). He also edited a number of anthologies, which immediately became controversial because of their non-Marxist content. One of these, *Ozbek ädäbiyati nämunäläri* (1928; specimens of Uzbek literature), is valuable even today in the study of early central Asian literature.

F. was a dominant figure of his time in the literary development and scholarship of central Asia, but only one of his numerous works seems to have been republished in the U.S.S.R. since his death, namely, *Qiyamät* (1923; judgment day), a novelette in Turki, which was rehabilitated, greatly altered, translated into Russian, and reprinted in Uzbek and Tajik, evidently in order to be construed as antireligious propaganda. It is, in fact, a subtle, wildly amusing satire on clericalism told in lively, idiomatic prose.

FURTHER WORKS: *Muqaddas Qan* (1915–17); *Begijan* (1916–17); *Abu Muslim* (1918); *Ulugh Beg* (1919); *Oghuz Khan* (1919–20); *Bidil* (1923–24); *Abul Faiz Khan* (1924); *Shäytanning tängrigä 'iysani* (1924); *Arslan* (1927); *Eng eski turk ädäbiyati nämunäläri: Ädäbiyatimizning ta'rikhi ochon mätiriyällär* (1927); *Äruz häqidä* (1936); *Tolkun* (1937)

BIBLIOGRAPHY: Erturk, M. H., "A. F.," *Milli Türkistan*, No. 80/81B (1952), 9–16; Hayit, B., "Die jüngste özbekische Literatur," *CAsJ*, 8 (1962), 119–52; Allworth, E., *Uzbek Literary Politics* (1964), pp. 53–58, 109–16, 201–8; Carrère-d'Encausse, H., "A. F.," *Encyclopaedia of Islam* (1965), Vol. II, pp. 932–33

EDWARD ALLWORTH

FITZGERALD, F(rancis) Scott

American novelist and short-story writer, b. 24 Sept. 1896, St. Paul, Minn.; d. 21 Dec. 1940, Hollywood, Cal.

The son of Edward Fitzgerald, a descendant of Francis Scott Key, the writer of "The Star-Spangled Banner," F. attended Princeton University (1913–17). His involvement in campus theatricals affected his academic standing, and he left Princeton to receive a commission in the U.S. infantry (1917). He married Zelda Sayre in 1920, shortly after the publication of his first novel, *This Side of Paradise* (1920). Their turbulent relationship is portrayed in much of F.'s fiction, with Zelda often serving as the model for his female characters.

The Fitzgeralds lived in Europe for extended periods, joining other prominent expatriates such as Ernest Hemingway (q.v.) and Gerald and Sara Murphy. To support their extravagant life style, F. frequently interrupted his work on his novels to write short stories that brought high fees from the popular magazines.

F.'s financial problems were increased by Zelda's recurrent attacks of mental illness, which began in 1929 and necessitated long periods of hospitalization. In 1935 F.'s chronic tubercular condition was reactivated by his anxiety and guilt over Zelda's now hopeless mental state and by his own excessive drinking. F. spent the last years of his life in Hollywood writing film scripts under a lucrative contract with Metro-Goldwyn-Mayer. He died of a heart attack.

F. became an immediate celebrity at the age of twenty-three with *This Side of Paradise*. The novel was acclaimed by F.'s youthful readers as the story of their generation—a generation shaped by World War I whose coming of age coincided with that unprecedented American phenomenon, the Jazz Age. F. became both spokesman for and typical product of his time. One of the weaknesses of *This Side of Paradise* is indeed the fact that F. is too close in age to his fictional character to evaluate the quality of Amory Blaine's experiences in his quest for selfhood. By the conclusion of the novel, Amory's transformation from an "egotist" to a "personage," we are told, is complete. F. does not, however, reveal by what means Amory has attained the wisdom to justify his final triumphant claim to self-knowledge. The epigraph announces that on "this side of Paradise" one finds "little comfort in the wise." For Amory's rebellious generation, F. suggests, the wisdom of their ancestors, which consists of "old cries" and "old creeds," provides small comfort. Despite its numerous flaws, the novel retains a reading audience because it is a compelling portrayal of an exceptional age in American history.

F.'s second novel, *The Beautiful and Damned* (1922), is his least successful. It explores the personal and social pressures that cause a person's disintegration. The fate of its protagonists, Anthony and Gloria Patch—young, wealthy, self-indulgent—dramatizes the effects of these corrosive pressures. The epigraph, "The victor belongs to the spoils," proclaims the moral lesson of *The Beautiful and Damned*. Although Anthony and Gloria finally acquire the Patch family fortune, the retribution exacted for their egotism and greed is fearful: Gloria, whose self-definition is in terms of her physical appearance, loses her beauty, and Anthony suffers a complete mental collapse.

F. intended the fate of these pitiful people to be an analogue to the moral and cultural debilitation of Western civilization. America, he perceived, was involved in a celebratory spree after World War I that would destroy the idealism of the American spirit of achievement. The very title of the novel is a deliberate perversion of the concept in Plato's *Symposium* of the beautiful and good. Whereas in the *Symposium* the movement is toward transcendence of the purely physical to the ultimate spiritual good, the lives of F.'s characters work downward from a perverted notion of beauty to a degree of debasement that is a travesty of the platonic concept.

The Great Gatsby (1925) is F.'s greatest achievement. Set in Jazz Age New York City and fashionable Long Island, the novel describes the loss of those romantic illusions that beguile with the promise of an "imagined glory." Jay Gatsby's world is sustained by such illusions. His lack of concern with the "true or false" of things has a deeper significance for F. than one man's failure to distinguish between reality and fancy. Defined in the novel by its narrator, Nick Carraway, indifference is a moral failure—a failure of society to recognize the imperatives of truth and justice.

In order to reestablish his romantic association with Daisy Fay, now married to Tom Buchanan, a man of social position and inherited wealth, Gatsby accumulates a fortune through questionable means. He fails in his quixotic quest for the "golden girl" personified in Daisy Fay Buchanan. But Nick Carraway, F.'s moral commentator, proclaims that only Gatsby, despite his shady associations and tainted wealth, has retained a pure conviction in his "incorruptible dream." In the lush last passages of the novel, F. compares Gatsby's dream with the Edenic vision of the New World beheld by the first Dutch settlers. He implies that the American dream of a utopian world was destroyed by materialism after World War I. It is only the Gatsbys who still believe in the wondrous promise of the past. But this is only the illusion, the "imagined glory."

Tender Is the Night (1934), F.'s most ambitious novel, was also his favorite. Although it lacks the technical perfection attributed to *The Great Gatsby*, it contains some of F.'s finest writing, and reveals an extraordinary maturity of perception of the underlying causes of human failure. His protagonist, Dick Diver, possesses exceptional talent and personal charm. F. intended him to be a man of superior potential without, however, the "tensile strength" of the truly great personality. Dick Diver's personal tragedy exemplifies F.'s fascination with the distance between the two worlds of the ideal and the actual. The novel is concerned with Dick's futile attempts to synthesize these two irreconcilable worlds in his personal, social, and professional relationships.

Dick Diver is a brilliant American psychiatrist who falls in love with Nicole Warren, a rich, beautiful mental patient. Yielding to Nicole's wistful offering of herself, Dick marries her in violation of his professional judgment. Under the constant pressure of Nicole's recurring insanity and the insidious presence of the Warren money, Dick's potential for a great career is lost. By the novel's end, Dick, the romantic idealist, is vanquished, forced into emotional bankruptcy; Nicole, the flawed but wealthy pragmatist, having battened on Dick's strength and love for ten years, emerges victorious.

With *Tender Is the Night*, F. hoped to prove, at last, that he was the best of the young American novelists. He was aiming at something radically different in form and structure, something that would provide a model for the contemporary novel. If *Tender Is the Night* does not measure up to his great ambition, it is, nonetheless, an impressive achievement.

F.'s last, unfinished work, *The Last Tycoon*, published posthumously in 1941, might have developed into his best novel. He had written six of the nine chapters projected in his outline when he died. The 1941 version, edited by Edmund Wilson (q.v.), includes the fragment, F.'s outline for the entire novel, and notes and drafts he was considering for its completion. Wilson notes that the manuscript represents that point where the artist had organized his material with a firm thematic intention that was not yet completely in focus.

Hollywood is the setting of *The Last Tycoon*, before the onslaught of the anarchic labor movements. Its protagonist, Monroe Stahr, is the last of the Hollywood moguls to be invested with unqualified authority. Stahr, F.'s most perceptively conceived male character, rises from the obscurity of a Bronx ghetto with a minimal education. Developing his natural talents of leadership, he becomes at age twenty-three the boy wonder of Hollywood.

There are two women in Stahr's life: Cecilia Brady, his partner's daughter, and his elusive love, the mysterious Kathleen Moore. The dynamic love story that F. had planned is not developed in the five encounters of the lovers in the manuscript. Cecilia serves a dual function as narrator-character through whom are presented the marvelously drawn minor characters who are woven into the backdrop of an ordinary day in a Hollywood studio. Cecilia is the most appealing character in the manuscript; the episodes in which she appears are presented with compelling immediacy. But, in most of the fragment, the narrative perspective is erratic. Even though F.'s notes indicate that he intended to refine his narrative technique in the final writing, it is improbable—in view of the complicated plans for the development of the several plots—that Cecilia, as narrator, would have achieved the credibility of Nick Carraway in *The Great Gatsby*.

F. is generally acclaimed as one of America's best short-story writers. The stories return the reader to the moral atmosphere of the novels, as F. explores once again his favorite themes.

He wrote parables such as "The Cut-Glass Bowl" (1920), which laments the perishability of physical beauty; "May Day" (1920), which warns against the corrupt social environment that encourages destructive human relationships. Stories like "Winter Dreams" (1922) and "Absolution" (1924) underscore the disenchantment that inevitably follows the pursuit of romantic illusions. "The Rich Boy" (1926), one of F.'s best stories, considers the debilitating influence of inherited money. True to his persistent belief that the very rich are different from the average American, F. frequently attributed failure to achieve selfhood to the possession of unearned wealth.

Hollywood provided some of F.'s themes of the 1930s. The young idealist, like Joel Coles of "Crazy Sunday" (1932), caught up in tawdry Hollywood intrigues, becomes a favorite subject, looking forward to its most extended presentation in *The Last Tycoon*. Emotional bankruptcy is another of F.'s preoccupations of the 1930s. "Family in the Wind" (1932) and "Babylon Revisited" (1931)—his finest short story—are concerned with the depletion of moral or physical energies caused by unrestrained drinking. Both stories also examine the plight of the middle-aged man who seeks to recapture the innocence of youth through his love for a young girl.

Not all the short stories are superior; in fact, many are hack work. But a number of them have the polish of F.'s best fiction, and at least a dozen rank high among the short stories of the 20th c.

F. contended that authors did not write novels with the intention of presenting a complete philosophical system. Yet, viewing F.'s works holistically, one detects an ultimate unity of theme that might be termed a philosophical perspective. F.'s novels are a re-creation of his own world. He admitted that his world view was dichotomous: he was both a romantic and a moralist. On the one hand, he clung to the illusion of life as romantic; on the other, he saw with puritanical clarity that self-indulgence courts self-destruction. F.'s male protagonists, from Amory Blaine to Monroe Stahr, are all projections of this conflict. The odd excitement of F.'s best fiction derives, in fact, from this inner tension.

Despite the structural flaws in his limited novelistic canon, F.'s place in American letters is assured. His fiction was rooted in the 1920s and early 1930s, but the human situations he examined so minutely with his own distinctly American vision defy the limitations of time and space.

FURTHER WORKS: *Flappers and Philosophers* (1920); *Tales of the Jazz Age* (1922); *The Vegetable; or, From President to Postman* (1923); *All the Sad Young Men* (1926); *Taps at Reveille* (1935); *The Crack-up* (1945); *The Portable F. S. F.* (1949); *The Stories of F. S. F.* (1951); *Afternoon of an Author* (1958); *The Pat Hobby Stories* (1962); *The F. Reader* (1963); *The Letters of F. S. F.* (1963); *The Apprentice Fiction of F. S. F., 1909–1917* (1965); *Letters to His Daughter* (1965); *Thoughtbook of Francis Scott Key Fitzgerald* (1965); *Dear Scott/Dear Max: The F.-Perkins Correspondence* (1971); *As Ever, Scott Fitz——* (1972); *Correspondence of F. S. F.* (1980); *The Price Was High: The Last Uncollected Stories of F. S. F.* (1981)

BIBLIOGRAPHY: Mizener, A., *The Far Side of Paradise* (1951; rev. ed., 1965); Turnbull, A., *S. F.* (1962); Callaghan, M., *That Summer in Paris* (1963); Eble, K., *F. S. F.* (1963); Miller, J. E., *F. S. F.: His Art and His Technique* (1964); Perosa, S., *The Art of F. S. F.* (1965); Piper, H. D., *F. S. F.: A Critical Portrait* (1965); Cowley M., and Cowley, R., *F. and the Jazz Age* (1966); Lehan, R. D., *F. S. F. and the Craft of Fiction* (1966); Graham, S., *Beloved Infidel* (1967); Shain, C. E., *F. S. F.* (1967); Sklar, R., *F. S. F.: The Last Laocoon* (1967); Stern, M. R., *The Golden Moment: The Novels of F. S. F.* (1969); Latham, A., *Crazy Sundays: F. S. F. in Hollywood* (1970); Bruccoli, M., and Bryer, J. R., *F. in His Own Time: A Miscellany* (1971); Cross, K. G. W., *S. F.* (1971); Gallo, R. A., *F. S. F.* (1978); Way, B., *F. S. F. and the Art of Social Fiction* (1980); Bruccoli, M. J., *Some Sort of Epic Grandeur: The Life of F. S. F.* (1981)

ROSE ADRIENNE GALLO

The Last Tycoon is thus, even in its imperfect state, F.'s most mature piece of work. It is marked off also from his other novels by the fact that it is the first to deal seriously with any profession or business. The earlier books of F. had been preoccupied with debutantes and college boys, with the fast lives of the wild spenders of the twenties. The main activities of the people in these stories, the occasions for which they live, are big parties at which they go off like fireworks and which are likely to leave them in pieces. But the parties in *The Last Tycoon* are incidental and unimportant; Monroe Stahr, unlike any other of S. F.'s heroes, is inextricably involved with an industry of which he has been one of the creators, and its fate will be implied by his tragedy. The moving-picture business in America has here been observed at a close range, studied with a careful attention and dramatized with a sharp wit such as are not to be found in combination in any of the other novels on the subject. *The Last Tycoon* is far and away the best novel we have had about Hollywood, and it is the only one which takes us inside.

Edmund Wilson, Foreword to F. S. F., *The Last Tycoon* (1941), p. ix

One of the most remarkable things about S. F. as a writer is the dual character of his self-knowledge, the curious way in which he combined the innocence of complete involvement with an almost scientific coolness of observation, so that he nearly always wrote about deeply felt personal experience, and nearly always as if the important use of personal experience was to illustrate general values. "Begin with an individual," he once wrote, "and before you know it you find you have created a type." As a general proposition, that may be exceedingly questionable, but as a comment on the character of F.'s best work it is very shrewd. This curious sense of experience is everywhere in Fitzgerald's work because it was the permanent foundation of his awareness of experience.

Arthur Mizener, Introduction to F. S. F., *Afternoon of an Author* (1958), p. 3

F.'s popularity shows no sign of waning; it seems certain that he will remain with Hemingway and Faulkner as the most interesting and rewarding of twentieth-century American fiction writers.

The legend of F.'s disorderly romantic life answers, and with a better writer, the intense American need for a mythical artistic hero like Poe. An interest in F.'s work can scarcely escape entanglement in the F. legend. Nevertheless, his work today seems to enjoy great favor, perhaps because he seems less mannered than Hemingway, less tortuous than Faulkner, and less clumsy than any of a dozen novelists in the naturalistic tradition. The excellence of his style tends to hold his reputation high while other reputations tumble. But at least two other matters operate in his favor. The first is the hard core of morality which makes him one with those writers of greatest strength in American fiction: Melville, Hawthorne, and James. Second, unlike a majority of modern American writers, he offers a fiction which is hard to imitate but from which much can be learned.

Kenneth Eble, *F. S. F.* (1963), p. 153

The Great Gatsby's excellence was immediately seen, but soon the carping began. Mencken wrote "a most enthusiastic letter" to F., in which he complained that "the central story was trivial and a sort of anecdote. . . ." In a characteristic blend of modesty, temerity and odd spelling, F. replied: "Without making any invidious comparisons between Class A and Class C, if my novel is an anecdote so is *The Brothers Karamazoff*."

Nevertheless, F. granted Mencken's point and agreed that it had been a mistake to becloud the relationship between Gatsby and Daisy from the time of their reunion until Gatsby's death. Yet F.'s error was his triumph. Had he dramatized that relationship he would have been validating a sham. There could be no fulfillment of Gatsby's tragic dream. . . .

The theme of F.'s novel is more inclusive and more shocking than we have known. Its subject is atrophy; the wasting away of the self as one grows into the world of sex and money and time; the wasting away of America as it grows from wilderness to civilization, of the universe as it grows by its impossible plan.

Humanly, the novel reflects the disillusionment and the failure of youthful dreams which is so marked a feature of man's lot. Culturally, it dramatizes, perhaps more cogently than any other

American novel, the cause and cost of America's identification with eternal beginnings. Cosmically, it suggests the apocalyptic vision with which we have become familiar in our literature, our intellectuals, and our newspapers.

It is the novel's greatest achievement to have painted this bleak picture with the brightest of colors. Never has the dying swan sung so sweetly or so surely. . . .

Finally, there is the incredible tightness in plotting, characterization and detail. In Joyce's sense of the word, *The Great Gatsby* is one of the few novels *written* in our language. In concentration of meaning, nuance, and effect, there are few books in any language with which to compare it.

Charles Thomas Samuels, "The Greatness of *Gatsby*," *MR*, 7 (1966), pp. 783, 793–94

If critical and popular opinion are to be taken as the criteria, *The Great Gatsby* is one of the few important works to come out of contemporary American literature. Moreover, F.'s third novel is a work of art which, like good wine, seems to get better with age. John Dos Passos has said in his note on F.: "It's the quality of detaching itself from its period that marks a piece of work as good." Judged by this rigorous standard, *The Great Gatsby* is very good indeed.

Reading it over again is both easy and pleasant, because it is one of the most compressed and concise of the great novels in any language. It can be compared in this respect to Turgenev's masterpiece *Fathers and Sons*, with which F.'s book has much in common. Aside from similarity of length, they are both representative of a whole civilization at a critical point in its history.

But the more one looks at the work both as a whole and as a collection of separable elements, the less it seems possible to account for its tremendous effect or to explain the inner mechanism by which this effect is secured.

T. S. Eliot, who read *Gatsby* three times, was never able to send F. the promised analysis to support the observation made in his letter that "this remarkable book . . . seems to me to be the first step that American fiction has taken since Henry James. . . . When I have the time, I should like to write to you more fully and tell you exactly why."

The sheer efficiency with which this little novel works upon the mind of the reader gives rise to the increasing respect it inspires. Within its strict confines, the writer has succeeded in capturing and giving form to his impressions of a vast and chaotic world. One is surprised at this realization, as one is surprised that some ladies' wrist watches, despite their phenomenally compact size, should accurately tell time. No American prose work of the twentieth century better exemplifies the epigram from the Greek Anthology: "Out of the jewel, grass is grown."

Milton Hindus, *F. S. F.: An Introduction and Interpretation* (1968), p. 35

Although in *Tender Is the Night* the psychological analyses of the characters have the upper hand, it is always in action that their true natures are revealed. . . . And if F., when he thought of rearranging *Tender Is the Night*, had a bitter exchange of letters with Thomas Wolfe in which he maintained the validity of the "novel of selected incident," the same concern with selection and structural symmetry was brought to bear in the "final version" as in the two other novels. . . .

In *Tender Is the Night* F.'s language is maturer and more complex, syntactically more elaborate. Less nervous and evocative, less syncopated and colored than in *Gatsby*, it spreads out in descriptions and analyses, in considerations and comments; it is more diffuse and full-bodied in its diction. Its pattern is here given by the long paragraph; its flow is discursive and spreading; it presupposes the "long time" and the calm development from sentence to sentence, from period to period. It is difficult to give a single specimen of it, because it is the extension of its rhythm, not the intensity of it, that counts.

Sergio Perosa, *The Art of F. S. F.* (1968), p. 129

Shortly before his death, in 1940, F. S. F. had the humiliating experience of walking into a large city bookstore and finding that none of his books were carried in stock and his name had been forgotten. But since then things have changed. The emergence of *The Great Gatsby* from a position of comparative obscurity a generation ago to its present position as a modern classic is one of the most remarkable events in recent American literary history. According to a recent New York *Times* report on paperback sales, more people are buying *The Great Gatsby* today than any novel by any writer of Fitzgerald's generation, including Faulkner and Hemingway. . . .

Few writers of his generation possessed a more passionate sense of time and place than F. . . . *The Great Gatsby* is not an historical novel. F. was written about the contemporary world of the early Twenties through which he had just lived. But because of the moral understanding he brought to his interpretation of that world, because of the concreteness of his description, we are brought closer to that world in the pages of his novel than in the more factual accounts of many orthodox historians. F.'s rendering of that world of almost fifty years ago is still relevant—to our understanding of the past, and to our understanding of the world today.

Henry Dan Piper, *F.'s "The Great Gatsby": The Novel, The Critics, The Background* (1970), p. 1

Speculation about the unwritten portion of the novel [*The Last Tycoon*] soon becomes futile. Although this problem is extremely interesting, we cannot speak with confidence about it. F.'s undated last outline provides only topics or ideas for the thirteen unwritten episodes. The most useful approach to the study of the novel is in terms of what Fitzgerald accomplished—not of what he was planning. His novel had developed in ways that were significantly different from his other work. Most notably, Monroe Stahr is a hero without a flaw. Unlike Amory Blaine, Anthony Patch, Jay Gatsby, or Dick Diver who are afflicted with character weaknesses, Monroe Stahr is intact up to episode 17, the last episode F. wrote. It is clear that he was to be defeated in the end, but F. plants no seeds of self-destruction in Stahr's character. Although Stahr's defeat is connected with his love for Kathleen, she is not the cause. Stahr's affair with Kathleen only provides Brady with a weapon to use against him.

F. was a life-long hero-worshipper, but he was not able to create an unflawed hero until he himself was in his forties. It is meaningful that Monroe Stahr is the first hero in a F. novel with a successful career; Amory and Anthony have no occupations; Gatsby's business activities are shadowy; and Dick Diver abandons his promising career. But Stahr is totally committed to his work and the responsibility that goes with it. He is F.'s only complete professional. Moreover, Stahr is immune to the emotional bankruptcy that is epidemic in F.'s work after 1930. A lonely young widower with a pervasive sense of loss, he is nonetheless not broken by loss, and he retains the capacity to love again. Stahr's one terrible mistake comes when he delays the decision to go away with Kathleen by one day—and during that day he loses her. If one is compelled to seek a flaw in Stahr, it is that he has an excess of reason or discipline; but it would be difficult to support this reading. . . .

Matthew J. Bruccoli, *The Last of the Novelists: F. S. F. and "The Last Tycoon"* (1977), p. 4

FLEISSER, Marieluise

German dramatist and short-story writer, b. 23 Nov. 1901, Ingolstadt; d. 2 Feb. 1974, Ingolstadt

F. studied German and theater arts in Munich, where she became acquainted with Lion Feuchtwanger and Bertolt Brecht (qq.v.). From 1926 until she returned for good to Ingolstadt, in 1932, she lived mostly in Berlin. There she was associated for a time with the group around Brecht and Erwin Piscator (1893–1966). During the Third Reich she was forbidden to publish, and her books were burned. After the war F. resumed writing in spite of great personal difficulties. She was awarded several prizes and, in 1965, became a member of the Bavarian Academy of Fine Arts.

F.'s name is closely associated with Ingolstadt, which provides the background for most of her works. Using the old Bavarian town as a prototype for small towns everywhere, she described and analyzed a way of life: the world of petty provincialism, with its narrow-mindedness and bigotry, created by people whose behavior is dictated by their roles in society, their inadequate education, and their inability to express themselves and thereby to get close to each other. Man's alienation from himself and the world becomes visible through the transparent medium of language.

In her play *Fegefeuer in Ingolstadt* (1926; second version, 1971; purgatory in Ingolstadt) some young people try desperately to break free of the stifling conventions in which they no longer believe. But since they have no positive convictions of their own to pit against those conventions, they find themselves reduced, in order to survive, to playing the callous game of the very society they reject. In a world characterized by the lack of charity, everybody inflicts upon the other what was inflicted on himself.

Pioniere in Ingolstadt (1928; second version, 1929; third version, 1968; pioneers in Ingolstadt) exhibits similar interpersonal patterns and modes of behavior. The play, with its sexual frankness, its depiction of the brutality of military life, and its derision of the bourgeoisie, clearly shows the influence of Brecht, and the Berlin performance of 1929, under the direction of Brecht, provoked quite a scandal, making her name known to a wider public. But it also furnished the Nazis with a reason to condemn her to temporary oblivion.

F.'s writings are lamentations, sad and angry and occasionally even cynical, over man's failure to realize his humanity, reflecting a world in which "the weak are abused." In a sense, her works can be read as documents of a spiritual biography, since her own experiences form the basis of most of her writing. But her dramatic and narrative works project more than just a personal portrait; they reveal the pettiness and cruelty of a deficient world, where man is man's wolf. Her plays seem to be a dramatization of Brecht's dictum: "The meanest thing alive, and the weakest, is man."

F., who characterized her talent as "basically epic," actually made her literary debut with short stories. Her first collection, *Ein Pfund Orangen, und 9 andere Geschichten der M. F. aus Ingolstadt* (1929; a pound of oranges, and 9 other stories by M. F. from Ingolstadt), displays an impressive mastery of narrative prose forms. The short story seems to have been the most appropriate vehicle for her talents. Her protagonists, inconspicuous people with inconspicuous fates, face the gradual disintegration of a meaningful reality with feelings of anguished helplessness. Her stories have justly been called "merciless idylls."

Praised by Walter Benjamin (q.v.) and the Berlin critic Alfred Kerr (1867–1948), called Bertolt Brecht's sister by the writer Curt Hohoff (b. 1913), F. stands as a link between Brecht and Ödön von Horváth (q.v.).

FURTHER WORKS: *Mehlreisende Frieda Geier: Roman vom Rauchen, Sporteln, Lieben und Verkaufen* (1931); *Andorranische Abenteuer* (1932); *Karl Stuart: Trauerspiel in fünf Akten* (1946); *Avantgarde* (1963); *Abenteuer aus dem Englischen Garten* (1969); *Gesammelte Werke* (3 vols., 1972)

BIBLIOGRAPHY: Rühle, G., ed., *Materialien zum Leben und Schreiben der M. F.* (1973); Dimter, W., "Die ausgestellte Gesellschaft: Zum Volksstück Horváths, der F. und ihrer Nachfolger," in Hein, J., ed., *Theater und Gesellschaft: Das Volksstück im 19. und 20. Jahrhundert* (1973), pp. 219–45; Kässens, W., and Töteberg, M., "'. . . fast schon ein Auftrag von Brecht': M. F.s Drama *Pioniere in Ingolstadt*," *Brecht-Jahrbuch* (1976), pp. 101–19; Sanger, C., "In the Avantgarde of Bertolt Brecht: M. F.'s *Pioniere in Ingolstadt*," in Nelson, C., ed., *Studies in Language and Literature*, Proceedings of the 23rd Mountain Interstate Foreign Language Conference (1976), pp. 517–22; Karasek, H., "Die Erneuerung des Volksstücks: Auf den Spuren M. F.s und Ödön von Horváths," in Arnold, H. L., and Buck, T., eds., *Positionen des Dramas: Analysen und Theorien zur deutschen Gegenwartsliteratur* (1977), pp. 137–69; Lutz, G., *Die Stellung M. F.s in der bayerischen Literatur des 20. Jahrhunderts* (1979); special F. issue, *TuK*, No. 64 (1979)

FRIEDHELM RICKERT

FLEMISH LITERATURE
See Belgian Literature

FO, Dario
Italian dramatist, b. 1926, San Giano

F.'s progressive political outlook was shaped by the socioeconomic status of his family—his fa-

ther was a railroad worker and his mother came from a peasant background—and by a vigorous tradition of working-class struggle in his native Lombardy. He was so determined in his convictions that while still very young he distinguished himself as a writer and actor of plays that expressed political commitment. Today he ranks as the leading militant Italian playwright.

F. first attracted the attention of the critics with *Il dito nell'occhio* (1953; a finger in the eye), a loosely structured harlequinade in which he combined the Marxist philosophy of Italy's young intellectual with gags, songs, and other theatrical devices reminiscent of the commedia dell'arte, the *avanspettacolo* (stage shows that used to be performed before movies until the end of World War II), and 19th-c. farce. Most of the works of his early period are one-act farces with complex comic plots full of twists and turns and unexpected reversals, mistaken identities, amorous triangles, family quarrels, and sexual equivocation.

F. spent a brief time as a film actor and set designer before returning to writing for the theater with a series of short plays that were produced in conjunction with La Compagnia Dario Fo–Franca Rame, a company he formed with the assistance of his wife. In the plays written and performed during this period, he increasingly clarified his political intent and directed himself toward specific targets. *La signora è da buttare* (1967; the lady is to be thrown away) remains the best play of this period. Written and staged at the moment when the war in Vietnam emerged as a motivation for mass mobilization and for a militant political campaign in Italy, the play criticizes American society as one manipulated by legalized crime and by prejudice, a society in which warmongering is a warranty of power.

Because of events of the 1960s, F. entirely rejected the principle of artistic creation as a marketable commodity in favor of a concept that views art as an instrument of social and political change. Consequently, he formed a noncommercial theater group and wrote plays for it that were not expressions of mere concern, but of militancy. The most original work of this period, *Mistero buffo* (1969; the comic mystery), consists of a number of monologues taken from medieval religious works and contemporary chronicles. The parts are linked by didactic commentaries to create a continuous dialectical exchange between past and present, culture and politics.

In 1970 F. dissociated himself from the

Communist leadership, whose criticism he had begun to attract because of his open attacks on the Party's bureaucracy and its failure to prepare the masses to face cultural and ideological responsibilities. From a dialectical theater, F. moved on to a rhetorical theater, to "collages" hurriedly constructed and staged in response to specific international, national, and local issues, such as the popular revolt in Chile in *Guerra di popolo in Cile* (1973; the people's war in Chile); the Palestinian question in *Fedayn* (1971; fedayeen); and the arrest of two supposedly innocent anarchists in *Morte accidentale di un anarchico* (1970; *Accidental Death of an Anarchist*, 1979). Moving as rapidly as the course of contemporary history, these last theatrical pieces depend upon improvisation and extensive revisions, with spectators becoming directly involved in the process before, during, and after every performance.

By bridging popular culture and radical thought, F. has established himself as a leading figure in the Italian theater of today.

FURTHER WORKS: *Morte e resurrezione di un pupazzo* (1972); *Ballate e canzoni* (1974); *Pum, pum! Chi è? La polizia* (1974); *Il Fanfani rapito* (1975); *Le commedie di D. F.* (5 vols., 1977)

BIBLIOGRAPHY: Sogliuzzo, A. R., "D. F.: Puppets for Proletarian Revolution," *TDR*, 16, 3 (1972), 71–77; Joly, J., "Le théâtre militant de D. F.," *Travail théâtral*, 14 (1974), 14–22; Cowan, S., "The Throw-Away Theatre of D. F.," *TDR*, 19, 2 (1975), 102–13; Cowan, S., "D. F., Politics and Satire: An Introduction to *Accidental Death of an Anarchist*," *Theater*, 10, 2 (1979), 7–11

MARIO B. MIGNONE

FOIX, J(osep) V(icenç)

Spanish poet, essayist, journalist, and critic (writing in Catalan), b. 31 Jan. 1893, Sarrià

F. came from a middle-class family. After graduating from high school, he entered law school, but left after a year. He then worked in the family pastry business and soon became involved in literary and artistic circles. From 1911 to 1920 F. wrote a poetic diary, which he later used as a main source for a number of his major writings. From 1917 on, he contributed to various influential Catalan periodicals.

F., who received the Honor Prize of Catalan Letters of 1973, is, together with Josep Carner (1884–1970) and Carles Riba (q.v.), considered one of the best of the "old guard" Catalan poets. He is the surrealist (q.v.)—or more precisely, superrealist—poet par excellence of Catalonia. (Whatever the difference between the two designations might be, the term "superrealist" is often used because of his marked leanings toward dreams and the subconscious.) *Desa aquests llibres al calaix de baix* (1964; store those books in the bottom drawer) brings together miscellaneous writings of the period 1921–31; the collection shows F.'s experiments with superrealist automatic writing.

F.'s first published book, *Gertrudis* (1927; Gertrudis), began a connected cycle of poetic prose collections, some of which were written much later. These poetic fragments, linked by the figure of Gertrudis (invented by F.), constitute a magnificent suite of visual images, distorted perceptions of reality. The alienated speaker ultimately destroys Gertrudis.

In *KRTU* (1932; KRTU), also a succession of visionary images, the solitude of the poet-speaker is set against a background of seascapes and cityscapes. The fragments of *Del "Diari 1918"* (1956; from the 1918 diary) approach a true narrative. In *L'estrella d'En Perris* (1963; Perris's star) the isolated poet witnesses mysterious miracles and enchantments taking place in unreal landscapes; Venus, the reassuring guiding star, functions as a kind of reality amid his uncertain, eerie adventures. The inspired surrealistic and nightmarish fragments of *Darrer comunicat* (1970; last communiqué) have political overtones. Basic in *Tocant a mà* (1972; within reach), which teems with dreamlike fantasies, is the mysterious magic wall separating the poet from discovery, from the source of his creative power.

Sol i de dol (1936; alone and mourning), chronologically F.'s third book, was the first of the category of poetry proper. Its seventy sonnets are inspired by Catalan and Italian classics. Here the search for self gives way to a general human yearning to fathom the meaning of existence and to transcend the limits of time.

Les irreals omegues (1951; the unreal omegas), F.'s most complex book, includes long free-verse poems using the decasyllabic line. In *On he deixat les claus . . . ?* (1953; where have I left the keys . . .?) he again explores the theme of personal reality and the concomitant alienation from exterior reality. Keys symbolize the poet's identity. *Onze Nadals i un Cap d'Any* (1960; eleven Christmas poems and one for the New Year) is a magnificently stylized reworking of traditional Catalan Christmas poetry.

F.'s essayistic prose—on art, politics, and other subjects—at its best displays a verbal skill unsurpassed in Catalan. And F. the poet's need to experiment brings him directly to one of the central issues of modern art: to rediscover its own essence while probing the meaning of existence. He may be eccentric at times, but his sensitivity and creative power make him one of the leading contributors to the literature of modern Spain.

FURTHER WORKS: *Revolució catalanista* (1934); *Cópia d'una lletra tramesa a Na Madrona Puignau, de Palau ça Verdera* (1951); *Plant d'En Josep-Vicenç* (1957); *Lletra a En Joan Papasseit, i d'altres texts* (1963); *Quatre nus* (1964); *Obres poètiques* (1964); *Escenificació de cinc poemes* (1965); *Catalans de 1918* (1965); *Els lloms transparents* (1965); *La pell de la pell* (1970); *Allò que no diu "La Vanguardia"* (1970); *Mots i maons o a cuascú el seu* (1971); *Els amants* (1973); *J. V. F. en els seus millors escrits* (1973); *Tres cents aforismes sobre les figuracions poncianes* (1974); *Obres completes,* Vol. I (1974)

BIBLIOGRAPHY: Terry, A., "Sobre les *Obres poètiques* de J. V. F.," *Serra d'or,* May 1968, 47–52; Badosa, E., Preface to *Antología de J. V. F.* (1969), pp. 9–44; Teixidor, J., et al., "En el 80 aniversario de J. V. F.," *Destino,* 27 Jan. 1973, 21–25; Manent, A., et al., "J. V. F.," *Serra d'or,* Jan. 1973, 20–51; Boehne, P. J., *J. V. F.* (1980)

ALBERT M. FORCADAS

FON LITERATURE
See Beninian Literature

FORD, Ford Madox
(until 1919 Ford Madox Hueffer) English novelist, critic, editor, and poet, b. 17 Dec. 1873, Merton; d. 26 June 1939, Deauville, France

Family background encouraged in F. a cosmopolitan outlook and artistic interests. His grandfather was the Pre-Raphaelite painter Ford Madox Brown, his uncle William Michael Rossetti. Their circle—including Dante Gabriel and Christina Rossetti, Algernon Swinburne, Edward Burne-Jones, and William Morris—formed part of the literary-artistic milieu in which F. grew up, an environment outside the mainstream of English culture. His father, Francis Hueffer, music critic for *The Times,*

was a German émigré; partly because of family connections in Germany and France, F. traveled on the Continent several times as a youth. Eventually he was to live for long periods abroad.

Gravitating toward the vocation of a writer, F. fell under the influence of Henry James (q.v.), then for several years was the close friend of Joseph Conrad (q.v.), with whom he collaborated on two novels. In 1908 he founded *The English Review,* the most important literary magazine of the period, which counted established writers like H. G. Wells, John Galsworthy (qq.v.), and Conrad among its contributors as well as publishing bright new talents like D. H. Lawrence, Wyndham Lewis (qq.v.), and Norman Douglas (1868–1952).

In 1915, at the age of forty-two, F. obtained a commission in the infantry and was sent to France. His military experience adversely affected his view of the English establishment and convinced him that the war had occasioned undesirable cultural changes. Attempting to pick up the emotional and financial pieces of his interrupted life, he spent several years as a cottage farmer in Sussex. Then, after a short stay in the south of France, F. moved with his family to Paris. At this time he changed his surname, in part because the German name had caused him annoyance during the war years, in part because the difficulty associated with his foreign name seemed a liability in selling his work. His founding in 1924 of *transatlantic review,* which published Hemingway, Joyce, Cocteau (qq.v.), and writers of similar stature, put him back in the center of the avant-garde literary community. From 1924 until 1930 F.'s career flourished, relatively speaking, due largely to the publication of the four novels making up the *Parade's End* tetralogy (1924–28).

The last decade of F.'s life was divided mainly between the U.S. (where he exerted considerable influence on Southern writers such as Allen Tate, Caroline Gordon, Robert Penn Warren, and Eudora Welty [qq.v.]) and southern France. In 1937–38 he was visiting lecturer in literature at Olivet College in Michigan. Although his books continued to appear, they sold poorly, and his financial circumstances during these last years were precarious.

F. was a prolific writer. His more than seventy books are characterized by great variety: they include fairy tales, novels, poetry, biography, art and literary criticism, sociological impressionism, propaganda, history, and reminiscence. The breadth of his oeuvre, together with his activity as an editor, compels us to regard him as a complete man of letters. Indeed, he seemed largely unconcerned about the fate of his books individually, while wishing to regard his cumulative activity as a contribution to the advancement of literature.

F.'s poetry reflects his evolving critical standards. His first five volumes were filled with casually written emotional verse derivative of 19th-c. nature poetry. But influenced by French prose writers like Stendhal and Flaubert and stimulated by talks with Ezra Pound (q.v.), he gradually became convinced that less restricted rhythms and more precise language would vitalize poetry by bringing it closer to real experience. F.'s "On Heaven" (1918), which compares heaven to a lover's meeting at a small café in Provence, illustrates his methods as well as his philosophy. Between 1908 and 1914, his ideas were adopted by the imagist (q.v.) poets, including F. S. Flint (1885–1960), Hilda Doolittle (q.v.), Richard Aldington (1892–1962), and Pound, and his imagistic poems were praised by Pound and T. S. Eliot (q.v.).

It is generally agreed that F.'s finest literary achievements were made as a novelist. Yet this assessment must be qualified, for of the thirty novels he wrote between 1892 and 1936, some were tossed off casually, and while numerous others reveal talent and competence, including historical romances such as *Ladies Whose Bright Eyes* (1911), *The Young Lovell* (1913), and the Katherine Howard trilogy (*The Fifth Queen* [1906], *Privy Seal* [1907], *The Fifth Queen Crowned* [1908]), only *The Good Soldier* (1915) and the *Parade's End* tetralogy (*Some Do Not* [1924], *No More Parades* [1925], *A Man Could Stand Up* [1926], *The Last Post* [1928]) are regarded as major contributions to the genre.

F.'s novels include historical romances, farces, comedies of manners, and studies of contemporary political and social life. But in spite of their great diversity, they are broadly linked by a dilemma common to their protagonists: an inability or refusal to come to terms with the society in which they live. Usually these protagonists espouse values from an earlier time, and thus are in conflict with their age. Often they are creatures of honor—compassionate, altruistic, self-effacing, instinctively responsible to their class or nation, exemplary in their contemporary wrongheadedness. Notwithstanding his sympathy toward them, F. shows the quixotic side of this stance and the harm it can cause. Underlying these situations is F.'s concern with the evolution of social forces and values.

In the dedicatory letter that introduces *The Good Soldier,* F. wrote that his previous novels, produced desultorily, were more or less pastiches, that not until *The Good Soldier* had he tried to put into a novel "all I knew about writing." His mature novelistic credo, which he detailed in *Joseph Conrad: A Personal Remembrance* (1924), had been forged gradually with particular debts to Continental writers like Flaubert, Maupassant, and Turgenev. They convinced him that style and technique were crucially important in artistic fiction, that the author must suppress himself and strive for objective, impartial realism, that the surface of experience should be rendered as a "succession of tiny unobservable surprises" through selection of *le mot juste.* To Henry James, F. owed a preoccupation with the technical manipulation of point of view, and commitment to dramatization. Of particular importance were the ideas F. had hammered out with Conrad. Straightforward chronological narration was to be rejected in favor of a more complicated but more lifelike "impressionistic" rendering of events. They believed that indirect, interrupted methods of telling are "invaluable for giving a sense of the complexity, the tantilisation, the shimmering, the haze, that life is." To accomplish this, they relied heavily on juxtaposition of event, image, scene, especially through impressionistic time shifts.

Embodying these principles, *The Good Soldier* is a dazzling display of craftsmanship; it is also—on a limited scale—a penetrating examination of Edwardian social morality and values. It deals with two couples who winter yearly at the same German spa, a microcosm of upper-class society. The action centers on the Englishman Ashburnham, a retired officer of solid public character who is privately a sentimental philanderer. When after a series of shallow infatuations he falls tragically in love with his young ward, each member of the foursome is revealed through his or her response to the progression of events.

Although the materials of the story are potentially lurid—adultery and suicide—F. does not exploit them as melodrama. Rather, he tells the story through Dowell, the rich American, whose involved impressionistic account is a pathetic attempt to find some meaning in these complex and disillusioning relationships. The seeming artlessness of Dowell's associative presentation of details has been contrived by F. to emphasize psychological complexity and to effect the most telling juxtaposition of major characters and their values. Meanwhile, the reader's curiosity is piqued by the gradual process of disclosing relevant information, a process that requires the reader to sort out chronological relationships. Marked by controlled comic irony, *The Good Soldier* has been called (originally by F.'s friend, John Rodker) the "finest French novel in the English language."

F.'s persistent concern with the techniques of fiction has received much critical attention; less well understood is his strong conviction that the novelist should be a historian of social forces and cultural shifts, informing and reshaping public attitudes by examining his age against the values of the past. In the *Parade's End* tetralogy F. brought this conception of the novelist's role to an impressive level of realization. The events recounted relate not merely to the fortunes of particular characters; they are interwoven with and symptomatic of the decline of the ruling class and its values—leisure, culture, responsibility, order, tradition—a breakup hastened by the Great War. Technically no less adroit than *The Good Soldier, Parade's End* presents a far broader picture of an age and reveals more powerfully the complexity of F.'s moral vision. Like Thackeray's *Vanity Fair*, with which it has been compared, it is filled with vivid characters whose social and moral behavior is penetratingly delineated in the context of a great historical and cultural watershed, but F.'s use of impressionistic techniques adds a dimension of psychological subtlety and realism not found in Thackeray.

Christopher Tietjens, the central character, is the quintessential F. hero. A paradoxical combination of disengagement and practicality, he is at once an 18th-c. Tory squire, a 20th-c. infantry captain, and a 17th-c. poet and saint. Tormented by an unfaithful wife, betrayed by friends, undermined professionally and socially, Tietjens is vulnerable to abuse because of his high-principled sense of noblesse oblige. Yet he manages to remain on an even keel amid social and moral confusion, imperturbable even in the chaos of trench warfare. He embodies the paradoxes of a good man trying to remain sane when so much conspires against decency and honor.

F. was a sensitive critic of literature, although anything but academic. His randomly dispersed critical statements, usually impressionistic in form, do insist that literature (and the arts) be assessed by intelligible standards. The principles of fiction which he advocated, mentioned earlier, have been widely influential. F. published volumes such as *The Critical Attitude* (1911), *Henry James: A Critical Study* (1914), and *The English Novel* (1929), but more important, his critical sense pervaded his

whole effort as a man of letters. It provided a foundation for the best of his own fiction and verse; it was vitally important to his achievement as an editor. This integration of criticism in his literary activity unquestionably extended his influence.

An account of F.'s contribution to letters must acknowledge his role as instigator and fostering spirit in the literary community. Like his friend Ezra Pound, he was not only a shrewd judge of talent but also by temperament inclined to provide encouragement and assistance to struggling writers. In numerous ways he helped create a social and critical climate among writers that he hoped would be conducive to cooperation. The two literary magazines he founded and edited served especially to advance promising new writers and to champion innovation not encouraged by the conservative establishment.

F.'s books of reminiscence, such as *Ancient Lights* (1911), which describes his growing up among the Victorian greats in his grandfather's household, *Joseph Conrad: A Personal Remembrance,* and *It Was the Nightingale* (1933), provide an informal view of great and not so great writers by an insider in the literary community. Impressionistically written, these books reveal F.'s engaging humor, his eye for detail, and his ability to render vividly the essence of incident and character. He was a great talker, and this form allowed him room to "talk" on paper. Yet he learned to unify the loosely related materials of such books around a central theme. His reminiscences are frequently inaccurate as to facts, as F. admitted, but he insisted that impressionistically they were absolutely true.

F.'s life and career were marked by paradoxes. He was a writer who never won widespread popular or even critical approval, although he exerted considerable influence on a number of important literary artists. It is frequently said of him that he was "a writer's writer": Graham Greene, William Carlos Williams, W. H. Auden (qq.v.), Allen Tate, and Caroline Gordon, among others, have praised his work. Oddly, he has been more appreciated in the U.S. than in his own country.

Easygoing and somewhat undisciplined in his character, he nevertheless produced a daily flow of prose and verse. Perhaps his greatest problem as a writer was that his facility with words led him to write too easily, too casually, and finally too much. As a consequence, the bulk of his work is uneven. Seldom did he demand fully of himself the discipline and restraint he advocated and which at his best he achieved.

Although *The English Review* and *transatlantic review* exposed F.'s limitations as a business manager and were short-lived, he was according to Graham Greene, the "best literary editor England has ever had." While he wrote few novels of major importance, his contribution to the theory of the novel puts him squarely in the important genealogy that leads from Flaubert through James and Conrad. He was a transitional artist, with a foot in both the 19th and 20th cs. A modernist in form, with his conservative values he seemed born a century —or two or three—too late.

FURTHER WORKS: *The Brown Owl* (1891); *The Feather* (1892); *The Shifting of the Fire* (1892); *The Questions at the Well* (1893, pseud. "Fenil Haig"); *The Queen Who Flew* (1894); *Ford Madox Brown* (1896); *Poems for Pictures* (1900); *The Cinque Ports* (1900); *The Inheritors* (1901, with Joseph Conrad); *Rossetti* (1902); *Romance* (1903, with Joseph Conrad); *The Face of the Night* (1904); *The Benefactor* (1905); *Hans Holbein the Younger* (1905); *The Soul of London* (1905); *Christina's Fairy Book* (1906); *The Heart of the Country* (1906); *An English Girl* (1907); *From Inland* (1907); *The Spirit of the People* (1907); *The Pre-Raphaelite Brotherhood* (1907); *Mr. Apollo* (1908); *The "Half Moon"* (1909); *A Call* (1910); *The Portrait* (1910); *Songs from London* (1910); *The Simple Life Limited* (1911, pseud. "Daniel Chaucer"); *High Germany* (1912); *The New Humpty-Dumpty* (1912, pseud. "Daniel Chaucer"); *The Panel* (1912); *The Desirable Alien* (1913, with Violet Hunt); *Mr. Fleight* (1913); *Collected Poems* (1913); *Antwerp* (1915); *When Blood Is Their Argument* (1915); *Between St. Dennis and St. George* (1915); *Zeppelin Nights* (1915, with Violet Hunt); *The Trail of the Barbarians* (1917); *A House* (1921); *Thus to Revisit* (1921); *The Marsden Case* (1923); *Women and Men* (1923); *Mister Bosphorous and the Muses* (1923); *The Nature of a Crime* (1924); *A Mirror to France* (1926); *New Poems* (1927); *New York Essays* (1927); *New York Is Not America* (1927); *A Little Less Than Gods* (1928); *No Enemy* (1929); *When the Wicked Man* (1931); *Return to Yesterday* (1931); *The Rash Act* (1933); *Henry for Hugh* (1934); *Provence* (1935); *Vive le Roy* (1936); *Collected Poems* (1936); *The Great Trade Route* (1937); *Mightier Than the Sword* (1938; Am., *Portraits from Life*); *The March of Literature* (1938); *The Bodley Head F. M. F.* (1962)

BIBLIOGRAPHY: Hunt, V., *I Have This to Say* (1926); Bowen, S., *Drawn from Life* (1941); *New Directions: Number Seven* (1942); Goldring, D., *South Lodge: Reminiscences of Violet Hunt, F. M. F. and the English Review Circle* (1942); Cassell, R. A., *F. M. F.: A Study of His Novels* (1961); Meixner, J. A., *F. M. F.'s Novels: A Critical Study* (1961); Wiley, P. L, *Novelist of Three Worlds: F. M. F.* (1962); special F. issue, *MFS*, 9, 1 (1963); Gordon, C., *A Good Soldier: A Key to the Novels of F. M. F.* (1963); Lid, R. W., *F. M. F.: The Essence of His Art* (1964); Ohmann, C., *F. M. F.: From Apprentice to Craftsman* (1964); MacShane, F., *The Life and Work of F. M. F.* (1965); special F. issue, *SR*, 74, 4 (1966); Hoffmann, C. G., *F. M. F.* (1967); Huntley, H. R., *The Alien Protagonist of F. M. F.* (1970); Mizener, A., *The Saddest Story: A Biography of F. M. F.* (1971); Stang, S. J., *F. M. F.* (1977); Stang, S. J., ed., *The Presence of F. M. F.: A Memorial Volume of Essays, Poems, and Memoirs* (1981); Moser, T. C., *The Life in Fiction of F. M. F.* (1981)

H. WAYNE SCHOW

When one finds Mr. F. M. F., the most able living novelist, devising a technique more complicated than Conrad's to disguise the same time-problem, one begins to wonder whether any novelist has found it possible to express the passage of time directly. . . . Mr. F.'s novels are novels of dramatic situations, situations of often wildly complicated irony. . . . Indeed the reviewers of the Sunday Press have frequently criticized Mr. F.'s method for what they consider its unnecessary complexity. They grant him vividness in his "big scenes"; they cannot understand that the vividness owes everything to the method. Mr. F. is unable to write narrative; he is conscious of his inability to write, as it were, along the line of time. How slipshod and perfunctory the joins between his dramatic scenes would seem if they were not put into the minds of the characters and their perfunctory nature "naturalized." The memory *is* perfunctory: you do not lose verisimilitude by such a bare record as this if you are looking back to events which have become history. . . . Mr. F. does not simply leave out; he puts in the links in his own good time, but they are properly subordinated to what he can do supremely well, dialogue and the dramatic scene.

Graham Greene, "The Dark Backward: A Footnote," *London Mercury*, Oct. 1935, 564–65

I call him Ford Madox Hueffer because that is the name he bore in the days of *The English Review*. He later changed his name to Ford Madox Ford; and under that name indefatigably continued to publish his oddly uneven work in considerable quantity and to give rise in the literary world to innumerable rumours. Hueffer is to me one of the enigmas of current literature. He had great talent, and much taste, to which he added considerable coarseness of spirit and a carelessness of statement which constantly spoil a reader's enjoyment of his work. He wrote much remarkable poetry, some historical romances which just missed being excellent, many novels on modern themes and situations which with much skill and passages beyond the reach of most living authors combined the coldness of the mortuary, criticism which for a paragraph here and there seems very like revealed truth and then drifts off into perversity, and memoirs of his own life and the lives of others which seem all the time to be boasting of his own unpleasantness.

He was editor of what was without doubt the most interesting periodical of our time, *The English Review*, in which were published . . . specimens of the work of almost all the established and arriving writers to 1908–11 (*The English Review* continued its work under another editor after the first glad Huefferian dawn), and in which living literature for the first time in English history was treated as quite important and quite exciting—much more important and much more exciting than students of English literature could imagine, and even more exciting than the contests of politicians or sportsmen. Books such as *The Fifth Queen* and *The Good Soldier* should be familiar to every investigator of what has been written in this century.

Frank Swinnerton, *The Georgian Literary Scene* (1935), pp. 195–96

He has been called a writer's writer; he had a deep insight into the techniques of composition, and his views influenced men so widely separated by time and nature as Ezra Pound and Joseph Conrad, and, at the other end of his life Ernest Hemingway, Allen Tate and Robie Macaulay. But the solid and subtle construction of his best books makes them fresh and attractive also to the general reader when many better-known works by F.'s contemporaries begin to seem dated and stale. . . . Above all, F. makes us see. We are never in doubt as to where the characters are, where the light comes from, what they can see through the window, where at a critical moment their hands are, what lies beyond the door. Sometimes their very movements of joint or neck are noted. They are seen as though on a stage; it is interesting to note that at about this time James was telling himself in his notebooks that he should visualize the action of his novels as though it were taking place on a stage-set.

Kenneth Young, *F. M. F.* (1956), pp. 7, 24

Hueffer realized that he was not a gentleman, but it gave him no particular pleasure; there were too many gentlemen and too few writers. Professionals, this was what writing needed; James and Conrad (with whom Hueffer had worked) were both professionals, and Hueffer gave the valuable hint that they had not even been read properly yet. The status of the writer in England was summed up for Hueffer during the demobilization of the army after the war, when the last of the eighteen categories to be released contained: "Travelling salesmen, circus performers, all writers not regularly employed on newspapers, tramps, pedlars. . . ." And like Pound, and for much the same reasons (Hueffer added the reason that Regent Street had been pulled down) Hueffer finally left London for Paris. The opening world had opened and closed again.

Hueffer's work both as novelist and critic still goes unrecognized, here if not in America, and this is a pity. The comments made above on the serious nature of Hueffer's critical concerns should suggest why at least some of his novels are interesting, not only for their great technical interest and skill, their sense of "form," and rendering, but also, to put it briefly, for their sense both of the constructive and destructive nature of a society so concerned with manners at a time when those manners are breaking up and throwing the individual upon his resources. In America his reputation has risen and the Tietjens novels have been reissued there.

Certainly he should serve as a model for editors of literary periodicals; his respect for the artist, the creative being, and his determination to nourish genius made him an invaluable figure.

Malcolm Bradbury, *"The English Review,"* London Magazine, Aug. 1958, 56–57

Parade's End has never yet been a popular success and few critics, I believe, have paid much attention to it. This neglect passes my comprehension. Of the various demands one can make of a novelist, that he show us the way in which a society works, that he show an understanding of the human heart, that he create characters in whose reality we believe and for whose fate we care, that he describe things and people so that we feel their physical presence, that he illuminate our moral consciousness, that he make us laugh and cry, that he delight us by his craftsmanship, there is not one, it seems to me, that F. does not completely satisfy. There are not many English novels which deserve to be called great: *Parade's End* is one of them.

W. H. Auden, "Il Faut Payer," *Mid-Century*, No. 22 (1961), 10

F.'s glory and mastery are in two or three of his novels. . . . He himself wrote poetry with his left hand—casually and even contemptuously. He gives sound and intense advice to a beginning poet: "Forget about Piers Plowman, forget about Shakespeare, Keats, Yeats, Morris, the English Bible, and remember only that you live in our terrific, untidy, indifferent empirical age, where not a single problem is solved and not a single Accepted Idea from the poet has any more magic. . . ." Yet he himself as a poet was incurably of the nineteenth century he detested, and to the end had an incurable love for some of its most irritating and overpoetic conventions. . . .

F. had no gift like Yeats for combining a conversational prose idiom with the grand style. I think he must often have felt the mortification of seeing the shining abundance of his novels dwindle away in his poetry to something tame, absentminded, and cautious. He must have found it hard to get rid of his jingling, hard to charge his lines, hard to find true subjects, and harder still to stick to them when found. Even such an original and personal poem as "On Heaven" is forever being beguiled from the road. Yet a magnificence and an Albigensian brightness hover over these rambling steps: F. and Pound were companions on the great road from twelfth-century Toulouse to twentieth-century London.

Buckshee is F., the poet, at his best. It too is uneven and rambling—uneven, rambling, intimate, and wonderful. . . . *Buckshee* coughs and blunders a bit in getting off, but in "Champetre," "Temps de Secheresse," and "Coda," F. finds the unpredictable waver of his true inspiration. In these reveries, he has at last managed to work his speaking voice, and something more than his speaking voice, into poems—the inner voice of the tireless old man, the old master still in harness, confiding, tolerant, Bohemian, newly married, and in France.

Robert Lowell, Foreword to F. M. F., *Buckshee* (1966), pp. xii–xv

FORSSELL, Lars
Swedish poet, dramatist, and critic, b. 14 Jan. 1928, Stockholm

F. was born into an upper-middle-class family. As a young man he lived and studied in the U.S. and France, experiences that did much to shape his literary tastes and preferences. His study of English evoked an admiration for Anglo-Saxon poetry, and in France he cultivated a love for the theater and cabaret entertainment. Although it was primarily for his poetry that F. was elected to the Swedish Academy in 1971, he has earned distinction writing plays, popular songs, film scripts, and essays on politics, art, literature, films, and sports.

F.'s second volume of poetry, *Narren* (1952;

the fool), established him as the master of lyric poetry of his generation. Equally adept at rhythmic, regular verse and irregular conversational verse, F. has shown a sensitive feel for blending expressively such contrasting elements and themes as tenderness, prankish humor, and existential fear.

In subsequent collections—*Telegram* (1957; telegram), *En kärleksdikt* (1960; a love poem), and *Röster* (1964; voice)—F. moved away from his earlier elaborate style, heavy with classical allusions, toward simplicity of form, improvisatory effects, and colloquial diction. The virtuoso precision of these volumes led one critic to call him a "sniper with words."

In the middle and late 1960s, a growing political consciousness in F.'s works made him one of the most controversial public figures in Sweden. Some of his critics see a conflict between his socialist sympathies and his failure to repudiate his upper-middle-class background. To charges that he is naïve in matters of ideology, he has replied that one has a duty to betray ideology in times when ideology has so consistently betrayed mankind.

Despite his reputation as a poet, F. thinks of himself primarily as a dramatist, and since 1953 more than a dozen of his plays have been performed in Sweden, Denmark, Norway, West Germany, England, Scotland, Ireland, and the U.S. In fact, his first collection of poetry, *Ryttaren* (1949; the equestrain), contained a short commedia dell'arte-style play on the theme of fear and death, *Narren som tillhörde sina bjällror* (the fool attached to his bells).

Like his early verse, F.'s first full-length play, *Kröningen* (1956; *The Coronation*, 1963), is on a classical theme: Euripides' Admetus is transformed into an absurd antihero, unable to deal with the demands of either life or death.

Antiheroes are also the central characters of F.'s next three plays. *Charlie McDeath* (1961; *Charlie McDeath*, 1965–66), a play in one act, is about a ventriloquist who exchanges places with his dummy. *Mary Lou* (1962; Mary Lou) is a long one-acter about an American female traitor who broadcasts for Hitler and lures a GI to his death. The antihero in the thoughtful comedy *Söndagspromenaden* (1963; *The Sunday Promenade*, 1968) is Justus Coriander, a fantast who tries to escape the bonds and demands of reality by leading his family off to imaginary places on weekly picnic strolls around their dining-room table. Set in turn-of-the-century Sweden, *Söndagspromenaden* is F.'s best-represented play in foreign productions.

Political themes are important in F.'s later

plays. *Galenpannan* (1964; *The Madcap*, 1973) and *Christina Alexandra* (1968; Christina Alexandra) have as their central characters the Swedish monarchs King Gustavus IV (1778–1837) and Queen Christina (1626–1689), respectively. Each protagonist tries unsuccessfully to assert personal moral values in a world corrupted by power politics.

Show (1971; show), staged in a distinguished production by Ingmar Bergman, is another drama about a social and political outsider, a Lenny Bruce-like entertainer who offends radicals and conservatives alike.

Haren och vråken (1978; the hare and the buzzard), a popular play throughout Scandinavia in the late 1970s, is an adaptation of Lope de Vega's (1562–1635) *Fuente ovejuna,* relocated to Stockholm in the revolutionary period on the eve of the assassination at a masked ball of King Gustavus III (1746–1792).

F.'s eminence as a poet-commentator is due in part to the ease and authority with which he moves through an astonishing range of genres —from passionate, lyrical poetry to stinging satirical songs to crisp, acerbic journalism—and in part to his ability to involve his audience in an intensely personal experience by confessing the world's fear, cruelty, and loneliness as his own.

FURTHER WORKS: *25 dikter* (trans. of Ezra Pound poems, 1953); *Chaplin* (1953); *F. C. Tietjens* (1954); *Cattus* (1955); *Snurra min jord* (1958); *Cantos I–XVII* (translation of Ezra Pound cantos, 1959); *Don Quixotes drömmar: Dikter 1949–1959* (1960); *Prototyper* (1961); *Torsten Andersson* (1963); *Det enda vi har är varandra: Dikter i urval* (1964); *Jack Uppskäraren och andra visor tryckta i år* (1966); *Samtal vid Ganges* (1967); *Upptåg: Flickan i Montréal, Drömmar i Omsk, Borgerlighetens fars* (1967); *Ändå* (1968); *Nedslag* (1969); *Borgaren och Marx* (1970); *Solen lyser på havet blå: Barnvisor* (1971); *Sigfrid Siwertz* (1971); *Oktoberdikter* (1971); *Försök* (1972); *Det möjliga* (1974); *Dikter (Den svenska lyriken)* (1975); *En bok för alla människor* (1975); *De rika* (1976); *Teater* (2 vols., 1977); *Jag står här på ett torg* (1979); *Stenar* (1980); *Brokigheten* (1980)

BIBLIOGRAPHY: Carlson, H. G., "The Anti-Hero in the Plays of L. F.," *Players,* 40, 2 (1963), 38–40; Carlson, H. G., "L. F.—Poet in the Theater," *SS,* 37 (1965), 31–57

HARRY G. CARLSON

FORSTER, E(dward) M(organ)
English novelist, essayist, and critic, b. 1 Jan. 1879, London; d. 17 June 1970, Coventry

F.'s architect father died when he was a baby and he was raised by his mother, grandmother, and paternal great-aunt Marianne Thornton, descendant of the Clapham Sect of evangelists and reformers, whose legacy later gave him the freedom to travel and to write. F. read at age four, composed stories at five, educated the maids at six; but, self-possessed in intellectual matters, he was delicate in constitution and sensitive to teasing. A lost lease to the family's country home occasioned F.'s move to Tonbridge ("Sawston" in the novels), where he experienced great unhappiness as a day student at the private school. F. found a new home at King's College, Cambridge, which he entered in 1897 with vague thoughts of becoming a schoolmaster. In the atmosphere of Cambridge skepticism (this was the era of Sir James Frazer [1854–1941] and *The Golden Bough* [1890]), and under the influence of his dons— especially the fiercely antiauthoritarian Nathaniel Wedd (1862–1940) and the philosophical Goldsworthy Lowes Dickinson (1862–1932) —F. shed his not very deep Christian faith and adopted in its stead a creed of personal relationships and appreciation of the arts. This creed, deriving from the philosophy of G. E. Moore (1873–1958), was reinforced by F.'s like-minded friends in the Society of Apostles and his later associates in the Bloomsbury group.

After completing his studies in the classics, F. struck out for Italy and Greece; there, his imagination stimulated, he decided to be a writer by profession. He interspersed work on his fiction with lecturing, tutoring, and editing; with contributions to the new liberal monthly *The Independent Review;* and with what became a twenty-year stint at the Working Men's College in London. F.'s tutoring of an Indian student led, in 1912, to his first "passage to India." Although F. had already published four novels in five years, he now became so haunted by his homosexual tendencies that he was able to produce only several unpublishable erotic stories (which he later destroyed) and the posthumously published novel *Maurice* (1971). During World War I, F. temporarily abandoned fiction and spent three years in Egypt with the Red Cross. After the war, a second trip to India as private secretary to the Maharajah of Dewas resulted in F.'s final completed novel: from 1924 until his death almost a half century later, he published no further major fiction. F. was well known for his defense of civil liberties in journals, on international councils, at obscenity trials, and over the airwaves, and was made a lifetime Honorary Fellow at Cambridge in 1946.

F.'s fictional works are moral guidebooks that juxtapose classes or cultures in order to enlarge perspective and achieve liberation from rigid social and national distinctions. In many of the short stories collected in *The Celestial Omnibus* (1911), *The Eternal Moment* (1928), *Collected Short Stories* (1947), and the posthumous *The Life to Come, and Other Stories* (1972), a pedant, aesthete, or snob meets a primitive, earthy, often lower-class individual. The crisis in these stories (most of them fantasies) comes at the moment a choice must be made between accepting the pagan, "foreign" element and thereby transfiguring one's existence or retreating into customary, stultifying modes of behavior.

These motifs figure more successfully in F.'s novels. *Where Angels Fear to Tread* (1905) revolves about the attempts of an Englishwoman's family at rescuing her from her marriage to an Italian and then, after her death in childbirth, at stealing her baby from its father. But it is the main character, Philip Herriton, who needs rescuing: from his snobbery and provincialism as well as from his resistance to active involvement in life. The novel contrasts the Sawston view of Italy, with its Authorized Sights, to the true vision that comes only off the beaten track, without the Baedeker. The guide to this vision is the baby's father, Gino Carrella, who offers Philip brotherhood and hence salvation. F. does not glorify Gino, nor does he gloss over the social and cultural impediments to a relationship. Nevertheless, F.'s sympathies clearly lie with instinct over etiquette, with native wisdom over acquired culture. Although Philip Herriton ultimately fails to connect, he at least has had a glimpse of the possibilities for heroic commitment to a less respectable but richer life.

The highly autobiographical *The Longest Journey* (1907) continues to ask the questions, What is our true home? What values should guide us? Contrasted homes and the values that they represent structure this tripartite book: Cambridge, Sawston, Wiltshire. The dedication to the novel is *Fratribus*, and the work hymns the brotherhood that F. knew with the Apostles; the problem for the main character, Rickie Elliot, as for Philip Herriton, lies in recognizing and acknowledging his true brother. Rickie, an

artist who writes of getting in touch with nature but cannot do so himself, is F.'s most ambitious portrait of the aesthete. He marries disastrously, in part because he wants a home to take the place of Cambridge, in part because he transforms his wife, as he had his mother before her, into an ideal of womanhood. The relationship that could save him from his wife's deathly Sawston mentality—smugness, materialism, orderliness, conventionality—is offered by Rickie's illegitimate half-brother, a Pan-like creature of the Wiltshire downs. But Rickie idealizes him, too, and therefore loses his chance at connection. Throughout, F. deals in ethical terms with G. E. Moore's refutation of Idealism. If facing reality is the test that Rickie Elliot takes and fails in this book about educational systems, the novel itself is realistic about the forces of darkness in 20th-c. society and optimistic about the possibilities for their defeat.

A Room with a View (1908) is F.'s second "Italian" novel and his sunniest: the Comic Muse presides, permitting no brutal fights or sudden deaths. The image of windows, important in the first two novels, receives primary emphasis here, as Lucy Honeychurch searches for her room with a view. Having lost her Baedeker and her very proper chaperone in Florence, Lucy finds new guides, the most notable being Mr. Emerson, whose original opinions throw open the windows on art and on love. His flouting of social, religious, and aesthetic conventions threatens the cultivated English society that F. targets here as elsewhere; and, after a few false "rescues" from Emerson's value system, and a few muddles (a favorite Forsterian word) that result from her lies and foolish proprieties, Lucy learns to trust her instincts for right and good. The forces of darkness are kept at bay in this novel by what F. believes to be the true marks of civilization: love and respect for otherness, open channels of communication (truth telling), and faith in humankind's inherent nobility.

F. examines the havoc that creeping urbanization and materialism wreak on the sense of connection to the land and people in such fiction as *The Longest Journey* and "The Machine Stops" (1909), his science-fiction rebuttal to H. G. Wells (q.v.). He explores the theme more fully in *Howards End* (1910), the work that established his reputation. In this novel about the making and valuing of money, and the substitution of the cash nexus for human bonds, the fate of the Wilcox country house symbolizes the direction that England will take. The marriage of Margaret Schlegel to a businessman, and Margaret's inheriting of Howards End, indicate F.'s belief that connection can be made between poetry and prose, between idealism and pragmatism, between England's past and her future. Margaret is the New Woman, Lucy Honeychurch one step down the road: outspoken, aggressive, and free, reconciling within herself the "masculine" and "feminine." The humanistic credo of the novel, "only connect," remains a wistful hope, its tentativeness underscored by the unconvincing love relationship between Margaret and her husband; by the extreme spirituality—indeed, the ghostliness—of the guide to action, Ruth Wilcox; and by the disturbingly lower-class characters hovering on the fringes. In response to his growing fear of disorder in the very fabric of life, F. triumphantly expresses order and control in this novel's complex system of leitmotifs and the determined lightness of its tone.

F.'s tone darkens considerably in *A Passage to India* (1924), which, unlike other contemporary works on the same subject, is highly critical of British imperialism. Although it has been faulted for its many inaccurate details, partly attributable to the decade that elapsed between drafts of the novel, its basic truth about Anglo-Indian relations is undeniable. The petty proprieties of class and country that proved dangerous to individual growth in F.'s earlier fiction are here writ large, in the policies of one nation toward another. Even more, by suggesting nature's indifference or even hostility toward man, F. raises unsettling questions about the efficacy of the good will and personal relations that constitute his creed of liberal humanism.

F.'s novels move gradually into silence. In his most lighthearted novel, *A Room with a View*, F. had drawn on his personal experiences at Cambridge to write of good friends engaging in lively conversation about noble ideals; but in *Howards End* the formerly talkative and witty heroine becomes ever less inclined to speak. *A Passage to India*, F.'s final novel, implies that human intercourse may be impossible and language in vain: the echo in the Marabar Caves reduces all sounds to one meaningless noise; and in these caves a misunderstanding between two people of different sex, religion, class, and nation has grave ramifications for the whole notion of human compatibility. F.'s love for the natural and primitive—in landscape and the psyche—is tempered here by a feeling of incomprehension approaching (but stopping short of) despair. *A Passage to India* simultaneously

recognizes the limitations of the humanistic creed, insists that the creed must nevertheless operate if we are to make any social and political progress, and hints at mysteries, both marvelous and frightening, lying beyond rational understanding. Because of its grand themes and its artistic unity and complexity, this novel is commonly regarded as F.'s finest work.

In *Maurice* and several of the stories in *The Life to Come* (1972), the "primitive" element that confronts F.'s protagonists is homosexuality. *Maurice* is a comparative failure: self-indulgent and thin, without F.'s saving irony, it is of interest mainly as a picture of British attitudes not long after Wilde; as a partial explanation of F.'s inability to draw convincing heterosexual relationships in his fiction; and as one reason for his eventual abandonment of that fiction. The erotic stories, like F.'s short stories in general, are successful only when they combine gentleness of touch with seriousness of theme.

Much of F.'s nonfiction has proven to be lasting and influential. *Aspects of the Novel* (1927), originally presented as lectures at Cambridge, is an idiosyncratic and engaging discussion of the novel as art form. Its distinctions between story and plot, pattern and rhythm, and "flat" and "round" characters have become commonplaces in literary criticism, and the book is an invaluable guide to F.'s own novels. The collections of his essays, book reviews, and radio braodcasts—*Abinger Harvest* (1936) and *Two Cheers for Democracy* (1951)—are unified stylistically by F.'s detached yet sympathetic tone and thematically by his preoccupation with rescuing the English character, and all of modern society, from its "Sawston" ways. In the second volume especially, F. speaks out against bullying institutions of any persuasion and for art as the only true ordering principle.

The Forsterian voice ensures F.'s place in literary history: at once casual and contentious, soft and strong, it argues without pomposity. In his reverence for instinct and nature, F. is a romantic; in his moralistic attention to man in society, a Victorian; in his skepticism, detachment, and reverence for art, a modern. F.'s beliefs are philosophic, not programmatic, and his "impracticality" has come to be valued as a testament to freedom from narrow systems. Although the fiction occasionally suffers from melodramatic plots, sentimentalized characters, archness of tone, and moralistic heavy-handedness, its strengths are numerous and their combination unique: a conversational, often playful style; the ability to surprise; the puncturing of cant and hypocrisy; a this-world spirituality; and a meticulous attention to craftsmanship.

FURTHER WORKS: *The Government of Egypt* (1920); *Alexandria: A History and a Guide* (1922); *Pharos and Pharillon* (1923); *Goldsworthy Lowes Dickinson* (1934); *Billy Budd* (1951; co-librettist for Britten's opera); *The Hill of Devi* (1953); *Marianne Thornton* (1956)

BIBLIOGRAPHY: McConkey, J., *The Novels of E. M. F.* (1957); Beer, J., *The Achievement of E. M. F.* (1962); Crews, F., *E. M. F.: The Perils of Humanism* (1962); Gransden, K. W., *E. M. F.* (1962); Wilde, A., *Art and Order: A Study of E. M. F.* (1964); Natwar-Singh, K., ed., *E. M. F.: A Tribute* (1964); Stone, W., *The Cave and the Mountain: A Study of E. M. F.* (1966); Thomson, G., *The Fiction of E. M. F.* (1967); McDowell, F. P. W., *E. M. F.* (1969); Stallybrass, O., ed., *Aspects of E. M. F.* (1969); Parry, B., *Delusions and Discoveries: Studies on India in the British Imagination 1880–1930* (1972), pp. 260–320; Gardner, P., ed., *E. M. F.: The Critical Heritage* (1973); Colmer, J., *E. M. F.: The Personal Voice* (1975); Rosenbaum, S. P., *The Bloomsbury Group: A Collection of Memoirs, Commentary and Criticism* (1975), pp.24–26, 163–69, and passim; McDowell, F. P. W., *E. M. F.: An Annotated Bibliography of Writings about Him* (1976); Das, G. K., *E. M. F.'s India* (1977); Furbank, P. N., *E. M. F.: A Life* (1978); Das, G. K., and Beer, J., eds., *E. M. F.: A Human Exploration* (1979)

JUDITH RUDERMAN

No one seizes more deftly the shades and shadows of the social comedy; no one more amusingly hits off the comedy of luncheon and tea party and a game of tennis at the rectory. His old maids, his clergy, are the most lifelike we have had since Jane Austen laid down the pen. But he has into the bargain what Jane Austen had not—the impulses of a poet. . . . At certain moments on the Arno, in Hertfordshire, in Surrey, beauty leaps from the scabbard, the fire of truth flames through the crusted earth; we must see the red brick villa in the suburbs of London lit up. But it is in these great scenes which are the justification of the huge elaboration of the realistic novel that we are most aware of failure. For it is here that Mr. F. makes the change from realism to symbolism; here that the object which has been so uncompromisingly solid becomes, or should become, luminously transparent. He fails, one is tempted to think,

chiefly because that admirable gift of his for observation has served him too well. He has recorded too much and too literally. He has given us an almost photographic picture on one side of the page; on the other he asks us to see the same view transformed and radiant with eternal fires. . . . [I]nstead of seeing . . . one single whole we see two separate parts. [1927]

Virginia Woolf, in Philip Gardner, ed., *E. M. F.: The Critical Heritage* (1973), pp. 321–24

[T]here is a good deal of attention to plot in the novels: but it is evidently not aimed at creating the normal relationship between author and reader. An author whose main concern is to entertain his audience will sometimes surprise them—but he will also take care not to jar them. At the point of surprise, the reader will begin to recognize that preceding events contained the seeds of the surprise. F.'s surprises, on the other hand, do sometimes jar—particularly those irruptions of death or violence which break suddenly into a prevailing atmosphere of domestic comedy. On examining the context of such passages, indeed, one sometimes discovers that F. has been deliberately leading his readers in a different direction: that the irruption of violence has actually been preceded by a letting down of tension in the narrative. The result is that sudden death enters the novel with the jarring quality that it has in real life. The harmonic pattern within which we are comfortably established suddenly gives way. There is a moment of unreality which we then recognize to be in point of fact a moment of reality—but the reality of everyday life, not of art. Such intrusions of an unartistic "reality" should in themselves convince the reader that this is no ordinary storyteller.

John Beer, *The Achievement of E. M. F.* (1962), pp. 11–12

The opening line of *Howards End*—"One may as well begin with Helen's letter to her sister"—is a perfect example of what one of Christopher Isherwood's characters refers to as F.'s tea-tabling. The remark is so casual and understated, the tone so relaxed and personal; here we are, almost before we know it, in the complicated world of the Schlegels and the Wilcoxes. Or the beginning of "Anonymity: An Enquiry," . . .: "Do you like to know who's a book by?" Do we? How flattering it is to have our opinion asked . . . and here we are again, this time in F.'s own world, involved in the process of discovery, sharing the sense of intimacy it is F.'s particular gift to create. This is the voice with which F. has spoken out over several decades for the importance of the individual . . .; the voice also with which he has attacked, wherever he found them, the abuses of authority and the perils of what he has called, in describing the English, "the undeveloped heart." And we are tempted, in an age of propaganda and advertisement, to listen to someone who refuses to speak in loud and commanding tones, who is hesitant, cautious, acutely aware, even self-conscious, who is—like ourselves.

Alan Wilde, *Art and Order: A Study of E. M. F.* (1964), pp. 1–2

Though F. and [D. H.] Lawrence differ extremely in superficial ways, the kinship between them is profound. They are both prophetic vitalists, hating the machine civilization that has cut men off from their roots, and revering what Aldous Huxley (like F. one of the few Bloomsburians on Lawrence's side) has called "the dark presence of otherness that lies beyond man's conscious mind." Perhaps only Conrad, Hardy, and—at a stretch—Meredith could share with F. and Lawrence what we might call the vision of the cave, the encounter with the chthonic underworld of human experience. . . . [I]t's too easy to think of F. only as the liberal humanist and forget his prophetic vision, the voice that gave heat and light to his humanity. . . . Lawrence is a Stephen to F.'s Rickie, his half-brother, and the prophet of that same "forgotten wisdom" which F. evokes with his Pans and Italians, caves and echoes. Their social criticism, too, stems from the same discontent. And nothing more clearly demonstrates F.'s independence from Bloomsbury, or any party line, than his frank and honest championing of a misunderstood and undervalued author.

Wilfred Stone, *The Cave and the Mountain: A Study of E. M. F.* (1966), pp. 381, 386–87

The assertion that F.'s people are either saved or damned, are either capable or not capable of vision, is true. The implication that this attitude points to hardness of heart and a kind of arrogance is false. . . . We may note that when F. comes forward as social philosopher or commentator in his nonfictional writing his vision of a sheep-or-goat humanity is severely modified; he is well aware of the dangers of arrogance. But in his fiction the drastic separation of good and evil is essential to the romance tradition in which he works. . . . To complain that he is unjust to the Anglo-Indians, unfair to the Wilcoxes (in fact he tries too hard to give them their due), and overly obvious in the short stories is to condemn an essential characteristic of the romance tradition and to ignore the fact that the conventions taken over from realistic fiction are being used for other than realistic ends.

George Thomson, *The Fiction of E. M. F.* (1967), pp. 48–49

. . . E. M. F. is our most musical novelist. And I don't mean that he just likes music or likes going to concerts and operas, or plays the piano neatly and efficiently (all of which he does), but that he really understands music and uses music in his novels, and fairly frequently. The musical *locus classicus* is, of course, *Howards End* . . . where a number of characters are presented in a tiny musical vignette—each of them reacting in a different way to a performance of Beethoven's Fifth Symphony. . . . The whole remarkable passage shows a most sensitive reaction to music, and allows the novelist to make some perceptive observations on Beethoven. . . . [T]he construction of F.'s novels often resembles that of the "classical" opera (Mozart–Weber–Verdi) where recitatives (the deliberately un-lyrical passages by which the action is advanced) separate arias or ensembles (big, self-contained set pieces of high comedy or great emotional tension). As examples of the latter, think of the bathing episode in *A Room with a View*, the Sunday school dinner at which Ansell confronts Rickie in *The Longest Journey*, and, perhaps greatest of all, the trial in *A Passage to India*.

Benjamin Britten, "Some Notes on F. and Music," in Oliver Stallybrass, ed., *Aspects of E. M. F.* (1969), pp. 81–83

F. once told us that he belongs to "the fag-end of Victorian liberalism," and the phrase is often taken with complete literalism and applied against him. As a result his intellectual and his literary destiny has been too readily linked with that strange death of liberal England which historians have dated around 1914, when the equation of economic individualism with social progress lost political force. . . . In this century critics have increasingly accepted modernist norms for the judgement of literature, even though, of course, many of our writers have not been modernists in the strict sense. F. is a paradox here; he is, and he is not. There is in his work the appeal to art as transcendence, art as the one orderly product, a view that makes for modernism; and there is the view of art as a responsible power, a force for belief, a means of judgement, an impulse to spiritual control as well as spiritual curiosity. The point perhaps is that F. is not, in the conventional sense, a modernist, but rather a central figure of the transition into modernism. . . . He is, indeed, to a remarkable degree, the representative of two kinds of mind, two versions of literary possibility, and of the tensions of consciousness that exist between them.

Malcolm Bradbury, "Two Passages to India: F. as Victorian and Modern," in Oliver Stallybrass, ed., *Aspects of E. M. F.* (1969), pp. 124–25

FOWLES, John

English novelist, b. 31 March 1926, Leigh-on-Sea

F. attended an English public school, where he excelled both as scholar and athlete and eventually became head boy. "At the age of eighteen," he later confessed, "I had the power to judge and punish six hundred to eight hundred other boys, and this gave me a distaste for power that has grown and grown." A lieutenancy in the British marines not only confirmed this distaste, but turned him into "a sort of anarchist" and away from the Establishment path.

F.'s intellectual liberation, however, really began at Oxford. Here, reading philosophy and French, he was profoundly influenced by the writings of French existentialism (q.v.) and those of the pre-Socratic Greek philosopher Heraclitus. After receiving his degree in 1950, F. spent the next thirteen years teaching in France, Greece, and England, and writing novels.

The Collector (1963), the first novel F. submitted to a publisher, caused only a minor stir in England but became both a critical and popular success in America. Its filming, two years later, brought F. international fame.

While the plot of *The Collector*—that of an artistic girl being imprisoned and wasting away in the home of a dreary, mean-spirited clerk and amateur lepidopterist—was partially inspired by a newspaper account of the 1950s, its principal theme goes back some 2,500 years. More than a psychological thriller or a study in class conflict, *The Collector* is a parable of the tension between the Few (*áristoi*, the good ones and intellectual elite) and the Many (*hoi polloi*, the unthinking, conforming masses). The novel questions whether the Many (like Clegg, the collector), who now seem to dominate society, will allow the Few (Miranda Grey) to live, in F.'s words, "authentically"; or whether the many will suffocate them. By living authentically, F. means (as do the French existentialists) not succumbing to anxieties but overcoming them, not running away from life but engaging it. The novel ties up this theme with that of free will, for the authentic character is one who, after self-discovery and acceptance of the past, believes in free will and achieves it. Miranda, through these psychological processes, becomes the novel's existential heroine, although she never escapes from Clegg.

F. enumerates his existential theories in *The Aristos: A Self-Portrait in Ideas* (1964, rev. ed. 1968). Cast as "one side of a dialogue," these somewhat eccentric notations touch on myth, philosophy, aesthetics, psychology, and history to generalize about our "universal situation": that is, where and what are we? F.'s conclusion to *The Aristos*—"to accept limited freedom . . . one's isolation . . . responsibility . . . to learn one's particular powers, and then with them to humanize the whole"—became the text for his two following novels.

The first of these, *The Magus* (1965), concerns Nicholas Urfe, who, uncertain of who he is or what he wishes to be, takes a teaching post on a remote Greek island, only to be drawn into a strange quest. The magus of the title, Maurice Conchis, engineers elaborate scenarios, masques, and psychological experiments to confuse Urfe's sense of appearance and reality. Urfe is finally led to the moment when he must choose whether or not to become a responsible person. F.'s skilled interweaving of mythic and literary allusion, his symbolic use of the tarot cards, his many fine descriptions, his proper balance between realism and fantasy, and his incredible turns of plot, make the novel a brilliant technical achievement. F. published a considerably revised version of *The Magus* in 1977.

From the point of thematic and technical interplay, however, *The French Lieutenant's Woman* (1969) is the most fascinating of F.'s works. Set in the 1860s, it ostensibly parodies one of the large canvases of Thomas Hardy (q.v.) or George Eliot by incorporating authorial digressions, gratuitous turns of plot, sexual innuendo, and contradictions between morals and manners. On the surface the novel tells a banal story: the thwarted love of a genteel, intelligent "evolutionist," Charles Smithson, for Sarah Woodruff, a passionate and imaginative governess and bohemian whose affair with a French naval lieutenant has ostracized her from society. Yet this is all about the book that is banal. Because he is writing from a contemporary perspective, with all the devices of the modern novel at his command, F. is able to freely juggle time and space to create patterns of truth and ambiguity about Victorian life. Combining fiction, criticism, and history, F. manipulates anachronisms, sociological reports, factual footnotes, quotations from Darwin, Marx, and the great Victorian poets, so that past and present ideologies are deftly juxtaposed. Still obsessed with the problem of freedom and authenticity, for his characters as well as for the novelist, F. provides two traditional endings for the novel—endings of which any Victorian might have approved—and then supplies modern denouements, less conclusive but more realistic. In *The French Lieutenant's Woman*, F. captures the sensibilities of the past, as well as subtly telling us a great deal about our present.

F.'s "variations on themes" and his theme of "variation" are further displayed in his curious fourth book, *The Ebony Tower* (1974). Neither a collection of stories nor a novel, this work is a forest of five intertwining fictions, where the quest to define one's freedom and existence becomes entangled with the bolder question of whether the modern writer—having descended from the ivory tower and now residing in an ebony one—is capable any longer of making such quests meaningful. Once again, the book is about Art and Life, but F. has partially lopped off the capitals to make both seem, more graspable than they were in *The Magus* and *The French Lieutenant's Woman*, and certainly less hermetic, fantastic, gimmicky, and recondite.

F.'s place as one of the greatest of contemporary novelists was secured at last by *Daniel Martin* (1977), his most thoughtful and formidable novel to date, one that uses art to tell us everything F. knows of life. Indeed, Martin's life emerges as the challenging and dominant theme itself. Detained in England for an inquest after a friend's suicide, Martin is thrown together with people he has not seen for years, led to places he has hoped to avoid. Confronting these, he is also forced to face the past: his boyhood in Dorset; his university days; his sexual initiations and transgressions; his marriage and adulteries; his promise as a playwright and his "selling out" to Hollywood. No mere flashbacks, but considered images that impinge on Martin's mind so that he is able to make of them flashforwards, these events and memories become tiny but significant illuminations that guide him toward rectifying his mistakes, "reifying" the abstraction that has been Daniel Martin. Added to this masterful unfolding of character, and the humane revelation of what direction life must take for authenticity and freedom, are F.'s familiar excursions into a wealth of ideas, each of which has pertinence to modern existence, all of which taken together add layer upon layer to the composite that is the hero/narrator. By the end of the novel's six hundred pages, nothing less emerges than a full-blown portrait of fine, earnest, humanistic sensibilities struggling to make themselves whole in an age of complexity and confusion.

F.'s intent as a writer of fiction has always been to strike the sane balance between art and life, at a time when both seem vulnerable to excess, and neither seems susceptible to control. His fictional works, very different in texture and technique from each other—and one a supreme achievement—are all concerned with man's potential to discover and fulfill himself.

FURTHER WORKS: *Poems* (1973); *Cinderella* (1976); *Shipwreck* (1976); *Islands* (1979); *The Enigma of Stonehenge* (1980)

BIBLIOGRAPHY: Churchill, T., "Waterhouse, Storey and F.: Which Way Out of the Room," *Crit*, 10, 3 (1968), 72–87; Allen, W., "The Achievement of J. F.," *Encounter*, Aug. 1970, 64–67; Karl, F., "Two New Novelists," *A Reader's Guide to the Contemporary English Novel* (1972), pp. 355–60; Palmer, W. J., *The Fiction of J. F.* (1974); Wolfe, P. *J. F.: Magus and Moralist* (1976); Myers, K. M., "J. F.: An Annotated Bibliography, 1963–76," *BB*, 33 (1976), 162–69; Magalaner, M., "The Fool's Journey: J. F.'s *The Magus*," in Morris, R. K., ed., *Old Lines, New Forces: Essays on the Contemporary British Novel 1960–1970* (1976), pp. 81–92; McSweeney, K., "Withering into the Truth: J. F. and *Daniel Martin*," *CritQ*, 20, 4 (1978), 31–38; Huffaker, R., *J. F.* (1980)

ROBERT K. MORRIS

FRAME, Janet

New Zealand novelist, short-story writer, and poet, b. 23 Aug. 1924, Dunedin

F. was brought up in a provincial society, that of Otago, a province in the south of New Zealand. Her family was poor and lived on the outskirts of Oamaru; this small town became the "Waimaru" of her novel *Owls Do Cry* (1957), which contains many autobiographical elements. In the 1940s she studied at the University of Otago in Dunedin. One critic, R. T. Robertson, has remarked that "the cultural milieu of New Zealand obeys what Northrop Frye has called Emerson's law, namely, that in a provincial society it is extremely easy to reach the highest level in cultivation, extremely difficult to take one step beyond that." It was F.'s attempt to take that step that led to the crises in her life between 1945 and 1955 and provided material for *Faces in the Water* (1961).

Although F. has written several volumes of short stories and one of poetry, she is best known as a novelist. She has said that she considers the best thing she ever wrote to be a fable written as a child entitled "Bird, Hawk, Bogie" (published in *Landfall,* 19 [1965], 40–47). This fable, in which the bird (inspiration and imagination) is eaten by the powerful, predatory hawk (materialistic, conformist society), which in the turn is eaten by the bogie (repressed imagination and individualism, which must eventually and inevitably return to avenge itself), provides the recurrent symbolism for all her work.

F. has one essential concern: the plight of the individual in a conformist society, a concern she shares with two other major Commonwealth writers, Doris Lessing and Patrick White (qq.v.). What characterizes the excolonial, provincial society for all three writers are an exaltation of the average and a fear of the nonconformist, of the imaginative, of what F. calls "open spaces of the mind."

From an early age F. was conscious of a division of society in which the imaginative people, the visionaries, the inhabitants of what she called "that" world were both feared and ostracized by the inhabitants of "this" world, a world of sterility, conformism, and materialism. Life/death, false/real, seeing/blind, sane/insane, treasure/rubbish are dichotomies recurring in all her work.

In her first novel, possibly her best, *Owls Do Cry,* she presents the two worlds, the movement of one person from the world of conformist society to the lonely world of the isolated individual, and the usual—perhaps inevitable—reaction on the part of the conformist society: to commit the nonconformist to a psychiatric hospital. F. consciously chose to become a citizen of "that" world, and it is a world in which she has remained up to the present day. The cost is high, as she shows in *Owls Do Cry* and even more in *Faces in the Water.* Over a certain period of time F. had repeated nervous breakdowns, caused essentially by her initial endeavors to conform, and these meant stays in psychiatric hospitals. *Faces in the Water* is a semiautobiographical account of such a hospital and the people who live in it, both patients and staff. It is a frightening indictment of such places, but it is much more than that, for it presents F.'s feeling that schizophrenia is not madness but an attempt on that part of the "ill" person to free the self from an oppressive society. Madness is a central metaphor in her work, and she can be considered one of the major novelists concerned with the knowledge-through-madness theme.

F. has widened her scope in her later novels to include both England and America, thereby showing that the malaise affecting 20th-c. man is not confined to New Zealand. She has always shown a keen social as well as psychological awareness and has recognized the role society plays in creating certain states of mind in its individual members. She may have rejected "this" world but not the people who inhabit it, for she sees them as victims, automatons robbed of their inner selves, prey to the forces of capitalism, reduced to producing-consuming machines. She reveals this social concern in *Intensive Care* (1970), an antiutopian novel describing a society after a nuclear World War III ruled by supertechnocrats whose "final solution" is the Human Delineation Act, designed, through computerized selection, to rid the world of its misfits. It is a horrifying vision made even more so by the reader's awareness of its real possibility.

F. is a difficult novelist. Rarely does she employ straightforward narrative or conventional characterization. Her language also presents problems, for in her endeavor to convey the at times almost unconveyable, she dislocates both syntax and words. But if she is difficult, she is also disturbing, for she possesses a more acute vision than most other 20th-c. writers of an utterly destitute world.

FURTHER WORKS: *The Lagoon* (1951); *The Edge of the Alphabet* (1962); *Scented Gardens for the Blind* (1963); *Snowman Snowman* (1963); *The Reservoir* (1963); *The Adaptable Man* (1965); *A State of Siege* (1966); *The Rainbirds* (1967; Am., *Yellow Flowers in the Antipodean Room,* 1969); *The Pocket Mirror* (1967); *Mona Minim and the Smell of the Sun* (1969); *Intensive Care* (1970); *Daughter Buffalo* (1972); *Living in Maniototo* (1980)

BIBLIOGRAPHY: Evans, P., "Alienation and Death: The Novels of J. F.," *Meanjin,* 32 (1973), 294–303; Delbaere, J., "Daphne's Metamorphoses in J. F.'s Early Novels," *ArielE,* 6 (1975), 23–37; New, W. H., *Among Worlds* (1975), pp. 149–54; Rutherford, A., "J. F.'s Divided and Distinguished Worlds," *WLWE,* 14 (1975), 51–68; Alcock P., "On the Edge: New Zealanders as Displaced Persons," *WLWE,* 16 (1977), 127–42; Evans, P., *J. F.* (1977); Delbaere, J., ed., *Bird, Hawk, Bogie: Essays on J. F.* (1978)

ANNA RUTHERFORD

E. M. FORSTER

ANATOLE FRANCE

SIGMUND FREUD

FRANCE, Anatole

(pseud. of Jacques-Anatole-François Thibault) French novelist, short-story writer, essayist, poet, and critic, b. 16 April 1844, Paris; d. 13 Oct. 1924, Tours

F. was born on Quai Malaquais (Paris) above the bookshop owned by his father, François-Noël Thibault, who used "France," the Angevin diminutive of François, as the name of his bookstore and then as his own surname, dropping Thibault. F. had a voracious appetite for books and was always involved with them, as critic, librarian, and eventually author of more than sixty volumes.

For the first half of his life, F. was a conservative, denouncing the government of the Paris Commune (spring 1871) in his novel *Les désirs de Jean Servien* (1882; *The Aspirations of Jean Servien*, 1912) as both evil and ridiculous, and favoring the return of order, which to him meant government by the elite. Although F. evolved politically toward socialism, his abhorrence of violence, even as a means of achieving a desirable end, never changed.

The Dreyfus affair forced F. to abandon his safe position as skeptical observer and openly take sides. He joined Émile Zola and socialist leader Jean Jaurès in coming to the defense of Captain Alfred Dreyfus, who was falsely convicted of espionage. F. incorporated elements of the Dreyfus affair in *L'anneau d'améthyste* (1899; *The Amethyst Ring*, 1919) and in *Monsieur Bergeret à Paris* (1901; *Monsieur Bergeret in Paris*, 1921), the third and fourth novels of his four-volume *Histoire contemporaine* (contemporary history)—the first and second volumes are *L'orme du mail* (1897; *The Elm Tree on the Mall*, 1910) and *Le mannequin d'osier* (1897; *The Wicker Work Woman*, 1910). In the last two novels of the tetralogy he exposed the basic anti-Semitism that lay behind the condemnation of Dreyfus, the only Jew on the French General Staff, and revealed the manner in which Dreyfus's supporters were persecuted.

Although F. had a wife and daughter, the most important woman in his life was Mme. Léontine Arman de Caillavet, a wealthy Jewish-born woman who ran a literary salon in Paris and who encouraged and prodded F. to write. F. lived openly with Mme. de Caillavet from the time of his divorce in 1893 until her death in 1910; the years they spent together were the most productive in F.'s career. Their stormy love affair, tormented by jealousy and possessiveness, is the source of F.'s most romantic novel, *Le lys rouge* (1894; *The Red Lily,* 1898). F. was elected to the French Academy in 1896 and won the Nobel Prize for literature in 1921. A national funeral was held upon his death in 1924.

F. began his career as a critic with *Alfred de Vigny* (1868), a study of the great writer (1797–1863), and as a poet with a collection of philosophical poems, *Les poèmes dorés* (1873; golden poems), dedicated to the Parnassian poet Leconte de Lisle (1818–1894). But it was not until the age of thirty-seven that F. gained wide recognition with the charming tale *Le crime de Sylvestre Bonnard* (1881; *The Crime of Sylvester Bonnard*, 1890). F. was immediately identified with its protagonist, the wise and tender skeptic, just as he would subsequently be identified with the young schoolboy Pierre Nozière, the protagonist of the autobiographical novels *Le livre de mon ami* (1885; *My Friend's Book*, 1913) and of *Pierre Nozière* (1899; *Pierre Nozière*, 1916), later with the good-natured, anarchistic Abbé Jérôme Coignard, the title character of *Les opinions de Jérôme Coignard* (1893; *The Opinions of Jérôme Coignard*, 1913), and finally with Monsieur Bergeret, the skeptical university professor in *Histoire contemporaine*. F. and his protagonists share an underlying pessimism tinged with a kindly indulgence toward human folly. F.'s superior, compassionate smile irritated extremists on the right and on the left, who sought to abolish the existing social order and establish a more perfect, "virtuous" society.

In the second half of his life, F. became a crusader much as Voltaire had been in the 18th-c. Like Voltaire, F. was an Epicurean, a seeker of intellectual and sensual pleasures, who delighted in beautiful works of art, fine furniture, the luxuries of modern times as well as the treasures of antiquity. In their satirical works, such as Voltaire's *Candide* and F.'s mock history of the French people, *L'île des pingouins* (1907; *Penguin Island*, 1909), both writers used broad Gallic wit and ribald Rabelaisian humor to poke fun at romantic notions of love and to deflate the pretensions of egotistical authorities of church and state. Mysticism was just as incomprehensible to F. as it had been to Voltaire. F.'s *Thaïs* (1890; *Thaïs*, 1892) and *Vie de Jeanne d'Arc* (2 vols., 1908; *The Life of Joan of Arc*, 1908) both deal with Christian themes in an antimystical manner. In *La révolte des anges* (1914; *The Revolt of the Angels*, 1914) F. portrays Satan in a sympathetic light as a Promethean hero.

Probably the most enduring works of F.'s maturity are the story "L'affaire Crainquebille" (1901; "Crainquebille," 1915) and the epic novel *Les dieux ont soif* (1912; *The Gods Are Athirst*, 1913). The short story was the ideal medium for F. since it obliged him to control his tendency toward lengthy digressions. "L'affaire Crainquebille"—which F. later made into a play, *Crainquebille* (1905; *Crainquebille*, 1915)—is the touching story of a poor push-cart peddler, unjustly accused of insulting a policeman, whose downfall is so pathetic that after his release from prison he intentionally shouts insults at a policeman in the hopes of being sent back to prison for food and shelter. The story of Crainquebille is symbolic of the persecution of Captain Dreyfus. By depicting society's need for a sacrificial victim and illustrating the injustice committed against the defenseless poor, F. clearly plants himself alongside the socialists as champion of the masses.

Yet this defender of the common people still had reservations about giving them power. In *Les dieux ont soif* F. exposed the corrupting influence of power, specifically as exercised during the French Revolution. The protagonist, Évariste Gamelin, a pure but overly zealous revolutionary, becomes a judge during the Reign of Terror. F. depicts the way in which this formerly gentle, sensitive intellectual, a painter by profession, is won over by the fanaticism of Robespierre and willingly sentences friends and relatives to death. For F., revolutions inevitably result in tyrannies just as oppressive as those they sought to displace.

The moral of F.'s works is one of tolerance and moderation. After his death, F. became unfashionable, especially from the viewpoint of the surrealists (q.v.). F.'s humanism, his irony, and even his pity did not appeal to a generation seeking a total break with classical style and culture. Outside France, however, F. has always been regarded as a model of French literary style, exemplifying clarity, irony, and sensitivity, the best characteristics of French wit.

FURTHER WORKS: *La légende de Sainte Radegonde, reine de France* (1859); *Jean Racine* (1874); *Racine et Nicole* (1875); *Les noces corinthiennes* (1876; *The Bride of Corinth*, 1920); *Idylles et légendes* (1876; *Golden Tales of A. F.*, 1926); *Jocaste et le chat maigre* (1879; *Jocasta and the Famished Cat*, 1912); *Abeille* (1883; *Honey-Bee*, 1911); *Marguerite* (1886; *Marguerite*, 1921); *La vie littéraire* (4 vols., 1888–92; *On Life and Letters*, 4 vols., 1911–14); *Balthasar* (1889; *Bal-*
thasar*, 1909); *L'étui de nacre* (1892; *Tales from a Mother of Pearl Casket*, 1896); *Aphorismes* (1893; *Epigrams on Life, Love, and Laughter*, 1924); *La rôtisserie de la Reine Pédauque* (1893; *At the Sign of the Reine Pédauque*, 1912); *Le jardin d'Épicure* (1894; *The Garden of Epicurus*, 1908); *Le puits de Sainte-Claire* (1895; *The Well of Saint Clare*, 1909); *Poésies; Les poemes dorés; Idylles et légendes; Les noces corinthiennes* (1896); *Au petit bonheur* (1898; *One Can But Try*, 1925); *Clio* (1889; *Clio*, 1922); *Filles et garçons* (1900; *Child Life in Town and Country*, 1910); *Opinions sociales* (2 vols., 1902); *Funérailles d'Émile Zola* (1902); *Sur la tombe de Zola* (1902); *Histoire comique* (1903; *A Mummer's Tale*, 1908); *L'Église et la république* (1904); *Crainquebille, Putois, Riquet, et plusieurs autres récits profitable* (1904; *Crainquebille, Putois, Riquet, and Other Profitable Tales*, 1915); *Sur la pierre blanche* (1905; *The White Stone*, 1910); *Vers les temps meilleurs* (1906; *The Unrisen Dawn: Speeches and Addresses*, 1928); *Le tombeau de Molière* (1908); *Les contes de Jacques Tournebroche* (1908; *The Merrie Tales of Jacques Tournebroche*, 1909); *Les sept femmes de Barbe-Bleue* (1909; *The Seven Wives of Bluebeard*, 1920); *Les poèmes du souvenir* (1911); *La comédie de celui qui épousa une femme muette* (1912; *The Man Who Married a Dumb Wife*, 1915); *Le génie latin* (1913; *The Latin Genius*, 1924); *Sur la voie glorieuse* (1915; *The Path of Glory*, 1916); *Ce que disent nos morts* (1916); *Le petit Pierre* (1918; *Little Pierre*, 1920); *Stendhal* (1920; *Stendhal*, 1926); *Pensées philosophiques* (1920); *Mémoires d'un volontaire* (1921); *Les matinées de la villa Saïd* (1921); *La vie en fleur* (1922; *The Bloom of Life*, 1923); *Dernières pages inédites* (1925); *Œuvres complètes* (26 vols., 1925–37); *La vie littéraire*, Vol. 5 (1949). FURTHER VOLUMES IN ENGLISH: *The Complete Works* (21 vols., 1908–28); *Great Novels of A. F.* (1914); *The Bride of Corinth, and Other Poems and Plays* (1920); *Golden Tales of A. F.* (1926); *The Six Greatest Novels of A. F.* (1936); *The Plays* (1925); *Under the Rose* (1926); *Prefaces, Introductions, and Other Uncollected Papers* (1927)

BIBLIOGRAPHY: Maurras, C., "A. F.," *RH*, 18 (1893), pp. 564–91; Brandes, G., *A. F.* (1908); Chesterton, G. K., "The Maid of Orleans," *All Things Considered* (1908), pp. 267–73; Guérard, A. L., *Five Masters of*

French Romance (1916), pp. 39–134; Brousson, J. J., *A. F. Himself* (1925); Valéry, P., "In Praise of A. F.," *The Dial,* Nov. 1927, 361–79; Chevalier, H. M., *The Ironic Temper: A. F. and His Time* (1932); Axelrad, J., *A. F.: A Life without Illusions* (1944); Tylden-Wright, D., "A. F.," *The Image of France* (1957), pp. 28–39; Sareil, J., *A. F. et Voltaire* (1961); Bancquart, M.-C., *A. F. polémiste* (1962); Jefferson, C., *A. F.: The Politics of Skepticism* (1965); Maurois, A., "Réhabilitons A. F.," *NL,* 26 May 1966, 1, 11; Bresky, D., *The Art of A. F.* (1969)

DEBRA POPKIN

FRANK, Bruno

German novelist, dramatist, and poet, b. 13 June 1887, Stuttgart; d. 20 June 1945, Beverly Hills, Cal., U.S.A.

F. first embarked upon the study of law before switching to the field of German language and literature, in which he took his Ph.D. in 1912. He subsequently traveled extensively in France and the Mediterranean countries. During World War I he served in Flanders and Poland. In 1924 he settled in Munich, where he enjoyed the life of a successful writer, being one of the more prominent figures in the city's cultural life. He left Germany in 1933, on the day following the burning of the Reichstag. He lived in exile in Austria, England, France, and Switzerland before finally coming to the U.S. in 1937.

Although a respected lyric poet before World War I, a very successful playwright until he joined the exodus of German writers, and, at all times, a novelist and short-story writer recognized at home and abroad, F. has not yet received the serious critical attention his work deserves. With his first publication, *Aus der goldenen Schale* (1905; from the golden bowl), he established himself as a precocious lyric poet. The poems, modeled on those of Rilke (q.v.), are predominantly intellectual and display an astonishing mastery of form. A more personal, often melancholy tone pervades the later collection *Die Schatten der Dinge* (1912; the shadow of things) and his *Requiem* (1913; requiem).

F.'s best-known dramas are *Zwölftausend* (1927; *Twelve Thousand,* 1928), a historical drama dealing with the recruiting of German mercenaries by the British for their fight against the rebellious American colonies; and *Sturm im Wasserglas* (1930; *Tempest in a Teapot,* 1936), a comedy in the tradition of the folk play, satirizing bureaucracy and politics in a small-town setting. F.'s plays are good theater, eschewing the intellectual agonizing of much of modern drama.

But F.'s favorite medium was fiction. His novels and stories are well written, exciting, and full of action. Their smooth and effective style shows a cultured and sensitive writer of considerable talent at work. F.'s subtle character studies reveal the compassion and understanding of a true humanist who, to quote W. Somerset Maugham, "was more apt to see the good than the evil in his fellow creatures." F. is at his best when dealing with the fates of historical characters. *Tage des Königs* (1924; *The Days of the King,* 1927) consists of three novellas about Frederick the Great, masterpieces in the historical genre that capture the lonely greatness and suffering of the man behind the legend. Far from being a chauvinistic portrayal, *Tage des Königs* represents a truly human picture of the king, a man of "humaneness, genius, and strength."

F.'s insights into the precarious political and cultural situation of his own time are reflected in his *Politische Novelle* (1928; *The Persians Are Coming,* 1937). It is the appeal of a man with a truly European outlook not to forsake the common cultural heritage of Europe and a warning against the threats posed by fascism, the soul-killing materialism of the West, and the collective uniformity of the East. Thomas Mann (q.v.), a good friend of F.'s, called it "just as ethically courageous and clear-sighted as it is poetic."

All of F.'s work reflects the profound unity of the man and the artist. He never followed any of the "isms" so typical of German intellectual life before 1933. His literary models were Turgenev, Flaubert, and Thomas Mann; his ideal was the type of the "humane gentleman." As an accomplished writer in the tradition of the great 19th-c. novelists, F. holds his own among the writers of the first half of our century.

FURTHER WORKS: *Im dunkeln Zimmer* (1906); *Gedichte* (1907); *Die Nachtwache* (1909); *Das Konzert* (1910); *Flüchtlinge* (1911); *Strophen im Krieg* (1915); *Die Fürstin* (1915); *Die treue Magd* (1916); *Der Himmel der Enttäuschten* (1916); *Bibikoff* (1918); *Die Schwestern und der Fremde* (1918); *Die Trösterin* (1919); *Die Kelter* (1919); *Gesichter* (1920); *Der Goldene* (1920); *Bigram* (1921); *Das Weib auf dem Tiere* (1921);

Leidenschaften (1921); *Trenck* (1926; *Trenck*, 1928); *Erzählungen* (1926); *Perlenkomödie* (1928); *Der Magier* (1929; *The Magician, and Other Stories*, 1946); *Nina* (1931); *Der General und das Gold* (1932); *Cervantes* (1934; *A Man Called Cervantes*, 1934); *Die Monduhr* (1935); *Der Reisepaß* (1937; *The Lost Heritage*, 1937); *Aus vielen Jahren* (1937); *Die junge Frau Conti* (1938; *Young Madame Conti*, 1938); *Die Tochter* (1943; *One Fair Daughter*, 1943); *Sechzehntausend Francs* (1943); *Ehre Vater und Mutter* (1944; *Honor Thy Father and Mother*, 1943); *Die verbotene Stadt* (1951); *Gesammelte Werke* (1957)

BIBLIOGRAPHY: Poore, C. G., on *A Man Called Cervantes, NYTBR*, 3 March 1935, 2; Cort, J. C., on *One Fair Daughter, Commonweal*, 10 Dec. 1943, 211; Hofe, H. von, "German Literature in Exile: B. F.," *GQ*, 18 (1945), 89–92; Weiskopf, F. C., on *The Magician, SatR*, 14 Dec. 1946, 27; Grimm, R., B. F., Gentlemanschriftsteller," in Weimar, S., ed., *Views and Reviews of Modern German Literature* (1974), pp. 121–32; Kamla, T. A., "B. F.'s *Der Reisepaß:* The Exile as an Aristocrat of Humanity," *Monatshefte*, 67 (1975), 37–47

FRIEDHELM RICKERT

FRANKO, Ivan

Ukrainian poet, novelist, dramatist, critic, scholar, translator, and journalist (also writing in Polish and German), b. 27 Aug. 1856, Nahuyevychi, Galicia (then Austro-Hungarian Empire); d. 28 May 1916, Lvov (Lviv)

Son of a village blacksmith, F. began to write imaginative works while still in school and made his debut as a poet in the journal *Druh* in 1874. Upon completing his secondary education, F. enrolled at the University of Lviv in 1875 and soon became a student activist advocating more social and political freedom for the Ukrainians in Galicia, then part of the Austro-Hungarian Empire. F.'s life was fraught with tragedy and misfortune: clashes with the Austrian authorities that led to his repeated arrest, unrequited love affairs, an unhappy marriage, continual conflicts with various circles of the Ukrainian and Polish intelligentsia, frustrated political and academic ambitions, poverty, and ill health—all left an indelible imprint on his work, both in terms of quantity and

quality. F. responded to adversity by writing indefatigably not only to make a living but also to come to terms with his personal dilemmas. Like Goethe, whose writings have been called "fragments of a great confession," he reacted to life's vicissitudes by transforming experience into art, but unlike the great German, he never had the time to subject his writings to a thorough editing. Thus, some of his works (notably his prose) reveal a hastiness of thought and a lack of polish that contrast sharply with his consummate poetic masterpieces such as *Moysey* (1905; *Moses*, 1938) or *Ivan Vyshensky* (1898; *Ivan Vyshensky*, 1981).

The voluminousness of F.'s work and its rich thematic and stylistic diversity preclude any clear-cut categorization of his literary output. Nonetheless, for the sake of clarity, his literary career may be divided into four periods. The first was one of patriotic romanticism (until 1876), and includes such early dramatic efforts as *Try knyazi na odyn prestol* (three princes for one throne) and *Slavoy i Khrudosh* (Slavoy and Khrudosh), written in 1874 and 1875 respectively and published posthumously in 1956. The dominant theme of these works is the quest for unity of the Kievan Rus pursued by strong, noble warriors who, as dramatis personae, display a spiritual kinship to the warriors in old Ukrainian literature and the heroic individuals of the German *Sturm und Drang* age. F.'s greatest historical drama is the more mature but still highly romantic *Son knyazya Svyatoslava* (1895; Prince Svyatoslav's dream). To this period also belongs F.'s first full-length novel, *Petryi i Dovbushchuky* (1875; the Petry and Dovbushchuk families), a tale from the life of Carpathian brigands, in which the influence of E. T. A. Hoffmann (1776–1822) is evident.

The second period of F.'s career, one of revolutionary realism, primarily comprises biting social satire and political poetry, influenced by the ideas of Mykhaylo Drahomaniv (1841–1895), a trenchant social and political thinker, as well as leading Western European authors. The latter part of this period coincides with F.'s "Polish decade" (1887–97), during which he worked for various Polish publications and wrote largely in the Polish language. Among the works of that period on social and revolutionary themes are poems "Kamenyari" (1878; "The Pioneers," 1948), "Hymn" (1882; "Hymn," 1963), the tale "Boa Constriktor" (1878; "Boa Constrictor," 1957), and *Panski zharty* (1887; *The Master's Jests*, 1979), a novella in poetic form dealing with the passing of serfdom in the Ukraine. This period, however, also includes such patriotic verse as "Ne pora" (1887; "National Hymn," 1963); the novel *Zakhar Berkut* (1883; *Zakhar Berkut,* 1944), a romantic synthesis of socialism and patriotism; and the collection of Decadent love poetry *Zivyale lystya* (1891; withered leaves). Also of importance are F.'s fairy tales, both original works and adaptations. Among the latter, the long narrative poem *Lys Mykyta* (1890; *Fox Mykyta,* 1978), read by children as a fairy tale and by adults as a biting satire, is an especially brilliant work.

The years 1898–1907, his third period, constitute what may be termed as F.'s period of symbolic realism; this marks the zenith of F.'s career as a poet and a scholar. Its more famous achievements are *My izmarahd* (1898; my emerald), a volume of moral and philosophical verse; *Semper tiro* (1906; Latin: always a beginner), a collection of poetry dealing with fundamental social and humanistic questions; *Ivan Vyshensky,* the poetic account of the tragedy of the Ukrainian religious leader (c. 1550–c. 1625) caught between asceticism and social activism; and his unquestioned masterpiece, the symbolic poem *Moysey,* built around the conflict between the leader and the masses he must lead. During this time, too, F. withdrew from political life, giving up his membership in the Rusin-Ukrainian Radical Party, which he had cofounded in 1892. He also severely limited his journalistic activities, especially his commitment to the Viennese paper *Die Zeit,* to which he had contributed both fiction and nonfiction since 1895, and devoted himself fully to Ukrainian letters.

The last period (1908–16) was marked by the tragic decline of F.'s powers as a writer and poet, brought about by a progressive paralysis that affected his mental state. He continued to work intermittently, mostly for the Shevchenko Scientific Society, in which he had been active since 1897, translating works from foreign literatures into Ukrainian, revising and editing his manuscripts, and doing some writing. Nonetheless, before his death, F. had some satisfaction in seeing himself acclaimed as *the* Ukrainian writer of his time and the mentor of a new generation of his people.

FURTHER WORKS: *Boryslav smietsya* (1882); *Z vershyn i nyzyn* (1887); *Smert Kayina* (1889); *V poti chola* (1890); *Ukradene shchastya* (1894); *Poemy* (1899); *Iz dniv zhurby* (1900); *Budka ch. 27* (1902); *Mays-ter Chyrnyak* (1902); *Zbirnyk tvoriv* (3 vols., 1903–5); *Tvory* (30 vols., 1924–29); *Vybrani tvory* (1930); *Tvory* (5 vols., 1930–32); *Vybrani tvory* (2 vols., 1934); *Vybrani tvory* (5 vols., 1935–36); *Vybrani opovidannya* (1947); *Vybir iz tvoriv* (1956); *Tvory* (20 vols., 1950–56); *Vybrani tvory* (1957); *Literaturna spadshchyna* (4 vols., 1956–67); *Tvory* (20 vols., 1956–62); *Beiträge zur Geschichte und Kultur der Ukraine* (1963); *Zibrannya tvoriv* (50 vols., 1976 ff.). FURTHER VOLUMES IN ENGLISH: *Selected Poems* (1948); *Poems and Stories* (1956); *Boa Constrictor, and Other Stories* (1957); *Stories* (1972); *Moses, and Other Poems* (1973)

BIBLIOGRAPHY: Manning, C. A., *Ukrainian Literature: Studies of the Leading Authors* (1944), pp. 76–88; Doroshenko, V., "I. F. as a Scholar," *UQ,* 12 (1956), 144–51; Rudnytzky, L. D., "I. F.—A Translator of German Literature," *Annals of the Ukrainian Academy of Arts and Sciences in the United States,* 12 (1969–72), 143–50; Čyževs'kyj, D., *A History of Ukrainian Literature* (1975), pp. 603–7; Mihailovich, V. D., et al., eds., *Modern Slavic Literatures* (1976), Vol. II, pp. 462–67; Kipa, A. A., "I. F.'s View of Gerhart Hauptmann," Sokel, W. H., et al., eds., *Probleme der Komparatisik und Interpretation: Festschrift für André von Gronicka* (1978), pp. 136–41; Rudnytzky, L. D., Introduction to I. F., *The Master's Jests* (1979), pp. 9–13

LEO D. RUDNYTZKY

FRENCH LITERATURE

The 20th c. has been a period of swift and radical change, which for the French nation has proved violent and costly. In the fifty or so years that elapsed between the national turmoil generated by the Dreyfus affair (1894–1906) and the establishment of the Fifth Republic (1958), which coincided with a bitter reassessment of France's international position in the nuclear age, French civilization was shaken to its foundations. In the 1960s the France which emerged from the shock of two world wars and from the syndromes that accompanied decolonialization, and which had to adapt to modern technology, and begin to integrate itself into a planned supranational European economy, seemed to have little in common with the France of the early 1900s. By 1980 France was a prosperous nation, one of the leaders, along with West Germany, in the slowly emerging Western European alliance.

The worldwide revolutionary character of the times was not manifest at the century's inception. In 1900, leaving behind it the critical phase of the Dreyfus controversy, France entered so marked a period of prosperity and equilibrium that it is still known as *"la belle époque."* The distinctive dynamism of the century—disintegrating traditional structures, fostering the emergence of uncertain new ones—was discernible in France at the time only in the first achievements of technology—films, the telephone, the automobile, the airplane—and in the arts. Mathematicians and researchers in French laboratories and clinics participated in the new scientific discoveries, whose impact, with that of Einstein and Freud (q.v.), was ultimately to be great; but these had not yet reached the general public.

By contrast, art had already, before World War I, made its own spectacular revolutionary leap—toward abstraction—and Paris, cosmopolitan and urbane, became the center of the art world, the chosen home, at one time or another, of Picasso, Juan Gris, Kandinsky, Chagall, Modigliani, De Chirico, Soutine, Brancusi. Painting moved rapidly by way of expressionism (q.v.), primitivism, and simultanism, from Fauvism (1905) to cubism (q.v., 1907), to a short-lived futurism (q.v.), toward its two-pronged postwar development—surrealism (q.v.) and the diverse forms of nonfigurative art. In architecture, the simple lines of functional building were being developed. Sculptors, influenced by the African mask, were on the path to the creation of autonomous volumes and mobiles. And composers like Satie and Stravinsky were making way for the postwar experiments with atonal, dodecaphonic, and finally concrete music. Visible everywhere, the "modern spirit" in the arts, scandalous to the bourgeois spirit of conservatism, was creative, adventurous, and exhilarating. It dominated the pre-World War I years and sealed an alliance between all the arts, including literature and the nascent cinema.

World War I inaugurated a phase of almost unbroken political revolution and international conflict. In the early 1900s, the French proletariat had shown signs of restlessness, but in a country still predominantly agricultural—in spite of a new wave of industrialization—the situation did not appear critical. It was in the realm of ideas, a bourgeois realm, that the future was adumbrated in ideologies which had crystallized early around the Dreyfus case and

which seemed, at first, designed merely to counterbalance one another. France in those years of prosperity could accommodate, although uneasily, the socialism of Jean Jaurès (1859–1914), founder of the new unified French Socialist Party, and the doctrinaire "integral nationalism" of Charles Maurras (1868–1952), leader of the reactionary rightist Action Française, and it could ignore Georges Sorel's (1847–1922) theory of revolution, based on the manipulation of the masses and the seizure by force of the controls of power, presented in *Réflexions sur la violence* (1908; *Reflections on Violence*, 1912). But between 1914 and 1950 ideological conflicts, international in character, compounded the difficulties of France's struggle for survival. France sometimes seemed close to civil war; was barely victorious, and at too great cost, in World War I; was defeated, occupied, and deeply humiliated in World War II. The exhilaration of *la belle époque* gave way to a growing anxiety. The rapid deterioration of social and political institutions, the exhaustion attendant upon what turned out to be thirty years of almost unbroken warfare, the atomic explosion at Hiroshima, which left the French with a feeling of horror and insecurity and the sense that they had fallen far behind in the fields of scientific and technological research—all contributed to an intellectual climate of serious, somewhat desperate, questioning. It lasted well into the 1960s, as the costly wars of decolonization in southeast Asia and Algeria compounded the violence of ideological controversy in France itself. The student revolt in 1968 brought the social unrest to a climax and inaugurated a new phase of economic and social planning in an effort to adapt obsolete socioeconomic and institutional structures to the realities of the modern world. In the dialogue between old and new, the women's liberation movement since 1970 has been the most prominent factor in political and cultural change.

Throughout the century, French literature, making of the process of creativity and change one of its major themes, mirrored in its diversity the broad spectrum of collective concerns and individual reactions. At the highest level of achievement, it drew from the writers' efforts at elucidation a validity and capacity for renewal that were to make the century one of the richest in its history. Among minor works, the rapid changes, the excessive tendentiousness, the ruptures and experiments created a bewildering sense of anarchy and confusion.

The French literary language, already enriched and made more flexible by the symbolists (q.v.), benefited greatly during those years, enlarging its vocabulary by the massive inclusion of new terms and, experimenting with a syntax that it disrupted, by the integration of forms prevalent in current French speech. It tended to narrow the gap between the spoken and the literary, the popular and the educated forms of language, while, by experiments in form, it emphasized the distance that separates literary expression from the proliferation of commercialized writing: journalism and popular fiction. Breaking down the barriers between the genres, transforming the traditional genres themselves beyond recognition, literary expression, often to the scandal or confusion of the reading public, became infinitely diversified if not fragmented. Yet perhaps because with the new organization of French education undertaken at the turn of the century, literature had become an honored institution, it is in literature that both the continuity of French tradition and its metamorphosis in the 20th c. can be discerned most clearly. In literature, as in the other arts, the concept of an "avant-garde," opening up the way to new forms of expression, became commonplace in the 1900s. But literary avant-garde movements, with the exception of the iconoclasm of Dadaism (q.v.), always referred back to literary sponsors chosen among writers of the past, creating for themselves a tradition while enriching the literary history of France, a task in which they were helped by an alert criticism.

In spite of the apparent confusion and fragmentation, the major literary achievements of the 20th c. first evolved from a carefully sought equilibrium between innovation and a recourse to the great masters of the past. Few writers of stature were not also critics. In a fast-changing country, literature tended to be a normative and stabilizing force, whose continuity was emphasized by the living presence throughout the first fifty years of the century of a few great figures born around 1870: Paul Claudel, Colette, André Gide, and Paul Valéry (qq.v.).

Writing, in the first half of the century, tended increasingly to involve the writer's whole person, to become the statement of a total outlook, an act that engaged the writer's responsibility. More than ever in the past, French readers looked to the writer for guidance, while the writer himself questioned the validity of his own occupation, examined the nature and genesis of literary creation and, ever more critically, its social role and function. But the status of literature itself, traditionally considered in France as the highest expression of its culture, became a more and more hotly debated issue after World War II. Within the Marxist perspective adopted by a majority of leftist intellectuals in the aftermath of the French defeat, it seemed urgent to replace established "bourgeois" norms by "new" or "revolutionary" texts. Not continuity but change—in fact rupture—became the leitmotif of those years. The French writer, in strong contrast to the inspired bard of romantic myth, became a conscious, indeed a self-conscious creator who called into question every facet of his craft, including his material, language itself. Writers thus unleashed what has been called a "terrorism" in literature, making of writing a complex and sometimes sibylline form of questioning.

Modern French literature does not always yield easily to classification by schools or movements. Although there was an ephemeral rash of "isms" in the early 1900s—synthetism, integralism, unanimism, Orphism, futurism, simultanism—only two movements, not exclusively French, nor exclusively literary, and never entirely in command, left their imprint on French letters: surrealism in the mid-1920s, and existentialism (q.v.) in the 1940s. Nor does the concept of generations greatly clarify the picture, the two world wars disrupting the orderly succession of generations, destroying or delaying certain talents while precociously fostering others. The history of literature is the history of the major writers, whose itinerary sometimes espouses the brusque oscillations of the time, sometimes not. One may, for the sake of convenience, distinguish three periods in the general evolution of French literature: the "modernist" period, which affected all the arts of the Western world from the early 1900s to the early 1930s; the metaphysical and social current, born of the turmoil of the 1930s; finally, during the 1950s, the upsurge of a critical and "scientific" mentality that heralded a postmodernist period as yet undefined.

The End of the Belle Époque

In the 1880s, the Decadents—to the confusion of the naturalists and to the consternation of the bourgeoisie—had invented a mythical "fin de siècle," a languorous twilight of the gods. The real mood of the fin de siècle, which began to crystallize in the 1890s, was more reassuring. Recovering, in 1900, from the more violent phase of the Dreyfus affair, an urbane, cosmopolitan society seemed ready to open its doors to the writers who, whether for or against Drey-fus, had shared and voiced its alarms. One by one a generation of great writers had disap-peared: Hippolyte Taine (1828–1893) and Ernest Renan (1823–1892), the ideological masters of two generations; the poets Jules Laforgue (1860–1887), Arthur Rimbaud (1845–1891), Paul Verlaine (1844–1896), and Stéphane Mallarmé (1842–1898); the fic-tion writers Guy de Maupassant (1850–1893), Émile Zola (1840–1902), and Alphonse Dau-det (1840–1897). Restraint, intelligence, clar-ity, common sense, and good manners seemed to be criteria common to good writing and good society. Reconciled with society, literature voiced the theme of "return": return to the classics, to nature, to tradition, to humanism, to ethics, to the Church. In fact, beneath a decep-tively brilliant and complacent surface, it was undergoing a great change.

Poetry

Poetry, still under the shadow of the great poets, was the most ubiquitous of genres. Be-tween 1900 and 1914 innumerable poets, grouped in small coteries, launched more than two hundred little magazines. Some, like *Vers et prose, La phalange,* and *Le divan,* prolonged the symbolist trend. Refining on symbolist theory, René Ghil (1862–1925) and Gustave Kahn (1859–1936), among others, developed its more superficial mannerisms—the disruption of syntax, the complex intellectualization of the form, the esoteric theme, the rare vocabulary —while, in complete solitude, Saint-Pol-Roux (pseud. of Paul Roux, 1861–1940) evolved his concept of poetry as "ideorealism," a theory that to some degree anticipated surrealism, in *Les reposoirs de la procession* (3 vols., 1893–1907; stations of the procession). Henri de Régnier (1864–1936), after his symbolist beginnings, turned to earlier poets like Ronsard for his models. Elsewhere, the reaction started by Jean Moréas (pseud. of Yannis Papadia-mantopoulous, 1856–1910)—whose École Ro-mane, a group founded in 1891, advocated a return to classical sources and forms—was gaining momentum, but not unity. Saint Georges de Bouhélier's (pseud. of Stéphane Georges de Bouhélier-Lepelletier, 1889–1942) *"naturisme"* advocated a return to simple uni-versal emotions—love of nature and mankind —and free lyrical expression; Fernand Gregh (1873–1960) advocated a new humanism. Whatever the theory, simpler forms of lyricism prevailed. Francis Jammes's (q.v.) intimate

verse, in works such as *De l'angélus de l'aube à l'angélus du soir* (1898; from the morning prayer to the evening prayer) and *Les géorqiques chrétiennes* (1912; Christian geor-gics), expressed in studiedly naïve terms the sane emotions of peasant life. Paul Fort (1872–1960)—in close to forty volumes of *Bal-lades françaises* (French ballads), published between 1896 and 1958—adapted to his neoro-mantic fancy popular ballad forms and themes, experimenting with the potentialities of the prose-poem; while Anna de Noailles (1876–1933), the most adulated of a group of women poets, sang easily, in works such as *Le cœur innombrable* (1901; the numberless heart) of love, death, and nature in cadences, stanzas, and rhetoric reminiscent of Victor Hugo. Deriv-ative or esoteric, poetry had become a minor genre.

Drama

In the last years of the 19th c. naturalists and symbolists alike had taken the theater to task—whether the commercial boulevard thea-ter or the state-subsidized Comédie Française —for its old-fashioned techniques, and, in the case of the boulevard, its stereotyped plays. Two little theaters had appeared: André An-toine's naturalistic Théâtre Libre, and, succes-sor to Paul Fort's Théâtre d'Art, Lugné-Poë's Théâtre de l'Œuvre. With the introduction of new dramatists—Strindberg, Hauptmann, Mae-terlinck (qq.v.), and of course Ibsen—the theater seemed to be stirring. By 1900 both the Théâtre Libre and the Théâtre de l'Œuvre had closed down, although only temporarily. The boulevard theater reigned unchallenged, content to live on the formulae that had made French theater famous since the 1850s. The boulevard conceived of theater as pure entertainment. It favored the *vaudeville,* which Georges Feydeau (q.v.) raised to the level of an art—light com-edy, with its standard stock-in-trade intrigues, quick repartee, and indulgent social satire, whose practitioners also included Tristan Ber-nard (1866–1947), Robert de Flers (1872–1927), and Robert de Caillavet (1869–1915)—and the Molièresque farces, bordering on the comedy of manners, of Georges Courteline (1858–1929) that exploited the foibles of bu-reaucracy, more particularly the military.

Serious theater continued to take the form of the well-made "problem play": Eugène Brieux (1858–1932) discussed motherhood, family life, or, as in *La robe rouge* (1900; *The Red Robe,* 1915), the corruption of justice; while

François de Curel (1854–1928) dramatized newer problems—the conflict of industrial workers and plant owners in *Le repas du lion* (1897; the lion's meal) and of science and religion in *La nouvelle idole* (1899; the new idol). Elevated in tone, moral in intent, socially acceptable in its solutions, the problem play moved along the well-oiled grooves of a set dramatic pattern. More popular, a so-called "theater of passion"—Georges de Porto-Riche (1849–1930), Félix Bataille (1872–1922), Henry Bernstein (1876–1953)—in an equally set mold, dramatized the conflicts between the passions—love, almost exclusively—and the rules of society. It was in fact not far removed from the *vaudeville,* dealing with the same themes: adultery, respectability, class taboos. To this theater Edmond Rostand (1868–1918), with his enthusiastically acclaimed *Cyrano de Bergerac* (1897; *Cyrano de Bergerac,* 1898) *and L'aiglon* (1900; *L'Aiglon,* 1927), neoromantic historical verse plays, brought a brief new luster and the only drama that survived, but added one more stillborn type of play to the roster. While elsewhere in Europe—in Russia, Germany, England—the fin-de-siècle movement of renovation was gaining momentum, the French theater remained what it had been: a brilliant, ritualized, and commercially rewarding social function organized for the entertainment of an elite and the greater glory of the star, the *monstre sacré* that the name of Sarah Bernhardt best exemplifies.

The Novel

The proliferation of novelists was as great as the proliferation of poets, all in some form or other inheritors of the great past. Bolstered by the establishment in 1903 of the Goncourt Prize, varieties of the realistic novel inherited from Flaubert, rather than from Zola, prevailed: historical or social frescoes, by Lucien Descaves (1861–1949), the Margueritte brothers, Paul (1860–1918) and Victor (1867–1942), Paul Adam (1862–1920), and the Rosny brothers, Rosny aîné (pseud. of Joseph-Henry Boëx, 1856–1940) and Rosny jeune (pseud. of Justin Boëx, 1859–1948); case histories, by Octave Mirbeau (1850–1917), Marguerite Audoux (1863–1937), and Charles-Louis Philippe (1874–1909); and innumerable novels of provincial life, by René Bazin (1853–1932) and Henry Bordeaux (1870–1963). But the masters of the younger generation introduced other overtones: a neoromantic exoticism and melancholy, inspired by

Pierre Loti (pseud. of Louis Marie Julien Viaud, 1850–1923) was perpetuated by Claude Farrère (pseud. of Charles Bargonne, 1876–1957), the Tharaud brothers, Jérôme (1874–1953) and Jean (1877–1952), and Louis Bertrand (1866–1941). More influential, Paul Bourget (1852–1935) had revived the novel of psychological analysis in a mood of moral righteousness eminently suited to a large bourgeois public. It proliferated to the point that it became synonymous with the term "French novel," a genre which, cultivated by Abel Hermant (1862–1950), Édouard Estaunié (1862–1942), René Boylesve (pseud. of René Tardivaux, 1867–1926), and Edmond Jaloux (1878–1949), reached a wide reading public.

More seminal was the transformation of the social-fresco novel in the hands of both Émile Zola at the end of his career, and of Maurice Barrès (1862–1923) into a vehicle for the dissemination of political doctrine—socialistic with Zola, nationalistic with Barrès. What distinguished the more vigorous, currently read novels of the period, the only ones that have survived, is their undisguised politicization and open didacticism. If Barrès's nationalistic trilogy *Le roman de l'énergie nationale* (1897–1902; the novel of national energy), Anatole France's (q.v.) socialistically slanted fictions, and Romain Rolland's (q.v.) vast ten-volume fresco, *Jean-Christophe* (1904–12; *Jean-Christophe,* 1910–13), have survived, it is as vehicles of thought rather than as novels.

Only one purely literary writer of stature, Colette, seems to have succeeded in truly reflecting the mood of the early 1900s. Free of ideology and didacticism, impressionistic in her style, rich in perception, Colette, after she abandoned the artificial perversity of her first novels, drew upon all that was best in the times: sophistication; a free sensuality; fascination with the joys, dangers, and complexities of sex; a taste for directness and intimacy. To these she brought a sensitivity to the world of sensation—light, color, smell, touch—that bound her closely to a quotidian universe in which she took keen delight. Her fame, slow to establish itself but unquestioned, rests on her command of a precise and fluid prose, an instrument exactly adapted to the expression of her limited and yet inexhaustible world.

Expository Prose

The fin de siècle had witnessed a complex and confused reaction against "scientism" and the methods and tenets of positivism, which had dominated the mid-19th c. Henri Bergson's (q.v.) critique of intelligence, his rehabilitation of intuition, and his emphasis on a measure of indetermination, hence of creative freedom in the shaping of the future; Nietzsche's exaltation of action and energy; and, among scientists, the critique of the scientific method itself—exemplified by Henri Poincaré's (1856–1912) *La science et l'hypothèse* (1902; *Science and Hypothesis*, 1905)—gave a new impetus to ideological discussion and to the resurgence of various forms of mysticism and religious conversion. A vigorous literature of debate was carried into every realm of thought. With the Dreyfus affair it took on dogmatic political overtones. Deplorable where national issues were at stake, it brought new ideas into circulation and reinvigorated a rather anemic prose. A generation of polemicists and essayists opened the way to the renascence of all forms of expository prose: Bergson, Charles Maurras (1868–1952), Léon Daudet (1867–1942), Charles Péguy (q.v.), Romain Rolland, André Gide, André Suarès (1868–1948), and Julien Benda (1867–1956) were the master-writers of a period that was no longer satisfied to accept the outmoded style, both abstract and ornate, of such pontifical critics as Ferdinand Brunetière (1849–1906), Jules Lemaître (1853–1914), and Remy de Gourmont (1858–1915).

New Orientations: The Prewar Years

Between 1905 and 1910, literature began to take on a new appearance; it was vigorous, deliberately modern, adventurous, ready to proclaim the advent of a new aesthetic attuned to the vast possibilities opening up in art as in the modern world. In the theater, the first real intimation of things to come hit the "tout-Paris" in 1909–10 with Diaghilev's Russian ballets starring Nijinsky and Pavlova, with the sumptuous stage sets and costumes of Léon Bakst. With *L'art théâtral moderne* (1910; modern theatrical art), Jacques Rouché (1862–1957), director of the Théâtre des Arts (1911–13), gave the first coherent survey of the theories and innovations of Konstantin Stanislavsky, Edward Gordon Craig, Adolphe Appia, and Max Reinhardt, and in 1913, Jacques Copeau, declaring open warfare on the boulevard, announced the opening of the Théâtre du Vieux Colombier, which, in the post-World War I years presided over the renovation of French theater. At Créteil, near Paris, a young group of writers and artists, the "Groupe de l'Abbaye," Tol-

stoyan in its inspiration, declared their intention of renovating art by going back to its source, the living community of men; while, in 1909, in close connection with them, Jules Romains (q.v.) launched his own program, "unanimism," the discovery, expression, and ultimately the guidance of the collective emotions and forces abroad in the exhilarating urban setting of modern life, born of Walt Whitman, Émile Verhaeren (q.v.), Zola, Tolstoy, and the sociologist Émile Durkheim (1858–1917). From Montmartre first, then from Montparnasse, cubism—creative, scandalous, sure of itself, and incarnate in the tall figure of the irrepressible poet Guillaume Apollinaire (q.v.)— brought a bevy of irreverent poets; while in his *Cahiers de la quinzaine*, stubborn, dogged, and obscure, Péguy was struggling toward a religious and patriotic commitment as far removed as was possible from the elegant dilettantism of Barrès, accumulating meanwhile a poetic work of considerable dimension, new in all its aspects. In 1906 there began to appear, in a Rouen paper, short chronicles signed "Alain." The *propos* (brief aphoristic pieces) of Alain (q.v.) proposing a method of thought, a discipline of free examination rather than a system, exercised a deflationary influence on the rhetorical prose of the warring dogmatisms. At the center of the movement was the young *Nouvelle revue française,* liberal and cosmopolitan in outlook, free from political commitment, and with the high standards of the literary tradition that had passed from Flaubert to Mallarmé. It brought to the fore, along with Gide, two writers whose work had slowly matured in relative obscurity—Paul Claudel (q.v.), and later Valéry —and sponsored the beginnings of a new generation of writers remarkable in their variety: Roger Martin de Gard, François Mauriac, Jean Giraudoux, Saint-John Perse (qq.v.), and Romains.

With the opening of the Vieux Colombier in 1913, the almost simultaneous publication of Apollinaire's *Alcools* (1913; *Alcohols,* 1964), Claudel's *Corona benignitatis anni Dei* (1915; *Coronal,* 1943), following upon the first production of his play *L'annonce faite à Marie* (1912; *The Tidings Brought to Mary,* 1916), Gide's *Les caves du Vatican* (1914; *Lafcadio's Adventures,* 1928), Martin du Gard's *Jean Barois* (1913; *Jean Barois,* 1949), Alain-Fournier's (q.v.) *Le Grand Meaulnes* (1913; *The Wanderer,* 1928), and, coming unexpectedly from another quarter, Marcel Proust's (q.v.) *Du côté de chez Swann* (1913; *Swann's Way,* 1922), it seemed that a new literary era had dawned, confident in its powers, undogmatic, eclectic, disciplined, rooted in the most solid of traditions, and at the same time open to all forms of innovation. When, in the *NRF*, its editor, Jacques Rivière (1886–1925), in an all-out attack on the ubiquitous novel of psychological analysis, called for a "novel of adventure," he was voicing the watchword of the day; adventure was in the air.

The Masters

Born around 1870, Gide, Claudel, Proust, and Valéry had started precocious literary careers in the hothouse atmosphere of the symbolist salons. From their early contact with a literary figure of the stature of Mallarmé, Gide, Claudel, and Valéry drew the sense of the nobility of the writer's calling that Proust shared. By the turn of the century all four men were aware that symbolism had outlived its creative potentialities, as had also the summary aesthetic of the naturalists. All four separately and in different ways worked over the years in relative obscurity and solitude, to develop their own aesthetic and forge their own idiom. By 1914, in their mid-forties, they had reached maturity. World War I, although it touched them deeply, did not affect their work. Each had created a style and universe specifically his own.

From his conversion to Catholicism Claudel drew a Thomist vision of a theocentric universe that gave his writings—essays and spiritual meditations, lyrical poetry and drama—their cosmic grandeur, authority, and vast sweep of language.

A close friend and disciple of Mallarmé, Valéry withdrew from literary life to observe and study the creative interplay of mind and language. To the postwar years he brought the lucid prose of his essays; the critical acuity of a mind trained in mathematical speculation; a theory of poetic creation; and a small number of quasi-perfect poems renewing the forms of classical prosody, embodying in their imagery and verbal harmonies the dynamic movement of the creative act.

Proust's vast novel *À la recherche du temps perdu* (7 vols., 1913–27; *Remembrance of Things Past*, 7 vols., 1922–32) is perhaps the greatest novelistic achievement of the 20th c., and its very dimensions for a time somewhat obscured its fundamental creative originality. It brought, besides new techniques that evolved from a new understanding of the working of the human mind, of the powers of memory and sensibility and the relations they establish with the outer world, a vision of literature as the highest form of knowledge, the only complete testimony as to the nature of human experience, an activity so imperious as to subordinate to its needs the very life of the writer.

The real master of the 1920s, however, was Gide, less perhaps for the skilled and subtle narrative forms with which since the turn of the century he had been experimenting, transforming the novel structure more radically even than Proust, but rather for what was called "Gidism"—his appeal to throw off outworn conventions, to become a responsible, authentic individual; his vision, foreshadowing the existentialist, of the human being's contingency in a purposeless universe; and his ethic of disciplined and rational freedom. A great and controversial figure, Gide dominated his time.

In the 1920s the young men who emerged from four years of war, with scant respect for the civilization that had organized and tolerated the hecatomb, with scanter respect for the feverish, cynical postwar Europe, could turn to these men with confidence. In the general collapse of all accepted values, literature as represented by them had stature, significance, and dignity. They had renovated all the traditional genres: the novel, drama, poetry, the essay. In their hands literary expression had acquired new dimensions, metaphysical, intellectual, ethical—incorporated into the work itself, determining its structure, not rhetorically inserted and imposed, and they used language with confidence and mastery.

The Innovators

It was not the literary masters, however, but the artists who gave the most fertile and characteristic impetus to literature. Their sense of art as a form of adventure, born of the unexpected potentialities of the medium itself, of art as the generator of its own language, was a new concept in the 1910s. Among the poets, a group called the "Fantaisistes"—Francis Carco (pseud. of François Carcopino-Tusoli, 1886–1958), Paul Jean Toulet (1867–1920)—was cultivating a light, often humorous, form of verse, drawing its effects from the free and unexpected play of imagery and word, compounded, in the work of Valery Larbaud (q.v.), an indefatigable client of the luxury express train, by the foreshortening of time and space, and in the writings of Blaise Cendrars (q.v.) by the violence of perceptions rolled in the flux of a dynamic stream-of-consciousness, perpetually renewed, perpetually in the process of creation. But it was the group of poets in close contact with the cubist painters —André Salmon (1881–1969), Max Jacob, Pierre Reverdy, Léon-Paul Fargue (qq.v.)— and more especially Apollinaire, the impresario of the cubists—who most nearly incarnate the creative versatility of the period, its dynamic itinerary from symbolism to new open forms of expression, its love of mystification, its commitment to art as a way of life, its superb and unself-conscious disregard of, rather than revolt against, society. Apollinaire, rather than Valéry, Claudel, or Péguy, was the great innovator of the period.

Renewal and Revolt: The Early 1920s

World War I favored the diffusion of a pious literature of social conformism, latent in a good deal of the writing that had predominated since the turn of the century. It survived for some time in the euphoria of victory, but by the early 1920s it had been driven from the boisterous center of the literary scene. The death of Barrès, France, and Loti, the rising influence of Gide, Claudel, Proust, and Valéry, the sensationalism, literary inflation, and anarchy of the time hastened its demise. It had been challenged early. In 1916 the production in Rome of *Parade*, a ballet in which the composer Erik Satie, Picasso, and Diaghilev had collaborated with Jean Cocteau (q.v.), and in 1917 the almost simultaneous production in Paris of *Parade* and *Les mamelles de Tirésias* (1917; *The Breasts of Tiresias*, 1961) were launched in open protest against the pall of conformism.

But the aestheticism of the protest was to be overshadowed when, in 1920, Dadaism, with Tristan Tzara (q.v.) as its leading spirit, moved to Paris from Zurich and started systematically to organize and exploit the joys of openly baiting and scandalizing the public. Among its precursors, Dada could recognize Alfred Jarry (q.v.), whose farce *Ubu roi* (1896; *Ubu Roi*, 1951), a deliberate assault on the sense of propriety of the audience, had created a scandal, which, by his way of life, Jarry had prolonged. Dada was, in a sense, openly miming the senseless violence camouflaged under the noble cadences of official speeches, tearing down false façades in a first upsurge of shock at the brutality of modern war, and countering by its violence the nihilism latent in a confrontation with what was later to be called the "absurd." Dada's assault on all the existing structures— political, social, religious, intellectual, cultural,

aesthetic—used as one among its weapons a disruption of language that made the experiments of Apollinaire and Cocteau seem circumspect. It challenged the legitimacy of literature, denounced its fictitious character and the nonauthenticity of language itself. It was Dada that unleashed terrorism in the world of letters, and although by 1922 its energies had spent themselves, its effects on French literature were deep and lasting.

By 1922, under the aegis of André Breton and Louis Aragon (qq.v.), surrealism was channeling the inventive impetus of the new spirit in an entirely new direction, while attaching it to a recognizable tradition: William Blake, Gérard de Nerval (1808–1855), Lautréamont (1846–1870), Rimbaud, Raymond Roussel (q.v.). Language, for the surrealists, when freed from the constraints of logic, became an instrument, a tool for the uncovering of "surreality," the network of relations linking human beings to one another and to the world. The mind, a vehicle of the unknown, appeared to the surrealists as an immense and barely explored realm. Putting to work Freudian concepts, the surrealists plunged into a systematic observation and stimulation of the subconscious working of their own minds. Their experiments with automatic writing and dreams, their cultivation of irrational states, affected the entire range of literary expression: the tenor, rhythms, and syntax of the language, as well as the methods of composition—alogical dream sequences, bizarre combinations of words, the symbolic use of objects, incongruous juxtapositions of images—processes that had been latent in the work of Jacob and Jarry. They massively injected into French literature, with an obscurity that official prewar literature had singularly lacked, an eerie form of black humor and the ability to treat all words—sexual, psychotic, ordinary—with sovereign equanimity. With Freud, they greatly contributed to opening wide to literature a subjective inner realism that had been approached heretofore more surreptitiously. By their severe contempt for commercial success and public opinion, by their insistence on living according to their concepts, by their combativeness, the surrealists served as a kind of counterpoint to the feverish, turbulent, inflated literary activity of the 1920s.

Versatile and restlessly inventive, a poet, dramatist, novelist, essayist, scenarist, actor, distinguished besides in the art of drawing, Jean Cocteau seems the veritable incarnation of the postwar period. From his scandalous beginnings with the ballet *Parade*, to his election to the French Academy, he lived the adventure of the iconoclastic art at whose genesis he had presided. Committed utterly to his work as artist, he made of artistic creation a discipline and a way of life, keeping his freedom intact. His is an independent figure that evades classification.

From Anarchy to Ideology

By the end of the decade, the surrealist group was disintegrating under the impact of new social pressures. Between 1926, when in *La tentation de L'Occident* (*The Temptation of the West,* 1961) André Malraux (q.v.) raised the question of the fate of Western civilization, and 1932, the date of Louis-Ferdinand Céline's (q.v.) *Voyage au bout de la nuit* (*Journey to the End of Night,* 1934) and Jean Prevost's (1901–1944) *Histoire de France depuis la guerre* (history of France since the war), the intellectual mood in France changed. Political tensions, the economic depression triggered by the Wall Street crash (1929), the rise of fascism, and the increasingly powerful influence of the successful Marxist revolution in Russia created a climate of tension immediately discernible in literature. "Return to order" was the leitmotif of Cocteau in these years, and of *L'ordre* (1929; order), the title of a novel by Marcel Arland (b. 1899) that launched a two-pronged attack on false order and false anarchy, echoed by Pierre Bost's (b. 1901) *Le scandale*; (1931; scandal). Robert Brasillach (1908–1945) announced the end of the postwar years, a formula echoed by Arland in the *NRF* in November 1931.

In 1929–30 "populism," a short-lived movement launched by Léon Lemonnier (1890–1953) and André Thérive (1891–1967), emphasized a growing preoccupation with social problems and an upsurge of neo-realism. In 1930 the surrealists finally split along political lines, Aragon, and with him the bulk of the group, adhering to Marxism. In a climate of increasing anxiety, the emphasis moved from the aesthetic to the social; European civilization, and more particularly bourgeois democracy, were pitilessly scrutinized—by Jean Guéhenno (1890–1978) in *Caliban parle* (1928; Caliban speaks), Emmanuel Berl (1892–1976) in *Mort de la pensée bourgeoise* (1929; death of bourgeois thought), Julien Benda in *La trahison des clercs* (1927; *The Treason of the Intellectuals,* 1928). Intransigent and aggressive, the embattled ideologies confronted each other, permeating the intellectual life of France once again, as at the time of the Dreyfus affair, but more sharply, more deeply fragmenting it. In this tense atmosphere, a few solid and viable literary works emerged from the froth and confusion of the 1920s. More than either poetry or drama, the novel and essay reflected the change in mood of the post-World War I years.

Poetry

Surrealism, as much perhaps through painters (Max Ernst, Francis Picabia, Fernand Léger, Joan Miró) and filmmakers (Luis Buñuel, Cocteau) as through its verbal experiments, renewed the modes of visual perception, the apprehension of an inner oneiric space in which objects were juxtaposed and organized in new ways. It led to a vigorous expansion of poetic expression and inspiration. From within the surrealist ranks came Robert Desnos, Paul Éluard (qq.v.), and Aragon. But the major poets of the time, while integrating into their works some of the devices and discoveries of surrealism, developed independently. Pierre Jean Jouve, Henri Michaux, Jules Supervielle, René Char (qq.v.), Pierre Reverdy, and Saint-John Perse each intensely personal, carried poetry to heights seldom attained since the romantic era. But it was not until the 1940s that the extent of depth of the poetic renascence was recognized.

Drama

In 1920 the Vieux Colombier reopened its doors. Within a couple of years, four outstanding directors followed suit: Charles Dullin, Louis Jouvet, Gaston Baty, and Georges Pitoëff. In turn they formed a bevy of young successors: Jean-Louis Barrault, Jean Vilar, André Barsacq. By the mid-1930s the reform of the stage had been accomplished, reaching the boulevard and the Comédie Française; theater was reinstated as a major art, and the actor's function was defined as a noble and selfless devotion to that art. The success of these theater people in turn inspired an opposition, new ideas, new procedures tried out in small avant-garde theaters, challenging the former experiments as soon as they tended to become stereotyped. French theater was so intensely alive by the mid-1930s that its impetus was not slowed down by the disaster of World War II.

In the euphoria of the 1920s, the boulevard revived a tradition that the sparkling egotistic wit of Sacha Guitry (1885–1957) and the broad humor of Marcel Pagnol (q.v.) refurbished. Despite the efforts of the new directors, drama in the early 1920s made a slow start, timidly trying out new themes in old molds; plays based on Freudian psychology (Henri-René Lenormand, 1882–1951); intimate dramas of emotion and irony (Marcel Achard, 1899–1974; Charles Vildrac, 1882–1971); dramas of melancholy sentiment and cynicism (Stève Passeur, 1889–1966); or with Jean-Jacques Bernard's (1888–1972) "theater of silence," plays of unspoken emotional intensity, belying an almost inarticulate dialogue. The farce, with Fernand Crommelynck's (q.v.) *Le cocu magnifique* (1921; *The Magnificent Cuckold,* 1966) and Jules Romains's *Knock; ou, Le triomphe de la médecine* (1924; *Doctor Knock,* 1925), made a vigorous reappearance, but was overshadowed by the influence on the French stage of Luigi Pirandello (q.v.), whose *Six Characters in Search of an Author,* marked an epoch but also inspired a rash of "Pirandellism."

It was not until 1928, with the production by Jouvet of Jean Giraudoux's first play, *Siegfried* (1928; *Siegfried,* 1930), that French drama broke away from the past. The renascence was brilliant. Breaking with the realistic conventions of drama, Giraudoux conceived of theater as a celebration, a festival of the senses and the mind, appealing through both spectacle and language to the sensibilities and imagination of the audience. With him a poetic theater, dealing in large human dilemmas and clothed in the colors of myth, took over the stage and prepared the way for other creative dramatists. While carrying through a series of experiments in dramatic form, Cocteau kept the stage open to new ideas and themes. Taking full advantage of the new freedom in technique, Armand Salacrou and Jean Anouilh (qq.v.) transferred to the stage, in the 1930s, the growing mood of anxiety of the hour; less successfully, Gabriel Marcel (q.v.), renewing the problem play, dramatized the intellectual and metaphysical problems besetting the modern mind. Along with the work of the major dramatists, a proliferation of minor plays by dramatists like Jacques Audiberti, the Belgian Michel de Ghelderode (qq.v.), Jules Supervielle, and Georges Neveux (b. 1900), brought to the stage both quality and excitement, developing a poetic theater of great diversity. The French stage, immensely enriched in its range of expression and its scope, became a vital center of aesthetic expression.

The Novel

The immediate postwar years favored an inflationary trend in the novel, due both to its prestige—Proust's immense novel continued to come out in successive installments between 1918 and 1927, while Gide published *Les faux-monnayeurs* (1926; *The Counterfeiters,* 1927)—and to its immense salability. Heralded by the success of the adolescent Raymond Radiguet's (q.v.) *Le diable au corps* (1923; *The Devil in the Flesh,* 1932) and *Le bal du comte d'Orgel* (1924; *Ball at Count d'Orgel's,* 1929), the novel continued its reign. Novels of travel, such as those by Paul Morand (q.v.), or of adventure, whether in exotic settings—Pierre Benoît (1886–1962), Henri Fauconnier (1879–1955)—in the stadium or arena—Henry de Montherlant (q.v.)—or in the underworld of Paris—Pierre Mac Orlan (pseud. of Pierre Dumarchey, 1882–1970), Francis Carco; novels of fantasy—Giraudoux; novels of childhood and adolescence—Cocteau's *Thomas l'imposteur* (1923; *Thomas the Imposter,* 1925) and *Les enfants terribles* (1929; *Enfants Terribles,* 1930); traditional novels of psychological analysis—Jacques Chardonne (pseud. of Jacques Boutelleau, 1884–1968), Marcel Arland, Jacques de Lacretelle (b. 1888); Catholic novels of psychological problems and spiritual anguish—Julien Green, Georges Bernanos (qq.v.), François Mauriac; novels of provincial life—Jean Giono, Marcel Jouhandeau (qq.v.), André Chamson (b. 1900), Henri Bosco (1888–1976). Georges Duhamel's (q.v.) five-volume *Vie et aventures de Salavin* (1920–32; *Salavin,* 1936), a semiepic, semirealistic allegory, traced the itinerary of a quixotic petit-bourgeois "stranger," attempting to give significance to a meaningless life in an indifferent world by trying out one by one and discarding the various traditional solutions open to him: friendship, religion, adventure, and finally saintliness. In *Les Thibault* (8 vols., 1922–40; *The Thibaults,* 1939; *Summer 1914,* 1941), Martin du Gard began to describe the prewar social history of a class through the evolution of two bourgeois families. The avalanche of novels—carefully written ones, brilliantly improvised impressionistic ones, exploratory novels charting the new psychoanalytical approaches to dreams, sexuality, and psychoses—receded in the tense political climate of the 1930s.

A renaissance of the neorealistic novel in the 1930s produced many minor writers—Eugène

Dabit (1898–1936), Guy Mazeline (b. 1900), Philippe Hériat (pseud. of Raymond Gérard Payelle, 1898–1971), Maxence Van der Meersch (1907–1951), and Elsa Triolet (1896–1970)—and one major one, Louis Aragon. The novels that have survived from the abundant production of the period are either characteristically imaginative individual works, each enclosed in its own sphere, each reflecting a unity of vision and consequently an ethic—the works of Mauriac, Bosco, Giono, Jouhandeau; the satirical fantasies of Marcel Aymé (q.v.); and, although less resilient, the multivolume sociohistorical fresco novels, which predominated in the 1930s: Romains's twenty-seven-volume *Les hommes de bonne volonté* (1932–46; *Men of Good Will*, 1933–46); Martin du Gard's seven-part *Les Thibault;* Duhamel's ten-volume *La chronique des Pasquier* (1933–45; *The Pasquier Chronicles*, 1938; *Cécile Pasquier*, 1940; *Two Novels from the Pasquier Chronicles*, 1949); and Aragon's panoramas of life before World War I that were to lead to his attempt at a "heroic and epic" novel of the proletariat, *Les Communistes* (6 vols., 1949–1951; the Communists). Mirroring the concerns of the times, these novels used traditional structure to interpret the recent historical past of the French nation: in humanitarian or ethical terms with Duhamel; in an optimistic and "unanimistic" perspective with Romains. Socialistic with Martin du Gard, Marxist with Aragon, these novels express the main trends of thought among the traditionally leftist "intellectuals"; fiction once again tended to be subordinated to ideology.

Expository Prose

In all the realms of French cultural life, in the 1920s and 1930s criticism abounded. The period could count the *Propos* of Alain, Valéry's *Variété* (5 vols., 1924–44; *Variety*, 2 vols., 1927, 1938); Claudel's *Positions et propositions* (1927, 1934; *Ways and Crossways*, 1933), Gide's articles, the *Approximations* (1926–37; approximations) of Charles Du Bos (1882–1939), the doctrinaire *Jugements* (2 vols., 1923–24; judgments) of Henri Massis (1886–1970), and, in the *NRF*, the chronicles of the solid and subtle literary critic Albert Thibaudet (1874–1936). Countering the dogmatism of Massis, Jacques Maritain's (1882–1973) intelligent neo-Thomism and Henri Bremond's (1865–1933) generous mysticism kept alive the dialogue between Christians and rationalists that had opened with the century, in the courteous dispassionate tone adopted by the *NRF* group for speculative thought.

With the upsurge of Marxism and fascism, political issues displaced more general ones, positions stiffened to the right and to the left, antagonisms erupted, and even the politically uncommitted *NRF* took political stands. The wide-ranging essay of the 1920s became more specialized: political, philosophical, or literary. Ranging from the fascist propaganda pamphlets Pierre Drieu la Rochelle (q.v.) and Robert Brasillach to the communist propaganda essays of Paul Vaillant-Couturier (1892–1937) and Louis Aragon, the political essay accommodated all shades of opinion and were produced by writers like Jean-Richard Bloch (1884–1947), Paul Nizan (q.v.), Benjamin Crémieux (1888–1944), Jean Guéhenno, Emmanuel Berl, Thierry Maulnier (b. 1909), Romains, Bernard Groethuysen (1880–1946), Bernanos, and Montherlant. The more traditional literary criticism, influenced by Thibaudet, produced a solid and brilliant group of essayists: Ramon Fernandez (1894–1944), Robert Kemp (1885–1959), Emile Henriot (pseud. of Émile Maignot, 1889–1961), André Rousseaux (b. 1896), René Lalou (1889–1960), and André Maurois (q.v.).

But more significant was the diffusion of the philosophical essay at the hands of the liberal Catholics—Maritain, Marcel, and Emmanuel Mounier (1905–1950)—attempting to counter a dominant Marxism through the diffusion of modern forms of Christian philosphy.

The Metaphysical Midcentury: 1930s to 1950s

Céline's *Voyage au bout de la nuit* is a landmark in the history of the French novel. Its narrative technique—a first-person epic narrative based on the rhythms and patterns of oral language—heralded the massive flow into French literature of new influences: Joyce (q.v.), whose *Ulysses* (1922) was translated in 1929; the American "behaviorists," Dos Passos, Hemingway, Steinbeck, and Faulkner (qq.v.). It is also a landmark in the history of French literature. Céline's desperate nihilism inspired his visionary description, on a worldwide scale, of the individual's existence as "absurd"—that is, as derisively insignificant and cruel in an indifferent, purposeless, social and natural world. The writers familiar to the reading public in the 1930s either offered forms of a humanistic ethic based on traditional values (Alain, Gide, Giono, Giraudoux, Duhamel, Romains, Martin de Gard) or like Maritain and François Mauriac, a Christian framework of reference; and with Aragon, a Marxist. But in the novels of Bernanos and Julien Green, both Catholic writers, or of Louis Guilloux (q.v.), in a non-Christian anarchist-socialist tradition—*Le sang noir* (1935; *Bitter Victory*, 1936)—a new and urgent note of anxious questioning had prevailed that by the 1940s became dominant. Literature became involved in a tense debate on the nature of man's fate seen in the light of history. The philosophies of history—Hegelian, Marxist, Spenglerian, and Christian—slowly took precedence over merely political ideology. The growing influence of Dostoevsky and Péguy stressed the metaphysical concern of the times.

As the 1930s moved inexorably toward disaster, the sense of the "absurd" began to pervade French letters: Kafka (q.v.) became widely known. The surrealists' literary experiments, based on a sense of the disparity between the real nature of the individual's relation to the world and its logical representations, had already disrupted traditional literary habits in syntax, composition, and psychological motivation. In the 1930s and 1940s, a heightened awareness of the "absurd" favored the systematic use of some of their techniques. An apparently purely descriptive literature transmitted with cold objectivity an incoherent, alogical image of human life, an image ferocious in Marcel Aymé's mechanically impeccable, arbitrary world; poetically gratuitous in Raymond Queneau's (q.v.) "antinovels"; emotionally charged with humor in Henri Michaux's poems; and tragic in those of René Char. But it was André Malraux who gave the literature of the period its prevailing style, its somber character, and its tense overtones, while Jean-Paul Sartre, Simone de Beauvoir, and Albert Camus (qq.v.) furnished its vocabulary (anguish, gratuitousness, freedom, the "absurd"), its method (phenomenological, existential description) and its ethic, an ethic of choice, commitment, and responsibility, which the life and testimony of Antoine de Saint-Exupéry (q.v.) seemed to exemplify. The obsessive dominant theme of the period is the tragic dilemma and solitude of individual consciousness confronting an incomprehensible universe, and the means whereby the dilemma can be transcended. Hence the metaphysical overtones of literature and the

preponderance of the philosophical and critical essay over creative writing.

The defeat and occupation of France in 1940 dispersed French writers—by exile or deportation or to prisoner-of-war camps—and split the intellectuals into two groups: a minority committed to collaboration with the Germans, a majority to more or less active resistance. The dispersal of the writers favored the creation of a number of new reviews, some of which proved ephemeral although they played a major role at the time: *Poésie, Confluences, Fontaine, L'arche,* and *Les chroniques de minuit.* Others prospered, and became influential: *La Nef, Les temps modernes, La table ronde, La revue française, Preuves.* After a short period of indecision at the time of the Liberation in 1944, a solid core of prewar reviews remained: the *NRF, Mercure de France, La revue de Paris, La revue des deux mondes, Études, Esprit, Europe,* and *Cahiers du Sud.* With the notable exception of the *NRF* and *Cahiers du Sud,* almost all those reviews reflected a social, political, or religious point of view. The fragmentation of the literary milieu was characteristic of the period, as was also, in the light of circumstances, the brusque decline, after 1944, of the influence of certain collaborationists, such as Charles Maurras, and the devaluation of their work (Drieu la Rochelle, Brasillach). Devaluations, independently of any political connotations, affected a whole series of authors who wrote in the 1930s, with the exception of the more urgently questioning Salacrou, Anouilh, Aragon, Bernanos, Michaux, Malraux, and Char. The disappearance of the great figures of the past—Giraudoux, Valéry, Gide, Claudel, and Colette—and the premature disappearance of younger men like Saint-Exupéry and Bernanos, created a vacuum that was filled by two men, Sartre and Camus.

Poetry

Under the double impact of Marxist aesthetics and a real and deep sense of collective suffering, poets, during the Occupation, moving away from the more esoteric themes and forms of the surrealist era, developed a poetry of circumstance, social and political in theme, and greatly simplified in form, a type that had begun to reappear in the late 1930s. Aragon, in *Le crève-cœur* (1941; heartbreak) revived traditional lyrical forms; Éluard in *Le livre ouvert* (2 vols., 1940–42; the open book) and *Poésie et vérité 1942* (1942; *Poetry and Truth, 1942,* 1944) and Char in *Feuillets d'Hypnos* (1946;

Leaves of Hypnos, 1973) greatly simplified their idiom, Jouve in *La vierge de Paris* (1944; the virgin of Paris) his tormented mysticism. A new generation of younger poets, such as Pierre Emmanuel and Jean Cayrol (qq.v.), made of poetry the vehicle for a fervent expression of the collective national distress. The unity of mood did not outlast the 1940s, which recognized four new masters: Francis Ponge, Jacques Prévert (qq.v.), Saint-John Perse, and Char. Ponge's *Le parti pris des choses* (1942, taking the side of things), a collection of prose-poems, describing with meticulous care and a subterranean form of fabulating humor, objects—natural and man-made—in the quotidian world, was admittedly an effort at bringing poetry away from its metaphysical speculations and back to the concrete. Ponge's method and approach dominated a current of what might be called phenomenological (descriptive) poetry, another of whose practitioners was Eugène Guillevic (b. 1907). Continuing the political-surrealist trend, Prévert exploited all the surrealistic devices—puns, incongruous juxtapositions of words, unexpected images—in satirical poems, often based on the well-known rhythms of popular, sentimental or nursery songs, politically slanted against all aspects of the Establishment, an attitude that reached its culmination with the quasi-Dadaistic revolt of Henri Pichette's (b. 1924) *Apoèmes* (1948; apoems). In exile in America, Saint-John Perse, silent since 1924, published one after another great epic poems, developing in ample stanzas, concerned with the eternal question of mankind's destiny in the cosmos. Char, in terse, contracted forms tending toward aphorism, expressed a new humanistic ethic, the concern too of Pierre Seghers (b. 1906), Jean Rousselot (b. 1913), and René-Guy Cadou (1920–1951). Whether politically, socially or humanistically oriented, or turned toward the non-anthropocentric world of things, poetry, in a number of individual idioms, tended to reestablish the continuity of rhythm, the organized sequence of words, and the organic unity of the poem that the surrealists had drastically rejected.

Drama

The theater, dependent upon stable social conditions, suffered attrition. In Paris a premium was put by the occupying forces on the boulevard theater of entertainment. The "cartel" of the four great directors was disrupted; Jouvet toured abroad; Pitoëff died in 1939;

Baty concentrated on marionettes; Dullin struggled to keep his theater alive in the face of insuperable financial difficulties, and, at the Comédie Française, Jean-Louis Barrault succeeded in giving a few fine performances, producing, notably, Claudel's *Le soulier de satin* (pub. 1930; *The Satin Slipper,* 1931). In 1945 a major reorganization of the state-subsidized theaters started a new period of expansion. The theater was decentralized, with government-subsidized dramatic centers in the provinces; young troups were encouraged and support given the Théâtre National Populaire directed by Jean Vilar. With the inauguration of the Festival of Avignon, Vilar started a movement toward outdoor, summer festivals: at Nîmes, Arras, Angers, etc. In Paris innumerable "little theaters," most of them temporary, gave a growing number of directors their chance: André Barsacq, Michel Saint-Denis, Jean Dasté, Georges Vitaly, and Roger Planchon.

After 1942 the decade produced three new dramatists of stature: Montherlant, Sartre, and Camus. Abandoning the novel, Montherlant made his debut with *La reine morte* (1942; *Queen after Death,* 1951), which was followed by Sartre's *Les mouches* (1943; *The Flies,* 1947), Camus's *Le malentendu* (1943; *Cross Purposes,* 1946), and Simone de Beauvoir's (q.v.) *Les bouches inutiles* (1945; useless mouths). Reaching against the poetic, nonrealistic drama of Giraudoux, Montherlant returned to psychological drama, creating stage characters, whether historical or modern, motivated by his own aristocratic, nihilist ethic and in conflict with their entourage. Sartre, brilliant and versatile, eschewing psychological drama, proposed an existential theater of "extreme" situations, in which characters, trapped as it were, must make a choice, commit themselves, act, and so determine their "becoming" while revealing their inner orientation. In keeping with his own theory of literature, Sartre proposed an "efficient theater," directed at the spectators, with the aim of revealing to them the nature of their own situation. Increasingly political in its orientation, Sartre's theater tended toward a neorealism, counterbalanced by a somewhat profuse rhetorical eloquence. Camus's plays centered on the conflicts created by the tragic and insoluble paradoxes inherent in his conception of "absurd" man. Drama became charged with philosophical, often tragic themes, and somber overtones, but did not basically alter in structure. At the turn of the mid-century, the French stage seemed particularly vigorous, simultaneously presenting plays by

Claudel, Giraudoux (posthumously), Cocteau, Anouilh, Salacrou, Montherlant, Sartre, Camus, and Marcel.

The Novel

It was Malraux who, in the late 1920s, set the novel on a new course with *Les conquérants* (1928; *The Conquerers,* 1929). He chose for his novels a background of revolutionary action in the immediate present, whether in Indochina, China, Germany, or Spain, and treated it with journalistic intensity and from the point of view of the revolutionary forces with whom he had worked closely. In the foreground a handful of characters, the heroes, engage in tense elliptical dialogues elucidating the reasons that threw them into action: they face prison, torture, and violent death. The human condition is the theme of their desperate meditations—and the title of the most influential of these novels, *La condition humaine* (1933; *Man's Fate,* 1934). Revolt and heroic action in Malraux's world are the answer to the indignity of man's fate in a purposeless universe. With *Courrier Sud* (1929; *Southern Mail,* 1933) and *Vol de nuit* (1931; *Night Flight,* 1932), Saint-Exupéry, in a more humanistic vein, brought fiction close to personal testimony, describing the heroism of the men who established the first commercial airlines. In both works fiction was a pretext rather than a purpose, used as a means to transmit the quality of a personal experience based on a total commitment.

In a different mood and setting, Sartre's *La nausée* (1938; *Nausea,* 1949) and collection of short stories, *Le mur* (1939; *The Wall, and Other Stories,* 1948), and Camus's *L'étranger* (1942; *The Stranger,* 1946) created fictional situations fashioned by an intellectual view of life; their heroes incarnate attitudes latent in the uneasiness of mind of a whole generation, which both writers sought to explore. *La nausée* and *L'étranger* are tales, told in the first person, of a metaphysical adventure.

But the "metaphysical novel" did not last through the 1950s. Malraux abandoned the novel after *Les noyers de l'Altenburg* (1943; *The Walnut Trees of Altenburg,* 1952); Sartre did not finish the fourth volume of *Les chemins de la liberté* (1945–49; *The Roads to Freedom,* 1947–51). After Simone de Beauvoir's *Les mandarins* (1954; *The Mandarins,* 1956) the metaphysical novel gave way to works of direct testimony, of which her four volumes of memoirs, published between 1958 and 1972,

and Sartre's *Les mots* (1964; *The Words,* 1964) are outstanding examples. Camus, with *La peste* (1947; *The Plague,* 1948), *La chute* (1956; *The Fall,* 1957), and a collection of short stories, *L'exil et le royaume* (1957; *Exile and the Kingdom,* 1958), and Maurice Blanchot (q.v.) in his more obscure esoteric tales, carried on the mode of metaphysical fiction for a time.

Expository Prose

Most characteristic of the period is the literature of philosophical disquisition and debate centered on the Marxist-existentialist conflict, dominated by Sartre's *L'être et le néant* (1943; *Being and Nothingness,* 1956), and fortified by his numerous essays. Beauvoir and Camus also gave new impetus to the philosophical essay. Marxist philosophers—Henri Lefebvre (b. 1910). Georges Politzer (1903–1943); existentialist philosophers—Sartre, Beauvoir, and Maurice Merleau-Ponty (1906–1961) among the atheistic, Gabriel Marcel among the Christian existentialists; Christian "personalists"— Emmanuel Mounier; and independent thinkers —Simone Weil (q.v.), Camus—kept up controversies, sometimes violent, that reached a climax with the publication of Camus's *L'homme révolté* (1951; *The Rebel,* 1954), one of many works that presented a critique of Marxism. Among these the most influential were Raymond Aron's (b. 1905) *Le grand schisme* (1948; the great schism) and *L'opium des intellectuels* (1955; *The Opium of the Intellectuals,* 1957), and Merleau-Ponty's *Les aventures de la dialectique* (1955; *Adventures of the Dialectic,* 1973). Literary criticism produced important works, characterized by a metaphysical, emphasis: *De Baudelaire au surréalisme* (1933; *From Baudelaire to Surrealism,* 1949) by Marcel Raymond (1897–1957) and *L'âme romantique et le rêve* (1939; the romantic soul and the dream) by Albert Béguin (1898–1957). In *Baudelaire* (1947; *Baudelaire,* 1949) Sartre proposed a new biographical approach based on the dialectics of existential psychoanalysis. The criticism of Maurice Blanchot and the speculations of Jean Paulhan (q.v.) on language and rhetoric, opened the way for a philosophical approach to literary criticism, which a lively debate on the nature of poetry, sparked by the militant poetic theories of the surrealists, emphasized; this approach can be seen in *L'expérience poétique* (1938; the poetic experience) by Roland de Renéville (b. 1903); *Clef de la poésie* (1944;

key to poetry) by Paulhan; *La poésie moderne et la sacré* (1945; modern poetry and the holy) by Jules Monnerot (b. 1908); *Les impostures de la poésie* (1943; the deceptions of poetry) by Roger Caillois (1913–1978).

But it was in the 1950s that, with Malraux's controversial but eloquent attempt to create a metaphysics of art—*Les voix du silence* (1951; *The Voices of Silence*, 1953), *La métamorphose des dieux* (1957; *The Metamorphosis of the Gods*, 1960)—the trend reached its climax, orienting criticism toward what has been called "metacriticism," a metaphysics of the creative process as such.

From the 1950s to the 1980s: A Rapidly Shifting Stage

The 1950s, with the emergence of a new generation, seem clearly to mark a turning point, a reorientation of literary currents. Both novel and drama broke away from the themes and forms of politically or philosophically committed literature; poetry showed a number of widely divergent trends, and nonfiction prose took on a literary rather than a philosophical coloring.

Narrative Modes

Novels of every type now flooded the market: historical, picaresque, erotic, sentimental. Among hundreds of names, only a few stood out: Vercors, Pierre Gascar, Françoise Mallet-Joris (qq.v.), Jean Cayrol. In reaction to the overbundant novelistic production, a publisher, Jérôme Lindon, selected for his Éditions de Minuit (midnight editions) a few original new writers. These "antinovelists," or "midnight," "new," or "experimental" novelists as they were called, did not constitute a school. They were in agreement on a certain number of points: the novel, in order to subsist, should incorporate further experimentations with technical innovations. Plot, character, psychological analysis, description, as traditionally practiced, would have to go. The novel should be politically "uncommitted," free of philosophical concerns extraneous to its purpose. Beyond this, those novelists shared no program, each exploring new forms and possibilities of narrative technique. Samuel Beckett, Alain Robbe-Grillet, Michel Butor, Nathalie Sarraute, Claude Simon, Raymond Pinget, Claude Ollier, and Marguerite Duras (qq.v.), besides producing novels both varied and challenging to the reader, created around the novel—the New

Novel (q.v.)—a flurry of criticism, and seemed to be preparing the way for new developments in the genre.

As the 1950s wore on, the novelists' concern with theories of narrative structure and semiology led to complex experiments in the production of abstract and arbitrary patterns, antirealistic and antianthropocentric in intent. "New" and "new, new" novels had a greater impact on literary criticism than on narrative fiction as such and never reached a broad reading public, which turned to science fiction, detective novels, history, and biography. One outstanding exception—a serious but widely read novelist—is Michel Tournier (q.v.).

In the late 1940s and into the 1950s autobiography emerged as a major narrative genre: Michel Leiris (q.v.), who had previously published *L'âge d'homme* (1939; *Manhood*, 1963) began his four-volume *La règle du jeu* (1948–1976; the rules of the game), and Sartre, Beauvoir, and Jean Genet (q.v.) all published important autobiographical works.

Drama

More immediately widely acclaimed was the appearance in the 1950s of what has been called "antitheater" or "Theater of the Absurd" (q.v.), a form of drama that drew some of its technique from a theoretician of the stage, Antonin Artaud (q.v.), a former actor and surrealist poet. Influenced by the Oriental stage, Artaud developed his ideas in a series of essays called *Le théâtre et son double* (1938; *The Theater and Its Double*, 1958), advocating a "theater of cruelty," whose aim should be to disrupt the composure of the audience, unleashing collective primitive emotions, thus releasing and exorcising those dark forces of life which, Artaud felt, were dangerously repressed by Europeans: eroticism, cruelty, terror, etc. It was more Artaud's dramaturgy than his ideas that influenced the antitheater of the 1950s: he advocated puppetlike actors, miming a violent action, using a stage "sign" language—where props, dance, and sound counted more than the words themselves. Samuel Beckett, and in their first works, Eugène Ionesco and Arthur Adamov (qq.v.), stripping the play down to its bare essentials, drew for their characters on the circus, mime, and the puppet show, and did away with plot, characterization, and rhetoric, developing a tragicomic drama of pattern and repetition. Jean Genet, in contrast, using a flow of language rich in imagery, developed a theater of ceremonial and ritual, based on mask and masquerade, while Georges Schehadé (b. 1910) continued the tradition of the poetic theater. By the 1960s, under the influence of Bertolt Brecht (q.v.), Adamov had developed toward a form of "epic theater"; Beckett, continually reducing his stage, was not renewing his themes. In spite of the success of Genet and Ionesco, the French stage was in search of new orientations, experimenting with various new forms of theater, radio plays (Raymond Pinget), and chamber plays (Jean Tardieu, q.v.).

The most original of the later playrights is Fernando Arrabal (q.v.), a Spaniard residing in France, whose violently baroque and erotic plays from *Pique-nique en campagne* (1961; *Picnic on the Battlefield,* 1967) to *La tour de Babel* (1976; the tower of Babel) escape classification. Two women writers, both novelists, Marguerite Duras and Nathalie Sarraute, have produced some of the more quietly innovative plays of the period. French conceptions of theater had changed in the 1960s and 1970s. Moving away from Paris, to summer festivals in centers such as Nancy and Avignon, and international in scope, theater freed itself from the restraints of the conventional stage and the expectations of an urban audience. For the forty or so companies that, in summer, play to some 150,000 spectators, theater is no longer wedded to a literary text. What counts is the quality and audacity of the stage productions. This may account for a certain dearth of playwrights.

Poetry

Postwar France showed an upsurge of lyrical talent, heralded in the 1940s by Pierre Emmanuel, undoubtedly the outstanding figure of his generation. The new poets—Yves Bonnefoy (q.v.), Alain Bosquet (b. 1919), André du Bouchet (b. 1924), Philippe Jacottet (b. 1925), André Marissel (b. 1928), Claude Vigée (b. 1921), Jean-Claude Renard (b. 1922), Robert Sabatier (b. 1923), Pierre Oster (b. 1933), Marc Alyn (b. 1937), and Edmond Jabès (q.v.)—reflect a wide diversity of tendencies and techniques. With the exception of Bouchet, influenced by Char, they all tend to use simpler, more direct forms of poetic expression and more traditional forms of prosody than their predecessors. Although no single trend predominates, the central concern of this poetry, born in the aftermath of war, is to probe the relation of the poet to a world under the shadow of destruction. The sense of peril and of beauty induced an elegiac and neoromantic mood, which is emphasized in many poets by a deliberate use of the rhythmical or-

ganization and rhetorical flow of the romantic poets, Victor Hugo most particularly. All have developed their own idioms, the most powerfully original being that of Edmond Jabès.

Two main tendencies mark the poetry of the 1960s and 1970s: the drive to renew the language and themes of French poetry without breaking with traditional rules of prosody; and experimentation with new forms, sometimes borrowed from other cultures (the Japanese tanka and haiku) or produced by the permutation of "generic" elements somewhat akin to the techniques of serial music, as seen in the works of Jacques Roubaud (b. 1932), Denis Roche (b. 1937), and the "antipoet" Marcelin Pleynet (b. 1933). Among the many poets untroubled by theory, Andrée Chédid (b. 1920), author of *Textes pour un poème* (1950; texts for a poem) has steadily published poems that place her among the two or three outstanding poets of the period.

Expository Prose

The turn of the midcentury showed a characteristic swing away from metaphysical and philosophical speculation toward literary criticism, and, with E. M. Cioran (b. 1911), found a successor to the great essay writer of the 1920s, Valéry. It has rightly been called an era of criticism.

Drawing on every other discipline—psychoanalysis (see Psychology and Literature), whether Freudian—Charles Mauron (1899–1966)—or Sartrian; on Marxist sociology and aesthetics as developed by György Lukács (q.v.)—Lucien Goldmann (1913–1970), Roland Barthes (q.v.); on anthropology—Georges Bataille (q.v.), and Roger Caillois—and structural anthropology and structuralism (q.v.)—Claude Lévi-Strauss (q.v.); on scientific phenomenological studies of the imagination—Gaston Bachelard (1884–1962)—criticism became "metacriticism," a phenomenology of the creative process, a heuristic—Gaëtan Picon (b. 1915), R.-M. Albérès (b. 1920); also important are the "thematic" critics Georges Poulet (b. 1902), Jean Pierre Richard (b. 1922), and Jean Starobinski (b. 1920). Problems of method predominated in university essays and discussions. Poets—Bosquet, Vigée, Bonnefoy, Emmanuel—reexamined the problem of the nature of poetry, its significance and function in the modern world. The New Novelists—Sarraute in *L'ère du soupçon* (1956; *The Age of Suspicion,* 1964), Butor in *Répertoire I* (1960; inventory I), Robbe-Grillet in *Pour un nouveau roman*

(1963; *For a New Novel,* 1965)—and the dramatists—Ionesco, for instance, in *Notes et contre notes* (1962; *Notes and Counter Notes,* 1964), also discussed methods and aims. In the early 1960s there were signs that, leaving aside some of its metaphysical ambitions, and less marked by political bias, French criticism, remarkably enriched, was beginning to move away from the turmoil and confusion of the preceding years. A good example of the shift in approach is Jean Rousset's (b. 1910) *Forme et signification: Essais sur les structures littéraires de Corneille à Claudel* (1962; form and signification: essays on literary structures from Corneille to Claudel).

The second half of the 20th c. may well be known, like the 18th c., for its *philosophes*—writers drawn from many disciplines—Claude Lévi-Strauss, anthropology; Jean-Paul Sartre, philosophy; Jacques Lacan (b. 1901), psychoanalysis; Emmanuel LeRoy Ladurie (b. 1929), history; Michel Foucault (b. 1926), sociology. These intellectuals set the ideological stage of the time, its moods, and themes.

Conclusion

In 1980, the French Academy made a momentous if belated decision: it elected its first woman writer, Marguerite Yourcenar (q.v.), novelist, essayist, playwright, and autobiographer. The election was a tribute to her and to the single most dynamic movement of the 1970s—social and literary—the women's liberation movement. Articulate, involved in passionate debate concerning the modalities of "women's writing," launching its often ephemeral reviews, running its own publishing house, Les Éditions des Femmes, it has made its presence felt in every facet of the intellectual and literary life of France. Since 1970 three generations of women, from different strata of society, whose work is characterized by its diversity and originality, have held the center of attention in literary Paris: Yourcenar, Sarraute, Beauvoir, Duras, Christiane Rochefort (b. 1917), Monique Wittig (b. 1935), and Hélène Cixous (b. 1937). To a certain extent they have filled the void left in the 1960s by Camus's death, Sartre's involvement in politics, and Malraux's withdrawal from the literary scene and his subsequent death, a void that in spite of their success the "new philosophes" of the late 1970s—Bernard Henri Lévy (b. 1948), André Glucksman (b. 1937)—have not filled. As one moves into the 1980s, literary activity in France continues at a hectic pace;

furthermore, never have so many of the great and lesser works of the past been available to younger readers; likewise, never have they had such quick access to contemporary world literature, put rapidly into circulation through translations. But, in this open, cosmopolitan world, except for the women, a younger generation was finding it difficult to fashion its own idiom.

A self-styled "avant-garde" grouped around new reviews (*Tel Quel; Change*), basing its activity on concepts and methodologies borrowed from other disciplines, more especially linguistics (see Linguistics and Literature) and psychoanalysis, sought to reorient, simultaneously, both the literary forms and the traditional concepts concerning the nature of literature implicit in critical analysis and interpretation. Accepting as their point of departure the axiom that a text is a "production," a nonreferential structure of words, refusing to privilege either content, "subject," or genre, moving from the analysis of linguistic codes to theories of textual production, they radically affected the vocabulary and goals of academic criticism. The theoretical and applied critical work by Julia Kristeva (b. 1941), the "deconstructive" criticism of Jacques Derrida (b. 1930), and the highly original texts produced by Philippe Sollers (q.v.) exemplify the tight coordination between theory, criticism, and production in the activities of the movement. In the 1970s one could sense a violent reaction against the abstractions and constraints of theoretical discourse, the recourse to a free flow of uncensored language that allegedly emanated directly from the unconscious—Pierre Guyotal's (b. 1941) *Éden, Éden, Éden* (1971; Eden, Eden, Eden) and Hélène Cixous's *Le troisième corps* (1970; the third body) and *Les commencements* (1970; the beginnings).

The most influential intellectual of the 1960s and 1970s, the mentor of this avant-garde, was Roland Barthes, a subtle essayist and critic, whose critical career embraced the successive theories of his time, applied, then transcended them. With *Plaisir du texte* (1973; *The Pleasure of the Text,* 1976), he abandoned the search for a scientifically based critical methodology. His later texts—*Roland Barthes par Roland Barthes* (1975; *Roland Barthes by Roland Barthes,* 1977), *Fragments d'un discours amoureux* (1977; *A Lover's Discourse: Fragments,* 1979)—place him in the tradition of French essayists inaugurated by Montaigne. It seemed plausible to conclude that the period of exacerbated literary experimentation was drawing to its end, while a new synthesis was in the making.

BIBLIOGRAPHY: Magny, C.-E., *Histoire du roman français depuis 1918* (1950); Chiari, J., *Contemporary French Poetry* (1952); Peyre, H., *The Contemporary French Novel* (1955); Brée, G., and Guiton, M., *An Age of Fiction: The French Novel from Gide to Camus* (1957); Grossvogel, D. I., *The Self-Conscious Stage in Modern French Drama* (1958); Chiari, J., *The Contemporary French Theatre* (1959); Mauriac, C., *The New Literature* (1959); Turnell, M., *The Art of French Fiction* (1959); Albérès, R.-M., *Histoire du roman moderne* (1962); Cruikshank, J., ed., *The Novelist as Philosopher: Studies in French Fiction* (1962); Pronko, L. C., *Avant-Garde: The Experimental Theater in France* (1962); Robbe-Grillet, A., *For a New Novel* (1965); Maurois, A., *From Proust to Camus* (1966); Moore, H. T., *Twentieth-Century French Literature* (2 vols., 1966); Fowlie, W., *Climate of Violence: The French Literary Tradition from Baudelaire to the Present* (1967); Guicharnaud, J., *The Modern French Theatre: From Giraudoux to Genet,* rev. ed. (2 vols., 1967); Nadeau, M., *The French Novel since the War* (1967); O'Brien, J., *The French Literary Horizon* (1967); Peyre, H., *French Novelists of Today* (1967); Sturrock, J., *The French New Novel* (1969); Bersani, L., *Balzac to Beckett* (1970); Mercier, V., *A Reader's Guide to the New Novel* (1971); Caws, M. A., *The Inner Theatre of Recent French Poetry* (1972); Fletcher, J., ed., *Forces in Modern French Drama* (1972); Roudiez, L. S., *French Fiction Today* (1972); Simon, J. K., ed., *Modern French Criticism* (1972); Brée, G., *Women Writers in France* (1973); Doubrovsky, S., *The New Criticism in France* (1973); O'Flaherty, K., *The Novel in France 1945–1965: A General Survey* (1973); Picon, G., *Contemporary French Literature: 1945 and After* (1974); Walzer, P.-O., *Littérature française: Le XXᵉ siècle I: 1896–1920* (1975); Popkin, D., and Popkin, M., eds., *Modern French Literature* (2 vols., 1977); Brée, G., *Littérature française: Le XXᵉ siècle II: 1920–1970* (1978); Brooks, R. A., ed., *A Critical Bibliography of French Literature: The Twentieth Century* (1979); Flower, J. E., *Literature and the Left in France* (1979)

GERMAINE BRÉE

Basque Literature

Until very recently the Basque language in France (spoken in the western Pyrenees region) was kept alive by the Catholic Church, which had created and sustained its literature.

Most of the major authors belonged to religious orders and wrote in the vernacular.

Jean Hiriart-Urruty (1859–1915) was the mentor of the modern generation of French-Basque writers. In 1887 he founded the weekly review *Eskualduna,* which he directed for thirty years and to which he contributed many articles. In a very rich but popular style he attacked the republican, anticlerical ideas of his time. His articles have recently been collected in two volumes: *Mintzaira, aurpegia: Gizon* (1971; tongue, face: man) and *Zezenak errepublikan* (1972; the bulls in the republic).

Among the early modern French-Basque writers, one of the best and most prolific was Jean Barbier (1875–1931), whose novel *Piarres* (2 vols., 1926, 1929; Piarres) is especially worth mentioning. The true protagonist is the Basque way of life of the early 20th c. The novel describes family life, work in the fields, holidays, games, death, and war.

Much of the most important French-Basque writing of the first half of the 20th c. was journalistic. Jean Etchepare (1877–1935) published frequently in the magazines *Eskualduna* and *Gure herria.* In addition he wrote two books: *Buruchkak* (1910; ears of wheat) and *Berebilez* (1931; by car). *Buruchkak* is a collection of articles in which he discusses religious education and morality from a viewpoint not well accepted by traditional Catholics. *Berebilez* narrates his travels in the Spanish Basque country. Etchepare was an outstanding stylist, employing, for the first time, the Basse-Navarre Basque dialect as a literary medium.

Bishop Jean Saint-Pierre (1884–1951) published impressions taken from the battlefields of World War I in *Eskualduna.* His style is direct and easily understandable. In 1921 he cofounded the magazine *Gure herria* and a year later received the "Kirikiño" literary award from the Academy of Basque Language for his efforts. His best articles were published together under the title *Les meilleures pages de Mgr. Saint-Pierre* (1952; the best pages of Monsignor Saint-Pierre).

Jules Moulier (pseud.: Oxobi, 1888–1958) is primarily known for his book *Alegiak* (1926; fables), a collection of fables written in verse. His humor is often bitter.

Later writers continued the journalistic tradition of their predecessors. The prolific writings of Pierre Lafitte (b. 1901) are devoted to the defense of Basque culture and the unification of the various Basque dialects. He has contributed extensively to *Eskualduna, Gure herria,* and *Herria* (which he founded).

More recent French-Basque writing has included some noteworthy drama and poetry. Pierre Larzabal (b. 1915) and Telesforo Monzón (1904–1981) are playwrights concerned with cultural, social, and political problems in the Basque country. Larzabal assisted Basque refugees from Franco's Spain, while Monzón, who had been a member of the Basque government in Spain before the civil war, lived the life of a political exile in the French Basque country. Both depict their experiences in their works. Larzabal has written about a hundred plays, most of which remain unpublished. The best-known are *Etchahun* (1953; good house), *Bordaxuri* (1962; the white hut), *Hiru ziren* (1962; they were three), *Senperen gertatua* (1964; what happened in Senpere), and *Hila esposatu* (1965; the dead married). His spare style reflects the austerity of the Basque character. Monzón is also a poet and musician, and thus his theater is rather lyrical. *Menditarrak* (1957; the mountaineers) and *Zurgin zaharra* (1956; the old carpenter) are two of his best plays.

The poet Jean Diharce (pseud.: Xabier Iratzeder, b. 1920), is abbot of the Benedictine monastery of Belloc; his translations of the biblical Psalms into Basque—*Salmoak* (1963; psalms)—have been used in the mass and religious songs. Of a totally different style are the works of the Paris-born Basque poet Jean Mirande (1925–1972), which reflect a lack of respect for reforms and conventions alike as the enemies of Basque culture. For him it is more important that poetry be aesthetically and stylistically elegant than that it address social and cultural issues.

Although it is difficult to foresee the future of French-Basque literature, it will most likely be of a political nature because of the Basque revival of the past twenty-five years.

BIBLIOGRAPHY: Lafitte, P., *Le basque et la littérature d'expression basque en Labourd, Basse-Navarre et Soule* (1941); Michelena, L., *Historia de la literatura vasca* (1960); Villasante, L., *Historia de la literatura vasca* (1961); Lecuona, Manuel de, *Literatura oral vasca* (1965); Cortázar, N. de, *Cien autores vascos* (1966); *Enciclopedia general illustrada del país vasco* (1966); Sarasola, I., *Historia social de literatura vasca* (1976); Mujika, L. M., *Historia de la literatura euskerika* (1979)

GORKA AULESTIA

Breton Literature

The Breton language, like Cornish and Welsh, is a Brythonic language derived from Celtic. In spite of centuries of French oppression, it is spoken by the inhabitants of western Brittany, whose ancestors emigrated from southwest Britain between the 4th and 6th cs.

The publication of the momentous and controversial *Barzaz breiz* (1839; Breton anthology), purported to be folk songs collected by Théodore Hersart de la Villemarqué (1815–1895), has had dramatic influence to this day in activating Breton authors, by kindling in them a sense of pride in their national and Celtic heritage.

A solitary Tangi Malmanche (1875–1953), forerunner of the Breton movement—which strives for cultural freedom and autonomy—and the greatest Breton playwright, writing in seclusion in Paris, reverted to the tales and traditions of Brittany for inspiration. His *Marvailh an ene naonek* (1900; the tale of the hungry soul), among others, was based on a single tradition, but most of his plays are interweavings of intricate patterns of beliefs and customs. All are composed in an excitingly innovative and virile style. In *Gurvan* (1923; Gurvan) there is a strong feeling of national consciousness arising from the hero's battles against the oppression of his cunning and ruthless Frankish neighbor, which loudly echoes the sentiments expressed in la Villemarqué's collection, in which Malmanche was well versed.

Revolutionary enthusiasm, when it fails to move the masses, often transmutes itself into disillusionment—particularly evident in Malmanche's plays and later in the poetry of Roparz Hemon (1900–1978).

Most 20th-c. Breton writers of note are inextricably associated with the Breton movement. *Gwalarn,* founded in 1925—the first literary magazine—was originally a supplement to the political periodical *Breiz atao,* whose title means "Brittany forever." Its aim, under the guidance of Roparz Hemon, was to produce works of distinction far superior to the sadly decadent peasant literature, and free from French influence. Instead of escaping from their cares to the land of fairies, *Gwalarn* writers found solace in prose portraiture of contemporary society, as in the short stories of Jakez Riou (1899–1937) and Roparz Hemon, and in Hemon's novel *Nenn Jani* (1974; Nenn Jani).

The influence of Irish and Welsh literatures is all-pervading. Plays by Hemon and by Fant Rozenn Meavenn (b. 1911) have been influenced by the Dublin Abbey Theatre Group, while poets such as Hemon and Gwilherm Berthou Kerverzioù (1908–1951) treat themes from Irish mythology. Welsh short-story writers influenced Fanch Elies (1896–1963), and later

Ronan Huon (b. 1922), of the new school of the journal *Al liamm*, founded in 1949, which continued the work of *Gwalarn*, suppressed after World War II by the French authorities.

Today, although preoccupation with world-wide contemporary moral and social injustices is increasingly noticeable in the works of the new generation, the strong sense of identity is as tenacious as ever.

BIBLIOGRAPHY: Le Mercier d'Erm, C., *Les bardes et poètes nationaux de la Bretagne armoricaine* (1919); Gourvil, F., *Langue et littérature bretonnes* (1952); Piette, J. R. F., "Modern Breton Poetry," *Poetry Wales*, 3, 1 (1967), 3–10, and 3, 3 (1967), 25–32; Denez, P., "Notes on Modern Literature in Breton," *AWR*, 19 (1971), 19–33; Piriou, Y.-B., *Défense de cracher par terre et de parler breton* (1971); Denez, P., "Modern Breton Literature," in Williams, J. E., *Literature in Celtic Countries* (1971); Durand, P., ed., *Breizh hiziv: Anthologie de la chanson en Bretagne* (1976)

RITA WILLIAMS

Occitan Literature

Occitan (frequently, but not accurately, referred to as Provençal outside France, and also known as *langue d'oc*) is a language of southern France comprising a number of dialects, including Provençal (in the restricted sense of the dialect of Provence). A great body of troubadour poetry was written during the Middle Ages in this language, but following a decree of Francis I in 1539 making French the language of his kingdom, Occitan was suppressed and produced few literary works until the 19th c., when the Félibrige revival movement, led by Joseph Roumanille (1818–1891), was founded in 1854.

The Félibrige movement, the fruit of a moral, aesthetic, and political retreat to the countryside, resulted in some major literary successes, but it did not lead to a general revival of the language. The Avignon School, the first incarnation of the Félibrige movement, produced an artist of noble ambitions in Théodore Aubanel (1829–1886), who sensitively expressed the clash between strict Catholicism and a pagan exaltation of the flesh. Above all, the Félibrige movement brought Frédéric Mistral (1830–1914) to world literature. This epic poet, with *Mirèio* (1859; *Mirèio*, 1872), *Calendau* (1867; Calendau),

and *Lou pouèmo dóu Rose* (1896; *Anglore: The Song of the Rhone*, 1937), succeeded in revitalizing for the modern world the rhythms, the splendor, and the spirit of the poetry of old. Mistral, called a "new Homer" after *Mirèio* and recipient of the Nobel Prize in 1905, came to symbolize an unfortunately illusory redemption of the condemned language.

The Félibrige, however, continued in its efforts to reawaken all the regions in which the *langue d'oc* was spoken. Among dozens of talented writers the best were the Gascon Michel Camélat (1871–1962), a wonderfully rough epic poet of the Pyrenees; the Provençal Joseph d'Arbaud (1872–1950), who developed an incantatory prose for Occitan; and Antonin Perbosc (1861–1944) from Quercy, who gave a new impetus to impersonal lyricism.

By around 1930 the Félibrige had outlived its effectiveness. It was at that time that a modern Occitan literature was founded on the pursuit of three fundamental and complementary goals: the perfection of a written language freed from French dominance; the elaboration (under Catalan influence) of the reasons for the demand for autonomy; and the desire for literary modernism (q.v.). The Society for Occitan Studies, which became the Institute for Occitan Studies in 1945, addressed itself to the first and third of these aims. Among prominent writers of this generation, Renat Nelli (b. 1906), a scholar of the Middle Ages and a poet of great strength influenced by Paul Valéry (q.v.), in *Arma de vertat* (1952; soul of truth) presented the experience of love with philosophical anxiety. Very different is Max Rouquette (b. 1908), a lyrical poet and a prose writer who with wonder but also sorrow vividly portrays Mediterranean Languedoc. Joan Mouzat (b. 1905) of Limousin is a learned poet, like the dazzling Paul-Louis Grenier (1879–1954), but Mouzat sometimes leaps into the realm of the fantastic. Léon Cordes's (b. 1913) poetry, fiction, and drama is firmly planted in his time and land.

The writers who came to prominence after World War II added to these achievements a strong desire to standardize the Occitan language, to treat the most varied subjects, and to turn their backs on regionalism. It is not for the author of this article (Robert Lafont, b. 1923) to discuss his own poems, plays, novels, and essays. Among other postwar writers, Henri Espieux (1923–1971) wrote poetry of a somber glow. The mystical, violent poet Bernard Manciet (b. 1923) moved from modernist, cosmopolitan odes to the mysterious prose of his novels of the Landes soil, such as *Lo gojat de novémer* (1954; the young man of November). Pierre Bec (b. 1921), whose poetry is very dense, has recently turned to dreamlike or realistic fiction, as in *Contes de l'unic* (1977; tales of the unique). The most important writer of this generation is Joan Boudou (1920–1975). Starting with folkloric prose, in the manner of the Félibrige, he was able, without abandoning regional subjects, to introduce into Occitan literature the great themes of the contemporary era: the loneliness of man at war; the dizzying gaze at the emptiness of destiny; the constant anguish over the absurd. He essayed the fantastic novel—*La santa Estela del centenari* (1960; the hundredth anniversary of Saint Estelle's Day); the historical novel—*La quimèra* (1974; the chimera); and the rural chronicle —*Lo libre de Catòia* (1966; the book of Catòia).

A very different group of writers appeared after 1956. Among its members is the poet Serge Bec (b. 1933), who denounced colonial wars in *Memòria de la carn* (1960; memory of the flesh). The novelist Pierre Pessemesse (b. 1931), who began with a chronicle of Provençal boyhood, *Nhòcas e bachòcas* (1957; wounds and bruises), portrayed an entire era in *De fuòc amb de cendre* (3 vols., 1973–78; fire and ashes). The poets Yves Rouquette (b. 1936) and Jean Larzac (b. 1937) moved from personal to political works. Christian Rapin (b. 1931) is a very accomplished poet, while Robert Allan's (b. 1927) verse is spontaneous and whimsical.

In 1968, a year of political and social turmoil in France, there was an upheaval in Occitan culture. The modern Occitan ballad—at the same time lyrical and aggressive—came into being through dozens of songwriter-singers; a new, militant drama stirred audiences; and formal experiments in other literary genres proliferated. Among writers who came to the fore, outstanding are Roland Pécout (b. 1948), at first a poet, then a writer of fiction portraying the modern world adrift; Roselyne Roche (b. 1946), whose poems chronicle the life of a woman; Florian Vernet (b. 1941), writer of absurdist works of fiction and drama; Jan dau Melhau (b. 1948), a rough novelist from Limousin; and the poet Joël Meffre (b. 1951).

Modern Occitan literature, now robust, is built on the very paradox of the mortal dangers threatening its language. These very dangers have led to an awakening: the need for the survival of Occitan language and culture has now penetrated the public consciousness.

BIBLIOGRAPHY: Camproux, C., *Histoire de la littérature occitane* (1953); Rouquette, J., *La littérature d'oc* (1968); Lafont, R., and Anatole, C., *Nouvelle histoire de la littérature occitane* (1971); Lafont, R., *Clefs pour l'Occitanie* (1971), pp. 131–51; Nelli, R., *La poésie d'oc* (1972); Armengaud, A., and Lafont, R., eds., *Histoire d'Occitanie* (1979), passim

ROBERT LAFONT

FRENCH-CARIBBEAN LITERATURE

When they arrived during the early 17th c., French settlers on the Caribbean islands of Haiti, Martinique, Guadeloupe, and later in French Guiana on the South American mainland, brought to their New World plantations the institutions and cultural norms of their homeland. The African slaves who were forcibly transported to these places maintained certain aspects of their ancestral cultures, while creating new forms in the context of plantation society. The literature of the French-speaking Caribbean therefore reflects the political problems, cultural ambiguities, and aesthetic challenges and achievements resulting from this encounter between varying traditions and systems of values. But only in Haiti does the literature manifest the presence of a definite national culture.

Haiti

Ever since their country's declaration of independence from France in 1804, Haitian intellectuals and men of letters have tended to imitate French models. The romantic, Parnassian, and symbolist (q.v.) modes have found their echoes in the writings of Haitian poets such as Oswald Durand (1840–1906), Justin Lhérisson (1873–1907), Georges Sylvain (1866–1925), and Damoclès Vieux (1876–1936). After the humiliating experience of the American occupation of the island from 1915 to 1934, writers turned inward, using indigenous cultural treasures in their works.

In their search for cultural particularity during the U.S. occupation, Haitian intellectuals discovered the roots of a national culture in folk traditions. The work of the Haitian ethnographer Dr. Jean Price-Mars (1876–1969), especially his study *Ainsi parla l'oncle* (1928; thus spoke the uncle), urged Haitian writers to find new subjects in the folklore, which is strongly imprinted with African cultural traits —the authentic patrimony of Haiti. Jacques

Roumain (q.v.), coeditor with Price-Mars of *La revue indigène*, applied the new perspective in his celebrated peasant novel *Gouverneurs de la rosée* (1944; *Masters of the Dew*, 1947).

A constellation of writers of the so-called "indigenous" school took up the challenge of Price-Mars and Roumain, and their work represents a true renascence in Haitian literature, analogous to the almost contemporary Harlem Renaissance in the U.S., with which it has close affinities. Normil Sylvain (1901–1929) wrote the group's manifesto in the first issue of *La revue indigène* (1927). He argued that writers should make their contribution to national pride and solidarity by singing the praises of their homeland. Philippe Thoby-Marcellin (q.v.), first in poetry and later in fiction, mirrored with sympathy the realities of peasant life. The poems of Émile Roumer (b. 1903) and Léon Laleau (b. 1892) describe Haitian flora and fauna, as well as the simple pleasures and hurts of Haitian peasants.

The indigenous trend inaugurated by the renascence writers was continued by the next generation, but there were other influences as well. The poetry of Magloire St. Aude (1912–1971), especially his *Dialogue de mes lampes* (1941; dialogue of my lamps), shows definite affinities with the dreamlike qualities of French surrealism (q.v.). The failure of the 1946 revolution brought a new tenor to Haitian literary expression. Disenchantment with the increasingly dictatorial regimes elicited a more militant and revolutionary tone. Many of the younger writers were forced into exile, and a new literature of the Haitian diaspora was thus created. Representatives of this generation include René Depestre (b. 1926), who writes from his adopted Cuba incisive critiques of the current Haitian regime and its French and American benefactors. Depestre's celebrated poem *Un arc-en-ciel pour l'occident chrétien* (1967; *A Rainbow for the Christian West*, 1972) shows traces of the indigenist search for values in Haitian culture. Jacques-Stéphen Alexis (1922–1961) applied his theory of "magic realism" (q.v.) in his novel *Les arbres musiciens* (1957; the musical trees), utilizing the aesthetic qualities of traditional Haitian religion, the vaudou.

Most recently Haitian writers have been attempting to push Alexis's "marvelous realism" to its logical extension in the creation of literature in an authentically Haitian language. The use of Creole in literature is a critical question, since this is the language used exclusively by over ninety percent of the Haitian people.

Frank Étienne (b. 1936) has written the first novel in Creole, *Désafi* (1975; disaffection). Haitian literature has therefore evolved from concern with French sources to preoccupation with finding the most effective means of expressing the soul of the Haitian people.

French Antilles and French Guiana

French colonies since the 17th c., Martinique, Guadeloupe and its dependencies, and French Guiana were accorded the status of Overseas Departments in 1946. Throughout their history there have been tensions between the white planter class and white administrators on the one hand, and, on the other, an underclass consisting in earlier times of slaves and freed men of color, and later the colored middle class and the lower class of urban dwellers and rural folk. There is no pervasive sense of national culture, even though there have been periodic attempts to develop such an awareness.

In poetry, the earlier writers, like their Haitian counterparts, followed French styles. Daniel Thaly (1880–1949) of Martinique, in *Le jardin des tropiques* (1911; tropical garden), and Jean-Louis Baghio'o (b. 1915) of Guadeloupe, in *Les jeux du soleil* (1960; sun games), focus on decor, excluding any significant consideration of social issues.

The publication of the manifesto *Légitime défense* (1932; self-defense) by the Paris-based Martinicans Étienne Lero (1910–1939), René Menil (b. 1902), and Jules Monnerot (b. 1906) signaled a new orientation in poetry. Accordingly, poetry would now manifest total liberation of non-Western sensibility, and address the real problems inherent in the colonial condition: Marxism and surrealism would be used in the service of the cultural revolution. Léon-Gontran Damas (q.v.) of French Guiana in his *Pigments* (1937; pigments) and Aimé Césaire (q.v.) of Martinique in his *Cahier d'un retour au pays natal* (1939; *Memorandum on My Martinique*, 1947; new tr., *Return to My Native Land*, 1969) contributed to this new perspective the Negritude (q.v.) notion of awareness and acceptance of the African heritage.

The spiritual return to Africa, however, did not meet with enthusiastic acceptance—least of all from the masses. Dissatisfied with the claims of Negritude, the Martinican Édouard Glissant (b. 1928) has been attempting to develop the theory of *Antillanité*, which takes into account the complex nature of Caribbean man and sees the resolution of the cultural impasse in the context of close relations with other Caribbean nations. Glissant's epic poem *Les Indes* (1956; the Indies) recounts the tragic encounter between Europeans and non-Europeans during the 16th c. as a necessary backdrop to the development of cultural awareness in the Antilles. Henri Corbin (b. 1932) of Guadeloupe is among the younger poets who have been influenced by Glissant's tragic sense.

The racial theme appears in the very first French Antillean novel, *Questions de couleur: Blanches et Noirs* (1923; questions of color: white and black), by Oruno Larra (1879–1942) of Guadeloupe. René Maran (q.v.) of Martinique also utilizes the theme of race. He does so, however, in the context of French colonial administration in French West Africa, especially in his novel *Batouala* (1921; *Batouala,* 1922), which won the Goncourt Prize in 1921. Major themes explored in later novels include slavery, rural life and man's relationship to the land, cultural alienation, and color prejudice.

Raphael Tardon (1911–1966) of Martinique is best known for his *Starkenfirst* (1947; Starkenfirst), which deals with the slave trade. Glissant's *Le quatrième siècle* (1964; the fourth century) traces the two opposing tendencies in Antillean history—conformity and assimilation versus resistance—and chronicles the gradual, although painful resolution of these tendencies with the physical merging of subsequent generations.

Joseph Zobel (b. 1915) of Martinique shows the contradictory relationship between man and the land: this relationship can be fruitful when the land belongs to the Martinican, as seen in *Diab'la* (1945; Diab'la), but it can be a source of suffering when the land belongs to the white plantation owner, a theme developed in *La Rue Cases-Nègres* (1958; *Black Shack Alley,* 1980). Glissant's novel *Malemort* (1975; bad death) pictures in dismal tones the pervasive erosion of Antillean culture, arising from the increasing alienation from indigenous sources. Maryse Condé (b. 1936) of Guadeloupe dramatizes in *Hérémakhonon* (1976; Hérémakhonon) the ineffectuality of the search for values by identification with Africa. Bertène Juminer (b. 1927) of Guiana examines the anguish of the intellectual elite who are assimilated into French culture but who feel the urgent need to be reconnected with their cultural roots in *Les bâtards* (1961; crossbreeds).

Female novelists have paid particular attention to color prejudice and sexual exploitation. Mayotte Capécia (1928–1953) of Martinique showed in *Je suis Martiniquaise* (1948; I am a Martinican woman) the mulatto woman's search for happiness through denial of her black identity. Jacqueline Manicom (1938–1976) of Guadeloupe, on the other hand, proposed in *Mon examen de blanc* (1972; my study of whiteness) that such a search leads not to the attainment of happiness, but rather to the bitter experience of racist humiliation.

Bereft of a readily observable and accepted national tradition, the French Antilles and Guiana manifest a continuing, self-conscious search for identity. The literature of the area reflects this pervasive quest for self-definition.

BIBLIOGRAPHY: Laroche, M., *Haiti et sa littérature* (1963); Garret, N., *The Renaissance of Haitian Poetry* (1963); Cartey, W., Introduction to Shapiro, N., ed., *Negritude: Black Poetry from Africa and the Caribbean* (1970), pp. 17–37; Kesteloot, L., *Black Writers in French: A Literary History of Negritude* (1974), passim; Kennedy, E., Introduction to *The Negritude Poets: An Anthology of Translations from the French* (1975), pp. xix–xxix; Corzani, J., *La littérature des Antilles-Guyane Françaises* (6 vols., 1978); Herdeck, D., et al., *Caribbean Writers: A Bio-Bibliographical-Critical Encyclopedia* (1979), pp. 261–547; Dathorne, O. R., *Dark Ancestor: The Literature of the Black Man in the Caribbean* (1981); Glissant, É., *Le discours antillais* (1981)

WILBERT J. ROGET

FRENCH GUIANA LITERATURE
See French-Caribbean Literature

FREUD, Sigmund
Austrian neurologist, founder of psychoanalysis, b. 6 May 1856, Freiberg (now Přibor), Moravia; d. 23 Sept. 1939, London, England

F.'s impact on writers and critics in the 20th c. is incalculable. This is so for various reasons: F. was a systematic, and at the same time complex, thinker, but he did not create a static psychological or sociological system; within his work there are numerous inconsistencies, some of them resulting from the evolution of his views between 1900 and 1938 on psychic structure, anxiety, and the vicissitudes of human instincts; his work has been distorted and oversimplified in translation and summary, and the

"Freud" of one writer or critic is often far different from the "Freud" of another. F. was not merely a revolutionary psychological thinker; he created a movement that evolved differently in different countries, even during his lifetime, and his own work cannot be considered coterminous with psychoanalysis as a historical phenomenon. F.'s own thinking exhibits the flexibility, restlessness, dogmatism, and openness of a man in search of inclusive laws of human psychological functioning. He cannot be justly summarized, and the history of his impact on writers and critics, mediated as it is by textual, personal, and national differences, is yet to be written.

Nevertheless, major aspects of F.'s thinking that have been widely influential in the literary world can be defined. These include (1) his theory of the essence and functions of dreams; (2) his ideas on symbolism; (3) his views on language; (4) his ideas on play, art, and the artist; (5) his specific views on various literary works and authors; and (6) his ideological bias. In these areas F.'s work exhibits a mixture of traditional philosophical, aesthetic, and scientific assumptions with radically challenging insights into the dynamic functions of psychic activity. While he accepted a naïve realism that regarded the external world as essentially indifferent to human desires, he also demonstrated the extensive role of "psychic reality" in determining the forms of experience and conflict. While he accepted the romantic idea that the function of art was self-expression, he also demonstrated that the strategies of art were the strategies of the human mind. And while he accepted and built on the language of 19th-c. science, with its metaphors of mechanisms, hydraulics, and impersonal forces, he also developed a language of explanation, interpretation, and meaning that is wholly psychological in its aims and methods.

Dreams

F. regarded *The Interpretation of Dreams* (1900)* as his most important work, and he continued to revise it until his death. "The interpretation of dreams is the royal road to a knowledge of the unconscious activities of the mind," he declared, yet he also wrote that dreams are "nothing other than a particular form of thinking, made possible by the condi-

---

* All titles in the text are in accordance with S. F., *Complete Psychological Works: Standard Edition* (24 vols., 1953–66), edited by James Strachey. Dates are those of original publication in German.

tions of the state of sleep." Dreams, then, provided F. with normal examples of psychic activity that also displayed itself in waking life, pathological symptoms, and creative works. He distinguished dreams from other mental activity by their primary function, which, he argued, is to preserve the sleeping state by transforming residual memories of daily experiences into compromise formations that fulfill unconscious wishes. Unconscious wishes are the motives for the dream, and the form of the dream, F. showed, can be explained as a set of defensive transformations that reveal the wish even as they disguise it. Dreams are, in short, meaningful symbolic expressions.

F.'s "formula" for defining the nature of dreams shows his characteristic way of thinking about mental life in general: "A dream is a (disguised) fulfillment of a (suppressed or repressed) wish." The dream is thought of as a substitute for the wish the dream reveals. Being resolutely dualistic in his thinking, F. divided the dream into manifest content and latent dream thoughts. The manifest dream is the dream as it is retained in conscious memory, and the latent dream thoughts are the unfulfilled unconscious wishes. F. assumed that the meaning of the dream as a symbolic expression could only be determined by a technique of interpretation that decomposes the manifest dream. The manifest dream is a paratactical structure and the process of interpretation uses the free associations of the dreamer to each element in this structure to translate it into a syntactic structure. Interpretation is required because the process of dream formation (the dream work) leaves protective gaps in the memory of the dreamer. The interpretation seeks to approach, but can never completely provide, a continuous "history" of the dreamer. F. decomposed the dream in order to recompose the unconscious continuity of the dreamer's psychic life. His method rests on the assumption that the wish transformed by the dream work can only be revealed in censored form because it represents or derives from erotic or aggressive impulses too extreme to tolerate, often left over from infancy. The manifest dream is a disguised synthesis of the dreamer's present experience and his infantile experience. Interpretation seeks to disclose this synthesis by deviously stripping the dream of its disguise.

F.'s interpretative aim was genetic, locating the essential meaning of the dream in its origin, the unconscious wish, but he also developed a structural theory by describing the techniques of the defensive process, the dream work. Dreams, he argued, are formed by a primary-process mode of thinking. This process is characterized by condensation, displacement, symbolism, and other techniques of distortion such as reversal of affect and splitting of representations united in the dream thoughts. The primary process disregards the material limits of reality in favor of the omnipotence of thoughts, and all the techniques of the dream work are forms of (disguised) affirmation, there being no negation in unconscious thought processes.

The process of interpretation translates primary-process ideation into secondary process, discursive language. The secondary-process mode is grammatical and rational, and takes considerations of external reality into account. F. considered the secondary process superior to the primary process because it recognizes the differences between fantasy and reality, thought and action, omnipotence and the limitations of the mind and body. He thought dreams delusional and regressive departures from the rational, however meaningful they are as symbolic expressions of unconscious wishes.

F. set no limits on the process of interpretation, because he recognized that each element of the manifest dream was potentially overdetermined. That is, one manifest dream image may be the condensed expression of many latent dream thoughts, and any one latent dream thought may manifest itself in many images. Any element in the dream may serve multiple functions. Although he compared the dream to a rebus and a hieroglyphic, F. did not advocate a one-to-one translation of manifest into latent contents, except in the case of certain symbols he regarded as universal, symbols of the parts of the human body, intimate personal relations, and ultimate human concerns, such as birth, death, and exposure. The dreamer, being an "entrepreneur," could use such symbols to invest his thought, but the meaning of his dream could not be limited to them.

Symbolism

Although F. treated dreams and other psychic expressions as symbolic activity, he reserved the name of symbolism for a special class of substitutive images or words. In this restricted usage a symbol is an unconscious identification of an image or word with a repressed idea of the body or of intimate bodily relationships or of instinctual fears and desires. A symbol is a distortion of the real, caused by intrapsychic conflict. Without such conflict there would be no need for the mislocation of affects involved in symbol formation, and hence no symbols in the strictly Freudian sense. If a

spear is a phallic symbol, this is so because the affect associated with the phallus is only acceptable to consciousness in disguised form.

F. regarded symbolism from a rationalist point of view, as a residue of primitive thinking. A phylogenetic mode of identifying words and things, especially sexual things, was, he believed, recapitulated in human ontogeny and retained in unconscious, primary-process thinking. His aim was to demythologize this primitive mode of thought in the interest of scientific progress. All symbols are illusions that require interpretation to break the link between words, things, and images, and the unconscious objects, wishes, or fears with which they are confused. For F., all symbols are to be interpreted "downward," toward the bodily and archaic roots from which they arise. Money, for example, is never in this strictly Freudian sense a symbol of wealth, but can be a symbol of feces. A ring does not symbolize marriage, but can symbolize the female genitals.

For F., the study of symbolism was an important link between psychoanalysis and other fields, such as philology, folklore, and the study of religion. He returned frequently to the study of symbols, in *Introductory Lectures on Psycho-Analysis* (1916–17), *New Introductory Lectures on Psycho-Analysis* (1933), and elsewhere, never abandoning his "downward" reading. In fact, he accumulated quite a number of "dream-book" symbolic translations, which he warned against being used as a substitute for free associations. Since F., the theory of symbolism has become the most widely known, used, and misused aspect of his thought, although many subsequent Freudians have expanded and revised the theory. Ernest Jones (1916) and Sandor Ferenczi (1912) stated the orthodox theory, and it has been reinterpreted and transformed by Melanie Klein (1930), Marion Milner (1952), Charles Rycoft (1956), Hannah Segal (1957), Jean Piaget (1951), Ernst Kris (1952), Norman O. Brown (1959), and others.

Language

F.'s emphasis was on language as an expressive phenomenon. He did not develop a theory of language as a symbolic system. Nevertheless, in interpreting dreams and free associations he made psychoanalysis into an almost purely verbal psychology. The subject of analysis is the precise language of the analysand, and the "peculiar plasticity of the psychical material" is revealed by the plasticity of language itself. F. compared the dream work to writing a poem:

he saw in both processes the aim of formulating an unconscious fantasy in disguise. "There is no need to be astonished at the part played by words in dream formation," he wrote. "Words, since they are nodal points of numerous ideas, may be regarded as predestined to ambiguity; and the neurosis (e.g., in framing obsessions and phobias), no less than dreams, make [sic] unashamed use of the advantages thus offered by words for purposes of condensation and disguise." Words, like clothes, take the shape of what they hide, and F. regarded them as the primary medium of unconscious disclosure.

One reason for F.'s emphasis on words was his assumption that they originate in images and that they can represent more primitive modes of expression and relationship. "Things that are symbolically connected today were probably united in prehistoric times by conceptual and linguistic identity," he wrote in *The Interpretation of Dreams*. In primary-process ideation, words assumed their "original" concrete functions, and F. showed how word representations could act like thing representations in widely disparate contexts, from delusions and dreams to jokes, poems, and ordinary social discourse. In *The Antithetical Sense of Primal Words* (1910), F. linked the strategies of reversal and antithetical meaning in ancient languages with the strategies of unconscious thinking in general, and he said that "we should understand the language of dreams better and translate it more easily if we knew more about the development of language." This is F. at his most "original." He believed that the unconscious wishes and strategies revealed in and by linguistic structures could be reduced to their beginning in some actual social situation, a prehistoric world in which symbolic events were literally acted out.

Such a belief is not required for us to recognize F.'s immense contribution to the understanding of literary forms and meanings. In *Jokes and Their Relation to the Unconscious* (1905) he investigated the techniques of the joking process, and he showed how jokes and the comic share the strategies of dreams and use condensation, displacement, and other transformations to encourage social identifications between tellers and auditors. In jokes the dream work becomes art work, sharable symbolic communication that uses the devices of literary form: puns, composite words, allusions, double entendre, metaphorical and literal meanings, synecdoche. The informing principle of the joke, he showed, is a sharable economy of psychic expenditure, and jokes thus depend as much for their effects on timing, rhythm, and tone as they do on choice of words. Jokes make language a medium of catharsis and a form of gratifying erotic and aggressive wishes. In short, the joke as F. analyzed it comprises a prototypical example of the strategies of literature in general and offers a way of relating these strategies to their social context.

After 1905 F. continued to explore the linguistic expression of psychic dynamics, and almost all of his works contain instances of verbal play in normal and pathological contexts. In "The Uncanny" (1919) he approached his subject through its linguistic expressions, showing how *unheimlich*, or unfamiliar and strange sensations, are rooted in the *heimlich*, or familiar and homelike. An analysis of "The Sandman" by E. T. A. Hoffmann (1776–1822) provided his central example of the aesthetics of the uncanny, but he also related it to Shakespeare, Sophocles, Heine, Schiller, and other writers. In *Humour* (1927) he returned to the subject of the comic, distinguishing humor from other comic expressions by its alliance with the parental consolations of the superego. In general, although F. offered no theory of language as a symbolic system, he showed many parallels between the structure of language and the structure of the mind.

Play, Art, and the Artist

Much of F.'s analysis of linguistic strategies in dreams, jokes, and literary works implicitly considers language a form of play. He showed how the human mind is inherently playful. "The opposite of play is not what is serious but what is real," he wrote in "Creative Writers and Day-Dreaming" (1908). F.'s most important discussion of play, in *Beyond the Pleasure Principle* (1920), presents the example of a child's game in which his absent mother is represented by small objects that are hidden and retrieved in a symbolic expression of the mother's loss and recovery. The child in play turns a passively experienced loss into an active repetition of the painful experience. F. interpreted the game as an act of symbolic mastery that reveals its origins even as it announces the renunciation of the instinctual satisfaction associated with the actual presence of the mother. The game has an economic motive; it provides pleasure in mastery where there was pain in loss, and it is also a substitute for the lost relationship. F. calls the child's game a "great cultural achievement" because it marks the transition from biological to symbolic expression, from instinct to ego control.

In "Creative Writers and Day-Dreaming" F. views the literary work as "a continuation of and a substitute for what was once the play of childhood." Art is thus a substitute for a substitute, and it is a continuation of play because it shares the aim of the child, which is to manipulate a symbolic medium to disguise and disclose unconscious erotic and aggressive wishes and conflicts. Art is at once a regressive activity and a way for the artist to transform past experiences into a present, though illusory, reality. In "The Claims of Psycho-Analysis to Scientific Interest" (1913) F. wrote: "Art is a conventionally accepted reality in which, thanks to artistic illusion, symbols and substitutes are able to provoke real emotions. Thus art constitutes a region halfway between a reality which frustrates wishes and the wish-fulfilling world of the imagination—a region in which, as it were, primitive man's strivings for omnipotence are still in full force."

F. saw three special aspects of the artist's personality: (1) the laxity of repression; (2) unusually strong instinctual drives; and (3) extraordinary capacity for sublimation. The artist needs and is able to use past, usually infantile, wishes provoked by occasions in the present to create "a picture of the future." Art is thus a synthetic as well as a regressive activity, and although the artist is like the child at play, he is also, for F., a person to be envied for his access to unconscious knowledge. "Creative writers are valuable allies," F. wrote in his study (1907) of Wilhelm Jensen's (1837–1911) "Gradiva," "and their evidence is to be prized highly, for they are apt to know a whole host of things between heaven and earth of which our philosophy has not yet let us dream."

F. believed that the power of the artist over his audience consisted in his ability to provoke and manipulate shared unconscious desires over which the artist had an extraordinary control that matched his extraordinary psychic conflict. The privacy of dreams and daydreams becomes in artistic productions a higher form of wish-fulfilling confession, precisely because the confession can be shared and, in some mysterious way, must be shared by the audience. Although F. did begin to develop a theory that could account for this confessional bond in his book on jokes (his explication of the role of identification), he did not expand on it systematically in later works. He regarded all his writings on the nature of the artist and his power as mere beginnings, tentative explorations of an area he thought psychoanalysis could not conquer for science. "Unfortunately, before the problem of the creative artist, analysis must lay down its

arms," he wrote in "Dostoevsky and Parricide" (1928).

Specific Works and Authors

Although F. renounced the hope of completely divulging the artist's secret powers, he did not hesitate to write both casual and extensive interpretations of specific works and writers. As early as 1897 he announced, in a letter to Wilhelm Fliess, the relationship between his discovery of the Oedipus complex and the unconscious appeal of *Oedipus Rex* and *Hamlet*. In *The Interpretation of Dreams* he repeated his conviction that these works anticipated and confirmed his most important discovery, the son's ambivalent relation to the father and his desire to possess the mother sexually.

Fuller interpretations followed. In "Psychopathic Characters on the Stage" (written 1905–6, pub. 1942), he discussed the cathartic power of dramatic illusions, using *Hamlet* again as an example. The play, he argued, offers us "forepleasures" that divert our attention from the real sources of its emotional power, repressed impulses we share with the hero. In 1906 F. wrote his most elaborate literary interpretation, *Delusions and Dreams in Jensen's "Gradiva"* (1907). Treating the protagonist as an actual person, F. constructed interpretations of his dreams, offering associations that Jensen did not offer. He described the parallels between the cure for delusions in the story and the analytic method he developed with Josef Breuer. He demonstrated that the delusion of the protagonist of "Gradiva" was a transformation of a repressed incestuous relationship between a brother and sister in their childhood.

The study of Jensen's "Gradiva" was followed by "Some Character Types Met with in Psycho-Analytic Work" (1916) and studies of Leonardo da Vinci (1910), Michelangelo's "Moses" (1914), Goethe (1917), and Dostoevsky (1928). In "Some Character Types" F. used characters from Shakespeare and Ibsen to illustrate forms of pathological character structure. His aim was to show the "complete agreement" between some literary characters and personalities encountered in clinical experience. He also explored the mechanisms by which the dramatist is able to "overwhelm us by his art and paralyze our powers of reflection." F. asserted that the "laws of poetical economy" are designed to overcome our resistance to the deeper motives of the work by providing superficial motives derived from them.

In each of the works on individual authors F. read visual or verbal expressions of the artist back into his unconscious or childhood biography, and the psychoanalytic method becomes a way of discovering the intention of the artist's work or life in its origin, a procedure that duplicates the interpretation of dreams. Leonardo is shown to have embodied the details of his childhood experience in the enigmatic figures of the "Mona Lisa" and the "Saint Anne"; Michelangelo, F. speculated, embodied an intense ambivalence in his "Moses," who seems frozen between rage and renunciation; Goethe revealed his childhood desire to eliminate a sibling rival in his "screen memory" of throwing crockery out of a window; and F. read Dostoevsky's posthumous papers, his epilepsy, and his gambling, each as an expression of his Oedipal struggle with his father.

F. was aware of the incompleteness of these works. Nevertheless, he believed throughout his life that artists shared the insights of psychoanalysis and that an essential part of his work was to translate their work into scientific explanation.

F.'s Ideological Bias

F. viewed the development of the individual in society as a process of restriction and renunciation of instinctual desires. His emphasis is almost always on the ways paternal social authority enforces the repression of childhood wishes. In describing the development of the individual and his relation to the cultural world, F.'s language is almost always that of battle, power, victory, and defeat. He compared character development to the progress of an army that leaves troops behind at points of potential conflict (fixation points), and he regarded these defensive maneuvers as the minimal price civilization claimed of the individual in exchange for participation in an order maintained by the power of the group. In *Civilization and Its Discontents* (1930), F. wrote: "Human life in common is only made possible when a majority comes together which is stronger than any separate individual and which remains united against all separate individuals." Human beings, he thought, are primarily hostile to one another. Pathological symptoms are the result of conflicts between the demands of civilization and the instinctual impulses too extreme for the individual to tolerate consciously, and, as such, they are only quantitatively different from the normal order of things.

F. derived his anti-instinctual view of civilization from the innate ambivalence of human beings. The child's conflict between love and hate for the father could only be resolved, he

thought, by the child's internalization of the father's threats of reprisal against forbidden actions. The child identifies with the feared aggressor and becomes civilized because he represses both his own desires and the memory of the conflict with the father's authority. The internalization of the father's authority is seen as an essential step in the acceptance of reality. It marks the transition from the pleasure principle to the reality principle, which teaches the child to seek gratifications in accord with the demands of the external world.

F.'s tendency to equate the demands of reality with the demands of the father derives from his Oedipal model of development. That is, although F. saw an explanation of the hostility and defiance of individuals toward society in the son's Oedipal struggle with paternal authority, his Oedipal theory actually determines his view of this antagonism. By viewing reality through the eyes of the son and the father, F. projected this antagonism onto society as a whole, and then explained social relations by recourse to their origins in father-son conflict. Then, society is seen as creating, in turn, the conditions for father-son conflict.

Another consequence of his emphasis on the father-son relationship is F.'s almost complete neglect of the role of the mother in the development of the child. His views are one-sided, and his relative neglect of the pre-Oedipal phases of the boy's development leaves him unable to account for the important phases of the girl's development that parallel the boy's. Hence, he had no context in which to describe the way children take in and integrate the anatomical difference between the sexes, only the limited concept of penis envy. In general, F.'s patriarchal bias led him to overemphasize the power of the Oedipus complex to account for both individual and social relationships.

He did, however, refer in late writings to the "oceanic" importance of the early mother-child relationship, and a major achievement of post-Freudian psychoanalysis has been the study and understanding of the formative role of pre-Oedipal development.

F.'s Influence on Writers

The impact of Freudian ideas has been felt by every major writer of the 20th c. Especially in America, "Freudianism" had become part of intellectual discourse and popular culture by the 1920s. In both Europe and America, however, F.'s influence varied immensely, depending on the particular writer's knowledge of F.'s works and judgment of their significance. F.'s ideas were assimilated to the interests of the century, and writers shared his focus on the inner life, the plasticity of language, the crises of Western society, and the meaning of civilization. "One could be influenced in this sphere," Thomas Mann (q.v.) wrote, "without any direct contact with his work, because for a long time the air had been filled with the thoughts and results of the psychoanalytic school."

Franz Kafka (q.v.) knew F.'s theories in detail, and his work comprises a profound exploration of the father-son relationship and the meaning of the law in society. Yet he regarded F.'s ideas as approximations of the truth, and he thought that biographical explanations of his work were "too facile." He had no faith in psychoanalysis as a therapy and distrusted F.'s rationalist bias. For Kafka, religion was not an illusion but a reality; for F. religion was to be overcome by scientific knowledge. Kafka and F., although they had much in common, adhered to profoundly different world views.

Thomas Mann, however, felt deep sympathy with F.'s thinking. He defended psychoanalysis as a legitimate scientific comprehension of the demonic aspect of the psyche, and he agreed with F.'s view that psychoanalysis was a work of ego-strengthening, "a reclamation work," as F. said, "like the draining of the Zuyder Zee." For Mann, F. had established the ground for "the building of a new anthropology . . . which shall be the future dwelling of a wiser and freer humanity." Mann also shared F.'s ideas about the links between ontogeny and phylogeny; he saw the timeless life of dreams as a link between the primitive and the mythical. History, for Mann, is shaped by mythical recurrence. In *Joseph and His Brothers* Mann embodied this view of history and dreams, and he openly acknowledged his affinity with F. in *F. and the Future.* F. stood for the heroic powers of the intellect in its struggle against the irrational forces devastating the West in these years.

Among writers in English, F.'s stature varied widely. James Joyce (q.v.) undoubtedly absorbed psychoanalytic ideas in his later linguistic polymorphousness, and there are many references, ironic and skeptical, to psychoanalysis in *Ulysses* and *Finnegans Wake.* Joyce's relation to F., however, is, like his relation to many other writers, incorporative rather than submissive, and his development of interior monologue and dream language reflects his own psyche more than the writings of psychoanalysts.

It was D. H. Lawrence (q.v.) who responded most extensively to F.'s theories. In *Psychoanalysis and the Unconscious* and *Fantasia of the Unconscious,* Lawrence attacked the intellectual, "cerebral" aspect of psychoanalysis. He thought that psychoanalysis was a fad, that F. advocated the removal of sexual inhibitions, and he rejected the theory of infantile sexuality. Lawrence advocated intuitive, vitalistic, spontaneous "blood" knowledge, as opposed to F.'s cognitive approach. He thought that the moral function of art was to express a passionate, undidactic appeal to bodily consciousness. Lawrence's attitudes reveal a profound rejection of F.'s scientific approach and an ambivalent attitude toward F.'s discoveries.

Other writers reveal a wide spectrum of responses to F. Dylan Thomas (q.v.) studied F.'s works and thought that "poetry must drag further into the clean nakedness of light more even of the hidden causes than F. could realize." W. H. Auden's (q.v.) *In Memory of S. F.* acknowledges the profound impact of F. on this century. Conrad Aiken (q.v.) studied F. as early as 1909 and realized that aesthetics had its source in the emotional life F. revealed. André Breton (q.v.) and the surrealists (q.v.) saw in F.'s new access to the dream world an ultimate ground of reality, and referred often to F.'s ideas. In his forewords Vladimir Nabokov (q.v.) unflaggingly addresses sarcastic "words of encouragement to the Viennese delegation" that would read biographical interpretations into literary works and sees the "little Freudian" as a "sleuth" who invades his privacy. Among poets, H. D. (Hilda Doolittle [q.v.]) is unique, in that she was analyzed by F. *Tribute to F.* records her analysis and her ambivalent respect for F.'s thought. Henry Miller (q.v.) saw psychoanalysis as a liberating force, but objected to its scientific focus. William Faulkner's (q.v.) style of representing the flow of consciousness undoubtedly owes much to the impact of psychoanalysis. Eugene O'Neill's (q.v.) dramatizations of the family reveal a deep affinity with F.'s thinking. Among contemporary Americans, Saul Bellow and Philip Roth (qq.v.) reveal personal acquaintance with psychoanalysis in their portrayals of Jewish character.

The continuing profound impact of F.'s personality and thought is best illustrated in D. M. Thomas's (b. 1935) *The White Hotel* (1981), a brilliant novel that includes F. as a character as it explores a woman's life and sensibility in the traumatic years of European crisis between 1909 and 1941. Thomas's imagination shows how Freudian influence transcends allegiance to F.'s particular theoretical views.

In general, F.'s influence, although pervasive, derives from the identification of his thought with the main currents of literary experiment, especially focus on dreams, the associative representation of consciousness, and confessional modes of writing. His influence on writers has derived, as he foresaw, more from shared concern with human character than from detailed study of his works, and, where he is rejected, more from antithetical styles of thinking than from rational counterargument.

F.'s Influence on Critics

From within the psychoanalytic movement and outside of it Freudian literary criticism has paralleled the development of psychoanalytic theory. F. and many of his followers turned to literature to explicate the unconscious dynamics of writers' and characters' minds. Of all writers, Shakespeare has received the most attention, and a very large body of psychoanalytic commentary has grown around his works. Ernest Jones's studies of *Hamlet* began appearing in 1910, and by 1949, when Jones's *Hamlet and Oedipus* was published, the impact of Freudian thought had produced major works on creative writers by analysts and literary critics.

Early psychoanalytic criticism focused almost exclusively on unconscious motivation, and on such motifs as incestuous desires, Oedipal rivalry, and childhood fixations in the lives and works of artists. Albert Mordell's *Erotic Motive in Literature* (1919) represents this emphasis. Although shunned as "reductive" by most literary critics, this style of criticism continued to be written by analysts, and the works of Sandor Ferenczi, for example, contain many references to and interpretations of literary themes. Otto Rank's studies of the incest motif in myth and literature and *The Myth of the Birth of the Hero* (1909) explore creative and pathological expressions of childhood fantasies and their cultural derivatives. In the 1930s Marie Bonaparte's *Psychoanalytic Interpretations of Stories of Edgar Allan Poe* (1933) was representative of the focus on symbolic decoding prevalent in Freudian interpretation.

The 1930s also saw the development of psychoanalytic ego psychology and serious discussion of Freudian aesthetics by major literary critics. Kenneth Burke's essay "F. and the Analysis of Poetry" (1939) explored F.'s interpretive strategies that treat the poem as a dream and concluded that they must be supplemented by mapping the literary work also as a "prayer" and a "chart" of associations, and by adding an interpretation of "matriarchal symbolizations" to F.'s patriarchal ones. Burke found F. "not dialectical enough," but has, for almost forty years, produced major criticism

that is often markedly psychoanalytic. The criticism of William Empson (q.v.), especially *Seven Types of Ambiguity* (1931), also shows the extensive influence of psychoanalysis in its interpretations of the linguistic designs of poetry.

Lionel Trilling's (q.v.) essay "F. and Literature" (1947) is perhaps the most positive affirmation of F.'s relevance for criticism written by a literary critic before 1950. "The Freudian psychology," Trilling wrote, "is the only systematic account of the human mind which, in point of subtlety and complexity, of interest and tragic power, deserves to stand beside the chaotic mass of psychological insights which literature has accumulated through the centuries." Trilling recognized that "the Freudian psychology is the one which makes poetry indigenous to the very constitution of the mind." Trilling's work has been a major force in American criticism, and through him informed psychoanalytic interpretation has reached a wide audience.

In the 1940s and 1950s Freudian criticism appeared at an accelerating pace. Frederick J. Hoffman's *Freudianism and the Literary Mind* (1945) chronicled the influence of F. on major writers. Edmund Bergler's *The Writer and Psychoanalysis* (1950) probed the infantile origins of the writer's fantasy life. In 1952 Ernst Kris's important book *Psychoanalytic Explorations in Art* greatly expanded the range of psychoanalytic theory in relation to painting and poetry and made extensive use of ego psychology as opposed to early focus on id psychology. In 1957 Simon O. Lesser's comprehensive psychoanalytic view of literature, *Fiction and the Unconscious*, appeared. Many Freudian studies, such as Phyllis Greenacre's *Swift and Carroll* (1955), applied contemporary theories to their subjects. In 1957 William Phillips collected major psychoanalytic statements in *Art and Psychoanalysis*. Although still not widely accepted, psychoanalytic criticism had become recognized as an academic reality in England and America.

In the 1960s the influence of psychoanalysis on critics continued to expand. Biographical studies—*Goethe: A Psychoanalytic Study, 1775–1786* (2 vols., 1963) by Kurt R. Eissler and *Joseph Conrad: A Psychoanalytic Biography* (1967) by Bernard C. Meyer—were published, and critical studies such as *Sins of the Fathers: Hawthorne's Psychological Themes* (1966) by Frederick C. Crews and *Allegory: The Theory of a Symbolic Mode* (1964) by Angus Fletcher represent the range of Freudian influence. In 1968 Norman N. Holland published *The Dynamics of Literary Response*, a systematically developed model of psychoanalytic interpretation. This book and Holland's *Psychoanalysis and Shakespeare* (1966) made him the foremost psychoanalytic literary critic in America. The 1960s also saw the publication of psychoanalytic criticism dealing with aesthetics, the problems of interpretation, and applied studies of individual writers in numerous anthologies.

Contemporary Freudian criticism draws largely on post-Freudian theories of pre-Oedipal development and on the view that literature is a complex, overdetermined phenomenon. Although F.'s views of art and the artist are influential, they have been supplemented by the reorientations of theory since his death. This combination of older and newer Freudianism can be seen in recent criticism, such as *Psychoanalysis and Literary Process,* edited by Frederick Crews (1970), Norman N. Holland's *Poems in Persons* (1973), and Mark Shechner's *Joyce in Nighttown* (1974). In Europe and America reinterpretations of F. continue to yield a wire range of critical styles. The influence of theorists like Erik Erikson, D. W. Winnicott, and Margaret Mahler can be seen in such works as *Representing Shakespeare: New Psychoanalytic Essays* (1980), edited by Murray M. Schwartz and Coppélia Kahn, Richard Wheeler's *Shakespeare's Development and the Problem Comedies* (1981) and Coppélia Kahn's *Man's Estate: Masculine Identity in Shakespeare* (1980)—to take only examples of Shakespearean criticism. Other works, such as Diana George's *Blake and Freud* (1980), interpret F. and poetic visions in relation to one another. A French style of Freudian interpretation has developed around the theories of Jacques Lacan, and it is producing new critical works, such as *The Fictional Father: Lacanian Readings of the Text* (1981), edited by Robert Con Davis. Prominent journals, such as *New Literary History, Diacritics,* and *Critical Inquiry* often feature Freudian interpretation. In its various forms, Freudian criticism remains very alive in intellectual discourse.

SELECTED WORKS: *Gesammelte Schriften* (12 vols., 1924–34; *Collected Papers of S. F.,* 5 vols., 1959); *Gesammelte Werke* (18 vols., 1952 ff.); *Briefe* (1960; *Letters of S. F.,* 1960); *S. F. und C. G. Jung: Briefwechsel* (1974; *The F.–Jung Letters,* 1974). FURTHER VOLUMES IN ENGLISH: *Complete Psychological Works: Standard Edition* (24 vols., 1953–66)

FURTHER BIBLIOGRAPHY: Phillips, W., ed., *Art and Psychoanalysis* (1957); Fraiberg, L., *Psychoanalysis and American Literary Criticism* (1960); Ruitenbeek, H., ed., *Psychoanalysis and Literature* (1964); Malin, I., ed., *Psychoanalysis and American Fiction* (1964); Ruitenbeek, H., ed., *Literary Imagination: Psychoanalysis and the Genius of the Writer* (1965); Manheim, L. and E., eds., *Hidden Patterns* (1966); Kaplan, M., and Kloss, R., *The Unspoken Motive: A Guide to Psychoanalytic Literary Criticism* (1973); Crews, F., *Out of My System: Psychoanalysis, Ideology, and Critical Method* (1975); Holland, N. N., *5 Readers Reading* (1975); Bersani, L., *A Future for Astyanax: Character and Desire in Literature* (1976); Gordon, D. J., *Literary Art and the Unconscious* (1976); Roazen, P., *F. and His Followers* (1976); Tennenhouse, L., ed., *The Practice of Psychoanalytic Criticism* (1976); Timpanaro, S., *The Freudian Slip: Psychoanalysis and Textual Criticism* (1976); Gay, P., *F., Jews, and Other Germans: Masters and Victims in Modernist Culture* (1978); Sherman, M. H., ed., *Psychoanalysis and Old Vienna: F., Reik, Schnitzler, Kraus* (1978); Brivic, S. R., *Joyce betweeen F. and Jung* (1979); Orlando, F., *Toward a Freudian Theory of Literature* (1979); Sulloway, F. J., *F.: Biologist of the Mind* (1979); Kaufman, W., *Discovering the Mind, Vol. 3: F. versus Adler and Jung* (1981); Meisel, P., ed., *F.: A Collection of Critical Essays* (1981)

MURRAY M. SCHWARTZ

See also Psychology and Literature

FREYRE, Gilberto

Brazilian anthropologist, social historian, essayist, and novelist (writing in Portuguese and English), b. 15 March 1900, Recife

Son of an educator and judge, F. completed his elementary and secondary studies at an American Protestant school in Recife, chosen by his father against the wishes of the Catholic family. He went to the U.S. to study at Baylor University in Texas and at Columbia University. His thesis, "Social Life in Brazil in the Middle of the 19th Century," is evidence of his early interest in Brazil's social history and especially the life of the slave. After travel and further study in Europe, he returned to Brazil. Since then, in addition to occasional lectures at a number of universities, he has devoted most of his time to writing.

F. is best known for his books on Brazilian patriarchal society—*Casa grande e senzala* (1933; *The Masters and the Slaves,* 1946)

and *Sobrados e mucambos* (1936; *The Mansions and the Shanties,* 1963). These two volumes, considered national classics, can be read as sociology, anthropology, social history, and social psychology; but they are also great works of literature, written in a conversational style. In the first volume he analyzed the complex, often violent Brazilian family life of the colonial period (1500–1822). He examined the three main ethnic groups—the native Indian, the Portuguese colonizer, and the African slave —in the hybrid, almost feudal, agrarian society that existed in Brazil for about 300 years. His detailed descriptions of every aspect of life, including customs, health habits, clothing, cooking, evoke in the reader a sense of the culture as a whole. We are shown every member of this society in his or her role—the white master, his wife, his concubines, the children, the black slaves, the nomadic Indians—and their relationships with each other.

F.'s ultimate theme in *Casa grande e senzala* is the exploration of the question that haunted Brazilians: Had miscegenation damaged and debased their country? F.'s unorthodox conclusion was that the mixed racial heritage of the people of Brazil was not a liability, but in fact a great asset; it enriched Brazilian culture. From both biologial and cultural points of view, Brazilians could be proud of their ethnic multiplicity.

Sobrados e mucambos focused on the decline of the all-powerful rural patriarch and the development of urban society from the late 1700s to the late 1800s, including the years 1822–89, when Brazil was an independent empire ruled by a monarchy. Here too F. treated in intimate detail the facts of everyday life. He traced the transition of power from the country to the city and the rise of mulattoes to positions of authority.

Brazil: An Interpretation (1945; written in English, and expanded in 1959 as *New World in the Tropics*) is an introductory manual to F.'s sociological ideas about Brazil. It is a synthesis of F.'s main theories about Brazil's unique tropical culture. He stressed Brazil's achievements: an integration of the races and regional diversity within political unity.

Dona Sinhá e o filho padre (1964; *Mother and Son,* 1967), which the author calls a "semi-novel," marked F.'s debut in fiction. It is of importance on two accounts. First, with its intersection of psychological planes and its use of actual newspaper clippings interspersed with the fictional narrative, it is structurally innovative. Second, through sociological knowledge and poetic insight, it deals humanely and objec-

tively with male homosexuality, a subject not previously treated in such a manner in the Brazilian novel.

F.'s latest published works reveal his expanded horizons. *O outro amor do Dr. Paulo* (1977; the other love of Dr. Paulo), his second semi-novel, is a combination of an exposé of Brazilians living in exile in late 19th-c. Paris, a narrative of their travels through Europe and their return to Brazil, and a slowly developing love story with a tragic ending. To move back in time and place, to impart veracity to characters, and to permit the inclusion of discussions and interpretations, F. utilized the technique of an informant, an elderly Brazilian exile who told the story of his friend in 1937 to F., who many years later puts it into book form. One suspects this work reveals much of F. himself as a writer and Brazilian.

Through his writings, F. has inspired Brazilians to reassess their history and culture and to change their attitude from self-disparagement to national pride. Although some have criticized his methods, ideas, and style, it cannot be denied that his works are statements of central importance about Brazil. He has been duly credited for his extraordinary contribution to Brazil's new pride in its racial mixture.

FURTHER WORKS: *Apologia pro generatione sua* (1924); *A propósito de Dom Pedro II* (1925); *Bahia de todos os Santos e de quase todos os pecados* (1926); *O estudo das ciências sociais nas universidades americanas* (1934); *Guia prático, histórico e sentimental da cidade do Recife* (1934); *Artigos de jornal* (1935); *Mucambos do Nordeste* (1937); *Nordeste* (1937); *Conferências na Europa* (1938); *Açucar* (1939); *Olinda: 2.° guia prático, histórico e sentimental de cidade brasileira* (1939); *Uma cultura ameaçada: A luso-brasileira* (1940); *Um engenheiro francês no Brasil* (1940); *O mundo que o Português criou* (1940); *Atualidade de Euclydes da Cunha* (1941); *Região e tradição* (1941); *Ingleses* (1942); *Continente e ilha* (1943); *Problemas brasileiros de antropologia* (1943); *Na Bahia em 1943* (1944); *Perfil de Euclydes e outros perfis* (1944); *Sociologia, I* (1945); *Ulisses* (1945); *Modernidade e modernismo na arte política* (1946); *Ordem, liberdade, mineiridade* (1946); *Ingleses no Brasil* (1948); *Joaquim Nabuco* (1948); *O camarada Whitman* (1948); *Guerra, paz e ciência* (1948); *Nação e exército* (1949); *Quase política* (1950); *José de Alencar* (1952); *Manifesto regionalista de 1926* (1952); *Aventura e rotina* (1953); *Um Brasileiro em terras portu-*

guesas (1953); *Um estudo do Prof. Aderbal Jurema* (1954); *Assombrações do Recife velho* (1955); *Reinterpretando José de Alencar* (1955); *Sugestões para uma nova política no Brasil: A urbana* (1956); *Integração portuguesa nas trópicos* (1958; *Portuguese Integration in the Tropics,* 1961); *Sugestões em torno de uma nova orientação para as relações internacionais no Brasil* (1958); *A propósito de frades* (1959); *A propósito de mourão, rosa e pimenta: Sugestões em torno de uma possível hispanotropicologia* (1959); *Em torno de alguns túmulos afro-cristãos de uma área africana contagiada pela cultura brasileira* (1959); *Ordem e progresso* (1959; abridged, *Order and Progress,* 1970); *Brasis, Brasil e Brasília* (1960); *Uma política transnacional de cultura paro o Brasil de hoje* (1960); *Sugestões de um novo contato com universidades europeias* (1961); *O Luso e o trópico* (1961); *The Portuguese and the Tropics,* 1961); *Arte, ciência e trópico* (1962); *O Brasil em face das Áfricas negras e mestiças* (1962); *Homem, cultura e trópico* (1962); *Talvez poesia* (1962); *Vida, forma e cor* 1962); *Brazil* (1963); *O escravo nos anúncios de jornais brasileiros do século XIX* (1963); *A Amazônia brasileira e uma possível lusotropicologia* (1964); *O estado de Pernambuco e sua expressão no poder nacional* (1964); *Retalhos de jornais velhos* (1964); *Forças armadas e outras forças* (1965); *Seis conferências em busca de um leitor* (1965); *The Racial Factor in Contemporary Politics* (1966); *O Recife, sim!: Recife, não* (1967); *Sociologia da medicina* (1967); *Como e porque sou e não sou sociólogo* (1968); *Contribuição para uma sociologia da biografia* (1968); *Oliveira Lima, Dom Quixote gordo* (1968); *A casa brasileira* (1971); *Nós e a Europa germânica* (1971); *Seleta para jovens* (1971; *The G. F. Reader,* 1974); *A condição humana e outros temas* (1972); *Pernambuco sim* (1972); *Estácio Coimbra, homem representativo do seu meio e do seu tempo* (1973); *Além do apenas moderno* (1973); *O brasileiro entre os outros hispanos* (1975; *A presença do açúcar na formação brasileira* (1975); *Tempo morto e outros tempos* (1975); *Obra escolhida* (1977); *Alhos & bugalhos* (1978); *Cartas do próprio punho* (1978); *Prefácios desgarrados* (1978); *Heróis e vilões no romance brasileiro* (1979); *O de casa!* (1979); *Tempo de aprendiz* (1979)

BIBLIOGRAPHY: Hanke, L., "G. F., Brazilian Social Historian," *Quarterly Journal of Inter-American Relations,* 1 (July 1939), 24–44; Stein, S. J., "F.'s Brazil Revisited," *HAHR,* 41 (1961), 111–13; Tannenbaum, F., Introduction to *The Mansions and the Shanties* (1963), pp. vii–xii; Mazzara, R. A., "G. F. and José Honório Rodrigues: Old and New Horizons for Brazil," *Hispania,* 47 (1964), 316–25; Skidmore, T., "G. F. and the Early Brazilian Republic: Some Notes on Methodology," *Comparative Studies in Sociology and History,* 6 (1964), 490–505; Loos, D. S., "G. F. as a Literary Figure: An Introductory Study," *RHM,* 34 (1968), 714–20; Martins, W., *The Modernist Idea* (1970), pp. 204–6, 294–99; Holloway, T. H., on *The G. F. Reader, Historian,* 38 (1976), 353–54

ELIZABETH R. SUTER

FRIEDELL, Egon

Austrian critic, essayist, and dramatist, b. 21 Jan. 1878, Vienna; d. 16 March 1938, Vienna

F. was the youngest son of Moriz Friedmann, a Jewish cloth manufacturer. Shortly after his birth his mother deserted her husband and three children. After the death of F.'s father in 1891 his governess took care of him, keeping house for him until her death in 1917. F. continued his education in Frankfurt, Baden near Vienna, Berlin, and Heidelberg, and after several unsuccessful attempts he finally graduated from secondary school at Bad Hersfeld in 1899.

Having left the Jewish fold in 1897, F. converted to Protestantism two years later. He studied German literature and philosophy at the University of Heidelberg, where he received the degree Doctor of Philosophy in 1904 on the basis of a dissertation on Novalis, the philosophic poet of early German romanticism. This degree qualified F., as he put it, to become artistic director of the Vienna cabaret Fledermaus (from 1905 to 1910). During those years he wrote several comedies, farces, and parodies in collaboration with Alfred Polgar (q.v.), including *Goethe* (or *Goethe im Examen,* 1908; Goethe taking a test), a witty sketch satirizing professorial pedantry in which F., also an actor, frequently played the title role over a period of three decades.

Until the outbreak of World War I, F. was codirector of the avant-garde Intimes Theater in Vienna. Between 1906 and 1924 he also produced translations or editions of Emerson, Hebbel, Georg Christoph Lichtenberg (1742–1799), Carlyle, Hans Christian Andersen, and Macaulay, as well as writings in the fields of literary history and drama criticism. In 1914 F. volunteered for military service but was rejected for physical reasons.

From 1924 on he was associated with Max Reinhardt, appearing in a variety of roles in Reinhardt's theaters in Vienna and Berlin. A few days after the Anschluss, F., who was about to be arrested by two SA men, committed suicide by jumping from a window of his bachelor apartment in Vienna, in which he had lived since 1900.

F.'s very versatility—he was a historian, a philosopher, a critic, an aphorist, an actor, a cabaret wit, a Falstaffian raconteur, a bohemian, and a dilettante in the grand manner—makes his stature somewhat difficult to assess. His first published work was his study *Novalis als Philosoph* (1904; Novalis as philosopher); it bore the name Friedell, though the name change did not become official until 1916. In 1912 F. published *Ecce Poeta*, a study of his friend Peter Altenberg (1859–1919), to whom F.'s collection of writings by and about him, *Das Altenbergbuch* (1922; the Altenberg book), is also devoted. F.'s unconventional five-act play *Die Judastragödie* (1920; the Judas tragedy), performed at the Vienna *Burgtheater* in 1923, portrays Judas as a tragic hero; it was followed in 1921 by an essayistic prose pendant entitled *Das Jesusproblem* (the Jesus problem). F.'s aphorisms appeared in 1922 as *Steinbruch* (quarry), and in the same year F. demonstrated his kinship with Johann Nestroy (1801–1862) by editing *Das ist klassisch!* (that's a classic!), a collection of the satirical dramatist's wit and wisdom.

F.'s magnum opus is *Kulturgeschichte der Neuzeit* (3 vols., 1927–31; *A Cultural History of the Modern Age*, 3 vols., 1930–32), a highly original, brilliant, aphoristic, stylistically notable intellectual and cultural history ranging from the Renaissance to World War I. It bears the subtitle "Die Krisis der europäischen Seele von der Schwarzen Pest bis zum Weltkrieg" ("The Crisis of the European Soul from the Black Death to World War I"). An equally ambitious two-volume *Kulturgeschichte des Altertums* (a cultural history of antiquity), on which F. started working in 1933, remained incomplete: *Ägypten und Vorderasien* (Egypt and the Near East) appeared in 1936 (and was reissued in 1947 as *Kulturgeschichte Ägyptens und des alten Orients* [a cultural history of Egypt and the ancient Orient]); *Kulturgeschichte Griechenlands* (a cultural history of Greece) was issued posthumously in 1940 and 1949.

FURTHER WORKS: *Der Petroleumkönig; oder, Donauzauber* (1908, with A. Polgar); *Soldatenleben im Frieden* (1910, with A. Polgar); *Von Dante zu D'Annunzio* (1915); *Kleine Philosophie* (1930); *Die Reise mit der Zeitmaschine* (1946; repr. as *Die Rückkehr der Zeitmaschine*, 1974); *F.-Brevier* (1947); *Das Altertum war nicht antik* (1950); *Kleine Portraitgalerie* (1953); *Aphorismen zur Geschichte* (1955); *Briefe* (1959); *Ist die Erde bewohnt?* (1961); *Aphorismen und Briefe* (1961); *Wozu das Theater?* (1965); *E. F.s Konversationslexikon* (1974)

BIBLIOGRAPHY: Polgar, A., "A Great Dilettante," *AR*, 10 (1950), 232–46; Haage, P., *Der Partylöwe, der nur Bücher fraß* (1971); Dencker, K. P., *Der junge F.* (1977)

HARRY ZOHN

FRISCH, Max

Swiss novelist and dramatist (writing in German), b. 15 May 1911, Zurich

After secondary school F. briefly studied German literature and art history at the University of Zurich. Following the death of his father he supported himself as a journalist for several years, during which he traveled extensively in Europe and the Balkans and completed his first novel. Temporarily giving up his literary pursuits, he studied architecture and received his diploma in 1941. For more than a decade he combined the tasks of an architect with a renewed commitment to literature, alternating intense periods of work at home in Zurich with frequent travel, especially to the U.S., Mexico, and Greece. He turned to writing full-time after the success of his novel *Stiller* (1954; *I'm Not Stiller*, 1958). Leaving Zurich, he lived in various rural communities and then in Rome before eventually settling in Berzona, in the Swiss canton of Ticino, where he still resides today.

Even in his earliest works of fiction, which show indebtedness to his compatriots Gottfried Keller (1819–1890) and Albin Zollinger (1895–1941), F. revealed preoccupations that place him in the tradition of 20th-c. novelists concerned with the disintegration of the self, such as Joyce, Kafka, Sartre, and Musil (qq.v.). His first published novel, *Jürg Reinhart* (1934; Jürg Reinhart), and particularly its more successful later adaptation, newly titled *J'adore ce qui me brûle; oder, Die Schwierigen* (1943; I adore what burns me; or, the difficult ones; the second version of 1957 reverses the title to *Die Schwierigen; oder, J'adore ce qui me brûle*), already introduce the major themes in his fiction: the need to transcend (Swiss) provincialism, the difficulty of maintaining human individuality in the modern world, the problems of alienation resulting from the collapse of traditional values and the revolution in technology, and the psychological bonds imposed by time. In *Die Schwierigen*, a *Bildungsroman*, the artist-protagonist Reinhart searches in vain for self-fulfillment; denied satisfaction in his own lifetime even after several fresh starts, he attains suprapersonal fulfillment when his son follows in his footsteps and reenacts the search. By emphasizing that single moments in time repeat themselves within the life of an individual as well as from generation to generation, F. shows that sequential events can be perceived as simultaneous in the human imagination.

The urge to seek out a life beyond the confines of place and time becomes the dominant propelling force for the protagonist of F.'s next novel, *Stiller*. Considered by many critics to be the author's most successful work of fiction, it combines the story of an artist in search of his authentic self with an almost Strindbergian portrayal of a marriage that is torturously destructive because husband and wife make absolute demands on each other. The sculptor Anatol Ludwig Stiller, frustrated by the narrow-mindedness and sterility of Swiss society and by his own artistic and marital inadequacies, escapes to the freedom of the U.S. and then attempts to preserve this freedom when he returns home after seven years by assuming a new identity as a "Mr. White." He is recognized at the border and arrested because of his fake passport, but he adamantly denies that he is Stiller. While in prison, he is asked to write down the objective "truth" about himself for the public prosecutor. During this attempt he gradually comes to terms with his past, realizing that his effort to liberate himself from the finished image (*Bildnis*) so insistently imposed on him by other people, including his wife, can succeed only by accepting and transforming it. By means of an ingenious narrative device F. skillfully captures Stiller's ambivalence about his identity, his experiences and failures, and his ability to communicate them: the novel begins with the first-person narrator "Mr. White" already in prison, writing about Stiller as a third person. Passages in the narrative present time by the obviously unreliable narrator alternate with third-person passages reconstructing the past. After "Mr.

White" and Stiller merge at the end of Part I, a "Postscript by the Public Prosecutor" lends a further, equally subjective perspective. Ironic juxtaposition of conflicting details injects touches of humor in this narrative texture of great depth and complexity.

The novel *Homo Faber* (1957; *Homo Faber*, 1959) has a similarly multilayered structure, but conveys the ambiguities and difficulties of self-definition quite differently. Another first-person narrator, the fifty-year-old UNESCO engineer Walter Faber, writes a chronological record of his present activities—constant travel in the U.S., Mexico, Central and South America, and Europe—interspersed with numerous flashbacks to incidents in his past, particularly during a period twenty-one years before when he was in love with an archaeologist named Hanna. Self-deceiving like Stiller, Faber has always defined himself in exclusively rational, scientific terms and is reassured by exactly those dimensions of existence that Stiller rebelled against: repetition, routine, predictability. Utterly lacking in spontaneity, he believes he can achieve absolute control over his life through sober, calculated analysis. Paradoxically enough, the very incalculable forces that Faber challenges or ignores eventually destroy him, just as he is beginning to appreciate them. His rigid preconceptions are undermined as he endures a series of catastrophic and shocking events, including an emergency airplane landing in a Mexican desert, an inadvertently incestuous affair with the daughter he didn't know he had, and an encounter with a horribly emaciated former professor. It is only after his daughter dies in a tragic accident and he learns he has stomach cancer that he finally realizes his blindness and even experiences a euphoric moment of insight: to be human means to be involved, emotionally as well as intellectually, in all facets of life, from love to hate, from bliss to terror. But change occurs too late; as he is wheeled into the operating room at the end of the novel, he senses he will not survive. Throughout the narrative F. endows Faber's report with a remarkable consistency of viewpoint, vividly evoking the defensiveness of a narrow technological mind threatened by an incomprehensible fate. The gradual evolution in style from laconic utterances fraught with scientific and technical vocabulary to artistic expansiveness convincingly reflects the engineer's increasing sensibility.

F.'s ability to reproduce varying psychological states of mind is displayed with almost manneristic virtuosity in the experimental novel

Mein Name sei Gantenbein (1964; *A Wilderness of Mirrors*, 1966). In a narrative structure reminiscent of the French New Novel (q.v.), the first-person narrator-protagonist seeks to prove the idea that every "I" can create his own role in life and thereby preserve absolute freedom. In the course of the virtually plotless novel, the narrative "I" invents a number of identities, including the intellectual, somewhat stuffy Enderlin, the architect Svoboda, and, his favorite, a man called Gantenbein who pretends to be blind in order to see how people really are. He discards or alters these identities at will, relentlessly exploring the possibilities of escaping from a finished, and therefore rigid, image of himself into all the fictions he is capable of imagining. As he repeatedly states, he tries on stories like clothes. While definite patterns of experience emerge, the narrator never quite grows into a character since he avoids commitment to any final role. Highly entertaining and humorous, the open-ended novel confirms in theme and structure, if only playfully, that the feared restrictions of identity and chronology can be overcome.

Montauk (1975; *Montauk,* 1976), a more conventional novel and F.'s most personal work of fiction, recounts a weekend spent by the first-person narrator Max, a sixty-four-year-old writer, with Lynn, a young American friend. Although he attempts to live purely for the moment during this weekend among the sand dunes of Long Island, Max cannot avoid interrupting the narrative present with the memories that constantly intrude on his consciousness and remind him of lost opportunities and the irrevocable passage of time. Because of the intimate style of much of this diarylike chronicle and numerous recognizably autobiographical elements, *Montauk* has often been read as pure autobiography, in spite of its structural and thematic similarities to earlier novels and the absence of any truly confessional passages. Autobiographical elements are characteristic for all of F.'s fiction, however. Indeed, his other novels can also be given the generic designation "diary novel" (*Tagebuchroman,* or "fictitious diary"). It must be emphasized that the first-person narrators in F.'s fiction, including the Max of *Montauk,* are without exception coherent, stylized characters. The author's real personal diaries—the military diary *Blätter aus dem Brotsack* (1940; leaves from my knapsack) and the two sets of journals, *Tagebuch 1946–1949* (1950; *Sketchbook 1946–1949,* 1977) and *Tagebuch 1966–1971* (1972;

Sketchbook 1966–1971, 1974)—make fascinating reading, but lack the stylization and artistic unity of his novels.

F.'s fiction tends to focus so exclusively on private, existential concerns that his plays, which treat both public and private issues, seem to many critics to be the work of an entirely different man. While the dramatist F. obviously learned much from Bertolt Brecht (q.v.), whom he actually worked with in Zurich, he is hardly a political revolutionary. Even his avowedly political parable plays explore general philosophical questions rather than specific political problems, and in ideology come closer to the works of Pirandello (q.v.), in structure to those of Thornton Wilder (q.v.).

Die chinesische Mauer (1947; rev. version, 1955; *The Chinese Wall,* 1961), *Biedermann und die Brandstifter* (1958; *The Firebugs,* 1959) and *Andorra* (1961; *Andorra,* 1962) are F.'s most important plays about political issues. *Die chinesische Mauer* seeks to define a concept of morality transcending the merely aesthetic culture characteristic of today's intellectuals. Set in China to achieve a kind of Brechtian alienation, the action concerns the collapse of Emperor Hwang Ti's vast political power, resulting from the emperor's resistance to change and his deafness to the "voice of the people." At a festive party celebrating the victory of his "Great Order," which is attended by various famous historical figures such as Columbus, Napoleon, and Philip II of Spain, an intellectual named the Man of Today criticizes absolute power, albeit in very theoretical terms, and warns about the dangers threatening mankind. But the intellectual cannot change anything with abstract pronouncements, no matter how articulate, and he consistently fails to act on his convictions. The play intends to expose the fatal tendency of history to repeat itself and the dichotomy of knowing and acting, but it lacks structural coherence, and its message disappears beneath its farcical surface.

In terms of theatrical effectiveness, both *Biedermann und die Brandstifter* and *Andorra* are far more successful. *Biedermann und die Brandstifter* presents a tightly constructed parable about the resistible rise of coercion and terror. The central figure, a bourgeois Mr. Regular Guy, does not oppose the arsonists who cunningly force their way into his house and set up gasoline barrels in his attic. In his cowardice and self-satisfied complacency, Biedermann foolishly rationalizes away all doubts about his visitors. When the inevitable catastrophe happens, he even praises the fire, for the destroyed building can be rebuilt with more comfort and superior materials. With much black humor a chorus of firemen parodying the verses of Greek tragedy comments on the action throughout.

The central theme of the more serious *Andorra* is racial prejudice, particularly anti-Semitism, but the drama obscures the true issues by overemphasizing the problem of self-image. The protagonist Andri is not Jewish at all, but actually the illegitimate son of a woman from the other side of the border and the Andorran schoolteacher who has "adopted" him. His cowardly father has passed him off as a Jew rescued from persecution abroad. Initially accepted by the Andorrans but then disparaged for being "different" when the country is threatened by foreign invasion, Andri gradually assumes the negative character traits people expect from him. His father tries in vain to tell him the truth, but he has become obsessed with his supposed Jewishness. When the foreign invaders take him away after a grotesque "Jew-inspection," his father, the real tragic figure of the play, hangs himself.

F.'s political parables remain curiously naïve and abstract because they fail to differentiate personal questions of self and image from issues of broader public relevance. More convincing are the plays restricted to private concerns, particularly the parodistic comedy *Don Juan; oder, Die Liebe zur Geometrie* (1953; *Don Juan; or, The Love of Geometry,* 1967), which illustrates how spontaneity may be killed by the images people create. F.'s Don Juan feels trapped in his own myth—he actually finds women tedious and much prefers the analytical purity of geometry. Although he occasionally succumbs to the women who pursue him, he arranges to stage publicly his descent into hell so that he can disappear and study geometry in peace. Ironically, at his place of refuge he falls in love and even fathers a child; the vitality of life has triumphed over geometrical abstractions.

The play *Biografie: Ein Spiel* (1967; *Biography: A Game,* 1969) again treats the theme of freedom of choice. The protagonist, Professor Kürmann (the name means "man who has a choice"), is given the opportunity by a figure called the Recorder of turning back his life to any point and effecting any changes he desires. Provided with an empty stage, actors, and props, Kürmann finds that he cannot alter the pattern of his experience, even by taking the radical step of joining the Communist Party; no matter how he begins and what revisions he makes, the scenes he stages inevitably turn out to reproduce his life.

In spite of his strong commitment to public concerns, then, F. is essentially an author of private sensibilities. With compassion and great subtlety he probes existential anxieties, repeatedly displaying an acute awareness of human transience and of the problematic nature of experience in a world that seems to have lost its axis. In the variety and stylistic originality of his works, in their elegance of form and humanity of substance, he proves himself to be a writer of major stature.

FURTHER WORKS: *Antwort aus der Stille* (1937); *Bin; oder, Die Reise nach Peking* (1945); *Nun singen sie wieder* (1946); *Santa Cruz* (1947); *Tagebuch mit Marion* (1947); *Als der Krieg zu Ende war* (1949; *When the War Was Over,* 1967); *Graf Öderland* (1951; *Count Oederland,* 1962); *Rip van Winkle* (1953); *Der Laie und die Architektur* (1954); *Herr Quixote* (1955); *Die große Wut des Philipp Hotz* (1958; *The Great Rage of Philip Holtz,* 1967); *Schniz* (1959); *Ausgewählte Prosa* (1961); *Stücke* (2 vols., 1962); *Zürich-Transit: Skizze eines Films* (1966); *Öffentlichkeit als Partner* (1967); *Erinnerungen an Brecht* (1968); *Dramaturgisches* (1969); *Wilhelm Tell für die Schule* (1971); *Dienstbüchlein* (1974); *Frühe Stücke* (1975); *Der Traum des Apothekers von Locarno* (1978); *Triptychon* (1978; *Triptych,* 1981); *Der Mensch erscheint im Holozän* (1979; *Man in the Holocene,* 1980)

BIBLIOGRAPHY: Stäuble, E., *M. F.* (1957; 3rd. ed., 1967); Bänziger, H., *F. und Dürrenmatt* (1960); Wellwarth, G., *The Theater of Protest and Paradox* (1964), pp. 161–83; Bradley, B., "M. F.'s *Homo Faber*: Theme and Structural Devices," *GR,* 41 (1966), 279–90; Hoffmann, C. W., "The Search for Self, Inner Freedom, and Relatedness in the Novels of M. F.," in Heitner, R. H., ed., *The Contemporary Novel in German* (1967), pp. 91–113; Weisstein, U., *M. F.* (1967); Demetz, P., *Postwar German Literature* (1970), pp. 112–25; Durzak, M., *Dürrenmatt, F., Weiss: Deutsches Drama der Gegenwart zwischen Kritik und Utopie* (1972); Kieser, R., "Man as His Own Novel: M. F. and the Literary Diary," *GR,* 47 (1972), 109–17; Marchand, W. R., "M. F.," in Wiese, B. von, ed., *Deutsche Dichter der Gegenwart* (1973), pp. 231–49; Pickar, G. B., "The Narrative Time Sense in the Dramatic Works of M. F.," *GL&L*, 28 (1974–75), 1–14, Grimm, R., and Wellauer, C., "M. F.: Mosaik eines Statikers," in Wagener, H., ed., *Zeitkritische Romane des 20. Jahrhunderts* (1975), pp. 278–300; Butler, M., *The Novels of M. F.* (1976); Knapp, G. P., ed., *M. F.: Aspekte des Prosawerks* (1978); Petersen, J. H., *M. F.* (1978); Kieser, R., "Taking on Aristotle and Brecht: M. F. and His Dramaturgy of Permutation," in Haymes, E. R., ed., *Theatrum Mundi: Essays on German Drama and German Literature* (1980), pp. 185–97

HELENE SCHER

F. experiences with great intensity the necessity to be his brother's keeper. The feeling of being a part of an indivisible world is present, though it is perhaps not as natural here as it is with Thornton Wilder. To the Swiss author, the family of man is not something to be taken for granted but something to be achieved. F.'s personal resiliency always brings him back to his fellow men—at times only to his fellow men in the halls of power—or, again, back to nature.

. . . F. . . . measures, so to speak, very much in spatial terms. The world at large enters the field of vision of Stiller, a quiet man caught up in small matters. He learns to accept his world with humility. The promises of the great are a snare and a delusion.

Hans Bänziger, *F. und Dürrenmatt* (1960), pp. 204–5

The psychological problem which fascinates F. is the inability of man to stand by himself, wholly independent of all other human beings. Man always strives to *be himself*. But, like Peer Gynt, he can do this only in his dreams. Man in search of himself is constantly either *dreaming* of running away to some idyllic paradise where he can live his own life away from all encumbrances and responsibilities, or he actually *is* running away. In either case he is invariably disillusioned, whether by awakening from the futile dream or by coming to the harsh reality of the wished-for paradise.

George E. Wellwarth, *The Theater of Protest and Paradox* (1964), p. 163

What F. has written here [in *Biedermann und die Brandstifter*] is not a propaganda piece against totalitarianism. The book searches more deeply. It "teaches" that we must resist at the very beginnings. But to tell the truth, its lesson comes really somewhat late, at least for Mr. Biedermann—and for Mr. Benes, Mr. Chamberlain, and Mr. Hin-

denburg. . . . Biedermann ultimately proves to be his own arsonist, setting fire to his own existence, but we recognize him as such only when we find him, a charred corpse, lying amid the ruins of his house. . . . Here too, then, as in his other pieces, the author does not offer us a ready-made solution to the problem he has raised. He merely confronts the public with the disturbing question, which ought not to leave us ever again—unless we are irredeemable Biedermanns—a question to which each of us can answer only with his life, a life in which word and world are one, a "true life."

Eduard Stäuble, *M. F.*, 3rd. ed. (1967), p. 121

In *Stiller, Homo Faber,* und *Mein Name sei Gantenbein* [F.] has created three of the most important novels of the past decade. Taken together, these books are perhaps the most meaningful recent German writing in their particular genre: the psychological novel.

Their significance does not lie so much in F.'s narrative technique. The structure and the plot development in *Stiller* and *Homo faber* are essentially traditional, and only in *Gantenbein* does F. move onto experimental, new narrative ground. He has developed a keenly sensitive and often highly imaginative style for illuminating the anguished consciousness of the contemporary intellectual in particular and of contemporary man in general. But while this brilliant style is evident in many single episodes and scenes of each novel, it is not employed consistently in any of the three. The significance of the works lies, rather, in the astonishing accuracy and depth of psychological insight with which the experiences of his typically modern heroes are viewed and presented. His characters are engaged—often against their will and rarely successfully—in what F. considers to be the most urgent concerns of living. And while these "urgent concerns" are not profound new discoveries, the psychological understanding that F. has for what motivates his characters is rare, indeed. Finally, since most of us can see ourselves in the central figures, the importance of the novels lies also in what they can help us to recognize about our own inner selves.

Charles W. Hoffmann, "The Search for Self, Inner Freedom, and Relatedness in the Novels of M. F.," in Robert H. Heitner, ed., *The Contemporary Novel in German* (1967), p. 94

There is something constantly alive and open about M. F.'s mind and work, and after more than thirty years of writing he continues to convey a distinct feeling of youthful energy, endless sympathy, and occasional naïveté. F. strikes me as a writer of renewed beginnings rather than of radical change: he does not sacrifice his interests easily, preferring rather to explore a few questions (involved with the essentials of modern human consciousness) in changing moods, figures, and genres; and if he does discover an answer, he is apt to reject it quickly in order to push his explorations still further. Much of his achievement consists of the revised and the tentative; fascinated by the vagaries of human life . . . he will often pursue an analogous theme in a diary note, a story, a novel, or a play. His individual works are imperfect, but individual imperfections are less important than the intense continuity of his search.

Peter Demetz, *Postwar German Literature* (1970), p. 112

The diary-writer's situation is basically and inevitably existentialist. By interpreting and analysing his daily experiences he is forced to reflect on the circumstances of his existence. It is not coincidental that all great theoreticians and philosophers of modern Existentialism were also authors of diaries. Yet while such writers as Kierkegaard, Bernanos, Sartre or Camus based their literary work on a philosophical theory we find in F.'s case a vehement refusal of "abstractions." The existentialist situation for F. becomes doubtful at the moment of the famous leap into the unknown: for this would presuppose the existence of an absolute truth. It is not the existentialist problem of nothingness which bothers F. His deepest concern, his obsession, is the question of truthfulness (*Wahrhaftigkeit*). There is probably no other contemporary non-religious writer whose entire work has been devoted to a similar degree to the subject-matter of truthfulness.

F.'s approach begins with the acknowledgment that there are truths but not truth. Instead he accepts the existence of a *Bewusstseinsschwerpunkt*, a centre of gravity which changes with the variable consciousness of man within the totality of time.

Rolf Kieser, "Man as His Own Novel: M. F. and the Literary Diary," *GR*, 47 (1972), 112

While by no means shirking *engagement*, F. has always been preoccupied with issues concerning the individual, primarily the painful problem of identity (which lies at the heart of his novel *Stiller*) and questions of human psychology. Beginning with *Mein Name sei Gantenbein*, he takes a keen interest in biography, which he regards as a cloak thrown around the psyche, changing its color, shape, and size according to the "will" of the subconscious. As F. expressed his thoughts in an imaginary interview with himself: what we commonly take to be the true *Geschichte* (history) of our lives is actually a body of *Geschichten* (stories) conforming to an *Erlebnismuster* (experiential pattern). This pattern, F. maintains, is the only source of stability in the individual; it is all that remains of what used to be called Self, character, or personality. As a logical conse-

quence, then, a biography is little more than the offshoot of a fictive existence (*der Ausläufer einer fiktiven Existenz*).

Ulrich Weisstein, Introduction to *Biografie: Ein Spiel*, text ed. (1972), p. v

But the sense of lost centricity . . . affects, in one way or another, all the characters who people F.'s narrative world. For they are eccentric individuals in that they are shown as living at odds with an environment which, far from exerting any central stabilising power, has itself a void at its core. The frightening nature of this void is disguised from the apparently centric majority only by habit and the repetitive shape of everyday routine. F.'s characters, indeed, are embedded . . . in the well-defined context of a modern bourgeois society which is depicted as deeply flawed. For by the conformity which it demands of its members, the roles which it expects them to perform, and the pressures to which it subjects them, this society is shown to be indifferent, if not inimical, to the maintenance and development of personal integrity. The linchpin of this social system is marriage, and F. uses the institution as a microcosm of the larger community beyond. It is not therefore surprising that marriage—and in particular the problematical nature of its supposed centripetence—is the fundamental experience to which all F.'s protagonists are exposed.

Michael Butler, *The Novels of M. F.* (1976), p. 10

FRISIAN LITERATURE
See section under Netherlands Literature

FROST, Robert
American poet, b. 26 March 1874, San Francisco, Cal.; d. 29 Jan. 1963, Boston, Mass.

F.'s life divides sharply into the thirty-nine years that preceded the appearance of his first book of poetry and the following half-century in which he became one of the most widely known poets of his time. Although indelibly identified with rural New England, F. was reared in California until he was eleven, when he returned to his father's native region. Not until his mid-twenties, when he took up poultry farming in Derry, New Hampshire, did he receive his first real exposure to country life. By then, he had attended Dartmouth and Harvard, although he never completed college, and had worked at various jobs, including teaching school, an occupation he returned to when his farming venture failed. In 1912 F. sailed for

England, where he made friends with Ezra Pound (q.v.) and the Georgian poets and published his first two books. The years following his return to America in 1915 brought both serious critical acclaim and popular appeal. His many accolades included four Pulitzer Prizes; academic appointments at Amherst, Michigan, Harvard, and Dartmouth, and countless lectures on other campuses; honorary degrees from Oxford and Cambridge; government-sponsored visits to other nations, and in 1961 an invitation to read "The Gift Outright" (1942) at the inauguration of President John F. Kennedy. F. cultivated the public image of the plain-speaking farmer-poet that endeared him to many, but behind this figure his biography reveals a complicated man haunted by self-doubt and familial conflicts.

F.'s first two books established his two major poetic genres. *A Boy's Will* (1913) introduces his lyric voice in a sequence of introspective poems loosely linked by the quest of the poet for his vocation. Although the style bears traces of conventional 19th-c. poetic diction, poems like "Mowing" and "Storm Fear" show F. discovering his distinctive idiom. *North of Boston* (1914), unquestionably his most distinguished single volume, reveals a masterful dramatic poet. Its dialogues, monologues, and dramatic narratives display his mature style; in "The Pasture" and "Mending Wall" one meets F.'s familiar Yankee persona, inclined toward understatement, mischievous humor, and a sly matter-of-factness. *Mountain Interval* (1916), *New Hampshire* (1923), and *West-Running Brook* (1928) contain fewer strictly dramatic works, but the dramatic element strongly colors both the longer narrative and philosophical poems and the enlarged lyric strain. *A Further Range* (1936), *A Witness Tree* (1942), *Steeple Bush* (1947), and *In the Clearing* (1962) fall short of the earlier volumes, but they contain some superb individual poems. The most comprehensive collection of his work is *The Poems of Robert Frost* (1969).

F.'s poetry transforms the country "North of Boston" into his personal imaginative territory, like Faulkner's (q.v.) Yoknapatawpha County. The merging of poet and place occurs not only in F.'s evocation of the landscape and the people, but most tellingly in the Yankee manner he adopts as his favorite way of seeing and speaking. The regional focus does not circumscribe his vision; from this vantage point, he looks outward on modern life and universal human experience. He is, in one guise, a modern pas-

toralist juxtaposing the declining New England rural order against that of an urban, technological, and cosmopolitan age, either directly—"New Hampshire" (1923)—or indirectly—"A Hundred Collars" (1913), "An Old Man's Winter Night" (1916). Yet F.'s multifaceted sensibility includes as well the nature poet, the speculative poet, and the tragic and the comic observer of the human situation.

Few modern poets have written so often and well about the natural world. From first to last, F. contemplates natural things and processes, and examines the equivocal human relationship to them. Human beings and nature act in harmony in many poems, and their nearness in a rural environment yields a sense of kinship, as in "The Tuft of Flowers" (1906), "Putting in the Seed" (1914), "Two Look at Two" (1923). The feeling of loss that attaches itself to the perpetual running down of things in the physical world is a recurrent theme in poems such as "Nothing Gold Can Stay" (1923), "The Oven Bird" (1916), and "Hyla Brook" (1916). But nature is not for F., as it was for Wordsworth or Emerson, the visible sign of a transcendent spiritual principle that unites the human and nonhuman realms; his outlook more closely resembles Melville's or Dickinson's. Whatever meaning people find in nature is the product of human consciousness; whatever moments of intimacy their relationship offers, nature is essentially indifferent to humankind. F. insists that human yearnings cannot obscure the hard truth of nature's otherness, even though this recognition may be desolating —"The Need of Being Versed in Country Things" (1920), "Bereft" (1927), "Neither Out Far nor In Deep" (1934). F.'s more typical stance, however, is nowhere better dramatized than in "The Wood-Pile" (1914), where a lone figure walking in a frozen swamp discovers only the abandoned handiwork of another person: the effort to locate oneself leads not to any communion with nature, but to what human beings make of the world through their individual actions.

F. spoke of four beliefs which he knew more intimately from living with poetry: "the self-belief," "the love-belief," "the art-belief," and "the God-belief." All four shape his view of humanity. The first two generate much of his poetry, finding expression both in his compassionate portrayals of personal conflict and suffering, and in his celebration of the courage, resiliency, and integrity of the human spirit. F.'s best-known lyric, "Stopping by Woods on a Snowy Evening" (1923), beautifully encapsulates the dialectic between solitary contemplation and the bond with others, which runs through his work from *A Boy's Will* forward. He believes, like so many American writers, that to discover the self, the individual must stand apart; the gesture of turning away is simultaneously a turning within. One continually encounters in his poems a fondness for solitude, the desire to strike out on one's own, and the value he places on independence and self-sufficiency. But the isolation of the self carries with it the burdens of loneliness and fear. In some of F.'s most moving lyric and dramatic poems—for example, "A Servant to Servants" (1914), "The Hill Wife" (1916), "Desert Places" (1934), and "Acquainted with the Night" (1928)—turning inward discloses the chaotic regions of the psyche.

If the solitary questing self, whether drawn to the woods or on imaginative flights out among the stars, is an essential human attribute, so, too, is love, which draws individuals back to familiar earthly things and into communion with someone besides themselves. F. relies less on a social bond among people in general than on the love between two persons, especially a man and a woman. The fulfillment that their mutual affection makes possible, both at its inception and as it endures, renews and sustains life—"The Generations of Men" (1914), "In the Home Stretch" (1916). The darker side of F.'s vision sees the failures of love when it is thwarted by emotional barriers that frustrate communication and empathy—"Home Burial" (1914), "The Subverted Flower" (1942). The themes of selfhood and love reach a culmination of sorts in F.'s late masterpiece, "Directive" (1946). The speaker provides directions back to a brook near a place where human activity and love once flourished but are no more; here, he says, one may "drink and be whole again beyond confusion." The poem invites any reader to set out imaginatively on this journey of self-recovery and self-possession; it must be undertaken alone, but the invitation is a gesture of love.

F. is hardly a religious poet in the usual sense. Nevertheless, the God-belief hovers in the background of several poems and occasionally occupies the foreground, as in his two late verse plays, *A Masque of Reason* (1945) and *A Masque of Mercy* (1947). F. is reticent and enigmatic when he approaches the question of God. He depicts God, by turns, as a distant and uncaring presence, as a well-intentioned human type, as the designer of a brutal universe, as a cosmic joker, and as a conventional afterthought. His intimations of the divine are hedged by a pervasive skepticism toward anything beyond the material cosmos, though the mysteries discerned there by science suggest analogues to the mysteries of religion—"For Once, Then, Something" (1920), "Sitting by a Bush in Broad Sunlight" (1928), "All Revelation" (1938). Even the masques, which, taken together, argue for a faith in a merciful Christian God, dramatize more forcefully the problematic nature of that faith. The foremost impression one gets from F. is that God is largely unknowable, and that perhaps He is whatever man makes of Him. "West-Running Brook" (1928) puts forward the idea that the source of all things is a spiritual reality to which the resistance to the deathward flow of time and change found in both nature and human beings bears witness. But, since the poem is a dialogue between a man and wife, this affirmation is firmly embedded in the immediate experience of their love and their imaginative contemplation of the brook.

What F. finds crucial is the ceaseless searching of the human mind, which is expressed in the God-belief and which is central to his belief in poetry. The human capacity to dream is the subject of two of his best-known poems, "After Apple-Picking" (1914) and "Birches" (1915). Here, as elsewhere, F. recognizes the human importance of the impulse to dream as it pushes against the limitations of finite existence. Yet the ideal or dream world is not a place apart; it closely adheres to the ordinary business of living—the labors of the apple harvest, the boyhood pleasure of swinging on birch trees. This outlook on human experience applies as well to the making of poetry. Where fact and dream converge is not only the point at which some of F.'s finest poems cohere, it is, for him, fundamental to the "literary belief" that brings a poem into being. The other questions of belief depend finally on the clarification of life that poetry makes possible. Every good poem creates "a momentary stay against confusion" that is simultaneously the significance of the poetic act and the act of living.

Writing in the period of modernist experimentation, F. stuck with conventional metrics and verse forms. He is a modern master of blank verse and the sonnet. An innovator in his own right, he fashioned within the framework of traditional forms a uniquely contemporary idiom that, without simply imitating the vernacular, is controlled by the rhythms and phrasings of ordinary speech and the shadings of voice tones. The style created through this medium is a highly flexible and sensitive register of the nuances of human experience, thought, and feeling. Its deceptive simplicity belies the complex range of meaning it expresses, largely through the subtle overtones of implication that emanate from the common things of rural life. Some, like houses, brooks, woods, and stars, take on symbolic weight through repeated use. This kind of suggestivity, however, seldom obtrudes upon the literal particularity of the represented experience. The same holds true for F. as a thinker. Although his tendency to deal more directly with ideas in his later verse has been frequently noted, he never systematically elaborates a philosophical position. He proceeds rather by certain ingrained habits of mind and ways of seeing life: his preoccupation with contraries in both nature and human nature, his abiding concern with boundaries and limits, his opposing inclinations toward clarifying himself and holding something back. All of these various traits, the formal reflection of F.'s belief that poetry should hew closely to immediate and tangible realities, contribute to a deeply personal but nonetheless distinctly modern style.

Unlike his American contemporaries T. S. Eliot, William Carlos Williams, Wallace Stevens (qq.v.), and Pound, F. is not a primary shaper of modern poetry and poetics, yet he is a major poet of our time. Both his admirers and detractors have sometimes underrated his achievement. He has been applauded simply as the poet of traditional American virtues and verities, and he has been accused of skirting present-day dilemmas by retreating to a bygone vantage point. Undeniably, he at times dismisses serious questions lightly, especially political and social ones, and the playful sententiousness of the later F. is frequently off-putting. Yet F.'s best poetry seriously engages the predicaments of modern life and testifies to the value of the ongoing effort to discover what it means to be human.

FURTHER WORKS: *The Letters of R. F. to Louis Untermeyer* (1963); *R. F.: Farm-Poultryman* (1963); *Selected Letters* (1964); *Selected Prose* (1966); *Family Letters of R. and Elinor F.* (1972)

BIBLIOGRAPHY: Thompson, L., *Fire and Ice: The Art and Thought of R. F.* (1942); Lynen, J. F., *The Pastoral Art of R. F.* (1960); Nit-

chie, G. W., *Human Values in the Poetry of R. F.: A Study of a Poet's Convictions* (1960); Sergeant, E. S., *R. F.: The Trial by Existence* (1960); Cox, J. M., ed., *R. F.: A Collection of Critical Essays* (1962); Brower, R. A., *The Poetry of R. F.: Constellations of Intention* (1963); Squires, R., *Major Themes of R. F.* (1963); Jennings, E., *F.* (1966); Thompson, L., *R. F.: The Early Years, 1874–1915* (1966); Gerber, P. L., *R. F.* (1967); Thompson, L., *R. F.: The Years of Triumph, 1915–1938* (1970); Barry, E., *R. F.* (1973); Cook, R. L., *R. F.: A Living Voice* (1974); Greiner, D. J., *R. F.: The Poet and His Critics* (1974); Lentricchia, F., *R. F.: Modern Poetics and the Landscapes of Self* (1975); Thompson, L., and Winnick, R. H., *R. F.: The Later Years, 1938–1963* (1976); Poirier, R., *R. F.: The Work of Knowing* (1977); Wagner, L. W., *R. F.: The Critical Reception* (1977); Borroff, M., *Language and the Poet: Verbal Artistry in F., Stevens, and Moore* (1979), pp. 23–40; Kemp, J. C., *R. F. and New England: The Poet as Regionalist* (1979); Harris, K. G., ed., *R. F.: Studies of the Poetry* (1979)

PETER W. DOWELL

I conceive that R. F. is doing in his poems what Lawrence says the great writers of the classic American tradition did. That enterprise of theirs was of an ultimate radicalism. It consisted, Lawrence says, of two things: a disintegration and sloughing off of the old consciousness, by which Lawrence means the old European consciousness, and the forming of a new consciousness underneath.

So radical a work, I need scarcely say, is not carried out by reassurance, nor by the affirmation of old virtues and pieties. It is carried out by the representation of the terrible actualities of life in a new way. I think of R. F. as a terrifying poet. Call him, if it makes things any easier, a tragic poet, but it might be useful every now and then to come out from under the shelter of that literary word. The universe that he conceives is a terrifying universe. Read the poem called "Design" and see if you sleep the better for it. Read "Neither Out Far nor In Deep," which often seems to me the most perfect poem of our time, and see if you are warmed by anything in it except the energy with which emptiness is perceived.

Lionel Trilling, "A Speech on R. F.: A Cultural Episode," *PR*, 26 (1959), 451

The vagueness and casual quality of the colloquialisms enables F. to hint at the underlying significance in just the right way. He does not wish to make his symbolism flatly mechanical, because the meaning will only be convincing if it grows naturally out of the realistic details of the scene. . . . Hence the importance of the speaker. He tells us of his own experience, and in experience one does not read the meanings of things like neatly written labels, but rather the significance glows dimly beneath the surface. F. is able to portray the speaker in the very act of seeing, because he presents the poem ["The Grindstone"] as a tentative exploration, an awareness of the hidden depths and dark areas of uncertainty. Ironically, the qualities which make colloquial idiom seem unsuited for serious literature are for F. the very means of showing the speaker's superior perceptiveness. The vagueness of the idiom serves as a way of subtly indicating the complications of what he sees. The casual attitude it suggests expresses the careful restraint of one who will not let his feelings confuse him in his cautious searching of reality.

John F. Lynen, *The Pastoral Art of R. F.* (1960), pp. 97–98

The figure the poems make is the figure of R. F. in a New England landscape. The figure and the scene are finally identical, for the poet's language *personifies* his region, making it an extension of himself and converting what was mere geographical space to personal property. F.'s New England is not the alien virgin wilderness occupied by savages and subdued by Puritans; instead it is second growth timber come back to claim land which has been lived over and left behind within the memory of living men; it is thus a grand metaphor for all the past which man throws aside as being at once unpromising and unprofitable. The poet literally enters this abandoned human landscape—human because it has been not only explored but also experienced, still retaining the domestic scars beneath its wilderness—and reclaims it for us all. The result of this imaginative enterprise which converts space to property is a relentless self-possession, bringing into the full range of consciousness as much of that half-remembered life as possible.

James M. Cox, Introduction to James M. Cox, ed., *R. F.: A Collection of Critical Essays* (1962), pp. 2–3

One finds it easy to suppose that R. F. has always been able to make the kind of poem for which he has been readily admired: the horse, the snow, the dark woods—all in a clear congruency, yet squeezed like clay until allegories of grief and joy spread from between the fingers. To do this is to contain and transform the environment, to make a permanent predicate of what merely happens. It is, ultimately, to conquer nature in the formalities of a drama where man faces some manner of temptation: he is tempted to disappear in the dark woods; he is tempted to climb to heaven. In effect,

the temptation is only mildly perverse, mildly self-destructive. The resistance to the temptation is, however, of some intensity, and the triumph lies in refusing to give up any degree of being human in order to become more natural. There is something odd in the triumph, for the conqueror and the conquered, man and nature, are assumed to be conspirators. They have an agreement. They mirror each other.

Radcliffe Squires, *The Major Themes of R. F.* (1963), p. 21

There is something pleasant about the solitude of the Wordsworthian speaker, connected it may be with the "pleasing" retirement of the eighteenth century, but more importantly with Wordsworth's sense that the deeper value of his experience depends on his separation from the world of men. Wordsworthian moments of solitude are positively thrilling, as when the mountain rises up "huge and black," or when it magically rolls by in earth's "diurnal round," or when the boy is clinging perilously to a cliff in a tremendous blast of wind. For this solitary voice—as the context usually makes clear—is never quite alone: it feels presences and powers, or hears other voices, admonishing or consoling—the many expressions of ministering nature. F.'s speaker, by being so surely fixed in the physical world, the neutralized nature of the late nineteenth and twentieth century, is much more surely alone. His matter-of-fact tone is based on matters of fact: thrushes sing deep in the woods at evening, the oven bird's "teacher-teacher" is heard in midsummer. The "call to lament" in "Come In" therefore reminds him that there is no one to lament with. For the traveler in "Stopping by Woods" to say he is "between the woods and frozen lake" is to say also how far he is from home.

Reuben A. Brower, *The Poetry of R. F.: Constellations of Intention* (1963), pp. 76–77

This pilgrim's-progress pattern became a matrix. It was used with conscious variations in most of F.'s books, all the way from *A Boy's Will* to *In the Clearing*. In this pattern there is the subtle suggestion that for F. the central problem of his life—artistic and non-artistic—was to find orderly ways of dealing with dangerous conflicts he found operative within himself or between himself and others. It was part of his delight to discover many different processes for dealing with these conflicts; but he liked to give his lyrics a surface effect of playful ease and serenity even when some of them dramatized his deepest uneasiness. Sometimes the effect of serenity was achieved, in his poems of escape, by his representing his own idealized attitude as being real, no matter how blatantly the biographical facts contradicted the poetry. Most of the time, however, he used his poems either as tools or as weapons for actually trying to bring under control and resolve those conflicts which he viewed as being so dangerous that they might otherwise engulf and destroy him.

Lawrance Thompson, *R. F.: The Early Years, 1874–1915* (1966), p. xxii

We come closest to the spirit of F.'s work whenever as readers we get into the action, the performance of the poem, joining him especially in those movements by which he keeps a poem from "tightening up." There are disclaimers embedded in assertions ("For once, then, something"); conciliating understatements that call for correction ("And to do that to birds was why she came," he says of Eve in "Never Again Would Birds' Song Be the Same"); evasive tactics in the use of words like "almost" and "somehow," of "unless" and especially "as if" ("As if the earth in one unlooked-for favor/Had made them certain earth returned their love," in "Two Look at Two"); predilections for negatives which evoke the reality being denied ("Not bluebells gracing a tunnel mouth–/Not lupine living on sand and drouth" in "A Passing Glimpse"); ascriptions of perception or capacity where none exist ("The aim was song–the wind could see" in "The Aim Was Song"); open-ended endings ("If design govern in a thing so small," "Design"). He is wonderfully exciting in the daring with which he chooses to show that a poem is "less than everything" because, given the nature of things and language, it is difficult enough to be "more than nothing."

Richard Poirier, *R. F.: The Work of Knowing* (1977), pp. 26–27

The characteristic diction of "Mending Wall" and other similar poems is one important aspect of a seemingly realistic style in which features of syntax, word order, and sentence structure drawn mainly from the common level also play their parts. In this style, too, the meanings of words and the content of successive statements are readily intelligible, even though the thematic interrelationships and implications of the statements may be subject to dispute. Nothing on the verbal surface is eccentric, illogical, or cryptic; there are no difficult metaphors or sophisticated plays on words: the references to stones as *loaves* and *balls* and the metonymy "He is all pine and I am apple orchard" are immediately understood because they are the sort of figures of speech we ourselves might use in conversation. All these aspects of style combine in an artful simulation of straightforward thought or speech which has at the same time a preternatural lucidity.

Marie Borroff, *Language and the Poet* (1979), p. 30

FRY, Christopher

(born Arthur Hammond Harris) English dramatist, translator, and screenwriter, b. 18 Dec. 1907, Bristol

F.'s home environment and early schooling exposed him to music and literature, and as a boy he frequently wrote short plays, poems, and farces. His first play to be produced, *Youth and the Peregrines,* was written when he was eighteen. F. was involved in theatrical activity in England during the 1930s, principally as an actor and director. After World War II he turned to playwriting and has had some two dozen plays produced on stage, film, and television.

F. has been instrumental in the movement to restore verse drama to the modern theater. Among his influences are the Bible, Shakespeare, and T. S. Eliot (q.v.), to whom he is often compared. His major plays, written in irregular blank verse, are set in remote periods and places, indicating his belief in the universality of his characters' concerns and in the unchanging nature of the human condition. Although some are called comedies, they all evidence a free mixing of the comic, the tragic, and the religious. All the plays reveal a distinctly Christian outlook; F. himself has divided them into the two categories of the secular and the religious, the latter group intended for staging in a church.

The best of his four religious dramas is *A Sleep of Prisoners* (1951), a long one-act play in which four soldiers, imprisoned in a church, fall asleep and enact biblical stories in their dreams. In each soldier's dream, the other three play out the Biblical roles in ways that profoundly affect the lives of all four after they awaken. Complex in structure, *A Sleep of Prisoners* is a highly theatrical and affecting drama.

F. created the genre of "seasonal comedy," in which the "scene, the season and the characters are bound together in one climate." By stressing the physical details of setting–the weather, the vegetation, the animal life–F. created action that is dominated by the mood and tone of the season in which it takes place. The four seasonal comedies–for spring, autumn, winter, and summer, respectively–are *The Lady's Not for Burning* (1949), *Venus Observed* (1950), *The Dark Is Light Enough* (1954), and *A Yard of Sun* (1970). The best known is *The Lady's Not for Burning*. It concerns a misanthropic soldier in the 15th c. who rescues a young girl accused of witchcraft from burning at the stake. Its witty dialogue is often brilliant and its characterizations are among the strongest in F.'s work.

Generally considered F.'s finest play, *A Phoenix Too Frequent* (1946) is a long one-act comedy based upon the "widow of Ephesus" legend, a narrative popular with writers from the time of Petronius. This play is F.'s most successful statement of a theme that dominates his works: self-realization and redemption through love. It exemplifies his finest work as a dramatic poet; its dialogue, rich in metaphor and imagery, is eminently stageworthy and fully revealing of character.

F.'s sole tragedy is *Curtmantle* (1961), one of three major modern plays recounting the story of Henry II and Thomas à Becket. Unlike the versions by Eliot and Jean Anouilh (q.v.), F.'s tragedy focuses on the English king as tragic protagonist and treats the martyr Becket as a secondary figure. *Curtmantle* is not among F.'s better plays.

F.'s translations of the plays of Anouilh and Jean Giraudoux (q.v.) are highly regarded and have done much to enhance the appreciation of those two French dramatists by English-speaking audiences and readers. Since the 1950s, F. has enjoyed some success as a writer for film and television, penning screenplays for the biblical epics *Ben Hur* (1959), *Barabbas* (1962), and *The Bible* (1966) and contributing to television such well-regarded scripts as *The Brontës of Haworth* (1975).

F.'s efforts to restore verse drama to the modern theater have frequently been coolly received and his own verse criticized for its linguistic excesses. He has been accused of superficiality, derivativeness, and verbosity. In his best plays, however, F. has created dramatic verse which is fully expressive of action and character and which is frequently dazzling in its imagery.

FURTHER WORKS: *The Boy with a Cart* (1939); *The Firstborn* (1946); *Thor, with Angels* (1949); *An Experience of Critics* (1952); *The Queen Is Crowned* (1953); *Sister Dora* (1977); *The Best of Enemies* (1977); *Can You Find Me* (1978)

BIBLIOGRAPHY: Spender, S., "C. F.," *Spectator*, 24 March 1950, 364; Stanford, D., *C. F.: An Appreciation* (1951); Schear, B., and Prater, E., "A Bibliography on C. F.," *TDR*, 4, 3 (1960), 88–98; Kerr, W., "C. F.," in Freedman, M., ed. *Essays in the Modern Drama* (1964), 294–99; Roy, E., *C. F.* (1968); Wiersma, S. M., *C. F.* (1970)

JACK A. VAUGHN

FRYE, Northrop

Canadian literary theorist and critic, b. 14 July 1912, Sherbrooke, Que.

F. received his B.A. from the University of Toronto in 1933, was ordained in the United Church of Canada in 1936, and took his M.A. at Merton College, Oxford, in 1940. He has taught English at Victoria College, Toronto, since 1939 and served as principal of the college from 1959 to 1966. Holder of numerous honorary degrees, in 1958 he was awarded the Lorne Pierce Medal for distinguished service to Canadian letters.

F.'s first book, *Fearful Symmetry: A Study of William Blake* (1947), was a major reinterpretation of the whole corpus of Blake's writing and exerted an enormous influence over all subsequent Blake criticism. Coming from a background of theological as well as literary training, F. saw Blake as a "poet of the Bible" and interpreted his works as in a tradition that included Spenser and Milton. F.'s major interest was in the symbolic and archetypal structure of Blake's work, or what has been called Blake's "mythology." Contrary to most previous critics, however, F. saw Blake's mythology not as private, but as a consciously constructed encyclopedic effort to contain within itself the tradition of poetic prophecy.

Between 1947 and 1957 F. published numerous essays in the process of creating his extraordinarily influential *Anatomy of Criticism* (1957). If the book on Blake became the seed of many subsequent works of practical criticism in the archetypal mode, the *Anatomy of Criticism* has had a similar influence in the area of literary theory, seeking to organize the whole study of literary criticism according to an elaborate scheme that includes a place for historical, ethical, archetypal, and rhetorical modes. Some commentators have claimed that F.'s book marks a definite, indeed a total, break with the main movement of Anglo-American critical theory as it expressed itself in the works of the New Critics (*see* Literary Criticism); others have seen it as an attempt to synthesize the various divergent schools of modern criticism; still others have thought F.'s work represents the culmination of a critical movement begun in romanticism.

The major influence on *Anatomy of Criticism* and all of F.'s subsequent theorizing is, however, William Blake, to whom F. returns for the fundamental symbols of his own thought. Central to *Anatomy of Criticism* is a theory that describes the literary symbol as existing on a scale between a "descriptive" extreme, where the symbol points outward to a referent, and a "literal" extreme, where the symbol is purely self-intentive, or "centripetal." A major part of the book presents an elaborate theory of archetypes, or myths. F.'s theory of archetypes brings in neither Plato nor Jung (q.v.), but declares an archetype (for his purposes) to be a repeated symbol that, appearing in different works, unifies our literary experience and makes a theory of *literature* thinkable. In F.'s theory of genres, there is an effort to establish grounds for the criticism of types of literature—the romance, for instance—that in previous criticism had been given relatively little systematic attention. One type of work that F. identifies and describes is the anatomy; thus he ironically includes his own book within the range of literature that it analyzes.

F.'s later work has developed ideas offered in *Anatomy of Criticism,* such as his view that "every deliberately constructed hierarchy of values in literature known to me is based on a concealed social, moral, or intellectual analogy," and that criticism should have to do with recognition, not evaluation. He has argued the usefulness of his "archetypal" criticism to the teaching of literature at all levels, and he has extended theory to practice, as in two short books on Shakespeare—*A Natural Perspective* (1965) and *Fools of Time* (1967); and one on Milton—*The Return of Eden* (1965).

More recently F. has explicitly brought his literary concerns into studies of what might be called the mythical structure of society (implicit in his earlier work). His theory of the competing cultural myths of "concern" and "freedom," developed in *The Modern Century* (1967) and *The Critical Path* (1971), leads to his advocacy of the notion of "open mythology," which for him would allow a culture to escape the stultification of a fixed mythic structure.

FURTHER WORKS: *Fables of Identity* (1963); *T. S. Eliot* (1963); *The Well-Tempered Critic* (1963); *The Educated Imagination* (1967); *A Study of English Romanticism* (1968); *The Stubborn Structure* (1971); *The Secular Scripture* (1976); *N. F. on Culture and Literature: A Collection of Review Essays* (1978); *The Great Code: The Bible and Literature* (1981)

BIBLIOGRAPHY: Kermode, F., "N. F.," *Puzzles and Epiphanies* (1962); Krieger, M., ed., *N. F. in Modern Criticism* (1966); Krieger, M., "The Critical Legacy of Matthew Arnold . . . ," *SoR,* 5 (1969), 457–74; Denham, R. D., "Science, Criticism, and F.'s Metaphysical Universe," *SCR,* 7, 2 (1975), 3–18; Fisher, M. R., "The Imagination as a Sanction of Value," *CentR,* 21 (1977), 105–17; Fletcher, A., "N. F.: The Critical Passion," *CritI,* 1 (1975), 741–56

HAZARD ADAMS

FUENTES, Carlos

Mexican novelist, short-story writer, critic, and dramatist (writing in Spanish and English), b. 11 Nov. 1928, Panama City, Panama

F.'s father was a Mexican career diplomat, Rafael Fuentes Boettiger; during his early years he lived with his family in various capitals in the western hemisphere. He later attended the prestigious Colegio de México in Mexico City and graduated with a law degree from the National University of Mexico. Another year was spent in Geneva, studying economics at the Institute of Higher International Studies. F. has held a number of positions in the Mexican government. During his university years he became a Marxist and since then has gained renown as an influential writer of the left in Latin America. In 1959 F. married the famous Mexican actress Rita Macedo.

F. began his writing career in the late 1940s but did not become well known until 1954 with the publication of a collection of short stories, *Los dias enmascarados* (the masked days), told in the vein of fantasy and satire. F.'s first novel, *La región más transparente* (1958; *Where the Air Is Clear,* 1960), created a sensation with its experimental techniques. It was an attempt to do for Mexico City what John Dos Passos (q.v.) had done for New York City in *Manhattan Transfer.* The novel was also viewed as a *roman à clef,* exposing the foibles of the upper class, a group to which F. and his family belonged. *La muerte de Artemio Cruz* (1962; *The Death of Artemio Cruz,* 1964), a brilliant tour de force told in the first, second, and third person, is probably F.'s best novel to date. In it, he follows the rise of a peon during the Mexican revolution to his eventual position as a captain of industry and the influential owner of a newspaper chain.

A third major novel, *Cambio de piel* (1967; *A Change of Skin,* 1968), won a prestigious prize in Barcelona, Spain, but censors would not allow its publication in that country. The most universal of F.'s novels, it treats such diverse topics as German guilt over World War II atrocities, the Jewish community in New York City, and the frustrated artist in Mexico.

More recent novels include *Terra nostra* (1975; *Terra Nostra,* 1976), a fanciful compendium of Spanish and Mexican history covering events from Roman times until the end of the world, in 1999, and *La cabeza de la Hidra* (1978; *The Hydra Head,* 1978), an espionage novel revolving around Jewish, Arab, and North American intrigues involving Mexico's newly discovered oil fields.

F.'s work in other genres consists of two plays and four volumes of collected essays. Although F. turned to theater relatively late in his writing career, he had previously produced numerous film scripts, and his novels have always been characterized by their sparkling dialogue. *Todos los gatos son pardos* (1970; all the cats are dark) is a mythical play re-creating the confrontation between Montezuma (1480?–1520) and Cortes (1485–1547) during the conquest of Mexico. *El tuerto es rey* (1970; the one-eyed man is king) is essentially a dialogue between two blind individuals, neither of whom realizes that the other cannot see, but each of whom is in desperate need for support from the other. The play can best be related to the Beckett (q.v.) school of contemporary theater.

During his first two decades of writing, F. published numerous articles in diverse foreign journals, as well as regular columns in two leftist magazines in Mexico, *Siempre* and *Política.* A sampling of his political essays can be found in *La revolución de mayo* (1968; the May revolution) and in *Tiempo mexicano* (1971; Mexican time), an interpretation of key events and personalities in recent Mexican history.

La nueva novela hispanoamericana (1969; the new novel in hispanic America) is a seminal work interpreting the rise of the Latin American "new novel." As a participant as well as a thoughtful critic, F. offers valuable insights into one of the most flourishing areas of 20th-c. fiction. His fourth volume of essays, *Casa con dos puertos* (1970; the house with two doors), is of more general cultural orientation and underlines F.'s vast intellectual background.

F. represents a unique link between the Latin American and the North American novel. He is at home equally in English and Spanish. He has read North American writers in depth and enjoys personal contact with William Styron, Norman Mailer, and Arthur Miller (qq.v.). In his writings perhaps his most valuable contribution has been twofold: to introduce innovative techniques into mainstream Latin American fiction and to define the Mexican national character, both in terms of its struggle with its inferiority complex as well as in the more universal

terms of the 20th-c. existentialist hero. He, Juan Rulfo, and Agustín Yáñez (qq.v.) are generally considered the three major novelists of contemporary Mexico.

FURTHER WORKS: *Las buenas conciencias* (1959; *The Good Conscience,* 1961); *Aura* (1962; *Aura,* 1965); *Whither Latin America?* (1963); *Cantar de ciegos* (1964); *Zona sagrada* (1967; *Holy Place,* in *Triple Cross,* 1972); *Cumpleaños* (1969); *Los reinos imaginarios* (1971); *Cuerpos y ofrendas* (1972); *Una familia lejana* (1980; *Distant Relations,* 1981). FURTHER VOLUME IN ENGLISH: *Burnt Water: Stories* (1980)

BIBLIOGRAPHY: Mead, R. G., Jr., "C. F.: Mexico's Angry Novelist," *BA,* 38 (1964), 380–82; Harss, L., and Dohmann, B., *Into the Mainstream* (1967), pp. 276–309; Sommers, J., *After the Storm* (1968), pp. 95–164; Reeve, R. M., "An Annotated Bibliography on C. F.: 1949–1969," *Hispania,* 53 (1970), 595–652; Guzman, D. de, *C. F.* (1972); Giacomán, H., ed., *Homenaje a C. F.* (1972)

RICHARD M. REEVE

FUGARD, Athol

South African dramatist (writing in English), b. 11 June 1932, Middleburg

F., of mixed Afrikaner and English parentage, grew up in Port Elizabeth. He first became involved in the theater in 1957, when he organized an experimental group in Cape Town. A year later his experience as a clerk in the Native Commissioner's Court in Johannesburg, dealing with "pass law" violations, led him to write plays based on the unhappy circumstances of Africans whom he met in the court. His first works, *No-good Friday* (perf. 1958, pub. 1974) and *Nogogo* (perf. 1958, pub. 1974), set in Sophia Town, Johannesburg's black "township," were written for a multiracial theater group he organized in 1958. The first is concerned with a black correspondence-school student whose efforts to improve his social condition by his studies are cut short by a confrontation with an extortionist. *Nogogo* is set in a "shebeen' (a cheap African saloon) run by a woman whose past as a miners' whore destroys her hopes for happiness with an enterprising but naïve salesman.

The first works by F. to achieve international recognition were his "Port Elizabeth plays": *The Blood Knot* (perf. 1961, pub. 1963), *Hello and Goodbye* (perf. 1965, pub. 1966), and *Boesman and Lena* (perf. and pub. 1969). *Hello and Goodbye* and *Boesman and Lena* were written for the Serpent Players, a drama group that some hopeful black actors in Port Elizabeth's "township" asked him to organize in 1963. The casts of these plays are small: two or three characters confront each other in tense, painful moments which reveal a humanity that cannot be completely overmastered by an antihuman racial milieu. *The Blood Knot* deals with two half brothers, sons of the same mother, who work to save for a farm where they can be free. Zachariah, the darker brother, learns that the "pen pal" he has discovered in a newspaper advertisement is the sister of a white policeman, and Morris, who is light-skinned enough to "pass" for white, realizes that the dream of the farm is hopeless but that the blood that links him to Zachariah is less of a "knot" than their love. *Hello and Goodbye*, the most despairing of the three plays, concerns a brother and sister waiting for their father to die so that they can claim an inheritance which, in fact, does not exist. *Boesman and Lena* are a "Coloured" husband and wife, homeless because "progress" has bulldozed their shanty-town; they camp by a roadside and berate each other until Lena finds a release in her pity for an old African who has been dumped in a field to die.

In 1967, influenced by the theories of the Polish experimental theater director Jerzy Grotowski (b. 1933) F. and his black actors began to experiment with improvisational theater. While F. provided the starting point for the two resulting plays and directed the process by which John Kani and Winston Ntshoni improvised the dialogue, the plays' texture and force emerged from the inner experiences of the actors; F. credited them as fellow "devisers" of the plays, *Sizwe Bansi Is Dead* (perf. 1972, pub. 1974) and *The Island* (perf. 1973, pub. 1974). These works avoid the pitfalls of didacticism, a real danger because of their subject matter (the "pass" law and the political prison on Robben Island, respectively), by transforming the real social ordeal of the doubly real people—the actors *and* their roles—into artistic and therefore meaningful structures.

F.'s most recent work uses more conventional artistic procedures, but *Dimetos* (perf. 1975, pub. 1977) is a daring experiment based on a few lines from the notebooks of Albert Camus (q.v.). Here F. for the first time abandoned a South African setting. Dimetos, a distinguished engineer, exiles himself to a distant province of an unspecified

country, refuses to return to "the city," and permits his emotions to become entangled in incestuous affections for his niece. Her suicide finally causes him to come to terms with his guilt, his irresponsibility, and his existential predicament.

Tsotsi, a powerful short novel written in 1959–60, was published in 1979. It is concerned with a Sophia Town thug who is orphaned as a child, survives by crimes ranging from theft to murder, and, before his violent death, begins to discover his humanity when he happens to find an abandoned baby. The novel is stark in its realism, the social conditions it describes are appalling, and the mastery of fictional techniques makes clear that if F. had not chosen the theater he probably would have had an equally distinguished career as a novelist.

F.'s career reveals a great courage to experiment, a willingness to take artistic risks, a remarkable capacity for avoiding mere didacticism, and profound sympathy for his human subjects. His ability to transform local South African conflicts into universal human predicaments suggests that his future career will continue the steady growth he has already demonstrated.

FURTHER WORKS: *People Are Living There* (1970); *The Coat* (1971); *Statements after an Arrest under the Immorality Act* (1974); *The Guest: An Episode in the Life of Eugene Marais* (1977, with Ross Devenish); *A Lesson from Aloes* (1978)

BIBLIOGRAPHY: Berner, R. L., "A. F. and the Theatre of Improvisation," *BA*, 50 (1976), 81–84; Tucker, A. C., "A. F. Interviewed," *Transatlantic*, Nos. 53–54 (1976), 87–90; Green, R. J., "Politics and Literature in Africa: The Drama of A. F.," in Hayward, C., ed., *Aspects of South African Literature* (1976), pp. 163–73; Benson, M., "Keeping an Appointment with the Future: The Theatre of A. F.," *TheatreQ*, 28 (1977–78), 77–83; "F. on Acting: Actors on F.," *TheatreQ*, 28 (1977–78), 83–87; O'Sheel, P., "A. F.'s 'Poor Theatre,'" *JCL*, 12, 3 (1978), 67–77

ROBERT L. BERNER

FUKS, Ladislav

Czechoslovak novelist and short-story writer (writing in Czech), b. 24 Sept. 1923, Prague

F. studied philosophy and psychology at the Charles University in Prague and in 1949 received his doctorate. For some time he worked in various nonliterary professions, but since 1960 he has devoted himself entirely to literature.

F. is one of the most significant of contemporary Czech writers of fiction; he has experimented with highly inventive and original ways of expressing the problems, formal and semantic, that preoccupy contemporary literature. His first novel, *Pan Theodor Mundstock* (1963; *Mr. Theodore Mundstock*, 1968), is set in Prague during the German occupation. It is an ironic treatment of tragedy with strong mythic overtones, and, like so many of F.'s works, it focuses on the inner life of the hero. A Prague Jew, a little man without particular attributes, awaits arrest and transportation to a concentration camp. While waiting, he attempts to prepare himself to withstand the cruelties of the camp by training himself for the rigors he expects. But he is run over by a German military truck on his way to the collection point for the transport.

Mé černovlasí bratři (1964; my dark-haired brothers) is a series of short stories all told in the first person by a young secondary-school student. They take place in the early years of the German occupation and depict the plight of the Jewish fellow students of the narrator, who are tormented by a cruel geography teacher.

F.'s second novel, *Variace na temnou strunu* (1966; variations for a dark string), continues the basic theme of *Pan Theodor Mundstock* and *Mé černovlasí bratři*, that of the threat of the German occupiers. The novel, about the psychological maturing of a boy from the ages of six through fourteen, is dominated by paradox and a sense of the absurd and is infused with strong surrealist (q.v.) and cubo-futurist (see Futurism) elements. Multiple temporal perspectives coexist in a complex system in which linearity is intertwined with simultaneity.

F.'s third novel, *Spalovač mrtvol* (1967; the cremator), which was subsequently made into a film, is cast as a modern horror story whose antihero is a crematorium official, Kopferkringl, who professes kindliness but is in fact a murderer. Again, the novel focuses upon a paradox: the protagonist does not appear to be an evil man; he seems to be harmless and obedient to law and order, and upholds all the normative platitudes, such as that man should not have to suffer. Yet he commits ghastly murders—not out of hate but because the circumstances of his time lead him to crime. He begins by killing his part-Jewish wife and children and ends by putting his crematorium experience to work in the gas chambers of the Nazi concentration camps. The repetitions of key episodes and phrases account for both a fragmentation of traditional reality and an intensification of the internal structure of the work.

F.'s most significant short stories are found in the collection *Smrt morčete* (1969; the death of the guinea pig); they are again set in the time of the German occupation. The longest and most significant story, "Cesta do zaslíbené země" (the trip to the promised land) is based on a biblical myth, which is grotesquely set against the reality of German-occupied Europe.

In the novel *Myši Natalie Mooshabrové* (1970; Natalia Mooshaber's mice) there is a striking culmination of the trends begun in F.'s earlier work. It is a synthesis of various modes of modern literature: the grotesque gothic horror story set in a Kafkaesque dream world; science fiction; and the New Novel (q.v.); these elements are, in turn, juxtaposed with the fairy tale and with archetypal myths. In this work, F. amalgamates the most variegated traditional genres into a new stylistic whole, freed from the conventions of both realistic and surrealistic texts.

F. is preoccupied with the fate of the Jews in German-occupied Europe. But he uses his subjects as a point of departure, for the Jews represent the human condition, and their fate is that of all mankind. Furthermore, the Nazi occupation must be seen as a metaphor for any oppressive system. For F. is concerned with the individual living in the alienated world of today, a world of violence and injustice.

FURTHER WORKS: *Příběh kriminálního rady* (1971); *Oslovení z tmy* (1972); *Návrat z žitného pole* (1974); *Pasáček z doliny* (1977); *Křištalový pantoflíček: Příběh z dětství Juliusa Fučíka* (1978)

BIBLIOGRAPHY: Elman, R., on *Mr. Theodore Mundstock*, *NYTBR*, 28 Jan. 1968, 5; Winner, T. G., "Some Remarks on the Art of L. F.," *RSI*, 17–19 (1970–72), 587–99; Winner, T. G., "Mythic and Modern Elements in the Art of L. F.: *Natalia Mooshaber's Mice*," in Birnbaum, H., and Eekman, T., eds., *Fiction and Drama in Eastern and Southeastern Europe* (1980), pp. 443–61

THOMAS G. WINNER

FULANI LITERATURE
See Mali Literature

FULLER, Roy

English poet and novelist, b. 11 Feb. 1912, Failsworth

F. was born and raised in a provincial, lower-middle-class milieu in Lancashire. When he was eight years old his father died, and two years later the family moved to Blackpool, where he was educated in the local high school. F. was anxious to escape to London, and at the age of sixteen he left school and was articled to a solicitor. Five years later he qualified as a lawyer and from 1933 to 1968 he followed both a legal and literary career.

The poetry that he has always chosen to write is to a large degree socially and politically motivated, and indeed the subject matter and the style of his work may reflect his dual commitment to both verbal and legal matters. In 1968 F. retired as a solicitor and was elected to a five-year term as a professor of poetry at Oxford. Since then he has kept up a steady stream of poems, reviews, essays, lectures, and novels. The consistency that marks the thirteen books of poems, three children's books, eight novels, and two collections of essays that he has published thus far attest to his steadiness and productivity as a writer.

F. is the only English writer who has been affiliated with and influenced by both the political writers of the 1930s (W. H. Auden, Stephen Spender, and C. Day Lewis [qq.v.]) and the "Movement" writers of the 1950s (Philip Larkin, John Wain [qq.v.], and Donald Davie [b. 1922]). He writes a poetry of high civility and intelligibility, and he most often speaks in his poems as a private man registering his response to public events. Auden has been the most important influence on F.'s development, affecting the style, the tone, and the subject matter of his work. As an essentially social poet, F. matured rapidly during World War II, and indeed the war marks the great watershed in his work, separating his first three books—*Poems* (1939), *The Middle of a War* (1942), and *A Lost Season* (1944)—from those that followed. Some of the early poems note the fears and forebodings of the ordinary citizen; others are soliloquies and epitaphs for the war dead. It is in this context that one poem announces, "Life at last I know is terrible . . ." ("What Is Terrible," 1944).

But F. survived the war, and after two books of juvenile fiction—*Savage Gold* (1946) and *With My Little Eye* (1948)—he turned his new poetry to civilian affairs. The voice that animates the postwar poems is still skillful, witty, and formal, still thoroughly political. The majority of F.'s work takes the stance of a middle-aged suburban man addressing in quiet, autobiographical tones the public life of his times. The central political ideology behind F.'s work is Marxist socialism, and the materialist conception of history infuses and informs both his poems and his novels. His imaginative concerns are essentially civic, and he has never swerved from the central Wordsworthian ideal that the poet is a man speaking to other men. But F.'s sensibility is more Augustan than romantic, more rational than emotive, and it is fair to say that his first concern is our shared social life. He has perhaps put his own case best in "Obituary for R. Fuller" (1949) when he writes: "If any bit of him survives/It will be that verse which contrives/To speak in private symbols for/The peaceful caught in public war." One of the major strengths of F.'s work is the way in which his private symbols do in fact reflect the life of a representative man inevitably implicated in the extraordinary events of his own time.

F.'s calm and thoughtful life's work addresses itself to a series of tumultuous events and ongoing social wars. He is one of our minor masters of the public mode.

FURTHER WORKS: *Epitaphs and Occasions* (1949); *The Second Curtain* (1953); *Fantasy and Fugue* (1954); *Counterparts* (1954); *Image of a Society* (1956); *Brutus's Orchard* (1957); *The Ruined Boys* (1959); *The Father's Comedy* (1961); *Collected Poems* (1962); *The Perfect Fool* (1963); *My Child, My Sister* (1965); *Buff* (1965); *Catspaw* (1966); *New Poems* (1968); *The Carnal Island* (1970); *Owls and Artificers: Oxford Lectures on Poetry* (1971); *Professors and Gods* (1973); *Tiny Tears* (1973); *An Old War* (1974); *From the Joke Shop* (1975); *The Joke Shop Annexe* (1975); *Poor Roy* (1977)

BIBLIOGRAPHY: Hamilton, I., "Professor of Poetry," *Listener*, 5 (1968), 761–62; Woodcock, G., "Private Images of Public Ills: The Poetry of R. F.," *WascanaR*, 4, 2 (1969), 21–34; Garfitt, R., "Intimate Anxieties," *London*, Dec.–Jan. 1975–76, 102–9; Austin, A., *R. F.* (1979)

EDWARD HIRSCH

FURPHY, Joseph

(pseud.: Tom Collins) Australian novelist and short-story writer, b. 26 Sept. 1843, Yering (now Yarra Glen); d. 13 Sept. 1912, Claremont

Except for a short period of formal schooling, F. was educated at home. Subsequently, he found employment in a variety of rural occupations. Drought forced him to take up more reliable work in his brother's foundry in Shepparton. It was during this period, and at the age of fifty, that F. began to write a novel based on his bush experiences.

Such Is Life: Being Certain Extracts from the Life of Tom Collins, described by its author as being of a "temper democratic; bias, offensively Australian," first confronted a bewildered reading public in 1903. It purports to be a plotless, realistic chronicle. However, its narrator, Tom Collins, because of his insensitivity and his fondness for philosophizing, fails to discern the lineaments of a romance between a jilted woman (whose face has been grotesquely disfigured by a fall from a horse) and her remorseful, melancholy, misogynistic lover. Unwittingly, Tom provides inaccurate information, which could reunite the lovers. So elaborate and subtly disguised is this submerged plot that many first-time readers of the novel fail to recognize it, as indeed did many of its early critics. It is not merely the comic potential of this hidden plot that F. exploits; rather, he uses his self-consciously literary narrator to explore the nature of fictional narrative, rejecting unequivocally the romance genre employed in such novels of Australian life as the English writer Henry Kingsley's (1803–1876) *Recollections of Geoffrey Hamlyn* (1859). *Such Is Life* also raises, in a piquantly ironic form, the philosophical question of why events occur. Tom contructs a theory (the "one-controlling alternative" theory), which is finally deterministic, but purports to be a compromise between predestination and free will; the events of the novel ironically undermine the theory, and suggest that the author believes that the moral man is the one who takes responsibility for his own actions.

The Buln-Buln and the Brolga (published posthumously in 1948), nominally a series of bush men's yarns and tall stories, further explores the relationship between fact and fiction. It poses the question of whether artistic reshaping of the facts distorts reality and is therefore morally culpable, or whether it imaginatively enhances reality. Tom, as unreliable narrator, favors the former viewpoint, but finds himself humiliated and outnumbered by exponents of the latter view. F. continually presents him as clownish, as incapable of morally evaluating his own actions, and as continually evading reality and intimacy by escapes into theory and literature.

Rigby's Romance: A "Made in Australia" Novel (first published in serial form in *The Barrier Truth* in 1905–6, and in novel form in 1946) belongs to the genre of argumentative utopian novels. F. uses the character of Jeff Rigby to expound on a subject close to F.'s heart: the Christian socialist state. Like the other novels, this one has an ironic framing narrative, involving another hopeless romance between the stump orator and his lovelorn American woman. In this novel, however, the narrative is secondary to F.'s didactic purposes.

Together with Henry Lawson (1867–1922), F. has been regarded as one of the chief exemplars of the tradition of bush nationalism in Australian literary history. However, because of his erudition (used invariably for ironic ends), his consciousness of belonging to the wider European literary tradition, his concern with moral and social issues and with philosophical and literary questions, his significance is more than merely regional. F. undoubtedly overestimates the patience and perceptiveness of the average reader to penetrate the extraordinarily comic and ironic personae of Tom Collins. Those readers prepared to engage in the intellectual gymnastics involved in reading *Such Is Life* may find that it resembles Laurence Sterne's *Tristram Shandy* in being comic in sensibility and ironic and jocular in mode of narration. But the novel is *sui generis:* it is a witty, daring, and literate novel, an unusual product of a raw colonial culture.

FURTHER WORK: *The Poems of J. F.* (1916)

BIBLIOGRAPHY: Phillips, A. A., "The Australian Image: (2) The Literary Heritage Re-assessed," *Meanjin,* 21 (1962), 172–80; Barnes, J., *J. F.* (1963); Kiernan, B., "Society and Nature in *Such Is Life,*" *ALS,* 1 (1963), 75–88; McKenzie, K. A., "J. F., Jacobean," *ALS,* 2 (1966), 266–77; Knight, N., "F. and Romance in *Such Is Life,*" *Southerly,* 29 (1969), 243–55

FRANCES DEVLIN GLASS

FUTABATEI Shimei

(pseud. of Hasegawa Tatsunosuke) Japanese novelist and translator, b. 4 April 1864, Tokyo; d. 10 May 1909, on shipboard in the Bay of Bengal

Born into the samurai class, F. entered the Russian division of the Tokyo School of Foreign Languages in 1881 and fell passionately in love with Russian literature. He made his reputation early with translations of stories by Turgenev and with *Ukigumo* (1887–89; *Ukigumo*, 1967), Japan's first modern novel. Despairing of surviving as a professional writer, he entered the government bureaucracy in 1889. He was also subsequently employed as a teacher and journalist. He resumed publication of translations in 1897, and two final works of fiction appeared early in the 20th c.: *Sono omokage* (1906; *An Adopted Husband,* 1919) and *Heibon* (1907; *Mediocrity,* 1927). He died on shipboard of an illness while returning home from Russia.

In constructing *Ukigumo* (whose title literally means "drifting clouds"), F. introduced limitations of time, space, and character previously unknown in Japanese fiction. Confining his novel to a detailed study of four characters within a two-week period, and limiting the action to a minute geographical area, he concentrated on probing into his characters' lives with an intensity generally absent in earlier fiction. Their problems are such as might be shared by any of his contemporaries, and the language they speak in internalized comments and to each other is the language of his time. Readers were able to approach F.'s narrative without the special knowledge required for much of the earlier fiction of Japan, and they responded eagerly to this new accessibility. It was a novel for and about the emerging, more equalitarian Japan, and it provided a model for subsequent generations.

Sono omokage deals with the agonies of an intellectual adopted into his wife's family, and *Heibon* is actually a series of short sketches—seemingly autobiographical—reflecting the weary and frustrated tone of the Japanese naturalist school.

In all of his fiction F. maintained an attractive balance between bittersweet humor and pathos. There are no major tragedies nor is there sustained slapstick. The reader finds instead a sense of appropriateness. Emotions are confined within plausible boundaries, and actions are no more or less than his contemporaries are likely to have experienced.

The language in which F. wrote his translations and fiction is remarkably vibrant and contributed significantly to the development of modern Japanese prose. Just as F.'s Russian models portrayed their own class and society —with all its limitations—so F. sought to hold the mirror of fiction up to his compatriots in Japan.

FURTHER WORKS: *Zenshū* (16 vols., 1953–54)

BIBLIOGRAPHY: Ryan, M. G., *"Ukigumo": Japan's First Modern Novel* (1967); Ryan, M. G., *The Development of Realism in the Fiction of Tsubouchi Shōyō* (1975)

MARLEIGH GRAYER RYAN

FUTURISM

Italian Futurism

Initially an Italian literary movement, futurism was founded by Filippo Tommaso Marinetti (q.v.) in February 1909 when he published, in French, his "Manifeste du Futurisme" ("The Founding and Manifesto of Futurism," 1971) in *Le Figaro* of Paris. Marinetti asserted that civilization was on the threshold of a new historical epoch, and he advocated the absolute rejection of the past with all its museums, libraries, and academies. The essential elements of poetry would henceforth be "courage, audacity, and rebellion"; its new aesthetic criteria were to be speed and aggression, concretized in automobiles, airplanes, and war. The "Manifesto technico della letteratura futurista" ("Technical Manifesto of Futurist Literature," 1971), published in May 1912, specified the means by which writers could achieve this revolution: adjectives, adverbs, punctuation, and syntax were proscribed. In their place, the writer would use substantives, verbs in the infinitive mood, and mathematical symbols; analogy would supplant syntax. Words would thus be freed (*parole in libertà*) from their historical and logical functions. Repudiating the psychological foundations of previous literature, Marinetti proposed concentrating on the physical—noise, weight, and smells—in order to realize a spontaneous, dynamic, and concrete poetry.

Futurism's emphasis on the sensuous and the dynamic appealed to painters, sculptors, and performing artists. Futurist manifestos, some by Marinetti, some by others, soon appeared on music, theater, and film. Indeed, even the literature of futurism had its theatrical aspect; as the critic Luigi Russo (1892–1961) noted, Marinetti's temperament was not that of a poet: he was an actor whose works must be declaimed rather than read.

The period 1909–15 was the heyday of futurism. It attracted, however briefly, some of Italy's finest writers: Corrado Govoni (1884– 1965), Aldo Palazzeschi (q.v.), Giovanni Papini (1881–1956), and Ardengo Soffici (1879–1964). It also spawned or influenced similar movements in other European countries. The roots of English Vorticism, founded in 1914 by Percy Wyndham Lewis (q.v.), are embedded in Italian soil. Russian futurism, although in many respects an autonomous phenomenon, was influenced by Marinetti's movement and perhaps by Marinetti himself: he appears to have visited Russia as early as 1910. Unlike the Italian movement, however, Russian futurism produced a significant body of literature.

Although futurism can be said to have disappeared only with Marinetti's death in 1944, its influence declined rapidly after Italy's intervention in World War I. The futurists had long and loudly proclaimed war to be the "hygiene of the world," but their bellicose attitude was not universally popular in Italy. Moreover, in 1914 Marinetti had become friends with Benito Mussolini, and the association between Fascism and futurism alienated many active and potential supporters of the movement. Futurist activities in the 1920s focused on the theater, film, and radio; the last performance took place on radio in 1933.

The significance of Italian futurism does not lie in its literary masterpieces—there are none. Yet its achievements are considerable. It freed Italian poetry definitively from its traditional language and its postromantic themes, thus opening the way for modern poets like Giuseppe Ungaretti and Eugenio Montale (qq.v.). Painting and sculpture of futurist inspiration fared much better: Umberto Boccioni (1882–1916), Giacomo Balla (1871–1958), Carlo Carrà (1881–1966), Gino Severini (1883–1966), and Luigi Russolo (1885–1947) all created distinguished works of art. The futurist music produced by mechanical "noise-intoners" presaged synthetic electronic music, while the futurist theater directly influenced Luigi Pirandello and Thornton Wilder (qq.v.). Although futurism has to a large extent been overshadowed by other avant-garde literary movements in Europe, there can be no doubt that it anticipated and made important contributions to Dadaism, surrealism, expressionism, and the Theater of the Absurd (qq.v.).

BIBLIOGRAPHY: Kirby, M., *Futurist Performance* (1971); Marinetti, F. T., *Selected Writings* (1971); Rye, J., *Futurism* (1972); Apollonio, U., ed., *Futurist Manifestos* (1973); Andreoli-De Villers, J.-P., *Futurism and the Arts: A Bibliography, 1959–73* (1975); Tindall, C., and Bozzolla, A., *Futurism* (1978)

LOUIS KIBLER

Russian Futurism

Russian futurism arose after the dissolution of Russian symbolism (q.v.) around 1910. It represents one of the major Russian contributions to the international avant-garde movement in art and literature. There were four main groups: Hylaea, also known as cubo-futurism, whose earliest activities date back to 1908–9; ego-futurism, organized in Petersburg in 1911 by the popular poet Igor Severyanin (1887–1941); The "Mezzanine of Poetry," a Moscow group initiated in 1913 by Vadim Shershenevich (1893–1942); and Centrifuge, started in 1913 in Moscow and including the poets Boris Pasternak (q.v.) and Nikolay Aseev (1889–1963).

By far the most important group was the cubo-futurists, organized by the poet and painter David Burlyuk (1882–1967), and including two of the greatest Russian poets of the 20th c., Velemir Khlebnikov and Vladimir Mayakovsky (qq.v.), as well as Alexey Kruchyonykh (1886–1968), Vasily Kamensky (1884–1961), and Benedikt Livshits (1887–1939). Livshits later wrote his memoirs, which contain a history of the movement: *Polutoraglazy strelets* (1933; *The One-and-a-Half-Eyed Archer,* 1978). The group's famous manifesto "Poshchyochina obshchestvennomu vkusu" (1912; "A Slap in the Face of Public Taste," 1980), an attack on bourgeois aesthetics and a call for revolution in the arts, set the tempo for its "militant year," 1913–14, which saw a stormy and provocational tour of seventeen provincial Russian cities and the presentation in St. Petersburg's Luna Park in December 1913 of two key futurist works: Kruchyonykh's opera *Pobeda nad solntsem* (1913; *Victory over the Sun,* 1971), with backdrops and costumes designed by Kazimir Malevich, and Mayakovsky's extraordinary verse drama *Vladimir Mayakovsky: Tragedia* (1913; *Vladimir Mayakovsky: A Tragedy,* 1968). The cubo-futurists were unanimous in disclaiming the influence of Italian futurism, rejecting its militarism and its emphasis on new content rather than formal innovation, and gave Marinetti (q.v.) a chilly, at times scandalous, reception when he visited Russia in 1914.

Cubo-futurist aesthetics emphasized the form of poetic language rather than its objective reference or ideational content, and wide-ranging verbal experimentation was its distinguishing characteristic. The futurists' debt to cubism (q.v.) is apparent in their call for "rough" poetic texture; their insistence on the break with realism and on the independence of art from reality (Khlebnikov's theory of the *samovitoe slovo*, "selfsome" or "self-oriented word"); their use of "shifts" or "dislocations" (*sdvigi*) on the metrical, semantic, and plot levels; and also their predilection for fragmentary composition. They advocated a new poetic language written "beyond the mind," or *zaum* ("transrational" or "supraconscious" language). For Kruchyonykh this concept meant a type of glossolalia, meaningless but expressive sequences of sounds, while for Khlebnikov it entailed the restructuring of the semantics of the language through the revival of dead etymological connections and the creation of new kinships between words based on the similarities in their sound, in particular the "poetic valency" or associative potential of their first consonant. Cubo-futurism was noted for the creation of neologisms and the deformation of existing words through the addition of unusual prefixes and suffixes, the mixing of lexical and stylistic levels, and the cultivation of a generally "anti-aesthetic" stance as regards both thematics and the poetic persona.

The futurists failed in their attempt to gain official recognition after the Russian Revolution, although their influence in the 1920s was considerable, as is reflected in the journals Mayakovsky edited, *Lef* (1921–23) and *Novy Lef* (1927–28). Their impact on the development of Russian poetry to the present day has been considerable, and the works of Khlebnikov and Mayakovsky, in particular, remain exemplary for Russian writers of an avant-garde persuasion.

BIBLIOGRAPHY: Markov, V., *Russian Futurism: A History* (1968); Barooshian, V., *Russian Cubo-Futurism 1910–1930* (1974); Jangfeldt, B., *Majakovskij and Futurism 1917–1921* (1976); Barron, S., and Tuchman, M. eds., *The Avant-Garde in Russia 1910–1930: New Perspectives* (1980); Proffer, C. and E., eds., *The Ardis Anthology of Russian Futurism* (1980)

STEPHEN RUDY

MAX FRISCH

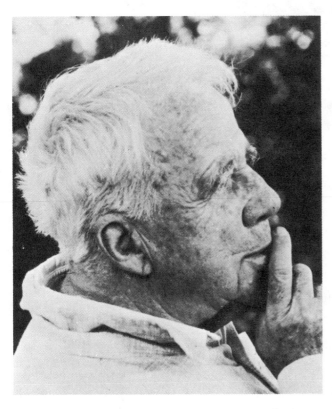

ROBERT FROST

CARLOS FUENTES

FEDERICO GARCÍA LORCA

GADDA, Carlo Emilio

Italian novelist, short-story writer, and essayist, b. 14 Nov. 1893, Milan; d. 21 May 1973, Rome

G. was born into a family of the well-to-do upper middle class, but because the family lost most of its money and G.'s father died when G. was a child, he was brought up by a mother who tried to keep up appearances and lived beyond her means. G. fought in World War I and in 1917 was taken prisoner by the Germans. In 1920 he received a degree in engineering, and until 1935 he worked at his profession in various countries. In 1926 he began the association with the Florentine review *Solaria* that marked his early career. Between 1950 and 1955 G. worked in Rome for RAI, the Italian radio and television network. He was awarded the Formentor Prize in 1957 and the International Prize for Literature in 1963.

For years G.'s fame as a writer remained confined within the circles of the literati who appreciated his refined belles lettres, memory pieces, and short stories collected in such volumes as *La Madonna dei filosofi* (1931; the philosophers' Madonna), *Il castello di Udine* (1934; the castle of Udine), *L'Adalgisa: Disegni milanesi* (1944; Adalgisa: Milanese drawings), *Novelle dal ducato in fiamme* (1953; tales of the burning duchy), and *Accoppiamenti giudiziosi* (1963; judicious couplings). Yet even in these works there are the qualities to be found in G.'s major books: a keen observation of human behavior and a tormented and merciless introspection (both conducted through psychoanalytic processes), interest in sociological and linguistic subjects (different social classes, various dialects, and technical jargon), and a masterful manipulation of literary style.

These qualities began to be appreciated by a wider public with the first publication in full of *Giornale di guerra e di prigionia* (1955; war and prison journal), a record of his World War I experiences, and above all of his two major novels, written much earlier and previously issued only in installments in literary journals, in 1946 and 1938 respectively: *Quer pasticciaccio brutto de via Merulana* (1957; *That Awful Mess on Via Merulana*, 1965) and *La cognizione del dolore* (1963; definitive ed., 1970; *Acquainted with Grief*, 1969).

Quer pasticciaccio brutto de via Merulana is a "detective novel," in the sense that a Poe or a Borges (q.v.) used the genre. The protagonist is a police commissioner in Fascist Rome who has to disentangle a murder and a jewel robbery. The mass of external facts, clues, and witnesses corresponds to the inner tangle of the commissioner's thoughts, motivations, emotions, and sentiments, and to the interrelationships between these and the corresponding ones of a dozen or so secondary characters from various Italian regions—with their related dialectal inflections.

La cognizione del dolore is the tragic story of Gonzalo's neurosis—the obscure resentment of and love/hate for his parents and their country estate, reminiscent of G.'s own family villa and a symbol of the bourgeoisie—coupled with the mysterious murder of his mother (for which he feels a terrible sense of guilt), and set against an imaginary South American landscape, which is nothing but a linguistic as well as geographic distortion of the Brianza region north of Milan.

Both novels are unfinished, and both are based on philosophical presuppositions that can be best ascertained in G.'s treatise *Meditazione milanese* (1974; Milanese meditation), in which the author, starting from Leibniz and Spinoza, explains his concept of reality as a tangle of relationships and his belief in literature as knowledge. Another important work for the understanding of G.'s sociopolitical and moral views is *Eros e Priapo: Da furore a cenere* (1967; Eros and Priapus: from fury to ashes); it starts off as a powerful satire and indictment of Mussolini and Fascism, considered as the result of the degeneration of bourgeois values, and ends up as both a disguised autobiography and an "erotic history of mankind."

G. is an extremely difficult author, and in fact, the American translator of his two novels, William Weaver, should be commended for the splendid job he did in rendering the originals.

G.'s grotesque expressionism is his stylistic (that is, personal) response to the crisis of a world that appears chaotic, "baroque," and dehumanized; it is the vehicle of his moral indignation against, and disillusionment with, the worst aspects of our society—vulgarity, violence, hypocrisy, greed, fascism. That is why G.'s best works, like those of his European counterparts, are so strong yet tender, so ferocious yet melancholic.

FURTHER WORKS: *Le meraviglie d'Italia* (1939); *Gli anni* (1943); *Il primo libro delle favole* (1952); *I sogni e la folgore* (1955); *I viaggi la morte* (1958); *Verso la Certosa* (1961); *I Luigi di Francia* (1964); *Il guerriero, l'amazzone, lo spirito della poesia nel verso immortale del Foscolo* (1967); *La meccanica* (1970); *Novella seconda* (1971); *Le bizze del capitano in congedo* (1981)

BIBLIOGRAPHY: Pucci, P., "The Obscure Sickness," *IQ*, 11, 42 (1967), 43–62; Ragusa, O., "G., Pasolini, and Experimentalism: Form or Ideology?" in Pacifici, S., ed., *From Verismo to Experimentalism* (1969), 239–69; Risset, J., "C. E. G.; ou, La philosophie à l'envers," *Critique* (Paris), No. 282 (1970), 944–51; Dombroski, R. S., "The Meaning of G.'s War Diary," *Italica,* 47 (1970), 373–86; Biasin, G.-P., "The Pen, the Mother," *Literary Diseases: Theme and Metaphor in the Italian Novel* (1975), pp. 127–55

GIAN-PAOLO BIASIN

GADDIS, William

American novelist, b. 29 Dec. 1922, New York, N.Y.

Although neither of his two novels has been a commercial sucess, G. has long been involved with commercial writing. After attending Harvard from 1941 to 1945, he was for two years a staff researcher for *The New Yorker*, and, after five subsequent years of world travel, he settled down to a career of writing speeches for corporation executives and of scripting industrial films, with occasional stints of teaching and public relations work. His first novel, *The Recognitions* (1955), was written largely during his years of travel, and grants from the National Institute of Arts and Letters, the Rockefeller Foundation, and the National Endowment for the Arts gave him sufficient leisure to complete his second novel, *JR* (1975). Little is known of G.'s life beyond these simple facts, however, for he is an intensely private person and avoids all publicity.

The Recognitions is an encyclopedic, thousand-page novel that depicts a world of elaborately compounded fictions—art and religion most notable among them. Indeed, the central character, Wyatt Gwyon, abandons thoughts of the priesthood to become an accomplished forger of Flemish old masters in a quest for authentic experience, and at the end of the novel he retreats to a Spanish monastery to scrape old masterworks down to the canvas in an effort to reach the tabula rasa beyond all fictions. Every character in the novel is a counterfeiter of some sort, and there is every kind of forgery in the book, suggesting that Wyatt's quest is manic and that man can know only an irreducible complex of fictions. Freighted with esoterica and with formidable difficulties for the casual reader, the novel has enjoyed only a cult following and the praise of a few major critics, but it continues to stake its claim as a major work of art, and it may yet be recognized as such.

JR is a slightly smaller and more accessible novel that chronicles the rise and fall of J. R. Vansant, a sixth-grader who parlays his way, seriocomically, to implausible eminence in the world of high finance. The satiric illuminations of the novel are many, but its focus is the detritus of contemporary language: G.'s characters bombard the reader, with jargon, clichés, and barbarisms of all kinds, and their elephantine dialogues virtually swamp the narrative line. Unlike *The Recognitions,* which asks serious, metaphysical questions under the surface of its madcap humor, *JR* stupefies the reader with its impenetrable linguistic surface, and the agonized questions of the first novel seem to be replaced in the second with a settled pessimism about man's ability even to ask a metaphysical question.

G.'s reputation is a limited one, since he is largely unread. Nonetheless, his novels are serious works in the modernist tradition, offering the compensation of their aesthetic order for the disorder that is their subject; they bear comparison with Thomas Pynchon's (q.v.) *Gravity's Rainbow* and Joseph Heller's (q.v.) *Something Happened,* and even with such a classic text of modernism as James Joyce's (q.v.) *Ulysses.*

BIBLIOGRAPHY: Benstock, B., "On W. G.: In *Recognition* of James Joyce," *WSCL*, 6 (1965), 177–89; Madden, D., "W G.'s *The Recognitions,*" in Madden, D., ed., *Rediscoveries* (1971), pp. 291–304; Tanner, T., *City of Words* (1971), pp. 393–400; Koenig, P. W.,

"Recognizing G.'s *Recognitions*," *ConL*, 16 (1975), 61–72; Salemi, J. S., "To Soar in Atonement: Art as Expiation in G.'s *The Recognitions*," *Novel*, 10 (1977), 127–36; Stark, J., "W. G.: Just Recognition," *HC*, 14 (1977), 1–12; Klemtner, S. S., " 'For a Very Small Audience': The Fiction of W. G.," *Crit*, 19 (1978), 61–73

ROBERT F. KIERNAN

GAELIC LITERATURE
See Irish Literature and Scottish Literature

GAŁCZYŃSKI, Konstanty Ildefons
Polish poet and satirist, b. 23 Jan. 1905, Warsaw; d. 6 Dec. 1953, Warsaw

Born into a solid urban working-class family, G. never evinced clear-cut political or class affiliations. As a young writer in newly reconstituted Poland after World War I, he worked for journals of both the left and right; indeed, even anti-Semitic papers were not unacceptable to him. He was associated for a while during the 1920s with "Quadriga," a leftist writers' group. In the 1930s he abandoned his former bohemian ways to become a professional poet and family man. During World War II he was a prisoner of war and did forced labor in a German factory. After he was liberated by the American forces he went briefly into exile in the West, but in 1946, homesick for his native land and language, he returned to Poland and his wife and daughter (who had given him up for dead). With typical flexibility, he maneuvered successfully through the thickets of Stalinist literary politics, achieving, despite some criticism from Party hacks and émigrés alike, a large measure of recognition and popularity before a heart attack ended his career prematurely.

G. boasted that he was the "Bacchus of democracy," and indeed, his poetry includes many popular elements, from street speech to commercial jargon. Above all, his writing is characterized by trenchant satirical thrusts at a great range of popular targets—intellectuals, other writers, occasionally politicians—all skewered in the name of the simple outsider. Yet G. did not condescend to his audience: his style is replete with classical imagery, literary allusions, foreign words and phrases (in the best Polish "macaronic" tradition), and complex metaphors. He did not hesitate to use even the grotesque, the macabre, or the absurd to make his poetic points. In his prewar poetry,

Koniec świata: Wizje świętego Ildefonsa; czyli, Satyra na wszechświat (1928; the end of the world: visions of St. Ildefonso; or, satire on the universe), *Bal u Salomona* (1933; party at Solomon's), and *Zabawa ludowa* (1934; popular pastime), G. dwelt largely on the theme of an impending disastrous conflict in Europe (a point of view known as "catastrophism" in Poland). For a number of years after the war his theatrical fragments called "Teatrzyk 'Zielona geś" (the minitheater "Green Goose") and his feuilletons, which appeared under the title "Listy z fiołkiem" (letters with a violet), published in the satirical journal *Przekrój*, mocked the false "humanism" so popular at the time. Although topical, G.'s satires are still widely read for the vigor of their wit and playful use of language.

G. also wrote in a lyric vein quite distinct from his satirical pieces. Particularly noteworthy in this regard are his *Noctes aninenses* (1939; nights at Anin); two poems written during the war, "Pieśń o żołnierzach z Westerplatte" (1939; song about the soldiers from the Westerplatte) and "Matka Boska stalagów" (1944; Our Lady of the stalags); *Zaczarowana dorożka* (1948; the magic carriage); and *Pieśni* (1953; songs). Although humor and contemporary concerns figure in these works, too, they differ from G.'s other writings in their calm simplicity and tenderness and their exhibition of G.'s love for man and appreciation of life.

In both lyric and satiric modes G. was a poet with a highly individualized voice. He has some stylistic affinities with the Polish poets of the premodern period, yet in many senses he is sui generis within the literary tradition of his language in the 20th c.

FURTHER WORKS: *Porfirion Osiełek; czyli, Klub świętokradców* (1926); *Utwory poetyckie* (1937); *Wiersze* (1946); *Niobe* (1951); *Wit Stwosz* (1952); *Wiersze liryczne* (1952); *Chryzostoma Bulwiecia podróż do Ciemnogrodu* (1954); *Satyra, groteska, żart liryczny* (1955); *Dzieła* (5 vols., 1957–60)

BIBLIOGRAPHY: Herman, M., *Histoire de la littérature polonaise* (1963), pp. 625–26; Miłosz, C., *The History of Polish Literature* (1969), pp. 409–11; Krzyżanowski, J., *A History of Polish Literature* (1978), pp. 603–4

HENRY R. COOPER, JR.

GALICIAN LITERATURE
See section under Spanish Literature

GALLEGOS, Rómulo

Venezuelan novelist and short-story writer, b. 2 Aug. 1884, Caracas; d. 4 April 1969, Caracas

G. was a schoolteacher for seventeen years. He began his literary career in 1909 as a cofounder of the review *La alborada,* which sponsored debates on themes of social protest. From 1913 on he published naturalistic fiction, and in his short novel *La rebelión* (1922; the rebellion) he took up specifically Venezuelan themes and motifs that he would never abandon. In the novel *La trepadora* (1925; the climber), which revealed the maturing of his narrative art, he defended the cause of the mulattoes in his country and endeavored to show the values of mestization (mixing of the races). In 1929 G. published *Doña Bárbara* (*Doña Bárbara,* 1931), his most important work. The Venezuelan dictator Vicente Gómez felt so threatened by this vibrant, reformist novel that G. had to go into exile. In Spain he wrote *Cantaclaro* (1934; a name meaning "a minstrel of the plains") and *Canaima* (1935; a name meaning "the spirit of evil"), both describing the epic struggle of the Venezuelan against nature as well as against other men.

After Gómez's death, G. returned to Venezuela and was appointed minister of education, a post he did not keep for long because of conservative opposition. In 1937 he published *Pobre negro* (poor black man), again defending a dispossessed race in his country. In 1941 he founded and began to lead the Democratic Action Party, while continuing to write novels of social protest. *Sobre la misma tierra* (1944; upon this very earth) exposed the oppression of the Indians living in the oil-rich region of Zulia. In 1947 he was elected president of his country, with eighty percent of the votes, but a right-wing coup d'état forced him into exile once again. While in Cuba he wrote *La brizna de paja en el viento* (1952; the piece of straw in the wind), which deals with opposition in Cuba to dictatorships; in Mexico he conceived what was to be his last, posthumously published, novel, *Pies sobre la tierra* (1971; feet upon the earth), which, using the example of Mexico, depicts agrarian reforms triumphant and the coming of a revolutionary constitutionalism to Latin America. He also made several visits to the U.S., especially to the University of Oklahoma. He returned to his home country upon the advent of democracy in 1958 and lived there until his death.

G.'s fame still rests on *Doña Bárbara.* This novel came at the most opportune moment,

when the peoples of Latin America were beginning to search for their identity, when nativism, a blend of local color with social and political protest, was triumphing, and when intellectuals, labor leaders, and revolutionaries kept ideological issues alive. *Doña Bárbara* depicts a double conflict: the struggle of man to tame a violent nature, and the epic efforts of civilizers bent on eliminating human barbarism. G. intelligently used all the resources of realism and nativism at his disposal. Thus, the novel simultaneously depicts a distinctly Venezuelan and a broader Latin American cosmos: customs, superstitions, epic hunts in the rivers, taming of wild horses, and political conflicts. But in spite of its many characters and massive structure, its plot is rather simple: it is basically about the clash of two wills, that of Doña Bárbara, a despotic feudal mistress (drawn from actual life), and that of Santos Luzardo, the civilizer. Underlying the plot is the universal theme of good versus evil and the permanent dilemma as to whether violence in the name of a good cause can be justified. The upright hero Luzardo solves the issue by first gaining popular support and then answering violence with violence, thus overcoming barbarism—a thesis that has haunted dictators ever since.

Doña Bárbara gained high praise everywhere, but it has also been criticized. The overemphasis on the ideal qualities of its hero has been the main weakness noted. But its message is powerfully presented, and that is what G. aimed for. Moreover, G. showed elsewhere that he could also conceive more realistic protagonists. The title character in *Cantaclaro* is a wandering minstrel endowed with warm humor who fights for social justice. And the novel is also a treasure trove of local lore.

G.'s literary production is pedagogical and it must be evaluated as such. By means of his art he sought to promote needed reforms, and this he did achieve. He died generally admired both in his homeland and throughout South America.

FURTHER WORKS: *Los aventureros* (1913); *El último Solar* (1920); *La coronela* (1928); *El forastero* (1942); *Obras completas* (1949); *Novelas escogidas* (1951); *Obras selectas* (1959)

BIBLIOGRAPHY: Spell, J. F., *Contemporary Spanish American Fiction* (1944), pp. 205–38, 266–86; Torres-Rioseco, A., *Grandes novelistas de la América hispana* (1949), Vol. I, pp.

43–77; Leo, U., *R. G.: Estudios sobre el arte de novelar* (1954); Dunham, L., *R. G.: Vida y obra* (1957); Chapman, A. G., "The Barefoot Galateas of Bret Harte and R. G.," *Symposium*, 18 (1964), 332–41; Araujo, O., *Narrativa venezolana contemporánea* (1972), pp. 157–203; Dunham, L., *R. G.: An Oklahoma Encounter and the Writing of the Last Novel* (1974)

EVELIO ECHEVARRÍA

GALSWORTHY, John

(pseuds.: John Sinjohn; A.R.P.-M.) English novelist, short-story writer, dramatist, essayist, and critic, b. 14 Aug. 1867, Kingston Hill, Surrey; d. 31 Jan. 1933, London

G. was born to wealth; his father was a successful London solicitor and director of companies. G. was educated at Harrow and then at Oxford, where he dutifully read law (although called to the bar, his interest in law was slight), lived the life of a wealthy young man in London, and traveled extensively. A crisis occurred when in 1895 he and Ada, his cousin's wife, became lovers. With her encouragement (after her divorce, G. and Ada married in 1905), he decided to become a writer.

Influenced by Turgenev, Maupassant, and Tolstoy, G. spent the years 1897–1901 learning his craft, and in the process produced two volumes of short stories and two novels. His third novel, *The Island Pharisees* (1904), was, despite weaknesses, a work of significant achievement. In 1906 G. established his importance beyond any doubt with *The Man of Property*, an acknowledged masterpiece and his first full-length treatment of the Forsytes, and with *The Silver Box* (also 1906) he began a distinguished career as a dramatist.

He returned to what would become his most famous subject—the Forsytes—in 1918 and earned an international reputation with his two Forsyte trilogies: *The Forsyte Saga*—consisting of *The Man of Property*, *In Chancery* (1920), and *To Let* (1921) plus two lyric interludes, "Indian Summer of a Forsyte" (1918) and "Awakening" (1920), all published together in 1922—and *A Modern Comedy*, consisting of *The White Monkey* (1924), *The Silver Spoon* (1926), and *Swan Song* (1928) plus two stories, "A Silent Wooing" (1927) and "Passers By" (1927). These works tell of the never-ending struggle between those who judge everything in terms of its material worth and those who know that there are intangible values that cannot be owned. The comfortable, ordered world of the Forsytes is not secure from the incursions of the unorthodox and of passion.

Further evidence of G.'s creative abilities is to be found in his seven non-Forsyte novels, his more than two dozen dramas, and his many short stories and essays. One of his finest non-Forsyte novels was *Fraternity* (1909). Exploring the interrelationships between the impotent world of well-intentioned intellectuals, the Dallisons, and the helpless world of the poor, the novel dramatizes the search for a better world; for some, better plumbing would free the poor and thereby save the world; for the senile Mr. Stone who is its prophet, Universal Brotherhood is the answer. *Strife* (produced 1909), *Justice* (produced 1910), and *Loyalties* (produced 1922) are three of his most compelling dramas. G. almost always created drama out of the mundane and ordinary: the theft of a cigarette box dramatizes that the law for the poor is not the same as the law for the rich (*The Silver Box*). Probably G.'s most famous scene is the one in *Justice* that without any dialogue shows Falder breaking down under the strain of solitary confinement.

After refusing a knighthood in 1918, G. accepted the Order of Merit in 1929 and the Nobel Prize for literature in 1932. Much of his fame rested on the mistaken belief that he was a sociological writer whose satiric analyses of man and society were photographically lifelike. Although this belief still prevails, present-day critical evaluation of his work displays a very different viewpoint: since the society he chronicled and the causes he espoused are now past history, G. is often dismissed as an out-of-date social historian. If, however, the emphasis on the sociological aspects of his writing is a mistaken one, it is evident that G.'s work should be examined anew and on its own terms as literature. His achievement is clearly greater than his present reputation would allow; indeed, he may justly be considered the last great Victorian novelist.

An important statement of G.'s artistic creed is "A Novelist's Allegory" (1909), which tells of an old man, Cethru, who as a nightwatchman aids passers-by as they traverse dark streets. Because the light from his lantern shone on some unpleasant scenes, Cethru is accused of criminal intent. In his defense the point is made that the lantern impartially reveals both good and evil and shows the true proportion of things to one another. In G.'s view the artist is important because he is the discoverer of truth or spiritual proportion. Beauty and art (profound embodiments of the spiritual, the humane, and the civilizing) are the cornerstones of his humanitarianism.

FURTHER WORKS: *From the Four Winds* (1897); *Jocelyn* (1898); *Villa Rubein* (1900); *A Man of Devon* (1901); *The Country House* (1907); *A Commentary* (1908); *A Justification of the Censorship of Plays* (1909); *A Motley* (1910); *The Spirit of Punishment* (1910); *Joy* (1910); *The Little Dream* (1911); *The Patrician* (1911); *The Inn of Tranquillity* (1912); *The Eldest Son* (1912); *The Pigeon* (1912); *Moods, Songs and Doggerels* (1912); *For the Love of Beasts* (1912); *The Dark Flower* (1913); *The Slaughter of Animals for Food* (1913); *The Fugitive* (1913); *The Mob* (1914); *The Army Veterinary Corps* (1915); *The Little Man, and Other Satires* (1915); *The Freelands* (1915); *A Bit o' Love* (1915); *A Sheaf* (1916); *Your Christmas Dinner Is Served* (1916); *Beyond* (1917); *Five Tales* (1918); *The Children's Jewel Fund* (1918); *The Land: A Plea* (1918); *Five Poems* (1919); *The Burning Spear* (1919); *Saint's Progress* (1919); *Addresses in America* (1919); *Another Sheaf* (1919); *Tatterdemalion* (1920); *The Foundations* (1920); *The Skin Game* (1920); *The Bells of Peace* (1921); *Six Short Plays* (1921); *A Family Man* (1922); *Windows* (1922); *Captures* (1923); *International Thought* (1923); *Works* (30 vols., 1923–36); *Memorable Days* (1924); *On Expression* (1924); *Abracadabra, and Other Satires* (1924); *The Forest* (1924); *Old English* (1924); *Caravan* (1925); *Is England Done For?* (1925); *The Show* (1925); *Escape* (1926); *Verses New and Old* (1926); *A Talk on Playing the Game with Animals and Birds* (1926); *Two Forsyte Interludes* (1927); *The Way to Prepare Peace* (1927); *Castles in Spain, and Other Screeds* (1927); *Mr. G.'s Appeal for the Miners* (1928); *Exiled* (1929); *The Roof* (1929); *A Rambling Discourse* (1929); *On Forsyte 'Change* (1930); *Two Essays on Conrad* (1930); *Maid in Waiting* (1931); *The Creation of Character in Literature* (1931); *Literature and Life* (1931); *Candelabra* (1932); *Flowering Wilderness* (1932); *Forsytes, Pendyces and Others* (1933); *Over the River* (1933; Am., *One More River*); *Autobiographical Letters of J. G.: A Correspondence with Frank Harris* (1933); *Author and Critic* (1933); *End of the Chapter* (1934); *Collected Poems* (1934);

Letters from J. G. 1900–1932 (1934); *The Winter Garden* (1935); *Glimpses and Reflections* (1937); *J. G.'s Letters to Leon Lion* (1968)

BIBLIOGRAPHY: Chevrillon, A., *Three Studies in English Literature: Kipling, G., Shakespeare* (1923), pp. 153–219; Marrot, H. V., *The Life and Letters of J. G.* (1935); Ross, W. O., "J. G.: Aspects of an Attitude," in Wallace, A. D., and Ross, W. O., eds. *Studies in Honor of John Wilcox* (1958), pp. 195–208; Eaker, J. G., "G. as Thinker in *The Forsyte Saga*," *Phi Kappa Phi Journal*, 51 (1971), 10–20; Gindin, J., "Ethical Structures in J. G., Elizabeth Bowen, and Iris Murdoch," in Friedman, A. W., ed., *Forms of Modern British Fiction* (1975), pp. 15–41 and passim; Stevens, H. R., "G.'s *Fraternity*: The Closed Door and the Paralyzed Society," *ELT*, 19 (1976), 283–98; Stevens, E. E., and Stevens, H. R., eds., *J. G.: An Annotated Bibliography of Writings about Him* (1980)

EARL E. STEVENS

GÁLVEZ, Manuel

Argentine novelist and essayist, b. 18 July 1882, Paraná; d. 14 Nov. 1962, Buenos Aires

G. received early religious training and was throughout his life an unswerving defender of Catholicism. He took his degree in law and, interested in social questions, he wrote his thesis on the problem of white slavery. He traveled extensively in his early years and was particularly impressed by Spain and its culture; one of his first works, *El solar de la raza* (1913; the roots of the race), stressed the significance of the Spanish heritage that Argentines enjoyed. In 1906 G. was named inspector of secondary schools, a post that he held for some twenty-five years. One of the most prolific Argentine writers of this century, G. dealt in a forthright way with a number of controversial subjects and is considered one of the most important realistic-naturalistic authors of his time.

G. began his writing career as a poet and dramatist, went on to journalism—producing countless magazine and newspaper articles—and was intermittently involved in a number of publishing enterprises designed to bring deserving writers into prominence. He was perhaps more interested than anyone else of his time in examining the role of the writer in his society.

As a young man, G. devised a plan to document, much in the manner of the Spanish novelist Benito Pérez Galdós (q.v.), the society and customs of his age. Argentina was his subject, and in the more than fifty years of his writing career he explored many aspects of Argentine history and culture.

His first novel, *La maestra normal* (1914; the normal-school teacher), re-creates the stifling, conservative atmosphere of Argentine provincial life and offers a deterministic account of a casual love affair and its consequences. G.'s explicit description of the romance between a convalescing Buenos Aires government employee and a small-town schoolteacher attracted a wide audience and was the first of his many commercially successful works. The novel remains engrossing and eminently readable.

El mal metafísico (1916; the metaphysical illness) is a roman à clef that treats Buenos Aires literary life and portrays, with very little disguise, a number of prominent personalities of the day. *Nacha Regules* (1919; Nacha Regules), which G. himself adapted for the theater, is another stark portrait of Buenos Aires society which, curiously, unlike most naturalistic writing, does not shun sentimentality and which adopts a surprisingly moralistic tone.

G.'s preoccupation with spiritual and carnal conflicts was displayed in a series of novels, of which perhaps the best-known is *Miércoles Santo* (1930; *Holy Wednesday*, 1934). G.'s interest in history is shown in two groupings of novels that are fictional treatments of the events of the disastrous Paraguayan War (1865–70) and of the turbulent regime of the 19th-c. Argentine dictator Juan Manuel de Rosas. The Paraguayan debacle is documented in three novels: *Los caminos de la muerte* (1928; the roads of death), *Humaitá* (1929; Humaitá), and *Jornadas de agonía* (1929; days of agony). Between 1931 and 1954 G. wrote eight novels about the Rosas dictatorship.

In all of his novels G. wrote a straightforward and unadorned naturalistic prose, uniform in distinctive stylistic features. There is a dynamic intensity to his novels that commands the reader's attention.

G. was a fervent nationalist, an attitude that is clearly evident in the subjects he chose for his novels and biographies, and that (since nationalism and fascism were closely linked in Argentina in the 1940s) also found expression in the sympathies he professed for the Axis, during World War II. G. remained active up to the end of his life. At the time of his death he was perhaps underrated or even rejected by some critics. But the merit of his work and the ceaseless dedication to his art he manifested during his long career cannot be dismissed.

FURTHER WORKS: *El enigma interior* (1907); *El sendero de humildad* (1909); *El diario de Gabriel Quiroga* (1910); *La inseguridad de la vida obrera; La vida múltiple* (1916); *La sombra del convento* (1917); *Luna de miel, y otras narraciones* (1920); *Tragedia de un hombre fuerte* (1922); *Historia de arrabal* (1922); *El cántico espiritual* (1923); *El espíritu de aristocracia, y otros ensayos* (1924); *La pampa y su pasión* (1926); *Una mujer muy moderna* (1927); *El hombre de los ojos azules* (1928); *El gaucho de los Cerillos* (1931); *El General Quiroga* (1932); *Vida de Fray Mamerto Esquiú* (1933); *Este pueblo necesita* (1934); *La Argentina en nuestros libros* (1935); *Cautiverio* (1935); *La noche toca a su fin* (1935); *Hombres en soledad* (1938); *Vida de Hipólito Yrigoyen* (1939); *Vida de don Juan Manuel de Rosas* (1940); *Vida de don Gabriel García Moreno* (1941); *Vida de Aparicio Saravia* (1942); *Calibán* (1943); *Vida de Sarmiento* (1944); *Amigos y maestros de mi juventud* (1944); *España y algunos españoles* (1945); *José Hernández* (1945); *Don Francisco de Miranda* (1947); *El santito de la toldería* (1947); *La ciudad pintada de rojo* (1948); *La muerte en las calles* (1949); *Tiempo de odio y angustia* (1951); *Han tocado a degüello* (1951); *Bajo la garra anglo-francesa* (1953); *Y así cayó don Juan Manuel* (1954); *Las dos vidas del pobre Napoleón* (1954); *El uno y la multitud* (1955); *Tránsito Guzmán* (1956); *Poemas para la recién-llegada* (1957); *Perdido en su noche* (1958); *Recuerdos de la vida literaria* (1961); *Me mataron entre todos* (1962)

BIBLIOGRAPHY: Torres-Rioseco, A., *Grandes novelistas de la América hispana* (1943), pp. 137–60; Spell, J. R., *Contemporary Spanish-American Fiction* (1944), pp. 15–63; Lichtblau, M., "The Recent Novels of M. G.," *Hispania*, 42 (1959), 502–5; Anzoátegui, I. B., *M. G.* (1961); Lichtblau, M., *M. G.* (1972)

DONALD A. YATES

GAMBIAN LITERATURE

Gambia is Africa's smallest country, situated along the banks of the Gambia River. A classic illustration of colonial indifference to natural boundaries, it is totally surrounded by its larger and wealthier French-speaking neighbor, Senegal. Having few resources, it is developing into a Caribbean-type winter resort for Scandinavians.

There is here only minimal basis for any identifiable or sustained national literature. Nevertheless it has, surprisingly, produced two major writers: William Conton (b. 1925) and Lenrie Peters (q.v.). Conton has lived long enough in Sierra Leone to have rather a marginal residual allegiance, and the themes of both writers are as much contemporary West African as definably Gambian.

William Conton made his name through one influential novel, *The African* (1960); its early date makes him a pioneer in contemporary African literature. The novel proffers a rather awkward mixture. It opens with a conventional portrayal of an African coping with the problems of being educated in Britain, includes several amusing, probably autobiographical, anecdotal incidents to give it reality, and concludes with events after the hero's return when, having achieved political success, he makes a curiously symbolic voyage to a mythic country, presumably South Africa. The novel cannot be critically admired for its technical qualities, but its influence has been considerable. Its fame is apparent from its translation into Arabic, Russian, and Hungarian. It is less regularly read at present, but it is so well known that it has encouraged several African writers to attempt similar exercises.

Lenrie Peters is a doctor by profession and spent many years away from Gambia earning degrees at Cambridge and the University of London. He is a far more subtle and sophisticated writer than Conton. His first novel, *The Second Round* (1965), is set in Sierra Leone, but it could be equally appropriately located in either country, having the common semiautobiographical plot. It details the difficulties, both social and personal, that confront the well-educated doctor on his return to his traditional life at home. Peters's handling of this idea is more sensitive to the psychological complexities of the protagonist's dilemma than is usual in African fiction. Most African novelists choose to blame the external social pressures for their hero's difficulties.

This topic of the anxiety and alienation of the returnee is a regular theme in Peters's volume of poetry, *Satellites* (1967). His verse is highly sophisticated and urbane, sometimes appearing only minimally African. It remains always keenly aware of the core of the African cultural dualism.

Gambia suffers, like all small countries, from the dispersal of its more able people to other places offering more rewarding opportunities. For this reason its literature is for some time likely to appear only as the works of isolated, if individually impressive, writers—too isolated and exceptional to form any markedly national tradition.

BIBLIOGRAPHY: Cartey, W., *Whispers from a Continent* (1969), passim; Dathorne, O. R., *The Black Mind* (1974), passim

JOHN POVEY

GAMSAKHURDIA, Konstantine
Georgian novelist, short-story writer, and poet, b. 15 May 1891, Abasha; d. 17 July 1975, Tbilisi

G. was born into a family of the Georgian nobility. In 1911, upon completing his schooling in Kutaisi, he traveled to Germany and entered the University of Königsberg. He transferred to the University of Munich in 1913 and finally to the University of Berlin, where, in 1919, he received his doctorate. G. returned to Georgia in the same year.

G.'s first work in his native language was published in 1914; the strong influences of Nietzsche, the individualist anarchism of Max Stirner (1808–1856), and the philosophy of Henri Bergson (q.v.) are evident in his early novellas, essays, and poetry. A period of impressionist writing followed, primarily novellas, and lasted until the Soviet invasion of Georgia in 1921. Choosing to remain in his native country despite the Communist takeover, G. was obliged to change his style once more, to suit the political climate: a collection of short stories in the realist manner appeared in 1924.

In 1925 G. published his first novel, *Dionisis ghimili* (Dionysus' smile), which reflected once again the early intellectual influences of his formative period in Europe. This book was unacceptable in the Soviet context of the time, and, in order to redeem himself ideologically, he wrote a three-volume novel, *Mtvaris motatseba* (1935–36; the theft of the moon), which described the conflicts between traditional Georgian society and the new Communist order during the bloody and tortured period of collectivization.

G. may be said to have created the school of historical fiction in Georgian literature. His books in this style are unparalleled in the Georgian language and rank with the best serious novels of this type in European and American literature as well. His first work in this genre was *Didostatis mardjvena* (1939; the right hand of the master). It describes the confrontation of the medieval King Giorgi with his nobles over questions of governmental authority, but includes a wealth of information regarding the culture and customs of the period. It also demonstrates a fine degree of psychological perception in the limning of the characters and their individual worlds.

G.'s tetralogy, *Davit Aghmashenebeli* (David the Builder) appeared from 1946 to 1954. This extraordinary novel is unquestionably the crowning achievement of G.'s creative life. Set in the 11th c., it builds an immense panorama around the struggles of the Georgian people and their king, David—called the Builder—to achieve national independence. Against this background, G. re-creates the complete cosmos of medieval Georgia, replete with totally convincing characterizations of great depth.

While unable to avoid in his art a certain pandering to the political requirements of life under a Soviet regime, G. nevertheless remains an author of huge stature and the greatest novelist of the 20th c. writing in Georgian. His work has been translated into all the major languages of the Soviet Union, as well as into other languages.

FURTHER WORK: *Vazis qvaviloba* (1956)

LEONARD FOX

GANDA LITERATURE
See Ugandan Literature

GARCÍA LORCA, Federico
Spanish poet and dramatist, b. 5 June 1898, Fuentevaqueros; d. 19 Aug. 1936, Viznar

G. L. was raised in the Moorish city of Granada, whose pageantry and people he would later celebrate in poetry and drama. Even as a child he was intrigued by puppets, toy theaters, and all sorts of dramatic situations that often became material for impromptu performances. He was a talented musician, taught by his mother and later by the composer Manuel de Falla, with whom he eventually collaborated. He also was an artist of wit and delicacy, qualities that would also mark his poetry and plays.

G. L. attended the University of Granada, where he earned a degree in law in 1923 after an interruption of several years, which he advantageously used by writing and living in Madrid's intellectual and creative hotbed, the Residencia de Estudiantes. There he met the best minds of his generation: Pedro Salinas, Jorge Guillén, Juan Ramón Jiménez (qq.v.), among writers; and the painter Salvador Dalí, with whom he had an intimate and stormy friendship.

When G. L. left Spain for a spell, he went to New York, where he lived on the campus of Columbia University in 1929–30. *Poeta en Nueva York* (1940; *The Poet in New York*, 1940; also tr. as *Poet in New York*, 1955) was the fruit of that trip.

After a short visit to Cuba, he returned to Spain and soon became the head of a traveling theatrical company, La Barraca, established by the government of the Second Republic, which brought classical plays and other worthy dramas to the provinces. In 1936, during the first weeks of the civil war, G. L. was killed by partisans of Franco. The circumstances of his death are still shrouded in mystery.

G. L.'s heinous murder angered not only the international literary community but also the world at large, for it robbed them of one of Spain's greatest talents. G. L. was a brilliant poet and dramatist, who not unlike Dylan Thomas (q.v.), used words magically. With the sheer musicality of a language that flowed spontaneously, he cast an unforgettable spell. His art was one of prophetic beauty.

In both his drama and poetry G. L. created a delicate balance between the traditional and the modern, between Spanish sensibility and mainstream European ideas, between folk mythologies and high culture. His work was fashioned with a new and daring imagery that was intended, oddly enough, for simple people, with whom he had always chosen to identity.

Although G. L.'s literary production was quite varied, his themes remained constant. His poetry and drama attested to a tacit anxiety about obtaining what seemed to be unobtainable. With primitive passion, G. L. wrote about a lost Eden, frustrated sexuality, the tragedy of ubiquitous death, and the necessity for individual freedom. His work, in short, was a working through of his own personal, literary, and social dilemmas.

G. L.'s first book of poetry, *Libro de poemas* (1921; book of poems) shows wit, daring, and impudence as it mocks the adult world with fablelike poems that are populated by animals. Although clearly a book of apprenticeship, it reveals the poet's promising talent and introduces many of the themes that he continued to develop. *Canciones* (1927; *Songs,* 1976), written between 1921 and 1924, is also ironic and sarcastic in tone. The poems are highly inventive and delicate and have echoes of Antonio Machado (q.v.) and Juan Ramón Jiménez.

The publication of *Poema del cante jondo* (1931; *Deep Song,* 1980), written in 1921, and *Primer romancero gitano (1924–1927)* (1928; *The Gypsy Ballads of G. L.,* 1953) firmly established the reputation of G. L. and made him *the* poet of Andalusia. The "deep song" of the title of *Poema del cante jondo* refers to the music and culture of the gypsies, which serve as a backdrop to the poems. G. L. openly accepts the spirit of folk ballads with which he writes sinister poems that sing of death and irretrievable loss. However, amid all this sinister tone and all the lost horsemen of these poems who never return from their journeys, there exist a lightness and playfulness characteristic of much of G. L.'s poetry.

In *Primer romancero gitano* G. L. strikes the perfect balance between the traditional and the modern. Again by using gypsy culture and mythology as a point of departure to express his tragic vision of life, G. L. avails himself of the standard meter and verse form of the Spanish ballad, which he fills with new and exciting metaphors reminiscent of the European vanguard.

Poeta en Nueva York, written 1929–30, marked a departure in G. L.'s poetry, which at first upset some of his admirers. It eschewed traditionally Spanish material, embracing motifs that were more mythical and at the same time more intimate. It is also G. L.'s great virtuoso performance in surrealism (q.v.). With shocking and at times grotesque imagery, G. L. undertakes a psychic journey that goes from personal chaos and alienation, caused by the decadent mores of a dehumanized metropolis, to a point of reintegration with the natural world. In this surrealistic journey of horror, anguish, and hope, G.L. praises Walt Whitman and a homosexuality based on true love and affection; he celebrates the black man, who, like the gypsy, although poor and suffering, has not lost his vitality or his roots in "primitive" culture. *Poeta en Neuva York,* in short, is an Orphic book of painful beauty.

Llanto por Ignacio Sánchez Mejías (1935; *Lament for the Death of a Bullfighter,* 1937), the moving and dramatic four-part elegy for the death of one of G. L.'s close friends, marked another high point in the poet's career. Sánchez

Mejías is a symbol of vitality and man's tragic encounter with death. The poem begins on a note of anguish and pain, which the poet underscores by using shocking surrealistic images and plaintive repetitions. It ends quietly with mellifluous verses of resignation and acceptance.

That G. L. had a flair for drama could be detected easily by an examination of his poetry. For G. L., poetry and drama were not separate. He believed that the theater should offer a complete spectacle, and in this sense, G. L. rebelled against the realistic theater of the middle class. He attempted to infuse the moribund Spanish theater of the 1920s with imagination, poetic vision, and folk speech. His undertaking was enormous, and initially he did not succeed with the general public, who at first misunderstood his work and did not appreciate his elegiac manner.

G. L.'s first play, *El maleficio de la mariposa* (pub. 1954; *The Butterfly's Evil Spell,* 1963), first performed in 1920, was too delicate and precious for Spanish audiences. It is an allegory in which a poet-cockroach falls in love with a wounded butterfly, who ultimately rejects the lowly insect. The love-struck cockroach thus fails to obtain his dream.

Nor were audiences in 1927 prepared for *Mariana Pineda* (pub. 1928; *Mariana Pineda,* 1962), G. L.'s only historical drama, which is set in Granada around 1830. This romantic play is like a faded print of lyric beauty, but lacks dramatic action. Mariana Pineda, a woman who is tragically in love and cries out for freedom, finally decides that it is better to die for a noble cause than to denounce her lover, Don Pedro Sotomayor, a leader of a liberal uprising. Against this historical background, G. L. explores the problems of liberty and repression that were so important to him.

G. L.'s experiments in the theater also involved puppet plays, of which he had been so fond as a child. *Títeres de Cachiporra: La tragicomedia de don Cristóbal y la señá Rosita* (pub. 1949; *The Tragicomedy of Don Cristóbal and Doña Rosita,* 1955), performed in 1931, and *El retablillo de don Cristóbal* (pub. 1938; *In the Frame of Don Cristobal,* 1944), written in 1931, are attempts to escape from the clichés of realism and excessive lyricism. They represent a turn toward a primitive, more action-filled theater.

G. L.'s principal surrealist dramas, · *El público* (fragments pub. 1934; *The Audience,* 1958), written in 1933 and only published in its entirety in 1974, and *Así que pasen cinco años* (1937; *If Five Years Pass,* 1941), also written in 1933, further showed the complexity of his theatrical sensibility. *El público* is an outrageous attack not only on commercial theater and its self-satisfied audiences but also on the entire social order. In his play, which his family and intimates begged him to destroy, G. L. publicly aired his problems with his own homosexuality. *Así que pasen cinco años* is an inordinately difficult but delightful play that uses a panoply of surrealist devices. It is an allegory of lost time in which life is seen as a cruel mockery, as are death and sexual frustration. Life is portrayed as being absurd and inharmonious, and man as its half-comprehending victim.

In spite of all his considerable previous achievements in the theater, G. L. is best known by most audiences, and solely by some, for his thematically linked trilogy of rural tragedies, beginning with the hauntingly poetic *Bodas de sangre* (pub. 1935; *Blood Wedding*, 1939), first performed in 1933. The play, which closely resembles a classical Greek tragedy, is a blend of drama and poetry, reality and unreality, played out against the elemental passions of Andalusian peasants. The perennial love triangle is given new urgency and dynamism. It is a gripping theatrical spectacle that transforms G. L.'s previous concerns with repressed vital passions and sexuality, omnipresent death, and the relationship between tradition and modernism into a satisfying and coherent dramatic unity.

Yerma (pub. 1937; *Yerma*, 1941), performed in 1934, the second play in the trilogy, is the tense drama of a man and woman whose marriage is barren, as suggested by the title of the play (*yerma* means "barren" in Spanish). The barrenness can be seen on several levels. Yerma's consuming desire but inability to have a child is echoed by her desire to have her indifferent husband love her. Her dual search leads only to frustration, which then leads to brutal violence—Yerma's murder of her husband.

La casa de Bernarda Alba (pub. 1945; *The House of Bernarda Alba*, 1947), written just before G. L.'s death, is the final play of the trilogy. It focuses on Bernarda and on her five daughters, who, while they hunger for freedom and an opportunity to express their own sexuality, are tyranically imprisoned by their mother. The lack of freedom and the closed system that Bernarda creates immediately brings to mind fascistic societies. G. L. starkly dramatizes the conflict and passions that the one available male, Pepe el Romano, stirs up. Although Pepe

is never seen, his presence is always felt. In fact, so skillfully does G. L. create this effect that some critics have called the play a homosexual reverie. The youngest, most sexual and rebellious daughter, who is having an affair with Pepe, although he is dutifully engaged to her oldest sister, commits suicide when she is made to believe that her mother has killed Pepe. It is a tragic but ironic ending to a drama that has been played out in stark simplicity.

Although cut down at the height of his career, G. L. is a writer of great stature. He reached far down into his own being, into man's innermost recesses. He identified with the downtrodden and the alienated, but his work was never meant as a consolation to them or to any other person; his work intensifies fears, scrapes the viscera, gnaws at the soul.

FURTHER WORKS: *Impresiones y paisajes* (1918); *La doncella, el marinero y el estudiante* (1928; *The Virgin, the Sailor and the Student*, 1957); *El paseo de Buster Keaton* (1928; *Buster Keaton's Promenade*, 1957); *Seis poemas gallegos* (1935); *Primeras canciones* (1936); *El amor de don Perlimplín con Belisa en su jardín* (1938; *The Love of Don Perlimplín for Belisa in His Garden*, 1941); *La zapatera prodigiosa* (1938; *The Shoemaker's Prodigious Wife*, 1941); *Doña Rosita la soltera* (1938; *Doña Rosita, the Spinster* (1941); *El diván del Tamarit* (1940; *Divan*, 1974); *Química* (1957; *Chimera*, 1944); *Obras completas* (1971). FURTHER VOLUMES IN ENGLISH: *Lament for the Death of a Bullfighter, and Other Poems* (1937); *Poems* (1939); *The Poet in New York, and Other Poems* (1940); *Selected Poems* (1941); *Selected Poems* (1943); *F. G. L.: Some of His Shorter Poems* (1955); *The Selected Poems of G. L.* (1955); *After L.* (1957); *L. (Selected Poems)* (1960); *Five Plays* (1963); *G. L. and John of the Cross* (1968); *Tree of Song* (1971); *L. and Jiménez: Selected Poems* (1973); *Divan, and Other Writings* (1974); *The Cricket Sings* (1980; bilingual); *Deep Song, and Other Prose* (1980)

BIBLIOGRAPHY: Honig, E., *G. L.* (1944); Crow, J. A., *F. G. L.* (1945); Barea, A., *L.: The Poet and His People* (1949); Bowra, C. M., *The Creative Experiment* (1949), pp. 189–253; Campbell, R., *L.: An Appreciation of His Poetry* (1952); Trend, J. B., *L. and the Spanish Poetic Tradition* (1956); Durán, M., ed., *L.: A Collection of Critical Essays* (1962); Lima, R., *The Theatre of G. L.*

(1963); Young, H. T., *The Victorious Expression: A Study of Four Contemporary Spanish Poets* (1964), pp. 139–216; Freedman, M., *The Moral Impulse* (1967), pp. 89–98; Umbral, F., *L.: Poeta maldito* (1968); Allen, R., *The Symbolic World of F. G. L.* (1972); Higginbotham, V., *The Comic Spirit of F. G. L.* (1976); Craige, B. J., *L.'s "Poet in New York": The Fall into Consciousness* (1977); Predmore, R. L., *L.'s New York Poetry: Social Injustice, Dark Love, Lost Faith* (1980)

MARSHALL J. SCHNEIDER

With each fresh addition to our knowledge of F. G. L., the poet's genius becomes more impressive. That extraordinary brilliance which struck one at once, in the first few of his poems to be translated, has turned out by no means to be an intermittent or accidental thing—it was sustained. Brilliance came as naturally to him, in fact, as dullness or preciosity to others; it was simply his speech. Nothing could be more remarkable, in this new collection, *Poet in New York*, than the apparently inexhaustible fertility of G. L.'s imagination. It was everywhere at once, it was prodigal, it was fantastic—the subjective and objective worlds rolled up and ignited in a single ball—the quotidian married singularly to the classic, the folksong crossed with the baroque. To call him a surrealist is a mistake, for to be a surrealist is to be something else than a poet, something less than a poet: surrealism is perhaps one of many names, merely, for the substratum out of which poetry is made. G. L. devoured all the properties of surrealism, stuffed his cheeks with them, like a conjuror, blew them out of his mouth again as poems—but so he did with everything else that he fed on. The papery guitars, the ingeniously misplaced eyes, the little traplike mouths cropping out of the sides of heads, and all the rest of that slightly sinister and somehow iodine-tinctured phantasmagoria of the followers of Loplop and synesthesia, these are certainly here, in the New York poems, but they have been made into poetry. [1940]

Conrad Aiken, "F. G. L.," *A Reviewer's ABC* (1958), pp. 276–77

With Synge, L. shares the creative mission of returning poetry to its basic dramatic function on the stage. In L.'s work it is impossible to speak of a consistently upheld view of life. His drama celebrates the life of instinct; which is to say, it does not come bearing a message. It comes in the ancient spirit of the magician and soothsayer—to astound; to entertain, and to mystify; it also comes in the spirit of the jongleur, to invent a world and people with whose pathetically valorous lives the audience is quick to identify itself. But it has no hidden didactic motives.

Synge's work is also notable for its artistic self-sufficiency, its renewal of the rich poetic language of the fold, and its re-creation of the primitive drama of feeling. . . . [Synge and L.] have alike the spontaneity of speech and poetic imagination which grows out of the heart of a fold untouched by the perversities of city life; with whom it is still possible to express pathos and tragedy in terms of the most elemental passions. When drama reaches behind the improvised curtain of middle-class Christian morality to the lives of such people and into their wild old pagan heritage, one comes upon the springs of a new classicism in the theatre, which Synge and L. exemplify. But the difference is that Synge, writing in prose, accepts the conventions of the tight coils of traditional stage techniques. L., on the other hand, a poetic dramatist reviving particular Spanish conventions on the stage and adding techniques of his own, shifts the stylistic emphasis very often from the prose speech of the characters to the verse and bright design of spectacle and musical conception.

Edwin Honig, *G. L.* (1944), pp. 214–15

The final value of Federico's theatre, and the one which most characterizes it, is this fundamental attitude of an author who likes to live; that is to say, to suffer and enjoy life's course as an inevitable universal drama. It seems as though in Federico, both in his life and in his writing, the man was not alive except in his moments of laughter and tears, in his extreme moments of joy and sorrow. Other times are entr'actes. . . .

Laughter and tears, tears above all, run through all his poetry. Federico is fundamentally an elegiac poet. And laughter and tears are the two poles of his theatre. This explains why all his work courses between tragedy and farce. His literary creatures, always poetic embodiments, are conceived either in a tragic sense or with the wry grimace of guignol characters. Poetry, laughter and tears are the ingredients of his dramatic invention.

Francisco García Lorca, Preface to *Three Tragedies of F. G. L.* (1947), pp. 2–3

G. L., a conscious artist despite his seeming spontaneity, imperiously felt the need to give his art, with its deep roots in the past, complete contemporary validity. He was and he wanted to be a man of his period, but without renouncing an atom of himself, in whom there were many links with the past which made him incompatible with the transitory fashions of the moment. He wished to avoid both the applause of the hide-bound majorities and the criticism of the ultramodern minorities, both of which only partially understood him, and find his own path in a harmony between the new and the age-old native qualities that were fused in him. This was what he did in his poetry and it is this that gave him a place that is in a sense unique among contemporary Spanish poets. . . .

GARCÍA LORCA

G. L. may be regarded as the most purely and essentially Spanish writer of our day and, consequently, the one hardest to translate and understand. Spanish through and through, his art resides in the words and not in the ideas; in the music, the gesture, the physical sensations and the irrational emotions, in a play of forms, rhythms and images which conceal beneath them the mystery of life and of death. It demands an effort on our part to understand him as he was, and to see his work as a poetic creation of pure art in which we find anew, stripped of history, of picturesque romanticism and genre realism, a clear, profound vision of the eternal Spain.

Federico de Onís, "F. G. L.," in A. M. I. Fiskin, ed., *Writers of Our Years* (1950), pp. 30, 35

Being a poet, he did not analyze or describe, he *felt*—and his feeling took the form of thematic images. There are a few which appear very soon, in the first poems [of *Poet in New York*], and are constantly repeated until they become leitmotifs: "things without roots," "flight and dissolution of forms," "forgetfulness of heaven," "lack of outlet," "struggle," and especially "emptiness," "vacuity," "hollowness," "void."

But perhaps more revealing than these recurrent themes and images, is the fact that all the elements of the book's style are organized in a dynamic and at the same time dialectic tension, as a result of seeing the world of reality torn by a permanent duality and conflict. This takes many forms: natural, religious, or conceptual: birth and death, heaven and earth, sin and redemption, geometry and anguish, spirit and passion, man in his constant clash with matter. All are related to a single all-embracing idea: the return to primitive, destructive instincts and passions let loose by a mechanical civilization, deprived of Grace, or, as it were, in rebellion against the spirit. The contrast is one between the primitiveness of human appetites without moral restraints, and of the perfection of technology: man, emptied of his spiritual content in a mechanized world, returns to barbarity. The result is a self-destructive confusion, as if the crumbling of this man-created chaos is necessary for the rising of a new life in which nature and the spirit will find harmony. The book is not so much an impression of New York as an indictment of modern civilization.

Ángel del Río, Introduction to F. G. L., *Poet in New York* (1955), pp. xxviii–xxix

The inspiration [for *Gypsy Ballads*] derives in part from G. L.'s lively compassion for the gypsies, who in his time were much tormented by the Civil Guard, a green-uniformed police with patent leather tri-cornered hats. In the celebrated "Ballad of the Civil Guard," these implacable guardians of law and order, their souls as black as their hats and their heads full of a vague "pistol astronomy,"

GARCÍA MÁRQUEZ

wreak brutal havoc upon a gypsy fiesta. To the bourgeoisie of G. L.'s time, as now, the gypsies seemed a useless, inferior, good-for-nothing lot. But G. L. saw in them the elements of poetry and recognized in their disheveled, passionate state a childlike quality. His insight is vindicated by the emotional response we still make to his gypsies, elevated from rags and misery to "bronze and dreams."

G. L. was able to raise the gypsies to the level of poetry by, as he put it, inventing a mythology for them. Unlike the sophisticated Greek and Roman myths, the tradition spun by G. L.'s fancy remained close to primitive roots.

Howard T. Young, *The Victorious Expression: A Study of Four Contemporary Spanish Poets* (1964), p. 165

While L.'s comic spirit is present in *Blood Wedding* and *Yerma*, his grim humor becomes increasingly critical in his last two more socially oriented plays. No longer engaged in purely personal conflict the heroines of *Doña Rosita, the Spinster* and [*The House of*] *Bernarda Alba* now struggle against a decadent morality that imprisons them in a tight cocoon. Doña Rosita becomes a passive member of a society of fools, while Adela [*Bernarda Alba*] and her sisters [in *The House of Bernarda Alba*] lose an emotional and psychological combat with the ferocious bully who is their mother. The highly wrought tension between humor and anguish in these two plays is too incongruous to be described by the rather nondescript term "tragicomedy." At the same time amusing and terrifying, *Doña Rosita, the Spinster* and *Bernarda Alba* recall L.'s puppet plays and the tragic farce *Perlimplín*. Like *Perlimplín*, these last two plays seem best described as, to borrow a phrase from Tennessee Williams, "slapstick tragedy."

L. is horrified by the hypocrisy and cruelty of established morality and expresses his dismay not only by creating rigid, one-dimensional characters, but also by adapting scenes and gestures from ancient farce for the purpose of serious criticism. Although not a polemical dramatist, L. never ceases to rebel against the web of social injustice, hurling satirical barbs at what he considers outmoded social attitudes that might be changed. His outlook on life, however, is darkly pessimistic. Using grim humor to depict social paralysis and decay, he joins other modern playwrights in suggesting that anguish in a morally bankrupt culture is absurd and meaningless.

Virginia Higginbotham, *The Comic Spirit of F. G. L.* (1976), p. 120

GARCÍA MÁRQUEZ, Gabriel
Colombian novelist and short-story writer, b. 6 March 1928, Aracataca

G. M. spent the first eight years of his life in Aracataca, near the Atlantic coast, in the home of his grandparents, whose store of myths, legends, and superstitions had a profound influence on him. After studying law at the University of Bogotá, he worked in several Colombian cities as a journalist, in Europe as a correspondent for the Bogotá daily *El espectador*, and in New York City for the Cuban news agency Prensa Latina. During most of the 1960s he lived in Mexico, where he wrote film scripts as well as his most famous book, *Cien años de soledad* (1967; *One Hundred Years of Solitude*, 1970). From 1967 until 1975 he resided in Barcelona, Spain, and in recent years he has spent considerable time in Mexico and Colombia.

The setting of many of G. M.'s works is Macondo, a small town modeled after Aracataca. His first novel, *La hojarasca* (1955; *Leaf Storm*, 1972), depicts life in Macondo during the first three decades of the 20th c., a period covering the town's founding by refugees from the Colombian civil wars (1899–1903), its economic boom brought on by the banana industry, and its subsequent decline. The interwoven plots and subplots are narrated in the form of monologues by three characters, all of whom are attending a wake following the suicide of the town's doctor. A man of mysterious origin and questionable character, the deceased appears to embody the forces of guilt and evil threatening the community. *La hojarasca* suffers from monotony and flatness because its three narrative voices lack individuality, but it does succeed in evoking an oppressive, fatalistic atmosphere of moral decay and physical stagnation.

Set against the backdrop of Colombia's civil strife during the 1950s, *El coronel no tiene quien le escriba* (1961; *No One Writes to the Colonel*, 1968) is a masterfully written novella about a retired colonel (inspired by G. M.'s grandfather) who waits in vain for his government pension. Impoverished and ailing, he falls victim to illusion when he inherits a gamecock from his recently slain son and decides to enter it in a contest with a bird from a neighboring community. The contrast between the naïve, good-natured protagonist and his skeptical, embittered wife provides a vein of humor that highlights the poignancy of the old man's plight. His unflagging determination in the face of adversity, moreover, characterizes him as an absurd hero whose valor is symbolically illuminated by the gamecock. This work's combination of stylistic precision, verbal economy, and

psychological insight has rarely, if ever, been surpassed in Latin American fiction.

The civil conflict of the 1950s plays a more important role in *La mala hora* (1962; *In Evil Hour,* 1979), in which the citizens of "el pueblo," already nervous because of political tensions, find themselves on the verge of panic when slanderous posters of unknown origin begin to appear in their midst. Ensuing events unveil a society of morally corrupt citizens whose irrational impulses and collective guilt find expression in the posters. The novel's spare, elliptical prose and disjointed montage structure serve to intensify the atmosphere of uncertainty and fear enveloping the community.

In his first collection of short stories, *Los funerales de la Mamá Grande* (1962; in *No One Writes to the Colonel, and Other Stories,* 1968), G. M. resumed his realistic sketches of Macondo, often leaving the details of his protagonist's interior drama to the reader's imagination, as, for example, in "La siesta del martes" ("Tuesday Siesta"), the tale of a courageous woman who stoically confronts the hostile curiosity of an entire town. Objective reality is abandoned, however, in the title story ("Big Mama's Funeral"), which makes use of myth, fantasy, and hyperbole to describe the death and fabulous funeral of an unforgettable ninety-two-year-old matriarch.

The shift to a more subjective plane of vision becomes increasingly evident in *Cien años de soledad,* a recapitulation of all G. M.'s previous works. This exceptionally fine novel, which has been acclaimed as a masterpiece by critics and reading public alike throughout Latin America, Europe, and the United States, relates the founding of Macondo by José Arcadio Buendía, the adventures of six generations of his descendants, and, ultimately, the town's destruction. It also presents a vast synthesis of social, economic, and political evils plaguing much of Latin America. Even more important from a literary point of view is its aesthetic representation of a world in microcosm, that is, a complete history, from Eden to Apocalypse, of a world in which miracles such as people riding on flying carpets and a dead man returning to life tend to erase the thin line between objective and subjective realities. The resultant impression of totality is further strengthened by the novel's ingeniously conceived spiral structure as well as by its narrative technique. In the final pages the narrator turns out to be not an omniscient author viewing the action from afar, as the reader has been led to believe, but one of the characters (the old gypsy Melquíades), whose manuscript and the fictional universe therein are obliterated by the hurricane "full of voices from the past." The illusion is thus conveyed of an all-encompassing novelistic world, both engendered and consumed from within.

The title—*Cien años de soledad*—alludes to the mental state of the characters, whose irrational single-mindedness and intense struggles against a hostile natural and social milieu leave them frustrated, alienated, and, as in the case of the last two adult Buendías, condemned to engender a baby with a pig's tail. Nevertheless, *Cien años de soledad* is not primarily a novel of social protest. Rather it is a poetic depiction of man's solitude in a labyrinthine universe he can never understand or dominate. G. M. takes his cue from the Argentine Jorge Luis Borges (q.v.), who stresses the fictive nature of literature because language reflects only the mind of the author, not objective reality. Thus the obliteration of Macondo in the final lines of the novel could be read as a sleight-of-hand disappearance of a purely imaginary world that ceases to exist when it is no longer perceived by the reader.

The fantasy so characteristic of *Cien años de soledad* is even more prevalent in *La increíble y triste historia de la cándida Eréndira y su abuela desalmada* (1972; *Innocent Eréndira, and Other Stories,* 1979), a collection of seven delightful tales, several of which were written for children. "Un señor muy viejo con unas alas enormes" ("A Very Old Man with Enormous Wings") describes an amusing sequence of events unleashed by an aging winged creature's fall to earth in a seaside village, but on a more intellectual level it assails capitalistic exploitation, parodies religion, and suggests the demise of innocence. The collection's title story displays themes, characters, and an organizational framework strongly reminiscent of Grimm's fairy tales.

G. M.'s most recent fictional endeavor, *El otoño del patriarca* (1975; *The Autumn of the Patriarch*, 1976), is a highly sophisticated novel about an unnamed dictator (the patriarch), who, at the time of his death, is somewhere between 107 and 232 years of age. The patriarch embodies the archetypal evils of despotism, but even more significant is his extreme, and often pathetic, solitude, which becomes increasingly evident with his advancing age and which emerges as the principal theme. Despite its political and psychological overtones, *El otoño del patriarca* can best be described as a lyrical novel, whose plot and char-

acter development are subordinate to formal design and symbolic imagery. The work's narrative content is conveyed by a wide variety of rhetorical devices, including its figurative language, rambling syntax, and constantly shifting point of view. In addition, frequent infusions of fantasy, hyperbole, and grotesque absurdities further enrich its texture and elicit reader reactions ranging from hilarity to horror. Hailed as a masterpiece by many critics, this brilliantly stylized portrait of solitude resulting from tyranny stands out as an ingenious experiment in fiction.

Although G. M. has expressed an avid interest in a multitude of writers, the most important influences on his works are probably Hemingway and Faulkner (qq.v.), the former for his detached, succinct mode of expression, and the latter for his creation of a single microcosmic universe populated by human failures.

G. M. is presently Latin America's most widely known and admired novelist. In its totality his fiction imparts not only the stark reality of an emerging, strife-torn continent but, through the humanistic and universalizing elements of myth, imagination, and aesthetic perception, an original vision of man and his world.

FURTHER WORKS: *Tres cuentos colombianos* (1954, with Guillermo Ruiz Rivas and Carlos Arturo Truque); *Isabel viendo llover en Macondo* (1967); *La novela en América Latina: Diálogo* (1968, with Mario Vargas Llosa); *Relato de un náufrago* (1970); *Ojos de perro azul* (1972); *Cuando era feliz e indocumentado* (1973); *El negro que hizo esperar a los ángeles* (1973); *Chile, el golpe y los gringos* (1974); *Cuatro cuentos* (1974); *Todos los cuentos de G. G. M. (1947–1972)* (1975); *Crónicas y reportajes* (1976); *Operación Carlota* (1977); *Periodismo militante* (1978); *Crónica de una muerte anunciada* (1981). FURTHER VOLUMES IN ENGLISH: *Leaf Storm, and Other Stories* (1972)

BIBLIOGRAPHY: Harss, L., and Dohmann, B., "G. G. M., or the Lost Chord," *Into the Mainstream* (1966), pp. 310–41; Peel, R. M., "The Short Stories of G. G. M.," *SSF,* 8 (1971), 159–68; Rodríguez Monegal, E., "A Writer's Feat," *Review 70* (1971), 122–28; Vargas Llosa, M., "G. M.: From Aracataca to Macondo," *Review 70* (1971), 129–42; Vargas Llosa, M., *G. M.: Historia de un deicidio* (1971); Goetzinger, J. A., "The Emergence of a Folk Myth in *Los funerales de la Mamá*

Grande," *REH*, 6 (1972), 237–48; Shorris, E., "G. G. M.: The Alchemy of History," *Harper's*, Feb. 1972, 98–102; Dauster, F., "The Short Stories of G. M.," *BA*, 47 (1973), 466–70; Gallagher, D. P., "G. G. M.," *Modern Latin American Literature* (1973), pp. 144–63; Guibert, R., *Seven Voices* (1973), pp. 303–37; Hall, L. B., "Labyrinthine Solitude: The Impact of G. M.," *SWR*, 58 (1973), 253–63; Luchting, W. A., "Lampooning Literature: *La mala hora*," *BA*, 47 (1973), 471–78; Coover, R., "The Master's Voice," *Amer. Review* (Bantam Books), No. 26 (1977), pp. 361–88; Lipski, J. M., "Embedded Dialogue in *El otoño del patriarca*," *TAH*, 2, 14 (1977), 9–12; McMurray, G. R., *G. G. M.* (1977); Williams, R. L., "The Dynamic Structure of G. M.'s *El otoño del patriarca*," *Symposium*, 32 (1978), 56–75; Zamora, L. P., "The Myth of Apocalypse and Human Temporality in G. M.'s *Cien años de soledad* and *El otoño del patriarca*," *Symposium*, 32 (1978), 341–55

GEORGE R. MCMURRAY

How he came by his meticulous purity of style is something of a mystery. Perhaps, one may think, he found a precedent in Colombian purism, which may have a positive side, after all. He denies it. His language is not Colombia, he says simply, but his grandmother. She was a great story teller. "She spoke this way." Her voice can often be heard like a whisper in the background, reminding G. M. of the magic childhood world he grew up in, which infests so many of his best pages. There are scenes, gestures, phrases, situations that recur with obsessive regularity in his work. There are sudden beams of blinding light that create a sort of magnetic field around them, charged with unfathomable implications. Their meaning remains deliberately enigmatic. "What gives literary value is mystery," says G. M., who always tries to tap "the magic in commonplace events." In everything he writes there is this "lost chord," as he calls it. It may be a cryptic hint, a glimpse of something caught in flight, undecipherable as a dream lost on waking. Whatever its origin or appearance, it alludes to a private mythology that inhabits him like a message from the deep.

Luis Harss and Barbara Dohmann, *Into the Mainstream* (1966), pp. 336–37

Rather than attempting to recapture the actual world of his childhood in every petty detail, G. M. has created a new world that bears comparison to Faulkner's Yoknapatawpha County; G. M. calls it Macondo. . . . G. M., like the French genius Marcel Proust, recalls the past not by massive conventional realism, but in terms of exquisitely selective insights into remembered characters, situations, and anecdotes. From this welter of odd bits from the past, an image of a whole society's past comes forth. G. M.'s vision is like that of a child, endowed with the magical coherence that only a child can project onto the chaos of reality. Macondo is pure myth filtered out of reality, an enclosed yet living world in fiction.

Alexander Coleman, *Cinco maestros: Cuentos modernos de Hispanoamérica* (1969), pp. 223–24

Anybody who has been enchanted by *The Arabian Nights*, as a child or adult, who has laughed with Rabelais, who has read Faulkner, will find his experiences revived and blooming in the pages of *Cien años de soledad*. Does it surprise, then, that despite so much having been written about the novel, despite the seminars, papers, discussions, etc., nobody so far seems really to have come to grips with it? Whatever one reads or hears about it reveals, I believe, an underlying helplessness in face of this intensely alive work, a kind of embarrassed, secret admission of critical arms thrown away, and of an at first hesitant, then joyful abandon to the seductive powers of the novel. And I by no means wish to claim my own words here to be an exception to this process, or myself to have kept my critical "cool." I doubt if anyone can keep it when reading *Cien años*.

Wolfgang A. Luchting, "G. G. M.: The Boom and the Whimper," *BA*, 44 (1970), 26–27

One Hundred Years of Solitude is about the Buendías and their descendants in much the same way that the Bible is about Adam and Eve and their descendants.

Macondo is a world, a place of greater possibility than the imaginary county of Faulkner, by whom G. M. has surely been influenced. The family of the Buendías . . . is the family of man, the first family, the people of Eden, Canaan, and the world. . . . In *One Hundred Years of Solitude* G. M. has produced a novel that twice delights us, a joy to the senses and the mind, a myth made of unforgettable irony.

It is also necessary to consider G. M. as a moralist, a political man; for myth, though it negates history by making circles of time and events, relates to the way we live; it is not made in a vacuum, but in the deeps of experience. G. M. writes of exploitation, colonialism, and revolution from the point of view of a man who was influenced in his childhood by a grandfather who lived out his days as one of the leavings of a revolution in a town called Aracataca, which was exploited and then abandoned by banana barons from the United States.

Earl Shorris, *Harper's*, Feb. 1972, p. 100

G. M. is one of those writers who enchants us as he deals with those perennial forces that rule our lives and cast us hither and thither. He also represents a highly encouraging phenomenon in world literature, which has been designated as the South American boom in literature. In an age when more and more often we hear that the novel is dying or dead, . . . it is worthwhile, I feel, to find such a countercurrent of fantasy and to bewingedly reflect thus upon the human lot awhile, and refreshed, thence to renew our efforts and even gingerly resume taking arms against a sea of troubles. . . .

It seems to me that G. M. marries realism and objectivity with a most singular sense of the fantastic and delicious fabulating gifts, often employing surrealistic clairvoyance to paint frescoes full of moral indignation and anger protesting against oppression and violence, degradation and deceit. Extolling pride, he clearly depicts certain ludicrous, even grotesque aspects, such as quixotic bravery and intransigent single-mindedness of purpose. It is a joy to encounter a poet who revels in his seductive powers as G. M. does. And yet he is so exact in his formulation and precise in his composition. In juxtaposing the twin elements of humor and tragedy G. M. often achieves contrapuntal heights where language and image are thoroughly fused.

Thor Vilhjálmsson, "Presentation of G. G. M.," *BA*, 47 (1973), 10–11

Cien años de soledad is a very Latin American *reading* of Borges, for it discovers Borges's relevance to Latin American—the relevance of his cyclical vision of time to the cyclical nature of Latin American history, the relevance of his sense that life is a dream, a fiction, to the dreamlike nature of Latin American politics, the relevance of his sense that the past is inseparable from the fictive words that narrate it to the tragic fact that Latin America's past is inseparable from the deliberately distorted words that have claimed to record it, the relevance, finally of Borges's demonstrations that our perceptions of things depend on our previous assumptions about them to the fact that in a continent shared by so many cultures there can be no common continental perception of anything.

D. P. Gallagher, *Modern Latin American Literature* (1973), p. 163

It is evident that *El otoño del patriarca* is not written in any conventional novelistic mode: with its grotesque extremes, its outlandish images, its exaggerated horrors, it is in fact a caricature of conventional fiction, presenting comic distortions and fantastic perversions of normal novelistic material. The social setting and plot of *Cien años de soledad* is abandoned. Patterns of poetic association,

images which project mental realities, fears, dreams, nightmares, and suggestive gestures replace the discursive movement of Melquíades' manuscript. Of course, *Cien años de soledad* is also a poetic novel, but the imagery is used less to project mental realities than to create a novelistic ambience suggestive of man's prodigious capacities for both good *and* evil, love *and* hatred. . . . Like the apocalyptists, G. M. seems to feel that only through grotesquely exaggerated and fantastical imagery can the political evils of his time be fully apprehended.

Lois P. Zamora, "The Myth of Apocalypse and Human Temporality in G. M.'s *Cien años de soledad* and *El otoño del patriarca*," *Symposium*, 32 (1978), 350–51

GASCAR, Pierre

(pseud. of Pierre Fournier) French novelist, short-story writer, and essayist, b. 13 March 1916, Paris

G. spent his childhood in a village in southwestern France. He served eight years in the army, five of them as a prisoner of war in Germany and in the Nazi-occupied Ukraine during World War II. A journalist after the war, he has traveled extensively: to China and, while working with the World Health Organization, to southeast Asia and Africa. He has written for radio and television and has been a literary critic and lecturer.

The short stories of *Les bêtes* (1953, pub. in one vol. with *Les temps des morts; Beasts and Men,* 1956), written when G. was a prisoner of war, depict the atavistic cruelty of men and animals in the suffering of a world at war; both realistic and fantastic, they are rich in surrealist (q.v.), mythic images of the mental darkness in which each man struggles against despair and resignation. In these, and in the other stories of this dark concentration-camp world, those in the collection *Les femmes* (1955; in *Women and the Sun,* 1965) and the novel *Le fugitif* (1961; *The Fugitive,* 1964), G. affirms his hope of an evolutionary metamorphosis of man.

Other early autobiographical works, *La graine* (1955; *The Seed,* 1959) and *L'herbe des rues* (1956; the grass of the streets) are lyric novels of a tightly controlled rythmic style. They are unsentimental accounts of rural life; the solitary child can "believe in stones," in the natural world, even in this loveless, indifferent milieu.

In his later works, G. abandoned fiction for the personal *récit* and the philosophical essay. His travels in the Third World, his reading in history, and his interest in psychology and the natural sciences provided material for these speculative works. In all of them, the material world and the dreams hidden behind it fascinate G.: the dream imagery of salt, blood, and monstrous grafted plants in *Chimères* (1969; chimeras), lichen in *Le présage* (1972; presage). In these works, G. elaborates his dominant themes: the future evolution of the natural world, man's need for natural forms, the destructive effects of science and of our false cult of rationality. In *Les sources* (1975; the springs), a commentary on the works of a French Renaissance philosopher-naturalist, Bernard Palissy (c. 1510–1589), G. finds the hope of the future world in the rediscovery of the primitive unity of the Whole, the harmony of all form and matter.

Although G. has not created imaginative fiction of wide scope, he excels as the "witness" and "dreamer" of our present and future world. He is both an exact observer and analyst and a disciplined poet of the subconscious and of nature.

FURTHER WORKS: *Les meubles* (1949); *Le visage clos* (1951); *Chine ouverte* (1955); *Les pas perdus* (1957); *Voyage chez les vivants* (1958); *La barre de corail* (1958; *The Coral Barrier*, 1961); *Soleils* (1960; in *Women and the Sun*, 1965); *Le feu mal éteint* (1961); *Camile Hilaire* (1961); *Chambord* (1962; *Chambord*, 1964); *Vertiges du présent* (1962); *Les moutons du feu* (1963; *Lambs of Fire*, 1965); *Le meilleur de la vie* (1964; *The Best Years*, 1967); *Les charmes* (1965); *Histoire de la captivité des Français en Allemagne* (1967); *Auto* (1967); *L'arche* (1971); *Rimbaud et la commune* (1971); *Quartier Latin* (1973); *Les bouchers* (1973); *L'homme et l'animal* (1974)

BIBLIOGRAPHY: Borbás, L., "Man and Beast in G.'s Tales," *KFLQ*, 6 (1959), 1–5; Obuchowski, C. W., "The Concentrationary World of P. G.," *FR*, 34 (1961), 327–35; Radke, J. J., "The Metamorphosis of Animals and Men in G.'s *Les bêtes*," *FR*, 39 (1965), 85–91; Chalfin, D. E., "*Women and the Sun*, by P. G.," *SSF*, 3 (1966), 266–67; Fabre-Luce, A., "L'incidence de l'imaginaire dans les nouvelles de P. G.," *FR*, 41 (1968), 839–48; Lorent, L. E., "P. G.: Charmes et chimères," *La revue nouvelle*, 51 (1970), 204–7; Albérès, R. M.,

"Le réalisme onirique de P. G.," *Littérature, horizon 2000* (1974), pp. 235–53

JUDITH RADKE

GASS, William H.

American novelist, short-story writer, and essayist, b. 30 July 1924, Fargo, N.D.

When G. was six months old his family moved to industrial Warren, Ohio, where he grew up, returning to rural North Dakota only for summer visits to relatives. G. received a B.A. from Kenyon College (Ohio) and a Ph.D. in philosophy from Cornell University. Beginning in 1955 he taught philosophy at Purdue University for several years and now teaches at Washington University in St. Louis, Missouri.

G. prefers to balance the contradictory impulses in art, which are to communicate and to make an artifact out of the medium. Both impulses are apparent in G.'s first novel, *Omensetter's Luck* (1966). But the simple story of Brackett Omensetter, the happy man, who does what he does because it feels good, becomes too complex in G.'s straining for language and narrative technique.

G.'s short fiction, which had appeared in little magazines since 1958, was published as *In the Heart of the Heart of the Country* (1968). Each story in this collection presents a mind walled up in its loneliness, desperately producing fantasies to take the place of love and to avert madness. The title story orients the whole collection to G.'s view of the relationship between art and life. It begins with a misquotation from William Butler Yeats's (q.v.) "Sailing to Byzantium," which juxtaposes G.'s midwestern town of "B" and Yeats's mythical city. But the country that in Yeats's poem is not for old men is also, in G.'s story, not for the young. What we think of as childhood, states his aging narrator, is a lie created by poetry. And where Yeats's man forswears bodily existence, G.'s man asserts that body equals being.

This assertion of the primacy of life over art is restated in *Willie Masters' Lonesome Wife* (1971). A sixty-page parody composed of footnotes, distortion of typefaces, and arty photographs, it satirizes the idea of art for art's sake and concludes by admonishing the reader: "You have fallen into art—return to life."

G.'s essays on language, philosophy, and literature, however, collected as *Fiction and the Figures of Life* (1971), argue the case for art. If all were to practice the artist's virtues, a richer state of being for humanity might be possible. But this G. regards as highly unlikely, a dim view of human possibility that runs through his work as an undercurrent of personal despair. Countering it is a delight in recording sensuous experience and a restless inquiry into the human condition. The essays develop G.'s belief that the novelist does not render the world; he creates one from the medium of which he is master—language. G. observes this creativity in the best contemporary writers and evaluates their achievement in making new orders of the world ("figured histories") for their readers. His judgment is divided. Beckett, Borges, and Barth (qq.v.), although they resist literal interpretation, are not merely puzzling but profound. Yet G. believes that these writers' "fear of feeling" inhibits their appeal to a reader's sensibilities. G. finds this fear also in Hawkes, Nabokov, Barthelme (qq.v.), and Robert Coover (b. 1932). On the other hand, Faulkner, Lowry, Lawrence, Bellow (qq.v.), and Stanley Elkin (b. 1930) command a reader's emotional as well as intellectual involvement.

G. has continued to publish more essays than fiction. His ability to translate the philosopher's concerns for the problems of language and being into the stuff of imagination is inhibited by a conflict in even his best work between medium as a means and medium as an end. This conflict qualifies the achievement of much mid-century American writing and accounts for the many writers who are interested in G. as a theorist-practitioner

Yet G. at his best, *On Being Blue* (1976), an essay on the semantic and imaginative implications of blueness, leaves no doubt about wherein his strength lies: it is in direct statements one after another, driven by high voltage intellectual energy, and kept in motion by a curious mind that is sometimes reminiscent of Robert Graves (q.v.), although with an unmistakable American toughness of language and attitude.

FURTHER WORK: *The World within the Word* (1978)

BIBLIOGRAPHY: Kane, P., "The Sun Burned on the Snow: G.'s 'The Pedersen Kid,' " *Crit,* 14, 2 (1972), 89–96; special G. issue, *Crit,* 18, 1 (1976); Merrill, R. B., "The Grotesque as Structure: *Willie Masters' Lonesome Wife,"* *Criticism,* 18 (1976), 305–16; Rueckert, W., "Love Lavished on Speech," *ChiR,* 29, 4

(1978), 53–59; Waxman, R. E., "Things in the Saddle: W. G.'s 'Icicles' and 'Orders of Insects,' " *RS,* 46 (1978), 215–22; Janssens, G. A. M., "An Interview with W. G.," *DQR,* 9 (1979), 242–59; McCaffery, L., "The G.–Gardner Debate: Showdown on Main Street," *LitR,* 23 (1979), 134–44

MANLY JOHNSON

GATTO, Alfonso
Italian poet and journalist, b. 17 July 1909, Salerno; d. 8 March 1976, Rome

Born to a family of sailors and small shipbuilders, G. did not finish his university studies. In his youth he worked as a bookseller, schoolteacher, proofreader, and journalist. In 1933 he moved to Milan, where he wrote articles on literature, architecture, and interior decoration. Jailed as an anti-Fascist in 1936, he became a Communist and joined the resistance in 1943. Like many other intellectuals, he eventually left the Communist Party, in 1951. Married to a painter, he spent the postwar years in Rome, working for various papers as journalist and editor until his death.

Like other writers of his generation, G. contributed to the best periodicals of the 1930s. He wrote for *Circoli* and *Letteratura,* and in 1938 he and Vasco Pratolini (q.v.) founded *Campo di Marte* to educate all classes in the appreciation of contemporary arts.

G.'s early poetry, written under Fascism, is influenced by hermeticism (q.v.) but does not completely belong to that school: critics have called it surrealist (q.v.) and even "neocubist." Other elements in his style are its typically southern musicality, imagery that is both three-dimensional and pliant, and a very cultivated intellectualism alternating with a certain amount of pathos.

G.'s early work is included in *Poesie* (1941; poems), which contains all the poetry he had published since 1932.

Political circumstances and the war caused his work to become more realistic and socially committed, as is evidenced in the war poems of *Il capo sulla neve* (1949; head on the snow). *La madre e la morte* (1960; mother and death), however, reflects a more personal and existential focus. His later books show a continuing preoccupation with social and ethical problems, a controlled sentimentality, and constant stylistic experimentation. The characteristics of his early poetry are slightly modified, being used now to give glimpses of the subconscious world in contrast to everyday reality. The result is a "magic" feeling unique to G.'s poetry.

G.'s best-known collections are *Osteria flegrea* (1962; Phlegraean inn), whose main theme is death, and *La storia delle vittime* (1966; history of the victims), which won the Viareggio prize. *Rime di viaggio per la terra dipinta* (1969; rhymes of travel through the painted earth) is noteworthy for its exceptionally skillful use of formal poetic techniques.

G.'s collected poetry has appeared in the prestigious *Lo Specchio* series. He has also written children's verse, the most important volume of which is *Carlomagno nella grotta* (1962; Charlemagne in the grotto). G. was one of the best and most passionately committed of the formerly hermetic poets; his work has earned him a secure niche in the history of 20th-c. Italian literature.

FURTHER WORKS: *Isola* (1932); *Atanasio Soldati pittore* (1934); *Morto ai paesi* (1937); *Poesie* (1939); *Disegni di Rosai* (1939); *Luigi Broggini scultore* (1940); *Ottone Rosai* (1941); *L'allodola* (1943); *Virgilio Guidi pittore* (1943); *La sposa bambina* (1943); *Amore della vita* (1944); *La spiaggia dei poveri* (1944); *Il duello* (1944); *Il sigaro de fuoco* (1945); *Il vaporetto* (1963); *Poesie d'amore* (1973); *Desinenze* (1976)

JOY M. POTTER

GE'EZ LITERATURE
See Ethiopian Literature

GENET, Jean
French novelist, dramatist, and poet, b. 19 Dec. 1910, Paris

Of all the writers of France, G. is the most disquieting. The appalling string of descriptive categories with which he is always introduced—illegitimate child, thief, beggar, male prostitute, pornographer, and convict—seems to bear no relationship to his achievement, which in addition to a handful of poems includes five prose works and five plays that hold a central position in modern literature. And yet G.'s life is the ostensible subject of his prose works and implicit even in his plays. While other writers, particularly modern ones, have blurred the boundaries between literature and autobiography, only G. has created a mythic version of his life that has

completely replaced whatever that life may have been in reality. Because G. spent so many years either incarcerated or wandering through the lowest strata of European society, and because he has provided so little new information in the rare interviews he has granted, a biography dealing in detail with the first half of his life is not likely to be written. The only accounts of G.'s unique transformation from hardened criminal to major writer would then remain his own and that of Jean-Paul Sartre (q.v.), whose existentialist (q.v.) interpretation of G.'s life, *Saint Genet: Comédien et martyr* (1952; *Saint Genet: Actor and Martyr,* 1963), is almost identical to G.'s own, and (appropriately enough) was published as the first volume of G.'s complete works.

Somehow the supposedly self-educated G. became one of the most elegant prose stylists in all of French literature. His first book, *Notre-Dame-des-Fleurs* (1944; rev. ed., 1951; *Our Lady of the Flowers,* 1963), begins in a prison cell, which G. has decorated with pictures of notorious criminals, and the narrative constantly returns to that cell, as G. awaits a hearing that may set him free. In his imagination, however, he is already free, as he weaves stories around the Parisian homosexuals and petty criminals who are the focus of his yearning and admiration. *Miracle de la rose* (1946; rev. ed., 1951; *Miracle of the Rose,* 1965) is a meditation on the meaning of imprisonment, on the reformatory where G. spent his adolescence, and especially on a convict named Harcamone, who like G. has moved from reformatory to prison but by committing murder has surpassed G. and moved even higher—to the scaffold. The "miracle" of the title is the transformation of Harcamone's chains to a garland of flowers, and by an equally miraculous imaginative process G. leaves his own body and ascends to paradise in the body of Harcamone at the moment of the murderer's execution. While in these two works fiction can be said to be blended with autobiography, the distinction between those two forms has vanished in *Pompes funèbres* (1948; rev. ed., 1953; *Funeral Rites,* 1969). As in his other works, G. alternates between a (real?) present and a fantasized past, but in this case his own identity is so tenuous that he moves as well from third to first person, sometimes in the middle of a sentence, and remains aware, even when he has "assumed the form of Erik . . . of the sharp, luminous presence within me of J. G."

In *Querelle de Brest* (1949; rev. ed., 1953; *Querelle,* 1974), G. does not appear as a character at all; in *Journal du voleur* (1949; *The Thief's Journal*, 1964) G. seems to move from fiction to autobiography—yet Richard N. Coe has turned up fragmentary evidence suggesting that even in G.'s memoirs the element of fiction should not be totally discounted. In any case, G. produced a "novel" and an "autobiography" only after showing in three other books that the two forms were in his case virtually identical. Not only does G. thus emphasize the fictional element in his own identity, but his prose works can be viewed as a series of attempts to destroy the whole notion of human identity. (Even *Querelle de Brest*, which is a relatively straightforward novel, deals with doubles and multiple personalities.) When the threat of prison no longer hung over him, G. moved on to the one form of literature in which an individual identity is absolutely essential—the drama—in order to abolish identity even there.

In between G.'s prose works and his full-length plays, however, came Sartre's massive psychoanalytical study *Saint Genet: Actor and Martyr*, which in addition to being one of the greatest critical studies of the century has a certain claim to being another work generated by G. himself, since virtually the only references in it are to G.'s works and to G. in conversation. Whether G. was the best possible example of Sartre's philosophy, because of the way he consciously chose to become what he already was in the eyes of others, or whether Sartre is simply so brilliant that it is impossible to read G. without borrowing Sartre's viewpoint, every subsequent writer on G. has followed in Sartre's footsteps, and written what is at times more a commentary upon Sartre than upon G. One critic has speculated that because Sartre's study is so overwhelming, its publication made G. himself incapable of writing any more prose of his own, but by 1952 G. had already written two short plays and had embarked upon yet another transformation—from novelist to dramatist.

Haute surveillance (1949; *Deathwatch*, 1954) takes place in a prison cell, and its theme is the inability of minor criminals to attain the exalted position of murderers, since murder is a grace given by destiny and not available to the unworthy. *Les bonnes* (1954; *The Maids*, 1954) deals on one level with the relationships between masters and servants, but, as Sartre has shown, G.'s two early plays are really variations of the same basic situation, both dealing with ritualized attempts to gain power—attempts that are ultimately unavailing. *Le balcon* (1956; rev. ed., 1960; *The Bal-*

cony, 1957) is set in a brothel where clients who play at being powerful figures have the opportunity to live out their fantasies of power in real life as the result of an abortive revolution. In this play G. uses the house of illusions as a metaphor for the world as a whole, where revolutionaries fail because they are unaware that rituals are more important than ideals.

Les nègres (1958; *The Blacks*, 1960) carries the notion of a play within a play one step further: the blacks onstage perform a play for an audience of black actors wearing white masks, but the "real" white audience in the theater is all the while being entertained by this spectacle in order to be kept ignorant of the "real" black revolution taking place outside the theater.

Les paravents (1961; *The Screens*, 1962) takes place during the Algerian revolution, although the play seems with the passing years to have so little to do with that specific historical reality that the scandal occasioned by its first performances in France (1966) seems almost irrelevant to the play's content. At the end of the play its major characters have burst through the screens on stage to reach a realm where every distinction between individuals has been abolished. In G.'s prose works extremes are reconciled—a Nazi makes love to a Frenchman and a murderer embraces a detective. In *Les paravents* extremes cannot be said to be reconciled because by the end of the play they no longer even exist, and characters who were on opposite sides while they lived sit together chuckling gently, with no bodies, no beliefs, no personalities at all.

G. claims to have been particularly impressed by the novels of Dostoevsky and Proust (q.v.), and indeed, their influence is apparent in his prose works, although the childhood paradise he recalls with longing is a reformatory and the Siberia toward which he yearns is a penal colony in French Guiana, where he hopes not to be regenerated but rather to be confirmed in criminality. The influences usually cited among dramatists are Artaud and Pirandello (qq.v.). G. shares with Artaud a contempt for the theatrical experience as it has become fossilized and meaningless in the Western world, and like Pirandello he constantly juggles with illusion and reality. As influences on G., however, these writers are problematic. G. is less a product of influences than a seminal figure who sums up in his work the major literary tendencies of his age. This is not to deny the scandal inherent in a figure whose three cardinal virtues are theft, homosexuality, and treason, and whose ten major works constitute a modern antidecalogue whose inverted values contain something to offend almost any reader. Although the thrust of G.'s work may be overwhelmingly destructive, however, his great merit is to have elevated nihilism to an ethical imperative. G. has written of the time a plaster bust in his home "miraculously broke, and I saw the bust was hollow. I had had to leap into the void in order to see it." That leap into the void is both the subject and method of G.'s works, and his pervasive image of that void is as an endless hall of mirrors, where it is impossible to distinguish essence from reflection. Under these circumstances his battle plan, like that of the lieutenant who leads his men in an attack upon an Algerian village in *Les paravents,* is to open fire first upon the mirrors.

FURTHER WORKS: *Poèmes* (1948); *Œuvres complètes* (1951 ff.); *Lettres à Roger Blin* (1966; *Letters to Roger Blin,* 1969). FURTHER VOLUME IN ENGLISH: *Treasures of the Night: The Collected Poems of J. G.* (1980)

BIBLIOGRAPHY: Sartre, J.-P., *Saint Genet: Actor and Martyr* (1963); McMahon, J. H., *The Imagination of J. G.* (1963); Brustein, R., *The Theater of Revolt* (1964), pp. 361–411; Driver, T. F., *J. G.* (1966); Coe, R. N., *The Vision of J. G.* (1968); Knapp, B. L., *J. G.* (1968); Thody, P., *J. G.* (1968); Coe, R. N., ed., *The Theater of J. G.* (1970); Cetta, L. T., *Profane Play, Ritual, and J. G.: A Study of His Drama* (1974); Choukri, M., *J. G. in Tangier* (1974); Naish, C., *A Genetic Approach to Structures in the Work of J. G.* (1978); Brooks, P., and Halpern, J., eds., *G.: A Collection of Critical Essays* (1979)

MICHAEL POPKIN

From a literary point of view, it is essentially irrelevant whether a writer indulges in this vice or that, or even whether or not he has been a common criminal. What matters is that, starting out from this or that given vice, or from whatever may have been the singular accidents of his life, his work open out upon the general experience of Man. If Proust had never depicted anything save the scene of M. de Charlus being whipped in a brothel, he would be no more significant than is M. J. G. himself: a highly specialized writer who places a great deal of talent in the exclusive service of his specialty. Proust painted *the* world, not simply *a* world. . . . Whereas M. J. G., himself no less than the heroes of *Deathwatch,* goes around and around in circles like a squirrel in a cage, imprisoned in the dungeon of a vice from which he cannot escape, even through the process of literary creation, since he can conceive of nothing outside the barbed-wire perimeter of his own tiny private hell. [1949]

François Mauriac, "The Case of J. G.," in Richard N. Coe, ed., *The Theater of J. G.* (1970), p. 77

The general impression of him, such as it is, seems to leave out the heart of the matter, which is that however repellent his preoccupations, and however childish the philosophical equipment that he shares with many of his betters in that line, he is with little question one of the most gifted French prose writers of this generation, and the only one to have created a world nearly comparable in compulsion if not in scope to that of Proust or Céline. He is successor to both of them, and their only one, though he has a closer ancestry among the poets of the nineteenth century.

Unfortunately, public prudery being what it is, it will probably be a long time before his reputation will be based on much more than hearsay in this country. It is hard to see how the books could be made generally available here except in mutilated form, or even how they could be mutilated, since G.'s sexual candor, to put it mildly, is not eruptive as in Sartre but entirely of the grain; to doctor his writing for commercial purposes would be to operate on every line.

Eleanor Clark, "The World of J. G.," *PR,* April 1949, 443–44

Since the pariah and God are alike external to nature, it will suffice for the pariah, in his cell, to dare invent being: he will be God. G. creates in order to enjoy his infinite power. . . .

Now that his dreams are written down, he is no longer either God or man, and he has no other way of regaining his lost divinity than to manifest himself to men. These fictions will assume a new objectivity for him if he obliges others to believe in them. And at the core of all his characters is the same categorical imperative: "Since you don't have faith enough to believe in us, you must at least make others adopt us and must convince them that we exist." In writing out, for his pleasure, the incommunicable dreams of his particularity, G. has transformed them into exigencies of communication. There was no invocation, no call. Nor was there that aching need for self-expression that writers have invented for the needs of personal publicity. You will not find in G. the "fateful gift" and "imperiousness of talent" about which the high-minded are in the habit of sounding off. To cultivated young men who go in for literature, the craft of writing appears first as a means of communication. But G. began to write in order to affirm his solitude, to be self-sufficient, and it was the writing itself that, by its problems, gradually led him to seek readers. [1952]

Jean-Paul Sartre, *Saint Genet: Actor and Martyr* (1963), pp. 479, 481–82

GABRIEL GARCÍA MÁRQUEZ

JEAN GENET

STEFAN GEORGE

MICHEL DE GHELDERODE

What strikes us in *The Blacks* is the great freedom and lightness of the invention, compared with the obsessive and claustrophobic heaviness of G.'s novels. It is as if the theater were the agency through which the damned G. obtains his redemption.

Redemption from what? From the muck of reality, from the obsession with everyday experience, from the insolence of the reprobate enclosed in his autobiography, determined to batten on the reproof of others without being able to answer them except by repeating to himself that he is a criminal and a pervert, segregated in Evil, and therefore inaccessible to the judgment of others. But simply by advancing onto the stage, by playing the game of the theater, there appears, instead, the possibility of a judgment that is not accompanied by condemnation and that is objective because it is purely intellectual; thus the imagination is liberated from autobiographical determinism. The novel was a prison that enclosed G. in his narcissistic obsession. The theater provided an opening onto the world and the love of others. [1966]

Nicola Chiaromonte, "The Ceremonial Theater of J. G.," *The Worm of Consciousness, and Other Essays* (1976), p. 180

Some of the decisive experiences of the European Left have been incorporated into [*The Screens*]. First of all: the possibility of a successful revolt in Algeria, and in other countries throughout the world as well. Then: victory alone will not guarantee men happiness and freedom, nor secure a place within the new order for those values which, as Ommu says, are not to be realized in action but are to become song. The play's three social orders correspond to three basic concepts of European socialist thought: the class society based on oppression; the society born of the successful revolt which does away with oppression but is still rooted in constraint; and the vision of a classless society with no restraints. This last serves the same need for socialist thought as the Kingdom of Heaven does in Christian eschatology.

Saïd and through him G. refuse to participate in these three orders. There is another path which must be followed if we wish to remain men. *The Screens* is the first French theater work to describe the possibilities that men still have intact and—paradoxical as this may sound—to put on stage a hero who, in and through his negativity, is ultimately positive. [1966]

Lucien Goldmann, "The Theatre of G.: A Sociological Study," in Kelly Morris, ed., *G./Ionesco: The Theatre of the Double* (1969), pp. 105–6

I sit and read *Miracle of the Rose* again. Fever, palpitations, shivers, just the way it was when I read it first, nineteen years ago. I was an adolescent of thirty-eight. I was discovering the happi-ness of adoration, the joy of admiration. Now I am an adolescent of fifty-seven, I am discovering the happiness of adoration, the joy of admiration. For whom had I caught that fever? For whom was I in a swoon? For Harcamone, the convict condemned to death. I reread G. and my heart beat faster. . . . I can open G. anywhere. The griefs and agonies in G. are my litanies. I am raised up like Harcamone; see how I hover over his majestic misfortunes, his sumptuous experiences, his rituals, his carnivals, his metempsychoses, and G.'s ultimate alchemy when he transforms imprisoning chains to flowering bracelets. . . . Every book he writes is a commemoration of transfigured sufferings. At his high mass I hurry to be early, to get a seat in the front row. [1970]

Violette Leduc, *Mad in Pursuit* (1971), pp. 73–74

I remember Ruth Benedict's remarking that, among the Zuñi Indians of the Southwest, almost every act, every moment of the day, was invested with some sort of ritual significance. This is what it is like in *Querelle*. Each character spends most of his time and energy on his "interior theatricals," obsessively measuring his "power" and "beauty" against those of everyone else.

I suspect that G. is popular simply because he coincides with current fashion. His best literary passages are too complex to win him a wide audience, but he has erected a paradoxical metaphysics around an extremely anti-Establishment position, and this alone is enough to win him a reputation. Add to that his "profound" obscurity and you have the formula for "genius."

Anatole Broyard, "Murder and Mimosas," *NYT*, 6 Sept. 1974, 31

For all that has been written about G. the man, he remains a figure of mystery: his truth—including the facts of his biography—seems inextricably interwoven with his fictionalized self-images. He clearly wishes to remain protean, ungraspable. And it is difficult to know what surprises he may yet produce as an artist—if any. His recent creative activity seems to have principally taken the form of political articles and the production of a film. It has been more than a decade since his last major work—*The Screens*—and it may be that his *opus* is substantially complete, ready for overall critical estimate. But it will be a long time before we arrive at a cool, "objective" verdict on G. He continues to be an unsettling force in culture, difficult to assimilate and to make peace with.

Peter Brooks and Joseph Halpern, eds., Introduction to *G: A Collection of Critical Essays* (1979), p. 6

GEORGE, Stefan

German poet, b. 12 July 1868, Büdesheim; d. 4 Dec. 1933, Minusio, Switzerland

G.'s life was peripatetic. After graduating from secondary school he traveled extensively (1888–92). He was often in Paris where he met leading French symbolist (q.v.) poets, especially Mallarmé and Verlaine. G. never married, but close friendships with congenial poets and scholars were central to his life and work, and there was a large circle of young people who regarded G. as their artistic and ethical model. G.'s crucial personal relationships were those with Ida Coblenz (1870–1942), who later married the poet and playwright Richard Dehmel (1864–1920), and with Maximilian Kronberger (1888–1904), named "Maximin" by G., who saw in the youth's physical and spiritual beauty an incarnation of mythic divinity.

From its outset, G.'s approach to poetry displayed two aspects: as a means of personal expression, and as a medium for cultural and ethical reform. His poetic ideals were exemplified in his translations (1891) of Baudelaire's *Flowers of Evil*, of works by other poets—published in *Zeitgenössische Dichter* (2 vols., 1905; contemporary poets—mainly French symbolists but also including Dante Gabriel Rossetti, Swinburne, the Danish writer J. P. Jacobsen (1847–1885), and D'Annunzio (q.v.), of Shakespeare's sonnets (1909), and of parts of Dante's *Divine Comedy* (1912). The journal of the arts, *Blätter für die Kunst,* published from 1892 to 1919, which G. edited and contributed to, and in which many of Hugo von Hofmannsthal's (q.v.) and G.'s poems were first published, reflects the evolution of his thinking about art and culture.

G.'s first three volumes of poetry, *Hymnen* (1890; *Odes,* 1949), *Pilgerfahrten* (1891; *Pilgrimages,* 1949), and *Algabal* (1892; *Algabal,* 1949), later always printed together, share the theme of the artist's isolation from nature and society. In the symbolist manner, using a variety of lyrical forms, the poet condenses and manipulates experience into vivid artifacts of the poetic imagination. Artistic alienation and uncertainty about the primacy of the objective versus the subjective world are a source of torment. In *Algabal,* however, the persona of the Roman emperor Heliogabalus transforms his barbarous imaginings into an empirical reality of life as a work of art; perversely sumptuous subterranean chambers and gardens, untrammeled voluptuousness, and murders of exquisite

aesthetic brutality characterize his existence. By denying the limits of nature and the validity of a reality outside himself, Algabal falls prey to the suicidal despair of solipsism. *Algabal* represents an artistic experiment, a venture into total subjectivity, a possibility that G. ultimately rejected.

The books that gained G. his widest public acceptance were *Die Bücher der Hirten- und Preisgedichte, der Sagen und Sänge und der hängenden Gärten* (1895; *The Books of Eclogues and Eulogies, of Legends and Lays, and of the Hanging Gardens,* 1949) and *Das Jahr der Seele* (1897; *The Year of the Soul,* 1949). In the earlier work, the universality and timelessness of human feeling are evoked by the retrospective projection of the poet's present experience into Arcadian antiquity, into a medieval world strongly colored by romanticism, and into a legendary realm in Persia. The poems are by turns lyrical, elegiac, and balladesque, recalling but never imitating characteristic forms of each time and place. In their intensity and compression, the love poems of *Das Buch der hängenden Gärten* are especially distinctive. *Das Jahr der Seele,* G.'s most popular collection, contains poems inspired by his unhappy relationship with Ida Coblenz, but transposed onto an apparently impersonal plane of artistic stylization. Characterized by fastidious formal craftsmanship, these verses express profound melancholy through motifs of landscape that are both immediate and transcendently symbolic. The dilemmas of the artist's relationship to experience as well as to form and of his mission in the world are also to be felt deeply here.

Around the turn of the century a significant change in the direction of G.'s thinking and efforts took place, which is most clearly perceptible in *Der Teppich des Lebens und die Lieder von Traum und Tod mit einem Vorspiel* (1899; *The Tapestry of Life and the Songs of Dream and Death with a Prelude,* 1949) and *Der Siebente Ring* (1907; *The Seventh Ring,* 1949). Here G. abandoned his subjective concerns in favor of a didactic, indeed prophetic function. *Der Teppich des Lebens* celebrates the powers of a heroically conceived mankind that have created the vitality and beauty of human culture. In *Der Siebente Ring* the stance becomes more aggressive. The section called "Zeitgedichte" ("Poems of Our Times") bitterly reproaches modern man for not acknowledging his sublime potential to grow beyond the conditions of necessity and for failing to recognize harbingers of a higher destiny, such as

Dante, Goethe, and Nietzsche, culminating in dire warnings of what will come if men remain blind to the life of the spirit, to their own innate divinity. For G., the life and death of "Maximin," celebrated in the central section of *Der Siebente Ring*, were exemplary proofs of the spiritual and corporeal perfection of which humanity is capable.

Der Stern des Bundes (1913; *The Star of the Covenant*, 1949) combines scathing condemnation of modern culture and thought with apodictic precepts for an elect brotherhood of the best of the nation's youth who are to propagate and realize in their time the ideal, which G. saw embodied in "Maximin." The prophetic role of the poet, much like Nietzsche's Zarathustra, is definitively elaborated in G.'s last collection, *Das Neue Reich* (1928; *The Kingdom Come*, 1949), in such major poems as "Der Krieg" ("The War"), "Der Dichter in Zeiten der Wirren" ("The Poet in Times of Confusion"), and "Geheimes Deutschland" ("Secret Germany"). The closing section of the volume is notable for lyrics of gnomic profundity and an arrestingly simple beauty.

As the proponent of the formal and ideological values of symbolism in Germany, G., despite his esotericism and exclusivity, was an influential and controversial personality. A dedicated opponent of dehumanizing materialism in culture, of epigonism and naturalism in art, he strove to keep alive the classical ideals of the supremacy of spirit over matter, of form over feeling. The forceful compression of G.'s style left a lasting mark on German lyric poetry, especially among the expressionists (q.v.). The rigorous and absolute standards for ethical conduct that G. set in his life and works are best exemplified by the fact that his close friend Count Claus Schenk von Stauffenberg (1907–1944), sacrificed his life as a conspirator in the plot to assassinate Adolf Hitler on July 20, 1944, a deed that has been described by Claude David as *the* gesture that puts G.'s thought into perspective."

FURTHER WORKS: *Die Fibel* (1901; *The Primer*, 1974); *Tage und Taten* (1903); *Schlußband* (1934); *Briefwechsel zwischen G. und Hofmannsthal* (1938); *S. G.–Friedrich Gundolf Briefwechsel* (1962). FURTHER VOLUMES IN ENGLISH: *The Works of S. G.* (1949; 2nd rev. and enl. ed., 1974); *S. G. in fremden Sprachen* (1973; contains English translations)

BIBLIOGRAPHY: Gundolf, F., *G.* (1920); David, C., *S. G.: Son œuvre poétique* (1952); Boehringer, R., *Mein Bild von S. G.* (1953); Goldsmith, U. K., *S. G.: A Study of His Early Work* (1959); Landmann, G. P., *S. G. und sein Kreis: Eine Bibliographie* (1960; 2nd rev. and enl. ed., 1976); Morwitz, E., *Kommentar zu dem Werk S. G.s* (1960); Landmann, E., *Gespräche mit S. G.* (1963); Schultz, H. S., *Studien zur Dichtung S. G.s* (1967); Winkler, M., *S. G.* (1970); Metzger, M. M. and E. A., *S. G.* (1972)

MICHAEL M. METZGER
ERIKA A. METZGER

GEORGIAN LITERATURE

Three main trends may be distinguished in Georgian literature during the 19th c.: romanticism (with the concomitant expressions of longing for individual and national freedom), best exemplified by the poet Nikoloz Baratashvili (1817–1845); nationalist realism, represented by numerous writers, most notably Ilia Chavchavadze (1837–1907) and Akaki Tsereteli (1840–1915); and a genre unparalleled in most European literatures with the exception of Albanian, namely, an idealized evocation of the traditional values of isolated mountain tribes, combined with elements of folklore and customary law. The two foremost writers in this genre were Alexander Qazbegi (1848–1893) and Vazha Pshavela (1861–1915). Pshavela's work in particular shows great depth of psychological insight and the endeavor to come to grips with philosophical and ethical problems in a manner not to be found in Georgian literature up to his time.

At the beginning of the 20th c., until about 1914, social concerns make up the primary thematic material of the school of "democratic poets," especially Irodion Evdoshvili (1873–1916). During World War I a group of young poets organized under the name Blue Horns produced work of fine sensitivity influenced by the ideas and style of French symbolism (q.v.). Their movement was a reaction to the realism that had dominated Georgian literature during the several preceding decades. The leading writer of this group was Galaktion Tabidze (q.v.), while the outstanding writer and philosopher Grigol Robakidse (q.v.) acted as its guiding spirit. Other noted poets who belonged to the Blue Horns—and who were later to adapt to the demands of the Soviet regime—included Valerian Gaprindashvili (1889–1941), Titsian Tabidze (1895–1937), Giorgi Leonidze (1899–1966), and Paolo Iashvili (1895–1937).

They and their fellow writers published extensively in the Blue Horn journals *Bakhtriani* and *Barikadebi*.

Georgia, which had been under Russian domination since 1801, declared its independence at the beginning of 1918, following the 1917 Russian Revolution. The new state and its social-democratic government were recognized *de jure* and *de facto* by most of the nations of the world, including Soviet Russia, and the next three years were extremely fruitful ones for young Georgian authors of all literary schools and persuasions. Impetus was given to artistic development by the foundation of a university in the capital, Tbilisi, and the official policies of freedom of press, speech, and expression, as guaranteed by the Georgian constitution, were utilized to advantage, resulting in a spate of literary creativity in all genres. The proliferation of literary and political journals and newspapers provided ample outlets for poets, prose writers, and dramatists. Much new and interesting work was also in evidence within the fields of children's literature, humor, and satire.

This remarkable burgeoning of creative expression in diverse modes was abruptly halted by the Soviet Russian invasion of Georgia in February 1921. The assault by the Red Army came despite mutual nonaggression treaties and other legal instruments signed by Lenin himself, which guaranteed the independence and sovereignty of Georgia. The newly established Soviet regime rapidly imposed the precepts of Socialist Realism (q.v.) on all genres of Georgian literature and put an end to experimentation. Coincident with the Russian invasion and lasting for a brief time into the 1920s was a futurist (q.v.) movement in Georgian literature. Similar in precepts to the Russian futurists, the Georgian group called for the destruction of classical forms and the propagation of a special type of language based on arbitrary usage and invented words having no objective reference. Authors who were later to become well known for more staid literary productions, such as Simone Chikovani (1903–1966) and Demna Shengelaia (b. 1896) were members of this movement, and their work was published in the journals H_2SO_4 and *Memartskheneoba*.

Soon after the consolidation of Soviet power in Georgia, the leading poets and novelists of the country were constrained to come to terms with the new political exigencies. Galaktion Tabidze, the greatest poet of his generation remaining in Georgia, was obliged to turn from symbolism and lyricism to the production of such poems as "Revolutsionuri Sakartvelo" (1931; revolutionary Georgia) and the cycles "Epoka" (1930; the epoch) and "Patsipizmi" (1930; pacifism), which embodied the Party line at the expense of individual creativity. Other members of the Blue Horn movement, such as the sensitive lyricist Paolo Iashvili, as well as Titsian Tabidze, Giorgi Leonidze, and Valerian Gaprindashvili, were pressed into service to the state and forced to produce propagandistic trivia. Not only were the extent of their subject matter and variety of style reduced to the barest minimum, but their earlier work was forbidden to be reprinted. For some, conditions of literary existence became too suffocating. Iashvili, for example, committed suicide in 1937 at the age of forty-two; Titsian Tabidze died in the same year and at the same age under mysterious circumstances; and in 1959 Galaktion Tabidze—according to popular report—committed suicide, although the authorities simply reported that he had fallen out of a window.

The only way around Party dogmatics after 1921 in Georgian literature lay in the utilization of historical themes and in the heroic folk genre of Vazha Pshavela. Of ideological necessity, certain "messages" had to be conveyed in this type of writing also, in particular the supposedly exploitative nature of the feudal system in medieval Georgia and the ever-present "class struggle." Despite these constraints, however, a number of well-written and interesting works, primarily novels, began to appear in the 1930s. The acknowledged master of the historical novel was Konstantine Gamsakhurdia (q.v.), whose massive work *Didostatis mardjvena* (1939; the right hand of the master), re-creating the life of Georgia in the 10th and 11th cs., established the genre on a firm footing; indeed, it remains one of the best examples of this type of writing in Georgian.

The official Party line on history and social development was promulgated during the 1930s by a large number of novels, such as Leo Kiacheli's (1884–1963) *Gvadi Bigva* (1938; Gvadi Bigva), a humorous work about peasant life; Alexandre Kutateli's (b. 1897) *Pirispir* (1933–43; face to face), a four-volume work woven of completely and deliberately falsified historical "facts" regarding the 1921 Soviet invasion of Georgia, its prelude, and its aftermath; and Ilia Lisashvili's (b. 1897) *Ketskhoveli* (1941; Ketskhoveli), about the origins and subsequent organization of the Communist movement in Georgia.

The dramatic arts during this period were represented by such playwrights as Polikarp

Kakabadze (1895–1972), whose comedy on social themes, *Qvarqvare Tutaberi* (1928; Qvarqvare Tutaberi) was widely performed and remains in the repertory of the Georgian theater; I. Vakeli (b. 1900), a "proletarian" author specializing in themes dealing with the lives of Georgian workers following the Communist takeover, but also treating historical subjects, as in his *Shamil* (1935; Shamil); and the Georgian-Jewish writer Hertsel Baazov (1904–1937), known for his play *Itska Rizhinashvili* (c. 1935; Itska Rizhinashvili), among others, and for his novel—unique in Georgian literature—*Petkhain* (1935; Petkhain), which depicted the life of the Jewish quarter of Tbilisi and gave an acute, if necessarily slanted insight into the conflicts between the traditional values and religious life of the Georgian Jews and the new realities imposed upon them by the Soviet regime. Baazov himself died in prison, victimized because of his father's open and avowed Zionism. Many other plays were written and produced in the 1930s, but few were marked by anything more than a slavish adherence to standard Communist ideology. Just like the other arts, drama was used simply as a vehicle to further the propagandizing of the Party line.

World War II created a need for highly patriotic and antifascist literature. As in the other republics of the Soviet Union, so in Georgia writers had to serve the country's requirements. Aside from the more usual displays of patriotic fervor in verse, fiction, and drama, several works of a more nationalistic and historical character appeared. (Indeed the two are inseparable in a Soviet context: nationalism may only be expressed in a historical framework as synonymous with antimonarchism or antifeudalism; its expression in a contemporary framework, that is, as related to conditions within the Soviet Union, is a punishable crime.) Such were an epic poem about the 18th-c. poet Davit Guramishvili (1705–1792) by Simone Chikovani (b. 1903) and a poem on the medieval Georgian king David the Builder by L. Gotua (b. 1905), who also wrote a historical play, *Mepe Irakli* (1944; King Irakli).

The years immediately following World War II saw relatively little change in the tenor of Georgian literature. While there was less conspicuously antifascist work produced, novels, as well as stories and poems with war themes continued unabated. Hymns and odes to Stalin were also composed in incredible numbers, as were other works incorporating the usual Party dogmatics. Once again, only literature utilizing historical motifs as a mode of expressing both creativity and national pride could be consid-

ered worthy of notice, such as M. Mrevlishvili's (b. 1904) play, *Nikoloz Baratashvili* (c. 1950; Nikoloz Baratashvili) about the great 19th-c. Georgian romantic poet who was called the "Byron of Georgia," and I. Vakeli's play, *Mepe Tamara* (c. 1950; Queen Tamara).

After Stalin's death and the subsequent, if temporary, relaxation of certain ideological restrictions under Khrushchev, Georgian literature exhibited an expansion of thematic material. Historical novels still remained the most important genre, little troubled by overt ideological considerations. Foremost among these is the remarkable tetralogy *Davit Aghmashenebeli* (1946–54; David the Builder) by Konstantine Gamsakhurdia, which re-creates the life and times of the greatest king of Georgia during the country's golden age in the early medieval period. Also worthy of mention are Grigol Abashidze's (b. 1914) *Lasharela* (1957; Lasharela) and *Grdzeli ghame* (1963; the long night), which describes the sufferings and heroism of the Georgians during successive invasions by the Persians and Mongols.

Among the first prose works to appear in Georgia that dealt with contemporary life and yet had no overbearing political message to impart were three novels by Nodar Dumbadze (b. 1928): *Me, babia, Iliko da Ilarioni* (1958; I, grandmother, Iliko, and Ilarion), *Me vkhedav mzes* (1962; I See the Sun, 1968) and *Mziani ghame* (1967; The Sunny Night, 1968). Although of slight literary stature, these short humorous works dealing with student life in present-day Tbilisi show a refreshing departure from ideological concerns and are meant quite simply to entertain—a consideration that had not concerned publishing in Georgia since 1921.

Georgian poetry also began to show signs of renewed vigor in the late 1950s, a trend that continues, although some constraints have become evident in recent years. Themes of Georgian, as opposed to Soviet, nationalism have become more marked and more open, for example, Irakli Abashidze's (b. 1909) cycles "Rustavelis nakvalebze" (c. 1960–66; on the traces of Rustaveli) and "Palestina, Palestina" (c. 1960–66; Palestine, Palestine). Among the younger generation of poets, perhaps the most important in terms of both literary expression and freedom of thematic material is Ana Kalandadze (b. 1924). Her work evokes nature in all its manifestations, as well as the more personal world of the experiences of love.

Dramatic writing in Georgia has remained the weakest literary form. Vakeli, Mrevlishvili, and others have continued to add to the repertory, but it is indicative of the state of the art that Robert Sturua, director of the prestigious and internationally acclaimed Rustaveli Theater of Tbilisi, stated in a 1980 interview with a Georgian newspaper that the standard of Georgian drama is such that he prefers to stage Shakespeare and Brecht (q.v.). Sturua did not mention the fact that the greatest play in Georgian, *Lamara* (c. 1925; Lamara) by Grigol Robakidse, produced to outstanding acclaim in the early 1920s, is still banned in Georgia, together with all other works by this extraordinary writer, despite the fact that *Lamara* is based on elements of Georgian folk tradition and contains nothing that could be considered subversive to the Soviet regime.

An extremely successful and well-produced television drama was given in Georgia in the late 1970s based on the novel *Data Tutashkhia* (1973–75; Data Tutashkhia) by the talented author Chabua Amiredjibi (b. 1921). Drawing upon historical material, the novel and play tell the story of an early-19th-c. folk hero who, like Robin Hood, fought the forces of oppression in Georgia together with a band of devoted confederates.

Despite the extraordinary ideological constraints placed upon Georgian authors since the advent of Soviet rule in 1921, two forces have continued to play a major role in tempering the character of Georgian literature: intense nationalism and the fiercely independent nature of the Georgian people. Working within the imposed framework of Communist literary norms, Georgian authors have found ways of enlarging the scope of their creative work by relying on these forces and imbuing their work with them. In the area of unofficial writing, comparatively little Georgian *samizdat* has reached the West, most of it in the photocopied journal *Sakartvelos moambe*. Although the contributions in this journal are not primarily literary in nature, being concerned with human rights particularly, the same two forces of nationalism and independence are very much in evidence. This unwavering tenacity of the Georgians to stress continually their cultural and historical uniqueness continues to find eloquent expression in the best work of their prose writers and poets.

LEONARD FOX

See also North Caucasian Literatures

GERMAN LITERATURE

The Political and Literary Background

The political configuration of the world and the social conditions of the human race changed radically during the century preceding World War II. The changes were more frequent and more abrupt in Germany than in any other Western country. Germany's unification and its victory in the Franco-Prussian War (1870–71) were followed by two decades of peace, prosperity, and increasing national pride under Bismarck, a trend that continued until World War I. The defeat of 1918 shattered the nation's political and economic stability. The founding of Germany's first democratic government, the Weimar Republic (1919), restored a semblance of order, but resentment over the terms of the Treaty of Versailles, as well as the economic chaos of the postwar years, undermined the stability of the republic and contributed to the growth of the Nazi and Marxist movements. The impact of the Great Depression was later added to these phenomena. The German republic died when Hitler assumed power in 1933. The state of the economy improved and by the end of the decade Hitler enjoyed the support of most Germans who had not fled the country or been imprisoned. The effects of the military collapse and unconditional surrender in 1945 greatly surpassed those of 1918. Now Germany faced not only economic privation and the loss of territory, but also national shame, as details of the Nazi policy of genocide became known. The division into eastern and western occupation zones widened into a gulf, and in 1949 two separate German states were founded, the capitalist German Federal Republic and the communist German Democratic Republic (both at the time still closely regulated by the Western Allies and the Soviets, respectively).

The volatile political situation strongly influenced the development of 20th-c. German literature. The years preceding World War I witnessed an increasing tension between writers of conservative, nationalistic persuasion and a smaller but untimately more significant group of progressives and socialists. The war produced both visionaries and authors with realistic perspectives, although there was little unity or consistency within either group. During the 1930s most writers of the first rank emigrated. Moscow, Los Angeles, and New York became the new centers of German literature, and small groups or isolated individuals sought safety throughout the world, from New Zealand to Brazil. With very few exceptions, the works written in exile were a direct reflection of the political situation, although the points of view and emphases differ according to the individual author's reason for leaving Germany (most were communists or Jews; some were anti-Nazi humanists). Even much contemporary literature constitutes a reaction to Germany's past history or current political situation. And finally, many promising young German writers met violent deaths, while serving in the armed forces in both world wars, or as victims of the Nazis. Especially significant was the loss, during World War I, of a number of writers who later could have been counted on to provide artistic leadership and continuity.

The political birth of the German nation in 1870 coincided with a literary nadir. A score of major authors were born during the first two decades of the 19th c., but few remained active in the 1870s, and only one, Theodor Fontane (1819–1898), lived past 1890. No writers who today enjoy widespread recognition were born between 1830 and 1860, with the exception of Friedrich Nietzsche (1844–1900), known primarily as a philosopher, and Wilheim Raabe (1831–1910) and Detlev von Liliencron (1844–1909), whose claim to "major" status is dubious at best. The resulting literary vacuum was first filled by two very different writers born in the 1860s, Gerhart Hauptmann and Stefan George (qq.v.).

Hauptmann's *Vor Sonnenaufgang* (1889; *Before Dawn*, 1909) created a sensation. To be sure, this play was indebted to German as well as foreign sources. Yet, given the weak position of German literature in the 1870s and 1880s, it is understandable that inspiration and direction were sought abroad, and during the 1880s several minor writers attempted to introduce French naturalism in Germany—the novels of Émile Zola were especially admired and imitated. Henrik Ibsen exerted a strong influence on the development of the drama. In addition, the theories of Charles Darwin were rapidly gaining attention. *Vor Sonnenaufgang*, the first major work of German naturalism, established a pattern for many dramas of the 1890s, in its careful attention to realistic detail, concern with the lower and middle classes, and portrayal of the disintegration of a family, with emphasis on the negative effects of heredity. The principal theoretician of German naturalism, Arno Holz (1863–1929), attempted to reduce art to an exact reproduction of life, as in the formula "art = nature − x," in which x is the inevitable subjective factor occasioned by the participation of the artist. Hauptmann produced, in addition to several minor naturalist dramas, two great ones, the historical tragedy *Die Weber* (1892; *The Weavers*, 1899) and the comedy *Der Biberpelz* (1893; *The Beaver Coat*, 1912). Otherwise, naturalism is only of historical interest, as a transitional stage between the vacuum of the preceding decades and the realistic, socially critical literature of the 20th c.

Simultaneous with Hauptmann's promulgation of a socially conscious literature written in the naturalist style were the radically different innovations of Stefan George. An avowed disciple of the French symbolists (q.v.), George had no precursors in Germany. In 1890 he published his first collection of verse, *Hymnen* (*Odes*, 1949), and by the end of the decade was recognized by a small and elite, but nonetheless important group as Germany's leading poet. His direct influence was limited, and his austere, finely chiseled verse found few imitators beyond his own circle. But his admiration for the symbolists and for Nietzsche came to be shared, at least to some extent, by many German writers of the 20th c. George's circle of intimates included several of Germany's leading intellectuals, including the literary critics Friedrich Gundolf (1880–1931) and Max Kommerell (1902–1944).

1900–20: From Impressionism to Expressionism

Much of the literature of the first two decades of the century constitutes a revolt against the premises, attitudes, and intellectual background of naturalism. Nietzsche replaced Darwin as the most important mentor for German writers. The terms impressionism, neoromanticism, symbolism, neoclassicism, and expressionism (q.v.) are often used to categorize various authors who participated in the revolt against the naturalists' emphasis on the ugly side of human nature and modern life. All are useful, although only expressionism, which dominated the 1910s, represents a coherent literary movement.

Poetry

Detlev von Liliencron, who established his reputation in the 1880s and continued to write into the 20th c., was the most accomplished of the impressionist poets. His poems, not unlike impressionist paintings, capture the essence of a scene. Sound and image are carefully integrated in his precisely wrought verse. The poetry of Richard Dehmel (1863–1920), who was originally sympathetic to both Nietzsche and the naturalists, combined social consciousness and eros, nature and spirit, an awareness of the ugly, chaotic aspects of life and the belief that art is capable of providing refinement and order. The irrationalistic impulse is even stronger in other poets, including Else Lasker-Schüler (1869–1945), a forerunner of expressionism, whose first collection, *Styx* (Styx) was published in 1902. Her poems are alternately whimsical and visionary; individual images assume an increasing degree of autonomy, and free verse tends to replace traditional forms. Other visionary poets of the period were Max Dauthendey (1867–1918), whose sensual poetry is rich in imagery; Theodor Däubler (1876–1934), best known for *Das Nordlicht* (1910; the northern lights), a lyrical epic poem of some thirty thousand lines; Alfred Mombert (1872–1942), the author of *Der himmlische Zecher* (1909; the heavenly carouser) and other collections of ecstatic verse; and Christian Morgenstern (q.v.), remembered today almost exclusively for his "gallows songs," *Galgenlieder* (1905; *Galgenlieder* 1964), which are in turn whimsical, grotesque, and parodistic.

Toward the end of the first decade of the century, the beginnings of the expressionist movement began to take shape. Marinetti's (q.v.) futurism (q.v.) influenced its development, as did the numerous works of aesthetic theory defending visionary "expressive" art over mimetic art. The journals *Der Sturm* (founded in 1910) and *Die Aktion* (founded in 1911), edited by Herwarth Walden (1878–1941) and Franz Pfemfert (1879–1959), respectively, were immediately recognized as the voices of modernist aesthetics. Among the first expressionist poets published in them were Jakob van Hoddis (1887–1942) and Alfred Lichtenstein (1889–1914). Georg Heym (1887–1912), Ernst Stadler (1883–1914), and the Austrian Georg Trakl (q.v.) were the most accomplished expressionist poets. Their early deaths —Heym's accidental, Stadler's and Trakl's in the war—had a profound detrimental effect on the development of the German lyric. Heym's verse, collected in *Der ewige Tag* (1911; the eternal day) and *Umbra vitae* (1912; Latin: shadow of life), utilizes strikingly original images to express a dark vision of impending cataclysm. The growth—and evils—of the city, and modern man's loss of substance are common themes. Heym's traditional meter and rhyme stand in sharp contrast to modernist images and content. Stadler's verse is no more mimetic than Heym's, but his vision is less pessimistic, and the effect of his long dithyrambic lines, which are reminiscent of Walt Whitman's, is not as dependent on the presence of autonomous images. Another important early expressionist was the physician Gottfried Benn (q.v.), now better known for his later works, whose first poems, *Morgue* (1912; morgue), created a sensation because of their morbid subject matter.

Soon after the beginning of the war one branch of expressionism turned to sociopolitical problems. The ecstatic verse of these poets expressed pacifist and socialist sentiments. One, Johannes R. Becher (1891–1958), was later to become president of the Academy of the Arts in East Germany. A smaller group moved in the opposite direction, toward linguistic experimentation. From the terse, ejaculatory style of August Stramm (q.v.) it is but a small step to the nonsensical antiart of the Dadaism (q.v.) of Hans Arp (1887–1966), Richard Huelsenbeck (1892–1974), and others. The diversity of the expressionist movement is illustrated by Kurt Pinthus's (1886–1975) anthology *Menschheitsdämmerung* (1919; dawn of mankind), in which twenty-three poets, from Däubler and Lasker-Schüler to Becher and Stramm, are represented.

The conservative tradition in poetry was very much alive during the first two decades of the century, although its representatives are today overshadowed by the progressive and avantgarde writers discussed above. Rudolf Alexander Schröder (1878–1962), who published religious and patriotic verse and translations of classical authors, was one of the most prolific and highly respected of these writers. The ballad, which was popular during the age of Goethe, enjoyed a renascence in the early 20th c. Börries von Münchhausen (1874–1945) and Lulu von Strauss und Torney (1873–1948) wrote some of the finest examples of this form.

Drama

At the beginning of the century the drama of Austria—Hugo von Hofmannsthal, Arthur Schnitzler (qq.v.)—overshadowed that of Germany. With the exception of Hauptmann, who remained a prolific and respected playwright, most German dramatists of the period—impressionists and neoclassicists—are largely forgotten today. One exception is Frank Wedekind (q.v.), an irreverent social critic whose scathing attacks against middle-class morality made him a hero of many progressives, especially those of the younger generation, as well as a favorite target of government censors. During the 1910s Germany (and especially Berlin) assumed a position of international prominence in the theater. The formal and stylistic innovations of the expressionist dramatists and the imaginative direction and stage craft of Max Reinhardt (1873–1943), an Austrian active in Berlin, and, some time later, Erwin Piscator (1893–1966), gained worldwide recognition.

The plays of Carl Sternheim (q.v.) constitute a transition from impressionism to expressionism. A modern Molière, Sternheim mercilessly lampooned the German middle class. Materialistic values and narrow-mindedness are the hallmarks of the bourgeois heroes of *Die Hose* (1911; *A Pair of Drawers*, 1927; new tr., *The Underpants*, 1960) and other popular plays.

The drama of expressionism, which was indebted to Wedekind and the Swedish August Strindberg (q.v.) as well as to Sternheim, leaves realism behind. The language is highly charged—an ejaculatory "telegram style" replaces realistic dialogue—and the structure is loose, as a series of "stations" replace traditional acts and scenes. Furthermore, the characters are not individuals but types. One of the dramas most representative of the movement is Reinhard Sorge's (1892–1916) *Der Bettler* (1912; *The Beggar*, 1963), in which the protagonist (identified only as "the poet" and "the son") attempts, unsuccessfully, to establish a new artistic and social order. Similar in many respects, although more traditionally structured, is Walter Hasenclever's (1890–1940) *Der Sohn* (1914; the son).

The call for a rebirth of mankind, sounded in Sorge and Hasenclever, remains important in later expressionist drama. A strong religious element is present in the plays of Ernst Barlach (q.v.). Georg Kaiser (q.v.), the leading dramatist of the era, typically retained the vision of the "new man" while utilizing a more traditional structure. Later expressionist dramas often added a political dimension to calls for moral rebirth. The most significant of these works is *Masse Mensch* (1921; *Masses and Man*, 1923) by Ernst Toller (q.v.), which portrays, in a highly expressionist style, the conflict between the necessity of revolution and the legitimate rights of the individual.

By the mid-1920s, expressionist drama had ceased to be a major force in German literature. Its influence, however, was immense; among the many major dramatists who later utilized and refined expressionist techniques are Bertolt Brecht, Thornton Wilder, Eugène Ionesco, Samuel Beckett, Max Frisch, and Friedrich Dürrenmatt (qq.v.).

Fiction

The development of poetry and drama from an ill-defined impressionist idiom to an exuberant expressionist style during the second decade of the century, was not paralleled in fiction. The expressionists generally found prose less suited to their purposes than poetry and drama (indeed, it has been said that expressionist prose is almost a contradiction in terms). Furthermore, Theodor Fontane provided a viable model for young novelists, a model that poets and dramatists did not have. The most important work to spring from this background was Thomas Mann's (q.v.) *Buddenbrooks* (1901; *Buddenbrooks*, 1924), a novel of truly epic proportions that traces four generations of a north-German family in a style that is realistic in detail but not without impressionist elements. Mann's novellas, including the six stories of *Tristan* (1903; Tristan) and *Der Tod in Venedig* (1913; *Death in Venice,* 1925), offer subtle studies of the conflict between the artistic and bourgeois worlds. These works represent the culmination of the impressionist tradition in Germany. Friedrich Huch (1873–1913) also wrote several successful novels in this style. Eduard Graf Keyserling (1855–1918) is perhaps the best known of the many other authors influenced by Fontane. His impressionistic novels and stories, set in northeastern Germany and dealing with tragic love relationships, enjoyed considerable popularity at the time.

Many novelists aligned themselves with neoromanticism. Typical of these writers is an interest in German history, Germanic mythology, and the supernatural; a favorite theme is the struggle of the individual, often an artist, for self-fulfillment. The foremost representative of this group is Ricarda Huch (q.v.), whose works include several historical novels; the novel *Vita somnium breve* (1903; Latin: life is a short dream), in which a young man is torn between his sense of responsibility to his family and his yearning for freedom and beauty; and an outstanding two-volume scholarly study, *Die Romantik* (1899, 1902; romanticism). The early works of Hermann Hesse (q.v.) are likewise firmly rooted in the neoromantic tradition. The novels of Jakob Wassermann (q.v.), which are rich in psychological insight, contain neoromantic elements.

This period also witnessed the rise of the novel of social and political commitment. Heinrich Mann (q.v.), the brother of Thomas, achieved his first success with a satirical attack against the bourgeoisie, *Professor Unrat* (1905; *Small Town Tyrant,* 1944) and later wrote directly political novels portraying, from a leftist perspective, the conflicts of Wilhelmine Germany.

For the most part the expressionists eschewed prose fiction. Notable exceptions are two collections of novellas (as they are inappropriately labeled in the subtitles) written in an expressionistic style by authors known primarily as lyric poets, Heym's *Der Dieb* (1913; the thief) and Benn's *Gehirne* (1916; brains).

1920-45: Weimar and Hitler

In spite of the economic and political instability, a rich and diverse German literature flourished in the Weimar Republic. As the vision of the expressionists began to fade in the mid-1920s, many authors turned to the realistic style of *Neue Sachlichkeit* (new factualism); but literary pluralism reigned, and Marxists, centrists, and members of the non-Nazi right alike produced memorable works. Upon Hitler's assumption of power in 1933 internal opposition to the Nazis ceased. The writers forced into exile ranged from apolitical assimilated Jews to active Marxists, who in many cases had previously had nothing in common. To be sure, they were not transformed into a homogeneous group upon leaving Germany. But as exiles they virtually all shared financial insecurity, a keen awareness of the significance of politics, and the sense of alienation and rootlessness brought about by being suddenly thrust into a foreign culture. Furthermore, as writers they suffered greatly from the loss of daily contact with the German language. All of these factors are consistently reflected, directly or indirectly, in their works.

Within Germany, only two kinds of literature were sanctioned: that which directly supported Nazi policies, and apolitical works. Enormous quantities of political literature were published, including fiction by Hans Grimm (1875–1959) and Hans Blunck (1888–1961), dramas by Hanns Johst (b. 1890) and Hans Rehberg (1901–1963), and poetry by Will Vesper (1882–1962) and Baldur von Schirach (1907–1974) extolling the virtues of the German people and nation or excoriating the Jews and Marxists. Nazi writers produced nothing of lasting value, and they are now of interest only to literary sociologists.

Many accomplished writers remained in Germany. A few, notably Gottfried Benn and Ernst Jünger (q.v.), were at first favorably disposed toward the Nazis, but the majority stayed for a variety of other reasons. Those who did not emigrate but were unsympathetic to Hitler came to be referred to, collectively, as the "inner emigration." Most wrote apolitical works, traditional in style and form (primarily religious poetry and historical novels with neutral settings). Some clandestinely composed anti-Nazi works that remained unpublished

until after the war. Occasionally a concealed attack against the regime slipped by the censors and appeared in print, such as Jünger's *Auf den Marmorklippen* (1939; *On the Marble Cliffs*, 1947) and portions of Hauptmann's House of Atreus tetralogy (1941–48).

Poetry

Little poetry of lasting significance was published in the Weimar Republic. Rudolf Alexander Schröder, Ina Seidel (1885–1974), Gertrude von Le Fort (1876–1971), and others, continued to write traditional, often religious verse. Konrad Weiss (1880–1940) and Oskar Loerke (1884–1941) penned some outstanding nature poetry. Among the works by younger writers, Brecht's *Hauspostille* (1927; *Manual of Piety,* 1966), a collection of satirical social criticism, stands out, along with the chansons of the talented and versatile Kurt Tucholsky (q.v.). The lyric did, on the other hand, prove to be an appropriate vehicle for many of the exiles, including the Jewish authors Else Lasker-Schüler, Karl Wolfskehl (1869–1948), and Yvan Goll (1891–1950). Among the members of the inner emigration who turned to the lyric were the religious poets Reinhold Schneider (1903–1958) and Albrecht Goes (q.v.), and Wilhelm Lehmann (1882–1968), whose mystical nature poetry received critical acclaim only after the war. Friedrich Georg Jünger (1908–1977), the brother of Ernst, wrote tightly structured verse based on classical models. The Jewish Gertrud Kolmar (q.v.), one of the outstanding poets of her generation, remained in Germany and continued to write until she was taken to a concentration camp. Most of her work was published posthumously.

Drama

The German theater maintained its dynamism and diversity during the short life of the Weimar Republic, as Kaiser, Toller, and others continued to write expressionist dramas into the 1920s, and Hauptmann's more traditional plays were enthusiastically received. The first important new face to emerge was Brecht. *Baal* (1918; *Baal,* 1963) and *Trommeln in der Nacht* (1918; *Drums in the Night,* 1961) contained expressionist elements, but Brecht soon abandoned this style in favor of a more directly political drama. *Die Dreigroschenoper* (1928; *The Threepenny Opera,* 1955) and *Aufstieg und Fall der Stadt Mahagonny* (1929; *The Rise and Fall of the City of Mahagonny,*

1976), anticapitalistic works set to music by Kurt Weill (1900–1950), and several short didactic plays with a specifically Marxist slant were produced between 1928 and 1933. *Die Matrosen von Cattaro* (1930; *The Sailors of Cattaro*, 1935) by Friedrich Wolf (q.v.) is the most significant of the numerous other dramas of the period reflecting a leftist position. Carl Zuckmayer (q.v.) enjoyed a reputation equal to Brecht's during the final years of the Weimar Republic. In the comedies *Der fröhliche Weinberg* (1925; the joyful vineyard) and *Der Hauptmann von Köpenick* (1931; *The Captain of Köpenick,* 1932) a realistic portrayal of simple people is combined with effective satire against nationalism and militarism.

Little noteworthy drama was written during the Hitler years. The theater in Germany was highly political, and the inner emigrants accordingly turned to other genres. The exiles, too, preferred other forms, the one significant exception being Brecht. In several major dramas written in exile, including *Mutter Courage und ihre Kinder* (1939; *Mother Courage and Her Children,* 1941) and *Der gute Mensch von Sezuan* (1938–41; *The Good Woman of Setzuan,* 1948), Brecht developed his concept of the antiillusionary drama.

Fiction

During the 1920s several established authors rose to new heights. Thomas Mann turned to the novel of ideas in *Der Zauberberg* (1924; *The Magic Mountain,* 1927), and Hermann Hesse, now under the influence of Nietzsche and C. G. Jung (q.v.), received critical and public acclaim for *Demian* (1919; *Demian,* 1923) and the novels that followed. Simultaneously, a new generation of novelists appeared who abandoned realistic chronological narration. This movement, to some extent influenced by such writers as James Joyce and John Dos Passos (qq.v.) and to some extent a parallel development, was stronger in Austria than in Germany. Major German examples include *Berlin Alexanderplatz* (1929; *Alexanderplatz, Berlin,* 1931) by Alfred Döblin (q.v.), and Hans Henny Jahnn's (q.v.) *Perrudja* (1929; Perrudja).

The realistic political and social novel was especially vigorous during the last years of the Weimar Republic. Erich Maria Remarque's (q.v.) *Im Westen nichts Neues* (1929; *All Quiet on the Western Front,* 1929) had no rivals as the most significant of the innumerable war (or antiwar) novels. Equally successful in Germany, if not internationally, was Hans Fallada's (1893–1947) *Kleiner Mann—was nun?* (1932; *Little Man, What Now?,* 1933), in which the life of average people during the inflationary period of the early 1920s is portrayed. A Marxist position is taken in Arnold Zweig's (q.v.) *Der Streit um den Sergeanten Grischa* (1927; *The Case of Sergeant Grischa,* 1928), Ludwig Renn's (1889–1979) *Krieg* (1928; *War,* 1929), and Anna Seghers's (q.v.) *Aufstand der Fischer von St. Barbara* (1928; *The Revolt of the Fishermen,* 1929). These three continued to write in exile and later assumed positions of leadership in the literary circles of the GDR. Seghers's concentration camp novel *Das siebte Kreuz* (1942; *The Seventh Cross,* 1942), her best-known work, was written and published in exile. Another important writer of the political left was Lion Feuchtwanger (q.v.), many of whose historical novels treat Jewish themes. Bruno Frank, Oskar Maria Graf, and Annette Kolb (qq.v.), all established authors prior to Hitler's assumption of power, continued to write in exile.

Ernst Jünger stands out among the conservative, nationalistic novelists of the 1920s. Others who were popular at the time and who, unlike Jünger, continued to write nationalistic works under Hitler, include Edwin Erich Dwinger (b. 1898) and Erwin Guido Kolbenheyer (1878–1962), a native of Budapest. Erich Kästner, Walter Bauer, Stefan Andres, Ernst Wiechert (qq.v.), and Werner Bergengruen (1892–1963) are important authors of the inner emigration.

1945–Present: New Directions

The military defeat of 1945 was followed by four years of political, economic, and artistic upheaval. Much that had been accepted under Hitler, from the currency and the form of government to philosophy and aesthetics, was banned by the allied occupational authorities. Even the German language itself seemed tainted to many, especially the exiles and members of the younger generation. The political situation in the Federal Republic stabilized in the early 1950s, as a strong democracy emerged under the leadership of Konrad Adenauer and the nation moved from destitution to prosperity—the so-called *Wirtschaftswunder* (economic miracle). The economy in Walter Ulbricht's GDR did not improve significantly until after the erection of the Berlin Wall in 1961.

Pro-Nazi writers were banned, but otherwise there was little cohesion in the West German literature of the late 1940s. Some critics referred to a *Nullpunkt* (zero point) of German literature in 1945 and advocated a *Kahlschlag* (clearing the thickets), a purification of the language and the concomitant rejection of the idealistic tradition. The former term is an expressive, but at best inadequate image; the latter captures the mood of one group of young writers but likewise fails to present a true picture of the complex West German literary scene. Traditional authors of the inner emigration continued to publish. Some of their works were apolitical, but others represented reactions to the German defeat and addressed the hotly debated subject of collective guilt. For the most part, only religious authors were able to find cause for optimism. A significant new dimension was added as the works of the exiles— Thomas Mann, Brecht, Zuckmayer, and others —began to appear in Germany for the first time since 1933. Almost immediately the influence of foreign writers banned under Hitler was felt, as such figures as Albert Camus, William Faulkner, Ernest Hemingway (qq.v.), and the French surrealists (q.v.) found admirers and imitators.

A new generation of writers soon made its presence felt. A leadership role was assumed by Hans Werner Richter (b. 1908). Together with Alfred Andersch (q.v.), Richter edited *Der Ruf* (1946–47), a liberal sociopolitical journal that served as the voice of Germany's disillusioned youth. When the occupational authorities revoked the journal's license, Richter called together several of his friends and colleagues. At the meeting, held in September 1947, the invited guests read from unpublished manuscripts and discussion followed. This marked the birth of the "Gruppe 47" (Group 47), which, under Richter's guidance, continued to meet once or twice a year until 1967 and during that time dominated the West German literary scene. Initially the group was a rather homogeneous collection of writers who shared Richter's preference for a realistic literature reflecting a socialist, but democratic point of view. Frank discussion invariably prevailed, and even established members were not spared. As the prestige of the group increased in the 1950s, so did the number of participants and the diversity of the works read at the meetings. By 1960 diversity had become the hallmark of the group, and the older writers who had been the angry young men of the 1940s came to be regarded as the "establishment" by some young participants.

Indeed, much had changed in West Germany during this time. The economic miracle was accompanied by an increasingly materialistic orientation and a sense of complacency in society at large. Many writers expressed first alarm and then disillusionment over the developments and began to attack the bourgeoisie with growing intensity. Few, however, turned to Marxism, for the Stalinist regime in the GDR did not seem to offer a viable alternative. Simultaneously, some authors began to experiment with the new modes of expression offered by concrete poetry, an international movement in which the importance of content, or plot, is greatly reduced and the sound and visual appearance of individual words assume a considerable degree of autonomy.

West German literature of the late 1950s and early 1960s was rich and pluralistic. Several new faces appeared who had little in common except their considerable talent and the speed with which they developed international reputations: Günter Grass, Uwe Johnson, Peter Weiss, Hans Magnus Enzensberger (qq.v.), and the cosmopolitan East Germans Johannes Bobrowski, Peter Huchel, and Christa Wolf (qq.v.). In the mid-1960s a new trend became noticeable. As a result of several factors, especially the hostility of students and intellectuals to the conservative university system, increasing concern over the Vietnam War, and a waxing sympathy to Marxism, many writers—young and old alike—began to espouse a revolutionary position in their works. Herbert Marcuse (1898–1979) was the idol of the younger generation, and the writings of Walter Benjamin and Theodor Adorno (qq.v.) exerted a strong influence, especially on intellectuals. In the 1970s a growing feminist movement also became a significant force.

From about 1965 on, the attention of many writers and critics turned to "realism," although there was (and is) little agreement on the nature of realist literature. Some proponents of a new realism understood the term in its popular meaning and utilized simple language and readily accessible themes in poetry, drama, and fiction alike. Walter Kempowski (b. 1929), for example, enjoyed several commercial and critical successes with his series of realistic autobiographical family novels. Dieter Wellershoff (b. 1925), Günter Herburger (b. 1932), and other members of the "Cologne School of New Realism" looked to the French New Novel (q.v.), while still others, taking a position from the debates of the 1930s in which Brecht and György Lukács (q.v.) were prominently involved, maintained that the complexities of the modern world can be adequately (and, hence, realistically) treated only by eschewing superficially realistic plots and style.

The development of the literature of East Germany was quite different. For a brief period after the end of the war, a degree of artistic freedom was allowed by the authorities, but after the founding of the GDR, writers were generally required to conform to Marxist ideals and aesthetic theories. Older, established figures dominated the scene: Arnold Zweig, Anna Seghers, Johannes R. Becher, and the maverick Bertolt Brecht, whose stature enabled him to maintain a modicum of independence. The situation changed somewhat in 1956, as the effects of the post-Stalin "thaw" were felt. Since that time, brief periods of tolerance on the part of the government have alternated with times of heavy-handed repression. Many of the best writers of the GDR were subjected to harassment, in spite of their professed allegiance to Marxism, and by late 1970s a significant number, including Wolf Biermann, Reiner Kunze (qq.v.), and Sara Kirsch (b. 1935) had emigrated to the West.

Poetry

Many of the first poets published in the West were older traditionalists, a majority of whom could be described as Christian humanists. With the horrors of the immediate past reflected in the elegiac tone of their verse, these poets faced the future with the muted hope of a moral rebirth of mankind. Important representatives of this group include Werner Bergengruen—*Dies irae* (1945; Latin: day of wrath) —Hans Carossa (q.v.), the younger Rudolf Hagelstange (b. 1912)—*Venezianisches Credo* (1945; Venetian credo)—and Hans Egon Holthusen (b. 1913), also a leading literary critic. Poetry of this kind soon lost favor, although it continued to be written well into the 1950s. A second type of lyric that was popular during the immediate postwar years was mystical nature poetry. The oldest and most influential member of this group, Wilhelm Lehmann, is a respected figure whose work seems destined to survive, although it is viewed as "escapist" by some critics. On the other hand, the works of many of his imitators lack substance and they are now rightly forgotten. Karl Krolow (q.v.), who later beecame one of Germany's most highly regarded literary figures, was one of the few younger poets of stature influenced by Lehmann.

There was little poetry that dealt in a direct and undisguised manner with the Nazi period during the years 1945–48. The first important exception is *Moabiter Sonette* (1946; *Moabit Sonnets,* 1978) by Albrecht Haushofer (1903–1945). Written in the Moabit prison in Berlin shortly before Haushofer's execution by the Nazis, these sonnets vividly convey the terrors of the time from the perspective of a political prisoner. The first postwar work of Nelly Sachs (q.v.), who barely managed to escape from Germany in 1940, is even more important. *In den Wohnungen des Todes* (1947; in the habitations of death) is a highly emotional reaction to the Holocaust from a Jewish perspective. Sachs continued to write until her death, and although her works became increasingly complex and mystical, the later poetry consistently reflects the themes present in her first poems. Günter Eich (q.v.) was another prominent poet of the period. Some of his poems deal directly with his experiences as a soldier and prisoner-of-war. His later work went through many phases, culminating in the short experimental prose poems, or texts, of *Maulwürfe* (1968; moles) and its sequel, *Ein Tibeter in meinem Büro: 49 Maulwürfe* (1970; a Tibetan in my office: 49 moles)

It would be difficult to overestimate the importance of the year 1948, when the first postwar books of several major figures appeared, including *Statische Gedichte* (static poems) by Gottfried Benn. Younger poets, fascinated by Benn's masterful use of language and poetic form, for the most part ignored the intellectual content of his work and began to imitate the form and language, with unfortunate results. Several of these poets gained brief fame during the 1950s, but practically all are forgotten today. Benn published several volumes of poetry in the following years and his influence grew rapidly. His essay *Probleme der Lyrik* (1951; problems of poetry) was the most significant theoretical document of the decade.

The years 1952–53 marked the debut of a group of important new poets, including Walter Höllerer, Hans Piontek (qq.v.), Peter Härtling (b. 1933), and Johannes Poethen (b. 1928), and three who are not, strictly speaking, West Germans, but who are in no sense regional authors: Paul Celan (q.v.), a native of Romania, Ingeborg Bachmann (q.v.), an Austrian, and Eugen Gomringer (b. 1925), a truly international figure who was born in Bolivia. Poethen and others, including Ernst Meister (1911–1979) and Max Hölzer (b. 1915), are generally classified, for lack of a better term, as "surrealist" poets. While they clearly do not follow rigidly the theories of the French surrealists, the work of the two groups does have much in common, most notably the use of metaphors and the dreamlike quality of the poems. Höllerer, Piontek, Walter Helmut Fritz (b. 1929), Hans-Jürgen Heise (b. 1930), Hilde Domin (q.v.), Christoph Meckel (b. 1935), and many other poets of this talented generation sought a personal idiom, free of rigid philosophical, literary, or political dogma; their work is modern, but not avant-garde. Meckel, a prolific as well as accomplished writer, is also a graphic artist who has illustrated many of his collections of prose and poetry.

Eugen Gomringer, one of the founders of concrete poetry, has been an influential figure. His own poems are among the most significant of their kind, and he has also written several important essays on experimental literature. The effect of his works, as well as those of his followers, is primarily the result of visual and acoustical elements. Franz Mon (b. 1926), the editor of the anthology *Movens* (1960; Latin: moving), stands close to Gomringer. Max Bense (b. 1910) is a leading theoretician of the avant-garde movement. Helmut Heissenbüttel (q.v.) also belongs in the group of concrete poets, although his "texts" and "combinations" are quite different in style and effect from Gomringer's work.

The late 1950s witnessed a significant development in the lyric: the emergence of the political poem. To be sure, Wolfgang Weyrauch (1907–1980) and others had written poems dealing with political questions soon after the war. But with few exceptions these poems expressed little more than the horror of the immediate past and a vague hope for the future. The younger generation of writers, however, began to examine their society in a very critical manner. At first these writers frequently utilized irony, and many poems tended strongly toward the grotesque. Grass and Enzensberger are the most important of this generation of political poets, whose numbers also include Wolfdietrich Schnurre (q.v.), Peter Rühmkorf (b. 1929), Horst Bingel (b. 1933), and Horst Bienek (b. 1930). Recent political poetry has tended to be more direct and vitriolic, beginning with the increasing student activism and general leftward drift of the mid-1960s and culminating in the vehement reaction against the Vietnam War.

If the political poem is one manifestation of many young writers' interest in realism, another can be seen in a new subjectivism similar to the prose of the Cologne school—Herburger, Nicolas Born (b. 1937), and Rolf Dieter Brink-

mann (1940–1975) have written this kind of verse. An interesting recent development is the "poetry of facts" of Arno Reinfrank (b. 1934), which attempts to integrate science and literature.

In East German poetry two themes emerged in the first postwar years: the evils of the Nazi past and the prospect of a bright future in a Marxist Germany. Initially, examples of the latter took the form of hymns of praise to Communist leaders and odes to the joys of work and productivity. The traditional verse of J. R. Becher was held up as a model for younger writers. Poets who were unable or unwilling to conform either fell silent, like Peter Huchel, or, like Stephan Hermlin (q.v.), turned to other genres. Soon the permissible subject matter was broadened to include more personal themes, such as love and nature, as they relate to human life in a social context. By the late 1950s some poets, emulating the laconic style of Brecht, were beginning to question the shortcomings and repressive policies of the government. Their number increased in the 1960s. The most prominent was Wolf Biermann, whose direct attacks against the regime contributed substantially to the imposition of stricter censorship. Others who to some extent shared Biermann's concerns, but expressed them in more subdued language, include Reiner Kunze, Günter Kunert (q.v.), and Rainer Kirsch (b. 1934). Volker Braun (b. 1939) and Karl Mickel (b. 1935) attempted, with some success, to reconcile the demands of society with the concerns of the individual. Wulf Kirsten (b. 1934), whose poetry is reminiscent of Bobrowski's, is one of the few poets of stature to have emerged in the GDR during the 1970s.

Drama

The West German drama was slow to recover from the devastating effects of the Nazi years. The only exile to make a significant contribution to the West German stage was Carl Zuckmayer, whose first postwar work was *Des Teufels General* (1946; *The Devil's General*, 1962), a gripping tragedy based on the life of Ernst Udet, an anti-Nazi general in Hitler's air force who ultimately committed suicide in 1941. The inner emigrants wrote few plays, and the younger authors similarly preferred other literary forms. Nonetheless, *Draußen vor der Tür* (1947; *The Man Outside*, 1952), Wolfgang Borchert's (q.v.) only drama, proved to be the most successful and sensational single work produced by anyone of his generation during the immediate postwar years. This expressionistic play about the despair of a returning soldier, for all its popularity, found no imitators, and Zuckmayer's later works were clearly inferior to *Des Teufels General*.

Despite the moderately successful attempts of several younger playwrights—Karl Wittlinger (b. 1922), Leopold Ahlsen (b. 1927), Wolfgang Altendorf (b. 1921)—and a few older ones—Hans Henny Jahnn, Ferdinand Bruckner (q.v.)—the West German drama of the 1950s in no way compares with that of Austria, Switzerland, or the GDR. The best plays of the 1950s were not written for the stage, but for the radio. The *Hörspiel* (radio play) attracted the attention of many talented playwrights, including Marie Luise Kaschnitz, Wolfgang Hildesheimer (qq.v.), Günter Eich, Erwin Wickert (b. 1915), Ernst Schnabel (b. 1913), and Fred von Hoerschelmann (1901–1976).

Toward the end of the 1950s, the drama began to show signs of a revival. Hildesheimer became the leading German proponent of the Theater of the Absurd (q.v.) with the three plays of *Spiele, in denen es dunkel wird* (1958; plays in which darkness falls). Two authors better known for their fiction, Siegfried Lenz (q.v.) and Günter Grass, wrote realistic and absurdist plays, respectively. In 1960 the first of Tankred Dorst's (b. 1925) many successful dramas was produced: *Die Kurve* (*The Curve*, 1968), a "farce" in the absurdist tradition. But not until 1963 did a West German drama become an international success, when Rolf Hochhuth's (q.v.) *Der Stellvertreter* (*The Deputy*, 1964), a polemical attack on the behavior of Pope Pius XII during the war, delighted (or shocked) audiences throughout the world. Hochhuth's reliance on documentary material set a trend that was to dominate the stage for the remainder of the decade. Heinar Kipphardt's (b. 1922) *In der Sache J. Robert Oppenheimer* (1964; *In the Matter of J. Robert Oppenheimer*, 1968) utilized a courtroom setting. After the brilliant tour de force *Marat/Sade* (1964; *Marat/Sade*, 1965), Peter Weiss similarly turned to the documentary drama with a courtroom setting in *Die Ermittlung* (1965; *The Investigation*, 1966), which has the trials of Nazi war criminals as its theme. Hochhuth and Weiss continued to write documentary dramas, and other authors, including Dorst and Enzensberger, were also attracted to this form.

Before the enthusiasm for the documentary theater had waned, several young playwrights became interested in a new kind of drama, one treating everyday life in a matter compatible with the new realism. These plays are indebted to the earlier *Volksstück* (folk play) of Marieluise Fleisser (q.v.) and the Austrian Ödön von Horváth (q.v.), and, in many cases, to the American Edward Albee (q.v.). Domestic settings, realistic dialogue, and situations ranging from banal to grotesque are characteristics of the dramas of Jochen Ziem (b. 1932), Martin Sperr (b. 1944), Botho Strauss (b. 1944), and F. X. Kroetz (q.v.). They are related to the films of Rainer Werner Fassbinder (b. 1946), who also wrote works for the stage. The most successful of these plays was *Die Zimmerschlacht* (1967; *Home Front*, 1972), by the versatile Martin Walser (q.v.).

The East German drama had a more auspicious beginning, due to the presence of Brecht. The master of his own theater, the Berliner Ensemble, he offered outstanding productions of works by German and foreign playwrights, as well as his own dramas. Erwin Strittmatter's (q.v.) *Katzgraben* (1954; Katzgraben) was the best of the many early plays that adhered closely to Socialist Realism (q.v.). Somewhat later two great talents appeared, Peter Hacks and Heiner Müller (qq.v.). Hacks wrote excellent comedies, and both attempted serious plays set in the GDR before running afoul of the authorities. Later they turned to safer subjects, especially the reworking of classical themes. Other noteworthy East German plays are *Frau Flinz* (1962), a comedy by Helmut Baierl (b. 1926), and *Die Kipper* (1972; the dumpers), a realistic drama by Volker Braun.

Fiction

In the immediate postwar years a plethora of novels by exiles and inner emigrants were published in Germany. For all their differences, virtually all dealt, directly or indirectly, with the Hitler years. In *Stalingrad* (1945; *Stalingrad*, 1948) Theodor Plievier (1892–1955) portrayed the horrors of battle with grim realism, and Ernst Wiechert's *Der Totenwald* (1946; *The Forest of the Dead*, 1947) is realistic both in its portrayal of life in a concentration camp and in the narrator's admission that a factual account cannot capture the essence of the experience. The terrors of the Third Reich are suggested symbolically in the negative utopias of *Heliopolis* (1949; Helopolis) by Ernst Jünger and *Die Stadt hinter dem Strom* (1949; *City beyond the River*, 1953) by Hermann Kasack (1896–1966), as well as in the most ambitious novel of the age, Thomas Mann's *Doktor Faustus* (1947; *Doctor Faustus*, 1948). A less pessimistic view is offered in

Das unauslöschliche Siegel (1946; the indelible seal) and *Märkische Argonautenfahrt* (1950; *The Quest,* 1953), by the Christian writer Elisabeth Langgässer (1899–1950). Several older authors began to write in the nonrealistic style of William Faulkner (q.v.), Joyce, and Dos Passos that had become popular in the free world during the 1930s. Among these are Langgässer, Ernst Kreuder (1903–1972), Wolfgang Koeppen, and Hans Erich Nossack (qq.v.). Whereas Kreuder never again equaled the success of his first postwar novel, *Die Gesellschaft vom Dachboden* (1946; *The Attic Pretenders,* 1948), Nossack and Koeppen each published several major works.

Younger authors for the most part preferred shorter fiction to the novel. The stories of Wolfgang Borchert, in which the anguish of his generation received poignant expression, were scarcely less popular than his drama. Most younger writers, on the other hand, developed a realistic style in the manner of Ernest Hemingway (q.v.). Heinrich Böll (q.v.), Wolfdietrich Schnurre, and Hans Bender (b. 1919) were concerned with the fate of individuals—soldiers, POWs, and civilians—caught up in the war and its aftermath. This group of short-story writers shared a leftist, but usually not Marxist perspective, a sense of revulsion over Germany's militaristic history, and a strong desire to prevent a recurrence of the evils of the past. In the 1950s they began to attack bourgeois materialism and complacency.

Conservative voices were not lacking. These writers represented a variety of positions, but in general shared a dislike of contemporary society. Instead of looking forward to increasing socialism as a solution, they stressed the importance of the individual and looked back to religious or philosophical values of the past. In *Der Fragebogen* (1951; *The Questionnaire,* 1955) Ernst von Salomon (1902–1972) offered an account of his life, from his devotion to the German cause in World War I to his internment by the Americans following World War II, in which he bitterly satirized the allies' denazification program. Albrecht Goes, a Protestant minister also known as a poet and essayist, produced two realistic novellas, *Unruhige Nacht* (1949; *Arrow to the Heart,* 1951) and *Das Brandopfer* (1954; *The Burnt Offering,* 1956), set during the Nazi period, in which the author's faith in God and, ultimately, human nature, shines through. The novels and short fiction of Heinz Risse (b. 1898) and Gerd Gaiser (1908–1976) reflect the authors' distrust of modern civilization, Risse from a humanistic Christian perspective and Gaiser from that of a

neoromantic youth movement of the 1920s. Gaiser's *Die sterbende Jagd* (1953; *The Last Squadron,* 1959), one of the most important German war novels, consists of a multitude of vignettes focusing on different members of the Luftwaffe squadron in Norway at the turning point of the air war with England. Many attitudes toward the war and the German cause are represented, and the single unifying thread is the pervasive feeling of nostalgia as the fighter pilot, the last of those warriors for whom battle is a ritual with a code of honor, loses his unique position and becomes just another instrument of mechanized modern warfare. Rudolf Krämer-Badoni (b. 1913) is another leading conservative novelist and critic.

The late 1950s and early 1960s witnessed the rise of a number of important writers whose novels are progressive in both form and content, but vary greatly in execution and intent. The first of these was Heinrich Schirmbeck's (b. 1915) *Ärgert dich dein rechtes Aug* (1957; *If Thine Eye Offend Thee,* 1960), a philosophical work of considerable thematic complexity in which the protagonist, a cyberneticist, struggles to reconcile the search for scientific truth with the dangers posed to civilization by the rapid advances of technology. The appearance of *Die Blechtrommel* (1959; *The Tin Drum,* 1962) made an international celebrity of its author, Günter Grass. This picaresque novel, which narrates the improbable adventures of a dwarf during the war and postwar years, is the very antithesis of Uwe Johnson's sober and reflective first novel, *Mutmaßungen über Jakob* (1959; *Speculations about Jacob,* 1963). Johnson, an immigrant from the GDR, indirectly explores—speculates about—the relationship between East and West, as his figures consider the enigmas that surrounded the life and death of the title character, Jakob Abs. Martin Walser should also be mentioned in this context, as should Heinrich Böll, who developed from the promising young author of realistic war stories of the late 1940s to the author of *Billard um halbzehn* (1959; *Billiards at Half Past Nine,* 1962) and *Ansichten eines Clowns* (1963; *The Clown,* 1965), novels of artistic maturity as well as social commitment. With the exception of Schirmbeck, who later turned primarily to theoretical essays on the relationship between science, literature, and society, these novelists have continued to produce works that have received both critical and popular acclaim. Another major figure who emerged at that time was Siegfried Lenz, whose works are somewhat more traditional.

It had long been a cliché in certain critical

circles that traditional fiction—novels and stories with a protagonist and recognizable linear plot—was experiencing a "crisis." This was evident in some German writers of the 1950s, most notably Arno Schmidt (q.v.) and Helmut Heissenbüttel, but only in the 1960s did avant-garde prose forms become widespread. The writers who were involved, for all their differences, shared a distrust of traditional forms and values, and their works display an attention to minute detail and an awareness of the banality of language. The novelists Dieter Wellershoff and Günter Herburger, and Jürgen Becker (b. 1932), the author of *Felder* (1964; fields) and *Ränder* (1968; margins), collections of short prose texts, soon came to be recognized as the leading representatives of this school. Hubert Fichte (b. 1935), a "German Jack Kerouac" (q.v.) wrote disjointed novels set in the youthful subculture, as did Peter Chotjewitz (b. 1934), one of the most versatile of the experimental prose writers. *Don Quichotte in Köln* (1968; Don Quixote in Cologne) by Paul Schallück (q.v.), is nontraditional, if less radical than the works of Fichte and Chotjewitz. In Gabrielle Wohmann's (q.v.) fiction an attention to the minutiae of daily life is combined with keen psychological insights into the difficulty of achieving satisfying human relationships. Many writers, including Alfred Andersch and Dieter Kühn (b. 1935), turned to a semidocumentary style in which factual material alternates with a connecting fictional narrative.

In the GDR, most fiction written during the 1950s was rather sterile Socialist Realism. The work of Anna Seghers is noteworthy, as is *Nackt unter Wölfen* (1958; *Naked among Wolves*, 1960) by Bruno Apitz (1900–1979), which is set in a concentration camp in 1945. At about the same time the traditional novel of Socialist Realism reached a pinnacle in *Ole Bienkopp* (1963; *Ole Bienkopp*, 1966) by Erwin Strittmatter, a new kind of prose fiction began to appear in the GDR. Beginning with Christa Wolf's *Der geteilte Himmel* (1963; *Divide Heaven*, 1970), East German writers started to examine their society more closely and more critically, discussing the relationship between social theory and practice, as well as that between the individual and society. The expansion of thematic scope was accompanied by a gradual departure from the rigid stylistic and structural requirements of doctrinaire Socialist Realism. *Die Aula* (1965; the auditorium) by Hermann Kant (b. 1926) and Christa Wolf's controversial *Nachdenken über Christa T.* (1969; *The Quest for Christa T.*, 1970)—especially the latter—are among the

most significant East German novels of the 1960s. Also important are works by Rolf Schneider (b. 1932), Jurek Becker (q.v.), Günter de Bruyn (b. 1926), Manfred Bieler (b. 1934), Günter Kunert, and Ulrich Plenzdorf (b. 1934), whose *Die neuen Leiden des jungen W.* (1973; *The New Sufferings of Young W.*, 1979), set in the GDR but based on a sustained allusion to Goethe's *The Sufferings of Young Werther*, was the literary sensation of the 1970s. The prose of Johannes Bobrowski, like his poetry, stands apart from the mainstream of East German Literature.

BIBLIOGRAPHY: Eloesser, A., *Modern German Literature* (1933); Lange, V., *Modern German Literature, 1870–1940* (1945); Bithell, J., *Modern German Literature, 1880–1950*, 3rd ed. (1957); Waidson H., *The Modern German Novel* (1959); Sokel, W., *The Writer in Extremis: Expressionism in 20th-Century German Literature* (1959); Garten, H., *Modern German Drama* (1959); Soergel, A., and Hohoff, C., *Dichtung und Dichter der Zeit* (2 vols., 1961–63); Hoffmann, C., *Opposition Poetry in Nazi Germany* (1962); Schwitzke, H., *Das Hörspiel: Dramaturgie und Geschichte* (1963); Gray, R., *The German Tradition in Literature* (1965); Hamburger, M., *From Prophecy to Exorcism: The Premises of Modern German Literature* (1965); Hatfield, H., *Modern German Literature* (1966); Hatfield, H., *Crisis and Continuity in Modern German Fiction* (1969); Demetz, P., *Postwar German Literature* (1970); Flores, J., *Poetry in East Germany* (1971); Durzak, M., ed., *Die deutsche Literatur der Gegenwart: Aspekte und Tendenzen* (1971); Koebner, T., ed., *Tendenzen der deutschen Literatur seit 1945* (1971); Domandi, A. K., ed., *Modern German Literature* (2 vols., 1972); Thomas, R., and Bullivant, K., *Literature in Upheaval: West German Writers and the Challenge of the 1960s* (1974); Gumpel, L., "*Concrete" Poetry from East and West Germany* (1976); Patterson, M., *German Theatre Today* (1976); Hutchinson, P., *Literary Presentations of Divided Germany* (1977); Willett, J., "*The New Sobriety": Art and Politics in the Weimar Period* (1978); Krispyn, E., *Anti-Nazi Writers in Exile* (1978); Huettich, H., *Theater in a Planned Society: Contemporary Drama in the GDR* (1978); Van D'Elden, K., ed., *West German Poets on Society and Politics* (1979); Bosmajian, H., *Metaphors of Evil: Contemporary German Literature and the Shadow of Nazism* (1979); Innes, C., *Modern German*

Drama (1979); Taylor, R., *Literature and Society in Germany 1918–1945* (1980)

JERRY GLENN

GHANAIAN LITERATURE

Ghana has one of the longest written literary histories in Africa, extending back into the 18th c., when Antonius Guilielmus Amo (c. 1703–c. 1750) studied in Germany and produced a powerful theological study in Latin, and Ottobah Cugoano (c. 1745–c. 1790) wrote a bitter antislavery tract in England.

During the 19th and early 20th cs., there was considerable publication in English, but most of these books were rather pedantic volumes of history or anthropology. Carl Reindof (1834–1917), Raphael Armattoe (1913–1953), and Adelaide Casely-Hayford (1868–1959) were typical. Their works emulate British styles and attitudes. These were sarcastically pilloried by Kobina Sekyi (1892–1956) in *The Blinkards,* a play produced as early as 1915. In addition, and this is not common in Africa, there has been a considerable publication in local languages—Fanti, Twi, Ewe—often sponsored by missionaries.

There was little that could properly be called creative literature until 1946, which saw the publication of Michael Francis Dei-Anang's (1909–1978) first collection of poetry, *Wayward Lines from Africa.* Although he must be regarded as the first Ghanaian poet, his work is strongly influenced by the conventions of British Victorian poetry. Such literary borrowing is characteristic of many lesser poets who published in this period, who emulated the colonial culture even while they made gentle professions toward nationalism.

Significant literature of international stature developed only in the years following the 1966 coup against Kwame Nkrumah's restrictive socialist government. Since then, writing in all genres by numerous gifted writers has been published. Their themes cover the subjects found regularly in other West African countries that have shared a similar colonial experience, but with a specifically Ghanaian emphasis.

Today many novels record the past fondly while describing the process of inevitable change. They often include substantial autobiographical details, especially of growing up in a traditional or transitional society. This theme is exemplified in such novels as Joseph Abruquah's (b. 1921) *The Catechist* (1965), Amu Djoleto's (b. 1929) *The Strange Man* (1967),

Asare Konadu's (b. 1932) *A Woman in Her Prime* (1967), and Francis Selormey's (b. 1927) *The Narrow Path* (1966). These novels often show reverence for traditional life even when they deal with the personal impact occasioned by its inescapable destruction. The conflict of generations in the division of spiritual beliefs brought about by Christianity, and in the division of mind brought about by education, are persistently expressed.

In contrast, there are the novels that deal with more recent history and focus upon the frenetic experience of the rapidly developing (and deteriorating) city life, which is simultaneously attractive and shocking. Cameron Duodu's (b. 1932) *The Gab Boys* (1967) typifies this theme, describing the delinquencies of unemployed school dropouts who lounge around town in their fancy gabardine trousers looking for excitement and trouble, an international subject surprising only in coming from Africa.

In this vein is one of the most powerful novels yet produced by an African: Ayi Kwei Armah's (q.v.) *The Beautyful Ones Are Not Yet Born* (1969), with its sardonic implication that those who have been born are marked by a spiritual ugliness. It is a scarifying attack on corruption during the Nkrumah regime, blazing with profound anger at the way in which independent Africa has been seduced by the modern toys of Western capitalism, just as were the old chiefs by gifts of beads and mirrors. This novel had international impact; it raised the whole standing of African fiction.

Armah went on to write four more distinguished novels: *Fragments* (1970), *Why Are We So Blest?* (1972), *Two Thousand Seasons* (1973), and *The Healers* (1975). His analysis blames the new elite not only for their greedy arrogance but for their deeper spiritual corruption deriving from their infatuation with things European and the shame they feel for their African heritage.

The only Ghanaian writer of similar stature is Kofi Awoonor (q.v.), whose political views have brought him to prison. His complex novel *This Earth, My Brother* (1971) repeats Armah's critical challenge to Ghana's rulers. Awoonor is also a critic and a poet. His poetry is marked by its originality and sensibility, and shows his unusual determination to maintain his Ewe inheritance in his English verse. He regularly takes the pose of oral narrator, his themes often derive from Ewe culture, and his style forces English to adapt to some of the forms of Ewe oral verse. In *Rediscovery* (1964) and *Night of My Blood* (1971) he confronts the continual problem of the cultural dualism that afflicts African writers. By asserting the importance of tradition, he separates himself from another major poet, Albert Kayper-Mensah (b. 1923), whose collection *The Drummer in Our Time* (1975) seems as close to Europe as to Africa.

The last fifteen years have seen a large new group of published Ghanaian poets. The most significant is Atukwe Okai (b. 1941), who, like Awoonor, is committed to his inheritance, an attitude demonstrably more fruitful than emulation of foreign writers. Okai has become highly popular as a public reader, thus restoring poetry to the oral mode. *Call of the Fonton-fron* (1971) occasionally lapses into mere rhetoric, but it indicates a direction that other Ghanaian poets followed.

There is the beginning of a Ghanaian drama. Drama can be argued to be relatively free from the stigma of primarily seeking international appeal, since it initially requires a local audience. Nevertheless, there is a clear distinction between plays written for educated audiences who patronize the theater, and the local vaudeville-type comedy of the ever-popular concert parties (traveling singing and acting troupes). Ama Ata Aidoo (b. 1942), well known for her realistic short stories, has written a conventional play on an important theme, the problems of the black American "returning" to Africa—*Dilemma of a Ghost* (1965). Joe de Graft (b. 1924), who is deeply involved in the theater, began his career as a dramatist with *Sons and Daughters* (1963), a conventional enough social comedy. However, he became more ingeniously experimental with *Through a Film Darkly* (1970), which suggested options for the African playwright to escape from the borrowed format of the formal well-made play. His ideas have been augmented in a different vein by Efua Sutherland (b. 1924), who helped found the Ghana Drama Studio. Her most famous published play is *Edufa* (1964), but she has written numerous other plays for local radio broadcast.

Ghanaian literature flourishes sufficiently to be able to support the irregularly published literary journal *Okyeame*. The country also sustains a printing industry that frees at least some authors from dependence on foreign publication. Locally published short novels may be considered unworthy of critical analysis, but they delight a broad readership. Cofie Quaye's (b. 1947) amusing if derivative detective stories, such as *Sammy Slams the Gang* (1970), and Asare Konadu's intense love stories like

Come Back Dora (1966) have a substantial sale. These books, which satisfy readers on a fairly elementary level of English literacy, may well form the basis for an indigenous readership out of which could grow a literature more truly Ghanaian than the writings of those who are admired abroad and whose audience is limited to an intellectual elite.

BIBLIOGRAPHY: Cartey, W., *Whispers from a Continent* (1969), passim; Roscoe, A., *Mother Is Gold* (1971), passim; Senanu, K. E., "Creative Writing in Ghana," in Kayper-Mensah, A. W., and Wolff, H., eds., *Ghanaian Writing* (1972), pp. 13–31; Dathorne, O., *The Black Mind* (1974), passim

JOHN POVEY

GHELDERODE, Michel de

(born Adhémar-Adolphe-Louis Martens) Belgian dramatist (writing in French), b. 3 April 1898, Ixelles; d. 1 April 1962, Schaerbeek

What little is known about G.'s biography can be found in *Les entretiens d'Ostende* (1956; partial tr., "The Ostend Interviews," in *Seven Plays*, Vols. 1 and 2, 1960, 1964), radio interviews in which G. also discussed his dramatic theories and practices. G.'s father was principal clerk of the Archives Générales and wanted his son to enter the civil service too. G. did earn his living for some twenty years as an archivist, but he also had a second life in the "realm of dreams," in his words. At sixteen, during his convalescence from a near-fatal illness, he wrote his first poems, and as a youth he haunted the marionette theaters of Brussels; these puppet performances were to influence his work profoundly. In 1918 he wrote his first play, *La mort regarde à la fenêtre* (death looks in at the window), in the manner of Poe, for a literary group to which he belonged. In it one can see the characteristics of G.'s later theater: tension caused by hyperbolic plotting; blatant visual antitheses used as a foreshadowing technique; and a strange morality.

G.'s first substantial play was *La mort du Docteur Faust* (1926; *The Death of Doctor Faust*, 1964). In 1926 the director of the Flemish Popular Theater commissioned a play, *Saint François d'Assise* (1927; Saint Francis of Assisi) from G. Adapting techniques from the popular arts, G. told his story not only through dialogue but through pantomime, dance, and acrobatics. The work was the beginning of a brief but fruitful association with this theater, in which his plays were performed in Flemish translation.

One of G.'s finest works, *Pantagleize* (written 1929, pub. 1934; *Pantagleize*, 1960), a "farce to make you sad," is a product of this period. It is about a Chaplinesque Everyman who by his innocent remark "What a lovely day!" unwittingly triggers a series of events that lead to a revolution and his own death. It is a modern morality play, exploring man's predicament in an indifferent universe.

Two historical dramas from this period are among his most successful works. *Christophe Colomb* (1928; *Christopher Columbus*, 1964), somewhat expressionist (q.v.), is a "dramatic fairy tale" that amusingly recounts, with many anachronisms, the adventures of Columbus in America. *Escurial* (1928; *Escurial*, 1957), set in 16th-c. Spain, deals with the rivalry of a king and his jester. Similar settings and characters, and indeed, the macabre ambience of the play, were to appear many more times in G.'s work.

A number of plays written for the Flemish Popular Theater were vehicles for the actor Renat Verheyen. When he died young in 1930, G. wrote *Sortie de l'acteur* (written 1930, pub. 1942; actor's exit) as a tribute; the "exit" of the actor is death, and the play is about the nature and mystery of theater itself.

Although G. wrote in French (and changed his name legally in 1929), he was of Flemish origin, and his spirit is distinctly Flemish. His inspirations were, along with the Elizabethan and Jacobean dramatists, the Flemish masters Breughel and Bosch, and the modern Belgian painter James Ensor, whose visions of masks and carnivals had a strong influence on G.'s work. A number of G.'s plays are based directly on Breughel's paintings, including *Les aveugles* (written 1933, pub. 1936; *The Blind Men*, 1960).

What he derived from this Flemish sensibility, particularly in his many plays set in medieval or Renaissance Flanders, was a sense of the grotesque, the macabre, and the satanic. A baroque, hallucinatory atmosphere pervades the plays, which are populated by dwarfs, hunchbacks, resurrected corpses, and devils. Sympathies are paradoxically elicited for unlikable figures. Horror, murder, decay, carnality, scatology, and death are all trademarks of G.'s theater. It could be called a theater of cruelty, although G.'s earlier works antedate the theoretical writings of Antonin Artaud (q.v.). In *L'école des bouffons* (written 1937, pub. 1942; the school for buffoons) Folial, the jester of *Escurial*, reappears, and suggests that the source of all true creativity is cruelty.

A prime example of G.'s violent, demonic spectacles is *Fastes d'enfer* (written 1929, pub. 1943; *Chronicles of Hell*, 1960), set in a decaying episcopal palace in medieval Flanders. A bishop, murdered by one of his unspeakably corrupt priests, returns from the dead, unable to rest until he has spat out the Host, which has been choking him. The play, palpitating with evil and cruelty, shocked Paris when it was produced at the Théâtre Marigny in 1949 by Jean-Louis Barrault, and a scandal ensued in which G. was accused of blasphemy and any number of other crimes, including lycanthropy. Other important plays in this mode are *Magie rouge* (written 1931, pub. 1935; *Red Magic*, 1964) and *Hop, Signor!* (written 1935, pub. 1938; *Hop, Signor!*, 1964).

G.'s dramas were almost unknown outside Belgium until 1947, when La Compagnie du Myrmidon presented *Hop, Signor!* in Paris. His fame increased with the *succès de scandale* of *Fastes d'enfer*, and G., who had been hitherto neglected, came to be recognized as a key figure in the avant-garde theater. Although by the late 1940s he was in bad health, he lived to see himself acknowledged as a forerunner of the Theater of the Absurd (q.v.) and as a playwright who particularly influenced the "cruel" theater of Jean Genet and Fernando Arrabal (qq.v.).

G. has great strengths but also some gaping flaws; at times his grotesqueries pall, the horror is exaggerated, and coarseness overtakes ribaldry. Yet his universe is unmistakably gripping. In G., the macabre is surrounded by true poetry.

FURTHER WORKS: *Le repas des fauves* (1918); *Piet Bouteille* (written 1918, pub. 1925; *Piet Bouteille*, 1964); *Le club des menteurs* (written c. 1920, pub. 1943); *Un soir de pitié* (written 1921, pub. 1929; *A Night of Pity*, 1964); *L'histoire comique de Keizer Karel* (1922); *La halte catholique* (1922); *Têtes de bois* (1924); *La farce de la mort qui faillit trépasser* (1925); *Les vieillards* (1925); *Le mystère de la Passion de Notre Seigneur Jésus-Christ* (1925); *Kwiebe-Kwiebus* (1925); *La corne d'abondance* (1925); *L'homme sous l'uniforme* (1925); *La tentation de Saint Antoine* (written 1925, pub. 1929); *Le massacre des innocents* (written 1926, pub. 1929); *Vénus* (1926); *Trois acteurs, un drame* (written 1926, pub. 1929; *Three Actors and Their Drama*, 1960); *La vie publique de Pantagleize* (1926); *Barabbas* (written 1928, pub. 1932; *Barabbas*, 1960); *Don Juan; ou, Les amants chimériques* (1928); *Les femmes au tombeau* (written 1928, pub. 1934; *The Women at the Tomb,* 1960); *Ixelles, mes amours* (1928); *La transfiguration dans le cirque* (1928); *Noyade des songes* (1928); *Duveloor; ou, La farce du diable vieux* (1931); *Arc-en-ciel* (1933); *Le chagrin d'Hamlet* (1933); *Chronique de Noël* (1934); *Les treize chansons de Pilou, chien* (1934); *D'un diable qui prêcha merveilles* (written 1934, pub. 1942); *Mademoiselle Jaïre* (written 1934, pub. 1942; *Miss Jairus,* 1964); *Sire Halewijn* (written 1934, pub. 1943; *Lord Halewyn,* 1960); *Le ménage de Caroline* (1935); *Le singulier trépas de Messire Ulenspiegel* (written 1935, pub. 1951); *La balade du Grande Macabre* (1935); *Masques ostendais* (1935); *Adrian et Jusemina* (1935); *La farce des ténébreux* (written 1936, pub. 1942); *La pie sur le gibet* (1938); *Le cavalier bizarre* (1938); *Sortilèges* (1941); *Le soleil se couche* (1942); *L'hôtel de Ruescas* (1943); *Mes statues* (1943); *Choses et gens de chez nous* (1943); *Voyage autour de ma Flandre* (1947); *Théâtre complet* (5 vols., 1950–57); *Théâtre d'écoute* (1951); *Le perroquet de Charles Quint* (1951); *La folie d'Hugo Van der Goes* (1951); *La Flandre est un songe* (1953); *Marie la misérable* (1955); *La grande tentation de Saint Antoine* (1958); *Secret: Poèmes* (1960); *Sortilèges, et autres contes crépusculaires* (1962); *Lettres à Catherine Toth et André Reybaz, René Dupuy, Roger Iglésis, Jean Le Poulain, Marcel Lupovici, Gilles Chancrin, Georges Goubert* (1962); *M. de G. et Henri Vandeputte, correspondance: Autour d'une amitié naissante* (1964); *Le sommeil de la raison* (1967)

BIBLIOGRAPHY: Grossvogel, D. I., *20th Century French Drama* (1961), pp. 254–310; special G. section, *TDR,* 8, 1 (1963), 11–71; Pronko, L. C., *Avant-Garde: The Experimental Theater in France* (1963), pp. 165–80; Vandromme, P., *M. de G.* (1963); Francis, J., *L'éternel aujourd'hui de M. de G.: Spectographie d'un auteur* (1968); DeCock, J., *Le théâtre de M. de G.: Une dramaturgie de l'anti-théâtre et de la cruauté* (1969); Wellwarth, G. E., *The Theater of Protest and Paradox,* rev. ed. (1971), pp. 111–26; Beyen, R., *G.* (1974)

KENNETH S. WHITE

GHOSE, Aurobindo

Indian poet, dramatist, and philosopher (writing in English and Bengali), b. 15 Aug. 1872, Calcutta; d. 5 Dec. 1950, Pondicherry

Educated in English-speaking schools in India and an honors graduate of Cambridge, A. was fluent not only in English and Bengali, but in Greek, Latin, Sanskrit, French, German, and Italian as well. His literary career divides roughly into two periods. The first is from 1893 to 1910, during which time he returned to India, taught in colleges in Baroda and Calcutta, and wrote numerous political and literary pieces for several English- and Bengali-language newspapers and journals. His first major collection of lyric poems, *Songs to Myrtilla,* appeared in 1895, followed by a number of other important works, including the narrative poem *Love and Death* (1921), several blank-verse plays, notably *Perseus the Deliverer* (1907), and the first draft of his magnum opus, *Savitri: A Legend and a Symbol,* published in its final form in 1950–51.

At this time A. came under the influence of the well-known Yogi Lele and started to practice yoga. An ardent nationalist, A. was implicated in a bomb-throwing incident in 1908, for which he was jailed. While awaiting trial he underwent a profound mystical experience in which he said he witnessed the presence of God (Narayana). As a result, he underwent a major personality change. Acquitted of terrorist charges, A. was released, but due to harassment by the British authorities, he retired to the French mandate of Pondichéry (now Pondicherry) in 1910, established an ashram, or spiritual retreat, and remained there for the rest of his life.

At Pondicherry A. completed many of his best-known works, including *The Ideal of Human Unity* (1919), *The Renaissance in India* (1920), *The Life Divine* (1940), *Collective* [sic] *Poems and Plays* (1942), *The Synthesis of Yoga* (1948), *Heraclitus* (1949), *The Human Cycle* (1949), and *Essays on the Gita* (1950). Numerous other works, while completed at various times in his life, were published long after they were written, many posthumously. In 1920 Madame Mirra Richard, subsequently known as "The Mother," joined the settlement, and in 1926, after A. underwent another profound mystical experience—a vision of the god Krishna—she took complete charge of the ashram. For the next twelve years A. went into virtual isolation but kept close contact with disciples through letters. Toward the end of his life he appeared before his devotees on special viewing, or *darshan,* days and continued to write prolifically and to translate Sanskrit works.

While his writings are in the main philosophical, A.'s literary pieces can be looked upon as extensions or elaborations of this larger philosophical view. Essentially A. views the cosmos as having undergone a process of devolution from the pure stage of Absolute Spirit (*sacchidanand,* or "existence-consciousness-bliss") to supermind, mind, and matter, where it languishes at present. According to A., the time has come for the cosmos to evolve once again to that original pristine state of deathlessness, perfection, and infinity. In this process man will become a God-man possessing not only physical but spiritual superpowers. Ultimately, man as well as the cosmos will achieve perfection.

Opinions vary widely as to the quality of A.'s writings. Some critics, many of them his devotees, contend that he is a sublime literary artist who matches, or even surpasses, Dante and Milton. Other submit that his writings are abstruse, muddled, and have received attention not because of any inherent literary merit, but rather because of the enthusiasm of A.'s zealous followers. Such judgments aside, A. has exercised a considerable influence on a large number of creative writers in both Indian vernacular literatures and in English literature written by Indians.

FURTHER WORKS: *Urvasie* (c. 1896); *Two Lectures* (1908); *An Open Letter to His Countrymen* (1909); *Ahana, and Other Poems* (1915); *The Ideal Karmayogin* (1919); *Uttapara Speech* (1919); *Dayananda: The Man and His Work* (1920); *Evolution* (1920); *Ideals and Progress* (1920); *War and Self-Determination* (1920); *The Age of Kalidasa* (1921); *The Brain of India* (1921); *A System of National Education* (1921); *The Yoga and Its Object* (1921); *Baji Prabhou* (1922); *Man: Slave or Free?* (1922); *The National Value of Art* (1922); *Speeches* (1922); *The Need in Nationalism, and Other Essays* (1923); *Rishi Bunkim Chandra* (1923); *The Mother* (1928); *Kalidasa* (1929); *The Riddle of This World* (1933); *Six Poems* (1934); *Lights on Yoga* (1935); *Bases of Yoga* (1936); *Sri A.: A Life* (1937); *Swami Dayanand Saraswati* (1939); *Bankim—Tilak—Dayananda* (1940); *Poems, Views and Reviews* (1941); *On Quantitative Metre* (c. 1942); *On the War* (1944); *Poems: Past and Present* (1946); *Words from Long Ago: The Mother* (1946); *Letters of Sri A.* (First Series, 1947; Second and Third Series, 1949; Fourth Series, 1951); *The Significance of Indian Art* (1947); *The Spirit and Form of Indian Polity* (1947); *The Doctrine of Passive Resistance* (1948); *More Lights on Yoga*

(1948); *After the War* (1949); *Chitrangada* (1949); *Conversations of the Dead* (1951); *Letters of Sri A. on The Mother* (1951); *The Phantom Hour* (1951); *Science and Culture* (1951); *Last Poems* (1952); *Life—Literature—Yoga* (1952); *The Problem of Rebirth* (1952); *Sayings of Sri A. and The Mother* (1952); *The Supramental Manifestation upon Earth* (1952); *Elements of Yoga* (1953); *The Foundations of Indian Culture* (1953); *The Future Poetry* (1953); *The Mind of Light* (1953); *Sri A. on Himself and on The Mother* (1953); *Bankim Chandra Chatterji* (1954); *Correspondence with Sri A.* (1954); *Kalidasa* (Second Series, 1954); *Views on National Problems* (First and Second Series, 1954); *On the Veda* (1956); *Vyasa and Valmiki* (1956); *Illion: An Epic in Quantitative Hexametres* (1957); *More Poems* (1957); *Vasavadutta* (1957); *On Yoga* (Second Series, 1958); *Thoughts and Aphorisms* (1958); *The Hour of God* (1959); *The Viziers of Bassora* (1959); *Eric: A Dramatic Romance* (1960); *On Nationalism* (1965); *Sri Aravinder mul bangla racavali* (1969); *Bande Mataram: Early Political Writings* (1972); *The Chariot of Jagganath* (1972); *Light to Superlight* (1972); *New Lamps for Old* (1974)

BIBLIOGRAPHY: Roy, A., *Sri A. and the New Age* (1940); Mitra, S., *Sri A. and Indian Freedom* (1948); Langly, G. H., *Sri A.: Poet, Philosopher and Mystic* (1949); Srinivasa Iyengar, K. R., *Sri A.: A Biography* (1950); Diwakar, R. R., *Mahayogi: Life, Sadhana and Teachings of A.* (1954)

CARLO COPPOLA

GIDE, André

French novelist, essayist, and dramatist, b. 22 Nov. 1869, Paris; d. 19 Feb. 1951, Paris

Born into a Protestant family with a Catholic branch, with relatives in both Provence and Normandy, G. insisted that his divided nature could be harmonized only through literary expression. After his father's premature death, he was raised by his Calvinist mother, whose influence was harshly repressive. His cousin and childhood confidant Madeleine Rondeaux, whom he married in 1895, shortly after his mother's death, replaced her psychologically, and G.'s love for her always remained idealized and asexual. His marriage also followed two trips to North Africa, where he had discovered the sensual delights of a primitive, "pagan" society and had been introduced to pederasty by Oscar Wilde. The dichotomy between sexual pleasure and the secularized Calvinism his pure love of "Em" (as he referred to his wife) represented, and G.'s effort to harmonize the two, is the subject of his best work.

His earliest works show the influence of Schopenhauer and of Mallarmé, to whose symbolist (q.v.) literary circle G. belonged. By the late 1890s the influences of Nietzsche and Goethe had helped liberate him from his early aestheticism. For the next twenty years he attempted in his writing to balance this liberating force with the severe restraints which were an integral part of his being and which gave his work a classical purity of form. G. had been one of the founders of the influential *Nouvelle revue française* in 1909, but he gained celebrity as a writer only in the early 1920s, with the publication of *Pages choisies* (1921; selected pages) from his earlier works and the open avowal of his homosexuality in *Corydon* (1924 [privately pub. 1911]; *Corydon*, 1950). *Voyage au Congo* (1927; *To the Congo,* in *Travels in the Congo,* 1929) and *Le retour du Tchad* (1928; *Back from the Chad,* in *Travels in the Congo,* 1929), where he exposed deplorable treatment of the natives and colonial corruption in French Equatorial Africa, launched a decade of involvement with social and political causes, including a brief, regretted flirtation with communism in the mid-1930s. G.'s creative writing continued, however, and he was awarded the Nobel Prize for literature in 1947.

G.'s earliest work, *Les cahiers d'André Walter* (1891; *The Notebooks of André Walter,* 1968), expresses the fundamental conflict between the "angel" and the "beast" within him. His fictional André, as G. himself did, preserves the purity of his love for "Emmanuèle" by renouncing it (the symbolist ideal), then fails, after her death, to maintain it against the demands of the flesh. Besides stating explicitly his erotic dichotomy, G. already uses here the narcissistic device of a hero trying unsuccessfully to finish a book on the same subject as G.'s book.

Paludes (1895; *Marshlands,* 1953) satirizes the stifling atmosphere of the symbolist literary salons G. had frequented before his liberating trips to North Africa. The protagonist sees the hollowness of this life where no one is capable of an original thought, or even of expanding his physical horizons (and writing a book about it), but he cannot break its grip. G., having

broken its grip, can return to it only with a satirical perspective.

G.'s real liberation, however, is expressed in *Les nourritures terrestres* (1897; *Fruits of the Earth,* in *Fruits of the Earth,* 1949), in which the angelic and the demonic are not in conflict, but are harmonized. Love of life, spontaneity, desire, pleasure, and freedom are interwoven with the themes of fervor, of the stripping away of acquired culture, and of the purity of the present moment. The longings of the body and the aspirations of the spirit have the same object: the concrete, immediate reality of God. G. unites eroticism and evangelism against the restrictions of conventional morality. His spontaneous, direct poetic rhetoric is an expression of revolt against form as well. This text, which contains the essential of G.'s "doctrine," went largely unnoticed, however, until World War I had effectively destroyed the basis for traditional morality and the withdrawal from society implicit in the symbolist attitude.

The play *Saül* (1897; *Saul,* 1952) was a kind of antidote to *Les nourritures terrestres* as *Paludes* had been to *Les cahiers d'André Walter*. It depicts the undermining of the power and authority of the biblical king by the "demons" of his own sensual weakness, and thereby warns of the dangers inherent in the complete individual freedom extolled in *Les nourritures terrestres*. G.'s Saul is a tragic figure dominated by erotic and religious drives similar to his creator's, which he cannot control and which destroy him and those he loves.

L'immoraliste (1902; *The Immoralist,* 1930), G.'s first *récit,* or short psychological novel, presents a subtler, less tragic hero, Michel, whom he could have become, as he said later, if he had not become himself. Michel discovers the value of life, as G. had, through convalescence from tuberculosis in North Africa. He successfully reconciles this new dimension with his traditional, civilized career as a scholar, at least for a time. His return to the stuffy Paris literary salons and his wife's illness and subsequent miscarriage, which occurs while he is being convinced of the necessity of choice by an old acquaintance resembling Oscar Wilde, force Michel, however, to recognize the fragility of the equilibrium he has established. Eventually Michel chooses a self-cultivation which is destructive of all that represents the traditional side of his character, including his wife (hence the title). Again G. attacks the traditional European bourgeois society, but also the unrestrained destructive freedom Michel claims for himself.

La porte étroite (1909; *Strait Is the Gate*, 1924) served as a counterweight to *L'immoraliste*. In this novel, which also contains many autobiographical elements, G. explored the consequences of excessive and misunderstood Calvinist piety, which cuts the youthful Jérôme and Alissa off from social and sexual reality and eventually destroys Alissa. Although *La porte étroite* was received more favorably than *L'immoraliste* in traditional social and literary circles, the book also criticizes the arranged marriage. More importantly, it presents us, like *L'immoraliste*, with a possible resolution, also rejected by G., of his moral-sexual dilemma, his need to separate totally spiritualized love and hedonistic sensuality.

In *La symphonie pastorale* (1919; *The Pastoral Symphony*, 1931), the last of G.'s *récits*, a Protestant minister who awakens to life a blind, deaf-mute adolescent girl, but who teaches her only the gospel of love, is unaware of his own motives, the sexual nature of his attraction to her, and of the effect of his actions on his family. When she regains her sight and becomes aware of her mentor's unwitting evil, of evil in the world in general, and of the sorrow she has caused, she commits suicide. The novel is a direct statement of some of G.'s religious meditations during World War I, but it is also a veiled allusion to his first "real" infidelity to his wife and an admission of the impossibility of maintaining a separation and balance between pure love and sensual pleasure.

There is much self-irony here, as there had been in *Les caves du Vatican* (1914; *Lafcadio's Adventures*, 1928). G. called this work a *sotie*, after the late medieval satirical farces, which presented exaggerated parodies of Church ceremonies and of other institutions, and it is structurally and psychologically more complex than the three *récits*. Here we meet Lafcadio, young and ostensibly rootless (no father or nationality)—G. as he (perhaps) would like to have been—and without responsibility. He discovers, however, first family relationships and then that his "gratuitous act" of throwing an unknown man from a railroad carriage does in fact entail responsibilities he could not have foreseen. Through the device of a supposed impostor in the Vatican and Lafcadio's interaction with three very different, but very bourgeois brothers-in-law (one of whom, it turns out, is his new-found half-brother and another the man he gratuitously pushed off the train), G. treats the problem of human potential, freedom, and responsibility in a more openly satirical manner than in the novels previously dis-

cussed. The three brothers-in-law each glimpse a potential freedom, then reject it, and Lafcadio's encounter with responsibility is left inconclusive.

In 1908 G. had discovered Dostoevsky, whose spirit may be glimpsed in *Les caves du Vatican*, and in 1922 he delivered a series of public lectures on the Russian novelist, while composing his most ambitious novel, *Les faux-monnayeurs* (1926; *The Counterfeiters*, 1927). G. recapitulates here and deepens the themes treated in his earlier novels: individual freedom and restraint, authenticity (all individuals and groups in the novel are to some extent counterfeiters), social and religious criticism, and the nature of literary expression (the protagonist is also writing a novel entitled *Les faux-monnayeurs*). As suggested in *Les caves du Vatican*, and partly because of his further study of Dostoevsky, G. now saw the novel as an organic development rather than as the means for analyzing a limited problem. Édouard, a middle-aged novelist, is related to or becomes involved with all the social groups and forces G. introduces: the diabolical Strouvilhou and his band of young adolescents distributing counterfeit coins; the morally repressive and religiously hypocritical Azaïs-Vedel clan; and their materialistic counterparts, the Profitendieu and Molinier families—all of whom are driving their children away from the values they claim to uphold; the girl Bronja, whose death is the destruction of purity; and the younger Boris, for whose suicide Édouard is at least partly responsible. Édouard, who cannot complete his novel because of his unwillingness to deal with concrete reality, has abandoned his fiancée, and young Bernard Profitendieu and Oliver Molinier, Édouard's nephew, become the focal points of his life. Bernard is a more refined Lafcadio, who will maintain his freedom "provided this leads him upward," and through Édouard and Olivier G. explicitly exalts pederasty for the first time in his fiction. All heterosexual relationships, from Bronja's and Boris's to that of his grandparents', are also in the process of dissolution. The growth and dissolution of relationships is well defined, but G. indicates at the end that his long "organic" novel is not necessarily complete, that it could be continued.

Besides breaking out of the limitations of the *récit*, G. has in effect largely resolved the personal problems explored in his earlier shorter fiction and sees them in a wider social context here. His espousal of social and political causes is explained in part by this recognition that the freedom-restraint conflict had become more social than individual. There was a concomitant decline in G.'s creative power, which was renewed, however, in *Thésée* (1946; *Theseus,* 1950), which he considered his literary testament. Here the symbolist sterility of André Walter, the destructive individuality of Michel, Alissa, and Lafcadio are replaced by Theseus' commitment to freedom and human progress. While G.'s sociopolitical program is unoriginal, Theseus retains much of his earlier heroes' spontaneous creative energy and uses it for the benefit of society. Theseus' encounter with the guilty, introspective Oedipus is a constructive confrontation between the two essential aspects of G.'s character. His positive creative energy must still overcome the sense of guilt at having betrayed his ideal of purity. The victory leaves Theseus serene, and in this sense the novel is a fitting capstone to G.'s long career.

Throughout his life, G. maintained a journal of his thoughts, readings, and literary activities and relationships, which were later published: *Journal 1889–1939, Pages de journal 1939–42, Journal 1939–49* (1939, 1944, 1950; *The Journals of A. G.,* 4 vols., 1947–51), as polished a literary work as any of his creative writings. His published correspondence with other writers, such as Francis Jammes, Paul Claudel, Paul Valéry, and Roger Martin du Gard (qq.v.), to mention only the most important, also reveals many of G.'s literary and psychological attitudes.

G.'s greatness lies in part in his liberating influence, especially through *Les nourritures terrestres,* on the generation reaching maturity during or immediately following World War I, including writers such as Aragon, Montherlant, Saint-Exupéry, Malraux, Sartre, and Camus (qq.v.). The Calvinist primacy of the individual conscience was here in concert with the liberation of body and spirit from the dying 19th-c. morality. But his greatness lies as much, if not more, in his ability to express his dilemmas, conflicts, and complications in a style and tone that rendered them typical of this generation, and to a great extent of any generation. His writings are not simply the cries of anguish of an individual and (because of his peculiar Calvinist-homosexual conflict) atypical tortured soul. This is particularly true of *L'immoraliste* and *La porte étroite,* which are perhaps his most successful creations, where the tensions created in the protagonists are conveyed in a tone substantially different from G.'s own, since he had resolved the conflicts differently. In the last analysis, his greatest strength is his literary artistry, although the moral force and influence of his writings is more immediately evident.

FURTHER WORKS: *Le traité du Narcisse* (1891; *Narcissus,* 1953); *Les poésies d'André Walter* (1892); *Le tentative amoureuse* (1893; *The Lover's Attempt,* 1953); *Le voyage d'Urien* (1893; *Urien's Travels,* 1952); *El Hadj* (1899; *El Hadj,* 1953); *Le Prométhée mal enchaîné* (1899; *Prometheus Misbound,* 1953); *Philoctète* (1899; *Philoctetes,* 1952); *Le roi Candaule* (1901; *King Candaules,* 1952); *Prétextes* (1903); *Amyntas* (1906; *Amyntas,* 1958); *Le retour de l'enfant prodigue* (1907; *The Return of the Prodigal,* 1953); *Oscar Wilde* (1910; *Oscar Wilde,* 1949); *Isabelle* (1911; *Isabelle,* 1931); *Nouveaux prétextes* (1911); *Bethsabé* (1912; *Bathsheba,* 1952); *Souvenirs de la cour d'assises* (1914; *Recollections of the Assize Court,* 1941); *Dostoïevsky* (1923; *Dostoevsky,* 1925); *Incidences* (1924); *Si le grain ne meurt . . .* (1926; *If It Die . . .,* 1957); *Le journal des Faux-monnayeurs* (1926; *The Journal of the Counterfeiters,* 1927); *Numquid et tu . . .?* (1926; *Numquid et Tu . . .?,* in *The Journals of A. G.,* 1947–51, Vol. II); *Essai sur Montaigne* (1929; *Montaigne,* 1929); *L'école des femmes* (1929; *The School for Wives,* 1929); *Robert* (1930; *Robert,* 1950); *La séquestrée de Poitiers* (1930); *Œdipe* (1931; *Oedipus,* 1950); *Divers* (1931); *Perséphone* (1934; *Persephone,* 1952); *Les nouvelles nourritures* (1935; *The New Fruits,* in *Fruits of the Earth,* 1949); *Geneviève* (1936; *Genevieve,* 1950); *Retour de l'URSS* 1936; *Return from the U.S.S.R.,* 1937); *Retouches à mon "Retour de l'URSS"* (1937; *Afterthoughts on the U.S.S.R.,* 1938); *Le treizième arbre* (1942); *Attendu que* (1943); *Interviews imaginaires* (1943); *Deux interviews imaginaires, suivis de Feuillets* (1946); *Francis Jammes et A. G.: Correspondance 1898–1938* (1948); *Préfaces* (1948); *Notes sur Chopin* (1948; *Notes on Chopin,* 1949); *Robert; ou, L'interêt général* (1949); *Paul Claudel et A. G.: Correspondance 1899–1926* (1949); *Feuillets d'automne, précédés de quelques récents écrits* (1949; *Autumn Leaves,* 1950); *Littérature engagée* (1950); *Lettres de Charles Du Bos et réponses d'A. G.* (1950); *Et nunc manet in te, suivi de Journal intime* (1951; *Madeleine,* 1952); *Ainsi soit-il; ou, Les jeux sont faits* (1952; *So Be It; or, The Chips Are Down,* 1959); *Correspondance avec Rainer Maria Rilke* (1952); *A. G.–Paul Valéry: Correspondance 1890–1942* (1955);

The Correspondence of A. G. and Edmund Gosse 1904–1928 (1959); *Correspondance d'A. G. à Henri de Régnier* (1963); *Correspondance A. G.–Arnold Bennett* (1964); *Correspondance d'A. G. et d'André Rouveyre* (1967); *A. G.–Roger Martin du Gard: Correspondance* (1968); *Correspondance A. G.–François Mauriac* (1971); *Correspondance avec Albert Mockel* (1975); *Correspondance Henri Ghéon et A. G.* (1976); *Correspondance A. G.–Jules Romains* (1976); *Correspondance A. G.–Jacques Émile Blanche* (1979); *Correspondance A. G.–Dorothy Bussy* (2 vols., 1979–80). FURTHER VOLUMES IN ENGLISH: *Imaginary Interviews* (1944); *Pretexts* (1959)

BIBLIOGRAPHY: Thomas, L., *A. G.: The Ethic of the Artist* (1950); Pierre-Quint, L., *A. G.: Sa vie, son œuvre* (1952); March, H., *G. and the Hound of Heaven* (1952); McClaren, J. C., *The Theater of A. G.: The Evolution of a Moral Philosopher* (1953); O'Brien, J., *Portrait of A. G.* (1953); Lafille, P., *A. G. romancier* (1954); Mallet, R., *Une mort ambiguë* (1955); Schlumberger, J., *Madeleine et A. G.* (1956); Brachfeld, G., *A. G. and the Communist Temptation* (1959); Hytier, J., *A. G.* (1962); Brée, G., *G.* (1963); Delay, J., *The Youth of A. G.* (1963); Fowlie, W., *A. G.: His Life and Art* (1965); Watson-Williams, H., *A. G. and the Greek Myth* (1967); Cordle, T., *A. G.* (1969); Guérard, A., *A. G.* (1969); Ireland, G. W., *A. G.: A Study of His Creative Writings* (1970)

CHARLES G. HILL

[G.'s] *récits* have often been misunderstood, primarily because they have been taken for more or less fictionalized confessions, secondly because they have been read without being "placed" in the ensemble of G.'s works, and finally because their hidden irony has not been discerned. G. explicitly states in one of his *Feuillets:* "With the single exception of my *Nourritures,* all my books are *ironic* works; *they are books of criticism. La porte étroite* is the criticism of a certain form of romantic imagination; *La symphonie pastorale,* of a form of lying to oneself; *L'immoraliste* of a form of individualism."

The *récits* therefore constitute a part of the same series of tendentious works to which the *soties* belonged. They too are satires, although G. has hedged a bit here (" 'Criticism' doesn't mean the same thing as 'satire' "), but of a special nature: they are serious and indirect satires. We all know that a portrait painted with great fidelity and complete submission to the model can be infinitely more cruel than caricature, especially since, being

truthful, it leaves no margin for the illusion of a systematic distortion against which the model could protest. G.'s *récits* are like those implacable portraits in which the painter's very love for his subject serves only to reinforce—emotionally—the severity of his vision by a deliberate accuracy. [1938]

Jean Hytier, *A. G.* (1962), pp. 120–21

G. is a stimulant, a dynamic, hence a potential poison: the invigoration of his doctrine consists in a muscular acceptance of the burden of a temperament, a valiant acquiescence in what is for the sensitive soul more difficult to tolerate than the blows of external fortune—the inward fatality, the thorn in the heart, the original sin: it precognises courage as the highest of the virtues, without particular regard for the ruthlessness it implies, and the human intellect and spirit, unsustained by any such notion as transcendental grace, as adequate sources of strength and instruments of progress. Courage is the insistent thread that connects the Dionysiac assertions of *Les nourritures terrestres, via* the intoxicated heroisms of a Michel, an Alissa, with the lucid, inflexible sobriety of a Thésée. That courage, without constituting greatness, is an ingredient in it, as stimulation is in nourishment, cannot be denied, and only priggish insensitiveness could emerge from immersion in G. without having felt the penetration of an intrepid spirit, the tonic of a rare intellect, without having received the heightened clarity of vision that comes from contact with an intense sensibility.

Lawrence Thomas, *A. G.: The Ethic of an Artist* (1950), pp. 258–59

As the creative fervor ebbed, as the communist venture proved illusory, as he began to feel tired and discouraged, he turned back to view his life and to attempt to discover its significance. Perhaps he was not after all so much of an innovator as he had thought. He had been, it was true, quickly sensitive to changes of literary climate. He had been one of the first to break with the abstractions of Symbolism and to proclaim the necessity for turning back to the "fruits of the earth." He had recognized that the suavely beautiful style, which charmed the esthetes of the late nineteenth and early twentieth centuries and which found its supreme exemplar in Anatole France, needed reinvigoration, and in *Les caves du Vatican* he had written a book which a postwar generation could embrace as its own. If, like many others, he had been deluded about communism, he was one of the first to confess his disillusionment. And he had said things about God and man that anticipated the Existentialists.

Harold March, *G. and the Hound of Heaven* (1952), pp. 386–87

ANDRÉ GIDE

MARNIX GIJSEN

JEAN GIRAUDOUX

The complexity of A. G.'s character and writings has long been legendary. He himself frequently wondered at it, and almost all his commentators, according to their views, have admired or deplored his abundant or devious, but ever surprising, resources. To some the epitome of French classicism, to others an outstanding example of current Alexandrianism, he has variously appeared as a profound religious thinker and a devil's henchman, an apostle of sincerity and a crafty purveyor of guile, a broad humanist and an egocentric introvert, a moral teacher and a calculating perverter of youth. His old friend, Charles Du Bos, who felt after years of subtle converse with G. that he had penetrated the secret, characterized him as a "lattice-work labyrinth."

Indeed, G.'s dynamic equilibrium—this is a word he uses with particular and frequent affection—rests upon a number of familiar antinomies, such as the soul and the flesh, life and art, ethics and aesthetics, ardor and austerity, expression and restraint, the individual and society, classicism and romanticism, Christ and Christianity, God and the devil.

Justin O'Brien, *Portrait of A. G.* (1953), pp. 10–11

G.'s personal ease and fine sense of balance, quite rare in the often crass brutality of our own time, may temporarily, perhaps, hide the firmness and integrity of his critical approach and its value as example and discipline. In the long run it will emerge as the very foundation of his reputation. From *Fruits of the Earth* to *New Fruits of the Earth*, G. eliminated all direct messages from his work. His extraordinary ability as author was to probe and reveal indirectly the devious ways of human consciousness in relation to everyday existence. And in this chosen realm G. concentrated upon a topic of no small consequence: the struggle of human beings with truths compulsively followed.

Germaine Brée, *G.* (1963), p. 3

Indeed, it was the Christian significance of Madeleine's presence that made André Gide exclude her from the atheistic universe of *Les Faux-Monnayeurs*. He wrote it at the time when the future of their relationship seemed conclusively compromised by his mad escapade with M[arc] A[llégret], the time at which he thought he had "lost" the "game" he could have "won only with her." And yet the mystical image had such force that, even in such a godless world, he embodied it in the figure of the angelic Bronja, whose death took away little Boris' only hope for salvation: "Without her how could he believe in the angels . . . ? Even heaven was now empty. Boris went back to the classroom as one might plunge into hell." More than a fictional episode, it was, at the heart of the book, the representation on a childish level of the drama that the fifty-year-old man was experiencing on an adult level.

Jean Delay, *The Youth of A. G.* (1963), p. 456

G.'s strength was in the "logic" of his nature, in that vital dialectic of desire and restraint, of instinct and culture, that marked the progress of his life from neurotic childhood to the stormy conflicts of his late years. His power as an artist began with his intense preoccupation with himself, with his search for that "superior, secret reason for living" that each man bears hidden within his being.

For every impulse he found an equally authentic counterimpulse. The search for love led him to the delight of the senses *and* to the passionate refusal of the sensual. His Christian education implanted in him the seeds of an ascetic moralist and a lyrical enthusiast. He could renounce neither, and therefore became both. He touched the extremes of his culture and experienced in the most intimate and positive way its tensions and contradictions. It was his recognition of the *typicalness* latent in his "complication" that completed his artistic power and assured his genius of its grasp on the minds of men. That, plus the determination reached at the time of *André Walter* to reveal his personality in all its complexity, to hold back nothing, and to make his work coextensive with his being; to make it the consciousness of his life and the validation of his hesitancies as well as of his desires.

Thomas Cordle, *A. G.* (1969), p. 165

[The value of G.'s novels lies in] their psychological interest and accuracy. Like Conrad, the young G. did not read Freud or his disciples. He nevertheless dramatized the unending buried struggle between conscious intention and unconscious need, the forms which uncalculated self-destructiveness may take, the minute workings of repression and sublimation, the "gratuitous acts" of unconscious identification. Intuitive knowledge and successful introspection served G. better than close study served others—as the wearied reader of Lawrence's *The Fox* or Huxley's *Point Counter Point* may verify. The largely fictitious psychology of Faulkner (which posits not merely a collective unconscious memory but a collective unconscious foreknowledge) is more amusing and dramatically perhaps more serviceable. And the old-fashioned introspections and associations of Proust certainly lend themselves better to poetic effect. But G.'s "humane nature" is the one with which we must live. He never consciously explored the unconscious, as a few of his contemporaries did. No doubt this is another limitation. But his intuitive psychology has been discredited at not a single point.

Albert Guérard *A. G.* (1969), p. 180

GIJSEN, Marnix

(pseud. of Jan-Albert Goris) Belgian novelist and essayist (writing in Flemish, French, and English), b. 20 Oct. 1899, Antwerp

G. received a strict Catholic education, first in a school run by nuns, about which he wrote in *Allengs, gelijk de spin* (1962; gradually, like a spider), later in a Jesuit college, depicted in *De man van overmorgen* (1949; the man of the day after tomorrow). Toward the end of World War I he worked as a journalist with strong anti-Walloon opinions. In the early 1920s, after serving in the army, he began his studies at the University of Louvain. After having finished his dissertation, *Étude sur les colonies marchandes méridionales à Anvers de 1488 à 1567* (1925; a study on settlements of merchants from the south in Antwerp, 1488–1567), G. traveled on a study grant to London, Paris, and Seattle. During these years his love for a young woman sustained him; she died in 1927. His memorial to her, *Klaaglied om Agnes* (1951; *Lament for Agnes,* 1975), is one of the most touching ones in Netherlandic literature. Here G. dropped his sarcasm, behind which, in most of his works, he tried to hide his vulnerability. After holding several diplomatic positions, G. was appointed assistant director of the Belgian Pavilion at the 1939 World's Fair in New York, where he was stranded at the outbreak of World War II. In 1940 he accepted the post of director of the Belgian Information Center in New York. After serving as general commissioner of the Belgian Pavilion at Expo '67 in Montreal, G. retired in 1968 and returned to Belgium.

G. began as a religious writer; in his nonfiction work *Loflitanie van den H. Franciscus van Assisi* (1920; litany of praise for St. Francis of Assisi) he defended Christian morality against the inroads of an immoral literature. But in his early forties he broke radically with the Catholic Church and became a convinced and stoic agnostic. In a much later nonfiction book, *Biecht van een heiden* (1971; confession of a pagan), G. lists among the causes of his apostasy what he saw as the intolerance of the Church toward other religions, and above all the incomprehensibility of the suffering of so many innocent creatures. Like Pushkin, whom he admired, G. has a keen sympathy for the downtrodden, who cannot free themselves from misery and suffering.

G.'s novels, the first of which did not appear until 1947—*Het boek van Joachim van Babylon* (*The Book of Joachim of Babylon,*

1951)—often center on the themes of love and death. In several of them he focuses on the contrast between the Old and New Worlds. Although G. lived in the U.S. for more than twenty years, he never became more than a European observer of American life and the American way of thinking. This attitude is seen not only in G.'s first novel set in America, *Goed en kwaad* (1950; good and evil), but as well in his later works, like *Harmàgeddon* (1965; Armageddon). Yet G. pictures life in the U.S. and especially the life of European immigrants in a vividly realistic way.

In other novels and short stories the setting is Flanders, and the narrative incorporates many reminiscences of the author's childhood and youth—for example, *Telemachus in het dorp* (1948; Telemachus in the village).

The main characters of G.'s novels are seen in their relation to society, to the opposite sex, and to themselves. Most of them are lonely outsiders for whom neither life nor the world has meaning. They seek forgetfulness in drink or study. They are portrayed without sentimentality, but so vividly that the reader feels as much sympathy for them as if he knew them personally. Most of G.'s novels are in the first person, and most contain autobiographical details, since he likes to write about himself, as in *Zelfportret, gevleid natuurlijk* (1965; self-portrait, flattering of course) and *De leerjaren van Jan-Albert Goris* (1975; Jan-Albert Goris's years of apprenticeship). It is his belief that the writer must be honest with himself and that every book should bear testimony. Hence, all of G.'s works establish a close relationship between author and reader.

G. has also written poems. In fact, before 1947 he had published only essayistic works and a collection of poems, *Het huis* (1925; the house), which was later followed by the collection *The House by the Leaning Tree* (1963; title in English). In his poetry G. is less hesitant than in his novels to show his feelings and proves to be a master in evoking specific atmospheres.

G.'s two plays, *Helena op Ithaka* (1967; Helen on Ithaca) and the one-act *Een gezellige avond* (1970; a pleasant evening), have not been very successful, probably because of their lack of action.

G. is considered to be the single most important modern writer in the Netherlandic language. His works, in which the mother, the child, the innocently oppressed, play an important role, show a moralistic bent. The main figures are independent individuals who differ from their fellow men and who adjust to society only with great effort. G.'s greatest merit, besides his mastery of the language, is the warmth and tenderness that lie behind a mask of irony and bitterness.

FURTHER WORKS: *De XII sonnetten van de schoonheydt van Brederoo* (1919); *Karel van de Woestijne* (1920); *Breeroo's lyriek* (1922); *Karel van Mander* (1922); *Ontdek Amerika* (1927); *Odysseus achterna* (1930); *Antwerpen* (1930); *Ons volkskarakter* (1932); *Le cœur des États-Unis* (1933); *Lierre* (1935); *Breviarium der Vlaamsche lyriek* (1937); *Josef Cantré, houtsnijder* (1937); *Albert Dürer: Journal de voyage dans les Pays-Bas* (1937; with G. Marlier); *Hans Memling te Brugge* (1939); *De literatuur in Zuid-Nederland sedert 1830* (1940); *Lof van Antwerpen* (1940); *Peripatetisch onderricht* (1940–42); *Belgium in Bondage* (1943); *Du génie flamand* (1943); *Vlaamsche lyriek* (1944); *The Miracle of Beatrice* (1944); *Strangers Should Not Whisper* (1945); *The Liberation of Belgium* (1945); *Rubens in America* (1945, with J. Held); *The Growth of the Belgian Nation* (1946); *Belgian Letters* (1946); *Modern Sculpture in Belgium* (1948); *Modern Belgian Wood Engravers* (1949); *Portraits by Flemish Masters in American Collections* (1949); *Drawings by Modern Belgian Artists* (1951); *De vleespotten van Egypte* (1952); *De kat in de boom* (1953); *Van een wolf, die vreemde talen sprak* (1953); *De lange nacht* (1954); *Wat de dag meebrengt* (1954); *De oudste zoon* (1955); *Some Scholarly Comments on the Saying of the Dutch Poet Leo Vroman "Liever heimwee dan Holland"* (1955); *Er gebeurt nooit iets* (1956); *Marie-ama van Antwerpen* (1957); *De stem uit Amerika* (1957); *Ter wille van Leentje* (1957); *Karel van den Oever* (1958); *Mijn vriend de moordenaar* (1958); *Lucinda en de lotoseter* (1959); *De school van Fontainebleau* (1959); *De diaspora* (1961); *Onze zuster Alice* (1961); *Van een kat die te veel pretentie had* (1963); *Kaddish voor Sam Cohn* (1964); *Candid Opinions on Sundry Subjects* (1964); *Karel Jonckheere* (1964); *Scripta manent* (1965); *De kroniek der poezie* (1965); *De parel der diplomatie* (1966); *Het paard Ugo* (1968); *August van Cauwelaert* (1968); *Het dier en wij* (1968); *Marie Gevers* (1969); *Del val van Zijne Excellentie Minister Plas* (1969); *Jacqueline en ik* (1970); *Gezegden* (1970); *De afvallige* (1971); *Een stad van heren* (1971); *Mi chiamano Mimi*

(1971); *Weer thuis* (1972); *De grote God Pan* (1973); *Orpheus* (1973); *De kroeg van groot verdriet* (1974); *Terug van weggeweest* (1975); *Van een wolf, een kat en een paling* (1976); *Uit het Brussels Getto* (1978); *Overkomst dringend gewenst* (1978); *Verzamelde werken* (1978)

BIBLIOGRAPHY: Hermanowski, G., *Die Stimme des schwarzen Löwen* (1961), pp. 83–87; Meijer, R. P., *Literature of the Low Countries,* new ed. (1978), pp. 361–62

JUDICA I. H. MENDELS

GINSBERG, Allen

American poet, b. 3 June 1926, Newark, N.J.

G. received his B. A. from Columbia University in 1949, after a period of academic probation due to mental instability. Later, he suffered relapses and at one point had himself committed. During the 1940s he formed friendships with the founders of the beat movement, among them William S. Burroughs, Jack Kerouac (qq.v.), and Neal Cassady (1926–1968). They greatly influenced his work, particularly Kerouac's notion of "spontaneous poetics." G. has also traveled widely, and his journeys within the U.S., to South America, Asia, eastern Europe, and the Arctic Circle, have found their way into his poetry.

Although G. first became known as a beat, the label limits him (as it does others) too much, and he underwent a long apprenticeship in traditional forms. Son of poet Louis G. (1895–1976), he began with rhymed and metered lyrics, published many years later as *The Gates of Wrath* (1973). While obviously derivative (the best influence is Blake's lyrics), the poems reveal a sharply accurate imitative ear, and many are accomplished, if not remarkable, in their own right.

At the same time, G. wrote free verse, based on William Carlos Williams's (q.v.) short line of American colloquial speech and published a decade later with an admiring introduction by Williams as *Empty Mirror* (1961). Here, many of G.'s characteristic preoccupations first appear: madness, the journey metaphor, the world not as the veil of divine eternity but as eternity itself, and the notion of poetry as recording. *Empty Mirror*, far more assured and original than *Gates of Wrath*, shows G. as a solid practitioner of the Williams lyric, but with a nightmarish quality of his own.

The appearance of *Howl, and Other Poems* (1956), which led to a well-publicized obscenity trial, turned G. into the biggest American poetic celebrity since Robert Frost (q.v.). Since then G. has seldom been out of the public eye. His participation in various movements—from the 1950s and 1960s drug counterculture to the Vietnam war protests—have been thoroughly documented by the popular press. Unfortunately, G.'s public persona has interfered with critical appreciation of his work. Critics tend to praise or condemn the poems as expressions of an attitude or political stand and have seldom analyzed G.'s craft. The most detailed examination of "Howl," one of the strongest postwar American poems, remains G.'s own *To Eberhart from G.* (1976).

Williams ended his introduction to *Howl, and Other Poems* by saying: "Hold back the edges of your gowns, Ladies, we are going through hell." The nightmare of *Empty Mirror* has intensified. With such literary ancestors as Christopher Smart (1722–1771), Walt Whitman, the prophetic Blake, and, through the last, Jeremiah and Revelations, "Howl" is essentially a series of lengthy catalogues held together by what G. calls a "fixed base," a phrase or syntactic unit repeated with each line. The first part presents an apocalyptic vision of "the best minds of my generation" destroyed by the horrors of contemporary life. The second part names the catastrophic cause, Moloch, identified with big money and Blake's destroying angel of reason, Urizen. The third part, however, affirms that redemptive human love is possible, even in hell—here, G.'s friendship with Carl Solomon, a fellow inmate in the Rockland mental hospital. The final part, "Footnote to Howl," is a hymn of praise, a true kaddish: because of human love, the world is holy, despite the nightmare.

Kaddish, and Other Poems (1961) contains fewer interesting poems than *Howl*. The title poem, however—on the poet's mother, her madness and death—is unsurpassed in G.'s work and represents an advance on "Howl" in its greater complexity of idea and feeling and subtler use of the "fixed base." "Kaddish" begins with G.'s sense of loss and moves on to document his mother's life and death. The second part ends with a "Hymmnn" to the blessedness of the universe, which includes death. The last three sections meditate on death's meaning but end with the sense of something great and unknowable, as opposed to the definite affirmation of "Howl."

G.'s later work can generally be divided into three types: prophecy, vision, and elegy. The influence of Blake, Whitman, Hart Crane (q.v.), and, marginally, Hindu vedas becomes more pronounced. Prophecy in G. is not so much prediction as a call to righteousness. Often it manifests itself in poems on political subjects, mainly in *Planet News* (1968) and *The Fall of America: Poems of These States* (1972). Yet G. is more an ethical or religious poet than a political one. The quality of these prophecies varies greatly. They seem best when most unresolved politically: "Kral Majales" (1965), "Wichita Vortex Sutra" (1966), and the magnificent "Ecologue" (1970) on the spiritual malaise of the times. The visionary poems—from those in *Kaddish* and *Reality Sandwiches* (1961) to those in *Mind Breaths* (1977)—at their best record not only the details of mystical experiences but the poet's sense of their all-importance and his simultaneous inability to articulate their meaning.

Probably influenced by Asian thought, G.'s anger—which lay behind many of his early poems—diminished, and he had to find some other means of sustaining interest, particularly in long works. His experimentation was only partially successful. G. also became interested in music-poetry, particularly blues, but the results were poetically and musically amateurish and without the quirkiness of a genuine primitive. Lacking the early impulse, many of his long poems are "loose, baggy monsters," merely recording phenomena. The visionary poems can become exercises in Hindu deity name-dropping. While G. may admire Eastern philosophies, he often seems not to believe them; in the most moving of his visions, Orientalia play a minor, scenic role.

G. has outlived many friends, and the elegy becomes increasingly important for him. "Don't Grow Old" (1976), on his father's death, suffers when compared to "Kaddish." "Back on Times Square, Dreaming of Times Square" (1958), "Elegy for Neal Cassady" (1968), and the beautiful "On Neal's Ashes" (1968), however, demonstrate mastery of this form and also G.'s continued ability in the short lyric.

FURTHER WORKS: *The Yage Letters* (1963, with William S. Burroughs); *Ankor Wat* (1968); *Airplane Dreams* (1968); *Indian Journals* (1970); *Improvised Poetics* (1971); *Iron Horse* (1974); *Gay Sunshine Interview* (1974); *Allen Verbatim: Lectures on Poetry, Politics, Consciousness* (1974); *The Visions of the Great Rememberer* (1974); *First Blues* (1975); *Sad Dust Glories* (1975); *Chicago Trial Testimony* (1975); *Journals: Early Fifties, Early Sixties* (1977); *As Ever: The Col-*

lected Correspondence of A. G. and Neal Cassady (1977); *Poems All over the Place, Mostly 'Seventies* (1978)

BIBLIOGRAPHY: Ferlinghetti, L., "Horn on *Howl*," *Evergreen*, 1, 4 (1957), 145–58; Ammons, A. R., "G.'s New Poems," *Poetry*, 104 (1964), 186–87; Kramer, J., *A. G. in America* (1969); Merrill, T. F., *A. G.* (1969); Tytell, J., *Naked Angels: The Lives and Literature of the Beat Generation* (1976)

STEVEN SCHWARTZ

GINZBURG, Natalia

Italian novelist, short-story writer, essayist, dramatist, and translator, b. 14 July 1916, Palermo

Born of a Catholic mother and a Jewish father, G. grew up with no religious training or affiliation. This was an important cause, she has said, of her lifelong sense of social isolation. She spent her childhood and adolescence in Turin (where her father was a professor of biology) until her marriage in 1938 to editor and political activist Leone Ginzburg, who died in 1944 while imprisoned by the Germans in Rome. After his death she worked as an editorial consultant for Einaudi publishers in order to help support her three children. In 1950 she married Gabriele Baldini, a professor of English literature at the University of Rome; he died in 1969. She has been awarded numerous literary prizes.

According to G., her first "real" story was "Un'assenza" (an absence), written at age seventeen and published in the Florence magazine *Solaria*. Like all of her later short stories, it has an intimate family setting and centers on an unhappy, anguished individual who is plagued by boredom. The subject here, as in G.'s other works, is the quiet tragedy of the failure of human relationships and, more specifically of the relationship of a couple.

Using a sparse, everyday vocabulary, G. has created a deceptively simple style. Most of her profoundly moving tales are constructed almost entirely of dialogue; frequently they are devoid of action. She excels in reproducing speech patterns and in creating characters through a few of their revealing phrases. What seems at first glance to be a mere recounting of the intimate trivia of daily life becomes, upon reflection, a deep probing of human psychology.

G.'s fiction is avowedly a mixture of reminiscence, observation, and invention. Much of it is written in the first person. In the preface to a 1964 edition of *Cinque romanzi brevi* (five short novels [also contains four short stories]), G. explains that in her first stories she had tried to avoid autobiographical writing. But soon she discovered the "pleasure of first person narrative" and then realized that unconsciously she had been inserting herself into her characters from the very beginning.

A young woman narrator who is disappointed and betrayed in her search for love and understanding figures prominently in three of G.'s best-known works: *La strada che va in città* (1942; *The Road to the City*, 1952), *È stato così* (1947; *The Dry Heart*, 1952), and *Le voci della sera* (1961; *Voices in the Evening*, 1963). The young woman finally reaches a point of quiet desperation that will continue throughout her life.

G.'s longest novel, *Tutti i nostri ieri* (1952; *A Light for Fools*, 1956), is centered on the life of a family during World War II. At the same time, it is the story of a generation that lived through Fascism, war, the German invasion, the Italian resistance, and finally the liberation.

Lessico famigliare (1963; *Family Sayings*, 1967), G.'s autobiographical novel, is the book in which she feels she attained her greatest freedom as a writer. As the title suggests, it is through the repeated words and phrases of the various members of her family that the recollections of her childhood, adolescence, and early adulthood are presented. But it is more than just the story of her family; it is also that of Italian society between the wars.

With the remarkable subtlety and economy that have prompted critics to compare her with Chekhov (q.v.), G. evokes most penetratingly in *Caro Michele* (1973; *No Way*, 1974) the loneliness and sadness of her characters, who, however, still yearn for happiness. Her most recent book, *Famiglia* (1977; family), is a volume of two novellas whose titles, *Famiglia* and *Borghesia* (bourgeoisie), suggest the two main themes of G.'s works. They are the stories of two middle-aged characters whose lives, hopes, and ambitions disintegrate and melt away before our eyes. Finally, both die of illness, and all traces of their lives soon disappear.

Three volumes of G.'s essays and articles have been published: *Le piccole virtù* (1962; little virtues), *Mai devi domandarmi* (1970; *Never Must You Ask Me*, 1973), *Vita immaginaria* (1974; imaginary life). As an essayist, she comments on all manner of subjects, ranging from current movies, books, and art to pedagogy and morals. Her observations are penetrating and stimulating; above all, they are humane.

FURTHER WORKS: *Valentino* (1951); *Sagittario* (1957); *L'inserzione* (1965; *The Advertisement,* 1969); *Fragola e panna* (1966); *La segretaria* (1967); *Ti ho sposato per allegria* (1968); *Paese di mare, e altre commedie* (1973)

BIBLIOGRAPHY: Pacifici, S., *A Guide to Contemporary Italian Literature* (1962), pp. 135–43; "Un-Italian Activities," *TLS,* 23 Feb. 1967, 149; Heiney, D., "N. G.: The Fabric of Voices," *IowaR,* 1, 4 (1970), 87–93; "The Unenchanted," *TLS,* 15 June 1973, 661; Quigly, I., "The Low in Spirit," *TLS,* 2 June 1978, 607; Piclardi, R. D., "Forms and Figures in the Novels of N. G.," *WLT,* 53 (1979), 585–89

JANE E. COTTRELL

GIONO, Jean

French novelist, dramatist, and essayist, b. 30 March 1895, Manosque; d. 8 Oct. 1970, Manosque

Born into a poor family—his father was a shoemaker, his mother operated a laundry—G. left school one year before graduation to accept a job as a bank clerk, so he could help support his family. To find relief from the tedium of his job, G. immersed himself in the literature of classical Greece and Rome. The horrors of World War I turned G. into a passionate and uncompromising pacifist. After the war, he returned to his bank job and also began to write. Success came to him in the late 1920s, enabling him to devote all of his time to his writing career. Because of his pacifist activities, G. was twice imprisoned, once at the outbreak of World War II, and again in 1944, when he was accused of collaboration with the Nazis. He was also blacklisted by the French Liberationist writers, and it took the intervention of André Gide (q.v.) to rehabilitate him. When G. finally made a successful comeback, he was a different writer, since his encounter with the Nazi version of "blood and soil" mythology had led him to a reevaluation of his own earlier attitudes. In 1954 he was elected to the Goncourt Academy.

When *Colline* (1929; *Hill of Destiny,* 1929) was published in book form, G. was hailed by Gide as the new "Vergil from Provence." It was the first work of the "Pan trilogy," which also includes *Un de Baumugnes* (1929; *Lovers Are Never Losers,* 1932) and *Regain* (1930; *Harvest,* 1939). These short novels are regionalist and unabashedly anti-intellectual. G. celebrates the simple, even primitive but noble people of the countryside in their intricate interrelationship with a nature both hostile and benevolent. The books can be seen as the protest of an extremely sensitive man against the artificiality of modern industrial civilization, with its barren cityscapes. G.'s Rousseauesque tendencies became even more dominant in his subsequent works: *Le chant du monde* (1934; *The Song of the World,* 1938), *Que ma joie demeure* (1935; *Joy of Man's Desiring,* 1949), and *Batailles dans la montagne* (1937; battles in the mountain). These works, considerably larger in scope, have been called epic novels. They take their inspiration from a kind of prophetic vision, which reflects the writer's quest for the ideal of a harmonious blending of man with nature.

G.'s idea of a simple life close to nature appealed to many people, and his house in Manosque became a place of pilgrimage. The annual meetings at his farm on the Contadour plateau between master and disciples began in 1935 and ended in 1939. During this Contadour period G. was more of a preacher than a writer. He was deeply disturbed by the growing tyranny of Mussolini, Hitler, and Stalin, and aggressively denounced all political ideologies in Europe. From an artistic viewpoint, however, this period of social involvement resulted in his weakest works.

After the war G. emerged with a new style, which in part can be attributed to his admiration for Stendhal and Machiavelli. In his "chroniques" (chronicles), as G. liked to call them, the effusive poetic descriptions of nature, so prevalent in his previous novels, are subordinated to a more objective depiction of characters. The events are related from the limited perspective of the first-person narrators, who are usually not the protagonists. This seemingly objective detachment on the part of the author himself constitutes an innovation in technique; it owed much to Faulkner (q.v.) and the American novel, with which G. was familiar, and paved the way for the New Novel (q.v.). The style of such "chronicles" as *Un roi sans divertissement* (1947; a lonely king)—film version, 1963—*Les âmes fortes* (1949; strong souls), and *Le moulin de Pologne* (1952; *The Malediction,* 1955) is simple and concise, concentrating on storytelling. Dialogue becomes an important aspect of this new style. The colorful, rather unusual and picturesque adjectives of his early works all but disappeared. The stories are a mixture of minute realism and fantastic adventures.

Probably the most famous of G.'s postwar novels is *Le hussard sur le toit* (1951; *The Horseman on the Roof*, 1954), the picaresque story of Angelo and his efforts to help combat a cholera epidemic and to alleviate the pains of its victims. It is part of the Angelo cycle, whose main characters are largely inspired by G.'s father, mother, and grandfather.

Besides his numerous novels, some youthful poetry, and many provocative essays, G. also wrote several plays, among them the well-known *La femme du boulanger* (1943; the baker's wife) and *Le voyage en calèche* (1947; traveling by calash). In both the much admired poetic spontaneity of his first period and the more spartan style of his later works, G. was a storyteller of extraordinary talent.

FURTHER WORKS: *Accompagnés de la flûte* (1924); *Présentation de Pan* (1930); *Manosque des plateaux* (1930); *Solitude de la pitié* (1930); *Naissance de l'Odyssée* (1930); *Églogues* (1931); *Le grand troupeau* (1931; *To the Slaughterhouse*, 1969); *Jean le bleu* (1932; *Blue Boy*, 1949); *Solitude la pitié* (1932); *Le serpent d'étoiles* (1933); *Les vraies richesses* (1936); *Rondeur des jours* (1936); *Le bout de la route* (1937); *Refus d'obéissance* (1937); *Le poids du ciel* (1938); *Lettre aux paysans sur la pauvreté et la paix* (1938); *Entrée du printemps; Mort du blé* (1938); *Précisions* (1938); *Provence* (1939); *Pour saluer Melville* (1941); *Triomphe de la vie* (1941); *L'eau vive* (1943); *Théâtre* (1943); *Les pages immortelles de Virgile* (1947); *Noé* (1947); *Fragments d'un déluge* (1948); *Fragments d'un paradis* (1948); *Mort d'un personnage* (1949); *Village* (1950); *Les grands chemins* (1951); *Arcadie, Arcadie!* (1953); *Voyage en Italie* (1953); *L'Écossais; ou, La fin des héros* (1955); *Une aventure; ou, La foudre et le sommet* (1955); *Notes sur l'affaire Dominici* (1955; *The Dominici Affair*, 1956); *La pierre* (1955); *Lucien Jacques* (1956); *Bernard Buffet* (1956); *Le bonheur fou* (1957; *The Straw Man*, 1959); *Provence* (1957); *Angelo* (1958; *Angelo*, 1960); *Domitien, suivi de Joseph à Dothan* (1959); *Sur les oliviers morts* (1959); *Chroniques romanesques* (1962); *Le désastre de Pavie* (1963; *The Battle of Pavia*, 1965); *Deux cavaliers de l'orage* (1965; *Two Riders*

of the Storm, 1967); *Provence perdue* (1968); *Ennemonde; ou, Autres caractères* (1968; *Ennemonde*, 1970); *Une histoire d'amour* (1969); *L'Iris de Suze* (1970); *Les récits de la demi-brigade* (1972); *Le déserteur, et autres récits* (1973)

BIBLIOGRAPHY: Chonez, C., *G. par lui-même* (1956); Robert, P. R., *J. G. et les techniques du roman* (1961); Brée, G., and Guiton, M., *The French Novel from Gide to Camus* (1962), pp. 107–13; Ullmann, S., *Style in the French Novel* (1964), pp. 217–31; Smith, M. A., *J. G.* (1966); Redfern, W. D., *The Private World of J. G.* (1967); Peyre, H., *French Novelists of Today*, rev. ed. (1967), pp. 123–54; Goodrich, N. L., *G.: Master of Fictional Modes* (1973)

BLANDINE M. RICKERT

GIPPIUS, Zinaida
See Hippius, Zinaida

GIRAUDOUX, Jean
French dramatist, novelist, and essayist, b. 29 Oct. 1882, Bellac; d. 31 Jan. 1944, Paris

G. was born in a small provincial town in the Limousin region of central France, which was to be the setting of his plays *Intermezzo* (1933; *The Enchanted*, 1950) and the posthumously published *L'Apollon de Bellac* (1946; *The Apollo of Bellac*, 1954) as well as several of his novels. A brilliant student, G. loved the classics of Greek and Roman literature and of 17th-c. France; after secondary school he went on to specialize in German literature, winning a scholarship to continue his German studies in Munich. G. visited the U.S. twice, first as a teaching assistant in the French Department at Harvard University (1906–7), and later during World War I, when, having been wounded at the front and decorated, he was sent by his government as an instructor of military tactics. He recorded his impressions of the U.S. in the essay collection *Amica America* (1918; America my friend).

G. pursued a double career as writer and diplomat. At the age of twenty-seven he entered the foreign service and was assigned to the press bureau. Twenty years later G. became Chief of Press in the Foreign Ministry under Premier Poincaré. He incorporated his impressions of France's leading political figures in his novels: In *Bella* (1926; *Bella,* 1927), G.'s friend Philippe Berthelot, the Secretary General for Foreign Affairs, is the inspiration for the character Dubardeau, while Raymond Poincaré is portrayed in an unfavorable light as the character Rebendart. In *Combat avec l'ange* (1934; struggle with the angel) G. depicts an idealized Aristide Briand in the character Brossard.

In 1939 G. was appointed Minister of Information in the Daladier cabinet, a position in which he felt extremely uncomfortable. Nevertheless, G.'s sense of duty prevailed and he remained in this post until the German Occupation, at which point he resigned, totally discouraged and disillusioned. He died shortly before the Liberation.

As novelist, essayist, and short-story writer, G. was highly regarded by the literary elite. But G.'s early fictional works were too sophisticated to appeal to the general public. His style is highly impressionistic, with plot and character analysis practically eliminated. His protagonists are young, highly cultured intellectuals, usually adolescent girls on the threshold of adulthood. They desire one last chance to escape the humdrum reality of everyday life before they make any permanent commitments. Typical of G.'s early fiction are the novels *Suzanne et le Pacifique* (1921; *Suzanne and the Pacific,* 1923) and *Juliette au pays des hommes* (1924; Juliette in the land of men). *Suzanne et le Pacifique* is set in 1914 at the start of World War I. Suzanne, who comes from G.'s native town of Bellac, is shipwrecked on a desert island in the Pacific, where dead bodies of German and British sailors are washed ashore. G. provides a happy ending for Suzanne when she finds her Prince Charming in the person of the Supervisor of Weights and Measures, a character partially inspired by G.'s own father, a tax collector. A similar character appeared thirteen years later to provide a happy ending for Isabelle in *Intermezzo.* In *Juliette au pays des hommes* the heroine visits several interesting men and explores the various possible existences she might lead before returning to marry her loyal fiancé Gérard. Like several other writers of his time, especially Gide and Cocteau (qq.v.), G. felt a special nostalgia for childhood and adolescence. The young and uncommitted are endowed with intuitive powers, beauty, and grace, while the middle-aged characters are generally stereotyped as dull, pretentious, and corrupt.

In addition to its importance as a prefiguration of *Intermezzo, Juliette au pays des hommes* is noteworthy for G.'s famous ironic definition of preciosity: "an evil that consists of treating objects like human beings, human

beings as if they were chaste gods, and gods as if they were cats or weasels." This definition of preciosity is precisely G.'s technique in his novels and plays. He elevates the status of everyday objects and ordinary human beings while mocking the gods—Jehovah as well as Jupiter.

It was not until he reached the age of forty-six that G. began to write for the theater. In collaboration with the actor-director Louis Jouvet, G. adapted his novel *Siegfried et le Limousin* (1922; *My Friend from Limousin,* 1923) for the stage under the title *Siegfried* (1928; *Siegfried,* 1930). In reworking his novel for the stage, G. was forced to tighten the structure of his work and eliminate the lengthy digressions that tended to make all his novels rather diffuse.

The story of Siegfried, a French amnesia victim who is nursed back to health and given a new identity by the Germans, is G.'s idealistic plea for Franco-German friendship and understanding. When Siegfried renounces the political power he could have enjoyed as a German and decides to resume his French identity and return to France as Jacques Forestier, Geneviève, the Frenchwoman he had loved, cries out, "Siegfried!"—indicating that she now loves the German in him. G. himself loved both France and Germany. His most cherished hope was for a reconciliation between those two great cultures. From G.'s point of view, France represented clarity, order, logic, and the great classics of Molière, Racine, and La Fontaine. G. considered Germany as representing the heroic, the rebellious, the unknowable, and the romantic, as best exemplified in the masterpieces of German music. In 1928 G. was still optimistic enough to believe that the two countries could live in harmony. Through human fraternity, G. thought, it would be possible to blend the best elements of both cultures.

The opening of G.'s drama *Siegfried* was the major theatrical event of the decade; critics hailed the play as marking the return of dramatic "literature" to the stage. It was praised for its verbal inventiveness and its poetic vision. Before the opening of *Siegfried,* the French naturalistic theater was at a low ebb, and the public was ready to turn to poetry and fantasy, which it found in abundance in G.

G.'s second play, the light comedy *Amphitryon 38* (1929; *Amphitryon 38,* 1939) was both a critical and popular success. Supposedly the thirty-eighth version of the classical legend of Jupiter's seduction of the faithful Alcmena, when he visits her disguised as her husband Amphityron, this play combines bedroom farce with serious discussions about human destiny.

In a verbal battle of wits, G.'s Alcmena clearly outsmarts the foolish, egotistical ruler of the universe, Jupiter. She finds nothing especially impressive about Jupiter's performance in bed and characterizes their night of lovemaking as merely pleasant, remembering other more exciting nights spent in the arms of her husband. Irony and paradoxes abound when Jupiter is tricked by his own disguise into feeling totally human—yet feeling more powerful in that form than he had felt as a god.

The failure of *Judith* (1931; *Judith*, 1955), G.'s third play and the only drama he labeled a "tragedy," left him bitter and apprehensive. Just as *Amphitryon 38* poked fun at the gods of antiquity, so *Judith*, a modern version of the killing of Holofernes by the Hebrew maiden Judith, mocks the story of purity and self-sacrifice in the Old Testament. For his next play, G. returned to familiar ground, to Bellac, for the setting of his comedy-fantasy *Intermezzo*, in which the heroine Isabelle must choose between a Ghost, who promises to initiate her into the secrets of the kingdom of the dead, and the more down-to-earth Supervisor of Weights and Measures, who promises to help Isabelle find beauty and poetry in everyday provincial life.

G.'s most important success, both in France and in the U.S., was the antiwar drama *La guerre de Troie n'aura pas lieu* (1935; *Tiger at the Gates*, 1955). At the peak of his creative powers, G. drew upon his own background not only as a scholar of the classics but also as a war veteran and as a diplomat experienced in the subtleties of peace negotiations. G.'s play focuses on the events leading up to the Trojan War and on the desperate efforts of the Trojan general Hector to avert a catastrophe. G.'s ironic theme here, as in his other serious dramas, is that despite their best efforts, human beings are powerless to control their destiny. The Trojan War will take place because it was preordained by the gods. Yet Hector's oration for the war dead, a brilliant and ironic indictment of war for depriving men of the joys of life, is more memorable than any other lines in the play.

During the 1930s G. became increasingly bitter and pessimistic. As his hopes for a reconciliation between France and Germany grew dimmer, the mood of his plays grew darker. *Électre* (1937; *Electra*, 1952) illustrates the devastation brought about by those who seek absolute justice and refuse to compromise. Electra, like Judith, young, pure, self-righteous and unyielding, refuses to forgive the now repentant Aegisthus for the murder of her father Agamemnon, although she realizes that Aegis-

thus' death will cause the destruction of the city of Argos and the slaughter of thousands of innocent victims who played no part in her father's assassination. The search for the absolute, the refusal to compromise and to accept life's imperfections, leads inevitably to death and destruction.

The same moral can be found in G.'s most delightful fantasy, *Ondine* (1939; *Ondine*, 1954). Based on a German legend popularized by Friedrich de la Motte-Fouqué (1777–1843), *Ondine* deals with man's quest for a perfect love and his failure to achieve a perfect union with his beloved. Much of the character of Ondine, the water sprite, was already sketched out in the chapter entitled "Stephy" (1929), which was incorporated into G.'s novel *Les aventures de Jérôme Bardini* (1930; the adventures of Jérôme Bardini). Ondine, a child of nature, eternally young, sincere, and beautiful, courts and woos the knight-errant Hans von Wittenstein, who is initially bedazzled by her charms. The failure of their love to survive in the artificial society of the royal court, and Hans's failure to appreciate the true value of Ondine's honesty and purity give the play its tragic overtones. Yet here, as in his other works, when a dramatic situation becomes too painful to bear, G. provides escape through comedy and fantasy, with secondary characters supplying humorous interludes.

G.'s most popular success came posthumously when Louis Jouvet directed G.'s *La folle de Chaillot* (1945; *The Madwoman of Chaillot*, 1947). In this farce a delightfully zany old lady and her equally nonconformist accomplices, all of whom are outcasts from society, take on the military-industrial establishment of Paris and actually win, saving the beautiful city from the threat of being torn apart and drilled for oil. The play is a scathing indictment of the greed, materialism, and mechanization of modern society. It is also a hymn to the beauties of everyday life. When Aurélie, the Madwoman of Chaillot, expresses her love for life to Pierre, the young man who has just been rescued from an attempt at suicide, the audience cannot help but be moved. If this destitute old woman can find joy in her meager existence, how much more joy there must be for those more fortunate than she! G.'s zest for life is contagious. According to him, all the living are lucky—lucky to be alive. Beauty and poetry exist. Modern man should not be too sophisticated to appreciate the simple pleasures of being alive.

An early environmentalist, G. awakens us to the beauties of our surroundings and to the need to preserve our towns from the onslaught of modern technology. In the one-act play *L'impromptu de Paris* (1937; the rehearsal in Paris), a theoretical discussion on the theater inspired by Molière's *L'impromptu de Versailles,* G. has Louis Jouvet and his troupe of actors express his own noble ambitions for the theater. As G.'s principal spokesman, Jouvet explains the way in which a good play can touch and transform the viewer, awakening his latent sensitivities. Before the viewer can understand and intellectualize, the play must appeal to his emotions and his imagination. In order for this quasi-mystical experience to take place, the play must move the viewer through its extraordinary style.

Throughout his career, G. was, above all, a great stylist. His elegant language and sparkling wit are the products of a man who, according to his friend the novelist Paul Morand (q.v.), never uttered a vulgar word in his life. His writings contain enough stylistic devices (metaphors, similes, litotes, parallels, and antitheses) to illustrate an entire manual of rhetoric, yet his style is very personal. Even today, G.'s verbal technique remains unequaled. It is especially for his style that he is regarded as the outstanding French playwright of the period between the two world wars, and one of the greatest dramatists of the 20th c.

FURTHER WORKS: *Provinciales* (1909); *L'école des indifférents* (1910); *Lectures pour une ombre* (1917; *Campaigns and Intervals,* 1918); *Simon le pathétique* (1918); *Adieu à la guerre* (1919); *Elpénor* (1919; *Elpenor,* 1958); *Adorable Clio* (1920); *La Pharmacienne* (1922); *La prière sur la Tour Eiffel* (1923); *Visite chez le Prince* (1924); *Hélène et Touglas; ou, Les joies de Paris* (1925); *Premier rêve signé* (1925); *Le cerf* (1926); *Les hommes tigres* (1926); *Églantine* (1927); *La grande bourgeoise; ou, Toute femme a la vocation* (1928); *Marche vers Clermont* (1928); *Le sport* (1928); *Divertissement de Siegfried* (1928); *Le signe* (1929); *Racine* (1930; *Racine,* 1938); *Fugues sur Siegfried* (1930); *Mirage des Bessines* (1931); *Je présente Bellita* (1931); *Berlin* (1932); *La France sentimentale* (1932); *Fin de Siegfried* (1934); *Tessa* (1934); *Supplément au voyage de Cook* (1937; *The Virtuous Island,* 1956); *Et moi aussi, j'ai été un petit Meaulnes* (1937); *Les cinq tentations de La Fontaine* (1938); *Cantique des cantiques* (1938; *Song of Songs,* 1961); *Choix des élues* (1938); *Pleins pouvoirs* (1939); *Le futur armistice* (1940); *Pour*

l'avenir français (1940; *The France of Tomorrow,* 1940); *Littérature* (1941); *L'Apollon de Marsac* (1942); *Le film de la duchesse de Langeais* (1942); *Sodome et Gomorrhe* (1943; *Sodom and Gomorrah,* 1961); *Le film de Béthanie: Texte de "Les anges du péché"* (1944, with Raymond Léopold Bruckberger and Robert Bresson); *Écrit dans l'ombre* (1944); *Armistice à Bordeaux* (1945); *Théâtre complet* (15 vols., 1945–54); *Sans pouvoirs* (1946); *Pour une politique urbaine* (1947); *Visitations* (1947); *Variantes* (3 vols., 1947–48); *De pleins pouvoirs à sans pouvoirs* (1950); *La Française et la France* (1951); *Pour Lucrèce* (1951; *Duel of Angels,* 1958); *Les contes d'un matin* (1952); *Œuvre romanesque* (2 vols., 1955); *Œuvres littéraires diverses* (1958); *La menteuse* [fragments] (1958); *Un prince* (1962); *Or dans la nuit: Chroniques et préfaces littéraires, 1910–1943* (1969); *La menteuse* [complete text] (1969; *Lying Woman,* 1972)

BIBLIOGRAPHY: Brasillach, R., "Le théâtre de J. G.," *Portraits* (1935), pp. 123–63; Rousseaux, A., "G.; ou, L'éternel printemps," *Âmes et visages du XXᵉ siècle* (1936), pp. 109–56; Sartre, J.-P., "M. J. G. et la philosophie d'Aristote: À propos de *Choix des élues,*" *NRF,* 54 (1940), 339–54; Magny, C.-E., *Précieux G.* (1945); Morand, P., *G.: Souvenirs de notre jeunesse* (1948); Sørensen, H., *J. G.: Technique et style* (1950); Jouvet, L., *Témoignages sur le théâtre* (1952), pp. 148–56, 185–213; May, G., "Marriage vs. Love in the World of J. G.," *YFS,* 11 (1953), 106–15; Mercier-Campiche, M., *Le théâtre de G. et la condition humaine* (1954); Albérès, R.-M., *Esthétique et morale chez J. G.* (1957); Inskip, D., *J. G.: The Making of a Dramatist* (1958); Debidour, V. H., *J. G.* (1958); Le Sage, L., *J. G.: His Life and His Works* (1959); Cohen, R., *G.: Three Faces of Destiny* (1968); Lemaitre, G., *J. G.: The Writer and His Work* (1971)

DEBRA POPKIN

M. G. is a man of fancy, fantasy and humor. His aesthetic is built upon unexpectedness and disproportion, and leaves us with the minor feeling Poe noted—a sense of difficulties happily surmounted. It moves in the direction of romanticism, not realism, of entertainment, not experience. The heart of his mental machinery is contained in the following sentence: his whole book is a dilation of that heart. "I tasted large scarlet mushrooms: in France I would have had spotted fever, numb fingers, twitching eyelids; but solitude vaccinated me against all these ills." One who believes that the function of literary art is to give a proportioned heightened representation of the actual cannot follow in the direction of M. G.

But to such a one the principal overtone of *Suzanne and the Pacific* may be valuable. Suzanne is adorably attached to modern civilization. Pitched on a desert island, she hunts for rice powders, perfumes, tobacco, feather dresses: she yearns for railway stations, daily newspapers, moving-pictures, metropolitan crowds; she finally makes her island a fragment of France. . . . M. G. is adept at turning the texture of modern sensations into literature, and in the exploitation of these new undigested materials, he is a comrade of the dadaists.

Gorham B. Munson, "A Specimen of Demi-Dadaisme," *New Republic*, 18 April 1923, 220

G. restores freedom to the French stage [in *Siegfried*]. He demands nothing either of the ballet, the cinema, or the music-hall. He asks everything of words, style, expression. His theater is a literary theater, a poetic theater, a return to dramatic literature; in the very heart of dramatic literature, he succeeds in asserting his originality. . . .

Siegfried marks a date, a point of departure, a new hope. It marks the theater's escape from naturalism, from too much psychology, through poetry (not expressionism or futurism). It marks the renaissance of style in the theater, the resurrection of drama in which each character has the right to finish his sentences, to utter monologues or even long declamations, the resurrection of theater from which intellectual ideology, verbal magic have not been banished, theater which allows ecstasy, expansiveness, enthusiasm, theater big enough to house the world, great enough to contain the struggle between modern consciences and the most burning questions.

Since Musset, no French author has approached the stage with so much ease and grace. With fewer paradoxes and less vehemence, the *Siegfried* of G. introduces into our theater the freedom and diversity which the English stage owes to Bernard Shaw. [1928]

Benjamin Crémieux, "J. G.'s *Siegfried*," in Justin O'Brien, ed., *From the N. R. F.* (1958), pp. 167–68

The role in J. G.'s universe delegated to Isabelle [in *Intermezzo*] is the one that the entire Middle Ages delegated to the young girl, that of the interpreter of the supernatural world. It is she who is tempted to exceed the limits of the earth—but not to betray the world. What she desires is not so much to die as to annex a new kingdom for life —and this kingdom happens to be the kingdom of the dead. . . . Although the wise supervisor reprimands her, dangerous tasks are always undertaken by young girls, and it is right that they should:

thanks to these young girls, our vision is expanded, our dreams find some foundation, and the most ambitious extravagances acquire some sort of real substance. Are the dead not ready to reenter the world of the living? . . .

Only young girls can suppose so, and perhaps they can even find proof. Isabelle is our Parsifal, declares the sentimental yet ironic supervisor. But as soon as a potential husband appears for Isabelle, the whole beautiful supernatural world she has seen will disappear. . . . She will be converted to the limited wisdom of the supervisor, and since she will no longer be able to know anything else, she will finally consent, with courageous calm, to turn her back upon the charms of ghosts and gods in order to rejoin humanity. It is a shame, no doubt—but that is the price of living.

Robert Brasillach, *Portraits* (1935), pp. 145–47

In order to enter fully into the universe of *Choice of the Elect*, we must first forget the world in which we live. I therefore pretended that I knew nothing at all about this soft, pasty substance traversed by waves whose cause and purpose are exterior to themselves, this world without a future, in which things are always meeting, in which the present creeps up like a thief, in which events have a natural resistance to thought and language, this world in which individuals are accidents, mere pebbles, for which the mind subsequently fabricates general categories. . . .

It would be a mistake, however, to regard M. G. as a Platonist. His forms are not in the heaven of ideas, but among us, inseparable from the matter whose movements they govern. They are stamped on our skin like seals in glass. Nor are they to be confused with simple concepts. A concept contains barely more than a handful of the traits common to all the individuals of a given group. Actually, M. G.'s forms contain no more, but the features that compose them are all perfect. They are norms and canons rather than general ideas. [1940]

Jean-Paul Sartre, *Literary and Philosophical Essays* (1955), pp. 43–44

As with *Siegfried*, the broad political panorama prevents [*The Trojan War Will Not Take Place*] from wallowing in seriousness. G. delighted in wit, wordplay, and theatrical legerdemain as before—concluding the play with an extraordinary device in which the curtain begins to fall and then rises again. The theatricalism enforces an objectivity over the crucial issue of war, and prevents the play from rigidly taking a side and becoming propagandistic instead of analytic, which it remains. . . .

The Trojan War [*Will Not Take Place*] is a play about war and against it. It is not mere pacifism—an oversimplification which G. would have abhorred, and it is far from one-sided. But the message is clear, and when the brilliance of the dialogue, the theatricalism of the setting, and the complex progression of the plot have receded in our minds, the bitterness at war's irrationality remains. Easily comprehensible in its major theme, *The Trojan War* [*Will Not Take Place*] is G.'s final despairing cry for peace, and it has become one of the rare masterpieces of the century.

Robert Cohen, *G.: Three Faces of Destiny* (1968), pp. 103–4

As G. advanced in age, his characters seemed to acquire more and more the value of pure symbols. . . .

This progressive degradation of the characters representing passionate reality seems to parallel the change for the worse that took place in G.'s personal views of the real itself. In the last years of his life G. was evidently overwhelmed by a feeling of disgust for the world in which we live. Although he fought as best as he could against that feeling in such works as *L'Apollon de Bellac* and *La folle de Chaillot*, his final outlook remained grim. A few of the "elect"—of whom Lucile is the last example in his plays—may be personally exempt from the taint of almost universal corruption, but they can escape defilement at the contact of the world and retain their essence of purity only by moving out of this world altogether.

During his youth, a happy G. had fondly believed that the ideal and reality could meet. In his mature age, he had toyed with the hundred possibilities of interplay between them. When he grew old, he reached the disconsolate conclusion that they are incompatible. Rather than debase the ideal, rather than submit to the loathsome claims of reality, he chose to retain the ideal intact—in death. This is the fundamental meaning of *Pour Lucrèce* and the last message of G. himself before his own end.

Georges Lemaitre, *J. G.: The Writer and His Work* (1971), p. 145

GIRONELLA, José María

Spanish novelist, essayist, and critic, b. 31 Dec. 1917, Darnius

G. grew up in a small village near Gerona in Catalonia, where he has lived most of his life. He never received any formal education and in his youth worked at a variety of odd jobs ranging from factory apprentice to bank clerk; he had ambitions to become a priest but abandoned this idea. At the outbreak of the civil war in 1936 he joined the Nationalist army;

during the war he wrote many letters and love poetry. In 1940, after the end of the war, he returned to Gerona and became a newspaper reporter; he also was a correspondent for *Informazione* in Rome. In 1947 G. and his wife left Spain illegally and traveled extensively. He suffered a nervous breakdown in 1951 while in Paris and sought cures at clinics in Vienna and Helsinki; he described his illness in *Los fantasmas de mi cerebro* (1958; in *Phantoms and Fugitives*, 1964). G. returned to Spain in 1952 but has continued to travel abroad periodically.

G.'s first novel, *Un hombre* (1946; *Where the Soil Was Shallow*, 1957), won the Nadal Prize. Somewhat autobiographical, it is an improbable circus tale that displays all the romantic zeal of a young writer trying to discover himself and his métier through literature. *La marea* (1949; the tide) is an "experimental" novel in which he successfully integrated history with a highly unlikely love story among Nazis set in Germany during World War II. It was virtually unnoticed by critics.

G.'s most famous work is *Los cipreses creen en Dios* (1953; *The Cypresses Believe in God*, 1955), which won the National Prize for Literature. It is a long novel of great scope. G. is a master storyteller, and as this novel shows, his forte lies in graphically explicating the panorama of the Spanish Civil War. *Los cipreses creen en Dios* and two sequels—*Un millón de muertos* (1961; *One Million Dead*, 1963) and *Ha estallado la paz* (1966; *Peace after War*, 1969), both of which are of lesser importance than the first book—trace the vicissitudes of the Alvear family from the period before the civil war to its aftermath. The Alvears are very much individuals, but their struggles also represent the struggles of all Spanish families who shared in the making of history during the civil war, and the characters take on a universal significance.

G. has written, among other things, several travel books on Japan, China, and Israel; a highly praised collection of short stories and essays entitled *Todos somos fugitivos* (1961; in *Phantoms and Fugitives*, 1964), whose central theme is escape—from reality, loneliness, death; and a best-selling novel in two volumes, *Condenados a vivir* (1971; condemned to live), which continues the Alvear family saga, tracing the lives of the characters through the decade of the 1940s. Yet nothing has equaled the quality and success of *Los cipreses creen en Dios*. Nevertheless, he is very prominent on the Spanish literary scene. He spearheaded efforts against government censorship of literature in the early 1950s and is also one of the first Catalan writers still residing in Spain to approach straightforwardly the "forbidden" subject of the civil war. He is also indisputably the first novelist to publish an explanation of the civil war generally acceptable to Spaniards.

FURTHER WORKS: *Ha llegado el invierno y tú no estás aquí* (1945); *El novelista ante el mundo* (1954); *Muerte y juicio de Giovanni Papini* (1959); *Mujer, levántate y anda* (1962); *Personas, ideas y mares* (1963; partial tr., *On China and Cuba*, 1963); *El Japón y su duende* (1964); *China, lágrima innumerable* (1965); *Gritos del mar* (1967); *En Asia se muere bajo las estrellas* (1968); *Conversaciones con Don Juan de Borbón* (1968); *Cien españoles y Dios* (1969); *Gritos de la tierra* (1970); *Los hombres lloran solos* (1971); *El escándalo de Tierra Santa* (1977); *Carta a mi padre muerto* (1978)

BIBLIOGRAPHY: Boyle, K., "Spain Divided," *Nation,* 11 June 1955, 506–7; Kerrigan, A., "J. M. G. and the Black Legend of Spain," *Books on Trial,* 14 (1956), 343–45; Devlin, J. J., "Arturo Barea and J. M. G.: Two Interpreters of the Spanish Labyrinth," *Hispania,* 41 (1958), 143–48; Urbanski, E. S., "Revolutionary Novels of G. and Pasternak," *Hispania,* 43 (1960), 191–97; Payne, R., on *Peace after War, SatR,* 17 May 1969, 49; Schwartz, R., *J. M. G.* (1972); Schwartz, R., *Spain's New Wave Novelists, 1950–1974: Studies in Spanish Realism* (1976), pp. 50–65

RONALD SCHWARTZ

GLADKOV, Fyodor Vasilievich

Russian novelist and short-story writer, b. 21 June 1883, Chernavka; d. 20 Dec. 1958, Moscow

G. was born into an impoverished peasant family of Old Believers (a sect of Russian schismatics). In his youth, he held various jobs before becoming a teacher in 1902. Except for his exile to Siberia (1906–9) for pro-Bolshevik activity, he taught until 1918. Following the October revolution he fought for the Bolsheviks and joined the Communist Party in 1920. In 1921 he turned to literature full time.

G. first began to publish as early as 1900. His initial formative period was influenced by Maxim Gorky's (q.v.) sympathetic depiction of rebellious tramps, and by symbolism (q.v.)—especially its cult of suffering and morbid eroticism. Both influences are seen in *Izgoi* (written 1909–11, pub. 1922; the outcasts), a collection of narratives that portray a socially variegated group of political exiles in Siberia. As would prove characteristic of G., authorial sympathies favored the steadfast workers over the seriously flawed intellectuals.

After the revolution, his proletarian orientation notwithstanding, G.'s prose reflected ornamentalism, an essentially nonproletarian, experimentalist trend begun by Andrey Bely (q.v.), and adopted by many aspiring Soviet authors. Ornamentalism increased the expressive potential of prose through metaphoric density, rhythmic and sound devices proper to poetry, and esoteric vocabulary. Ornamentalism was prominent in G.'s tale *Ognenny kon* (1923; the fiery steed), which also reflected a common view (later heretical) that the Russian Revolution was a national, organic event beyond the control of individuals or parties. G. would ultimately renounce *Ognenny kon.*

In 1923 G. joined The Forge, a group of writers who extolled the proletariat and burgeoning technology. The group's principles, together with ornamentalism, would be prominent in G.'s most famous work, the novel *Tsement* (1925; *Cement,* 1929), which focuses upon the efforts of a Communist, Gleb Chumalov, to resume production in a cement factory that closed during the civil war. Gleb overcomes worker apathy and hostility, red tape, sabotage, and various technical problems, but his social victories are offset on a personal level by the death of his daughter and estrangement from his wife Dasha, who, during Gleb's military service, changed from a dutiful housewife to a fully emancipated woman and promiscuous social activist. Through Gleb and Dasha, G. raised, but did not resolve, the question of emancipation for Soviet women and its implications for the family. The same holds true for G.'s handling of the plight of Soviet intellectuals; the problem of maintaining revolutionary fervor in the face of concessions to free enterprise under the NEP (New Economic Policy); and internal Party justice (the purge scenes and the "personality cult" surrounding Badin, a ruthless Party leader).

Tsement became popular, not just because it was topical and proletarian, but also because its stylistic richness and racy characters were interesting. From the later 1920s until his death, however, G. repeatedly weakened *Tsement* by revising it to reflect Socialist Realist (q.v.) principles of stylistic neutrality, maximal clarity, puritanism, and Party loyalty. Similarly questionable, if less extensive, revisions affected most of G.'s other works, including his unfinished, serially published construction novel *Energia* (1932–38; energy).

The most interesting of G.'s later works is his autobiographical cycle: *Povest o detstve* (1949; a tale of childhood); *Volnitsa* (1950; a free gang); *Likhaya godina* (1954; a woeful year), and the unfinished *Myatezhnaya yunost* (1956; *Restless Youth*, 1958). The cycle is thoroughly Socialist Realist in that it shows the prerevolutionary order as inhumane, corrupt, and historically doomed, while amid religious bigotry and oppression, Russian toilers show promise of revolt in the name of truth, freedom, and social justice. While character and social relationships are basically pat, G. often makes his narratives engrossing through the immediacy of dramatic episodes, colorful language, and the beauty of the natural world.

The retrospective incursion of Socialist Realist criteria into so much of G.'s corpus makes the assessment of his legacy highly problematical. Talented enough to earn the esteem of both Gorky and Bely, he was representative of many Soviet artists of the 1920s who tried to combine a sincere commitment to revolutionary ideals with the search for artistic originality. When political criteria became paramount in Soviet literature from the late 1920s onward, he gradually and dutifully accommodated them with dire effect upon the intrinsic interest of his works. Nevertheless, G.'s *Tsement*, a Soviet classic, many of whose themes, while tempered by revisions, are still relevant in the Soviet Union, has been translated into all major languages of the world, and represents its author's main continuing claim to international renown.

FURTHER WORKS: *Staraya sekretnaya* (1926); *Malenkaya trilogia* (1927); *Novaya zemlya* (1931); *Pyanoe solntse* (1932); *Beryozovaya roshcha* (1940); *Klyatva* (1944); *Sobranie sochineny* (8 vols., 1958); *Myatezhnaya yunost, ocherki, stati, vospominania* (1961)

BIBLIOGRAPHY: Brown, E. J., *Russian Literature since the Revolution* (1963), pp. 162–71; Struve, G., *Russian Literature under Lenin and Stalin, 1917–1953* (1971) pp. 132–34; Busch, R. L., "G.'s *Cement*: The Making of a Soviet Classic," *SEEJ*, 22 (1978), 348–61; Vavra, E., Afterword to *Cement* (1980), pp. 313–25
ROBERT L. BUSCH

GLATSTEIN, Jacob

(Glatshteyn, Yankev) Yiddish poet, critic and essayist, b. 20 Aug. 1896, Lublin, Poland; d. 19 Nov. 1971, New York, N.Y., U.S.A.

G. received a sound traditional Jewish religious education as well as instruction in secular subjects. As a child he was first exposed to the writings of the Yiddish classics by his father, whose decisive influence G. acknowledged in later life. He began to write at an early age. At thirteen he traveled to Warsaw, like many other aspiring Yiddish writers of the day, to show his work to Yitskhok Leybush Peretz (1852–1915).

In 1914, in response to mounting anti-Semitism, G. emigrated to the U.S., arriving in New York, the city that became his permanent home. That same year he published his first piece, a short story. G. experienced a difficult period of adaptation to his new environment and ceased writing Yiddish for a time. In 1918, while studying law, influenced by the works of Rabindranath Tagore (q.v.) and Kahlil Gibran (1883–1931), he began to write poetry in English. A young Yiddish poet, Nokhem Borekh Minkoff (1893–1958), introduced G. to the then-flourishing Yiddish literary community, which prompted his return to writing Yiddish. The outstanding Yiddish poets Moyshe Leyb Halpern (q.v.) and H. Leivick (1886–1962) encouraged him. In 1919 G. made his poetic debut. Together with Aaron Glanz-Leyeles (1889–1966) and N. B. Minkoff, he launched the "Inzikh," or introspective movement in American Yiddish poetry—the name derived from the group's journal, *In zikh* (inside the self).

To insure his livelihood, G. turned to journalism, an occupation he had previously shunned as unfit for a poet. He began a long and respected career as a columnist, commenting on most significant events in Jewish literary and cultural life as well as on world literature.

In 1934 G. returned to Poland to visit his dying mother in Lublin. This journey resulted in two autobiographical travel narratives, *Ven yash iz geforn* (1938; *Homeward Bound*, 1969) and *Ven yash iz gekumen* (1940; *Homecoming at Twilight*, 1962), notable for their innovative poetic prose permeated by a sense of impending doom.

G. is recognized first and foremost for his poetic achievement. At the outset of his career a principal theorist of the introspectivist group, G. was influenced by Ezra Pound and T. S. Eliot and by imagism (qq.v.). The Inzikh program emphasized the concrete image and pre-ferred association and suggestion to direct statement and logical development. G. helped introduce free verse into Yiddish poetry in order to capture the rhythms of everyday speech and to convey the sounds of the modern metropolis. In his first two volumes, *Yankev Glatshteyn* (1921; Jacob Glatstein) and *Fraye ferzn* (1926; free verse), he asserted his personality and the principles of the Inzikh program.

G. did not remain bound to introspectivist theory or to any literary dogma, but his penchant for the rhythms of the spoken language, his bold imagery, his use of association and suggestion, and his gift for irony are continuing elements that characterize his entire poetic oeuvre.

From the beginning of his career as a poet, G. was in love with the vitality of language and particularly with his medium, the Yiddish language. His brilliant word play, his invention of nonce words and neologisms, although more evident in the earlier stage of his career, persist as striking features of his poetry.

The Holocaust transformed G. into one of the great elegists of eastern European Jewry. He treasured and memorialized the goodness and justness of its life and the humanism of its culture. Yet, significant strains of G.'s post-Holocaust poetry remain personal and private. When G. accepted the burden to bear witness to the Holocaust, in his *Gedenklider* (1943; memorial poems), *Shtralndike Yidn* (1946, radiant Jews), and *Dem tatns shotn* (1953; my father's shadow), previously unsympathetic critics who mistrusted the rebellious individualist now embraced G. as the spokesman of a national culture.

FURTHER WORKS: *Kredos* (1929); *Yidishtaytshn* (1937); *Emil un Karl* (1940); *Yosl Loksh fun Khelm* (1944); *In tokh genumen* (1947); *Fun mayn gantser mi* (1956); *In tokh genumen* (1956); *In tokh genumen* (2 vols., 1960); *Di freyd fun yidishn vort* (1961); *Mit mayne fartogbikher* (1963); *A yid fun Lublin* (1966); *Af greyte temes* (1967); *Kh'tu dermonen* (1967); *Gezangen fun rekhts tsu links* (1971); *In der velt mit yidish* (1972); *Prost un poshet* (1978). FURTHER VOLUMES IN ENGLISH: *Poems* (1970); *The Selected Poems of J. G.* (1972)

BIBLIOGRAPHY: Faerstein, C., "J. G.: The Literary Uses of Yiddish," *Judaism*, 14 (1965), 414–31; Howe, I., "Journey of a Poet," *Commentary*, Jan. 1972, 75–77; Lapin, S., "J. G.: Poetry and Peoplehood," *American Jewish Yearbook*, 73 (1972), 611–17; Tabatshnik, A., "A Conversation with J. G.," *Yiddish*, 1 (1973), 40–53; Hadda, J. R., *Yankev Glatshteyn* (1980)

EUGENE ORENSTEIN

GOES, Albrecht

German narrative writer, poet, and critic, b. 22 March 1908, Langenbeutingen

A Lutheran pastor, son and grandson of Swabian ministers, G. resigned from the ministry in 1953 to devote most of his time to writing, except for a few regularly delivered sermons. He has written poetry and symbolic plays since about 1930. During World War II he served as an army chaplain. Two of his prose narratives are direct echoes of his wartime experience; *Unruhige Nacht* (1949; *Arrow to the Heart*, 1951) and *Das Löffelchen* (1965; the little spoon). In *Unruhige Nacht* G. displayed great gifts for the dispassionate evocation of stark reality coupled with compassion and a deep sense of humanity. *Das Löffelchen*, although written in the same terse, lean prose, is much more passionate and becomes an outcry against barbarity; G.'s sense of the tragic imbues the vivid scenes, painted even more forcefully than in the earlier work. The novella *Das Brandopfer* (1954; *The Burnt Offering*, 1956) is the moving yet sparely told story of a German butcher's wife who feels compulsion to atone for the Nazis' treatment of the Jews; she experiences that "love that contains the world."

G.'s interests are manifold. He is a precise and knowledgeable literary and music critic and art lover, and an able guide to archaeological treasures, his disclaimer of competence outside a few limited areas notwithstanding. Above all, his ethics are a model of unpretentious, straightforward development of essential themes both in religion and in civil life. His role as a mediator between East and West Germany should not be underestimated—above politics, he is universally respected in both Germanys. G. often expresses the voice of German conscience much in the way critics have found Vercors (q.v.) to incarnate French conscience. His stature stems from reflection and from quiet strength in confused times. G. received thousands of letters from radio listeners to his oft-repeated exhortation to all Germans during the 1950s and 1960s, reminding them of their duties to those wronged under the Hitler regime.

Whereas some of these letters initially took issue with G.'s urging that the guilt must not be forgotten, over the years practically unanimous approval of his viewpoint prevailed. Never raising his voice, either in his writings or his radio addresses and sermons, G. thus got his message across to young Germans. Hence he has an unusual position, above politics but within the mainstream of democratic life.

Some of his shorter writings have been incorporated in two substantial volumes containing poems, solemn addresses, literary criticism, musical analysis, and musings of an exquisite connoisseur. The first, *Aber im Winde das Wort* (1963; words in the wind) represents twenty years of writing; it also contains the two earliest stories. Its dominant note is the fine-grained humanistic tradition that G. knows how to rekindle, bridging the painful "hiatus" of the years of dictatorship. Some of the reminiscences are humorous, others on the sentimental side; others again are timeless testimony to the highest values of culture and ethics. In *Tagwerk* (1976; daily task) G. once again felicitously blends personal impressions of some of the world's great thinkers and artists with incisive views on Mozart, Martin Buber (q.v.), and many others whom he revered and whose influence he readily acknowledges.

Perhaps the most striking of all his published works is an imaginary obituary of himself (in *Tagwerk*), in which he squarely faces his responsibility as both a writer and a minister, never equivocating when challenged to state his position as either. The good citizen, the solid thinker, in all his genuine modesty, finds vigorous ways to declare his unorthodox views of religion and art and relates his poetic and fictional work to the spiritual activity quite simply and beautifully. Another fine illustration of his art is also to be fond in *Tagwerk* in "Lautloser Dialog" (silent dialogue), an unfictionalized account of a dramatic episode from the war concerning army nurses, a chaplain (the narrator), and the narrator's father.

G. maintains a sober yet noble tone of fine, subtle, and tactful simplicity. But it is the refined simplicity of a virtuoso of word and thought, whose message is as intellectually convincing as it is gripping and enlightening.

FURTHER WORKS: *Verse* (1932); *Die Hirtin* (1934); *Der Hirte* (1934); *Heimat ist gut* (1935); *Lob des Lebens* (1936); *Die Roggen-fuhre* (1936); *Vergebung* (1937); *Der Zaun-gast* (1938); *Mörike* (1938); *Über das Gespräch* (1938; rev. ed. 1957); *Begegnungen* (1939); *Leuchter und Laterne* (1939); *Der Nachbar* (1940); *Die guten Gefährten* (1942); *Die Begegnung* (1944); *Ein erster Schritt* (1945); *Der Weg zum Stall* (1946); *Auf der Flucht* (1946); *Schwäbische Herzens-reise* (1947); *Da rang ein Mann mit ihm* (1947); *Die Herberge* (1947); *Der Mensch von unterwegs* (1948); *Die fröhliche Christ-tagslitanei* (1949); *Von Mensch zu Mensch* (1949); *Gedichte 1930–1950* (1950); *Unsere letzte Stunde* (1951); *Christtag* (1951); *Freude am Gedicht* (1952); *Vertrauen in das Wort* (1953); *Krankenvisite* (1953); *Heilige Unruhe* (1954); *Worte zum Sonntag* (1955); *Erfüllter Augenblick* (1955); *Ruf und Echo* (1956); *Das dreifache Ja* (1956); *Der Neckar* (1957); *Hagar am Brunnen* (1958); *Der Gastfreund* (1958); *Wort zum Fest* (1959); *Stunden mit Bach* (1959); *Wagnis der Versöhnung* (1959); *Das St. Galler Spiel von der Kindheit Jesu* (1959); *Die Gabe und der Auftrag* (1962); *Die Weihnacht der Bedrängten* (1962); *Alle unsere Tage* (1963, with Waldemar Austiny); *Im Weitergehen* (1965); *Erkennst du deinen Bruder nicht?* (1965); *Dichter und Gedicht* (1966); *Nachtgespräche* (1967); *Der Knecht macht keinen Lärm* (1968); *Ein Winter mit Paul Gerhardt* (1973); *Dunkler Tag, heller Tag* (1977); *Lichtschatten du* (1978)

BIBLIOGRAPHY: Lehmann, W., *A. G., Träger des Lessingpreises der Freien Hansestadt Hamburg* (1953); Janzen, W., *A. G. zu seinem 60. Geburtstag* (1961); Rollins, E. W., and Zohn, H., eds., *Men of Dialogue: Martin Buber and A. G.* (1969); McInnes, E., "Abandonment and Renewal: Reflections on the Novellas of A. G.," *FMLS*, 7 (1971), 183–96; Robinson, A. R., "An Approach to A. G.," *ML*, 52 (1971), 161–66; Klein, U., "A. G.," *Bibliographische Kalenderblätter*, 3 (1973), 42–46

KONRAD BIEBER

GOETEL, Ferdynand

Polish novelist, journalist, and dramatist, b. 15 May 1890, Sucha, Austro-Hungarian Empire; d. 24 Nov. 1960, London, England

G.'s father, a train conductor, died when G. was six, and his widowed mother had to rely on relatives' help in raising her two boys. G. drifted from school to school in Cracow and Lvov, studied architecture in Vienna, then moved to Warsaw in 1912 and tried his hand —at first unsuccessfully—at literature while earning his living by tutoring. At the outbreak of World War I in 1914, as an Austrian citizen in Russian-ruled Warsaw, he was deported by the Russians to Tashkent, where he was employed at building bridges, until the revolution, when he was drafted into the Red Army; during the civil war he served in the Caucasus. He returned to Poland, via Persia and India, in 1921.

In 1945, after the defeat of the Germans in Poland, G. left the country for Italy, where he joined the Polish army, and then went to England. He spent the last years of his life in London, fighting advancing blindness, and earning his living by writing for émigré papers.

G.'s war experiences and his later travels to Egypt, Iceland, and India between 1926 and 1932 served as background for his best-known works: *Kar Chat* (1923; *Messenger of the Snow*, 1930), *Serce lodów* (1930; *The Heart of the Ice*, 1931), and *Z dnia na dzień* (1926; *From Day to Day*, 1931). The last, an experimental novel, is written in the form of a double diary. Its entries alternate between the present —the everyday life in Cracow of a successful writer, returned from the wars to his wife and little daughter—and the past—the story of his love affair with an orphaned Polish girl, owner of a farm to which, as a prisoner of war in Asia, he was assigned as a laborer by Russian military authorities.

G.'s work has lyric, epic, and dramatic elements, although he wrote only one play, a tragedy, *Samuel Zborowski* (1929; Samuel Zborowski), based on the stormy career and death of a 16th-c. Polish nobleman. His lyricism is evinced in the ill-starred love stories of his plots. The epic element is seen in G.'s male protagonists, whose strenuous adventures are sharply etched against a backdrop of political upheaval—war and revolution in *Kar Chat* and *Z dnia no dzień*—or inclement nature, as in *Serce lodów*.

G.'s style, like his heroes, is robust and realistic. He tends to present the complexities of life in simple terms, avoiding psychologizing and detailed descriptions of either events or his protagonists' states of mind. He feels nature deeply—especially its exotic grandeur in central Asia, the Caucasus, and Iceland, as well as the effect it has on men subjected to its cruelty and indifference. This feature of G.'s talent has led some critics to suggest the influence on his work of Joseph Conrad (q.v.) and the Scandinavian writers, just as the "novel within the novel" form of *Z dnia na dzień* was said to be inspired by André Gide's (q.v.) *The Counter-*

feiters. Yet G. is an innovator in his own right who has left his mark on the Polish literature of the interwar period.

FURTHER WORKS: *Przez płonący Wschód* (1921); *Pątnik Karapeta* (1923); *Egipt* (1927); *Humoreski* (1927); *Wyspa na chmurnej północy* (1928); *Ludzkość* (1930); *Podróż do Indii* (1933); *Pod znakiem faszyzmu* (1939); *Cyklon* (1939); *Kapitan Luna* (1947); *Tatry* (1953); *Nie warto być małym* (1959); *Anakonda* (1964)

BIBLIOGRAPHY: Galsworthy, J., Foreword to *From Day to Day* (1931), pp. v–vi; Zaleski, Z. L., *Attitudes et destinées* (1932), pp. 342–44; Lorentowicz, J., "Polens literarische Staatspreisträger," *Slavische Rundschau*, No. 1 (1938), 19–21; Coleman, A. P., "F. G. Today," *BA*, 12 (1939), 420–23; Kridl, M., *A Survey of Polish Literature and Culture* (1956), p. 497; Miłosz, C., *The History of Polish Literature* (1969), p. 423; Krzyżanowski, J., *A History of Polish Literature* (1978), pp. 622–23

XENIA GASIOROWSKA

GOLDING, William
English novelist, b. 19 Sept. 1911, St. Columb Minor

While still an Oxford undergraduate, G. published a volume of poetry; it was not until twenty years later, however, that his first novel appeared. In the meantime he had spent four years working in a small London theater, had served five years in the Royal Navy, and had become a schoolmaster (he continued to be one until 1961).

G. has compared himself to an archaeologist: as the latter explores the dark places under the earth, he explores the dark places of the human soul. He is not simply describing the human tragedy but looking for its source—in that human nature of which modern man is appallingly ignorant. His response to liberal and optimistic interpretations of the human condition is to parody them. In *Lord of the Flies* (1954) he takes a schoolboy classic, R. M. Ballantyne's (1825–1894) *Coral Island*, (1857) and reverses what happens in it; his group of boys on a desert island does not live in harmony and happiness but degenerates into savagery. A gripping story whose meaning is debatable, *Lord of the Flies* had an enormous success both in England and the U.S. G.'s characters remain within the world of childhood, yet they suggest or foreshadow a range of adult roles—from Ralph, who tries to create and maintain order, to Jack, who surrenders to a compulsion to hunt and kill. "I should have thought that a pack of British boys . . . would have been able to put up a better show than that," says the naval officer who rescues them; but his rebuke is full of unconscious irony, given the adult world G. has him represent—a world devastated by nuclear war. The Lord of the Flies is Beelzebub, Prince of Devils, the source of evil outside oneself; through his Swiftian parable G. shows that man is a fallen being, with a propensity to worship the wrong gods.

Similarly, in *The Inheritors* (1955) G. overturns H. G. Wells's (q.v.) *Outline of History* (1920), "the rationalist gospel *in excelsis.*" For Wells, Neanderthal man was a gorillalike monster, possibly cannibalistic; G. shows him as innocent and kindly, so that it is with the coming of Homo sapiens that the fall into complexity, ambiguity, and self-division occurs. In *Pincher Martin* (1956; Am., *The Two Deaths of Christopher Martin)* the central character, a sailor, is a parody Prometheus, a parody Robinson Crusoe, a parody Lear (in the critic Samuel Hynes's view), who loves no one but himself but seems the indomitable individualist, the archetypal survivor—until we suddenly learn that he has been dead all the way through the book. In *The Spire* (1964) the dean of a medieval cathedral has a Promethean ambition: to crown his cathedral with a four-hundred-foot spire. In spite of weak foundations, tainted money, human suffering, and his own suspicion that his motives are corrupt, he succeeds in building a beautiful spire that seems to reach to infinity.

Only in *Free Fall* (1959) did G. deal with an ordinary man, not a Promethean, in an ordinary social situation. Still, out of this situation mythic dimensions emerge, since his hero is looking back over his past to find "the beginning of responsibility, the beginning of darkness, the point where I began." The title suggests both a fall in space and a fall from grace, a scientific and a religious approach to existence; the question the hero must ultimately face is whether there is any pattern to existence at all. Interior darkness is also the theme of *Darkness Visible* (1979), G.'s first full-length novel in twelve years. The beginning is extraordinary: out of fire raging during the London blitz a boy comes walking, his face hideously burned; "a maimed creature whose mind has touched for once on the nature of things," he puts his ability to recognize the darkness in the souls of others to forceful use.

Rites of Passage (1980) portrays, with astonishing realism, life aboard an ancient ship of the line at the end of the Napoleonic Wars, but again, the main interest of the novel is in the interior world. It shows once again that past, present, and future serve G. equally well in his exploration of the dark places of the human heart.

Martin Green has written that G. is not importantly original in thought or feeling because his handling is too predictable and too exaggerated. This is one of the possible criticisms; but nothing could be farther from the truth. If G. deals with age-old moral, religious, and metaphysical questions, he devises very imaginative and original fictional situations by which to examine them. And the answers are never easy; as his best critics have shown, the reader who thinks that a G. novel can be summed up in a simple moral maxim has not begun to understand him. One of his main strengths is his ability to enter into a character, to see him from the inside, as it were—with the objective view probably being given only at the end, and the reader suddenly realizing that he has been accepting the character's perspective all the way through. G. is undoubtedly one of the most interesting, and demanding, of contemporary novelists.

FURTHER WORKS: *Poems* (1934); *Envoy Extraordinary*, in *Sometime, Never: Three Tales of Imagination* (1956); *The Brass Butterfly* (1956); *The Hot Gates* (1965); *The Pyramid* (1967); *The Scorpion God* (1971)

BIBLIOGRAPHY: Hynes, S., *W. G.* (1964); Oldsey, B. S., and Weintraub, S., *The Art of W. G.* (1965); Kinkead-Weekes, M., and Gregor, I., *W. G.: A Critical Study* (1967); Babb, H. S., *The Novels of W. G.* (1970); Tiger, V., *W. G.: The Dark Fields of Discovery* (1974); Medcalf, S., *W. G.* (1975); Biles, J. I., and Evans, R. D., eds., *W. G.: Some Critical Considerations* (1978)

D. J. DOOLEY

GOMBROWICZ, Witold
Polish novelist and dramatist, b. 4 Aug. 1904, Małoszyce; d. 24 July 1969, Vence, France

G. was born into a landowning family. From 1923 to 1926 he studied law at the University of Warsaw. In August 1939 G. took a pleasure trip to Argentina, but he remained there for twenty-four years owing to the outbreak of World War II and the postwar developments in eastern Europe. He returned to Europe in 1963, and after spending a year in Berlin he settled in Vence.

Two key words for understanding G.'s works are "immaturity" and "form," both repeatedly used by G. The short stories in *Pamiętnik z okresu dojrzewania* (1933; memoir from adolescence) and his first novel, *Ferdydurke* (1937; *Ferdydurke*, 1961) are devoted to the definition and investigation of what G. perceived as perpetual and inevitable human immaturity. In his view, human beings incessantly engage in the game of hiding their own lack of a full understanding of the world while exposing this lack in others. G.'s short stories sketch out instances of that struggle: the hobo against the miser, the misfit against the well-adjusted person, the innocent debutante against her worldly-wise fiancé. *Ferdydurke* begins as a story of a thirty-year-old writer who has been patronized and patted on the head by the "cultural aunts and uncles" (that is, so-called guardians of culture) until he lost his resistance and allowed others to overwhelm him with their claim to know everything better. Eventually he rebels against his captors and exposes the flimsy foundations of their alleged superiority.

Ferdydurke introduces the concept of form and the formal impulse. The latter is an impulse all human beings have to create a communicative network among themselves and to structure the reality around them. The form thus produced both structures the reality and distorts it; it also separates one person from another. People are entrapped by, and hide behind, the form they have produced. G.'s intuitions about form resemble what the French psychologist Jacques Lacan has observed about the distortion of the "I," communication, and language.

The sadomasochistic dependence of one man on another is the ultimate concern of G.'s novels and plays. They contain portraits of people who at first seem to have achieved a certain degree of autonomy and rationality but on second look turn out to be ridiculously dependent on the existence and opinions of others. They are incapable of thinking thoughts and desiring things that others had not thought and desired. They hate others and themselves for that and their actions are motivated by this hate.

Ferdydurke first identified the phenomenon of immaturity and interdependence masquerading as maturity and independence. G.'s next novel, *Trans-Atlantyk* (1953; trans-Atlantic), written in Argentina, pokes fun at the ridiculous lengths to which people go to emphasize their separateness and superior knowledge. The two branches of the Polish émigré community in Argentina—the aristocratic and the proletarian—do everything in their power to discredit the other in the eyes of the outsiders and of other Poles. *Pornografia* (1960; *Pornografia*, 1965) explores sexual dependency and the lying associated with it. In this novel, two eldely gentlemen arrange a sexual encounter between two teenagers, and eventually cement with a murder the teenagers' lascivious friendship and their own, too. In *Kosmos* (1965; *Cosmos,* 1966), for which he was awarded the International Publishers' Prize in 1967, Leo Wojtys lives a seemingly independent life amid his family and friends. Like the heroes of *Pornografia,* he is a lecher and a voyeur, and his secret enjoyments depend on the presence of others.

G.'s plays likewise expose man's cruelty to himself and others. In *Iwona, księżniczka Burgunda* (1938; *Ivona, Princess of Burgundia,* 1969), the presence at the royal court of the ugly and awkward girl Ivona makes everyone so self-conscious and uneasy that eventually Ivona has to be murdered so that the comfortable harmony of royal society can be restored. The theme of *Slub* (1953; *The Marriage,* 1969) is a gradual discovery by the Polish soldier Henryk, who fights the Nazis in France during World War II, of the pressure of others on what people think about themselves. Henryk tries to rid himself and his family of this pressure but eventually he submits to it. In *Operetka* (1966; *Operetta,* 1971) the concern with human immaturity and interdependence takes a different form. An uneducated shopkeeper's daughter, Albertine, saves the society depicted in the drama from despair and disintegration by the vigor of her youth and beauty. *Operetka* contains a suggestion that in man's immature drives and desires there is hidden an ability stubbornly to seek after knowledge, wisdom, and joy.

G.'s modernistic novels and plays share several structural features. The novels use the first-person narrator, who in turn is usually overshadowed by the "stage director," a character who surpasses the narrator in mental acumen and experience. The novels' plots are centered around a sadomasochistic contest between the narrator and the stage producer, and between these two and other characters in the novel. The omnipresence of the sadomasochistic feelings in G.'s novels accounts in large measure for the eccentricities of his plots and the ensuing difficulty of summarizing them. While the action of G.'s novels takes place in an everyday world, in the plays we encounter the world of royalty and aristocracy. Members of this supposedly highly refined society use vulgarisms and dialect words unsuitable to people of their station. The device of mismatching a character with his speech contributes to the parodic atmosphere of G.'s plays.

Several intellectual traditions can be discerned in G.'s writings. From Nietzsche he derives his preoccupation with the individual's desire for self-assertion. His early Catholic training contributed to his perception of human beings as irrevocably deprived of self-sufficiency. His absurdist plots bespeak an awareness of existential philosophy and of post-Freudian psychology. His sadomasochism brings him close to the writings of the Marquis de Sade and to the novels of his countryman Jerzy Kosinski (q.v.). On the other hand, his belief in the capacity of human beings for joy and development makes his fictional world different from the humorless French New Novel (q.v.) and from the Theater of the Absurd (q.v.).

In many ways, G.'s works stand in opposition to the Polish literary tradition, which has favored gentility rather than parody and noble ideas rather than sadomasochism. G. belongs to that tradition, however, in that all his works respond in some way to a specific work of the past, or a specific tendency of Polish literature. G. saw himself as a voice of negation indispensable for the dialectic of literary development. In that, his own views and those of his critics have often coincided.

FURTHER WORKS: *Opętani* (1939; *Possessed of the Secret of Myslotch*, 1981); *Dziennik* (3 vols., 1962, 1966, 1971); *Rozmowy z G.* (1969; *A Kind of Testament*, 1973); *Varia* (1973); *Wspomnienia polskie; Wędrówki po Argentynie* (1977)

BIBLIOGRAPHY: Roux, D. de., *G.* (1971); Jelenski, C., and Roux, D. de, eds., *G.* (1971); Volle, J., *G.: Bourreau-martyr* (1972); Schmidt, K., *Der Stil von W. G.s "Trans-Atlantyk" and sein Verhältnis zur polnischen literarischen Tradition* (1974); Bondy, F., and Jelenski, C., *W. G.* (1978); Thompson, E., *W. G.* (1979)

EWA THOMPSON

GÓMEZ DE LA SERNA, Ramón

Spanish novelist, biographer, essayist, humorist, and dramatist, b. 3 July 1888, Madrid; d. 12 Jan. 1963, Buenos Aires, Argentina

A highly experimental writer, greatly esteemed by members of avant-garde literary groups from the end of World War I to the beginning of the Spanish Civil War, G. published more than one hundred volumes of travel books, short stories, novels, plays, impressions, and humorous essays, and thousands of articles. He excelled at experimentation in what he defined as a world of disintegrating conventionalisms, especially in his *greguerías*, short semiaphoristic statements.

An early interest in art led him to write biographies of Goya, El Greco, Velázquez, and other painters, but he also published many other biographies and literary portraits. Beginning in 1911, he developed a special style, intuitive, often penetrating, and poetic, involving description of personal gestures, physical movements, and anecdotal material. G. stressed special traits in each of his subjects, such as Oscar Wilde's outrageous impudence or George Bernard Shaw's (q.v.) vegetarianism. He also utilized expanded metaphorical constructions, "to pierce the outer layer of reality and to probe into a deeper, more intimate reality." Among his best biographies are *Goya* (1928), an intuitive interpretation of the works of an artist in whose *Caprichos* G. saw a relationship to his own *greguerías; Azorín* (1930), in which he imitated Azorín's (q.v.) style to show that author's place in history together with that of the famous Generation of '98; and *Ramón María del Valle-Inclán* (1944), about the Spanish writer Valle-Inclán (q.v.), with whose extravagant and volatile personality G. could easily identify.

G. wrote several autobiographies, the best of which is *Automoribundia* (1948; autodeathography), which relates his birth, hungers, frustrations, triumphs, defeats, and disappointments, and whose title he explained as "how a man progresses toward death," a subject that always fascinated him.

His novels, quite often filled with sensual and bohemian types, reveal an unreal, absurd, and often humorous world. *El doctor inverosímil* (1921; the unlikely doctor), based on an earlier short story of the same name, depicts a doctor who fancies himself a medical Sherlock Holmes and uses psychiatric techniques to discover the reason for his patients' allergies. Humorous but perceptive, the novel reflects G.'s fascination with human illness and pathology.

El torero Caracho (1926; the bullfighter Caracho), one of his most popular novels, relates the rise from poverty of Caracho, his rivalry with another bullfighter, Cairel, and their brutal, if heroic deaths, in defense of some spectators. *Cinelandia* (1923; *Movieland,* 1930) penetrates the reality behind Hollywood as it explores its promiscuity, parties, thrill seekers, and stars.

G. also experimented with a series of novels he labeled "nebulous." *El incongruente* (1922; the incongruent one) is an innovative, surrealistic novel of the absurd about a man who lets life live him instead of living life, set in a fantasy world without real time or space. *¡Rebeca!* (1936; Rebeca!), a fragmented, dehumanized novel, treats of an erotic odyssey in search of the ideal woman, whom the protagonist himself has invented. Realizing that reality is more productive, he marries a Jewish lady, an autobiographical re-creation of G.'s own life. These novels, as well as his many novelettes and short stories, quite often deal with the morbid, grotesque, and fantastic and include murder, adultery, and a variety of sexual obsessions.

G. is most famous for his *greguerías*, a word he coined in 1909, short and pithy rearrangements of reality that try to define the incongruities and trivialities of life. At times shocking, they capture fugitive impressions and sensations and express subconscious associations involving God, time, nature, and death. In some twenty volumes written between 1914 and 1960 he indulged in a kind of humorous, lyrical, magic anticreation. He defined these brief insights as "what beings shout confusedly from their subconscious," stating that in these ephemeral fusions of extremes he was trying to define the indefinable: "Thunder, a trunk falling down the stairway of heaven"; "In her wristwatch the time was so small she never had enough of it for anything."

G. created an endless variety of almost unclassifiable, humorous, and lyrical works that broke all the taboos of his day. He attempted new aesthetic and verbal games, showing great facility as one of the early experimenters with surrealism (q.v.) and the absurd, and he influenced the development of Spanish literature and its 20th-c. literary genres.

FURTHER WORKS: *Entrando en fuego* (1905); *Morbideces* (1908); *El drama del palacio deshabitado* (1909); *Utopía* (1909); *El laberinto* (1910); *El teatro en soledad* (1912); *Ex-votos* (1912); *El lunático* (1912); *El Rastro* (1915); *La viuda blanca y negra* (1917); *El circo* (1917); *Senos* (1917); *Pombo* (1918); *Muestrarios* (1918); *El alba y otras cosas* (1918); *Variaciones* (1920); *Virguerías* (1920); *Libro nuevo* (1920); *Disparates* (1921); *La tormenta* (1921); *Leopoldo y Teresa* (1921); *El miedo al mar* (1921); *El secreto del acueducto* (1922); *La hija del verano* (1922); *El olor de las mimosas* (1922); *La gangosa* (1922); *El gran hotel* (1922); *Ramonismo* (1923); *La quinta de Palmyra* (1923); *El novelista* (1923); *El chalet de las rosas* (1923); *La malicia y las acacias* (1923); *La sagrada cripta del Pombo* (1924); *Por los tejados* (1924); *En el bazar más suntuoso del mundo* (1924); *Aquella novela* (1924); *Caprichos* (1925); *La fúnebre falsa* (1925); *Hay que matar el Morse* (1925); *Gollerías* (1926); *La mujer de ámbar* (1927); *Seis falsas novelas* (1927); *El hijo del millonario* (1927); *El caballero del hongo gris* (1928); *El dueño del átomo* (1928); *La hiperestésica* (1928); *Efigies* (1929); *Los medios seres* (1929); *La nardo* (1930); *Ismos* (1931); *Elucidario de Madrid* (1931); *Policéfalo y señora* (1932); *Flor de greguerías* (1933); *Siluetas y sombras* (1934); *El Greco* (1935); *Las escaleras* (1935); *Los muertos y las muertas, y otras fantasmagorias* (1935); *El cólera azul* (1937); *Mi tía Carolina Coronado* (1940); *Retratos contemporáneos* (1941); *Lo cursi, y otros ensayos* (1943); *Ruskin, el apasionado* (1943); *Don Diego de Velázquez* (1943); *José Gutiérrez Solana* (1944); *Doña Juana la Loca* (1944); *Oscar Wilde* (1944); *Lope de Vega* (1944); *Nuevos retratos contemporáneos* (1945); *Ventura García Calderón* (1946); *El hombre perdido* (1947); *Trampantojos* (1947); *Cuentos del fin del año* (1947); *Explicación de Buenos Aires* (1948); *Cartas a las golondrinas* (1949); *Las tres gracias* (1949); *Interpretación del tango* (1949); *Quevedo* (1953); *Greguerías completas* (1953); *Edgar Poe, el genio de América* (1953); *Lope viviente* (1954); *Nostalgias de Madrid* (1956); *Cartas a mí mismo* (1956); *Obras completas* (2 vols., 1956, 1957); *Nuevas páginas de mi vida* (1957); *Biografías completas* (1959); *Piso bajo* (1961); *Retratos completos* (1961); *Total de greguerías* (1961); *Guía del Rastro* (1961); *Diario póstumo* (1972). FURTHER VOLUME IN ENGLISH: *Some Greguerías* (1944)

BIBLIOGRAPHY: Cardona, R., *Ramón: A Study of G. and His Works* (1957); Gómez de la Serna, G., *Ramón: Vida y obra* (1963); Mazzetti, R., "Some Comments on the Biographical Sketches of R. G.," *KRQ*, 17 (1960), 275–86; Mazzetti, R., "The Use of Imagery in the

Works of R. G.," *Hispania,* 54 (1971), 80–90; Camon Aznar, J., *R. G. en sus obras* (1972); Mazzetti, R., *R. G.* (1974); Jackson, R., "The Status of the Greguería of R. G.," *MFS,* 22 (1976–77), 237–42

KESSEL SCHWARTZ

GONZALEZ, N(estor) V(icente) M(adali)

Philippine novelist, short-story writer, and poet (writing in English) b. 8 Sept. 1915, Romblon

As a child, G. was taken by his father, who was a teacher, to pioneer Mindoro Island, whose farmers and fishermen have dominated his fiction ever since his autobiographical novel, *The Winds of April* (1940), won a prize in the Commonwealth Literary Contest in 1940. After a Rockefeller-funded postwar visit to U.S. writing centers, G. returned to teach creative writing at the University of the Philippines.

For his defense of traditional Philippine values, G. received the Republic Award of Merit (1954), the Republic Cultural Heritage Award (1960), and the Rizal Pro Patria Award (1961). Since 1969 G. has taught Third World literature at the University of California, Hayward, and in several essays he has offered lessons learned from other developing nations as advisories to his countrymen.

Social change, in G.'s fiction, tends to be subtle to the point of near invisibility, because his frontiersmen take their tempo from natural cycles. Yet although there is a seemingly static quality to the folk life represented in *Seven Hills Away* (1947), a pattern of slow change and movement toward new horizons emerges from these sketches. Women and children are often the narrators in his fiction. G.'s deceptively simple style not only authenticates the quiet manner of ordinary folk but makes their daily encounters with birth and death seem less staggering to the reader.

But while the poor are admired for their honesty and resilience, G. also reveals the destructiveness of their slash-and-burn method of farming, which makes hard field work still harder. Still, their family closeness protects them from the loneliness of those—in the second half of *Look, Stranger, on This Island Now* (1969)—who leave the land entirely and are corrupted in the mainland metropolis. Not only the greedy merchant but also the self-styled intellectual are criticized for the increasing separation between themselves and the peasantry. Ernie Rama, antihero of *The Bamboo Dancers* (1959), is portrayed as a wandering Fisher King whose apathy is both his wound and the

symptom of the modern wasteland, which is contrasted to the values of communitarian responsibility indigenous to the Philippines' traditional agrarian culture.

FURTHER WORKS: *Children of the Ash-Covered Loam* (1954); *A Season of Grace* (1956); *Selected Stories* (1964); *Mindoro and Beyond* (1979)

BIBLIOGRAPHY: Casper, L., *New Writing from the Philippines* (1966), pp. 42–55; Galdon, J., ed., *Philippine Fiction* (1972), pp. 153–59; Galdon, J., *Essays on the Philippine Novel in English* (1979), pp. 108–24

LEONARD CASPER

GONZÁLEZ MARTÍNEZ, Enrique

Mexican poet, b. 13 April 1871, Guadalajara; d. 19 Feb. 1952, Mexico City

G. M. began his literary career at the age of fourteen with a translation of Milton's sonnet on his blindness, for which he was awarded a prize. In 1886 he enrolled in medical school at the University of Guadalajara and graduated in 1893. In 1895 he moved with his family to the state of Sinaloa, where his father became director of a school in Culiacán. While practicing medicine, G. M. also contributed to a number of provincial literary magazines. His first collection of poetry, *Preludios* (1903; preludes), was warmly received. In 1907, in collaboration with Sixto Osuna (dates n.a.), he published *Lirismos* (lyrical poems) and founded the journal *Arte.* In 1911 G. M. moved to Mexico City to embark on a university and diplomatic career, became a member of the Mexican Academy, and joined the influential "Atheneum of Youth," a group of young writers and intellectuals responsible for the rebirth of humanism and the break with positivist thought in early-20th-c. Mexican literature. At various points in his life he represented Mexico as ambassador to Spain, Argentina, and Chile. He was also instrumental in the founding of the prestigious National College in 1943 and was awarded the Manuel Ávila Camacho Prize in 1944.

Although literary historians have found it difficult to classify the work of G. M. because of the poet's ambivalent relationship to Spanish American modernism, (q.v.) the American Hispanist John Brushwood has divided G. M.'s work into three main periods. To the early period (1895–1920), which marks the time of his discovery of himself as a poet and is characterized by an emerging awareness of his relationship to the universe, belong *Silénter* (1909; silently), *Los senderos ocultos* (1911; the hidden paths), *La muerte del cisne* (1915; the death of the swan), and *Jardines de Francia* (1915; gardens of France).

"Tuércele el cuello al cisne" ("Wring the Neck of the Swan," 1958); published in *Los sendros occultos,* is perhaps G. M.'s best-known poem and is characteristic of his preoccupation with the importance of poetry during this period. In this sonnet G. M. replaced the elegant swan, the symbol of modernist extravagance, with the figure of the pensive owl. Many critics consider the poem to signal the end of the modernist period in Spanish American letters.

G. M.'s second period, which runs from about 1921 to 1934, corresponds to the period of his work in the diplomatic corps and shows a subtle change in direction. His two principal books from this time, *El romero alucinado* (1923; the bedazzled pilgrim) and *Las señales furtivas* (1925; the subtle tokens), evince a certain indebtedness to vanguard thought seen in his experimentation with new poetic forms and his use of images related to the modern world. In the last stage of G. M.'s career (1935–52) he returned to the themes and techniques of his first period. These late poems are marked by a pervasive sadness and melancholy and considerable restraint in form and technique. The most important collection of this period is *Poemas truncos* (1935; unfinished poems).

Serving as a transition between modernism and postmodernism, G. M. was a major figure in the history of Mexican literature. It was not innovation but rather constancy, universality, and fidelity to his art that best characterize the work of G. M., who exerted an important stabilizing influence on poetry in Mexico throughout the first half of the 20th c. He also played an important role as a model to the members of the renowned "Contemporaries," the generation of the late 1920s who strived to express Mexican themes within a framework of cultural universality.

FURTHER WORKS: *La hora inútil* (1916); *El libro de la fuerza, de la bondad y del ensueño* (1917); *Parabolas* (1918); *Poemas de ayer y de hoy* (1918); *La palabra del viento* (1921); *Poesía 1909–1929* (1929); *Ausencia y canto* (1937); *El diluvio de fuego* (1938); *Poemas 1938–1940* (1940); *Bajo el signo mortal* (1942); *Poesías completas* (1944); *El hombre del buho* (1944); *Segundo despertar* (1945); *Villano al viento* (1948); *Babel* (1949); *La apacible locura* (1951); *Narciso* (1952); *Cuentos y otras páginas* (1955)

BIBLIOGRAPHY: Goldberg, I., *Studies in Spanish American Literature* (1920), pp. 82–92; Avrett, R. "E. G. M., Philosopher and Mystic," *Hispania*, 14 (1931), 183–92; Paz, O., *An Anthology of Mexican Literature* (1958), pp. 34–35; Topete, J. M., *El mundo poético de E. G. M.* (1967); Brushwood, J., *E. G. M.* (1969)

EDWARD MULLEN

GONZÁLEZ PRADA, Manuel

Peruvian essayist and poet, b. 5 Jan. 1844, Lima; d. 22 July 1918, Lima

Born into an aristocratic family, G. P. displayed a rebellious spirit at an early age. Against parental opposition he planned to study engineering in Europe; thwarted in this desire, however, he remained in Lima and attended San Marcos University, where he devoted himself to literature. Peru's disastrous defeat by Chile in the War of the Pacific (1879–83), in which G. P. participated, played a decisive role in arousing his concern for the problems underlying his country's weaknesses.

The fruit of these concerns was a series of highly charged speeches and essays, later published in *Pájinas libres* (1894; free pages). G. P.'s residence in Europe (1885–91) brought him in contact with the latest radical thinkers and movements of the Old World, and influenced the essays of *Horas de lucha* (1908; hours of struggle) as well as subsequent works. While never directly involved in politics, G. P. soon became a mentor of Peru's growing group of young revolutionaries. In his later years, especially between 1912 and 1918, when he held the seemingly innocuous post of Director of the National Library, his office became a gathering place for a group of firebrands that included such future leaders as Victor Raúl Haya de la Torre (1895–1979) and José Carlos Mariátegui (1895–1930).

In *Pájinas libres* G. P. undertook a merciless diagnosis of his country's ills. Peru's military collapse, its corruption, its lack of national will, and the obscurantism of its intellectuals is traced to the negative influence of the army, the Church, and the governing elite. Since Spain, the mother country, determined the character of these institutions, the Hispanic legacy becomes the ultimate target of G. P.'s attacks. By contrast, he repeatedly asserts that Peru's Indian masses, often accused of being lazy, dullwitted, irresponsible—in a word, "inferior"—are simply the victims of exploitation. Once given opportunities to develop and improve their condition the Indians, he believed, could well become the force for a totally regenerated nation.

In his second collection, *Horas de lucha*, G. P. continued to press for the reform of Peruvian society and for the redress of injustices done to the Indian. But he also explored Latin American problems in the broader context of the intellectual currents to which he had been exposed during his European travels. Among these ideologies, anarchism gradually assumed increasing importance in his thinking; and, in his posthumously published collection *Anarquía* (1936; anarchy), it became a central theme.

In addition to his political essays, G. P.'s contributions to Spanish American poetry are substantial. Like his prose, his verse was innovative and individualistic. His introduction of little-used French and German metrical forms links him to the work of the modernist (q.v.) poets, yet unlike this group he shunned the ivory tower and often dealt with social issues. The poetry of his mature years is especially interesting: it reveals G. P.'s deep frustrations, bitterness, and nihilism.

On balance, G. P.'s diagnoses of sociopolitical ills is much more specific than the remedies he suggests. It is clear that he had a strong positivistic faith in science and technology; it is also apparent that he desired the separation of church and state, the redemption of the Indian, and a more equitable distribution of wealth. He was certainly a precursor of 20th-c. Latin American radicalism, especially of *Aprismo* (derived from the acronym APRA, which stands for Alianza Popular Revolucionaria Americana), an indigenous-oriented political movement that gained considerable power in the Andean region during the late 1920s and 1930s. Despite his leftist orientation, G. P. had a fine understanding of the way in which revolutionary ideals age, become rigid, and eventually die: as he observed in *Horas de lucha*, "Every triumphant revolutionary degenerates into a conservative."

FURTHER WORKS: *Minúsculas* (1901); *Presbiterianas* (1909); *Exóticas* (1911); *Baladas peruanas* (1915); *Grafitos* (1917); *Trozos de vida* (1918); *Bajo el oprobio* (1933); *Obras* (8 vols., 1933–40); *Nuevas páginas libres* (1937); *Figuras y figurones* (1938); *Libertarias* (1938); *Baladas* (1939); *Propaganda y ataque* (1939); *Antología poética* (1940); *Prose menuda* (1941); *El tonel de Diógenes* (1945); *Florilegio: Poesía, ensayo, crítica* (1948)

BIBLIOGRAPHY: Sánchez, L. A., *Don Manuel* (1930); González Prada, A., *Mi Manuel* (1947); Mead, R. G., "G. P., Peruvian Judge of Spain," *PMLA*, 68 (1953), 696–715; Zum Felde, A., *Indice crítico de la literatura hispanoamericana: El ensayo y la crítica* (1954), pp. 271–88; Chang Rodríguez, E., *La literatura política de G. P., Mariátegui, y Haya de la Torre* (1957); Davis, H. E., *Latin American Thought* (1972), pp. 117–19; Sánchez, L. A., *Mito y realidad de G. P.* (1976)

MARTIN S. STABB

GORDIMER, Nadine

South African novelist (writing in English), b. 20 Nov. 1923, Springs

G. was educated in the Transvaal and attended the University of the Witwatersrand in Johannesburg. Her home is in Johannesburg, the setting of most of her fiction. Although she has not lived outside South Africa for any extended period, she has traveled extensively in Africa, Europe, and North America, and has made many appearances as a lecturer abroad, particularly in the U.S.

G.'s writing career extends over thirty years of political turbulence in her native country. Her novels and short stories are predominantly concerned with the effects on individual lives and sensibilities of the political situation in southern Africa. "In South Africa, society *is* the political situation," she stated in an interview with Alan Ross in *London Magazine* (May 1965).

Her fiction reflects the changes in the life of the region since 1949, when her first collection of stories, *Face to Face*, was published. She shows a startling clarity of perception as she chronicles the corrosive effects of life in authoritarian, segregated South Africa, with its taboos, restrictions, and intricate apparatus of police power. The world she knows intimately is that of the white, English-speaking middle class. In describing the strange reality of comfortable, isolated white society she usually links closely observed details with overriding emotional effects: aridity, a sense of fear or powerlessness, distrust, lost spontaneity.

Her short stories have changed as the situation in South Africa has deteriorated. In *The Soft Voice of the Serpent* (1952) and *Six Feet of the Country* (1956) many tales reveal injustices caused by white supremacy. "Decent" and "humane" whites are shown to be themselves emotional casualties of the discriminatory system in which they are involuntarily involved. The later collections, *Not for Publication* (1965) and *Livingstone's Companions* (1971), depict the growing powerlessness of opposition to the tentacular police state. As effective political action from both whites and blacks is crushed, opportunistic political gesturing takes its place. Not all the stories carry political overtones, however. Several are short, closely focused evocations of moods, attitudes, or moments in the emotional lives of their protagonists.

G.'s novels show a similar development. *The Lying Days* (1953) is a *Bildungsroman*. Its protagonist is a young woman who decides to remain in South Africa in spite of her sense of guilt and foreboding after the Afrikaner Nationalists come to power in 1948. The novel has many beautifully observed descriptions of the decorum-ridden mining community in which the heroine grows up. The stresses of life in a segregated society are depicted in both *A World of Strangers* (1958) and *Occasion for Loving* (1963). In the former an Englishman finds himself unable to maintain friendships with both middle-class Johannesburg whites and a black acquaintance from the "townships." In the latter an illicit love affair between a black man and a white woman ends bitterly for all those involved.

Political events themselves inform *The Late Bourgeois World* (1966). The central character is a young white divorcee who is asked for help by a friend in the black underground. Her fear at his request and her memory of the futile sabotage attempts of her ex-husband provide constant tension and menace while she goes about her bland daily round in white Johannesburg.

G. maintains an interest in politics in *A Guest of Honour* (1970). Its setting is not, however, South Africa, but a newly independent African country whose problems are revealed through the experiences of a former English official, returned as a guest of the new government.

Two recent novels are again set in South Africa. *The Conservationist* (1974) has at its center a successful industrialist. His sense of possession is troubled by memories of unsuccessful personal relations and by the obtrusive presence of blacks on his weekend farm. They have a more natural claim on the land and community than he. *Burger's Daughter* (1979) is a poignant account of the unsuccessful attempt by the daughter of a renowned Afrikaans Communist to live an apolitical life after her father's death in prison.

Burger's Daughter, dealing with the Soweto riots of 1976 and black-power rejection of all white assistance and good faith, encapsulates the intractability of the tainted society described by G. with haunting clarity throughout her creative life.

FURTHER WORKS: *Friday's Footprint, and Other Stories* (1960); *The Black Interpreters* (1973); *Selected Stories* (1975); *Some Monday for Sure* (1976); *A Soldier's Embrace* (1980); *July's People* (1981)

BIBLIOGRAPHY: Haugh, R. S., *N. G.* (1974); Hope, C., "Out of the Picture: The Novels of N. G.," *London*, 15, 1 (1975), 49–55; Smith, R., "The Johannesburg Genre," in Smith, R., ed., *Exile and Tradition* (1976), pp. 116–31; Green, R. J., "N. G.: The Politics of Race," *WLWE*, 16 (1977), 256–62; Parker, K., "N. G. and the Pitfalls of Liberalism," in Parker, K., ed., *The South African Novel in English* (1978), pp. 114–30

ROWLAND SMITH

GORDON, Caroline

American novelist and short-story writer, b. 6 Oct. 1895, Todd County, Ky.; d. 11 April 1981, Chiapas, Mexico

G. graduated from Bethany College in West Virginia in 1916. After newspaper work she married the poet Allen Tate (q.v.) in 1924 (they were divorced in 1959). She won the O. Henry Prize in 1934, and at various times lectured on creative writing at Columbia and Purdue and the universities of North Carolina, Washington, Kansas, and California at Davis. She spent the last years of her life in Mexico.

G.'s fictional techniques are derived from the tradition of Gustave Flaubert and of Henry James, Ford Madox Ford, and Joseph Conrad (qq.v.), and are reflected in her theories about writing, which inform her critical study, *How to*

Read a Novel (1957). Her interest in narrative point of view, particularly the Jamesian central intelligence, is revealed continually in her stories and novels, which possess carefully balanced structures, consistent narrators, unified tones, and concrete exactitude in diction. The clarity and order of her language and the coherence of her structure represent her idea that the artist must perceive a unified pattern within the apparent flux of a chaotic reality.

From the beginning of her career G. argued for the importance of order, authority, tradition, and myth. She told largely the same story many times in her works: the destruction of the old South necessitated an ordering myth of salvation, not one that advocated the material values of progress and commerce but one that revitalized the agrarian ethic of the past. Her first novel, *Penhally* (1931), studies the Southern family unit at a time of cultural crisis; Chance Llewellyn, a hero of agrarianism, kills his materialistic brother, an advocate of the new South of progress and change.

Nature is a source of knowledge for man in many of her novels and stories, but it is often antagonistic as well as benevolent. The characters of *Green Centuries* (1941), in their westward migration as pioneers, suffer for their pursuit of the unknown and their escape from the past and themselves. Likewise, the 20th-c. families of *The Garden of Adonis* (1937) and *The Women on the Porch* (1944) fight hard to defend a past way of life, but their rootlessness turns their love into lust. This carnality figures in many of G.'s novels; her men, even those who strive for tradition and order, frequently fail to turn to the women who might focus their vision on the love that engenders charity, compassion, and understanding. Aleck Maury, the hero of many of her stories and her second work, *Aleck Maury, Sportsman* (1934), can find salvation only tentatively in the agrarian life style. There is a higher morality in G.'s fiction, the consequence of her own conversion in 1947 to Roman Catholicism, which offers the order and authority of a traditional religious ethic as a prop against the disorder of modern man's fragmented sensibility. *The Strange Children* (1951) and *The Malefactors* (1956) portray G.'s idea that the religious myth is the source of man's salvation.

G.'s work gives evidence of skillful narrative technique and a constant search for a meaningful ethic in a world that has lost its traditional values. Unlike her stories, her novels sometimes fail to cohere into something larger than the sum of their parts, because her craftsmanship is overly conscientious. Yet her work has achieved great success and recognition as part of the Southern renaissance for its intelligence, integrity, and scope.

FURTHER WORKS: *None Shall Look Back* (1937); *The Forest of the South* (1945); *A Good Soldier: A Key to the Novels of Ford Madox Ford* (1963); *Old Red, and Other Stories* (1963); *The Glory of Hera* (1972); *Collected Stories* (1981)

BIBLIOGRAPHY: Cowan, L., "Nature and Grace in C. G.," *Crit*, 1 (1956), 11–27; Thorp, W., "The Way Back and the Way Up: The Novels of C. G.," *BuR*, 6 (1956), 1–15; McDowell, F. P. W., *C. G.* (1966); Rocks, J. E., "The Mind and Art of C. G.," *MissQ*, 21 (1967–68), 1–16; Brown, A., "The Achievement of C. G.," *SHR*, 2 (1968), 279–90; Landess, T. H., ed., *The Short Fiction of C. G.* (1972); Stuckey, W. J., *C. G.* (1972)

JAMES E. ROCKS

GORKY, Maxim

(pseud. of Alexey Maximovich Peshkov) Russian novelist, dramatist, and essayist, b. 28 March 1868, Nizhny Novgorod (now Gorky); d. 18 June 1936, Gorky (near Moscow)

G., hailed as Russia's first proletarian writer, was not of proletarian origin but of the lower middle class. Orphaned at an early age—he lost his father when he was four and his mother at ten—he was sent out into the world by his impoverished grandfather while still a youth. With little formal education G. found various odd jobs: as a servant, a cobbler's apprentice, an errand boy in an icon shop, among others. He also wandered around Russia. Endowed with an astonishing memory and great concentration, G. acquired a very broad education on his own, but he never lost a feeling of inadequacy as a result of his lack of formal training. He became involved in clandestine revolutionary activity beginning with the *narodniki* (populist) circles of Kazan in the 1880s, later moving close to the Russian Socialist Democratic Labor Party (RSDLP), which benefited from his financial assistance and literary contributions.

G. (his pseudonym means "Maxim the Bitter") became famous practically overnight after the publication of *Ocherki i rasskazy* (sketches and stories) in 1898. By 1902 his name was well known both at home and abroad. In that year he became director of the publishing house Znanie and in that position was able to assist many young Russian writers. He took an active part in the 1905 revolution and was imprisoned. Following his release and the suppression of the Moscow uprising in December 1905, G. left Russia for western Europe and the U.S. His task was to propagandize for the revolutionary cause and to collect money for the RSDLP. But he failed in his mission and in 1906 settled on the island of Capri, Italy, where he remained until 1913.

For G., the Capri years were important to both his political and literary work. He became more deeply involved in the affairs of the RSDLP, attended the Fifth Party Congress in London, wrote for the Party's publications, and began an extensive correspondence with Lenin, who admired G.'s literary talents and valued the writer's support but was critical of his political vacillations. In 1913 the two men broke over G.'s preaching the doctrine of "god-building," which was an attempt to graft a religious superstructure onto Marxist ideology. The strain between Lenin and G. was compounded by G.'s joining the Vperyod (Forward) group, which had broken away from Lenin's Bolshevik faction in 1909.

A tsarist amnesty proclaimed on the three-hundredth anniversary of Romanov rule permitted G. to return to Russia. There he founded the publishing house Parus and the political-literary journal *Letopis*. In 1914 he took a stand against Russia's participation in World War I on pacifist grounds. G.'s attitude toward the February 1917 revolution was one of confusion followed by fear of chaos, anarchy, and disorder. In April he founded the daily *Novaya zhizn* and in a series of articles entitled "Nesvoevremennye mysli" (untimely thoughts) he criticized the Bolshevik party and Lenin for attempting to bring about a socialist revolution in backward Russia.

By 1918 G. had come to an accommodation with the new regime and, as head of numerous societies and associations, assumed the role of curator of Russia's cultural heritage and protector of artists and intellectuals. At Lenin's behest G. left the Soviet state in 1921, settling first near Berlin and later in Sorrento, Italy. He visited the Soviet Union in 1928 and then intermittently until 1933, when he moved back permanently.

Stalin exploited G.'s popularity and used him to rubber-stamp his activities; G. became editor of numerous publications and wrote articles praising Soviet achievements. In 1934 he was chosen chairman of the first All Union Congress of Soviet Writers and is credited with formulating the literary doctrine known as Socialist Realism (q.v.). G. died while Stalin was initiating the policy of large-scale purges. The causes of G.'s death are still a matter of controversy.

G. the writer emerged on the literary scene at a crucial period in Russian history. His career spanned the prelude and postlude of the revolution. He believed that literature had to have social significance, that it had to teach and guide; hence the didactic features present in the majority of his works.

In G.'s early works, mainly stories and tales, he sought his heroes among the gypsy nomads of the Black Sea area, fishermen and peasants on the loose, all living outside the society they felt alienated from. The romantic protagonists of the steppes in "Makar Chudra" (1892; "Makar Chudra," 1901) and "Starukha Izergil" (1895; "The Old Woman Izergil," 1905) were, however, soon replaced by characters inhabiting damp cellars, outskirts of cities, ports, and flophouses. "Chelkash" (1895; "Chelkash," 1902), while still in the romantic mode, portrays a drunken harbor thief. "Byushye lyudi" (1897; "Creatures That Once Were Men," 1906) was G.'s first story in a more realistic style.

G. knew his characters well from his observations during his travels through Russia. He captured their speech, the local slang. The realistic portrayal of the poverty, ignorance, and suffering of the lower strata was novel and attracted wide audiences.

While presenting misery and violence in a harshly realistic manner, G. also wrote of humaneness and beauty. He saw evil as resulting from social injustice and from the general backwardness of Russia. His tramp-heroes, striving for freedom and liberty, are filled with warmth and compassion, regardless of the sordidness of the milieu. Such characters appear in his most famous play, *Na dne* (1902; *The Lower Depths*, 1912), first performed at the Moscow Art Theater in a production directed by Konstantin Stanislavsky. Living in a flophouse, the characters are trodden down by life—and by society. Totally degraded, they drink, gamble, fight, and despair. The central conflict of the play is between the need for messages of hope and consoling illusion, which are dispensed by the pilgrim Luka, and the need to face the truth without comforting lies, the choice offered by the eloquent thief Satin.

G.'s other plays before the revolution focus on the bourgeoisie rather than on the lower levels of society. In *Meshchane* (1902; *The Smug Citizen*, 1906) G. ridicules greed, pettiness, and the tedious existence of the petite bourgeoisie and would-be intelligentsia. In *Dachniki* (1905; *Summer Folk*, 1905), *Deti solntsa* (1905; *Children of the Sun*, 1912), *Varvary* (1906; *Barbarians*, 1945), *Vragi* (1906; *Enemies*, 1945), *Vassa Zheleznova* (1910; *Vassa Zheleznova*, 1945), *Zykovy* (1913; *The Zykovs*, 1945), and others, G. portrays self-made and ambitious but crude, ruthless, and materialistic middle-class people who exploit workers and peasants, and effete intellectuals who are cut off from the masses. G. sees hope in the rise of the new intellectual, dedicated to helping the proletariat and to effecting a revolution, hope in the struggle of the proletariat itself against its masters.

In G.'s early novels, *Foma Gordeev* (1899; *Foma Gordeyev*, 1901) and *Troe* (1900; *Three of Them*, 1902), portraying the nascent merchant class, G. excels in characterization on a larger scale than in his earlier fiction. But these novels suffer from too much detail, loose structure, and didacticism.

G.'s most celebrated novel, *Mat* (1906; *Mother*, 1907), is regarded as a classic in Russian revolutionary literature; it became a model for many Soviet novelists. It depicts a woman who, as she becomes involved in the revolutionary cause her son serves, loses her timidity and becomes a fulfilled person. Although not of the highest literary merit, *Mat* is important because of its message and its having introduced the new class of industrial worker as a character in Russian literature.

G. came to maturity as a writer during his Capri years. Of the novels composed there, *Ispoved* (1908; *A Confession*, 1909) is particularly interesting. Written in a biblical style, it is full of folkloric touches and poetic images. The main theme is religious faith: its distortion by the established church and its deep roots in the people. The people become the "god" of the new religion and also the "god-builder." Among other important works written on Capri were the novella *Gorodok Okurov* (1909; the town Okurov) and the novel *Zhizn Matveya Kozhemyakina* (1910; *The Life of Matvei Kozhemyakin*, 1959). In both works G. depicted the life he knew well—that of the Russian lower-middle class at the turn of the century—and continued the sociological and psychological

analysis of that class, which he had begun in *Foma Gordeev*.

In 1913 the first volume of his autobiographical trilogy, *Detstvo* (*My Childhood*, 1914), appeared, and it was soon hailed as a masterpiece. The second and third volumes, *V lyudyakh* (1914; *In the World*, 1917) and *Moi universitety* (1922; *My University Days*, 1923), were also greeted with acclaim. In many ways G. surpassed his fictional works in this three-volume autobiography. Many of the same themes appear: human cruelty, the need for action, the backwardness of Russia. But, ironically, he is more objective here, with his material under greater control, than in his novels written before it. While writing about himself, G. wrote about things universal: love, compassion, violence, and hatred. In spite of his gloomy childhood and adolescence, G. does not lose sight of the bright and beautiful that existed alongside cruelty and ugliness. The autobiography is rich in the variety of its characterizations; and it is not devoid of humor.

G.'s reminiscences of his fellow writers—Chekhov, Andreev, Blok (qq.v.), Vladimir Korolenko (1853–1921)—added to the literary reputation secured by his autiobiography. Although he had written literary portraits early in his career, the later ones—especially *Vospominania o Lve Nikolaeviche Tolstom* (1919; *Reminiscences of Leo Nikolaevich Tolstoy*, 1920), perhaps the best portrait of Tolstoy written by any of his contemporaries—complement his autobiography in their great vividness. G. provided insights into giants of Russian literature that no biographer could, for he knew and understood them better. To these memoirs should also be added G.'s portraits of Lenin. The book-length essay *V. I. Lenin* (1924; *Days with Lenin*, 1932), although G. had to revise it several times following its initial publication, remains a fascinating portrait of the revolutionary leader written shortly after his death.

G. was often reproached for failing to depict life in postrevolutionary Russia. And indeed, only his propagandistic works address themselves to the Soviet period. In his major works written after 1917 he again turned to the period leading up to the revolution. In his late plays —*Yegor Bulychov i drugie* (1932; *Yegor Bulichov and Others*, 1937), set immediately before the revolution; and its sequel, *Dostigaev i drugie* (1933; *Dostigayev and Others*, 1937), set during the revolution—G. portrays the decline and fall of a wealthy family. In the novel *Delo Artamonovykh* (1925; *Decadence*, 1927;

later tr., *The Artamonov Business*, 1948), which shows a control over structure lacking in his earlier novels, three generations of a merchant family symbolize the corrupt Russian bourgeoisie. *Zhizn Klima Samgina* (4 vols., 1927–36; *The Life of Klim Samgin: The Bystander*, 1930; *The Magnet*, 1931; *Other Fires*, 1933; *The Spectre*, 1938)—which remained unfinished at G.'s death in 1936—is more ambitious but less artistically successful than *Delo Artamonovykh*. It chronicles the period from 1870 through the revolution, focusing on the failings of the intelligentsia.

G.'s significance as a writer and his place in world literature lie in his ability to combine the great Russian literary tradition of the 19th c. with the spirit of the 20th. Although he cannot be ranked as an artist with such writers as Pushkin, Tolstoy, Dostoevsky, or Turgenev, he was an important innovator as well as a synthesizer. His mode could be called "synthetic realism," combining as it does romantic and naturalistic elements. His great gifts are characterization and the ability to convey through his art important ideas about society and people's personal lives. Finally, G. had an immense influence on an entire generation of Soviet writers.

FURTHER WORKS: *Goremyka Pavel* (1894; *Orphan Paul*, 1946); *Zhizn nenuzhnogo cheloveka* (1908; *The Spy: The Story of a Superfluous Man*, 1908); *Poslednie* (1908); *Leto* (1909; *Summer*, 1909); *Chudaki* (1910); *Skazki ob Italii* (1911–13; *Tales of Italy*, 195?); *Po Rusi* (1915; *Through Russia*, 1921); *Stati za 1905–1916 g.* (1918); *Revolyutsia i kultura: Stati za 1917 god* (1920); *Starik* (1921; *The Judge*, 1924); *Sobranie sochineny* (21 vols., 1923–28); *Zametki iz dnevnika: Vospominania* (1924); *O literature: Stati i rechi* (1933; *On Literature*, 1960); *Sobranie sochineny* (25 vols., 1933–34); *O religii* (1937); *Istoria russkoy literatury* (1939); *Arkhiv G.* (14 vols., 1939–1973); *Sobranie sochineny* (30 vols., 1949–55); *Literaturnye portrety* (1959; *Literary Portraits*, n.d. [1960?]); *Sobranie sochineny* (18 vols., 1960–63); *O pechati* (1962); *Polnoe sobranie sochineny* (1968 ff.). FURTHER VOLUMES IN ENGLISH: *Malva, and Other Tales* (1901); *The Outcasts, and Other Stories* (1902); *Twenty-six Men and a Girl, and Other Stories* (1902); *Tales from G.* (1902); *Creatures That Once Were Men* (1908); *Orloff and His Wife: Tales of the Barefoot Brigade* (1909); *Tales of Two Countries* (1914); *Chelkash, and Other Stories* (1915); *Stories of the Steppe* (1918); *Tales* (1923); *Fragments from My Diary* (1924); *The Story of a Novel, and Other Stories* (1925); *On Guard for the Soviet Union* (1933); *The Last Plays of M. G.* (1937); *Culture and the People* (1939); *A Book of Short Stories* (1939); *Seven Plays by M. G.* (1945); *Reminiscences* (1946); *Literature and Life: A Selection from the Writings of M. G.* (1946); *The History of the Civil War in the USSR* (1946); *Unrequited Love, and Other Stories* (1949); *Articles and Pamphlets* (1951); *Letters of G. and Andreev, 1899–1912* (1958); *A Sky-Blue Life, and Selected Stories* (1964); *Untimely Thoughts: Essays on Revolution, Culture, and the Bolsheviks, 1917–1918* (1968)

BIBLIOGRAPHY: Dillon, E. T., *M. G.: His Life and Writing* (1902); Vogüé, E. de, *M. G.: L'œuvre et l'homme* (1905); Kaun, A., *M. G. and His Russia* (1931); Roskin, A., *From the Banks of the Volga: The Life of M. G.* (1946); Holtzman, F., *The Young M. G.: 1868–1902* (1948); Alexinsky, G., *La vie amère de M. G.* (1950); Wolf, F., *M. G.* (1953); Pozner, V., *Erinnerungen an G.* (1959); Gourfinkel, N., *G.* (1960); Muchnic, H., *From G. to Pasternak* (1961), pp. 29–103; Hare, R., *M. G.: Romantic Realist and Conservative Revolutionary* (1962); Levin, D., *Stormy Petrel: The Life and Work of M. G.* (1965); Weil, I., *G.: His Literary Development and Influence on Soviet Intellectual Life* (1966); Borras, F. M., *M. G. the Writer: An Interpretation* (1967); Wolfe, B. D., *The Bridge and the Abyss: The Troubled Friendship of M. G. and V. I. Lenin* (1967); special G. issue, *Y/T*, 2 (1976)

TOVA YEDLIN

G. must be taken, for better or for worse, as a didactic writer. He is always imbued with a social idea, which he is anxious to convey to his readers, and his literary output may be approached with regard to the proportion and intensity of the message preached in each individual work. It hardly need be suggested that the quality of his work is in inverse proportion to the degree and obviousness of its didacticism. Yet one should remember that it was this latter trait that enhanced his value in the eyes of the masses and their fighting vanguard, and lent him the public significance which cannot be discounted by any purely aesthetic considerations.

Alexander Kaun, *M. G. and His Russia* (1931), p. 553

G. is truly a great landscape painter and, more important, a passionate landscape lover. He finds it difficult to approach a person, to begin a story of a chapter of a novel without first glancing at the sky to see what the sun, the moon, the stars and the ineffable palette of the heavens with the ever-changing magic of the clouds are doing.

In G. we find so much of the sea, the mountains, forests and steppes, so many little gardens and hidden nooks of Nature! What unusual words he invents to describe it! He works at it as an objective artist: now as Monet, breaking down its colours for you with his amazing analytical eye and what is probably the most extensive vocabulary in our literature, now, on the contrary, as a syntheticist who produces a general outline and with one hammered phrase can describe an entire panorama. But he is not merely an artist. His approach to Nature is that of a poet. . . .

In order to create Nature's majestic and beautiful orchestrations for his human dramas, G. uses most skilfully the frailest similarities and contrasts between human emotions and Nature, which at times are barely discernible. [1932]

Anatoli Lunacharski, *On Literature and Art* (1965), pp. 222–23

He preferred to praise rather than pity, and to speak of man's conquests of, rather than his submission to, Nature. Impatient with theory, complexity, "psychologizing," he saw existence in the light of his unambiguous dogma. and, like the solicitous father of very small children, told lies to bolster their morale. All men appeared to him in the guise of the snake and falcon of his fable; he wanted all of them to be falcons, never doubted that they could be, and toward the end of his life had the joy of seeing them so transformed, as he thought. It was an ardent zeal, a generous humanistic faith that, to his mind, was more "loving" than Tolstoy's egotistic passion. . . . He was "engaged" in life, in the French sense of *engagé;* as a writer his business was to "serve," to rouse, to work for improvement, to be actively involved in the moment; unlike Tolstoy, he did not look upon human beings as moral entities but only as social organisms: they either destroyed or built communities, and their role in society determined their value as men.

Helen Muchnic, *From G. to Pasternak* (1961), pp. 98–99

He concentrated on the sordid details, primarily those of a physical nature: hunger, drunkenness, pain, filth, the lack of all physical essentials. With the exception of Dostoevsky. there is no other Russian writer of the nineteenth century who dealt as much as G. did with physical violence and murder. Whatever the psychological explanation may be in terms of G.'s personality, it would be next to impossible to detect any grin of sadistic pleasure in his gruesome descriptions of wives mangled by their husbands, of vagabonds beaten up by police. From his early childhood he had been deeply affected by all the excesses of violence around him: the fury of blows, the floggings, the madness of drunken brawls. He had become aware of physical violence as a main feature of Russian life, and its exposé remained one of his principal objectives; he denounced it not only as an Asiatic heritage, a survival of the Tartar yoke, but also as a result of ignorance and oppression: the cruelty of the common people was bred by their misery and was a release as well as a compensation for their slavery.

Marc Slonim, *From Chekhov to the Revolution* (1962), p. 136

His best earlier stories had thrown a highlight on strong and self-reliant characters at loggerheads with their drab environment, by no means only tramps, but also princes, landowners, and legendary figures. . . . While he had neither morally whitewashed nor tried to rationalize their unpredictable, impulsive conduct, he was clearly fascinated by their integrity, by their refusal to be dragged down by convention-bound society. After all these glowing pictures of buoyant energetic men and women, G. changed over paradoxically to an apologia for weak or broken individuals. Sometimes they are the same people as before, seen at the later stage of life. The characters in *The Lower Depths* have all started boldly, and then been broken on the wheel. But G. could more easily start to justify sympathetic but defeated people, because some of his favourite heroes had been men of quite ordinary capacities, struggling to play gigantic roles beyond their strength. It was inevitable that many of his defiant tramps and ultra-individual misfits, if they could not die bravely before their youthful vigour was exhausted, should sink into the dull abasement of the doss-house.

Richard Hare, *M. G.* (1962), pp. 60–61

G. was always prepared to rework his plays to modify or clarify their meaning (notably *Enemies* to which he gave a significantly different political slant for its Soviet revival in 1933), but he never returned to *The Lower Depths* and it remains as it was originally written—ambiguous and inconclusive. When he wrote it in 1902 he had no choice: the conflict between truth and compassion, between harsh facts and the beautiful lie was within himself. Soon he sought to resolve it by embracing the activist cause of Marxism and by pursuing the truth in a series of socially committed works of which *Enemies* is perhaps the least compromising. Yet his characters remained . . . "facts of life," complex human beings who transcend dogmatic

JACOB GLATSTEIN

WILLIAM GOLDING

WITOLD GOMBROWICZ

MAXIM GORKY

schematization. In *Enemies* even the unscrupulous factory boss, Mikhail Skrobotov, is treated with a compassion that G. manages still to reconcile with the inescapable social truth of the play.

If *The Lower Depths* is G.'s most humane, hence most inconclusive play, it is by no means a play apart: like all his work it proceeds from the man himself, reflecting his own complexity and his own honest doubt. About one thing only G. was never in doubt: as Satin says "Man! There's the truth for you! What is man? It isn't me—or you—or them . . . no! It's you and me and them and the old man and Mahomet . . . all rolled into one." To that extent he was a political writer. [1972]

Edward Braun, Introduction to M. G., *The Lower Depths* (1973), p. xiv

GOYTISOLO, Juan

Spanish novelist, essayist, and critic, b. 5 Jan. 1931, Barcelona

Early in his childhood, G. experienced the horrors of the Spanish Civil War. His mother was killed in 1938 during a Nationalist bombardment of Barcelona, and the family was forced to abandon the city and take refuge in a small village in Catalonia until the war was over, when they returned to Barcelona, where G. continued his formal education. Between 1950 and 1953 G. studied law in Barcelona and Madrid and began testing his narrative skills. During this time he founded the "Turia" literary group with the distinguished novelist Ana María Matute (q.v.) and others, and wrote three short stories, a novelette, and his first full-length novel, *Juegos de manos* (1954; *The Young Assassins*, 1959). The publication of this work marked his first formal step into the world of the novel and the end of his aspirations to practice law.

Before leaving Spain to establish permanent residence in Paris in 1957, he published *Duelo en el paraíso* (1955; *Children of Chaos*, 1959), wrote *El circo* (1957; the circus) and *Fiestas* (1958; *Fiestas*, 1960), enhancing his reputation, at home and abroad, as one of the most talented novelists in 20th-c. Spain.

Stylistically, G.'s novelistic output shows two distinctive phases. The first, which includes the novels mentioned above, plus *La resaca* (1958; the undertow) and *La isla* (1961; *Island of Women*, 1962), is characterized by rather traditional construction, manipulation of time and space, and portrayal of character. Detailed, objective descriptions and dialogue are used to capture the moral and physical reality of Spain

immediately before, during, and after the Spanish Civil War, which in these novels becomes the cause for the characters' moral degradation and the vivid evidence of a fanatical society where there is no room for justice or tolerance. Most of the characters are children and adolescents who, following their parents' behavior, resort to deception and murder as the only choices in order for them to survive. Although objective depiction of events is prevalent in this phase, there is also lyricism, used especially to embody the dreams of those striving to escape the cruelty of the world in which they are trapped.

In the mid-1960s G.'s initial objective realism, evident also in most of the writings of other authors of his literary generation, began to move in a new direction, toward more imaginative technical experimentation. Three major works belong to this new phase: *Señas de identidad* (1966; *Marks of Identity*, 1969), *Reivindicación del Conde don Julián* (1970; *Count Julian*, 1974) and *Juan sin tierra* (1975; *Juan the Landless*, 1977). They are the product of a mature novelist whose primary commitment is to his genre, the novel, more than simply to society, as seen in his earlier works. In these three later novels G. progressively creates a more ambitious and challenging world where language becomes the central force for poetic experimentation in point of view, time, space, character development, and structural design. As fragmentation leads to ambiguity, ambiguity leads to reader participation in the creation of the work whose open structure turns it into a never-ending source of meanings. More than novels of traditional form, they are malleable texts wherein the three protagonists search for new identities while destroying their present ones. To do this they must attack everything that is held sacred by Spaniards and Westerners: religion, social institutions, conventional morality, and so on, and irony, parody, and sarcasm become the main weapons. Nothing is left intact in this process of annihilation.

Even though these works form a three-part unity of self-discovery, each maintains its distinctive individuality of form and content.

Álvaro Mendiola, in *Señas de identidad*, while listening to Mozart's Requiem in his family's home near Barcelona, looks through some old family albums, letters, and newspaper clippings that had been kept for a long time in drawers and forgotten and that now are about to take him back to his personal past, and to the past of his country. At first, this rummaging appears to be only a trivial pastime, but later it turns into an obsessive exploratory journey whereby the character—in a series of interior monologues, intense, fragmented recollections, and collages, with the author using multiple narrative points of view—brings to light the horrors of Spanish society before, during, and after the Spanish Civil War, including his recent and bitter experiences of his self-imposed exile in Paris between 1952 and 1953, when the opposition forces to the Franco regime began to disintegrate for lack of internal unity. Even though the exploratory journey into Álvaro's past leads him nowhere, except to more anguish and deeper alienation, the sincerity of his efforts, to strip himself of the identity imposed on him by the society he criticizes, becomes the redeeming trait of the character.

In *Reivindicación del Conde don Julián* G. intensified his attacks on the system. This time he utilizes as the central force of the novel the legend of Don Julián, who is said to have allied himself with the Arabs, in the invasion of Spain in 711, in retaliation to his daughter's seduction by Roderick, the last Gothic king of Spain. The protagonist is a lonely Spaniard, exiled in Tangiers, who, having transformed himself into a Moor and with the inspiration of Count Julián's rebellious spirit and treason, in an interior monologue that lasts twenty-four hours, in his imagination invades Spain and systematically destroys its religious, political, and literary institutions. This symbolic destruction is also the destruction of his present identity, which enables him in turn to create a new one and redefine his individuality. Under the guidance of the Marquis de Sade, Lautréamont, and Jean Genet (q.v.), and with skillful manipulations of intricate imagery and surreal fragmentations of plot, time, and space, he commits a variety of atrocities: he rapes Queen Isabella I, embarks on a surreal trip through her vagina, sodomizes a child (representing the protagonist's own past), and breaks all rules of decency. He assaults every political and religious institution, and, as if that were not enough, finishes off, one by one, with all the literary classics of Spanish literature, including Lope de Vega, Calderón de la Barca, Miguel de Unamuno (q.v.), and most of the writers of the so-called Generation of '98. Cervantes and Luis de Góngora are among the few masters he shows respect for and saves from his literary massacre. Furthermore, he honors them by following their example in developing an autonomous, highly metaphoric, complex text wherein the destruction of an entire literary corpus (as in *Don Quixote*) becomes the subject and the method of literary creation.

Unlike the two previous novels, in *Juan sin tierra* the protagonist, transformed into a modern wandering Jew (hence the title), through a complex succession of dreams contained in numerous narrative units, systematically attacks not only Spain, but also all the commonly held sacred values of Western civilization: family, religion, social institutions. By engaging in this violent attack, which is conceived and executed within a general framework of vengeance, hatred, and perversion, the character, once again, seeks to annihilate his present self and replace it with another, free of guilt and shame. His guiding principle for self-realization is clear: the more he destroys society's values (and thus his present self) the more he develops his new identity. And the more he vilifies himself, the more effective the destruction becomes. In time and space the novel reaches apocalyptic proportions. His self-destruction extends not only to his childhood but all the way to the moment he was conceived by his mother. And the more he travels in terms of space the more complete and satisfying his aggression becomes.

Juan sin tierra is the culmination of G.'s thematic aggression and artistic experimentation. It is perhaps one of the most powerful texts in 20th-c. literature. Compared to this work, *Makbara* (1979; *Makbara*, 1981) is wanting in stylistic power and imagination. G.'s attack on modern capitalist society in *Makbara* lacks the intensity and the artistic subtlety of the three preceding novels.

G. has also written literary theory and criticism. In three critical works—*Problemas de la novela* (1959; problems of the novel), *El furgón de cola* (1967; the caboose), and *Disidencias* (1977; dissidences)—G. develops perceptive and controversial commentaries on the novel in general and on specific literary works written by old and new, Spanish and foreign, authors.

G.'s novelistic art, especially that of his second phase, has placed him among the most innovative Hispanic authors of this century. His rich poetic imagination and his daring manipulation of language is comparable only to those of such Spanish American writers as Guillermo Cabrera Infante, Carlos Fuentes, and Mario Vargas Llosa (qq.v.).

FURTHER WORKS: *Campos de Níjar* (1959); *Para vivir aquí* (1960); *Fin de fiesta* (1962; *The Party's Over*, 1967); *La chanca* (1962);

Pueblo en marcha (1963); *El problema del Sahara* (1979)

BIBLIOGRAPHY: Schwartz, K., *J. G.* (1970); Sobejano, G., *Novela española de nuestro tiempo* (1970), pp. 260–92; special G. issues, *Norte,* Nos. 4–6 (1972); Ortega, J., *J. G.: Alienación y agresión en "Señas de identidad" y "Reivindicación del Conde don Julián"* (1972); Romero, H., "Los mitos de la España sagrada en *Reivindicación del Conde don Julián,*" *JSSTC,* 1 (1973), 169–85; Ríos, J., ed., *J. G.* (1975); Levine, L. G., *J. G.: La destrucción creadora* (1976); Cabrera, V., "Movilidad y repetición narrativas en *Juan sin tierra,*" *TAH,* 1, 9 (1976); 7–9; Spires, R., "La autodestrucción creativa en *Reivindicación del Conde don Julián,*" *JSSTC,* 4 (1976), 191–202; Ríos, J., ed., *Juan sin tierra* (1977); Robatto, M. A., *La creación literaria de J. G.* (1977); Pérez, G., *Formalist Elements in the Novels of J. G.* (1979)

VICENTE CABRERA

Signs of Identity, G.'s most outspoken attack on the Franco regime, presents biographies of birth and death, suffering and sorrow in the Spanish police state where, during twenty-five years of "peace," man had beaten, arrested, and killed defenseless fellow citizens for the crime of having defended their legal government, the Republic. No progress, says G., will be able to wipe away the humiliations, the injustices, the persecution, the destroyed lives, of those years.

G. examines Spanish history from the 1930's on, the days of José Antonio Primo de Rivera, Ledesma, and others, recalling the public works programs, the depression, the Popular Front, the violence and unrest among starving peasants and their battles with the Civil Guard; he more forcefully condemns Franco for the spiritual and physical murder of his countrymen who are born, multiply, and die in silent resignation. Andalusia recalls a cemetery to him in its eternal misery: "A woman in mourning carried a jug on her head and even the mangy dog swatting flies with his tail seemed an exact replica of others seen a thousand times in a Southern town."

Kessel Schwartz, *J. G.* (1970), pp. 98–99

With Count Julian, J. G. has succeeded in giving us a meticulous and clear-minded account, both brilliant and full of salutary laughter, of a first voyage into the interior of a volcano. . . . It is a thorough, lyrical, passionate account of a task of systematic destruction. . . . Without doubt—and there has been no lack of those who have said it —Count Julian follows a typically Spanish tradition because of the haughtiness of its excess and the corrosive bite of its humor. It is almost a century since Valle-Inclán cried: "Poets, guillotine your swans," and since he promised to work relentlessly "to dig the grave in which to bury the hollow and pompous Spanish prose which can no longer be ours. . . ." The anonymous character who haunts the last novel of J. G. re-creates, in effect, this situation of exile and marginality of the writer in Spanish society, who is obliged, generation after generation, to wage the same struggle, to renew the same subversion of values.

Jorge Semprun, on *Reivindicación del Conde don Julián, L'express,* 26 July–1 Aug. 1971, 67–68

Señas de identidad is the detailed and intimate, yet broad and panoramic exploration of a personal crisis. Álvaro Mendiola, the author and protagonist . . . portrays his own experience as a member of a specific generation of young Spaniards who were born during the thirties, and for whom the Civil War is one of their childhood memories. He is the descendant of a tradition-bound family of industrialists and landowners whose values he despises. But it is not until he is a young man struggling to orient himself ideally and intellectually to the causes of social and economic justice for Spain's working classes at home and in exile that he becomes aware of the extent to which he is cast in the mold of the social class he is opposing. It is not a question of his intellect or even his moral values resembling those of his family, for he appears to have set himself fiercely against everything they stand for in those respects. There is something deeper and far subtler that he has inherited from his elders that seems in spite of everything to determine his consciousness at the deepest level: it is a sense of life, a mythology, a "Weltanschauung" which he can scarcely identify rationally that has brought him to this critical impasse.

Reed Anderson, *"Señas de identidad:* Chronicle of Rebellion," *JSSTC,* 2 (1974), 3

Count Julian represents for Spain what a combined critical consciousness of black, Indian, Chicano, Women's Liberation and Gay Power attitudes would represent in the United States. There is a difference, however. The contesting minorities in the United States have questioned a success story. G. is questioning a failure. The risks he takes are proportionately greater. . . . Count Julian is the most terrible attack against the oppressive forces of a nation that I have ever read. Nothing that black has written against white, or woman against man, or poor against rich, or son against father, reaches quite the peak of intense hatred and horror that G. achieves in this novel. That he does it with magnificent beauty and perfect craftsmanship only adds to the power of his invective against his "harsh homeland." It is quite a feat, and quite a risk, for the novelist works with words, yet he is conscious that "violence is mute."

Carlos Fuentes, on *Count Julian*, *NYTBR*, 5 May 1974, 6–7

Juan sin tierra is inspired by one of the most difficult concepts in literature—irony—by that "perception of life in terms of incongruities occurring between appearances and reality," even though "reality" here must be used in quotation marks. Sometimes the ironic undertone seems to be mere humor, but if one is to read a few more lines apparently in the same vein, irony stands out to the point that it overwhelms the entire book. Much more compact than *Conde Don Julián* (I use this name instead of the complete title because of the joy the English translation, *Count Julián* produces in me), more open than *Señas de identidad*, *Juan sin tierra* is perhaps J. G.'s best book. No critical analysis could ever supplant the pleasure of its reading, which, as in any good fable, forces us to forget reading its maxim; yet there is no other book that is so Spanish, so relevant to the Spaniard and, at the same time, so irreverent to Spain. The book's only heroine is the Spanish language —but do I have to remind anyone that "heroine" (in Spanish) means both heroine and heroin?

Guillermo Cabrera Infante, "El fin como principio," in Julián Rios, ed., *Juan sin tierra* (1975), pp. 228–29

Because of its radical difference not only to novels in general but to G.'s previous works, *Juan sin tierra* could be classified as an entirely new genre in the vein of *Finnegans Wake*. Samuel Beckett's comment about Joyce's magnum opus is pertinent: "It [the novel] is not to be read—or rather it is not only to be read. It is also to be looked at and listened to. His writing is not about something; it is that something itself." G.'s work had elements of a travelogue, a book of memoirs, and even a diary "to see clearly," as Roquetin said in [Sartre's] *La nausée*. The intentions of the author appear to be that of engaging the reader in a voyage of self-discovery in which fact and fiction, the present, the past, and the future are intermingled. Furthermore, the frequent use of the second-person singular point of view contributes, as in *Don Julián*, to the amalgamation of the protagonist and the reader. Unlike *Don Julián*, however, the author, who shows himself in the act of writing, indicates that he is the narrator-protagonist and fuses himself with the protagonist and reader.

Genaro J. Pérez, "Form in J. G.'s *Juan sin tierra*," *JSSTC*, 5 (1977), 137–38

GOZZANO, Guido

Italian poet, b. 19 Dec. 1883, Turin; d. 9 Aug. 1916, Agliè Canavese

From an upper-middle-class family, G. received a traditional education and lived most of his life in his native region of Piedmont, alternating between Turin and his country estate in Agliè. He studied law but followed his natural bent for journalism and literature. His collections of poems *La via del rifugio* (1907; the road to shelter) and *I colloqui* (1911; *The Colloquies*, 1981) were favorably received and established him, in his twenties, as one of the authentic voices in Italian poetry of the early 20th c.

His short life was marked by a long fight against tuberculosis, an illness that resisted years of medical care and may have been partially responsible for the melancholy and disillusioned outlook that characterizes G. as a representative of the *Crepuscolari*, the poets of the "twilight" school.

In 1912 G. undertook a long voyage to India and Ceylon, hoping to regain his health. His impressions of that venture were published as letters in the Turin newspaper *La stampa* and later collected in *Verso la cuna del mondo* (1917; toward the cradle of the world) with a preface by the critic Giuseppe Antonio Borgese (1882–1952). G. also left an unfinished poem on butterflies, one of his favorite subjects of study and naturalistic observation, in which he treats a traditionally didactic genre with a fundamentally lyrical inspiration. Of considerable value for the understanding of his life and work is his correspondence with Amalia Guglielminetti, with whom he had a difficult relationship.

G.'s disenchantment with reality and often also with literature made him yearn for the simple values and bourgeois settings of past years. In poems such as "Paolo e Virginia" (1910; Paolo and Virginia) and "La signorina Felicita" (1909; Miss Felicity) he expressed emotions and insights in a freshly colloquial style whose natural fluency succeeded in opening new paths beyond D'Annunzio's (q.v.) high diction and refined style. But it is the ironic self-awareness of his style that distinguishes G. from all the poets of his time, including the *Crepuscolari*, whose world he contemplates and cherishes while implicitly confessing and regretting the impossibility of a full acceptance of it beyond a carefully modulated and balanced compromise between detachment and sympathy, melancholy and cheerfulness, participation and irony.

G. also wrote fables, tales, and verse for children, as well as an outline for a film on St.

Francis of Assisi that bespeaks an uncommon gift for visual imagery.

FURTHER WORKS: *I tre talismani* (1914); *La principessa si sposa* (1917); *L'altare del passato* (1918); *L'ultima traccia* (1919); *Lettere d'amore di G. G. e A. Guglielminetti* (1951); *Poesie e prose* (1961). FURTHER VOLUME IN ENGLISH: *The Man I Pretend to Be: "The Colloquies" and Selected Poems* (1981, bilingual)

BIBLIOGRAPHY: Bracegirdle, M., "D'Annunzio and G.," *IRLI*, 6 (1977), 95–103; Williamson, E., Introduction and Biographical Note, in Lind, R. F., ed., *Twentieth Century Italian Poetry* (1974), pp. 34–69, 367–88

A. ILLIANO

GRACQ, Julien

(pseud. of Louis Poirier) French novelist and essayist, b. 27 July 1910, Saint-Florent-le-Vieil

G. studied in Paris at the École Normale Supérieure and the École des Sciences Politiques, receiving his degree in history in 1934. He then taught history at various secondary schools throughout France and, from 1947 to his retirement in 1970, at the Lycée Claude Bernard in Paris. During World War II he served in the French army. He now lives in Paris.

A disciple of André Breton (q.v.), whom he admired and on whom he wrote a study, G. was deeply influenced by surrealism (q.v.). His novels could be called vast prose poems exploring the strangely mysterious, giving new life to old myths in stories abounding in quaint enchanted castles with secret passages, desolate shores, and dense impenetrable forests. Although written in a surrealistic vein, these novels show no trace of "automatic writing." On the contrary, G.'s style is sumptuous, with a rich and suggestive vocabulary. His elegant prose, characterized by slow-moving, long, involved sentences, seems to delay forever the coming of the enigmatic "Event."

Unlike the surrealists, G.'s foremost preoccupation is with destiny and the tragic sense of life. In *Au château d'Argol* (1938; *The Castle of Argol*, 1951), three exceptional characters (all strangely beautiful, all educated on Hegel and able to comprehend life's deepest intricacies) live an intense spiritual adventure in a remote enchanted castle in Brittany. The themes and scenery were undoubtedly inspired by

Wagner's *Parsifal*. In fact, G. himself conceives of his narrative as a "demonic version" of the Grail legend. But other myths—man's fall and the Faust legend—also play a significant part in the intricately woven fabric of the novel, which explores the dialectical nature of good and evil, spirit and flesh.

G.'s most famous novel, *Le rivage des Syrtes* (1951; the shore of the Syrtes), won the Goncourt Prize, which G., however, refused. The book is another interesting interpretation of the Grail myth, and shows affinities with Ernst Jünger's (q.v.) *On the Marble Cliffs*, of which G. said he would have enjoyed claiming authorship. Like Jünger's "Marina," G.'s imaginary "Orsenna" is a highly civilized state, whose inner decay, nevertheless, is unmistakable. Yet, in spite of the prevailing "indecent affirmation of life" characteristic of the people of Orsenna, "who were never given to value the tragic," there exists at the same time a secret desire for the possibly redeeming catastrophe. Aldo, G.'s protagonist, is aware of this undercurrent and, seized by an irresistible inner urge, becomes the traitor or redeemer of Orsenna by provoking fate. He deliberately crosses the line of demarcation between Orsenna and its enemy of three hundred years, uncivilized Farghestan, thus bringing about a resumption of hostilities, which could very well lead to Orsenna's annihilation. But it is neither pure lust for adventure nor simply a destructive instinct that drives him to his act; they are only part of a more encompassing desire to experience life once more to its fullest, even though it may be for the last time. The thirst for purification and the desire for redemption are inextricably fused with any death wish.

G.'s literary production is not limited to novels. It includes short stories, prose poems, a play, and several volumes of critical essays. But his reputation is based above all on his novelistic work. His novels are long meditations on man's fate, revealing a strong and disturbing obsession with death, reminiscent of classical tragedy. The traditional concept of characters and plot has been shattered. In each novel a multitude of dark forces are at play; little by little they seem to converge and intensify until the final catastrophe, which more often than not remains only suggested. The main characters are "marked" beings who act as catalysts to those forces, bringing with them inevitable disaster.

G.'s work stands decidedly apart from the main currents of contemporary French literature. It is characterized especially by those traits that link surrealism with romanticism—

German romanticism and Hegelian idealism in particular.

FURTHER WORKS: *Un beau ténébreux* (1945; *A Dark Stranger*, 1951); *Liberté grande* (1947); *André Breton: Quelques aspects de l'écrivain* (1948); *Le roi pêcheur* (1948); *La littérature à l'estomac* (1950); *La terre habitable* (1951); *Prose pour l'étrangère* (1952); *Un balcon en forêt* (1958; *Balcony in the Forest*, 1959); *Préférences* (1961); *Lettrines* (1967); *La presqu'île* (1970); *Les eaux étroites* (1977); *Lettrines 2* (1978)

BIBLIOGRAPHY: Leutrat, J.-L., *J. G.* (1967); Matthews, J. H., "J. G. and the Theme of the Grail in Surrealism," *RR*, 58 (1968), 95–108; Dobbs, A.-C., *Dramaturgie et liturgie dans l'œuvre de J. G.* (1972); Peyronie, A., *La pierre de scandale du "Château d'Argol" de J. G.* (1972); Gaudon, S., "J. G.'s *Un balcon en forêt*: The Ambiguities of Initiation," *RR*, 67 (1976), 132–46; Denis, A., *J. G.* (1978); Francis, M., *Forme et signification de l'attente dans l'œuvre romanesque de J. G.* (1979)

BLANDINE M. RICKERT

GRADE, Chaim

Yiddish poet, novelist, and memoirist, b. 5 April 1910, Vilna, Lithuania

Son of a Hebrew teacher and grandson of a grenadier in Napoleon's invading army of 1812, G. was raised in a household devoted to the observance of traditional Judaism as well as the acquisition of secular knowledge. But he abandoned Orthodoxy in his early manhood. In the face of the Nazi onslaught, he took with him only a Hebrew Bible and a German translation of Dante's *Divine Comedy* and fled first to Vilna, the Jerusalem of Lithuania, from Russia, where he was living, and later to Soviet Central Asia. In Lithuania he emerged as a leader of the "Young Vilna" group of Yiddish writers. This self-assertive and eager pleiad of young literati shunned the accepted rules of writing, denounced the common wisdom about the essence and purposes of literature—preferring introspection and the pursuit of idiosyncrasy—and refused to assume the mantle of "professional writers."

After World War II G. left the Soviet Union, sojourned briefly in Paris, and in 1950 settled in the U.S. He established himself in the canon of modern Yiddish literature by the quality of his narrative skill, both puissant and gentle; by his relentless perception of the human psyche when it is faced with philosophical dilemmas; and by the tender sensitivity he exhibits for the millennial treasure of his beloved language. He was the only Yiddish poet invited to read at the literary festival held in the White House in January 1980.

In post-World War II Yiddish belles lettres, G. and Avrom Sutzkever (q.v.) stand as the two contemporary bards of the Holocaust, which truncated their people and brought their language to the threshold of annihilation. The national motif undergirds much of G.'s elegiac poetry. He summons the Jewish people, as a latter-day prophet "tossed between oblivion and life," to awaken, live, and continue.

The second national (and personal) trauma that enflames his creative imagination is the destruction in the early 1950s of the flower of Yiddish literati in Moscow. G. has immortalized these writers in his "Elegiye oyf di sovetish-Yidishe shrayber" (1962; "Elegy for the Soviet Yiddish Writers," 1969), already recognized as a classic in the repertory of modern Yiddish poetry.

The Musar, or Moral Discipline, movement was initiated in 19th-c. Lithuania by Rabbi Israel Salanter, who preached the need for higher Jewish learning to bring about moral perfection. G.'s epic poem *Musarnikes* (1939; the ethical ones) chronicles life in a yeshiva of this type, tracing the way a young Orthodox Jew gropes among the perplexities of faith, only to emerge as a determined humanist and affirmer of life.

G.'s writing is haunted by three figures from his youth: his father, his mother, and his mentor, Rabbi Chazon Ish. These three personages, together with the author himself, appear and reappear in various guises in his major works, *Tsemakh Atlas* (2 vols., 1967–68; *The Yeshivah*, 2 vols., 1976–77); *Di agune* (1961; *The Agunah*, 1974); and his novelette, *Der brunem* (1958; *The Well*, 1967). These works demonstrate a zest for subtle characterization and an impressive architectonic skill that limns the ethical, philosophical, and theological currents that have percolated through Lithuanian Jewry for the past two hundred years.

Inspired by an abiding affection for the centuries-old way of life of East European Jewry, G. lays open with a surgeon's skill the strengths and weaknesses of both the sages and the pious ordinary folk of this now vanished world. In a series of remarkable panoramas, he fills out their biographies, finding the merit and salvation of these lives in their quest for the spiritual and in their self-oblation.

Only in the 1960s did G. allow his works to be translated. Since then critical interest and appreciation of his talent have grown and his reputation has become international. He has received the Bimko Prize for *Di mames tsuve* (1949; partial tr., *The Seven Little Lanes*, 1972), and the Lamed Prize for his volume of short stories, *Di mames shabeysim* (1955; my mother's Sabbaths), his first volume of prose.

A man of East and West, possessed of cosmopolitan sophistication, he is at the same time the leading student of the Torah among today's writers in Yiddish. Reworking the themes of shtetl life, Talmudic and biblical riches, Hasidic and Musarnik lore, his oeuvre constitutes an ongoing dialogue between the Jew who believes despite the Holocaust and the poet, seeking faith and understanding. G. illustrates, in the words of one critic, the Pauline principle by which the spiritual man slays the carnal.

FURTHER WORKS: *Yo* (1937); *Has: Lider un poemen* (1943); *Doyres* (1945); *Oyf di khurbes* (1947); *Farvaksene vegn: Lider un poemes* (1947); *Pleytim* (1947); *Shayn fun farloshene shtern* (1950); *Der shulhoyf* (1958); *Der mentsh fun fayer* (1962); *Yerushalayim shel mayle un Yerushalayim shel mate* (1965); *Parmetene erd* (1968); *Mayn krig mit Hersh Raseyner* (1969); *Oyf mayn veg tsu dir* (1969); *Di kloyz un di gas* (1974); *Der shtumer minyen* (1976)

BIBLIOGRAPHY: Madison, C., *Yiddish Literature* (1968), pp. 315, 325; Biletzky, I. C., *Essays on Yiddish Poetry and Prose Writers of the Twentieth Century* (1969), pp. 233–42; Liptzin, S., *The Maturing of Yiddish Literature* (1970), pp. 261–67; Hecker, I., "C. G.: The Challenge to God" and "C. G.: A Portrait of the Man," *Judaica Book News* (1979), 15–22; Slotnick, S. A., "C. G.'s Central Concern," *Jewish Book Annual*, 37 (1979–80), 106–115

THOMAS E. BIRD

GRAF, Oskar Maria

German novelist and short-story writer, b. 22 July 1894, Berg, on Lake Starnberg; d. 28 June 1967, New York, N.Y., U.S.A.

The son of a village baker and a farmer's daughter, G. first learned his father's trade; but at age sixteen he went to Munich, where he began to write and participated in the anarchist movement. During World War I he was drafted and, after he had refused to carry out an unrea-sonable command, was thrown into prison. He pretended to be insane and was committed to an asylum. After his release, he worked at a number of odd jobs in Munich and took part in the revolution of 1918–19.

G.'s literary career in Germany coincided with the fate of the Weimar Republic. After Hitler's rise to power he went into voluntary exile, first to Vienna (until 1934), then to Brno, Czechoslovakia (until 1938—his stay was interrupted by an extended trip to the Soviet Union in 1934), and finally New York. After World War II, he wanted to visit Germany again, but not until he had become an American citizen. Because he refused to sign the clause that would require a person to bear arms on behalf of the U.S., his process of naturalization was not completed until 1958.

Although his first publications were poetry, G. is now primarily known as a prose writer. *Frühzeit* (1922; early youth), the first part of his autobiography, while it received little notice in Germany, was published in two Russian editions in 1925. G.'s reputation was established when he added a second part to this work and published both parts together under the title *Wir sind Gefangene* (1927; *Prisoners All*, 1929). As an open confession of the author's personal past and of his having witnessed the historical events leading up to the Munich revolution, the work self-critically examines the role of a confused German intellectual during the time of political and social crisis. G. took a firm stand against war in *Einer gegen alle* (1932; *The Wolf*, 1934), a novel about a German soldier who cannot adapt to a peacetime society. In another novel, *Bolwieser* (1931; *The Station Master*, 1933), G. showed how a self-indulgent German petit bourgeois becomes the victim of his own weakness.

During his exile G. depicted a number of characters who either directly or indirectly aided Hitler in his usurpation of power. The novel *Anton Sittinger* (1937; Anton Sittinger), for example, centers around a retired postal employee who has always voted for the party that happened to be in power; after the Nazi victory, the protagonist almost finds himself on the wrong side, but he has been saved once more by his shrewd, opportunistic wife, who has secretly enrolled him in Hitler's party. The tragic consequences of an apolitical position are depicted in the novel *Unruhe um einen Friedfertigen* (1947; agitation around a peaceful man). Here the main character is a German Jew who has tried to make himself secure by skillfully concealing his background; but he is brutally killed by the Nazis when his identity is revealed in connection with an unforeseen inheritance.

The personal and the historical aspects of G.'s oeuvre achieved their highest degree of artistic integration in the biographical novel *Das Leben meiner Mutter* (1946; published first in English as *The Life of My Mother*, 1940), in which Germany's history from the time of Bismarck until the beginning of the Hitler tyranny is reflected in the story of a simple Bavarian woman and her (G.'s) family. Another work in which autobiographical elements are depicted against the background of a historical situation is *Die Flucht ins Mittelmäßige: Ein New Yorker Roman* (1959; escape into an average life: a New York novel). The plot centers around refugees from the Third Reich whose exile has become a permanent state after the war.

In Germany G.'s reputation rests perhaps more on his short stories than on his longer prose works. His frequently reprinted collection of Bavarian peasant stories, *Das bayrische Dekameron* (1928; the Bavarian Decameron) abounds in earthy, humorous, and erotic situations reflecting the cultural and linguistic milieu of the author's upbringing. In the *Kalendergeschichten* (1929; calendar tales) G. made a lasting contribution to a specifically German form of the short story that can be traced back to the 19th-c. authors Johann Peter Hebel (1760–1826) and Jeremias Gotthelf (1797–1854). Like his literary ancestors, G. wrote about the day-to-day problems of simple people, but he revealed his more modern position by letting his characters become the victims of an unjust political system and frequently of their own greed and social ignorance.

G.'s active social conscience and his personal integrity of character are the ever-present elements in all of his works. The strongest of his works are those in which he depicted people's lack of social maturity and political justice; he was less successful as a writer when he tried to show how human and social conditions should be improved. With his partly autobiographical, partly fictitious political novels and short stories, he has become a part of the best tradition of European realistic literature.

FURTHER WORKS: *Die Revolutionäre* (1918); *Amen und Anfang* (1919); *Ua-Pua . . . !* (1921); *Maria Uhden* (1921); *Zur freundlichen Erinnerung* (1922); *Georg Schrimpf* (1923); *Bayrisches Lesebücherl* (1924); *Die Traumdeuter* (1924); *Die Chronik von Flechting* (1925); *Die Heimsuchung* (1925); *Fin-* *sternis* (1926); *Licht und Schatten* (1927); *Wunderbare Menschen* (1927); *Im Winkel des Lebens* (1927); *Dorfbanditen* (1932); *Notizbuch des Provinzschriftstellers O. M. G. 1932* (1932); *Der harte Handel* (1935); *Der Abgrund* (1936); *Der Quasterl* (1938); *Der Quasterl, und andere Erzählungen* (1945); *Das Aderlassen* (1947); *Die Eroberung der Welt* (1949); *Mitmenschen* (1950); *Menschen aus meiner Jugend auf dem Dorfe* (1953); *Der ewige Kalender* (1954); *An manchen Tagen: Reden, Gedanken und Zeitbetrachtungen* (1961); *Der große Bauernspiegel* (1962); *Altmodische Gedichte eines Dutzendmenschen* (1962; *Old-Fashioned Poems of an Ordinary Man*, 1967); *Größtenteils schimpflich* (1962); *Er nannte sich Banscho* (1964); *Gelächter von Außen* (1966); *O. M. G.: Beschreibung eines Volksschriftstellers* (1974); *Reise in die Sowjetunion 1934* (1974)

BIBLIOGRAPHY: Genschmer, F., "O. M. G. since World War I," *GQ*, 20 (1947), 57–61; Heydt, A. von der, "O. M. G.," *GQ*, 41 (1968), 401–12; Recknagel, R., *Ein Bayer in Amerika: O. M. G. Leben und Werk* (1974); Pfanner, H. G., *O.M.G.: Eine kritische Bibliographie* (1976); Johnson, S. K., *O. M. G.: The Critical Reception of His Prose Fiction* (1979); Pfanner, H. F., "O. M. G.: Exile in Permanence," in Spalek, J. M., and Bell, R. F., eds., *Exile: The Writer's Experience* (1981)

H. F. PFANNER

GRASS, Günter

West German novelist, dramatist, and poet, b. 16 Oct. 1927, Danzig (now Gdańsk, Poland)

G. came from an ethnically mixed, lower-middle-class background in the (former) Free City of Danzig—an ancestry and environment that finds extensive direct reflection in his writing. His father owned a grocery store. His mother was of Kashubian origin (the Kashubians are a Slavic people indigenous to the rural area around Danzig, quite distinct from the Poles both as to language and culture). G. was five years old when the Nazis seized power in Germany. While a student in the Danzig schools, he was a member of Hitler youth groups. He left school in 1943 to do paramilitary duty. He was drafted into the army in 1944 and was wounded in April 1945. While recovering from his wounds he was captured by the Americans.

Freed in 1946, G. supported himself for the next two or three years by working on farms, in a potash mine, and as a stonemason's apprentice, until he enrolled as a student of painting and sculpture in the Düsseldorf Academy of Art. In 1952 he moved to West Berlin to continue his art studies. In both Düsseldorf and Berlin he also wrote lyric poetry, some of which he read before Group 47, an influential group of writers. He moved temporarily to Paris in 1956, where he wrote his hugely successful first novel, *Die Blechtrommel* (1959; *The Tin Drum*, 1962). At about the same time and shortly afterward he wrote several dramas, which, like his verse, achieved only modest public acclaim. After establishing his fame with the "Danzig Trilogy," of which *Die Blechtrommel* was the first part, G. became active in politics, championing the cause of Willy Brandt and the Social Democrats, and inveighing—as in his writing—against the prominence and influence of former Nazis and against the state of mind in West Germany that preferred the delights of conspicuous consumption to the agonizing acceptance of responsibility for Nazi crimes. In G.'s view, Nazism is to be equated absolutely with the German petite bourgeoisie.

By 1977, after a decade of political activism and world travels, both substantially incorporated into his writing, G. was beginning again to accord a primacy to more purely literary work, although his political tenets and his literary creations remain very closely connected.

Die Blechtrommel, awarded the distinguished Group 47 Prize before it was published, was an instant critical and commercial success. It thrust G. into a worldwide prominence that has scarcely diminished to the present. Like G.'s subsequent works, *Die Blechtrommel* resists facile interpretation, and indeed G. regards interpretation, especially the academic variety, as superfluous. Critics nonetheless have offered quite elaborate explications, worked out, for example, on the basis of myth, or the picaro tradition, or the New Testament. These perspectives, as well as that of psychology, are not without advantage in providing insights into the novel. More recent criticism, however, aided by an increasing G. oeuvre, inclines to regard the novel as primarily historical or even—with certain reservations—as realistic. G. himself calls it a "realistic novel."

The history under consideration, the realism, including generous autobiographical detail reinforced by later personal reconnaissance, is the history and realism of Danzig at the beginning of and during the Nazi terror and that of West Germany during the Adenauer years—the latter of which G. also finds little reason to be sanguine about. Thus, Oskar Matzerath, the owner of the tin drum, a present on his third birthday, wills his own stunted stature, that of a three-year-old, as a protest against the misery of his human existence. The drum and drumming are consonant with, among other things —for example, sex—the military tenor of the Nazi years, and at least to this extent we are to regard Oskar as a petit-bourgeois representative of Nazism. With the capitulation of the Nazis in May 1945, Oskar resumes growing. He develops a hunchback, however, a deformity that may signal Oskar's warning response to the questionable direction of the Adenauer regime, with its rehabilitated Nazis and its turn to the prosperous consumer society. In postwar West Germany, Oskar's feeling of guilt—the guilt of the petit bourgeois about Nazism—is such as to make him an outsider, to a pathological degree. For as we know from the start, he is writing his memoirs, with their sweep of revelation, while in an insane asylum, perhaps not permanently, but confined for observation. His memoirs constitute one level of straightforward, if amazing chronological narration, while his confinement represents a second level of time, equally chronological. The relationship of time levels and of the narrator to the author will become more complex in the later G.

G. wrote the second part of the Danzig Trilogy, the novella *Katz und Maus* (1961; *Cat and Mouse*, 1963), after he made what he later regarded as a false start on the third part, the novel *Hundejahre* (1963; *Dog Years*, 1965). *Katz und Maus* dwells on the experiences and adventures of lower-middle-class youth in Danzig from 1939 to 1944, related by one of their number, Pilenz. More specifically, it is Pilenz's story of Mahlke, whose status as an outsider is emphasized from the beginning by his overdeveloped Adam's apple, that is, "Maus." Mahlke's career parallels the Nazi effort in World War II—launching, successes, and collapse. Like Oskar Matzerath, Mahlke is later afflicted with guilt. His more youthful days were characterized by a fierce devotion to the Virgin Mary and by swimming out to a sunken Polish minesweeper in the bay and making himself at home—quite literally—there. Mahlke's end consists in humiliation at his former school in being refused a forum, even as a wearer of the Iron Cross; and finally, in a trip to the familiar minesweeper, from which, for whatever reason, he does not emerge.

The long novel *Hundejahre* amplifies and focuses more sharply the concerns of G. that found voice in the earlier parts of the Danzig

Trilogy: the Nazi crimes and the postwar prosperity and acceptability of former Nazis. The crimes against the Jews are focused in the love-hate relationship between Walter Matern and the half-Jew, Eduard Amsel, also known as Brauxel (spelled variously). This relationship is one of the two chief subjects. The second is suggested by the title of the novel: it is, in fact, Hitler's own dog, the ancestry of this dog, and the dog's seeking, in May 1945—and finding—his fortune west of the Elbe, that is, in West Germany. The plight of Walter Matern in the West as a former Nazi and present guilty outsider resembles that of Oskar Matzerath. G. names former Nazis and Nazi apologists evidently less encumbered by guilt than the fictional Matern, who in the 1950s are doing quite well in Adenauer's Germany.

The great diversity and idiosyncratic sweep of *Hundejahre* is emphasized structurally by G.'s device of attributing committee authorship to the novel. Early episodes in the 1930s, celebrating the childhood friendship of Amsel and Matern, are narrated by an omniscient author, Brauxel-Amsel; the second part is carried forward by means of love letters from their friend Harry Liebenau to his cousin Tulla Pokriefke (a network of identical characters inhabit the component works of the Danzig Trilogy); the narrative point of view of the postwar episodes is that of Walter Matern. All three fictive writers bring their completed and frequently shocking segments together in 1962, thus replicating the compositional efforts of G. himself.

In the play *Die Plebejer proben den Aufstand* (1966; *The Plebeians Rehearse the Uprising*, 1967) G. turned from the familiar prewar Danzig and postwar West Germany to the Berlin of the 1950s, where he himself was by then living. Bertolt Brecht (q.v.) appears in the play as the Boss—an art-oriented Boss who declines to leave his theatrical preoccupations to support the East Berlin workers' uprising. The uprising is not, however, aimed at revolution, but reform. Berlin is likewise the scene, and reform the theme, of a drama *Davor* (1969; *Max: A Play,* 1972) and an intrinsically related novel, *Örtlich betäubt* (1969; *Local Anaesthetic,* 1969), which G. wrote simultaneously; the play is an expansion of the central portion of the novel. On a historical canvas not unlike that of the Danzig Trilogy, G. has superimposed a new historical picture, that of the disenchanted student radicals of the mid-1960s. Abandoning the grand sweep of the trilogy, G. presents a tightly controlled, highly dialectical argument, with little action. In fact, the dilu-

tionary effect of objectification on potential action is an important theme, which stands in a dialectical relationship to the principal theme: that revolution dialectically induces inaction and failure, and that reform is thus to be preferred. Failure to perceive that this conclusion does not stand in exclusive relation to the above line of reasoning, but relates as well to G.'s passionate denunciation of the complacent consuming, gadget-worshiping society, may account for the otherwise curious fact that *Örtlich betäubt* achieved greater success in the U. S. than any of G.'s other works.

In *Aus dem Tagebuch einer Schnecke* (1972; *From the Diary of a Snail,* 1973) G. for the first time revealed himself completely in his writing. He did so by using the device of a fictive colloquy with his children, a "diary" of his travels and involvement—and commitment —as a campaigner for the Social Democrats and Willy Brandt in the 1969 election. Interwoven with this account of G., the campaigning reformer, is a story by G., the writer, based on the history of the Danzig Jews in the Nazi era, vignettes from the life of one Hermann Ott, also called Doubt. Doubt collects snails and as a non-Jewish friend and supporter of Jews takes refuge from the Nazis with a Kashubian who wants to become a German. The snail metaphor, developed with astounding virtuosity, pervades, and is central to, the fictional history. It represents G.'s political philosophy and his notion of the only possible way toward progress: "being a little quicker than the snail. . . ." The slow, unaggressive snail is the symbol of peaceful evolution working out its path between the violent and aggressive extremes of Communism and Fascism. The recommended attitude of skepticism and the character, Doubt, —into whose role G. sometimes steps—even challenge G.'s self-acknowledged lapses into political partisanship, the latter fueled by his contemplation of ex-Nazis in high places to the accompaniment of public insouciance. In this novel G. the father, the fiction writer, and the political reformer successfully inform a single written work.

The lengthy novel *Der Butt* (1977; *The Flounder,* 1978) marked the return of G. to primarily literary endeavor after a decade in which politics and literature were symbiotic. As to authorial approach, however, *Der Butt* has much in common with *Aus dem Tagebuch einer Schnecke.* The narrator and the author are to a great extent identical. And that narrating author illustrates—to adults as well as children—what he has on his mind that he wants to communicate. Such illustration in *Der Butt* is, however, complex and elaborate.

G. elevates to thematic significance his long interest in cooking, research into which brings him up against—or to awareness of—the historical role of cooks, who turn out to be women cooks. A series of nine such cooks, each representing one month of the term of pregnancy, from in and around Danzig, and from different eras, and the men with whom history associates them, illustrates the sexual role conflicts besetting the narrator and his consort through the ages, Ilsebill. Another arena of conflict based on sex role is composed of the tribunal of—taken as a group, less than admirable—feminists in Berlin who are sitting in judgment on the talking flounder caught by three of their number. The flounder, here confined to a tank as a prisoner, is based on the flounder in the Grimms' fairy tale "The Fisherman and His Wife," in which a fisherman is granted favors for his wife by a talking flounder, who is actually an enchanted prince. G. develops the flounder as the initiator of, and eloquent spokesman for, the male-dominated society that millennia ago succeeded the society in which women were dominant. G.'s flounder, in accord with G.'s political principle of reform (or at least, change), is however, far from rigid and ultimately declares himself ready to champion the feminists' cause.

The novel has three endings, coinciding with possible live birth at seven or eight months, as well as at nine months. The first two endings, with man resigned, or with woman replicating the errors of man, are followed by an open ending, a birth. Not necessarily a happy ending—there are disquieting signs—but an ending with dialectical possibilities: there may be a third way. G. still seems concerned about reform, but his area of concern has transcended politics.

In 1961 G., who had made his literary debut some years earlier as a poet, explained that his poetry and plays, as well as his fiction, were built on dialogue. No doubt his concept of the underlying role of dialogue facilitated his transition to plays and fiction, in both of which genres is to be found the elaboration of originally poetic pictures and metaphors. G.'s verse is itself occasional—as he insisted—object-oriented metaphors, the objects often being removed from their conventional context and aligned with other objects so as to produce unconventional and striking relationships. G.'s later verse approaches surrealism (q.v.). He has no use for the poetry of abstraction and individual lament, nor for that of didacticism. As with his politics

and his novels and plays, G. eschews the antagonism of the extremes.

G. declared that his "master" was Alfred Döblin (q.v.), but it is more appropriate to give credit to G.'s own literary originality, power, and versatility. It may be that Döblin foreshadowed some of the devices G. used in *Die Blechtrommel*, but it is difficult to speak of any continuing literary influence. More to the point, in the longer run, is Döblin's preceptoral role as a writer-politician. Certainly G. has pursued both those careers vigorously; despite objections by purists, his literary work is not lessened thereby. G. is something of a latter-day Renaissance man: novelist, poet, dramatist, sculptor, politician, illustrator, book designer. G.'s politics have exposed him to a special intensity and variety of criticism, both of his art and of the politics (and social credos) that he does not hesitate to couch in his art. Preferring moderate reform, he offers an easy target to the extremes. From both the artistic and political point of view, he not only faced down old Nazis when that was perhaps not so difficult to do, but faced up to the excesses of the new left when for an artist that was a rather lonely office. In any case, G. has been an author of world rank for two decades; his powers are quite undiminished and, indeed, seem to be still developing.

FURTHER WORKS: *Die Vorzüge der Windhühner* (1956); *Beritten hin und zurück* (1958; *Rocking Back and Forth*, 1967); *Noch zehn Minuten bis Buffalo* (1958; *Only Ten Minutes to Buffalo*, 1967); *Hochwasser* (1960; *Flood*, 1967); *Gleisdreieck* (1960); *Die bösen Köche* (1961; *The Wicked Cooks*, 1964); *Die Ballerina* (1963); *POUM; oder, Die Vergangenheit fliegt mit* (1965); *Onkel, Onkel* (1965; *Mister, Mister*, 1967); *Ausgefragt* (1967; *New Poems*, 1968); *Über das Selbstverständliche: Reden, Aufsätze, Offene Briefe, Kommentare* (1968; *Speak Out!: Speeches, Open Letters, Commentaries*, 1969); *Briefe über die Grenze* (1968, with Pavel Kohout); *Tschechoslowakei 1968* (1968); *Über meinen Lehrer Döblin, und andere Vorträge* (1968); *Gesammelte Gedichte* (1971); *G. G.: Dokumente zur politischen Wirkung* (1971); *Mariazuehren* (1973; *Inmarypraise*, 1974); *Liebe geprüft* (1974); *Der Bürger und seine Stimme: Reden, Aufsätze, Kommentare* (1974); *Denkzettel: Politische Reden und Aufsätze 1965–1976* (1978); *Das Treffen in Telgte* (1979; *The Meeting at Telgte*, 1981); *"Die Blechtrommel" als Film* (1979, with

Volker Schlöndorff); *Kopfgeburten; oder, Die Deutschen sterben aus* (1980); *Aufsätze zur Literatur* (1981). FURTHER VOLUMES IN ENGLISH: *Selected Poems* (1966); *Four Plays* (1967); *Poems of G. G.* (1969); *In the Egg, and Other Poems* (1977)

BIBLIOGRAPHY: Cunliffe, W. G., *G. G.* (1969); Tank, K. L., *G. G.* (1969); Willson, A. L., ed., *A G. G. Symposium* (1971); Woods, J. M., "G. G.: A Selected Bibliography," *WCR*, 5, 3 (1971), 52–56, and 6, 1 (1971), 31–40; Diller, E., *A Mythic Journey: G. G.'s "Tin Drum"* (1974); Everett, G. A., Jr., *A Select Bibliography of G. G. (From 1956 to 1973)* (1974); Leonard, I., *G. G.* (1974); Mason, A. L., *The Skeptical Muse: A Study of G. G.'s Conception of the Artist* (1974); Miles, K., *G. G.* (1975); Reddick, J., *The "Danzig Trilogy" of G. G.* (1975); O'Neill, P., *G. G.: A Bibliography, 1955–1975* (1976); Rothenberg, J., *G. G.: Zeitgeschichte im Prosawerk* (1976); Rölleke, H., *Der wahre Butt* (1978); Brode, H., *G. G.* (1979); Neuhaus, V., *G. G.* (1979)

RICHARD H. LAWSON

Every myth takes place within a given culture, at some point in history, but then, as in a literary work such as *The Tin Drum*, myth is posited as an attempt to transcend history by shifting focus from measurable time and specific events to paradigmatic ritualized forms of a timeless order. It is precisely here, in the conjunction and pressure of mythogenesis colliding with secular reality, that the author of *The Tin Drum* most fully exercises his genius. The historical context of *The Tin Drum* is of course obvious and should not be ignored, for that is *the* significant moment of time which is to be transcended by sacred repetition and purpose. But our concern here is with the embracing sweep of the novel, the attempt to reconceive and experience myth as divine history and witness its triumphs and failures in relationship to profane history, to the "powerhouse of change."

Edward Diller, *A Mythic Journey: G. G.'s "Tin Drum"* (1974), pp. 3–4

[G.] has worked to become a major novelist in the German tradition; he has come to grips with both German literary tradition and German history, having seen how changed historical circumstance has profoundly disrupted, but not wholly destroyed that tradition. Out of this awareness, he has realized in his early novels a wealth of comic fantasy that is quite distinctive for German literature; he has created narrators who are acutely conscious of their art of storytelling and who use all the tricks of that art with remarkable energy and inventiveness. Recently, he has worked towards an art which more sharply criticizes itself; correspondingly, his artist-heroes and narrators have been more conspicuously portrayed as failures, juxtaposed with a social reality they have difficulty understanding or accepting.

Ann L. Mason, *The Skeptical Muse: A Study of G. G.'s Conception of the Artist* (1974), p. 128

Dialectical thinking constitutes the most striking structural element in G.'s compositions. In *The Tin Drum* it extends to the individual images as well as to their overall pattern. The drum has its dialectical opposite in the Black Witch. Oskar's drumming is an attempt to synthesise the two extremes of morality and amorality, of construction and destruction. This general duality also governs the details of the novel, down to its smallest episodes. The drum itself is made up of contradictions, for it can be put to good and bad purpose, radiate love as well as hatred, even if its primary function is positive. The negative aspect of Oskar's gifts, the purely destructive impulses, are symbolised by his glass-shattering voice. Such polarity between light and dark is followed through in juxtaposing Goethe and Rasputin, Apollo and Dionysus, Jesus and Satan, and is further evoked in the colour symbolism of white and black.

Irène Leonard, *G. G.* (1974), p. 84

In his novel *From the Diary of a Snail* G. describes how Hermann Ott, confined to a cellar for the duration of the war, entertains his hosts by solo performances of classic dramas of the German theatre. To differentiate between characters, he employs a series of old hats, making discarded headgear the basis of his art. G.'s poetry anticipates Ott's cellar presentations. Like Ott the snail-collector, G. the poet wears a variety of hats; he takes on the roles of lyric poet, educationist, jester, moralist, realist, surrealist, traditionalist, experimentalist. His poems can evoke the lightheartedness and delicacy of a Paul Klee or the nightmarishness and abrasiveness of a Georg Heym. They can be playful celebrations of innocence or grim reflections of experience. They can reproduce the exterior world or exist in a realm of their own. Where G.'s art is more subtle than that of Ott is in his ability to wear all the hats at the same time, to fuse the disparate personalities into one. The artist does not vanish when the political activist speaks: the jester does not disappear in the presence of the moralist. It is the characteristic feature of G.'s poetry that it finds a way to make each cap, separately and simultaneously, fit.

Keith Miles, *G. G.* (1975), pp. 25–26

In G. G.'s work the lyric forms a universal constant. Not only is the lyric—together with sculpture and graphics—G.'s earliest form of artistic expression, but right up to the many poems in *The Flounder* he has never given it up. His lyrical oeuvre is correspondingly extensive. At the same time, the lyric is the genre with which he has the most intimate connection. It is the germ cell of his dramatic and narrative works.

Volker Neuhaus, *G. G.* (1979), p. 158

Central to the novel [*The Flounder*] is the question of the disturbed role-relationships between the sexes. To that extent the book is historically and directly allied to the questions—much discussed in the western world in the mid-seventies—of female emancipation and the related shock to male self-perception. Ilsebill and the narrator are profoundly disturbed at their insight that the traditional rules of conduct are now obsolete; the well-indoctrinated role-stereotypes no longer function. The male illusion of superiority is at the brink of collapse—and on a global scale, because the planning rationale as well as the exploitive appropriation of the world are leading to political and ecological catastrophe. For her part, woman on the way to emancipation has not yet progressed beyond shaking the foundations of her previous understanding of herself and her role. On both sides, there are no new, substantial positions in sight.

Hanspeter Brode, *G. G.* (1979), p. 180

GRAVES, Robert

English poet, novelist, critic, essayist, biographer, translator, and mythographer, b. 26 July 1895, London

G.'s father, Alfred Percival Graves, was a Gaelic scholar and an inspector of schools; his mother, Amalie von Ranke Graves, was related to the German historian Leopold von Ranke (1795–1886). G.'s education, therefore, began early in his parents' excellent library. His formal education included attendance at Charterhouse and at Oxford University. As an officer in the Royal Welsh Fusiliers, G. was seriously wounded in France during World War I. He taught one year at the University of Cairo, and lectured at Oxford and elsewhere in Europe and in the U.S. With the American poet Laura Riding (b. 1901) he established the Seizin Press (1928) and published the critical magazine *Epilogue* (1929). He has been married twice, has eight children, and has lived most of his life since 1929 in Majorca, except when lec-

turing or when political upheavals required evacuation of British citizens.

G. considers himself primarily a poet. His earliest adolescent poems were heavily freighted with 19th-c. romantic diction and gothic subject matter. He quickly became his own best critic, however, and continually refined his craftsmanship. His early poems were first published during World War I in *Over the Brazier* (1916), *Goliath and David* (1916), and *Fairies and Fusiliers* (1917).

The horrors of trench warfare had a profound effect upon his poetry for the next ten years. He, like other poets in this situation, such as his friend Siegfried Sassoon (q.v.) suffered from serious neuroses connected with their war experience. Dr. W. H. R. Rivers, a Freudian psychologist and a specialist in war neurasthenia, influenced G.'s theory of poetry during this period. G. agreed with Rivers that poems deal symbolically with emotional conflicts and can help to achieve a resolution of such conflicts, both for the writer and for the reader who has similar difficulties. G. later discarded the idea of poetry as therapy, but during the period immediately following the war his poetry was often haunted by images of guilt and fear. He seldom wrote about war experience itself, but often translated his emotional turmoil into more traditional gothic imagery. Some of the most representative poetry of this kind is in *The Pier-Glass* (1921). The title poem, for instance, uses a haunted-house ambience; "The Castle" re-creates the sensations of nightmare and entrapment in a medieval setting. One of the best poems of this period, "Down," also in this collection, achieves a striking combination of associations—the mythical geography of the underworld, the childhood experience of dropping a stone down an abandoned well, the subconscious mind, madness, and death.

After 1929, when he published his autobiography, *Goodbye to All That,* one of the best descriptions of trench warfare to come out of World War I, G. turned his back upon his past in more ways than one. His poetry gradually became more objective, more devoted to exploring philosophical ideas, the complexities of love, and the ambiguous qualities of language itself, as a means of both striving for truth and disguising reality. "The Cool Web" (1927), for instance, suggests that language is a way of mitigating the intensity of raw experience.

G.'s later poetry, stemming from his brilliant, though idiosyncratic, combination of literary and mythological research in *The White Goddess* (1945), deals mainly with the experience of love, expressed within the mythological framework he discovered both in archaic poetry and in ancient fertility religions. He became the oracle of the Goddess, who is both the artist's Muse and the Triple Goddess of moon, earth, and underworld who controls birth, love, and death. G. experienced a burst of poetic power that resulted in some of the best love lyrics written in this century. Including periodic collections of those poems he wished to preserve, G. has published forty-seven volumes of poetry. About two thirds of these followed the publication of *The White Goddess* and are, in some measure, influenced by the Goddess mythology.

G.'s interest in ancient myth was not confined to poetry, but led to the writing of several prose works displaying an impressive knowledge of ancient lore combined with an imaginative flair for comparative and causal analysis. His mode of explaining origins of myth in his two-volume study, *The Greek Myths* (1955), is quite eclectic. He admits sources, for instance, in both religious ritual and historical event (two views of myth origin that are sometimes thought to be mutually exclusive). He consistently avoids psychological explanations of either the Freudian or Jungian schools. In general terms, he attributes the famous myths of the Olympian gods to the process of changing from the worship of goddesses (variations of the Triple Goddess noted above) to the cult of masculine deities introduced by invading patriarchal tribesmen from the north. Thus, the notorious rapes and seductions attributed to the Achaean sky god Zeus establish his superiority over the resident female dieties of Greece. And the all-powerful goddesses became wives, mistresses, or daughters to Father Zeus.

Critics often find fault with G.'s methodology in these books. G. was influenced by a number of 19th- and early-20th-c. anthropologists, such as Sir James Frazer (1854–1941), Robert Briffault (1876–1948), J. J. Bachofen (1815–1887), Jane Harrison (1850–1928), and Margaret Murray (1863–1963). G.'s theory that not only religion, but society itself, was originally matriarchal in structure seemed the revival of supposedly outmoded theories explored in 1861 in Bachofen's *Mother Right*. Yet the primacy of matriarchy or, at least, the early dominance of the female principle in religion, has received renewed attention since G. proposed it. Part of this response may be attributable to the recent rise of feminist critics,

some to post-Jungian psychologists like Erich Neumann (1905–1960), author of *The Great Mother* (1955), some to new archeological evidence, such as that put forth in *The Cult of the Mother Goddess* (1959) by E. O. James (1888–1972). Academic scholars hesitate to acknowledge indebtedness to G. because of his tendency to fill in the gaps of historical fact with generous dollops of intuition. Yet his widespread impact on general interest in mythology and matriarchal values seems undeniable.

G. collaborated with Joshua Podro (dates n.a.) on *The Nazarene Gospel Restored* (1953) and with the Jewish scholar Raphael Patai (b. 1910) to produce *The Hebrew Myths: The Book of Genesis* (1964). The former brought shocked responses from some biblical scholars, but one prominent theologian, Reinhold Niebuhr (1892–1971), praised the volume as a "work of careful scholarship."

G. is probably best known to the general public for his novels based on history or myth. He received both the Hawthornden Prize and the James Tait Black Memorial Prize for *I, Claudius* and *Claudius the God* (both 1934). These studies in the dynamics of power in ancient Rome enjoyed a resurgence of public interest in the 1970s through an engrossing television series based on them, produced by the BBC. His subjects for historical novels are extremely varied: the career of a Byzantine general (*Count Belisarius*, 1938), the American Revolution from the point of view of a British soldier (*Sergeant Lamb of the Ninth*, 1940), John Milton as a bigoted and tyrannical husband (*The Story of Marie Powell, Wife to Mr. Milton*, 1943), a 16th-c. expedition to colonize the Solomon Islands (*The Islands of Unwisdom*, 1949). G. also wrote novels based on myth, such as *The Golden Fleece* (1944) and *Homer's Daughter* (1955). His most striking and original vehicles for myth are *King Jesus* (1946) and an entertaining futuristic fantasy, *Seven Days in New Crete* (1949). *King Jesus* fuses the Goddess mythology with Hebrew legend to create a new myth about Jesus. G.'s novels will not stand among the world's great literature, but his best, such as *I, Claudius*, *King Jesus*, and perhaps *Count Belisarius*, will surely retain their fascination for a long time to come.

G.'s reputation will probably come to rest most surely on his poetry, some of which is among the best written in the 20th c. He has always disdained fashionable literary movements and demonstrated again and again how every true poem is original not imitative, each poem determining its own diction, rhythm, and form. The impact of his voluminous prose, both fiction and nonfiction, is considerable, not just for itself alone, but for the example of an erudite, rebellious, original thinker who has revitalized our appreciation of the past.

SELECTED FURTHER WORKS: *Country Sentiment* (1922); *On English Poetry* (1922); *Whipperginny* (1922); *The Meaning of Dreams* (1924); *Poetic Unreason, and Other Studies* (1925); *Poems 1914–1926* (1926); *Poems 1914–1927* (1927); *A Survey of Modernist Poetry* (1927, with Laura Riding); *The English Ballad: A Short Critical Survey* (1927); *Lawrence and the Arabs* (1927); *Mrs. Fisher; or, The Future of Humour* (1928); *Poems 1926–1930* (1931); *But It Still Goes On* (1931); *Poems 1930–1933* (1933); *The Real David Copperfield* (1933); *Antigua, Penny Puce* (1936); *Collected Poems* (1938); *No More Ghosts* (1940); *The Long Week-end: A Social History of Britain 1918–1939* (1940, with Alan Hodge); *Proceed, Sergeant Lamb* (1941); *The Reader Over Your Shoulder* (1943, with A. Hodge); *Poems 1938–1945* (1945); *Collected Poems 1914–1947* (1948); *The Common Asphodel* (1949); *Occupation: Writer* (1950); *Poems and Satires* (1951); *Poems* (1953); *Adam's Rib* (1955); *Collected Poems* (1955); *¡Catacrok!* (1956); *English and Scottish Ballads* (1957); *Jesus in Rome: A Conjecture* (1957, with Joshua Podro); *They Hanged My Saintly Billy* (1957); *5 Pens in Hand* (1958); *Steps* (1958); *Collected Poems* (1959); *Food for Centaurs* (1960); *Collected Poems* (1961); *More Poems* (1961); *Selected Poetry and Prose* (1961); *New Poems* (1962); *The Big Green Book* (1962); *The Siege and Fall of Troy* (1962); *Nine Hundred Iron Chariots* (1963); *Man Does, Woman Is* (1964); *Mammon* (1964); *Collected Short Stories* (1964); *Majorca Observed* (1965); *Mammon and the Black Goddess* (1965); *Love Respelt* (1965); *Collected Poems* (1965); *The Crane Bag* (1969); *The Green-sailed Vessel* (1971); *Poems 1968–1970* (1970); *Difficult Questions Easy Answers* (1973); *New Collected Poems* (1977)

BIBLIOGRAPHY: Seymour-Smith, M., *R. G.* (1956); Cohen, J. M., *R. G.* (1960); Day, Douglas, *Swifter than Reason* (1963); Higginson, F. H., *A Bibliography of the Works of R. G.* (1946); Hoffman, D., *Barbarous Knowledge: Myth in the Poetry of Yeats, G., and Muir* (1967), pp. 129–222; Stade, G., *R. G.* (1967); Kirkham, M., *The Poetry of R. G.* (1969); Mason, E., *Focus on R. G.,* No. 1 (Jan. 1972); Vickery, J. B., *R. G. and "The White Goddess"* (1972); Fussell, P., *The Great War and Modern Memory* (1975), passim; Matthews, T. S., *Jacks or Better* (1977), passim; Snipes, K., *R. G.* (1979)

KATHERINE SNIPES

GREEK LITERATURE

Greek literature has the longest and the most persistent tradition in the Western world, one that sweeps over three millennia and embraces every form of literature known to man, many of these forms having been invented by the ancient Greeks themselves. There is a continuity in the history of Greek literature, as there are elements of discontinuity, but the modern author is aware of a weighty tradition, which he may accept or reject, but he more often than not reacts to his Greek tradition in some way, using it to compose his own work in a way that will be meaningful to him and his times. The Greek tradition is, of course, not limited to the classical but includes the Byzantine (one must remember that the Byzantine Empire, which was culturally Greek, lasted for eleven hundred years and was a world-state) and the period of the Turkish domination (1453–1821), and shows definite Western influence from various European sources and the Greek War of Independence.

In connection with the development of modern Greek literature it must be pointed out that with the birth of the modern Greek nation there arose in sharply defined terms the question of the use of language. It was only natural that with political freedom there would be some effort to return to the classical heritage, and the easiest way to do this practically (or so it seemed) was to return to the classical language (albeit with some modifications). The modern classical language, or *katharevousa*, was an important factor in the development of modern Greek literature. It came into direct conflict with the popular language, or *dhimotiki* (demotic), which owed much to the Greek folk song and which contained a good number of foreign elements. Opponents of *dhimotiki* pointed out that this "vulgar" language was not fit to express Greek literature. The "language problem" plagued Greek writers and readers for some time, even resulting in riots when the

New Testament appeared in the demotic language in 1901. Two years later other riots broke out because the *Oresteia* of Aeschylus was translated into the vernacular and so presented. But in the recent past there has not been the violent quarreling over what language the literature of modern Greece should employ. The demotic has won the day because it has developed naturally and has shown beyond any reasonable doubt that it can express great ideas, great thoughts, and even the Greek tradition.

Poetry

Two literary schools should be noted before proceeding to 20th-c. writers. The Old School of Athens (flourished 1821–49), whose head and founder was Alexandros Soutsos (1803–1863), generally employed *katharevousa* and was characterized by an excessive romanticism. The greatest representative of the second half of this period was Achilles Paraschos (1838–1895), whose themes were patriotism, love, and death.

The greatest figure of the Ionian School (flourished 1850–1880) is a man who was basically bilingual (Italian and Greek) and who became the national poet of modern Greece, Dionysios Solomos (1798–1857). Solomos is significant for many reasons in the history of modern Greek literature, but it cannot be overlooked that his choice of the *dhimotiki* as his linguistic vehicle of expression was a major breakthrough whose impact would be felt for generations to come and would make really creative poetry possible. Solomos combined the classical and romantic spirit and demonstrated that he was no mere verse technician but a poet who had succeeded in bringing Greek literature into the mainstream of European literature.

In 1880 the New Poetic School of Athens was founded. Often called the Greek Parnassians, these men reacted against romanticism and were encouraged by *To taxidhi* (1888; the voyage) of Ioannis Psykharis (1854–1929), which, although ostensibly a travel book, actually promoted the cause for *dhimotiki,* as did the work of the great folklorist Nikolaos Politis (1852–1921), who gathered together the folk songs of the Greek people in a monumental enterprise that was to have repercussions far beyond his own field of research. The New School of Athens, among whose members were Kostis Palamas (q.v.), Yorghos Dhrossinis (1859–1949), Ioannis Polemis (1862–1925), Nikolaos Kambas (1857–1932), and Yorghos

Straitigis (1860–1938), gave ample evidence that the tide was turning in favor of demotic.

Yorghos Dhrossinis devoted his entire life to poetry. His verse is distinguished by great dignity but is at times too detailed and superficial. His poems are really poetical sketches with a simple idea made into a poem marked by fineness and delicacy. Ioannis Polemis cultivated a rather facile poetry. Sometimes, however, he produced poems of tender simplicity. Writing in *katharevousa* and demotic, Nilolaos Kambas did not express violent passions but rather emotions conerned with the small pains and joys of everyday life. Unpretentious, his poetry is said to have murmured with a soft smile. Yorghos Straitigis wrote in *katharevousa* and demotic. His later collections seem pallid and weak in inspiration and form.

The most important figure of this new school was Kostis Palamas, who was twice nominated for a Nobel Prize. He was knowledgeable in mythology, history, poetry, and philosophy, and aware of the social and spiritual problems of his own and previous generations, and in his poetry revealed both European and Eastern influences. His most famous and most important work is probably also his most obscure, the epic-lyric poem *O dhodhekaloghos tou ghiftou* (1907; *The Twelve Words of the Gypsy,* 1964), in which the gypsy musician, initially presented as a symbol of freedom and art, slowly becomes the Greek patriot, and finally becomes the cosmopolitan Hellene, the citizen of the world. *I floghera toy vasilya* (1910; *The King's Flute,* 1967) is a historical epic in Byzantine dress that celebrates the continuity of Hellenism from the medieval Christian and ancient pagan traditions. His collection *I asalefti zoi* (1904; *Life Immutable,* 1919) shows French influences.

The importance for modern Greek literature of Palamas must not be underestimated. He exerted his influence not only on his contemporaries but on practically all of Greek poetry that has followed. Ioannis Ghryparis (1872–1942), Konstandinos Hatzopoulos (1871–1920), Miltiadis Malakasis (1869–1943), Lambros Porfyras (1879–1932), Zakharias Papandoniou (1877–1938), and Kostas Karyotakis (q.v.) all show that Palamas was important in their development and expression, for it was with this group that German and French symbolism (q.v.) made its impact felt; even free verse was introduced into modern Greek literature.

Ghryparis knew the language of the people well, and he was able to make good use of popular medieval literature, while absorbing the influence of French Parnassianism. Later he turned to the symbolists, and his verse became freer and more musical, his images more suggestive. Influenced by German literature and life, Hatzopoulos attached himself to the German social movement, which he attempted to propagate in Greece by connecting social ideology with the innovative trends of demoticism. Following the teaching of the symbolists, he produced a musically charming verse that is a vague, elegiac reverie lacking concrete detail. The verse of Malakasis has great robustness but lacks lyric depth. Porfyras, a few of whose poems are symbolist, possesses a delicacy of feeling and tender sympathetic melancholy, although his powers of expression are not as great as those of Hatzopoulos. A learned man, Papandoniou was first of all a stylist, prolific in poetical production but careless in thought and expression; he wrote essays, biographies, travel literature, and criticism. Still, he has a sympathetic comprehension of life and nature. Often called the most representative writer of his generation, Karyotakis wrote serious poetry expressing an intense desire for a fulfilled life and a total consciousness of reality. His verse also shows a pervading feeling of futility and loss, which became starker and starker and led to his suicide.

Although the 20th c. is marked by the triumph of the *dhimotiki* in poetry, one of the greatest Greek and also European poets of the early 20th c., an inhabitant not of Greece but of Alexandria, Egypt, did not employ the demotic tongue but rather a modified form of *katharevousa*. C. P. Cavafy (q.v.), looked back at the decadent Hellenistic world in which he found the landscape, so to speak, through which he could express himself and depict the decadent individual behind many masks, the human condition as it appeared to him. In no other Greek poet are the tragic aspects of life so sensually expressed or sensuality so tragically depicted. Out of touch with the mainstream of Greek literature, Cavafy ironically recorded high and low life in ancient or modern Alexandria and in the medieval world of the Byzantine Empire.

Another major poet was the flamboyant Angelos Sikelianos (q.v.) who together with his American wife reintroduced the Delphic idea by establishing the Delphic Festivals of 1927–30. Described by some as a poet of pantheism; clearly marked by Dionysiac mysticism; philosophic in his approach to nature, tradition, and history; beautiful, rich, incisive, and lucid in his use of language and vocabulary —Sikelianos created some of the finest poetry ever composed in Greek. Two aspects have been observed in the poetry of Sikelianos: the lyrical positing of the natural world with the human body as a part of it, and the knowledge that the natural world is replete with tragedy and suffering, with the essence of man's real life to be found elsewhere.

The modern Greek author who is perhaps better known throughout the Western world than any other is Nikos Kazantzakis (q.v.). His *Odyssia* (1938; *The Odyssey: A Modern Sequel*, 1958) had tremendous impact on other literatures through its many translations. With the English translation of this poem in 1958 by Kimon Friar the literary world was made aware of Kazantzakis's bold attempt to restore epic poetry as a legitimate and meaningful form in modern literature. The poem is drenched in sex, violence—and philosophy. The poetry ranges from the nauseatingly vulgar to the ethereally sublime. It is a search for an answer to the eternal question of "Who am I and what am I doing here?" in which Kazantzakis attempts to find order in a world infested with so much disorder and violence.

A contemporary of Kazantzakis, the poet Kostas Varnalis (q.v.), wrote originally in *katharevousa* but after returning from Paris dedicated himself to writing only in demotic. The author of the first completely leftist poem in Greek literature, he became Greece's greatest socialist poet. He praises the "kingdom of work," hates war, and protests against slavery and fascism. Initially influenced by the Parnassians and symbolists, his later poetry is marked by a strong Dionysiac flavor and a deep sense of music. Playful and humorous, he can also be satirical and even savage.

Greece's first Nobel Prize winner was George Seferis (q.v.), considered by many Greece's leading modern poet. The actual number of his poems is small, but they are extremely significant. When the Swedish Academy awarded him the 1963 Nobel Prize for literature, it acknowledged one whose lyric poetry combined the best in the Greek and Western traditions. It transcends the particular, the ephemeral, and attains the universal, the permanent. Seferis is acutely aware of the triumphs and tragedies of both ancient and modern Greece, and of his own roots in Asia Minor. The musicality of Seferis's poetry, and his deep insight into the human predicament have given modern Greek poetry and literature the international recognition that it has long deserved.

The award of the Nobel Prize to Odysseus Elytis (q.v.) in 1979 marked the second time in sixteen years that a Greek poet received this honor. The Swedish Academy praised his "poetry, which, against the background of Greek tradition, depicts with sensuous strength and intellectual clearsightedness modern man's struggle for freedom and creativeness," and also noted that "sensuality and light irradiate Elytis's poetry. The perceptible world is vividly present and overwhelming in its wealth of freshness and astonishing experiences." Elytis himself regards "poetry as the only thing that can preserve man's spiritual integrity."

In *To Axion Esti* (1959; *The Axion Esti,* 1974) Elytis attempts to set a new moral order in a complex tapestry of prose, liturgical forms, odes, and his pattern of rhyme and strict syllabic stress. Elytis, the poet of the sun, sea, earth, youth, and the beauty of nature, believes that it is the poet's duty to cast drops of light into darkness. This he has done and continues to do.

Yannis Ritsos (q.v.), the author of seventy-seven volumes of poetry, as well as plays, essays, and translations, has been translated into forty-four languages. He is probably Greece's major poet of the left. A sense of dislocation, inertia, and silence pervade much of Ritsos's landscape. Tyranny, oppression, torture, and degradation are reflected in the nightmarish imagery and absurdities of his poetry. Pain is everywhere; humanity is debased. Ritsos intensely feels the tragedy of mankind. A poet of the Greek people, he is also a poet of all.

Nikiforos Vrettakos (b. 1911), another prolific poet, hates injustice and believes that art must be the expression of love and goodness. Christian and democratic, he tends to moralize at times. Nikos Gatsos (b. 1915), the author of only a single long poem, *Amorghos* (1943; *Amorgos*, 1961), exerted great influence on the writers of his generation. In his poetry surrealism (q.v.), the Bible, and the tradition of Greek folk songs are combined in an elegiac way. The poet Takis Sinopoulos (b. 1917), trained as a physician, was also a painter, translator, and critic. His poetry reinterprets ancient Greek themes and evokes, perhaps more than any other contemporary author, the horrors of life during the 1940s—both the Nazi occupation and the civil war. For Sinopoulos, the world is a ravaged land of black trees, inhabited by the wandering dead, where the sunlight is blinding, destructive, and merciless.

Fiction

Much of contemporary Greek fiction has been concerned with the relation of the individual to society. It critically and often satirically questions the very basis of that society. The Asia Minor disaster, World War II and the Nazi occupation, and the civil war after World War II had a strong impact on writers. Man's inhumanity to man—be it of the Turks, the Nazis, or the Greeks themselves, of either the right or left—frequently occurs in the fiction of modern Greece.

Gregorios Xenopoulos (q.v.) was the most distinguished Greek novelist of the early modern generation. His realistic novels, set in his own time, skillfully blend a fine narrative technique with sharpness of observation. Alexandros Papadiamantis (q.v.), also of the older generation, is still considered Greece's best short-story writer. Papadiamantis vividly portrayed the life, and problems, of the simple people of his native island of Skiathos before the turn of the century and that of the lower-class Athenians. He had a profound Christian faith, a love of nature, and a sympathy for the downtrodden. He created many memorable characters and sought to penetrate the cosmic mystery that encases the tragic human condition.

The novels of Nikos Kazantzakis have excited a great deal of attention in literary circles. *O telefteos pirasmos* (1955; *The Last Temptation of Christ*, 1960) is a novel of great intensity and power; it was condemned by the Greek Orthodox Church. It re-creates the figure of Christ as a man. For Kazantzakis, Christ is the prototype of the free man who by force of will transmutes matter into spirit. His Christ is a personal experience that has no connection with any ecclesiastical tradition.

In *O Kapetan Mihalis* (1953; *Freedom or Death*, 1956) Kazantzakis concentrates on the background and character of the Cretan rebellion of 1889, which was directed against the Turkish overlords—a rebellion that ended unsuccessfully for the Greeks. But more than this, Kazantzakis gives a detailed characterization of the people who make up the various racial and religious elements of the population living in and about the city of Megalokastro (where half the action of the novel takes place)—a picture of both oppressors and oppressed, of Turks, Greeks, Armenians, and Jews.

The title character of *Vios kai politia toy Alexi Zorba* (1946; *Zorba the Greek,* 1953) has been described as a kind of subconscious or alter Kazantzakis. Zorba is undoubtedly a primitive, sensual man, but the important thing to note is that he does not survive in the novel. Only the artist, the analytical Kazantzakis, survives.

O Hristos xanastavronete (1954; *The Greek Passion*, 1953) is a magnificent and powerful novel. Through the Christian Passion story, Kazantzakis examines good and evil in the world; through vividly depicted characters he presents the reader with a concretization of the philosophical and theological problems of good and evil.

Stratis Myrivilis (q.v.), author of *I panaghia i ghorghona* (1949; *The Mermaid Madonna*, 1959), is one of the most highly respected literary figures. His powerful war novel *I zoi en tafo* (1914; rev. ed., 1930; *Life in the Tomb*, 1977), written in the form of a journal of a sergeant in the trenches, is probably the most widely read work of fiction in Greece.

Fotis Kontoglou (1897–1965), better known as an icon painter, made a stirring debut as a writer with *Pedro Cazas* (1913; Pedro Cazas), the story of a Spanish corsair drawn from popular sources and written with unusual force and a tense, vibrant language.

Pandelis G. Prevelakis (q.v.), one of the leading contemporary novelists, also ranks high as an art critic. In the tradition of his fellow Cretan Kazantzakis, Prevelakis uses the Cretan theme in novels such as *To hroniko mias politias* (1938; *The Tale of a Town*, 1976).

Significant attention has recently been given to the novels of Anghelos Terzakis (q.v.). He is representative of Greek fiction after Kazantzakis. As one critic has recently put it, Terzakis, who is much interested in the uncertain aspects of life between the two world wars, probes into the social and psychological characteristics of the modern family, its problems and tribulations. Terzakis concentrates on the microcosm of the family or a certain number of characteristic individuals who cannot successfully cope with the world about them. By dealing with the specific and concrete, Terzakis uncovers the souls of his characters, revealing their desperation and failure.

Elias Venezis (q.v.), awarded the Greek National Prize for Literature in 1939, has written travel impressions and histories as well as novels and short stories. A depth of perception and feeling for events of everyday life and a dreamlike atmosphere characterize his works, and symbolism, lyricism, and a deep love of humanity mark his novels. Rooted in the soil, charming, nostalgic, his novels are often loosely structured and at times emotionally overloaded.

Yorghos Theotokas (q.v.), a lawyer by profession, was dedicated to literature and also to the theater. He was much concerned with the sociological problems of the middle class and the anxieties and ideological conflicts of the youth of the post-World War II generation. In his novels he searches for the inner man and shows his acute awareness of the critical times in which he lived.

I. M. Panayotopoulos (q.v.), a prolific writer who together with George Seferis was awarded the Palamas Prize in 1947, has written more than thirty volumes, including novels, poetry, literary and art criticism, essays, and travel literature. His early poetry was characterized by neoromanticism and symbolism; his later poems express a burning desire for newer, more personal expression. In his novels and short stories he evinces an introspective response to life that gives meaning and depth to the present but does not look to the future, which contains only old age and decay.

Stratis Tsirkas (b. 1911), born in Cairo, Egypt, is the author of the trilogy *Akyvernites politeies* (cities adrift)—*O kyklos* (1960; the circle), *Ariani* (1962; Ariani), *Nykteridha* (1965; the bat)—which deals with World War II in the Middle East, and especially with the mutinies of the Greek expeditionary forces. Called the Greek Faulkner (q.v.), Tsirkas concerns himself with the ambiguity of historical destiny and with political drama, the concept of freedom, and man's inherent contradictions. A contemporary of Tsirkas, Petros Haris (q.v.), is essentially a short-story writer and essayist. The editor of the most important literary magazine in Greece, *Nea estia*, his fiction is marked by warm lyrical impressions of life and by sympathetic reminiscences. He probes the inner world of his characters for the special moment of painful discovery.

Takis Doxas (b. 1913) writes novels and short stories depicting life in the Greek provinces. His characters consist of the oppressed peasants and provincials for whom life holds little or no hope, and who symbolize the spiritual agony of contemporary man.

Two outstanding writers of fiction of more recent times are Andonis Samarakis and Vassilis Vassilikos (qq.v.). In simple, direct prose, Samarakis writes about the common city dweller for whom the boredom of contemporary life alternates with the increasing threat of totalitarianism. His protagonists are often frustrated middle-aged men who take political stands in antiheroic ways. Using flashback and detective-fiction techniques, Samarakis always speaks out for the humanity of mankind. Vassilikos, internationally known as the author of *Z* (1966; *Z*, 1968), is one of Greece's most prolific and most outspoken novelists, the author of more than fifty books that have been translated into twenty languages. In his work one can trace the development of his own psyche and the conflicts and contradictions of his nation and his age.

Drama

Modern Greek drama is much concerned with the relation of the individual to society. It is critical and satirical, often in a highly metaphorical way.

Spyros Melas (1883–1966), one of the older established playwrights, was a very prolific writer and a demoticist par excellence. He wrote social and historical dramas influenced by Ibsen, as well as satirical comedies.

The plays of Anghelos Terzakis have had considerable success, and two of them have been performed by university groups in the U.S. Since 1937 he has served the National Theater of Greece as secretary, director, instructor, and general manager. At the center of his plays are investigations about the difficulties and tormenting doubts of contemporary man.

Iakovos Kambanellis (q.v.) satirizes contemporary social and political life. He is very much in the tradition of American realist drama of the 1930s through the 1950s, while producing a form of impressionistic celebration of Greek folk traditions. In a rich demotic Greek, Kambanellis manages to capture the life and spirit of the Greek people and show Greek history as cyclical—alternating between tyranny and revolution, idealism and selfishness.

Kostas Mourselas (b. 1934), a quiet man whose satires are fierce, cries out against man's capacity for depravity in contemporary urban existence. Blending tragicomedy and satire, and proceeding from simple and often humorous situations to increasingly complicated and serious dilemmas, Mourselas is concerned with humanistic values. He has been a leading figure in resuscitating the Greek theater through his interest in the individual and his relation to contemporary society. In Mourselas the tragic becomes comic.

Yorghos Kampanellis (b. 1922) presents Greek history as a ritual repetition of a modern myth showing internecine strife, revolt, and betrayal. Myth and history become a cyclical nightmare of glory destroyed by treachery and ending in defeat and subjugation. Kampanellis's use of myth has strong political implications.

Yorghos Skourtis (b. 1940), using the popular folk art of the shadow theater, utilizes these caricatures of human personalities as the archetypes of the Greek experience.

Modern Greek literature was in a real sense reborn around 1930. It could be said that Greek literature came of age then and caught up with Western Europe. Greek literature in the 20th c. has shown itself to be a living literature with a living tradition, aware of the glorious Greek past but not its slavish imitator. Rather, modern Greek writers are striking out on their own with vigor, originality, and a full awareness of the world and the times in which they live.

BIBLIOGRAPHY: Trypanis, C., *Medieval and Modern Greek Poetry* (1951); Sherrard, P., *The Modern Greek Threshing Floor* (1956); Keeley, E., and Sherrard, P., eds., Introduction to *Six Poets of Modern Greece* (1961), pp. 3–27; Gianos, M. P., *Introduction to Modern Greek Literature* (1969); Bien, P., and Keeley, E., eds., *Modern Greek Writers* (1972); Bien, P., *Kazantzakis and the Linguistic Revolution in Greek Literature* (1972); Dimaras, C. T., *A History of Modern Greek Literature* (1972); Friar, K., *Modern Greek Poetry: From Cavafis to Elytis* (1973); Politis, L., *A History of Modern Greek Literature* (1973); Mackridge, P., ed., "Greece: The Modern Voice," special issue, *RNL*, 5, 2 (1974); Doulis, T., *Disaster and Fiction: The Impact of the Asia Minor Disaster of 1922 on Modern Greek Fiction* (1977); Sherrard, P., *The Wound of Greece: Studies in Neo-Hellenism* (1979); Raizis, M. B., *Essays and Studies from Professional Journals* (1980); Lorenzatos, Z., *The Lost Center, and Other Essays in Greek Poetry* (1980)

JOHN E. REXINE

See also Cypriot Literature

GREEN, Henry

(pseud. of Henry Vincent Yorke) English novelist, b. 29 Oct. 1905, Tewkesbury; d. 13 Dec. 1973, London

After Eton, G. went to Oxford, where he wrote a novel, *Blindness* (1926), astonishingly sophisticated for an undergraduate. The theme expands from the accidental blinding of a sensitive young man somewhat like James Joyce's (q.v.) Stephen Dedalus to the discovery that blindness is universal in this wasteland world. As Angus Wilson (q.v.) has said, G. had discovered a theme that obsessed him: the disintegration of old ways of living. "The truth is," G. himself wrote, "these times are an absolute gift to the writer. Everything is breaking up." His response was not to retreat into aestheticism like Joyce and Virginia Woolf (q.v.), but to leave Oxford and go to work in his father's foundry in Birmingham, "with my wet podgy hands." Out of his life as a shop apprentice came his second novel, *Living* (1929). Christopher Isherwood (q.v.) described it as the best proletarian novel ever written; amused, G. said that he just wrote what he heard and saw. Although he eventually became managing director of the family firm, he remained much more sympathetic in his novels to ordinary working people than to members of his own class. He was aware of the drabness of ordinary lives, yet he described them with humor and without either condescension or political bias.

G. specialized in claustrophobic situations, emotional Black Holes of Calcutta. In *Party Going* (1939) the setting is a London railway hotel in which a group of idle rich young people is marooned. In *Caught* (1943) it is London before and during the blitz; his own experiences with the Auxiliary Fire Service enabled him to explore the tensions in a group of people, chiefly of the lower class, thrown together because of the war. In *Concluding* (1948) it is a training institute for young girls in some future welfare state, where individuality is dangerous deviationism.

In G.'s masterpiece, *Loving* (1945), it is a country house in Ireland during World War II; the novel begins with "Once upon a day" and ends with "Over in England they married and lived happily ever after," but the fairy-tale framework provides scope for comic juxtapositions and ironic reversals. Ogres figure prominently—they are the I.R.A.; a ring that is lost and found, as in many a fairy tale, brings trouble rather than gifts and blessings; peacocks and doves lend enchantment to the scene but, as the critic Edward Stokes writes, they become complex symbols of pride, vanity, beauty, sex and greed. The King of the Castle is missing; the Queen, Mrs. Tennant, is fearful of the Germans, the Irish, and her own servants; and a Prince Charming, Captain Davenport, comes riding on a bicycle to commit adultery with the golden-haired princess, whose husband is away on active service. If the morals of the upper class are no better than they should be, the servants below stairs are capable of surprising us. When the butler Raunce falls in love with the housemaid Edie, he changes from a lecherous and conniving person to a moral, responsible, and conventional one. Loving may mean romantic enchantment, as in Raunce's vision of his beautiful fiancée at the end; most of the time and for most of the characters, however, it means thralldom rather than happiness.

If Evelyn Waugh (q.v.) was the satirist of his generation and Graham Greene (q.v.) the moralist, it has been said, G. was the artist. He described his writing as an advanced attempt to break up the old-fashioned type of novel; he kept himself out of his books, and, as his one-word titles show, he pared things down to essentials, even leaving out definite and indefinite articles. In his first eight novels, the dialogue was economical and pointed; nevertheless there were enough poetic descriptive passages and dense symbolism to remind readers of Virginia Woolf. Some critics thought that in *Back* (1946) and *Concluding* poetry had taken over, to the exclusion of everything else. As if in reaction, in his last two novels, *Nothing* (1950) and *Doting* (1952), he left out almost all description and made dialogue carry the whole burden of narration and character portrayal. Brilliant experiments though these novels were, he had squeezed out the poetry, and squeezed out too much of life.

The rest was silence. Perhaps he felt like a modernist betrayed, when the traditional novel form was revived in the 1950s. Perhaps he had nothing to say to the world of the Angry Young Men. Or perhaps, like many a humorist, he walked on thin ice; John Updike (q.v.) speculated that he had made a "personal withdrawal into the despair that always fringed his pellucid world." Whatever the reason, he published no novels at all during the last twenty years of his life. Nevertheless, in spite of his withdrawal and the temporary eclipse of his reputation, he remains one of the few important English novelists of his time.

FURTHER WORK: *Pack My Bag* (1940)

BIBLIOGRAPHY: Dennis, N., "The Double Life of H. G.," *Life*, 4 Aug. 1952, 83–94; Stokes, E., *The Novels of H. G.* (1959); Russell, J., *H. G.: Nine Novels and an Unpacked Bag* (1960); Weatherhead, A. K., *A Reading of H. G.* (1961); Bassoff, B., *Toward Loving: The Poetics of the Novel and the Practice of H. G.* (1975); Ryf, R. S., *H. G.* (1967); Odom, K. E., *H. G.* (1978)

D. J. DOOLEY

GREEN, Julien

American novelist, diarist, and dramatist (usually writing in French), b. 6 Sept. 1900, Paris, France

Youngest child of American Southerners living in Paris, G. experienced expatriate isolation from birth. The only native French speaker in his English-speaking family and the only boy in a household of Southern belles, he created his own private world. Into this world he brought his beloved mother's horror of sex and her love of religion (both associated with English) and his own passionate nature (safely expressed only in French). After his mother's death in 1914, he followed his father into the Catholic Church. This religion, however, did not accommodate his sensuality, for he had discovered another cause for isolation—homosexuality. It added to his alienation while studying at the University of Virginia in the early 1920s. Unwilling to risk sacrificing his homosexuality, he became a lapsed Catholic in the Paris literary scene of the 1920s and 1930s. However, he reconverted to Catholicism in 1939. Exiled to the U.S. during World War II, he returned to Paris in 1945. Yet he has maintained his American citizenship and in 1971 became the first American elected to the French Academy. Despite his unhappiness with Vatican II for eliminating the Latin liturgy, which had protected him from the language of sin (French) and guilt (English), he now seems serene with the realities of his riven self.

From these polarities initially caused by an accident of birth and an atypical childhood, G. has transformed his private fantasy world into a special fictional one. His protagonists, whether American or French, male or female, adolescent or middle-aged, are exiles. They never find their true homeland, never find anyone who speaks their true language. Their sensuality, whether expressed overtly as sexual aggression or covertly as religious fanaticism, never finds satisfaction. With their life the battleground of flesh and spirit, they seek death. Only Denis, the young hero who relates his homosexual awakening in *L'autre sommeil* (1930; the other sleep), is willing to accept mere intimations of immortality. Directly autobiographical, *L'autre sommeil* combines experiences G. had in both the U.S. and France. More typical of G.'s formula are his two best novels, *Moïra* (1950; *Moïra*, 1951) and *Chaque homme dans sa nuit* (1960; *Each in His Darkness*, 1961). Here the autobiographical heroes in heterosexual disguise play out their compulsions of eroticism and mysticism in the South Atlantic seaboard settings that were G.'s when he was expatriated to his official fatherland. G. punishes Joseph of *Moïra* by sending him to the police; he raped and killed Moïra (a word meaning fate in Greek, and Mary—or salvation—in Gaelic). G. punishes Wilfrid of *Chaque homme dans sa nuit* by having him shot by the young man whose overtures he had rebuffed. These "trans-

lated" heroes are not so credible as G.'s self-characterization in his *Journal*, which covers the years 1928–70 (9 vols., 1938–72; selections in *Personal Record* [1939,] and *Diary* [1964]) seven autobiographies (five written in French, two in English). Here his authenticity and sincerity put him in the moralist tradition of his friends and mentors, André Gide, François Mauriac (qq.v.), and Jacques Maritain (1882–1967). The diary and autobiographies, valuable to cultural historians, are even more interesting to linguists, since Green, sometime translator and foreign-language scholar, is acutely aware of how the language he uses influences what he says and who he is.

G.'s plays, coming midway in his career, owed their limited success to his reputation in other genres. *Sud* (1953; *South*, 1955) takes place the weekend before the start of the U.S. Civil War and features a triangle of a transcendentalist girl, the Yankee lieutenant she loves, and the Confederate officer he loves. The dialogue, a direct transcription of American Southern speech, is only of linguistic interest.

As a foreign writer of French, G. is very conservative in style and content. His distraught characters think in impeccable French. Their reprehensible conduct is off-camera. The apparent strangeness comes from G.'s literal translation of American diction and idiom and from his assimilation of the Anglo-American literary tradition. Like Poe and Hawthorne, he connects physical darkness with spiritual blindness. Like the Brontës, he blurs the distinction between fictional reality and dream. Like Dickens, he uses the consciousnesses of characters too young or too disturbed for a balanced perspective. Like many Anglo-American writers down through his generation, he finds his chief symbols and motifs in the King James Version of the Bible—in his case, translated. In short, his work, like his life, has been productively poised between two major cultures, making him one of the foremost bilingual authors of his generation.

FURTHER WORKS: *Pamphlet contre les catholiques de France* (1924); *Mont-Cinère* (1926; *Avarice House*, 1927); *Le voyageur sur la terre* (1926; *Christine, and Other Stories*, 1930); *Adrienne Mesurat* (1927; *The Closed Garden*, 1928); *Suite anglaise* (1927); *Un puritain homme de lettres* (1928); *Léviathan* (1929; *The Dark Journey*, 1929); *Épaves* (1932; *The Strange River*, 1932); *Le visionnaire* (1934; *The Dreamer*, 1934); *Minuit* (1936; *Midnight*, 1936); *Varouna* (1940;

Then Shall the Dust Return, 1941); *Memories of Happy Days* (1942); *Si j'étais vous . . .* (1947; *If I Were You*, 1949); *L'ennemi* (1954); *Le malfaiteur* (1955; *The Transgressor*, 1957); *L'ombre* (1956); *Le bel aujourd'hui* (1958); *Partir avant le jour* (1963; *To Leave before Dawn*, 1967); *Mille chemins ouverts* (1964); *Terre lointaine* (1966); *Les années faciles* (1970); *L'autre* (1971; *The Other One*, 1973); *Qui sommes-nous* (1972); *Ce qui reste du jour* (1972 [Vol. 9 of *Journal*]); *Jeunesse* (1974); *La liberté* (1974); *La nuit des fantômes* (1976); *Memories of Evil Days* (1976); *Le mauvais lieu* (1977); *Ce qu'il faut d'amour à l'homme* (1978); *Dans la gueule du temps* (1979)

BIBLIOGRAPHY: Saint-Jean, R. de, *J. G. par lui-même* (1967); Rose, M. G., *J. G.: Gallic-American Novelist* (1971); Burne, G. S., *J. G.* (1972); Kostis, N., *The Exorcism of Sex and Death in J. G.'s Novels* (1973); Piriou, J.-P. J., *Sexualité, religion et art chez J. G.* (1976); Dunaway, J. M., *The Metamorphoses of the Self in the Works of J. G.* (1978); Piriou, J.-P. J., ed., *Une grande amitié: Correspondance de J. G. et Jacques Maritain* (1979)

MARILYN GADDIS ROSE

GREENBERG, Uri Zvi

Israeli poet (writing in Hebrew and Yiddish), b. 22 Sept. 1896, Bilikamin, Austro-Hungarian Empire; d. 8 May 1981, Tel Aviv

Born in Galicia and descended from a line of rabbis, G. began his career as a bilingual poet in Lvov (then Lemberg) and associated with such Yiddish writers as Perets Markish (q.v.) and Melikh Ravitsh (b. 1893). His earliest poems were published in 1912, the first in Yiddish, the second in Hebrew; in them he already articulated a sense of special mission. He was one of the founders of a Jewish literary expressionism (q.v.), which in his case was to become more specifically nationalistic. His World War I experiences are echoed in his first volume of poems (in Yiddish), *Ergits oyf felder* (1915; somewhere in the fields), and later, after he had moved to Warsaw in 1921, in such poetic works as *Mefista* (1921; Mephisto) and in pieces in the new journals *Kaliastre* and *Albatross*. He advocated the impregnation of contemporary literature with contemporary reality: "Therefore there should be cruelty in the song." Poetry (including and especially Jewish

poetry) must come down to earth and address men's immediate concerns in contemporary language. Expressionism broke with the traditional subject matter of Yiddish verse, as well as with its cadences, rhythms, and diction.

G., unlike many of his fellow Yiddishists, saw Zionism as the only salve to the ills of the Jewish people; after spending a year in Berlin, he emigrated to Palestine in 1924, at the end of the third *aliyah* (wave of immigration). This move signaled, too, his almost exclusive adoption of Hebrew as a literary language. The Yiddishists, in G.'s words, sought out the Gentile *emes* (Yiddish for "truth") in association with the revolution, whereas he went to the Jewish *emet* (Hebrew for "truth") in Erets Yisrael. He "expressed" and represented "Hebrew man" in his first volume of Hebrew verse, *Emah gdolah veyareach* (1924; great dread and a moon), as worker and prophet in the re-created homeland. From an early stage, G. adopted a politically maximalist stance (that is, he supported the demand for a Jewish state to be established on both sides of the Jordan River). He moved toward a total identification with the so-called Revisionists, the political party formed in the mid-1930s to work for immediate Jewish statehood. This point of view is a major theme in his poetry.

In addition to the dozen or so volumes of Hebrew verse, the works in Yiddish (now collected in two volumes) and the programmatic material (that stating his ideological position and his view of the direction of Hebrew literature), a great deal of G.'s writing remains as yet unpublished, a situation of his own volition. He always saw himself as out of step with the contemporary literary scene in Israel, which he regarded as a trivial marketplace, not truly representing the historical moment. All phases of G.'s work attempt to express the story of our times, the Holocaust, the Jewish nation, and his own particular mission in their regard. Thus, he was sui generis, the paramount Jewish expressionist.

FURTHER WORKS: *Hagavrut haolah* (1926); *Klape tishim vetishah* (1927); *Chazon achad haligyonot* (1928); *Anakreon al kotev haitsavon* (1928); *Kelev bayit* (1929); *Ezor magen unum ben hadam* (1930); *Sefer hakitrug vehaemunah* (1937); *Min hachachlil umin hakahol* (1950); *Mitoch sefer haigul* (1951); *Rechovot hanahar* (1951); *Minofim rechoke mahut* (2 vols., 1952–53); *Lisif sela etam* (2 vols., 1967–68); *Gezamelte verk* (2 vols., 1979)

BIBLIOGRAPHY: Alter, R., "A Poet of the Holocaust," *Commentary*, Nov. 1973, 57–63; Arnson, C., "U. Z. G.: The Early Years," *MHL*, 1 (1975), 4–7; Yudkin, L. I., *U. Z. G.: On the Anvil of Hebrew Poetry* (1980)

LEON I. YUDKIN

GREENE, Graham

English novelist, short-story writer, journalist, and essayist, b. 2 Oct. 1904, Berkhamsted

G. was educated at Berkhamsted School, where his father was headmaster, and at Balliol College, Oxford. After graduation he worked as an assistant editor for the London *Times* until the publication of his first novel, *The Man Within* (1929). Two unsuccessful novels in the style of Joseph Conrad (q.v.) followed, and G. was about to abandon writing when, as a last try, he changed his style and produced a fast-paced thriller, *Stamboul Train* (1932; Am., *Orient Express*), which gave him a new impetus and direction. His fiction thereafter alternated between "entertainments," as he called them, and more serious novels which reflect the influence of Ford Madox Ford and Henry James (qq.v.), and which, although cast in the mold of pursuit fiction, deal seriously with social issues. G. converted to Roman Catholicism in 1926, and Catholic themes mark the four novels that made him famous: *Brighton Rock* (1938), *The Power and the Glory* (1940), *The Heart of the Matter* (1948), and *The End of the Affair* (1951).

Throughout his life G. has been a great traveler. A trek across northern Liberia is reported in *Journey without Maps* (1936), and he investigated religious persecution in Mexico in *The Lawless Roads* (1939; Am., *Another Mexico*). From 1941 to 1943 he served with the British Secret Service in Sierra Leone. After the war, as an independent journalist, he visited political hot spots throughout the world which provided background for most of his subsequent novels: Indochina for *The Quiet American* (1955), the Congo for *A Burnt-Out Case* (1961), Haiti for *The Comedians* (1966), Paraguay for *The Honorary Consul* (1973).

A humorous vein surfaced in *Our Man in Havana* (1958) and reached its apogee in *Travels with My Aunt* (1967). In *The Human Factor* (1978) he remained true to the thriller genre he has perfected, but as a traveler returned full circle, to his native Berkhamsted, where much of this spy novel is set.

G. is a prolific writer. Besides novels he has published several volumes of short stories, most included in *Collected Stories* (1973). He has written five plays and the screenplays of several of the many films based on his novels. In the 1930s and early 1940s he wrote over five hundred reviews of books, films, and plays, mainly for *The Spectator*. A selection of his literary essays appears in *Collected Essays* (1969) and of his film criticism in *The Pleasure Dome* (1972; Am., *The Collected Film Criticism of G. G.*). Autobiographical writings, besides his travel books, include *In Search of a Character* (1961), *A Sort of Life* (1971), and *Ways of Escape* (1980).

In a modern idiom G. continues the tradition of Robert Louis Stevenson, a distant relative. The strange, the dangerous, and often the uncivilized and subtropical have always fascinated him; when his scene is urban, it is most often the shifty, seedy world of the petty criminal and the hunted spy, a setting critics have labeled "Greeneland." Superficially, his novels are suspense fiction, treating contemporary subjects from a melodramatic angle with techniques close to those of film. But although the early novels may be read as an alarmed commentary on social decadence as Europe lurched toward war, they already bear the stamp of the special perspective G. was to cultivate throughout his fiction. He always took the side of the underdog, the unregenerate, the eccentric, the individual. His pursuit fiction was criminal-centered; his Catholic novels skirted heresy; his journalism espoused unpopular causes; his comedies were sad, and his politics paradoxical.

What G. develops in his novels is a consistent view of the human condition. He has given it aphoristic expression in several places. Describing the impulse that drove him to write, he says that he he discovered very young that "human nature is not black and white but black and grey." He praises the "virtue of disloyalty" as freeing the novelist from accepted opinions and giving him the "extra dimension of understanding." Recalling Browning's Bishop Blougram's chessboard, he says that one must be able to write "from the point of view of the black square as well as of the white." He takes as perhaps the only sign of a Christian civilization "the divided mind, the uneasy conscience, the sense of personal failure." And as the epigraph he would choose for his complete work, he again cites Bishop Blougram: "Our interest's on the dangerous edge of things."

This controversial attitude is embodied in all G.'s writing, early and late. The title of his first novel is taken from Sir Thomas Browne's (1605–1682) "There's another man within me that's angry with me." Heroes of the novels of the 1930s, like remittance man Minty in *England Made Me* (1935; Am., *The Shipwrecked*), the hired killer Raven in *A Gun for Sale* (1936; Am., *This Gun for Hire*), and the adolescent gang leader Pinkie in *Brighton Rock,* are social outcasts whom G. follows with sharp psychological penetration and deep sympathy. The corruption that these characters are tainted with is extra-personal; the world they live in is so much more corrupt than they. Minty's spoiled youth, Raven's harelip and institutional childhood, Pinkie's slum upbringing are all crippling handicaps, like social or physical equivalents of original sin. The violence of these characters is just the excrescence of a larger international, not to say universal, violence. If they are doomed or damned, the responsibility is widely shared. G. challenges his reader to withhold quick judgment, to take the comprehensive view, to allow that "between the stirrup and the ground" there remains a possibility of understanding and pardoning these dark wayward heroes.

G.'s saints are just as complex and contradictory as his sinners. In fact, the two categories are barely distinguishable. The whiskey priest, hero of *The Power and the Glory*, is a drunkard, father of an illegitimate child, a wanted man in the eyes of the state, in his own eyes a failure. His heroism consists mainly in his flight from the police, in his tired persistence in continuing surreptitiously to administer the sacraments, in exposing others to the danger of protecting him. His sanctity lies in his sense of his own unworthiness, in the office he so humbly and badly fills, and in his martyr's death. G. strips conventional notions of sainthood of their usual connotations and illustrates Charles Péguy's (q.v.) statement that the sinner is at the heart of Christianity.

This thesis is taken as epigraph for *The Heart of the Matter*. Scobie, Assistant Police Commissioner in Sierra Leone during World War II, is a just man, a devout Catholic, a devoted husband. But his justice is corrupted by pity, and he is led inexorably to a triple betrayal of trust: as a police officer, as a husband, and as a Catholic—falling successively into corruption, adultery, and suicide.

A simplistic view of G.'s "Catholic" novels of the late 1930s and 1940s (and one that G. has aired on occasion himself) is that Pinkie is slated for Hell, the whiskey priest for Heaven, and Scobie for Purgatory. But such classifica-

tions belie G.'s compassionate concern for all his characters and his ultimate appeal to the "appalling strangeness of the mercy of God."

In the 1950s G.'s emphasis switched from religion to politics. *The End of the Affair* and his first play, *The Living Room* (1953), are his last "Catholic" works, the novel bright, the play dark in tone. Thereafter the religious concerns of his characters take second place to political preoccupations. Yet there is a continuity to G.'s vision, for whether he is investigating in his fiction Papa Doc Duvalier's repressive rule in Haiti (*The Comedians*), American involvement in Indochina (*The Quiet American*), a hostage drama in Paraguay (*The Honorary Consul*), or Communist counterespionage in Britain (*The Human Factor*), his main concern has always been the problem of faith, religious or political, in an increasingly complex and faithless world. The intention G. attributes to *A Burnt-Out Case,* "to describe various types of belief, half-belief and non-belief," might be taken as the broad canvas for all his work, if one remembers not to narrow the definition to religious belief alone.

Whatever the political scene and whatever the dialectics of political choice involved, G. also remains true to his earliest commitment as a novelist. His loyalty always goes to the individual ahead of the state, the party, the cult. Querry in *A Burnt-Out Case* fights against the stereotype others would make of him as a famous Catholic architect. Wormold in *Our Man in Havana*, because he is an eccentric individual, not a cipher in a system, turns his secret-service mission into farce. Although defeated by Duvalier's nightmarish police, the unimportant and slightly ridiculous characters in *The Comedians* triumph in human terms. Castle, hero of *The Human Factor*, becomes involved as a double agent on personal rather than ideological grounds; this novel, unlike most spy novels, focuses on the humdrum, unsensational aspects of life as a spy, and the drama results from the conflict between the impersonal intricacies of superstate politics and private loyalties.

The frontier land of G.'s fiction is a place of contradictory responsibilities, of dangerous choices, and of constant revision of judgments and attitudes. It is not just Greeneland but a place very like the difficult world we live in. The virtues his characters bring to cope with it, sometimes successfully in comedy, sometimes unsuccessfully in tragedy, are not heroic ones but are those of tolerance, humor, and intense personal loyalties.

G.'s reputation as a novelist is secure. His fiction meets T. S. Eliot's (q.v.) criteria for greatness: "variety, abundance and complete technical competence." To this one might add "poetic quality" in the sense Ford Madox Ford defines it: "not the power melodiously to arrange words, but the power to suggest human values." This accomplishment is backed by outstanding contributions in many fields. He was one of the most brilliant film critics of the 1930s. He is the most-filmed British novelist of his generation. As a director of the publishing houses Eyre & Spottiswoode (1944–48) and The Bodley Head (1958–68), as well as in a personal way, he has been very generous with his help to younger writers. His literary criticism has been described as a dark lantern throwing intense light from a particular angle on the subjects it focuses on. His plays are interesting corollaries to his fiction, his journalism is daring, and his political commitments are provocative. Over a long career G. has given vivid dramatic expression to universal concerns, presenting them in a popular, entertaining, yet always intellectually stimulating way and in a style that has shed its early melodramatic excesses to become classically simple, dense, and direct.

FURTHER WORKS: *Babbling April* (1925); *The Name of Action* (1930); *Rumour at Nightfall* (1931); *It's a Battlefield* (1934); *The Basement Room, and Other Stories* (1935); *The Confidential Agent* (1939); *British Dramatists* (1942); *The Ministry of Fear* (1943); *Nineteen Stories* (1947); *Why Do I Write?* (1948); *The Third Man* (1950); *The Lost Childhood, and Other Essays* (1951); *Essais catholiques* (1953); *Twenty-One Stories* (1954); *Loser Takes All* (1955); *The Potting Shed* (1957); *The Complaisant Lover* (1961); *A Sense of Reality* (1963); *Carving a Statue* (1964); *May We Borrow Your Husband?* (1967); *Lord Rochester's Monkey* (1974); *The Return of A. J. Raffles* (1975); *Doctor Fischer of Geneva; or, The Bomb Party* (1980)

BIBLIOGRAPHY: Rostenne, P., *G. G.: Témoin des temps tragiques* (1949); Madaule, J., *G. G.* (1949); Mauriac, F., *Mes grands hommes* (1951), pp. 245–53; Rischik, J., *G. G. und sein Werk* (1951); Allott, K., and Farris, M., *The Art of G. G.* (1951); de Pange, V., *G. G.* (1953); Mesnet, M.-B., *G. G. and the Heart of the Matter* (1954); Wyndham, F., *G. G.* (1955); O'Faolain, S., *The Vanishing Hero* (1956), pp. 71–97; Atkins, J., *G. G.* (1957); Zabel, M. D., *Craft and Character* (1957), pp. 276–96; Matthews, R., *Mon ami G. G.* (1957); Kunkel, F. L., *The Labyrinthine Ways of G. G.* (1959); Lewis, R. B. W., *The Picaresque Saint* (1961), pp. 220–74; Pryce-Jones, D., *G. G.* (1963); Evans, R. O., ed., *G. G.: Some Critical Considerations* (1963); De Vitis, A. A., *G. G.* (1964); Stratford, P., *Faith and Fiction: Creative Process in G. and Mauriac* (1964); Lodge, D., *G. G.* (1966); Turnell, M., *G. G.* (1967); Cargas, H., *G. G.* (1969) Vann, J. D., *G. G.: A Checklist of Criticism* (1970); Boardman, G. R., *G. G.: The Aesthetics of Exploration* (1971); Wolfe, P., *G. G. the Entertainer* (1972); Phillips, G. D., *G. G.: The Films of His Fiction* (1974); Veitch, D. W., *Lawrence, G., and Lowry: The Fictional Landscape of Mexico* (1978)

PHILIP STRATFORD

"Novels" and "Entertainments" are both written in the same grim style, both deal mainly with charmless characters, both have a structure of sound, exciting plot. You cannot tell from the skeleton whether the man was baptized or not. And that is the difference; the "Novels" have been baptized, held deep under in the waters of life. The author has said: "These characters are not my creation but God's. They have an eternal destiny. They are not merely playing a part for the reader's amusement. They are souls whom Christ died to save." This, I think, explains his preoccupation with the charmless. The children of Adam are not a race of noble savages who need only a divine spark to perfect them. They are aboriginally corrupt. Their tiny relative advantages of intelligence and taste and good looks and good manners are quite insignificant. The compassion and condescension of the Word becoming flesh are glorified in the depths.

Evelyn Waugh, "Felix Culpa?" *The Tablet,* 5 June 1948, 352

He appears to share the idea, which has been floating around ever since Baudelaire, that there is something rather *distingué* in being damned; Hell is a sort of high-class night club, entry to which is reserved for Catholics only, since the others, the non-Catholics, are too ignorant to be held guilty, like the beasts that perish. We are carefully informed that Catholics are no better than anybody else; they even, perhaps, have a tendency to be worse, since their temptations are greater. . . . But all the while—drunken, lecherous, criminal, or damned outright—the Catholics retain their superiority since they alone know the meaning of good and evil. . . .

This cult of the sanctified sinner seems to me to be frivolous, and underneath it there probably lies

GÜNTER GRASS

JUAN GOYTISOLO

GRAHAM GREENE

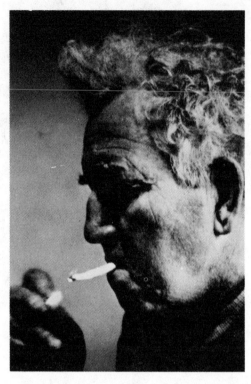

ROBERT GRAVES

JORGE GUILLÉN

a weakening of belief, for when people really believed in Hell, they were not so fond of striking graceful attitudes on its brink.

George Orwell, on *The Heart of the Matter, New Yorker*, 17 July 1948, 66

G. G., then, employs a distinctive form: he also exhibits a distinctive concern. Just as Balzac came back again to avarice and Stendhal to ambition, so, in book after book, G. G. analyses the vice of pity, that corrupt parody of love and compassion which is so insidious and deadly for sensitive natures.

. . . Behind pity for another lies self-pity, and behind self-pity lies cruelty.

To feel compassion for someone is to make oneself their equal; to pity them is to regard oneself as their superior and from that eminence the step to the torture chamber and the corrective labour camp is shorter than one thinks.

For providing us with such exciting reading and at the same time exposing so clearly a great and typical heresy of our time, G. G. deserves our lasting gratitude.

W. H. Auden, "The Heresy of Our Time," *Renascence*, 1 (Spring 1949), 24

This hidden presence of God in an atheistic world, this subterranean circulation of grace, fascinates G. G. far more than the majestic façades that the temporal Church still raises up above the people. If there exists a Christian who would not be troubled by the collapse of the visible Church, he is certainly . . . G. G. . . .

[*The Power and the Glory*] providentially addresses itself to the generation that the absurdity of a mad world has seized by the throat. To the young contemporaries of Camus, and Sartre, desperate prey of a mocking liberty, G. will perhaps reveal that this absurdity is in truth that of a boundless love.

François Mauriac, *Mes grands hommes* (1951), pp. 250–51

There is a sentence by Gauguin, quoted approvingly by G., that comes near to expressing his main obsessional outlook: "Life being what it is, one dreams of revenge." A terror of life, a terror of what experience can do to the individual, a terror at a predetermined corruption, is the motive force that drives G. as a novelist. With different degrees of plausibility in his various books G. is continually saying that happiness is unusual and anxious routine nearer the disappointing 'natural' state of man, that experience saddens, that we must bear rather than rejoice because, in Matthew Arnold's words, of a "something that infects the

world." Failure, ugliness, the primitive are in some sense truer than success, beauty and civilization with their deceptive gloss.

Kenneth Allott and Miriam Farris, *The Art of G. G.* (1951), pp. 15–16

All G. G.'s best work can only be read as "a sort of poem," an exciting blend of realism as to its detail and poetry as to its conception. It is not only the brainless and predestined quality of his characters that makes them move so fast: they have been conceived under the emotional pressure of poetic inspiration which flies them as high as maddened kites. In this sense, G.'s characters really are hunted men, the hounds of heaven at their heels. It is one significant reason why they are least interesting when they pause. Then they come down to earth, to common life, and common life is a range of experience beyond G.'s powers, since it is outside his interest.

Sean O'Faolain, *The Vanishing Hero* (1956), pp. 93–94

He would have made an admirable Pierrot in the eighteenth-century Commedia dell' Arte, concealing under his rather woebegone mask a great capacity for cynical humour. He was often exuberant: he could be positively blithe. Nor have the exuberance and the blitheness vanished. And even at the present period, when I reread his books—those sombre chronicles of sin and suffering, where every form of pleasure is naturally suspect, every love-affair inescapably doomed, and a breath of Evil mixes with the fog that swirls the lonely street lamps—I sometimes feel that I am confronting the spirited schoolboy in a more accomplished and more portentous guise. I cannot resist the suspicion that he gets a good deal of fun—lighthearted schoolboyish fun—from causing his own and his reader's flesh to creep, and that he half enjoys the sensations of disgust and horror that he arouses with such unusual terror.

Peter Quennell, *The Sign of the Fish* (1960), p. 64

G. often turns away from the relatively civilized to inspect human life in its cruder and more exposed conditions: in a dark corner of Brighton, the jungles and prisons of Tabasco, the coast of West Africa—all places where, as Scobie tells himself in *The Heart of the Matter*, "human nature hasn't had time to disguise itself"; places where there openly flourished "the injustices, the cruelties, the meanness that elsewhere people so cleverly hushed up." In these primitive scenes we encounter the *dramatis personae* of G.'s recurring drama and of his troubled universe: the murderer, the priest, and the policeman, . . . they tend more and more to resemble each other. The murderer Pinkie is knowingly a hideously inverted priest; the policeman Scobie becomes involved with crime and criminals; the lieutenant in *The Power and the Glory* has "something of a priest in his intent observant walk," while the priest in turn has queer points of resemblance with the Yankee killer whose photograph faces his in the police station. The three figures represent, of course, the shifting and interwoven attributes of the Greenean man: a being capable of imitating both Christ and Judas; a person who is at once the pursuer and the man pursued; a creature with the splendid potentiality either of damnation or salvation.

R. W. B. Lewis, *The Picaresque Saint* (1961), pp. 241–42

GREENLAND LITERATURE
See Eskimo Literature

GRIEG, Nordahl
Norwegian poet, novelist, dramatist, and journalist, b. 1 Nov. 1902, Bergen; d. 2 Dec. 1943, Berlin, Germany?

G. provides a severe test of the tenet that a writer's works should be judged independently of the individual who wrote them. It is likely that G.'s works have been both overly praised and unfairly deprecated in reaction to the man, a man truly of large and varied dimensions. He was, at the same time, an ardent patriot, a dedicated communist, a concerned pacifist, a solider, and ultimately a military martyr.

To the extent that Norway has a patrician class, G. may be said to be of that stock. G.'s given names—Johan Nordahl Brun—were those of a forebear who was an eminent 18th-c. cleric and writer. G.'s surname derives from lineage with the great composer. G.'s father held a university position as a teacher of music while his mother was of a politically active family.

At the age of seventeen, G. went to sea, and began a hectic career of adventure, travel, writing, and political action. The first literary result of his stint as a seaman was *Rundt Kap det gode Håp* (1922; *Around the Cape of Good Hope,* 1979), a book of sea poems with the flavor, the style, and the popularity of John Masefield and Rudyard Kipling (qq.v.).

A counterpoint to the general romanticism of the sea poems was struck by the explicit realism of the quasi-autobiographical novel he published two years later, *Skibet går videre* (1924;

The Ship Sails On, 1927). This book has been translated into at least nine languages and was the precipitating event leading to the worldwide campaign by the International Red Cross against the venereal disease problem in port cities.

G.'s first important political statement was *Barrabas* [sic] (1927; Barabbas), a play in which he presented the choice of pacifism or violence, the cross or the sword, in the struggle for freedom. It was a hastily constructed but daringly experimental work that presented Barabbas as a violent rebel against Roman rule who was needed more than was Jesus in the grand strategy of the Pharisees.

The play *Vår ære og vår makt* (1935; *Our Power and Our Glory,* 1971) is a flawed but powerful indictment of war and war profiteers. It deals with the corrosive forces eating at Norway as a "neutral" country during World War I. The theatrical techniques and stage effects drew heavily on the experience G. gained during his two-year stay in Russia (1932–34).

G.'s most successful play is *Nederlaget* (1936; *Defeat,* 1944), a depiction of the Commune revolution in Paris in 1871. Without equivocation the play makes clear that freedom must be won through struggle. The theatrical technique represents a maturation of that employed in *Vår ære og vår makt*; additionally, *Nederlaget* is less stylized, has a sharper dramatic development, and depicts people more realistically.

With the Nazi invasion of Norway, all pacifistic doubts were resolved. G. joined the military service and participated in the dramatic removal of Norway's gold reserves to England. Above all, he wrote and read over Radio Free Norway resistance poetry that played a vital role in strengthening the common purpose and the common will to survive during the dark days of the Occupation. The war poetry was published in a number of books after his death. G. was killed when the bomber on which he was an observer did not return from an attack on Berlin.

For all his enduring popularity in Norway, G. is little known outside of Scandinavia. However, the continued republication of his works attests to the fact that he will remain read and respected in his native land, which he loved so well.

FURTHER WORKS: *Stene i strømmen* (1925); *Kinesiske dage* (1927); *En ung mands kjærlighet* (1927); *Norge i våre hjerter* (1929); *De unge døde* (1932); *Atlanterhavet*

(1932); *Men imorgen* (1936); *Spansk sommer* (1937); *Ung må verden ennu være* (1938); *Dikt i utvalg* (1944); *Flagget* (1945); *Friheten* (1945); *Håbet* (1946); *Veien frem* (1947); *Samlede verker* (7 vols., 1947); *Samlede dikt* (1948); *Lengselen* (1957); *Langveisfra* (1964); *Morgen over Finnmarksvidden* (1967); *Skuespill/ N. G.* (1975); *Norge, og andre dikt* (1976). FURTHER VOLUME IN ENGLISH: *War Poems of N. G.* (1944)

BIBLIOGRAPHY: Barrett, K., "Between Curtains," *TA*, 22 (1938), 384–86; Lescoffier, J., "N. G.," *Mercure de France*, 291 (1939), 721–23; Koht, H., "N. G.," *ASR*, 30 (1942), 32–40; special G. issue, *WZUG*, 12 (1963); Dahlie, H., "Lowry's Debt to N. G.," *CanL*, 64 (1975), 41–51

HAROLD P. HANSON

GRÍMSSON, Stefán Hörður
Icelandic poet, b. 31 March 1919, Hafnarfjörður

G. is self-educated and well read in literature and philosophy. He belongs to the group of writers and artists who finally brought modernism (q.v.) to Iceland during World War II.

G.'s first volume, *Glugginn snýr í norður* (1946; window to the north), showed a clear connection with the traditional poetry of the 1930s, both in form and content. Many of the poems have fragments of narration and deal with social criticism as well as with love. Their style is often heavy and ornamental. There are, however, some poems that are predominantly modernistic and free in form.

In his second volume, *Svartálfadans* (1951; dance of the black fairies), G. completely broke with the past and found his own personal expression through modernistic poetic imagery. Gone are the narrative fragments; instead, the poems contain concentrated imagery, and are simple and concise. Images of nature are often used to express the poet's sensitivity and personal philosophy. There is less direct social criticism than in his first book, and what there is is often symbolically veiled or hidden in philosophical speculation on human nature.

Hliðin á sléttunni (1970; the gates [or side] of the plain) is a logical continuation of *Svartálfadans*. The poetic quality has increased, the style is simpler and more transparent; at the same time the thought is more profound

and more complicated. The images, at first glance, seem clear and even ordinary; but they usually are laden with complex symbols and allusions. The poems in this slim volume are largely expressions of a deeply felt personal philosophy, but some also contain sharp social criticism and reveal G.'s fear for the future of mankind.

G. is not a prolific poet. In the three volumes published together in 1979 under the title *Ljóð* (poems) there are only sixty-six poems. But he is undoubtedly one of the most accomplished poets of contemporary Iceland. His development has been toward an even simpler form, and he has succeeded in deepening his poetic vision and giving it mythical dimensions.

NJÖRÐUR P. NJARÐVÍK

GRUŠAS, Juozas
Lithuanian dramatist, short-story writer, and novelist, b. 16 Nov. 1901, Žadžiunai

G., from a family of small farmers, graduated from the University of Kaunas in 1931. From 1928 to 1939 he earned his living as a teacher, and for a time he also edited a weekly Christian newspaper. In 1940–41 he was the editor of the state publishing company of Lithuania. After the second Soviet occupation of Lithuania he worked as a literary consultant for the theater of Šiauliai. Since 1944 he has lived in Kaunas, engaged solely in creative writing.

In all of G.'s writing, from traditional, realistic short stories to modern, psychological plays to surrealistic prose sketches, two themes remain constant. The first is life seen as a constant struggle between the inhibitions of an ethical conscience and the destructiveness of uncontrolled passions; the second is his pity for the weak and downtrodden.

In his short stories G. deals with variations on the theme of the psychology of a victim. In the stories in two of his best collections, *Rūstybės šviesa* (1969; the light of anger) and *Laimingasis—tai aš* (1973; the luckiest of all —myself), the main characters are the victims of society and circumstances—the humiliated poor, the cripples leading a marginal life among the normal people, those who live in the shadows and are often brutalized by those who cannot stand their suffering. The stories also portray emotionally starved and weak characters who are victimized by the passions of others. In both cases G. is interested not so much in the social structures that isolate the victim as in the relationship between the aggressor and the victim. Additionally, G. often analyzes the character who lives in a world of illusion and is considered mad by the standard of sanity in the "normal" world; the madman is his archetypal victim. The real enemy of humanity is the intolerance of those who refuse to see the truth beyond logic.

G. is known in Lithuania above all as a dramatist. His plays fall roughly into three categories. The first group are realistic plays that deal with moral dilemmas. The central conflict of these plays is the difficult choice: between family loyalty and social responsibility, as in *Tėvas* (1942; father); between a scientist's duty to scientific progress and the possible consequences of scientific advances on future generations, as in *Profesorius Markas Vidinas* (1963; Professor Markas Vidinas); between the integrity of an individual and the revelation to his son of a truth that will destroy the son's beliefs, as in *Adomo Brunzos paslaptis* (1967; the secret of Adomas Brunza).

The second type of play is a mixture of moralistic allegory and Theater of the Absurd (q.v.). In *Meilė, džiazas ir velnias* (1967; love, jazz, and the devil) a group of young people, rejecting the values of their parents, search for self-definition. To achieve this they try to impose their will on the outside world, but the result is only a series of pointless, brutal actions that result in the destruction of the only character they respect.

The plays in the third category are large-scale historical dramas. *Herkus Mantas* (1957; Herkus Mantas), *Barbora Radvilaitė* (1971; Barbora Radvilaitė), *Švitrigaila* (1976; Švitrigaila), and *Rekvijum bajorams* (1978; a requiem for the nobles) all deal with the theme of the tragedy of historical characters who must reconcile public and personal levels of existence. The moral problem they confront is often that they desire noble ends while being fully aware of the bloody means they demand.

The psychological realism of G.'s works has never wavered from its original premise—to see human destiny in a scheme of moral imperatives. His knowledge of the human soul has always revealed to the reader his greatest moral imperatives: vivid indignation in the face of injustice and great respect for its victims.

FURTHER WORKS: *Ponia Bertulienė* (1928); *Karjeristai* (1935); *Sunki ranka* (1937); *Nenuorama žmona* (1955); *Dūmai* (1956); *Gintarinė vila* (1979)

ILONA GRAŽYTĖ-MAZILIAUSKAS

GUADELOUPE LITERATURE
See French-Caribbean Literature

GUATEMALAN LITERATURE
See Central American Literature

GUÐMUNDSSON, Tómas
Icelandic essayist and poet, b. 6 Jan. 1901, Grímsnes

Already as a high-school student in Reykjavík G. attracted notice for poems he had written. He earned a law degree from the University of Iceland in 1926, and then practiced law in Reykjavík. He also worked for the Bureau of Statistics for a time, but after 1943 dedicated himself wholly to writing. He edited the literary magazine *Helgafell* from 1942 to 1955 and another magazine, *Nýtt Helgafell*, from 1956 to 1959. He has translated several books into Icelandic including works by Giuseppe Tomasi di Lampedusa and Erich Maria Remarque (qq.v.).

G.'s first volume of verse, *Við sundin blá* (1925; beside the blue channels), has the markings of the new romantic life-worship introduced into Icelandic poetry around 1920 through the works of Stefán frá Hvítadal (1887–1933) and Davíð Stefánsson (1895–1964). Most of the poems in this book concern the pleasures of youthful love, although there is often an undercurrent of nostalgia for the past—a tone of sadness that grew in intensity in G.'s later verse. On the whole, these early poems have a thoughtful and intellectual quality, while the romantic sentiment tends to be somewhat detached. The intellectual humor that was to play such a prominent role in his later poetry can hardly be detected in this first volume.

With *Fagra veröld* (1933; beautiful world), G. established himself as a mature poet. The book was a tour de force that gained him immense popularity, among other reasons because many of the poems were about Reykjavík, Iceland's still young capital, and life there—a subject largely ignored by poets up to that time. G. opened the eyes of Reykjavík residents to the beauty of their own town. *Fagra veröld* at the same time shows a make-believe world far from the reality of economic depression and class conflicts that dominated the headlines when the book appeared. As a reward for singing its praise, the city of Reykjavík gave the poet a stipend that enabled him to travel in southern Europe, and some of the poems in his next volume, *Stjörnur vorsins* (1940; the stars of springtime), evolved from the experiences of that trip. Although this book has more pure lyricism in it than any of G.'s other works, it also contains poems on social concerns such as race bigotry and the rise of Nazism in the 1930s. The terrors of World War II, however, affected him more profoundly than any other political events, as is clearly seen in *Fljótið helga* (1950; the sacred river), the most pessimistic, philosophical, and religious book of verse that G. wrote.

His latest collection of verse, *Heim til þín, Island* (1977; return to Iceland), largely contains poems dedicated to various festive occasions—reflecting his status as Icelandic poet laureate. Also in this volume are several personal poems, expressing concern over approaching death along with nostalgia for a vanished youth, and disappointment with life's limitations.

G.'s poetry has in many respects a classical quality, yet it is shot through with romantic worship of beauty and nostalgic longing. His poetic forms are varied, but long lines of colloquial diction are typical of much of his work. His fondness for paradox gives his humor an intellectual cast, but his greatest achievement is perhaps that he was the first mature poetic spokesman for Icelandic city dwellers; he adapted the traditional diction of verse to suit emerging life styles by using an idiom close to the rhythms of colloquial speech.

SVEINN SKORRI HÖSKULDSSON

GUILLÉN, Jorge

Spanish poet and critic, b. 18 Jan. 1893, Valladolid

After receiving his secondary education at the Institute of Valladolid, G. studied at the Maison Perreyve of the French Fathers of the Oratory in Fribourg, and at the universities of Madrid and Granada. In 1917 he began at the Sorbonne a long academic career that took him to Murcia, Oxford, Seville, Middlebury College in Vermont (after 1938, when he became a voluntary exile from war-torn Spain), McGill University in Montreal, and finally, Wellesley College in Massachusetts (1940–57). Since 1947 he has also been a visiting professor at various universities in North and South America, having delivered the Charles Eliot Norton Lectures in Poetry at Harvard in 1957 and

1958. He received the first Cervantes Prize in 1976, the most important Hispanic literary prize, after being nominated for it by both Spanish and Argentine academies. He now lives in Málaga.

On his seventy-fifth birthday, the collected poems of G. up to that time were published as *Aire nuestro* (1968; our air). In this volume of 1700 pages the poetry written during forty-seven years is gathered into one carefully planned composition. *Aire nuestro* is made up of the following books published earlier: *Cántico: Fe de vida* (1928, 1936, 1945; 1st complete ed., 1950; canticle: certificate of life); the three-volume *Clamor: Tiempo de historia* (clamor: time of history)—Vol. I, *Maremágnum* (1957; pandemonium), Vol. II, *... Que van a dar en la mar* (1960; ... that flow down to the sea), Vol. III, *A la altura de las circunstancias* (1963; rising to the occasion); and *Homenaje: Reunión de vidas* (1967; homage: a reunion of lives).

For many years G. was known as the author of one book, *Cántico*, which grew and was perfected from one edition to another. "It has an overall architectural design like Baudelaire's *Les fleurs du mal*, with a mathematically conceived order of Dantean severity" (Hugo Friedrich). "In Spanish poetry there is probably no creation more austere than *Cántico*, or any work more simple, dedicated to one single theme.... The composition of *Cántico* is that of a rose" (Joaquín Casalduero). What these critics say about *Cántico* can also be said about *Aire nuestro*, an even more amazing achievement of organic growth and architectural planning.

G. has inherited something of the dynamic fervor of Saint John of the Cross (1542–1591) and the classical clarity of Fray Luis de León (1527–1591). Yet G.'s *Cántico* is dedicated to the celebration of this world and its real wonders. As a matter of fact, the spiritual beyond is right here, according to "Más allá" ("Beyond," 1965), the opening poem in *Cántico*. Air is celebrated all through these poems as the giver of life, light, happiness. Air reveals to us what is real while being the perfect symbol of spirituality, even of eternity itself. G.'s technique owes much to the French poets from Baudelaire to Valéry (q.v.), but he has infused their approach with a spirit all his own. In its *élan vital*, G.'s poetry has more affinities with Gerard Manley Hopkins and with Boris Pasternak (q.v.) than with the masters of French symbolism (q.v.).

Because of G.'s highly concentrated style,

one that is often even elliptical and that forgoes nonessentials, he may seem difficult. Brief questions, abrupt answers, ecstatic exclamations mark his style; nouns are given preference over verbs, and the present is the preferred tense. These features of G.'s poetry have led to charges of abstraction, intellectualism, and hermeticism by critics who were unable to penetrate the style to discover the meaning. G.'s form is as disciplined as his style. He moves with masterful assurance from *décimas* (stanzas of ten octosyllabic lines) to romances, from sonnets to poems in free verse, and summarizes his main themes in contrapuntally built longer poems such as "Más allá," "Anillo" ("Ring," 1965), and "Vida extrema" (extreme life), all in *Cántico*.

Cántico embodies G.'s vision in its most original form. It presents the reader with, in G.'s words, an "affirmation of being and living." Chance, chaos, evil, suffering, death are held in the background in order to voice the more effectively G.'s "jubilant existentialism" (Eugenio Frutos), which celebrates the elemental life of childhood, youth, adulthood transfixed in an eternal present.

Cántico exhibits a spiritual discipline that does not surrender to anxiety, despair, or negation in contemplating reality in all its aspects. It strive for a vital equilibrium and hence does not overlook joy and hope as fundamentals of human existence. *Cántico* is one of the rare books of consolation in modern poetry. Yet there is nothing facile about G.'s luminous affirmation, which has to be wrested again and again from the encroaching shadows of absurdity, ever present and threatening.

The emergence of *Clamor* in no way annulled the faith in life proclaimed by G.'s *Cántico*. Many of the poems in *Clamor* are continuations of poems in *Cántico*. Thus, *Clamor* acts as a clarification of and a complement to *Cántico*, one in which the negative aspects of life are brought to the fore. G., now older, evinces a natural gift for the elegy. The "In Memoriam" of *Clamor* moves one as strongly by its restrained but intense evocation of lost love as one is moved by the cycle "Salvación de la primavera" ("A Springtime Salvation," 1965) in *Cántico*, which has been described as Spanish love poetry at its most ecstatic.

Clamor in general is immersed in time and the present age through references to places, autobiographical episodes, facts, and anecdotes. Satire, epigrams, narrative, and politically engaged poems, such as "Potencia de Pérez"

("The Powers of Pérez," 1979) are new departures in G.'s work. Almost a book within a book is formed by the many *tréboles*—the three-to-four-line "cloverleaves" that distill the themes of *Clamor* with haiku-like lyricism or nail them down with epigrammatic force.

Homenaje constitutes the cornerstone of the structure of *Aire nuestro*. New facets enter into G.'s poetry, while the main preoccupations of the previous two works are woven together. The central section of *Homenaje* is titled precisely "El centro" (the center) and contains the third great cycle of G.'s love poems, dedicated to his second wife, which reveals a Goethean ability to be renewed in love. This love poetry is deceptively simple, yet full of freely given love, of grace, and of human dignity.

In other poems in *Homenaje* G. looks back upon a lifetime of friendships with poets and years of reading and teaching literature. The section called "Al margen" (in the margin) is made up of poems of homage (or protest) written in response to various works—from Genesis to his own *Cántico*. "Atenciones" (attentions) are verse portraits of writers, among whom are Juan Ruiz (1283?–1350?) and G.'s friends Pedro Salinas and García Lorca (qq.v.). "Variaciones" (variations) is a section made up of translations/imitations from Tasso and Shakespeare to Valéry and Yeats (q.v.).

Homenaje reflects not only G. the voracious reader but also the exile and traveler who literally made the world his home. France, Italy, Greece, Portugal, and North and South America are celebrated in occasional verse. Indeed, in this volume G. proves himself to be a major writer of minor poems, one who equals the artistry and wit of a Mallarmé in this demanding genre.

Y otros poemas (1973; rev. and expanded, 1979; and other poems) gathers verse from 1966–75 in a volume the size of one of the three preceding books of *Aire nuestro* and further enriches the three modes embodied in them. *Final* (1981) is the concluding book of the monumental design of *Aire nuestro*.

Although *Aire nuestro*, through a web of mottoes, references, and quotations, belongs at the heart of the Spanish literary tradition, it is just as aware of the great European poetry, past and present. Ingratitude does not mar G.'s generous humanism, nor does admiration for other poets handicap his originality. Perhaps only the poet who is completely assured of his own vision of the world can be so open to the achievement of others.

The richness of variations that makes up

Aire nuestro springs from the one fundamental intuition that sees human life as a constant impulse toward form, as an appeal to human inventiveness to create and re-create order out of absurdity. It is not any extraordinary order that G. has in mind. The "energy of normality" that enables us to perceive the "minimal miracles" in everyday living, the only one we have, will do. A secular mystic, G. has realized in his *Aire nuestro* that *ars vivendi* for which he praises the city of Paris, because "ceaselessly inventing itself, it inheres in its being."

FURTHER WORKS: *La poética de Bécquer* (1943); *Federico en persona* (1959); *El argumento de la obra* (1961; "Introduction," in *Affirmation*, 1968); *Lenguaje y poesía* (1962; *Language and Poetry*, 1961); *En torno a Gabriel Miró* (1970); *Hacia "Cántico": Escritos de los años 20* (1980). FURTHER VOLUMES IN ENGLISH: *Cántico: A Selection* (1965; undated ed., 1977); *Affirmation: A Bilingual Anthology 1919–1966* (1968); *G. on G.: The Poetry and the Poet* (1979)

BIBLIOGRAPHY: Pleak, F. A., *The Poetry of J. G.* (1942); Casalduero, J., *J. G.: Cántico* (1946; rev. and expanded eds., 1953, 1974); Gullón, R., and Blecua, J. M., *La poesía de J. G.* (1949); Darmangeat, P., *J. G.; ou, Le cantique émerveillé* (1958); Muela, J. G., *La realidad de J. G.* (1962); Ivask, I., and Marichal, J., eds., *Luminous Reality: The Poetry of J. G.* (1969); Dehennin, E., *Cántico de J. G.* (1969); Ciplijauskaité, B., *Deber de plenitud* (1973); Debicki, A. P., *La poesía de J. G.* (1973); Ruiz de Conde, J., *El "Cántico" americano de J. G.* (1974); Prat, I., *"Aire nuestro" de J. G.* (1974); Yudin, F. L., *The Vibrant Silence in J. G.'s "Aire nuestro"* (1974); Ciplijauskaité, B., *J. G.* (1975); Macrí, O., *La obra poética de J. G.* (1976); [Wellesley College], *Homenaje a J. G.* (1978)

IVAR IVASK

In spite of what some people said, and even still say today, regarding influences and preferences, it became sharply clear in this book [*Cántico*] that the poetry of J. G. was undoubtedly the most personal and highly individualized poetic statement that had ever been made by any Spanish poet. Regardless of the opinion of many critics, this was poetry which was sparklingly clear, optimistic and jubilant like the circumference of a circle drawn without lifting the hand—exultant, vivid and admirable. Some apparently found it difficult to understand its formal content. Not everyone understands the beauty of a circle when it is not formed by a compass but by a trembling hand which is able to trace it with complete perfection and with one stroke of the pen. This was not prefabricated poetry, as Juan Ramón [Jiménez] sarcastically suggested in his attack. It was poetry that grew directly from the objects it described in a dynamic ecstasy before the world; a transparent world in which even the shadows were clearly outlined and bathed in light. A poet who is eternally young, elastic and forever confident, G. has been nourished by his canticle which has continued to surge upward until today. From its zenith, it can capture better than any other Spanish poetry the realities of the earth and also the very special and terrible reality of Spain. [1959]

Rafael Alberti, *The Lost Grove* (1976), pp. 266–67

Such is the spectacle that G.'s poetry offers. From the outset, perfection is attained, and from the outset too, it is revealed. Here, there is therefore neither progress, nor opposition, nothing but the recording of objective splendor. From this point of view, G.'s poetry separates itself distinctly from the rest of European poetry. It does not begin from the interior but from the exterior. It places that which is, not in the central hollow of the consciousness, but in the peripheral manifestation of a tangible reality. Everything is there, and everything begins from there. It is nevertheless true that the exterior perfection of the being having been immediately verified, the poet runs the risk of having nothing left to say. Everything has been said once, and for all. But G.'s attitude is not to be confounded with that of the Eleatics. It is not satisfied to recognize the splendor of the external being. It seizes and describes its efficacy. Yes, without a doubt the being is that which is placed outside. It develops itself on all sides in curves which close in on themselves; but, in closing, these curves enclose the point at which their action converges. The perfection is not static. It is an organization of the cosmos directed toward a center. . . .

A singular relationship which seems to reverse the habitual direction of thought. What? Everything no longer springs forth from the interior? What? It is no longer *from the center* that life is born and is propagated? Coming from within the soul, as with Rilke, or from the divine center, as with Eliot, will not a whole series of rays or of eccentric circles issue forth and cover space? On the contrary, with G., it is concentrically that space is traversed and that the beneficent forces converge to pour out their influence on the object on which their rays finally meet and coincide. So G., counter to all the poetry preceding him, rediscovers not only the sense of ambient fecundity, of the cosmic generosity, but also, by a corollary movement, the feeling of the receptivity, the happy humility of the being which finds itself overwhelmed by a luminous and dispensing nature. To the simple presentation of an objective center there is

297

now substituted the revelation of a median consciousness. Not a flower, a tree, a town, but myself. Myself at the center of the world, I who receive all from the world.

Georges Poulet, *The Metamorphoses of the Circle* (1966), pp. 348–49

G. occupies a central place in modern Spanish poetry. It is central in a paradoxical way; his work is an island, yet at the same time it is the bridge uniting the survivors of Modernism and the Generation of '98 to the Generation of 1925. . . . He is the least intellectual poet of his generation, by which I do not mean that he is the least intelligent. Perhaps just the opposite: he exercises his intelligence in his poems, not outside them. Like all intelligence, his is critical; like all creative criticism, it is invisible: it is not in what he says but in how he says it and above all in what he does not say. Silence is part of language and an authentic poet is distinguished more by the temper of his silences than by the sonority of his words. G.'s intelligence is not speculative; it is knowledge in action, a sentient wisdom; a feeling for weight and heat, the color and meaning of words, not excluding the almost incorporeal monosyllable. . . . G.'s transparency reflects the world, and his word is perpetual will for embodiment. Seldom has the Castilian language achieved such corporeal and spiritual plenitude. Totality of the word. G. has been called the poet of being. That is precise, on the condition that being is conceived of, not as idea or essence, but as presence. In *Cántico* being actually *appears*. It is the world, the reality of this world. Multiple and unique presence, a thousand adorable or terrible appearances resolved into one powerful affirmation of pleasure. Joy is power, not dominion. It is the great Yes with which being celebrates itself and sings of itself. [1966]

Octavio Paz, *The Siren and the Seashell* (1976), pp. 153, 155–57

J. G., who is beyond dispute the greatest living Spanish poet, seems at first sight to stand definitely outside the literary tradition of Spain. He never strives after local color as so many . . . of his countrymen do; he is not self-consciously Spanish. Gradually, one begins to realize that he harks back to a tradition that came before Gongorism or Euphuism, the Platonic tradition of Fray Luis. . . . Literature in our time is only too full of dark mazes and of harrowing involutions; the poems of J. G., though signally and splendidly modern, breathe a serenity and a tenderness that have something of the godlike about them. Precision and infinitude, as of music, are their constant gift to the reader.

Jorge Luis Borges, in J. G., *Affirmation* (1968)

Although in "La salida" G. celebrated "the joyful accuracy of the sudden muscles of instinct," he never allowed his instinct or his senses to accelerate into a feverish pose or distort his vision of the universe as a compact and marvellously normal sphere encircling a man humbly grateful to be inside it. In *Cántico*, as G. himself has pointed out, there is "No fusion, no magic," only "the enrichment of him who lives by exalting his life." What *Cántico* offers is poise, control, harmony and a classic simplicity of form, feeling and diction. It is no accident that in describing G.'s poetry as precise, intact, sparse, incisive and balanced, one is using some of the words G. himself favoured as he tried constantly to achieve the aim expressed in the final dedication to the 1950 edition of *Cántico*: "to consummate the fullness of being in the faithful fullness of words." The timeless dignity and measured eloquence of his tribute to the gift of life make *Cántico* transcend the age in which it was written.

C. B. Morris, *A Generation of Spanish Poets 1920–1936* (1969), p. 142

The tone of serene contemplation in many of G.'s poems results, in fact, from the effort of achieving a vital contact and integration with the world, a sometimes hard-won meshing of observer and observed. G.'s restrained fervor is never passive, for his work as a whole pursues a difficult goal: to embrace and comprehend all human activity.

. . . We do not have to look far for analogues in other languages and other eras. Whether it be Coleridge's concrete universal, Eliot's objective correlative, or William Carlos Williams' mere things, this sense of poetry is not unfamiliar. The rigorous intellectual attention that G. brings to sensual experience, however, distinguishes him among modern poets. To some small degree it is the Spanish literary tradition that allows him to unite the humble table and the abstract notion of "reality" so gracefully and so immediately; but by the same token, the Anglo-American literary tradition may hinder the English-speaker's appreciation of G.'s dexterity and seriousness in doing this.

Thus we do well to look to the formal texture of G.'s poetry for the sense of physical presence which is so vital and impressive in his work. G.'s mastery of exacting metrical forms, predominant especially in his early work, and his acute sense of formal effects at the most minute level of sound and sense, dignify those commonplace things and events that hold for him the values of vitality and coherence. He perceives experience as a kind of radiance of these values, and fixes them in poems whose metrical and musical shape expresses a contained ecstasy. If the phrase seems a paradox, let it then suggest the tension between the form and matter characteristic of many poems in *Aire nuestro*.

. . . He uses metaphor not to mystify the reader,

but rather to assess the just proportions of precise observation. Though often a poet of things, he is also interested explicitly in ideas and emotions. His metaphors, then, frequently yoke not two disparate objects, but a level of emotional intensity with an essential perception. . . . In some of his later poetry G. can very nearly dispense with metaphor entirely.

Reginald Gibbons and Anthony L. Geist, trs., Preface to *G. on G: The Poetry and the Poet* (1979), pp. 6–9

GUILLÉN, Nicolás
Cuban poet, b. 10 July 1902, Camagüey

G., a mulatto, used Negritude (q.v.) and left-wing ideology to forge a distinctive poetry that is a blend of Afro-Cubanism (q.v.) and social consciousness. His early verse was in the romantic-modernist vein, but he first came to the attention of the poetic world with *Motivos de son* (1930; *son* [a Cuban dance] motifs), eight poems based on an Afro-Cuban dance form and filled with primitive rhythms, dialect, humor, and black sensuality.

In *Sóngoro Cosongo* (1931; Sóngoro Cosongo), whose title comes from a verse in *Motivos de son,* G. stresses the mulatto aspects of Cuba. Continuing his series of satirical Cuban caricatures, he portrays the pimp, the street vendor, the boxer, and so forth, in verse imbued with black music and sensuality; but he also portrays black tragedy and superstition. In his first two volumes, then, he created a magical, ironic atmosphere and interpreted both the joys and sorrows of his compatriots.

In his next collection, *West Indies Ltd.* (1934; title in English), G. intensified his portrait of the black as a social victim, although he did not completely abandon his folkloric vision of the world. Here he explores relationships between the races and in revolutionary terms attacks the political situation and the exploitation of all Cubans. As he expresses his hatred, pain, and outrage at U.S. imperialism in ironic, sarcastic, and even violent imagery, at the same time he engages in a revolutionary search for human identity. In this and later collections he tries to destroy, in his petrified society, the very stereotypes that he had previously helped create by concentrating on Cubans as social beings exploited by foreign capitalism.

In the antimilitaristic *Cantos para soldados y sones para turistas* (1937; songs for soldiers and dances for tourists) G. sees the soldier as a pawn of imperialistic forces, one victim among many. He contrasts the poverty of blacks with the wealth of American tourists, whose gambling, drunkenness, and sexuality he mocks.

Having been exiled and having suffered because of his political beliefs, G. produced his most virulent social poetry in *La paloma de vuelo popular* (1958; the dove of popular flight) whose themes include prison, slavery, racism, the integration troubles in Little Rock, Arkansas, the activities of Senator Joseph McCarthy, and proletarian solidarity.

In his *Elegías* (1958; elegies), some of which have an epic quality, G. recalls his youth in Camagüey and writes of his Cuban heritage and of actual victims of racism. He employs striking color imagery to add intensity to his human sentiment and search for idealism.

Tengo (1964; *Tengo,* 1974) celebrates his pride at the triumph of the Castro revolution. Along with themes of national independence, revolutionary passion, and hatred of the past, he includes a note of tenderness for his country and people.

In *El gran zoo* (1967; *Patria o Muerte!: The Great Zoo, and Other Poems,* 1972) G. softens propaganda about exploitation and racial prejudice to produce an antirhetorical, playful, and almost whimsical symbolic tour of a stylized Cuban zoo. A kind of fable of human behavior as seen through the eyes of animals, from crabs to tigers, the collection stresses lighthearted fantasy.

G., perhaps Cuba's greatest living poet, whatever his political proclivities, has attempted to serve his artistic conscience. Master of avant-garde techniques and startling imagery, he tempers them with a simplicity that furthers his political passions and social purposes as he identifies his black and Cuban roots.

FURTHER WORKS: *Cerebro y corazón* (1922); *España: Poema en cuatro angustias y una esperanza* (1937); *El son entero: Suma poética* (1947; partial tr.: *Cuba Libre,* 1948); *Balada* (1962); *Antología mayor* (1964); *Poemas de amor* (1964); *La rueda dentada* (1972); *El diario que a diario* (1972); *Prosa de prisa* (3 vols., 1975); *El corazón que vive* (1975); *Poemas manuables* (1975); *Antología mayor* (1978). FURTHER VOLUMES IN ENGLISH: *Selected Poems* (1946); *Man-Making Words: Selected Poems* (1972)

BIBLIOGRAPHY: Augier, A., *G.: Notas para un estudio biográfico crítico* (1965); Cartey, W. G., *Three Antillean Poets: Emilio Ballagas,*

Luis Palés Matos, and N. G. (1965); Tous, A., *La poesía de N. G.* (1971); Márquez, R., Introduction to *Patria o Muerte!: The Great Zoo, and Other Poems* (1972), pp. 1–29; Sparrow de García Bario, C., *The Black in Cuban Literature and the Poetry of N. G.* (1975); Davis, S., *Development of Poetic Techniques in the Works of N. G.* (1977); Johnson, H., "N. G.'s Portraits of Blacks in Cuban Society," in Chang-Rodríguez, R., and Yates, D. A., eds., *Homage to Irving A. Leonard: Essays on Hispanic Art, History and Literature* (1977), pp. 197–207

KESSEL SCHWARTZ

GUILLOUX, Louis

French novelist and essayist, b. 15 Jan. 1899, Saint-Brieuc

Born in Brittany, the son of a cobbler, G. studied philosophy and also medicine before starting out as a journalist. His first novel, *La maison du peuple* (1927; the house of the people), shows him as a keen, yet warmhearted observer, capable of evoking human drama against the background of social struggle. A sense of mystery pervades the clipped and powerful prose of *Dossier confidentiel* (1928; confidential file), the narrative of the boyhood and slow but determined self-assertion of a lonely individual.

His most accomplished work, *Le sang noir* (1935; rev. ed. 1964; *Bitter Victory*, 1936) is rated one of the great French novels of this century, along with Malraux's (q.v.) *Man's Fate* and Sartre's (q.v.) *Nausea*. It is the story of a philosophy teacher at a lycée in western France whom his students derisively called "Cripure"—a pun on his pet subject, Kant's *Critique of Pure Reason*—who has failed dismally, intellectually and also in life. He is "stuck" with a woman well beneath his station; he braves society on her account but is spineless on more important, ethical matters concerning his students' lives. The novel portrays the atmosphere of a town in France during World War I, with its smug, conformist society. There are glimpses of human passion, of genuine and of mock devotion to causes, and of monsters engendered by the hero's imagination—to wit, the famous theme of the "cloporte" (inadequately translatable as "wood louse," because it is quite akin to Kafka's [q.v.] unhappy creature in *Metamorphosis*). Cripure is duty-bound to shoulder responsibilities toward his young charges that are more than merely edu-

cational; he must advise them in an exceptionally critical time. At times ruthless when asked what a young man should do about his obligations in wartime, he is nevertheless torn between an easy answer—"Go and fight"—and his deeper understanding of the situation, which has made him a pacifist. When it comes to speaking up against the draft, he throws up his arms in despair. G. adapted the plot of the novel as a play, *Cripure* (1962) maintaining the essential preoccupation with ideals betrayed through everyday compromise, and putting the monsters into a ballet.

Le pain des rêves (1942; the bread of dreams) deals with the hardships of a family poor in worldly goods but rich in perception and affection. *Le jeu de patience* (1949; the jigsaw puzzle) is a vast panorama of G.'s hometown as it goes through the two worlds wars and many social upheavals. Again G. sketches a gripping indictment of social injustices, enlivened by the colorful portrayal of Frenchmen of all classes and numerous waves of refugees from all parts of Europe. The title is amply justified by the clever use of flashbacks and of glimpses into the future, yet the frequent shifting from one set of historical and political circumstances to another never becomes confusing.

Les batailles perdues (1960; lost battles), perhaps G.'s most ambitious endeavor, is disappointing in its verbose and sometimes repetitious development of characters. *La confrontation* (1967; the confrontation) is noteworthy, however, for its complete change of pace and style. Even though it uses techniques decidedly unoriginal, strongly reminiscent of Camus's (q.v.) *The Fall*, it achieves an artistic success of sorts by deemphasizing plot to the benefit of a dreamlike vision. While the novel's mystery—which involves the search for an elusive heir to a treasure—is never completely solved, the quest is worthwhile because its results in the discovery of the self for several of the characters. The almost compulsive soliloquy of the narrator, less tortuous but also less compelling than in Camus's book, leads to a liberation of the individual that opens vistas of universal happiness through contemplation.

G. has also distinguished himself as a translator and, lately, as an essayist on literary and artistic subjects. His stature is growing, although few of his works have yet been translated.

FURTHER WORKS: *Compagnons* (1930); *Hyménée* (1932); *Le lecteur écrit* (1933); *Angelina* (1934; new ed., 1950); *Histoires de brigands* (1936); *Souvenirs sur Georges Palante* (1939); *Absent de Paris* (1952); *Parpagnacco; ou, La conjuration* (1954); *Le muet mélodieux* (1957); *Merveilles des Châteaux de Bretagne et de Vendée* (1970; with Claude Fregnac); *Salido* (1976, with O. K. Joël); *Carnets 1921–1944* (1978)

BIBLIOGRAPHY: "Interview avec L. G.," *NL*, 17 Dec. 1935, 1; Clark, E., "Death of a Thinker: A Note on the French Novel, 1925–1940," *KR*, 3 (1941), 322–34; "The World of L. G.," *TLS*, 26 March 1954, xii; Brombert, V., *The Intellectual Hero: Studies in the French Novel, 1886–1955* (1961), pp. 119–33; Braudeau, M., "L. G., témoin discret," *L'express*, 4 Nov. 1978, 28–29

KONRAD BIEBER

GUIMARÃES ROSA, João

See Rosa, João Guimarães

GUINEA-BISSAU LITERATURE

The tiny west African country of Guinea-Bissau lags far behind other Portuguese-speaking African nations in imaginative writing. In colonial times the small enclave was little more than a neglected trading outpost of the far-flung Portuguese empire. The absence of anything approaching the indigenous bourgeoisie that in other lusophone African colonies gave rise to small but significant elites of black and mixed-race intellectuals explains why little Portuguese-language and Creole writing emerged in preindependence Guinea-Bissau.

Not to be discounted, of course, is the rich oral expression in indigenous languages and in the region's Portuguese-based Creole. But what little Portuguese-language writing did appear in colonial times was chiefly quasi-ethnographic and mainly produced by Europeans and Cape Verdeans.

Fausto Duarte (1903–1955), a Cape Verdean who lived most of his life in Guinea-Bissau, can, by default, be called the first important writer of Guinea-Bissau. His five novels, published between 1935 and 1945, depict indigenous cultures in somewhat exotic terms.

In 1974 Guinea-Bissau gained its hard-fought independence amidst a surge of cultural and literary activity. A prime mover was Mário de Andrade (b. 1928), a distinguished Angolan intellectual and writer who was eventually appointed Guinea-Bissau's Minister of Culture. Andrade played an important role in the publi-

cation of *Mantenhas para quem luta!* (1977; hail to those who struggle!), a landmark anthology of poems in Portuguese by fourteen Guineans, most in their twenties. This historically important collection was followed by *Antologia dos jovens poetas* (1978; the young poets' anthology), comprising thirty-eight poems, almost equally divided between those in Portuguese and those in Creole.

With independence, the Creole lingua franca came to play a major role in literacy campaigns and primary education. Moreover, a project aimed at collecting Creole oral traditions resulted in *'N sta li 'n sta la* (1979; I'm everywhere) and *Junbai* (1979; togetherness), both attractively illustrated, bilingual (Portuguese/Creole) collections of traditional riddles and stories.

In November of 1980 the cultural-literary impetus suffered a setback when the government was overthrown. The cultural leadership of Andrade ended, and several promising writers fled into exile. This setback notwithstanding, a national literature has definitively come into being in Guinea-Bissau.

BIBLIOGRAPHY: Bull, B. P., *Le Créole de la Guiné-Bissau* (1975); Hamilton, R. G., *Voices from an Empire: A History of Afro-Portuguese Literature* (1975), pp. 358–62; Moser, G. M., on *'N sta li 'n sta la*, *RAL*, 11 (1980), 402–3

RUSSELL G. HAMILTON

GUINEAN LITERATURE

Although Guinea, which achieved independence from France in 1958, consists of twenty-four ethnic groups, three predominate: the Malinké in Upper Guinea, the Peul in Middle Guinea, the Soussou in Lower Guinea. With this mosaic of ethnic diversity, Guinea acknowledges eight national languages: Poular, Soussou, Malinké, Kissi, Guerzé, Coniagui, Toma, and Bassari. A program initiated in 1962 encourages Guineans to learn to read and write in their national tongues, using a modified Latin alphabet for transcribing their oral languages. Devoutly Muslim, the Peuls have used Arabic script to translate the Koran into Poular and to write religious poetry and prose. French, the legacy of colonialism, is the tool of communication for all administrative, commercial, and technical tasks, and, as the lingua franca of educated Guineans, is the official language. Yet it is understood by barely one fifth of the population.

The first modern Guinean literary works appeared in the 1950s, all of them in French, with the exception of the writings of Modupe Paris (b. 1901), a Guinean who studied in the U.S. and published his autobiography, *I Was a Savage* (1957), in English.

Guinean literature bears the stamp of history, both modern and traditional. Mamadou Traoré's (b. 1916) *Vers la liberté* (1961; toward liberty) and Sadan-Moussa Touré's (b. 1932) *Les premières guinéades: Contes, légendes de chez nous* (1961; the first Guineads: stories, legends of our homeland) celebrate Guinean independence in verse. Condetto Nenekhaly-Camara's (b. 1930) two plays, *Continent-Afrique* (African continent) and *Amazoulou* (Amazulu), published in one volume in 1970, present historical figures; the first play portrays Antar, a 6th-c. Arab warrior, and the second, Chaka, the 19th-c. Zulu king. Alpha Sow (b. 1935) has published an anthology of Peul folklore, *Chroniques et récits du Fouta Djalon* (1968; chronicles and tales of the Fouta Djallon mountains).

The Guinean literary scene has been largely dominated by Camara Laye (q.v.), whose first novel, *L'enfant noir* (1953; *The Dark Child*, 1954), was awarded the Charles Veillon Prize in 1954 and brought international recognition to its author. This work, profoundly poetic, recounts the life of a boy growing up in an African village, learning about his ancestors, appreciating his father's skills as a goldsmith. Camara's next novel, *Le regard du roi* (1954; *The Radiance of the King,* 1956), highly symbolic, presents a French protagonist unequipped for life in black Africa. Political difficulties with President Sekou Touré sent Camara into exile from 1965 until his death in 1980, first to Ivory Coast, then to Senegal, an exile made all the more painful when Sekou Touré detained Camara's wife in Guinea for several years. After leaving Guinea, Camara published *Dramouss* (1966; *A Dream of Africa,* 1968), a novel highly critical of Guinea's present political regime. Shortly before his death, he published an ethnographic work, *Le maître de la parole* (1978; the wordmaster), a transcription in French of the Malinké epic recounting the legend of Soundiata.

Djibril Tamsir Niane (b. 1920) had also published a version of this epic, entitled *Soudjata; ou, L'épopée mandingue* (1960; *Sundiata: An Epic of Old Mali,* 1965), in which he relates the tales of the crippled boy who grew up to rule the Mali empire (1230–55). Although the two versions are similar, Niane and Camara had based their work upon the accounts of different *griots,* or Malinké oral historians. In his introduction, Niane defines the role of the griot: "In the very hierarchical society of Africa before colonization, where everyone found his place, the griot appears as one of the most important men in this society, because it is he who, for want of archives, records the customs, traditions, and governmental principles of kings." Niane, who has griot ancestors, has also collaborated with the French historian Jean Suret-Canale (b. 1921) on an illustrated history of West Africa, *Histoire de l'Afrique occidentale* (1960; history of West Africa), and written two plays, *Sikasso* (1971; Sikasso) and *Chaka* (1971; Chaka), both with historical subjects.

As interested in Malinké history and tradition as Niane, but choosing a different vehicle of expression, Fodéba Keita (b. 1921), also of griot background, has composed music, poetry, and dance based on traditional sources. Keita's Ballets Africains, the Guinean national dance troupe, toured the globe in the early 1960s. After serving in the government from 1968 to 1971, Keita was imprisoned and disappeared. He is presumed dead.

One can only hope that Guineans in the future will have greater freedom of expression—both artistic and political—than they do at present, and that their rich oral tradition will continue to provide inspiration. It is unfortunate that talented artists such as Camara and Keita fell victim to repression. It is everyone's loss that their talents were not nurtured in their homeland.

BIBLIOGRAPHY: Gleason, J., *This Africa: Novels by West Africans in English and French* (1965); Brench, A. C., *The Novelists' Inheritance in French Africa: Writers from Senegal to Cameroon* (1967); Larson, C., *The Emergence of African Fiction* (1972); Olney, J., *Tell Me Africa: An Approach to African Literature* (1973); Blair, D., S., *African Literature in French* (1976); Cook, D., *African Literature: A Critical View* (1977); Owomoyela, O., *African Literatures: An Introduction* (1979)

MILDRED MORTIMER

GÜIRALDES, Ricardo

Argentine novelist, short-story writer, and poet, b. 13 Feb. 1886, Buenos Aires; d. 8 Oct. 1927, Paris, France

G. belonged to a wealthy family of landowners, and was thus acquainted with Argentine country life. In Paris, which he visited many times and where he died, he became acquainted with avant-garde writers, who had a decisive influence on his literary career. In Buenos Aires and in Montevideo, Uruguay, he was befriended by postmodernist Latin American poets: Conrado Nalé Roxlo (b. 1898), Raúl González Tuñón (b. 1905), Leopoldo Marechal, and Jorge Luis Borges (qq.v.).

G.'s first work, the collection of poems *El cencerro de cristal* (1915; the crystal bell), placed him at the forefront of avant-garde writers in Latin America. The same year he published a book of short stories, *Cuentos de muerte y de sangre* (1915; tales of blood and death), basically romantic. Although outright failures with the reading public, both works showed G. to be a master of language. *Raucho* (1927; Raucho), a semiautobiographical novel, followed and then *Rosaura* (1922; Rosaura) and *Xaimaca* (1923; Xaimaca). The latter two works, sentimental and melancholy, also showed G. as an innovator in language, since he experimented constantly with the techniques initiated by the postmodernist and by the European and Spanish American avant-garde movements. In 1923, with Jorge Luis Borges and Pablo Rojas (1896–1956), G. founded the review *Proa,* which encouraged the presentation of themes drawn from Argentine life but expressed by means of "all the technical discoveries of postwar Paris." But G. soon retired to his estate to write a novel he had begun to conceive around 1919. This was *Don Segundo Sombra* (1926; *Don Segundo Sombra: Shadows on the Pampas,* 1935), his last work.

As is the case with many Spanish American writers, G.'s fame rests on a single work. *Don Segundo Sombra* brought its author instant success. It tells the story of an orphan who follows Don Segundo Sombra, an old gaucho, who initiates him into the life of the roaming cowboys of the pampas at the time of their imminent disappearance, since progress was destroying their precious freedom and forcing them to become farmhands. The novel is, then, the portrait of a virile frontier life about to recede into the past, and the scenes it contains thus have the feeling of a fond farewell: encounters at a country store, dances, folkloric tales, cock fights, long herding cavalcades, stampedes, and knife duels. G.'s style, polished to perfection, is a harmonious blend of avant-garde metaphoric elegance and gaucho popular language. The novel can be classified as a *Bildungsroman* describing the upbringing of a lad under the guidance of a wise elder; it has been said that it reveals the influence of Cervantes's *Don Quixote,* Mark

Twain's *Adventures of Huckleberry Finn,* and Rudyard Kipling's (q.v.) *Kim.*

The genesis of this novel must ultimately be found in Domingo Faustino Sarmiento's (1811–1888) essay *Facundo: Civilization and Barbarism* (1845), in which the gaucho, the savage master of the plains, is portrayed in his hour of triumph. A sequel to the biography of the pampas is José Hernández's (1834–1886) *Martín Fierro* (1872, 1879), the Argentine epic poem that describes the gaucho when, defeated by progress, he has to submit to assimilating to a life on the farms or in the cities. The freedom-loving cowboy thus dies, and G.'s novel met the need to portray this type when he was becoming nothing but a mere shadow of an epic past. But *Don Segundo Sombra* is a quite complex novel, since it also afforded a glimpse into the future. G. published it when Latin Americans had begun the quest for their identity. And *Don Segundo Sombra* made clear that a firm identity rested only on the bonds between man and the land. This novel thus buries the world of a breed of men who had had such an identity and foreshadows the advent of another, the world of the alienated man of today.

FURTHER WORKS: *Poemas místicos* (1928); *Poemas solitarios* (1921–27); *Seis relatos* (1929); *Pampa: Poemas inéditos* (1954)

BIBLIOGRAPHY: Chapman, A. G., "Pampas and Big Woods: Heroic Initiation in G. and Faulkner," *CL,* 11 (1959), 61–77; Weiss, G. H., "Technique in the Works of R. G.," *Hispania,* 43 (1960), 353–58; Previtali, G., *R. G. and "Don Segundo Sombra": Life and Works* (1963); Ghiano, J. C., *Introducción a R. G.* (1967); Beardsell, P. R., "French Influences on G.," *BHS,* 46 (1968), 511–44; Saz, S. M. de, "G. and Rudyard Kipling," *Neophil,* 55 (1971), 270–84; Echevarría, E., "Nuevo acercamiento a la estructura de *Don Segundo Sombra,*" *RI,* 40 (1974), 629–37

EVELIO ECHEVARRÍA

GUJARATI LITERATURE
See Indian Literature

GULLBERG, Hjalmar
Swedish poet, b. 30 May 1898, Malmö; d. 19 July 1961, Bökebergsslätt

G., born out of wedlock, was left by his mother in the care of foster parents, whose name he adopted. In 1927 he received an advanced degree in literature from the University of Lund, which awarded him an honorary doctorate in 1944. From 1936 on G. was program director for drama of the Swedish National Broadcasting Corporation. In 1940 he became a member of the Swedish Academy.

In his very first collection of poetry, *I en främmande stad* (1927; in a strange city), G. displayed a very personal style, which harked back to the high-spirited, witty rhymings of his student days. He borrowed his means of expression from a variety of sources ranging from religious hymns to contemporary journalistic jargon and gave his poems an elegant, at times flippant form through unconventional rhymes, deliberate anachronisms, and startling contrasts by mingling the sublime and the trivial. Although aware of the danger of this style's becoming a mannerism, G. never completely abandoned his fondness for ironic juxtapositions in form and content. Behind his attitude of a detached and skeptical observer and a cosmopolitan tourist in life, G. expressed religious and metaphysical concerns and a sense of his poetic calling. *Andliga övningar* (1932; spiritual exercises) and *Att övervinna världen* (1937; to conquer the world) abound in Christian symbols, from Bethlehem to Golgotha, and show a leaning toward mysticism and a wish to escape from the world in self-effacement and death.

In *Kärlek i tjugonde seklet* (1933; love in the twentieth century) G. caught the modern erotic sensibility in a series of love poems in which a sober medical or psychoanalytical terminology alternates with expressions of sensuous exultation, melancholy reflections on partings, and bitter regrets.

The previously mentioned *Att övervinna världen*, as well as *Fem kornbröd och två fiskar* (1942; five loaves and two fishes) show an increased awareness of the political situation in Europe. G., who had been staying in Berlin at the time of Hitler's takeover, displays an unremitting opposition to the fascist ideologies of violence.

After an unproductive period during the 1940s G. returned with *Dödsmask och lustgård* (1952; death mask and garden of delights). G.'s fascination with ancient Greece and his familiarity with its myths and literature (as a translator he brought a number of classical Greek dramas to the Swedish public) had always been evident in his poetry. In contrast to the earlier sun-drenched Apollonian visions of Hellas, the later collections emphasize the dark,

tragic aspects of Greek antiquity, and the figures of Dionysus, Orpheus, and Christ merge into one embodiment of the timeless sufferings of man and his gods.

G.'s last collection of poetry, *Ögon, läppar* (1959; eyes, lips), marks a high point in his production. Written during his agonizingly protracted illness, the poems are whittled down to a naked simplicity and stripped of illusions in the face of death. The collection contains some of G.'s most moving love poems dedicated to the woman who had been his companion during his last years.

Except for some early experimentations in free verse, G. remained within the discipline of established verse forms. His poetry derives its strength from the tensions between a modern skeptical sensibility, a classical traditionalism, and a yearning for religious commitment.

FURTHER WORKS: *Sonat* (1929); *Ensamstående bildad herre* (1935); *Terziner i okonstens tid* (1958). FURTHER VOLUME IN ENGLISH: *"Gentleman, Single, Refined," and Selected Poems, 1937–1959* (1979)

BIBLIOGRAPHY: Vowles, R. B., "H. G., An Ancient and a Modern," *SS*, 24 (1952), 111–18; Sjöberg, L., Foreword to *"Gentleman, Single, Refined," and Selected Poems, 1937–1959* (1979), pp. xi–xvii

LARS G. WARME

GUMILYOV, Nikolay Stepanovich

Russian poet, literary theorist, and dramatist, b. 3 April 1886, Kronstadt (now Kronshlot); d. Aug. 1921, Petrograd? (now Leningrad)

G.'s father was a doctor in the Russian navy. G. was educated at the Imperial Lyceum at Tsarskoe Selo (now Pushkin) and in St. Petersburg. While at school he met the future poet Anna Akhmatova (q.v.), whom he married in 1910. After finishing secondary school in Russia, he enrolled at the Sorbonne in 1906 or 1907. In 1907 G. made his first of several trips to Africa. The subject of Africa was to remain important throughout his creative work.

Before the revolution G. played a central role in the literary life of St. Petersburg as one of the chief theorists and proponents of the Acmeist school of poetry. During the first years of World War I G. saw action in Prussia and Poland. Between the March and October 1917 revolutions he traveled as a lieutenant to Paris, where he stayed for six months, then went to

London for three months. He returned to Petrograd in May 1918.

On August 3, 1921, G. was arrested by the Petrograd Secret Police for alleged involvement in a counterrevolutionary conspiracy. His execution was announced on September 1, 1921, about one week after it had taken place. His burial place remains unknown.

G.'s first three books of poems—*Put konkvistadorov* (1905; path of the conquistadors), *Romanticheskie tsvety* (1908; romantic flowers), and *Zhemchuga* (1910; pearls)—contain, at least in germinal form, all the major themes that were to occupy G.'s more mature work: the search for an ideal love, the conflict between earthly passion and spirituality, the theme of adventure, including wandering, conquest, and battle. All three books were written under the heavy influence of the major writers of Russian Decadence, Bryusov, Bely, and Balmont (qq.v.). They have been criticized for their overabundance of exotic colors, decorative imagery, and bombastic tone.

Chuzhoe nebo (1912; foreign skies) marked the end of G.'s apprenticeship to Bryusov and the other Decadents. It was the culmination of of his participation in the Poets' Guild and the Acmeist school. The tenets of Acmeism included balance, precision, clarity, craftsmanship, respect for tradition, and restraint. The movement opposed the dominant though declining school of Russian symbolism (q.v.), an opposition articulated by G. and Sergey Mitrofanovich Gorodetsky (1884–1967) in articles about the nature of the word in poetry. Acmeism did not deny the appropriateness of spiritual themes for poetry. It defended, however, the place of *this* world, with its own colors, forms, weight, and time, in modern poetry. It argued for the direct, clear, referential properties of language.

With its almost complete lack of fantasy, with its more direct expression of personal lyricism, with its simple and more straightforward style, *Chuzhoe nebo* is G.'s most Acmeist work. It is significant that G. included five of his translations of Théophile Gautier in this book of poems. That spiritual themes are not excluded from the Acmeist canon is demonstrated by the central place religious impulses occupy in this book. Yet even here the accent is on earthly experience and the poet's struggle to reconcile his quest for spiritual purity with his belief in the transcendent value of intense physical experience.

Kolchan (1916; the quiver) and *Shatyor* (1921; the tent) develop a tendency in G.'s work toward a more strongly expressed subjective artistic personality. The themes of love, battle, exotic travels, and religion, all important in *Kolchan,* are found in its central autobiographical poem "Pyatistopnye yamby" (1913; iambic pentameters). G.'s attraction to Africa, expressed in *Shatyor,* complements his own deeply felt attraction to extreme situations that tested and provoked elemental human drives: poetry, war, kingly rule, and erotic passions.

G.'s last two books, *Kostyor* (1918; the pyre) and *Ognenny stolp* (1921; the fiery pillar), are concerned with the fantastic, with the ineffable, and with ideal love. They are, in a sense, a return to the metaphysical concerns of symbolism. The romantic conception of love as a link between the earthly and the ideal runs throughout G.'s work, but it becomes central to the love lyrics of *Kostyor.* The experience of love becomes a way of access to the world of the ideal, but the beloved remains the remote "blue star," a shadowy female presence, always ultimately unattainable, always the source of erotic frustration.

The appearance of Russia as a theme is connected with the increasing interpenetration of the lyrical world of the poet with the world around him. This process reaches a climax in two fantastic poems from his last books: "Muzhik" ("The Muzhik," 1972) in *Kostyor* and "Zabludivshysya tramvay" ("The Lost Tram," 1972) in *Ognenny stolp.* "Muzhik" is a vision of half-pagan peasants marching out of primeval Russian bogs and forests against an alien urban civilization imposed by St. Petersburg. "Zabludivshysya tramvay" concerns itself with the fate of Russia and the Orthodox religion and with the poet's own personal concern for his love.

G. also wrote six dramatic works, three of them little more than one-act sketches. Only *Otravlennaya tunika* (written 1917–18, pub. 1952; *The Poisoned Tunic,* 1972), a tragedy, can be considered a true, full-length play, and it stands comparison with his better lyric and narrative poetry.

G.'s work occupies a significant place in the history of modern Russian poetry. Although he has never been extensively published in Soviet Russia, he continues to be a significant presence for Russian poets both within the U.S.S.R. and in the emigration.

FURTHER WORKS: *Akteon* (1913); *Gondla* (1917); *Ditya Allakha* (1917); *Farforovy pavilon* (1918); *Mik: Afrikanskaya poema* (1918); *Ten ot palmy* (1922); *Pisma o russkoy poezii* (1923); *Sobranie sochineny* (4 vols., 1962–68). FURTHER VOLUMES IN ENGLISH: *The Abinger Garland* (1945); *Selected Works* (1972); *N. G. on Russian Poetry* (1977)

BIBLIOGRAPHY: Strakhovsky, L., *Three Poets of Modern Russia* (1949), pp. 5–52; Maline, M., *N. G., poète et critique acméiste* (1964); Monas, S., "G.: Âkme and Adam in St. Petersburg," in *N. G., Selected Works* (1972), pp. 3–26; Sampson, E. D., *N. G.* (1979)

GERALD PIROG

GUNNARSSON, Gunnar

Icelandic poet, dramatist, essayist, and novelist (writing in Danish and Icelandic), b. 18 May 1889, Fljótsdalur parish; d. 21 Nov. 1975, Reykjavík

G.'s father was a farmer. The early death of his mother left deep psychological scars on him, as many passages in his writings clearly suggest. His father was poor, so the boy received little formal education.

G. made his literary debut with two collections of verse: *Vorljóð* (1906; spring poems) and *Móðurminning* (1906; remembering mother). In order to get some education and to establish himself as a writer, he went to Denmark in 1907, enrolling there at the folk high school of Askov, where he studied until 1909. He lived in Denmark until 1939, when he returned to Iceland.

As a writer in Danish, G. first published a volume of poems entitled *Digte* (1911; poems), but his breakthrough work was the tetralogy of novels *Borgslægtens historie* (4 vols., 1912–14; abridged tr., *Guest the One-Eyed*, 1920)—consisting of *Ormarr Ørlygsson* (1912; Ormarr Ørlygsson), *Den danske frue på Hof* (1913; the Danish lady at Hof), *Gæst den enøjede* (1913; Guest the one-eyed), and *Den unge ørn* (1914; the young eagle). This "history of the family at Borg" is a neoromantic family chronicle set in Iceland for which G. created a special character type that was to recur frequently in his subsequent fiction: the solid and dependable Icelandic farmer. In this case, however, the farmer's two sons belong to different worlds; one is a dreamer and a noble-minded artist, torn between the call of his art and the call of the soil where he has his roots, while his brother is a demonic evildoer whose

misdeeds stem from blind instinct. The conflicts in the story grow out of the tension between these two polarities—a dualism that was to become one of the prime characteristics of G.'s fiction.

World War I was a severe blow for G., demolishing, as he saw it, his ideological world view, and the next phase of his literary career evinces deep pessimism as well as a struggle with psychological and ethical problems. Thus, his novel *Livets strand* (1915; the shore of life) focuses on the tragic life of a clergyman caught in a bind between the principle of human reason and his faith in divine providence. *Varg i veum* (1916; wolf in sacred places) concerns the ruin of a young man who has rebelled against bourgeois standards of decency. *Salige er enfoldige* (1920; *Seven Days' Darkness,* 1930) takes place in Reykjavík in seven days while the Spanish flu is raging—against a backdrop of a volcanic eruption.

Departing after 1920 from the pessimistic psychological tack, G. returned to material from his youth and place of origin, with his five-volume fictionalized autobiography *Kirken på bjerget* (1923–28; the church on the mountain; tr. of Vols. I–III, *Ships in the Sky,* 1938, and *The Night and the Dream,* 1938). *Kirken på bjerget* is at once the story of the maturing of a young writer and a significant contribution to cultural history, since it is also an account of rural life in Iceland at the turn of the century.

In the period 1920–40 G. was also a very productive essayist. He lectured extensively in the Nordic countries, and also in Germany, where he won acceptance and became a significant influence as a writer. The unification of the Nordic countries is a central concept in his essays, while they deal, broadly speaking, with Icelandic culture and Icelandic problems. A selection was published as *Det nordiske rige* (1927; the Nordic state).

G. supplemented the thoroughgoing self-examination of *Kirken på bjerget* by charting in a similar way the nature and fate of the Icelandic nation—a work he envisioned as a twelve-volume series of historical novels, although he never completed it. The first was *Edbrødre* (1918; *The Sworn Brothers,* 1920), about the first two settlers in Iceland. In *Jord* (1933; earth), G. moved on to the establishment of an organized state in the early history of the nation; this book contains a strong element of religious mysticism, with ancient Nordic paganism shown as being typified by a reverence for life, simple worship, and belief in fate. A similar mystical feeling also runs deep in *Hvide-*

Krist (1934; white Christ), which focuses on events leading to Iceland's conversion to Christianity around the year 1000. *Gråmand* (1936; the man in gray) treats of the incipient dissolution of the Icelandic Commonwealth during the 13th c., while *Jón Arason* (1930; Jón Arason) is both the story of the last Catholic bishop in Iceland and a survey of the nation's transition to a new religious order during the Reformation (the first half of the 16th c.).

Not all of G.'s works are so concerned with Icelandic history. *Svartfugl* (1939; *The Black Cliffs*, 1967), for example, which is based on a murder case in about 1800, is a novel shot through with religious mysticism, but also a psychological probing of the evil in human nature. Another novel, *Vikivaki* (1932; folk dance), G.'s most enigmatic work of fiction, is an absurdist fantasy about the responsibility of a writer toward his art and toward humanity.

After his return to Iceland, G. wrote and published his books in his native language. While he had projected a five-volume series of novels on life and social developments in Iceland during the first half of the 20th c., he completed only two: *Heiðaharmur* (1940; grief in the mountains) and *Sálumessa* (1952; requiem). His last work was *Brimhenda* (1954; the sonata of the sea), a short novel.

The hallmarks of G.'s fiction are strong individualism, psychological insight, and religious mysticism—as well as creation of characters of an unusual range. Although the bulk of his literary output is the work of an expatriate, G. derived his subject matter exclusively from his native soil, and his descriptions of life in Iceland have great immediacy, at the same time viewing what is characteristically Icelandic from an artistic distance.

FURTHER WORKS: *Sögur* (1912); *Små historier* (1916); *Små skuespil* (1917); *Drengen* (1917); *Små historier II* (1918); *Ringen* (1921); *Dyret med glorien* (1922); *Den glade gård, og andre historier* (1923); *Island* (1929); *En dag til overs, og andre historier* (1929); *Rævepelsene* (1930); *Verdens glæder* (1931); *De blindes hus* (1933); *Sagaøen* (1935); *Advent* (1937; *Advent*, 1939 [repub. as *The Good Shepherd*, 1940]); *Das Rätsel um Didrik Pining* (1939); *Trylle og andet småkram* (1939; *Trylle and Other Small Fry*, 1947); *Siðmenning og siðspilling* (1943); *Árbók 45* (1945); *Árbók 46–47* (1948); *Vestræn menning og kommúnismi* (1954); *Rit* (21 vols., 1941–63); *Skáldverk* (19 vols., 1960–63)

BIBLIOGRAPHY: Einarsson, S., *A History of Icelandic Literature* (1957), pp. 285–87

SVEINN SKORRI HÖSKULDSSON

GUSTAFSSON, Lars

Swedish poet, novelist, dramatist, essayist, and critic, b. 17 May 1936, Västerås

G. spent his childhood in Västmanland, mostly in the city of Västerås but also in the country district of northern Västmanland: both locales recur frequently in his works. G. studied philosophy at Uppsala University, receiving a "fil. lic." (doctorate) degree in 1961 and a Ph.D. in 1978. G. edited the influential *Bonniers litterära magasin* from 1961 to 1972. He was elected to the Academy of Art, West Berlin, in 1974. G.'s world travels are reflected in many of his works, such as *Världsdelar* (1975; continents), *Kinesisk höst* (1978; Chinese fall), and *Afrikanskt försök* (1980; African attempt). G.'s several extended visits to the U.S. have inspired poems in *Bröderna Wright uppsöker Kitty Hawk* (1968; the Wright brothers visit Kitty Hawk), and the novella *Tennisspelarna* (1977; the tennis players), set at the University of Texas in Austin, where G. taught in 1976 and again in 1979.

G.'s fusion of international and home-district backgrounds in his works makes him at once cosmopolitan and regional, a combination used to masterly effect in *Kärleksförklaring till en sefardisk dam* (1970; declaration of love to a Sephardic lady), a long poem that ranges from Västmanland to Berlin to the Sinai desert. G.'s early reputation was mainly that of a lyric poet. *Sonetter* (1977; sonnets) marked G.'s return to poetry after almost a decade of writing prose. The fixed-form poetry of *Sonetter*, skillful and intricate sonnets and sestinas, are departures from G.'s earlier free verse. However, the melancholy theme of homelessness in the world again dominates. In *Artesiska brunnar cartesiska drömmar* (1980; artesian wells Cartesian dreams) G. uses strongly rhythmic free verse in poems that pose philosophical riddles or explore the theses of philosophers such as Descartes and Kant.

G.'s play *Den nattliga hyllningen* (homage at night), published in *Två maktspel* (1970; two power plays), received particularly favorable attention in Germany and Switzerland. Although set in 19th-c. Västerås, the play deals with contemporary misuses of power.

G.'s doctoral thesis, *Språk och lögn* (1978; language and lies), and his more popularly written *Filosofier* (1979; philosophies) evidence an interest in semantic problems like those explored by Ludwig Wittgenstein (1889–1951) and Noam Chomsky (b. 1928), an interest that found earlier expression in his essays, especially those in *Utopier* (1969; utopias).

G.'s greatest achievement to date is a series of five novels with the overall title *Sprickorna i muren* (1971–78; the cracks in the wall): *Herr Gustafsson själv* (1971; Mr. Gustafsson himself) is an autobiographical novel dealing with G.'s time as an editor and with a prolonged stay in West Berlin. *Yllet* (1973; wool) focuses on problems of depopulation and dehumanization in rural Västmanland. *Familjefesten* (1975; the family party) is concerned with political power and corruption in Swedish society. *Sigismund* (1976; Sigismund) develops the themes of the power of the subconscious and of science-fiction fantasy first introduced in *Yllet*. After the inferno and purgatory of the first four novels, *En biodlares död* (1978; *Death of a Beekeeper,* 1981) supposedly takes us to paradise, which turns out to be absence of pain as experienced by the dying protagonist; true paradise can only be shown in fantasy, in a science-fiction section entitled "När Gud vaknade" (when God awoke).

G. is one of the most productive and versatile of contemporary Swedish writers, and because his works address problems common to all Western societies, he is also one of the Swedish writers of his generation best known outside his country.

FURTHER WORKS: *Vägvila* (1957); *Poeten Brumbergs sista dagar och dod* (1959); *Bröderna* (1960); *Nio brev om romanen* (1961, with Lars Bäckström); *Följeslagarna* (1962); *Ballongfararna* (1962); *Enförmiddag i Sverige* (1963); *The Public Dialogue in Sweden* (1964); *En resa till jordens medelpunkt och andra dikter* (1966); *Den egentliga berättelsen om herr Arenander* (1966); *Förberedelser till flykt, och andra berättelser* (1967); *Utopier* (1969); *Konsten att segla med drakar* (1969); *Varma rum och kalla* (1972); *Kommentarer* (1972); *Den onödiga samtiden* (1974, with Jan Myrdal); *Strandhugg i svensk poesi* (1976; *Forays into Swedish Poetry,* 1978); *Den lilla världen* (1977); *Konfrontationer* (1979); *I mikroskopet* (1979); *För liberlismen* (1981); *Lyckliga människor* (1981). FURTHER VOLUMES IN ENGLISH: *Selected Poems* (1972); *Warm Rooms and Cold* (1975)

BIBLIOGRAPHY: Höllerer, W., "L. G.," *Ein Gedicht und sein Autor: Lyrik und Essay* (1967), pp. 7–35; Sjögren, L., "Eine Seltsame Landschaft: Über die Lyrik L. G.s," *Akzente,* 17 (1969), 424–35; Sandstroem, Y., "The Machine Theme in Some Poems by L. G." *SS,* 44 (1972), 210–23; Sandstroem, Y., "Three Poems from the New World: Translation and Commentary," *The American-Swedish '72,* pp. 31–36; Rovinsky, R., " 'The Machines': Translation and Commentary," *American Review,* 21 (1974), 116–25; Mortensson, J., "G.'s Bee-Keeper," *Swedish Books,* 2 (1979), 6–7

YVONNE L. SANDSTROEM

GÜTERSLOH, Albert Paris

(pseud. of Albert Konrad Kiehtreiber) Austrian novelist and poet, b. 5 Feb. 1887, Vienna; d. 16 May 1973, Baden

Educated for the priesthood, G. refused to take the vows; instead he studied painting (with Gustav Klimt) and acting; in 1907 he went to Berlin, where he worked with Max Reinhardt as a stage designer and director. There he wrote his first novel, *Die tanzende Törin* (1911; shortened version, 1913; the dancing fool), an early example of expressionist (q.v.) prose. In 1929 he was appointed professor at the Vienna School for Applied Arts. After the Anschluss in 1938 he was forced to resign his professorship and to do factory and office work. In 1945 he became a professor at the Vienna Academy of Fine Arts; he served as its rector from 1954 to 1955. In 1952 he was awarded the Austrian State Prize for painting; in 1961 he received the same award for literature.

Although G.'s early prose works are significant contributions to the development of expressionism, his writing cannot be explained in terms of any particular modern school or literary movement. His art is the result of his unusual life and his diverse talents. A strong inclination toward theological-philosophical speculation is equaled by the painter's sensuous delight in surfaces and textures. By means of his humor G. overcame dialectically the tensions between his talents and interests, the spiritual and the sensual, the divine and the human. His writing also reflects a love of the baroque—its vitality, exaggeration, obscurity, and lucidity, and its view of the world as a stage. In this preference G. is profoundly Austrian.

G.'s very unusual autobiography, *Bekenntnisse eines modernen Malers: Quasi un'allego-*

ria (1926; confessions of a modern painter: almost an allegory), can serve as an introduction to his life's work. *Kain und Abel* (1924; Cain and Abel) is called a legend, but *Die Vision vom Alten und vom Neuen* (1921; the vision of the old and the new) and *Innozenz; oder, Sinn und Fluch der Unschuld* (1922; Innozenz; or, the meaning and curse of innocence) are also closer to allegory and legend than to realism.

The subtitle of the last mentioned—the meaning and curse of innocence (which could also be translated as "purity")—characterizes well the central preoccupation of these shorter works as well as an important theme of the novels *Die tanzende Törin, Der Lügner unter Bürgern* (1922; The Fraud, 1965), and *Eine sagenhafte Figur* (1946; a legendary figure). These three works focus on the theme of the fate of spiritual purity in an impure, material world. The stories of *Die Fabeln vom Eros* (1947; the fables of Eros) actually move more and more out of the realm of allegory, legend, and fable and into that of realistic narrative.

G. is most accessible to the reader in his late collection of stories *Laßt uns den Menschen machen* (1962; let us create man) and the major novel *Sonne und Mond: Ein historischer Roman aus der Gegenwart* (written 1935–62, pub. 1962; sun and moon: a historical novel from the present). It is one of the great original novels of Austrian self-interpretation. The story is centered upon Austria, yet manages easily to soar almost everywhere in time and space; it is a delightful pretext for the author to give us the sum total of his wisdom and insight gathered in a lifetime of seventy-five years. Count Lunarin has inherited a ramshackle castle near the village of "Recklingen." No sooner has Lunarin, the "moon" of the novel, arrived in the village than he meets a former love of his and takes off again, yet not without first selecting a caretaker for his castle during his absence of just three days. The three days, however, stretch into a full year and the manager, a rich and capable farmer named Till Adelseher, is simply forced —and tempted—to rebuild the run-down castle from his own funds. Till's "sunlike" conscientiousness exceeds by far the rights bestowed upon him by his absent master. After a year the count returns and makes a present of the refurbished castle to his eager manager, but takes from him the woman Till loves.

On one level of meaning, the novel can be read as an allegory of Austria between 1913 and 1938, on another as being about the idea of kingship and the question of succession; birth

stands against virtue, ontological man is played against logical man. But these are only a few of the subtle implications of this major work. G.'s humor and wit, his linguistic and metaphoric inventiveness all come to his aid in building a baroque castle that is the very opposite of Kafka's (q.v.) abstractly constructed *The Castle.*

FURTHER WORKS: *Egon Schiele* (1911); *Die Rede über Franz Blei; oder, der Schriftsteller in der Katholizität* (1922); *Der Maler Alexander Gartenberg* (1928); *Musik zu einem Lebenslauf* (1957); *Gewaltig staunt der Mensch* (1963); *Zur Situation der modernen Kunst* (1963); *Der innere Erdteil* (1966); *Zwischen den Zeiten* (1967); *Die Fabel von der Freundschaft* (1969); *Miniaturen zur Schöpfung* (1970); *Paradiese der Liebe* (1972); *Treppe ohne Haus* (1974); *Beispiele* (1977); *Briefe an Milena 1932–1970* (1980)

BIBLIOGRAPHY: Doderer, H. von, *Der Fall G.: Ein Schicksal und seine Deutung* (1930); Blei, F., *Schriften in Auswahl, Nachwort von A. P. G.* (1960), pp. 288–94; *A. P. G.: Autor und Werk* (1962); Basil, O., Eisenreich, H., and Ivask, I., *Das große Erbe: Aufsätze zur österreichischen Literatur* (1962), passim; Ivask, I., "Sonne und Mond," *BA*, 37 (1963), 304–5; Thurner, F., *A. P. G. Studien zu seinem Romanwerk* (1970); Prokop, H. F., "A. P. G.: Bibliographie," *LuK*, 68 (1972), 483–92; Hutter, H., *A. P. G. Beispiele: Schriften zur Kunst/Bilder/Werkverzeichnis* (1977)

IVAR IVASK

GUYANESE LITERATURE
See English-Caribbean Literature

GUZMÁN, Martín Luis
Mexican novelist, essayist, journalist, and editor, b. 6 Oct. 1887, Chihuahua; d. 22 Dec. 1976, Mexico City

G. spent his childhood in Mexico City and Veracruz. At the age of fifteen he enrolled in the National Preparatory School, famous for its programs in mathematics and the sciences. He received a degree in jurisprudence from the National University of Mexico in 1913.

The life, literary work, and journalistic career of G. parallel and reflect the beginning, consummation, and consolidation of events of the Mexican Revolution in successive stages of its trajectory. He was a member of the Atheneum of Youth, a firm supporter of the political leader Francisco Madero, and a partisan and adviser of General Francisco (Pancho) Villa. For political and ideological reasons he spent the years 1915–20 and 1924–36 in exile, principally in Spain but also in the U.S. In Spain he edited the periodicals *El sol* and *La voz* and wrote and also published two of his most famous works: *El águila y la serpiente* (1928; *The Eagle and the Serpent*, 1930) and *La sombra del caudillo* (1929; in the leader's shadow). *La sombra del caudillo,* an authentic story of intrigue and violence set in the 1920s in the period of political dominance in Mexico of Álvaro Obregón, is probably Spanish America's best political novel.

Back in Mexico City to stay in 1936, G. founded the review *Romance* (1940–41) and in 1942 *Tiempo,* which ranks as Spanish America's most prestigious news weekly. He was elected to the Mexican Academy in 1954. In 1958 he received the National Prize for Literature. As a politician he served in both houses of the Mexican legislature.

In the years following his return to Mexico G. wrote and published a five-volume work titled *Memorias de Pancho Villa* (1938–51; *Memoirs of Pancho Villa,* 1965), employing the style in which Villa talked. While some critics consider this work to be his masterpiece, most G. scholars assign this distinction to *El águila y la serpiente.* G.'s contrast of the eagle, representing "idealism," with the serpent, representing "Calibanism," provides a graphic and universal image of the polarities involved in the experience of the Mexican Revolution.

Contrasts constitute basic and unifying structural components of G.'s major works. Images of light and shadow are used in the presentation of characters and situations: Pancho Villa is portrayed as having a flawed personality but as being well motivated in intent and potentially a serviceable idealist; the Mexican Revolution is seen as a dynamic aspiration and hope culminating in a truncated opportunity and result; postrevolution politics is depicted as a viscous web of venal interests and violence undermining the thrust for national regeneration and reconstruction.

Because of his distinctive style and his insights into recent historical events and personalities, G. is considered one of the best prose writers in Spanish of the 20th c.

FURTHER WORKS: *La querella de México* (1915); *A orillas del Hudson* (1917); *Mina el*

mozo: Héroe de Navarra (1932); *Filadelfia, paraíso de conspiradores* (1933); *Kinchil* (1946); *El liberalismo mexicano en pensamiento y acción* (15 vols., 1947–50); *Apunte sobre una personalidad* (1954); *Islas Marías, novela y drama* (1959); *Obras completas* (2 vols., 1961)

BIBLIOGRAPHY: Morton, F. R., *Los novelistas de la revolución mexicana* (1949), pp. 115–40; Carballo, E., *Diecinueve protagonistas de la literatura mexicana del siglo XX* (1965), pp. 61–99; Carter, B. G., "El contraste como eje literario de *El águila y la serpiente,*" *Revista mexicana de cultura,* 28 Feb. 1965, 1–2; Brushwood, J. S., *Mexico in Its Novel* (1970), pp. 200–203; Ocampo de Gómez, A., and Prado Velázquez, E., *Diccionario de escritores mexicanos* (1967), pp. 166–68; Langford, W. M., *The Mexican Novel Comes of Age* (1971), pp. 39–42; Alegría, F., *Historia de la novela hispanoamericana* (1974), pp. 146–49

BOYD G. CARTER

GYLLENSTEN, Lars

Swedish novelist and essayist, b. 12 Nov. 1921, Stockholm

Concurrently with his literary work, G. has pursued a medical career. He received his medical degree in 1948 and then resumed research in histology at Caroline Institute, the famous teaching hospital in Stockholm, where he worked as a teacher and researcher after 1953. He left this post in 1973 to devote himself completely to writing. G. was elected to the Swedish Academy in 1966 and has been its permanent secretary since 1977.

G.'s first published work was a parody of 1940s' surrealist poetry, *Camera obscura* (1946; Latin: dark room, punning on "obscure"), written with his friend Torgny Greitz (b. 1913) and published under the pseudonym Jan Wictor. *Camera obscura* received a great deal of attention—it did not altogether come across as the hoax it was intended to be—but it remains G.'s only excursion into poetry.

In his novels G. is a consistent experimenter, both in form and in the attitude toward life displayed in the different works. The role of the narrator in particular has been interesting to G., some of whose earlier novels, in particular *Barnabok* (1952; child book) can be seen as a reaction to the "absent author" device (whose most renowned exponent is James Joyce [q.v.]) characteristic of many Swedish novels of the 1940s and 1950s. G. instead stresses the novel as art form, as conscious manipulation of and experimentation with several possible realities, rather than as a "slice of life" representing this reality. G.'s technical experiments also take the form of so-called collage novels, in G.'s case a collection of texts not assembled from different quarters, but written and arranged by the author himself. The most typical and most fragmented of these collage novels is *Juvenilia* (1965; Latin: writings of/about youth). His nonfiction prose, as well, for example, *Diarium spirituale* (1968; Latin: spiritual diary) and *Lapptäcken–Livstecken* (1976; patchwork quilts–signs of life), consisting of G.'s own work notes, comments, and reflections, make a collage impression.

Like Ibsen and Kierkegaard (the latter profoundly influenced G.), G. often explores a particular personality type and attitude toward life to plumb its opposite in a following work. Thus, in *Barnabok* an essentially infantile reaction to life is presented, while *Senilia* (1956; Latin: writings of/about old age) exhibits a more mature personality type but with a distancing attitude toward life that brings its own difficulties. Several critics have seen *Barnabok* and *Senilia* as thesis and antithesis, with *Juvenilia* as synthesis, an attempt to reconcile the opposing attitudes of the two earlier novels.

Like many modern authors, such as Thomas Mann (q.v.) and Joyce, both of whom influenced his work, G. often uses myth. Thus the Jonah myth serves as a frame of reference in *Barnabok*, the Pasiphaë myth in *Senatorn* (1958; the senator). In later works myth is used for a deeper purpose, as revealing permanent truth about the human condition. *Palatset i parken* (1970; the palace in the park) uses the Orpheus myth as its thematic basis.

G.'s realization that, as he says in *Lapptäcken–Livstecken*, his exploration of humanity can provide neither final answers nor final victory has resulted in his consistently questioning stance and also contributed to the difficulty of his novels, for the problems he deals with admit neither easy answers nor easy treatment. G. is one of the most important and influential of contemporary Swedish novelists, as well as one of the most rewarding.

FURTHER WORKS: *Moderna myter* (1949); *Blå skeppet* (1950); *Carnivora* (1953); *Sokrates död* (1960); *Desperados* (1962); *Kains memoarer* (1963; *The Testament of Cain*, 1967); *Nihilistiskt credo* (1964); *Lotus i Hades* (1966); *Ur min offentliga sektor* (1971); *Mänskan, djuren, all naturen* (1971); *Grottan i öknen* (1973); *I skuggan av Don Juan* (1975)

BIBLIOGRAPHY: Sjöberg, L., "L. G.: Master of Arts and Science," *ASR*, 55 (1967), 158–62; Isaksson, H., *L. G.* (1978); Warme, L., "L. G.'s *Diarium spirituale*: The Creative Process as a Novel," *Scan*, 19 (1980), 165–80

YVONNE L. SANDSTROEM

HAANPÄÄ, Pentti

Finnish novelist and short-story writer, b. 14 Oct. 1905, Piippola; d. 1 Oct. 1955, Piippola

During his lifetime H. was the object of several persistent misconceptions: that he held communist sympathies; and that he was a kind of natural genius—a writer who came by his talent without the help of family background, training, or wide reading. In fact, both his grandfather and father were published authors, and H. himself conscientiously prepared for a literary career by wide reading, even in the English language. As to his communist sympathies, these were in large part attributed to him by a populace made conservative by the Finnish civil war of 1918, during which communist revolutionary activities were seen as a threat to Finnish independence. Except for brief travels, he lived quietly and simply in Piippola, a town in northern Finland. He is presumed to have died by suicide.

The predominant tone of H.'s writing is one of disillusion. He subjects life to rational scrutiny and finds no reliable source of happiness. Human relations, in his view, both private and social, produce only frustration. H.'s one comfort is in nature; he finds something approaching joy in its peace, beauty, and steadfastness. Consequently H.'s favorite character is the lumberjack, whose life is free and who is attuned to the seasons and the forces of nature.

The destruction of this natural freedom is the theme of most of H.'s writings. In his most controversial work, the collection of short stories *Kenttä ja kasarmi* (1928; the field and the garrison), H. criticized the peacetime military for moral decay. The book aroused such a violent outcry that no publisher would publish H.'s works for the next seven years. In the enthusiastic promilitary atmosphere of Finland in the 1920s, any criticism of the army, the instrument and symbol of national independence, was interpreted as socialism or communism. Seen from today, these stories seem to address only H.'s constant subject: the violation of human liberty by social institutions.

H. depicted the military in several other works, notably the novels *Vääpeli Sadon tapaus* (written 1935, pub. 1956; the case of Sergeant Major Sato), *Korpisotaa* (1940; war in the wilderness), and *Yhdeksän miehen saappaat* (1945; the boots of nine men). These works all have a war setting, but in them the author condemns war itself.

In 1931, while under the publishing boycott, H. wrote his best novel, the posthumously published *Noitaympyrä* (1956; the vicious circle). It is about a lumberjack who, in spite of his misgivings about society, gets a job, advances to foreman, but quits in protest against company pressures. He experiences the hardships of unemployment and poverty. He then meets an unusual and well-educated man from the south and spends a summer of freedom with him in remote Lapland. The companion, however, has an automobile accident and ultimately commits suicide. The protagonist, left alone, makes a quick decision: he walks over the border to the Soviet Union and disappears. His act is presented not as a solution but as an act of despair.

H.'s reputation rests chiefly on his short stories, of which he published twelve collections. He is a true master of short fiction, many of his novels being in effect only series of short episodes. His stories, with their colorful and expressive language, are written in a style that gives the reader a feeling of actually listening to a master teller of tales. In fact, H. is said to have used the largest vocabulary of any Finnish author. It is clear, however, that H. is not just a great storyteller; he is also very conscious of literary technique. If one were to single out one collection above the others, it would probably be *Jutut* (1946; stories).

With his skeptical, appraising pessimism, H. viewed injustice and oppression as ills for which no remedy can exist. Social arrangements cannot accommodate human individuality. With his monumental pessimism, relieved typically by a harsh humor, and his focus on simple people, H. is the last of Finland's peasant writers.

FURTHER WORKS: *Maantietä pitkin* (1925); *Kolmen Torapään tarina* (1927); *Tuuli käy heidän ylitseen* (1927); *Hota-Leenan poika* (1929); *Karavaani* (1930); *Isännät ja isäntien varjot* (1935); *Lauma* (1937); *Syntyykö uusi suku* (1937); *Taivalvaaran näyttelijä* (1938); *Ihmiselon karvas ihanuus* (1939); *Nykyaikaa* (1942); *Heta Rahko korkeassa iässä* (1947); *Jauhot* (1949); *Atomintutkija* (1950); *Iisakki Vähäpuheinen* (1953); *Kiinalaiset jutut* (1954); *Akkuna ja maantie* (1956)

BIBLIOGRAPHY: Ahokas, J., *A History of Finnish Literature* (1973), pp. 228–34

K. BÖRJE VÄHÄMÄKI

HAAVIKKO, Paavo

Finnish poet, dramatist, novelist, and short-story writer, b. 25 Jan. 1931, Helsinki

H.'s father was a Helsinki businessman, and he himself has managed to combine a career in publishing with that of a writer. After spending some time in the real estate business, H. joined one of the major Finnish publishing companies, Otava. He became a member of the board at the age of thirty-seven, soon after his appointment as literary editor, a post he still holds. He is also a director of Yhtyneet Kuvalehdet Oy (United Illustrated Magazines). His business experience is reflected in the themes of money and power in his work. H. married Marja-Liisa Vartio (1924–1966), a prominent Finnish writer, in 1955. He is now married to Ritva Rainio (b. 1929), who is also well known in literary circles. H. did not attend a university, but he received an honorary Doctor of Philosophy degree from Helsinki University in 1969.

H. appeared as a full-fledged modernist with his first collection of poems, *Tiet etäisyyksiin* (1951; ways to faraway), setting the pace for a whole generation of young writers and helping decisively to bring Finnish poetry up to date. Highly individual in thought and language, he has been prolific both as a poet and a writer of prose.

The themes of his poetry are language and poetry itself, love and death, and—especially more recently—history and power. These themes are brought together in *Talvipalatsi* (1959; *The Winter Palace*, 1968), a long poem that has been said to have had an impact on contemporary Finnish poetry comparable to that of T. S. Eliot's (q.v.) *The Waste Land* on English and American poetry.

H. has said that everything is history. The world of Rome or Byzantium is where man's destiny was worked out; man made blind mistakes at these moments, and he is repeating them today. But he may blend myth with history, as in the long narrative poem *Kaksikymmentä ja yksi* (1974; twenty and one), which draws heavily on the Finnish folk epic *Kalevala* for both style and theme. In history, as in H.'s poetry, permanence is an illusion. Life slips by without our noticing it. Speech flows in a flowing world. But man is not aware of this impermanence, nor is he aware that each historical event is unique. He believes in his own power. H. often chooses people of high rank as the symbols of impermanent power—kings, statesmen, wealthy merchants, the Empress Zoe in her Byzantine court.

H.'s poetry is characterized by a free, strong, rhythmic line, with the impact and flexibility of speech. He makes surprising connections, and his poems often operate on several levels simultaneously.

In his numerous stage and radio plays H. continues the theme of power, often with a historical setting. His early works are close to those of the Theater of the Absurd (q.v.). There are strong elements of grotesque, black comedy in *Ylilääkäri* (1968; *The Superintendent*, 1978), where a Freud-like father figure, superintendent of a hospital in 1906, plays sadistic games with his subordinates and his wife's relations. In what is perhaps his best play, *Agricola ja kettu* (1968; Agricola and the fox), Finland is caught between Sweden and Russia, between King Gustavus Vasa and Ivan the Terrible (the two rulers are played by the same actor). In the libretto of an opera, *Ratsumies* (1974; *The Horseman*, 1974), with music by the Finnish composer Aulis Sallinen, H. returns to a similar theme.

During the 1960s, H. wrote several novels. They are objective, spare, along the lines of the French New Novel (q.v.). In "Lumeton aika" (snowless time), the most important story in the collection called *Lasi Claudius Civiliksen salaliittolaisten pöydällä* (1964; a glass at the table of Claudius Civilis' conspirators), H. sets the scene in a Finland of 1963 in which he imagines the Communists have taken over fifteen years previously. The story deals with the relation between man's public role and his private self. His latest examination of Finland is a historical "comment on the unknown history of an unknown nation 1904–1975" called *Kansakunnan linja* (1977; national line), which has aroused considerable discussion. H. sees the nation as a business enterprise, struggling to keep ahead in the world. He differs from "official" historians in suggesting that Finland got through World War II successfully because unlike many other small countries she

313

preserved her freedom to make decisions according to the situation.

From his wide production over almost thirty years, H. emerges as a complex, deep-reaching poet with a superb command of language. He has been accused of cynicism (which he strongly denies), ambiguity, and a certain coldness. But he is generally recognized as an important and stimulating thinker and as the leading living Finnish poet today.

FURTHER WORKS: *Tuuliöinä* (1953); *Synnyinmaa* (1955); *Lehdet lehtiä* (1958); *Münchausen* (1960); *Yksityisiä asioita* (1960); *Toinen taivas ja maa* (1961); *Vuodet* (1962); *Runot 1951–1961* (1962); *Puut, kaikki heidän vihreytensä* (1966); *Puhua, vastata, opettaa* (1972); *Neljätoista hallitsijaa* (1970); *Runoja matkalta salmen ylitse* (1973); *Sulka* (1973); *Harald Pitkäikäinen* (1974); *Kuningas lähtee Ranskaan* (1974); *Runot 1949–1974* (1975); *Runoelmat* (1975); *Viiniä, kirjoitusta* (1976); *Ihmisen ääni* (1977); *Näytelmät* (1978); *Soitannollinen ilta Viipurissa 1918* (1978); *Viisi pientä draamallista tekstiä* (1981). FURTHER VOLUME IN ENGLISH: *Selected Poems* (1968)

BIBLIOGRAPHY: Hollo, A., Introduction to P. H., *Selected Poems* (1968); Laitinen, K., "How Things Are: P. H. and His Poetry," *BA*, 43 (1969), 41–46; Binham, P., "Dreams Each within Each: The Finnish Poet P. H.," *BA*, 50 (1976), 337–41; Dauenhauer, R., "The View from the Aspen Grove: P. H. in National and International Context," in Dauenhauer, R., and Binham, P., eds., *Snow in May: An Anthology of Finnish Writing 1945–1972* (1978), pp. 67–97; Binham, P., "Poet's Playground: The Collected Plays of P. H.," *WLT*, 53 (1979), 244–45

PHILIP BINHAM

HACKS, Peter

East German dramatist, poet, and essayist, b. 21 March 1928, Breslau (now Wrocław, Poland)

H. spent his youth in Silesia, a part of Germany that was annexed by Poland following World War II. After the war, H. studied sociology, philosophy, modern literature and theater in Munich, where he received a doctorate in 1951 for a dissertation on drama of the Biedermeier period (c. 1815–48). He was active in West German theater and radio until 1955, then moved to East Germany for political reasons. In the late 1950s he was associated with the Berliner Ensemble, and from 1960 to 1963 he worked as a dramatist for the Deutsches Theater. He has been actively involved in the East German Academy of Arts and the presiding council of the East German branch of the International PEN Club.

H. was influenced by models as diverse as Shakespeare, Aristophanes, and the modern agitprop tradition. He learned much from Bertolt Brecht (q.v.) and has further developed the historical and folk-drama forms that are characteristic of Brecht's works. Especially visible in H.'s dramas is the use of Brecht's technique of employing songs to replace monologues, to explain attitudes, and to connect ideas. The resulting product is an oeuvre of realistic drama comprising comedies that achieve their effect through masterful construction and didactic plays that convince through artfully employed naïveté.

In his early works, H. contrasted a Marxist view of history with myths and legends of bourgeois tradition. His first successful play, *Eröffnung des indischen Zeitalters* (1954; opening of the Indian era; repub. as *Columbus; oder, Die Weltidee zu Schiffe*, 1970; Columbus; or, the world idea aboard ship), presented Columbus as a leader into a new age of scientific reason and introduced him into East German literature as a symbol for man on his way to the new society. Among other important early works are *Die Schlacht bei Lobositz* (1956; the battle at Lobositz), a satire of Prussian militarism intended as an attack against West German remilitarization; and *Der Müller von Sanssouci* (1957; the miller of Sanssouci), a satirical assault on the legend of Frederick the Great, in which H. introduced for the first time his concept of the "giant" as a key historical figure.

Near the end of the 1950s H. turned away from historically remote materials and focused directly upon specific problems in the evolution of East German society. The ensuing plays became extremely controversial and were rejected by Marxist critics as lacking a properly positive sense of reality. Enormous tension arose because H.'s portrayals were uncomfortably realistic, his criticisms of the society were valid, and his attitude was nonsubmissive.

The best drama of this period is *Moritz Tassow* (1961; Moritz Tassow), a realistic, dialectically argumentative verse comedy about a revolutionary swineherd, in which H. attacked the state's insensitivity to individual needs.

With its blatant detail and colorful secondary characters, *Moritz Tassow* significantly elevated the quality of the East German peasant drama while satirizing such postwar developments as the land reform and the farm commune. The play also contains an innovation of special importance for East German drama: the introduction of an antihero in the figure of the ideal socialist Mattukat.

In the late 1960s H. responded to sharp criticism against his direct portrayals of East German reality by returning to politically safer substance from history and mythology. Typical of works created since 1965 are *Omphale* (1970; Omphale), in which a Hercules legend becomes a vehicle for exploring the problem of male and female social roles, and *Adam und Eva* (1973; Adam and Eve), an interpretation of the biblical account of the fall of Adam employed as a poetic allegory for the dialectic self-determination of man.

Among H.'s recent plays, *Ein Gespräch im Hause Stein über den abwesenden Herrn von Goethe* (1976; a conversation in the Stein home about the absent Mr. Goethe), a hilarious satirical comedy about the relationship between Goethe and Charlotte von Stein, will surely come to be viewed as one of his best works. It clearly reemphasizes that H.'s dramatic strength lies in his ability to employ the devices of drama to shatter illusions and compel his audience toward personal introspection. This ability has made him the most important contemporary dramatist in the German Democratic Republic.

FURTHER WORKS: *Das Volksbuch vom Herzog Ernst; oder, Der Held und sein Gefolge* (1953); *Der gestohlene Ton* (1953); *Das Fell der Zeit* (1954); *Das Windloch* (1956); *Geschichte eines alten Wittibers im Jahre 1673* (1956); *Theaterstücke* (1957); *Die Kindermörderin* (1957); *Die unadlige Gräfin* (1958); *Literatur im Zeitalter der Wissenschaften* (1960); *Die Sorgen und die Macht* (1960); *Falsche Bärte und Nasen* (1961); *Frieden* (1962); *Das Turmverlies* (1962); *Die Form ist das Politikum* (1962); *Zwei Bearbeitungen* (1963); *Die schöne Helene* (1964); *Stücke nach Stücken: Bearbeitungen 2* (1965); *Der Flohmarkt: Gedichte für Kinder* (1965); *Polly; oder, Die Bataille am Bluewater Creek* (1965); *Der Schuhu und die fliegende Prinzessin* (1965); *Fünf Stücke* (1965); *Lieder zu Stücken* (1967); *Kasimir der Kinderdieb* (1967); *Margarete in Aix* (1967); *Amphytrion* (1968); *Vier Komödien* (1971); *Noch einen Löffel Gift, Liebling?* (1972); *Die Katze wäscht den Omnibus* (1972); *Das Poetische* (1972); *Der Bär auf dem Försterball* (1972; The Bear at the Hunter's Ball, 1976); *Gedichte* (1972); *Ausgewählte Dramen* (2 vols., 1972, 1976); *Kathrinchen ging spazieren* (1973); *Lieder, Briefe, Gedichte* (1974); *Die Dinge in Buta* (1974); *Die Sonne* (1974); *Meta Morfoß* (1975); *Das Pflaumenhuhn* (1975); *Oper* (1976); *Das Jahrmarktsfest zu Plundersweilern* (1975); *Das Jahrmarktsfest zu Plundersweilern; Rosie träumt* (1976); *Die Maßgaben der Kunst* (1977); *Das musikalische Nashorn* (1978); *Sechs Dramen* (1978)

BIBLIOGRAPHY: Glenn, J., "Hofmannsthal, H., and Hildesheimer: Helen in the Twentieth Century," *Seminar*, 5 (1969), 1–20; Laube, H., *P. H.* (1972); Schleyer, W., *Die Stücke von P. H.* (1976); Schütze, P. F., *P. H.* (1976); Scheid, J. R., *"Enfant Terrible" of Contemporary East German Drama: P. H. in His Role as Adaptor and Innovator* (1977); Gerber, M., "After the Revolution—What Then? P. H.'s Theory of a Socialist Classicism," *UDR*, 13, 2 (1978), 3–11

LOWELL A. BANGERTER

HAGIWARA Sakutarō

Japanese poet, essayist, and literary theorist, b. 1 Nov. 1886, Maebashi; d. 11 May 1942, Tokyo

The son of wealthy parents, H. was able even as a young man to devote himself full time to writing poetry. He never finished college, but studied Western authors on his own and was especially attracted to Poe, Nietzsche, Schopenhauer, and Dostoevsky. His first collection of poems, *Tsuki ni hoeru* (1917; Howling at the Moon, 1978), immediately established him as a highly imaginative poet. During the next twenty-five years he published five volumes of poetry, eight collections of essays, four books of aphorisms, one novelette, and three treatises on poetry. He also helped to found several literary magazines, and taught at Meiji University in Tokyo from 1934 until the year of his death.

Tsuki ni hoeru gained lavish critical acclaim because it represented the first successful attempt to give, in colloquial Japanese, a poetic form to existential anxiety. The poems skillfully articulated what H. called a "physiological fear," a fear that, lying deep in man's physical existence, ceaselessly threatens his mental well-being. A modern man afflicted with this fear feels something rotten in the core of his being and vainly looks up toward the sky for salvation. In H.'s metaphor man is a dog fearful of his own shadow and forever howling at the moon.

In H.'s second collection of poems, *Aoneko* (1923; *Blue Cat*, 1978), this anxiety gives way to ennui, gloom, and despair. The central image of the book is a tired, melancholy cat sitting lazily and indulging in fantasies. Man, having lost all hope in life, no longer howls at the dream world; he is completely within it. The nihilism pervading the book was partly derived from Schopenhauer, but in giving verbal expression to it H. made masterful use of a dull rhythm characteristic of colloquial Japanese.

Hyōtō (1934; the iceland), H.'s last major book of poetry, marks a return from the dream world to the realities of daily life. The predominant tone of these poems is neither fear nor melancholy; it is the anger of a man ostracized by contemporary society because of his extrasensitivity as a poet. For H., this anger was too intense to express in colloquial Japanese. Making effective use of sonorous literary Japanese, he vented his rage at the people who failed to understand him. Modern Japan seemed like an iceland.

As he grew older, H. turned increasingly to prose. In *Nekomachi* (1935; *The Cat Town*, 1948) he tried to bridge the gap between poetry and prose; in his words, he created a novelette "in the form of a prose poem." The experiment, however, was not entirely successful. Describing a journey into an imaginary land, the book is much like *Aoneko*, but without its evocative power.

H. fared better in writing aphorisms and critical essays. An avid reader of classical poetry, he compiled the anthology *Ren'ai meika shū* (1931; a treasury of love poems), in which he provided his own interpretive analysis of each poem. The analysis was most successful in dealing with poems that sang of longing for a remote, metaphysical lover. His study of an 18th-c. haiku poet, *Kyōshū no shijin Yosa Buson* (1936; Yosa Buson, the poet of nostalgia), likewise is a personal interpretation of poems of longing and nostalgia.

H.'s talent for literary theory found its best expression in *Shi no genri* (1928; principles of poetry). "Through a uniquely dreamlike method," he wrote, "poetry articulates the essence of the self that looms in the twilight zone of consciousness." "A uniquely dreamlike method" meant symbolic representation ("imagerization" was H.'s equivalent for it), and H.

considered the Japanese language as lending itself especially well to the symbolist mode, because it was imagistic by nature. On the other hand, he lamented the paucity of musical qualities in modern Japanese.

H. made two major contributions to modern Japanese poetry. First, with his consummate skill with words he demonstrated that vernacular Japanese could be used in an artistically satisfying way. Other poets before him had made use of the vernacular in their works, yet their diction was essentially little different from everyday speech. With H., modern Japanese became a *poetic* language for the first time. Second, he was the first Japanese author who successfully created poetry out of the existential anxiety typical of a modern intellectual. Nietzsche and Schopenhauer had been known in Japan before his time, but no one else had taken their pessimism so much to heart as H. did. For better or for worse, Japanese poetry has come markedly closer to that of Europe through H.'s effort.

FURTHER WORKS: *Atarashiki yokujō* (1922); *Chō o yumemu* (1923); *Junjō shōkoyoku shū* (1925); *Shiron to kansō* (1928); *Kyomō no seigi* (1929); *Junsei shi ron* (1935); *Zetsubō no tōsō* (1935); *Rōka to shitsubō* (1936); *Shijin no shimei* (1937); *Mu kara no kōsō* (1937); *Nippon e no kaiki* (1938); *Shukumei* (1939); *Kikyōsha* (1940); *Minato nite* (1940); *Atai* (1940). FURTHER VOLUME IN ENGLISH: *Face at the Bottom of the World, and Other Poems* (1969)

BIBLIOGRAPHY: Piper, A., "Das Shi als Ausdruck des japanischen Lebensgefühls in der Taishōzeit: H. S. und Takamura Kōtarō," *Nachrichten der Gesellschaft für Natur- und Völkerkunde Ostasiens*, 77, 79–80 (1955–56), 8–21, 110–30; Wilson, G., Introduction to *Face at the Bottom of the World, and Other Poems* (1969), pp. 11–32; Tsukimura, R., "H. and the Japanese Lyric Tradition," *JATJ*, 11 (1976), 47–63; Sato, H., Introduction to *Howling at the Moon* (1978), pp. 11–26

MAKOTO UEDA

HAITIAN LITERATURE
See French-Caribbean Literature

al-HAKĪM, Tawfīq
Egyptian dramatist, novelist, and short-story writer, b. 9 Oct. 1898 (or 1902?), Alexandria

After graduating as a lawyer in Cairo, H. was sent by his father to Paris in 1925 to continue his legal studies and submit a doctoral thesis. Instead of devoting his energies to his studies, however, he was strongly attracted to the theater and deeply influenced by Shaw, Pirandello (qq.v.), and Ibsen, whose plays he read or saw. In 1928 he returned to Egypt without a doctorate, but with the skill and inspiration of a promising writer.

Although he had written some music-hall plays before leaving for France, H. came into prominence only after publishing his first novel, *'Awdat al-rūh* (1933; the return of the spirit), in which he tried to describe and account for the sudden awakening of nationalist feelings that led to the 1919 revolution. In this novel, which is in part based on H.'s own experiences, a symbolic layer is superimposed on the essentially realistic, day-to-day story. *'Awdat al-rūh* was meant to be a literary expression of the then-popular notion according to which Egypt has always retained a distinctive national and cultural identity.

Yawmiyyāt nā'ib fī al-aryāf (1937; *The Maze of Justice*, 1947) is a distinctive novel written in the form of diary and draws on H.'s personal experience as a public prosecutor in provincial towns. Autobiographical material is also found in his novel *'Usfūr min al-sharq* (1938; *A Bird from the East*, 1966), which depicts the emotional and intellectual reactions of an Easterner in his first encounter with the West. In spite of the personal material in these three novels, however, H. has repeatedly warned literary critics not to take them as autobiographical documents. Like all novels, he insists, they are fictional works of art and should, therefore, be read as such.

His fame as a novelist notwithstanding, it is in the realm of drama that H.'s talent is best manifested. He wrote scores of social plays and playlets in which the dialogue, often in colloquial Arabic, is full of wit and dramatic tension. But H. is at his best in intellectual plays, which he introduced into Arabic literature. As dramas of ideas, they ought to be considered in the light of H.'s world outlook. Man, he believes, is constantly at war with forces stronger than himself. In his perseverance lurk the secret of his greatness and the source of his tragedy. The heroes of *Ahl al-kahf* (1933; *The People of the Cave,* 1971), which is based on the Koranic version of the Christian legend of the Seven Sleepers of Ephesus, are engaged in a hopeless struggle against time, whereas Shahriyār, the hero of his *Shahrazād* (1934;

Scheherazade) aspires to free himself from the confinements of space.

H.'s tragic heroes are also subject to an inner conflict between various dualisms, such as life and art, as in his play *Pygmalion* (1942; Pygmalion), or strength and wisdom, as in *Sulaymān al-hakīm* (1943; Solomon the wise).

H. also wrote a number of experimental plays. In *Yā tāli' al-shajara* (1962; *The Tree-Climber*, 1966), he borrows some of the devices employed by the dramatists of the Theater of the Absurd (q.v.), although he does not share their sense of loss and despair: he still has faith in a meaningful and well-ordered universe. A play within a play is found in *Al-Ta'ām li-kull fam* (1963; food for every mouth), in which the characters in the outer play undergo exhilarating experiences under the impact of what happens in the inner one. In *Bank al-qalaq* (1967; the bank of anxiety), which is set against the political background of 1960s Egypt, the dramatic episodes are interspersed with narrative ones.

Although H. is often referred to as an artist shut up in his ivory tower, his literary production displays an acute awareness of Egypt's cultural and social problems, as well as deep concern over the present situation of mankind.

FURTHER WORKS: *Ahl al-Fann* (1934); *Muhammad* (1936); *Masrahiyyāt T. al-H.* (1937); *Al-Qasr al-mashūr* (1937); *Taht shams al-fikr* (1938); *'Ahd al-Shaytān* (1938); *Ash'ab* (1938); *Prāxā* (1939); *Rāqisat al-ma'bad* (1939); *Nashīd al-anshād* (1940); *Himār al-H.* (1940); *Sultān al-zalām* (1941); *Min al-burj al-'Ājī* (1941); *Taht al-misbāh al-akhdar* (1942); *Zahrat al-'umr* (1943); *Al-Ribāt al-muqaddas* (1944); *Shajarat al-hukm* (1945); *Himārī qāla lī* (1945); *Qisas T. al-H.* (1949); *Al-Malik Ūdīb* (1949); *Masrah al-mujtama'* (1950); *Fann al-adab* (1952); *'Adāla wa fann* (1953); *Arinī al-Lāh* (1953); *'Asā al-H.* (1954); *Ta'ammulāt fī al-Siyāsa* (1954); *Al-Aydī al-nā'ima* (1954); *Al-Ta'āduliyya* (1955); *Īzīs* (1955); *Al-Safqa* (1956); *Al-Masrah al-munawwa'* (1956); *Lu'bat al-mawt* (1957); *Ashwāk al-salām* (1957); *Rihla ilā al-ghad* (1957); *Adab al-hayāt* (1959); *Al-Sultān al-hā'ir* (1960; *The Sultan's Dilemma*, 1973); *Sijn al-'umr* (1964); *Rihlat al-rabī' wa al-Kharīf* (1964); *Shams al-nahār* (1965); *Laylat al-zifāf* (1966); *Masīr sarsār* (1966); *Al-Warta* (1966); *Qālabunā al-masrahī* (1967); *Qultu dhāt yawm* (1970); *Ahādīth ma'a T. al-H.*

(1971); *T. al-H. yatahaddath* (1971); *Majlis al-'adl* (1972); *Thawrat al-shabāb* (1972); *Rāhib bayn nisā'* (1972); *Hadīth ma'a al-Kawkab* (1974); *Al-Dunyā riwāya hazliyya* (1974); *'Awdat al-wa'y* (1974); *Al-Hamīr* (1975); *Wathā'iq fī tarīq 'Awdat al-wa'y* (1975); *Safahāt min al-tārīkh al-adabī* (1975); *Mukhtār tafsīr al-Qurtubī* (1977); *Bayn al-fikr wa al-Fann* (n.d.). FURTHER VOLUME IN ENGLISH: *Plays, Prefaces, & Postscripts of T. al-H.,* Vol. I (1981)

BIBLIOGRAPHY: Landau, J. M., *Studies in the Arab Theater and Cinema* (1958), pp. 138–47; Long, C. W. R., "T. al-H. and the Arabic Theatre," *MES*, 5, 2 (1969), 69–74; Haywood, J., *Modern Arabic Literature* (1971), pp. 197–204, 219–34; Starkey, P., "Philosophical Themes in T. al-H.'s Drama," *JArabL*, 8 (1977), 136–52; Fontaine, J., *Mort—Résurrection: Une lecture de T. al-H.* (1978); Long, R., *T. al-H.: Playwright of Egypt* (1979)

DAVID SEMAH

HALAS, František

Czechoslovak poet, essayist, and translator (writing in Czech), b. 3 Oct. 1901, Brno; d. 27 Oct. 1949, Prague

H.'s father, a textile worker, was a repeatedly jailed left-wing radical. H. himself was active in the Communist Party from his early youth. He worked in a Prague publishing house and was coeditor of various left-wing avant-garde journals. During the Nazi occupation he was involved in the Resistance. After the war H. became a high official at the Ministry of Information, head of the Writers' Syndicate, and member of the National Assembly. Not long after the Communist takeover of 1948 he died in angry despair at what he called his "whored-up dreams."

H.'s first book of verse, *Sépie* (1927; sepia), loosely associated him with the then-leading Czech avant-garde group of poets, who were influenced by French Dadaism and surrealism (qq.v.). H.'s serious concerns and his unique style, however, soon excluded him from a movement chiefly distinguished by brilliant verbal gamesmanship.

Nevertheless, this early alliance marked H.'s later work with an enduring love of metaphor and of the densely charged image. His painstaking quest for the potent word, combined with his continuous striving for simplicity, ultimately resulted in verses in which bare nouns are gathered together and juxtaposed not only with each other but also with the all-meaningful bare spaces between the words, the white silences, containing all colors. Often he mates words in violent conjunctions, reminiscent of the 17th-c. metaphysical "conceit." His mixture of colloquialisms, neologisms, and folk and archaic terms is also typically baroque, as is his use of assonance and dissonance in preference to rhyme. Against the songlike, fluid quality of mainstream Czech poetry, H. built rocklike, static, harsh, gratingly rhythmic lines. Although he could, and occasionally did, write melodious stanzas—notably in his collections *Tvář* (1931; face) and *Hořec* (1933; gentian) and in some of his best translations, such as those of the Polish poets Adam Mickiewicz (1798–1855) and Juliusz Słowacki (1808–1849)—most of his work is constructed from monumental, majestic blocks of verse.

After the Munich betrayal of Czechoslovakia in 1938 H. discarded his private voice to become the voice of the silenced land, of its fierce yet tenuous hopes, its anxieties, its anger. His forceful *Torzo naděje* (1938; torso of hope) was read, memorized, and repeated throughout the period of the Nazi occupation, and again during the 1968 invasion of Czechoslovakia by the Warsaw Pact armies.

Even after his death H. continued to serve his country. He became the pivot of the Czech writers' rebellion against Stalinist dogma. The prolonged battle over H. started during the Writers' Congress of 1956, where voices were raised in his defense, and continued until the explosive Writers' Congress of 1967, the eloquent harbinger of the Prague Spring. The controversy was, above all, over H.'s undoubted preoccupation with darkness and death, so irritating to the mindless optimism of the official culture. H.'s work was repeatedly assailed as "morbid" and "macabre" and as exhibiting "desolate nihilism," "sickly pessimism," and "blackest despair." Yet the darkness that fascinated H. is the life-giving darkness of the earth, "where the stream of primeval life trembles and quickens the rhythm of life, of faith, of memories"—a line from the posthumously published *Magická moc poesie* (1958; magical might of poetry). In these essays particularly, H. made clear that he was speaking of the seed that must be plunged into the dark in order to live and of "the roots that grope in the darkness of the earth for life-saving nourishment."

Like his style, H.'s vision of death-in-life and life-in-death is reminiscent of 17th-c. baroque poetry. The fateful, the unavoidable fusion of life and death is what concerns H. This is no nihilism, but precisely the opposite. The strength and energy animating his verse are built on his refusal to evade the eternal presence of death in life.

Despair appeared only at the end, overwhelming H.'s last poems, written in secret, at a time when the political system he had helped to bring to power dropped its mask, revealing its inhuman face. In his posthumously published verse—for instance, in *A co?* (1957; so what?) —he seems literally to be gasping for air.

H. is one of the giants of modern Czech poetry. His passionate honesty and his dogged search for truth made his poetry a battlefield between hope and mounting disillusionment. It also reflects the tragic destiny of his native land.

FURTHER WORKS: *Kohout plaší smrt* (1930); *Tiše* (1932); *Staré ženy* (1935; *Old Women,* 1947); *Dokořán* (1936); *Časy* (1939); *Naše paní Božena Němcová* (1940; *Our Lady Božena Němcová,* 1944); *Ladění* (1942); *V řadě* (1948); *Počítadlo* (1948); *Halas dětem* (1954; *A Garland of Children's Verse,* 1968); *Potopa* (1956); *Básně* (1957); *Potopa; Hlad* (1965); *Hlad* (1966); *Obrazy* (1968)

BIBLIOGRAPHY: Otruba, M., and Pešat, Z., eds., *The Linden Tree: An Anthology of Czech and Slovak Literature* (1962), p. 180; French, A., *The Poets of Prague* (1969), passim; Blackwell, V., "The Rock and the Roots," *BA,* 43 (1969), 13–17; Novák, A., *Czech Literature* (1976), pp. 321–22

VERA BLACKWELL

HALPERN, Moyshe Leyb

Yiddish poet, b. 2 Jan. 1886, Zloczów, Austro-Hungarian Empire; d. 31 Aug. 1932, New York, N.Y., U.S.A.

Born in eastern Galicia, H. attended both the traditional Jewish religious elementary school and a modern Polish-Jewish school. At age twelve he was sent to Vienna to study applied art. During a nine-year sojourn in the Hapsburg capital, H. familiarized himself with modern German literature and began to write verse in German. Returning to Zloczów in 1907, he was persuaded by the young Yiddish poets Samuel Jacob Imber (1889–1942) and Jacob Mestel (1884–1958) to write in his mother tongue. At

this time H. published his first Yiddish poems in the Galician Yiddish press.

In 1908 H. immigrated to New York. His arrival coincided with the debut of The Young, the insurgent literary group that first gave a distinctively modern voice to American Yiddish literature. H. contributed to the group's publications and was acclaimed as its most forceful and daring poet. His first collection of poems, *In Nyu-York* (1919; in New York), assured him recognition as a major Yiddish poet. Its subject matter and imagery are permeated by his sense of alienation in the modern metropolis, and the plight of modern man is brought into sharp focus through the eyes of the immigrant.

H. became a regular contributor to the Yiddish communist daily *Frayheyt* from its inception in 1922. After a brief period of popularity in radical circles, unable to submit to restraints or party discipline, H. terminated his association with *Frayheyt* in 1924. That same year his second book of verse, *Di goldene pave* (1924; the golden peacock), appeared.

Although originally associated with The Young, H. departed on his own, violently rejecting the self-conscious aestheticism characteristic of this group. He is considered the enfant terrible of modern Yiddish literature. His is a poetry of the grotesque, of disjunctive rhythms, coarse idioms, bold-faced images, and imprecations. Yet H. loved to cavort and clown in his poems. Nevertheless, the lyric voice is not lost in his tempestuous poetry. H. created the persona of "the rascal Moyshe Leyb," which achieved broad recognition and an almost autonomous existence, even during his own lifetime.

FURTHER WORKS: *Lider* (2 vols., 1934)

BIBLIOGRAPHY: Liptzin, S., *The Flowering of Yiddish Literature* (1963), pp. 216–18; Madison, C. A., *Yiddish Literature: Its Scope and Major Writers* (1968), pp. 302–5; Howe, I., and Greenberg, E., eds., *A Treasury of Yiddish Poetry* (1969), pp. 34–36; Wisse, R., "A Yiddish Poet in America," *Commentary,* July 1980, 35–41

EUGENE ORENSTEIN

HAMSUN, Knut

(pseud. of Knud Pedersen) Norwegian novelist, dramatist, and poet, b. 4 Aug. 1859, Lom; d. 19 Feb. 1952, Nørholm

H. is generally recognized as Norway's greatest novelist, and, after Ibsen, the nation's second most important literary figure. Although H. was born in Gudbrandsdal, the fertile valley that runs through the spine of south-central Norway, his family moved when H. was three years old to Hamarøy in Nordland. Here his father, an itinerant tailor and sometime farmer, worked the farm called Hamsund, which H.'s maternal uncle had purchased. In these northern reaches, where nature was most harsh and demanding, H. developed his love of the earth by observing the rush of the Arctic seasons and the grandeur of the mountains and forests.

At the age of nine, H. was sent to the uncle to live and work in the store, where he was cruelly disciplined. It seems likely that this experience developed the feeling of defiance and bitterness that permeates his writings, and also his distrust of older people and age itself. After unsuccessful efforts to run away, H. succeeded eventually and returned to Gudbrandsdal for his confirmation; but when he had this certification of his maturity and independence, he returned to Hamarøy to work at a wide variety of odd jobs.

At the age of eighteen, he published his first book under the name of Knut Pedersen, and two more books the following year under the name of Knut Pedersen Hamsund. A printer's error later on dropped the final *d* on Hamsund, and H. accepted this as a felicitous accident. Although he published various newspaper articles, he was not to be accepted by a major publishing house until another grueling and frustrating decade had elapsed. In the meantime he worked at more trades in Norway and was in the U.S. twice for two-year periods.

In 1888 H. returned to Europe with a manuscript entitled *Fra det moderne Amerikas åndsliv* (1889; *The Intellectual Life of Modern America*, 1969). In this bitingly witty work he excoriated the shallowness and materialism of the U.S. He viewed it and Britain as the least cultured nations of the world because of the industrial mechanization that had left the two countries without meaning, without purpose, and without souls.

H.'s first masterpiece was *Sult* (1890; *Hunger*, 1899). It is a completely egocentric book, largely autobiographical. Detailing the kaleidoscopic and often nearly delirious perceptions of a homeless man close to starvation, the novel is a piece of pure art without any hint of social message. While it is realistic enough as to subject, namely indigence and loneliness in the big city, its technique is unalloyed impressionism. In many ways it is stream-of-consciousness

prose, antedating Joyce (q.v.) and later writers, but the spirit is Dostoevskian.

H. then embarked on a widely discussed lecture tour in which he attacked the Brahmins of Norwegian literature, most notably Ibsen, for preoccupation with utilitarian literature written for a social purpose. While the lectures were not met with universal approval, it is impossible to overestimate the impact that *Sult* and the lecture series had on Norwegian belles lettres.

Consistent with his lectures and with the literary thrust he had initiated in *Sult*, H. published the enigmatic *Mysterier* (1892; *Mysteries*, 1927). H.'s primary motif of the erratic wanderer, who makes no appeal for sympathy or even understanding, propels the novel. Perhaps more than any of his other writings, *Mysterier* allowed H. to display his contempt for politicians, his antipathy toward the old, his exaltation of the individual, and his admiration of the Nietzschean superman.

Many critics consider *Pan* (1894; *Pan*, 1920) to represent H.'s most magnificent writing. The leading character is akin with other wandering strangers in H.'s work, but he is a stronger, more primordial force. However, what truly distinguishes *Pan* is the lyrical description of the magic beauty of the Norwegian north country. Perhaps nowhere in literature has H.'s description of the colors, the lights, and the vastness of the sub-Arctic in the summertime been matched. H. expresses an urgent longing for the melding of man and nature, for a return to a more elemental, meaningful life.

The other side of the same coin is expressed in the two coupled novels *Børn av tiden* (1913; *Children of the Age*, 1924) and *Segelfoss by* (1915; *Segelfoss Town*, 1925). The books are social satires depicting the evolution of a patriarchal farming community into a capitalistic town. The societal development is portrayed with far less of the subjective lyrical style that H. employed in his other works. Nevertheless, the two novels constitute a witty, savagely ironic contribution to literary art. In their realism they reveal a deep pessimism about a society that apparently belongs to self-centered men of no imagination and no horizons.

Markens grøde (1917; *Growth of the Soil*, 1920), which led to his being awarded the Nobel Prize in 1920, is his most widely read and universally acclaimed work. Just as H. distrusted and disapproved of modern civilization, which he regarded as a sickness of mankind, he honored the individual farmer-pioneer who extracted both his physical and his psychological nourishment from the soil. Writing with a powerful lyric style reminiscent of the Bible, H. created an indelible picture of the persevering and uncomplaining farmer for whom the soil is sufficient reason for being. H. himself farmed, and he, like Robert Frost (q.v.), chose to regard himself as a farmer as much as a writer.

Because of the intrinsic difficulty of translating poetry, and because of the small corpus of poems that H. permitted to be published (he tells of two major burnings), he is little known as a writer of poetry to the non-Nordic world. Nevertheless he must be ranked among Norway's finest poets.

His one major poetic contribution is *Det vilde kor* (1904; the wild choir), which with a few additions and changes was published again in *Samlede verker* (1916; collected works). H. was a craftsman of language, and while he was uncharacteristically modest about his poetic ability ("I am no Robert Burns," he confessed), his poetry was on an artistic level with his prose. The lyric quality that pervades *Markens grøde* is magnified in *Det vilde kor*. The mad humor and passionate recklessness of *Sult* are distilled and condensed in his poetry. All the arrogance, tenderness, and sardonic sense of humor that appear in H.'s novels are paralleled in his poems.

H.'s last years were tragic, although it is not likely that he regarded them as such. His support of Nazi Germany during World War II was unfortunate but not surprising. He hated the British (he was merely contemptuous of Americans), and he had favored the German cause in World War I. H.'s basic philosophy was Nietzschean, and his vision of the solitary independent wanderer was warped somehow into its direct antithesis, the Nazi ideal. Most of H.'s wartime writings consisted of political polemics and appeals to Norwegians to accept and even support the Germans.

After World War II, H. was arrested and tried as a traitor. He could have easily had his case passed over had he been willing to live with the widely held view that he was senile. Instead he goaded and prodded the government, and displayed little sign either of senility or contriteness. After he was convicted and fined, he published *På gjengrodde stier* (1949; *On Overgrown Paths*, 1967), a journal of his thoughts from the time of his initial arrest to his conviction and sentencing. It is a poignant, rueful, but in no way pathetic statement.

In 1952, at the age of ninety-two, H. died. He departed with wit and wits intact. During his life span he had seen the establishment of an independent Norway, two world wars, and a great depression. He had received adulation, and had been condemned as a traitor and rene-

gade. Had he merely lived his biblically allotted three score and ten, instead of more than four score and ten, he would have died completely honored and revered. But whatever judgments are made of his politics, as a writer he was a towering figure who made a magnificent contribution not only to Norwegian literature, but to the world.

FURTHER WORKS: *Den gådefulde* (1877); *Et gjensyn* (1878); *Bjørger* (1878); *Lars Oftedal* (1889); *Redaktor Lynge* (1893); *Ny jord* (1893; *Shallow Soil*, 1914); *Ved rigets port* (1895); *Livets spil* (1896); *Siesta* (1897); *Aftenrøde* (1898); *Victoria* (1898); *Munken Vendt* (1902); *I æventyrland* (1903); *Dronning Tamara* (1903); *Kratskog* (1903); *Sværmere* (1904; *Dreamers,* 1921); *Stridende liv* (1905); *Under høststjærnen* (1906; *Under the Autumn Star,* 1922); *Benoni* (1908; *Benoni,* 1925); *Rosa* (1908; *Rosa,* 1926); *En vandrer spiller med sordin* (1909; *A Wanderer Plays on Muted Strings,* 1922); *Livet ivold* (1910; *In the Grip of Life,* 1924); *Den sidste glæde* (1912; *Look Back on Happiness,* 1940); *Konerne ved vandposten* (1920; *The Women at the Pump,* 1928); *Dikte* (1921); *Sidste kapitel* (1923; *Chapter the Last,* 1929); *Landstrykere* (1927; *Vagabonds,* 1930; new tr., *Wayfarers,* 1981); *August* (1930; *August,* 1931); *Men livet lever* (1933; *The Road Leads On,* 1934); *Ringen sluttet* (1936; *The Ring Is Closed,* 1937); *Samlede verker* (17 vols., 1936)

BIBLIOGRAPHY: Larsen, H. A., *K. H.* (1922); Wiehr, J., *K. H., Smith College Studies in Modern Languages,* 3, 1–2 (1921–22); Gustafson, A., *Six Scandinavian Novelists* (1940), pp. 226–85; Hamsun, T., *Mein Vater* (1940); Mendelssohn, P. de, *Der Geist in der Despotie* (1953); Hamsun, M., *Der Regenbogen* (1954); McFarlane, J. W., "The Whisper of the Blood," *PMLA,* 71 (1956), 563–94; Lowenthal, L., *Literature and the Image of Man* (1957), pp. 190–220; Naess, H., "The Three H.s: The Changing Attitude in Recent Criticism," *SS,* 32 (1960), 129–39; Naess, H., "H. and America," *SS,* 39 (1967), 305–28

HAROLD P. HANSON

HANDKE, Peter

Austrian novelist, dramatist, poet, and essayist, b. 6 Dec. 1942, Griffen

H.'s work first appeared while he was studying law at Graz (1961–65), where a group of like-minded coevals, including the playwright

Wolfgang Bauer (b. 1941) and the novelist Gerhard Roth (b. 1942) staged plays and literary events and contributed to the magazine *manuskripte*. In the mid-1960s H. moved to Frankfurt-am-Main, West Germany, where his first play was performed and his first novel published (both in 1966). With a move to Paris in 1969 and another one back to Frankfurt in 1971 came a greater concentration on writing fiction; by the end of the 1970s, having returned to his native Austria (Salzburg), he had eight novels to his credit but had apparently stopped writing for the theater—although he was writing (and directing) more for the screen. He was awarded the German Academy's prestigious Büchner Prize in 1973.

H. has essayed most forms of writing, but it was as an anticonventional playwright (coupled with a provocative public persona) that he made his initial impact. In his first play, *Publikumsbeschimpfung* (1966; *Offending the Audience*, 1969), four actors inform the audience that what they are watching is not a play but simply a stage with four people on it; they then alternately insult the audience and compliment them on their "performance," a strategy that often provoked extreme audience reaction. There followed three less outrageous plays— *Selbstbezichtigung* (1966; *Self-Accusation*, 1969), *Weissagung* (1966; prophecy), and *Hilferufe* (1967; *Calling for Help*, 1971)— which nonetheless shared with *Publikumsbeschimpfung* a lack of plot, character, and dramatic construction. The aim of these plays, said H., was not to "revolutionize, but to make [the audience] aware"—of themselves and of certain realities.

This was also the aim of *Kaspar* (1968; *Kaspar*, 1969, H.'s first—and probably best —full-length play, and the first to feature a dramatic character. Using as a model the real-life Kaspar Hauser, who mysteriously turned up in Nuremburg in 1828 at the age of sixteen, but with the mind of a child, H. created an abstract parable to "make audiences aware" of how accepted modes of expression are imposed on an individual, thus circumscribing his originality. Kaspar, a speechless innocent, is indoctrinated into becoming an orderly, articulate member of society. But his final lapse into incoherence indicates a Wittgensteinian realization that, in learning a language, one has to accept the values implicit in it, and that it is therefore impossible to form thoughts independent of that value system.

After *Das Mündel will Vormund sein* (1969; *My Foot My Tutor*, 1971), a compel-

ling one-act scenario in which two half-masked men perform odd rituals of domination and subservience, H. explored an idea suggested by a ballad about a horseman who rides unsuspectingly across a thinly frozen lake only to die of fright when subsequently told of the danger he had been in. The characters in *Der Ritt über den Bodensee* (1971; *The Ride across Lake Constance*, 1972) are all skating on the thin ice of "normal" behavior, which H. depicts as a random collection of stock theatrical speeches and gestures. The tension arises from the fact that these mechanical figures are constantly on the brink of breaking through the clichés to something unknown and untried but, H. implies, more exciting than stale normality.

This uncompromising piece was followed by H.'s most conventional play—apparently his last—*Die Unvernünftigen sterben aus* (1974; *They Are Dying Out*, 1975), about a consumer-goods capitalist who cannot reconcile his emotional sensitivity with the demands of business life. The treatment is fresh, but the theme is well tried, and the dramatic conventions are clumsily handled. H. had seemed surer on less familiar terrain.

Just as Wittgenstein haunts Handke's plays, his influence is also present in H.'s novels, most noticeably in their tendency to approach a phenomenon over and over again from different angles in search of its absolute reality (a preoccupation, along with a rejection of conventional character and plot, that H. shares with Alain Robbe-Grillet [q.v.] and other New Novelists). As with the plays, the initial critical reaction was hostile, but H.'s deadpan, ultraobjective accounts of characters in extreme states of mind moving through "normal" yet alien landscapes have won increasing acclaim—and numbers of readers.

In *Die Angst des Tormanns beim Elfmeter* (1970; *The Goalie's Anxiety at the Penalty Kick,* 1972) a murderer—the goalkeeper of the title—is on the run from a pointless, spur-of-the-moment killing. *Der kurze Brief zum langen Abschied* (1972; *Short Letter, Long Farewell,* 1974) is the first-person account of a young Austrian writer's picaresque journey across the U.S. in search of his estranged wife, a journey that allows H. to interlard lengthy quotations from books, plays, films, dreams, memories, and the surface phenomena of American life, thus paying homage to a number of his literary heroes, among them William Faulkner (q.v.), Raymond Chandler (1888–1959), and Patricia Highsmith (b. 1921).

Die Stunde der wahren Empfindungen

(1975; *A Moment of True Feeling*, 1977) concerns another murderer, a press attaché at the Austrian embassy in Paris, but despite nods in the direction of Kafka (q.v.) the careful depiction of tedium becomes itself dangerously tedious. In *Die linkshändige Frau* (1976; *The Left-handed Woman,* 1978), based on an original screenplay that Handke himself had filmed, an apparently happily married young mother, having suddenly asked her husband to leave her, has to cope both with her newfound independence and with a sense of disorientation, which is described in a style exactly matching the dispassionate eye of a camera.

In the middle of this sequence of novels, spurred by his mother's suicide, H. wrote an unsentimental yet affecting memoir of her life —not unlike that of his fictional characters. Called a "story," *Wunschloses Unglück* (1972; *A Sorrow beyond Dreams,* 1974) is told with beguiling simplicity but nonetheless embraces a complex interplay between factual content and fictional conventions. It represents H.'s technique at its best.

H. has also published poetry, essays, short stories, radio dramas, a television play, and a long journal of the eighteen months of his domicile in Paris, *Das Gewicht der Welt* (1978; *Fantasies and Prejudices,* 1979). Whatever the medium, however, H.'s concern is to demonstrate that experience is a succession of ready-made, preordained components, whose deadening effect must be painstakingly countered. Hence the persistent dialectic in his work between conventional and unconventional forms. Although his work can be difficult, in the breadth and variety of his experimentation and the uniqueness of his best fiction and drama, H. is one of the most exciting and original of the postwar generation of European writers.

FURTHER WORKS: *Die Hornissen* (1966); *Der Hausierer* (1967); *Begrüßung des Aufsichtsrat* (1967); *Die Innenwelt der Außenwelt der Innenwelt* (1969); *Deutsche Gedichte* (1969); *Wind und Meer* (1970); *Quodlibet* (1970); *Chronik der laufenden Ereignisse* (1971); *Ich bin ein Bewohner des Elfenbeinturms* (1972); *Als das Wünschen noch geholfen hat* (1974; *Nonsense and Happiness,* 1976); *Langsame Heimkehr* (1979); *Die Lehre der Sainte-Victoire* (1980); *Kindergeschichte* (1981); *Über die Dörfer* (1981)

BIBLIOGRAPHY: special H. issue, *TuK,* No. 24 (1969; 2nd ed., 1971); Heintz, G., *P. H.* (1971); Hern, N., *P. H.* (1972); Rischbieter, H., *P. H.* (1972); Scharang, M., ed., *Über P. H.* (1972); Gilman, R., *The Making of Modern Drama* (1974), pp. 267–88; Mixner, M., *P. H.* (1977); Taëni, R., "On Thin Ice: P. H.'s Studies in Alienation," *Meanjin,* 36 (1977), 315–25; Nägele, R., and Voris, R., *P. H.* (1978); Klinkowitz, J., "Aspects of H.: The Fiction," *PR,* 45 (1978), 416–24; Jurgensen, M., ed., *H.: Ansätze, Analysen, Anmerkungen* (1979); Schlueter, J., *The Plays and Novels of P. H.* (1981)

                                         NICHOLAS HERN

HANLEY, James

Anglo-Irish novelist, dramatist, essayist, biographer, and poet, b. 3 Sept. 1901, Dublin, Ireland

H., a very prolific author, was born into a poor Irish family. He left school when he was thirteen but educated himself by voracious reading and extensive travels by shipping out to sea for ten years. He worked at a variety of jobs: as a journalist, a railway porter, and race-course cashier. He lived in Wales for a number of years and now resides in London.

Two themes dominate H.'s writings: men in ships at sea, and men and women self-imprisoned in their private worlds of dreams and despair. H.'s world is crowded with marginal people, outcasts, loners, and strangers. In portraying their broken business of living, H. relentlessly conducts a complex but compassionate investigation to reveal the rugged individuality of their lives, whether they are adrift at sea, trapped in a Welsh rooming house, or frightened and huddling in a damp cellar in a London blitz.

Boy (1931), H.'s first novel of the sea, is an angry, realistic novel about the brutalization of an adolescent on a merchant steamer. It stirred a literary and social controversy, was suppressed under the British obscenity laws, and became a cause célèbre.

H.'s magnum opus is *The Furys Chronicle* —a five-volume family saga consisting of *The Furys* (1935), *The Secret Journey* (1936), *Our Time Is Gone* (1940), *Winter Song* (1950), and *An End and a Beginning* (1958)—about the fortunes of a lower-class Liverpool-Irish family. H.'s social concerns, his theme of men at sea, and his uncompromising realism in the portrayal of a people and a place are all harmoniously orchestrated in this work. Fanny Fury is one of the most fully realized women in contemporary fiction, while the portrait of John Kilkey is an impressive study of a pacifist.

Hollow Sea (1938), one of H.'s personal favorites, is an intense study of men under personal and professional pressure while involved in a secret wartime mission on a ship. *The Ocean* (1941) tells the story of six sailors in a lifeboat after their ship has been torpedoed by a German submarine. Through a series of flashbacks, H. tells the grim tale of survival at sea. *Sailor's Song* (1947) is the story of a wounded and delirious sailor afloat on a raft. His remembrance of things past before he drifts into death is narrated in a spare, poetic style. In *The Closed Harbour* (1953), set in Marseille, an outcast sailor has lost his honor and his ship: without his ship he disintegrates, and H. analyzes the strange umbilical relationship that exists between a sailor and his ship. *Levine* (1956) is a tale of two human wrecks, Felix and Grace, and their stormy relationship. Felix is a fascinating study of a man without a country and with no identity except in his memory.

After *Say Nothing* (1962), a novel about a man who takes up lodging with a strange couple that in its depiction of noncommunication and its imagery drawn from prison portrays what life is like for the totally damned, H. did not write fiction for ten years. But he took up play-writing for radio, television, and the stage. His plays indicate a temperamental affinity with Strindberg, Beckett, and Pinter (qq.v.).

H.'s recent novels, *A Woman in the Sky* (1973), *A Dream Journey* (1976), and *A Kingdom* (1978), reveal an artist at the height of his powers. In these works H. uses a plain but chiseled prose and much dialogue. Thus, the novels read like plays.

Although H. has been admired by many leading writers and has consistently received good reviews, he has had only a small cultish audience. Of his own writing H. has said, "It's like a prisoner, being a writer." As for the writing of a novel, he has said that it is "a series of blind gropings in a dark tunnel."

FURTHER WORKS: *Drift* (1930); *The Last Voyage: A Tale* (1931); *Men in Darkness: Five Stories* (1931); *Ebb and Flood* (1932); *Stoker Haslett: A Tale* (1932); *Aria and Finale, and Other Stories* (1932); *Captain Bottell* (1933); *Quartermaster Clausen* (1934); *At Bay* (1935); *Stoker Bush* (1935); *Half an Eye: Sea Stories* (1937); *Broken Water: An Autobiographical Excursion* (1937); *Grey Children A Study in Humbug and Misery* (1937); *People Are Curious* (1938); *Between the Tides* (1939); *No Directions* (1943); *Sailor's Song* (1943); *At Bay, and Other Stories* (1944); *Crilley, and Other Stories* (1945); *What Farrar Saw* (1946); *Emily* (1948); *Towards Horizons* (1949); *A Walk in the Wilderness* (1950); *The House in the Valley* (1951); *Collected Stories* (1953); *Don Quixote Drowned* (1953); *The Welsh Sonata: Variations on a Theme* (1954); *Chaliapin* (1967); *John Cowper Powys: A Man in the Corner* (1969); *The Face of Winter* (1969); *Herman Melville: A Man in the Customs House* (1971); *Another World* (1972); *The Darkness* (1973); *Against the Stream* (1981)

BIBLIOGRAPHY: Stokes, E., *The Novels of J. H.* (1964); "A Novelist in Neglect: The Case for J.H.," *TLS*, 11 June 1971, 675–76; Morris, R. K., "Saved and Damned by Imagination," *Nation*, 11 May 1974, 601–2; Howe, I., "An Original and Abrasive Novelist," *NYTBR*, 19 Dec. 1976, 1, 26; Mathewson, R., "H.'s Palimpsest," *New Leader*, 2 Jan. 1977, 17–18; Gibbs, L., *J. H.: A Bibliography*

K. BHASKARA RAO

HANSBERRY, Lorraine

American dramatist, b. 19 May 1930, Chicago, Ill.; d. 12 Jan. 1965, New York, N.Y.

H. developed as a writer during the 1950s and early 1960s, a period of racial tension and the nonviolent civil rights movement, both of which influenced her work. Although born to a prosperous black Chicago family, of which she was the youngest child, she could not ignore racism. After two years at the University of Wisconsin she moved in 1950 to New York City and settled in Greenwich Village, where a small group of dedicated friends encouraged her playwriting.

In 1959 H.'s first play, *A Raisin in the Sun*, opened on Broadway to rave reviews. The first black woman to have a play produced on Broadway, H. was also the first Afro-American whose work won the New York Critics' Circle Award for the best play of the year. The popularity of the play is quite understandable. Timely, moving, well crafted, it exposes the consequences of racism while generally avoiding platitudes, slogans, and one-dimensional characters. H. can sketch a white racist with understanding and treat her black protagonists, the Younger family, critically as well as sympathetically. Based on an actual incident when the

Hansberrys moved into a white neighborhood, *A Raisin in the Sun* pits Lena, the strong matriarch, against Walter Lee, her weak, self-indulgent son who "comes into manhood" when he refuses the white community's bribe to leave. His pan-Africanist sister, Beneatha, and her Nigerian boyfriend, Asagai, reinforce the importance of black pride and unity. Although the characters are black, the subjects—cultural pride, family responsibility, individual honor, and self-respect—are universal. Translated into over thirty languages, performed throughout America and Europe, adapted as a film and in 1973 as the successful musical *Raisin, A Raisin in the Sun* has gained international recognition as a major American drama.

H.'s versatility is evident in her second play, *The Sign in Sidney Brustein's Window* (1964), completed shortly before her death. Set in Greenwich Village, the play focuses on Sidney Brustein, a frustrated Jewish intellectual, and on his neurotic family and his friends. With the exception of Alton Scales, a black engaged to Sidney's sister-in-law, the characters are all white; the problems are human, only peripherally racial. By testing her characters' commitment and decency, H. shatters common stereotypes. Thus, a black can be bigoted, a racist tolerant, and a reform politician corrupt. The play touches on homosexuality and prostitution, but centers on Sidney Brustein, who, like Walter Lee Younger, matures and accepts responsibility for people and principles. In contrast to *A Raisin in the Sun, The Sign in Sidney Brustein's Window* was not initially well received. Criticized for its didacticism, slow pace, and flat characters, the play nearly closed after opening night, but the devoted producers, cast, and theater lovers kept it on Broadway until H. died, of cancer, three months later.

After her death, Robert Nemiroff, H.'s former husband (they had been secretly divorced), edited and published her unfinished manuscripts. *Les Blancs* (1972), the play H. was working on when she died, reflects her continued support for African nationalism. Consistently realistic, she recognized the problems confronting new nations and leaders, but believed in the struggle for independence. Her protagonist, Tshembe Matoseh, a British-educated African married to a white woman, symbolizes the complexities of race relations and the conflict between personal and communal obligations. His insights, growth, and commitment to freedom reflect H.'s values and life. In *To Be Young, Gifted and Black* (1969), autobiographical dramatized readings compiled by Nemiroff from her speeches, letters, journals, and plays, H. emerges as an intelligent, witty, courageous woman who dedicated her talent to the furthering of justice.

Although she completed only two plays, H. created memorable characters who defy stereotypes and transcend limited environments. Her treatment of racism, African nationalism, and social change foreshadowed the turbulent late 1960s and its protest movement.

FURTHER WORKS: *The Drinking Gourd* (1960); *The Movement: A Documentary of a Struggle for Equality* (1964)

BIBLIOGRAPHY: Davis, O., "The Significance of L. H.," *Freedomways,* 5 (1966), 396–402; Baldwin, J., Preface to *To be Young, Gifted and Black* (1969), pp. xi–xv; Miller, J., "L. H.," in Bigsby, C. W. E., ed., *The Black American Writer* (1969), Vol. II, pp. 157–70; Weales, G., "Losing the Playwright," *Commonweal,* 5 Sept. 1969, 542–53; Farrison, W. E., "L. H.'s Last Dramas," *CLAJ,* 16 (1972), 188–97; Brown, L. W., "L. H. as Ironist: A Reappraisal of *A Raisin in the Sun,*" *JBlS,* 4 (1974), 237–47; special H. issue, *Freedomways,* 19, 4 (1979)

EVELYN AVERY

HANSEN, Martin A.

Danish novelist, short-story writer, and essayist, b. 20 Aug. 1909, Strøby; d. 27 June 1955, Copenhagen

Born into a family of religious small farmers, H. was deeply influenced in his youth by the blend of simple Christian and traditional rural values that characterized the last vestiges of the dying peasant culture in Denmark. In the late 1920s and the early 1930s, while a student and subsequently as a young teacher in Copenhagen, he turned away intellectually from his religious, social, and political roots, espousing atheism and Darwinism and becoming a communist sympathizer. But by the 1940s, he had gradually become convinced of the inadequacy of the ideologies he had accepted. World War II in particular shattered his faith in rationalism, disclosing, it seemed to him, the lack of an all-embracing meaning in life.

Paradoxically, most of H.'s best fiction was written between 1939 and 1947, as he struggled to cope with Europe's external chaos and his own disillusionment. The conflict between his nihilistic perception of reality and the values

325

of his rural-Christian past became the dialectical basis for his mature fiction. His personal response to that conflict, best described as existential, would provide the passionate, humanly engaged perspective that informs his work. This perspective is seen in the dialectical structures of *Jonatans rejse* (1941; Jonathan's travels), a satiric picaresque novel in which a smith, having captured the devil in a bottle, sets out to bring him to the king, and of *Lykkelige Kristoffer* (1945; *Lucky Kristoffer*, 1974), perhaps H.'s finest novel, which describes the episodic quest of an idealistic, improverished young nobleman who leaves his provincial home and journeys to Copenhagen during the religious wars of the Reformation. In both novels the protagonists are naïve and either intuitive or idealistic, creatures of heart, faith, and simple virtues. Both protagonists have as foils companions committed to reason, intellect, science, atheism, men whose more sophisticated vision weakens their moral fiber.

This intense period of creativity climaxed with the publication of three novellas in the volume entitled *Tornebusken* (1946; the thorn bush), and with *Agerhønen* (1947; the partridge), a collection of short stories. While greatly varied in style, setting, and point of view, these stories repeatedly present people in complex existential situations, people who are in the process of examining their lives, making choices, and wrestling with the burdens of moral awareness.

After the war, H. gave up teaching and supported himself and his family exclusively with writing. In the widespread ideological debate that flourished in postwar Denmark, his was an influential voice seeking to define those aspects of the cultural tradition that were still vital and steadying in the chaos of modernity. This effort reached a high point with the publication of *Orm og tyr* (1952; serpent and bull), an impressive cultural history that examines the complementary relationships of pagan and Christian religions in Scandinavia. Yet his best known and most widely translated novel, *Løgneren* (1950; *The Liar*, 1954), harked back to the intense existential ambiguities of his earlier work. Originally a radio narrative, *Løgneren* is a compelling psychological revelation of its protagonist-narrator; it delineates the complex ethical struggle of a sensitive schoolmaster on a small ice-locked island as he vacillates between demonic self-indulgence and disciplined self-denial; it demonstrates H.'s mastery of lyrical and symbolic form.

With few exceptions, H.'s fiction vividly depicts the milieu in which he grew up, the farms and villages of rural Denmark. His characters' lives are linked to birds and seasons, fields and plants, water and weather. His fiction implies the need for a natural religiousness, suggesting the value of being in touch with natural cycles, with the land, with animals, and with people at a level more profound than mere rational awareness. Yet he does not show rural life as simply idyllic.

H.s fiction is characterized by disarmingly simple, unpretentious language. Its rhythms are typically those of oral storytelling. A rich vein of humor, often warmly playful, occasionally grimly ironic, pervades his work. The impression of simplicity is also conveyed by H.'s vigorous narration; he is a natural storyteller who engrosses readers quickly and sustains their interest at a high level until he reaches often startling conclusions. Yet readers caught in the web of H.'s engaging narrative surface gradually become aware that his fictions are far more subtle than they at first seem. This paradoxical yoking of simplicity and complexity in characterization, moral vision, and artistic form is one of the most striking features of his work.

In his twenty years as a writer, H. produced a substantial body of work. Now generally acknowledged as the foremost Danish writer of his generation and among the greatest Danish writers of this century, H. focused in a spiritually troubled time the cultural, ethical, and existential concerns of his countrymen in such a way as to appeal widely to both sophisticated readers and the more general public alike. His work has significantly influenced modern Danish literature. The gradual growth of his reputation outside Denmark since his premature death is evidence that his best fiction transcends his own time and place.

FURTHER WORKS: *Nu opgiver han* (1935); *Kolonien* (1937); *Tanker i en skorsteen* (1948); *Leviathan* (1950); *Dansk vejr* (1953); *Kringen* (1953); *Paradisæblerne, og andre historier* (1953); *Rejse på Island* (1954); *Konkyljen* (1955); *Midsommerkrans* (1956); *Efterslæt* (1959). FURTHER VOLUMES IN ENGLISH: *Against the Wind* (1979)

BIBLIOGRAPHY: Vowles, R. B., "M. A. H. and the Uses of the Past," *ASR*, 46 (1958), 33–40; Printz-Påhlson, G., "*The Liar*: The Paradox of Fictional Communication in M. A. H.," *SS*, 36 (1964), 263–80; Schow, H. W., Kierkegaardian Perspectives in M. A. H.'s *The Liar*," *Crit*, 15, 3 (1974), 53–65; Ingwersen, N., Introduction to *Lucky Kristoffer* (1974), pp. 5–22; Ingwersen, F. and N., *M. A. H.*

(1976); Schow, H. W., Introduction to *Against the Wind* (1979), pp. 1–12

H. WAYNE SCHOW

HANSEN, Thorkild

Danish documentary novelist and critic, b. 9 Jan. 1927, Copenhagen

Following studies in literature at Copenhagen University, a literary debut in 1947, and a stay in Paris from 1947 to 1952, H. worked as a journalist and literary critic on several Copenhagen newspapers. His deep interest in history and archeology led to his participation in archeological expeditions to Kuwait (1960), Sudan (1961), Hudson Bay, Canada (1964), and Guinea (1965). These expeditions laid the foundation for his literary production.

H. had his artistic breakthrough with *Pausesignaler* (1959; interval signals), a collection of travel notes and philosophical reflections, in which he rejects all ideological standpoints in favor of factual, undogmatic reporting of concrete reality. Drawing the full consequence of his demand for factual as opposed to fictitious narration, H. embraces a new genre in Danish literature—the documentary novel—in *Det lykkelige Arabien* (1962; *Arabia Felix,* 1964), which tells of a Danish expedition to Arabia during the 18th c. Through on-the-spot studies, archival research, and the use of diaries kept by the expedition leader, H. was able to draw a personal portrait of the explorer set against a geographical background with an exceedingly vivid atmosphere. In *Jens Munk* (1965; *The Way to Hudson Bay,* 1970), which deals with a Danish admiral and seafarer who in the 17th c. unsuccessfully sought the Northwest passage, H. likewise combined precise documentation, with his personal narrative technique, utilizing comedy, satire, and pathos. H.'s next published work, a three-volume study of the Danish slave trade between the Gold Coast and the sugar plantations of the West Indies, *Slavernes kyst* (1967; the slave coast), *Slavernes skibe* (1968; the slave ships), and *Slavernes øer* (1970; the slave islands), combines characteristics of the epic novel, the essay, and historical writing.

Another form of achieving closeness to reality is found in *De søde piger* (1974; the sweet girls)—the first in a projected ten-volume series. It consists of H.'s own diary entries from the years 1943–47. Although structured as a novel, the book gives a documentary close-up of a past era as well as providing background to the development of H.'s literary career. H. himself has labeled the book a documentary *Entwicklungsroman* (novel of development). His latest work, *Processen mod Hamsun* (1978; the trial of Hamsun), published simultaneously in the three Scandinavian countries, is a piece of historical documentation with the Norwegian author Knut Hamsun (q.v.) as the main character and hero. It has been criticized for its subjectivity and its defense of a man who collaborated with the Nazis during the occupation of Norway (1940–45). The underlying tenet is, however, a probing of the incompatibility of art and politics, and the rejection of the political man makes it a highly provocative work in our time.

In Danish literature H. stands outside modernism, and on the border between history and fiction. His use of the documentary novel, a genre that builds on authentic material from reality in contrast to the subjectivity of most modern novels, has given H. international fame. His success is also due to his exceptional ability to live up to the epic demand—his knack for telling a plain, unvarnished tale.

FURTHER WORKS: *Minder svøbt i vejr* (1947); *Resten er stilhed* (1953); *Syv seglsten* (1960); *En kvinde ved en flod* (1961); *Jens Munks minde-ekspedition* (1965, with Peter Seeberg); *Vinterhavn* (1972)

MARIANNE FORSSBLAD

HARDY, Thomas

English poet and novelist, b. 6 June 1840, Higher Bockhampton; d. 11 Jan. 1928, Dorchester

H.'s long life extended from the early years of Queen Victoria's reign to the restless period between this century's two world wars. He was writing fiction during the time of Dickens, Trollope, and George Eliot, and he published poetry in the decade of T. S. Eliot's (q.v.) *The Waste Land* and Hemingway's (q.v.) *The Sun Also Rises.*

From his family and his early surroundings H. gained a deep perspective on the past. He was born in the thatched cottage of the family's lifehold estate in Dorset, near a wild waste that H. would celebrate as the timeless Egdon Heath. He grew up in a region bristling with Roman rings and still more ancient tumuli; when he returned to his native section as a successful novelist, he built his home within sight of an early burial mound.

At the time of H.'s birth, the family fortunes

had declined somewhat from a long tradition of gentility. His father, a master mason and building contractor, was also a church musician, and from him H. learned the trade of stonecutting and a love of music. The rich folkloric materials that were to permeate his writings were absorbed from the live traditions of ballads and tunes, mummers' spectacles, local superstitions, and tales told by his elders, particularly his paternal grandmother.

H.'s mother, whose tastes included Latin poets and French romances, provided for his education. Although H.'s formal schooling ended when he was fifteen, he continued the study of languages on his own, and eventually was able to read the *Iliad* and the New Testament in Greek. At fifteen, H. began teaching Sunday school in the Stinsford Parish Church, and for a time it seemed possible that he would go to a university and prepare for holy orders; but instead he was apprenticed for a period of six years to a Dorchester architect, John Hicks. Next door to Hicks's office was a school kept by William Barnes, a poet who taught H. the value of local dialect. Both Hicks and Barnes drew around them a circle of young men of intellectual promise; association with these and with Horace Moule, of Queen's College, Cambridge, did much to stimulate H.'s critical powers and to awaken his literary ambition.

Still, it seemed that H. was settled for life in a provincial career of restoring churches, when in 1862 he traveled from the rural isolation of Dorset to London, there to work as an assistant in the architectural firm of Arthur Blomfield. Although he applied himself enough to win two architectural prizes, the next five years also included visiting art galleries, attending Dickens's public readings, and enjoying Shakespeare and opera. During these years he was reading Charles Darwin, Herbert Spencer, T. H. Huxley, and John Stuart Mill, whose positivism moved him to a reluctant agnosticism. He attended evening classes in French at King's College; he read Greek drama, the Elizabethan and romantic poets, and Tennyson and Swinburne, and gave informal lectures on poetry to Blomfield's staff; and he wrote poems, many of them grim, all of them rejected by editors. Most of these poems would appear years later in successive volumes of verse. His only published work at this time was a piece of prose fiction, "How I Built Myself a House," in *Chambers's Journal* (March 18, 1865).

In July 1867 H. left London for the family home in Dorset, and resumed work briefly with Hicks in Dorchester. It was at this time that H.

entered into a temporary engagement with Tryphena Sparks, a sixteen-year-old relative on his mother's side. The relationship, which was long concealed from the public, deeply affected H. and formed an emotional base for much of the content of his fiction and poetry, although he mentioned her by name in only one poem.

In July 1868 H. sent the manuscript of a novel, *The Poor Man and the Lady*, to Alexander Macmillan, who rejected its social satire as excessive. The next March he visited George Meredith, then a reader for Chapman and Hall, who persuaded H. to suppress the work and instead to try a novel "with more plot." The result was *Desperate Remedies* (1871), published anonymously at H.'s expense. An extravagant blend of romance and crime, the book was a failure.

Meanwhile, H. had been working at church renovation with G. R. Crickmay of Weymouth, and while on an assignment in St. Juliot, Cornwall, had met Emma Lavinia Gifford. A young woman with social aspirations, and some literary skill herself, she encouraged H. to consider literature as his "true vocation." Although he continued his architectural work, including another stint in London, he moved doggedly toward a professional writing career.

In 1872 appeared *Under the Greenwood Tree,* also anonymously. A slight work, whose idyllic scenes and rustic humor are unclouded by calamitous events, this novel was nevertheless an earnest of H.'s eventual achievement in depicting the "emotional history" of the region he called Wessex (after the ancient kingdom of Alfred the Great).

About this time Emma Gifford was assisting H. in the preparation of the manuscript of *A Pair of Blue Eyes*, which ran serially in *Tinsley's Magazine* and was published in book form in 1873. The serial publication, in Leslie Stephens's *Cornhill Magazine,* of *Far from the Madding Crowd* (1874) and its favorable reception in book form insured H.'s exchange of architecture for a career as a writer. The same year he and Emma Gifford traveled to London where they were married, over the objection of her father.

H. wrote *The Hand of Ethelberta* (1876) during a period when the couple lived in London and traveled on the Continent. At this time H. began making notes for a treatment of the Napoleonic wars as "grand drama."

During 1877, while residing in a cottage overlooking Dorset's River Stour, H. wrote *The Return of the Native* (1878). This novel was a masterful creation of classic austerity, presenting willful human beings who struggle against themselves and against an indifferent fate that dooms them through chance combinations of their own impulses and the witless whims of external nature.

By 1885 the couple had settled near Dorchester at Max Gate, a house designed by H. and built by his brother, Henry. With the exception of seasonal stays in London and occasional excursions abroad, this was H.'s home for the rest of his life.

The product of H.'s pen in the 1880s was uneven. *The Trumpet-Major* (1880), reflecting his persistent interest in the story of England's struggle with Napoleon, was followed by his weakest novel, *The Laodicean* (1881), and by *Two on a Tower* (1882). These were succeeded by a masterpiece, *The Mayor of Casterbridge* (1886), the study of a "man of character" whose fate evolves along Sophoclean lines, whose psychology H. plumbed to its unconscious depths before the world had been supplied with the convenient charts of Sigmund Freud (q.v.).

The Woodlanders (1887) showed the influence of H.'s recent reading of Schopenhauer's *The World as Will and Idea*, although the novel's plot emphasis is upon social tragedy arising from class discrimination and unjust divorce laws.

Another masterpiece, *Tess of the D'Urbervilles,* which ran serially in a bowdlerized form before its publication in 1891, seemed to confirm H.'s claim to reader affection and critical esteem—in spite of the fact that he had presented his heroine as "a pure woman" destroyed by Victorian prudery, hypocrisy, and intolerance. Another novel, *The Well-Beloved* (not published in book form until 1897) was running serially; the author and his wife were reveling in London invitations to "crushes, luncheons, and dinners"; and H. was collecting his third volume of short stories, *Life's Little Ironies* (1894). Then in 1895, the storm broke, following publication of *Jude the Obscure.*

This book, like *Tess of the D'Urbervilles* a consequence of H.'s exploration of a dark side of his family connections in Berkshire, set forth the gloomy tale of a stonemason whose tangled sexual relationships in and out of marriage wreck his scholarly ambitions and eventually drive him to a miserable death. The novel was met with public outrage, and critics on both sides of the Atlantic abused the author as degenerate, called the work itself disgusting, impious, obscene. H.'s wife, who hitherto had

helped in the preparation of his novel manuscripts, had bitterly opposed the project, and their own marriage, already in difficulty, suffered from the fallout.

The uproar over *Jude the Obscure* so offended H. that he never wrote another novel. Instead he turned to his first love, poetry, and before the century was over he had published *Wessex Poems* (1898). He acknowledged in a brief preface that many of the fifty-one poems had been written "long before"—only four had been previously published; some had been revised or reclaimed from the prose of the novels. Notable inclusions were the early poems "Hap," lamenting that the world seems ruled by two "purblind Doomsters," Casualty and Time; and "Neutral Tones," an etching in words expressing despair at extinct love.

Reception of this first volume of verse was inconclusive, but H. persevered, and *Poems of the Past and the Present*, issued late in 1901, was an immediate success. The book's ninety-nine poems included early ballads and love poems as before; but there were also more recent pieces: the "In Tenebris" trio, "I Have Lived with Shades," "The Darkling Thrush," "The Subalterns," and a sampling of poems reflecting H.'s opposition to the South African war. The transformation of the artist from novelist to poet was assured; in the next three decades H. would establish himself as one of the most productive poets of the 20th c.

In 1902 H. began work on his long-meditated "epic-drama of the War with Napoleon," *The Dynasts.* As early as 1875 he had conceived the idea of a succession of ballads treating episodes in the career of Bonaparte. Five of these ballads were printed in *Wessex Poems.* Now, working intensely over the next five years, H. produced a massive poem in three parts, nineteen acts, and 130 scenes. The three parts were published, successively, in 1904, 1906, and 1908. This "spectacular poem," H. himself admitted, was more epic than drama. Its blank-verse passages are generally undistinguished, the dialogue and diction are too often leaden. But the prose speeches of the common folk, the songs and other lyrical transitions, including, for example, the Trafalgar chorus, are impressive.

The scope of H.'s epic intention is equally impressive. Part I opens in 1805 with the English in high and low places discussing the threat of a French invasion of southern England, describes Napoleon's coronation, the battle of Austerlitz, and Nelson's triumph at Trafalgar and his death (in the arms of Captain Sir Thomas Hardy, H.'s ancestor), and concludes with the death of Pitt. Part II presents the defeat of the Prussians at Jena, the meeting of Napoleon and Czar Alexander at Tilsit, the war in Spain, Napoleon's abandonment of Josephine, and his marriage to Maria Louisa. Part III presents his Russian disaster in 1812, his multiplying defeats and his abdication, Elba, and Waterloo.

Perhaps H.'s most original conception was an adaptation of traditional epic machinery: the creation of "supernatural spectators of the terrestrial action," including the Spirit of the Years, the Spirit of the Pities, and the Spirits Sinister and Ironic, together with their choruses and other Intelligences. Unlike divinities in classical epics, these "impersonal abstractions" are detached from active involvement in human affairs. But like mortals, they are subordinate to the Immanent Will, the unconscious force that moves the world. The running comment of the Intelligences, delivered from their vantage point in the Overworld, adds a cosmic dimension to the work, providing a series of choral interpretations of the action and, at the same time, paradoxically reducing Napoleon and the other "dynasts" from the rank of heroes and, by implication, diminishing the significance of all human endeavor.

Now approaching seventy years of age, H. busied himself with the preparation of *Time's Laughingstocks, and Other Verses* (1909), a collection of ninety-six poems, some still dating back more than forty years, more composed in the new century: "The Revisitation," "A Trampwoman's Tragedy"; a number of love lyrics and country songs; "Panthera," based on an apocryphal story of Jesus' parentage and death; and a powerful antiwar poem, "The Man He Killed."

Honors were beginning to come to H. On the death of his friend George Meredith in 1909, he succeeded to the presidency of the Society of Authors. In 1910 King George V conferred on him the Order of Merit. Yeats (q.v.) was among those who journeyed to Max Gate in 1912 to present him with the gold medal of the Royal Society of Literature.

Then, in November 1912, H. was shaken by Emma Hardy's sudden death. *Satires of Circumstance, Lyrics and Reveries* (1914) contains "Veteris vestigia flammae," a group of twenty-one poems—some of H.'s very finest lyrics—that reveal H.'s retrospective view of their early love and the gradual deterioration of the marriage; and more than a hundred poems in later volumes continue themes relating to this

complex relationship. *Satires of Circumstance* also contains "The Convergence of the Twain," an ironic elegy on the sinking of the *Titanic*; "Channel Firing," a prophetic piece printed just three months before the outbreak of World War I; and bleak philosophic meditations like "A Plaint to Man."

H. had married his secretary, Florence Emily Dugdale, early in 1914. The remaining fourteen years of his life were lived in relative serenity. His productivity continued at an astonishing rate. *Moments of Vision and Miscellaneous Verses* (1917) and *Late Lyrics and Earlier* (1922) each contained more than 150 poems, among them "In Time of 'The Breaking of Nations'" and "And There Was a Great Calm." The latter volume was prefaced by a lengthy "Apology" in which H. defends himself against the repeated charge of pessimism and states a provisional faith in "evolutionary meliorism," bolstered by the frail hope that "the human and kindred animal races" may keep pain to a minimum "by loving-kindness operating through scientific knowledge, and actuated by the modicum of free will conjecturally possessed by organic life when the mighty necessitating forces—unconscious or other . . . happen to be in equilibrium. . . ."

From about 1920 through 1927 H. was working on his autobiography, which was disguised as the work of Florence Hardy, published in two volumes (1928 and 1930), later as the one-volume *Life of T. H.: 1840–1928* (1962).

Human Shows, Far Phantasies, Songs and Trifles (1925) was the last book of poems published in H.'s lifetime. *Winter Words in Various Moods and Metres* (1928) was ready for the press when he died. In all, H. had written close to a thousand poems, not counting *The Dynasts* or his verse drama *The Famous Tragedy of the Queen of Cornwall*, which he wrote and saw produced in 1923 when he was eighty-three years old.

Following H.'s death in his eighty-eighth year, his heart was buried in Stinsford churchyard and his ashes were buried in Westminster Abbey. His pallbearers included, besides the Prime Minister, Rudyard Kipling, Bernard Shaw, J. M. Barrie, John Galsworthy, A. E. Housman (qq.v.) and Edmund Gosse (1849–1928).

H.'s position as a novelist of the first rank seems secure; his place among 20th-c. poets, while undergoing reassessment, seems a permanent one. The poet Philip Larkin (q.v.) allotted more pages and many more poems to H.

than to any other poet in the 1973 *Oxford Book of Twentieth Century English Verse.*

In the light of the midcentury onslaught on realism, H.'s long-dispraised stress on accident and coincidence may be seen as his strategy for depicting the absurd. The Wessex of the novels and the poetry, like Faulkner's (q.v.) Yoknapatawpha, may be understood as a region in which the artist explores, in metaphor and symbol, the geography of the human mind.

The measure of H.'s influence on both fiction and poetry has been debated. H. G. Wells (q.v.) as a youthful writer derived ideas for one of his social comedies from the serial version of *Jude the Obscure.* The same novel fascinated D. H. Lawrence (q.v.) who drew upon it and other Wessex novels in his treatment of character and locale, and in "A Study of Thomas Hardy" (*Phoenix*, 1936) revealed how much H. occupied his thoughts at the time he was writing *The White Peacock* and *The Rainbow.* Ezra Pound (q.v.), who praised H.'s poetry for its clarity of expression, sent the older poet copies of his own verse for criticism. W. H. Auden (q.v.) confessed that he was under the spell of H.'s poetry for a period, and acknowledged that he owed H. an important debt of technical instruction. John Crowe Ransom (q.v.), calling H. a "late Victorian" poet, remarked on his closeness to the succeeding generation "by reason of his naturalism and rebellion against the dogma."

Television adaptations of H.'s short stories and recent films based on *Far from the Madding Crowd* and *Tess of the D'Urbervilles* have helped to keep H.'s name before the public. Those who read the books themselves are thereby engaged with a world that was already disappearing in H.'s day, and also with an artistic temperament and a noble intelligence that have added luster to the human spirit.

FURTHER WORKS: *Wessex Tales* (1888); *A Group of Noble Dames* (1891); *A Changed Man and Other Tales* (1913); *The Play of St. George* (1921); *Life and Art: Essays, Notes and Letters* (1925); *An Indiscretion in the Life of an Heiress* (1934); *The Letters of T. H* (1954); *T. H.'s Notebooks and Some Letters from Julia Augusta Martin* (1955); *"Dearest Emmie": T. H.'s Letters to His First Wife* (1963); *The Architectural Notebooks of T. H.* (1966); *T. H.'s Personal Writings: Prefaces, Literary Opinions, Reminiscences* (1966); *One Rare Fair Woman: T. H.'s Letters to Florence Henniker, 1893–1922* (1972); *The Literary Notes of T. H.* (1974); *The Com-*

plete Poems of T. H. (1976); *The New Wessex Edition of the Stories of T. H., Including Hitherto Uncollected Stories* (3 vols., 1977); *The Collected Letters of T. H., Vol. 1, 1840–1892* (1978); *The Personal Notebooks of T. H., with an Appendix including the Unpublished Passages in the Original Typescript of "The Life of T. H."* (1979); *From H. at Max Gate: A Series of Letters* (1979); *The Variorum Edition of The Complete Poems of T. H.* (1979); *The Collected Letters of T. H., Vol. 2, 1893–1901* (1980)

BIBLIOGRAPHY: Weber, C. J., *H. of Wessex: His Life and Career* (1940; 2nd ed., 1965); Guerard, A. J., *T. H.* (1949; rev. ed., 1964); Brown, D., *T. H.* (1954; rev. ed., 1961); Hardy, E., *T. H.: A Critical Biography* (1954); Purdy, R. L., *T. H.: A Bibliographical Study* (1954); Hynes, S. L., *The Pattern of H.'s Poetry* (1961); Orel, H., *T. H.'s Epic Drama: A Study of "The Dynasts"* (1963); Wing, G., *H.* (1963); Carpenter, R. C., *T. H.* (1964); Howe, I., *T. H.* (1967); Wright, W. F., *The Shaping of "The Dynasts": A Study in T. H.* (1967); Pinion, F. B., *A H. Companion: A Guide to the Works of T. H. and Their Background* (1968); Marsden, K., *The Poems of T. H.: A Critical Introduction* (1969); Bailey, J. O., *The Poetry of T. H.: A Handbook and Commentary* (1970); Miller, J. H., *T. H.: Distance and Desire* (1970); Brooks, J. R., *T. H.: The Poetic Structure* (1971); Millgate, M, *T. H.: His Career as a Novelist* (1971); Stewart, J. I. M., *T. H.: A Critical Biography* (1971); Davie, D., *T. H. and British Poetry* (1973); Gerber, H. E., and Davis, W. E., *T. H.: An Annotated Bibliography of Writings about Him* (1973); Gittings, R., *Young T. H.* (1975); Hawkins, D., *H.: Novelist and Poet* (1976); Orel, H., *The Final Years of T. H., 1912–1928* (1976); Page, N., *T. H.* (1977); Gittings, R., *T. H.'s Later Years* (1978)

CARL D. BENNETT

The Wessex novels . . . cover an immense stretch; inevitably they are full of imperfections—some are failures, and others exhibit only the wrong side of their maker's genius. But undoubtedly, when we have submitted ourselves fully to them, when we come to take stock of our impression of the whole, the effect is commanding and satisfactory. We have been freed from the cramp and pettiness imposed by life. Our imaginations have been stretched and heightened; our humour has been made to laugh out; we have drunk deep of the beauty of the earth. Also we have been made to enter the shade of a sorrowful and brooding spirit which, even in its saddest mood, bore itself with a grave uprightness and never, even when most moved to anger, lost its deep compassion for the sufferings of men and women. Thus it is no mere transcript of life at a certain time and place that H. has given us. It is a vision of the world and of man's lot as they revealed themselves to a powerful imagination, a profound and poetic genius, a gentle and humane soul.

Virginia Woolf, "The Novels of T. H.," *The Second Common Reader* (1932), p. 257

H.'s characters are full of moral conflicts and of decisions arrived at by mental processes. Certainly, Jude, Gabriel Oak, Clem Yeobright, above all, Henchard, are men who have decisions to make, and if they do not make them entirely on the plane of reason, it is because H. was interested most in that hairline dividing the rational from the instinctive, the opposition, we might call it, between nature, and second nature; that is, between instinct and the habits of thought fixed upon the individual by his education and his environment. Such characters of his as are led by their emotions come to tragedy; he seems to say that following the emotions blindly leads to disaster. Romantic miscalculation of the possibilities of life, of love, of the situation; of refusing to reason their way out of their predicament; these are the causes of disaster in H.'s novels. Angel Clare is a man of the highest principle, trained in belief, religion, observance of moral law. His failure to understand the real nature of Christianity makes a monster of him at the great crisis of his life. The Mayor of Casterbridge spends the balance of his life in atonement and reparation for a brutal wrong committed in drunkenness and anger; his past overtakes and destroys him. H. had an observing eye, a remembering mind; he did not need the Greeks to teach him that the Furies do arrive punctually, and that neither act, nor will, nor intention will serve to deflect a man's destiny from him, once he has taken the step which decides it.

Katherine Anne Porter, "Notes on a Criticism of T. H.," *SoR*, 6 (1940), 159–60

One by one the striking things about H.'s art as a story-teller fall naturally into place as functions of balladry. There is the reliance, especially at the outset, upon the sharp definition of scene and background. There is the easy alliance of the grotesque and disproportionate with the substantial and natural, and the unselfconscious boldness with which they are offered. There are the slighter rhythms and movements of the story suggesting that the sung stanza is never far behind. There are the neat, rounded, and intertwining groups of events, the simple and decisive balancing of characters. There is the vivid sense of the meaning of scenery, the human and the natural involving one another. There is the narrative method whereby encounter (whether of person with person, or person with Fate) is the life of the tale. The ballad situations and the ballad coincidences are carried off partly by boldness and verve; partly by an art which holds all spare attention concentrated upon the vividness of the presentation itself.

Douglas Brown, *T. H.* (1961), p. 111

As a writer of novels T. H. was endowed with a precious gift: he liked women. There are not, when one comes to think of it, quite so many other nineteenth-century novelists about whom as much can be said. With some, the need to keep returning in their fiction to the disheveled quarters of domesticity causes a sigh of weariness, even at times a suppressed snarl of discontent; for, by a certain measure, it must seem incongruous that writers intent on a fundamental criticism of human existence should be sentenced to indefinite commerce with sex, courtship, adultery and family quarrels. H., by contrast, felt no such impatience with the usual materials of the novel. Though quite capable of releasing animus toward his women characters and casting them as figures of destruction, he could not imagine a universe without an active, even an intruding, feminine principle. The sexual exclusiveness of nineteenth-century American writing would have been beyond his comprehension, though probably not beyond his sympathy.

Throughout his years as a novelist H. found steadily interesting the conceits and playfulness of women, the elaborate complex of stratagems in which the sexual relationship appears both as struggle and game. He liked the changefulness, sometimes even the caprice, of feminine personality; he marveled at the seemingly innate capacity of young girls to glide into easy adaptations and tactical charms. And he had a strong appreciation of the manipulative and malicious powers that might be gathered beneath a surface of delight. Except perhaps with Sue Bridehead, he was seldom inclined to plunge into the analytic depths which mark the treatment of feminine character in George Eliot's later novels; but if he did not look as deeply as she did into the motivations of feminine character, he was remarkably keen at apprehending feminine behavior. He had observed and had watched, with uneasy alertness. The range of virtuosity which other writers had believed possible only in a stylized high society or sophisticated court, H., in his plain and homely way, found among the country girls of southwest England.

Irving Howe, *T. H.* (1967), pp. 108–9

H.'s multiple vision of experience brings him close to the modern Absurdist form of tragi-comedy or comi-tragedy. . . . The Kafka-like distortions of figure or scene . . . stress the ironic deflation of

KNUT HAMSUN

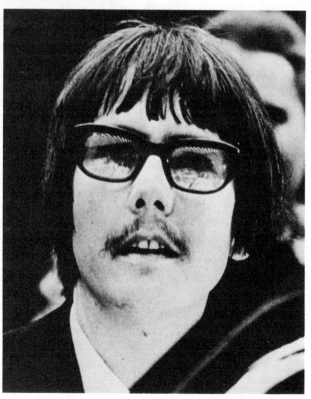

PETER HANDKE

THOMAS HARDY

JAROSLAV HAŠEK

romance, heroism, and tragedy by the objective incursion of absurdity; without, however, denigrat-
ing the value of romance, heroism, and suffering.
. . . In all his work H.'s personal voice, with its
humane values, its Gothic irregularities, its human
contradictions and rough edges, its commonness
and uncommonness, strains against the rigidities
of traditional patterns and expectations. The first
two paragraphs of *The Mayor of Casterbridge*, for
example, can provide the mixture to be found in
all the other novels, *The Dynasts*, and most of the
poems—the amalgam of homely simplicity, awkward periphrasis, triteness, and sharp sensuous vision that invests an ordinary scene with the significance of myth and Sophoclean grandeur. The dissonance of the multiple vision dramatically enacts
H.'s metaphysic of man's predicament as a striving, sensitive, imperfect individual in a rigid, non-
sentient, absurd cosmos, which rewards him only
with eternal death.

Jean R. Brooks, *T. H.: The Poetic Structure*
(1971), pp. 13–14

. . . H.'s poetry, with its tentative contexts and interrupted perspectives, invites condescension, in
the neutral sense of the word. H. seldom writes
with the authority of Yeats, or even Browning. He
does not manhandle his reader, but instead asks
him (politely) to excuse the potentially inexcusa-
ble, to tolerate or to ignore entirely whatever
seems too jagged or wayward. . . . He is beset by
omens and haunted relentlessly, and it is remarkable that these visitations should be so empty of
any suggestion of guilt. H., for all his obsessions,
is a healing poet. He forgets heroically and loses
cleanly. . . . Regret is no stranger to him, but his
regret is not for what he has done or left undone
but for the passing of what was good and beautiful. His only sadness is that life, though it must be
loved as all we have, is, after all, too small for us.
In saying these things, we excuse his faults, for we
have found in him a great and difficult sanity. . . .

James Richardson, *T. H.: The Poetry of Necessity*
(1975), pp. 77–78, 131–32

. . . His novels, although so little concerned to
cheer us up, are not in their total effect dispiriting
—as is today so much of the literature of despair
and of the absurd. We see man as a minute "vital-
ization" amid the dust of the stars, and individuals
as crawling specks on a Roman road, an immemorial heath, a brutal terrain of hacked turnips.
. . . H. himself offered as his ultimate apologia the
proposition that if a way to the better there be it
exacts a full look at the worst. He often provides
us with the worst in a distillation so extreme as to
strain our sense of the verisimilar, but the proposition itself does speak to our condition. . . . In part
it is a psychological statement, affirming the classical theory of catharsis. The confronting of spectacles of pity and terror is purgative, so that we *feel*

better . . . provided the personages we are invited
to contemplate are moral beings much like ourselves. . . . His people are moral agents, constantly
aware of the paradox that, in a neutral universe,
significance and dignity are theirs because they see
good and evil around them and own a duty to
conduct their lives, however senselessly tormented,
in terms of that perception.

J. I. M. Stewart, "The Major Novels," in Margaret
Drabble, ed., *The Genius of T. H.* (1976), pp.
65–66

What defeats the attempt to discriminate the better from the worse among H.'s poems is not just
the great number of the poems, and their various-
ness. It is not even the impossibility, for the most
part, of categorizing the poems as "early" or
"late"; nor the almost equal difficulty of categorizing them according to genre, except in the broadest and most impressionistic way. These impediments to taking H. the poet as a whole, the good
with the bad, do not come about by accident. Behind them is the curious paradox that H., who imposes himself so imperiously upon his medium,
imposes himself on his reader hardly at all. On
every page, "Take it or leave it," he seems to say;
or, even more permissively, "Take what you want,
and leave the rest."

This consciousness of having imposed on his
reader so little is what lies behind H.'s insistence
that what he offers is only a series of disconnected
observations, and behind his resentment that he
should be taken as having a pessimistic design
upon his reader, when in fact he so sedulously respects the reader's privilege not to be interested,
not to be persuaded. It is on this basis—his respect of the reader's rights to be attentive or inat-
tentive as he pleases—that one rests the claim for
H. as perhaps the first and last "liberal" in modern
poetry. And it is because we are so unused to liberalism as a consistent attitude in a poet, that we
have so much difficulty with the poetry of H.

But the outcome is that every new reader of
H.'s poetry finds there what he wants to find. And
in the event this means, for the most part, that
each reader finds in the poems what he brings to
them; what he finds there is his own pattern of
preoccupations and preferences. If this is true of
every poet to some degree, of H. it is exceptionally true.

Donald Davie, *T. H. and British Poetry* (1972),
pp. 28–29

HARIS, Petros

(pseud. of Yiannis Marmariadis) Greek short-
story writer, critic, essayist, poet, and editor, b.
1902, Athens

A versatile man of letters, H. has for more than
two generations been at the literary and cultural

center of Greece. He studied law at the University of Athens but made literature his lifelong career. Among his many posts, H. served on the board of the National Theater, as president of its Committee on Artistic Affairs, and on the National Board of Literature. As editor of *Nea Estia* from 1933 on H. exerted widespread influence and provided a regular forum for the finest Greek writers. The many honors he received culminated in his election to the Athens Academy in 1946. His travel book *Politeies kai thalasses* (1955; cities and seas) won the annual First National Award.

In *Nea Estia* and elsewhere H. published many essays on literary subjects. However, he is primarily noted for short stories that range from reminiscences of the past to revelations of character during moments of self-discovery. H. published six volumes of short fiction, beginning with *Teleftaia nichta tis yis* (1924; last night on earth). Along with other demotic writers he departed in his stories from the traditional "heroic style" in favor of a new realism. Both by precept in his essays and by example in his fiction H. helped to set high standards for the genre.

The title story of *Phota sto pelagos* (1958; lights on the sea) is set on a tiny island during the German Occupation. H. personifies freedom as a phantom ship that appears at night and is seen first by Vangelis, a retarded youth, who is not believed. He awakens the islanders by ringing the church bell. Then others who are more reliable also see the ship, and they also ring the bell. The ship of freedom can be glimpsed by individuals, but not by groups—not until liberation. And so the islanders ring the bell, and wait.

As a poet H. coauthored *Dialogoi kai poeimata* (1926; dialogues and poems) with I. M. Panayotopoulos (q.v.). He published travel articles in *Nea Estia*, as well as books on his travels, which took him as far as China. He also translated into Greek works such as *The Red and the Black* by Stendhal and *The Blue Bird* by Maeterlinck (q.v.). As an essayist commenting on literature, art, and life, H. wrote six volumes; the last of these books was *E zoe kai e techni* (1963; life and art).

As editor of *Nea Estia*, the most prestigious Greek journal, he maintained the high standards that helped to spark a literary renascence in modern Greece.

FURTHER WORKS: *K. G. Kariotakis* (1943); *Makrinos kosmos* (1944); *Krisimis oras* (1944); *Otan e zoe yinete oneiro* (1945, 1947); *Eleftheroi pnevmatikoi anthropoi* (1947); *Ellenes pezographoi* (1953); *Paleoi kai neoi dromi* (1956); *E Kina exo apo ta teichi* (1961); *Metapolemikos kosmos* (1962); *Dromos ekato metron* (1962); *Otan oi agioi katevainon sti yi* (1965); *E megali nichta* (1969)

BIBLIOGRAPHY: Gianos, M. P., *Introduction to Modern Greek Literature* (1969), pp. 22, 222
ALEXANDER KARANIKAS

HARRIS, Wilson

Guyanese novelist, critic, and poet, b. 24 March 1921, New Amsterdam

The originality and maturity of H.'s first novel, *Palace of the Peacock* (1960), and his consistent exploration and expansion of his themes in the novels he has produced since can be explained by the fact that that novel did not appear until he was thirty-nine and had put in a long apprenticeship. Before he went to England, H. worked as a surveyor in the 1940s and 1950s, becoming intimate with the peoples, rivers, and forests of his native Guyana. His speculations about the relationship of man to his landscape no doubt began then. During that time H. contributed poems and stories regularly to the Guyanese journal *Kyk-Over-Al*, in which his fascination with the bonds between myth and history and with the remarkable connections between the mythologies of different cultures can be observed. These early interests, experiences, and perceptions recur in his fiction, and many of his characters are autobiographical. Fenwick of *The Secret Ladder* (1963) and Wellington of *Genesis of the Clowns* (1977) are both Guyanese surveyors; and Da Silva of *Da Silva da Silva's Cultivated Wilderness* (1977) is, like H., a South American artist of mixed racial background working in London.

H. himself has described his work as "groping towards something . . . within a deepening cycle of exploration." It is possible to see this process beginning in *Palace of the Peacock* and continuing throughout his fiction. The journey the characters in that novel undertake to the heart of the South American continent is reminiscent of the one in Conrad's (q.v.) *Heart of Darkness* and is symbolic of a journey into their own histories and mythologies, a step necessary for self-awareness, which in turn will permit them to identify with life everywhere and throughout time.

In the early novels the jungles of South America are symbolic of the eternal present, the context in which man must learn to see himself. In later novels the art of painting is used to suggest this sense of eternity. H. attempts to encourage his readers to abandon their preconceptions, and to see the entirety and complexity of life afresh. He keeps reminding man that he possesses a "living closed spiritual eye" whose perceptions are more trustworthy than those of his "dead seeing material eye." Such juxtaposition of apparently incongruous ideas is one of the main devices H. uses to urge modern man to look at life constructively. This vision and the technique intrinsic to it is H.'s contribution to contemporary fiction.

FURTHER WORKS: *Fetish* (1951); *The Well and the Land* (1952); *Eternity to Season* (1954; new ed., 1978); *Far Journey of Oudin* (1961); *The Whole Armour* (1962); *Heartland* (1964); *The Eye of the Scarecrow* (1965); *The Waiting Room* (1967); *Tradition, the Writer and Society* (1967); *Tumatumari* (1968); *Ascent to Omai* (1970); *The Sleepers of Roraima* (1970); *History, Fable and Myth in the Caribbean and Guianas* (1970); *The Age of Rainmakers* (1971); *Black Marsden* (1972); *Fossil and Psyche* (1974); *Companions of the Day and Night* (1975); *The Tree of the Sun* (1978)

BIBLIOGRAPHY: James, C. L. R., *W. H.: A Philosophical Approach* (1965); Hearne, J., "The Fugitive in the Forest," in James, L., ed., *The Islands in Between* (1968), pp. 140–54; Sparer, J. L., "The Art of W. H.," in La Rose, J., ed., *New Beacon Reviews* (1968), pp. 22–30; Ramchand, K., *The West Indian Novel and Its Background* (1970), pp. 164–74; Gilkes, M., *W. H. and the Caribbean Novel* (1975); Maes-Jelinek, H., *The Naked Design: A Reading of "Palace of the Peacock"* (1976); Maes-Jelinek, H., "'Inimitable Painting': New Developments in W. H.'s Latest Fiction," *ArielE*, 8, 3 (1977), 63–80

                                    ANTHONY BOXILL

HARTLEY, L(eslie) P(oles)
English novelist, short-story writer, and critic, b. 30 Dec. 1895, Whittlesea; d. 13 Dec. 1972, London

H. assumed his rank as a distinguished novelist rather late in life, after early successes in short stories and book reviewing. His first full-length novel, *The Shrimp and the Anemone* (1944), the initial volume of his later acclaimed trilogy, comprising also *The Sixth Heaven* (1946) and *Eustace and Hilda* (1947) (the latter title standing for the trilogy), appeared when H. was forty-nine years old. Thereafter, H.'s career developed with remarkable smoothness, and his literary output achieved near prolificacy, with an especially large number of novels appearing in the last five years of his life.

Educated at Harrow and Oxford, and blessed with a considerable family fortune, H. lived the existence of a gentleman writer, concentrating in his fiction on upper-middle-class gentility with delicate, yet precise, psychological and moral delineations. A lifelong bachelor, H. often peopled his novels and short stories with slightly sinister, ambiguous servants who were necessary adjuncts for such a single man's domestic arrangements. H. invested many of his characters with his own moral concerns, his passion for Venice and for rowing, his somewhat diffident Christianity, and often something of his own charm, wit, and style.

H.'s fiction represents a distinctive synthesis of a dual tradition in the novel: romance derived from his much-beloved Nathaniel Hawthorne and realism indebted to Henry James (q.v.), with nods in the direction of some English favorites like the Brontës and Jane Austen. Much of H.'s best work features a rich symbolic structure that hints at fable and allegory behind his plausible and generally realistic narratives. For example, in the *Eustace and Hilda* trilogy H. shows how a brother and sister fulfill the destructive relationship, despite their genuine love for each other, of the shrimp and the anemone, into whose world the siblings as children intrude in the first scene of the initial volume.

H. often sought spiritual and metaphysical meanings besides clarification of social and psychological details, thereby suggesting metaphors for the condition of life in the 20th c. His most successful and best-known novel, *The Go-Between* (1953), offers a double perspective on the century as an aged narrator looks back from midcentury at events from his boyhood. Victim of his own distorting fantasy, like numerous protagonists in H.'s fiction, Leo Colston suffers permanent emotional damage when reality overtakes him and his grandiose conception of the inhabitants of a grand country house where for a short time one summer he, the usual outsider, felt himself to be the charmed insider.

A similar traumatized character whose adolescent vulnerability in the face of premature initiation into adult life has serious consequences is the protagonist of *The Brickfield* (1964). Like Elizabeth Bowen (q.v.), H. displayed special sensitivity in his portrayal of adolescents whose innocence becomes corrupted by the mature world.

H.'s pathos of misapprehended motives and situations on the part of children and adolescents frequently yielded to comedy of manners when adult protagonists pursue willful fantasies rather than face reality. The prototype was *The Boat* (1949), wherein a middle-aged bachelor novelist devoted to sculling brings his own war in the midst of World War II to a quiet English village in which the gentry had reserved the neighboring waters for fishing.

One of the most moving, although neglected, novels in the H. canon is *The Hireling* (1957). Here H. reveals an increasingly Lawrentian element in his figure of the attractive working-class male who obliquely woos the widow Lady Franklin.

H. turned to political satire and cautionary fable, criticizing the modern welfare state and celebrating individuality, in his dystopian novel *Facial Justice* (1960). Similarly, H. treated recent social experiments in modern Britain with irony and comic outrage in *The Betrayal* (1966) and *The Collections* (1972). As an old man, H. produced novels of a somewhat lighter tone and less symbolic structure. In subject matter, however, H. became more daring, with the introduction of incest and homosexuality as subjects in later novels.

Few 20th-c. English novelists can match H.'s portrayals of the romantic temperament caught in the cross-fire of the Edwardian past and the complex, equivocal present, or his humor and compassion in his deft exploration of the English class system, especially in his studies of masters and servants. H. remains an attractive minor master of a distinctly English restrictiveness, one of those rare artists who has something to say about culture and civilization and who can express sensibility and insight with ingratiating humor, well-turned style, and moral energy.

FURTHER WORKS: *Night Fears, and Other Stories* (1924); *Simonetta Perkins* (1925); *The Killing Bottle* (1932); *The Traveling Grave, and Other Stories* (1948); *My Fellow Devils* (1951); *The White Wand, and Other Stories* (1954); *A Perfect Woman* (1955); *Two for the River* (1961); *The Novelist's Responsibility: Lectures and Essays* (1967); *The Collected Short Stories* (1968); *Poor Clare* (1968); *The Love-Adept* (1969); *My Sisters' Keeper* (1970); *The Harness Room* (197); *Mrs. Carteret Receives, and Other Stories* (1971); *The Will and the Way* (1973); *The Complete Short Stories* (1973)

BIBLIOGRAPHY: Melchiori, G., "The English Novelist and the American Tradition," *SR*, 18 (1960), 502–15; Bien, P., *L. P. H.* (1963); Hall, J., "Games of Apprehension: L. P. H.," *The Tragic Comedians: Seven Modern British Novelists* (1963), pp. 111–28; Bloomfield, P., *L. P. H.* (1970); Webster, H. C., "L. P. H.: Diffident Christian," *After the Trauma: Representative British Novelists since 1920* (1970), pp. 152–67; Mulkeen, A., *Wild Thyme, Winter Lightning: The Symbolic Novels of L. P. H.* (1974); Jones, E. T., *L. P. H.* (1978)

EDWARD T. JONES

HAŠEK, Jaroslav

Czechoslovak poet and novelist (writing in Czech), b. 30 April 1883, Prague; d. 3 Jan. 1923, Lipnice

H.'s father, a rather unsuccessful teacher and later an office clerk, died when H. was thirteen. Although intelligent, H. did not exert himself at school and became a pharmacist's assistant for a while; better results from his studies at a commercial school in Prague brought him a job in a bank, but he could not keep it because of his often irresistible wanderlust. Walking penniless through large areas of central and southeastern Europe, H. gained some valuable experience. His World War I record is marred by his changing allegiance; he first worked as a patriotic journalist with Czech troops stationed in Russia, but later he collaborated on Communist propaganda as a member of the Bolshevik Party. After the war, when he returned to Prague to work as a professional writer, he was not very welcome, and even less so when he had to answer a charge of bigamy (which was true).

H. was a gifted writer and a very colorful character, who loved hoaxes and horseplay; convivial and anarchistic as he was, and an excellent raconteur, he could entertain his friends for hours. Yet, the coarseness of his humor and his total irreverence caused embarrassment to

Czech literary critics who made an effort to appreciate his work, and it was instead foreigners who first called attention to the special quality of his greatest creation, the good soldier Švejk.

In his early amusing stories H. explored the character of simple folk; this subject matter eventually led him to develop the type of a lower-class man defying his oppressors by simple cunning. The good soldier Švejk appears in stories published as early as 1912–*Dobrý voják Švejk, a jiné podivné historky* (the good soldier Švejk, and other strange tales). There he is a grotesque dog dealer, doing his national service and ridiculing the Hapsburg military bureaucracy by his pretended mental deficiency, which brings about his desired release from the army. This, however, is the prewar Švejk. Not even the Švejk in *Dobrý voják Švejk v zajetí* (1917; the good soldier Švejk in captivity) is the fully crystallized Švejk of H.'s masterpiece, *Osudy dobrého vojáka Švejka za světové války* (4 vols., 1921–23; *The Good Soldier Švejk and His Fortunes in the World War*, 1973). H. himself had to experience war in order to endow his great character with such cynicism and grotesqueness; his creation attests to H.'s strong disapproval of war.

Švejk is no fighter; in fact, his feigned obedience and eagerness to carry out orders only show up their absurdity and result in highly comic situations. Fully aware of his superiors' weaknesses, Švejk uses his boundless imagination to exploit them for his own benefit; his innocent smile and his good humor even in the most precarious situations infuriate his superiors, and in the long run, slowly but steadily, he undermines the whole bureaucratic system. This method of passive resistance stems from the subjugated position of the small Czech nation within the Austro-Hungarian Empire: noncooperation and sabotage were the only means of defense against oppression. Although the term "Švejkism" was later used to connote the Czechs' passive resistance in general, Švejk is not really a typical Czech; rather, he resembles "any 'little man' who gets caught up in the wheels of a big bureaucratic machine" (C. Parrott). As a comic character, Švejk embodies the wide range of H.'s humor: high comedy, sarcasm, satire, and irony, as well as simple folk wisdom. For these H. must be given credit, even if his Rabelaisian humor and the irresponsibility of the "hero" provoked objections on moral grounds from some critics. As a novel, the work is rather loose and episodic in structure, as is natural for H.'s gift as a raconteur; yet, the hero is a clearly delineated and very unusual protagonist.

H.'s other works also reveal his exuberant imagination, his wit, and his love of hoax; if he had, in real life, no misgivings about confounding the public by selling dogs with dyed furs and forged pedigrees, or advertising the sale of "two thoroughbred werewolves"–hoaxes he actually perpetrated–he could go even further in his fiction, as in *Můj obchod se psy* (1915; my dog business), *Průvodčí cizinců, a jiné satiry z cest i domova* (1913; *The Tourist Guide*, 1961), and *Tři muži se žralokem, a jiné poučné historky* (1921; three men with a shark, and other instructive stories).

However objectionable H.'s famous character and his own real-life behavior may have been, as a writer H. had a genius of a special kind; Švejk deserves a place in the gallery of great characters of world literature. Under the coarse surface, H.'s humor brings home quite subtly some very serious truths about human nature.

FURTHER WORKS: *Májové výkřiky* (1903, with L. H. Domažlický); *Trampoty pana Tenkráta* (1912); *Kalamajka* (1913); *Dva tucty povídek* (1920); *Pepíček Nový, a jiné povídky* (1921); *Dobrý voják Švejk před válkou, a jiné podivné historky* (1922); *Mírová konference, a jiné humoresky* (1922); *Paměti úctyhodné rodiny* (1925); *Šťastný domov* (1925); *Za války i za sovětů v Rusku* (1925); *Zpověď starého mládence* (1925); *Ze staré drogerie* (1926); *Všivá historie* (1926); *Podivuhodná dobrodružství kocoura Markuse* (1927); *Když kvetou třešně* (1927); *Můj přítel Hanuška* (1928); *Fialový hrom* (1958); *Zrádce národa v Chotěboři* (1962); *Dějiny strany mírného pokroku v mezích zákona* (1963). FURTHER VOLUME IN ENGLISH: *The Red Commissar* (1981)

BIBLIOGRAPHY: "The King of Bohemia," *TLS*, 7 Sept. 1962, 665–66; Peter, P., *H.s "Schweik" in Deutschland* (1963); Vlach, R., "Gogol and H.: Two Masters of 'Poshlost,'" *Études slaves et est-européennes*, 7 (1963), 239–42; Frynta, E., *H., the Creator of Schweik* (1965); Procházka, W., *Satire in H.'s Novel "The Good Soldier Schweik"* (1966); Enright, D. J., "The Survival of Švejk," *Listener*, 30 Aug. 1973, 284–85; "The Art of Survival," *TLS,* 21 Sept. 1973, 1083–84; Parrott, C., *The Bad Bohemian* (1978)

B. R. BRADBROOK

HAUPTMANN, Gerhart

German dramatist and novelist, b. 15 Nov. 1862, Obersalzbrunn; d. 6 June 1946, Agnetendorf

H.'s ancestors had lived in Silesia since 1600, where many of them had been weavers, but his father owned a resort hotel. His school years were unhappy and unsuccessful; he spent 1878–79 working on his uncle's farm, where the pietism of his relatives heightened a natural leaning toward mysticism. He turned to sculpturing, and spent two years at the Art Academy in Breslau and another year of desultory study at the University of Jena before setting up a sculptor's studio in Rome. Typhoid fever forced him to return home. At Jena he had listened to lectures on philosophy, archaeology, and literature. Through his brother, who was a student in the natural sciences, H. came under the influence of the German exponent of Darwinism, the popular lecturer Ernest Haeckel. The scientific determinism of the age, combined with a youthful zeal for social reform, challenged the religious orthodoxy of his boyhood. This unresolved conflict helps to explain the polarity of his literary work.

H.'s engagement to the wealthy Marie Thienemann in 1881 and his marriage in 1885 provided the financial support that made his literary career possible. His earliest poetic efforts are now available in a facsimile printing *Früheste Dichtungen* (1962; earliest poetry), but his serious concern with literature began after an unsystematic study of Greek literature, history, and philosophy and wide reading in the German classics and modern authors. After his marriage he lived first in Berlin and then in its suburb Erkner. He established contacts with the leaders of naturalism. Performances of Ibsen's *Ghosts* and Tolstoy's *The Power of Darkness* made him study the dialogue and the effectiveness of these dramas. At his own expense he published *Promethidenlos* (1885; the Promethean's fate), a Byronic epic, and a collection of lyrics, *Das bunte Buch* (1888; the many-colored book), and contributed to magazines two realistic stories, "Fasching" (1887; carnival), and "Bahnwärter Thiel" (1888; "Flagman Thiel," 1933).

The success of his first drama, *Vor Sonnenaufgang* (1889; *Before Dawn*, 1909), signaled the beginning of a new era for the German theater. It was performed by the Freie Bühne, the German equivalent of Antoine's Théâtre Libre in Paris, where Ibsen's social dramas had already avoided official censorship. The shock-ing details of the life of a dissolute peasant family, presented with grim realism, aroused the audience. Indignant protests against the revolting presentation of a sordid environment and the vicious consequences of hereditary alcoholism mingled with vociferous acclaim for the courageous young dramatist. The ponderous style of the day was suddenly swept away and a painstakingly accurate reproduction of the speech and mannerisms of every character introduced a new technique to the drama.

More plays followed in rapid succession: *Das Friedensfest* (1890; *The Coming of Peace*, 1900) and *Einsame Menschen* (1891; *Lonely Lives*, 1898), both family tragedies; and *Die Weber* (1892; *The Weavers*, 1899), the masterpiece of German naturalism, in which the historic uprising of 1844, a protest against the mechanical looms that destroyed the simple livelihood of Silesian weavers, is vividly recreated. In *Die Weber* five seemingly independent acts form a crescendo in dramatic action in which the numerous characters are carefully individualized but in their totality become the tragic protagonists of the suffering masses. Despite H.'s objective presentation of the misery and wretchedness that he had witnessed in visiting some areas of his province, he was accused of tendentious writing by the imperial government, which tried unsuccessfully to prevent public performances.

Der Biberpelz (1893; *The Beaver Coat*, 1912), using similar dramatic techniques and realistic characterizations, is a social satire and ranks high as a comedy. *Florian Geyer* (1895; *Florian Geyer*, 1929), a drama of the Peasant War, attempted to present the social, cultural, and linguistic background of the 16th c. with such an abundance of characters and epic breadth that the audience was overwhelmed. A complete failure at its first performance, it won understanding and appreciation after the collapse of Germany at the end of World War I, when the tragedy of political disunity had become meaningful.

A year earlier, in *Hanneles Himmelfahrt* (1894; *Hannele*, 1894), H. had combined the sordid atmosphere of the village poorhouse with a sensitive, psychological analysis of the bruised and tortured spirit of an adolescent girl who finds solace in a sensuous dream world of religious symbolism. The neoromantic aspects surprised the critics, who had called H. a "naturalist," but gave further proof that H.'s art transcended all labels. An almost complete surrender to romanticism is reflected in *Die versunkene Glocke* (1897; *The Sunken Bell*,

1898), his most popular dramatic success. Its folklore and fairy-tale elements, combined with the sentimental love story of a struggling artist, delighted an audience surfeited with drab realism, but its fame was ephemeral.

More permanent, perhaps even the most enduring of the tragedies depicting the brutality of life that destroys the individual, are *Fuhrmann Henschel* (1899; *Drayman Henschel*, 1913), *Rose Bernd* (1903; *Rose Bernd*, 1913), and *Michael Kramer* (1900; *Michael Kramer*, 1914), which might be grouped together as tragedies of isolation. Henschel and Rose Bernd are simple peasant types who are goaded and hounded to death. They are guided by instinct rather than reason, and in despair become the victims of their loneliness. H.'s sympathetic understanding of these characters, whose inevitable destruction is presented with restraint and artistic veracity, is unmatched in modern drama. In *Michael Kramer* the tragedy is transferred to an artist's family, where the son possesses the divine spark but lacks moral fiber, and the father has artistic integrity but limited talent. The son yearns in vain for a love that might redeem his soul and restore him to society. Despair drives him to self-destruction. *Der arme Heinrich* (1902; *Henry of Aue*, 1914) reveals the only solution: redemption through love. This drama contains some of H.'s finest poetry and psychologizes this miraculous legend of Middle High German literature.

H. continued to return to older themes in literature, which he reinterpreted with a sympathetic understanding of the demonic conflicts of the soul: *Elga* (1905; *Elga*, 1906), *Kaiser Karls Geisel* (1908; *Charlemagne's Hostage*, 1915), *Griselda* (1909; *Griselda*, 1909), *Der Bogen des Odysseus* (1914; *The Bow of Odysseus*, 1917), *Winterballade* (1917; *A Winter Ballad*, 1924), and *Veland* (1925; *Veland*, 1929). Despite its realistic background, *Und Pippa tanzt!* (1906; *And Pippa Dances*, 1907) is perhaps the finest expression of H.'s yearning for beauty, symbolized by this fragile, exotic creature pursued by all men.

After years of marital difficulties H. was divorced in 1904 and married Margarete Marschalk, a gifted young violinist. A journey to Greece three years later yielded not mere travel impressions in *Griechischer Frühling* (1908; Greek spring) but a profound appreciation of the Dionysian spirit of the Hellenic world, in which human sacrifice is the bloody root of tragedy. Henceforth H.'s dramatic work freed itself more and more of the artifice of the modern theater and its popular realism. He attempted to recapture the essence of what he called *das Urdrama*, the simplest and yet most dramatic conflict of the individual, split and torn asunder by antagonistic facets of his own personality.

H.'s narrative work, though secondary in importance, gives further proof of the breadth and scope of his literary genius. The novel *Der Narr in Christo Emanuel Quint* (1910; *The Fool in Christ, Emanuel Quint*, 1911) chronicles the life of a simple peasant who literally relives the experiences of the historical Jesus. H.'s deeply religious nature comes to grips with modern scientific skepticism and his own anticlerical leanings. The religious ecstasy of a modern mystic, combined with asceticism and naïve faith, reflect H.'s own feeling for a religious experience almost incompatible with the temper of modern society. The profound sympathy and psychological insight of the narrative are tempered with a faint irony that suggests the inadequacy of both mysticism and rationalism. Diametrically opposed in spirit is *Der Ketzer von Soana* (1918; *The Heretic of Soana*, 1923), a Rousseauan paean of praise to the goodness and fullness of life governed by natural instincts. The sensuous beauty of the landscape of Ticino and the pagan assertion of the senses make it a hymn to Eros. Stylistically and structurally it is H.'s most perfect narrative work.

Public recognition came soon after the first theater successes. The Imperial Academy in Vienna gave H. its highest award, the Grillparzer Prize, three times (1896, 1899, 1905) for *Hanneles Himmelfahrt*, *Fuhrmann Henschel*, and *Der arme Heinrich*. Only the personal antagonism of the emperor prevented his receiving the German drama award, the Schiller Prize, for which he was repeatedly recommended. In 1905 Oxford University bestowed on him the honorary degree of doctor of letters; other honorary degrees followed from the universities of Leipzig (1909) and Prague (1921), and from Columbia University (1932). Most important of all was the international recognition that came with the Nobel Prize (1912). The Weimar Republic gave him its highest decoration and celebrated his sixtieth birthday as a national event. The Third Reich ignored him, but his dramas continued to be performed. After World War I H. published the dramas *Der weiße Heiland* (1920; *The White Saviour*, 1924) and *Indipohdi* (1920; *Indipohdi*, 1924), which represent something of a flight from reality into an exotic world of fantasy. *Der weiße Heiland* depicts the cruel conquest of Mexico and the tragedy of the guileless and trusting Montezuma, who falls victim to the avarice of the Christian invaders. *Indipohdi* reflects H.'s disillusionment and despair during the war years; inspired and suggested by Shakespeare's *The Tempest*, it was meant as H.'s farewell to the world of the drama. The epic *Till Eulenspiegel* (1928; Till Eulenspiegel), written in hexameters, tells the adventures of a former aviator who wanders in despair through postwar Germany in the guise of the legendary prankster of German folk literature. H. not only portrays the chaotic conditions of his fatherland but takes his hero back through history in a series of visionary episodes that include a blissful existence in the realm of ancient Greece before his return to the chaotic real world, where he plunges to his death in the Swiss Alps.

After years of preoccupation with the study of Shakespeare and the "Hamlet problem" H. published a revision of the text, wrote the drama *Hamlet in Wittenberg* (1935; Hamlet at Wittenberg)), and a novel, *Im Wirbel der Berufung* (1936; in the turmoil of the vocation), concerned with the theater and the staging of *Hamlet*. *Das Buch der Leidenschaft* (1930; the book of passion), a novel in diary form, is a veiled confession of the emotional stress occasioned by his divorce and remarriage; *Das Abenteuer meiner Jugend* (1937; the adventure of my youth) is a detailed autobiographical account of his formative years and early literary struggles. The story "Das Meerwunder" (1934; the chimera) moves far beyond the realm of reality, and its almost surrealistic style reflects H.'s despair at man's inhumanity and betrayal of the brotherhood of man. The tortured cry "I don't want to be a part of the human race," which becomes the watchword of the protagonist, symbolizes H.'s repugnance at the Hitler era. Written during the war years, the epic *Der große Traum* (1942; the great dream) depicts a series of grandiose visions of the eternal conflict between the forces of darkness and light. Again H.'s speculative thinking, tinged with the philosophy of the gnostics, attempts to transcend human limitations. The tragedy of medieval witchcraft and the Inquisition, *Magnus Garbe* (1942; Magnus Garbe), had its origin in H.'s interest in the age of the Reformation and the Anabaptists, and was completed by 1915; but its unmitigated gloom, the "bitterest tragedy of mankind," as the poet called it, made him postpone its publication until the end of his life. The House of Atreus tetralogy, the tragedy of Agamemnon and his family, consists of the concluding drama *Iphigenie in Delphi* (1941; Iphigenia in Delphi),

the opening drama *Iphigenie in Aulis* (1944; Iphigenia in Aulis), and the connecting one-act dramas *Agamemnons Tod* (1948; Agamemnon's death) and *Elektra* (1947; Electra), the last two published after H.'s death. All the horror and despair that the war years had aroused find full expression in this cycle of crime, passion, and bloodshed. The curse of Tantalus and his race endangers and destroys humanity. Mankind longs helplessly for salvation. Only human sacrifice makes any sort of atonement possible.

H.'s last work, the unfinished novel *Der neue Christophorus* (1943; the new Christopher), is again the story of suffering humanity, to be redeemed by Erdmann, who represents the eternal rebirth of mankind. Shortly after the end of World War II and the occupation of Silesia by the Russians, who showed respect and friendship for the aged poet and protected him and his property against the indignities of Polish looting, H. died—at the very moment when orders were given for the mass evacuation of all Germans from that province. H., whose greatest fear at the end of his life had been the threat of deportation, virtually died with the anxious words "Am I still in my house?" on his lips.

His versatile talent in creating real human beings, his subtle exposition of milieu, and his lifelike dialogue gave his work a dominant place in German literature for fifty years after his sensational success in 1889, and made H. the representative figure of that epoch. Despite excessive adulation or temporary neglect, his work is firmly established and reflects the complexity, doubts, uncertainties, and relativism of our time. It represents the highest artistic expression of what may eventually be regarded as a transitional age. The contradictions and irrational forces of human nature are revealed sympathetically and understandingly. The simplicity and yet the universality of his work, the sympathetic understanding of suffering humanity, received high recognition and praise from his greatest contemporaries, Rilke and Thomas Mann (qq.v.).

FURTHER WORKS: *Schluck und Jau* (1900; *Schluck and Jau,* 1915); *Der rote Hahn* (1901); *Das Hirtenlied* (1904; *Pastoral,* 1917); *Die Jungfern vom Bischofsberg* (1907; *The Maidens of the Mount,* 1915); *Die Ratten* (1911; *The Rats,* 1913); *Gabriel Schillings Flucht* (1912; *Gabriel Schilling's Flight,* 1915); *Atlantis* (1912; *Atlantis,* 1912); *Festspiel in deutschen Reimen* (1913; *Commemoration Masque,* 1917); *Lohengrin*

(1913); *Parsival* (1914); *Peter Brauer* (1921); *Anna* (1921); *Phantom* (1922; *Phantom,* 1922); *Ausblicke* (1922); *Die blaue Blume* (1924); *Die Insel der großen Mutter* (1924; *The Island of the Great Mother,* 1925); *Dorothea Angermann* (1926); *Wanda* (1928); *Spuk* (1930); *Um Volk und Geist: Ansprachen* (1932); *Die goldene Harfe* (1934); *Die Tochter der Kathedrale* (1939); *Ulrich von Lichtenstein* (1939); *Mignon* (1947); *Die Finsternisse* (1947); *Die großen Beichten* (1966); *Gesammelte Werke* (6 vols., 1906); *Gesammelte Werke* (6 vols., 1912); *Gesammelte Werke* (12 vols., 1922); *Gesammelte Werke: Ausgabe letzter Hand* (17 vols., 1942); *Sämtliche Werke* (11 vols., 1962–74) FURTHER VOLUMES IN ENGLISH: *The Dramatic Works* (9 vols., 1912–29)

BIBLIOGRAPHY: Holl, K., *G. H.: His Life and His Work* (1913); Fechter, P., *G. H.* (1922); Schlenther, P., and Eloesser, A., *G. H.* (1922); Reichart W. A., "Fifty Years of H. Study in America (1894–1944): A Bibliography," *Monatshefte,* 37 (1945), 2–28; Muller, S., *G. H. and Goethe* (1949); Weisert, J. J., *The Dream in G. H.* (1949); Garten, H. F., *G. H.* (1954); Behl, C. F. W., *G. H.: His Life and Work* (1956); Sinden, H., *G. H.: The Prose Plays* (1957); Shaw, L. R., *Witness of Deceit: G. H. as Critic of Society* (1958); Grueneberg, E., *Demon and Eros in Some Plays of G. H.* (1960); Michaelis, R., *Der schwarze Zeus* (1962); Reichart, W. A., "H. Study in America: A Continuation Bibliography," *Monatshefte,* 54 (1962), 298–309; Knight, K.G., and Norman, F., eds., *H. Centenary Lectures* (1964); Guthke, K. S., "Nihilism and Modern Literature: The Case of G. H.," *Forum* (Houston), 5, 1 (1967), 4–13; Usmiani, R., "Towards an Interpretation of H.'s *House of Atreus,*" *MD,* 12 (1969), 286–97; Tschörtner, H. D., *G. H. Bibliographie* (1971); Lea, H. A., "The Specter of Romanticism: H.'s Use of Quotations," *GR,* 49 (1974), 267–83; Mellen, P. A., *G. H. and Utopia* (1976); Gousie, L., "G. H. and German Surrealism," *GR,* 53 (1978), 156–65; Dussère, C. T., *The Image of the Primitive Giant in the Works of G. H.* (1979)

WALTER REICHART
UPDATED BY FRIEDHELM RICKERT

G. H. . . . has not only a true tone, but also true courage and true *artistic skill* to match this courage. It is foolish to assume that naturalistic coarseness is always tantamount to artlessness. On the contrary, if properly employed . . . it attests to the highest artistry. . . .

He altogether appears to me as the fulfillment of Ibsen. All I had been admiring in Ibsen for years, the "reach into life, it is a teeming ocean," the novelty and the boldness of the problems, the ingenious simplicity of the language, the talent for characterization, together with the most rigorous organization of the action and the elimination of anything not directly related to the plot itself—all of this I also found in H. Moreover, all the things I disliked about Ibsen . . . I did *not* find in H. He is not a realist who sporadically suffers from whimsical fits of philosophical romanticizing but a realist in good style, which is to say that from beginning to end he is always the same. [1889]

Theodor Fontane, *Sämtliche Werke* (1969), Vol. II, pp. 819–20

G. H. was a great man, one of the greatest—and G. H. was a weak man who failed in the decisive hour of the German genius, at a moment, when it became the duty of the great spiritual leaders to make their decision known. When, in 1933, darkness descended upon Germany, G. H. remained silent. . . . No, there is no excuse for his silence; and indeed, we would do neither him nor ourselves any favor whatsoever, if we were to attempt, by way of embellishing touches, to brighten up the distressing image presented by the aged G. H. He was no equal to the greatness of his task; he chose to remain a bystander at a loathsome spectacle from which to emphatically turn away would have been his duty, even though it is true —and it is true a thousand times—that he himself remained the same, and that no inner ties bound him to the barbarians among whom he lived.

Oskar Seidlin, *Monatshefte,* 38 (1946), 332

H. lacks an essential ingredient: an awareness of evil, of man's productive demonism. Thus he is not truly and essentially a psychologist, that is, a discoverer and portrayer of areas of the soul hitherto unexplored and often characteristic of a specific period, in the exact and decisive sense in which, for instance, Shakespeare and some of his contemporaries and, later, Stendhal and Strindberg were psychologists. He is not so much an explorer of the soul as an apologist for it. . . . In H. there is none of the splendid—so to speak, total—harmony and unity, the dialectical and contrapuntal fugal treatment of all themes, that appears in its full glory in the drama of Schiller, Kleist, and Racine. This is undoubtedly connected with the fact that this genius who makes no assumptions has absolutely no relationship to history. For him all history finally becomes happening.

Hans Hennecke, *Dichtung und Dasein* (1950), p. 129

Although H., particularly in the latter part of his life, contributed to every genre of literature, he will always be known first and foremost as a dramatist. It was in drama that his greatest faculty, the creation of live characters, found its fullest scope. . . . H. sees drama in all human existence; life, for him, is in its essence an unceasing strife—a strife that rends the heart of man from the first moment of his conscious existence. . . . Hence genuine drama is for H. in the first place a drama of the mind, of character, and not of action. . . .

This basic conception of drama partly explains why H.'s principal characters are throughout passive. They do not act; things happen to them. Their tragedy springs not so much from an excess of action, or of passion, as from an insufficiency, an incapacity to cope with the exigencies of life. Their keynote is suffering. However, H.'s intrinsic philosophy is not one of fatalism. His central theme, shaped in countless variations, is redemption through suffering. In the end, when tragedy has taken its course, the victim, though felled by the force of circumstances, emerges as the true conqueror.

Hugh F. Garten, *G. H.* (1954), pp. 12–13

The earlier plays . . . remain his finest single accomplishment, and if there have been frequent references to Ibsen and Shaw in these pages it is because he has no other rivals in modern literature in the field of realistic prose drama. . . . H.'s work has breadth, a unique power of creating men and environment, and an attitude which makes it as progressive as that of his often more argumentative contemporaries. His first service to his own and succeeding generations is his ability to paint human beings from many spheres of society, from the lower classes as well as the middle, and with equal understanding and concern for both. But his second service is that, though his plays lack the intellectual quality of those of Ibsen or Shaw, he touches in his own way on just as wide a range of problems, social and economic, religious and political. And his whole attitude implies a desire for reform wherever it appears to him that the society of his day has become rigid in its ideals, careless of the lives of its individual members, or blind to the inevitability of change.

Margaret Sinden, *G. H.* (1957), pp. 230–31

H. shared the slogans and arguments employed by most writers of his time and, in particular, . . . he participated in their attack on the so-called *Kulturlüge*, or Lie of modern society.

H.'s action against the cultural lie was motivated by the two-fold conviction that man's problems lie within society and that an accurate representation of social conditions would lead almost of itself to an improvement of the situation. One

needed only to inform the ignorant about abuses they had not yet become aware of, and appeal to the conscience of those who were still using social instruments for their own gain. In spite of this basic assumption, however, . . . H. had little confidence in direct reform. Even when the reformer appears as protagonist . . . he does so only to reveal the wrongs which H. wished to condemn and to serve as an example of the futility or impracticability of his particular way of reform. Each of these reformers represents a point of view which H. had already rejected for himself.

Leroy R. Shaw, *Witness of Deceit* (1958), p. 97

H.'s dramatic work, various and abundant (he has written more than forty dramas), is not without consistency. The tetralogy of the last decade is not too far removed from the early plays that he wrote in the 1890's. H. has simply advanced from the immediate—although no less universal—problems of individuals and their environment to broader issues of mankind, irrespective of time and place. However, the deep compassion and feeling for humanity have remained the same. This is indeed the distinguishing mark of H.'s dramatic work: social sympathy, social pity, social compassion. His social feeling is not intellectual; it is intuitive. Thanks to this elemental feeling for his fellow men, H. has remained the foremost social poet of Germany. And thanks to this deep feeling for humanity he is counted among those modern dramatists who, like Ibsen, Strindberg, and Shaw, have outlasted the changes of time and fashion.

Horst Frenz, Introduction to G. H., *Three Plays* (1977), pp. xiii–xiv

HAUSA LITERATURE
See Nigerian Literature

HAVEL, Václav
Czechoslovak dramatist, essayist, and poet (writing in Czech), b. 5 Oct. 1936, Prague

In accordance with the Communist regime's guidelines during the 1950s for suppressing all bourgeois elements, H., the son of a wealthy property owner and thus a member of the bourgeoise, was refused acceptance to any institution of higher learning. After his military service he found employment in Prague theaters, first as a stagehand. Later he became the dramatic consultant of the theater Na Zábradlí, which in 1963 staged his first play, *Zahradní slavnost* (1964; *The Garden Party*, 1969). Also in 1963, at the age of twenty-seven, he was accepted as a student at the Academy of

Dramatic Arts in Prague, from which he graduated in 1967. In 1968 H. was involved in the Czechoslovak reform movement. His work has been under complete ban since the reimposition of strict controls in 1969. H. took part in various civic initiatives protesting against the infringement of human rights in Czechoslovakia in the 1970s. Throughout this period he was subjected to police harassment and arrests. In October 1979 he was sentenced to four and a half years' imprisonment for his activities as a member of the Committee for the Defense of Unjustly Prosecuted Persons (VONS).

In *Zahradní slavnost* H. adopted some of the devices of the Theater of the Absurd (q.v.) to satirize modern bureaucratic routines and their dehumanizing tendencies, as well as some features of the Czech national character, namely the unprincipled adaptability to circumstances shown by the middle classes. The play was an immediate success both at home and abroad.

In his next play, *Vyrozumění* (1966; *The Memorandum*, 1967), staged two years later by the same theater that did *Zahradní slavnost*, he examined in a more complex way the effect that patterns imposed by the mechanics of bureaucracy have on society and on the individual mind. The plot turns around the introduction of an artificial language that is supposed to allow for greater precision in communication. H. uses this absurd idea to expose the emptiness of established clichés devoid of any real meaning. As no one can understand the monstrous new language, the ridiculous attempt to improve efficiency results in a complete breakdown of human relationships. It is finally rejected, only to be replaced by another, equally incomprehensible system, but fostered by people who see in it a means to advance their careers. The play also contains an implied criticism of the weakness and ineffectuality of certain liberal humanist attitudes, as represented by one of the main characters.

The theme was taken even further in *Ztížená možnost soustředění* (1968; *The Increased Difficulty of Concentration*, 1972), produced again by the theater Na Zábradlí. This time it is mainly the language and postures of the modern social sciences that come under attack. In the course of the play, the protagonist, a man who appears quite unable to cope with the problems of his marriage and his love affairs, dictates a radio lecture that discusses the complexity of contemporary life and uses fashionable sociological terminology. The gradually revealed failings of his personality, his inability to resolve anything, and his degeneration into an intellectual and psychological automaton, are reflected in a computer used by a farcical research team observing him.

The plays written in the 1970s, *Spiklenci* (1970; the conspirators), *Horský hotel* (1976; mountain hotel), and *Žebrácká opera* (1976), an adaptation of John Gay's (1685–1732) *The Beggar's Opera,* were widely produced outside Czechoslovakia, but did not achieve the same degree of success as his earlier work. He was more successful when he turned for his subjects to the greatly changed conditions of life in his country in a series of one-act plays: *Audience* (1975; *Audience*, 1978), *Vernisáž* (1975; *Private View*, 1978), and *Protest* (1978?; *Protest*, 1980). The three are connected by the character of a dissident playwright in trouble with the authorities, whose principled stand provokes hostile reactions from others, who had adapted to the prevailing circumstances. In the first, the playwright, now working as a laborer in a brewery, is asked by the head maltster to provide written reports on himself, which the maltster could pass on to the secret police. His refusal to comply results in an outburst of pent-up frustrations from the maltster. In *Vernisáž*, his mere presence lays bare the shallowness of the good life enjoyed by a couple who had sacrificed their conscience in favor of material advantages. A fellow writer, who has managed to do well under the new regime, is similarly exposed in *Protest*. In these plays the microcosm of an individual situation reflects the larger problem of moral corruption under pressures imposed by a totalitarian state.

H. was the most original dramatist to appear in Czechoslovakia in the 1960s, and during the following decade his work was among the most interesting to come from eastern Europe. Although the 1960s plays were evidently inspired by a peculiarly Czech brand of bureaucratic absurdity, the social evils and individual follies that they exposed are universal. Even after H. had been silenced at home, his plays continued to provide an artistic testimony of human values being distorted by political oppression, while the dramatist himself has set an example of personal integrity and civic courage.

FURTHER WORKS: *Autostop* (1961, with Ivan Vyskočil); *Nejlepší rocky paní Hermanové* (1962, with Miloš Macourek); *Protokoly* (1966)

BIBLIOGRAPHY: Blackwell, V., "The New Czech Drama," *Listener,* 5 Jan. 1967, 10–12; Grossman, J., "A Preface to H.," *TDR*, 11, 3

(1967), 117–20; Mihailovich, V. D., et al., eds., *Modern Slavic Literatures* (1976), Vol. II, pp. 91–96; Tynan, K., "Withdrawıng with Style from the Chaos," *New Yorker,* 19 Dec. 1977, 41–111; Trensky, P. I., *Czech Drama since World War II* (1978), pp. 104–24 and passim; Goetz-Stankiewicz, M., *The Silenced Theatre: Czech Playwrights without a Stage* (1979), 45–87 and passim

IGOR HÁJEK

HĀWĪ, Khalīl

Lebanese poet and critic, b. 1 Jan. 1925, Shwayr

H.'s early education was in Christian missionary schools, where he learned French and English and began an ambitious reading program in Western literature. He studied Arabic literature and philosophy at the American University of Beirut (1947–52) and in 1959 received a doctorate in Arabic literature from Cambridge University. While at Cambridge, he came under the influence of F. R. Leavis (q.v.), who introduced him to the major schools and techniques of Western literary criticism.

In 1940 H. published his first poems in the Lebanese dialect, but he soon abandoned the use of dialect in favor of Modern Standard Arabic. H.'s first poem in Modern Standard, "Ilāh" (1947; a god), elicited favorable critical response.

H.'s fine master's thesis, *Al-'Aql wa al-īmān bayn al-Ghazzālī wa Ibn Rushd* (1952; reason and faith: between al-Ghazzālī and Averroes), and his highly acclaimed *Kahlil Gibran: His Background, Character, and Works* (1963), written in English, mark the consummation of his education in philosophy and literary criticism.

To date, H. has published five volumes of poetry—*Nahr al-ramād* (1957; the river of ashes), *Al-Nāy wa al-rīh* (1960; the wind and the flute), *Bayādir al-jū'* (1965; the threshing-floors of hunger), *Al Ra'd al-jarīh* (1979; the wounded thunder), and *Min jahīm al-kūmīdya* (1979; from comedy's inferno)—as well as numerous long poems and critical essays on Arabic, French, and English poetry. He is also the editor of the *Encyclopedia of Arabic Poetry*, of which four volumes appeared in 1974.

H.'s poetry represents something new in Arabic literature in both form and content. Writing in *al-shi'r al-hurr* (mistakenly referred to as "free verse"), a form of verse that substitutes the unity of foot to the unity of meter, H. suc-

cessfully exploits those meters that are used in folk songs and are most familiar to people's ears. This metrical quality, along with his fresh, simple diction, has had great influence on his contemporaries. Moreover, H. succeeds, where other poets before him failed, in eliminating narration from his poetry by transforming legends and folktales into fundamental symbols that simultaneously evoke intellectual and emotional associations.

His poetry is universal in that it addresses the existential questions and the problems of the present-day Arab world within a universal and philosophical context, striking a happy balance between the intellectual and the emotional. Some critics note his tendency toward pessimism and his profuse use of dark and violent images, but others attribute this quality to his unwavering engagement with the problems of his world and his commitment to the truthfulness of his visions.

BIBLIOGRAPHY: Badawī, M., *A Critical Introduction to Modern Arabic Poetry* (1975), pp. 245–50; Haydar, A., and Beard, M., "Two Interpretations of H.'s 'The Cave,' " *Edebiyat*, 3, 2 (1978), 57–71; Jabra, J. I., "The Rebels, the Committed and Others," *MEF*, 1 (1967), 19–32; Jayyūsī, S., *Trends and Movements in Modern Arabic Poetry* (1977), passim

ADNAN HAYDAR

HAWKES, John

American novelist, b. 17 Aug. 1925, Stamford, Conn.

H.'s childhood and adolescence were spent in such widely dispersed parts of the U.S. as New York City and Juneau, Alaska. After serving as an American Field Service ambulance driver in Italy and Germany during World War II, he attended Harvard, where he studied creative writing under Albert J. Guerard (b. 1914) and completed his first two novels, *The Cannibal* (1949) and *Charivari* (1949). Since 1958 he has been a professor of English at Brown University.

H.'s vision of life is one of the bleakest among contemporary American novelists. His fictional practice has been to portray individuals acting out their obsessions in a hallucinatory landscape, living with terrifying vividness their libidinal dreams of self-fulfillment and self-destruction. Employing surrealistically the subterranean fears and fantasies of human nature, he strips life of the illusions used as insulation from the reality of self and the horrors of history. Only the saving graces of a richly poetic prose and of a comic inventiveness make his sadomasochistic exposures of human desire acceptable, and sympathetic.

Uncompromisingly experimental, he parallels a narrative concentration on random violence and sexual grotesquerie with disjunctions of time and space and violations of verisimilitude. His rebellious originality, rejecting traditional fictional forms, has produced unconventional, even ferocious, parodies of the western—*The Beetle Leg* (1951)—the picaresque tale—*The Goose on the Grave* (pub. in one vol. with *The Owl*, 1954)—and the detective thriller—*The Lime Twig* (1961). And his effort to thwart conventional thematic response to narrative realism has led him to create landscapes of the mind, fictive settings ostensibly signifying Renaissance Italy, postwar Germany, contemporary France, postwar England, the American West, and mythical lands and islands in the Mediterranean and Caribbean, which are disconcertingly familiar and yet bewilderingly strange, tantalizingly resistant to recognition as places. Significant in this regard has been his shift to the first person, whereby his protagonist-narrator has become his own mythographer. With *The Lime Twig* and *Second Skin* (1964) H. has gradually modulated these surrealistic extremes in favor, relatively speaking, of a more realistic surface and of a more dramatic and narrative coherence. Still, H.'s difficultness prevails, and the severity of his imagination has tended to restrict readers to a small but admiring group of writers and academics.

In *The Blood Oranges* (1971), *Death, Sleep & the Traveler* (1974), *Travesty* (1976), and *The Passion Artist* (1979), H. has increasingly concentrated his attention on the entangling relationship in the human psyche of love and death, sexuality and imagination, impotence and sterility. An allied leitmotif is the relationship of victim and victimizer, who act out their dark terrors of the psyche against a background of society's normal comings and goings. With his moral passion for exposing the destructive instincts in the night journey of the human soul, H. is the Savonarola of American novelists. He has called himself a New England puritan in rebellion against the puritanical version of life with its law, dictum, and insistence on human perversity. His "sex-singers" and "passion artists" are a rebellious expression of his contrary lyrical espousal of Eros; but the havoc he imagines them causing, and even courting for themselves—Eros locked in wedlock with

Thanatos—reflects an equally stubborn residual survival in H., despite his extreme maintenance of icy authorial detachment, of the puritanical moral code.

There has always been criticism of the excesses of H.'s style, with its overwritten and overblown language, and objection to his reduction of narrative to brilliant but isolated and unassimilated events. As if deaf to such carping, H. has gone his independent original way; and as novel has followed novel, he is hailed ever more justifiably by a growing number of readers as a major contemporary novelist.

FURTHER WORKS: *The Innocent Party: Four Short Plays* (1966); *Lunar Landscapes: Stories & Short Novels 1949–1963* (1969)

BIBLIOGRAPHY: special H. and John Barth issue, *Crit*, 6, 2 (1963); Graham, J., ed., *Studies in "Second Skin"* (1973); Busch, F., *H.: A Guide to His Fictions* (1973); Greiner, D., *Comic Terror: The Novels of J. H.* (1973); Kuehl, J., *J. H. and the Craft of Conflict* (1975); Santore, A. C., and Pocalyko, M., eds., *A J. H. Symposium* (1977); Hryciw, C. A., *J. H.: An Annotated Bibliography, with Four Introductions by J. H.* (1977)

MAX F. SCHULZ

HAYASHI Fumiko

Japanese novelist, short-story writer, and poet, b. 31 Dec. 1904, Shimonoseki; d. 2 June 1951, Tokyo

Daughter of an itinerant peddler, H. spent most of her childhood traveling from town to town, living always in flea-ridden inns. What she remembered most vividly about those days was perpetual hunger. She found solace, however, in writing poetry and reading. H. managed to put herself through high school by working as a factory hand and as a maid. Upon graduating, she went to Tokyo, only to experience the most bitter hardships of her life. Since childhood, roving had become almost second nature; she never settled in one place and constantly switched jobs (waitress, clerk, peddler, maid). She changed lovers just as swiftly.

Between her jobs and love affairs she found time to write poetry and children's stories. She also kept a diary, excerpts of which were serialized in the women's literary magazine *Nyonin geijutsu*, in 1928, under the title *Hōrōki* (journal of a vagabond). When *Hōrōki* was published in book form in 1930 it immediately attained tremendous popularity. It depicts a young heroine who manages to live with impressive honesty and cheerfulness in the lowest stratum of society. It is candidly narrated, devoid of pessimism and sentimentality. The montagelike sequence of diary entries creates a natural time flow of events, and H.'s style is compellingly vivid and intensely lyrical.

The success of *Hōrōki* put an end to H.'s precarious mode of life; she was able to travel to China and, in 1931, to Europe. She spent much time in Paris frequenting museums, concert halls, and theaters. Returning home in 1932, she wrote a number of short stories that gradually established her place in literary circles.

In 1935 H. wrote her first successful novel, *Inazuma* (lightning), whose characters were modeled on the members of her own family. During the Second Sino-Japanese War (1937–45), she was dispatched to China as a special correspondent by the newspaper *Mainichi*. She also served as a member of the Japanese wartime press corps in the South Pacific in 1942. These experiences gave further scope and depth to her later writings. During the remainder of the war she lived in the country and concentrated on writing children's stories.

In 1948 H. published one of her finest stories, "Bangiku" ("Late Chrysanthemum," 1960). It delineates with consummate skill the subtle, shifting moods of a retired geisha who is visited by a former lover. But on arrival the man confides that the purpose of his visit is to solicit financial assistance. Struggling to hold onto her receding romance, she receives a second blow on learning that the money is for extricating him from a tangled affair with a young woman.

Ukigumo (1951; *Floating Cloud*, 1957) was acclaimed as H.'s major work. The heroine Yukiko leaves for Indochina, trying to forget a rape incident. There she falls in love with Tomioka, and together they return to Japan. Spurned by him, she vainly tries to revive Tomioka's affection and gradually degenerates to the point of prostitution. Tomioka, having failed in business, leaves for Yaku Island. Enfeebled with tuberculosis, Yukiko follows him to the island only to die while he is away in the mountains. Just before her death Yukiko abandons herself to beautiful memories of their days in Indochina. A dark pessimism prevails in this work, but H.'s controlled detachment and penetrating insight into the fallen, wandering Yukiko generate a genuine pathos and an added dimension to the world of H.'s hobo protagonists.

Few of her contemporaries can rival H.'s skill in vividly evoking a particular atmosphere. Perhaps more important, she felt and understood the loneliness of displaced women, creating female characters, alienated but always alive, who speak with a universal voice that transcends their milieu and their homeland.

FURTHER WORKS: *Hatō* (1939); *Shitamachi* (1948; *Tokyo*, 1957); *Chairo no me* (1949); *Meshi* (1951); *H. F. zenshū* (23 vols., 1951–52)

BIBLIOGRAPHY: Morris, I., ed., *Modern Japanese Stories* (1962), pp. 349–50; Janeira, A. M., *Japanese and Western Literature: A Comparative Study* (1970), pp. 172–74; Johnson, E. W., "Modern Japanese Women Writers," *LE&W*, 18 (1974), 98–99

KINYA TSURUTA

HEANEY, Seamus

Irish poet, b. 13 April 1939, County Derry, Northern Ireland

H. was born and raised on a farm in Northern Ireland. He moved to Belfast in 1957, took his B.A. in English at Queen's University (1961), taught in local Belfast schools and colleges (1962–66), and then returned as a lecturer to Queen's University (1966–72). He has been a guest lecturer in the U.S. at both Berkeley and Harvard, but since 1972 he has lived primarily in the Republic of Ireland, first in County Wicklow and then in Dublin. Nevertheless, he remains a Northern writer, and his work is firmly rooted in the rural, Catholic, County Derry soil of his boyhood. Inevitably, he also continues to remember and brood upon the political troubles of a strife-torn Northern Ireland.

H. has published five books of poetry to date: *Death of a Naturalist* (1966), *Door into the Dark* (1969), *Wintering Out* (1972), *North* (1975), and *Field Work* (1979). "Digging," the first poem in H.'s first book, established both the ground and the artistic mode of operation for his future work. Almost all of his books echo with deep personal memories of a grandfather cutting turf, a father digging his spade into gravelly ground. This patient hardworking digging becomes a metaphor for the literary process itself: "Between my fingers and my thumb/The squat pen rests./I'll dig with it." By reading poets like Patrick Kavanagh, Robert Frost, and Ted Hughes (qq.v.), H.

learned to trust his rural background and to believe that it is possible to write of local things without being restricted by them. Thus, the language of his finest poems attends closely to the traditional life of thatcher and farmer. He is a poet who meditates often on the depth and elemental force of the green world.

But H.'s digging also goes beyond the merely provincial. As his work has progressed, he has dug deeper and deeper into Ireland's past, trying to find the linguistic and archeological roots of an older northern world, a common Irish heritage. The central symbol in H.'s work is the bog, the wide unfenced country of rural Ireland that reaches back millions of years. It is in the bog, whose "wet centre is everywhere" ("Bogland," 1969), that he seeks to find the different layers of the Irish past, the material and cultural remains of an ancient race, the older Norse and Viking worlds. H.'s difficult task is to find the archetypal center of the Irish world.

Each of H.'s books has marked his quiet but steady poetic development. In the past ten years he has emerged as one of a handful of indispensable contemporary Irish poets.

FURTHER WORKS: *Poems: 1965–1975* (1980); *Preoccupations: Selected Prose, 1968–1978* (1980)

BIBLIOGRAPHY: Press, J., "Ted Walker, S. H., and Kenneth White: Three New Poets," *SoR*, 5 (1969), 673–88; Kiely, B., "A Raid into Dark Corners: The Poems of S. H.," *HC*, 7, 4 (1970), 1–12; Buttel, R., *S. H.* (1975); McGuinness, A. "'Hoarder of Common Ground': Tradition and Ritual in S. H.'s Poetry," *Éire*, 13, 2 (1978), 71–92; Zoutenbier, R., "The Matter of Ireland and the Poetry of S. H.," *DQR*, 9 (1979), 4–23; Druce, R., "A Raindrop on a Thorn: An Interview with S. H.," *DQR*, 9 (1979), 24–37

EDWARD HIRSCH

HÉBERT, Anne

Canadian poet, novelist, and dramatist (writing in French), b. 1 Aug. 1916, Sainte-Catherine de Fossambault, Que.

Daughter of the influential critic Maurice Hébert (1888–1960), and cousin of the poet Hector de Saint-Denys Garneau (1912–1943), H. grew up in a home where literature was important. She has been awarded major literary prizes, both Canadian and French, and in 1960

became a member of the Royal Society of Canada. She has worked for Radio Canada (1950–53) and the National Film Board (1953–60). Since 1954 she has spent increasing amounts of time in France, where since 1958 her works have mainly been published.

Although H. has written short stories, film scripts, novels, and plays for the stage, television, and radio, she is known primarily as a poet. Her first volume of poetry was *Les songes en équilibre* (1942; dreams in equilibrium), but her best work is *Poèmes* (1960; poems), which contains the previously published *Le tombeau des rois* (1953; *The Tomb of the Kings*, 1967) as well as "Mystère de la parole" (mystery of the word). The latter is prefaced by an essay, "Poésie, solitude rompue" (poetry, a broken solitude), from which it becomes apparent that H. sees herself as having the mission to offer her readers a new reality, one that will feed them like bread and wine. In practice, in her austerity, which is sometimes mistaken for simplicity (although her verse is by no means simple), she frequently offers water rather than wine, and the water is that of tears. In distress and deprivation there is communion. She writes in free verse, using dense, closely packed images, achieving an almost surrealistic effect. Her main themes are sorrow and joy, love, solitude, and death. The image of water predominates, recurring as rain, tears, the sea, and rivers.

Next in importance to her poems are the title story in her collection of short stories, *Le torrent* (1950; *The Torrent*, 1972), and her novels, *Les chambres de bois* (1958; *The Silent Rooms*, 1974) and *Kamouraska* (1970; *Kamouraska*, 1973). In "Le torrent," a story about a young man's alienation owing to his mother's determination to make him atone for the sin she committed in bearing him, she castigates the morbid sense of sin that is a product of the old traditions of Quebec. Added to this is another French-Canadian phenomenon, the feeling of the weight of the past, inhibiting freedom of action in the present and the future. *Le tombeau des rois* and *Les chambres de bois*, about a young woman who ultimately escapes from a husband who has a horror of sex, offer the hope that the weight of the past may be lifted.

In *Kamouraska,* the story of a woman who conspires with her lover to murder her husband, this hope offers little promise. In a quiet frenzy, the protagonist struggles with her memories of a past that she has done her best to negate, in the name of respectability, but whose truth refuses to be suppressed. She is a symbol of alienation, passionately desiring a fulfillment that cannot be achieved by a woman in 19th-c. Canada.

Les enfants du sabbat (1975; *Children of the Black Sabbath*, 1977), a tale of witchcraft, incest, and intercourse with the devil, set in a French-Canadian convent, was poorly received in Quebec, where it seemed out of touch with present-day preoccupations. The novel *Héloïse* (1980; Héloïse) is the story of a young couple living in Paris who are destroyed by two vampires, male and female. Set in the period around 1900, it is her only fictional work to date that does not deal with Quebec.

Recent studies on H. focus on her poetry, and it is for her poetic qualities that she is chiefly respected.

FURTHER WORKS: *Théâtre: Le temps sauvage; La mercière assassinée; Les invités au procès* (1967); *Dialogue sur la traduction* (1970, with Frank Scott). FURTHER VOLUMES IN ENGLISH: *Saint-Denys Garneau and A. H.* (1962; bilingual)

BIBLIOGRAPHY: Collin, W. E., "Letters in Canada, 1953," *UTQ*, 23 (1954), 325–26; Purcell, P., "The Agonizing Solitude: The Poetry of A. H.," *CanL*, No. 10 (1961), 51–61; Pagé, P., *A. H.* (1965); Le Grand, A., *A. H., de l'exil au royaume* (1967); Lacôte, R., *A. H.* (1969); Major, J. L., *A. H. et le miracle de la parole* (1976); Bouchard, D., *Une lecture d'A. H.: La recherche d'une mythologie* (1977); Lemieux, P. H., *Entre songe et parole: Structure du "Tombeau des rois" d'A. H.* (1978)

BARBARA J. BUCKNALL

HEBREW LITERATURE
See Israeli Literature

HEDAYAT, Sadeq
Iranian short-story writer, novelist, and essayist, b. 17 Feb. 1903, Tehran; d. 9 April 1951, Paris, France

H. was born into a family of landowners; among his ancestors were many prominent statesmen and men of letters. In his twenties he was sent to Belgium and France to study. After having considered numerous scientific and academic professions, he committed himself to writing.

On returning to Iran, H. published his first collection of short stories, *Zendeh be-gur* (1930; buried alive). He joined a group of progressive intellectuals, but instead of mingling with friends he immersed himself in the study of Iran's history, folklore, and traditional beliefs, and in writing about them. This search into the past led him to study Zoroastrian, Hindu, and Buddhist philosophy and to travel to India in the 1930s.

Very little is known about H. as an individual; he preferred to live modestly and in solitude. However, it is known that he cared for the underprivileged and the humble people of his country and that he was an ardent patriot. At the same time he was obsessed with isolation, alienation, dead ends, barriers, walls, prisons, madhouses, and the idea of self-destruction—obsessions that led eventually to his suicide. These themes are well reflected in his second and third collections of stories: *Seh qatreh khun* (1932; three drops of blood) and *Sayeh rowshan* (1933; chiaroscuro).

Despite his preoccupation with Iran at this stage, it is abundantly clear that H. had not ceased being involved in the artistic realities of Europe and America. The prose works of Stefan Zweig, Chekhov (qq.v.), Poe, and Maupassant, and the writings of contemporary philosophers were still stirring his imagination. Having the sensitivities of Iranian art as a heritage, and having adopted the existentialist (q.v.) convictions of Sartre and of Kafka (qq.v.), the latter of whose "In the Penal Colony" he translated into Persian with extensive notes, H. was confronted with existential torment.

The thread of H.'s obsessions with man's veiled search, culminating in his despair at his unfulfilled yearnings in the face of an absurd universe, can be followed throughout his work. The subverting of temporal and spatial concepts in the plot of his masterpiece, *Buf-e kur* (1937; *The Blind Owl*, 1957; new tr., 1974), creates a surreal atmosphere in which the allegorically unenlightened, unseeing owl (an animal possessing human wisdom in Persian tradition) searches, questions, and entreats, only to discover terror and frenzy in the realization that he will find only silence. In *Buf-e kur* one can trace the predominant influence of Rilke, Freud (qq.v.), Poe, and Kafka on H.'s own personality. Like his contemporary Western writers, H. is concerned with the psychological implications of man's existence and of his interaction with his fellows. He constantly probes into the uneven forces that govern life's unrelieved misery, irrespective of social class, but he writes mostly about the little people, with their problems, sorrows, hates, and weaknesses—sympathetic yet repulsive. His characters include the slang-speaking mule attendant, the laborer who is a local hero among the poor by virtue of his bullish strength, the brooding scullery maid, and the sullen streetwalker to whom the measure of a man's love is the stoutness of the blows with which he pummels her.

The satirical tone in some of his short stories is an indirect criticism of a society that obstructs the education and advancement of the masses. H. is particularly sympathetic toward the backward condition of women. His love for Iran and for its heritage is an important element in his work. We are constantly confronted with the displaced Iranian, adrift in the West, as an allegory of the eternal conflict of East and West, a conflict to which he was also subject.

Despite the unevenness of H.'s work he has compelled Iranian authors to look further than politics and sociology, without abandoning them. Through his pioneering position and literary distinction he has exerted an extraordinary influence on Iranian writers, especially since World War II. The work of H. signaled the victory of prose in the face of serious claims that the Persian language had no merit when used to adorn nonpoetic expression. And that is probably why he has acquired a status as the most important Persian author of the 20th c. With H., Persian prose at last earned a place in the body of world literature.

FURTHER WORKS: '*Alaviyeh Khanom* (1933); *Vagh Vagh Sahab* (1933); *Sag-e velgard* (1942); *Haji Aqa* (1945; *Hāji Āghā*, 1979). FURTHER VOLUME IN ENGLISH: *S. H.: An Anthology* (1979)

BIBLIOGRAPHY: Kamshad, H., *Modern Persian Prose Literature* (1966), pp. 137–208; Kubičkova, V., "Persian Literature of the 20th Century," in Rypka, J., et al., *History of Iranian Literature* (1968), pp. 410–12; Bashiri, I., *H.'s Ivory Tower* (1974); Katouzian, H., "S. H.'s 'The Man Who Killed His Passionate Self': A Critical Exposition," *IranS*, 10, 3 (1977), 196–206; Hillmann, M. C., ed., *H.'s "The Blind Owl" Forty Years After* (1978); Yarshater, E., Introduction to *S. H.: An Anthology* (1979), pp. vii–xiv

PETER J. CHELKOWSKI

HEIJERMANS, Herman

Dutch dramatist, novelist, and journalist, b. 3 Dec. 1864, Rotterdam; d. 22 Nov. 1924, Zandvoort

H. is the Netherlands' most important modern playwright, and the only Dutch dramatist since Joost van den Vondel (1587–1679) to win international renown. Born into a Jewish family and son of a journalist, he took up journalism and playwriting at the age of twenty-eight, after twice failing in business ventures. These early days of his literary career in bohemian Amsterdam are recounted with folksy candor in his autobiographical novel *Kamertjeszonde* (1898; sin in rented rooms). He joined the Socialist Party in 1896, embarking on a lifelong commitment to assailing the social ills of the age, especially the exploitation of the poor. A prolific writer of newspaper sketches, comedies, and naturalistic dramas in the vein of Hauptmann (q.v.) and Ibsen, H. achieved his greatest international triumph with the play *Op hoop van zegen* (1901; *The Good Hope*, 1928), a moving portrayal of North Sea fisher folk overwhelmed by powers beyond their control or understanding. Its impact in the Netherlands was such that a new law for the protection of sailors and their dependents was enacted.

H.'s plays of the 1890s reveal a grim world of religious persecution and intolerance. More than the loosely woven plots, it was H.'s characters that held audiences spellbound: a pious Russian Jew caught in the horror of a pogrom —*Ahasverus* (1893; *Ahasverus*, 1929); a Jewish rag merchant eager to sell into marriage a son who is alienated from his corrupting environment—*Ghetto* (1899; ghetto).

At the turn of the century H. wrote a series of short, unmistakably socialist plays. *De machien* (1899; the machine) focuses on a factory owner forced by the industrial revolution to invest in machinery, and on his hapless workers who must toss a coin to determine who will be laid off. He also addressed domestic problems, notably the double standard in sexual mores among the affluent bourgeoisie, and parent-offspring relationships. In *Het zevende gebod* (1900; the seventh commandment) a tubercular student is disowned by his self-righteous father because of an unacceptable liaison. *Schakels* (1903; *Links*, 1927) features an old-fashioned industrialist beleaguered by his rapacious children.

While H. was a harried manager-producer-director of a theatrical company from 1912 to 1922, his output diminished, and what did appear was often written in a lighter vein, such as the satire *De wijze kater* (1918; the wise tomcat).

In his minor works H. succumbed to the Dutch penchant for realistic visual details and thereby created a kind of genre tableau. In his finest plays he showed a gift for indignation, for humor, and for delineating character. The people of his dramatic world move in authentic milieus. Their speech, often a rough-hewn, comic jargon, reflects all the nuances of their background. No mere representatives of their class, they are imbued with individual vitality.

FURTHER WORKS: *Dora Kremer* (1893); *Trinette* (1893); *Interieurs* (1897); *Nummer tachtig* (1898); *Puntje* (1889); *Het antwoord* (1899); *De onbekende* (1899); *Toneel en maatschappij* (1899); *Een Mei* (1900); *Het pantser* (1902); *Ora et labora* (1903); *Het kind* (1903); *Het kamerschut* (1903); *Sabbath* (1903); *In de Jonge Jan* (1903); *Diamantstad* (1904); *Buren* (1904); *Saltimbank* (1904); *Kleine verschrikkingen* (1904); *Bloeimaand* (1905); *Allerzielen* (1905); *Gevleugelde daden* (1905); *Feest* (1906; *Jubilee,* 1923); *Biecht eener schuldige* (1906); *Berliner Skizzenbuch* (1908); *De grote vlucht* (1908); *Een wereldstad* (1908); *Wat niet kon* (1908); *Vreemde jacht* (1909); *Uitkomst* (1909); *Drijvende Klompjes* (1909); *Joeps wonderlijke avonturen* (1909); *Beschuit met muisjes* (1910); *Vierundzwanzig Stunden in der Irrenanstalt* (1910); *De schone slaapster* (1911); *De opgaande zon* (1911; *The Rising Sun,* 1926); *Glück auf* (1911); *De roode flibustier* (1911); *De meid* (1911); *Robert, Bertram & Comp.* (1914); *Eva Bonheur* (1919); *De vliegende Hollander; of, De grote weddenschap* (1920); *De dageraad* (1921); *Brief in schemer* (1921); *De buikspreker* (1921); *Een heerenhuis te koop* (1921); *Droompaard* (1923); *Van ouds "De Morgenster"* (1924); *Droomkoninkje* (1924); *De moord in de trein* (1925); *Vuurvlindertje* (1925); *Duczika* (1926)

BIBLIOGRAPHY: Panter, P. [Kurt Tucholsky], "H. H.," *Die Weltbühne,* 20, 49 (1924), 849–51; Engel, F., "H. H.," *Berliner Tageblatt,* 24 Nov. 1924, 2; Raché, P., "H.s Leben und Werk," *Berliner Tageblatt,* 24 Nov. 1924, 2; Barnouw, A. J., "H. H.," *Theatre Arts,* Feb. 1925, 109–12; Flaxman, S. L., *H. H. and His Dramas* (1954); de Jong, E., *H. en de vernieuwing van het Europese drama* [summary in English] (1967)

PETER BRUNING

HEISSENBÜTTEL, Helmut

West German literary critic and author of avant-garde texts, b. 21 June 1921, Rüstringen bei Wilhelmshaven

Following active service in World War II, H. studied literature, architecture, and art. He became a publisher's reader and in 1959 assumed the directorship of the radio essay department of South German Radio. He was awarded several literary prizes, including the Büchner Prize (1969).

H.'s belletristic works are often discussed under the rubric "concrete poetry," although they defy categorization, and even description. His first books, *Kombinationen* (1954; combinations) and *Typographien* (1956; typographies), belong in the tradition of Dadaism (q.v.) and such modernist writers as Apollinaire and Gertrude Stein (qq.v), and are characterized by a reduction of normal grammatical patterns, which leads to striking ambiguities. A primary concern with language itself remains central to the six volumes bearing the title *Textbuch* (1960–67; textbook). Some of these texts are called prose and others poetry, but virtually all are suggestive rather than discursive and lack traditional form and content.

H.'s next literary works are called "projects": Project 1, *D'Alemberts Ende* (1970; D'Alembert's end), an avant-garde novel, and Project 2, *Das Durchhauen des Kohlhaupts* (1974; chopping through the cabbage head), a collection of texts and radio plays. *D'Alemberts Ende* narrates a brief period at the end of the life of the fictitious critic D'Alembert; facts, episodic elements of plot, and commentary are juxtaposed and blended. In *Das Durchhauen des Kohlhaupts* language per se is of somewhat less importance than in the works of the 1960s; content and plot lines are more recognizable and the comments on contemporary social problems less ambiguous.

H. is considered by many to be among Germany's leading postwar literary critics and theoreticians. In *Über Literatur* (1966; on literature) and *Briefwechsel über Literatur* (1969; correspondence about literature), the latter coauthored with the like-minded critic Heinrich Vormweg (b. 1928), H. stresses the primacy of language over emotion, the necessity of breaking with the romantic tradition, and the role of the contemporary writer as a resister, an irritant, in a regulated society.

H. is one of contemporary Germany's most controversial literary figures. His insistence, in belletristic and essayistic works alike, on the necessity of making a complete break with the tradition, has been received with lavish praise, bewilderment, and scornful derision. Nonetheless, his position as one of the avant-garde's leading spokesmen is secure.

FURTHER WORKS: *Ohne weiteres bekannt* (1958); *Texte ohne Komma* (1960); *Mary McCarthy: Versuch eines Autorenportraits* (1964); *Was ist das Konkrete an einem Gedicht?* (1969); *Memorabiler Lochtext* (1970); *Das Texbuch* (1970); *Die Freuden des Alterns* (1971); *Zur Tradition der Moderne* (1972); *Ruprecht Geiger* (1972); *Gelegenheitsgedichte und Klappentexte* (1973); *Der fliegende Frosch und das unverhoffte Krokodil* (1976); *Mümmelmann oder die Hasendämmerung* (1978); *Eichendorffs Untergang und andere Märchen* (1978); *Wenn Adolf Hitler den Krieg nicht gewonnen hätte* (1979); *Die goldene Kuppel des Comes Arbogast; oder, Lichtenberg in Hamburg fast eine Geschichte* (1980); *Das Ende der Alternative* (1980).
FURTHER VOLUME IN ENGLISH: *Texts* (1977)

BIBLIOGRAPHY: Döhl, R., "H. H.," in Weber, D., ed., *Deutsche Literatur seit 1945* (1968), pp. 546–76; Bezzel, C., "A Grammar of Modern German Poetry," *Foundations of Language*, 5 (1969), 470–87; Waldrop, R., "H. H., Poet of Contexts," *GR*, 44 (1969), 132–42; Demetz, P., *Postwar German Literature* (1970), pp. 84–88; Endres, E., "H. H.," in Wiese, B. von, ed., *Deutsche Dichter der Gegenwart* (1973), pp. 469–80; Burns, R., *Commitment, Language, and Reality: An Introduction to the Work of H. H.* (1975); special H. issue, *TuK*, No. 69/70 (1981)

JERRY GLENN

HELLER, Joseph

American novelist and dramatist, b. 1 May 1923, Brooklyn, N. Y.

After serving as a bombardier in the U.S. Army Air Corps stationed in Corsica during World War II, H. returned home, enrolled at New York University, and began writing short stories, some of which were published in *Esquire* and *The Atlantic* (1947–48). He took an M.A. at Columbia University and was a Fulbright scholar at Oxford in 1949–50. After teaching English for a few years, he worked in advertising and promotion at a number of major magazines, until the tremendous success of *Catch-22* (1961), which he had written in his spare time, enabled him to quit his job. (The original opening chapter of the novel appeared under the title "Catch-18" in *New World Writing*, No. 7, in 1955.)

Catch-22 is a novel based in part on H.'s war experiences. The protagonist, a life-loving, comic, rebellious bombardier named Yossarian, will do almost anything to avoid being killed in the war and by those who are running it: the officer who, hoping for promotion, keeps raising the number of missions the men must fly, and Milo Minderbinder, who will do anything (including bombing his own squadron) to save from ruin the financial empire he has built from his blackmarket business. Yossarian's struggle to survive amid such forces represents the individual's predicament in a world whose systems of order have turned destructive. H.'s satire shows how those in power put their own ends above the value of human life. H.'s criticism thus is aimed less at war itself than at those who subvert our institutions to their own advantage.

To capture the absurdity and chaos produced by this subversion, H. employs a disordered narrative chronology, and to suggest Yossarian's entrapment in this chaos H. uses repetition of scenes: the men seem caught up in a pattern of destruction that negates both life and individuality. It is therefore not surprising that most of the characters are flat, comic, and cartoonlike, rather than fully developed personalities. The large number of characters (over forty), the war setting, and the rapid changes of scene and sequence give *Catch-22* an epic sweep, while the novel's humor adds emotional force to H.'s attack on the society he portrays. This Black Humor (q.v.) is increasingly blended with horror and death, until it becomes grotesque comedy, evoking pain rather than laughter.

Yossarian eventually escapes this insane world epitomized by the military regulation "Catch-22," which forces him to fly the bombing missions if he is sane, but defines "sanity" as the healthy desire not to fly them. The phrase "catch-22" has entered the English language to signify an individual's entrapment in a no-win situation, particularly one created by an institutional regulation.

In *Something Happened* (1974) H. attacks the corporate bureaucracies of American business. But the protagonist does not share Yossarian's zest for life or his energetic protest against a dehumanizing system; instead, Bob Slocum, a weary, middle-aged executive, cynically resigns himself to a success he secretly despises. His high salary, social status, and material acquisitions have brought not satisfaction but unhappiness, which is shared by his family.

Slocum's monologue attempts to discover how such unhappiness "happened." Although *Something Happened* satirizes the corporate hierarchy, its deepest concern is with what "happens" to the person who internalizes the corporation's ideals and demands so completely that they usurp his individual identity and humanity.

After exploring the unhappy life and consciousness of an upper-management executive within the power structure of American finance, H. turned in *Good as Gold* (1979) to a discontented outsider. Bruce Gold, a cynical college professor who plans to write a book on the American Jewish experience, feels outside the mainstream of American political and social power because he is Jewish. As a result, he jumps at the sudden promise of a high government appointment in Washington, even if it means divorcing his wife to marry the daughter of an influential gentile millionaire. By alternating family scenes with Gold's experience in Washington, H. satirizes American political power and portrays his protagonist's behavior as neither better nor worse than that of Everyman, who under the same circumstances would probably act as "good" as Gold.

H.'s play *We Bombed in New Haven* (1967) was written in part to express his protest against the American role in the Vietnam war. But in this play-within-a-play, where the actors self-consciously explain that they are only "acting" the part of soldiers in a play about war, the focus is not a specific war but instead the denial that makes war possible—the denial of death.

Although *We Bombed in New Haven* attests to H.'s versatility, his strength lies in his novels' depiction of the interplay between the individual and the institutional systems wielding power in America: the military, the corporations, and the federal government. H.'s work exhibits an increasing pessimism about what any individual can do about society's drift toward corruption and decay—besides retreating to a private safety. H.'s contribution to the novel lies in his innovative combination of elements in *Catch-22*—humor and horror, repetition, fragmented chronology, and a multiplicity of bizarre characters—to achieve a form expressive of chaos and absurdity.

FURTHER WORKS: *Catch-22: A Dramatization* (1971); *Clevinger's Trial* (1973); *A Critical Edition of "Catch-22"* (1973)

BIBLIOGRAPHY: Tanner, T., "A Mode of Motion," *City of Words* (1971), pp. 72–84;

Kiley, F., and McDonald, W., eds., *A "Catch-22" Casebook* (1973); Nagel, J., ed., *Critical Essays on "Catch-22"* (1974); Aldridge, J., on *Something Happened, SatR*, 19 Oct. 1974, 18–21; Plimpton, G., "The Craft of Fiction, LI: J. H.," *Paris Review*, No. 60 (1974), 126–47; Dickstein, M., "Black Humor and History: The Early Sixties," *Gates of Eden* (1977), pp. 91–127; Aldridge, J., on *Good as Gold, Harper's*, March 1979, 115–18

MELANIE YOUNG

HELLMAN, Lillian

American dramatist and memoirist, b. 20 June 1905, New Orleans, La.

H. moved to New York City with her family when still a child, although her frequent visits to relatives in New Orleans would later provide her with much literary material. She attended New York University but left before graduating and in 1924–25 was a manuscript reader for the publishing firm of Horace Liveright, where she was introduced to the literary world. In 1925 H. married humorist and playwright Arthur Kober (1900–1975), and began to write, and later went with him to Hollywood, where she was a scenario reader while continuing to write stories, articles, and reviews. (H. wrote several screenplays later in her career.) They were divorced in 1932; previously she had met the mystery writer Dashiell Hammett (1894–1961), with whom she formed an intimate attachment that lasted until his death.

H. achieved immediate success with her first play, *The Children's Hour* (1934), which introduces the recurring theme in her work—that of the pressures of a corrupt and hypocritical society on its "good" victims. Two young women who run a small girls' school are destroyed by malicious rumors of "unnatural" affection, although the subject of lesbianism is treated very gingerly.

H.'s most important play, *The Little Foxes* (1939), brilliantly develops the conflict between good and evil, greed and love, against a background of Southern society in the process of industrialization. The predatory Hubbard family, especially Regina, are the "eaters of the earth," the "little foxes who spoil the vines" in their ruthless pursuit of money and power. Although in 1939 the play was interpreted as a specific attack on capitalism, it has come to be regarded as a condemnation of avarice and lust for power in general. In *Another Part of the Forest* (1947) H. takes the Hubbard family back to twenty years before the events of *The Little Foxes* and presents them as they were then—consumed by hatred and selfishness.

Watch on the Rhine (1941) depicts an American family that is suddenly shaken out of isolation and indifference to the war in Europe when the daughter arrives with her German refugee husband and children. H. here attacked the complacency of those who allow evil to flourish and tried to awaken the American conscience to the European tragedy.

Among H.'s later plays, *Toys in the Attic* (1960) is most notable. Set in the South and reminiscent at times of Tennessee Williams (q.v.), it is less involved with social issues than her other plays. Rather, it is a perceptive psychological study of a weak and irresponsible man dependent on two older spinster sisters who try to survive on dreams doomed to remain unfulfilled.

Years after she stopped writing plays H. has emerged in a new role as the author of several highly acclaimed volumes of memoirs, which are not only autobiographical narratives but also explorations of her emotions and moral perceptions vis-à-vis her family and her relationships with her friends and colleagues. *An Unfinished Woman* (1969) proceeds more or less chronologically and includes moving portraits of Hammett and her friend Dorothy Parker (1893–1967). *Pentimento* (1973) presents reminiscences and more portraits (including the famous "Julia") unified by the theme of, in H.'s words, "seeing and then seeing again. . . . I wanted to see what was there for me once, what is there for me now." The controversial *Scoundrel Time* (1976) is an account of her experiences during the investigations of the House Un-American Activities Committee in the late 1940s and early 1950s.

H.'s political liberalism is reflected in her plays and her memoirs, but her ability to focus on subjects other than social evils saves her from being an agitprop writer. In most of her work she depicts personal lives being worked out against a backdrop of social change or historical crisis. Although H. the dramatist has often been accused of overusing the machinery of melodrama and the well-made play, in her best work the contrivance is expert and efficient. Her total moral commitment, as well as her skill at psychological characterization, makes her a major figure in the realistic mode of modern American drama.

FURTHER WORKS: *Days to Come* (1936); *Four Plays* (1942); *The North Star: A Motion Picture about Some Russian People* (1943); *The Searching Wind* (1944); *Montserrat* (adaptation of Roblès's *Montserrat*; 1950); *The Autumn Garden* (1951); *The Lark* (adaptation of Anouilh's *L'alouette*; 1956); *Candide* (libretto for operetta based on Voltaire's *Candide*; 1957); *Six Plays* (1960); *My Mother, My Father and Me* (1963); *The Collected Plays* (1972); *Three* (1979); *Maybe: A Story* (1980)

BIBLIOGRAPHY: Clark, B. H., "L. H.," *CE*, 6, 3 (1944), 127–33; Phillips, J., and Hollander, A., "The Art of the Theater; L. H.: An Interview," *Paris Review,* No. 33 (1965), pp. 65–95; Gould, J., *Modern American Playwrights* (1966), pp. 168–85; Adler, J., *L. H.* (1969); Moody, R., *L. H.: Playwright* (1972); Falk, D. V., *L. H.* (1978); Lederer, K., *L. H.* (1980)

RITA STEIN

HEMINGWAY, Ernest

American novelist, short-story writer, and journalist, b. 21 July 1899, Oak Park, Ill.; d. 2 July 1961, Ketchum, Idaho

In his youth H. had already begun the travels which are reflected in his work and which also shaped it to suggest an allegorical pilgrimage of a modern Odysseus. From the American youth Nick Adams, protagonist of many early short stories, to the Cuban Santiago of the late novel *The Old Man and the Sea* (1952), H.'s protagonists share a concern with performing well under the mental and physical stresses of richly varied lives. From his family's summer home in northern Michigan, where H. began to learn the skills of hunting and fishing from his physician father, to France, Spain, Italy, East Africa, and the Gulf of Mexico, where he and his heroes savored life and experienced death, H. made both a personal and literary pilgrimage.

H. came of age at the historical watershed of World War I, when a new literature began confronting new psychological and philosophical problems. While the subtle conflicts within his own family may have exerted long-lasting influence, he was unquestionably a child of the 20th c. At eighteen he was already a newspaper reporter for the prestigious Kansas City *Star*, covering a tough city beat, and as a volunteer in a Red Cross ambulance unit in Italy in 1918 he received his violent initiation to life "in our time" when he was blown up by an Austrian mortar shell and narrowly escaped death. While this traumatic event may not have been essential and critical to his artistic development, it does provide a metaphor for much of his subsequent work. In his fiction, many of his protagonists are the wounded, sometimes sacrificed heroes, not simply of a historical world in crisis, but of a mythic world emotionally felt by a wide-ranging audience that has crossed intellectual as well as national boundaries. Those of H.'s heroes who survive become, as he put it, "strong at the broken places," but the first reaction of the maimed body and sensibility was a withdrawal from life and then a gradual return to it as a sensitive observer of life. Like many of his heroes, H. was a wanderer on the face of the earth, an outsider with a keen eye for what places and feelings were really like. Strictly speaking he was not an intellectual who valued ideas in and of themselves. In the tradition of American pragmatism, the true or moral was what worked. ". . . I know only that what is moral is what you feel good after . . ." (*Death in the Afternoon*, 1932). While he could be a courageous supporter of a political cause (such as the Loyalists' in the Spanish Civil War or the incarcerated Ezra Pound [q.v.]), more often than not his best work was that of the skeptical critical pragmatist attacking the entrenched, the self-satisfied, the hypocritical.

As far as he had abstract values, they seem to have been fairly traditional. In spite of his position as an innovative stylist, there is an important truth in Gertrude Stein's (q.v.) observation (recorded in her *Autobiography of Alice B. Toklas*) that ". . . after all, you are ninety percent Rotarian. Can't you, he said, make it eighty percent." For instance, although married four times, he seems to have had a strong and conventional sense of the values of marriage and family. As for his craft of writing, he regarded it as seriously as the great craftsmen Gustave Flaubert and Henry James (q.v.) of an earlier generation, and he could be a hard taskmaster in the tradition of the Protestant work ethic. He was stoical and skeptical but enduring as long as the power of his art of writing provided the necessary articulation of his experience and imagination that were also suggestive of the common lot of mankind.

After the war H. returned to journalism but also began his career in creative writing. While he was European correspondent for the Toronto *Star*, virtually unknown and newly a husband and father, he quit his job and devoted himself to his creative writing until he had achieved professional skill and status.

H.'s first two slender books, *Three Stories and Ten Poems* (1923) and *in our time* (1924), were both published in Paris in very small editions for very few readers, but his readers and counselors were of the most influential and helpful sort, including Gertrude Stein, Ezra Pound, Sherwood Anderson, and F. Scott Fitzgerald (qq.v.). In 1925 the expanded *In Our Time* was published in the U.S. and signaled the beginning of a successful and illustrious career. But as his literary reputation grew, so did his personal fame as a sportsman and bon vivant. Many of the stories spread about his life were apocryphal, but some of them were credible enough to make the man himself as widely discussed as his work. Unfortunately for the sake of accuracy, much of his fiction was read as autobiography; and unfortunately for the sake of the seriously conceived and carefully written fiction, it was often read as hard-boiled adventure and enjoyed or depreciated on this ground alone. In fact, far from being a largely autobiographical writer celebrating the cult of experience, H. was a dedicated craftsman who read omnivorously and intelligently, so that he had the rare combination of being a writer of wide and often dramatic experience who was also a sensitive aesthete. Gertrude Stein, an early mentor, perceived that ". . . he looks like a modern and he smells of the museums" (*Autobiography of Alice B. Toklas*).

Some initial reactions to his first serious novel, *The Sun Also Rises* (1926), illustrate the problem. It was read as a roman à clef and a collective biography of the post-World War I "lost generation," the disillusioned, suffering, yet attractive young men and women whose values and faiths, like some of their very bodies, were also blown up in the war. H. denied that he or his sexually incapacitated hero Jake Barnes was "lost," but many readers submerged or overlooked the traditional values like love and courage that H. championed; glamorous nihilism and toughness were more the vogue of the 1920s, and the timeless theme keynoted by the epigraph from Ecclesiastes, the theme of the abiding earth and the indifference of life, the *élan vital,* to self-pitying romantics, was perhaps lost on many readers until the corpus of his work grew and revealed the underlying existential strength of his perceptions. Beyond them was the style that married so well to the bittersweet themes.

Jaded, disoriented, valueless, the characters hear neither drums nor prayers, but those like the narrator Jake Barnes and his hard-living lover *manqué* Lady Brett Ashley have a certain awareness and generosity of spirit that makes them superior to the other pitiful expatriates who are the "lost generation." By the assertion of love and courage and with a protective irony and humor, the admirable characters survive with dignity if not with victory. The novel affirms that "the earth abideth forever," but for the humans who inhabit it, life can seem chaotic and brutal, stupid and comical. In the closing lines, the antiheroine slips into self-pity: "'Oh, Jake,' Brett said, 'we could have had such a damned good time together,'" and the antihero, the man who does not act so much as react, the man to whom things are done, replies, "'Yes. . . . Isn't it pretty to think so?'"

This novel and the next, *A Farewell to Arms* (1929), were written in an understated, informal, but carefully controlled and objective or closely dramatic prose style, even though both novels are first-person narrations. Along with the bulk of the short stories, this early work best exemplifies the style that was of great influence in shaping modern prose fiction. The early H. distrusted abstract terms, but still this style was rich in imagery and symbolic action that suggested a tentative ethic or moral code. Certain character types suggested implicit principles: on one hand was the so-called "code hero" who denied or ignored traditional faiths or found them inadequate in coping with a meaningless world. This recurrent character type turned to self-imposed and often stringent rituals that obviated metaphysics or faith. On the other hand were either the careless and undisciplined men with no ritual controls or men living by corrupted beliefs, such as chauvinism or romanticism, that were irrelevant to H.'s efforts to give shape to those values a violent world and careless people had mutilated. Between these extremes, both rather simplistic and naïve, stood the H. protagonist who was drawn to the admirable and controlled life of the code hero but who was also too complex and sensitive to accept the planned discipline of, for example, a matador's or professional hunter's life.

By making his "separate peace" in a senseless world at mad war, Lt. Frederic Henry in *A Farewell to Arms* briefly enjoys an idyllic love affair, but inexorable fate destroys the committed and uncommitted alike; there is no escape. The protagonist has volunteered for ambulance service with the Italian army in World War I, but, typically, he has no particular commitment to any political cause: "I was always embarrassed by the words sacred, glorious, and sacri-

fice and the expression in vain. . . . There were many words that you could not stand to hear and finally only the names of places had dignity. . . . Abstract words such as glory, honor, courage, or hallow were obscene beside the concrete names of villages, the numbers of roads, the names of rivers, the numbers of regiments and the dates." This reduction is an extreme reaction to the general and the abstract, which are the bane of the artist trying to re-create beauty as well as the thinker trying to rediscover truth.

Thus, while the narrator studiously avoids such abhorred abstractions and rarely interrupts his description and narration with exposition, the discourse is always heavy with meaning. The brilliant description of the military action in the brief first chapter foreshadows the doom of the conclusion in which the lovers have deserted the war and its dangers only to find death and grief in the supposed haven of each other's, not the military's, arms. The narrator does, however, learn from his defeats, and he does dryly pontificate: "If people bring so much courage to this world the world has to kill them to break them, so of course it kills them. The world breaks every one and afterward many are strong at the broken places. But those that will not break it kills. It kills the very good and the very gentle and the very brave impartially. If you are none of these you can be sure it will kill you too but there will be no special hurry." Abstract words like *good* and *brave* have a simple dignity that has not been debased, and they are current in the H. vocabulary.

The style of H.'s later work changed somewhat to a prose more loosely structured and yet more complex than before. This change has been variously judged by his critics. Similarly, his subjects and themes evolved into socially and politically conscious contemporary problems. At the time of the swing to the political left by many writers in the U.S. during the 1930s, H. was widely applauded for his championing of the economic "have-nots" and his apparent loss of detachment in *To Have and Have Not* (1937). But this novel was one of his weakest in its stylistic achievement; its experimental techniques were not fully realized, partly because the novel as planned was radically changed in the editorial process to avoid potentially libelous passages. (H. frequently used real names and people in his fictions.)

For Whom the Bell Tolls (1940) also aligned the wandering H. hero—this time in civil-war Spain—with the left, but H.'s liberalism was far from orthodox. His conclusion in this novel, his most ambitious and judged by some critics as his best, was that neither political programs nor action in their behalf offered a substitute for the individual's need to obtain salvation for himself through tragedy, love, and self-knowledge. The hero, Robert Jordan, fights for the Spanish Loyalists against the Fascists; but this widely acclaimed novel was for many years not published in the Soviet Union, although H.'s other work had been given a sympathetic audience there.

H. wrote in a different mode in this long novel that has epic characteristics. The author who was stereotyped as writing a clipped "hard-boiled" prose became expansive in the story of the last few days of an American's life, but typically the hero dies in a futile ironic effort to aid in the larger war. His sacrifice is meaningful only in personal terms: he has been true to himself, he has demonstrated his courage ("grace under pressure"), and he has loved "truly and well." Far from glorifying war or political action, H. again underlines their awful ambiguities. Isolated on a mountainside with a band of guerrillas who form a microcosm, the hero suffers and dies for them, morally ambiguous real people, neither his compatriots nor uniformly laudable but nevertheless part of mankind: "any mans *death* diminishes *me*, because I am involved in *Mankinde;* And therefore never send to know for whom the *bell* tolls; It tolls for *thee*" (from John Donne; epigraph to the novel).

H. participated in World War II, first as a modern privateer on antisubmarine duty in the Caribbean and then as a European war correspondent and sometime leader of an irregular armed patrol during the liberation of France. His next novel, *Across the River and into the Trees* (1950), was partly based on his World War II experiences and had for its hero an aging U.S. Army colonel who was having an affair with a young Italian countess in Venice. The story lacks the drama of H.'s previous work, and its critical reception was generally unsympathetic, it being read as a discursive apologia and an embarrassing self-parody of his successful style of the 1920s and 1930s. While it lacked the force of earlier work, it, too, has interesting thematic dimensions and perhaps was misunderstood because it was a shift in mood and subject of a still developing, exploring author moving into an unexpected region and upsetting some critical preconceptions.

The Old Man and the Sea was even more radically different from his preceding work; but this deceptively simple, short fable of the courage, faith, love, and endurance of a poor Cuban fisherman was widely acclaimed. It both won H. a Pulitzer Prize and helped win him the Nobel Prize for literature in 1954. Although he had conceived other ambitious projects, this novella was to be his last book published in his lifetime.

After months of failure fishing in the Gulf Stream, a culmination of the losses of an ordinary yet dignified life, the fisherman finally hooks a huge marlin and fights it heroically for three days until in the majesty of the beautiful, dreadful sea, the hunter and hunted merge, tied together by the fishing line. But as if in a paradigm of man's fate, the victorious Santiago has his prize fish taken from him by rapacious sharks who mutilate and then devour the marlin, leaving the exhausted fisherman with nothing but a skeleton to show for his epic struggle. Yet he has survived, endured, and enlarged the feelings of true heroism. The gaunt, ascetic, isolated, beset man living in harmony with an indifferent environment again suggests how existential struggle can ennoble.

H.'s short stories are not numerous, but a significant number are of the highest quality, and a few critics think his short stories are more important than his novels. They are sometimes little more than tightly written sketches, sometimes nothing less than complex and infinitely rewarding narratives like "The Short Happy Life of Francis Macomber" (1936), "The Snows of Kilimanjaro" (1936), "Big Two-Hearted River" (1925), "In Another Country" (1926), "The Undefeated" (1926), "Soldier's Home" (1925), and "A Clean Well-Lighted Place" (1933). His gifts for the telling image, economy of plot, and brilliant dialogue are sometimes best seen in short stories like these.

H.'s nonfiction is of widely varying quality and seriousness, but it includes some of his best work: *Death in the Afternoon* (1932), an unsurpassed book on bullfighting, also contains important statements on his aesthetics; *Green Hills of Africa* (1935) is a novelistic but factual narrative of his hunt for big game on safari in East Africa; it too contains important commentary on the art of writing; *A Moveable Feast* (1964), his posthumously published reminiscences, mainly set in Paris in the 1920s, includes sketches of Ezra Pound, Gertrude Stein, and F. Scott Fitzgerald written in an extremely lively and insightful if sometimes subjective style. His other posthumously published work—a novel, *Islands in the Stream* (1970) and *The Nick Adams Stories* (1972), containing some previously unpublished fiction—were neither edited, completed, nor authorized by H. and have value mainly to the literary mortician, although the former contains some exciting and beautifully written passages.

The publication of *Selected Letters, 1917–1961* (1981), letters he himself never wanted published, rekindled the sport of H.-baiting among readers and reviewers who have new "evidence" to cloud the perception of the fiction by the smoke of the personality who was at turns loving and kind, egomaniacal and hateful, creative and imaginative, contradictory and ultimately self-destructive. With the powers of body and mind waning, the self-made hero chose suicide, but the continuing stream of posthumous works and publications about him keep his ghost ever present.

Along with William Faulkner (q.v.), H. is often considered the major writer of fiction in American literature of the 20th c. For some readers, H.'s value stops at a grudging appreciation of his style and at a belief that he is anti-intellectual and even adolescent. But as the exact quality of that style comes to be better understood and is seen as an organic medium for the expression of symbolic meaning and human understanding, his reputation grows.

FURTHER WORKS: *The Torrents of Spring* (1926); *Men without Women* (1927); *Winner Take Nothing* (1933); *The Spanish Earth* (1938); *The Fifth Column, and the First Forty-nine Stories* (1938); *Complete Stories* (1954); *By-Line: E. H.* (1967) *E. H.: Eighty-eight Poems* (1979)

BIBLIOGRAPHY: Baker, C., *H.: The Writer as Artist* (1952; 4th ed., 1972); Young, P., *E. H.* (1952; rev. ed., 1966); Fenton, C. A., *The Apprenticeship of E. H.: The Early Years* (1954); Baker, C., ed., *H. and His Critics: An International Anthology* (1961); DeFalco, J., *The Hero in H.'s Short Stories* (1963); Rovit, E., *E. H.* (1963); Asselineau, R., ed., *The Literary Reputation of H. in Europe* (1965); Lewis, R. W., *H. on Love* (1965; new ed., 1973); Baker, S., *E. H.: An Introduction and Interpretation* (1967); Hanneman, A., *E. H.: A Comprehensive Bibliography* (1967; *Supplement*, 1975); Hovey, R. B., *H.: The Inward Terrain* (1968); Stephens, R. O., *H.'s Nonfiction: The Public Voice* (1968); Bruccoli, M. J., ed., *The Fitzgerald/H. Annual* (1969 ff.); Baker, C., *E. H.: A Life Story* (1969); Benson, J. J., *H.: The Writer's Art of Self-Defense* (1969); Wylder, D. E., *H.'s Heroes* (1969); Watts, E. S., *E. H. and the Arts* (1971); Grebstein, S. N., *H.'s Craft* (1973); Astro, R., and Benson, J. J., eds., *H. in Our Time* (1974); Benson, J. J., ed., *The Short Stories of E. H.* (1975); Hemingway, M., *How It Was* (1976); Reynolds, M. S., *H.'s First War: The Making of "A Farewell to Arms"* (1976); Donaldson, S., *By Force of Will: The Life and Art of E. H.* (1977); Oldsey, B., *H.'s Hidden Craft: The Writing of "A Farewell to Arms"* (1979)

ROBERT W. LEWIS

Not that life isn't enjoyable. Talking and drinking with one's friends is great fun; fishing in Big Two-Hearted River is a tranquil exhilaration. But the brutality of life is always there, and it is somehow bound up with the enjoyment. Bullfights are especially enjoyable. It is even exhilarating to build a simply priceless barricade and pot the enemy as they are trying to get over it. The condition of life is pain; and the joys of the most innocent surface are somehow tied to its stifled pangs.

The resolution of this dissonance in art made the beauty of H.'s stories. He had in the process tuned a marvelous prose. Out of the colloquial American speech, with its simple declarative sentences and its strings of Nordic monosyllables, he got effects of the utmost subtlety. F. M. Ford has found the perfect simile for the impression produced by this writing: "H.'s words strike you, each one, as if they were pebbles fetched fresh from a brook. They live and shine, each in its place. So one of his pages has the effect of a brook-bottom into which you look down through the flowing water. The words form a tessellation, each in order beside the other."

Edmund Wilson, *The Wound and the Bow* (1947), pp. 215–16

. . . His writing career argues cogently that whatever philosophical validity the H. code may have possessed, its pragmatic functioning for him was cardinal and irrefutable. It enabled him to take over the role of what we might call "*jongleur* of pain" that he imagined so poignantly in his description of Belmonte in the Pamplona bull ring. He exhausted himself beyond his natural means, but he maintained that "grace under pressure," which, for him, was one of the conditions from which immortality might come.

But rather than end on such a subdued note, let us remember that if his range was narrow, it was not shallow. Art is long and it is large and it can also be deep; and if the sum of H.'s achievement was to project in compelling symbols his own human situation, his popularity attests to the fact that his was not a unique human condition. Too fragmented to make a rebellious vain rush against life and too proud to accept the inevitability of defeat and resignation, H. found in himself and communicated to countless readers a stance of heroism—positive, unillusioned, and defiantly humanistic.

Earl Rovit, *E. H.* (1963), pp. 172–73

Things like the "H. style," the "H. hero," the "manner" and "attitude" of H. are very widely recognized. Back in the minds of all literate Americans there is a place where this man etched a few lines. He is a part of our reading past, and the cleavage between what has happened to us directly, and what has happened to us in books, is not so deep as some think.

H. made a difference. There are people who do not admire his work, but even these are perfectly ready to admit—if only that they may deplore the fact—that he is "important." It is hard to think of a contemporary American who had more influence on modern writing, or on whom both general readers and literary critics are more likely to agree that the experience of his fiction is worth having, or, in his own time, of a writer more widely publicized. And yet despite all the attention, H.'s work, which is what we should ultimately remember him for, is still by no means as well understood as it might be.

Philip Young, *E. H.: A Reconsideration* (1966), pp. vii–viii

What carried H. along his path was a total dedication to art and an unrelenting will to make his writing true. Perhaps his range of vision can be seen in some respects as limited, but his aim was penetration, not comprehensiveness. H., unlike many of his contemporaries, was there during the wars, the evacuations, the social convulsions. Despite the attempt by many to minimize the importance of such direct experience with most of the major events of his time, and despite the exhibitionism that often colored H.'s attempts to expose himself to danger, this effort to sense the actual event and to reproduce its emotional effect artistically as precisely as possible is exactly what we need in an age when even war itself has become a spectator sport and our sensitivity to the suffering of others has dimmed.

The emotional intensity which led H. into his excesses also led him to his victories and fostered those qualities of character that made his victories possible: self-discipline, self-honesty, and a very real courage. He was locked in mortal combat all his life with an opponent, art, which grants no

quarter and never allows total victory. The artist can be, will be, and must be destroyed by such a conflict, but he need not be defeated.

Jackson J. Benson, *H.: The Writer's Art of Self-Defense* (1969), p. 191

So much has been written on the H. "hero" that it might seem unproductive to undertake another examination of this literary phenomenon. But I believe that one of the longstanding problems of H. criticism has been the failure to disentangle the H. personality, as evidenced in his life and in his nonfictional statements, from the characters that he has created for his novels. Coupled with this tendency to link H. with his protagonists, despite his own often vehement objections, has been an equal proclivity to view the H. protagonist as a recurring hero in a progression of novels so that the critical treatment of the H. hero has become almost an exercise in fictional biography. Nick Adams grows into Jake Barnes into Frederic Henry into Robert Jordan into Richard Cantwell; all are considered to be one character at different ages. The result, unfortunately, has been that the recurring biographical hero has provided almost the sole critical focus for the interpretation of separate novels which are unique artistic creations, distinctive not only in the concept of the hero and his environments but in artistic techniques as well. That critical focus, it seems to me, has frequently forced a preconceived and rigid pattern upon the interpretation of some of H.'s novels. This is particularly unfortunate, for such a view does not allow a demonstration of H.'s artistic versatility, his experimentation, and his increasing skill as a writer.

Delbert E. Wylder, *H.'s Heroes* (1969), pp. 3–4

The primary intent of his writing, from first to last, was to seize and project for the reader what he often called "the way it was." This is a characteristically simple phrase for a concept of extraordinary complexity, and H.'s conception of its meaning subtly changed several times in the course of his career—always in the direction of greater complexity. At the core of the concept, however, one can invariably discern the operation of three esthetic instruments: the sense of place, the sense of fact, and the sense of scene.

The first of these, obviously a strong passion with H., is the sense of place. "Unless you have geography, background," he once told George Antheil, "you have nothing." You have, that is to say, a dramatic vacuum. Few writers have been more place-conscious. Few have so carefully charted out the geographical groundwork of their novels while managing to keep background so conspicuously unobtrusive.

Carlos Baker, *H.: The Writer as Artist*, 4th ed. (1972), pp. 48–49

GERHART HAUPTMANN

ERNEST HEMINGWAY

HERMANN HESSE

ROLF HOCHHUTH

His image as an anti-intellectual was one that H. himself encouraged through his rugged appearance, his adventurous outdoor life, and his open contempt for any language that smacked of the pretentious. A writer, he believed, always got in trouble when he started thinking on the page, and in Big Trouble when he went in for Big Thinking. "The essential of big writing," he commented in 1930, "is to use words like the West, the East, Civilization, etc." He'd discovered, to bring the abstractions down to earth, that "when you stand with your nose toward the north, if your head is held still, what is on your right will be east and what is on your left will be west," and though you could write "very big" putting those words in capitals, it was "very liable not to mean anything."

The easy mistake to make about H., and about his writing, is to take both at surface value alone. Margaret Anderson, who knew Ernest during his expatriate days in Paris, concluded that the one adjective to describe him was "simple." Malcolm Cowley, on the other hand, chose "complicated" as the one word which best summed him up, and Cowley, who knew Ernest for many years, came far nearer the mark, for H. was a complicated man, with a difficult, a quirky, and frequently a contradictory mind.

Scott Donaldson, *By Force of Will: The Life and Art of E. H.* (1977), pp. xii–xiii

HEPPENSTALL, Rayner

English novelist, critic, and translator, b. 27 July 1911, Huddersfield

H. was educated in his native Yorkshire and was graduated from the University of Leeds in 1932 after attending the University of Strasbourg, France, in 1931. The towns of his boyhood are described in detail in his novel *The Woodshed* (1962), Strasbourg and its cathedral in the novel *The Connecting Door* (1962). In *The Greater Infortune* (1960) H. described life in London immediately preceding World War II, interweaving the chronology of events in the life of his protagonist and the chronology of political events; in the earlier *The Lesser Infortune* (1953) he described his army life.

H. was a producer for BBC Radio in London from 1945 to 1967. In this position, as well as in his free-lance writing, he has been in contact with many key figures in arts and letters, and he writes with expertise on various arts.

His knowledge of French literature and his interest in France are predominant in his work. He has translated or adapted works from French and treats French culture in several of his books. He has had a long friendship with J. I. M. Stewart (the mystery writer Michael Innes, b. 1906) since his student days at Leeds, and he has himself written several books on crime in France and in England. His most recent novel, *The Shearers* (1969), is a fictionalization of an actual French murder trial, transplanted to England.

H. is a cultural historian in his emphasis on events preceding and during World War II, in his literary histories, his crime histories, and his reminiscences of such figures as George Orwell (q.v.). He often uses first-person narration to link events in the manner of a diarist. In both his fictional and his nonfictional works, H. emphasizes the process of dating events and verifying these dates. Yet his concern with the chronology of events is rather for its surface pattern than for any inherent or constructed drama.

The keynote of H.'s fictional style is his presentation of sensual detail. In his first novel, *The Blaze of Noon* (1939), the protagonist is blind. The preface points to the direct influence of Montherlant's (q.v.) novel series, *The Girls,* and indeed, H.'s subject is not the disability of blindness but the experience of physical love. He expresses a free sexuality which, although hedonistic, is not libertine. His protagonists commit adultery without guilt, but they do not seduce. His novels reject conventional moral judgment and advocate, at least by implication, dismissal of both sentimentalism and vulgarity.

H.'s work as a whole is a significant contribution to 20th-c. letters. What has not been recognized yet is his important achievement in novelistic technique. He is an originator and transmitter of innovations in construction and style in his method of treating levels of reality and time in *The Connecting Door* and in his handling of stream-of-consciousness and interior monologue (q.v.), especially in *The Shearers.* He translated work by and wrote two studies of Raymond Roussel (q.v.), who is only now beginning to attract attention as a forerunner of the New Novel (q.v.) and its descriptive technique, which H. uses in his presentation of rooms and streets in *The Woodshed* and again in *The Connecting Door.* The latter, furthermore, is important as an antinovel. Even in his earliest fiction, H. was influenced by French writers, and he realized in the English language technical novelistic achievements that were in part the results of French literary influence and in part new developments. H. was disposing of conventional plot and characterization before such writers as Robbe-Grillet (q.v.) were doing so; in his later fiction, he not only transmitted but contributed to technical advances made by French writers. H.'s work is unlike that of any of his English contemporaries, although his literary criticism shows his understanding of English literary trends. He is particularly interesting as a recorder of English life and as a channel by which French style comes into the English world of letters.

FURTHER WORKS: *Middleton Murry: A Study in Excellent Normality* (1934); *First Poems* (1935); *Apology for Dancing* (1936); *Sebastian* (1937); *Blind Men's Flowers Are Green* (1940); *Saturnine* (1943; revised and expanded as *The Greater Infortune*); *Poems 1933–45* (1946); *The Double Image: Mutations of Christian Mythology in the Work of Four French Catholic Writers of To-day and Yesterday* (1947); *Léon Bloy* (1954); *Four Absentees* (1960); *The Fourfold Tradition: Notes on the French and English Literatures, with Some Ethnological and Historical Asides* (1961); *The Intellectual Part* (1963); *Raymond Roussel: A Critical Guide* (1966); *Raymond Roussel: A Critical Study* (1967); *A Little Pattern of French Crime* (1969); *Portrait of the Artist as a Professional Man* (1969); *French Crime in the Romantic Age* (1970); *Bluebeard and After: Three Decades of Murder in France* (1972); *The Sex War and Others: A Survey of Recent Murder, Principally in France* (1973); *Reflections on the Newgate Calendar* (1975

BIBLIOGRAPHY: Bowen, E., "The Blaze of Noon" (1939), *Collected Impressions* (1950), pp. 53–55; Monod, S., "R. H. and the *Nouveau Roman*," in Mack M., and Gregor, I., eds., *Imagined Worlds* (1968), pp. 461–75; Nye, R., "R. H.," in Vinson, J., ed., *Contemporary Novelists*, 2nd ed. (1976), pp. 625–28

JUDITH LEIBOWITZ

HERBERT, Zbigniew

Polish poet, dramatist, and essayist, b. 29 Oct. 1924, Lvov (now in the U.S.S.R.)

H. was an active member of the Polish resistance during the Nazi occupation. After World War II he studied in Cracow at the Academy of Fine Arts and then at the Academy of Commerce, from which he received a master's degree in economics in 1947. In 1950 he earned a law degree from the Nicolas Copernicus University in Toruń and stayed on there for a time to study philosophy. Between 1965 and 1971 he lived abroad.

H.'s poems reflect his war experience, although they seldom deal directly with the tragic scenes he witnessed. His poems began to appear in periodicals in 1950, but H. did not publish his first collection of poetry, *Struna światła* (1956; the chord of light), until the political thaw made greater freedom of expression possible. In a later collection, *Studium przedmiotu* (1961; study of the object), he discreetly refers to this fact in "Szuflada" ("Drawer," 1968). His second collection of poetry, *Hermes, pies i gwiazda* (1957; Hermes, dog and star), had come quickly on the heels of the first one.

H. does not easily fit into any rigid classification. Although usually considered the most classical of his contemporaries, H., like most of them, disdains traditional rhyme and meter (some of his poems are in prose). He has his own brand of classicism, and he has developed to an extraordinary degree the dramatic monologue, which he makes the vehicle for ironic and questioning reflections on the world about him.

H.'s eyes are not closed to the political realities amid which he lives, and much of his poetry has political overtones, but he never deals directly with political events. The tension in his work transcends the political plane; it is a Platonic tension between the ideal and the real that permeates his poetry, which he sees not as an end but as a means in the service of the good. He strives for a world without suffering.

H.'s recent collection of poems, *Pan Cogito* (1974; Mr. Cogito), has already been translated into about fifteen languages. (English translations of most of the poems of this book are included in *Selected Poems*, 1977.) Mr. Cogito, whose name reminds us of the Cartesian point of departure, serves the poet as a device in his search for the identity of the self. H.'s hero is a very ordinary human being rather than a great thinker, and his weaknesses and failures become his greatest assets. In the opening poem, Mr. Cogito observes his face in the mirror; in this and in some other poems, Mr. Cogito asks himself who he is. In *Studium przedmiotu,* it was a pebble that was close to attaining perfection. H. does not attempt to bring "pebbly" qualities to the human world. Instead, feeling the sense of communion with a stone, in "Poczucie tożsamości" ("Sense of Identity," 1977), he humanizes the inanimate objects. The poet's wisdom lies in his ability to accept defeat. As in his earlier poem, "Dojrzałość" (1957; "Maturity," 1968), so in many of the poems in *Pan Cogito* H. tells us without a trace of didacticism that we have to accept reality. He never pontificates. H. sounds most powerful when he does not raise his voice. In *Pan Cogito* H. departs only once from his low-key, subdued tone, in the very last poem, "Przesłanie Pana Cogito" ("The Envoy of Mr. Cogito," 1977). H. calls for courage when reason leaves us, for anger when we hear the voice of the beaten, and for scorn for the informers, executioners, and cowards. The poem ends with a call to march on, faithful to our ideals. Yet even in this departure, H. shows that he is only human and that there is a limit to his anger. Instead of defeating his purpose by breaking away from his tone, H. wins us and scores, in a roundabout way, another victory.

Like Tadeusz Różewicz (q.v.), with whom he is often compared, H. has endeavored to reach a wider audience through the stage. *Drugi pokój* (1958; the other room) exemplifies in a dramatic form his searching analysis of complex human relationships. There is, however, a fundamental difference between Różewicz and H. The former represents the war generation, which had lost the earlier morality and did not replace it with new moral values. H. keenly feels that there is a real need for "tablets of values" (a reference to the tablets of the Ten Commandments) in the contemporary world, and considers nihilism as the most serious menace of our modern culture.

One result of H.'s travels in France, England, Greece, and Italy is *Barbarzyńca w ogrodzie* (1962; the barbarian in the garden), a collection of essays examining a variety of aesthetic and historical problems. Coming from eastern Europe, the author plays the role of the "barbarian," while the West is represented by the "garden."

Deeply humanitarian, H. rarely becomes moralistic. His tragic view of life is balanced by his own brand of subtle irony. Highly intellectual, H.'s poetry is always filtered through a lyrical sensibility that transforms ideas into imagery and mood.

It may be premature to designate any contemporary Polish poet as the greatest of his generation; H. is already widely recognized as the most original. The freshness of his approach to classical themes is matched by form that reconciles the traditional and the modern. Czesław Miłosz (q.v.), in *The History of Polish Literature* (1969), has said of H.'s poetry that it is a distillation of the crushing experiences shared by all Poles during World War II, but that its meaning is universalized into a valid contribution to world poetry in this century.

FURTHER WORKS: *Napis* (1969); *Dramaty* (1970); *Poezje wybrane* (1970); *Wiersze zebrane* (1971). FURTHER VOLUMES IN ENGLISH: *Selected Poems* (1968); *Selected Poems* (1977)

BIBLIOGRAPHY: Kijowski, A., "Outcast of Obvious Forms," *PolP*, 9 (1966), 34–41; Lieberman, L., "A Confluence of Poets," *Poetry*, 114, 1 (1969), 40–58; Alvarez, A., "Z. H." (1967), *Beyond All This Fiddle: Essays 1955–1967* (1969), pp. 142–47; Miller, S., "The Poetry of Z. H.," in Cheuse, A., and Koffler, R., eds., *The Rarer Action* (1970), pp. 244–57; Piontek, H., "Die Lyrik H.s," *Männer die Gedichte machen* (1970), pp. 66–77; Matuszewski, R., "Tradition Triumphant," *PolP*, 14 (1971), 25–29; Carpenter, B., and Carpenter, J., "The Recent Poetry of Z. H.," *WLT*, 51 (1977), 210–14

JERZY J. MACIUSZKO

HERMETICISM

Although hermeticism is often loosely used to describe tendencies in modern poetry in a number of literatures, it properly identifies a fundamental tendency in modern Italian literature, mostly in poetry. The term derives from Hermes Trismegistus (first two centuries B.C. OR A.D.), the putative author of occult, mystical writings.

Not a movement but a moment and an atmosphere, hermeticism had no programmatic manifesto, it followed no recognized leader, it formed no homogeneous group. Therefore, the identification of memberships, dates, and evolutionary stages within its history is often problematic. In its most ample scope, hermeticism describes a new manner of considering the function of poetry and its modalities, developed during the period 1915–50, to which a large body of contemporary writers adhered in varying degrees and with different results: Giuseppe Ungaretti, Eugenio Montale, Salvatore Quasimodo, Alfonso Gatto, Mario Luzi, Carlo Betocchi, Piero Bigongiari (qq.v.), Leonardo Sinisgalli (1908–1981), and others.

Hermeticism has its roots in the "pure poetry" of French symbolism (q.v.), and is related to schools of poetry in France, Germany, Spain, Russia, and the English-speaking world —including imagism and surrealism (qq.v.). Yet hermeticism is typically Italian, with its own inner needs and recognizable characteristics. Hermeticism responded to exigencies within its national culture by continuing the process of the renovation of poetry begun by Giovanni Pascoli, Gabriele D'Annunzio, Benedetto Croce (qq.v.), the Crepuscolari poets, and futurism (q.v.).

The fulcrum of hermetic poetry is typically the word—a word that is no longer descriptive, oratorical, representational, but essentially evocative. Its aim is to suggest without naming, to allude without describing. The poetry that results is of lyrical fragments, where brevity and essentialness are defining prerogatives of an almost ascetic utterance. The controlling function of analogy in hermetic poetry, while revealing a crisis of knowledge in the accepted modes of communication, also attests to an effort to recover a lost innocence by an exploration beyond facts and appearances into the innermost recesses of existence and essences. A similar intention is evident in the "poetics of objects," where, with some suggestions from T. S. Eliot's (q.v.) objective correlative, reality becomes symbolic of a human condition.

In hermeticism the role of the poet is redefined. He operates from a framework of solitude, intended not as the exclusive prerogative of an elitist caste but as a precondition for the chaste inwardness of his exploration. His operation is characterized by a sensitive awareness of the creative act, which results in a meticulous work of poetic elaboration, and by an intensely autobiographical preoccupation, in which poetry, while being a process of inner deciphering, becomes at the same time also a definition of the mood of the time.

It has often been said that hermetic poetry was a political gesture prompted by a refusal to join in the exaltation of the Fascist era, and thus that the choice of autobiographical solitude should be viewed as a sign of protest. The factors, however, that determined its genesis would seem to imply the gratuitousness of such historical interpretation, although for some of these poets their artistic posture provided, after the fact, an aesthetic pretext for their political noninvolvement.

BIBLIOGRAPHY: Williamson, E., "Contemporary Italian Poetry," *Poetry*, 79 (1951–52), 159–81, 233–44; Ragusa, O., "French Symbolism in Italy," *RR*, 46 (1955), 231–35; Cecchetti, G., "The Poetry of the Past and the Poetry of the Present," *FI*, 10 (1976), 159–77

ANTONINO MUSUMECI

HERMLIN, Stephan

(pseud. of Rudolf Leder) East German poet and short-story writer, b. 13 April 1915, Chemnitz

Reared and educated in Berlin, H. joined the Communist Youth League in 1931, then published antifascist propaganda until 1936. After extensive travels he fought with the Loyalists in the Spanish Civil War. During World War II he lived in exile in France and Switzerland. In 1947, following two unhappy years in West Germany, he moved to East Germany, joined the Socialist Unity Party, and was elected vice president of the German Writers' Union. He also worked as an editorial adviser for the monthly periodical *Aufbau*.

In 1961 H. became secretary of the poetic arts division of the East Berlin Academy of Arts, but was relieved of that office in 1963 for supporting young, politically deviant writers. Appropriate penance later enabled him to regain some of his lost stature, but in the late 1970s he again ran afoul of the regime by protesting against the expatriation of Wolf Biermann (q.v.) and the expulsion of nine dissidents from the East German Writers' Union.

H. is unusual among modern East German poets. While important contemporaries sought to divorce themselves from bourgeois tradition, H. studiously became the eclectic's eclectic. The debts owed most especially to the French surrealists (q.v.) Paul Éluard and Louis Aragon (qq.v.) and the German expressionist (q.v.) Georg Heym (1887–1912) cannot be overemphasized. These writers gave him important models for form, syntax, and language, as well as for imagery, mood, and theme. Yet, with all his synthesizing, H. imbued his work with an ideological commitment to communism that thrust him into the mainstream of East German literature and set him apart from his precursors.

H.'s first collection of poems, *Zwölf Balladen von den großen Städten* (1944; twelve ballads of the great cities), contains works that are typical of his oeuvre as a whole and among the best he has written. These ballads anticipate the tone and themes of *Zweiundzwanzig Balladen* (1947; twenty-two ballads), for which H. received the (West German) Heinrich Heine Prize in 1948. They are marked by bold, often harsh imagery, conscious stylization, and the use of an elaborate esoteric and technical vocabulary. The focus is the urban world as a demonic setting for nightmares of universal destruction and collapse. And yet the poems are not pessimistic. They feature a peculiar duality between awareness of impending disaster and hope for regeneration. Each poem ends projecting a feeling of community and faith in the future.

The vitality and virtuosity of the poems of the 1940s are painfully lacking in the propagandistic *Mansfelder Oratorium* (1950; Mansfeld oratorio) and *Der Flug der Taube* (1952; the flight of the dove). *Mansfelder Oratorium*, however, was so politically successful that it became required reading in East German schools.

Although H. is primarily a poet, he has written some of the best fiction that has come from East Germany. The surrealistic dreams and illusions of the novella *Der Leutnant Yorck von Wartenburg* (1946; Lieutenant Yorck of Wartenburg), for example, reflect great narrative skill and psychological insight.

Unfortunately, H. no longer writes the vivid, sophisticated literature of his earlier years. Even *Abendlicht* (1979; evening light), an interesting collection of personal reminiscences, is only an echo of what was formerly one of the most important voices in modern political literature.

FURTHER WORKS: *Wir verstummen nicht* (1945, with Jo Mihaly and Lajser Ajchenrand); *Die Straßen der Furcht* (1946); *Ansichten über einige neue Schriftsteller und Bücher* (1947, with Hans Mayer); *Reise eines Malers in Paris* (1947); *Russische Eindrücke* (1948); *Die Zeit der Gemeinsamkeit* (1950); *Die Zeit der Einsamkeit* (1950); *Die erste Reihe* (1951); *Die Sache des Friedens* (1953); *Ferne Nähe* (1954); *Beethoven* (1954); *Dichtungen* (1956); *Nachdichtungen* (1957); *Begegnungen 1954–1959* (1960); *Gedichte* (1963); *Gedichte und Prosa* (1965); *Die Städte* (1966); *Die Zeit der Gemeinsamkeit; In einer dunklen Welt* (1966); *Erzählungen* (1970); *Scardanelli* (1970); *Lektüre 1960–1971* (1973); *Poesiealbum* (1973); *Die Argonauten* (1974); *Städteballaden* (1975); *Gesammelte Gedichte* (1979)

BIBLIOGRAPHY: Reich-Ranicki, M., "S. H., der Poet," *Deutsche Literatur in West und Ost* (1963), pp. 386–410; Huebener, T., *The Literature of East Germany* (1970), pp. 98–105; Flores, J., "S. H.: 'Volkstümlichkeit' and the Banality of Language," *Poetry in East Germany* (1971), pp. 27–71; Anderle, H. P., "S. H.," in Wiese, B. von, *Deutsche Dichter der Gegenwart* (1973), pp. 384–94; Ertl, W., "*Der Flug der Taube*: S. H.'s Attempts to Adjust to the Cultural-Political Demands in the GDR in the Early Fifties," *UDR* 13, 2 (1977), 49–62; Ertl, W., *S. H. und die Tradition* (1977)

LOWELL A. BANGERTER

HERNÁNDEZ, Miguel

Spanish poet and dramatist, b. 30 Oct. 1910, Orihuela; d. 28 March 1942, Alicante

Born into a poor peasant and laboring family, H. worked as a goatherd and at other farm tasks, a country life that was essential to his poetic development. During the Spanish Civil War he fought for the Republic. Imprisoned and for a time condemned to death, he suffered unbearably from hunger, cold, tuberculosis, and pulmonary complications, from which he died.

H. wrote several dramas, among them a neo-Catholic morality play, *Quien te ha visto y quien te ve y sombra de lo que eras* (1934; he who has seen thee and he who sees thee and the shadow of what you were), which treats of innocence and guilt, desire and the flesh, grace, and redemption and pardon through Christ. Following his pastoral orientation, H. exhibits in his religious feeling a natural sensuality that verges on the mystic.

H. combined the popular, classical, and traditional, the physical and the temporal in his poetry. In his dramatic and pantheistic *Perito en lunas* (1933; moon connoisseur), written in ottava rima, H., undoubtedly influenced by some of the poets of the Generation of 1927, employed hermetic, dehumanized, and artificially elaborate metaphorical constructions. At the same time he stressed the ambivalent role of nature, whatever its violent or chaotic aspects, depicting Mother Earth as something that both destroys and engenders.

In *El rayo que no cesa* (1936; the never-ending lightning), consisting of twenty-seven sonnets and three long poems, H. emphasized more human and personal themes, especially those of love and death. Pantheistic and existential, these poems, which utilize symbols such as the bull and the orange, also show his sensuality, frustration, sadness, sorrow, and anguish and horror at the thought of his own death and man's tragic destiny. Included in this volume is H.'s moving elegy to his intimate friend, Ramón Sijé, who died in 1935.

In his next collection, *Viento del pueblo* (1937; winds of the people), more realistic than metaphysical, H. exalted heroes in epic song but also dwelled on the horrors of war. Patriotic and passionate, social and sarcastic, these poems, which won H. a share of the National Prize for Poetry, paint a picture of poverty and sorrow, although the poet, compassionate and tender, refuses to despair. This collection has an immediacy and honesty far removed from the baroque aesthetics of his first collection, as religiosity yields to revolutionary fervor.

El hombre acecha (1939; man in ambush), in press but never published in book form during his lifetime, painfully reflects on wounded war victims and Spain's tragedy. H. laments the blood and sacrifice caused by war, but he also proclaims his proletarian solidarity. Spontaneous and socialistic, these poems show us man, stripped of his pretensions and cultural veneer, and prey to his brutish instincts as he ambushes his fellow man.

Cancionero y romancero de ausencias (1938–41; *Songbook of Absences*, 1972), poetry written in jail, contains H.'s most personally moving traditional and popular poetry. He muses on the paradox of temporal existence, expresses undying love for his family, and shares with others his memories and belief in brotherhood, freedom, peace, and truth. Despairing at imminent death, H. denounces war as a solution for human problems, but to the very end uses symbols of forest, sun, and wheat, extolling physical existence close to the earth he loved.

For all his culture and utopian idealism, H. was essentially a deeply telluric and autobiographical poet who sang of love, both sexual and spiritual, fulfilled and unrequited, and nature, almost with mystical fervor. His is a personal, almost confessional, poetry filled with sadness and solitude, light and color, wind and shadow, sun and earth, blood and death, renunciation and purification. He eventually abandoned his religious faith but never his belief in humanity; and his poetic gifts, had he lived, would have placed him among the greatest names in Spanish literature.

FURTHER WORKS: *El silbo vulnerado* (1934); *Teatro en la guerra* (1937); *El labrador de más aire* (1937); *El pastor de la muerte* (1938); *Sino sangriento* (1939); *Los mejores versos de M. H.* (1954); *Dentro de luz, y otras prosas* (1957); *Los hijos de la piedra* (1959); *Obras completas* (1960); *Poemas de amor* (1969); *Obras completas* (1973); *Obra*

poética completa (1976). FURTHER VOLUME IN ENGLISH: *M. H. and Blas de Otero: Selected Poems* (1972)

BIBLIOGRAPHY: Zardoya, C., *M. H.: Vida y obra* (1955); Cano Ballesta, J., *La poesía de M. H.* (1962); Puccini, D., *M. H.: Vida y poesía* (1970); Berns, G., "Familiar and Natural Violence in the Early Poetry of M. H.," *HR*, 38 (1970), 386–404; Ifach, M. de G., *M. H.* (1975); Nichols, G., *M. H.* (1978)
                                    KESSEL SCHWARTZ

HERRERA Y REISSIG, Julio

Uruguayan poet, b. 1 Aug. 1875, Montevideo; d. 18 March 1910, Montevideo

Although H. journeyed to countless faraway regions in his imagination, he spent his entire life in Montevideo except for a brief interlude in neighboring Buenos Aires, Argentina. From childhood he was immersed in a world of refinement, for his patrician family gave him wealth and rich surroundings. Unfortunately, he was also afflicted from birth with a heart condition, which killed him at the age of thirty-four.

H. stands out as one of the most original of the group of modernist (q.v.) poets who flourished in Latin America at the beginning of the 20th c. His earliest poems (1897–99), immature and romantic, nonetheless attest to an incipient verbal gift. In his second transitional stage—in *Las pascuas del tiempo* (1900; the feasts of time) and *Los maitines de la noche* (1902; the matins of night)—H. discovered modernism and plunged wholeheartedly into this new modality, absorbing the French influences in vogue, chiefly the symbolists (q.v.) and Decadents, and also Rubén Darío's (q.v.) *Prosas profanas* (1896). His final, mature period of poetic productions displays a true brilliance. *Los éxtasis de la montaña* (2 vols., 1904, 1910; ecstasies of the mountain), *Los parques abandonados* (1908; the abandoned parks), *La torre de las esfinges* (1909; the tower of the sphinxes), and *Las clepsidras* (1910; the water clocks) reflect much of the taste and tenor of the modernist movement: a striving and straining for originality of expression; an emphasis on vivid colors, plasticity of form, and musicality of verse; voluptuous, frivolous, and hedonistic tones, and a delight in the exotic.

The ivory-tower poet par excellence, H. actually spent much of his time from 1902 to

1908 in a real tower he had constructed atop his house, where he wrote and received his friends to read poetry and discuss aesthetics. There he escaped from a hostile bourgeois society into his own reality, turning to exotic sources for much of his inspiration—the opulent, sensual world of classical mythology, the dark, satanic spheres of the French Decadent poets—shunning the facile and obvious, and seeking out the subtle and bizarre. Like a glittering dragonfly, he went skimming over the modernist garden, flashing and iridescent at times, but also elusive. His extraordinary imagination loved to heap metaphor upon metaphor, often producing a dazzling kaleidoscope of images.

But all is not exquisite refinement in his verse. The Uruguayan countryside, for example, with its atmosphere of simple domestic life, serves as a setting for a large number of his poems. H., the urbanite, takes solace in a pastoral, rural vision. Nonetheless, he is well aware of the uglier aspects of country life and is capable of presenting them in scenes of sharply drawn, grotesque imagery, as in his poem "La cena" (1910; the supper).

H. handled various metrical forms and both long and short poems with grace and ease, but he had a particular gift for the sonnet. In addition to his several well-known volumes consisting entirely of verse in that form, he translated Albert Samain's (1858–1900) collection *Aux flancs du vase* (1898) from the French.

Faithful to the modernist cult of beauty, H.'s poetry continues to impress with its predominately aesthetic qualities. Despite certain Parnassian excesses, his poems still command attention and admiration for their exquisite lyricism, verbal richness, and originality.

FURTHER WORKS: *La vida* (1900); *Ciles alucinada* (1903); *Sonetos vascos* (1906); *Berceuse blanca* (1910); *Obras completas* (5 vols., 1911–13); *Prosas* (1918); *Poesías completas* (1941)

BIBLIOGRAPHY: Torre, G. de, Introduction to *Poesías completas* (1941), pp. 7–35; Bula Píriz, R., *H. y R.: Vida y obra; Bibliografía; Antología* (1952); Gicovate, B., *J. H. and the Symbolists* (1956); Seluja, A., Olivieri, M., and Pérez Pintos, D., *Homenaje a J. H. y R.* (1963); Miraz, R., *H. y R.: Antología, estudio crítico y notas* (1975)

GEORGE D. SCHADE

HESSE, Hermann

German novelist, short-story writer, poet, and essayist, b. 2 July 1877, Calw; d. 9 Aug. 1962, Montagnola, Switzerland

The son of devout parents, H. was exposed from childhood to a broad range of religious and philosophical doctrines. The early models that eventually became important for the world view reflected in his writings range from elements of his immediate Pietistic heritage to the various directions of Eastern thought with which his parents had become familiar while in India. In preparation for a career as a theologian, H. was sent to the Latin Grammar School in Göppingen, and then to the Protestant seminary at Maulbronn. His antipathy for the seminary was so great, however, that he ran away in the spring of 1892. Nor did he subsequently adapt any more readily to secular schools. Following abortive mechanic's and shopkeeper's apprenticeships, H. successfully completed a training program in the book trade. From 1899 to 1903 he worked as a bookdealer in Basel, Switzerland. When his first novel, *Peter Camenzind* (1904; *Peter Camenzind,* 1961), brought him success as an author, H. settled in Gaienhofen on Lake Constance. A journey to India in 1911 was the first in a series of important, if disappointing and even painful, personal experiences that shaped H.'s creative life during and after the years of World War I. The war itself was especially odious to H., although during that time he worked with German prisoners and edited a newspaper for them, the *Deutsche Internierten-Zeitung.* Under the pressures of the prolonged illness of his oldest son and the mental illness of his wife, H. suffered a nervous breakdown. In 1916 he began a two-year period of psychoanalytic therapy administered by a disciple of C. G. Jung (q.v.), an experience that had significance for his subsequent literary works. When his unhappy marriage ended in divorce in 1919, H. moved to Montagnola, becoming a Swiss citizen in 1923. Among the honors H. received for his writings were the Goethe Prize of the City of Frankfurt and the Nobel Prize, in 1946, and the Peace Prize of the German Bookdealers' Association, in 1955.

Viewed as a whole, H.'s fiction and poetry are most accurately described as literature of experience. They document H.'s belief that the role of the writer is neither to explain his age, nor to better it, nor even to teach, but rather to employ the revelation of the author's own sufferings and dreams in opening to the reader the world of images, of the soul, of experience. Accordingly, the course of H.'s literary development was shaped, modified, determined by the areas of personal confrontation and involvement that impressed themselves most deeply upon his day-to-day existence. The abiding influence of his parents, their ideas and attitudes, called forth in H.'s works repeated expression of reverence for tradition, for middle-class values, for order. The most significant literary focus of his preoccupation with tradition is the realm of personal religious and spiritual experience. H.'s deep love of nature also influenced his writings in several ways. It contributed to a consistent effectiveness and beauty of landscape description that paralleled his considerable achievements in landscape painting. Moreover, it allowed literary models created by earlier nature-oriented writers—among them, Gottfried Keller (1819–1890)—to provide positive stimulus for the development of his own descriptive technique. On a third level, his feeling for nature led him to seek an appropriate philosophical relationship to it. As a result, he was drawn very early to the writings of Friedrich Hölderlin (1770–1843), Eduard Mörike (1804–1874), and the German romantic poets. The influence of romanticism lent to H.'s works the flavor of a search for a universality that comprehends and resolves the manifold and contradicting aspects of the human spirit. Unlike the romantics, however, who sought to define the problems of man's existence in terms of man's spiritual unity—or lack thereof—with the rest of the universe, H. directed his literary attention toward the more basic problem of man's internal nature. For the works written after 1916, his encounter with Jungian psychoanalysis gave more precise direction to H.'s quest for man's identity. His mature narratives reflect especially an interest in Jung's ideas about introversion versus extroversion, the collective unconscious, idealism, specific symbols, and the fundamental duality of man. Application of Jung's theories enabled H. to explore the traditional problem of Faustian man in much greater depth than had Goethe or subsequent German writers. Under Jung's influence, H. began to view all of the tragedy of human existence as a product of man's fragmented spiritual nature. Because of H.'s profound skepticism with respect to contemporary life—induced in part by his view of World War I and its aftermath—his characters only rarely achieve the goal of their individual struggles for self-realization: harmonious inner unity.

H. began his literary career as a lyric poet.

His *Romantische Lieder* (1899; romantic poems) and subsequent collections of verse exhibit many qualities that also characterize his stories and novels. Strongly influenced by romanticism and the folk-poetry tradition, H.'s lyric creations are sensitive, pensive, and melodic. Although their language is simple and unassuming, the poems have a power of expression seldom equaled in 20th-c. German poetry. In what they convey to the reader, H.'s lyrics are an important complement to his narrative prose through their projection and realization of the goals toward which his characters strive. Perhaps no other modern German poet has so forcefully achieved in his work a productively positive, unclouded resolution of the tension between idealistic striving and the narrow limits of reality. The concept of love is the creative unifying principle upon which this poetic harmony is based. It is an immortal love that appears behind the afflictions and trials of life as a deeply elemental quality of existence itself. The element of love, viewed as true reality buried beneath the façade of appearances, is H.'s personal guide to the secret wellspring of life, his poetic path to inner unity and to God.

Like Goethe, H. saw himself as a wanderer and seeker. He projected that view of his own nature into his major literary figures. All of H.'s novels feature variations on the theme of the quest for personal fulfillment and self-realization. Peter Camenzind, the restless, insatiable wanderer of H.'s first novel, is a sensitive man whose consciousness seeks to assert and articulate itself in the feeling of a precarious connection to the world. Camenzind is the prototype of what later became a relatively standard character in H.'s works: the struggling artist who finds fulfillment in the experience of life rather than in his art. The conflicts of H.'s own childhood and youth in provincial Swabia inform much of Camenzind's relationship to the world of his encounters. And yet it is not the psychological penetration of the central character that gives this particular work its artistic power. Rather, it is the intensely personal, vibrantly captivating portraits of nature that draw the reader into the work with irresistible force. The visible dominance of nature throughout the work demands that H.'s hero experience fulfillment only in his ultimate return to the natural state symbolized in his final role as a farmer.

The positive, healthy state of nature is contrasted sharply with the destructive influence of civilized culture in H.'s novel *Unterm Rad* (1906; *The Prodigy*, 1957). A literary examination of H.'s Maulbronn experience, which reflects his disgust with the constrictions of traditional education, *Unterm Rad* was the first of H.'s novels to analyze the tensions between the spiritual-intellectual side of the artistic individual and the paralyzing institutions of bourgeois society. In his portrayal of conflicting components of human personality in the contrasting figures of Giebenrath and Heilner, H. established problem and character patterns that are central to subsequent novels. Certain polarities that H. identified as contending aspects of his own nature generate the story's tension, for example, in *Gertrud* (1910; *Gertrude and I*, 1915) and *Roßhalde* (1914; *Rosshalde*, 1970), two novels in which H. depicted conflicts between life in art and the demands of marriage.

With the remarkable novel *Demian* (1919; *Demian*, 1923), for which he received—and returned—the Fontane Prize, H. began a series of works that document his so-called "inward journey," a deeply psychological literary reaction to the negative stimuli of the war years. Under the influence of Jung, for whom the only true reality is within the self, H. came to regard the external social and political chaos of his time as a mirror of his own internal confusion. Accordingly, in *Demian* and subsequent works, H. sought to penetrate to his own identity in a process of psychological sorting and discovery. The results are the most powerful of H.'s novels.

The overwhelming strength of *Demian* lies in its portrayal of the semimystical dream-world experience of the demonic abysses of the human soul. The life of the first-person narrator, Emil Sinclair, which H. intended as a protracted symbol for the uncertainty of the era, is visibly Faustian. Sinclair lives a fear-filled existence, torn between the clarity and purity of the morally ordered world of his bourgeois home and the darkly sinful, sensually seductive realm of the servant girls and workers. The process of his internal struggle is one of self-judgment leading to a cathartic rebirth. Demian, the shadowy alter ego of Sinclair's dreams, enables Sinclair to find himself by teaching him to unite the opposing aspects of existence into a harmonious whole. The strong influence of Goethe's *Faust* upon the resolution of the central problem is especially apparent in Sinclair's association with Demian's mother, an embodiment of Sinclair's dream ideal of love who is symbolically related to the "mother" archetypes of the second part of *Faust*.

In its conception and approach, *Demian* is H.'s most important preliminary study for the internationally popular novel *Der Steppenwolf* (1972; *Steppenwolf*, 1929), in which the author carried the Faustian problem of man's fragmented nature to the extreme. One of H.'s most inventive and complex novels, *Der Steppenwolf* represents a further development of the narrative style employed by Thomas Mann (q.v.) in *The Magic Mountain*. *Der Steppenwolf* describes the "inward journey" of Harry Haller, a man in whom are combined the dilemmas of Faustian duality multiplied a hundredfold and the timeless situation of the suffering outsider in search of a place for himself within a society to which he does not belong. In numerous respects Haller is a composite of earlier H. figures, and as such a many-sided symbol for H. himself. Nevertheless, unlike predecessors such as Emil Sinclair, Haller only glimpses the end of his quest—symbolized here in the "immortals," another variation on Goethe's ideal archetypes. In the magical theater sequence, in which truth emerges from illusion, Haller's belief in the immortals enables him temporarily to transcend the limitations of time and to scan the hidden corners of his own soul. Yet the inability to assimilate the entire world into his being causes him to fall short of permanent internal harmony. In the psychological and expressionistic imagery employed to underscore the workings of opposing civilized and animalistic tendencies in Harry Haller's character, H. exposed the neuroses of his entire generation.

Der Steppenwolf exhibits literary power and depth unequaled in H.'s other major "inward journey" novels of the period: *Siddhartha* (1923; *Siddhartha*, 1951), a lyric novel set in the time of Buddha that describes the path to internal harmony via asceticism—a major literary fruit of H.'s journey to India in 1911; *Narziß und Goldmund* (1930; *Death and the Lover*, 1932; new tr., *Narcissus and Goldmund*, 1968), H.'s most balanced novel, featuring attempted resolution of the polarities of existence in Goldmund's lifelong quest for the archetypal "mother"; and *Die Morgenlandfahrt* (1932; *The Journey to the East*, 1957), a narrative that reworks themes from *Der Steppenwolf* in its portrayal of the figurative pilgrimage to the East of a timeless brotherhood of individuals in search of the light of truth.

Just as H.'s novels document the progress of the author's own search for identity, inner unity, and self-understanding, so they also present the course of his attempts to arrive at an ultimate symbolic representation of the real nature and destiny of man. Both of those strivings found their culmination in the symbolism of the

futuristic utopia portayed in H.'s final masterpiece, *Das Glasperlenspiel* (1943; *Magister
Ludi*, 1949; new tr., *The Glass Bead Game*,
1969). In the symbol of the Castalian Order
bead game of the early twenty-third century, a
transcendent form of spiritual and intellectual
discipline and meditation featuring a synthesis
of universal values from all the arts and sciences, H. described his vision of a possible state
of culturally ordered existence based upon
self-denying spiritual austerity that might
evolve in the ashes of a civilization destroyed
by irresponsible mass production, narrow nationalism, and militarism. The major literary
themes and problems of H.'s novels and stories
are examined once more in an analysis and criticism of culture that is generated around the
bead-game symbol, and in what is actually a
discussion of the possibility and the desirability
of Castalia's eventual existence. With grand
irony, H. employed the account of Josef
Knecht's life—his early studies, introduction to
the bead game, entry into the Castalian Order,
final mastery of the game, withdrawal from the
Order in search of active rather than contemplative humanism—to reveal the incompatibility of a static cultural ideal with the creative vitality of the individual, thereby proclaiming his
own true identity and defining the real values
toward which his search for self-understanding
had led him.

In the framework of his oeuvre as a whole,
H.'s shorter fiction can be viewed as minor experiments with variations on the "inward journey" concept. Some of them are closely related
to the author's nonliterary activities. In "Kling-
sors letzter Sommer" (1920; "Klingsor's Last
Summer," 1970), for example, H. employed
the style of his own painting to reveal how the
artist Klingsor produces with Van Gogh-like
passion and color an expressionistic panorama
of his personal inner landscape. Other short
works explore themes treated more successfully
in H.'s novels. "Klein und Wagner" (1920;
Klein and Wagner) carries the problem of psychological polarity to a destructive extreme in
the tale of a man who lives a Jekyll and Hyde
existence as a conscientious official/unscrupu-
lous murderer. "Kinderseele" (1920; the soul
of a child) is an additional document of H.'s
early preoccupation with the problems of the
adolescent who is torn between middle-class
morality and sin. With only one or two exceptions, H.'s short stories are artistically less satisfying than his novels.

Many qualities of H.'s creations cause him to
stand out among German writers of the 20th c.

Despite his obvious reliance upon elements of
tradition and his literary kinship to other important modern novelists, especially Thomas
Mann, the lyrical quality of his prose and the
vitality and color of his nature studies set him
apart from other authors. At the same time, the
intense psychological penetration of his characters and the originality with which he approached traditional themes and the timeless
problems of his own era combine to make him
an important spokesman not only for his own
"lost generation" but also for future generations
that must still make their own journey to individual and social fulfillment.

FURTHER WORKS: *Eine Stunde hinter Mitter-
nacht* (1899); *Die hinterlassenen Schriften und
Gedichte von Hermann Lauscher* (1902);
Gedichte (1902); *Boccaccio* (1904); *Franz
von Assisi* (1904); *Diesseits* (1907); *Nach-
barn* (1908); *Unterwegs* (1911); *Umwege*
(1912); *Aus Indien* (1913); *In der alten
Sonne* (1914; *In the Old Sun,* 1914); *Knulp*
(1915; *Knulp,* 1971); *Musik der Einsamen*
(1915); *Am Weg* (1915); *Brief ins Feld*
(1916); *Schön ist die Jugend* (1916; *Youth,
Beautiful Youth,* 1955); *Kleiner Garten*
(1919); *Märchen* (1919; *Strange News from
Another Star, and Other Tales,* 1972); *Zara-
thustras Wiederkehr* (1919); *Gedichte des
Malers* (1920); *Wanderung* (1920; *Wandering,* 1972); *Blick ins Chaos* (1921);
Ausgewählte Gedichte (1921); *Italien*
(1923); *Sinclairs Notizbuch* (1923); *Psycho-
logia Balnearia; oder, Glossen eines Badener
Kurgastes* (1924; repub. as *Der Kurgast,*
1925); *Kurzgefaßter Lebenslauf* (1925);
Prosa (1925); *Piktors Verwandlungen*
(1925); *Bilderbuch* (1926); *Die Nürnberger
Reise* (1927); *Betrachtungen* (1928; *Reflections,* 1974); *Krisis* (1928; *Crisis,* 1975);
Eine Bibliothek der Weltliteratur (1929);
Trost der Nacht (1929); *Der Weg nach Innen*
(1931); *Kleine Welt* (1933); *Fabulierbuch*
(1935); *Das Haus der Träume* (1936); *Stunden im Garten* (1936); *Gedenkblätter*
(1937); *Neue Gedichte* (1937); *Orgelspiel*
(1937); *Die Gedichte* (1942); *Berthold*
(1945); *Der Pfirsichbaum* (1945);
Traumfährte (1945); *Der Europäer* (1946);
Krieg und Frieden (1946; *If the War Goes On,*
1971); *Frühe Prosa* (1948); *Briefe* (1951);
Späte Prosa (1951); *Gesammelte Dichtungen*
(6 vols., 1952); *Zwei Idyllen* (1952); *Engadi-
ner Erlebnisse* (1953); *Beschwörungen*
(1955); *Gesammelte Schriften* (7 vols.,
1957); *Bericht an die Freunde* (1961); *Trak-*

tat vom Steppenwolf (1961; *Treatise on the Steppenwolf*, 1975); *Cavaliere Huscher und andere Erzählungen* (1963); *Ein Blatt von meinem Baum* (1964); *H. H.–Thomas Mann: Briefwechsel* (1968; *The H./Mann Letters*, 1975); *Mein Glaube* (1971; *My Belief*, 1974); *Gesammelte Briefe* (1973). FURTHER VOLUMES IN ENGLISH: *Poems* (1970); *Autobiographical Writings* (1972); *Stories of Five Decades* (1972); *Tales of Student Life* (1976); *Pictor's Metamorphoses, and Other Fantasies* (1982)

BIBLIOGRAPHY: Ball, H., *H. H.* (1947); Schmid, M., *H. H.* (1947); Brunner, J. W., *H. H.: The Man and His World as Revealed in His Works* (1957); Mileck, J., *H. H. and His Critics* (1958); Rose, E., *Faith from the Abyss: H. H.'s Way from Romanticism to Modernity* (1965); Ziolkowski, T., *The Novels of H. H.* 1965); Ziolkowski, T., *H. H.* (1966); Serrano, M., *C. G. Jung and H. H.* (1966); Boulby, M., *H. H., His Mind and Art* (1967); Baumer, F., *H. H.* (1969); Field, G. W., *H. H.* (1970); Zeller, B., *Portrait of H.* (1971); Reichert, H. W., *The Impact of Nietzsche on H. H.* (1972); Ziolkowski, T., ed., *H.: A Collection of Critical Essays* (1973); Norton, R. C., *H. H.'s Futuristic Idealism* (1973); Glenn, J., *H. H.'s Short Fiction* (1974); Sorell, W., *H. H.* (1974); Casebeer, E. F., *H. H.* (1976); Mileck, J., *H. H.: Biography, Bibliography* (1977); Mileck, J., *H. H.: Life and Art* (1978); Liebmann, J., ed., *H. H.: A Collection of Criticism* (1978); Freedman, R., *H. H.* (1978); Fickert, K. J., *H. H.'s Quest* (1978)

LOWELL A. BANGERTER

The secret of H.'s work lies in the creative power of his poetic similes, in the "magic theater" of the panoramas of the soul that he conjures up before the eyes and ears of the world. It lies in the identity of idea and appearances that, to be sure, his work—like any work of human hands—can do no more than suggest. But in H.'s work the asymptotic approximation reaches a point that few beside him can claim to have reached. In suggesting this identity H. H. becomes the mediator of what cannot be said, the prophet of what remains silent, and time and again his creative spontaneity vanquishes the arbitrariness of existence through his "ability to live by the strength of a faith."

Hugo Ball, *H. H.* (1947), p. 271

His struggle with the basic problems of his life, with the dichotomy of mind and soul, thus leads the poet toward a biocentric world view instead of the logocentrism that has dominated the attitudes of modern European man since the time of the Renaissance.

In the narrative *Die Morgenlandfahrt . . .* there is evidence of an impending change in H.'s attitudes, and in the poem "Besinnung" that change is first given a conceptually clear formulation. Meditation becomes H. H.'s major concern. It assures him the harmonious style of the life of reason imbued with a vital warmth, whose major stress, however, undergoes in *Glasperlenspiel* a progressively apparent shift from the element of warmth to that of reason. The world view of the aging poet, whose power of imagination revolves around the central harmony, becomes progressively logocentric. The Castalian harmony is not—as Goethe's was—an organic growth. It is the fruit of self-discipline, forced into being by a strict monastic code, by meditation, by ascetic self-control exercised under the rules and regulations of sober vigilance, and by the most meticulous exclusion of all external influences from the inner core of the soul. This Castalian harmony is a mask that conceals the face of the wolf of the steppe.

The romanticist H. has thus a classicist H. as his next-door neighbor, and the more the poet approaches the classical ideal of harmony, the more logocentric his world view becomes.

Max Schmid, *H. H.* (1947), p. 223

The extraordinary consistency of his opposition to the political course of his country from 1914 until 1945—in which the *total* attitude is not gradually evolved but stands there clear and whole from the outset—is an impressive (and rare enough) phenomenon in German intellectual life of this period. But always the message is in fact that of *Demian*. The tract *Zarathustra's Return* (1919), for instance, which tries and inevitably fails to recapture the authentic Nietzschean note, preaches the attainment of individuality and freedom through the acceptance of fate, exhorts German youth to eschew self-pity, and requires them to seek their god not in external slogans but in their own hearts.

Within the heart, however, lies chaos—especially the dissolution of every pseudo-objective moral canon; and the acceptance of chaos is combined with the exercise of a most sensitive conscience—this is the antinomy on which thenceforward H.'s moral outlook is based. The process which he calls "*Erwachen*" (awakening) shatters the shell of convention and opens the Way Within (*Weg nach Innen*); and this Way, ambiguously and profoundly, leads at one and the same time to the stringency of extreme responsibility and to anarchic freedom of the self.

Mark Boulby, *H. H.* (1967), p. 83

When considered as an ensemble, the novels from *Demian* to *Journey to the East*, with their various emphasized antinomies, bear a more balanced and less contradictory relationship with each other than one might otherwise expect. Many of the critical controversies concerning them have stemmed from the fact that commentators have tended to look upon each as a separate and final utterance rather than as the illumination of this or that facet of an interconnected and developing complex of ideas and problems. In regard to H.'s ideas on the future it can similarly be said that within an intriguing and sometimes bewildering melange of overlapping and intertwining concepts having to do with times and states to come, one can distinguish basic common directions.

A primary time-related characteristic shared by all of these novels is their renunciation of stasis, which evidences itself in the concept of dynamic, sequential occurrence as the chief impulse of both the plots and, particularly, of their open endings. As the product, so to speak, of this sequentiality the future stands in a sense as a goal in itself—a goal in no place clearly defined, and yet as palpable as any higher spiritual ideal can be.

Roger C. Norton, *H. H.'s Futuristic Idealism* (1973), p. 69

The Steppenwolf, one of H.'s most popular novels, . . . is as disconcerting as it is powerful in its structure and in the strength with which it indicts an era of jazz and loud-mouthed lies, a sham world in which the sensibilities of man are tested and crucified. Like H., the Steppenwolf is an outsider living on the edge of reality. Wrestling with his despair, groping for his innocence and his beliefs in a life of lost values, he seeks to find himself. His bearings are those of a bourgeois, but the stamp of his soul spells the anathema of the outsider. The city in which the novel's hero, Harry Haller, seems to be lost, is a symbol of unrelatedness. Someone puts a pamphlet into his hand, "The Treatise on the Steppenwolf," in which he finds the analysis of himself. There is his split nature, being man and wolf, kind and wild, full of love and tenderness as much as baring his wickedness and savagery. God and the Devil are in these people, "the capacity for happiness and the capacity for suffering; and in just such a state of enmity and entanglement were the wolf and man in Harry."

Walter Sorell, *H. H.* (1974), pp. 45–46

H.'s attachment to nature was intimate and long. Nature was his childhood wonderland and his boyhood playground; she became for him the refuge she is for his Peter Camenzind, and the source of solace and spiritual rejuvenation she is for his St. Francis of Assisi; her ephemeral beauty was a poignant reminder of man's mortality, and

her authenticity exemplified H.'s conception of self-will . . . and his associated ideal of self-living. Nature was also a lasting creative inspiration, remained a common theme in H.'s writing and painting, and became his most characteristic backdrop and metaphor. Water is primordial matter, rivers are life in all its flux, and fish a prehuman stage of evolution; forests are preculture and the roving wolf is man's instinctual self; gardens are a paradise, flowers and butterflies epitomize life's lasting beauty and its evanescence, and birds are associated with the soul; nature's seasons are man's stages of life and night is the mother- and day the father-principle; trees are life's stoic outsiders, mountains its imperturbable observers, and clouds are the blue flower of H.'s early romanticism, a symbol of man's eternal longing and of his soul's endless quest for a *Heimat* home.

Joseph Mileck, *H. H.* (1978), p. 121

H.'s inner landscape had become the arena of his life, the stage on which his anxieties were directly exposed. He molded a form that he thought commensurate with this condition and found an adequate symbol in the modern city.

Steppenwolf was the first and actually the only work by H. in which the entire action takes place in a contemporary metropolis. In almost all of his other work the scene was nature or the Middle Ages or a symbolic Orient. For this choice of the city he was to be attacked by many of his followers, but it agreed with his experience. The combination of Zurich and Basel that he used to develop his symbolic city was designed to expose the individual and collective neuroses H. viewed as symptomatic of his time. Its dehumanized mass culture he had already condemned in his travelogue *Journey to Nuremberg* . . . in which he had assailed the degradation of ancient Nuremberg by commerce and industry. The tone of the city is set by the . . . "music of doom." Among its tenements, in its boulevards lit up by electric lights, its automobiles and clanging streetcars, its modish shops and bars, H. sensed the temptation to which sensual man is subject, as well as the premonition of his anonymous death.

Ralph Freedman, *H. H.* (1978), pp. 277–78

HIKMET, Nazım

Turkish poet, dramatist, and novelist, b. 1902, Salonika (now Thessaloniki, Greece); d. 3 June 1963, Moscow, U.S.S.R.

H. studied briefly at the French-language Galatasaray Lycée (Istanbul) and at the Turkish naval academy (Istanbul), which he left because of poor health. From 1922 to 1924 he studied economics and sociology at the Oriental University in Moscow. There he came under the influence of Yesenin, Mayakovsky (qq.v.), and the constructivists.

In 1928, by then a member of the Turkish Communist Party, H. returned to Turkey, where he worked on a newspaper and at various other jobs. In 1938 he was arrested on charges of sedition, convicted by a military tribunal, and sentenced to a prison term of twenty-eight years. After extensive pressure on the Turkish government from intellectuals in Turkey and abroad, he was released in 1950. In 1951 he returned to the Soviet Union. He lived there and in other socialist countries until his death.

In 1950 H. shared the Soviet Union's International Peace Prize with Pablo Neruda (q.v.). Since then, his poetry has been translated into many languages. The only complete edition of his poems came out in Bulgaria in the 1960s. The multivolume complete works project, started in Turkey in 1968, remained incomplete by the early 1980s. His plays have enjoyed success in the Soviet Union and other communist countries, and, although those of his plays that were published and produced in Turkey in the 1960s were received with little critical enthusiasm, his earlier plays, of the 1930s, were more popular there. In France and Greece, his poetry and plays enjoy wide popularity. In the 1970s H. received critical praise from some prominent American poets. In Turkey vast numbers of books and articles about H. and his work were published in the late 1970s and early 1980s.

H. was the dominant force in the evolution of socially engaged poetry since the early 1920s in Turkey. He introduced free verse to Turkish poetry; his work merges lyrical, dramatic, and rhetorical elements. Essentially Turkish, yet also universal, he is a romantic as well as a rationalist.

H.'s revolutionary poems first appeared in a variety of periodicals in the 1920s. Soon, volume after volume was appearing rapidly. The last of these before his imprisonment, *Şeyh Bedrettin destanı* (1936; *The Epic of Sheik Bedreddin*, 1977), narrates the actions of an early-15-c. Anatolian religious sect. Committed to ideas of communal ownership, equality, and the brotherhood of man, the group took up arms against the Ottoman sultan, but was defeated by the sultan's armies. The volume is the high point of H.'s achievement and perhaps the best long poem written in Turkish in the 20th c.

The five-volume *Memleketimden insan manzaraları* (1966–67; humanscapes from my country), a sprawling episodic saga of the 20th c. in twenty thousand lines, was to be his magnum opus. Many of the sections and passages in this ambitious work are representative of the best in H.'s art, although the work as a whole did not score an impressive success.

As a playwright, H. made a strong impact with his innovative play *Kafatası* (1932; the skull) and consolidated his reputation with *Unutulan adam* (1935; the forsaken man), which demonstrates the dubiousness of fame and the frequent discrepancy between one's success in the world and one's unhappiness in private life. Applying the techniques of Brecht's (q.v.) epic theater, H. created characters that are vehicles for his ideology rather than persons of psychological and emotional depth. The actors create their parts on the stage, directed by the author, whose voice cuts into the action.

H.'s satirical comedy *Ivan Ivanovič var miydi yok muydu* (1956; has Ivan Ivanovich lived at all?) enjoyed popularity when it was performed in Moscow in 1956. It has been compared, by Tristan Tzara (q.v.), to Mayakovsky's *The Bedbug*. Written shortly after Stalin's death, in the de-Stalinization period, it is a virulent attack on the cult of personality, on bureaucracy, and on the new hierarchy that replaced the old. The play lampoons in particular the prevailing official literary criticism in the Soviet Union. If H. took issue with the deficiencies of the Soviet system, he did so out of concern about the dangers by which he saw the cause of communism threatened.

H.'s novels do not compare in quality to his poetry and plays. But his collection of tales, *Sevdalı bulut* (1968; the cloud in love), and his anthology of newspaper columns, *İt ürür kervan yürür* (1965; the dog barks, the caravan moves on), include many effective pieces. His three volumes of collected letters, posthumously published, are not to be overlooked; he emerges in them as a master letter writer.

H. proclaimed in the early 1930s that "the artist is the engineer of the human soul." Although he claimed that he was "only concerned with the literary aspects of Marxism and communism," it was his poetry that is to be credited with inspiring an ever-growing number of communist activists in Turkey. Few poets in the long history of Turkish literature have had a political or literary influence comparable to that of H., internationally the best known of Turkey's poets.

FURTHER WORKS: *Jokond ile si-ya-u* (1929); *835 satır* (1929); *Varan 3* (1930); *1 + 1 = 1* (1930); *Sesini kaybeden şehir* (1931); *Bir ölü evi* (1932); *Benerci kendini niçn öldürdü*

(1932); *Gece gelen telgraf* (1932); *Portreler* (1935); *Taranta babu'ya mektuplar* (1935); *Kurtuluş savaşı destanı* (1965; rev. ed., *Kuvâyı milliye,* 1968); *Şu 1941 yılında* (1965) *Saat 21–22 Şiirleri* (1965); *Kan konuşmaz* (1965); *Yeşil elmalar* (1965); *Ferhad ile Şirin* (1965); *Sabahat* (1965); *İnek* (1965); *Dört hapishaneden* (1966); *Yeni şiirler* (1966); *Rubailer* (1966); *Ocak başında—yolcu* (1966); *Yusuf ile Menofis* (1967); *Yaşamak güzel şey be kardeşim* (1967); *Kemal Tahir'e mahpusaneden mektuplar* (1968); *Oğlum, canim evladim, memedim* (1968); *Son şiirleri* (1970); *Va-Nu'lara mektuplar* (1970); *Henüz vakit varken gülüm* (1976); *Türkiye işçi sınıfına selâm* (1978). FURTHER VOLUMES IN ENGLISH: *Poems by N. H.* (1954); *Selected Poems* (1967); *The Moscow Symphony, and Other Poems* (1970); *The Day before Tomorrow* (1972); *Things I Didn't Know I Loved: Selected Poems of N. H.* (1975); *The Epic of Sheik Bedreddin, and Other Poems* (1977)

BIBLIOGRAPHY: Halman, T. S., "N. H.: Lyricist as Iconoclast," *BA,* 43 (1969), 59–64; Baybars, T., translator's notes to "N. H.: Poems," *Delos,* 4 (1970), 192–97; special H. issue, *Europe,* Nos. 547–48 (1974); Dohan, M., "The Poetry of N. H.," *LAAW,* 26 (1975), 24–35; Des Pres, T., "Poetry and Politics: The Example of N. H.," *Parnassus,* 6, 2 (1978), 7–25

TALAT SAIT HALMAN

HILDESHEIMER, Wolfgang

German dramatist, novelist, and short-story writer, b. 9 Dec. 1916, Hamburg

H. spent his formative years in many places: a German-born Jew, he was educated in Holland, England, Palestine (Jerusalem), and Austria, as well as Germany, and worked as a carpenter, scenic designer, painter, and graphic artist. From 1939 to 1945 he worked for the British as an intelligence officer in Palestine; from 1946 to 1949 he served as interpreter at the Nuremberg war crimes trials. Coming late to a literary career, he began to write in Germany in 1950. Since 1957 he has lived in Poschiavo, Switzerland. Along with many of the older postwar German writers, such as Heinrich Böll and Günter Grass (qq.v.), he was a member of Group 47. In addition to other honors, he received the prestigious Georg Büchner Prize in 1966.

H. achieved renown as a prose stylist with his volume of short stories, *Lieblose Legenden* (1952; loveless legends). Characterized by a surrealist sense of the ridiculous and an original droll wit, the collection satirizes cultural pretensions and other absurdities of everyday life and language: in a café, a simple man casually purchases a locomotive; another man brings live owls to Athens, the German equivalent of bringing coals to Newcastle. By taking an improbable premise to its final consequences with unremitting logic, H. creates a world in which familiar habits and norms suddenly become precarious.

H. turned primarily to dramatic works in 1953. His initial success was with the radio play, *Prinzessin Turandot* (1953; Princess Turandot), a reworking of the legend already treated by Gozzi and Schiller. It was adapted for a full stage production by the noted director Gustaf Gründgens, and premiered as *Der Drachenthron* (1955; the dragon throne). In his collection of short plays, *Spiele, in denen es dunkel wird* (1958; plays in which darkness falls), word play and visual gags—which bespeak the influence of Ionesco (q.v.)—form parables to convey the disconnectedness of life. Through a professor's confrontation with a hypothesized primeval bird, H.'s best-received play, *Die Verspätung* (1961; the delay) tests the limits of human imagination, a theme reminiscent of Pirandello (q.v.) H. is considered Germany's foremost representative of the Theater of the Absurd (q.v.).

H. achieved international acclaim with his novel *Tynset* (1965; Tynset). During a sleepless night, the first-person narrator reads a Norwegian train schedule. The name of one town, Tynset, becomes a kind of refrain in his interior accounting, a series of meditations and memories that revolve around the themes of murder and religious faith, and include his experience of the Nazi period. Ultimately, the troubled insomniac has no hope, and no recourse outside of his own mind and its activity in isolation.

As an essayist, H. has written on Beckett (q.v.) and the Theater of the Absurd, and on Joyce (q.v.) and Büchner in *Interpretationen* (1969; interpretations). This essayistic bent culminated in his massive and controversial biography *Mozart* (1977; *Mozart,* 1981). Challenging the clichés of Mozart scholarship, he advances his own, psychoanalytically founded analysis of the great genius. A fresh, vivid picture emerges, governed in each detail by H.'s unsentimental intelligence. No carefree darling of the muses, H.'s Mozart is a dark, eccentric figure, one who ultimately eludes understanding.

H. has also distinguished himself as a translator (of Djuna Barnes's [q.v.] *Nightwood*, plays by Sheridan), opera librettist (*Das Ende einer Welt* [1953; the end of a world], music by Heinz Werner Henze), and drama critic.

More than anything else, it is his diversity as an artist that distinguishes H. Aside from literature, the scope of his expertise includes music, theater, and the visual arts. In this sense he is a consummate man of culture, a connoisseur. In all the forms of his artistic activity his work is informed by an intellectual clarity. The occasional murkiness of his prose style is lightened by his flashing wit. This honed edge of his intelligence can be pixyish, somber, or forcefully analytical, depending on the context. His detached cleverness sometimes leads to facile conclusions in his earlier works; in his later works, it is in the service of a greater depth and personal involvement.

FURTHER WORKS: *Das Ende kommt nie* (1952); *Aktion Dschungel* (1952); *Paradies der falschen Vögel* (1953); *An den Ufern der Plotinitza* (1954); *Das Atelierfest* (1955); *Ich heiße Robert Guiscard* (1955); *Ich trage eine Eule nach Athen* (1956); *Begegnung im Balkanexpreß* (1956); *Die Bartschel-Idee* (1957); *Der schiefe Turm von Pisa* (1959); *Nocturno im Grand-Hotel* (1959); *Herrn Walsers Raben* (1960); *Unter der Erde* (1962); *Quo vadis?* (1962); *Nachtstück* (1963); *Vergebliche Aufzeichnungen* (1963); *Betrachtungen über Mozart* (1963); *Monolog* (1964); *Das Opfer Helena* (1965); *Mary Stuart* (1971); *Zeiten in Cornwall* (1971); *Masante* (1973); *Hauskauf* (1974); *Biosphärenklänge* (1977); *Exerzitien mit Papst Johannes* (1979)

BIBLIOGRAPHY: Esslin, M., "W. H.," *The Theater of the Absurd* (1969), pp. 224–26; Glenn, J., "Hofmannsthal, Hacks and H.: Helen in the 20th Century," *Seminar*, 5 (1969), 1–20; Rodewald, D. von, *Über W. H.* (1971); Parkes, S., "West German Drama since the War," in Hayman, R., ed., *The German Theater* (1975); pp. 129–51; Faber, M., "W. H.'s *Mozart* as Meta-Biography," *Biography*, 3 (1980), 201–8

MARION FABER

HILL, Geoffrey

English poet, b. 18 June 1932, Bromsgrove

H. must have had what one of his poems (hymn V in *Mercian Hymns,* 1971) calls a "rich and desolate childhood" in the English West Midlands. The same poem speaks of his being taken as "a king of some kind, a prodigy, a maimed one." This sense of both rapture and despair animates and informs his first apprentice pamphlet, *Poems* (1952), published while he was still a student at Keble College, Oxford. These poems showed him to be an audacious new English talent. Through the years H. has won a number of prizes for his small canon of painstaking and well-shaped poems, including the Gregory Award (1961), the Hawthornden Prize (1969), and the Heinemann Award (1972). For some years he has been a senior lecturer in English at the University of Leeds.

H. has published four full-length collections of poetry to date: *For the Unfallen* (1959), *King Log* (1968), *Mercian Hymns,* and *Tenebrae* (1979). He is a bleak, skillful, and profoundly religious poet, one of the few writers of his generation who is heir to a Christian visionary tradition that extends from John Donne's *Holy Sonnets* and Christopher Smart's "Jubilate Agno" through T. S. Eliot's (q.v.) *Four Quartets* and Allen Tate's (q.v.) *Sonnets at Christmas.* The first poem in *For the Unfallen,* "Genesis," announces that "there is no bloodless myth will hold," and thereafter H.'s fierce, compressed lyrics continually reenact the painful sacrifice of Christ. But most often in H.'s work men are not set free by that sacrifice: the Deity is terse, distant, difficult, and unappeasable, and the various personae of the poems are bewildered survivors. Thus, they witness their own abandonment, forced to watch what often appears as meaningless sacrifice, themselves untransfigured. For H. is a martyrologist. His first subject is human violence and pain, and he discovers the reenactment of sacrifice in the atrocities of war: the Wars of the Roses, the American Civil War, the two world wars. The argument of his poems is that the 26,000 who died in the Battle of Towton in 1461 (see "Funeral Music," 1968) and the 23,000 buried at Shiloh Church in 1862 (see "Locust Songs," 1968), command our belated witness. The grim music of H.'s poetry vigilantly remembers the long suffering and torment of the dead. He is one of the sublime poetic excavators of our unbearable holocausts.

At the center of H.'s work is the sense of a responsibility to a shared human past. The poems invoke the blood-bespattered muse of history. But the poems also know the irony of their own helplessness, their commitment to a reality that evades language. The poet labors at speech in a world where the Logos has lost its meaning, and his laborious task, however difficult and doomed to failure, is to reinfuse meaning into the discredited Word. The task is Promethean, but H. faces it squarely, questioning his own enterprise, but mustering great strength in the process. At the same time, the poems consider their own motives, accusing their maker of voyeurism, of being too in love with the sublime appeal of sacrifice. Finally, however, H.'s poems transcend their own reflexivity. The real quest is to establish "true sequences of pain," and indeed, it is "proper to find value/In a bleak skill, as in the thing restored" ("The Songbook of Sebastian Arruz," 1968). All of H.'s complex subjects are transfigured and illuminated by the intense light of his "bleak skill."

H. is one of the most important poets of his generation. He is also one of the few poets of a presiding Christian imagination still writing poetry of the highest order. He is a religious poet of great intensity, and his rich and desolate poems command our full attention.

FURTHER WORKS: *Somewhere Is Such a Kingdom: Poems 1952–1971* (1975)

BIBLIOGRAPHY: Ricks, C., "Cliché as 'Responsible Speech': G. H.," *London*, Nov. 1964, 96–101; Martin, W., "Beyond Modernism: Christopher Middleton and G. H.," *ConL*, 12 (1971), 420–36; Bloom, H., "Introduction: The Survival of Strong Poetry," in *Somewhere Is Such a Kingdom* (1975), pp. xiii–xxv; Hirsch, E., "Flesh and Blood," *SR*, 85 (1976), pp. xcvi–xcviii; special H. issue, *Agenda*, 17, 1 (1979); Brown, M., "Flesh of Abnegation: The Poems of G. H.," *SoR*, 15 (1979), 64–77
EDWARD HIRSCH

HIMES, Chester

American novelist and short-story writer, b. 29 July 1909, Jefferson City, Mo.

H.'s father taught industrial skills at southern black colleges. The family later moved to Cleveland, and H. entered Ohio State University in 1926 with the intention of studying medicine. He did not do well: he turned to sex, liquor, gambling, and crime. In November 1928 H. was arrested for armed robbery, and in 1929, at the age of nineteen, was sent to the Ohio State Penitentiary. While in prison, he began to write short stories about crime, criminals, and life in prison. *Esquire* published the first of several in 1934. After his release in 1936, H. wrote for the Federal Writers' Project and sold more stories to *Esquire* and *Coronet*.

H.'s early novels—*If He Hollers Let Him Go* (1945), *Lonely Crusade* (1947), and *The Third Generation* (1954)—treat the themes of black bourgeois life, interracial sex, and the psychological importance of the degree of blackness—that is, the darkness or lightness of skin; in the first two novels he also deals with the American labor movement. Using this subject matter, he emphasized the bitterness in the efforts of blacks to come to terms with their roots and their environment, especially in *The Third Generation,* which is autobiographical.

Seventeen years after his release from prison, H. wrote a novel based on his seven years there —*Cast the First Stone* (1953). *The Primitive* (1955), very autobiographical, H. considers his best novel. It relates the drunken interracial love affair of a black failed author and a white woman executive.

H. moved to Paris in 1953 and later to the south of Spain. His critical and popular acceptance was far greater in France than in America. The French translation (1958) of *For Love of Imabelle* (1957) won a prize in France. This was the first of a string of detective stories, and H. was, in fact, known in France primarily as a detective-story writer. The series featured two black detectives assigned to Harlem, Grave Digger Jones and Coffin Ed Johnson. The best known of this series in America is *Cotton Comes to Harlem* (1965; first pub. in French translation 1964): thieves steal from thieves as everyone scrambles for $87,000 hidden in a bale of cotton. This novel was made into a Hollywood film (1970), the success of which rekindled some American interest in H.'s work in general.

Blind Man with a Pistol (1969; retitled *Hot Day, Hot Night*), H.'s eighth detective novel, picks up the trail of the same detectives but turns to harsher tones, and the mood is in many ways reminiscent of H.'s earliest novels. H. handles the violence of frustrated, angry people and the cast of shadowy Harlem characters with skillful surrealism comparable to sections of Ralph Ellison's (q.v.) *Invisible Man.*

An atypical novel, *Pinktoes* (1961), shows H.'s ability to write satire, and to be more hilarious than harsh. It is a farcical portrayal of Harlem street life, a catalogue of the exploiters and the exploited. Harlem's hustlers, pimps, prostitutes, gamblers, and store-front preachers —its flamboyant characters—are brought together with downtown whites by a fat, loveable, black party-giver who believes that the best way to better interracial understanding is for people to know each other sexually.

During much of the 1970s H. was ill, living in Spain. This decade saw the publication of his two-volume autobiography, *The Quality of Hurt* (1973) and *My Life of Absurdity* (1976). His reputation has been made in France and rests on his series of detective novels; in his native U.S. he unfortunately remains largely unread.

FURTHER WORKS: *The Crazy Kill* (1959); *The Real Cool Killers* (1959); *All Shot Up* (1960); *The Big Gold Dream* (1960); *Une affair de viol* (1963); *The Heat's On* (1966); *Run Man Run* (1966); *Black on Black: Baby Sister, and Selected Writings* (1973)

BIBLIOGRAPHY: Micha, R., "Les paroissiens de C. H.," *TM*, 20 (1965) 1507–23; Margolies, E., "Race and Sex: The Novels of C. H.," *Native Sons: A Critical Study of Twentieth-Century Negro American Authors* (1968), pp. 87–101; Margolies, E., "The Thrillers of C. H.," *SBL*, 1, 2 (1970), 1–11; special H. issue, *Black World,* March 1972; Nelson, R., "Domestic Harlem: The Detective Fiction of C. H.," *VQR*, 48 (1972), 260–76; Lundquist, J., *C. H.* (1976); Milliken, S., *C. H.: A Critical Appraisal* (1976)

DAVID BAKISH

HINDE, Thomas

(pseud. of Sir Thomas Willes Chitty) English novelist, b. 2 March 1926, Felixstowe

Son of the headmaster of a boys' school, H. went to Winchester, served three years in the Royal Navy, and then read modern history at Oxford. After a variety of jobs—including a brief period operating the Big Dipper at Battersea Fun Fair and seven years as a public relations officer for Shell Oil—he settled into a writing career, with intervals of university lecturing. He inherited his title on the death of his father in 1971.

His first novel, *Mr. Nicholas* (1952), employed the bitter conflicts within one family to epitomize the social changes going on all over England. The domineering father, Mr. Nicholas, expects his son Peter, an Oxford undergraduate, to be interested in cricket and the Conservative Party; the conflict between them brings out the fading nature of middle-class ideals of gentility, and the strong resentment of the younger generation against anything that

appears bogus. H. sounded a new note with this novel, a note soon to be taken up by Kingsley Amis, John Wain (qq.v.), and the other "Angry Young Men"; he himself, however, was not angry but cool, detached, and observant.

As one critic has said, *Mr. Nicholas* was so good that its very excellence seemed to put a curse on H.'s career. His greatest gift has been described as an ability to suggest emptiness. Even Samuel Beckett (q.v.) cannot make such a theme consistently interesting. The difficulties H. had with it became apparent in his second novel, *Happy as Larry*. Larry Vincent, a typical antihero of the 1950s, drinks heavily, drifts from job to job, and is aimless and irresponsible; he can find no values in society worth upholding, and none even worth attacking. As a consequence, he is not sufficiently important or engaging to make the novel seem worthwhile.

H. has extended his range beyond the rural England he knows best to African and American settings; *High* (1968) and *Generally a Virgin* (1972) both deal with campus life in American universities. Yet he is more interested in states of mind than in setting and plotting; his plots are sometimes thin and obvious. Remaining detached and impersonal, he concentrates on the job at hand, often the depiction of the mind of a first-person narrator who is warped and limited. In *The Day the Call Came* (1964), for example, the contemporary popularity of spy stories provides a background; this call comes to and is the product of a disturbed mind, but the point apparently being made is that the only call a modern man can receive and acknowledge is a call to murder someone, without a reason why. The closest H. can come to a major theme is perhaps to parody it.

Despite his intelligence and his disciplined approach to the novelist's art, familiar criticisms continue to be made—that his central characters are shadowy figures, that he takes a theme on the grand scale and underplays it to a whisper, and that he has not found the major subject for which his talents fit him. In a sense, he has not gone beyond *Mr. Nicholas*; at his best he gave a brilliant rendering of life in the 1950s.

FURTHER WORKS: *For the Good of the Company* (1961); *A Place Like Home* (1962); *The Cage* (1962); *Ninety Double Martinis* (1963); *Spain* (1963); *Games of Chance* (1965); *The Village* (1966); *Bird* (1970); *Agent* (1974); *Our Father* (1975); *On Next to Nothing: A Guide to Survival Today* (1976, with Susan Hinde); *The Great Donkey Walk* (1977, with Susan Hinde); *Daymare* (1980); *Sir Henry and Sons* (1980)

BIBLIOGRAPHY: Allsop, K., *The Angry Decade* (1958), pp. 69–73; Podhoretz, N., *Doings and Undoings* (1958), pp. 171–73; Gindin, J., *Postwar British Fiction* (1962), pp. 94–95; Allen, W., *Tradition and Dream* (1964), pp. 278–79; "Forms of Insanity," *TLS*, 27 Oct. 1966, 973; "Sherry Pie," *TLS*, 9 June 1972, 649

D. J. DOOLEY

HINDI LITERATURE
See Indian Literature and Pacific Islands Literature

HINDKO LITERATURE
See Pakistani Literature

HIPPIUS, Zinaida
(also spelled Gippius) Russian poet, short-story writer, dramatist, and critic (also writing in French), b. 20 Nov. 1869, Belev; d. 9 Sept. 1945, Paris, France

Born into a cultured family of Western European stock, H. received a broad education from private tutors. Vivacious and beautiful, she married Dmitry Merezhkovsky (q.v.), a prominent symbolist (q.v.) theorist, novelist, and poet. From 1905 to 1917 their apartment in St. Petersburg was a mecca for like-minded poets and philosophers.

Greatly concerned with the Orthodox church, which they believed had allied itself with the earthly forces of autocracy and hypocrisy, H. and her husband founded a new faith. Universal love in Christ was to be the ruling principle, and the members wrote the liturgies and prayers for the services, which were patterned after the love feasts of the early Christians. These religious activities, described in their writings and memoirs, were continued in Paris, where the Merezhkovskys emigrated in 1919. Despite their great dedication, the church attracted few followers and did not survive their deaths.

H. subscribed to the symbolist creed that the purpose of art, particularly poetry, is to fuse the material and otherworldly spheres and so to lead man to a higher level of awareness. H. suffered great anguish when mystical ecstasy gave way to despair at the impossibility of union with God; many of her finest poems are distillations of those moments of agony, when isolation and self-disgust overwhelmed her. Because of this poetry, in which she describes her soul as "shameless, base, and sluggish," H. has sometimes been labeled a Decadent. Beside these poems, however, are to be found startling, vivid lyrics composed at the height of divine guidance and religious ecstasy. This dichotomy is basic to H.'s *Weltanschauung* and characteristic of the figures in her narratives and in her lyrical persona.

H.'s striving for otherworldliness and for a universal religion is the underlying theme of all her work. Her early poems—for example, "Belaya odezhda" (1904; "A White Garment," 1978)—are structurally and thematically like prayers, owing a great deal to the Orthodox liturgy. "Svet" (1922; "The Light," 1978), with its repeated long, dark vowels and its mood of prostrate supplication, is a litany of her unworthiness and failure to attain Christian simplicity and purity of heart.

H.'s technical skill was prodigious, and her daring yet polished lines contributed much to the liberation of Russian poetry from traditional prosody. To suggest the structure of a prayer, song, or verbal exchange, or to enhance the emotive force of her lyrics, she freely combined different rhythms or rhyme schemes.

Allegorical imagery is central to much of her poetry. In "O drugom" (1904; about something else) she offers herself as a candle before God. The poem itself as it is laid out on the printed page resembles a candle burning in a holder.

H.'s prose writings are primarily short stories. Although they are not on a level with her poetry, they too are spiritual and philosophical. The stories in such collections as *Novye lyudi: Rasskazy, pervaya kniga* (1894; new people: stories, first book) and *Zerkala: Vtoraya kniga rasskazov* (1898; mirrors: second book of stories) show characters struggling to free themselves from mundane concerns, petty pursuits, and loneliness, and to attain a synthesis of the intellectual, artistic, and spiritual spheres of life. The Dostoevskian dilemma—how to reconcile God's perfect wisdom and mercy with the evil in the world—persists in her stories as in her poems. Not surprisingly, H.'s characters often seem rather abstract, and some stories lapse into tendentiousness.

Under the pseudonym Anton Krayny, among others, H. wrote highly personal, trenchant, and perspicacious reminiscences of literary acquaintances. In one such sketch, "Moy lunny drug" (1925; my moonlight friend), she recalls her friendship with Alexandr Blok (q.v.) and their common efforts to attain spiritual fulfillment through poetry.

Although H. considered her religious activities the most worthwhile accomplishment of her life, she is better recognized for her highly innovative, polished, passionate lyrics and for her imaginative handling of age-old philosophical questions.

FURTHER WORKS: *Pobediteli* (1898); *Svyataya krov* (1902); *Tretya kniga rasskazov* (1902); *Sobranie stikhov: 1889–1903* (1904); *Aly mech: Rasskazy: Chetvyortaya kniga* (1906); *Chyornoe po belomu: Pyataya kniga rasskazov* (1908); *Le tsar et la révolution* (1908); *Literaturny dnevnik, 1899–1907* (1908); *Makov tsvet* (1908); *Sobranie stikhov: Kniga vtoraya, 1908–1909* (1910); *Chyortova kukla: Zhizneopisanie v 33-kh glavakh* (1911); *Literaturny dnevnik* (1911); *Lunnye muravi: Shestaya kniga rasskazov* (1912); *Roman-Tsarevich* (1913); *Kak my voinam pisali i chto oni nam otvechali* (1915); *Zelyonoe koltso* (1916; *The Green Ring,* 1920); *Poslednie stikhi: 1914–1918* (1918); *Dnevnik Z. N. G.* (1921); *Nebesnye slova i drugie rasskazy* (1921); *Tsarstvo Anti-Khrista* (1921); *Varshavsky dnevnik* (1921); *Stikhi: Dnevnik, 1911–1921* (1922); *Zhivye litsa* (1925); *Sinyaya kniga: Peterburgsky dnevnik 1914–18* (1929); *Chto delat russkoy emigratsii* (1930); *Siania* (1938); *Dmitry Merezhkovsky* (1951); *Dnevnik 1933 goda* (1968); *Epokha Mira Iskusstva* (1968); *Posledny krug* (1968); *Contes d'amour, 1893–1904* (1969); *Korichnevaya tetrad* (1970); *O byvshem* (1970); *Vybor?* (1970); *Zhenshchiny i zhenskoe* (1970); *Reklama: Otryvok s romana* (1971); *Stikhotvorenia i poemy* (1972); *Pisma k Berberovoy i Khodasevichu* (1978). FURTHER VOLUMES IN ENGLISH: *Selected Works of Z. H.* (1972); *Intellect and Ideas in Action: Selected Correspondence of Z. H.* (1972); *Between Paris and St. Petersburg: Selected Diaries of Z. H.* (1975)

BIBLIOGRAPHY: Maslenikov, O., *The Frenzied Poets: Andrey Biely and the Russian Symbolists* (1952), pp. 128–45; Pachmuss, T., *Z. H.: An Intellectual Profile* (1971); Matich, O., *Paradox in the Religious Poetry of Z. G.* (1972); Zlobin, V., *A Difficult Soul: Z. G.* (1980)

MARY CARROLL SMITH

HJARTARSON, Snorri
Icelandic poet, b. 22 April 1906, Hvanneyri

H.'s father was the principal of a school, and H. grew up in a prosperous and cultured home. He enrolled in secondary school in Reykjavík, but contracted tuberculosis and never completed the course of study. After spending some time in Danish sanatoriums recuperating, H. studied to be a painter in Copenhagen and later in Oslo in 1931–32.

H.'s first published work was a novel in Norwegian, *Høit flyvver ravnen* (1934; high flies the raven), which dealt with a young Icelandic artist and his struggle in choosing between dedicating his life to art and following an ordinary profession. Although this novel won favorable notices, H. was to write no other work of fiction; he returned to Iceland and became a librarian in Reykjavík, a position he held from 1939 to 1966.

Despite his limited output of verse—only four books: *Kvæði* (1944; poems), *Á Gnitaheiði* (1952; on Gnita Heath), *Lauf og stjörnur* (1966; leaves and stars), and *Hauströkkrið yfir mer* (1979; autumn twilight) —H. has been a leading voice in Icelandic poetry since World War II. When the modernist school burst upon the scene in Iceland in the 1940s with free forms and complex symbolism, he struck a compromise between old tradition and new style. Thus he uses conventional rhyme schemes but varies them at times. His imagery is modernistic, and shows influences from his background in painting. By reconciling Icelandic tradition in poetry and modernism, he set an example followed by many other contemporary poets in Iceland, of whom Hannes Pétursson (b. 1931) is the best known. H.'s own development, however, has been such that his last poems show the greatest concentration of images and the highest degree of freedom in form of all his works.

Icelandic history and the nature of the country are central motifs in many of H.'s poems, especially those contained in the first two collections. His descriptions of nature are rich in color and of exalted tone; the landscapes often serve to communicate a state of mind. Such pictures, however, are less pronounced in his two last books, where they function more like a backdrop or as a means of underscoring thoughts or sentiments. Longing and the search for happiness are recurring themes in H.'s poetry, but as he sees it, happiness can be achieved only by undergoing severe trials.

Á Gnitaheiði, the least introspective of H.'s books of verse, is a good example of the worry and uncertainty that prevailed during the cold-war period. In the face of the concerns that confront him, the poet celebrates Icelandic national cultural values. *Lauf og stjörnur*, on the other hand, is the most private of his verse collections, characterized by pessimism and disillusionment. Still, art and other achievements of the human spirit are seen here as affording a measure of relief. Many of the poems in this book deal with time and the transitory nature of life, but the poet can accept the prospect of approaching death as long as he can savor the pleasures that art and nature's beauty can afford him.

In his latest book of verse, *Hauströkkrið yfir mér*, H. reconciled himself to the human condition, replacing his prior sense of futility with basic acceptance. The language in this collection is his most direct. H. was awarded the Nordic Council's literary prize in 1981 for this volume of poetry.

SVEINN SKORRI HÖSKULDSSON

HŁASKO, Marek

Polish novelist and short-story writer, b. 14 Jan. 1934, Warsaw; d. 14 June 1969, Wiesbaden, West Germany

Born into a middle-class family, H. spent his childhood in Warsaw, but World War II prevented him from receiving a regular education. After the war he attended secondary school and worked as a truck driver. Encouraged by friends, he submitted his first short story in a contest for new talent and saw it published. The start of his literary career coincided with the beginnings of the Polish "thaw" in the mid-1950s, and by 1957 he had achieved immense popularity as the spokesman for the disenchanted younger generation. He ran afoul of the censorship and defected in 1958 while traveling in western Europe, moving first to Israel (although he was not Jewish), and, after a few years, to the U.S. But after settling in the U.S., he ceased writing. Later he moved to West Germany, where he committed suicide in a state of deep depression.

H.'s favorite motif is that of love destroyed by the shabbiness of the characters' physical surroundings and by the cynicism and brutality of the world. It is most brilliantly developed in the novel *Ósmy dzień tygodnia* (1956; *The Eighth Day of the Week*, 1958), which deals with the plight of a young couple who cannot consummate their love because of lack of privacy in war-ravaged Warsaw. In the novel

Cmentarze (1958; *The Graveyard*, 1959), published in Paris after his defection, H. depicts the corruption of ideals and human relationships in Stalinist Poland, skillfully combining nightmarish and humorous elements in an excellent example of sustained grotesquery that is perhaps his finest artistic achievement.

Another novel, *Następny do raju* (1958; *Next Stop—Paradise,* 1960), exemplifies H.'s preoccupation with violence as a major factor in life. Set in the mountains of southwestern Poland, this story of a group of truck drivers working under the most inhumane conditions emphasizes the contrast between the brutal truth of their daily struggle for survival and the falseness of official slogans with which the Communist Party tries to embellish their work. One by one the drivers are killed in unnecessary accidents while the Party boasts about their alleged contribution to the welfare of society. Such ironic contrasts also underly most of H.'s stories dealing with the living conditions in the postwar period, and led to the ban imposed on the publication of his work for almost twenty years in Poland.

In a series of novels and short stories written in Israel H. developed the theme of alienation combined with a gradual erosion of traditional values such as faith and love. In these works his world has become even more brutal and merciless. In a short autobiographical account, *Piękni dwudziestoletni* (1966; the handsome young men of twenty), H. explored the roots of his new philosophy, tracing them to his experiences in the socialist system, which has corrupted his generation back in Poland.

H.'s novels show the influence of Kafka (q.v.); elsewhere, however, Hemingway's (q.v.) example is supreme: H. cultivates an extreme economy of style and infuses his stark naturalism with a strain of lyricism. H. has made a lasting impact on the entire generation of young Polish writers of the 1960s.

FURTHER WORKS: *Pierwszy krok w chmurach* (1956); *Opowiadania* (1963); *Wszyscy byli odwróceni; Brudne czyny* (1964); *Nawrócony w Jaffie; Opowiem wam o Esther* (1966); *Sowa, córka piekarza* (1968); *Opowiadania* (1976)

BIBLIOGRAPHY: Anon., "Notes about the Author," *East Europe*, 2, 9 (1957), 11; Kryński, M. J., "M. H.—the Lyrical Naturalist," *PolR*, 6, 4 (1961), 11–21; Blöcker, G., *Kritisches Lesebuch* (1962), 63–87

MAGNUS JAN KRYŃSKI
JERZY R. KRZYŻANOWSKI

HO Ch'i-fang
Chinese poet, journalist, critic, and essayist, b. 1912, Wanhsien, Szechwan Province; d. 24 July 1977, Peking

Destined to become one of the more influential cultural figures in the People's Republic of China, H. began his literary career as a holdout among his youthful peers who advocated increased social involvement. Born into a wealthy Szechwan family at a time when warlords and bandits were ravaging the country, he developed an intense abhorrence of war and a keen distrust of political authority. His taste in poetry, which tended toward romanticism, was nurtured during his studies at Peking University (1931–35), when he came under the influence of the work of French symbolist (q.v.) Paul Valéry (q.v.) H.'s earliest poems were published in the literary quarterly *Wen-hsüeh chi-k'an* and subsequently included in a volume by him and two of his schoolmates, entitled *Han-yüan chi* (1936; the garden of Han). His first individual volume, a collection of essays entitled *Hua-meng lu* (1936; record of painted dreams), won the prestigious Ta Kung Pao literary award, not because of the themes of romantic love and the musings of a young artist but because of the poet's polished diction and vivid imagery. He then embarked on an often agonizing journey from noninvolvement and individualism to ardent patriotism and eventually to socialism. Falling under the influence of Romain Rolland (q.v.), H. began to use poetry as a weapon of political struggle; in 1937 he traveled to Yenan, where he soon became a dedicated Marxist. Up until his death in 1977, just as the Cultural Revolution was ending, he remained an unwavering supporter of Mao's literary policy and, as such, an influential member of the cultural hierarchy.

Although primarily remembered as a poet, H. also made his mark as a journalist during the Sino-Japanese War (1937–45), when he spent much time traveling with and observing Communist troops. His philosophical convictions spawned a succession of polemical works, satirical essays, and propaganda pieces that placed him firmly among the upholders of Maoist literary theories.

Owing to his fine traditional training in Chinese literature, a keen eye for nature, and an early appreciation of Western romanticism, H. wrote highly refined poetry. A deft application of symbols and rich imagery characterized his verse, particularly that of his university days. Although it occasionally lapses into sentimentality, his early verse is appealing in its sparseness of language and the captured essence of natural beauty. Following his conversion to Marxism, H. published a volume of poems, *Yeh-ko* (1945; nocturnal songs), that focused on his new experiences among the soldiers and villagers and reflected his newly acquired outlook on the role of the writer. He soon renounced this attempt as too feeble, however, sensing that his poetic language was still mired in his intellectual, romantic past. Over the next decade he wrote no poetry, immersing himself instead in a study of the people of New China and of their folk songs. His reemergence in the mid-1950s was accompanied by active participation in public debates over literary orthodoxy and by a corpus of poems in praise of socialism.

FURTHER WORKS: *K'o-yi chi* (1938); *Huan-hsing jih-chi* (1939); *Yü-yen* (1945); *Hsing huo chi* (1945); *Wu Yü-chang t'ung-chih ko-ming ku-shih* (1949); *Hsing huo hsin-chi* (1949); *Kuan-yü hsien-shih chu-yi* (1950); *Hsi-yüan chi* (1952); *Kuan-yü hsieh-shih ho tu shu* (1956); *San-wen hsüan-chi* (1957); *Mei-yu p'i-p'ing chiu pu-neng ch'ien-chin* (1958); *Lun "Hung lou meng"* (1958); *Ch'ih-mu te hua* (1961); *Shih-ko hsin-chang* (1962); *Wen-hsüeh yi-shu te ch'un-t'ien* (1964); *Huang-hun* (1970). FURTHER VOLUME IN ENGLISH: *Paths in Dreams: Selected Prose and Poetry of H. C.* (1976)

BIBLIOGRAPHY: Goldman, M., *Literary Dissent in Communist China* (1967), pp. xii, 30–32, and passim; Boorman, H. L., and Howard, R. C., *Biographical Dictionary of Republican China* (1971), Vol. II, pp. 58–60; Průšek, J., *Dictionary of Oriental Literature* (1974), Vol. I, p. 49; Gálik, M., "Early Poems and Essays of H. C.," *AAS*, 15 (1979), 31–64

HOWARD GOLDBLATT

HOCHHUTH, Rolf
West German dramatist and essayist, b. 1 April 1931, Eschwege

Brought up in a middle-class Protestant family, H. did not finish secondary school, preferring to work as a clerk in a bookstore while pursuing his interest in literature and history by voracious reading. He later worked as an editor for a publishing house until the success of his first play.

H. became famous overnight when his first play, *Der Stellvertreter* (1963; *The Deputy*, 1964), provoked a storm of controversy. In this play H. accuses Pope Pius XII of partial responsibility for the deaths of European Jews during World War II because he did not publicly protest the Nazi persecutions. The vehement international response to H.'s accusation —an open letter from the Vatican, demonstrations at performances in Basel and New York, and a spate of articles and books arguing pro and con—focused primarily on historical questions and tended to obscure considerations of literary merit.

In *Der Stellvertreter* H. contrasts Pope Pius XII with a fictitious protagonist, the idealistic young Jesuit Riccardo Fontana. Upon learning about the mass exterminations in the concentration camps, Riccardo attacks the politically circumspect but morally dubious nonintervention policy of the Vatican. In a climactic scene he confronts the Pope with the demand for a politically effective protest to Hitler. The Pope responds with a coldly analytical discussion of political and economic considerations, and then issues an elegantly stylized statement devoid of any concrete position. Riccardo accuses him of inhumanity and decides to take upon himself the role of Christ's deputy among the suffering: he pins the yellow Star of David on his cassock and joins a transport to Auschwitz. Desperately trying to help the victims, Riccardo repeatedly challenges the satanic camp administrator and eventually dies a martyr's death.

Written in free verse, which is often rhythmically tortuous or overly grandiloquent, *Der Stellvertreter* presents its controversial theme in the traditional framework of a classical five-act drama. Brutally realistic scenes alternate with lofty moral disputations, and fictitious characters and situations are combined with carefully selected historical data, the latter meticulously documented in over fifty pages of printed text. Unlike the documentary theater of Heinar Kipphardt (b. 1922) and others, however, the scholarship of this background material is only instrumental to H.'s objective—that of expressing his intensely felt moral outrage. Essentially a modern morality play with a historical core, *Der Stellvertreter* suffers from its divergent ideological and documentary intentions. Black-and-white, unconvincing characterizations and polemical confrontations tending toward sensationalism or cheap melodrama undermine the author's insistent claim for historical objectivity.

In the drama *Soldaten: Nekrolog auf Genf* (1967; *Soldiers: An Obituary for Geneva*, 1968), H. examines another controversial issue from World War II—Winston Churchill's role in the Allied decision to fire-bomb German cities. While the author expressly states that the play was written to demonstrate the need for a new international convention to regulate aerial warfare, it has been misunderstood as a vicious attack on Churchill and was even banned in England for a time. Structurally, *Soldaten* encloses a three-act, realistic inner play entitled "The Little London Theater of the World" within a morality-play frame dominated by the modern Everyman Peter Dorland. Dorland, a guilt-ridden former bomber pilot in the RAF who was involved in the devastation of Dresden, struggles to come to terms with his own moral responsibility by staging a play about Churchill, rehearsed before the ruins of Coventry Cathedral. In this central play Dorland insists on Churchill's fundamental moral culpability not only for the politically expedient saturation bombing of noncombatants in German cities, but also for the similarly motivated prearranged death of General Sikorski (1881–1943), premier of the Polish government in exile.

While H. again offers much documentary evidence, here in the form of extensive (and often superfluous) stage directions, the frame play of *Soldaten* motivates the controversial attitudes expressed in the inner play by identifying them as Dorland's personal interpretation of historical events. Churchill emerges as a powerful and complex man who realizes that political circumstances have forced him into an insoluble moral dilemma; he grows into an almost tragic figure as he accepts his agonizing responsibilities. *Soldaten* has stylistic and structural flaws, yet its more sophisticated understanding of the political pressures of a historical situation and its moving and skillful characterization of Churchill make it dramatically more successful than *Der Stellvertreter*.

H.'s subsequent dramas—*Guerillas* (1970; guerrillas); the comedies *Die Hebamme* (1971; the midwife) and *Lysistrate und die NATO* (1973; Lysistrata and NATO); and *Die Juristen* (1980; the legal profession)—do not achieve even the limited literary persuasiveness of his first two plays. In these later works, which display a simplistic understanding of current events, H. extrapolates conceivable although utopian developments from actual contemporary situations. In *Guerillas* U.S. Senator Nicolson makes an abortive attempt to instigate a social revolution from within the American political establishment; in *Die Hebamme* the midwife Sophie outwits bureaucracy to help the homeless social outcasts of West Germany; in *Lysistrate und die NATO* women on a Greek island employ the ancient antiwar method recommended by Aristophanes to keep their husbands from leasing their land for use as a U.S. military base; and in *Die Juristen* a powerful judge is forced to confront his dishonorable past (long forgotten summary sentences passed in Nazi courts), and his exposure helps to effect reforms in the present-day West German judicial system. All these situations present ideas that are curiously naïve and characters that are one-dimensional. H. nevertheless continues to draw large audiences and provoke debate with his plays, and his impact on public opinion remains so significant that the publication in the weekly newspaper *Die Zeit* of an excerpt from a novel based on his *Juristen* material (*Eine Liebe in Deutschland* [1978; *A German Love Story*, 1980]) contributed directly to the resignation of a prominent West German politician.

The flaws of H.'s work should not detract from his achievements as a public figure and moral conscience. With *Der Stellvertreter* and *Soldaten* he provoked many writers into active political involvement and initiated the important literary trend of the documentary theater (Kipphardt, Peter Weiss [q.v.], and others). Whatever the literary qualities of his plays and frequent journalistic essays, H. possesses an almost uncanny knack for uncovering fraud and hypocrisy. His courage to deal publicly with controversial moral and political issues has had a profound impact on postwar German cultural life.

FURTHER WORKS: *Die Berliner Antigone* (1964); *Die Hebamme, Erzählungen, Gedichte, Essays* (1971); *Krieg und Klassenkrieg: Studien* (1971); *Zwischenspiel in Baden-Baden* (1974); *Tod eines Jägers* (1976)

BIBLIOGRAPHY: Raddatz, F. J., ed., *Summa iniuria; oder, Durfte der Papst schweigen: H.s "Stellvertreter" in der öffentlichen Kritik* (1963); Bentley, E., ed., *The Storm over "The Deputy"* (1964); Schmidt, D. B. and Schmidt, E. R., eds., *The "Deputy" Reader: Studies in Moral Responsibility* (1965); Zipes, J., "Documentary Drama in Germany: Mending the Circuit," *GR*, 42 (1967), 49–62; Thompson, C., *The Assassination of Winston Churchill* (1969); Demetz, P., *Postwar German Literature* (1970), pp. 137–46; Zipes, J., "The Aesthetic Dimensions of the German Documentary Drama," *GL&L*, 24 (1970–71), 346–57; Taëni, R., *R. H.* (1977); Ward, M. E., *R. H.* (1977); special H. issue, *TuK*, No. 58 (1978)

HELENE SCHER

HOCHWÄLDER, Fritz

Austrian dramatist, b. 28 May 1911, Vienna

H. first worked as a craftsman in wood and leather; he is a skilled cabinetmaker and upholsterer, largely self-educated. When Hitler occupied Austria in the spring of 1938 his political convictions and his "non-Aryan" origin drove him into exile. He succeeded in getting into Switzerland. Here he met the great German expressionist (q.v.) playwright Georg Kaiser (q.v.), a fellow exile in Zurich who exercised a decisive influence on his work. And it was here in Switzerland that H. wrote his first important play, *Esther* (1940; Esther), a satirically updated version of the biblical story with obvious references to Hitler in the character of Haman.

H.'s breakthrough came with *Das heilige Experiment* (perf. 1943, pub. 1947; *The Strong Are Lonely*, 1954); it was first performed in Biel, Switzerland, and went on to achieve considerable international success. This play, freely based on actual historical events, deals with the fate of the Jesuit state in Paraguay, that fascinating attempt to create a perfect theocratic society, a Christian-communist state in the virgin territories of 18th-c. South America. The "holy experiment" is a success—so much so that the Indians, exploited and oppressed by the Spanish colonial settlers, flock to it. The settlers have denounced the Jesuit fathers at the court of the king of Spain for all sorts of malpractices; the play opens with the arrival of the king's investigator. The subsequent trial is a masterly discussion about the nature of society. The Jesuits are proved innocent of all accusations, but, in a brilliant dramatic turn, it is for that very reason that the ecclesiastical authorities order them to dismantle their new state, for all social experiments based on a theory, and rigidly organized accordingly, contain the seeds of totalitarianism and tyranny. *Das heilige Experiment* thus deals with a highly topical subject in a manner that lifts it out of its immediate context and gives it lasting validity. It also displayed to the best advantage H.'s peculiar talent of combining intellectual depth with supreme theatrical craftsmanship, a brilliantly original use of the technique of the well-made play.

H.'s subsequent successes showed this talent in a variety of original variations. *Der öffentliche Ankläger* (1947; *The Public Prosecutor,* 1958) is a prime example of H.'s sheer technical ingenuity. Here he solves the problem of how to construct a plot about a public prosecutor who prepares and argues a convincing case against a criminal only to discover at the end of the trial that the defendant he has doomed to the guillotine is himself. This variation of the age-old Oedipus theme seems almost impossible to bring off. Yet H.—by making ingenious use of the historical situation and character of Fouquier-Tinville, the hated prosecutor of the Terror of the French Revolution—accomplishes this feat: Fouquier-Tinville has so often coached and prepared false witnesses that he quite willingly obeys Tallien, a member of the Directoire, who asks him to prepare such a case against a personality so powerful that any inkling of his being under accusation would entail his striking first.

In *Donadieu* (1953; Donadieu) the problem of forgiveness of political crimes and atrocities, so burningly real in post-World War II Europe, is tackled with ingenuity and deep humanity in presenting an incident from the wars between Catholics and Huguenots in 17th-c. France. Donadieu recognizes the man who slaughtered his family, but ultimately renounces the opportunity of avenging himself on him.

H. returned to the Oedipus theme, which exercises an immense fascination on him, in a play, originally written for television but subsequently also staged, *Der Befehl* (1967; *The Order,* 1970), in which an Austrian policeman ordered to investigate a wartime crime committed by the Germans in Holland ultimately discovered that it was he himself who killed the Dutch child in the course of an operation that was such a routine event in the occupation duties of Gestapo men that he had completely forgotten it.

In a completely different vein H. explored the possibilities of creating a modern equivalent to the medieval mystery play: in *Donnerstag* (1959; Thursday) he attempted to put a modern individual, a product of our industrialized and overmechanized society, into the situation of Faust, who is tempted to sell his soul to the devil.

H. has also written a number of successful comedies and farces, notably his bitterly satirical re-creation of Gogol's *The Government Inspector* transferred to a post-Nazi Austria, *Der Himbeerpflücker* (1965; *The Raspberry Picker,* 1970). Here Gogol's original situation is ingeniously varied and updated. The citizens of the small Russian town of Gogol's play mistake a petty gambler for a government inspector and heap favors on him to bribe him to overlook their corruption. In H.'s play a petty criminal is taken by the citizens of a small Austrian community to be a major war criminal, whom they, as ex-Nazis to whom the Hitler years were the happiest of their lives, want to pamper and revere, only to discover to their horror that he is anything but the admired concentration camp butcher—he is just a petty thief, and Jewish to boot.

H.'s mastery of traditional dramatic techniques may have made him seem, in the 1960s and 1970s, less experimental and avantgardist, and more conventional than many of the playwrights then fashionable. But in fact, it may well be that his constant attempts to solve ever more difficult problems of the technique of drama in ever more daring and ingenious ways will reveal him, in a longer perspective, to have been more advanced and experimental than many of his contemporaries. Even more impressive in H.'s dramatic oeuvre is his uncompromising moral integrity, his commitment to the highest values of humanity, decency, and civilized standards of conduct. There are few playwrights of H.'s generation of whom that can be said with such complete conviction.

FURTHER WORKS: *Jehr* (1932); *Die unziemliche Neugier* (1934); *Liebe in Florenz* (1936); *Hôtel du Commerce* (written 1944, pub. 1954); *Der Flüchtling* (1945); *Meier Helmbrecht* (written 1946, pub. 1956); *Die verschleierte Frau* (1946); *Der Unschuldige* (1949; rev. 1958); *Virginia* (1951); *Die Herberge* (1956); *1003* (1964); *Lazaretti; oder, Der Säbeltiger* (1975; *Lazaretti; or, The Saber-Toothed Tiger,* 1980); *Dramen* (3 vols., 1975–79); *Im Wechsel der Zeit: Autobiographische Skizzen und Essays* (1980). FURTHER VOLUME IN ENGLISH: *The Public Prosecutor, and Other Plays* (1980)

BIBLIOGRAPHY: Garten, H. F., *Modern German Drama* (1959), pp. 244–46; Loram, I., "F. H.," *Monatshefte,* 57 (1965), 8–16; Wellwarth, G. E., *The Theater of Protest and Paradox,* rev. ed. (1971), pp. 207–21; Harper, A. J., "Tradition and Experiment in the Work of F. H.," *NGS,* 5 (1977), 49–57; Schmitt, J., "The Theater of F. H.: Its Background and Development," followed by "F. H. Bibliography," *MAL* 11, 1 (1978), 49–73; Innes, C., *Modern German Drama* (1979), pp. 213–15;

Esslin, M., "Introduction: H., Mastercraftsman of Ideas," in F. H., *The Public Prosecutor, and Other Plays* (1980), pp. vii–xix

MARTIN ESSLIN

HOEL, Sigurd

Norwegian novelist, essayist, and critic, b. 14 Dec. 1890, Odal; d. 14 Oct. 1960, Oslo

The son of an elementary-school teacher in eastern Norway, H. showed an early aptitude for mathematics and natural science, and from 1909 to 1912 distinguished himself as a brilliant student at the University of Oslo. Until 1918 he taught at a high school in Oslo, and from 1919 to 1924 served as secretary of the Oslo Academy of Science. In 1931 and 1932, while living in Berlin during the time his wife was studying there to become an analyst, H. gained firsthand acquaintance with what Nazism stood for. A decade later he was forced to take refuge in Sweden, where he continued to work in secret for the Norwegian cause and to prepare notes and manuscripts for subsequent publication.

Apart from his own masterful writings, H. has made two other great contributions to the literary life of Norway: his many years of service to Gyldendal Publishing House as chief literary adviser and his twenty-two years of editorship of *Den gule serie* (the yellow series). As early as 1929 his interest in contemporary authors of other countries prompted him to introduce Norwegian readers to the translated works of such writers as Faulkner, Hemingway, Steinbeck, Wilder (qq.v.), and others. The series quickly won enduring popularity.

With his first collection of short stories, *Veien vi gaar* (1922; the road we take), H. was nationally acclaimed as one of Norway's most promising young writers. His real breakthrough, however, came with the publication of *Syndere i sommersol* (1927; *Sinners in Summertime*, 1930), a witty, satirical story of postwar youth, who while accusing their elders of self-deception, themselves fall victim to their own duplicity.

Infidelity in marriage, one of H.'s frequent themes, is the focus of the boldly experimental novel *En dag i oktober* (1931; *One Day in October*, 1932). Set in Oslo, it exposes unfaithfulness in a number of bourgeois families. In spite of detailed analysis of emotional dispositions and behavioral reactions, here, as in some of H.'s other writings, the reader is left to draw his own conclusions about the characters' guilt or innocence.

Although most of H.'s books deal with urban life, he also wrote sensitive and convincing stories of childhood. *Veien til verdens ende* (1933; the road to the end of the world) is at once simple and profound. In following the joys and disappointments of Anders, a young farm boy, from the ages of three to fifteen, the author reveals memories of his own early years with warmth and intimacy.

A major psychological novel of the interwar years is *Fjorten dager før frostnettene* (1934; fourteen days before the frosty nights). The influence of Freud (q.v.) is clearly reflected in this novel as well as in many of H.'s narratives and essays, in which he shows that the feelings of lack of fulfillment in adults are traceable to fear- and anxiety-ridden years of childhood.

Møte ved milepelen (1947; *Meeting at the Milestone*, 1951), a distinctly psychological novel, is designed to throw light on the nature of Nazism, the contention being that Nazism is not merely a political phenomenon of a particular country at a particular period in history. It is a certain type of mentality, a tyrannical temperament extant in many people at all times, which under special circumstances may be stimulated to action, thereby bringing about catastrophic consequences. H. went so far as to propose that Nazi tendencies may be attributed to a highly authoritarian education smothering a child's impulses and claims to freedom and equity. He also analyzes the personal and sociological conditions that may have inclined some Norwegians to embrace Nazi ideology and turn traitors.

A collection of speeches and essays from the 1933–45 period, *Tanker i mørketid* (1945; thoughts in the time of darkness), deals with various subjects, such as the persecution of the Jews, the propaganda of Goebbels, and Norwegian literary output during the Occupation. These discourses give a critical, realistic picture of the structure of a society that cripples and corrupts spiritually and morally, thereby making people easy prey to the dictatorship of bigots.

H.'s deep understanding of human foibles, and his empathy with people engaged in soul-searching trials have placed him in a central position in the history of Norwegian literature.

FURTHER WORKS: *Syvstjernen* (1924); *Ingenting* (1929); *Don Juan* (1930); *Mot muren* (1930); *Sesam, sesam* (1938); *Om flyktningen* (1939); *Prinsessen på glassberget* (1939); *Arvestålet* (1941); *Tanker fra mange tider* (1948); *Samlede romaner og fortellinger* (1950); *Jeg er blitt glad i en annen* (1951); *Tanker mellem barken og veden* (1952); *Stevnemøte med glemte år* (1954); *Troll-ringen* (1958); *Tanker om norsk diktning* (1955); *Ved foten av Babels tårn* (1956); *Essays i utvalg* (1962)

BIBLIOGRAPHY: Jorgenson, T., *History of Norwegian Literature* (1933), pp. 534–35; Kielland, E., "The Literary Scene in Norway (S. H.)," *ASR*, 39 (1951), 42; Grunt, O. P., "S. H.," *ASR*, 41 (1953), 31–38; Beyer, H., *History of Norwegian Literature* (1956), pp. 317–19

AMANDA LANGEMO

HOFMANNSTHAL, Hugo von

Austrian poet, dramatist, essayist, and novelist, b. 1 Feb. 1874, Vienna; d. 15 July 1929, Rodaun

H. became involved in the cultural life of Vienna at an early age. While attending the secondary school he published poetry and essays in Austrian and German periodicals. The artistic maturity of his earliest writings won him immediate literary acclaim. In 1891 he began a stormy fifteen-year friendship with the German poet Stefan George (q.v.), and between 1892 and 1906 many of H.'s poetic works appeared in George's journal *Blätter für die Kunst.*

In 1892 H. entered the University of Vienna. An unsatisfying encounter with law school was followed in 1894 by a brief period of military service. H. returned to the university in 1895, and four years later he received a doctorate in Romance philology. After his marriage in 1901 he settled in Rodaun, near Vienna. Rodaun remained his home for the rest of his life, although frequent travels abroad had important impact on his literary creations. Italy became his second home, and there he wrote several important early works.

Two artistic friendships were extremely significant for H.'s creative development after the turn of the century. In 1903 he met Max Reinhardt, who became instrumental in H.'s increased involvement in the theater. Reinhardt's production of H.'s *Elektra* (1904; *Electra*, 1908), a free rendition of Sophocles's play, gave H. his first taste of popular success with drama and paved the way for the productive collaboration with Richard Strauss that began in 1906. A revised *Elektra* was the first of six librettos that H. wrote for Strauss's operas.

During the years of World War I H. served briefly in the Austrian army and then in the Austrian War Ministry. Deeply moved by the collapse of the monarchy, he then involved himself with the preservation and restoration of German and Austrian culture. In 1917 he helped found the Salzburg Festival, and during the 1920s he edited collections of writings by earlier German-language authors in an effort to reintroduce them to the reading public. Until his death H. remained completely committed to the whole spectrum of creative art that informed the cultural heritage he loved so much.

H.'s lyric poems attracted wide attention as products of supreme mastery of poetic technique. Although his verse depended on ideas and prosody from a broad range of models and traditions, he is best classified as an impressionist. His most important poems deal with incidentals, with transitoriness, with the unique spiritual state in all its finest differentiations, nuances, halftones, and hues. Visual themes are treated most effectively. Special emphasis is given to perfecting and purifying literary language and form of expression.

During his "lyric decade" (1890–1900) H. contributed to Austrian literature poems of lasting beauty that outshine the total oeuvre of many poets, and capsulized in verse the major aspects of his approach to life. His poems are a combination of vision and interpretation of the world and its phenomena.

Central to the world view presented in H.'s poetry is the concept of "preexistence." Preexistence is man's state outside mortal life: before birth, after death, when he is temporarily apart from life in dreams. In the framework of absolute existence, mortality is a transitory condition that is meaningless without reference to preexistence. H.'s poetic treatment of death, for example, merges present, past, and future into an eternal "now." Man follows a course from mortality to preexistence and back again, passing through a sequence of life forms in a never-ending process of purification.

In defining in his poetry the essence of mortality, H. employed three major metaphors for life: the dream, the game, the drama. In his dream imagery, H. explored life as a creative process within people. The drama metaphor reveals life as a set of roles played and interpreted within the absolute framework of preexistence. One important variation of life-as-drama occurs in H.'s elegies that treat the actor as symbolic man and dwell on the actor's power to give life to his roles. H. used the game metaphor to focus on strengths and weaknesses of man as an individual. Life is presented as a gamble that man often loses, and the game becomes a symbol for unfulfilled life. H.'s three metaphors are extremely important for his perception of the nature of the poet. He viewed the poet as a synthesis of man the dreamer, man the actor, and man the game-player: the ultimate creator who causes others to create by finding what is within themselves.

The most important goal of H.'s writing was the explanation and the education of the self. Nowhere is that more evident than in his many essays. H. cultivated the essay as a literary form throughout his life, examining a broad spectrum of topics ranging from Beethoven to Eugene O'Neill (q.v.), from Czechoslovakia to Africa, from classical antiquity to Buddhism, and treating each subject with remarkably careful attention.

The essays vary considerably in form. Some are even written as dialogues, others as letters. In each instance H. chose a style suited to the content. Most of the essays are creative rather than analytical. They are rich in imagery and feature language that is often poetic, even rhythmic, full of color and nuance.

H.'s most famous essay, "Ein Brief" (1902; "The Letter of Lord Chandos," 1952), is a fictitious letter of Phillip Lord Chandos (an imaginary person) to Sir Francis Bacon. It examines the plight of the poet who has lost the facility to express himself coherently, because he can no longer cope at all with language. The letter describes a process of psychological fragmentation, in which language disintegrates into incohesive, meaningless parts, thereby eroding all possibility of being understood. "Ein Brief" is commonly interpreted as H.'s attempt to cope with a crisis in his own literary productivity. Yet the essay does nothing to suggest that H. was experiencing the same problems as the fictional Chandos. Its images are bright, colorful, and vibrant. The selection of words and organization of ideas are flawless. Each sentence, each phrase is constructed with care and precision and is impregnated with life and meaning. Its impeccable style and its deep insight into problems of creativity and of effective use of language make the Chandos letter a landmark of the modern European essay.

Among H.'s most interesting creations are a few masterfully executed works of narrative prose. Offering deep psychological insight into the human situations, these stories focus on engaging variations on the themes of the search for personal identity and the confrontation with self.

"Das Märchen der 672. Nacht" (1895; "Tale of the Merchant's Son and His Servants," 1969) is a rather cold, uncomfortable, although highly polished and poetic tale. In exploring the problem of a young man who tries to withdraw from society and ultimately causes his own destruction, H. created a horror story reminiscent of the narratives of Franz Kafka (q.v.). The account is a dreamlike portrayal of a psychologically real sitation in which the protagonist is forced to face a reality from which he cannot escape.

The better-known *Reitergeschichte* (1908; *Cavalry Patrol*, 1939) is set in historically real circumstances: the war waged by the Austrians in 1848 against the Italian liberation army. The description of events leading to the execution of Anton Lerch for insubordination is a starkly brilliant psychological analysis of the emergence of the baser self. Like "Das Märchen der 672. Nacht," *Reitergeschichte* takes the form of an eerie nightmare in which a symbolic confrontation with self proves fatal.

H.'s unfinished novel, *Andreas; oder, Die Vereinigten* (1932; *Andreas; or, The United*, 1936), portrays coming to grips with one's self as a constructive process. Openly patterned after Goethe's *Wilhelm Meister, Andreas* equates the search for identity with the general process of maturation. The novel describes an educational journey from Vienna to Venice in 1778. In the course of his development, the protagonist must cope with love, negative aspects of life, and art. Andreas encounters life as an array of fragments, and his major task is to integrate its elements into a harmonious whole. He gains insight into himself and his relationship to others by freely assuming identities related to H.'s poetic metaphors for life. The resulting experiences expand both the world within him and his external sphere of influence. Unfinished portions of the novel suggest that H. also intended to explore sophisticated psychological problems, such as schizophrenia, while portraying Andreas's development.

Theatrical works are H.'s most well remembered contribution to modern Austrian literature. To H., theater was life as he experienced it. *Der Tor und der Tod* (1894; *Death and the Fool*, 1913), his best-known and best-loved short lyric play; *Das kleine Welttheater* (1897; *The Little Theater of the World*, 1961); and *Jedermann* (1911; *The Play of Everyman*, 1917), based on the old English morality play, belong to a series of dramas that focus on H.'s stage metaphor for life. The most important drama in this group is *Das Salzburger große*

Welttheater (1922; *The Salzburg Great Theater of the World,* 1963), which borrowed its central metaphor from Calderón's *The Great Theater of the World.* The scheme of Calderón's drama was especially attractive to H. because it allowed him to develop his notion of "preexistence" more clearly than he had done in the opera *Die Frau ohne Schatten* (1916; prose narrative, 1920; *The Woman without a Shadow,* 1957).

A major component of H.'s life-is-theater dramas is social criticism. His comedies are especially forceful in that respect. *Der Schwierige* (1921; *The Difficult Man,* 1963) and *Arabella* (1933; *Arabella,* 1955), for example, convey strong criticism of Viennese society while developing the idea that man as an actor plays his best and happiest role when playing himself.

Variations of H.'s game-player metaphor received significant elaboration in a group of plays that includes *Gestern* (1891; yesterday), *Der Abenteurer und die Sängerin* (1909; the adventurer and the singer), and *Christinas Heimreise* (1910; *Cristina's Journey Home,* 1916). The respective protagonists of these dramas are Casanova types. *Der Abenteurer und die Sängerin,* H.'s first major dramatic expansion of the game-player metaphor *per se,* presents a precise picture of the adventurer as a basic human type.

Later variations on the game-player theme employ specific games to make statements about man's nature. In *Der Unbestechliche* (first act only, 1923; complete play, 1933; the incorruptible man) the main character views life as a game of billiards. The success of his approach makes him a symbol for the man who understands life for what it is and plays the game accordingly. For other, more tragic H. heroes, life is a gamble that cannot be won.

Dramas in which H. developed his life-is-a-dream metaphor explore the idea that the dreamer is a creator of an alternate reality. The most important of these plays, *Der Turm* (1925; 2nd version, 1927; *The Tower,* 1963), is an outgrowth of many years' work with material from Calderón's *Life Is a Dream.* It became H.'s final major tragedy. With pessimistic overtones arising from H.'s experience of World War I, *Der Turm* portrays life as a nightmare, examining the problem of the innocent individual in a chaotic world that has forsaken all spiritual values. It is a symbolic representation of H.'s own "prophetic dream" of the future of his own society.

For H., the main task of the modern writer was to provide the reader with access to all of human experience. Through his poetry, essays, dramas, and narratives, by editing collections of earlier writings, and in his commitment to the cultural life of the German-speaking countries, H. accomplished much toward the achievement of that goal, thereby earning a place among the most significant literary figures in Austrian history.

FURTHER WORKS: *Die Hochzeit der Sobeide* (1899; *The Marriage of Sobeide,* 1920); *Theater in Versen* (1899); *Der Kaiser und die Hexe* (1900; *The Emperor and the Witch,* 1961); *Studie über die Entwicklung des Dichters Victor Hugo* (1901); *Der Schüler* (1902); *Ausgewählte Gedichte* (1903); *Unterhaltungen über literarische Gegenstände* (1904); *Das gerettete Venedig* (1905; *Venice Preserved,* 1915); *Das Märchen der 672. Nacht, und andere Erzählungen* (1905); *Kleine Dramen* (1906); *Oedipus und die Sphinx* (1906; *Oedipus and the Sphinx,* 1968); *Der weiße Fächer* (1907; The *White Fan,* 1909); *Die gesammelten Gedichte* (1907); *Die prosaischen Schriften* (3 vols., 1907, 1917); *Vorspiele* (1908); *Die Frau im Fenster* (1909; *Madonna Dianora,* 1925); *König Oedipus* (1910); *Alkestis* (1911); *Der Rosenkavalier* (1911; *The Rose-Bearer,* 1912); *Ariadne auf Naxos* (1912; *Ariadne on Naxos,* 1922); *Der Bürger als Edelmann* (1912); *Deutsche Erzähler* (4 vols., 1912); *Josephslegende* (1914; *The Legend of Joseph,* 1914); *Österreichischer Almanach auf das Jahr 1916* (1916); *Dame Kobold* (1920); *Reden und Aufsätze* (1921); *Buch der Freunde* (1922); *Deutsches Lesebuch* (2 vols., 1922–23); *Die grüne Flöte* (1923); *Florindo* (1923); *Prima Ballerina* (1923); *Deutsche Epigramme* (1923); *Augenblicke in Griechenland* (1924; *Moments in Greece,* 1952); *Achilles auf Skyros* (1925); *Die Ruinen von Athen* (1925); *Früheste Prosastücke* (1926); *Schillers Selbstcharakteristik* (1926); *Drei Erzählungen* (1927); *Wert und Ehre deutscher Sprache* (1927); *Der Tod des Tizian* (1928 [written 1892]; *The Death of Titian,* 1914); *Die ägyptische Helene* (1928; *Helen in Egypt,* 1928); *Ad me ipsum* (1930); *Loris* (1930); *Die Berührung der Sphären* (1931); *Wege und Begegnungen* (1931); *Das Bergwerk zu Falun* (1933; *The Mine at Falun,* 1961); *Nachlese der Gedichte* (1934); *Briefe 1890–1901* (1935); *Der Briefwechsel H.-Wildgans* (1935); *Dramatische Entwürfe* (1936); *Briefe 1900–1909* (1937); *Das Leben ein Traum* (1937); *Festspiele in Salzburg* (1938);

Briefwechsel zwischen George und H. (1938); *Gesammelte Werke in Einzelausgaben* (15 vols., 1945 ff.); *Erlebnis des Marschalls von Bassompierre, und andere Erzählungen* (1950); *Richard Strauss und H. v. H. Briefwechsel* (1952; *Correspondence between Richard Strauss and H. v. H.*, 1927); *H. v. H. und Eberhard von Bodenhausen: Briefe der Freundschaft* (1953); *H. v. H. und Rudolf Borchardt Briefwechsel* (1954); *H. v. H. und Carl J. Burckhardt Briefwechsel* (1956); *Sylvia im "Stern"* (1959); *H. v. H. und Arthur Schnitzler Briefwechsel* (1964); *H. v. H. und Helene von Nostitz-Wallwitz Briefwechsel* (1965); *Die Lästigen* (1965); *H. v. H. und Edgar Karg von Bebenburg Briefwechsel* (1966); *Briefe an Marie Herzfeld* (1967); *H. v. H. und Leopold von Andrian Briefwechsel* (1968); *H. v. H. und Willy Haas: Ein Briefwechsel* (1968); *H. v. H. und Harry Graf Kessler Briefwechsel 1898–1929* (1968); *Reitergeschichte: Erzählungen und Aufsätze* (1969); *H. v. H. und Josef Redlich Briefwechsel* (1971); *H. v. H. und Richard Beer-Hofmann Briefwechsel* (1972); *H. v. H. und Ottonie von Degenfeld Briefwechsel* (1974); *Komödien* (1974); *Sämtliche Werke* (1975 ff.); *H. v. H. und Rainer Maria Rilke Briefwechsel* (1978); *Gesammelte Werke in zehn Einzelbänden* (10 vols., 1979 ff.). FURTHER VOLUMES IN ENGLISH: *The Lyrical Poems of H. v. H.* (1918); *Selected Prose* (1952); *Poems and Verse Plays* (1961); *Selected Plays and Libretti* (1963); *Three Plays* (1966)

BIBLIOGRAPHY: Schaeder, G., *H. v. H.* (1933); Naef, K. J., *H. v. H.s Wesen und Werk* (1938); Hammelmann, H., *H. v. H.* (1957); Hederer, E., *H. v. H.* (1960); Fiechtner, H. A., ed., *H. v. H.* (1963); Norman, F., ed., *H* (1963); Coghlan, B. L., *H.'s Festival Dramas* (1964); Burckhardt, C. J., *Erinnerungen an H.* (1964); Wunberg, G., *Der frühe H.* (1965); Weber, H., *H. v. H. Bibliographie des Schrifttums 1892–1963* (1966); Ritter, F., *H. v. H. und Österreich* (1967); Alewyn, R., *Über H. v. H.* (1967); Pickerodt, G., *H.s Dramen* (1968); Goldschmit, R., *H.* (1968); Bauer, S., ed., *H. v. H.* (1968); Kobel, E., *H. v. H.* (1970); Bangerter, L. A., *Schiller and H.* (1974); Mauser, W., *H. v. H.* (1977); Bangerter, L. A., *H. v. H.* (1977)

LOWELL A. BANGERTER

In all the facets of his thoughts on poetics the same underlying trend can be observed, a trend toward a fuller engagement with reality, noticeable in the demand for . . . harmony, order and plasticity. . . . However, these imaginary conversations and letters do more than elucidate some basic problems of aesthetics . . . in their essence they constitute an act of self-clarification. It is nothing less than the quintessence of H.'s experience, as we know it from his early lyric period, now reviewed and revised. It is the old problem of personality, its identity and continuity that occupies him throughout these essays.

The receptivity of the young poet who surrendered to the impressions and experiences of the moment was such that at times he was threatened with a loss of any sense that he himself was a continuous entity in time, capable of enduring and assimilating these experiences. . . . This is the poet of *Gestern* who expresses by the very title of his playlet that that residue of personality beyond the immediate here and now of experience is felt as an obsolete remnant, an appendage that cannot be removed from the consciousness but which does not truly belong there.

Mary E. Gilbert, "H.'s Essays 1900–1910: A Poet in Transition," in Frederick Norman, ed., *H.* (1963), pp. 44–45

Time is the measure of mutability; and nothing is more patent than H.'s oppressive awareness of the transience of earthly things. . . . His very first playlet, *Gestern*, is an ironic comment upon the failure of his hero to come to terms with this basic fact. The awareness of time is a threat at all . . . levels. . . . For the neoplatonic mystic whose gaze is fixed on the eternal and unchanging essences, it is a confirmation that he is right in turning away from a world of shadows; there is an echo of this in the text from St. Gregory of Nyssa with which H. prefaced *Ad me Ipsum*. . . . An experience of time is one thing, an acceptance of its implications is another. To accept is to bind oneself, to have a fate; and this, for the lyric poet, can lead to crisis. . . . H.'s life was an endeavor to come to terms with the problems of time and eternity. The corrosive effect of time was a permanent threat; it was the meaning and possibility of eternity which had first to be thrashed out, starting with that painful process which led from the testing and rejection of a false notion of eternity as time open at both ends to that transcendence of change which can be achieved by the acceptance of a fate and metamorphosis through love.

John Bednall, "From High Language to Dialect: A Study in H.'s Change of Medium," in Frederick Norman, ed., *H.* (1963), pp. 101–2

He had much of that cosmopolitanism of outlook, both political and cultural, which has for long been a distinguishing feature of Vienna, standing from Roman times at a crossroads in Europe, the gateway to the Balkans, to the Slavonic East and the Near East, to the Germanic North and to the Mediterranean South.

Sensitive to currents flowing into Vienna from all directions, H. presents a finely balanced dualism, for this supranational side of his intellectual character appears with equal strength alongside his abiding love for simple rural custom, folk language and traditions, which are depicted in his work with marked sympathy. This dualism . . . was with time to become a dominating characteristic. . . .

The young H. was . . . one of those phenomena which an old civilization brings forth without effort from time to time. H., even more perhaps than Mozart or Richard Strauss, sprang fully armed at all points into the intellectual world. . . . At the age of seventeen, while still a schoolboy, H. was using the German language with an ease, a coruscating magic and wealth of overtone and suggestion whose like had not been experienced since the death of Goethe.

Brian Coghlan, *H.'s Festival Dramas* (1964), pp. 7–8

In terms of plot, then, *Andreas* appears to be just one more historical novel of picaresque adventures set in foreign lands. Yet what a plot summary conceals are the work's two most singular aspects: its extraordinarily modern, spatial structure and its highly symbolic mode of narration. Fully half of the eighty completed pages of the fragment deal, in the form of a flashback, with Andreas' adventures in the Alps; the episodes with Romana and Gotthilff, in other words, are given to us through the internal focus of Andreas' memory, as he sits musing for an hour or so in his room in Venice. In the Venetian scenes, on the other hand, style and narrative standpoint strike the reader as disturbingly modern and surrealistic, for the technique employed is very similar to that of both E. T. A. Hoffmann and Kafka, and the themes involved are those of reality-confusion, projected psychological disturbances and split personality.... Through its symbolic form and style, the action throughout the novel is thus effectively shifted from the outer landscape of epic narrative . . . to the complex inscape of twentieth century fiction. . . . Andreas' development does not press ever outward toward a Goethean fulfillment of the total personality, but rather inward . . . to an ultimate renewal and reassertion of the self.

David H. Miles, *H.'s Novel "Andreas"* (1972), pp. 109–10

Many of these early works of H. were illustrated with Jugendstil nature scenes. In these intricate and elaborate designs a natural world was depicted in which each separate organism is organically connected with some other entity, a plant

stalk joins up with the tail of a peacock, a brook becomes the leaf of a tree. It is a vision of the universe as a magically harmonious dream garden, beyond the divisive power of time. Precisely this is however the incomprehensible—for events do pass by, the present does not remain present, an organic part of our own being has gone through the process of being forgotten. The writer realizes that the single body of himself, his childhood, and his ancestors is made possible only through the liquid flow of time, the gliding motion which causes present to become past, and the ancestors to die physically only to remain alive in the body of the children. H. cannot rid his magic garden of the process of history. He feels in the identification of himself with the bodies of the past the drive of time: it is a realization he is reluctant to come to, but it occurs over and over in his struggle to draw some conclusion regarding his magic lyric powers.

Peter A. Stenberg, "*Der Rosenkavalier*: H.'s Märchen of Time," *GL&L*, 26 (1972), 25

When H. no longer needed to explore and define the shifting transitional stages of his inner maturation, and when his concern with more general themes had reached a degree of complexity that burst the bounds of the lyric genre, he had little left to say that could best be said in the medium of poetry. The later poem "Reiselied" (1898) shows that technically speaking he could still write poetry very well indeed, but it is a poem without human complexities, a symbolic summing up of his own poetic ideal of Arcadian serenity and gentle beauty. . . . If we posit the view that by the end of his lyric phase poetry had outlived its usefulness for H., we have a more convincing answer to the question of why he stopped writing in the genre than the answer most frequently given, namely that he lost faith in the power of language to do justice to experience. . . . The preeminence given to the "language crisis" has of course been largely based on the questionable . . . assumption that the famous "Chandos Letter" was an autobiographical utterance. If H. did suffer a "Sprachkrise" this did not prevent him from giving consummate linguistic expression to that very crisis, nor did it impair his powers of language in any of his contemporary or subsequent writings.

David E. Jenkinson, "The Poetry of Transition: Some Aspects of the Interpretation of H.'s Lyrics," *GL&L*, 27 (1974), 301

HÖLLERER, Walter

West German poet, novelist, critic, and editor, b. 19 Dec. 1922, Sulzbach-Rosenberg

After service on the Mediterranean front during World War II, H. earned his doctorate in comparative literature and became a professor in

Frankfurt and, later, Berlin. In the 1970s he taught at the University of Illinois.

The poems of H.'s first book, *Der andrere Gast* (1952; the other guest) reveal the author's familiarity with the literary tradition. Although many poems are rhymed and some are written in classical meters, his voice is strikingly original, especially in the use of images. The Mediterranean landscape often appears, in reference to antiquity as well as to the war. H.'s next three volumes of poetry, *Gedichte; Wie entsteht ein Gedicht* (1964; poems; how does a poem originate), *Außerhalb der Saison* (1967; off season), and *Systeme* (1969; systems), move further and further away from traditional forms, and *Systeme*, in appearance, although not in content, resembles concrete poetry.

If the early poems capture the essence of a single mood or scene, the later ones reflect H.'s growing interest in the complexities of contemporary society and his desire to address them in his works. Each of H.'s collections is progressive but not avant-garde, in relation to other verse written at the same time.

The novel *Die Elephantenuhr* (1973; the elephant clock) is a long, complicated work in which H.'s conception of the chaos and fragmentation of the contemporary world is reflected in the apparently chaotic style, structure, and plot. The protagonist is ultimately confined in a mental institution, where the manuscript is ostensibly written.

Few people have made a greater overall contribution to the contemporary German literary scene than H., who has also been active as a scholar, critic, editor, and literary theorist. One of the founding editors of *Akzente* in 1954, he remained a coeditor of this important periodical until 1967. In 1956 he edited *Transit*, one of the most significant anthologies of modern German poetry, and five years later became one of the founding editors of the journal *Sprache im technischen Zeitalter*. In his theoretical essays H. consistently takes a progressive position, but demands a solid intellectual basis and an understanding of different national literary traditions.

FURTHER WORKS: *Zwischen Klassik und Moderne* (1958); *Modernes Theater auf kleinen Bühnen* (1965); *Alle Vögel alle* (1978)

BIBLIOGRAPHY: Leonhard, K., "W. H.," in Nonnemann, K., ed., *Schriftsteller der Gegenwart* (1963), pp. 157–62; Heselhaus, C., "Völlig versteckt im Frühwind (3)," in Domin, H., ed., *Doppelinterpretationen* (1966), pp.

221–32; Lorbe, R., "W. H.: Schneeblauer Wind," *Lyrische Standpunkte* (1968), pp. 135–42; Hinck, W., "Ein Boot ist immer versteckt," *Frankfurter Anthologie*, 3 (1978), 223–25; Van D'Elden, K. H., ed., *West German Poets on Society and Politics* (1979), pp. 141–61

JERRY GLENN

HOLT, Kåre

Norwegian novelist, b. 27 Oct. 1917, Våle

The son of a railroad worker, and coming of age in the economically depressed 1930s, H. early became actively involved in the labor movement and worked as a journalist in the labor press. Eventually he was able to earn his living as a free-lance writer and novelist. H.'s novels center, on the one hand, on a social theme—the struggle between the haves and the have-nots—and, on the other, on an existential one—at what point does man cease to be a product of heredity and environment and begin to be able to exert free will and assume responsibility for his actions.

H.'s artistic breakthrough was *Det store veiskillet* (1949; at the crossroads). On the eve of the Nazi invasion of Norway a young man is cornered in a desperate situation, and on the basis of the ensuing choice of action H. develops three different life stories for the boy. The novel is a psychological study of the collaborator, the traitor, and the hero, but above all H. treats the problem of choice and, as he sees it, man's ethical responsibility for his actions.

H.'s next important work was a thoroughly researched historical trilogy depicting the rise of the labor movement: *Det stolte nederlag* (1956; the proud defeat), *Storm under morgenstjerne* (1958; storm under morning star), and *Opprørere ved havet* (1960; rebels by the sea). The three novels are written with great poetic force and superb craftsmanship. *Kongen* (1965–69; the king) H.'s next novel, also a trilogy, portrays the medieval Norwegian king Sverre, a legendary rebel and impostor whose rise from poverty to power in H.'s view does not lead to the democratic revolution that King Sverre claimed in his own official saga. *Kongen* is a major novel in postwar Norwegian fiction, it is rich in historical detail and powerful in its psychological portrayal of human loneliness and the corruption of power. *Kappløpet* (1974; *The Race*, 1975) emphasizes the less heroic aspects of the life and psyche of the Norwegian national hero, the polar explorer Roald

Amundsen, and caused a great stir among patriotic readers. H.'s thorough research, his great narrative talent, and his claim to poetic license, however, soon silenced his critics.

Similar debates (with similar results) occurred after his novels on the 18th-c. admiral Tordenskiold and the 17th-c. missionary to Greenland, Hans Egede, *Sjøhelten* (1975; hero of the sea) and *Sønn av jord og himmel* (1978; son of earth and heaven), respectively. These books strip the glamour from their protagonists, emphasizing human tragedy and human folly. H.'s studies of historical personages are at the same time critical and compassionate. They demonstrate his deep-seated suspicion of the corrupting influence of power as well as his fundamental belief in humanistic values.

FURTHER WORKS: *Tore kramkar* (1939); *Tore finner vei* (1940); *Spillemann og kjøgemester* (1941); *Hurra for han som innstifta da'n* (1945); *Udåden* (1945); *Demring* (1946); *Cleng Peerson og Nils med luggen* (1948); *Nattegjester* (1948); *Brødre* (1951); *Hevnen hører meg til* (1953); *Mennesker ved en grense* (1954); *Rømlingen Oskar og Maria fra Hulesjøen* (1959); *Den gamle veien til Kierlighed* (1961); *Perlefiskeren* (1963); *Oppstandelsen* (1971); *Kristine av Tunsberg* (1971); *Ansikter i sagaens halvlys* (1971); *Farvel til en kvinne* (1972); *Folket ved Svansjøen* (1973); *De lange mil til Paradiset* (1977); *Gjester fra det ukjente* (1980); *Mørke smil* (1981); *Biter av et bilde* (1981)

KJETIL A. FLATIN

HONCHAR, Oles
Ukrainian novelist and short-story writer, b. 3 April 1918, Sukha

H. was born into a family of farm workers. In 1937 he completed his studies in journalism in Kharkov, and, following a brief career in journalism, he enrolled (in 1938) at Kharkov University. He served during World War II with distinction. In 1946 he entered the University of Dnepropetrovsk, where he studied literature and philology. The recipient of several major literary awards, he served (1958–66) as the chairman of the Writers' Union of the Ukrainian S.S.R., then as its first secretary (1966–69).

H.'s artistic development has paralleled a growth in national self-awareness. Despite his status as a pillar of Communist society he has dealt in a forthright manner with moral dilemmas in his wartime and war-focused pieces, and with the question of cultural vandalism by unsympathetic bureaucrats in his postwar writing.

Several novels concern the moral and ethical dilemmas posed by war. His trilogy *Praporonostsi* (2 vols., 1947–48; *The Standard Bearers*, 2 vols., 1948–50), deals with the officially promulgated messianic notion that informed the Soviet Union's postwar policies in Europe. It chronicles the pursuit of the defeated Wehrmacht to Prague by the Soviet army, following the Battle of Stalingrad. *Tavria* (1952; Tauris) describes the growth of class consciousness among the Ukrainian proletariat. The novel is directed against the "bourgeois nationalists" and their sympathizers. *Perekop* (1957; *Perekop*, 1958) gives a panorama of the postrevolution civil war in the Ukraine. The novel ends with the fall of Perekop into the hands of the Bolsheviks.

In sharp contrast to these works are H.'s shorter novels, *Shchob svityvsya vohnyk* (1955; so the fire may gleam) and *Masha z Verkhovyny* (1959; Masha from the Highlands), both essentially love stories, Soviet-style, that is, sad and tender in tone, with no attempt to include the physical side of love.

H.'s writing during the 1960s demonstrates more self-assertiveness and awareness of Ukrainian traditions. In *Tronka* (1963; *The Sheep Bell*, 1964), a "novel in twelve novellas," H. portrays contemporary people attempting to achieve a viable synthesis of earlier life styles with today's, contrasting the old shepherd and his way of life with that of the narrator, a pilot. He praises Soviet man, but also critically examines some negative traits of life under socialism.

The novel that has come to be recognized as his masterpiece, *Sobor* (1968; the cathedral), is an indictment of the Russian authorities and their Ukrainian minions who are oblivious to the values of the Ukrainian past and ruthless in uprooting them. *Sobor*, although initially praised by the literary establishment, came under scrutiny and was eventually banned and its author censured.

Tsyklon (1970; *Cyclone*, 1972) glorifies the Party and served to rehabilitate H., reestablishing his credentials with the Soviet authorities. The title has a double meaning: the storm of Nazism and the natural flood disaster that moves in from the Atlantic. These themes provide the basis for a philosophical discussion of the destructive forces in man and nature.

No writer publishing in the Ukraine today demonstrates a keener or more subtle awareness of man's dependence on the past and his responsibility to the future than H., who is, moreover, a continuer of the Ukrainian classical literary heritage. Whole passages in his recent writing appear to derive directly from the work of the great poet Taras Shevchenko (1814–1861).

H. has taken as his civic and literary task a serious, longterm, unrelenting assessment of his nation's present and past, distinguishing the healthy impulses from the pernicious, and postulating spiritual absolutes as the inescapable answer to current problems.

FURTHER WORKS: *Alpy* (1947); *Zemlya hude* (1947); *Holubay Dunay* (1948); *Modry kamen* (1948; "The Wise Stone," 1955); *Novely* (1949); *Zlata Praha* (1949); *Mykyta Bratus* (1951; "Mykyta Bratus," 1955); *Pivden* (1951; "The South," 1955); *Doroha za khmary* (1953; *The Road to the Mountains,* 1953); *Partyzanska iskra* (1956); *Tvory* (4 vols., 1956–60); *Chary-Komyshi* (1958; "The Magic Reeds," 1955); *Lyudyna i zbroya* (1960; *Man and Arms,* 1961); *Zirnytsi* (1960); *Yaponski etyudy* (1961); *Ilonka* (1972); *Pro nashe pismenstvo* (1972); *Bryhantyna* (1973); *Bereh lyubovi* (1976). FURTHER VOLUME IN ENGLISH: *Short Stories* (1955)

BIBLIOGRAPHY: Shabliovsky, Y., *Ukrainian Literature through the Ages* (1970), p. 216; Mihailovich, V. D., et al., *Modern Slavic Literatures* (1976), Vol. II, pp. 467–69; "A Note on O. H.," *Journal of Graduate Ukrainian Studies,* 1, 1 (1976), 45–47; Sverstiuk, Y., "A Cathedral in Scaffolding," in Luckyj, G. S. N., ed., *Clandestine Essays* (1976), pp. 17–68; Rudnytzky, L., "O. H.'s *Cathedral,*" *Mitteilungen: Arbeits- und Förderungsgemeinschaft der ukrainischen Wissenschaften,* 15 (1978), 96–125

THOMAS E. BIRD

HONDURAN LITERATURE
See Central American Literature

HOPE, A(lec) D(erwent)
Australian poet and literary critic, b. 21 July 1907, Cooma

After graduating from the Universities of Sydney (1928) and Oxford (1930), where he read philology, H. taught in Sydney and lectured at Sydney Teachers' College and Melbourne

University. In 1951 he was appointed professor of English at Canberra University College (later the Australian National University), where he remained until his retirement in 1968. From 1969 to 1972 he was a Library Fellow at A.N.U. and in 1972 was awarded an O.B.E.

Although H. published in journals, his was a coterie audience until his first book, *The Wandering Islands* (1955). This collection, which received wide acclaim and immediately placed him in the vanguard of contemporary Australian poetry, is notable for its formalism, its satire of modern mass culture, and its themes of isolation, anxiety, and guilt. Subsequent volumes, *Poems* (1960), *New Poems 1965–1969* (1969), and *A Late Picking: Poems 1965–1974* (1975), continue themes and formal preoccupations set down in *The Wandering Islands*, but from *New Poems* on, a depth and range of feeling was realized that was only hinted at in the first volume: the demonic pride gives way to a communal poetry of humility and love. *A Late Picking* draws imagery from astronomy and physics, further exploring the efficacy of journeying into the unknown, a central concern of H.'s poetry from the outset. His *Dunciad Minor: An Heroick Poem* (1970) takes for its target an Australian critic, but its broad references to modern critics and criticism leads it beyond the local to an indictment of what H. takes to be an accelerating loss of faith in reason and a corresponding erosion of a uniform theological and intellectual (poetic and critical) tradition.

H. also wrote numerous essays on poetry and on literature in general, in which he elaborated his formalism, fitted Australian writing into a larger pattern of writing in English, and asserted the function of the poet "to participate in and support the order of the world." H. also wrote monographs on Australian literary history and on Australian writers, and published a long study of the Scottish poet William Dunbar (1460?–1520?), *A Midsummer Eve's Dream: Variations on a Theme by William Dunbar* (1970). Dunbar's greatness, H. argues with relevance to his own work, lies in his "amplitude of reference to great issues in human life and human history."

Central to H.'s poetry is a tension between his "classical" concern for form and a late-romantic view of man and the poet, recognizing questions of isolation and guilt and positing the artist as a synthesizer struggling to find order and relation, to restore connections to personal and social life. What appeared at first to be savage and ironic in his poetry, can, in the context of his later work, be seen as more truly celebratory, "even when what is asserted is itself a tragic or a terrifying truth." H. turns to the cultural reservoir of European literature for his sources, speaking in a public voice the "great commonplaces"; thus, his narratives, landscapes, and characters carry analogical significance beyond the particular case.

H. has established himself as one of the most significant poets in Australian literature, noted for his eloquence and candor. His formalism never falters, but, like his themes, speaks of his modernism, for in it we sense the need to impose order on chaos.

FURTHER WORKS: *Australian Poets Series—A. D. H.: Selected Poems* (1963); *Australian Literature 1950–1962* (1963); *The Cave and the Spring: Essays on Poetry* (1965); *The Literary Influence of Academies* (1970); *Henry Kendall: A Dialogue with the Past* (1971); *Collected Poems 1930–1970* (1972); *Selected Poems* (1973); *Native Companions: Essays and Comments on Australian Literature 1936–1966* (1974); *Judith Wright* (1975); *A Book of Answers* (1978); *The Pack of Autolycus* (1978); *The Drifting Continent, and Other Poems* (1979); *The New Cratylus: Notes on the Craft of Poetry* (1979)

BIBLIOGRAPHY: Goldberg, S. L., "The Poet as Hero: A. D. H.'s *The Wandering Islands*," *Meanjin*, 16 (1957), 127–39; Wright, J., "A. D. H.," *Preoccupations in Australian Poetry* (1965), pp. 181–92; Heseltine, H. P., "Paradise Within: A. D. H.'s *New Poems*," *Meanjin*, 29 (1970), 405–20; Brissenden, R. F., "Art and the Academy: The Achievement of A. D. H.," in Dutton, G., ed., *The Literature of Australia* (1976), pp. 406–26; Kramer, L., *A. D. H.* (1979); Hooton, J., *A. D. H.: A Bibliography* (1979)

JAMES WIELAND

HORA, Josef

Czechoslovak poet (writing in Czech), b. 8 July 1891, Dobříň u Roudnice; d. 21 June 1945, Prague

Following his parents' separation, H. was raised by his mother's family. Having graduated from law school in 1916, H. moved to Prague, where he joined the staff of *Právo lidu*. When the Communist Party was founded, he joined and transferred to its organ, *Rudé právo*, which he left in 1929, disappointed with the leadership.

Next he joined *České slovo,* the organ of the Czechoslovak Socialist Party. From 1929 to 1932 H. published *Plán*, a journal of literature, art, and science, and, in 1935, he founded a series of monographs called *Postavy a dílo* (men and creative work), to which he contributed a monograph (1935) on Karel Toman (pseud. of Antonín Bernášek, 1877–1946), a Czech poet and translator. When war was imminent, he became one of the organizers of the antifascist movement in Czechoslovakia. The last years of his life H. spent seriously ill in his Prague apartment, where he died shortly after the liberation.

H.'s first collection of poetry, *Básně* (1915; poems), shows the influence of prewar symbolists (q.v.), but it already reveals H.'s creative program, namely, the reflection of the world and himself in a subjective record. Vitalism, characterized by an enthusiasm for the joy and beauty of life, the trend prevalent at the time, found expression here and in H.'s next collection, *Strom v květu* (1920; a tree in bloom). But in the second book, vitalism is combined with admiration for civilization. The motifs of nature and civilization intertwine, as do the personal and the social tones of these poems.

H.'s concern with social themes grew, and *Pracující den* (1920; the working day), one of H.'s greatest literary achievements, can best be described as proletarian poetry. Here his description of social wrongs and poverty attained a level of hymnic celebration of work and became a call for justice. The belief in justice and the dualism of the intimate and the social is also the theme of *Srdce a vřava světa* (1922; the heart and the turmoil of the world). H.'s next volume, *Bouřlivé jaro* (1923; the tempestuous spring), gives evidence of a crisis of creativity: the poems, decrying the abuses of technological civilization and the ambivalence of justice, have neither the intensity of experience nor the daring imagery of his earlier work.

Itálie (1924; Italy) and *Struny ve větru* (1927; strings in the wind) were inspired by H.'s visits to Italy and the Soviet Union, respectively. The former volume represents the peak of vitalist lyricism not only in H.'s works, but also in Czech poetry as a whole. Impressionistic images and poetic fancy blend in superb melody. The latter collection marks a new period in H.'s work. Whereas in *Itálie* the objective and the subjective elements are still in balance, in *Struny ve větru* there is greater subjectivity: the poet is now disgusted with social reality, and as a means of escape he tends to use an inner, more spiritual lyricism and to stop and ponder over "time and silence"—the time of the painful crisis of the 1930s and the silence of nature in his own countryside.

H.'s leaning toward metaphysics gained momentum, and in collections like *Tonoucí stíny* (1923; drowning shadows, *Dvě minuty ticha* (1934; two minutes of silence), and *Tiché poselství* (1936; a silent message) H. demonstrated a melancholy about the futility of life and an inconsolable fear of transitoriness. These feelings brought him to the romantic pessimism of the Czech poet Karel Hynek Mácha (1810–1836), whom he acknowledged as his master in *Máchovské variace* (1936; Mácha variations). Eventually, under pressure of the impending Nazi occupation, H. paradoxically regained some of his faith in life. His *Jan houslista* (1939; Jan the violinist) clearly shows H.'s ardent love for his homeland. This work is strongly influenced by Pushkin's *Eugene Onegin,* which H. masterfully translated.

Although H. also wrote essays and criticism, his main achievement lies in his poetry, and as the foremost of the Czech lyric poets writing after World War I, he had a tremendous influence on the young generation of the period from the 1930s to the end of World War II.

FURTHER WORKS: *Socialistická naděje* (1922); *Hliněný babylón* (1922); *Z politické svatyně* (1924); *Probuzení* (1925); *Hladový rok* (1926); *Mít křídla* (1928); *Smrt manželů Pivodových* (1928); *Deset let* (1929); *Tvůj hlas* (1930); *Chvíle v Estonsku* (1932); *Popelec* (1934); *Domov* (1938); *Dech na skle* (1938); *Zahrada Popelčina* (1940); *Život a dílo básníka Aneliho* (1945); *Zápisky z nemoci* (1945); *Proud* (1946) *Pokušení* (1946); *Pozdravy* (1949); *Dílo J. H.* (1927–40); *Dílo J. H.* (1950–61)

BIBLIOGRAPHY: French, A., *The Poets of Prague* (1969), passim; Harkins, W. E., Supplement, in Novák, A., *Czech Literature* (1976), pp. 316–18

PETER Z. SCHUBERT

HORVÁTH, Ödön von

Austrian dramatist and novelist, b. 9 Dec. 1901, Fiume (now Rijeka, Yugoslavia); d. 1 June 1938, Paris, France

The son of a Hungarian diplomat, H. moved frequently during his youth, living in a number of cities of the Austro-Hungarian Empire. His mother tongue was German, but from his exposure to the other languages of the monarchy, he developed a sharp ear for usage and for the mixtures of idioms characteristic of that part of the world.

After desultory studies at the University of Munich, H. turned to writing. *Buch der Tänze* (1922; book of dances) was a commissioned project, a series of poetic texts to serve as the basis for pantomine performances. Dissatisfied with the florid style, H. later borrowed money to buy up all remaining copies and have them destroyed.

In 1924 H. moved to Berlin, where he participated in the exciting cultural life of the city and achieved considerable renown as a playwright. On the recommendation of Carl Zuckmayer (q.v.), he was awarded the prestigious Kleist Prize for young dramatists in 1931. In 1933, after the Nazi takeover, he left for Vienna, returning to Berlin briefly in 1934 to work on film scripts and study the phenomenon of Nazism firsthand. During the next four years, which H. spent in Vienna, he continued to write plays but found it increasingly difficult to get them performed. The German annexation of Austria in 1938 forced H. to flee. He was killed on the Champs Élysées in Paris in a freak accident: a tree limb fell on him during a storm. In addition to *Buch der Tänze,* H. left eighteen completed plays, three novels, a number of short prose works, and numerous fragments; most of these works were not published during his lifetime.

H. designated his first notable play, *Revolte auf Côte 3018* (1927; rebellion on slope 3018), which was revised as *Die Bergbahn* (1927; the mountain railway), a *Volksstück,* or "play for and about the common folk"; H. here drew upon the conventions of a traditional genre, but revised the content, language, and dramaturgy to reflect how the character and situation of the *Volk* had changed since the genre's heyday in the 19th c. The play centers around a group of workmen constructing a mountain railway in the Bavarian Alps. Under pressure from the financial backers, the engineer in charge insists that work continue despite a winter storm. An accident results, providing the catalyst for a revolt by the workers. This early play, ideologically closer to Marxism than any of H.'s subsequent works, shows a certain stylistic affinity to expressionism (q.v.) in the staging devices. But H.'s chief concern is language. All the characters, including the uneducated construction workers, have been infected by *Bildungsjargon,* the pretentious jargon shot through with advertising and propaganda clichés, which H. regards as both a symptom and a cause of the modern moral and political crisis.

With *Italienische Nacht* (1931; Italian night), his first play to attract great attention, H. continued his revision of the *Volksstück*. It depicts a confrontation between a small-town Social Democratic club and the local fascist group. Political obtuseness and cowardice are conveyed through language or through the juxtaposition of speech and action. The one Marxist character spouts theory without following it up in practice, and the Social Democrats hide behind phrases to avoid acknowledging the real menace to democracy posed by the fascists. Berlin audiences loved the play, which they mistook for a harmless comedy.

In his masterpiece, *Geschichten aus dem Wiener Wald* (1931; *Tales of the Vienna Woods,* 1977), H. used a large cast of Viennese to show various aspects of the petit-bourgeois mentality, which he saw as characteristic of his times. The characters cherish sentimental delusions about themselves but are actually motivated by resentment and aggression, the result of political and economic impotence. Through a deft combination of language, visual imagery, music, and action, H. stripped away the clichés that make up the popular image of Vienna. The city becomes a symbol of a moribund society, the waltz a dance of death that determines the structure of the play.

Two more *Volksstücke*, written just before Hitler came to power, reflect the economic misery caused by the Depression and the concomitant breakdown in human solidarity and compassion. In *Kasimir und Karoline* (1932; Kasimir and Karoline) H. used the backdrop of the Munich *Oktoberfest* to highlight the ugly desperation of the chauffeur Kasimir, whose girlfriend Karoline deserts him when he loses his job. As Kasimir and Karoline roam through the fair, hoping for new connections that will improve their prospects, they reveal the moral bankruptcy and the social alienation that helped prepare the way for Hitler, with his message of German race pride and his promise of economic recovery. *Glaube Liebe Hoffnung* (1932; faith hope love) illustrates the destruction of an individual by a judicial system biased against the unfortunate. Elisabeth, having been fined for peddling without a license, finds herself driven from one minor deception to another. When her new lover, a policeman, learns of her "past," he drops her, out of fear of jeop-

ardizing his career. Her suicide makes plain the absence of faith, hope, and love in a society whose institutions are as rotten as its foundations.

After several years of writing plays that no major theater dared perform, H. turned to the novel, writing two in rapid succession: *Jugend ohne Gott* (1938; *The Age of the Fish*, 1939) and *Ein Kind unserer Zeit* (1938; *A Child of Our Time,* 1939). In a plain, sometimes rhythmic prose that combines elements of *Bildungsjargon* with streaks of uncritical sentimentality, these novels portray the effects of totalitarianism and its roots in the individual. The narrator of the first novel is a schoolteacher who witnesses the spread of corruption among his pupils. The second novel presents the interior monologue of a young man who finds pride and identity in becoming a soldier. Both works may be seen as psychological analyses of the fascist mentality. In addition, the two novels, like most of the plays written after 1933, display a distinctly religious cast. Fascism, whose psychological and economic origins H. perceived with remarkable accuracy, appears in his later works as an overwhelming manifestation of evil, in the face of which the remaining good folk must go into hiding, like the early Christians in the catacombs. Divine grace, not an improvement in economic conditions, becomes the prerequisite for salvation.

Because of his untimely death and the Nazi ban on publication and performance of his works, H. was nearly forgotten. In the 1960s, however, a few television performances of his plays in West Germany awakened interest in H., not only for his acute observation of pre-Hitler social conditions but also for his precise recording of linguistic alienation and its relationship to political manipulation. Within the space of a few years, H. became a modern classic, performed throughout the German-speaking countries and ranked by a number of critics with Bertolt Brecht (q.v.).

Although the plots and linguistic references of H.'s works grow out of the specific atmosphere of the 1920s and 1930s, H.'s writings are better understood today than when they first appeared. Abuse of language by the Nazis and by subsequent political movements on both the right and the left has recently come under increasing scrutiny. H.'s recognition of the phenomenon of prefabricated speech links him with several of his contemporaries, who are likewise only now receiving the recognition they deserve: Karl Kraus, Kurt Tucholsky, and Marieluise Fleisser (qq.v.). In the English-speaking world, George Orwell's (q.v.) examination of language abuse is closely related to H.'s concerns. H.'s influence on such young playwrights as Peter Handke, Franz Xaver Kroetz (qq.v.), Wolfgang Bauer (b. 1941), and Martin Sperr (b. 1944) and the filmmaker Rainer Werner Fassbinder (b. 1946), is unmistakable.

In his choice of unheroic, ordinary people as characters, H. holds up a mirror to modern mass society. His works provide a powerful warning against jargon of all kinds, and against the mentality that seeks refuge from thought in clichés. His masterful, provocative portrayal of the verbal and characterological deformities typical of the modern industrial age makes H. a significant figure in 20th-c. literature.

FURTHER WORKS: *Mord in der Mohrengasse* (written c. 1923, pub. 1970); *Sportmärchen* (1924–26); *Zur schönen Aussicht* (1927); *Sladek; oder, Die schwarze Armee* (1928; rev. as *Sladek der schwarze Reichswehrmann,* 1929); *Der ewige Spießer* (1930); *Die Unbekannte aus der Seine* (written 1933, pub. 1961); *Hin und Her* (written 1933, pub. 1969); *Himmelwärts* (1934); *Mit dem Kopf durch die Wand* (1935); *Der jüngste Tag* (1937); *Figaro läßt sich scheiden* (written 1936, pub. 1961); *Don Juan kommt aus dem Krieg* (1937); *Ein Dorf ohne Männer* (1937); *Pompeji, Komödie eines Erdbebens* (1937); *Gesammelte Werke* (4 vols., 1970–71)

BIBLIOGRAPHY: Weisstein, U., "Ö. v. H.: A Child of Our Time," *Monatshefte,* 52 (1960), 343–52; Strelka, J., *Brecht–H.–Dürrenmatt: Wege und Abwege des modernen Dramas* (1962); Kahl, K., *Ö. v. H.* (1966); Loram, I., "Ö. v. H.: An Appraisal," *Monatshefte,* 59 (1967), 19–34; Hildebrandt, D., "Der Jargon der Uneigentlichkeit: Zur Sprache Ö. v. H.s," *Akzente,* 19 (1972), 109–23; Jarka, H., "Sprachliche Strukturelemente in Ö. v. H.s Volksstücken," *CollG,* 4 (1973), 317–39; Kurzenberger, H., *H.s Volksstücke: Beschreibung eines politischen Verfahrens* (1974); Winston, K., *H. Studies: Close Readings of Six Plays* (1977); Winston, K., "Ö v. H.: A Man for This Season," *MR,* 19 (1978), 169–80; Krischke, T., *Ö. v. H.: Ein Kind seiner Zeit* (1980)

KRISHNA WINSTON

HOSTOVSKÝ, Egon

Czechoslovak novelist (writing in Czech), b. 23 April 1908, Hronov; d. 7 May 1973, Millburn, N.J., U.S.A.

After studying philosophy at the universities of Prague and Vienna, H. worked as an editor in various publishing houses. In 1937 he became an official in the Czechoslovak diplomatic service. During World War II he was assigned to Paris and later New York. In 1949, following the Communist takeover of the previous year, he resigned in protest from his position as chargé d'affaires at the Czech embassy in Oslo; from then on he lived in the U.S., earning his living as a script writer for Radio Free Europe.

H.'s books written before and during the war deal with alienation, loneliness, guilt—real or imagined—fear of life, and the inability of their heroes, many of them Jewish like H. himself, to communicate. The problem of Jewish assimilation in the Czech milieu, the motif of the Dostoevskian double, the theme of "the insulted and the humiliated" all play important parts in his works. Many of his writings imply or reflect the struggle of good and evil forces both within and among men. A typical H. hero, clumsy, well-meaning, frustrated, can be found in his novel *Případ profesora Körnera* (1932; the case of Professor Körner). The author shows here an unusual ability to analyze the thinking and emotions of a Jewish intellectual, who is tormented by an inferiority complex and by the problem of assimilation and reacts by escaping into a world of dreams and illusions. In the novel *Žhář* (1935; the arsonist), for which H. received the prestigious State Prize for Literature, a triple arson in a small town is conceived as a symbol of the common danger and uncertainty threatening the world in the prewar period. The chaos of Europe in the late 1930s is mirrored in the novel *Sedmkrát v hlavní úloze* (1942; *Seven Times the Leading Man,* 1945), a tale, partly realistic, partly fantastic, concerned with the acceptance or rejection of Nazism by a group of intellectuals in Prague just before the fall of Czechoslovakia.

In his writings after 1948 H. added political events and espionage to his earlier subject matter, very likely as reflections of the cold war. These new themes can be seen as a possible parallel to the works of Graham Greene (q.v.), whose influence (unlike that of Dostoevsky and Kafka [q.v.]), H. was willing to admit. The first book of this period was *Nezvěstný* (1955; *Missing,* 1952), whose protagonist, a Czech diplomat, finds himself in the center of interest of both Western and Eastern intelligence services during the 1948 Communist takeover in Prague. The autobiographical elements in this novel, as in many others, are rather obvious. Another "espionage" novel, *Půlnoční pacient* (1959; *The Midnight Patient*, 1954) is set in New York, as is *Dobročinný večírek* (1958; *The Charity Ball*, 1957), a satire peopled with refugees from east-central Europe and having a dubious "charity" as its central feature.

H.'s most significant work is *Všeobecné spiknutí* (1969; *The Plot*, 1961). It is a first-rate narrative, a brilliantly executed psychological tale in which fantasy, adventure, and philosophy are mingled in a nearly surrealistic and yet credible way. It was unfortunately ignored by most American critics, probably owing to a poor translation. Again, it is partly autobiographical, the hero being a former Czech diplomat and writer long resident in the U.S.

In the memoirs *Literární dobrodružství českého spisovatele v cizině aneb o ctihodném povolání kouzla zbaveném* (1966; literary adventures of a Czech writer abroad, or about an honorable profession deprived of charm), H. wrote with unusual frankness and often with painful self-irony about his parents, siblings, and himself living in the Czech countryside, and his failure to achieve world success as a writer. His only dramatic work, *Osvoboditel se vrací* (1972; the liberator is coming back), was never produced on stage. It portrays a fictitious land, probably Czechoslovakia, where a civil war has just ended and everyone crossed over to the victorious rebels who now expect their leader, the "liberator," to return from abroad, not knowing that he is bringing but another tyranny to his country and his family alike.

H.'s probing of subconscious drives, the sensitivity with which he treats his heroes, his rich inventiveness, and his craftsmanship remain unsurpassed in Czech literature. Next to Karel Čapek (q.v.) he is the best-known Czech writer outside Czechoslovakia.

FURTHER WORKS: *Zavřené dveře* (1926); *Stezka podél cesty* (1928); *Ghetto v nich* (1928); *Danajský dar* (1930); *Ztracený stín* (1932); *Černá tlupa* (1933; *The Black Band,* 1950); *Cesty k pokladům* (1934); *Dům bez pána* (1937); *Tři starci* (1938); *Kruh spravedlivých* (1938); *Listy z vyhnanství* (1941; *Letters from Exile,* 1942); *Úkryt* (1943; *The Hideout,* 1945); *Cizinec hledá byt* (1947); *Osaměli buřiči* (1948; *The Lonely Rebels,* 1951); *Tři noci* (1964; *Three Nights,* 1964); *Epidemie* (1972)

BIBLIOGRAPHY: Prescott, O., on *The Plot, NYT,* 3 Feb. 1961, 23; Sturm, R., ed., *E. H.: Vzpomínky, studie a dokumenty o jeho díle a osudu* (1974, multilingual); Kunstmann, H., *Tschechische Erzählkunst im 20. Jahrhundert* (1974), pp. 129–42

RUDOLF STURM

HOUSMAN, A(lfred) E(dward)

English poet and classical scholar, b. 26 March 1859, Fockbury; d. 20 April 1936, Cambridge

From his birthplace H. could see to the northwest the hills of Shropshire for which his celebrated book of sixty-three lyrics, *A Shropshire Lad* (1896), is named. The eldest son of a Victorian middle-class family, H. was fondly devoted to his mother, whose death on his twelfth birthday had a considerable effect on him. After attending Bromsgrove School and, as he tells us in an autobiographical sketch, becoming attached to paganism by reading John Lemprière's (1765?–1824) *Classical Dictionary* (1788), he matriculated in 1877 at St. John's College, Oxford, where he met Moses J. Jackson. There is good reason to believe that his strong homosexual affection for Jackson was instrumental in his failure of the Greats at Oxford in 1881, since he was distracted from his studies. Disappointed, he went from Oxford to the menial drudgery of a clerk in the Patent Office in London. For the next ten years he spent his evenings in the British Museum perfecting scholarly papers on Aeschylus, Sophocles, Ovid, and other classical writers. These pursuits led in part to his appointment as Professor of Latin, University College, London, in 1892. Meanwhile, his work on Manilius and Juvenal began to appear, and in 1911 he was made Kennedy Professor of Latin at Cambridge and held the position until his death.

H.'s poetic output was meager, his reputation resting primarily on *A Shropshire Lad* and two other thin volumes, *Last Poems* (1922), and *More Poems* (1936). His reputation as a classical scholar is based primarily on his edition of Manilius's *Astronomica* (Books I–V, 1912–30), but also on his editions of Juvenal's *Satires* (1905), and of Lucan (1926). H. was a conservative textual scholar, his reviews of other scholars were caustic and often narrow, characteristic of the emphasis placed on the importance of textual studies (as opposed to literature and history) in England and Germany. Monastic, eccentric, austere, H. withdrew into his rarefied world of intellectual arrogance, to pursue his work with zealous passion.

But during his London years H. experienced the "continuous excitement" that culminated in *A Shropshire Lad*, one of the great lyric achievements of the 19th c. The bittersweet quality of the lyricism reflects the trauma of H.'s personal disappointments, his repressive withdrawal, and his stoic commitment to textual scholarship.

In *Last Poems* and *More Poems* H. continued his melancholic lament, the emphasis remaining on regret and loss. Often sentimental, the lyrics are nonetheless remarkably controlled, an attempt by H. to make his poetry essentially classical. Yet in trying to capture in English the brevity of such Latin masters as Horace and Juvenal, Housman overemphasized control. It is not unusual, therefore, in a lyric of H.'s for technique (the liberal use of the monosyllable, for example) to be the essence of the poem, narrowly reducing the poet's potential ability to deal with the ambiguous and complex.

Despite his many followers, H.'s poetry has often been labeled as adolescent, simplistic (in theme as well as form), pessimistic, banal, self-indulgent, and antiintellectual. As summed up by Ezra Pound (q.v.), his message was one of woe. But more recently Housman has attracted the sharper eye of the newer critics and other admirers who praise his metrical skill, his subtle tonality, his classical symmetry, his consummate craft, his skillful use of irony, and his theme of courage and stoic endurance.

Like Blake in his *Songs,* Housman has suffered from being too easily accessible. His clipped, colloquial speech patterns, incisiveness and felicity of phrasing, often too palatable to cursory readers, obscure the elegance and grace of his language and his masterful use of literary convention.

FURTHER WORKS: *Collected Poems* (1939); *Manuscript Poems* (1955); *Selected Prose* (1961); *Collected Letters* (1971)

BIBLIOGRAPHY: Housman, L., *A. E. H.* (1937); Richards, G., *H.: 1897–1936* (1941); Watson, G. L., *A. E. H.: A Divided Life* (1957); Marlow, N., *A. E. H.: Scholar and Poet* (1958); Ricks, C., ed., *A. E. H.: A Collection of Critical Essays* (1968); Leggett,

B. J., *The Poetic Art of A. E. H.* (1977); Graves, R. P., *A. E. H.: The Scholar Poet* (1980)

JULES SEIGEL

HOWE, Irving

American literary critic, cultural historian, and social commentator, b. 11 June 1920, New York, N.Y.

H. attended New York City public schools and from an early age adopted the attitudes of the socialist movement: thirst for change, skepticism about the dominant culture, and a taste for polemic. He studied at City College in New York, received a B.S. in 1940, and did graduate work for a short time at Brooklyn College. After a stint in the army, he took up an academic career and taught at Brandeis, Stanford, and Princeton universities. He became a professor of English at the City University of New York in 1963 and continued his work as editor of the socialist magazine *Dissent*; the latter position, which he has held since the 1950s, has contributed to his authority and influence in the world of letters as well as in contemporary political discourse.

Passionate about ideas, steeped in a tradition of dialectic, literary without being ivory-towered, H. is a representative leader of the New York intellectuals. In his words, this means being "an anti-specialist . . . a *Luftmensh* of the mind, a roamer among theories." H.'s style—the "thrust and parry" of debate—is pungent, often ironic, and sometimes blunt. His essays frequently display the "brilliance" he describes as a hallmark of New York critics: "free-lance dash, peacock strut, daring hypothesis, knockabout thrust."

As a literary critic, H. is concerned with the social and political problems of a text, its informing conceptions, and its place within a culture. *Politics and the Novel* (1957) is a unified study of ideology and the artist: it traces the emergence of the political novel and sees it as postdating 19th-c. stable conceptions of society. The political novelist explores disorder and the modern tension between ideas and personal emotions. He must "melt" political ideas into the behavior of characters and function as a "nimble dialectician" in dealing with abstractions and people.

The troubled, ambivalent modern consciousness emerges as a theme in this book and becomes a central concern in *Decline of the New*

(1970); here H. ranges over many works, examining the origins and breakup of the modernist literary tradition. Modern literature, arising as a rebellious response to 19th-c. progress and positivism, has been institutionalized in our time. Its restlessness and protest are now cultural clichés. H. therefore wants the modern temper to be scrutinized and its worn-out ideas retired. At the same time he is concerned about what comes next. Will postmodernist literature find arresting subjects and a way to express them? Or will the literary mind become "a docile attendant to an automated civilization"?

The burden of such questions informs *The Critical Point* (1973). H. typically measures the modernist vision—especially its irrationality and glorification of the sick self—and proposes that we look beyond it. As a socialist he seeks the "City of the Just"; as a literary critic he reminds us that at least one 20th-c. writer, James Joyce (q.v.), had a humane and skeptical vision that transcended the nihilism of his age. H.'s pursuit of de-alienation continues in *Celebrations and Attacks* (1979), a volume of reviews written over a period of thirty years. Here he begins by explaining Jewish immigrants' struggle for a relationship with American literary tradition; he then measures a variety of contemporary authors by using his criteria of artistic complexity and social responsibility.

This latter standard is the theme of *Steady Work* (1966), a collection of social and political essays from the 1950s and 1960s. He focused on threats to democratic radicalism—whether the ease of "welfarism" or the arrogance of the New Left. H. is especially disturbed by mass society—a passive, consumer-oriented, infinitely assimilative society that could dull men's devotion to change. In seeking "secular transcendence," H. champions the ideals of pluralism and autonomy. *World of Our Fathers* (1976) is written from the same perspective: this massive, richly textured account of Jewish emigration from Europe, the new life and culture created in America, and the struggle to preserve identity is presented as a kind of secular transcendence. At once a sociologist, literary historian, and chronicler of individual lives and movements within the Jewish community, H. demonstrates his range, feeling, and stylistic expansiveness as he deals with a part of his own past.

In an age inundated by bizarre theories of literature and society, H.'s unusual directness makes him especially valuable. His place among the New York intellectuals has been especially important, but not without its qualifying circumstances. As a literary critic he is less subtle and elegant than Lionel Trilling (q.v.); his political commitments sometimes give an edge to his analysis of a work. He has little of the juicy, heart-on-sleeve quality that makes Alfred Kazin (b. 1915) a poetic and highly personal recorder of American Jewish life. And his ideas are less startling and original than those of Leslie Fiedler (q.v.) on literature or Paul Goodman (1911–1972) on society. Nevertheless, H. remains a stimulating, sane, and lucid witness to the spectacle of modern literature and the politics of change.

FURTHER WORKS: *The U.A.W. and Walter Reuther* (1949, with B. J. Widick); *Sherwood Anderson* (1951); *William Faulkner* (1952; 3rd ed., 1973); *The American Communist Party* (1958, with Lewis Coser); *A World More Attractive* (1963); *Thomas Hardy* (1967); *Trotsky* (1978)

BIBLIOGRAPHY: Adler, R., on *A World More Attractive, New Yorker*, 4 July 1964, 60; Capouya, E., on *Steady Work, Commonweal*, 9 Dec. 1966, 295; Solotaroff, T., "I. H. and the Socialist Imagination," *The Red Hot Vacuum* (1970), pp. 133–41; Wood, M., on *Celebrations and Attacks, NYRB*, 8 Nov. 1979, 34; Donoghue, D., on *Celebrations and Attacks, NYTBR*, 11 March 1979, 9

DAVID CASTRONOVO

HRABAL, Bohumil

Czechoslovak short-story writer, novelist, and poet (writing in Czech), b. 28 March 1914, Brno

H. spent his childhood in Nymburk, where his father was the manager of a brewery. It was also there that he experienced the influence of his eccentric uncle Pepin, an incessant talker, who came for a two-week visit and stayed on for forty years. Just before World War II H. began to study law in Prague, but when Czech universities were closed by the Nazis, he took up various jobs, starting in the Nymburk brewery and ending as dispatcher in a small railway station. Although he completed his law studies after the war, he chose to work as a commercial and insurance agent rather than a lawyer. Later he worked in a steel mill, in a scrap-paper warehouse, and as a stagehand in a Prague theater. Since 1963 he has been a full-time writer.

H. had to wait long to see his first book published. In 1958 a volume of short stories was at the printer, but as a result of the ideological tightening up following the publication of Josef Škvorecký's (q.v.) *The Cowards*, H.'s book was not printed. The author was just a year short of fifty when the volume, *Perlička na dně* (1963; the pearl at the bottom), finally appeared to critical acclaim. By this time, non-ideological writing was no longer taboo, but the main novelty of H.'s short stories was the author's peculiar, often grotesque vision. Far from being exemplary, the characters presented in H.'s stories are people from the lower social strata, who compensate for the triviality of their lives by embellishing banal incidents with humorous exaggeration and transforming them into brilliantly unique experiences. Often these tall tales are both inspired by and told over a mug of beer. The atmosphere is reminiscent of early silent movies and the method used by the author is purely anecdotal, as he places in his tales the momentous side by side with the commonplace in a montage without a hint of hierarchical order.

The same zany lust for life, reflected in an eccentric, hyperbolical mirror, has characterized all H.'s writing. *Perlička na dně* was followed by another volume of short stories, *Pábitelé* (1964; the palaverers), and then *Taneční hodiny pro starší a pokročilé* (1964; dancing lessons for seniors and the advanced), an old man's life story told in a single unfinished sentence.

H. had by now acquired many enthusiastic admirers, but his unselective approach to the realities of life had also offended some more conservative members of the reading public. Even in his next book, *Ostře sledované vlaky* (1965; *Closely Watched Trains*, 1968)—the most conventional of H.'s works and the closest to the traditional novel in form—the heroism of a young man's deed during World War II is preceded and deflated by a discussion of his intimate problems. This short novel was made into a very successful film (the screenplay, written by H. and Jiří Menzel, was published in English as *Closely Watched Trains*, 1971).

In the aftermath of the suppression of the 1968 reform movement, two complete editions of H.'s books, *Domácí úkoly* (home works) and *Poupata* (buds), both printed in 1970, were destroyed. After having publicly expressed support for the new authorities, however, the author was later allowed to publish again, but only the more conventional of his works, which have hardly added to his previous achievement. In *Postřižiny* (1976; the haircutting) he draws in a series of scenes and in the usual grotesque fashion a lovable portrait of an early emancipated woman, and both *Slavnosti sněženek* (1978; celebration of snowdrops) and *Krasosmutnění* (1979; beautiful mourning) turn to the past for most of their subjects.

Some of H.'s books that could not be published in Czechoslovakia have been circulating in the West as duplicated manuscripts or as private editions. These unpublished works, such as *Obsluhoval jsem anglického krále* (MS. 1971; I waited on the king of England) and *Příliš hlučná samota* (MS. 1976; a too noisy solitude), are definitely superior; they show a tendency to impose an ideational order on the sequence of images and action episodes of which they are composed, and thus to increase the coherence of the text.

H. has become one of the best-known modern Czech writers, and his comic tales of urban folklore, which he claims only to have recorded in a surrealistic collage, have been enjoyed throughout the world. But there is a great amount of literary sophistication behind the façade of tavern bragging, and the naïveté is often as deceitful as that of the primitive painters whose imagination H. in many respects shares. What impresses most is H.'s fresh and striking vision, which creatively transforms triteness into a miracle of the everyday.

FURTHER WORKS: *Inzerát na dům, ve kterém již nechci bydlet* (1965); *Automat Svět* (1966); *Toto město je ve společné péči obyvatel* (1967); *Morytáty a legendy* (1968); *Městečko, kde se zastavil čas* (MS. 1978); *Každý den zázrak* (1979). FURTHER VOLUME IN ENGLISH: *The Death of Mr. Baltisberger* (1975)

BIBLIOGRAPHY: Mihailovich, V., et al. eds., *Modern Slavic Literatures* (1976), Vol. II, pp. 113–17; Gibian, G., "The Haircutting and I Waited on the King of England: Two Recent Works by B. H.," in Harkins, W. E., and Trensky, P. I., eds., *Czech Literature since 1956: A Symposium* (1980) pp. 74–90

IGOR HÁJEK

HSÜ Chih-mo

Chinese poet, diarist, essayist, and translator, b. 15 Jan. 1897, Hsia-shih, Chekiang Province; d. 19 Nov. 1931, Tsinan, Shantung Province

In his own lifetime the fame of H. as a poet rested as much on his life, which epitomized a fearless attack on conventions and a relentless pursuit of freedom, love, and beauty, as on his work. The son of a wealthy banker, he first sought reform in China through a study of law and politics at Peiyang University (later known as Peking University), of banking and sociology at Clark University in Massachusetts (1918–19), and of political science at Columbia University, where he obtained a master's degree in 1920. As early as 1915 he had come under the strong influence of the most liberal reformist thinker of his time, Liang Ch'i-ch'ao (1873–1929). He left the U.S. for England, and it was at King's College, Cambridge, that H. discovered his affinity with literature and began to write poetry.

At this time he also discovered love. Before leaving China, H. had been married to an educated, modern girl from a prominent family, and the young bride had followed him to Cambridge. But H. carried on a secret love affair with Lin Hui-yin, the seventeen-year-old daughter of a friend. He clamored for a divorce which was granted in 1922, but because of objections of family and friends, he did not marry Miss Lin.

For several years following his return to China in 1922, H. wrote and taught; he was rocketed to national fame when he became the interpreter for the Indian poet Rabindranath Tagore (q.v.) on his 1924 tour of China. At about the same time, he became the center of a cause célèbre by falling in love with yet another prominent woman, the wife of a young Chinese military officer. To cure himself of this attachment and to allay gossip, H. took a trip through Europe in 1925; but he returned to Peking to insist upon his right to marry the woman he loved, which he did in 1926. These several episodes of his love life found curious parallels in the life of the English poet he admired most, Shelley; and they accomplished as much in shocking the traditional Chinese society and tearing down the old conventions as did his bold and lyrical treatment of his experience in his writings.

In 1925, the year his first volume of poetry, *Chih-mo ti shih* (poems of Chih-mo), was published, H. became the editor of the literary supplement of the newspaper *Ch'en pao*. For this magazine, a year later, he started the now famous poetry journal *Shih-k'an*, which ran for eleven issues. (It resumed publication in 1931 as an independent journal with the aid of Wen I-to [q.v.].) Also for the pages of *Ch'en pao*, to introduce Western-style plays to China, he started a drama section. Together with Wen I-to, H. became the founder in 1928 of the monthly *Hsin-yüeh*, or *Crescent*. In the manifesto of the new journal H. called for a union of music (rhythm), painting (color), and architecture (form and structure) as the sine qua non of *pai-hua* (vernacular) poetry. The *Crescent* poets countered the popularity of the Whitmanesque free verse by insisting upon the supremacy of form and the fusing of classical diction with colloquial speech. With unerring sensitivity to the rhythm of spoken Chinese, H. successfully experimented with metrics, producing a poetry that is simple, direct, and never bookish. One particularly famous poem, "Ai ti lin-kan" (love's inspiration), included in the posthumously published collection *Yün-yu* (1932; wandering in the clouds), a dramatic monologue of over four hundred unrhymed lines that effectively rely upon enjambment and the natural rhythm of vernacular speech, became a classic of the new poetry. His imagery is highly visual and often ethereal, again bespeaking a kinship with Shelley. While some of his early poems were mildly satiric, most of his works reflect the basic romantic attitude concerning the attainability of a dream or an ideal in an imperfect, transitory world. Some of the poems written during the last two years of his life, however, are imbued with a deep sense of despair. "Huo-ch'ê ch'in chu kuei" (night train)—included in *Yün-yu*—a poem in sixteen stanzas with two decasyllabic lines in each, and designed to appear in print like parallel railroad tracks, is H.'s most philosophical—and most pessimistic—work.

During the last years of his life H. held teaching posts at several universities in Shanghai, Nanking, and Peking. He was killed in a plane crash. Like Shelley, whose life was also cut short, H. seems for modern Chinese poetry the "beautiful angel" whose "luminous wings" symbolize a poet's constant search for order and cadence, for beauty and truth.

FURTHER WORKS: *Lo-yeh* (1926); *Fei-leng ts'ui ti i-yeh* (1927); *Pa-li ti lin-chua* (1928); *Tzu-p'ou wen-chi* (1928); *Pien-k'un Kang* (1928, with Lu Hsiao-man); *Meng-hu chi* (1929); *Lung-p'an hsiao-shuo chi* (1929); *Ch'iu* (1931); *Ai-mei hsiao-cha* (1947, with Lu Hsiao-man)

BIBLIOGRAPHY: Birch, C., "English and Chinese Meters in H. C.'s Poetry," *Asia Major*, New Series, 7 (1959), 258–93; Lin, J. C., *Modern Chinese Poetry: An Introduction* (1972), pp. 100–132; Lee, L. O., *The Romantic Generation of Modern Chinese Writers* (1973), pp. 124–74

IRVING YUCHENG LO

HU Shih

(birth-name: Hu Hung-hsing) Chinese poet, literary reformer, and scholar (writing in Chinese and English), b. 17 Dec. 1891, Shanghai; d. 24 Feb. 1962, Taipei, Taiwan

H. changed his name to mean "to fit into" after being inspired by T. H. Huxley's (1825–1895) *Evolution and Ethics.* He studied under the American philosopher John Dewey (1859–1952) at Columbia University, from which he received a doctorate in philosophy in 1917. He then taught at Peking University and other colleges. H. lectured extensively in Europe and the U.S.—he received numerous honorary degrees—and was the Chinese ambassador to the U.S. from 1938 to 1942. He returned to China in 1946 but came back to the U.S. in 1948 and worked as a librarian at Princeton University. During the 1950s he was condemned by the Communist Chinese government as a lackey of U.S. imperialism. In 1958 H. became president of the Academia Sinica in Taiwan.

In the field of literature, H. is better known for advocating reforms and for his scholarship in vernacular literature, than he is for his creative writing. A skeptic and critic of traditional Chinese mores, he wrote a story entitled "Chen-ju tao" (1906; the surrealist isle) in which Chinese superstitious practices were attacked. Another short story, "I-ko wen-t'i" (1919; a problem), and the play *Chung-shen ta-shih* (1919; marriage), a farce, were both quite superficial in dealing with social issues.

In his youth, H. called for the reform of the literary tradition. In essays like "Wen-hsüeh kai-liang ch'u-i" (1917; a modest proposal for literary reform), he declared basically that the *wen-yen* (literary written language) should be abolished and that the practical *pai-hua* (spoken language) should be adopted for all writing, and he published *Ch'ang shih chi* (1919; the experiment), a collection of poems written in the vernacular. The work itself was very immature, as H. admitted; nonetheless, its publication signified the quest and victory of the *pai-hua* literary movement over the time-honored *wen-yen* literary tradition.

H.'s contribution to the new literature movement also lies in his scholarship. His *Pai-hua wen-hsüeh shih* (1928; history of vernacular literature) proved the existence of a vernacular tradition in Chinese literature. Unfortunately, the book's contents ended prematurely with the 9th c. In addition, H. published numerous research studies that dealt with matters of the authorship and textual and historical significances, as well as the literary merits of almost all the well-known Chinese vernacular fictional works. Until very recently, for example, his research on *Dream of the Red Chamber,* which linked it to the family history of its author, Ts'ao Hsüeh-ch'in (1717–1764), dominated all studies on the novel. The fact that vernacular fiction is now respected in Chinese literature is due mainly to H.'s efforts.

H. also promoted the writing of *chuan-chi wen-hsüeh* (biographical literature), claiming that China has yet to produce an interesting and readable biography. He tried writing some himself, including one of his mother, and an autobiography.

As a believer in reforming China through "wholesale Westernization" and "wholehearted modernization," H. is admired and condemned for the destruction of the Chinese literary tradition and for his pro-Western outlook. Nevertheless, his importance in modern Chinese literature is undeniable: known as the "father of the literary revolution," H. was a pioneer in the dawning of a new era of literary expression in China.

FURTHER WORKS: *Chung-kuo che-hsüeh shih ta-kang, shang p'ien* (1919; *The Development of the Logical Method in Ancient China,* 1922); *China's Own Critics: A Selection of Essays* (1931); *The Chinese Renaissance* (1934); *H. S. yen-lun chi* (2 vols., 1953–55); *H. S. liu-hsüeh-jih-chi* (1959); *H. S. wen ts'un* (rev. ed., 1961)

BIBLIOGRAPHY: Forster, L., *The New Culture in China* (1936), pp. 221–34; Chow, T., *The May Fourth Movement* (1960), pp. 271–79; Shih, V., "A Talk with H. S.," *ChinaQ,* 10 (1962), 149–65; Grieder, J., *H. S. and the Chinese Renaissance: Liberalism in the Chinese Revolution, 1917–1937* (1970)

MARLON K. HOM

HUCH, Ricarda

(pseuds. in first works: Richard Hugo, R. I. Carda) German poet, novelist, short-story writer, critic, essayist, and historian, b. 18 July 1864, Brunswick; d. 17 Nov. 1947, Kronberg

H. came from a merchant family with strong artistic inclinations. Her brother Rudolf (1862–1943) and her cousins Felix (1880–1952) and Friedrich (1873–1913) Huch were writers. H. had to move to Zurich,

Switzerland, to obtain her high school certificate and her Ph. D. in history at the university, since women were not yet admitted as regular students in Germany. After working as a librarian and a high school teacher in Zurich and Bremen she married an Italian dentist, Ermanno Ceconi, and lived with him in Trieste and Munich. After an amicable divorce, she married her lifelong love, her cousin Richard Huch, but the marriage ended in complete failure. In her later years, H. lived with her daughter's family and followed her to Berlin, Heidelberg, Freiburg, and Jena. She died near Frankfurt shortly after her move to the Western-occupied zones.

H. received the Goethe Prize of the city of Frankfurt (1931) and was the first woman to be elected to the Prussian Academy of the Arts (1927), a position she courageously resigned in 1933, protesting the expulsion of writers such as Heinrich Mann and Alfred Döblin (qq.v.) by the Nazi regime. Having been close to the Lutheran opposition and the anti-Hitler conspirators of July 20, 1944, she planned a collection of biographies of German Resistance fighters, a project completed after her death by Günther Weisenborn (*Der lautlose Aufstand* [1953; the silent rebellion]).

A contemporary of the major naturalist writers—Gerhart Hauptmann, Frank Wedekind (qq.v.), Arno Holz (1863–1929)—H. was independent of, even opposed to, this movement. She is generally classified as a leading writer of neoromanticism, but she herself rejected that label. A kinship with the flowery, manneristic style of writing called *Jugendstil* is evident in her early works. Later, she strove for a blending of the tradition of Goethe and Gottfried Keller (1819–1890) with modern sensitivity.

After a number of early publications, H. became known to a wider audience through her first novel, *Erinnerungen von Ludolf Ursleu dem Jüngeren* (1892; memories of Ludolf Ursleu, Junior). Against a Hanseatic-merchant background similar to that of Thomas Mann's (q.v.) *Buddenbrooks*, this work traces the demise of a family succumbing to the fatal, overwhelming passion of love. H.'s tragic characters try to follow their inner calling in an unsympathetic world of rigid conventionality and decadence. In her next novel, *Aus der Triumphgasse* (1902; from Triumphal Lane), it is poverty—encountered by H. herself in Trieste, where the story is set—that prevents the characters from fulfilling themselves. *Vita somnium breve* (1903; Latin: life is a short dream; 4th ed., 1909, retitled *Michael Unger*) returns to

H.'s native milieu. The same basic conflict is treated in a more fairy-tale-like manner in *Von den Königen und der Krone* (1904; of kings and crown), where the descendants of a supposedly royal family prove unable to protect and preserve the legendary crown in the era of modern capitalism, reaching out in vain for a future ideal. While failing, H.'s heroes gain an awareness of themselves, of their time, tradition, and potential, and ultimately of God. With a pessimistic view of the present age, H. combines a faith in the vital forces of humanity in a more Christian than Nietzschean sense.

A major work of this early period is H.'s study of German romanticism, *Die Romantik* (2 vols., 1899, 1902; romanticism). In opposition to the then dominant school of positivism, H. tried to express the essence and meaning of the romantic movement, concentrating on the romantics' ways of life, religion, and modes of expression, and presenting a series of model biographies. *Die Romantik* was received as a manifesto of neoromanticism, but it contains as much criticism as praise.

During the second phase of her work, H. turned mainly to history, writing both historical novels and essays. Her interest in the Italian unification movement of the 19th c. resulted in the novels *Die Geschichten von Garibaldi* (2 vols., 1906–7 [a projected third part was never written]; *Garibaldi and the New Italy*, 1928–29); *Das Leben des Grafen Federigo Confalonieri* (1910; the life of Count Federigo Confalonieri), considered by many critics to be her best novel; and the essay *Das Risorgimento*, later retitled *Menschen und Schicksale aus dem Risorgimento* (1908; men and destinies of the Risorgimento).

Her chief interest remained the history of the Holy Roman Empire, whose social structures —such as local self-government, social and political action on a personal, not a bureaucratic or abstract level, a stable yet flexible class system—she preferred to modern government, in its various democratic, socialist, or dictatorial forms. The ultimate breakdown of the Holy Roman Empire during the Thirty Years' War (1618–48) was described by H. in her most ambitious novel, *Der große Krieg in Deutschland* (3 vols., 1912–14; the great war in Germany; later retitled *Der Dreißigjährige Krieg* [the Thirty Years' War]). For H., Freiherr vom Stein, the Prussian reformer of 1807, about whom she wrote in *Stein* (1925; Stein), wanted to restore the old Empire in a new form, but his heritage lost out against mechanistic capitalism and liberalism from 1848 on, a view she propounded in *Alte und neue Götter: Die Revolution des 19. Jahrhunderts in Deutschland* (1930; old and new gods: the revolution of the 19th century in Germany). Her three-volume history of Germany, *Deutsche Geschichte* (1934, 1937, 1949; German history), synthesized this view of history. H.'s clear opposition to the Nazi view of history prevented the publication of the last volume until after World War II.

During H.'s third and last period of creativity, historical writings alternated with essays conveying her *Weltanschauung*. The roots of her conception of humanity and human history can be found in early German romanticism and the works of C. G. Carus (1789–1869). In *Entpersönlichung* (1921; depersonalization) she described how human development from a preconscious harmony with the environment leads to states of consciousness and self-consciousness involving an unavoidable alienation of the individual from the environment and a breaking-up of the whole personality, although in different forms for men and women, because of their essentially different characters. H. called for a return to life forces as found in the writings of Martin Luther—*Luthers Glaube: Briefe an einen Freund* (1916; Luther's faith: letters to a friend); the Bible—*Der Sinn der Heiligen Schrift* (1919; the meaning of the Bible); and the writings of Goethe.

H. remained a poet all her life and also wrote a large number of stories. Her detective novel *Der Fall Deruga* (1917; *The Deruga Trial*, 1927), although written for money, is one of the most valuable examples of the genre. *Der wiederkehrende Christ* (1926; Christ returning) exemplified H.'s criticism of her age in a less convincing satirical manner.

H.'s strong personality has elicited a number of biographies. Most criticism so far has focused on the relationship between her life and her work. A critical assessment of H.'s ideas and achievement and of her place in German literary history is urgently needed.

FURTHER WORKS: *Gedichte* (1891); *Die Hugenottin* (1892); *Evoë* (1892); *Der Mondreigen von Schlaraffis* (1896); *Drei Erzählungen* (1897); *Fra Celeste* (1899); *Gottfried Keller* (1904); *Seifenblasen* (1905); *Neue Gedichte* (1907); *Der Hahn von Quakenbrück* (1910); *Der letzte Sommer* (1910); *Natur und Geist als die Wurzel des Lebens und der Kunst* (1914); *Wallenstein* (1915); *Jeremias Gotthelfs Weltanschauung* (1917); *Michael Bakunin und die Anarchie* (1923); *Graf Mark und*

die Prinzessin von Nassau-Usingen (1925); *Im alten Reich: Lebensbilder deutscher Städte* (1927–29); *Frühling in der Schweiz* (1938); *Weiße Nächte* (1943); *Herbstfeuer* (1944); *Urphänomene* (1946); *Der falsche Großvater* (1947); *Briefe an die Freunde* (1960); *Gesammelte Erzählungen* (1962); *Gesammelte Werke* (11 vols., 1966–74)

BIBLIOGRAPHY: Hoppe, E., *R. H.* (1936; rev. ed., 1951); Flandreau, A., *R. H.'s Weltanschauung as Expressed in Her Philosophical Works and in Her Novels* (1948); Baum, M., *Leuchtende Spur* (1950); Leopold, K., *R. H.'s "Der letzte Sommer": An Example of Epistolary Fiction in the Twentieth Century* (1962); Baumgarten, H., *R. H.: Von ihrem Leben und Schaffen* (1964); Emrich, W., Foreword to *Gesammelte Werke*, Vol. I (1966), pp. 9–130; Kappel, H.-H., *Epische Gestaltung bei R. H.* (1976)

WULF KOEPKE

HUCHEL, Peter

German poet and editor, b. 3 April 1903, Berlin; d. 30 April 1981, Staufen

H., who grew up in Mark Brandenburg, studied literature and philosophy in Berlin, Freiburg, and Vienna. In the mid-1920s he began to publish poetry in periodicals and in 1932 received the literary prize of the leftist journal *Die Kolonne*. H. voluntarily cancelled the planned publication of a collection of poetry in 1933 as a protest against the Nazi regime. Following military service during the war he worked for the East German radio. In 1949 he became editor-in-chief of *Sinn und Form*, which soon came to be recognized as the most liberal journal in East Germany, and one of the outstanding literary periodicals in Europe. His refusal to adapt his editorial policy to the principles of Socialist Realism (q.v.) led to his dismissal in 1962, following which he lived in Potsdam in virtual isolation. He was allowed to emigrate in 1971, settling eventually in West Germany. He received numerous literary prizes in the GDR in the early 1950s and in the West in the 1960s and 1970s.

H.'s poetry is firmly rooted in the world of nature. He has often been compared with Oskar Loerke (1884–1941) and Wilhelm Lehmann (1882–1968), and some of his early poems, collected in *Gedichte* (1948; poems) and *Die Sternenreuse* (1967; the star basket), do in fact have much in common with the writers of the "nature-magical school": the mysteries and majesty of a landscape are celebrated, as a scene is described in minute detail, often with little or no reference to human beings. Other early poems, however, reveal the poet's sense of social consciousness. Nature is again used as a setting, and description is not lacking, but here the emphasis is placed upon the people who are surrounded by nature, especially children, and servants and other representatives of the lower classes. The mood is frequently idyllic, but occasionally elegiac. H. is often praised by critics for his effective use of rhyme, meter, assonance, and alliteration in these early poems.

Never a prolific poet, H. wrote very little verse during the Nazi years, and some of these poems were lost during the war. Nature continued to play an important role in the extant works of H.'s second period. The tone, however, is quite different. Images of snow and ice replace the summer and autumn imagery of the earlier poetry. The feeling of desolation is underscored by a decrease in the regularity of rhyme and meter. H. enthusiastically welcomed the early postwar reforms of the East German government, and much of his poetry from the years 1945 to 1952 reflects his support of the government and his hope for the future. The Land Reform Law of 1945, which dissolved the large estates and distributed the land among the lower classes, was celebrated in "Das Gesetz" (1950; the law), which, like a few other works of this period, closely corresponds to the criteria of Socialist Realism.

Soon, however, H. lost faith in the policies of the regime, primarily because of the failure of the lot of the working class to improve and the government's lack of tolerance for artistic experimentation. The poetry of the 1950s and early 1960s, collected in *Chausseen Chausseen* (1963; highways highways), became increasingly hermetic and melancholic, reflecting the poet's growing sense of isolation and resignation. Rhyme and regular meter virtually disappeared, and, as in the poetry of the war years, snow and ice are among the most common images. The poems of *Gezählte Tage* (1972; counted days), written during H.'s period of isolation, are even more pessimistic. Veiled references to the political situation of the GDR and to the author's position as an exile in his own country are frequent. *Die neunte Stunde* (1979; the ninth hour), which contains poems written after H.'s emigration, is dominated by the presence of death. The tone, however, is now one of stoical resignation, as is reflected in the controlled use of language and images.

Although he published relatively little, H. remained until his death one of Germany's foremost literary figures, admired for his personal integrity no less than for his literary achievements. In recent years many critics have come to consider him the most important German-language poet of his time.

FURTHER WORK: *Gedichte* (1973). FURTHER VOLUME IN ENGLISH: *Selected Poems* (1974)

BIBLIOGRAPHY: Flores, J., *Poetry in East Germany* (1971), pp. 119–204; Mayer, H., ed., *Über P. H.* (1973); Scher, H., "Silence in the Poetry of P. H.," *GR*, 51 (1976), 52–61; Vieregg, A., *Die Lyrik P. H.s* (1976)

JERRY GLENN

HUGHES, Langston

American poet, novelist, short-story writer, dramatist, anthologist, translator, and editor, b. 1 Feb. 1902, Joplin, Mo.; d. 22 May, 1967, New York, N.Y.

When he was very young H.'s parents separated, eventually to be divorced. Until his thirteenth year he lived largely in Lawrence, Kansas. He spent his high-school years in Cleveland, Ohio. After graduation he sojourned for a year in Mexico with his father, who had found in Mexico a release from American racism. But H.'s father also worshiped moneymaking. He wanted H. to be an engineer. From his father's bounty H. did accept a year at Columbia. At the end of the year, however, breaking permanently with his father, H. subsisted in, and around, New York on his own for another year, then went to sea. Successive jobs as a waiter and doorman supported him for a season in Paris. Having worked his way home on a ship and already recognized as a poetic luminary of the Harlem Renaissance, he matriculated at Lincoln University in Pennsylvania, which granted him a bachelor's degree in 1929. During the early 1930s he traveled widely in America and Russia and saw the Far East. An assignment as a war correspondent took him to Spain during the civil war. But New York City was his home for virtually the last thirty years of his life.

In *The Confident Years* (1953) Van Wyck Brooks calls H. the "most adventurous and versatile of Negro authors." A quarter of a century has produced nothing to contradict Brooks's judgment. It was H.'s poetry that first brought him fame. His "The Negro Speaks of Rivers" written on a train taking him to Mexico, may be the most quoted of all poems by black poets. The poetry of *The Weary Blues* (1926) assimilated techniques associated with the secular music of black folk to the medium of verse even while its content reflected the lives of that same folk, especially in terms of how those lives were adjusting their Southern agrarianism to the alien environment of the urban North. *Fine Clothes to the Jew* (1927), more poetry, followed. But then came the novel *Not without Laughter* (1930). Starting with *The Ways of White Folks* (1934), H. was to publish three collections of the sixty-six short stories he wrote, preeminently in the 1930s and exclusive of his Simple tales.

As an adolescent in Cleveland he had participated enthusiastically in every phase of the activity of the celebrated, though nonprofessional, Karamu Players. The first play of his to be published was *The Gold Piece* (1921). His *Mulatto,* revised without his knowledge and decidedly not to his liking, ran on Broadway in 1935. In the 1930s and early 1940s he founded Negro little theaters in Harlem, Los Angeles, and Chicago. And he wrote more than twenty plays, musicals, and hybridizations of plays and musicals, as well as a special kind of play, of his own invention, which he called the gospel song-play.

His autobiography of his youth, *The Big Sea* (1940) is indispensable for students of the Harlem Renaissance. It is supplemented by *I Wonder as I Wander* (1956). He translated a novel by the Haitian writer Jacques Roumain (q.v.) and poetry by Nicolás Guillén, Federico García Lorca, and the Nobel laureate Gabriela Mistral (qq.v.). For juveniles he did a series of "Famous" biographies, beginning with *Famous American Negroes* (1954) and the "First Book" histories, starting with *The First Book of Negroes* (1952). He turned out a steady stream of articles on many subjects, wrote, with the actor Clarence Muse (1889–1979), the screenplay for the Hollywood film *Way Down South* (1942) and, by himself, the lyrics for the musical version of Elmer Rice's (q.v.) *Street Scene.* He also wrote radio scripts, a television script, and the lyrics for at least forty popular songs.

H. may have crowned his career with the character Simple, whom he created in 1942 for his column in the *Chicago Defender.* Simple grew, in effect, into every black person's Everyman; the Simple stories are now most conveniently available in five collections garnered from the more than fifteen years of columns H. wrote.

H.'s poetry and prose both tend to impress a reader with their apparent simplicity. Both for the most part, read easily. Moreover, both never seem to center on epic figures or to attempt epic themes or epic manners—and certainly both never extend to epic lengths. Yet neither in poetry nor prose does H. ever seem to be inconsequential either as an artist or as a critic of society. His apparent simplicity is therefore much more apparent than real, and betokens a genuine and tremendous effort on his part not to be obscure or grandiose or to pretend to profundities for which he feels he should not try to stake a claim. On the other hand, it does not indicate a want of aesthetic discipline or the absence of a respectable addiction to contemplative thought. One has but to recognize the formal accuracy of H.'s blues or to be made aware of the intense study he gave to models of the short story to guess the truth, that he was a conscientious artist who worked hard at achieving his passionate desire, forms of expression palatable to ordinary people, yet serious and significant as commentaries on the life of man. He has been rightly called an authentic voice, probably without a peer, of, and for, the Negro folk.

He once testified unequivocally to a very inquisitive Senate committee that he was not, and never had been, a Communist. Even so, he was sometimes, also, an ardent voice of sociopolitical protest. He affected an avoidance of the complex, the difficult, the unpleasant, and the unpopular only in the manner of his art. In its substance—or, at least, in what he wanted that substance to communicate—he often did precisely the opposite. There, upon numerous occasions, he did come to grips with troublesome issues, helped by his rich sense of humor and, not too infrequently, by ingenious resorts to irony.

FURTHER WORKS: *Dear Lovely Death* (1931); *The Negro Mother* (1931); *The Dream Keeper, and Other Poems* (1932); *Scottsboro Limited* (1932); *Popo and Fifina: Children of Haiti* (1932, with Arna Bontemps); *A New Song* (1938); *Shakespeare in Harlem* (1942); *Freedom's Plow* (1943); *Jim Crow's Last Stand* (1943); *Lament for Dark Peoples, and Other Poems* (1944); *Fields of Wonder* (1947); *One-Way Ticket* (1949); *Simple Speaks His Mind* (1950); *Montage of a Dream Deferred* (1951); *Laughing to Keep from Crying* (1952); *Simple Takes a Wife* (1953); *The First Book of Rhythms* (1954); *Famous Negro Music Makers* (1955); *The First Book of Jazz* (1955); *The Sweet Flypaper of Life* (1955, with Roy DeCarava); *The First Book of the West Indies* (1956);

A Pictorial History of the Negro in America (1956, with Milton Meltzer); *Simple Stakes a Claim* (1957); *Famous Negro Heroes of America* (1958); *The L. H. Reader* (1958); *Tambourines to Glory* (1958); *Selected Poems* (1959); *The First Book of Africa* (1960); *Ask Your Mama: 12 Moods for Jazz* (1961); *The Best of Simple* (1961); *Fight for Freedom: The Story of the NAACP* (1962); *Something in Common, and Other Stories* (1963); *Simple's Uncle Sam* (1965); *Black Magic: A Pictorial History of the Negro in American Entertainment* (1967, with Milton Meltzer); *The Panther and the Lash: Poems of Our Times* (1967); *Black Misery* (1969)

BIBLIOGRAPHY: Redding, S., *To Make a Poet Black* (1939), pp. 113–17; Emanuel, J., *L. H.* (1967); O'Daniel, T., ed., *L. H., Black Genius: A Critical Evaluation* (1971); Dickinson, D. C., *A Biobibliography of L. H., 1902–1967* (1972); Wagner, J., *Black Poets of the United States* (1973), pp. 385–474; Jackson, B., and Rubin, L., *Black Poetry in America* (1974), pp. 51–58; Barksdale, R. K., *L. H.: The Poet and His Critics* (1977)

BLYDEN JACKSON

HUGHES, Richard

Anglo-Welsh novelist and dramatist, b. 19 April 1900, Weybridge; d. 28 April 1976, Bangor, Wales

Born in England of Welsh parentage, H. went to Charterhouse and Oxford. While still an undergraduate, he had a volume of poems published and a play produced on the London stage. Nevertheless in his early twenties he did write other plays (including the first "listening play," or play for radio), together with stories collected in *A Moment of Time* (1926) and poems collected in *Confessio Juvenis* (1926). Then he began writing the novel that made his name. It appeared first in the U.S. as *The Innocent Voyage* (1928), and then in England under its more familiar title, *A High Wind in Jamaica* (1929).

A gripping story, this novel contains extraordinary evocations of life in Jamaica and aboard a sailing ship in the middle of the 19th c. After a hurricane has destroyed their home, the Bas-Thorntons decide to send their five children home to school in England. But the ship is captured by pirates, and the children spend weeks on a schooner sailing the Spanish Main. Most of the story is told from the children's perspective, particularly that of ten-year-old

Emily; as H. himself said, he tried to get two kinds of thinking into the novel, the adult's and the child's. They are often in ironic contrast; the children miss connections, but the adults' expectations of the children are often wildly wrong. The rescue of the children leads to a deceptively conventional "happy ending" in which, because of the way in which Emily's evidence is misinterpreted by a judge and jury, the pirate leaders are hanged for a murder they did not commit. Suspense and melodrama, humor and horror, are completely at the narrator's command, to summon up as he wishes; but what stands out particularly is his portrayal of the minds of children at various stages of maturity.

H.'s next novel did not appear for almost another decade; once again it was a striking success. *In Hazard* (1938) is a tense story about a ship caught in a tropical hurricane. Easily and confidently, H. explains at the beginning how modern technology has taken away the terrors of the sea. Then, having established this atmosphere of confidence and security, H. destroys it; nature plays games with the ship, toying with it for six days and blowing the funnel clean away. For the crew it is a learning and a testing experience. As in Conrad (q.v.), the focus is on the moral qualities that the sea—and life—demands, that is, on virtuous behavior in extreme conditions.

H. published no more novels for twenty-three years. During World War II he held an important position in the British Admiralty; later he collaborated with the historian J. D. Scott (b. 1917) on a section of the Official History of the War dealing with war production (1955). Not until 1956 did he begin writing *The Human Predicament*, an ambitious fictional chronicle of his own times planned to be in four volumes. The first, *A Fox in the Attic*, came out in 1961. It begins with Augustine Penry-Herbert carrying a drowned girl out of a marsh in Wales; because of the suspicion surrounding her death he is forced to leave his home and visit relatives in Germany. So he begins on what amounts to a personal quest, and H. on an examination of why the world is heading for catastrophe and barbarism. The novel contains an effective mingling of real and imaginary people and events; in particular, it shows how patterns of events that people cannot see penetrate deeply into their own psyches. Nevertheless, Augustine is far too passive and uncomprehending to serve as a focus; for example, he understands nothing of the political machinations leading to Hitler's abortive Munich beer hall *putsch*.

In the only other part of his saga H. completed, *The Wooden Shepherdess* (1973), he brings in the American scene as well as the English and the German; he is not entirely successful with the American setting and characters. He also finds it more difficult to assimilate and convey the necessary background information in this novel, even though there are gripping and convincing episodes such as the account of the Night of the Long Knives in Germany. Since *The Human Predicament* is unfinished, and since it is not easy to see how H. could have brought it to a successful conclusion, especially in view of the inadequacies of his central character, it must be judged an ambitious failure.

H. wrote only four novels in a long lifetime. The last two are difficult to evaluate, since they are parts of an incomplete chronicle. The first two, however, are masterpieces of their kind, and because of them he will not soon be forgotten.

FURTHER WORKS: *Gipsy Night, and Other Poems* (1922); *Lines Written upon First Observing an Elephant Devoured by a Roc* (1922); *The Sisters' Tragedy* (1922); *Meditative Ode on Vision* (1923); *The Sisters' Tragedy, and Other Plays* (1924); *Ecstatic Ode on Vision* (1925); *R. H.: An Omnibus* (1931); *The Spider's Palace* (1931); *Don't Blame Me!* (1940); *Liturgical Language Today* (1962); *Gertrude's Child* (1966); *Gertrude and the Mermaid* (1968); *The Wonder-dog: The Collected Children's Stories of R. H.* (1977); *In the Lap of Atlas* (1979)

BIBLIOGRAPHY: Symons, J., "Politics and the Novel," *Twentieth Century*, 170 (1962), 147–54; Bosano, J., "R. H.," *EA*, 16 (1963), 58–62; Henighan, T. J., "Nature and Convention in *A High Wind in Jamaica*," *Crit*, 9 (1966), 5–18; Thomas, P., "The Early Writings of R. H.," *AWR*, 20 (1971), 36–57; Swinden, P., *Unofficial Selves: Character in the Novel from Dickens to the Present* (1973), pp. 181–202; Thomas, P., *R. H.* (1973)

D. J. DOOLEY

HUGHES, Ted

English poet, dramatist, critic, and short-story writer, b. 17 Aug. 1930, Mytholmroyd

The youngest son of a carpenter, H. spent his early youth among the Yorkshire moors and mountains, which later provided both subject and background for much of his poetry. From 1950 to 1954 he attended Cambridge on scholarship, studying anthropology and archaeology. In 1956 H. married the American poet Sylvia Plath (q.v.). H. now lives in Devon.

In his first book of verse, *The Hawk in the Rain* (1957), H. offered a sardonic appraisal of man's function in the universal scheme. Deceptive, helpless, frustrated human beings are measured against predatory beasts, whom H. sees as their counterparts. The natural manifestations of power and ferocity of the beast evoke the admiration of the poet, whereas he has only contempt for the studied violence of man. *The Hawk in the Rain* was immediately recognized as the work of a potential genius, even though the poems are flawed by some straining for effect, and by forced diction and imagery.

Lupercal (1960) is concerned primarily with history, both religious and political, and with myth and ritual. H. limns human transience against the indestructible continuity of history. The volume contains three of H.'s finest poems, "Hawk Roosting," "Thrushes," and "Pike." Each exalts the ruthless efficiency with which the subject performs what is, according to its kind, a demonstration of its natural propensities. Throughout *Lupercal* H. catalogues the intransient nonhuman energies that overmaster man's pitiable pretensions to historical continuity or personal immortality.

Wodwo (1967) is a collection of poems, stories, and a play intended "to be read together, as parts of a single work." The epigraph from *Sir Gawayne and the Green Knight* identifies the wodwo as a wood dweller and suggests the quest, initiation, and metamorphosis motifs developed in the volume. Hallucinatory and deathly images contrast oddly with the wistful figure of the wood sprite. Organic nature is called upon to suffer tortures as the dismembering force of Death rends its victims into sacrificial bits.

In the short stories of *Wodwo*, such as "The Rain Horse," "The Harvesting," and "Sunday," man is seen in curious relationship to the animals who are mastered. At the climactic moment man becomes one with his victim, tasting its anguish. The animals are exquisitely rendered, both in their struggle and defeat. In each case man is diminished in stature, checked in his attempt to establish control.

Crow (1971) presents a mordant view of civilization trapped in "the war between vitality and death." The very choice of protagonist—Crow—expresses a desperate and frenetic vitality that is generated and sustained only by an irrational determination to survive. In the H.

world, anguish creates. Birth is a sundering experience with Death, its concomitant, stalking at the womb's door. Crow challenges the supremacy of Death, and the battle is on between the horrific vitality of Crow and the excruciating mutilations that Death can effect. Like Crow emerging from his progenitor Scream, the volume's energy derives from the presence of sound. This emphasis points toward the stylistic development that H.'s work was undergoing. His dramatic experiment, *Orghast* (performed 1971), goes after nothing less than a new language whose meaning emerges entirely from sound.

With *Season Songs* (1975), H. moved from the relentless nihilism of *Crow* to participate in the revivifying rhythms of the changing seasons. Birth and death, fruition and decomposition, in this collection are but recurrent processes in nature's continuing impulse toward a unified state of being. Intended at first for "young readers," the seasonal songs express the simple wonder of the perennial youth whose perception is profound in its childlike directness.

Gaudete (1977) has been heralded as one of the major innovative poetic accomplishments of the decade. Once again H. pushes language beyond its traditional limits as he plunges now into the phantasmagorical world of the psyche. Reverend Lumb is spirited away from his small, puritanical parish to minister to the deformed goddess of a mythical world. Meanwhile, a changeling Lumb, placed on earth to perform the clergyman's duties, seduces—in direct contrast to his celibate alter ego—his women parishioners by promising that one of them will give birth to a messiah fathered by him. Reverend Lumb, after a series of mutilating initiation rites, experiences his renascence into the world of the body and of elemental nature, even in its most unlovely forms. After the annihilation of the promiscuous changeling, the transformed Reverend Lumb returns to earth and in the role of priest-poet composes verses of praise to the goddess of nature. *Gaudete* suggests that the "loyalty of heart" divided between the flesh and the spirit is harmful.

Cave Birds: An Alchemical Cave Drama (1978) was inspired by a set of bird drawings by Leonard Baskin. Envisioning the birds as characters, H. wrote individual poems for each drawing and incorporated them into a poetic drama. He added to the bird poems another series of verses in which the same story is presented with a human protagonist. The work is a formidable attempt to synthesize the visual and verbal arts.

Moortown (1979) consists of four different sequences. The "Prometheus on the Crag" section was written at the same time as *Orghast*, which is also based on the Prometheus myth. Chained to his crag, Prometheus represents man trapped in the "numbness of his humanity"; Prometheus endures his mutilation and is reborn. Another sequence, "Earth-Numb," describes the futility of striving for fulfillment. In "Adam and the Sacred Nine" the nine muses assuming different bird forms finally succeed in revivifying Adam after his Fall. With the coming of the ninth bird, the Phoenix, Adam rises. The title sequence "Moortown," which is the center of the collection, dwells on the brutal aspects of farm life. With relentless realism, H. focuses on "fox corpses . . . beaten to their bare bones," on cattle suffering the pitiless process of dehorning with "mouth drooling, the eye/Like a live eye caught in a pan, like the eye of a fish imprisoned in air." The unceasing gore underscores the indomitable will to endure, for in the H. universe the act of survival becomes the supreme challenge and justification.

Throughout his work, H. brilliantly objectifies the tumultuous quality of nonhuman forces. He is not a romantic nature lover even though his favorite protagonists and personae are animals. H. is well aware of the rapacious urges that quicken all forms of existence. His particular genius lies in the ability to apprehend and to convey the sentient qualities of being itself. For H., the writing of poetry demands the experiential involvement of the total person. Each word possesses a sensory life of its own that must be felt and controlled by the poet. H. believes that poems, like animals, are each one "an assembly of living parts, moved by a single spirit." An extraordinarily versatile craftsman, H. charges traditional poetic forms and devices with compelling energies. Not always successful in controlling his tempestuous imagination, H. still manages in his best work to shape style and subject into tangible forms of meaning.

FURTHER WORKS: *Meet My Folks!* (1961); *Selected Poems* (1962, with Thom Gunn); *The Earth Owl and Other Moon People* (1963); *How the Whale Became* (1963); *Nessie, the Mannerless Monster* (1963); *The Burning of the Brothel* (1966); *Recklings* (1966); *Scapegoats and Rabies: A Poem in Five Parts* (1967); *Animal Poems* (1967); *Poetry in the Making: An Anthology of Poems and Programmes from "Listening and Writing"* (1967; Am., *Poetry Is*, 1970); *Five Autumn Songs for*

Children's Voices (1968); *The Iron Man: A Story in Five Nights* (1968); *Poems* (1968, with Gavin Robbins); *Seneca's Oedipus* (1969); *A Crow Hymn* (1970); *A Few Crows* (1970); *The Martyrdom of Bishop Farrar* (1970); *The Coming of the Kings, and Other Plays* (1970; Am., *The Tiger's Bones, and Other Plays for Children*, 1974); *Crow Wakes* (1971); *Poems* (1971, with Ruth Fainlight and Alan Sillitoe); *Eat Crow* (1971); *Shakespeare's Poem* (1971); *In the Little Girl's Angel Gaze* (1972); *Selected Poems 1957–1967* (1972); *Eclipse* (1976); *Chiasmadon* (1977); *Sunstruck* (1977); *Moon-Bells* (1978); *Orts* (1978); *Calder Valley Poems* (1978); *Under the North Star* (1981)

BIBLIOGRAPHY: Rosenthal, M. L., *The New Poets: American and British Poetry since World War II* (1967), pp. 224–33; May, D., "T. H.," in Dodsworth, M., ed., *The Survival of Poetry* (1970) pp. 133–63; Lodge, D., "*Crow* and the Cartoons," *CritQ*, 13 (1971), 37–42, 68; Bauson, J., "A Reading of T. H.'s *Crow*," *CP*, 7 (1974), 21–32; Bedient, C., *Eight Contemporary Poets* (1974), pp. 95–118; Hahn, C., "*Crow* and the Biblical Creation Narratives," *CritQ*, 19 (1977), 43–52; Heaney, S., "Now, and in England," *CritI*, 3 (1977), 471–88; Sagar K., *The Art of T. H.* (1978); Faas, E., *T. H.: The Unaccommodated Universe* (1980); Hirschberg, S., *Myth in the Poetry of T. H.* (1981); Gifford, T., and Roberts, N., *T. H.: A Critical Study* (1981)

ROSE ADRIENNE GALLO

HUIDOBRO, Vicente

Chilean poet, essayist, novelist, and dramatist (writing in Spanish and French) b. 10 Jan. 1893, Santiago; d. 2 Jan. 1948, Cartagena

H. was born into a wealthy upper-class family and educated by the Jesuits. As a young man, H. suffered a spiritual crisis that had a profound effect on his development as a poet as well as on his political beliefs. His revolt against his aristocratic Catholic upbringing led to a break with his family. When he left for Paris in 1916, H. had already published six books of poetry and had begun to reveal the tenets of a new poetic aesthetic that he and the French poet Pierre Reverdy (q.v.) would call "creationism." In Paris H. began to contribute to avant-garde literary magazines such as *Sic*.

He was a cofounder with Reverdy and Guillaume Apollinaire (q.v.) of the famous magazine *Nord-Sud*. During his first two years in France he published six books of poetry, including three written in French. On a trip to Madrid in 1918, he encouraged experimentation by other Hispanic poets: Gerardo Diego (b. 1896), Juan Larrea (b. 1895), and Jorge Luis Borges (q.v.). And as a result, the Hispanic vanguard poetry—called ultraism (q.v.) because of its attempt to expand metaphor to its ultimate limits—was born. Thus, H. played a role similar to that of Rubén Darío (q.v.) for Spanish American modernism (q.v.), as the principal propagator of avant-garde ideas and techniques throughout Latin America. He returned to Chile for one year in 1925 and became the editor of a short-lived newspaper as well as a presidential candidate sponsored by the Chilean Federation of Students in the national elections (he did not win). H. then returned to France and diversified his literary output to include several unconventional novels with innovative language and form. He also wrote two short plays. In 1936 H. participated in the Spanish Civil War on the side of the Republic. As the Republic's fall became imminent, H. returned, in 1938, to Chile, where his most important novel, *Sátiro; o, El poder de las palabras* (1939; Satyr; or, the power of words), was published. At the outbreak of World War II H. enlisted in the French army. He performed heroically and received a serious head wound that eventually led to his death. His last poems were collected and published posthumously by his daughter under the title *Ultimos poemas* (1948; last poems).

Although H.'s early poetry was mainly modernist in technique and modeled on the works of Darío and Ramón del Valle-Inclán (q.v.), he had already begun his search for new poetic forms and language. After H. lost his Christian faith, his search for an artistic revolution included a metaphysical quest to satisfy a spiritual yearning that tormented him throughout the rest of his life. *Canciones en la noche* (1913; songs in the night), contained the first Spanish-language *caligrammes,* in which the spatial configuration of the words on a page converted the poem into a veritable pictograph. The most important books of H.'s early poetry were *Adán* (1916; Adam) and *El espejo de agua* (1916; the mirror of water) because they constitute the first application of creationist theory to H.'s own poetry. *Adán* is a harbinger of H.'s mature poetry and is structured on the archetypal image of the fallen man who is also, like the poet, the originator of a new language that describes the world he inhabits. *El espejo de agua* is famous especially for the poem "Arte poética" (poetic art), in which H. likens the poet to a "small god" who creates his own realities and discerns the occult relationships between disparate objects. The poem represents a manifesto of all the essential principles of creationism.

H. had written an earlier literary manifesto in prose called *Non serviam* (1914; Latin: I shall not be a slave), in which he boldly asserted the idea that the poetic creator should not be the slavish imitator of the products of natural creation but should emulate the creative act itself and give birth to truly original creations. Inspired in part by Emerson's notion that poetic creation need not be constrained by adherence to preconceived rules and conventions, H. viewed the poem as an autonomous reality and generator of its own forms of expression. H. also attempted to redefine "poetry" according to the original Greek meaning of the word, which means "to create." Creation would be the poet's sole objective.

Creationism flourishes in *Poemas árticos* (1918; *Arctic Poems,* 1974) and *Ecuatorial* (1918; equatorial); each book corresponds to one of the two most pervasive tendencies in his work. The former emphasizes the tendency toward experimentation and a break with poetic tradition, while the latter reveals a more personal side of H.'s poetry and also a marked social concern for the plight of man in war-ravaged Europe. *Poemas árticos,* a book of forty-four poems, is particularly noteworthy for its radical treatment of the perennial themes of poetry through a rupture with punctuation and the conventional stanzaic form of the poem. The entire poem, not only individual verses, affects the reader's sensitivity through the spatial representation of words in columns with capitalization of some of the words, reiteration, and the inclusion of futuristic elements of the modern technological world (such as airplanes, steamships, cigarettes), which are used as poetic images or symbols for the first time. The reader was forced to view the poem as an artistic whole and as a unique visual design that underlines its full significance. Both the verbal and spatial impact of the whole poem determines its essential meaning.

Altazor: El viaje en paracaídas (1931; Altazor: the trip in a parachute) is H.'s masterpiece. This long poem joins the poet's intimate quest for personal salvation through the religion of poetry to his search for a new poetic language. As a consequence of this literary and personal inquiry, words are stripped of conventional meaning and morphologically transformed into a series of nonsense syllables, which produce a new language. This new, created language is recondite for the reader but charged with emotive significance for its creator. As Altazor, the poet's alter ego, plummets to earth aware of his inevitable confrontation with death, he dramatizes one of the universal literary themes of the 20th c.: the existential predicament of an alienated and anguished soul in search of self-identity and fulfillment. The poem is structured on the archetype of the Fall and is divided into seven cantos in which Altazor retells his life, relates the importance of woman in creation, and becomes a word magician who dismantles conventional language and syntax. Altazor's tragic spiritual disintegration and vulnerability are shown to stem from personal disillusionment and an awareness that he cannot totally free himself from a dependence on the traditional word. In this poem, as in most of H.'s poetry, the pictorial aspect stands out, along with plays on words and concepts, onomatopoeia, paradox, and the "created word" that results from the transposition of halves of old words fused together to form new ones.

The poet's last two major poetic words, *Ver y palpar* (1941; seeing and touching) and *El ciudadano del olvido* (1941; the citizen of oblivion), are intensely personal and contain autobiographical elements. H.'s reiterative technique to heighten emotional effects is the most salient stylistic feature of both books. In both there is also less word play and emphasis on the graphic and spatial dimensions of the poem as a verbal design with underlying symbolic meaning than in H.'s earlier works.

Most critics now rank H., the Peruvian César Vallejo (q.v.), and H.'s fellow Chilean, Pablo Neruda (q.v.), as the most important and influential voices of 20th-c. Spanish American poetry. H. was undoubtedly Latin America's first avant-garde poet and boldly removed the last obstacles to freedom of expression in poetry. H. also transformed the genre into a truly spatial and pictorial art form akin to painting.

FURTHER WORKS: *Ecos del alma* (1911); *La gruta del silencio* (1913); *Pasando y pasando* (1914); *Las pagodas ocultas* (1914); *Horizon carré* (1917); *Tour Eiffel* (1918); *Hallali* (1918); *Saisons choisies* (1921); *Finis Britan-*

niae (1923); *Automne régulière* (1925); *Tout à coup* (1925); *Manifestes* (1925); *Vientos contrarios* (1926); *Mío Cid Campeador* (1929; *Portrait of a Paladin,* 1931); *Temblor de cielo* (1931); *Tres novelas ejemplares* (1931); *Gilles de Raíz* (1932); *En la luna* (1934); *La próxima* (1934); *Papá; o, El diario de Alicia Mir* (1934); *Cagliostro, novela-film* (1934; *Mirror of a Mage,* 1931); *Obras completas* (2 vols., 1964). FURTHER VOLUME IN ENGLISH: *Selected Poetry* (bilingual, 1981)

BIBLIOGRAPHY: Holmes, H. A., *V. H. and Creationism* (1934); Forster, M. H., "V. H.'s *Altazor*: A Reevaluation," *KRQ,* 17 (1970), 297–307; Goiç, C., *La poesía de V. H.,* 2nd ed. (1974); Caracciolo Trejo, E., *La poesía de V. H.* (1974); De Costa, R., ed., *V. H. y el creacionismo* (1975); Wood, C. G., *The Creacionismo of V. H.* (1978); special H. issue, *RI,* 45, 106–7 (1979)

JAMES J. ALSTRUM

HULDÉN, Lars

Finnish poet (writing in Swedish), b. 5 Feb. 1926, Jakobstad (Pietarsaari)

H. has described as a formative poetic influence the verbal games he played by himself and with other youths of his native region Österbotten (Pohjanmaa). The games, quests for the perfect expression in a given situation, were no doubt reinforced in H.'s home, with its literary tradition. His father, Evert, was a noted poet. But H.'s preoccupation with the verbal led most immediately to an academic career; he currently occupies a chair in Nordic languages at the University of Helsinki. In this position he has contributed to scholarship on C. M. Bellman (1740–1795) and J. L. Runeberg, (1804–1877), two influential poets whose spirits can be observed in H.'s own works.

Österbotten has always been a primary source for H.'s inspiration. His first book, *Dräpa näcken* (1958; kill the kelpie [water sprite]), and those immediately following blend nostalgia and a nearly burlesque narration of the lore and the customs of that region. His style is mundane, reflecting his down-to-earth subjects, and can be seen as a position taken against a trend in Finno-Swedish poetry toward increasingly abstract themes. H. is a versatile writer who has also produced songs and dramatic works; the short-story collection *Hus* (1979; houses), marked his debut as a prose writer. But poetry forms the bulk of his production, and it is as a poet that he occupies

the prestigious Poet's Residence in Borgå (Porvoo).

Much of H.'s production is lyrical, expressed in numerous forms, athough narrative poems and 2-line units of verse dominate. Its mark is a perception of specific events as a microcosm mirroring an irrational world where irony and compassion must stand guard. While the early works have frivolous overtones, H.'s later poetry, beginning with *Herr Varg!* (1969; Mr. Wolf!), often takes somber turns, even morbid ones, as in the collection of epitaphs, *Läsning för vandrare* (1974; reading for wanderers). An equilibrium is reached in *Herdedikter* (1973; shepherd songs), where H. alternates lyrical poems and terse commentary verses, the former epigrammatic, the latter objective as footnotes. A deceivingly simple style depends on unobtrusive metaphorical imagery, yielding poetry of incisiveness and surprising sublimity.

Expressions from H.'s native dialect frequently appear in his works suggesting a dilemma vis-à-vis dialect and standard Swedish. In *Heim/Hem* (1977; home), the obstacle, if it is one, is removed as H. presents a bilingual collection. In these compassionate poems dialect poetry reaches new heights in Finno-Swedish literature. It is too early to tell whether *Heim* represents a threshold in H.'s development, but the next collection, *J. L. Runeberg och hans vänner* (1978; J. L. Runeberg and his friends), in standard Swedish, approaches the elegance of *Heim.* In *J. L. Runeberg och hans vänner* H.'s refined talent for adopting the spirit of poetry other than his own is most fully developed; it is as if the two poets from Österbotten, both transplanted to Borgå, though in different ages, were performing a preordained duet.

Because H.'s poetry seems so effortless, it may give an impression of being hasty, or tied to seemingly insignificant phenomena, but the simplicity masks irony, sophistication, and a deep concern for the fate of mankind. In Swedish Finland, where a long tradition of modernism (q.v.) may have run its course, H.'s poetry gives a fresh alternative through a concrete vision.

FURTHER WORKS: *Speletuss* (1961); *Spöfågel* (1964); *Enrönnen* (1966); *Två raseborgsspel* (1974); *Island i december* (1976); *Visbok* (1976); *Dikter vid särskilda tillfällen* (1979)

BIBLIOGRAPHY: Jones, W. G., "L. H.," *BF,* 11 (1977), 140–45

KIM NILSSON

HUNGARIAN LITERATURE

The classic-romantic populist movement that began with a bang in the 1840s, when the reform generation burst on the literary scene, ended with a whimper amid the placid artificiality of the century's end. The reform generation fought for political emancipation as well as for the revitalization of Hungarian literature. At the end of the century its political and, particularly, its literary programs were hopelessly outdated. The lull caused by the gradual exhaustion of traditional literary form was, however, of short duration. In the first years of the 20th c. the creative forces of the rising generation regained sufficient momentum to give entirely new dimensions to Hungarian literature.

The process of revitalization was triggered mainly by poets. This was hardly surprising since poetry, particularly lyrical poetry, was the traditional genre in which the literary genius of Hungary usually manifested itself. As in the age of enlightenment and in the reform period, poetry thus provided the most effective means through which the hopes and aspirations of the new generation were to be expressed.

The group formed around the periodical *Nyugat*, founded in 1908 by the critics Ignotus (pseud. of Hugo Veigelsberg, 1869–1950) and Ernő Osvát (1877–1929), did not, of course, consist entirely of poets. But although the group included fine writers such as Zsigmond Móricz, Margit Kaffka, and Frigyes Karinthy (qq.v.), it was chiefly through *Nyugat* poets, headed by Endre Ady (q.v.), that the movement exerted the galvanizing effect that was to result within the next decades in the radical transformations of the literary scene. This was due, in addition to the traditional response to poetry, to Ady's almost demoniacal ability to present in strikingly new forms the revolutionary message that was to change—so he hoped, at least—the spiritual and political physiognomy of the "vast fallow lands of Hungary."

When *Nyugat* was founded, Ady had already published two volumes—*Uj versek* (1906; new poems) and *Vér és arany* (1907; blood and gold)—containing some of his major poems (many of these have been translated by Anton N. Nyerges in *Poems of Endre Ady,* 1969). The influence of French symbolism (q.v.)—Ady had spent some time in Paris—is evident, particularly in his early poems. Nevertheless, Ady was too individualistic and too original to be classified as the representative of any one literary school. While he preferred to express himself by means of symbolist techniques, as shown by his famous poems "Az ős kaján" (1907; "The Demon Guile," 1969) and "A fekete zongora" (1907; "The Black Piano," 1969), biblical and folkloric influences are also clearly discernible in the sometimes moody, sometimes apocalyptic lines in which he described the tragic search of an oversensitive but dedicated man for truth, justice, love, faith, and inner peace. His poems, abounding in an overpowering imagery, melodious resonance, and almost balladlike density, represented the quintessence of the "new songs of new times," which the members of the *Nyugat* group were singing while setting out to give a new form and concept to Hungarian literature.

In contrast to Ady's tumultuous individualism, Mihály Babits (q.v.), the second most influential poet of the *Nyugat* group, displayed a classic discipline that brought fully into relief the immaculate perfection of his artistry. Desző Kosztolányi (q.v.) expressed, with the self-assurance, and often with the audacity, of the virtuoso, the changing moods of his generation. Erudition, refinement, and an impressive faculty to translate into poetical terms the sensitivities of a lonely soul were the hallmarks of Árpád Tóth's (q.v.) poetry. Regardless of their allegiance to various schools, ranging from Parnassianism to symbolism, from Pre-Raphaelitism to early futurism (q.v.), all the poets of the *Nyugat* group, such as Gyula Juhász (q.v.), Oszkár Gellért (1882–1967), Milán Füst (1888–1967), Simon Kemény (1883–1945), Anna Lesznai (1885–1966), and Ernő Szép (1884–1953), united originality of expression with astounding versatility in their search for new poetical forms and techniques.

One of the great accomplishments of the group was the widening of literary horizons through close contacts with Western European and American literature. Most poets gathering around *Nyugat,* particularly Babits, Kosztolányi, Tóth, and later Lőrinc Szabó (q.v.), were exceptionally gifted translators whose masterly renderings of Yeats, Jammes, Verhaeren, Rilke, George (qq.v.), Wilde, Byron, Keats, Shelley, Rossetti, Baudelaire, Verlaine, Rimbaud, Mallarmé, Poe, and Whitman contributed considerably to refining literary tastes and adding further momentum to the great literary renaissance.

Social protest, so strongly expressed in Ady's revolutionary poetry as well as in the lyrical output of poets such as Tóth and Juhász, provided the main theme for the novelists who appeared on the literary scene in the decade preceding World War I. The social, economic, and psychological plight of the peasantry was described with forceful realism by Móricz, considered the most significant Hungarian prose writer of the 20th c. While village life—*Sárarany* (1910; golden mud); "Hét krajcár" (1909; seven pennies)—the Hungarian past —*Tündérkert* (1922; fairy garden)—and the eccentricities of the country squires—"Úri muri" (1928; squirish feast)—provided the raw material for Móricz's penetrating sociopsychological analyses, the drab monotony of petit-bourgeois existence, and the sullen hopelessness of the proletariat inspired the caustic protests voiced in the novels and short stories of Lajos Nagy (q.v.). In Karinthy's books of imaginary travels—*Utazás Faremidóba* (1916) and *Capillária* (1921)—translated together as *Voyage to Faremido; Capillaria* (1965)—the fantastic, interwoven with the absurd, became the vehicle for witty social satire, while his collection of parodies—*Így írtok ti* (1912; so you write)—concealed highly spirited literary criticism under a façade of whimsical playfulness.

It is fairly safe to say that the *Nyugat* group represented, in both a political and a literary sense, leftist-radical tendencies (radicalism in the European sense, that is, moderates on the left-center). To the right of the radical opposition stood the proponents of 19th-c. liberalism, such as the poet József Kiss (1843–1921), the novelist and playwright Sándor Bródy (q.v.), and the highly versatile Jenő Heltai (1871–1957). Kiss, whose literary weekly *A hét* had paved the way for *Nyugat*, showed great skill and sincerity in broadening the poetic scope of classic-romantic traditions. Bródy contributed considerably to the development of a new literary idiom marked by strong naturalistic tendencies, as seen in *A tanitónő* (1908; the schoolmistress). Heltai, who began his career as the author of songlike poems and amusing novelettes, acquired, after World War I, solid literary stature with his psychological novel *Álmokháza* (1929; house of dreams) and the play *A néma levente* (1936; the mute knight). Géza Gárdonyi's (1863–1922) impressive historical frescos, *Isten rabjai* (1908; slaves of God) and *Egri csillagok* (1901; stars of Eger), were highly appreciated by critics as well as the public.

In the period 1908–18 the increasing activities of the literary avant-garde did not fail to call forth a vigorous reaction from conservative nationalists, headed by the influential Jenő Rákosi (1842–1929). The polemics between defenders of literary orthodoxy and their progressive opponents, such as the critics Zoltán Ambrus (q.v.), Aladár Schöpflin (1872–1950), and György Lukács (q.v.), created an exceptionally tense literary atmosphere in which the clash of ideological and particularly aesthetic currents added further stimulus to the creative processes. In the conservative camp the leading literary figure was Ferenc Herczeg (1863–1954), a novelist—an outstanding work is *Pogányok* (1902; pagans)—and playwright—*Bizánc* (1904; Byzantium)—whose psychological insight, stylistic skill, and highly developed sense for both humor and drama commanded the respect even of his most resolute opponents.

Curiously, the playwrights who succeeded about this time in putting Budapest on the theatrical map took little or no part in the momentous debates. The reason for this was that essentially they had no program to defend, no ideology to propagate, no message to deliver. Dezső Szomory (1869–1944), from a literary point of view perhaps the most interesting figure in this group, dedicated all his talents to the search for artistic perfection, which he sought to attain by projecting the opaque elements of the subconscious through the medium of a highly colored, impressionistic imagery, as in, for example *II. József* (1918; Joseph II). Ferenc Molnár (q.v.) was at his best when describing the secret tragedies of metropolitan life, for instance, in his novel *A Pál-utcai fiúk* (1907; *The Paul Street Boys,* 1927), and plays like *Széntolvajok* (1918; coal thieves) and *Liliom* (1909; *Liliom,* 1921). Sincere, moving, and abounding in poetic tenderness, these masterly reconstructions of the world of children, vagabonds, and thieves provide far better evidence of Molnár's exceptional literary talents than his technically flawless comedies like *Játék a kastélyban* (1926; *The Play's the Thing,* 1927) and *Az ördög* (1907; *The Devil,* 1908). A very similar technical virtuosity and dramatic flair contributed to making Menyhért Lengyel's (1880–1974) *Tájfun* (1907; *Typhoon,* 1911) a great success.

By the early 1920s the literary revolution triggered by the *Nyugat* group had run its course. But while humanistic-cosmopolitan ideas propagated by the periodical lost much of their significance as a result of the social and intellectual upheavals that followed World War I, the revolutionary-populist content of Ady's and Móricz's writings provided a rich source of inspiration for younger poets and novelists. The most original representative of the revolutionary-populist mystique was Dezső Szabó (1879–1945), whose torrential style and polemical zest in such works as *Az elsodort falu* (1919; the swept-away village) and *Segítség* (1925; help) added an entirely new and powerful note to Hungarian prose. The tendency to consider the peasantry as the main source of national regeneration was clearly reflected in the novels of János Kodolányi (1899–1969) and Pál Szabó (1893–1970). The leading figure in this group was Gyula Illyés (q.v.), who succeeded in lending both persuasiveness and originality to all genres—poetry, drama, fiction, and journalism—to which he dedicated his impressive talents.

While the interest of writers gathering around the so-called village sociographers (*falukutatók*) remained focused on rural life, particularly on the plight of the agrarian proletariat, other novelists chose different terrains for their psychological and social explorations. Gyula Krúdy (q.v.), who belonged to the first *Nyugat* generation, used almost surrealist (q.v.) techniques in evoking with nostalgic tenderness the moods of the past and in recalling dreamlike episodes in the lives of strange, lonely men and women as in *A vörös postakocsi* (1914; *The Crimson Coach*, 1967). In contrast to Krúdy's delicately emotional approach, Sándor Márai (b. 1900) followed a rigorous intellectual method in his brilliant analyses of the bourgeoisie in *Idegen emberek* (1930; foreign people) and *Vendégjáték Bolzanóban* (1940; guest performance in Bolzano). Mihály Földi (1894–1943), a physician by profession, used Freudian techniques to depict intricate psychological problems in *Sötétség* (1918; darkness) and *Szahara* (1920; Sahara). Ferenc Móra's (1894–1934) tender and amusing character sketches revealed great literary skill joined with a genuinely humanistic outlook in *Ének a búzamezőkről* (1927; *Song of the Wheatfields*, 1930). Lajos Zilahy's (q.v.) well-constructed plays, like *Süt a nap* (1924; the sun shines) and novels like *Két fogoly* (1927; *Two Prisoners*, 1931) and *Ararát* (1947; *The Dukays*, 1949) reflected an intense awareness of the social and psychological developments that preceded the moral and political disintegration of central and eastern Europe.

The remarkable autobiography, *Egy ember élete* (8 vols, 1928–39; the life of a man), of Lajos Kassák (q.v.), the first Hungarian poet of stature to experiment with futurist and expressionist (q.v.) techniques, provided in highly articulate literary terms a valuable human document on the corrosive processes that were threatening 20th-c. Hungarian society. The critic, novelist, and playwright László Németh (q.v.) adopted the technique of the great Western realists to offer in a highly individualistic style a critical analysis of Hunga-

ry's political and social institutions. His novels —such as *Iszony* (1947; *Revulsion*, 1965) and *Égető Eszter* (1956; Eszter Égető)—his plays —such as the historical drama *Galilei* (1956; Galileo)—and his essays abound in original, although often confusing ideas expressed with great verbal artistry.

The same extraordinary diversity that distinguished Hungarian poetry in the beginning of the century remained the characteristic feature of the new literary era. Gyula Illyés, József Erdélyi (1896–1979), and Ferenc Juhász (b. 1928) represented the populist trend; Lőrinc Szabó, Miklós Radnóti (q.v.), and Sándor Weöres (q.v.) followed in the footsteps of the first *Nyugat* generation by seeking to broaden in a highly individualistic manner the classic-romantic forms of poetical expression. Catholic poets such as László Mécs (1895–1979) and Sándor Sík (1889–1963) successfully translated into lyrical terms their spiritual yearnings and experiences. Unconnected with any group or literary school, Attila József (q.v.) emerged as the greatest poet of this period. Uniting a moving, almost naïve sensitivity and an inexhaustible artistic imagination with a melodious flexibility of expression and a passionate commitment to human dignity and justice, József succeeded in expressing with equal ease and credibility moods and attitudes ranging from serene introspection and quiet nostalgia to indignant social protest.

Social criticism, which had been one of the leitmotifs of 20th-c. Hungarian literature, was turned into parodistic farce by the Party hacks who dominated literature in the years following the establishment of the Communist regime in Hungary. Curiously enough, the intellectual terror that lasted from 1948 to 1956 provided the best evidence of the resilience of Hungarian writers, who succeeded in preserving the traditional vigor of their creative powers even in the literary Sahara of the era of compulsory Socialist Realism (q.v.). In fact, writers, led by Gyula Illyés, in the postwar era the dean of modern Hungarian letters, played a leading role in preparing the intellectual climate for the uprising of 1956. Having hailed the advent of "redemptory socialism," most prominent poets of that era took considerable risks, both before and after the Russian intervention, by denouncing the despotic measures the regime had taken in trying to conceal the glaring defects of the Stalinist system.

The inner conflict triggered by a clash between socialist ideals and harsh realities colors the poems of László Benjámin (q.v.) written in the mid-1950s. After experimenting with expressionist techniques, Zoltán Zelk (b. 1906) returned to more traditional poetic forms to reaffirm with great sensitivity his commitment to an undogmatic world view, seen in the collections *Tűzből mentett hegedű* (1963; violin saved from fire) and *Zuzmara a rózsafán* (1964; hoarfrost on the rose tree). Uniting sensuous originality with great artistic virtuosity, György Faludy (b. 1913), in *Őszi harmat után* (1947; after the autumn dew) and *Emlékkönyv a rőt Bizáncról* (1961; memorial volume of red Byzantium), succeeded in keeping alive the traditions of the first *Nyugat* generation. Gyula Illyés's poem "Egy mondat a zsarnokságról" (1956; "One Sentence on Tyranny," 1968) galvanized public opinion on its publication and is now considered a lasting monument of modern Hungarian poetry.

The role played by writers and poets such as Illyés and Faludy in the 1956 events added considerable momentum to the literary revival that took place in the following decade. The revival was most noticeable in lyric poetry, which has always been the literary genre in which Hungary's national genius expressed itself most eloquently and convincingly. Moreover, in the 1960s and 1970s, poetry left wider room for subjectivity and experimentation than other literary genres. No less important was the country's emergence from almost complete cultural isolation. The works of Yeats, Pound, Eliot, and Dylan Thoms (qq.v.) became available, and some of their poems were even published in translation. The effects of that cultural cross-fertilization are clearly discernible in the works of the younger poets.

The public, long subjected to the cultural devastation of Socialist Realism, responded enthusiastically to the poetic revival. According to official statistics, between 1957 and 1972, 804 volumes of poetry by then living poets was published in addition to 57 anthologies.

The spiritual, moral, and intellectual tensions of the post-Stalinist period are clearly reflected by the efforts of most contemporary Hungarian poets to bring into accord conflicting moods and orientations. Their deep disappointment over the defects of the socialist experiment has been gradually mitigated by hope for a better future, while commitment to collectivity became sufficiently flexible to leave room for subjective concerns and inclinations. The search for a middle ground on which the conflicting ideological, social, and psychological trends could be successfully reconciled is manifest in the works of Ferenc Juhász, whose over-

powering imagery, abounding in folkloristic and mythical elements, evident in *Harc a fehér báránnyal* (1965; struggle with the white lamb) and *A Szent Tűzözön regéi* (1969; the tales of the Sacred Fire-Flood), expresses the individual's fears and perplexities in a dangerously restless world. Inspired by Christian ethics, János Pilinszky (q.v.) voiced with disciplined artistry his protest against war and oppression in *Nagyvárosi ikonok* (1970; big-city icons) and *Szálkák* (1972; splinters).

Distinguished by fascinating virtuosity, the poems of Sándor Weöres reflect the whole gamut of human emotions, ranging from playful insouciance to a soberly sympathetic understanding of man's existential problems. In the poems of István Vas (b. 1910) a rationalist-humanist philosophy in the Greco-Roman tradition irradiates the melancholy themes of senescence and death. Like Babits, Tóth, and Kosztolányi, Vas too has greatly enriched Hungarian literature with masterly translations ranging from the tragedies of Shakespeare, Racine, and O'Neill (q.v.) to Maeterlinck's and Apollinaire's (qq.v.) works. In contrast to Vas's elegiac mood, Mihály Váci (1924–1968) gave free rein to revolutionary passions in asserting his faith in the prophetic vocations of poets in his collections *Kelet felől* (1965; from the East) and the posthumously published *Sokaság fia* (1970; son of multitude). László Nagy (b. 1925), one of the most impressive poets of his generation, experimented with various techniques, including surrealism, before fashioning the highly original style in which he expresses moods ranging from subdued pessimism to a rapturous celebration of the joys of life, as in *Himnusz minden időben* (1965; hymn in all times).

The evolution of modern Hungarian prose writing reflects the same tensions that characterized the poetic revival. Prose writers, however, faced difficulties greater than poets did in trying to overcome the limitations imposed on them by Party ideologists, who continue to consider Socialist Realism as the norm of literary acceptability. The difficulties were partly overcome by trying to reinterpret the meaning of realism. Thus, a new trend emerged that is often described as "new realism"—an amalgam of "traditional" and "popular" realism. Popular realism is distinguished from traditional realism by its preoccupation with sociopolitical problems affecting the working classes.

Whatever the label attached to their style, most Hungarian writers continue to focus their attention on one or another of the great issues that came to the fore amid the radical changes that took place in Hungary after World War II. Tibor Déry's (q.v.) novel *Feletet* (2 vols., 1950–52; answer) triggered a long and impassioned ideological debate because of the author's allegedly "subjective" views on the evolution of the worker's movement in Hungary. Before defecting to the West, Tamás Aczél (b. 1921) published several novels—*A szabadság árnyékában* (1948; in the shadow of freedom), *Vihar és napsütés* (1949; storm and sunshine) —which were well recived by critics as well as the public. The playwright Gyula Háy (b. 1900), a veteran Communist who was to take an active part in the 1956 freedom uprising, showed great skill in using the stage for sustaining the Marxist view of history in such plays as *Isten, császár, paraszt* (1946; God, emperor, and peasant), which had first been produced in Germany in 1932.

József Lengyel (b. 1896), another veteran Communist who had spent long years in Stalin's prison camps, described with documentarylike precision the crimes and aberrations of the Stalin era in his short stories and in such novels as *Igéző* (1961; *The Spell*, 1968) and *Elévült tartozás* (1964; prescribed debt). József Darvas (b. 1912), had revived his childhood memories in portraying village life—in *A legnagyobb magyar falu* (1937; the greatest Hungarian village); in his later works he explored the psychological and social significance of individual responsibility in works such as *Részeg eső* (1963; drunken rain). The impact of historical upheavals on individual morality is the main theme of Ferenc Sánta's (b. 1927) writings, which are inspired by a deep-rooted humanism; two of his best works are *Az ötödik pecsét* (1963; the fifth seal) and *20 óra* (1964; 20 hours). The life of "small people" living on the peripheries of the big cities, and their inability to adapt themselves to social and economic progress, is critically analyzed by Endre Fejes (b. 1923) in his novel *Rozsdatemető* (1962; *Generation of Rust*, 1970), which triggered an animated literary debate. So did György Konrád's (b. 1933) novel *A látogató* (1969; *The Caseworker;* 1974), which underscored the difficulty of solving ethical problems by sociological means.

In spite of the dominant trends that called for investing every literary work with social significance, many writers sought to add new dimensions to "realism" by infusing into it psychological and even allegorical elements. In analyzing the existential problems of individuals as they try to find their place in successive Hungarian societies, Magda Szabó (b. 1917) uses with great skill modern literary devices, including the interior monologue in such novels as *Freskó* (1958; fresco) and *Az őz* (1959; the deer). György Moldova (b. 1934) portrays with sympathy, flavored with a touch of bitter humor, the solitary eccentrics who appear in works like *Az idegen bajnok* (1963; the foreign champion) and *A sötét angyal* (1964; the dark angel). In his novels, short stories, and plays inspired by a cool but imaginative rationalism, István Örkény (b. 1912) seeks to reveal a reality that remains hidden behind the grotesque or even absurd façade of everyday life: *Házastársak* (1951; spouses), *Jeruzsálem hercegnője* (1966; the princess of Jerusalem), and *Egyperces novellák* (1968; one-minute short stories) are among his best works of fiction.

Literary debates on important subjects such as the nature of realism or socialist aesthetics are greatly stimulated by the publication of several literary periodicals of outstanding quality: *Kortárs, Nagyvilág, Alföld, Jelenkor*. In addition to contributing to the clarification of aesthetic and other theoretical issues, these debates attest to the continuing vitality of Hungarian letters in spite of the ideological restrictions to which all creative endeavors are subjected.

BIBLIOGRAPHY: Farkas, J. von, *Die Entwicklung der ungarischen Literatur* (1934); Gömöri, G. *The Hungarian Literary Scene, 1957–1959* (1959); Cushing, G. F., Introduction to *Hungarian Prose and Verse: A Selection with an Introductory Essay* (1956), pp. xi–xxxv; Fenyő, M., "The *Nyugat* Literary Magazine and Modern Hungarian Literature," *NHQ*, 3, 3–4 (1962), 7–19; Sivirsky, A., *Die ungarische Literatur der Gegenwart* (1962); Klaniczay, T., et al., *History of Hungarian Literature* (1964); Reményi, J., *Hungarian Writers and Literature* (1964); Gömöri, G., "Hungarian Literature," in Ivask, I., and Wilpert, G. von, eds., *World Literature since* 1945 (1973), pp. 357–71

ANN DEMAITRE

See also sections on Hungarian writing in the articles on Czechoslovak, Romanian, and Yugoslav literatures

HUSAYN, Tāhā

Egyptian novelist, short-story writer, critic, literary historian, and educator, b. 14 Nov. 1889, Maghāgha; d. 28 Oct. 1973, Cairo

H.'s loss of sight at a very early age had a deep effect on his life and his writing. In 1902 he went to Cairo and became a student at al-Azhar, Egypt's venerable institute of religious studies, but his disappointment with the traditional system of education brought him into conflict with his conservative teachers. At the newly established Egyptian University H. made his first acquaintance with modern scholarship. His thesis on the famous Arab poet Abī al-'Alā' al-Ma'arrī (973–1057), *Dhīkrā Abī al-'Alā'* (1915; the memory of Abī al-'Alā') earned him the first Ph.D. to be granted in Egypt. In France H. obtained from the Sorbonne his second Ph.D. for a dissertation on Ibn Khaldūn (d. 1406), the great Arab philosopher of history. Back home in 1919, he embarked on a university teaching career, and from 1950 to 1952 he was Minister of Education. He received honorary degrees from several European universities.

The publication of H.'s defiant book *Fī al-shi'r al-jāhilī* (1926; on pre-Islamic poetry), in which he claimed that the poetry attributed to the pre-Islamic period was forged in a later period and questioned some religious beliefs, placed him in the center of a public storm, and the teachers of al-Azhar accused him of heresy and tried to have him prosecuted. In retrospect, it is the intellectual courage displayed in his critical approach, rather than his actual conclusions, that earned H.'s study its prominent place in Arabic scholarship.

H. was a prolific writer whose output consists of six novels, as well as short stories, epigrams, and artistic paraphrasing of ancient Arabic poems. He also wrote books on Islamic history and Arabic literature, critical essays, translations of classical Greek and French plays, and innumerable journalistic articles on social and political topics.

H.'s autobiography, *Al-Ayyām* (3 vols., 1925, 1939, 1967; *An Egyptian Childhood*, 1932; *The Stream of Days*, 1948; *A Passage to France*, 1976), may be considered one of the finest works in modern Arabic literature. In addition to the insight it provides into the inner world of the blind youth, it sheds valuable light on Egyptian social and cultural life. The idiosyncratic style, which makes full use of the resources of the Arabic language, is extremely evocative. Its imagery shows that H.'s attitude toward people and things is determined by his reaction to the sounds they make rather than their appearance. This book, with its emotional appeal, helped mold the sensibilities of two generations of readers.

H.'s novel *Shajarat al-bu's* (1944; the tree of misery) depicts the life of a traditional family with great sympathy, whereas the short stories in *Al-Mu'adhdhabūn fī al-ard* (1949; the sufferers on earth) are symptomatic of growing resentment against social injustice prior to the 1952 revolution.

In his work as a literary historian and critic, a certain line of evolution is discernible. H. came to believe that criticism is an art, not a science. His book on the poet al-Mutanabbī (d. 965), *Ma'a al-Mutanabbī* (1936; with al-Mutanabbī), in which he laid greater emphasis on his personal taste, contrasts sharply with his earlier book on al-Ma'arrī, in which he tried to apply a rigid scientific method.

Although the Arabic cultural heritage ranked high in his esteem, H. was an admirer of Western civilization, and of French culture in particular. These meant for him not only material prosperity and scientific achievements, but also freedom of thought and respect for human rights. In his famous *Mustaqbal al-thaqāfa fī Misr* (1938; *The Future of Culture in Egypt*, 1954) he reiterated his adherence to the cause of Westernization, and exhorted the Egyptians to adapt themselves to the requirements of modern life.

An ardent lover of freedom, H. was opposed to a politically committed literature. His own writing, however, was motivated by a deep sense of mission and responsibility. His contribution, therefore, cannot be evaluated merely in terms of aesthetic excellence; it should also be taken in the context of the role he played in the emergence of a new culture. During his lifetime H. gained general recognition as the most outstanding figure in modern Arabic literature.

FURTHER WORKS: *Étude analytique et critique de la philosophie sociale d'Ibn Khaldun* (1917); *Qādat al-fikr* (1925); *Hadīth al-arbi'ā'* (3 vols., 1925, 1926, 1945); *Fī al-Adab al-jāhilī* (1927); *Ma'a Abī al-'Alā' fī sijnihi* (1930); *Fī al-sayf* (1933); *Hāfiz wa Shawqī* (1933); *'Alā hāmish al-sīra* (3 vols., 1933, 1939, 1943); *Du'ā' al-karawān* (1934); *Adīb* (1935); *Min ba'īd* (1935); *Min hadīth al-shi'r wa al-nathr* (1936); *Al-Qasr al-mashūr* (1937); *Al-Hubb al-dā'i'* (1942); *Ahlām Sharazād* (1943); *Sawt Abī al-'Alā'* (1944); *Fusūl fī al-adab wa al-naqd* (1945); *Jannat al-shawk* (1945); *'Uthmān* (1947); *Rihlat al-rabi'* (1948); *Mir'āt al-damīr al-hadīth* (1949); *Al-Wa'd al-haqq* (1950); *Jannat al-hayawān* (1950); *Alwān* (1952); *Bayn bayn* (1952); *'Alī wa banūhu* (1953);

Khisām wa naqd (1955); *Naqd wa islāh* (1956); *Ahādīth* (1957); *Min adabinā al-mu'āsir* (1958); *Mir'at al-Islām* (1959); *Min laghw al-sayf* (1959); *Al-Shaykhān* (1960); *Min laghw al-Sayf ilā jidd al-shitā'* (1961); *Khawātir* (1967); *Kalimāt* (1967)

BIBLIOGRAPHY: Cachia, P., *T. H.: His Place in the Egyptian Literary Renaissance* (1956); Hourani, A., *Arabic Thought in the Liberal Age, 1798–1939* (1962), pp. 324–40; Semah, D., *Four Egyptian Literary Critics* (1974), pp. 109–50

DAVID SEMAH

HUXLEY, Aldous

English novelist, essayist, and critic, b. 26 July 1894, Godalming; d. 22 Nov. 1963, Los Angeles, Cal., U.S.A.

H. was born into an eminent British family of letters and science. His grandfather was the renowned biologist Thomas Henry Huxley, who popularized Darwinism; his granduncle was the poet-essayist Matthew Arnold, and his grandaunt was the novelist Mrs. Humphrey Ward; his father, Leonard, was an essayist and the editor of *Cornhill* magazine; his brother, Sir Julian, a noted biologist; and his half brother, Andrew Huxley, won the Nobel Prize for physiology in 1963. H. maintained an interest in science throughout his life, and indeed he first decided on a career in medicine, but a serious eye affliction that nearly blinded him forced him to abandon his medical studies and instead turn to the study of literature. He published his first two books of poetry, *The Burning Wheel* (1916) and *The Defeat of Youth* (1918), while still a student at Oxford. It was during this time that he met D. H. Lawrence (q.v.), with whom he had a lifelong friendship and who influenced his early philosophy. He married Maria Nys in 1919 while on the editorial staff of *The Athenaeum*, and in 1920 published a volume of short stories, *Limbo*, and a third volume of poetry, *Leda*. In 1921 he published his first novel, *Crome Yellow,* and his literary career was well launched.

H. has written numerous volumes of nonfiction, ranging from the early travel book *Jesting Pilate* (1926), in which he examines the cultures of the East, to biographies such as *Grey Eminence* (1941), a study of Cardinal Richelieu's assistant François Leclerc in which H. indicates his dissatisfaction with orthodox

Christianity, and *The Devils of Loudun* (1952), in which he explores the psychological and spiritual implications of nuns seemingly possessed by devils; and to philosophical essays such as *Ends and Means* (1937), in which he views the inadequacies of modern Western civilization, and *The Perennial Philosophy* (1945), in which he suggests personal mysticism as the means of salvation for modern man, and *The Doors of Perception* (1954) and *Heaven and Hell* (1956), which analyze his experiences under the influence of mescaline (he believed that the heightened perceptions induced by this hallucinatory drug lead to visionary revelations, either mystical or artistic). Yet H.'s literary reputation is mainly that of a novelist. However, there is a continuity and an interrelationship between H.'s fiction and his nonfiction in the development of his philosophy and his art.

H. once described himself as an essayist who sometimes wrote novels: there is an essential truth in this remark made somewhat facetiously late in his career when he was writing more nonfiction than fiction: all of H.'s novels are novels of ideas, a genre that derives its form in part from the dramatic essay in which a symposium of ideas is presented; thus, for example, ideas and attitudes on politics, religion, and education expressed in the essays in *Proper Studies* (1927) are dramatized in the novel *Point Counter Point* (1928). H., through his character Philip Quarles, defines the novel of ideas also in relation to allegory: "The character of each personage must be implied, as far as possible, in the ideas of which he is the mouthpiece. Insofar as theories are rationalizations of sentiments, instincts, dispositions of soul, this is feasible." In his early novels (through *Brave New World,* 1932) H. maintains a philosophical skepticism about the differing ideas and attitudes, and he achieves the necessary artistic balance through satire, using the technique of counterpoint to play one idea or attitude against another. In his later novels, beginning with *Eyeless in Gaza* (1936), H. is no longer skeptical, and characters such as Miller and Beavis in *Eyeless in Gaza,* Propter in *After Many a Summer Dies the Swan* (1939), and Barnack and Rontini in *Time Must Have a Stop* (1944) become mouthpieces for H.'s mysticism.

Crome Yellow (1921), *Antic Hay* (1923), and *Those Barren Leaves* (1925), his first three novels, of which *Antic Hay* is the best, form a continuity of characterization, ideas, and situations found in *Point Counter Point;* together they are a satiric portrait of the 1920s with that decade's skepticism, hedonism, and clash of ideas and values. Gumbril, Jr., and Mrs. Viveash in *Antic Hay* are the earlier counterparts of Walter Bidlake and Lucy Tantamount in *Point Counter Point*, sophisticated young men and women of the 1920s, hedonistic, certain that the old values of the prewar generation died in the war but uncertain of anything else beyond pleasure-seeking and personal freedom; Coleman the cynic and Shearwater the scientist but incomplete man are prototypes of Spandrell and Lord Edward Tantamount. The changing patterns of the characters' relationships, suggested by the title (a rustic dance in which the partners weave in and out), is the same technique of counterpoint used to dramatize the conflict of ideas or the instability of human relationships in a world where intellectual values themselves are unstable. In *Point Counter Point* H. provides a norm (the artist Mark Rampion) against which the lives and ideas of the other characters are counterpointed, whereas in *Antic Hay* no single viewpoint dominates. Rampion, who expounds Lawrentian ideas in *Point Counter Point*, is happily married, the only character in the novel who has a satisfactory love relationship; thus his naturalistic philosophy of life and his criticism of modern science and industrialism and of orthodox Christianity for creating incompleteness and disharmony in modern life and human relationships are given added credence. Burlap represents the perversion of spirituality in the modern world, and Illidge and Webley represent the perversion of political action; even Philip Quarles, who essentially agrees with Rampion, is satirized for his over-intellectualism. Yet in the end H. withholds from Rampion in his debate with Spandrell the ultimate answer to the meaning of life. Thus H. remains sufficiently detached from even the Lawrentian philosophy of life, which he obviously admired at this time, by not presenting it as a final solution and means of human salvation; for while it may work as a practical solution to the problem of living in the modern world, it does deny the soul. Inherent in the inadequacy of Rampion's philosophy of life to explain the soul is the clue to H.'s later adoption of mysticism as a way out of the modern wasteland.

Brave New World (1932), an antiutopian novel, is the last of H.'s novels in which his philosophical skepticism balances opposing ways of life; Mustapha Mond's controlled society, with its modern technological advances

utilized solely for the purpose of achieving material happiness, and John Savage's "primitive" belief in the tragic condition of man are both equally untenable ways of life. Although the former eliminates war, disease, and suffering, it creates a monstrously hedonistic society devoid of humanistic and spiritual values; it is the direction in which modern society is moving, provided mankind does not annihilate itself in atomic warfare, H. indicates in the foreword he wrote to the 1946 American edition of the novel, a theme he expands upon in the volume of essays *Brave New World Revisited* (1958). While John Savage's world of traditional values, the world of Shakespeare's plays from which the ironic title of this novel is taken, has its poetry, spiritual visions, and deeper human relationships, it also has its wars, poverty, suffering, and unhappiness because the artistic and spiritual vision and the significant human relationship are dependent on man's acceptance of his tragic condition. Nowhere is H.'s changed philosophical viewpoint better illustrated than in his fictional "brave new world revisited," *Island* (1962), a utopian novel in which an isolated island of sanity exists in this still wasteland world, an island where the people devote their lives to the contemplative life, utilizing such scientific knowledge as necessary to the good life, such as hallucinatory drugs to induce or intensify spiritual and creative visions.

In 1932 H. met the English theologian and mystic Gerald Heard (1889–1971), who had an important influence on his acceptance of mysticism, but H. was not suddenly converted to mysticism by his association with Heard; the whole direction and development of his thought, as it was for T. S. Eliot (q.v.), was a quest for certainty, and behind the urbane, sophisticated mask of intellectual wit and satire was the moralistic indignation of an Old Testament prophet. All of H.'s later works of fiction, from *Eyeless in Gaza* to *Island*, are dramatic essays expounding his own personal philosophy; H. is no longer the detached, skeptical novelist but an explicit philosopher, a partisan rather than an observer in the drama of ideas. Thus H.'s later novels are less satisfactory artistically because in writing them H. the philosophic essayist overshadows H. the satiric novelist.

H.'s mystical philosophy as developed in these later novels and in his volumes of essays, particularly *The Perennial Philosophy*, is a search for what Heard called "the eternal gospel," the essential truths that are found in all great religions. As Anthony Beavis in *Eyeless in Gaza* states, everything that causes separation and division is evil, whether it be of the body, mind, or soul; everything that creates unity and harmony is good. Since the human condition of modern man is divisive and separatist in all aspects of human endeavor—social, political, religious, and psychological—the individual must seek to achieve inner peace by transcending time through the contemplative life. Time, which is associated with the ego, must have a stop. This is the realization Sebastain Barnack comes to in *Time Must Have a Stop.* "It is axiomatic," H. stated explicity the following year in *The Perennial Philosophy* "that the end of human life is contemplation, or the direct and intuitive awareness of God." Modern man, however, beset by a confusion of moral standards, by a standardization of material life, and by social and political regimentation, is lost in the wasteland of technology, totalitarianism, and militant religious orthodoxy. He follows the ape of bodily passions, not the essence of being, which is the spirit, H. shows in *Ape and Essence* (1948); he worships the genius of science, not the goddess of love, H. suggests as his allegorical theme in *The Genius and the Goddess* (1955). It is the mission of what Heard called "men of the margin," modern prophets, to act as voices in the wilderness pointing the way to the promised land of spiritual fulfillment and happiness, the "island" of inner peace. Thus in his later novels H., through his characters who act as spokesmen for his philosophy, assumes the role of such a prophet.

FURTHER WORKS: *Chapbook* (1920, with T. S. Eliot); *Mortal Coils* (1922); *On the Margin* (1923); *Little Mexican* (1924); *The Gioconda Smile: A Play* (1924); *Along the Road* (1925); *Selected Poems* (1925); *Two or Three Graces* (1926); *Essays, New and Old* (1926); *Arabia Infelix* (1929); *Do What You Will* (1929); *Holy Face* (1929); *Vulgarity in Literature* (1930); *Brief Candles* (1930); *The Cicadas* (1931); *Music at Night* (1931); *The World of Light* (1931); *Texts and Pretexts* (1932); *Beyond the Mexique Bay* (1934); *The Olive Tree* (1936); *Stories, Essays, and Poems* (1937); *The Art of Seeing* (1942); *Verses and Comedy* (1946); *Science, Liberty, and Peace* (1946); *Collected Edition* (1947); *Themes and Variations* (1950); *Joyce, the Artificer* (1952, with Stuart Gilbert); *Adonis and the Alphabet* (1956; Am., *Tomorrow and Tomorrow and Tomorrow*); *Collected Short Stories* (1957); *Collected Essays* (1959); *On Art and Artists* (1960); *Literature and Science*

(1963); *The Crows of Pearblossom* (1968); *Letters of A. H.* (1969); *Collected Poetry* (1971); *Moksha: Writings on Psychedelics and the Visionary Experience, 1953–1963* (1977)

BIBLIOGRAPHY: Atkins, J. A., *A. H.: A Literary Study* (1956); Ghose, A., *A. H.: A Cynical Salvationist* (1962); Huxley, J., ed., *A. H., 1894–1963* (1965); Huxley, L. A., *This Timeless Moment: A Personal View of A. H.* (1968); Bowering, P., *A. H.: A Study of the Major Novels* (1969); Meckier, J., *A. H.: Satire and Structure* (1969); Watts, H. H., *A. H.* (1969); Brander, L., *A. H.: A Critical Study* (1970); Holmes, C. M., *A. H. and the Way to Reality* (1970); Birnbaum, M., *A. H.'s Quest for Value* (1971); Firchow, P., *A. H., Satirist and Novelist* (1972); May, K., *A. H.* (1972); Bedford, S., *A. H.: A Biography* (1974); Kuehn, R. E., ed., *A. H.: A Collection of Critical Essays* (1974)

CHARLES G. HOFFMANN

The search for "a more desirable way of life," what H. has called a philosophy based on "all the facts of human experience," is the underlying motif of all the major novels. The very meaninglessness of the life he saw about him was in itself a challenge; and it is not without significance that *Eyeless in Gaza,* H.'s single complete expression of the conversion theme, his first novel to restore the meaning, stands central to his work as a whole. Everything he wrote earlier is in a sense preparatory, everything subsequent a tailing off, except for the final utopian vision of *Island.* After *Crome Yellow* the theme of moral regeneration, leading to Anthony Beavis's conversion, is latent in all the novels of the nineteen twenties. . . . After *Eyeless in Gaza,* the exemplary characters, the "virtuous, adultly non-attached personages," hold the centre of the Huxleyean stage.

Peter Bowering, *A. H: A Study of the Major Novels* (1968), pp. 19–20

H.'s major achievement, especially when compared with that of previous discussion novelists such as Thomas Love Peacock and W. H. Mallock, consists in the development of a structure for his novels that in itself carries out and supports his satire. The structural technique he prefers continually exposes the egotism of his characters. It satirizes their fragmentary existence while also suggesting they are parts of a recoverable whole. By structure this essay means the planned framework of a novel, the overall arrangement of the entire work or of a particular scene and, finally, the technical method by which the structure is attained. In *Point Counter Point,* the format is supposedly a musical one but the characters or instruments that come together in the discussion scenes fail to produce anything but discord. . . .

In effect [in *Point Counter Point*], theme has become structure. What is being satirized and what makes the novel go are one and the same: the eccentricity of its characters. What the novel is about and the way it is put together have merged.

Jerome Meckier, *A. H.: Satire and Structure* (1969), pp. 41–42

For the H. of *After Many a Summer Dies the Swan* and *Time Must Have a Stop*, the persons who achieve superior existence are those who have gone beyond the trammels of personality, the fear of death, and the constriction of being this man or that man at a particular time and place. All who plunge into the great sea of being, who merge with primal unity, have only one way to swim. Furthermore, in contrast with the graceful and easy motion that this sea makes possible, the ordinary movements of man must seem a floundering. And the depiction of such floundering—in novels and in essays that make an analysis of human behavior —is marked, in H., by a kind of impatient reportage, lively when the sheer grotesqueness of human folly amuses the writer and dull when the writer is oppressed by the basic tediousness of human behavior.

It may be added that H.'s insight into man— that he is the creature who must supplement or fulfill his animal and rational natures by some sort of vision that is the same for all who enjoy it—is peculiarly limiting to a novelist.

Harold H. Watts, *A. H.* (1969), p. 149

To one school of ontology the world as a whole is unintelligible, whatever order we may discern in its parts. . . . From *Eyeless in Gaza* on, H. assumes the opposite. He takes it on faith that there is a Nature, an Order of Things, which we must both assume and within our limits try to grasp. We can confirm this immanence in our day-to-day existence if we are willing to use all our available resources, and subject all but the basic assumption to a pragmatic, existential test. *Island* is H.'s equivalent to Yeats' *Vision*. Both writers began as divided men, and poets; both were alert to contraries for most of their lives; both were ultimately reconciled to them; both were able to make final assertions of joy. *A Vision*, however, is a more symbolic work, *Island* a far more literal one. Both symbolize a belief in ultimate order, but *Island* offers a human order here and now. Contraries are resolved on the plane of the divine, yet the divine resolution can be—it really is—immanent in our lives.

Charles M. Holmes, *A. H. and the Way to Reality* (1970), p. 199

Wherein then lies the value in giving serious consideration to H.? Precisely in his being able to articulate the intellectual and moral conflicts being fought in the collective soul of the twentieth century. D. H. Lawrence would express his reactions viscerally but failed to look through a microscope, as H. reminds us. James Joyce could disentangle himself from the nets in which he felt caught, but he did not seem aware of the oases to be found in Eastern meditative systems. E. M. Forster knew of passages to other cultures but preferred to regard art as self-sufficient rather than as catalytic. Virginia Woolf knew the agony of private torment but did not realize the healing that can emerge from societal involvement. It was H. of all these twentieth-century English writers who best reflected and coordinated the divisions of the modern world; he best expressed its *Weltanschauung* in its most universal sense. Thomas Henry Huxley, A. H.'s grandfather, was called "Darwin's bulldog" because he so tenaciously clung to and advocated Darwin's theories; similarly, A. H. may become best known for being both an observer of and a contributor to the shifting values of our world.

Milton Birnbaum, *A. H.'s Quest for Values* (1971), p. 4

In the useful terminology employed by Erich Auerbach in *Mimesis,* H. is a hypertactic writer, Lawrence a paratactic one; H. is the Hellene who must see and elaborate all the connections which go to make up an experience, Lawrence the Hebrew who intimates and suggests rather than states; H. is the Platonic rationalist who finally prefers history to fiction, Lawrence the Aristotelian who knows that art can be truer than life.

Not that the one is wrong and the other right. They are merely different, with each having his particular virtues and concomitant vices. And surely it is good that it should be so, that there should be many great traditions and not merely a single exclusive (not to say, narrow-minded) one. If the bent of the modern mind is still more toward an appreciation of the paratatic or "congenital" type of novelist, this should not mean that its sympathies might not extend occasionally to writers of the opposite kind.

Peter Firchow, *A. H., Satirist and Novelist* (1972), p. 8

[H.] was a religious man who felt twentieth-century problems in the quick of his being long before many people became fashionably and often rather spectatorially aware of them. I doubt if it is possible to think of one contemporary spiritual or social crux which H. was not urgently concerning himself with forty years ago. The general assumption that his answer after the mid-thirties was mystical is true, though it may give rise to misunderstandings. He never became a fully fledged mystic, but remained a professional writer (the two vocations probably are incompatible). His profound interest in the mystical, continually reinforced or modified by the most up-to-date finding of psychologists (for, unlike most literary men, he was not content with smatterings of Freud, Jung and Adler) did not force out enthusiasm for the reform of institutions. He was what many aspire to be, the complete liberal, being the embodiment, except in physical capacities, of his grandfather's famous definition of a liberal education.

Keith M. May, *A. H.* (1972), p. 226

ÖDÖN VON HORVÁTH   HUGO VON HOFMANNSTHAL

RICARDA HUCH

TED HUGHES

ALDOUS HUXLEY

EUGÈNE IONESCO

IBUSE Masuji

Japanese novelist, short-story writer, essayist, and poet, b. 15 Feb. 1898, Kamo

Born into an old family of independent farmers, I. spent his childhood in the country. In 1917 he moved to Tokyo and for several years studied literature and painting. Although he specialized in French literature, he became interested in Russian writers, chiefly in Tolstoy and Chekhov (q.v.).

In 1923 I. published his first successful story, "Yūhei" (confinement). The story, a satirical allegory of intellectual and artistic pretense, is better known by its revised title, "Sanshōuo" ("Salamander," 1971). In another early story, "Yofuke to ume no hana" (1925; "Plum Blossom at Night," 1971), I. blended a self-mocking humor with a dreamy, symbolist (q.v.) mood.

The allegorical or symbolist overtones of these early works suggest Western influences, but in 1926, with "Koi" ("Carp," 1971), I. turned to the more traditional techniques of his homeland. Using the highly subjective Japanese "I-novel" mode, in which narrator and author are one, he interwove fiction and reality, literary symbols and actuality. In sharp contrast, however, with other I-novelists who concentrate solely on expressing their own feelings, he used the technique as a means of restraining the emotion-filled memories precipitated by a friend's death.

During the 1930s, I.'s thematic interest shifted to the rustic countryside of southern Japan where he was born. A painstaking craftsman, he had always spent more time revising and polishing his stories than taking sides in ideological polemics.

The symbolic return to his native soil inspired some of I.'s best stories and novellas, such as "Tangeshitei" (1931; "Life at Mr. Tange's," 1971), a loving, humorous evocation of two colorful rustics, master and servant, in a remote mountain valley.

In these works, I.'s expression acquired its full, mature flavor. Skillful use of dialect, subtle contrasts in dialogue, nuances of mood and setting, a wry humor and sparse characterization through gesture and manner of speech, are the distinguishing traits of this style.

As the military clique rose to power and Japan was moving toward World War II, I. steadily worked on the most remarkable of his works on historical themes, *Sazanami gunki* (1930–38; a war diary). The historical background of the novella is the actual escape and the final defeat of the Heike clan in the 12th c.; the story itself portrays the initiation of a sensitive young Heike samurai into a brutal world.

I.'s last major prewar work, the novella *Tajinko mura* (1939; "Tajinko Village," 1971), presents a broad portrayal of the life of a village; it is also a fond farewell to a gentler way of life that cannot last.

I. did not write much during the war; his unwilling induction into the army as a war correspondent probably inspired his biting satire of the debilitating influence of army drills in "Yōhai taichō" (1950; "Lieutenant Lookeast," 1971).

Although I. returned to publishing short stories and novellas in the years following World War II, he was preparing for his longest and most important novel, *Kuroi ame* (1966; *Black Rain*, 1969), which deals with the atomic ordeal of Hiroshima. A quiet elegy for a city and its population, *Kuroi ame* emerges as a significant work of art distinct from the many sentimental or political accounts of the bombing.

I. avoided portraying the disaster in its totality, but rather set the beauty of the southern landscape, the ancient customs of the people, their colorful foibles, the little, everyday details of their lives, against the absurd brutality of the atomic holocaust. All his previous techniques and thematic interests served him well here. He needed not only his characteristic sympathy for the simple life and an intimate knowledge of popular lore, but also the calm tone and detached poise of a chronicler that he had acquired in his earlier historical writings. He also needed the skill to handle a vast documentary montage of eyewitness accounts and authentic journals.

Using the rich resources of his literary tradition, I. cautiously experimented with a number of prose techniques and styles, trying to expand the limits of the novel. He enlivened the conventional I-novel, grafted onto the ancient stock of romantic nature-lyricism a robust, epic quality, and introduced a dry, original humor into the often too serious and sometimes too sentimental art of modern Japanese prose writing.

FURTHER WORKS: *Shigotobeya* (1931); *Kawa* (1932); *Zuihitsu* (1933); *Keirokushū* (1936); *Shūkin ryokō* (1937); *John Manjirō hyōryūki* (1937; *John Manjiro: The Cast-Away, His Life and Adventures,* 1940); *Shiguretō jokei* (1941); *I. M. zuihitsu zenshū* (3 vols., 1941); *Chūshū meigetsu* (1942); *Gojinka* (1944); *Wabisuke* (1946); *Magemono* (1946); *Oihagi no hanashi* (1947); *I. M. senshū* (9 vols., 1948); *Kashima ari* (1948); *Shibireike kamo* (1948); *Honjitsu kyūshin* (1950); *Kawatsuri* (1952); *I. M. sakuhinshū* (5 vols., 1953); *Hyōmin Nanakamado* (1955); *Usaburō* (1956); *Kanreki no koi* (1957); *Ekimae ryokan* (1957); *Nanatsu no kaidō* (1957); *Chinpindo shujin* (1959); *Tsurishi, Tsuriba* (1960); *Kinō no kai* (1961); *Shuzai ryokō* (1961); *Bushū hachigatajō* (1963); *Mushinjō* (1963); *I. M. zenshū* (12 vols., 1964); *Gendai bungaku taikei* (1966); *Shinchō nihon bungaku* (1970); *Tsuribito* (1970); *I. M. zenshū* (14 vols., 1975). FURTHER VOLUME IN ENGLISH: *Lieutenant Lookeast, and Other Stories* (1971)

BIBLIOGRAPHY: Lifton, R., "Black Rain," *Death in Life* (1967), pp. 543–55; Kimball, A., "After the Bomb," *Crisis in Identity and Contemporary Japanese Novels* (1973), pp. 43–59; Liman, A. V., "I.'s Black Rain," in Tsuruta, K., and Swann, T., eds., *Approaches to the Modern Japanese Novel* (1976), pp. 45–72

ANTHONY V. LIMAN

ICAZA, Jorge

Ecuadorian novelist and dramatist, b. 10 July 1906, Quito; d. 26 May 1978, Quito

I. worked for a time as a government employee, bookseller, and director of the National Library. Beginning his literary career as a dramatist, he wrote seven plays, of which the most challenging was *Flagelo* (1936; flogging), a revolutionary literary manifesto written in colloquial language, utilizing sexual symbolism, and depicting and attacking the degradation of the Indians by the whites.

Barro de la sierra (1933; mountain clay), I.'s first short-story collection, displayed most of the themes and concepts that were to appear in later works. The stories dwell on the defects of the *latifundio* system (of great landed estates) and the evils of Church and State; his indignation over social injustice is supported by Freudian analysis. One of his subjects is the fate of an Indian village deprived of water by a greedy landowner and the relationship of mestizo half-brothers. In later story collections, I. also fused magic realism (q.v.) with folklore elements.

Huasipungo (1934; *The Villagers,* 1964) may well be the most brutal portrayal of Indian misery ever written. In a series of indicting incidents I. portrays the plight of the suffering Indians as he dissects their unhappy existence. Deprived of their *huasipungos,* or inherited land, by those in power, the Indians can neither fathom white psychology nor plan resistance. With the aid of the priest and the local political boss, the landlord, Alfonso Pereira, forces the Indians to build a highway. When they revolt, the police kill all those who stay to fight. I. thus depicts the Ecuadorian government's complete disregard for human life and dignity. Although laced with local color, Indian traditions, and Quechua vocabulary, the novel, perhaps impressionistically exaggerated, conveys an appalling picture of human degradation. With good reason it has been called the "*Tobacco Road* of the Ecuadorian highlands."

Cholos (1938; half-breeds) concentrates on caste distinctions and social barriers. A more complex and poetic and more structured novel than *Huasipungo,* it concerns three half brothers: one white, one of mixed blood, and one Indian. I. examines the complicated caste relationships and racist impulses of those who hate both the Indians and their white masters, whom they nonetheless envy and try to emulate. I. uses the same amalgam of social problems, traditions, and customs as before, but here he emphasizes individual guilt over political degradation. He combines the complicated psychology of the protagonist Alberto Montoya and his attempt to climb the social ladder with a visionary prophecy of racial union as the hope for the future. In spite of its cloying symbolism, the novel is a very persuasive portrayal of Ecuadorian society.

El chulla Romero y Flores (1958; the upstart Romero y Flores) concentrates on the city mestizo. I. depicts a city filled with beggars, crooks, drunks, and prostitutes and examines Romero's attempt to escape both his bloodlines and poverty. I. vividly exposes Romero's inner conflicts and his resolution of them against a background of sexuality, religious bigotry, discrimination, exploitation, and political corruption. Romero, a naïve but roguish small-time bureaucrat, tormented by his inability to accept what he is, finally acknowledges his heritage and seeks salvation through moral regeneration.

Los atrapados (1972; the trapped) consists of three volumes: *El juramento* (the oath), *En la ficción* (in fiction), and *En la realidad* (in reality). In this novel I. employs dream, hallucination, and free association to reinforce his mixture of autobiography and fiction. A pastiche of previous works, with less inflammatory anger, it deals with racial prejudice and social change. As I. becomes aware of his literary abilities, he decides to use them for his people, especially the Indians with whom he had always felt attuned. He attempts to fulfill his vow, but his characters, who in a sense have free will and who fear for their own identity, impede his psychological and literary objectives. I. attempts to discover the total reality of his country's problems and to penetrate Ecuadorian masks, but he finds that reality a mutable and essentially iniquitous entity.

I., considered Ecuador's greatest novelist, portrayed shocking scenes of human degradation; he offered symbolic union of classes (the three brothers of *Cholos* walking arm in arm toward the rising sun, for example) and the elimination of landed estates as solutions to problems that appear to have none, given the human depravity he seems to accept as the norm. In this sense, his social realism, even allowing for his occasional probing study of the individual citizen, fails to convince or arouse empathy. From I.'s pessimistic point of view, the common man, obviously, will never control his destiny, nor will the exploitation I. depicts appreciably change. Although his conclusions are not cogent because his totally black and bleak portrayal of human brutishness fails to convince readers, I. nevertheless manages to move us by his conviction and by the vividness of his documentation of man's inhumanity to man.

FURTHER WORKS: *El intruso* (1928); *Comedia sin nombre* (1929); *Por el viejo* (1929); *Como ellos quieren* (1931); *Cuál es* (1931); *Sin sentido* (1932); *En las calles* (1935); *Media vida deslumbrados* (1942); *Huairapamushcas* (1948); *Seis relatos* (1952); *Seis veces la muerte* (1953); *Viejos cuentos* (1960); *Obras escogidas* (1961); *Relatos* (1969)

BIBLIOGRAPHY: Dulsey, B., "J. I. and His Ecuador," *Hispania*, 44 (1961), 99–102; Ferrandiz Alborz, F., "El novelista ecuatoriano J. I.," in J. I., *Obras escogidas* (1961), 9–71; Vetrano, A. J., *The Ecuadorian Indian "Cholo" in the Novels of J. I.: Their Lot and Language* (1966); Sacoto, A., *The Indian in the Ecuadorian Novel* (1967), 129–228; Cueva, A., *J. I.* (1968); Vetrano, A. J., "Imagery in Two of J. I.'s Novels, *Huasipungo* and *Huairapamushcas*," *REH*, 6 (1972), 293–301; Sackett, T., *El arte novelística de I.* (1974)

KESSEL SCHWARTZ

ICELANDIC LITERATURE

At the beginning of the century Icelandic literature, after a short period of realism, took a turn to neoromanticism, which became more or less a dominant factor for about three decades, especially in poetry. Icelandic society was changing from a completely rural one to a more urban one based on a small-scale fishing industry. This change can clearly be seen in the works of two pioneers of the Icelandic novel. Jón Trausti (1873–1918) was still preoccupied with the life of the farmer, while Einar H. Kvaran (1859–1938) dealt with the way of life in the small capital of Reykjavík. In many ways Kvaran can be regarded as a typical Icelandic writer of the turn of the century. He was one of the leaders of the realistic movement in Iceland, but he soon turned against it to a kind of progressive romanticism. He later came under the influence of spiritualism, and after that his writing mostly concerned the Christian duty of forgiving and the immortality of the soul.

The term "progressive romanticism" implies optimism, which characterized the first quarter of the century. In 1918 Icelanders won their independence after ages of Danish colonial rule, and both in the last phase of the struggle for independence and in the first years afterward they had a feeling of bold self-assurance and great expectations for a bright future of technological wonders. World War I did not change this feeling, since it had very little impact in Iceland. This optimism was strongly expressed by the poet Einar Benediktsson (1864–1940), one of the two most important poets of the neoromantic school. In flamboyant, rhetorical poems, in which nature imagery and the portrayal of human situations are used as entries into philosophical or metaphysical discussions, often of a slightly didactic nature, Benediktsson pointed out the limitless possibilities of a newly freed nation on the road to technological and industrial progress based on the great Icelandic sources of energy, above all hydroelectric power. His grand visions, mixed with a kind of pantheism, have made him one of the most popular poets of the century in Iceland. The other great neoromantic poet, Jóhann Sigurjónsson (q.v.), was quite different. In his short, concentrated poems the images speak for themselves. His dense imagery was something completely new, and he stands out as perhaps the most important shaper of modern Icelandic poetry. Immensely popular during the 1920s were Stefán frá Hvítadal (1887–1933) and Davíð Stefánsson (1895–1964). Their main contribution was to write poetry in an easygoing style, close to everyday language, although their work sometimes had the tendency to sink into sentimentality.

In his time, around the turn of the century, Jóhann Sigurjónsson was not only one of Iceland's most important poets, he was also the most important playwright and a leading figure among the group of Icelandic poets and writers who moved to Denmark, started writing in Danish in order to make a living, and for a while became important to Danish literary life. For the most part they wrote about life in Iceland, a fact that seems to have given their work an exotic flavor in the eyes of Continental readers. Jóhann Sigurjónsson was the first Icelandic writer in modern times to gain a European audience, especially through his plays, in which he portrayed Icelandic life using themes from folklore and history. The most successful of this group, however, was the novelist Gunnar Gunnarsson (q.v.), who won international fame with his writings about Iceland past and present; his autobiographical novel *Kirken på bjerget* (5 vols., 1923–28; the church on the mountain; tr. of Vols. I–III, *Ships in the Sky*, 1938, and *The Night and the Dream*, 1938) is his most outstanding achievement. A third important writer of this group is the playwright and novelist Guðmundur Kamban (1888–1945), whose characters, unlike those of his colleagues, were not necessarily Icelandic. Most of Kamban's writings deal with either of two subjects: marriage, and criminals and their punishment. He was extremely critical of the institution of marriage, and he also wrote extensively about what makes a man become a criminal and about the inhumane penal system.

Since World War I had very little effect in Iceland, a so-called postwar literature hardly exists. Important literary movements like expressionism, surrealism, and futurism (qq.v.) were represented only sporadically in individual works. Thus, the latter half of the 1920s could be called a period of hesitation, when a recently freed people groped for a new form of expression, a time when neoromanticism was still dominant but drawing toward a close.

During the 1930s Icelandic literature steered a much clearer course. The world economic depression hit Iceland hard and caused profound changes in the structure of its society. Since farming was no longer profitable, farmers gave up in great numbers and streamed into fishing villages and towns, where soaring unemployment caused general unrest. The trade unions were greatly radicalized, and there were serious labor conflicts and strikes. These conditions also radicalized literature in Iceland. The socialist literary periodical *Rauðir pennar* became the voice of young radical writers and poets, and the publishing company Mál og Menning was formed on an idealistic, noncommercial basis to spread radical literature.

Above all, the 1930s were the decade of the Nobel Prize winner Halldór Laxness (q.v.). In three great novel cycles he analyzed different aspects of Icelandic society from a more or less Marxist point of view: he describes the fishing villages, the poor farmers, and the situation and the role of the poet in society. The second most important writer of the 1930s was Þórbergur Þórðarson (q.v.), who made his breakthrough as a major writer with his collection of essays and stories *Bréf til Láru* (1924; a letter to Lára). His most important contribution to a radical literature are two autobiographical works: *Íslenzkur aðall* (1938; *In Search of My Beloved*, 1967) and *Ofvitinn* (2 vols., 1940–41; the eccentric), both written with a shrewd, biting humor and irony. Among the emerging writers of fiction of the time, Ólafur Jóhann Sigurðsson (q.v.) both in novels and short stories dealt with the hard life of the farmers during the depression, but also excelled in beautiful lyrical descriptions of nature.

Poetry also became radicalized during the 1930s, although not all of it. In the middle of the depression Tómas Guðmundsson (q.v.) published a collection of poems with the surprising title of *Fagra veröld* (1933; beautiful world), an immensely popular book full of subtle lyricism, occasional mild humor, and nostalgic dreams. Most of the other important poets, however, dealt more directly with the harsh realities of poverty and unemployment. Jóhannes úr Kötlum (q.v.) began in the 1920s as a neoromantic, and developed into a revolutionary poet who wrote emotional, rhetorical appeals for immediate action. He later came under the influence of modernism (q.v.). Steinn Steinarr (q.v.) started off in the early 1930s as a revolutionary poet who used daring and original imagery and a bitter, ironic humor. His political interests, however, gradually gave way to profound skepticism and pessimism, his poetry becoming more and more introverted. His preoccupation with experiments in form made him one of the forerunners of modernism in Iceland. Guðmundur Böðvarsson (1904–1974) was a self-educated farmer who expressed his hopes with the inborn wariness of a farmer. His socialism was often closely related to patriotism, a link that became quite common after Iceland joined NATO. He was more reasoning than rhetorical, and more often warned rather than preached.

World War II changed Iceland completely, although it was not fought there. In 1940 Iceland was occupied by the British, who withdrew, however, the following year and were replaced by American forces. Iceland had suddenly become strategically important. The foreign forces needed a lot of workers, and unemployment vanished overnight. In 1944 the Icelandic Republic was declared. At the end of the war Iceland had become quite rich, the country was industrialized, and the ideological struggle of the 1930s, except in the field of foreign affairs, diminished. Laxness wrote a much debated novel, *Atómstöðin* (1948; *The Atom Station*, 1961), but apart from that, directly political literature was on the decline, and Laxness himself became less and less interested in ideological questions.

The postwar years, with their radical changes and booming economy, provided an ideal ground for modernism, which particularly flourished in poetry. The members of the modernist group published their own literary periodical, *Birtingur.* Icelandic poetry had been very traditional and formally conservative; the modernists, therefore, had to revolutionize form, although they met great resistance from a very conservative public. Although greatly influenced by T. S. Eliot and Ezra Pound (qq.v.), they still belonged to the political left and wrote extensively against NATO and the American forces in Iceland. They changed Icelandic poetry completely, freed it from formal bonds, and based it on imagery, often combined with complicated use of metaphors, personification, and allusion. Images became the most important element instead of rhymed discussions, which were prevalent in earlier poetry. The modernist poets—Einar Bragi (b. 1921),

Hannes Sigússon (b. 1922), Jón Óskar (b. 1921), Sigfús Daðason (b. 1928), and Stefán Hörður Grímsson (q.v.)—dominated Icelandic poetry in the 1950s.

Along with the modernists, another group of poets was gaining strength. These were poets who combined certain elements of modernism, above all its stress on imagery, with the more traditional forms of classical Icelandic poetry. They have never completely deserted the rules of rhyme and alliteration, but rather use them in a personal way as a part of their own poetic language. They are bound together not only by this formal element, however; their themes also link them. Very Icelandic in their poems, these poets are preoccupied with Icelandic nature, history, folklore, mythology, and language, and with the struggle of a small cultural unity to survive intact in a world of growing internationalism. To this group belong Snorri Hjartarson (q.v.), Hannes Pétursson (b. 1931), and Þorsteinn frá Hamri (b. 1938).

Thor Vilhjálmsson (q.v.) is the most important modernist prose writer. His development is based on a revolt against the classical epic tradition of Icelandic prose. In his novels and travel books, written in a style full of complex imagery, the main theme is the modern, alienated European intellectual's search for identity. But Vilhjálmsson stands quite alone among Icelandic novelists. Other important prose writers have mainly dealt with the way of life in Iceland, the forces that have shaped Icelandic society, and what may happen to it. Indriði G. Þorsteinsson (b. 1926), in his most important novels, has described the changes in Icelandic society in the 1930s and during and after World War II. Jakobína Sigurðardóttir (b. 1918) has written political satires of great strength, and Svava Jakobsdóttir (b. 1930) deals mostly with the position of women and the tendency of both individuals and the nation to lean on others instead of going one's own way. Guðbergur Bergsson (q.v.) has written novels about people of a small village near the American base in Keflavík. In these books, written with subtle humor and an edge of sarcasm, he shows how people slave to keep a standard of living they never have time to enjoy, and presents a consciously distorted picture of a gray and monotonous reality. He has been influenced by Latin American writers, and is a creator of a sort of grotesque realism that shows the Icelandic people a mirror image of themselves that they might not care to see.

Professional theater in Iceland is only thirty years old. Since Icelanders wrote plays in Danish at the beginning of the century, it is only recently that professional playwrights have developed. The most important of them are Jökull Jakobsson (1933–1978) and Guðmundur Steinsson (b. 1925), who have both dealt with various aspects of the modern Icelandic way of life and its problems, although in different ways. Jökull was a literary playwright who stressed the word. Guðmundur, on the other hand, is a very theatrical playwright who stresses action rather than language.

BIBLIOGRAPHY: Einarsson, S., *History of Icelandic Prose Writers 1800–1940* (1948); Beck, R., *History of Icelandic Poets 1800–1940* (1950); Einarsson, S., *A History of Icelandic Literature* (1957); Carleton, P., *Tradition and Innovation in Twentieth Century Icelandic Poetry* (1967); Jónsson, E., "Icelandic Literature," in Ivask, I., and Wilpert, G. von, *World Literature since 1945* (1973), pp. 372–77

NJÖRÐUR P. NJARÐVÍK

IDRĪS, Yūsuf

Egyptian short-story writer, dramatist, and novelist, b. May 1927, al-Bayrūm

After a childhood spent in the Nile delta, I. came to Cairo to attend university. He studied medicine, and upon graduation (1951) became a medical inspector in the Department of Health. He had already been writing short stories for amusement as a student, and the requirements of his medical position that he visit the poorer quarters of Cairo served to strengthen and expand his innate ability to portray the living conditions of the poor in realistic detail. His first collection of short stories appeared in 1954 and was an instant success; between 1954 and 1958 he published five collections and three plays. His increasing fame as a writer led him to give up his medical career, and he has since worked as a full-time creative writer and journalist. During the 1970s he wrote relatively little, contenting himself with occasional articles for the newspaper *Al-Ahrām*; these pieces may not contain quite as much of the direct social and political criticism that made I. an enfant terrible earlier in his career and led to his imprisonment on more than one occasion, but they still succeed in penetrat-

ing to the core of the Egyptian character and in reflecting the concerns and aspirations of his fellow countrymen of all classes.

The short-story collections of the 1950s, beginning with *Arkhas layālī* (1954; the cheapest nights), describe in vivid and often gruesome detail the conditions of Egypt's poorest classes both in the towns and the countryside. In the majority of cases, the reader is introduced to the character within his surroundings and shown the routine of his life; little has changed by the end of the story. The title story of his first collection is typical. A man emerges from evening prayer in the mosque and has to wade through scores of children in order to proceed in any direction. He curses them and the hole in heaven through which they come. His mind is spinning because of a cup of strong tea he has been given. After despairing of finding any of his friends with whom he might spend the evening, he heads for home and makes love to his wife, if only to keep warm. In due time he is being congratulated yet again on the birth of a child. The way in which I., the doctor and short-story writer, projects the overwhelming problem of Egypt's birth rate with such force and clarity is exactly the quality that has made his works at once so popular and so important in the history of this genre.

During the 1960s I. began to write symbolic and surreal tales. Examples of these are "Al-Aurta" ("The Aorta," 1978) from *Lughat al-ay ay* (1965; the language of screams), a horrifying parable concerning the callousness of human beings spurred on by the herd instinct; "Alif al-ahrār" ("The Omitted Letter," 1978) from *Ākhir al-dunyā* (1961; the end of the world), an amusing yet poignant tale of bureaucratic man as victim; and "Mu'jizat al-'asr" (the wonder of the age) from *Al-Naddāha* (1969; the clarion). Another feature of I.'s recent writings has been a concern with the role of sex in society, explored, for example, in "Bayt min lahm" ("House of Flesh," 1978) from the collection *Bayt min lahm* (1971; house of flesh).

I.'s contributions to the novel and drama are also numerous, but, with a few notable exceptions, they tend to show a certain lack of affinity on the writer's part with longer genres. For example, by far his most successful play is *Al-Farāfīr* (1964; *The Farfoors*, 1974; also tr. as *Flipflap and His Master*, 1977), a brilliant attempt at combining elements of Egyptian popular dramatic forms with the modern techniques of the Theater of the Absurd (q.v.).

Yet, the work suffers from an excess of padding and farce that lessens the total impact. Of I.'s novels, perhaps only *Al-Harām* (1959; the taboo), with its themes of moral hypocrisy among villagers faced with an annual visit of transhumants (people who move seasonally from one area to another in search of pasturage for their animals) avoids this same lack of cohesion or excessive concern with politics.

One of the most interesting aspects of I.'s craft is his style, which has reflected an adventurous spirit of growth during his career. When he began to publish his stories, I.'s language was criticized severely. Far from paying any attention to such views, I. has persisted in his distinctive style to such a degree that his most recent works are a blend of the written and spoken languages. I. himself admits that he writes in an impulsive fashion, and this may well account for his greater success in short stories than in other genres. As a short-story writer and as a brilliant and controversial innovator in language and form, I. is guaranteed a major place in the history of modern Arabic literature.

FURTHER WORKS: *Jumhūriyyat Farahāt* (1956); *Al-Batal* (1957); *A laysa kadhālika?* (1957); *Al-Lahza al-harija* (1957); *Hādithat sharaf* (1958); *Al-'Ayb* (1962); *Al-'Askarī al-aswad* (1962); *Al-Mahzala al-ardiyya* (1966); *Al-Mukhattatīn* (1969); *Al-Baydā'* (1970); *Al-Jins al-thālith* (1971). FURTHER VOLUMES IN ENGLISH: *In the Eye of the Beholder: Tales from Egyptian Life from the Writings of Y. I.* (1978); *The Cheapest Nights* (1978)

BIBLIOGRAPHY: Beyerl, J., *The Style of the Modern Arabic Short Story* (1971), passim; Cobham, C., "Sex and Society in Y. I.," *JArabL*, 6 (1975), 80–88; Somekh, S., "Language and Theme in the Short Stories of Y. I.," *JArabL*, 6 (1975), 89–100; Allen, R., Introduction to Y. I., *In the Eye of the Beholder* (1978), pp. vii–xxxix; Mikhail, M., *Images of Arab Women* (1979), pp. 77–89, 91–111

ROGER M. A. ALLEN

IGBO LITERATURE
See Nigerian Literature

ILF, Ilya
(pseud. of Ilya Fainzilberg) Russian novelist and essayist, b. 5 Oct. 1897, Odessa, Ukraine; d. 13 April 1937, Moscow

PETROV, Yevgeny
(pseud. of Yevgeny Kataev) Russian novelist and essayist, b. 13 Dec. 1903, Odessa, Ukraine; d. 2 July 1942, near Sevastopol, Ukraine

Both I., the son of a bank clerk, and P., the son of a history teacher and younger brother of Valentin Kataev (q.v.), grew up in Odessa. Both began their literary careers as journalists; both moved to Moscow in 1923. They did not, however, become acquainted until 1925, when they were working on the railwaymen's newspaper *Gudok*. In 1927 they formed a literary partnership that was to last until I.'s death.

I. and P.'s first significant joint effort was the hilarious satirical novel *Dvenadtsat stulev* (1928; *Diamonds to Sit On*, 1930). The novel was a great popular success, and a sequel, *Zolotoy telyonok* (1931; *The Little Golden Calf*, 1932), soon followed. In 1935 I. and P. visited the U.S. and made a transcontinental automobile trip. Their impressions of American life are described in their witty, satirical book *Odnoetazhnaya Amerika* (1936; *Little Golden America*, 1937). The two writers also coauthored a large number of satiric stories, sketches, and feuilletons, which appeared in Soviet journals and newspapers under different pseudonyms, most notably "Tolstoyevsky." Grieved by the death from tuberculosis of his close friend and collaborator, P. wrote little fiction in the next few years. In 1940 he became editor of the journal *Ogonyok*. When World War II broke out, he became a war correspondent; his reports from the front were collected and published posthumously under the title *Frontovoy dnevnik* (1942; front-line diary). P. was killed in an airplane crash returning from besieged Sevastopol.

I. and P. are best known for *Dvenadtsat stulev* and *Zolotoy telyonok*, which are perennial favorites with Russian readers. Both novels are picaresque and revolve around the adventures of one Ostap Bender, who longs to become a millionaire in a society where it has become impossible to satisfy such an ambition. Bender, a cunning, imaginative rogue, is one of the most memorable characters in Soviet literature. His audacity and ingenuity continually delight and amuse the reader. In *Dvenadtsat stulev*

Bender searches high and low for diamonds that have been hidden in one of a set of twelve chairs. His treasure hunt takes him throughout Russia, and this device allows I. and P. to show us glimpses of provincial towns and large cities and to introduce a wide variety of characters —Soviet bureaucrats, journalists, former noblemen, provincials, Muscovites. *Dvenadtsat stulev* has an appropriate ideological ending: Bender is killed by a diamond-hunting rival; the diamonds are found and sold, and the money is used to build a club for workers. The unforgettable picaro, however, is brought back to life in the sequel, *Zolotoy telyonok*. Here he succeeds in becoming a millionaire but discovers that money in a Communist society brings him no power. Again the hero's adventures are played out against scenes of Soviet life. While equally entertaining, the satire here is more biting. Its target is Soviet bureaucracy, philistinism, and greed.

The wonderful humor in I. and P.'s novels —the absurd comic situations and clever use of language—accounts for their continued popularity. There have been numerous stage and film versions of their books in the Soviet Union and a movie adaptation of *Dvenadtsat stulev* in the U.S. (Mel Brooks's *The Twelve Chairs,* 1970). Although much of I. and P.'s satire is topical, their works contain pithy observations about human foibles that give them universal appeal and meaning. Officially criticized for insufficient ideological militancy, I. and P.'s works express a deeply humane and warmhearted attitude toward life.

FURTHER WORKS: *Svetlaya lichnost* (1928); *1001 den; ili, Novaya Shakherezada* (1929); *Kak sozdavalsya Robinzon* (1933); *Ravnodushie* (1933); *Silnoe chuvstvo* (1933); *Direktivny bantik* (1934); *Bezmyatezhnaya tumba* (1935); *Chuvstvo mery* (1935); *Chudesnye gosti* (1935); *Poezdki i vstrechi* (1936); *Tonya* (1937). I.: *Zapisnye knizhki* (1939). P.: *Radosti Megasa* (1926); *Bez doklada* (1927); *Sluchay s obezyanoy* (1927); *Stsenarii* (1943)

BIBLIOGRAPHY: Zavalishin, V., *Early Soviet Writers* (1958), pp. 342–44; Struve, G., *Russian Literature under Lenin and Stalin, 1917–1953* (1971), pp. 165–67; Wright, J., "Ostap Bender as a Picaroon," *PPNCFL,* 25, Part 1 (1974), 265–68; Friedberg, M., Introduction to I. and P., *The Twelve Chairs* (1961), pp. v–xii

SONA STEPHAN HOISINGTON

ILLYÉS, Gyula

Hungarian poet, essayist, dramatist, and novelist, b. 2 Nov. 1902, Rácegres-puszta

Born into a mixed marriage—his father was a Catholic, his mother a Calvinist—and amid feudal surroundings (his parents were estate servants), I. was exposed to the best blend of tradition and rebellion. Early in his youth, he joined the revolutionary army; when the short-lived dictatorship of the proletariat in Hungary collapsed (1919) and I. was forced into exile, he was barely seventeen. After short stays in Vienna and Berlin, I. arrived in Paris, where he found a second home. While working as a miner, a bookbinder, and also as a teacher, he studied at the Sorbonne. His exposure to French culture made a deep and lasting impression on him. Surrealism (q. v.) was the literary fashion of the time, and I.'s first poems, appearing in émigré papers, bore its stamp, with an undertone of revolutionary zeal.

Returning to Hungary in 1926, I. went to work as a clerk, but his driving passion was writing. The grand old man of Hungarian literature, Mihály Babits (q.v.), offered him space in the avant-garde monthly *Nyugat*; I.'s poems were received with skeptical interest. Here was a young poet who addressed himself to burning Hungarian problems with a surrealistic style. The country reeked of feudalism: a thousand aristocrats and a dozen bishops owned more than half of the land; the agrarian laborers were semiserfs; and the independent peasantry as well as the industrial workers were in the shackles of the Horthy regime. In his writings I. presented the oppressed life of the peasantry vividly, warmly, and also sarcastically.

In his first work, a collection of poems, *Nehéz föld* (1928; heavy earth), he lamented the plight of the poor peasants and expressed his dismay with the feudal establishment. But he dealt it his strongest blow with the nonfiction prose work *Puszták népe* (1936; *People of the Puszta,* 1967). In this masterfully written book, I. recollected the events of his youth on one of the *pusztas* (feudal hamlets) where the peasants lived in subhuman conditions. This book aroused the national conscience and shattered the romantic belief that the peasantry would regenerate the Hungarian nation. A strong movement was born—populism for radical reform. I. fought so hard for the rights of the peasants to a better life that in 1945 he was elected to the Hungarian Parliament.

After the Communist coup d'état in 1947, I.'s individualistic and anti-Marxist views made him the target of Communist zealots, and he was silenced for a while. But in the mid-1950s, when the writers again appeared on the scene as the stormbirds of the revolution, he courageously declared: "I, who gave voice to the voiceless,/Let me express the mute torment again . . . ." And during the 1956 revolt he published a poem (written in 1951) that is regarded as the Hungarian poem of the century: "Egy mondat a zsarnokságról" ("One Sentence on Tyranny," 1968). It is a majestic indictment of the torture suffered by spirit and intellect in a totalitarian state.

After the uprising was crushed, I. was silenced again and was even investigated by the Hungarian secret police. Yet he was not muted. First he continued to write for his literary drawer; later, in a somewhat more relaxed climate, for the public.

In the third phase of his life, I. perhaps mellowed, but he gave up none of his beliefs. Using the stage for his message, I. exposed man's ambitions. Most of his dramas deal with the Hungarian past. His principal theme is that the cause of all human tragedy is lack of freedom and the misinterpretation of the meaning of liberty.

Haunted and anguished throughout his life by the fate of his people, I. is obsessed with the future of the Hungarian nation. In one of his dramas, *Tiszták* (1969; puritans), set in French Provence, I. worries about the small ethnic groups who are not regarded as important or needed on the world stage. The play is about the Provençals of the Middle Ages who are lectured by a papal visitor for their heretical views and told that they, like many of the ancient nations, could disappear from the face of the earth if they do not give up their stubborn insistence on "freedom."

FURTHER WORKS: *Sarjurendek* (1931); *Három öreg* (1932); *Hősökről beszélek* (1933); *Ifjuság* (1934); *Oroszország* (1934); *Szálló egek alatt* (1935); *Petőfi* (1936; *Sándor Petőfi,* 1973); *Rend a romokban* (1937); *Magyarok* (1938); *Külön világban* (1939); *Ki a magyar?* (1939); *Lélek és kenyér* (1940); *Összegyüjtött versek* (1943); *Csizma az asztalon* (1941); *Mint a darvak* (1942); *Válogatott versek* (1943); *A tű foka* (1944); *Egy év* (1945); *Honfoglalók között* (1945); *Hunok Párizsban* (1946); *Kiáltvány a parasztság művelődése ügyében* (1946); *Szembenézve* (1947); *Tizenkét nap Bulgáriában* (1947); *Összes versei* (1947); *Franciaországi változások* (1947); *A*

lélekbúvár (1948); *Két kéz* (1950); *Két férfi* (1950); *Ozorai példa* (1952); *Válogatott versek* (1952); *Tüz-viz* (1952); *Föltámadott a tenger* (1952); *Fáklyaláng* (1953); *Tűvetevők* (1953); *Dózsa György* (1956); *Hetvenhét magyar népmese* (1956); *Három dráma* (1957); *Kézfogások* (1957); *Uj versek* (1961); *Nem volt elég* (1962); *Másokért egyedül* (1963); *Ingyen lakoma* (1964); *Tűz vagyok: Petőfi élete* (1964); *Hajszálgyökerek* (1971); *Iránytüvel* (1975); *Szives kalauz* (1975); *Összegyüjtött versek* (1977); *Összegyüjtött drámák* (1977); *Uj testamentum* (1977); *Az Éden elvesztése* (1978); *Beatrice* (1979); *Homokzsák* (1979). FURTHER VOLUMES IN ENGLISH: *Once upon a Time: Forty Hungarian Folktales* (1964); *A Tribute to G. I.* (1968); *Selected Poems* (1971)

BIBLIOGRAPHY: Klaniczay, T., et al., *History of Hungarian Literature* (1964), pp. 254–57; Reményi, J., *Hungarian Writers and Literature* (1964), pp. 383–87; Gömöri, G., *Polish and Hungarian Poetry* (1966), pp. 70–75; Follain, J., "The Poetry of G. I.," Tabori, P., "Ten Encounters with G. I.," and Kabdebo, T., "Notes on G. I.," in Kabdebo, T., and Tabori, P., eds., *A Tribute to G. I.* (1968), pp. 7–8, 9–19, 137–45; Beládi, M., "The Seventy Years of G. I.," *NHQ,* 48 (1972), 83–89; Ferenczi, L., "G. I., Poet of a Nation," *NHQ,* No. 68 (1977), 54–65; Nagy, K., "G. I.'s Poetry of Hope" *CARHS,* 5, 2 (1978), 53–61

IMRE KOVACS

ILOKO LITERATURE
See Philippines Literature

IMAGISM

Imagism began as a literary movement early in the 20th c.; its critical manifesto, "Imagisme" (the final *e* was later dropped) appeared in *Poetry* in 1913. The term was coined by Ezra Pound (q.v.) in part as a counter to the host of literary "ismes" attracting attention on the Continent, but also to distinguish poems written in accordance with a stringent technical criterion and a theory of the image. Pound may have been the foremost publicist and practitioner of imagism, but his ideas were influenced by T. E. Hulme (1883–1917) and Ford Madox Ford (q.v.), both of whom he met in London in 1909.

The main impetus for the movement was the desire to break free from the current, worn-out poetic modes, to create a poetry independent of the uncritical imitations of late Victorian romanticism. Imagists objected to sentimentality and provincialism, to vague and pretentious language, to commonplace and ill-defined ideas, and to predictable and artificial metrical forms. They advocated (1) direct treatment of the subject, (2) precision and concentration of language, (3) invention of new rhythms, and (4) adherence to a "Doctrine of the Image." Pound found precedents for his aesthetic in such eclectic sources as classical, Oriental, and medieval poetry.

The imagist doctrine was based on a double concept of the image. Not merely a visual sense impression, the image involves the perception of relationships. It forms in the moment of awareness, what Pound called the moment of metamorphosis, when one thing is understood to be like another. Faces in the gloom are perceived as "petals on a wet, black bough." On a more complex level, imagism works by ideogram; concrete particulars are juxtaposed in order to suggest commonality. The imagist avoids abstractions and instead cites specific examples, for instance: cherry, flamingo, rust, and sunset. The reader is left to infer their relationship, in this case, redness. The world is thus viewed as dynamic patterns of correspondences, and the very act of reading imagist poetry mirrors the creative process.

In their determination to reform poetry, the imagists were attempting to meet the challenge posed by science. In a skeptical age, scientific rationalism had claimed that it was the only reliable approach to knowledge, the final arbiter of truth. By combining the scientific methods of accurate observation and precise definition with the traditional poetic methods of analogy and intuition, the imagists sought to restore the credibility of poetry as a significant source of information about human experience.

Hilda Doolittle (q.v.), Richard Aldington (1892–1962), and F. S. Flint (1885–1960) were founding members of the group. They were represented along with only eight others, including James Joyce and William Carlos Williams (qq.v.), in Pound's anthology *Des Imagistes* (1914). Amy Lowell (q.v.) adopted the term and began publicizing imagism in America. Her three anthologies, *Some Imagist Poets* (1915, 1916, 1917), were limited to the work of three American and three British poets: Hilda Doolittle, John Gould Fletcher (1886–1950), and herself as well as Aldington, Flint, and D. H. Lawrence (q.v.).

Believing that Amy Lowell had misunderstood the doctrine of the image and neglected his critical principles, Pound dissociated himself from her group, calling it "Amygism." In 1914 the poetics of imagism were translated by Pound into vorticism, a new movement emphasizing the dynamic energy of art and including such writers and artists as Wyndham Lewis (q.v.) and Henri Gaudier-Brzeska (1891–1915). Thus, imagism continued to inform Pound's work and to exert a considerable influence on modern poetry.

BIBLIOGRAPHY: Lowell, A., *Tendencies in Modern American Poetry* (1917); Hughes, G., *Imagism and Imagists* (1931); Coffman, S., *Imagism* (1951); Pound, E., "A Retrospect," *Literary Essays of Ezra Pound* (1954), pp. 3–15; Kenner, H., "Imagism," *The Pound Era* (1972), pp. 173–91

JO BRANTLEY BERRYMAN

INDIAN LITERATURE

Traditionally, India has been regarded more as a cohesive cultural entity than as a single political one, a "nation of confederate sovereignty" —with the cohesiveness of a "unity in diversity." In the past four centuries two foreign powers invaded India—the Moghuls and the British—established two empires, and left behind their contributions to the composite Indian culture.

Because of the numerous political changes in the Indian subcontinent—the variety of governing authorities in British India, the creation of the independent states of India and Pakistan in 1947, the declaration of Bangladesh as an independent nation in 1971—and the realignment of Indian states along linguistic lines and also across linguistic regions, it is difficult, or rather too early, narrowly to define what is state or national literature.

Dravidian, the oldest language family on the subcontinent, has produced four literary languages in the south: Tamil, the oldest; Kannada; and subsequently Telugu from Kannada, and Malayalam from Tamil. In the north the Dravidian dialects, coalescing with the dialects of Indo-Aryans, contributed to the growth of the language of composite Dravido-Aryan culture and became known as Sanskrit. A great many Dravidian dialects of northern India have survived in limited areas.

Sanskrit, the mother of Indo-Aryan languages, one of the oldest languages belonging to the Indo-European language family, and the classical language of Hinduism, gave rise to a number of dialects, which have become the modern Indo-Aryan languages of north India, viz., Assamese, Bengali, and Oriya in the east; Maithali, Hindi, Nepali, and Marathi in the center; Rajasthani Gujarati, and Sindhi in the west; and Punjabi and Kashmiri in the north. (A dialect of Oriya transplanted to Sri Lanka became known as Sinhala.)

Sanskrit occupies a unique place in Indian culture because of its pervasive influence on all the Indian religions (including Buddhism, Jainism, Sikhism), and on all the Indian languages, both Indo-Aryan and Dravidian. Sanskrit is recognized as the language of subcontinental cultural unity and also as the source for new creative, critical, and research vocabulary, like Greek and Latin in European culture. Sanskrit, therefore, functions not only as a sacred language of a continuing tradition but also as a secular language of culture. It is being cultivated as a living official language in the form of Modern Sanskrit, like Hebrew in Israel.

When the imperial Moghuls and the imperial British superimposed Persian and English as the languages of the court and administration, Indians acquired proficiency in these studied second languages, first as a means for securing patronage and jobs, and second for producing extraterritorial literature.

Urdu, on the other hand, emerged as a mongrel speech of the soil in the 17th c. in the marketplaces and the military camps around Delhi. Urdu is basically Hindi in structure, Turkish and Persian in vocabulary, written in Arabic script. Because of the script, it is often erroneously identified as a "Muslim language." Urdu became the medium of Indo-Moghul synthesis and was vigorously cultivated for literary expression by 18th-c. Indians regardless of religion. During the freedom movement, however, Urdu became more and more subjected to Persian and Arabic influences by Muslim writers, thus making it less intelligible to non-Muslim Indians. Urdu is one of the official languages of India; it is also the state language of Pakistan.

In terms of languages and literature, the Indian subcontinent may be compared to the European continent. What is national literature in Europe is state literature in India, and what is national literature in India is the literature of the European continent.

Indian literature has been studied in terms of individual languages, and there are as many surveys as there are languages producing literature. In a nation that has eighteen major official languages used for administration as well as for literary writing, about a hundred minor languages, each spoken by over a million people, and two thousand dialects, the question of national literature becomes more of a composite idea than the usual philological approach to language and its literature.

The literary tradition in India has had a three-layered existence: there is regional literature in regional languages; pan-Indian literature in the dominant language of the civilization—Sanskrit, Pali, Tamil, or English—without reference to the regional language; and a continuously flourishing oral literature among the Adivasis, the tribal hill people, which in recent years has been studied as Adivasi literature (the proto-Dravidian, pre-Aryan peoples, scattered throughout the subcontinent, have not only been granted cultural autonomy but have also been encouraged to cultivate their arts and literature).

Among the major influences affecting the mental climate of the Indian subcontinent in the 20th c. are the "English education" and exposure to European culture; the internal movements for reformation and renascence; the impact of Marxist ideas and the Russian Revolution; the freedom movement and the traumatic experiences of Gandhi's nonviolent-resistance doctrine of Satyagraha (Sanskrit: "truth-fire" or "truth-force"), and, in recent decades, UNESCO's "Major Project for the Mutual Appreciation of Cultural Values of East and West."

Among all these movements perhaps no single one has been as overpowering as the "English education." It produced generations of Indians aware of the European tradition and alienated from their own culture. But this education also led to an intense nationalism in the early decades of the century. While English education has been a blessing in making possible instant communication of literary moods, attitudes, techniques, and values from European and American literature, the mental subordination has also prevented Indian creative minds from generating major literary movements of their own. Jawaharlal Nehru, who had the best of English educations, having reeducated himself in the British prisons during nine terms, saw that Indians were so mentally conditioned that they perceived the world with "English eyes and English prejudices." Some writers are now beginning to see that a true renascence can only come to India not through imitation but through assimilation within the consciousness of national tradition.

Rabindranath Tagore

With the award of the Nobel Prize for literature in 1913, the Bengali Rabindranath Tagore (q.v.), who also wrote in English, became known internationally as the major literary figure of modern India. He was the first Asian writer to receive that prize.

At the beginning of the 20th c., India produced two outstanding men of striking personalities who resurrected distinct aspects of the Indian culture and ways of life: Gandhi, with his spiritual austerity and renunciation, ventured into social reform and practical action to achieve political independence; while Tagore, asserting the intellectual aristocracy of the Upanishadic tradition, aimed at personal, intellectual, and artistic freedom.

During his long and active life, Tagore was prodigious in his literary creation. In his poems he dramatized man's quest to understand the spirit within and its relation to the Supreme Spirit in the manner of the *rishis*, or sages, of the Upanishads, breathing the mystics' "divine frenzy." The spirit of humanism pervades his plays. His fiction presents conflicts arising from the changing mores within the traditional orthodox society, but he is never without compassion for the individual.

Tagore became an institution in India, like Goethe in Europe. Non-Bengali Indians read Tagore in translation in other Indian languages or in English. Yet there did not emerge a distinct Tagore school in literature. The influence of Tagore lies in his quickening of the literary impulse in other Indian writers, his serving as a catalytic guru who gave others confidence to write about Indian life and portray Indian values and conflicts. Even Indo-English writers who were slavishly copying European authors began to assert their identity, taking cues from Tagore's bold independence. Tagore's romanticism, however, soon gave way to the new wave of social realism that began to affect the literary scene in India in the 1930s, in the form of the Progressive movement.

Poetry

The spirit of nationalism generated in the 19th c. pervaded Indian poetry in the early decades of the 20th. Following Tagore's enlightened nationalism, many poets expressed deeply felt patriotic sentiments and perceptions of national ideals in varying moods and shades. Outstanding among them were Subramania Bharati, Vallathol Narayana Menon, Sarojini

Naidu, Muhammad Iqbal, and Aurobindo Ghose (qq.v.).

The Tamil poet Bharati's patriotism merged with his mysticism. In his poetry, he moved freely from the love of Mother India to the worship of the "Mother of Livingkind." Patriotism and freedom became essentially a state of being in a dynamic person, aware of spiritual possibilities. Some of Bharati's lyrics also depict the perennial values of the household, the tender graces of childhood, and the delicate beauty of womanhood.

Vallathol Narayana Menon, Malayalam poet and critic, was a classical scholar steeped in Sanskrit poetry. His patriotic feelings developed into a deep and abiding love for ancient Indian culture and its poetry. It was his mission to make the classical vision part of contemporary consciousness. Along with his associates, Kumaran Asan (1873–1924) and Ullur Parameswara Aiyar (1877–1949), he ushered in the modern era in Malayalam poetry. His poems move from a romantic to a realistic approach to life.

Sarojini Naidu, educated in India and England, was one of the most gifted Indo-English poets India produced in the 20th c. Acquiring felicity of expression in English, her third language, she used it with consummate skill, creating exquisite lyrics marked by haunting rhythms and lilting Oriental melodies. Like her predecessor Toru Dutt (1856–1877), who died before she could fulfill her promise, in her early life Sarojini Naidu demonstrated how a young woman could write poetry with ease and emotion and still be Indian, whereas most Indo-English poets up to her time were simply imitating British poets. Critics found in her early verse poetic qualities in "heaped measure" and praised her poems for enriching the English language. In her last volume, *The Broken Wing* (1917), her lyricism bordered on mystical ecstasy. Although she lived thirty-two years after this volume was published, she did not write verse during the long political struggle of that era, in which she was very active. Apparently she realized that for true poetic creation one needs to write in one's mother tongue.

Muhammad Iqbal, a Muslim poet writing in Urdu and Persian, is regarded by Pakistanis as their national poet. His early poems, written in Urdu, celebrated Indian nationalism and the freedom movement. These poems, written before he left Punjab for England, echo the sentiments and vocabulary of the Persian Sufi mystics and the English romantic poets. Iqbal's European visit restructured his thinking. He discovered that European nationalism resulted in jingoistic adventures into other people's land and that colonialism gave rise to intense economic monopoly and rivalry. Disillusioned, he turned to theological nationalism, claiming that Islam was the answer for the people of southwestern Asia. To make his pan-Islamic dream known to other Muslim countries, he abandoned Urdu and began writing in Persian.

Among 20th-c. Indian poets, Aurobindo Ghose (later Sri Aurobindo) alone is a true Vedic seer-poet; he resurrected a whole way of life from the substratum of Indian culture, a way of life in which literary expression became only incidental to mystic visions and enlightenment. Because he spent his early years in England, insulated from Indian schools, culture, and language, English became, for all practical purposes, his mother tongue.

In the 1890s Ghose felt that the Indian freedom movement was misled by a feeble group of empire-supporting Indian politicians who rather timidly advocated some moderate demands for reform within the colonial system. The British considered all his writings as seditious. During one of his imprisonments, he experienced mystical visions, which completely altered his attitude to life. In French-controlled Pondicherry he became a master yogi and established an ashram. In his writings Sri Aurobindo formulated a metaphysics and a system of spiritual discipline that he called "purna yoga" (integral yoking), or reintegrating experience and human personality.

He also wrote five plays in blank verse, but these are more dramatic poems than plays. In all these works his major theme is that love is divine and has redemptive power, which, he predicts, will one day deliver the world. In his later works Sri Aurobindo developed a technique for his visionary poems, which he discussed in *The Future Poetry* (1953)—something bordering on telepathic communication of meaning through rhythmic sound in concentrated imagery, like the Vedic mantras.

Apart from the major pan-Indian poets, there were many other regional poets, who, absorbing the various influences coming to India in the 1930s, began to express themselves in their own languages in a variety of moods and techniques. Although they are too numerous to cover comprehensively, some significant ones deserve to be singled out.

Early 20th-c. Hindi literature was dominated by the *Chhaya-vada* movement, or Indian romanticism, with an attitude of wonder at nature and with Vedantic synthesis as a theme. Progressive ideas were ushered in by the *Pragati-vada* movement, or Indian realism, which pointed to the ruthless amorality of nature and sympathized with the sufferings of the exploited and downtrodden. The pioneers of the *Chhaya-vada* movement were Suryakant Tripathi (pseud.: Nirala, 1896–1961) and Sumitranand Pant (b. 1900). Although the novelist Premchand (q.v.) gave *Pragati-vada* a progressive, liberal slant, it soon became the closed shop of an explicitly Marxist-oriented group, Yashpal (b. 1904), Nagarjun (b. 1911), and Rameshawar Shukla (pseud.: Anchal, b. 1915) are some of the leading writers of this group.

Mohan Singh's (b. 1905) early poems in Punjabi were considered progressive; his later poetry has a definite Marxist stamp. Amrita Pritam (b. 1919), a successful woman poet, is popular on both sides of the India-Pakistan border in the Punjab. Her works are remarkable for their spontaneity and musicality.

A group of Marathi poets set out to reclaim poetry from the extravagances into which it had fallen and to make it speak to everyday issues. A. R. Deshpande (pseud.: Anil, b. 1901) advocated free verse to liberate Marathi poetry from its stiltedness. B. S. Mardekar (1909–1956), influenced by Eliot and Pound (qq.v.), wrote sensitive poetry expressing the bleak life of a frustrated man.

In eastern India, the "people's poets" writing in Oriya, Sachidananda Routray (b. 1916) and Anant Patnaik (b. 1913), were mouthpieces of the Progressive Party's attitudes and values. Writing in Bengali, Buddhadev Bose (b. 1908) called for Westernization as a means of modernization, while the more radical Sudhindranath Dutt (1901–1960), who considered himself a "nihilist," advocated free inquiry into all values, traditional or modern. Kazi Nazrul Islam (q.v.) began his literary career with short stories, but gained fame with his heroic poems and popular songs glorifying the freedom movement. With his uncompromising opposition to oppression and injustice, he became a "people's poet" in both western and eastern Bengal (now Bangladesh).

The swing to realism in Telugu poetry was led by Srirangam Srinivas Rao (pseud.: Sri Sri, b. 1910). He had no admiration for the Taj Mahal, for instance, but saw it only as a monument to forced labor and exploitation of artists. Dattatreya Ramachandra Bendre (b. 1896), a pioneer in modern Kannada poetry, drew on folklore and traditional ballads in his approach to social realism. In Malayalam, G. Shankar

Kurup (b. 1901) combined symbolism with social realism.

Indo-English poets experimented with a variety of techniques taken over from British and American poetry. Outstanding among them are Nissim Ezekiel (b. 1924) and the outspoken woman poet Kamala Das (b. 1934). Most assertive among the champions of Indo-English literature is P. Lal (b. 1928), with his Writers' Workshop in Calcutta.

Modern Sanskrit poetry is showing vitality. Important achievements are Jitendra Nath Bhattacharya's (dates n.a.) two short eulogies on Gandhi and Tagore, G. C. Jhala's (dates n.a.) elegies and descriptive verses, and Mathuranatha Kavi Sastri's (dates n.a.) poems about nature and modern technology. Some Sanskrit poets have revived classical subjects, while others have written on contemporary political events. In *Bharati gita* (19??; song of India) Lady Lakshmi Ammal (dates n.a.) calls on Mother India to energize her children to a fruitful renascence. In *Satyagraha gita* (1932; song of satyagraha) Kshama Rao (dates n.a.) romantically treats political developments in graceful epic measures. What is most significant in these works is that Modern Sanskrit—having achieved a flexibility, a style distinct from classical diction, imagery, and mood—is emerging as a secular language capable of expressing modern aesthetic concerns.

Drama

Modern drama in India has had to compete with regional popular and folk theater. In some states folk theater has an unbroken tradition of dramatizing events from the Indian classics, sacred and secular; these dramatic presentations are like the miracle and mystery plays of medieval Europe. Most often they are unscripted and depend upon the ability of the actors to develop and sustain the well-known story through extemporaneous dialogue. These plays frequently include song, dance, and mime. In Kerala and Karnataka there are traditional dance-dramas, called Kathakali and Yakshagana respectively, with elaborate costuming, skillful dancing, and stylized acting. In states like Mysore and Orissa, where royalty formerly gave patronage to classical learning, many classical plays in the original language or in modern translations appealed to sophisticated audiences.

When the modern Indian theater emerged in the early decades of the 20th c., it evinced a strong passion for nationalism and a still stronger zeal for social reform. Such a transformation was precipitated by the spread of English education, and through it, the study of European drama.

Rabindranath Tagore dominated the Bengali stage early in the century, with comedies, tragedies, farces, symbolic plays, and operalike dance dramas. He also introduced new techniques of acting. The spirit of humanism pervades his plays. The Bengali dramatist Mukunda Das (dates n.a.) introduced the Swadeshi political philosophy, which called for India to produce its own goods rather than being merely a market for industrialized countries, into one of his plays, *Jatra-wala* (1905; pilgrim). Saratchandra Chatterji's (q.v.) dramatizations of some of his novels were popular on the Bengali stage because of their acute social criticism.

The Bengali theater influenced the neighboring Assamese and Oriya stages. Lakshminath Bezbarua (1868–1938), who married into the Tagore family, brought Tagore's innovations to Assamese drama. His romantic plays depict feudal ways of life. Jyoti Prasad Agarwal (dates n.a.) wrote lyrical plays about romantic love, incorporating music and dance. Writing in Oriya, Godavaris Mishra (1888–1956) and Ashwani Kumar Ghosh (dates n.a.) introduced modern techniques and themes. They turned from mythological stories to social, historical, and biographical subjects. Kalicharan Patnaik (b. 1900), a musician and poet, wrote lyrical plays.

In western India, the commercial city of Bombay generated a lively audience, which helped activate the Gujarati and Marathi theaters. A powerful Gujarati dramatist is the prolific Manilal Tribhuvandas (pseud.: Pagal, dates n.a.), who wrote about a hundred plays, dealing mainly with social problems, filled with earthy humor. Umashankar Jethalal Joshi (b. 1911), in a series of one-act plays, depicted the variety of Gujarati village life.

Many successful plays were written by enterprising Marathi dramatists. K. P. Khadilkar (pseud.: Kakasaheb, 1872–1948) established a dramatic society in Poona in 1905, for which he wrote many plays. In *Keechaka-vada* (1910; the slaying of Keechaka) Khadilkar allegorically satirized the Governor-General, Lord Curzon. The play was banned by the British authorities but was revived by the Congress ministry in 1937. Khadilkar's powerful historical plays were eclipsed by the musical plays of Shreepad Krishna Kolhatkar (1871–1934), who combined satirical comedy and romantic tangles with avowed social criticism. The Marathi stage reached maturity in the plays of Bhargavaram Vithal Varerkar (pseud.: Mama Varerkar, 1883–1964). He was a tireless experimenter in theme and technique; he dealt with such diverse topics as politics, the evils of the dowry system, the forced conversion by Christian missionaries, and the problems of the untouchables. His later plays are in a more realistic mode. Motiram Gajanan Rangnekar (b. 1907) introduced elegant drawing-room comedies to the Marathi stage, with lively dialogue and only a few songs.

Urdu is deficient in drama, since the language was generally a vehicle for Muslim sentiment and there is no Islamic dramatic tradition. After 1930, when Indian dramatists started using social and political themes for plays, Urdu writers saw the potential of the theater. Much Urdu talent, however, was channeled into the more popular and lucrative film and radio industries after the establishment of the broadcasting system in 1935.

In the absence of a vigorous dramatist, the Hindi stage had languished. In the early 20th c. some experiments were made in verse and fantasy plays, but without much success. Among dramatists who later attempted to gain an audience are Upendranath Ask (b. 1910), Ramkumar Varma (b. 1905), Lakshminarayan Mishra (b. 1903), and Bharatabhushan Agarwal (b. 1919). Mohan Rakesh (q.v.), after publishing a number of novels and short stories, turned to the theater and wrote controversial but innovative plays: *Asadh ka ek din* (1958; *A Day in Ashadh,* 1969) and *Lahon ke rajhans* (1962; *The Swans of the Great Waves,* 1973) treat classical themes, while *Adhe adhure* (1969; *Halfway House,* 1971) portrays the disintegration of traditional Indian family life under the impact of independence and an industrial economy.

T. P. Kailasam (1884–1945) was an innovator on the Kannada stage. He used humor to expose current social prejudices. Kailasam also wrote plays in English, dramatizing events from the epics. Verse plays by the poets D. R. Bendre and Govinda Pai (b. 1883) were enthusiastically produced by amateur dramatic groups. In recent times Girish Ragunath Karnad (b. 1938), a Rhodes scholar at Oxford (1960–63), returned to India to write for the Kannada stage. He has been in the forefront of the New Drama in India. His *Yayati* (1961; Yayati) is an existentialist (q.v.) play retelling an Indian classical legend in terms of contemporary life and dealing with the problem of individual responsibility. *Tughlaq* (1964; Tughlaq) explores the paradox of the idealistic 14th-c. sultan of Delhi, Muhammad bin Tughlaq; his rule in north India became a spectacular failure, but his ideas were nevertheless far in advance of his time. The novelist Kota Shivaram Karanth (q.v.) has also made important contributions to the Kannada stage.

Sanskrit dramatists were not far behind in presenting contemporary conflicts and concerns. *Manoharam dinam* (1941; lovely day) by A. R. Hebare (dates n.a.) presents schoolboys maneuvering to make the principal declare a school holiday. Contemporary women's domestic problems were dramatized in *Aranya-rodana* (1949; forest roaring) by Sita Devi (dates n.a.). Tiru Venkatacharya (dates n.a.) presents the conflict of an irate officer at home and in his office in *Amarsha mahima* (1951; sway of temper). Surendra Mohan Panchatirtha's (dates n.a.) play *Vanik-suta* (1955; merchant's daughter) depicts the wooing of a young rich widow by a Hindu and a Buddhist. The theme of romantic love was used by Sundersena Sarma (dates n.a.) in *Prema vijaya* (1943; triumph of love). C. Venkataramanayya (dates n.a.) composed a long allegorical play *Jiva-sanjivani nataka* (1949; drama of life after life) on the efficacy of Ayurvedic medicine.

There is a paucity of good actable Indo-English plays, although many writers have written English plays in both verse and prose. Harindranath Chattopadhyaya (b. 1898), brother of Sarojini Naidu, wrote a number of plays on contemporary life, collected in *Five Plays* (1937). His *Siddhartha: The Man of Peace* (1956) is a historical drama about the Buddha.

The dancer Bharati Sarabhai's (b. 1912) first play, *The Well of the People* (1943), is a symbolic, poetic pageant. A widow, unable to make a pilgrimage to the holy places in the Himalayas, decides to spend all her savings on a well for the *harijans* (untouchables) in the village. Her second play, *Two Women* (1952), portrays the dual personalities of each woman —what she is and what she would like to become—and contrasts the modern and traditional aspects of their lives.

S. Fyzee Rahamin's (dates n.a.) play *Daughter of Ind* (1940) treats the love of an untouchable girl for her master, an idealistic Englishman. Pratap Sharma's (b. 1939) *A Touch of Brightness* (1968) portrays the degradation and corruption in the infamous red-light district in Bombay called "The Cages." Asif Currimbhoy (b. 1928) experimented with a variety of techniques. *The Tourist Mecca* (1961) portrays star-crossed lovers who in the end passively accept separate continued existence. Currimbhoy frequently blends the satirical and the serious.

Fiction

Fiction is the dominant genre in 20th-c. Indian literature. It is also, unlike in Europe, one of the oldest, going back as far as the 4th c. B.C.

With the exposure to European fiction, Indian writers adopted its forms and techniques and produced innumerable volumes of short stories and novels. At the beginning of the 20th c. fiction writers for the most part patronizingly depicted social situations. But in the 1930s, social realism began to take hold, and the majority of Indian writers of fiction may be classified as "social chroniclers," exposing a decadent society emerging from feudalism into the industrial age.

Premchand popularized social realism in India. He wrote in Urdu until 1914, then switched to Hindi. He was at his best in his many short stories. In the novel *Godan* (1936; *The Gift of a Cow*, 1968) he describes the problems of peasant India with striking realism. Premchand is regarded as the Gorky (q.v.) of India because of his reformist zeal.

Kota Shivaram Karanth used social realism to present the life of tribal people in the southwest coastal region of Karnataka; he also wrote many lyrical novels in Kannada.

The fictional representation of tribal life was carried forward by Gopinath Mohanty (q.v.). In his novels and short stories in Oriya, he uses a rich and powerful folk idiom to depict the common people against Orissa's picturesque setting.

In Bengal, writers like Saratchandra Chatterji abandoned Tagore's sweet music of humanity to portray realistically urban middle-class characters. Bibhuti-Bhusan Banerji (q.v.) concentrated his vision on a Bengali rural family in stark poverty in his haunting novel *Pather panchali* (1929; *Pather Panchali: Song of the Road*, 1968). Manik Bandopadhyaya (1908–1956), born in East Bengal (now Bangladesh), presents such nontraditional characters as cheaters and the sexually frustrated. *Putul nacher itikath* (1936; dance of the dolls) depicts characters who are thoroughly disillusioned. *Padma nadir majhi* (1936; *Padma River Boatman*, 1973) portrays the life of boatmen, fishermen, palm-tappers, weavers, and peasants.

The most aggressive champion of social realism is Mulk Raj Anand (q.v.), who in his tremendous output of fiction in English has proved himself an indefatigable polemicist. He won early recognition with *Untouchable* (1935) and *Coolie* (1936). Focusing on the destitute and downtrodden, Anand exposes social injustices, and shows great compassion for the unfortunate victims.

Another powerful writer who has achieved international fame is the Malayalam Thakazhi Sivasankara Pillai (b. 1914); with great skill he portrays varied life styles in the state of Kerala. *Tottiyte makan* (1947; *The Scavenger's Son*, 1970) deals with three generations of scavengers, attacking the social degradation to which they have been subjected. *Rantitangazhi* (1949; *Two Measures of Rice*, 1967), which established Pillai as the foremost novelist in Malayalam, presents the struggles and humiliations of members of outcaste communities who work in the rice fields of Kuttanad. In his novels of maturity Pillai abandons the overriding concern with social realism to concentrate on individuals caught in the web of social conflicts. His most outstanding novel, *Chemmeen* (1956; *Chemmeen*, 1962), portrays the love of a daughter of a Hindu fisherman and a son of a Muslim fish merchant. Social realism is tempered by romance and a deeper human interest.

P. Vaithialingam Akilandam (pseud.: Akilon, b. 1923), writing in Tamil, is another prolific writer of both short stories and novels. His recent novel *Pon malar* (1978; *Flower of Gold*, 1978) tells a touching story of a woman's awesome capacity for self-sacrifice.

Expatriate Indian writers, writing in English, seem to telescope Indian life and its varied conflicts and concerns. Balachandra Rajan (b. 1920), in such novels as *The Dark Dancer* (1958) and *Too Long in the West* (1961), deals mainly with experiences of returning Indians in the process of being reabsorbed into Indian life. John A. Karkala's (b. 1923) *Nightless Nights* (1974) and *Joys of Jayanagara* (1980) are about the problem of rootlessness of Indians living in two worlds. Arthur S. Lall's (b. 1911) *House at Adampur* (1956) and *Seasons of Jupiter* (1958) explore the problem of cultural identity.

A noted writer, G. V. Desani (q.v.), displays a quaint sense of humor and even quainter style in *All About H. Hatterr* (1948). His bold experimentation with language, reminiscent of

Joyce (q.v.), annoyed some and delighted many. Another successful novelist, Kamala Markandaya (q.v.), has attempted an East-West synthesis in works such as *Nectar in a Sieve* (1954), *Some Inner Fury* (1955), *A Silence of Desire* (1960), and *A Handful of Rice* (1966).

The Gandhian revolution was a traumatic experience on the subcontinent, and no writer was left untouched by it. Although the movement was based on the ideals of nonviolence, it was bedeviled by religious conflict, and the partition in 1947 was accompanied by bloody riots and massacres in which millions were killed and millions more left homeless. Both the idealism of the freedom movement and the passions of partition were portrayed in numerous works of fiction. Anant Gopal Sheorey (b. 1911), writing in Hindi, produced an outstanding novel, *Jwalamukhi* (1956; *Volcano*, 1965), which deals with the convulsions of August 1942 with Gandhi's "Quit India" movement; he movingly depicts the sufferings of a great nation on the verge of freedom. Birendra Kumar Bhattacharya's (b. 1924) *Iyanuingam* (1961; Iyanuingam), written in Assamese, presents the volatile situation in eastern India during World War II. Nanak Singh's (b. 1897) Punjabi novel *Ik miyan do talwar* (1961; two swords in one sheath) describes the Ghadar Party, a revolutionary group organized by young Sikhs to throw off the British yoke. The novel re-creates a time when Hindus, Muslims, and Sikhs were united against the common foreign enemy.

The period leading up to and following partition is vividly portrayed in Khushwant Singh's (q.v.) novel of horror, written in English, *Mano Majra* (1956; reprinted as *Train to Pakistan*, 1961). Raja Rao's (q.v.) *Kanthapura* (1938), also written in English, on the other hand, presents a much richer cultural life underneath the sufferings during the nationalist strivings of the 1930s, pointing to the redemptive nature of the suffering. Govind Malhi's (b. 1921) Sindhi novels, from *Ansoo* (1952; tears) to *Desi sen kajan* (1963; one must marry in one's fold), depict the life of Sindhi refugees after the partition and their attempt to rehabilitate themselves.

One of the most delightful writers among Indian novelists, whose strength lies in his humor, is R. K. Narayan (q.v.), who writes in English. In his short stories and novels he depicts the world of an imaginary south-Indian town, Malgudi. Among his fine later novels are *Waiting for the Mahatma* (1955), *The Guide* (1958),

which was also filmed, *The Man-Eater of Malgudi* (1961), *The Sweet-Vendor* (1967), and *A Painter of Signs* (1976).

Shripad Narayan Pendse (b. 1913), a Marathi novelist, portrays the picturesque Konkan coastal region from Bombay to south of Goa and creates memorable comic characters—quarrelsome social misfits who refuse to submit to conventions. Pendse is a feminist; his women demand the right to love and be loved, rather than being mere appendages to their mates. His most popular novel is *Garambicha Bapu* (1952; *Wild Bapu of Garambi,* 1969), dealing with an eccentric old village man.

Ahmed Ali (b. 1912) started writing short stories in Urdu but later switched to English for his novels. *Twilight in Delhi* (1940) portrays the decadence and decline of a Muslim aristocratic family in Delhi at the turn of the century. *Ocean of Night* (1964) is a haunting romantic tale, depicting the life and values of the declining wealthy leisure class and the rise of the newly rich, with their lack of culture.

Vishnu Sakharam Khandekar (q.v.), a Marathi writer, attempts to retell legends of the past in modern terms. His outstanding work of fiction, which powerfully retells an episode from the *Mahabharata*, the ancient Sanskrit epic, is *Yayati* (1959; *Yayati*, 1978).

Raja Rao has achieved honor among Indian novelists for being both profoundly rooted in the Indian tradition and at the same time aware of the cultural springs of the Western tradition. Writing in Kannada, French, and English, he belongs to the intellectual and artistic tradition of the scholar-poet, producing lyrical fiction in the manner of metaphysical fables. *Comrade Kirillov* (1976) is a fine example of his distinctive qualities.

In recent decades many novelists writing in English have produced accomplished work. Manohar Malgonkar (q.v.), in portraying Indian feudal aristocracy or former British military officials, shows a nostalgic fondness for the values of the vanishing past. *A Bend in the Ganges* (1964) deals with the idealism of the freedom movement and the tragedy of partition. Bhabani Bhattacharya (b. 1906) has successfully portrayed contemporary social conflicts: *So Many Hungers* (1947) shows the havoc caused by the Bengal famine of 1943–44; *He Who Rides the Tiger* (1954) is a rather vicious satirical portrait of a bogus holy man.

A new trend in Indo-English literature is the rise of women writers. Among the novelists, two are outstanding. Anita Desai's (b. 1937) first novel, *Cry, the Peacock* (1963), presents a young Indian woman of artistic sensibilities in conflict with her older, worldly husband. In *Voices in the City* (1965) she takes up the interior desolation of contemporary Indian youth who are abandoning traditional values. Kamala Das, also a poet, writes in Malayalam as well as in English. *My Story* (1976), her unorthodox autobiography, written in poetic prose, shocked and dazzled the Indian literary world because of its sensuality. It was followed by the novel *Alphabet of Lust* (1976), about the adventures of a married woman poet in the world of politics; it presents uninhibited ideas about male-female relations.

Another woman writer, who during her residence in India created fiction with the felicity of an insider, is Ruth Prawer Jhabvala (q.v.). Born in Germany of Jewish parents and raised and educated in England, she lived in India for some time after marrying an Indian architect. In her novels she mirrors Indian life in Delhi, portraying with irony and brilliant satire some of the social conflicts of Indians as well as expatriate British and European characters lingering in India in quixotic dreams. Jhabvala has shown an extraordinary ability to see two worlds from an ambivalent position. Yet because of her background she cannot be regarded as an Indo-Anglian writer. Rather, she is an outstanding contemporary representative of a distinct line of Anglo-Indian writers, including Rudyard Kipling, E. M. Forster (qq.v.), and Paul Scott (1920–1978), who wrote of the Indian experience from a non-Indian point of view.

Indian literature in the composite sense is still evolving, mainly because the concept of a truly national literature is yet to develop. The paucity of translations, both within India among the various languages and abroad, has been a hindrance. The Sahitya Akademi (National Academy of Letters) in New Delhi has launched a systematic translation program and has encouraged a comparative approach to the literature of India, and its efforts may produce a more balanced presentation of the major and significant works among the mass of writing that is produced every decade. Additionally, UNESCO's translation program has helped to popularize some of the major authors from the various language regions of India. In view of the complexities of the literary scene, a survey of 20th-c. Indian literature is unavoidably somewhat limited.

BIBLIOGRAPHY: Kumarappan, B., ed., *The Indian Literature of Today: A Symposium* (1947); Publication Division, Government of India, *Indian Drama* (1956); Publication Division, Government of India, *Literature in Modern Indian Languages* (1957); Sahitya Akademi, *Contemporary Indian Literature: A Symposium* (1957; rev. ed., 1959); Kabir, H., *Modern Indian Literature* (1959); Sen, S., *History of Bengali Literature* (1960); Mansinha, M., *History of Oriya Literature* (1962); Srinivasa Iyengar, K. R., *Indian Writing in English* (1962); Chatterji, S., *Languages and Literatures of Modern India* (1963); Bakhtiyar, I., ed., *The Novel in Modern India* (1964); Barua, B. K., *History of Assamese Literature* (1964); Sadiq, M., *A History of Urdu Literature* (1964); Derrett, M.E., *The Modern Indian Novel* (1966); Dwivedi, R. A., *A Critical History of Hindi Literature* (1966); Kabir, H., *The Bengali Novel* (1968); Kripalani, K., *Modern Indian Literature: A Panoramic Glimpse* (1968); Sitapati, G. V., *History of Telugu Literature* (1968); Clark, T. W., ed., *The Novel in India: Its Birth and Development* (1970); Chaitanya, K., *A History of Malayalam Literature* (1971); Dimock, E. C., Jr., et al., eds., *The Literatures of India: An Introduction* (1974); Machwe, P., and Chelishew, E., eds., *Problems of Modern Indian Literature* (1975); Williams, H. M., *Studies in Modern Indian Fiction in English* (2 vols., 1975); Machwe, P., *Four Decades of Indian Literature* (1976); Machwe, P., *Modernity and Contemporary Indian Literature* (1977); Singh, R. S., *The Indian Novel in English* (1977); Williams, H. M., *Indo-Anglian Literature, 1800–1970: A Survey* (1977); special Indian issue, *RNL*, 10 (1979)

JOHN B. ALPHONSO-KARKALA

INDONESIAN LITERATURE

In 1928 the Second Congress of Indonesian Youth proclaimed Malay, which had been for centuries the lingua franca of the region, the language of the Indonesian nationalist movement. The language, since known as Indonesian (*Bahasa Indonesia*), is today the republic's official language and the principal vehicle for innovative literary expression.

The history of modern Indonesian literature must be viewed against the traditional literatures in regional languages. Many traditional theatrical genres remain vigorous. Djakartan *lenong* drama and Javanese *ludrug* are predominantly urban and contemporary in character, while Balinese *gong* drama, Javanese *ketoprak*, Sundanese *gending karesmen*, and Minangkabau *randai* present performances modernized to varying degrees of mainly historical stories.

Attempts at writing modern literature have been made in most of Indonesia's major regional languages, with Javanese and Sundanese exhibiting the greatest fecundity. Writing in these languages differs in some fundamental respects from that in Indonesian. Literature in Indonesian is governed by the values of the urban middle class, is influenced by foreign literatures, appears in expensive, hard-to-get books, and is written in a language most people do not use in their homes and do not learn until they go to school. By contrast, literature in the regional languages tends to deal more with life in rural areas or provincial towns, is stylistically more lively and linguistically more accessible to readers for whom the language concerned is their mother tongue. Regional literatures make more unself-conscious reference to the corpus of symbols, allusions, and literary conventions peculiar to certain regions and already familiar to readers there. Regional literature appears predominantly in magazines, which makes it cheaper and easier to obtain.

In Indonesian

Fiction

Fiction in Indonesian began toward the end of the 19th c. Three main streams contributed to its genesis: popular tales (*penglipur lara*) and narrative verse (*syair*) in Malay, Chinese romances of love and the martial arts, and melodramatic romances in Dutch. Early novels were predominantly romantic melodramas spiced with sensational crimes and supernatural occurrences, but soon a more serious strain of social criticism and nationalist sentiment appeared.

In 1908 the Netherlands Indies government established a state commission for reading matter in vernacular languages, later known as the Balai Pustaka publishing house. In the 1920s and 1930s Balai Pustaka encouraged the writing of fiction, but its editors carefully vetted manuscripts for what they regarded as politically or morally contentious content and insisted on a somewhat pedantic style.

Despite alterations at the insistence of Balai

Pustaka, *Salah asuhan* (1928; a wrong upbringing) by nationalist activist Abdoel Moeis (1898–1959) remains the outstanding achievement of early Indonesian fiction. Racism and the question of cultural identity are the themes pursued with fluent passion in this narrative of a Dutch-educated Indonesian whose admiration for European society renders him contemptuous of his own people. The interaction of Indonesian and European value systems is, in fact, a consistent theme in preindependence novels.

In *Layar terkembang* (1936; sails unfurled), Sutan Takdir Alisjahbana (q.v.) contrasts two sisters, one independent, earnest, and an activist in the women's welfare movement, the other carefree, dreamy, and feminine in the traditional fashion. Takdir criticizes what he sees as the debilitating tendency of Indonesians to glorify the achievements and institutions of the past. *Belenggu* (1940; shackles) by Armijn Pane (1908–1970) also juxtaposes two women, one Western-educated and busily involved in social welfare work, the other a self-sacrificing prostitute who excels in the domestic arts and in singing traditional songs.

Possibly the most original and brilliantly executed work of preindependence fiction is *Sukreni, gadis Bali* (1936; Sukreni, virgin of Bali) by Anak Agung Pandji Tisna (1908–1978). Utilizing the symbols and conventions of traditional Balinese theater, Pandji Tisna portrays the destructive effect of contemporary commercial ethics on Balinese society. The fragility of traditional values is also the theme of *Atheis* (1949; *Atheis*, 1972) by Achdiat Karta Mihardja (q.v.), in which a young man from rural west Java finds that his mystically tinged Islamic faith crumbles before the materialism, Marxism, and atheism of urban radicals.

The Japanese occupation (1942–45) and Indonesia's armed struggle for independence from the Netherlands (1945–49) swept away the romanticism and dilettante nationalism of the contributors to the elite literary journal *Pujangga baru*. Disillusionment and a note of tough realism became evident in the fiction of the late 1940s and 1950s. The short-story writer Idrus (1921–1979), together with the novelist and short-story writer Pramoedya Ananta Toer (q.v.), wrought a revolution in prose style, replacing prewar formality and archness with an expressive but terse and colloquial style.

For both Idrus and Pramoedya, the Japanese occupation and the revolutionary war provided both the setting for their major works and the touchstone against which the characters in these works are tried. Idrus's influential early stories, laced with cynicism and sardonic humor, are collected in *Dari Ave Maria ke jalan lain ke Roma* (1948; from Ave Maria to another road to Rome). Pramoedya's novels are unmatched for their somber exploration of man's alienation and disillusion in the midst of war. *Keluarga gerilya* (1950; guerrilla family) depicts a family that, like Indonesian society, is split geographically and in political allegiance by the revolutionary war. *Bukan pasar malam* (1951; *It's Not an All Night Fair*, 1973) explores the essential loneliness of the human condition, catching the mood of dislocation and dispiritedness that marked the immediate post-revolutionary period.

While the revolutionary war and nationalism remained prominent themes in the fiction of the 1950s, writers increasingly turned their attention to the young republic's burden of social ills. The kaleidoscopic *Senja di Jakarta* (pub. 1964; *Twilight in Jakarta*, 1963) by Mochtar Lubis (b. 1922) is a mosaic of images contrasting Djakarta's corrupt rich with its helpless poor. Achdiat's collection of short stories *Keretakan dan ketegangan* (1956; fissures and tensions) turns a jaundiced eye on the country's hypocritical politicians and nouveaux riches.

From the late 1950s to the mid-1960s literary life was dominated by the conflict between leftist insistence on the social and political utility of art, and liberal insistence on the possibility of divorce between art and organized politics. Before the October 1, 1965 incident (a power grab in which right-wing forces emerged victorious), leftist pressure forced many liberal writers into silence, but after 1965 the tables were turned. A number of writers with leftist sympathies disappeared or were imprisoned and their works banned.

Curiously, the ideological conflict of the 1960s left popular fiction largely untouched. Fueled by newly created mass literacy and accompanied by a decline in the authority of elite literary magazines, popular publishing boomed in the late 1960s and throughout the 1970s. A leading figure in this boom was Motinggo Boesye (b. 1937), whose many novels combine a highly readable narrative style with mild sexual titillation and satirical observation of the urban middle class. Fiction by women writers swelled in quantity and quality. *Pada sebuah kapal* (1973; on a ship) by Nh. Dini (b. 1936) chronicles with rare sensitivity a young woman's disengagement from allegiance to traditional social and marital roles.

The question of national identity, hitherto an almost inevitable element in fiction, virtually disappeared in the works of younger writers but remained prominent in those of the older generation. Sutan Takdir Alisjahbana's *Kalah dan menang* (1978; defeat and victory) explores Indonesia's cultural options against the background of Japan's wartime occupation, rejecting fascism and the authoritarianism of tradition for liberal values adopted from Western Europe. In a short novel, *Sri Sumarah* (1975; Sri Sumarah), Umar Kayam (b. 1932) vividly and sympathetically conveys the spirit of traditional Javanese culture and affirms its continuing relevance in the emerging national culture. Alienation attendant upon cultural deracination and urban life styles brought the appearance of absurdist fiction. *Ziarah* (1969; *The Pilgrim*, 1975) by Iwan Simatupang (1928–1970) is a Kafkaesque study of the encounter between the anarchic artist and the social reality of Indonesia.

Following his release from prison in 1979 Pramoedya Anant Toer published *Bumi manusia* (1980; man's earth), a novel of epic proportions that traces in its central figure the first stirrings of a distinctly modern Indonesian consciousness in the early years of this century. Despite, or perhaps because of, its enthusiastic popular reception, the book was banned by the government in mid-1981.

Poetry

Distinctly innovative poetry began to appear in Indonesia in the 1910s. The European sonnet form was especially popular, but the influence of traditional verse forms remained strong. The poetry of the 1920s and 1930s was marked by an intense and largely reflective romanticism.

Arguably Indonesia's greatest modern poet, and certainly the most prominent figure in preindependence poetry, was Amir Hamzah (1911–1946), whose work is collected in two small volumes, *Nyanyi sunyi* (1937; songs of silence) and *Buah rindu* (1941; fruits of longing). Amir's best poetry expresses the agony of doubt about his Islamic faith.

The iconoclastic verse of Chairil Anwar (q.v.) released Indonesian poetry from the bonds of traditional forms and literary language, exerting a profound influence on postindependence poetry. His works convey a powerful, vitalistic individualism.

Sitor Situmorang (b. 1923) was strongly influenced by Chairil. A sojourn in Europe inspired his early work, represented most notably in the collection *Surat kertas hijau* (1953; a letter on green paper), which reveals an unquiet personality burdened with moral doubts and guilt, nostalgic for the Indonesian homeland. Like Pramoedya Ananta Toer and a number of other writers, Sitor became attracted to socialism in the late 1950s, and his poetry changed markedly. His *Zaman baru* (1961; new era) records the impact upon him of a visit to China. The anguished subjectivism of his earlier work disappeared, to be replaced with unequivocal praise of socialist ideals and achievements.

Zaman baru typifies the unadorned, politically committed verse of the 1960s. After the demise of the Indonesian Communist Party in 1965, the spare and strident poetry of protest against exploitation of workers and peasants gave way to equally strident protests against the illiberalism, economic bungling, and rhetorical humbug of the preceding years. Much poetry of the 1960s and 1970s was strikingly public in character, and no poet more dominated the public scene in the 1970s than the charismatic Rendra (b. 1935). His collections *Blues untuk Bonnie* (1971; *Indonesian Poet in New York,* 1971) and *Pamflet penyair* (1978; *State of Emergency,* 1980) are preeminently declamatory. They contain hard-hitting, sometimes crudely worded attacks on misuse of authority and the degradation of the poor at the hands of the rich.

Drama

Most plays of the 1920s and 1930s were ponderous historical dramas or allegories of nationalist struggle and colonial oppression. The Japanese occupation produced an upsurge of interest in more realistic dramas of everyday life, but neither these plays nor those of the prewar period are today of any more than academic interest.

Utuy Tatang Sontani (1920–1979) was the first Indonesian dramatist to gain wide recognition. His early plays, most notably *Bunga rumah makan* (1948; ornament of the restaurant) and *Awal dan Mira* (1952; Awal and Mira), are concerned with the possible avenues for dignified living open to ordinary individuals in the midst of a society obsessed with false and empty values. After aligning himself with the political left Utuy wrote *Si Sapar* (1964; Sapar) and *Si Kampeng* (1964; Kampeng), two short plays that treat class differences and exploitation, employing a style in which caricature is of paramount importance.

Drama in the 1970s was dominated, on the one hand, by the immensely popular satirical plays of Rendra, and, on the other, by the absurdist works of Arifin C. Noer (b. 1941) and Putu Wijaya (b. 1944). Rendra's *Kisah perjuangan suku Naga* (1975; *The Struggle of the Naga Tribe,* 1979) is a brilliantly funny condemnation of the Indonesian elite's economic and cultural dependence on foreigners. The play is thoroughly modern, but it draws upon the conventions of the traditional Javanese shadow play, thereby emphasizing in its form the theme of cultural autonomy that lies at its heart. Arifin C. Noer's *Kapai-kapai* (1970; *Moths,* 1974) is a crazy pastiche of episodes, sometimes macabre and mystical, dramatizing one man's suffering and his escape into unreality.

In Javanese

Fiction in Javanese (the language of central and east Java) is characterized by three somewhat overlapping streams. The *priyayi* (aristocratic and official class) stream is dedicated largely to the defense of aristocratic values and status in the face of social mobility and creeping egalitarianism. It is indebted to the belletristic writing of the Javanese courts and emphasizes refinement, etiquette, mystical knowledge, and mastery of formal Javanese. *Rangsang Tuban* (1913; song of Tuban) by Padmasusastra (1843–1926) is an early masterpiece of this type. Ostensibly a historical novel, it in fact gives complex expression to *kabatinan,* the characteristically Javanese form of mysticism. *Serat Riyanta* (1920; Riyanto's story) by Sulardi (1888–19??), often called the first true novel in Javanese, utilizes the conventional love romance to express aristocratic ideals. In *Ngulandara* (1936; wanderlust), Margana Djajaatmadja (dates n.a.) affirms the superiority of the *priyayi* by fashioning a contemporary transmutation of the traditional Panji romance of courtly love, while *Anteping tekad* (1975; unshakable determination) by Ag. Suharti (b. 1920) defends the *priyayi* ethic in a non-Javanese, postindependence context.

The second stream of writing, the popular, seems to be preoccupied with forging a sense of security and identity in the newly emergent lower middle class. Written, since its rise in the 1930s, at the informal level of Javanese, popular fiction has been much indebted to popular novels in Indonesian, especially those by Chinese-Indonesian authors. Popular theater, too, has been influential in this stream. The novel *Sala peteng* (1938; darkness in Solo) by Mt. Suphardi (b. 1913) has a plot strikingly similar to those of Javanese *ludrug* stage melo-dramas. The theme of unwitting incest, common in popular Javanese fiction, suggests that *Sala peteng* and similar novels are appealing for the preservation of the traditional family unit in the midst of fragmenting social change. The prolific giants of the postindependence romance were Any Asmara (b. 1913) and Widi Widajat (b. 1928), both of whose works are highly formulaic and strongly influenced by the conventions of oral narrative and popular theater.

Writers in the third, or "modernist," stream have sought to develop a prose style at once expressively literary yet close to colloquial usage. Unlike *priyayi* and popular writers, they evince strong interest in individualized characterization and taut structure. The romantic but frequently somber short stories of St. (Sulistyou-tami) Iesmaniasita (b. 1933), in her collections *Kidung wengi ing gunung gamping* (1958; nocturne in the limestone hills) and *Kalimput ing pedhut* (1976; veiled in mist), are noteworthy for their vivid portraits of village and urban middle-class women. *Lara lapane kaum republik* (1967; agony and sacrifice in the republican cause) by Suparto Brata (b. 1932) is a down-to-earth and wryly humorous story of the revolution. Sudharma K. D. (1934–1980) and Esmiet (b. 1938) address the problem of economic development in the Javanese cultural context. Esmiet's *Tunggak-tunggak jati* (1977; trunks of teak) examines the impact upon a rural community of the alliance between an unscrupulous Chinese businessman and corrupt community leaders.

Innovative poetry in Javanese has developed vigorously since Indonesia's independence. It has been dominated by St. Iesmaniasita and by Muryalelana (b. 1932), whose verse is mostly inward-looking. Modern stage drama has not developed significantly in Javanese, but the radio plays of Soemardjono (b. 1925), some of which are adaptatations from European sources and others romances of his own creation, gained a huge following in the 1960s and 1970s.

In Sundanese

Preindependence fiction in Sundanese (the language of inland west Java) is almost synonymous with the name of Mohammad Ambri (1892–1936). His interest in rural life, particularly rural religious practices, is the common thread of his novels. *Ngawadalkeun nyawa* (1932; self-sacrifice) gives an absorbing portrait of life in a rural Islamic academy (*pesantren*), while *Munjung* (1932; homage) demon-strates how Sundanese villagers make sense of cash-based commerce by relating it to the demonic figures of the spirit world.

Mohamad Ambri's prose style has exercised an enormous influence on later writers. Some of his novels consist almost entirely of dialogue, in colloquial, unadorned, yet remarkably expressive language. Among postindependence writers indebted to him is Ki Umbara (pseud. of Wirdja Ranulaksana, b. 1914), whose collection of short stories *Diwadalkeun ka siluman* (1965; sacrificed to demons) explores some of the darker corners of Sundanese folk religion. By contrast, the novel *Manehna* (1965; she) by Sjarif Amin (pseud. of Mohamad Koerdie, b. 1907) is a lyrical, sometimes painfully nostalgic evocation of the Sundanese world of the author's youth.

Haji Hasan Mustapa (1852–1930) wrote poetry in traditional forms, but brought to his work a new spirit of individualism and innovation. Like Mohamad Ambri, he did not hesitate to make creative use of colloquial Sundanese, raising the poetic forms of folk narrative and children's songs to a new level of seriousness. Only in the 1950s did Sundanese poetry directly face contemporary society and achieve release from traditional verse forms. In the work of Sajudi (dates n.a.) Sundanese poetry found a powerful voice. In his collection *Lalaki di tegal pati* (1963; a man on the field of battle) he pays tribute to the heroic spirit of old Sunda, but also writes lyrically of love, patriotism, and the sufferings of the weak in postindependence Indonesian society. Allusions to the Sundanese past and a prominent note of romanticism are evident too in the works of Surachman R. M. (b. 1936) and the prolific Wahyu Wibisana (b. 1935). Wayhu Wibisana, together with Utuy Tatang Sontani and short-story writer Rachmatullah Ading Affandie (usually abbreviated R. A. F., b. 1929), have gained some recognition as playwrights, but by and large modern stage drama in Sundanese has been infertile.

In Minangkabau and Balinese

Of the other regional literatures, west Sumatran Minangkabau and Balinese writing have displayed promising stirrings of innovation. The traditional Minangkabau *kaba*—a romantic narrative in rhythmic prose—has been transformed by a few writers into a popular comic genre making satirical comment on contemporary life. Innovative verse has flourished in the lyrics of popular songs.

In the Balinese language two novels have appeared: *Nemu karma* (1931; punished by fate) by Wayan Gobiah (dates n.a.) and *Mlancaran ka Sasak* (1939; rev. ed. 1978; journey to Lombok) by Gde Srawana (dates n.a.). Both are romances, the former marked by the theme of karmatic retribution, the latter remarkable for its humor and its lively, earthy style. Stimulated by government and privately sponsored competitions, Balinese writers turned their attention to the short story in the late 1960s and 1970s. The stories in the collection *Katemu ring Tampaksiring* (1975; meeting at Tampaksiring) by Made Sanggra (b. 1926) examine the fate of the poor in Bali, but also touch on the persistence of traumatic memories in those who experienced the revolutionary war. In the anthology of poetry *Ganda sari* (1973; scent and blossoms) Made Sanggra and Nyoman Manda (b. 1938) display an idealistic but almost prosaic interest in the impact of economic development on Balinese society.

In Chinese-Indonesian

Chinese have lived in Indonesia from earliest historical times. In the second half of the 19th c. migration from China swelled, and many of the descendants of these migrants adopted the languages and cultures of their new home while still maintaining a distinctly Chinese identity. In the first half of the 20th c. the Chinese dialect of Indonesian became the vehicle for a lively literature.

Toward the end of the 19th c. Chinese-Indonesian writers adopted the traditional Malay *syair* verse form, using it for narratives of contemporary events and for romantic stories. An early and accomplished exponent of the *syair* was Lie Kim-hok (1853–1912), whose *Sair cerita Siti Akbari* (1884; the story of Siti Akbari), a legendary romance set in India, became the most admired work of the genre. Lie Kim-hok's many detective stories also played a key role in establishing the viability of prose fiction in this dialect. The finest Chinese-Indonesian novelist was Liem King-hoo (dates n.a.); in *Berjuang* (1934; struggle) and *Masyarakat* (1939; community) he analyzes the character and social role of Indonesia's Chinese, urging them to search for a humane, socialistic alternative to capitalism.

Indonesia's independence brought the death of the Chinese-Indonesian dialect as a literary language, but the spirit of Chinese-Indonesian literature lived on in the immensely popular works of Asmaraman Sukowati (previously

Kho Ping Hoo, b. 1926) and Marga T. (previously Tjoa Liang Tjoe, b. 1943). Marga's *Gema sebuah hati* (1976; echoes in a heart) is a romantic and melodramatic novel depicting the lives of Chinese-Indonesian students caught in the conflicting loyalties and political turmoil of Djakarta in 1965.

In Dutch

Although Dutch was for hundreds of years the upper-echelon language of administration and commerce in Indonesia, indigenous Indonesians did not find it a congenial vehicle for literary expression. Among the few exceptions was Kartini (1879–1904), whose eloquent letters of protest against colonial paternalism and the feudal oppression of women were collected and published posthumously in *Door duisternis tot licht* (1911; *Letters of a Javanese Princess*, 1921). The most substantial work of fiction in Dutch by an Indonesian author is the novel *Buiten het gareel* (1940; out of harness) by Suwarsih Djojopuspito (1912–1978). It is a sensitive portrayal of day-to-day strains in the marriage and work of an educated woman.

Romance, interest in Oriental exotica, and, most recently, intense nostalgia for the colonial past are the hallmarks of the Indies novel by Dutch writers. A few outstanding works, however, echo the impassioned brilliance of Multatuli's (pseud. of Eduard Douwes Dekker, 1820–1887) *Max Havelaar* (1860; *Max Havelaar*, 1868; new trs., 1927, 1967) and capture the essence of Dutch colonial society with its special Indies character and its ambivalent attitude toward its Indonesian subjects. One such work is the novel *De stille kracht* (1900; *The Hidden Force*, 1922) by Louis Couperus (q.v.), which superbly catches the superciliousness of Dutch officialdom in confrontation with the incomprehensible yet tangible power of Javanese culture. The works of Madelon Hermina Székely-Lulofs (a.k.a. Madelon Lulofs, 1899–1958), among them the popular *Rubber* (1931; *Rubber*, 1933) and *Koelie* (1932; *Coolie*, 1936), attack colonialism, especially as it manifested itself in the exploitative plantation enterprises of North Sumatra. The novel of nostalgia is raised to high art in the works of Maria Dermoût (1888–1962). Her *De tienduizend dingen* (1956; *The Ten Thousand Things*, 1958) is a justly praised evocation of colonial society in a remote corner of eastern Indonesia. The pithy short stories of Vincent Mahieu (a.k.a. Tjalie Robinson, pseuds. of Jan Boon, 1911–1974) are collected in *Tjies* (1954; pea rifle) and *Tjoek* (1960; constriction). Using dialect and the imagery of hunting and boxing, they conjure up the tough world of the Indonesian Eurasian.

The poet Notosoeroto (1888–1951), a Javanese, and Getrudes Johannes Resink (b. 1911), a Eurasian, were influenced by the neoromanticism of late-19th-c. European verse. But Notosoeroto's collection *Wayang-liederen* (1931; songs of the shadow play) and Resink's *Kreeft en steenbok* (1963; Cancer and Capricorn) both reveal an outlook profoundly colored by Javanese mysticism.

(See also Netherlands Literature.)

BIBLIOGRAPHY: Raffel, B., *The Development of Modern Indonesian Poetry* (1967); Nieuwenhuys, R., *Oost-Indische Spiegel* (1973); Aveling, H., *A Thematic History of Indonesian Poetry: 1920–1974* (1974); Balfas, M., "Modern Indonesian Literature in Brief," in Spuler, B., ed., *Handbuch der Orientalistik*, Vol. 3, Part 1 (1976), pp. 41–116; Freidus, A. J., *Sumatran Contributions to the Development of Indonesian Literature, 1920–1942* (1977); Johns, A. H., *Cultural Options and the Role of Tradition: A Collection of Essays on Modern Indonesian and Malaysian Literature* (1979); Ras, J. J., *Javanese Literature since Independence* (1979); Teeuw, A., *Modern Indonesian Literature* (2 vols., 1979)

GEORGE QUINN

INGUSH LITERATURE
See North Caucasian Literatures

INNER MONGOLIAN LITERATURE
See Mongolian Literature

INTERIOR MONOLOGUE
See Stream of Consciousness

IONESCO, Eugène
French dramatist, essayist, short-story writer, and novelist, b. 13 Nov. 1912, Slatina, Romania

Born of a Romanian father and a French mother, I. was a year old when his mother brought him to Paris. His first language was French. When he was nine years old, he and his younger sister were sent by their parents to spend some time in the care of a kind peasant family in the village of La Chapelle-Anthenaise in Mayenne, where he attended the local school. For I. the years at La Chapelle-Anthenaise were Edenic. In the mind of the adolescent, and later of the mature writer, the peaceful hamlet acquired archetypal dimensions.

When I. turned thirteen, the family left France to join his father, an attorney, in Bucharest. Shortly afterward his parents were divorced, but the boy, although he sided with his mother, had to remain with the parent who was able to provide for his life and education. In Romania, I. perfected his knowledge of his father's language, completed his secondary-school training, and entered the University of Bucharest. He began to teach French when he was eighteen and also embarked on his literary career, publishing poetry and essays in various reviews. His first book of essays, *Nu* (no), was published in 1934. As a young man growing up in Romania, I. learned to recognize the signs of political and intellectual fascism; he seemed to develop an immunity to the malady he would later call "rhinoceritis."

In 1936 I. married, and the couple left Romania in 1938 when I. received a government scholarship to study at the Sorbonne, where he was planning to write a thesis on the theme of death in modern poetry, starting with Baudelaire. War broke out and the couple sought refuge in the south of France, living in the country, then in hiding in Marseille. Returning to Paris in 1945, I. worked as a proofreader. This was a period of great financial hardship, and yet also a time when the young married pair felt happy in a world at peace. I. no longer thought of himself as a writer. He was to become a dramatist "by accident," as he himself often says.

In 1948 I. decided to add a third language to the ones he acquired as a child. He embarked on the study of English, using the Assimil conversation method. As I., the would-be student of the English language, began to transcribe the obvious, almost simple-minded sentences into his notebook, he was struck with the fact that things one takes for granted might indeed have a quality of strangeness, that indeed the world, and our being in the world which we do not question, are phenomena that can fill one with amazement. This realization filled him with metaphysical angst, and he had to lie down. When he returned to his working table he continued to transcribe the Assimil sentences, but now both the characters and the dialogue began to run away with themselves, to acquire a kind of autonomous existence. The result was a neosurrealist comedy, actually "a tragedy of language," as I. states. *La cantatrice chauve* (1949; *The Bald Soprano*, 1958), an "antiplay," was staged by Nicholas Bataille on May 11, 1950, at the Théâtre des Noctambules. It went unnoticed and unattended until some established writers, such as the dramatist Jean Anouilh (q.v.) and the avant-garde novelist Raymond Queneau (q.v.), supported it, and embarked on a systematic campaign to attract an audience and a number of critics. They succeeded beyond anyone's expectation. It is a classic of the Theater of the Absurd (q.v.).

Although I.'s most favorable critics saw the play as a satire on bourgeois society, *La cantatrice chauve* was already a metaphysical farce. Apsychological, derisive, absurdist, it is a celebration of Dionysian rebirth, of the power of language once it has been stripped of its clichés. The Martins and the Smiths may be interchangeable automatons, but the Dionysian couple, the Fireman and the Maid, the latter composing a poem on the power of fire, are savage forces that precipitate the staid and boring world of routine into a frenzy of deconstruction, and of ultimate freedom.

La cantatrice chauve was quickly followed by *La leçon* (1953; *The Lesson*, 1958), *Jacques; ou, La soumission* (1953; *Jack; or, The Submission*, 1958), and *L'avenir est dans les œufs* (1958; *The Future Is in Eggs*, 1960). *La leçon* is a terrifying picture of the erotic thrust of tyrannical power. As in *La cantatrice chauve*, language is here the protagonist and the hero-villain. The Professor will kill the girl student with a knife as word and object. The murder is a rape, and the knife a phallus. The student's preparation for her *"doctorat total"* is a grotesque mating dance. It is the lecture on philology that unleashes the Professor's murderous sexuality. The play has been called a parable of destruction by habit and magic.

I.'s masterpiece of the first period is probably *Les chaises* (1954; *The Chairs*, 1958). In it the real and the imaginary coincide in a single semicircle of proliferating chairs, seats for imaginary guests of the old couple. The play reveals the fundamental mechanism of the imagination. It also suggests absence through the presence of the empty chairs; it is a stage poem about the ontological void. Although the Old Man hopes to leave a message after a mock-heroic double suicide with his wife, the Orator turns out to be afflicted with a form of aphasia. There will be no message. The only reality lies in the tenderness of the Old Woman for her

husband, and in the Old Man's vision of the Emperor, "the King of Kings," as I. has revealed in private conversation. It is important not to miss the mystical level of *Les chaises*.

A mystico-comical ascension, a liberation from a stultifying marriage, are portrayed in *Amédée; ou, Comment s'en débarrasser* (1954; *Amédée; or, How to Get Rid of It*, 1958). A mysterious corpse, stretched out on the conjugal bed of Amédée and his wife Madeleine, is afflicted with a strange malady, growth. As its legs begin to protrude into the living room, the only room where the married couple lives and works, it is clear that soon it will become uninhabitable. We are never told when, how, or why the cadaver got into the apartment; its presence is a phenomenological evidence. It suggests, however, a stifling atmosphere, the break-up of a marriage. Madeleine urges her weak, passive husband, an unsuccessful playwright—clearly I. is caricaturing himself—to "get rid of it." One detects also a parody of the detective play, one of I.'s cherished Sophoclean devices. As Amédée, the God-beloved fool, lowers the incriminating, cumbersome body out the window, into the street, then, running out of the house, tries to drag it in the direction of the Seine, the corpse, grown light, floats up, carrying away a delighted runaway husband. The stage is filled with lights, fireworks, the atmosphere of the carnival. Never has the euphoria of freedom regained been more eloquently concretized upon the stage.

A reverse apprehension, that of weightiness and of secret guilt informs *Victimes du devoir* (1954; *Victims of Duty*, 1958). Here a strong Oedipal motif underlies the action as Madeleine (wife/mother) and the Detective (father/ analyst/judge/detective) force Choubert, the protagonist, to question his "unfinished symphony" by plumbing his inner depths. The gaps in Choubert's memory are to be filled with the crusts of the stale bread he is forced to chew by the Detective-Executioner. An unexpected guest arrives, the ectoplasmic projection of the wicked parents, Nicolas d'Eu, whose name suggests a regal incognito (Nicolas II). Madeleine, elated, turns into a frantic hostess, balancing a proliferating number of coffee cups. Her frenzied entrances and exits, her juggling act, remind the audience of the whirling dervish dance of the Old Woman in *Les chaises*. Here, what Antonin Artaud (q.v.) called the "anarchy of humor" borders on the demonic.

One of I.'s most joyous plays, despite a strong hint of an inevitable apocalypse, is *Le piéton de l'air* (1963; *A Stroll in the Air*, 1968). The protagonist is an astronaut who has no need of spaceships since he can levitate out of pure joy, a shamanic exercise in the powers of the spirit. He rises where world and anti-world interpenetrate, while an inhabitant of this antiworld wanders among earthlings, clearly lost. Unlike Amédée, who is borne aloft by the corpse-balloon, the stroller treads air as we do water. He moves into outer space *under his own power*. The exultant mood of *le piéton* yields to angst once he begins to circle the earth. He sees from above that our planet is the only verdant place in the universe, and that it is surrounded by "deserts of ice, deserts of fire." Man is indeed a creature caught between the infinity of smallness and the other infinity, that of vastness. I.'s protagonist is happy to return to those he loves upon the earth, and to live a little longer in a state of truce.

I. is a libertarian, perhaps even a gentle anarchist. Two plays reveal this aspect of his philosophy: *Tueur sans gages* (1958; *The Killer*, 1960) and *Le rhinocéros* (1959; *Rhinoceros*, 1960). The first of these presents I.'s "hero in spite of himself," Bérenger, the dramatist's Everyman. A timid, honest, secretly lyrical, deeply committed human being, Bérenger wanders by error—taking the wrong tramway—into an ersatz paradise, the "radiant city." This architectural marvel can offer its dwellers no protection against the universal human condition of mortality symbolized by the murderous will of a *tueur sans gages* (killer without wages)—I. invented this term—who, unlike a *tueur à gages* (a hired assassin), kills gratuitously, for no reason of gain or profit—in fact, irrationally. Bérenger is aghast when the killer's existence is revealed to him by the Architect, an efficient technocrat who takes the scandal of mortality and the presence of evil in his stride. At the end of the play I.'s antihero finds himself facing a puny creature; he realizes that this is the Killer. The final scene of the play is a dialogue-monologue in the course of which the murderer never answers; he just snickers. As Bérenger talks on, attempting to fathom the mentality of one who destroys for the sake of annihilation, he finds only arguments for his own demise. To argue with nihilism is to enter the void, to embrace Nothingness. Although Bérenger is armed—he carries old-fashioned pistols—the Killer's short knife and long-lasting determination are bound to triumph. Unable to kill the Killer, even in self-defense, Bérenger seems to accept his fate.

The Bérenger of *Le rhinocéros* is another incarnation of his namesake. The protagonist of the later play may be outwardly a weak man, even a tippler, and a sentimentalist, but he will have the immense courage of retaining his humanity in the face of universal metamorphosis to bestiality and brutality. Rhinoceritis is the disease of conformity. Bérenger seems to be immune, and yet, sadly, he will remain quite alone at the end of the play, the last human being among creatures whose thick green skin and hoarse, bellowing voices he begins to envy. I. has said in conversation: "There was a time when it seemed to me that everyone had become a fascist, all members of my family, my friends, my colleagues. It was somehow up to me, little me, to resist." *Le rhinocéros* is the stage image of this resistance.

I.'s third profoundly political play is *Macbett* (1972; *Macbett*, 1973). This play is a cartoon version of Shakespeare's *Macbeth*, a grotesque rendition of the ways in which absolute power corrupts absolutely.

Death, the process of dying, trying to search for the meaning of life, such are the great universal themes of I.'s most ambitious later works. He wrote *La soif et la faim* (1966; *Hunger and Thirst*, 1968) for performance at the Comédie Française. In this allegorical drama, Jean, the protagonist, deserts his wife and child to go in quest of the ideal. He is mistaken as to the roads he chooses, and even as to his desires. His thirst cannot be slaked, nor his hunger sated. Finally he will reach a dubious inn, run by fake monks. The monastic society smells of the concentration camp. He will be held prisoner for an indeterminate amount of time, and will be condemned to serve at table, dressed in monk's habit. Time is fragmented into infernal minutes, their numbers appearing on illuminated screens. Now, in this Purgatory, Jean understands the mistake he made when he left home to look for a happiness that was there for him to find. It is too late.

The image of the process of dying finds its most eloquent expression in an earlier play, perhaps I.'s masterpiece, *Le roi se meurt* (1963; *Exit the King*, 1965). Here the same Bérenger has become Bérenger I, the sovereign of a decaying country. Early in the play, he is informed by Marguerite, his first wife, that he is to die soon, at the end of the play. The court physician, who is also the astrologer and the executioner, confirms this prognosis. The king at first refuses to believe this, despite the signs of his own decrepitude, and of the disintegration of his country, but after a while it becomes evident that the end is near. The play echoes the lamentations of Job, and of Shakespeare's Richard II. The final monologue of the shrewish Marguerite, who slowly changes into a divinity of death, is based on Plato's account of the end of Socrates, and on *The Tibetan Book of the Dead. Le roi se meurt* is a tone poem on the process of dying and a paean to life. The death of Bérenger I is not only that of an individual, but the decline of our civilization, the end of the planet earth. It is a comic apocalypse.

Two dream plays form a diptych: *L'homme aux valises* (1975; *Man with Bags*, 1977), a play in which the voyage becomes an allegory of man's search for his identity, and *Thème et variations; ou, Voyages chez les morts* (1980; *Journey among the Dead*, 1980). The latter is a series of conversations between Jean, the protagonist, and his dead relatives, including his mother and father. Ancient guilts, remorses, and debts are brought up to the surface. I.'s infernal voyage echoes that of Odysseus to the land of the Cimmerians and that of Aeneas and Dante. W. H. Auden (q.v.) once said: "Art is breaking bread with the dead." This play shows us that the way is always open for the living to make contact with their ancestors.

Although he is best known as a playwright, the creator of the genre that could be called metaphysical farce, I. is also an important essayist. *Notes et contre notes* (1962; *Notes and Counter Notes*, 1964) is a lucid collection of *pensées* on modern dramaturgy. His other volumes of essays include *Journal en miettes* (1967; *Fragments of a Journal*, 1968); *Présent passé passé présent* (1968; *Present Past Past Present*, 1971), *Antidotes* (1977; antidotes), a collection of essays on politics and philosophy, *Un homme en question* (1979; a man in question), and the earlier *Découvertes* (1970; discoveries), an illustrated volume of childhood remiscences for which I. composed drawings reminiscent of those of Paul Klee. *Découvertes* is one of the most charming and important books by I.; it translates that sense of wonder which is at the basis of his apprehension, and without which there would have been no *La cantatrice chauve*.

The man who became a member of the French Academy in 1971 has remained also a prankster. He likes to say that as a writer he belongs to the "cabaret school of literature." His ancestors are Charlie Chaplin, the Marx Brothers, and Buster Keaton. But this eternal child is a reader of Plato and Plotinus. For him, nothing is actual; one must rend the veil of appearance. It is through language that we get at the truth. I. wishes to invent a language that will translate the original world, the world of "before" which is that of pure thought. To do so the dramatist often deconstructs speech, as at the end of *La cantatrice chauve* and also of *Voyages chez les morts*. Not unlike Dante, I. longs for Paradise, where language was never the seed of doubt and misunderstanding because it coincided with Being, with God.

FURTHER WORKS: *Le salon de l'automobile* (1953; *The Motor Show*, 1963); *Théâtre* (7 vols., 1954–81); *L'impromptu de l'Alma* (1958; *Improvisation; or, The Shepherd's Chameleon*, 1960); *Le nouveau locataire* (1958; *The New Tenant*, 1958); *Le maître* (1958; *The Leader*, 1960); *La vase* (1961; "Slime," 1966); *La photo du colonel: Récits* (1962; *The Colonel's Photograph, and Other Stories*, 1969); *Délire à deux* (1963; *Frenzy for Two or More*, 1968); *Le tableau* (1963; *The Picture*, 1965); *La colère* (1963; *Anger*, 1968); *Scène à quatre* (1963; *Foursome*, 1963); *La lacune* (1966; *The Gap*, 1969); *Entretiens avec Claude Bonnefoy* (1966; *Conversations with E. I.* 1970); *Jeux de massacre* (1970; *Killing Game*, 1974); *Discours de réception d'E. I. à l'Académie Française et réponse de Jean Delay* (1971); *Ce formidable bordel!* (1973; *What a Bloody Circus!*, 1975); *Le solitaire* (1973; *The Hermit*, 1974); *Voyages chez les morts* (1981); *Le blanc et le noir* (1981). FURTHER VOLUMES IN ENGLISH: *The Killer, and Other Plays* (1960); *Hunger and Thirst, and Other Plays* (1969)

BIBLIOGRAPHY: Fowlie, W., *Dionysus in Paris* (1960), pp. 229–37; Pronko, L. C., *Avant-Garde: The Experimental Theatre in France* (1962), pp. 59–111; Sénart, P., *I.* (1964); Pronko, L. C., *E. I.* (1965); Benmussa, S., *I.* (1966); Donnard, J. H., *I. dramaturge; ou, L'artisan et le démon* (1966); Guicharnaud, J., *Modern French Theater from Giraudoux to Beckett*, rev. ed. (1967), pp. 215–29; Jacobsen, J., and Mueller, W. R., *I. and Genet: Playwrights of Silence* (1968); Abastado C., *I.* (1971); Coe, R. N., *I.: A Study of His Plays*, rev. ed. (1971); Tarrab, G., *I. à cœur ouvert* (1971); Wulbern, J. H., *Brecht and I.* (1971); Vernois, P., *La dynamique théâtrale d'E. I.* (1972); Lamont, R. C., ed., *I.: A Collection of Critical Essays* (1973); Saint, T., *E. I.; ou, À la recherche du paradis perdu* (1973); Esslin, M., *The Theater of the Absurd*, rev. ed. (1973); pp. 100–65; Jacquart, E..

Le théâtre de dérision: Beckett, I., Adamov (1974); Bondy, F., I. (1975); Hayman, R., E. I. (1976); Lamont, R. C., and Friedman, M. J., eds., The Two Faces of I. (1978)
ROSETTE C. LAMONT

La cantatrice chauve [The Bald Soprano] goes back to 1950, and yet it has managed to remain unaltered through the nine intervening years. The other day, I found it more spare and bare than ever before, and still funnier. This "antiplay" has become a play, as one might have easily predicted, one that makes fun of other dramatists' works, and of itself as well; it constitutes the most burlesque parody of conversation that I have ever been given to encounter, whether in the salon or on the stage, also of "dramatic situations," and, more generally, of the peculiar mania that afflicts one and all, the utter inability to keep quiet.

The thought has crossed my mind—who is not afflicted by occasional doubt?—that if I had had such a good time discovering The Bald Soprano, the work of some unknown, presented at the now defunct Théâtre des Noctambules, it might have been due to its novelty and singularity. The production at La Huchette, and frequent rereadings as well, have served to reassure me. In fact I laughed more heartily than on the first day. Nicolas Bataille's staging, inseparable from the play itself, has managed to retain these precious qualities of surprise, of grace in the midst of the absurd, banality within insanity, qualities which had appeared so striking, and had congested the brains of pure Cartesians when the play first opened. . . .

Today, E. I. remains true to himself with an ever increasing discipline, one that does not exclude the aesthetic and the amusing. Neither the overstrung sycophants who attempt to push him in the direction of abstraction and systematization, of "a philosophy of language," nor the detractors who try to bludgeon him as soon as he makes an appearance, have been successful in distracting him from his goal, which is to make the audience laugh at its own intimate void, its own zaniness.

Jacques Lemarchand, "Les débuts de I.," Cahiers des saisons, No. 15 (1959), pp. 215, 218

The horror of proliferation—the invasion of the stage by ever-growing masses of people or things —which appears in The Future Is in Eggs is one of the most characteristic images we find in I.'s plays. It expresses the individual's horror at being confronted with the overwhelming task of coping with the world, his solitude in the face of its monstrous size and duration.

This is also the theme of The Chairs . . . often considered one of I.'s greatest achievements. . . . A play like The Chairs is a poetic image brought to life—complex, ambiguous, multi-dimensional. The beauty and depth of the image, as symbol and myth, transcends any search for interpretations.

Of course it contains the theme of the incommunicability of a lifetime's experience; of course it dramatizes the futility and failure of human existence, made bearable only by self-delusion and the admiration of a doting, uncritical wife; of course it satirizes the emptiness of polite conversation, the mechanical exchange of platitudes that might as well be spoken into the wind. There is also a strong element of the author's own tragedy in the play—the rows of chairs resemble a theatre; the professional orator who is to deliver the message, dressed in the romantic costume of the mid-nineteenth century, is the interpretative artist who imposes his personality between that of the playwright and the audience. But the message is meaningless, the audience consists of rows of empty chairs—surely this is a powerful image of the absurdity of the artist's, the playwright's, own situation.

Martin Esslin, The Theatre of the Absurd (1961), pp. 99–100

The type of theatre against which I. usually inveighs is the ideological theatre which claims social usefulness as its main function. This, he says, is nonsense . . . and it is more illuminating to read a psychological treatise than to visit a psychological theatre, for the latter is insufficiently psychological. . . . I. does not maintain that ideas have no place in the theatre. He draws a line between ideas and ideology. . . . He makes a distinction between ideas which are universal in character and those which are local and specific, such as political ideas.

Bernard F. Dukore, "The Theatre of I.: A Union of Form and Substance," ETJ, 13, 3 (1961), pp. 174–75

What was being displayed to those tiny audiences who attended the first performances of The Bald Soprano and The Lesson was, as Jean Vannier has written, "a drama of language, wherein human speech is put on exhibition." The clichés of the first play, which I. was inspired to write by his dizzying encounter with an English phrase-book, and the deadly logical flights of the second, were the dramas themselves, not simply means of advancing some anteriorly conceived "action" or of illustrating character or even, as the chief dignified misreading of I. would have it, of mocking the orderly processs of social existence and celebrating an absurd counterpart. . . .

I., however, had a future, and it was to go beyond the exigencies and fatalities of language, although they were always to remain a condition of his work. His later plays are richer and more complex; in them new lyrical and philosophic modes develop, humor becomes less a matter of linguistic sport than of the tension between appearance and reality, the dramatic consciousness spreads to include fuller states of being and more inclusive atti-

tudes toward the horrifying, the banal, the metaphysically unjustifiable. In his greatest plays—
Amédée, Victims of Duty, Killer without Wages
—I. has written works of the same solidity, fullness and permanence as his predecessors in the
dramatic revolution that began with Ibsen and is
still going on. [1963]

Richard Gilman, *Common and Uncommon
Masks: Writings on Theatre—1961–1970* (1971),
pp. 87–88

I.'s people—unlike Beckett's or Genet's—are
lonely where, according to any materialist philosophy, they have no right to be: in a social situation.
In their families, their sitting-rooms, their offices,
surrounded by relatives, *concierges,* policemen and
visitors, they discover willy-nilly an additional dimension to be lonely in. And this brings us back,
finally, to I.'s dilemma in relation to the current
avant-garde—the "Happening" and the drama of
participation. For the "enclosed" situation of I.'s
heroes (and hence the structure of his plays) has
nothing accidental about it; it is essential to the
deepest elements in his vision of the world. They
are enclosed *in* a society: to escape that prison,
there is only one way out—into the solitude of a
dimension of which society has no knowledge.
Whereas the drama of participation sees the problem exactly in reverse: it is the stage-"character"
who is solitary, imprisoned in his theatre, enslaved
by the dictatorial will of his dramatist and his producer, locked away inside the dungeon of his individualism and his vain private dreams. His escape
is outwards, into the street, into the pub and the
park, into the world. For the Living Theatre, society offers the escape from solitude. For I., solitude offers the escape from society. It does not
look as though the dilemma has any obvious solution.

Richard N. Coe, *I.: A Study of His Plays,* rev. ed.
(1971), p. 164

Critics have attempted to distinguish various periods in I.'s inspiration, and thus varied styles in his
dramaturgic writing. In reality, the dramaturgy he
espouses issues from a single way of looking at
himself, the way in which each human being envi-
sions the existential fact of being alive. The diver-
sification of stage expression flows from the necessity to express varied, though limited, relations
created by the interaction of an individual with the
ambient universe. . . . These relations with beings
and things may be many, but they are all viewed
in the light of an archetypal feeling, that of
amazement, the astonishment that invades a
human consciousness when it grapples with the
mystery of its existence. If I. seems to question
language, knowledge, society, and death, it is in
order to deepen and probe the modes of these relations, and the final relation of all these with
nonbeing: in turn, the object, the other, the oth-

ers, and the beyond. I.'s dramaturgy lays the foundation of the *derisive* genre, an amalgam of the
laughable and the bitter. A haunting, obsessive
doubt hovers over the public: man and the universe are reduced to a simple, desperate interroga-
tion.

Paul Vernois, *La dynamique théâtrale d'E. I.*
(1972), p. 2

I., the absurdist playwright, is like Pär Lagerkvist,
the cubist playwright, in that he discovers classicism, with its constants of balance, tension, primitivism, and archetypality, to be the vehicle and not
the fellow-traveler of certain modes or genres.
Lagerkvist's classicism incorporates cubism and
tragedy; I.'s incorporates absurdism and tragicomedy. The two dramatists share an aversion to
being classified by critics. In each case the aversion is qualified: Lagerkvist upholds classicism
and virtually defines it as cubism; I. is willing to
be identified as a classicist. But I. is not willing to
be labeled as a dramatist limited to any one of the
modes which contribute to his classicism—for example to comedy, tragedy, or absurdism. With
proper qualification of the critical terms that bear
application to Ionescan drama, it is feasible to
conclude that I., well attuned to the absurdity exposed in Aeschylean and Sophoclean tragedy, has
transmuted this exposure into true tragicomedy
and has become the classic dramatist of the theatre of the absurd.

Roy Arthur Swanson, "I.'s Classical Absurdity," in
Rosette C. Lamont and Melvin J. Friedman, eds.,
The Two Faces of I. (1978), p. 147

IQBAL, Muhammad
Indian poet and philosopher (writing in Urdu,
Persian, and English), b. 9 Nov. 1877, Sialkot
(now in Pakistan); d. 21 April 1938, Lahore
(now in Pakistan)

I. started to write poetry seriously while a student at Scotch Mission College, Sialkot, and
earned a considerable reputation as a poet in
Urdu prior to leaving for England in 1905 to
study at Trinity College, Cambridge. He also
studied law in London and received a Ph.D. in
philosophy from the University of Munich in
1907. Returning to India, he distinguished himself both as a statesman and poet-philosopher,
in recognition of which he was knighted in
1922. An activist in the Muslim League, I. articulated in 1930 his famous plea for a separate
state for Muslims in northwest India. In 1932
he traveled throughout Europe and met a number of intellectual and political leaders, including Henri Bergson (q.v.) and Benito Mussolini.

I. continued to champion the cause of Muslims in India and to write poetry until his death.

In order to reach a Muslim audience beyond India, I. wrote his first major poem, *Asrar-e khudi* (1915; *The Secrets of the Self*, 1920), in Persian. In this work he enuciated his concept of the self (*khudi*), the living principle of the universe, the foundation of all human endeavor. To I.'s thinking, life is not a static but rather a dynamic, evolutionary process of "becoming." The only way in which one can activate this process is to affirm and enlarge the self. This self, whether of individuals or nations, grows and expands as long as it is held in a state of tension, which, in turn, produces action, adventure, and inquiry. The urge to maintain such a tension is love (*ishq*), a concept that bears a close resemblance to Bergson's *élan vital*. To relax this tension is to create inertia, weakness, a negation of life—in short, evil. Such evil manifests itself in the form of *saval*, or questioning, which appears in various guises, such as borrowing another person's or country's money, ideas, customs, mores, and so forth. By imitating, I. states, one shows a lack of resourcefulness and of courage to accept the challenge of life and living. His thinking was revolutionary in Muslim intellectual circles, which were dominated by the principles of classical Muslim mysticism and its notions of fatalism and quietism.

In his second collection of Persian poems, *Rumuz-e bekhudi* (1919; *The Mysteries of Selflessness*, 1953), I. counterbalances the sense of egoism and individuality of *Asrar-e khudi* with the ideas of brotherhood and service in Islam. His masterpiece is another Persian poem, *Javid nameh* (1932; *The Pilgrimage of Eternity*, 1961). Modeled on Dante's *Divine Comedy* and Milton's *Paradise Lost*, the work depicts the poet's ascent through the various spheres of heaven until he experiences a vision of the Divine. His guide through this pilgrimage is the 13th-c. Persian mystic-poet, Jalaluddin Rumi.

I.'s first collection of Urdu poems, *Bang-e dara* (1924; call of the highway), contains poems from two distinct periods: those written between 1895 and 1905 in India, which are essentially nationalistic in outlook, and others composed between 1905 and 1908 in Europe, which deal with love themes in various guises. The earlier poems are often couched in lush nature imagery drawn from I.'s Indian surroundings. Among the latter group of poems is the famous "Khizr-e rah" (guide of the road), in which I. warns Indians against being dazzled by Western modes of government and law, espe-

cially as vehicles with which to solve the problems of the East.

The second Urdu collection, *Bal-e Jibril* (1936; wing of Gabriel), contains many of I.'s most famous poems, including "Masjid-e Qartabah" (mosque of Cordova), which commemorates his emotional visit to the cathedral of Cordova, Spain, a structure that had been a mosque prior to 1236. Another is "Lenin khuda ke huzur men" (Lenin in the presence of God), a dramatic confrontation between the apostle of Marxism and the Divine.

I.'s major English work is *The Reconstruction of Religious Thought in Islam* (1930), which crystallized his political thinking and articulated the intellectual position of Muslim separatists in their pursuit of a Muslim homeland in India, to be called Pakistan. I. stresses the need for reform in Islam much the same way Christianity required change just prior to the advent of Protestantism. While progressive in advocating change, I. is conservative in expounding methods for the actualization of these reforms.

I. is considered the spiritual father of Pakistan, which was established in 1947. In Persian literature he is accorded a place of honor among modern poets; in Urdu he is revered as the greatest poet of this century by Urdu speakers in both Pakistan and India, where many of his verses have entered the language as adages and sayings. His message of self-reliance and Islamic activism both shaped and reflected the Indian nationalist movement during the 1920s and 1930s, especially for Muslims, who look upon him even today as their leading intellectual figure of the 20th c.

FURTHER WORKS: *The Development of Metaphysics in Iran* (1908); *Payam-e mashreq* (1923; *The Tulip of Sinai*, 1947); *Zabur-e ajam* (1927; *Persian Psalms*, 1948); *Pas che bayad* (1936); *Musafer* (1936); *Zarb-e kalim* (1937); *Armaghan-e hijaz* (1938). FURTHER VOLUMES IN ENGLISH: *A Voice from the East: The [Urdu] Poetry of I.* (1922); *[Urdu] Poems from I.* (1955)

BIBLIOGRAPHY: Singh, I., *The Ardent Pilgrim* (1951); Bilgrami, H., *Glimpses of I.'s Mind* (1954); Vahid, S., *I.: His Art and Thought* (1959); Dar, M., *Introduction to the Thought of I.* (1961); Schimmel, A., *Gabriel's Wing* (1963); Malik, H., ed., *I.: Poet-Philosopher of Pakistan* (1971); Memon, M., ed., *I.: Poet and Philosopher between East and West* (1979)

CARLO COPPOLA

IRANIAN LITERATURE

The thousand-year-old classical Persian literature has been admired not only in countries of western and central Asia and the Indian subcontinent but also in Western Europe, especially during the romantic movement. It was praised and even considered one of the four main bodies of world literature by such writers as Goethe. In the long history of the Iranian people the Persian language and its literary idiom have played a pivotal role around which the nation and the culture have revolved.

The revolt in Iran at the end of the 19th c. and the beginning of the 20th c. finally brought forth the constitution of 1906, which changed the absolute monarchy into a constitutional one. Although the literati of the country actively participated in trying to implement this innovation, it proved to be easier in theory than in practice. This was true also in the application of drastic and decisive reform measures in the establishment of a modern literary idiom in Iran.

During the Pahlavi rule of Iran (1925–79) the constitutional process suffered a setback. Although great strides were made toward the modernization and Westernization of the country, literature was not encouraged unless it served the monarchy. With the steady erosion of political freedom in Iran, literary repression prevailed, but it could not really inhibit the writers.

In the view of the majority of Iranian writers, the imposition on the Iranian nation of the regime of the Islamic Republic, after the revolution brought down the Pahlavis, is a further setback. The goals and workings of the Islamic Republic are in contradiction to the ideas and ideals for which the majority of writers fought since the mid-1950s.

Fiction

Up to the end of the 19th c. stylized prose forms and emphasis on theology, philosophy, and history had long prevailed. There had been no creative fiction. As in poetry, rhetorical considerations had become the object, the goal, rather than the vehicle. Originality was frowned upon, and attempts at writing novels in the Western manner were both unsuccessful and unacceptable.

During the upheaval of the constitutional period the need for a new form of expression became apparent. Even reporting of daily events in the mushrooming press required a new prose style. Translations of Western works were very

helpful models. Under the influence of Alexandre Dumas père, Victor Hugo, and Jules Verne, writers of fiction chose the historical novel as the vehicle for their social and political comments.

Hasan Badi's (dates n.a.) *Dastan-e bastan* (1921; an old legend) provided a transition to the more modern approach. Having studied in Western sources the history of the Achaemenids, the first historical Persian dynasty, Badi produced a historical novel that, while dealing with a traditional subject, succeeded in a new way by using fully rounded characters and a unified plot; he also appealed to the current patriotism. By contrast, *Daliran-e Tangestani* (1932–33; the heroes of Tangestan) by Hussein Roknzadeh Adamiyat (dates n.a.), while by no means a fine creative work, was acclaimed for its anticolonial sentiments.

The short story patterned on Western examples proved to be a more suitable vehicle for Persian prose. *Yeki bud, yeki nabud* (1921; once upon a time) by Mohammad 'Ali Jamalzadeh (b. 1896) should be considered not only the literary manifesto of the author but also a Magna Carta for the written word in the Persian language. The volume contains six stories, which represent the first artistically successful attempt at social comment. Jamalzadeh portrayed the signs of a decayed system—corrupt religious and governmental ideologies, the need for social reform—and he condemned the men who perpetuated social ills. His criticism was tempered by his humor, his vivid descriptions, his caricatures of common life, and his lucid language. Although *Yeki bud, yeki nabud* had to overcome opposition from religious and governmental circles, Jamalzadeh's use of the short story as an artistic and effective tool assured his canonization as the guiding spirit for the next generation of Persian writers.

The most outstanding of these was Sadeq Hedayat (q.v.), who epitomized the confluence of post-World War I Western influence and the evolution of Persian fiction. He was concerned with the psychological implications of man's existence and human interactions, and preoccupied with silent and malign unseen forces which seemed predominant and to which he finally succumbed by committing suicide in 1951. In writing about the seamy elements of Iranian street life, he showed omnipresent compassion for the futility and frailty of human life, as in *Buf-e kur* (1937; *The Blind Owl*, 1957; new tr., 1974). His stories are of the gutters and slums as well as of the students and minor officials.

Hedayat was an ardent patriot. His love for

Iran and for its heritage is an important element in his work. He was also a great collector of Iranian folk tales, which he often used in his creative writing. Hedayat was probably the most important Persian writer of the 20th c. With him, Persian fiction at last earned a place in the body of world literature. Thirty years after his death his presence is still strongly felt, not only among the literati and the intellectuals but especially among the youth of Iran, for whom Hedayat is an idol.

One of his many followers is Sadeq Chubak (q.v.), although his style differs from that of Hedayat. Chubak, the realist, writes of similar everyday situations of flesh and blood, but without the metaphysical overtones of Hedayat and with an underlying optimism. He, too, reproduces realistic pictures of Iranian locales and people by using their own language with aggressive vigor. His technique is like a snapshot of an event, but it has a distressing emotional and intellectual impact. It proceeds single-mindedly to its climax unencumbered by compound sentences, peripheral descriptions, or inconsequential dialogue. Chubak likes to exploit certain common social stereotypes and colloquial language, triggering predetermined images and emotional reactions that render lengthy exposition unnecessary. A full range of stock characters and behavioral patterns of varying complexity are thus incorporated in a few sentences. His writing is an intricate counterplay between the lyric and the macabre, the poetic and the horrible. Although the literary content, symbolism, and setting of Chubak's short stories and novels are very Iranian, they never lose their universal appeal.

The works of several outstanding writers of fiction, in addition to their literary value, are eternal monuments to the fight for artistic and political freedom, social justice, and tolerance. Buzurg Alavi (q.v.) is especially noted for short stories vividly portraying oppression, injustice, and suffering. Jalal Al-e Ahmad (1923–1969) exposed in his fiction the problems of Iranian society. His social criticism is written in a straightforward, unadorned prose, as in *Modir-e madraseh* (1958; *The School Principal*, 1974). His essays in literary criticism were of great value in introducing that genre to Iran.

Another writer with a very sharp pen who understood his role as artist and social critic was Samad Behrangi (1939–1968). Because of his outspoken political, economic, and social criticism, most of Behrengi's writings were offically banned by the Shah's security police.

His short stories are mostly about children and for children. A selection in English translation appeared under the title *The Little Black Fish* (1976). Beh'azin (pseud. of Mahmud Etemadzadeh, b. 1915) also had a great impact on modern Iranian fiction. His masterful short stories mainly portray the humble peasants of his native Caspian province.

In 1961 a very long novel was published by the then-unknown writer 'Ali Mohammad Afghani (b. 1925): *Showhar-e Ahu Khanom* (Ahu Khanom's husband). This event was considered by Iranian literary critics as a turning point in contemporary literature, because of the novel's perceptiveness and penetration.

The period extending from Jamalzadeh and his followers until today has been quite aptly termed the "age of prose." Persian prose has matured in the last six decades. After fighting with poetry for its existence as a valid art form, it has now equaled it in expression and popularity.

Poetry

Poetry, with its elevated position, although very popular among all classes of Iranians, had for a long time become a staid and rigid system. The 'aruz (classical prosody) acquired a prestige demanding total obedience. Poetic diction also solidified at the expense of ideas.

One of the first great masters who tried to bring poetry into synchronization with the 20th c. was Mohammad Taqi Bahar (1886–1951), known as the "king of poets." He did not try to divorce himself from the style that had been prevalent for centuries but, instead of putting the emphasis upon perfection of form, stressed content and simplicity of language. He was one of the first Persian poets to write about his private life—portraying his family, his work, his associates; and about city life, with its streets, public bathhouses, bazaars, mosques, squares, and especially its people. He was also one of the first to introduce a simplified vocabulary and common expressions into poetry.

However, the appearance of a free-verse poem entitled *Afsaneh* (1921; the legend), by Nima Yushij (pseud. of 'Ali Esfandyari, 1895?–1959), should be thought of as a point of departure from the centuries-old domination and despotic rule of 'aruz over Persian poetry. Nima Yushij destroyed the strongest and longest-surviving elements of classical poetry—its meter and rhyme. It was a revolution. The country was divided between the *nowparastan* —worshipers of the new—and the *kohnepa-*

rastan—worshipers of the old. Although young poets joined forces with Nima Yushij, it took a long time and many battles in the pages of literary journals until the free-verse poets achieved recognition. This recognition was won thanks to such poets as Fereydoun Tavallali (b. 1919), who can still attract more traditional audiences through his mastery of the poetic image.

After World War II the main impulse in poetic creativity became antitraditional in its attitudes toward politics, social life, and literature. Many people could not understand the sociopsychological causes of this revolutionary eruption. From the mid-1950s on, modernist poetry proliferated. Younger poets carried modernism further. But not all of them pursued a headlong course. Some returned to more traditional verse, which obviously could not remain unchanged after such an experience; some were content with what they had gained; and some went to the extreme of the new wave. The extremists insisted that poetry remain free from social, political, and moral commitments, or even a commitment to logic.

In the history of modern Persian poetry, the other end of the spectrum—the lyrical poetry of Nader Naderpour (b. 1929)—should not be neglected, despite his predilection for classical diction. In a sense, he represents an important link to the past, binding modern poetry to its great tradition.

Among the modernists, two early followers of Nima Yushij were Manuchehr Sheybani (b. 1923) and Esmail Shahrudi (b. 1925). With clarity of expression, Sheybani presents the pre-Islamic, Zoroastrian world of light and darkness, truth and falsehood.

According to many critics, Forugh Farrokhzad (q.v.) is not only the most important poet since Nima Yushij but also Iran's best poet after the great classical period of the 15th c. In her poetry she violates not only the norms of form but also those of expression by freely stating her feelings unencumbered by symbolic representations and metaphor. Her uncensored personal communications are startlingly plain, but in a way innocent. *Tavvalod-e degar* (1964; another birth), the last volume before her untimely death in an automobile accident, is a personal and artistic climax—a victory for a woman who could free herself from the fetters of the alienation and frustration of that male-dominated society and a victory for artistic achievement in modern Persian poetry.

Another leading modern poet of Iran, who like Farrokhzad strove for the Sufi-like integration of man and a transcendent unity of being, was Sohrab Sepehri (1928–1979). His poetry, like his painting (Sepehri was one of the best painters of modern Iran, and exhibited in many countries), is like contemplation and meditation about nature, which is seen by his inner "eye of the heart." While his art is definitely Persian, it never loses its universality; although it is very modern and avant-garde, it is also timeless. The most representative collection of Sepehri's poetry is *Hasht ketab* (1976; eight books).

The living masters who have been most influential on the youngest generation of modern poets of Iran are Ahmad Shamlu (b. 1925) and Mehdi Akhavan-Sales (b. 1928). Shamlu, ceaseless searcher for new means of poetic expression, is like a prestidigitator whose hat is full of ever fresh and extraordinary metrical and verbal resources. But he is not a trickster who tries to impress his audience. On the contrary, he is probably the most honest Iranian poet, the one most committed to the totality of Iran's past, present, and future. At the same time, his innovative lyrics tie modern Persian poetry to that of the rest of the world.

The poetry of Akhavan-Sales has been governed by what may be termed homeostatic dynamics: discarding certain values of the past that were hindering political, social, cultural, and especially literary development, and striving at the same time to preserve some of the old values, and if possible adapt them to the new circumstances of a rapidly changing society. His poetry, although very modern, is nevertheless an exponent of the continuity of the past.

Siavash Kasrai (b. 1927) combines lyricism with an epic breadth. Manuchehr Ateshi (b. 1931) reflects in his poetry the rugged landscape of the desert near the Persian Gulf and the toughness of the nomadic tribes. Mohammad 'Ali Sepanlu (b. 1938), like many contemporary Iranian short-story writers, tries to weave into his poetry the spoken language and everyday situations.

The majority of today's poets, despite all the innovations and experiments, do not forget that poetry has been a point of reference, a mirror of Iran's history and myths and an expression of national identity.

Drama

There has been no established literary corpus of Persian creative drama. On the other hand the only indigenous drama in the world of Islam is Persian *ta'ziyeh*, a ritual theater that derives its form and content from deep-rooted religious traditions. Its genius is that it combines immediacy and flexibility with universality. But since there is no fixed text, it has not been considered literature. There are *ta'ziyeh* manuscripts, but they are mostly written as individual parts for each performing character, and therefore they are not intended to be read separately.

At the end of the 19th c. *ta'ziyeh* was on the brink of giving birth to a secular theater in Iran. Unfortunately, this birth did not occur, since the trend was toward Western-style drama. Until recently, however, all the attempts at imitating Western drama were very poor. The playwrights were not completely aware of the dramatic functions and forces of the play. But since the 1960s literary dramatic activity has flourished. It is probably the fastest-growing literary genre, despite the fact that the political restrictions on freedom of expression have probably hampered drama more than any other form.

There are two main schools of playwriting in Iran. One is familiar with Western drama but borrows very little from it, other than structure. These dramatists turn to Iranian folklore and traditional entertainment, and they employ familiar stock characters. The main representative of this school is Bahram Beyzai (b. 1938).

The other school bases itself to a great extent on Western patterns, especially the work of such post-World War II dramatists as Beckett and Ionesco (qq.v.). The action is set in predominantly Iranian locales. The best representative of this group is Gowhar Murad (pseud. of Gholam-Hossein Sa'edi, b. 1935). His plays—outstanding among which are *Chub be dastha-ye Varazil* (1965; the stickwielders of Varazil) and *Ay ba kulah ay bi kulah* (1968; oh fool, oh fooled)—are marked by political symbolism and allegory.

Like fiction and poetry, modern drama in Iran for the most part takes its subjects from everyday life and employs colloquial speech.

BIBLIOGRAPHY: Brown, E. G., *Press and Poetry of Modern Persia* (1914); Avery, P., "Developments in Modern Persian Prose," *MW*, 45 (1955), 313–23; Kamshad, H., *Modern Persian Prose Literature* (1966); Kubičkova, V., "Persian Literature of the 20th Century," in Rypka, J., et al., *History of Iranian Literature* (1968), pp. 353–418; Yarshater, E., "The Modern Literary Idiom," in Yarshater, E., ed., *Iran Faces the Seventies* (1971), pp. 284–320; Ricks, T., ed., special Iran issue, *LitR*, 18, 1 (1974); Hillmann M. C., ed., special Iran issue, *LE&W*, 20, 1–4 (1976); Chelkowski, P., "The Literary Genres in Modern Iran," in Lenczowski, G., ed., *Iran under the Pahlavis* (1978), pp. 333–64; Karimi-Hakkak, A., Critical Introduction to *An Anthology of Modern Persian Poetry* (1978), pp. 1–27; Hillmann, M. C., "Revolution, Islam, and Contemporary Persian Literature," in Jabbari, A., and Olson, R., eds., *Iran: Essays on a Revolution in the Making* (1981), pp. 121–42

PETER J. CHELKOWSKI

For non-Persian writing in Iran, see under Azerbaijani Literature and Kurdish Literature

IRAQI LITERATURE

Starting with the closing decades of the 19th c., Iraq, first as an Ottoman province and then as an independent country (1921), began to witness modernistic trends in its literature. Such trends were guided by a twofold objective: first and more importantly, to revitalize and further develop, in response to modern needs, the primary traditional genre in Arabic, poetry; and second, to enrich Arabic literature with new genres and techniques.

Poetry

In poetry two distinct phases of development may be identified. The first, which lasted until 1945, was primarily concerned with the scope and content of traditional poetry, while the second, beginning in the late 1940s, made drastic departures in content and form. During the first phase, numerous poets sought, with varying degrees of success, to rid poetry of its highly contrived style, its outmoded ceremonial role, and its limited range of themes. Outstanding among them was Jamīl al-Zahāwī (1863–1936), a liberal poet noted for his encyclopedic turn of mind and his fascination with European scientific, social, and philosophical achievements. With him poetry became a vehicle of enlightenment defiantly conveying unpopular ideas and themes ranging from rejection of many time-honored beliefs and practices—social, religious, and political—to espousal of scientific and revolutionary concepts—Darwinism, human rights, women's emancipation. Al-Zahāwī's innovations also included experimentation with structural forms.

The second important poet of this phase, Ma'rūf al-Ruṣāfī (1875–1945), displayed in his poetry a similarly rebellious spirit but with greater artistry, vivid realism, and more emphasis on the emotional than the cerebral approach. Like al-Zahāwī, he addressed himself to social ills and national issues of his time. Both al-Ruṣāfī and al-Zahāwī also wrote numerous prose works indicating their wide range of intellectual pursuits.

By far the greatest poet of this period is Muhammad Mahdī al-Jawāhirī (b. 1900), who has re-created the rich language of the golden age of Arabic poetry. Although betraying an ideological vacillation, he is best noted for his political verse, which promotes progressive causes in Iraq and other parts of the Arab world. Other themes pursued less frequently but with similar mastery revolve around nature and love.

The second phase began in 1947 with successful efforts by a new generation to evolve a poetics more flexible than the traditional structure of Arabic verse, and with a wider range of techniques and subject matter, including extensive use of soliloquy, allusions to inspiring myths, historical symbols, and voices that transcend national boundaries. Among the leading poets of this phase are Nāzik al-Malā'ika (b. 1923), Badr al-Sayyāb, Abd al-Wahhāb al-Bayyātī (qq.v.), Buland al-Haydarī (b. 1926), Sa'dī Yūsuf (b. 1934), and Hasab al-Shaykh Ja'far (b. 1939). Al-Malā'ika is noted for her role as both a poet and a theoretician instrumental in developing this form, as indicated in her collections published since 1947 and in her critical works. Her highly subjective poetry evokes a world haunted by a sense of futility and unfulfilled romantic yearnings, but when she deals with national crises she displays a highly optimistic tone and a defiant spirit, as seen in her collection *Li al-salāh wa al-thawra* (1978; to prayer and revolution). Al-Sayyāb blends elegance of form and density of imagery to depict the tribulations of a prophetic hero inspired by a vision of rebirth and renewal.

Of all other poets of the period, al-Bayyāti seems most versatile and persistent in evolving his poetic vision or refining his techniques. Through the years he has shifted his emphasis from a romantic portrayal of his society, to sympathy for an open commitment to revolutionary causes, and then to a highly lyrical and surrealistic approach rich with symbolism. Nevertheless, his poetry continues to express, with a remarkable degree of consistency, his uncompromising revolutionary stance and his optimistic view of man's relentless struggle for the ideal.

Other significant poets who have contributed to the new form are Buland al-Haydarī, whose work is marked by existentialist (q.v.) themes tinged occasionally with Marxist overtones;

Shādhil Tāqa (1929–1974), noted for his preoccupation with the Arab nationalist and partisan (Ba'thist) struggle; and Sa'dī Yūsuf, who is unusual in his devotion to localized and unpretentious themes and his conversational poetic idiom. The vitality of contemporary Iraqi poetry is evident in the efforts of new poets to shun the material world and concentrate primarily on abstract or metaphysical questions. An increasing number of women poets have added a new dimension through their portrayal of women's feelings as they seek to assert their rights. Additionally, the traditional form of poetry as a medium best suited for oral communication, especially in a political context, has continued to show resiliency. Most noteworthy among the new traditionalists is Shafīq al-Kamālī (b. 1929), known for his attempts to recapture a lost Arab glory and for his untempered pride in Arab virtues.

Fiction

In contrast to poetry, drama and fiction have been handicapped by a lack of native roots and by Iraq's relatively slow and limited response to these genres. Aside from a few exceptional cases that display artistic refinement and maturity, most nonpoetic Iraqi works tend to suffer from some thematic and structural flaws.

Among the leading novelists of the first generation are Mahmūd al-Sayyid (1903–1937), noted for his socialist bent; Ja'far al-Khalīlī (b. 1904); and Dhu al-nūn Ayyūb (b. 1908). Ayyūb is known for his novel *Duktūr Ibrāhīm* (1939; Dr. Ibrahim), which unmasks the moral bankruptcy of a Western-educated intellectual. A more recent work, *Wa 'alā al-dunyā al-salām* (1972; farewell to the world), maintains the same didactic tone in depicting violent political upheavals taking place in an unnamed Arab country (but clearly Iraq) between 1960 and 1967.

This preoccupation with the political tension prevalent in the country pervades the works of other writers who emerged in the post-World War II period, and inevitably reflects the novelist's ideological point of view. Ghā'ib T. Farmān (b. 1927), for example, attempted in *Khamsat aswāt* (1968; five voices) to offer an inside story of five leftist intellectuals struggling against the royal regime before 1958. With the Ba'thists assuming power in 1968, Iraqi fiction began to exhibit a Ba'thist orientation. Committed novelists sought to portray the struggle of the party in recent years, as in *Al-Ayyām al-tawīla* (2 vols., 1978; long days) by 'Abd al-amīr Ma'alla (b. 1942). Perhaps most successful among the new novelists are Abd al-Rahmān al-Rubay'ī (or al-Rabī'ī, b. 1939) and Abd al-Rahmān Munīf (dates n.a.). Al-Rabī'ī's *Al-Qamar wa al-aswār* (1976; the moon and the walls) captures the tension in his native southern city of Al-Nasiriyya a few years before the 1958 revolution, identifying courses of action suggested by different ideologies: Islamic, socialist, and nationalist. Only toward the end does the novel introduce the Ba'th as an ideology capable of fulfilling the protagonist's aspirations. In his subsequent novels, dealing with later periods, he tends to emphasize the heroic acts of Ba'th party members who remain faithful to the end, although his recent works, such as *Al-Washm* (1974; tattoo), have turned to the subject of political prisoners (under the pre-Ba'th regimes) who falter or confess under physical and mental torture. More moving and nightmarish is Munīf's *Sharq al-Mutawassit* (1975; east of the Mediterranean), which reveals the anguish of the political prisoner in graphic detail rarely encountered in modern Arabic literature.

Some gifted short-story writers who emerged in the postwar period include 'Abd al-Malik Nūrī with *Nashīd al-ard* (1954; song of the earth); Fu'ād al-Takarlī (b. 1927) with *Al-Wajh al-ākhar* (1960; the other face); Mahdī al-Saqr (dates n.a.) with *Ghadab al-madīna* (1960; the wrath of the city); and Mūsā Kuraydī (b. 1940) with *Khutuwāt al-musāfir nahw al-mawt* (1970; the traveler's steps toward death). These writers have contributed toward the maturity of Iraqi fiction not only because of their subtle characterization and skillful use of dreams, stream of consciousness, and other devices, but also because of their humane concern with the inner world of their characters.

Drama

There are only a few noteworthy plays, mostly written in the Iraqi Arabic vernacular. The early works of Yūsuf al-'Ānī (b. 1927), largely guided by Socialist Realism (q.v.), tended to dramatize daily concerns of his characters against a background of political injustice or social constraints. In later works he progressed from simplistic solutions for problems to a more subtle vision. His *Al-Miftāh* (1968; the key) uses a nonsensical folkloric formula to suggest the absurdity of the human condition. Nūr al-dīn Fāris (b. 1934) is chiefly

concerned with the injustices of his society's feudal class structure, as in *Ashjār al-tā'ūn* (1965; the trees of the plague). 'Ādil Kāzim (dates n.a.), who uses the literary language as his medium and materials derived from the Bible and Mesopotamian mythology, explores the perpetual tension between the ruler and the ruled, and sympathetically depicts man's yearning for justice and freedom, advocating self-sacrifice and commitment as redeeming values. Jalīl al-Qaysī (date n.a.) displays a similar preoccupation with positive human values.

A number of plays in verse, mostly of the traditional form, have been written, notably by Khālid al-Shawwāf (b. 1924), who follows the conventional approach of relating historical events to the contemporary Arab situation. His *Al-Zaytūna* (1968; the olive tree), is set during the early years of Muhammad's mission, when the Arabs were divided and subjugated by Persia and the Byzantine Empire; its central idea is that only by depending on their native sources of inspiration were the Arabs able to forge and maintain an independent, united, and creative culture.

BIBLIOGRAPHY: Harris, G. L., ed., *Iraq: Its People, Its Society, Its Culture* (1958); Izzidien, Y., *Poetry and Iraqi Society: 1900–1945* (1962); Altoma, S. J., "Postwar Iraqi Literature," *BA*, 46 (1972), 211–17; Altoma, S. J., *Modern Arabic Literature: A Bibliography of Articles, Books, Dissertations, and Translations in English* (1975), passim; Badawi, M. M., *A Critical Introduction to Modern Arabic Poetry* (1975), passim; Boullata, I. J., ed., *Critical Perspectives on Modern Arabic Literature* (1980), passim

SALIH J. ALTOMA

For Kurdish writing in Iraq, see Kurdish Literature

IRISH LITERATURE

The literature of Ireland in the 20th c. is a complex amalgam of cultural traditions, styles, individual temperaments, and ideas that have been enriched by the pressures of political and social events. Two traditions—the Gaelic and the Anglo-Saxon—have been in dynamic tension for centuries: the Gaelic language and culture struggled for survival in the 19th c., and managed to stay alive in our own time. The Anglo-Saxon tradition was changed by William

Butler Yeats, John Millington Synge (qq.v.), Lady Gregory (1852–1932), and others who created a literature in English that was distinct from that of England and America. Irish writers forged an intensely national literature from Celtic myth and folklore, from convulsive political and social circumstances—including centuries of English domination, the deaths of patriots like Robert Emmett (1778–1803) and Charles Stewart Parnell (1846–1891), a famine, a rebellion in 1916 and civil war in the 1920s—and from the heritage of earlier Irish authors. Yeats left a record of his country's literary indebtedness in his poetry: in "To Ireland in the Coming Times" (1893) he invoked "Mangan, Davis, Ferguson" as shapers of the collective Irish consciousness. The poet James Clarence Mangan (1803–1849) made the Celtic tradition in poetry available to English readers in his verses and translations. Sir Samuel Ferguson (1810–1886) collected Irish folk songs and made the "Celtic Twilight" a motif in literature. And Thomas Davis (1814–1845), who published political essays in the 19th c., called for pride in native culture and a sense of national unity. These forerunners, however, are only part of the heritage behind 20th-c. Irish literature. Yeats, James Joyce, George Moore (qq.v.), and others openly acknowledged their debts to the European and English symbolists (q.v.) and realists of the 19th c. The Irish Literary Renaissance of the early 20th c.—as well as the continued creative work of our time—was nurtured by native writers and forces as well as by international currents.

Drama

One early force driving the Renaissance forward was the theater movement started by Yeats, Edward Martyn (1859–1923), George Moore, and Lady Gregory. Their Irish Literary Theatre produced Yeats's The Countess Cathleen in 1899, a drama with controversial religious overtones. In the same year, Douglas Hyde (1860–1949), a poet and scholar, contributed the first important Gaelic play, Casadh an tsúgáin (1899; The Twisting of the Rope, 1901). Thereafter, the direction of the Irish theater was a matter of dispute: should drama deal with folk and peasant themes, or should it move into other areas? In the short run the folk themes prevailed. By 1902 a new theater society emerged; this Irish National Dramatic Company (in 1903 it become the Irish National Theatre Society) produced Synge's In the Shadow of the Glen (1903) and Padraic Col-

um's (1881–1972) Broken Soil (1903), both plays that explored the lives of peasants. Synge's work appeared in the Abbey playhouse, provided by a subsidy from Miss A. E. F. Horniman; in 1907 The Playboy of the Western World, a comic "extravaganza" at once satiric and outrageous, rocked the Dublin theater world, causing riots and skyrocketing its author into international prominence. Synge's savage wit at the expense of the peasant mentality and his use of rhythmic native speech constituted a major breakthrough in the national theater—a lyric rebellion against convention.

A major wit and critic of society, George Bernard Shaw (q.v.), was outside the folk atmosphere of the theater movement: his John Bull's Other Island (produced 1904, pub. 1909), commissioned by Yeats, is a cerebral but highly humorous treatment of English-Irish political relations and Shaw's only work involved with the Irish situation.

During the early years of the century, Lady Gregory's tamer plays of peasant life were also produced. Spreading the News (1904), a slender comedy of small-town gossip, is representative of her gift for capturing folkways and humors. In the same year George Russell's (q.v.) Deidre was performed by the Ulster Literary Theatre, the Belfast branch of the dramatic movement. The peasant and mythic-heroic strains thus remained dominant. Yeats practiced both. The Pot of Broth (1902) and The King's Threshold (1904) illustrated his range and also gave him much needed training in shaping literary forms. He cursed plays "that have to be set up in fifty ways" but continued to write for the theater in a variety of styles; later in the century he turned to the stark, passionate language of Purgatory (1939) and experimented with the form of Japanese Noh plays.

The time following the 1916 uprising was a difficult one for the theater. It was not until the appearance of Sean O'Casey (q.v) that the drama had a figure of the magnitude of Yeats and Synge. O'Casey's intense plays of political and social strife were at once genre portrayals of urban life and epic treatments of a people's history. Transfiguring the language of Dublin's slums into a comic-ironic poetry, O'Casey chronicled the 1916 rebellion in The Plough and the Stars (1926). In Juno and the Paycock (1924) and The Shadow of a Gunman (1923) he examined the tragic impact of civil war on heroic and petty characters. A revolutionary himself, O'Casey is nevertheless humanistic and skeptical in these plays: human suffering is his

459

central concern, not ideology. His later expressionist (q.v.) experiments in *The Silver Tassie* (1928) did not receive the welcoming reception of these first three tragedies, and he subsequently broke with the Abbey Theatre.

Denis Johnston (q.v.) also took an expressionist direction in his plays. The Dublin Gate Theatre, devoted to experimental drama and far more adventurous than the Abbey, produced *The Old Lady Says "No!"* (1929).

Meanwhile, another writer of problem social plays, Paul Vincent Carroll (q.v.), came to prominence in the late 1920s and brought the spirit of Ibsen into Irish literature in an explicit way. While drawing on myth and legend for his imagery in *Shadow and Substance* (1937) and *The White Steed* (1939), he nevertheless wrote pungent exposés of provincial hypocrisy and violence that often featured the character of a heroic and rebellious bearer of truth.

Contemporary dramatists have continued to study the ways in which the "Irish situation" affects the individual. Brendan Behan (q.v.), an IRA veteran and "graduate" of a borstal (prison), explored the human aspects—sometimes even the humor—of capital punishment in *The Quare Fellow* (1954). His best play, *The Hostage* (1958), combines Irish social protest with richly imaginative dialogue. Brian Friel (b. 1929) also uses humor to deal with the condition of Ireland: in *Philadelphia, Here I Come* (1964) he studies a young Irishman on the eve of emigration. Friel's gifts and his dramatic craftsmanship are also notable in *Lovers* (1968), two one-act plays that embody the yearnings of limited people seeking fulfillment in modern Ireland. Hugh Leonard (b. 1928) has worked in a similar vein, especially in *Da* (1978), a father-son battle of wills that uses the motif of a young man trying to escape from his Irish past.

Poetry

One of the central concerns of the drama—how to represent the meaning of native experience—is even more pronounced in poetry. Yeats himself moved through several different phases in trying to embody his sense of what Ireland meant to universal experience. He began in the Pre-Raphaelite mode, painting mythological pictures with "glimmering girls" and yearning lovers. Lyrics such as "Who Goes with Fergus" (1893) deal with "love's bitter mystery" in a beautifully escapist manner. After his early period of theater work, he was dissatisfied with the vagueness of his style and

also wanted to "hammer" his thoughts "into unity." Strong, ironic lyrics of political disillusionment and love are characteristic of Yeats in the 1910s. By the 1920s his style became structurally more complex, idiomatic in diction, passionate, and meditative; he raged at Ireland through his character Crazy Jane and brooded on the country's seeming dissolution in the time of civil war.

At the end of his life Yeats addressed Irish poets in "Under Ben Bulben" (1939), his poetic last will and testament. He wanted them to "sing the peasantry," to be disciplined in their craft, and to remember the "seven heroic centuries" of Irish culture.

Austin Clarke (q.v.) is one of several major figures who shared Yeats's devotion to craft in representing Irish life and tradition. In poems from the 1920s he used Irish myth; in "A Sermon on Swift" (1968) he used the figure of Jonathan Swift to portray the bitter ironies of life in Dublin. Throughout the course of a long career he wrote finely shaped verse protesting political hatred and the cruelty of bourgeois society. Patrick Kavanagh (q.v), another poet of great range and depth, was a wit, an inspired lyric poet, and an explorer of Ireland's spiritual ills. In "The Paddidad" and "Who Killed James Joyce?" from *Come Dance with Kitty Stobling, and Other Poems* (1960), he attacks literary prostitutes, so-called poets and other purveyors of blarney and balderdash. The title poem in the volume is a vaunting lyric about imagination and passion. Kavanagh's most ambitious poem, *The Great Hunger* (1942), is about the modern "famine" in which life is "dried in the veins" of rural people "strangled" by work and convention.

Younger poets, while maintaining an obsession with social and political themes, have become increasingly dense and complex in texture. Thomas Kinsella's (b. 1928) elusive poems, especially those in *Nightwalker, and Other Poems* (1967), are less emotional than those of the older generation. Richard Murphy's (q.v.) work, however, is intricate while having a bardic, alliterative quality. His poem of political disillusionment, *The Battle of Aughrim* (1968), expresses the peasant's oppressed sense of Irish history. Also political is the work of John Montague (b. 1929), who deals with the great disasters of modern Ireland: in *The Rough Field* (1972) he explores the fate of the Gaelic language, and in "The New Siege" (1970) he gives the Northern Catholic perspective on violence in a framework that juxtaposes 17th- and 20th-c. events.

Seamus Heaney (q.v.) also treats life in Ulster —especially the hardships of farmers. "Requiem for the Croppies" (1969), a moving poem about the agricultural workers' revolt against the English in 1798, is an assertion of the enduring spirit of rebellion.

While not yet in the first ranks of Irish writers, Gaelic poets have made a continuing contribution. Padraic Pearse (1879–1916), the executed leader of the 1916 uprising, wrote a few lyrics, but was actually more interested in philosophizing about an Irish language "which would be noble and dignified, not merely indigenous." In the 1920s and 1930s, according to the critic David Greene, Gaelic "verse was at a standstill." This was in part due to the lack of models for young poets to imitate. Later Máirtin Ó Direáin (b. 1910) wrote lyrics that eloquently denounced the oppression of landlords. By 1950 Seán Ó Tuama produced an anthology called *Nuabhéarsaíocht* (new verse). Since then Gaelic poetry has taken several directions. Seán Ó Ríordáin (b. 1917) is deeply philosophical and interested in aesthetics. Maire Mhac an tSaoi (b. 1922) is a Dublin woman whose love lyrics are especially intense. While uncertain, the future of Gaelic verse is not without rising prospects. Michael Hartnett (b. 1941) has written *A Farewell to English* (1975), a fiery denunciation of Anglo-Saxon culture and an assertion that "Gaelic is our final sign/that we are human. . . ." He has vowed to write only in Irish henceforth.

Fiction

The movement for "de-Anglicizing" Ireland —which can be traced to Douglas Hyde's essay "The Necessity for De-Anglicising Ireland" (1892)—caused a number of prose writers to turn away from the oppressor's language. Among these are Pádraic Ó Conaire (1883–1928), who recorded urban experience in well-constructed short stories, some of which dealt with rebellion. A younger disciple, Séamus Ó Grianna (1891–1969) also wrote a novel of the upheaval, *Mo dhá Róisín* (1920; My Two Rosaleens). But the late 1920s saw a new form: "life stories" written by Blasket Island people who were not writers by profession. Tomas Crithin's (1856–1937) *An toileanach* (1929; *The Islandman,* 1934), Muiris Ó Súilleabháin's (1904–1950) *Fiche blian ag fás* (1933; *Twenty Years A-Growing,* 1933), and Peig Sayers's (1873–1958) *Peig* (1936; *Peig,* 1939) record the texture of a folk society and are notable for their feeling for elemental

things. But the highest achievements in Gaelic prose were in the modernist style. Máirtin Ó Cadhain (b. 1907) wrote *Cré na cille* (1949; graveyard), a complex venture into Joycean verbal experiment. Brian O'Nolan—alias Flann O'Brien (q.v.), alias Myles na Gopaleen—began his career as a satirist writing in English, but extended his wild parodies of the Irish character into Gaelic in *An béal bocht* (1941; *The Poor Mouth,* 1961) and various newspaper pieces.

Despite the importance of Gaelic, the major prose tradition in 20th-c. Ireland is in English. It is an immensely rich body of works with two strains: the realistic-symbolic and the explicitly experimental. The former strain is seen early in the century in George Moore's *The Untilled Field* (1903), a collection of stories about the frustrations and social decay of North Mayo life that is both suggestive in language and true to everyday experience. The unadorned style in this collection anticipates Joyce's "scrupulous meanness" in *Dubliners* (1914). Joyce used the facts of Dublin life and made ordinary scenes into "epiphanies" that constituted a "moral history" of the community.

Other writers used this subtle blend of realism and suggestion. Seamus O'Kelly's (1881–1918) posthumously published *The Weaver's Grave* (1920) is a haunting treatment of aged peasants that is grounded in the harshness of rural Ireland and emblematic of the universal search for death. Frank O'Connor (q.v.), a master of the well-crafted story, ranged over the comic trials of growing up poor and Catholic at the same time that he dealt with the mysteries of political violence and romantic love. Sean O'Faoláin (b. 1900) documented political troubles and did so in a lyrical style. Liam O'Flaherty (b. 1897) is a prolific novelist of strong political bent whose best-known work, *The Informer* (1925), is about the civil war. James Plunkett's (b. 1920) *Strumpet City* (1968), a panoramic study of Dublin in 1916, continues the realistic tradition of social awareness. An important collection of short stories by Benedict Kiely (b. 1919), *States of Ireland* (1980), is a testament to the vitality of a genre and also a link with the great tradition of George Moore and Frank O'Connor. In stories of private conflict and public turmoil, Kiely employs humor, meticulous character description, and a deeply humane perspective.

The realistic tradition has also been marked by intense concern for individual psyches. Elizabeth Bowen (q.v.), in fiction the preeminent figure of the Anglo-Irish Ascendancy, was an elegant anatomist of emotions. *The Death of the Heart* (1938) and her stories capture the moods of the Protestant gentry and in some ways are part of the mainstream of English fiction. Mary Lavin (b. 1912) is a deft and prolific short-story writer who studies the natures of a range of Irish people with great humor, irony, and insight. Her *Collected Stories* (1971) reflect work done since the 1940s and have caused V. S. Pritchett (q.v.) to liken her to the Russian masters. Sensitive psychological portrayal is also the characteristic of Brian Moore (q.v.) in *The Lonely Passion of Judith Hearne* (1955), a study of the collapse of a tormented Belfast woman. Edna O'Brien's (q.v.) fiction has mined similar territory, especially in a series of novels dealing with the emotional turmoils of young women. *The Lonely Girl* (1962) is conventional in style, but one of her later novels, *Night* (1972), has an almost surrealistic texture that evolves from the second prose tradition—the experimental.

James Stephens (q.v.) used a blend of myth, philosophy, and humor in *The Crock of Gold* (1912), but Joyce went far beyond this excursion into fantasy. His *A Portrait of the Artist as a Young Man* (1916) is the first major work of Irish prose to depart from the external life and plumb the depths of the self through dream, symbol, and stream-of-consciousness (q.v.). An advance stylistically on *Dubliners*, it employs a fugal technique to deal not with Dublin society, but with the developing consciousness, spiritual upheaval, and artistic destiny of the protagonist, Stephen Dedalus. In *Ulysses* (1922) Joyce opened out his vision with other central characters, gave it mythic dimensions, concentrated the action in a day, and wove internal lives together into a grand design representing human desire in the modern world. *Finnegans Wake* (1939) fragments and resynthesizes language, as it deals not with a day, but a night of dreams, archetypal recollections, and Irish myths.

Joyce's work seemed a dead end to many critics: where, after all, was there to go after refashioning language and penetrating to the recesses of the self? A member of Joyce's circle in Paris, Samuel Beckett (q.v.), who achieved international recognition with his play *Waiting for Godot* (1954), took up the challenge. While Joyce celebrated plenitude, Beckett took "lessness," destitution, and decay as his themes. A dry-witted voyager into the lives of mental patients, misfits, and bums, Beckett has fashioned a desperate universe where the only meaning seems to be the fruitless act of communicating. Linguistically unhoused, Beckett wrote *Murphy* (1938) in English and after the war turned to French in his trilogy, *Molloy* (1951; *Molloy*, 1955), *Malone meurt* (1951; *Malone Dies,* 1956), and *L'innomable* (1953); *The Unnamable*, 1958). These novels are among the greatest of our age: writing about a surreal place that has much in common with Ireland, Beckett journeys with his decrepit antiheroes into territories far stranger than those of *Ulysses* and *Finnegans Wake*.

While less philosophical than Joyce and Beckett, Flann O'Brien also tried to upend literary convention and form to create his own world of reveries and extended jokes. *At Swim-Two-Birds* (1939) is an outrageous parody of Celtic myth and bardic afflatus; at the same time it pokes fun at the act of writing novels. O'Brien kept native concerns and local color alive in his work—and kept his readers laughing at them. Some similar punning and skylarking can be seen in Brigid Brophy's (q.v.) *In Transit* (1969), a novel about consciousness, the craziness of modern civilization, and the language itself. The American-born J. P. Donleavy (b. 1926) has joined the Irish joking contest in his picaresque novel *The Ginger Man* (1955; rev. ed., 1958).

Essayistic Prose

Modern Irish literature has been rich in memoirs and belles lettres. The early years of the Irish Renaissance have been treated in an anecdotal and controversial manner by George Moore in his trilogy *Hail and Farewell* (1911–14). Yeats's *Autobiography* (1938), a collection written in the 1910s and 1920s, is a record of a poet's development, his relationship to his country and age, and more generally his awareness of Irish literary destiny. In a lighter vein Oliver St. John Gogarty's (1878–1957) *As I Was Going Down Sackville Street* (1937) is a witty remembrance of Dublin and its personalities. On the political and social questions, Frank O'Connor's *An Only Child* (1961) charts the growth and struggle of a Republican in time of civil war, while Sean O'Casey's massive autobiography, beginning with *I Knock at the Door* (1939), is a highly wrought story of his own consciousness and troubled times. In *Bowen's Court* (1942) Elizabeth Bowen used an even larger canvas to study her family history—and in a wider sense the world of the Anglo-Irish Ascendancy. Irish literary criticism owes much to Yeats and O'Connor as well as to more recent figures. Daniel Corkery

(1878–1965), a scholar of language and creative writer, taught Frank O'Connor Gaelic and left his imprint on criticism with *Synge and Anglo-Irish Literature* (1931). Lately, Conor Cruise O'Brien (b. 1917) has written essays with a strong social and political orientation while Denis Donoghue (b. 1928) has worked as a prolific and learned critic of literary modernism.

The spirit of the early Irish Renaissance—Synge's lyrical boldness, Yeats's and Joyce's passion for craftsmanship and hatred of convention—is kept alive in our time by writers who characteristically use irony, humor, realistic statement and experiment to represent Ireland's heritage of strife and suffering. Forged in a time of mounting cultural and political oppression, modern Irish literature has never lost its rebellious mission.

BIBLIOGRAPHY: Boyd, E. A., *The Contemporary Drama of Ireland* (1917); Morris, L. A., *The Celtic Dawn: A Survey of the Renascence in Ireland, 1889–1916* (1917); Boyd, E. A., *Ireland's Literary Renaissance* (1922); O'Connor, N. J., *Changing Ireland: Literary Backgrounds of the Irish Free State, 1889–1922* (1924); Colum, P., *The Road Round Ireland* (1926); Law, H. A., *Anglo-Irish Literature* (1926); Brugsma, R. P. C. B., *The Beginnings of the Irish Revival* (1933); Gwynn, S., *Irish Literature and Drama* (1936); Alspach, R. K., *A Consideration of the Poets of the Literary Revival in Ireland, 1889–1929* (1942); O'Sullivan, T. F., *The Young Irelanders* (1945); Clarke, A., *Poetry in Modern Ireland* (1951); Kelly, B. M., *The Voice of the Irish* (1952); Ussher, A., *Three Great Irishmen—Shaw, Yeats, Joyce* (1953); Ellis-Fermor, U. M., *The Irish Dramatic Movement*, 2nd ed. (1954); Taylor, E. R., *The Modern Irish Writers* (1954); Howarth, H., *The Irish Writers, 1880–1940* (1958); Kain, R. M., *Dublin in the Age of William Butler Yeats and James Joyce* (1962); Mercier, V., *The Irish Comic Traditon* (1963); Browne, R. B., Roscelli, J. W., and Loftus, R., eds., *The Celtic Cross: Studies in Irish Culture and Literature* (1964); Loftus, R. J., *Nationalism in Modern Anglo-Irish Poetry* (1964); Thompson, W. I., *The Imagination of an Insurrection, Dublin, Easter, 1916: A Study of an Ideological Movement* (1967); O'Connor, F., *A Short History of Irish Literature* (1967); Brown, M., *The Politics of Irish Literature* (1972); Greene, D., *Writing in Irish Today* (1972)

DAVID CASTRONOVO

ISHERWOOD, Christopher

Anglo-American novelist and memoirist, b. 26 Aug. 1904, High Lane, England

Born into the landed gentry in Cheshire, I. was educated at Repton School and Corpus Christi, Cambridge. After leaving Cambridge without a degree in 1925, he renewed his friendship with W. H. Auden (q.v.), his former classmate at St. Edmund's preparatory school. He lived in Berlin from 1930 to 1933; there he felt released from the social and sexual inhibitions that stifled his development in England. Disillusioned with left-wing politics and with English insularity, he emigrated to the United States in 1939 and declared himself a pacifist. Settling permanently in Los Angeles, I. began writing film scripts. In 1940 the influence of a Hindu monk and surrogate father, Swami Prabhavananda, prompted his conversion to Vedantism. He became a U.S. citizen in 1946. In 1971 he publicly revealed his homosexuality and became an active participant in the gay liberation movement.

I.'s earliest novels, *All the Conspirators* (1928) and *The Memorial* (1932), depict English middle-class malaise in the 1920s and reveal his mastery of narrative technique and ironic perspective. In the Berlin stories—*Mr. Norris Changes Trains* (1935; Am., *The Last of Mr. Norris*) and *Goodbye to Berlin* (1939)—I. created some of the most memorable characters in modern fiction, perfected his apparently naïve first-person narration, and brilliantly portrayed a city decaying from within. *Goodbye to Berlin* is among the most significant political novels of the 20th c., exploring the Nazi nightmare with startling insight and prophetic accuracy.

I.'s collaboration with Auden on three experimental verse dramas in the 1930s yielded less satisfactory work. The only really distinguished product of the Auden-I. collaboration is *Journey to a War* (1939), a travel book based on their 1938 trip to China.

His later novels, from *Prater Violet* (1945) through *A Meeting by the River* (1967), are enriched by the Vedantic influence. *Down There on a Visit* (1962) is a disturbing study of the Protean self, an unsentimental dissection of the author's past. *A Single Man* (1964), I.'s finest novel, masterfully balances worldly and religious concerns to create a double vision of the mundane and the transcendent. Beautifully written in a style that alternates between poetic intensity and ironic understatement, the book is a technical tour de force in which every nuance is perfectly controlled.

I.'s explicitly autobiographical works—*Lions and Shadows* (1938), *Kathleen and Frank* (1971), *Christopher and His Kind* (1976), and *My Guru and His Disciple* (1980)—succeed largely because of his novelistic gift of portraying his earlier selves as incomplete versions of his current consciousness.

I. may be the most self-absorbed of contemporary writers; yet his novels and autobiographies are never self-indulgent. They confront questions of alienation and isolation, of sexuality and spirituality, of maturity and transcendence. Born of scrupulous self-examination, I.'s penetrating vision illuminates the conflicts of our time.

FURTHER WORKS: *The Dog beneath the Skin* (1935, with W. H. Auden), *The Ascent of F 6* (1936, with Auden), and *On the Frontier* (1938, with Auden); *The Condor and the Cows* (1949); *The World in the Evening* (1954); *An Approach to Vedanta* (1963); *Ramakrishna and His Disciples* (1965); *Exhumations* (1966); *Frankenstein: The True Story* (1973, with Don Bachardy)

BIBLIOGRAPHY: Heilbrun, C. G., *C. I.* (1970); Wilde, A., *C. I.* (1971); Hynes, S. L., *The Auden Generation* (1976); Piazza, P., *C. I.: Myth and Anti-Myth* (1978); Finney, B., *C. I.: A Critical Biography* (1979); Funk, R. W., *C. I.: A Reference Guide* (1979); Summers, C. J., *C. I.* (1980)

CLAUDE J. SUMMERS

ISHIKAWA Takuboku

Japanese poet, critic, and diarist, b. 20 Feb. 1886, Hinoto village, Iwate prefecture; d. 13 April 1912, Tokyo

The only son of a Zen priest in a rural community in northern Japan, I. developed a strong, individualistic personality. From his student days on, he engaged in literary activity, dropping out of school in 1902 in order to go to Tokyo to become a writer. His first verses, in the form of *tanka* (or *waka,* thirty-one-syllable poems), were published in the influential periodical, *Myōjō,* and I. benefited from the tutelage of the editor, Yosano Tekkan (1873–1935), and his wife, the poet Yosano Akiko (1878–1942). In February 1903, I. became ill and was forced to return to his home in northern Japan. From this time until his death from tuberculosis, he struggled against abject poverty and failing health.

I.'s first collection of verse, *Akogare* (1905; longing), demonstrated a strong romantic bent, but thereafter his poetry took on an independent direction. With *Ichiaku no suna* (1910; *A Handful of Sand,* 1934) he established himself as a leading writer of *tanka,* to which he imparted a new tone of realism. He endeavored to write "poems that are down to earth, poems with feelings unremoved from actual life," and he abhorred all traces of imitativeness. The 551 verses of *Ichiaku no suna* were integrated to form a unified whole, imparting a sense of growth and progression to the collection and giving somewhat the effect of a spiritual autobiography in verse. Through *Ichiaku no suna* and his posthumously published book of verse, *Kanashiki gangu* (1912; sad toys), I. infused a powerful new current of life into the old tradition of *tanka.* His verses continue to be anthologized in Japanese school texts, and later *tanka* poets have accepted his innovations, which changed the very nature of this form of poetry.

In the last years of his life, after the trial behind closed doors and execution (which followed immediately) of the Japanese anarchist philosopher Kōtoku Shūsui (1871–1911), I. was increasingly moved by socialist ideals, as verses such as the following reveal: "Still quite far away/I believed it all to be;/But the terrorists'/Plaintive and heart-rending cry/ Day by day now draws nearer." In 1910–12, in association with Toki Zemmaro (1885–1980), *tanka* poet, essayist, and scholar of Japanese literature, I. attempted to publish a socialist literary magazine. The venture failed, but their friendship, ardor for socialism, and efforts to establish a proletarian *tanka* group continued undiminished. One week before I.'s death, Toki Zemmaro delivered the manuscript for *Kanashiki gangu* to the publisher and used the twenty-yen advance to buy medicine to comfort his dying friend.

I.'s diaries and miscellaneous writings, as well as his verse, are admired for the stark revelation of his search for love and his struggle against poverty, despair, and death. His *Romaji nikki* (1948–49; partial tr., *The Romaji Diary,* 1956), the especially noteworthy journal that I. kept in the spring of 1909, stands out as one of the memorable works of 20th-c. Japan. It reveals a completely modern three-dimensional man, capable of introspection and displaying fierce, self-destructive honesty.

One of the first modern voices in Japanese poetry, I. is best remembered for the way in which he utilized the traditional *tanka* form to articulate new problems of the modern age. Despite the brevity of his life, I.'s subsequent influence on *tanka* poets such as Saitō Mokichi (1882–1953), Nishimura Yōkichi (1892–1959), and Watanabe Junzō (1894–1972) marks him as one of the significant innovators and as one of the enduring voices in 20th-c. Japanese literature. I.'s writings reveal not a tranquil world of soft rain sounds and delicate relations but rather the shrill outcry of a tortured young soul, pouring forth a red-hot stream of uncontrollable passion.

FURTHER WORKS: *Yobiko to kuchibue* (1913); *Takuboku zenshū* (8 vols., 1978). FURTHER VOLUMES IN ENGLISH: *The Poetry of I. T.* (1959); *Takuboku: Poems to Eat* (1966).

BIBLIOGRAPHY: Takamine, H., *A Sad Toy: A Unique and Popular Poet, Takuboku's Life and His Poems* (1962); Keene, D., *Landscapes and Portraits* (1971), pp. 131–70; Hijiya, Y., *I. T.* (1979)

LEON M. ZOLBROD

ISRAELI LITERATURE

Because Israel declared itself an independent state only in 1948, any literature before that date is technically non-Israeli. In practice, however, May 1948 is not a particularly significant literary watershed. The official language of the new state was to be Hebrew, and Israeli literature inherited the long tradition of Hebrew literature, whose origins are biblical and whose written output extended over several millennia and to all those parts of the world where Jewish communities and culture flourished.

More specifically, Israeli literature is in the tradition of the new Hebrew literature of modern times, encapsulating two major trends: (1) the secularizing, although partially national, tendency of the Jewish Enlightenment (late 18th c. and following) and (2) the tendency toward a return to the ancient Palestinian homeland, where the reborn cuture could flourish unhampered. The Hebrew Enlightenment struggled for increased lexical and syntactic scope, and for an extension of literary genres beyond the medieval and traditional bounds. A breakdown of old forms of community and religion in the wake of secularization and social unrest was noted by the greatest of the new Hebrew masters, sometimes with enthusiasm and sometimes with foreboding. In the late 19th c.

satirists such as the Yiddish and Hebrew novelist Mendele Mokher Sforim (1836–1917) both attacked characteristic social patterns and mourned the passing of the old. The leading poet of the generation, Chayim Nachman Bialik (q.v.), blended his own sense of existential tragedy with a description of the national character of the Jewish people to create the effects of an ineradicable pathos.

Until the World War I the chief centers of modern Hebrew creativity were in the Diaspora, particularly in eastern Europe. But the ravages of that war, the Bolshevik revolution, and the Russian civil war effectively destroyed the old-style Pale of Settlement and the *shtetl* within. This process was to be completed during World War II and the Holocaust of European Jewry. Meanwhile, the World War I victory of the British, who had offered the Balfour Declaration of November 1917, stimulated the movement of Jews to Palestine. The wave (now the third such wave) of the period following the war more than doubled existing Jewish settlement, and, in spite of major setbacks, the so-called *yishuv* (Jewish community of Palestine) established itself as a state on the way. The ongoing disaster of European Jewry reinforced this tendency, so that by 1939, a state, now challenged by systematic Arab opposition, could begin to emerge. Other centers of Hebrew creativity were dying in three major areas: (1) in western Europe, where the Holocaust was to trap the Jews, and, of course, their culture; (2) in eastern Europe, where Communism was throttling the "counterrevolutionary" language of Hebrew, together with other independent sources of Jewish expression; and (3) in the U.S.A. (which had become the home of the single largest Jewish population in the world), where cultural and linguistic assimilation was proceeding apace. In the new circumstances, only Palestine/Israel was a possible Hebrew center.

With Israeli independence Hebrew could now flourish not just as a literary language but as a current vernacular and the official medium of expression in the new state. Meanwhile, Hebrew writers of the early part of the century had established themselves in Palestine, so that by the 1920s a self-conscious Palestinian-Hebrew literature had been created. Avraham Shlonsky (1900–1973), Uri Zvi Greenberg, and Natan Alterman (qq.v.)—all poets nourished in eastern Europe—moved to Palestine in this period with the third wave. S. Y. Agnon (q.v.) returned to Palestine in 1924 after an earlier stay there before World War I.

465

The Oriental Hebrew novelist Yehuda Burla (1887–1969) was Palestinian-born, as was the poet Esther Raab (b. 1899). On the one hand, there was a natural drawing on the local soil by the native writer, and, on the other hand, some of the immigrant writers, in different ways, sought to assume a Palestinian identity by obliterating traces of the Diaspora. The earlier warnings issued by Yosef H. Brenner (1881–1921) against the Palestinian genre as such might have exerted their influence on the writers of the second wave (from 1909 onward —the first was in the early 1880s), but the third wave saw Palestine and a specifically local literature established as a major focus. In "Masada" (1929; Masada), a long poem by Yitzhak Lamdan (1900–1954), the poetic narrator idealized labor in the tones of a Russian revolutionary poet; Greenberg donned prophetic garb; Agnon turned to the Palestinian epic; and Chayim Hazaz (1898–1972) incorporated the Palestinian scene in his narrative subject matter.

In the poet Saul Tchernichowsky (q.v.) we find an interesting fusion of universalism and nationalism. The poet regarded himself as "a strange plant" among the Jewish people, a rebel renegade admiring Greek and Canaanite strength rather than Jewish weakness. Thus, he argued for a more masculine Jewish assertiveness and nationalism. He emigrated to Palestine in 1931, at a stage where he could still be shaped by the new environment in his creativity. His writing marks out a program for the life of the individual and the nation. Its combination of heresy and ethnicity sat well with the conditions of emergent Israel.

So by 1948, the literary character of the country was established, just as the social and political molds had also settled. Some of the most notable exponents of Israeli literature had begun writing earlier. The Sabra novelist Yizhar Smilansky (b. 1916) began to publish in 1938, seeking a richer lexical and syntactic language for the expressive consciousness of his narrative pivot. However long his story, the plot is always sparse. His central concerns are the landscape, the moral issue, the indecisive hero, and the language itself. But the plot is characteristically unresolved by any action. The poetry of Chayim Guri (b. 1921), which started to appear at the close of the War of Independence, focuses on war, the hero, his beloved, his bloody memories—a very local scene. Many of the heroes in the novels and stories of Moshe Shamir (b. 1921) are not only native-born, but see themselves as a different species from the Diaspora Jew. The new Israeli is characterized as simple, direct, active, healthy, single-minded, and strong, in contrast to the divided, urban, tortured Diaspora Jew. Shamir, like others, set up a small journal, *Yalkut hareim,* and the general description of this writing as "Palmach literature" (named after the striking arm of the Haganah—defense forces) owes its origins to this sense of comradeship and a single, collective purpose. The subject matter for treatment was, in general, emergent Israel: absorption of immigrants, the war, the kibbutz, the issues of the new state. The concerns were practical and ideological, of public polity rather than the individual.

The 1950s witnessed changes on various fronts. Poets became more introspective and skeptical, doubtful of the collective thrust, and began uncertainly to look over their shoulder to their forebears and earlier Jewish existence. Yehuda Amichai (q.v.) made much of the contrast between the generations, highlighted by the surprising image become metaphor. Amir Gilboa (b. 1917), whose initial power derived its original expression from the public Jewish situation and Israeli independence, articulated uncertain introspection in his later poetry. Natan Zach (b. 1930) has always been concerned with the private world of the poet and with the delicate structure of interpersonal relationships. Pinchas Sadeh (b. 1929), seeing "life as a parable," started to produce a rather un-Israeli type of confessional prose, whose concerns were the self, truth, and God. Intense religious experience has not been a prominent subject of Israeli authors, although the poet known simply as Zelda (b. 1913) has more recently begun to express an ecstatic certainty of God's presence in the constant face of death. But away from public commitments, the heroes of Israeli novels of the 1950s and 1960s are seen in flight from their official or imagined roles. Shamir's work moved in this direction. The characters of the novelist Aharon Megged (b. 1920) are sometimes disillusioned, making their way from the kibbutz to the city, as in *Chedvah vaani* (1954; Chedvah and I) or away from the enslavement to the national myth, as in *Hachai al hamet* (1965; living on the dead).

Israeli existence was, of course, multitinted. But ideologies had not only been promoted as in conflict, but sometimes as peculiar and exclusive to the new Israel. One such ideology was aired in the periodical *Alef,* which was founded in the 1940s to advocate a sort of Hebrew Semitic Union unconnected with Diaspora Jewry and which continued to press for a secular Middle Eastern state. Another, although less certain, ideology appeared in a forum entitled *Likrat*, distributed from 1952 on—it had neither a leftist nor rightist orientation. These were alternative voices to the predominant public policy of strong Zionism. But these voices were often muted as the literature of the State of Israel in general became less sure of itself and its direction less certain. Israel was and is characterized by division and has become increasingly "normalized," that is, the people are now more concerned with their own personal situation. So too has its literature become less publicly oriented, although the Land of Israel—Erets Yisrael—naturally remains, at least subliminally, its subject—and its object, too, in the sense that the literature expresses ideological aspirations for the country.

One aspect of the revival of Israel in the context of Hebrew literature is the emergence of the Cinderella of literary genres into the limelight. Hebrew drama had always been relatively weak—for lack of a living vernacular, for lack of a stage, and for lack of a tradition in the genre. The two best Israeli dramatists are Nissim Aloni (q.v.), who is also a short-story writer, and Hanoch Levin (b. 1943). Aloni has written naturalistically of his youth in his fiction, and built poetic fantasies in his plays. Perhaps this removal from current reality illustrates a difficulty of Hebrew drama. Levin, on the other hand, is a satirist, whose low-keyed characters comment on Israeli obsessions and political and social attitudes. At first execrated as unpatriotic, particularly with the staging of *Malkat haambatyah* (1972; queen of the bathtub), Levin is now in the acceptable mainstream of the Israeli stage. His predominant character bases his life on expectation rather than fulfillment, and so illuminates the nature of human aspirations.

More recent years have seen moves backward in time, to earlier history formative of the present, and forward, to a concern with total contemporaneity. Aharon Appelfeld (b. 1932), in fiction such as *Badenhaim ir nofesh* (1975; *Badenheim 1939*, 1980), writes mainly of Israel's prehistory, of a European Jewry in its twilight world, reaching for assimilation on its path to destruction, and of the world of the survivors in Israel rooted in that past. It is both the world of the author's childhood and the public Israeli world of an often unacknowl-

edged infancy. The novelist A. B. Yehoshua (b. 1937), author of *Bitchilat kayits 1970* (1971; *Early in the Summer of 1970*, 1977) and *Hamahev* (1977; *The Lover*, 1978), among others, has stated that his object is to render contemporary Israeli man and his paradoxical dilemmas. Amos Oz (q.v.) has sought symbols of the Israeli situation, images of terror and siege that haunt ordinary people, whose interior lives are really quite extraordinary. He, too, has attempted to recover his own childhood world and the pre-1948 Palestinian world in a collection of novellas *Har haetsah haraah* (1976; *The Hill of Evil Counsel*, 1978).

Many of Israel's younger fiction writers, then, view Israel within a larger context: either in its condition of terror and siege, or in relation to a past, which, although gone, still lives in the present. Israel may be small and isolated, but it is revealed in its literature as relating to history and current politics.

The current scene abounds with experimentation in mimesis. Amalia Kahana-Carmon (b. 1926) has long been writing intensely rendered stream-of-consciousness stories, often as if they were narrated by a child or by an adult with a childlike point of view who is fixated on another individual. Yaakov Shabtai (b. 1934) produced a series of short narrative extravaganzas, then a long novel written in one paragraph, *Zichron dvarim* (1977; memory of things), moving from one death at its opening, to another at its close, the first of Goldmann's father, the second the suicide of the son; it moves as well from the banal to the tragic with apparently effortless control. Shabtai has also contributed to the drama with a political satire based on the biblical story of Ahab and Jezebel called *Ochlim* (1979; eating). Yona Wallach (b. 1935) has attempted to reproduce the effect of trance in her poems, which seek to etch unusual experience; a very frail individual stands at their center. Confessional autobiography of the type of Pinchas Sadeh's, although without Sadeh's religious mysticism, and with a fair admixture of humor, has been produced by Dan Ben-Amots (b. 1923), either directly, reporting his own history and thought à la Henry Miller (q.v.), or through someone else, only thinly disguising the authorial voice.

One of the most striking recent achievements of Israeli fiction writers is a reconstruction of the European background told, as it were, by a Berlin-born Israeli narrator: the novel by David Schütz (b. 1941) called *Haesev ve-*

hachol (1978; the grass and the sand). Although the narrator Emmanuel controls the novel, different voices speak within, giving their account of events and the family. It is Emmanuel whose initiative it is to return to his "home" and attempt a resolution of his past with his present, of himself with his family and background, with a history going back to the middle Europe of the turn of the century.

A very complex picture emerges in a survey of the Israeli literary scene. By now, the dominant language is Hebrew, although literature in other languages is produced by, for example, long-standing English-speaking expatriates, or by more recent Soviet immigrants. A Hebrew literary tradition has been inherited and modified, sometimes by writers with little knowledge of or sympathy with that tradition. Hebrew is a language rich in traditional and liturgical associations but young as a vernacular. Its writers are of several generations and vastly different cultural and geographical backgrounds. But they jostle together in the turbulent current of Hebrew literature: the young and the old, the Israeli-born and the recent immigrant, the Zionist conservative and the radical, the Oriental and the European Jew, the religious and the secular Jew, the hopeful and the disillusioned.

BIBLIOGRAPHY: Klausner, J., *A History of Modern Hebrew Literature* (1932); Ribalow, M., *Modern Hebrew Literature: A Volume of Literary Evaluation* (1959); Epstein, G. L., and Zeldner, M., *Modern Hebrew Literature* (1965); Mintz, R. F., ed., Introduction to *Modern Hebrew Poetry: A Bilingual Anthology* (1968), pp. xxiii–liv; Rabinovich, I., *Major Trends in Modern Hebrew Fiction* (1968); Alter, R., *After the Tradition* (1969), pp. 163–256; Halkin, S., *Modern Hebrew Literature: From the Enlightenment to the Birth of the State of Israel* (1970); Yudkin, L. I., *Escape into Siege: A Survey of Israeli Literature Today* (1974); Sandbank, S., Introduction to Anderson, E., ed., *Contemporary Israeli Literature: An Anthology* (1977), pp. 3–17; Alter, R., "Afterword: A Problem of Horizons," in Anderson, E., ed., *Contemporary Israeli Literature: An Anthology* (1977), pp. 326–38; Hamalian, L., and Yohannan, J. D., eds., "The Israeli Background," *New Writing from the Middle East* (1978), pp. 189–95; Abramson, G., *Modern Hebrew Drama* (1979); Yudkin, L. I., *Jewish Writing and Identity in the Twentieth Century* (1982)

LEON I. YUDKIN

For Yiddish writing in Israel, see Yiddish Literature

ITALIAN LITERATURE

A survey of 20th-c. Italian literature must begin with such turn-of-the-century writers as Giovanni Verga, Giovanni Pascoli, and Gabriele D'Annunzio (qq.v.), whose innovations in technique and content have exerted a vast influence on the writers of our century.

Verga is now considered—especially for the two novels of his maturity, *I Malavoglia* (1881; *The House by the Medlar Tree*, 1890) and *Mastro-don Gesualdo* (1889; *Mastro-Don Gesualdo*, 1893)—one of the greatest masters of modern European literature. He was a practitioner of *verismo* (truthfulness-to-life)—a poetic of the poor and humble—which emphasizes impersonality: "The work itself [he wrote] must have the imprint of a real event; the work of art will seem to have been made by itself. . . ." In the novels on which his fame rests, Verga succeeded in putting himself "under the skin" of his characters in order to speak with and through their brains, hearts, and language. His Sicilianism is evident throughout—in syntax, rhythm, inflection, words, solecisms, proverbs—because Verga's major goal was to write what he "picked up along the paths of the countryside, almost with the same simple and picturesque words of a popular narration." *I Malavoglia* and *Mastro-don Gesualdo* were the first two books of a projected sequence of five novels—the other three were never written—to be called *I vinti* (the defeated ones). He wanted to give the reader "the naked and unchanged facts, instead of having him look for them between the lines of a book." Massimo Bontempelli (q.v.)—the writer of "magic realism" (q.v.)—perceptively observed at the centennial of Verga's birth in 1940 that "he opened the doors of the twentieth century years before D'Annunzio closed the doors of the nineteenth."

Pascoli, the father of modern Italian poetry, was another antitraditionalist whose main concern was to re-create the lives, feelings, and language of humble people. Perhaps it is true, as Pier Paolo Pasolini (q.v.) claimed, that modern Italian poetry is an elaboration of Pascoli. Certainly, we find a complexity of psychological depth and existential predicament in him that we later find in poets from the *Crepuscolari* (twilight poets) to Eugenio Montale (q.v.).

Pascoli works in a manner of deliberate primitivity, and his poetics have been called "pregrammatical" or "biological." His "Il fanciullino" (1897; the little boy) is the basic essay for understanding his work. Although man grows older, he still carries in his heart the simplicity and humility of a little boy who sees everything with innocent awe and astonishment and who speaks in his own infantile language to "animals, trees, stones, and stars." This is not to say that Pascoli is not a poet of considerable consciousness, and Pasolini rightly states that "an irrational power forces Pascoli to a stylistic firmness and to an *intentional* power that lead him to stylistic tendencies very different [from those of his contemporaries]." He was particularly interested in the preservation of dialectal forms, and at the end of his *Canti di Castelvecchio* (1903; songs of Castelvecchio) he printed a dictionary of dialect words. He was a precursor of the national popular literature, which Antonio Gramsci (1891–1937) always advocated, although it must be also said that an autobiographical thread runs through all Pascoli's work: his family, his home, his people, his patriotism, his pessimism, and his obsession with death.

Unlike Verga and Pascoli, D'Annunzio has been an object of both praise and repudiation in Italy and the rest of Europe not only for his writings but also for his audacious military enterprises, his extravagant life, and his support of Fascism (although he later came to reject Mussolini and to write an epigram against Hitler). What looks like the sheerest bombast becomes upon reconsideration a document of an artist's life and work. That he was given to the hyperbole of the superman is true beyond doubt: verse, he wrote, "can represent the superhuman, the supernatural, the superadmirable. . . ." But he was not without a certain modesty, and in "Contemplazione della morte" (1912; Contemplation of death), speaking of his last encounter with Pascoli, he candidly admits that "no modern craftsman possessed Pascoli's art. . . . Nobody knew better than he [Pascoli] that art is nothing but practical magic. 'Teach me some secret,' I asked him." Montale, not just a great poet but an incisive critic, well knew that D'Annunzio's influence "is present in all [writers] because he experimented or touched all the linguistic and prosodic possibilities of our time. In this sense, not to have learned anything from him is the worst sign."

Verismo—elsewhere called realism or naturalism—is a significant element in many modern Italian writers. Matilde Serao (1850–1927), the Neapolitan "verista," anecdotal and impressionistic in her best novels, explored the poorest, most squalid places in order to portray the tragic existence of a people who have borne the social injustice of centuries.

Ada Negri (1870–1945), another analyst of suffering and humiliation, characterized the poor so accurately in her novels because she saw in them her "own suffering and humiliation." Sibilla Aleramo (pseud. of Rina Faccio, 1876–1960), in her largely autobiographical novel *Una donna* (1906; *A Woman at Bay*, 1908), examines the struggle of a woman in a society dominated by men. In her consciousness of the impact of women in social and artistic endeavors, Aleramo was the chief forerunner of Italian feminist literature.

The Nobel Prize-winning Grazia Deledda (q.v.) portrays her native Sardinia as an almost mythical country: in the autobiographical *Il paese del vento* (1931; country of the wind) or in that fable of childhood *Cosima* (1937; Cosima), Sardinia emerges as a place of fantastic natural beauty whose people live in subjection to their violent instincts and passions. Salvatore Di Giacomo (q.v.), who mostly wrote in Neapolitan dialect, was another brilliant representative of southern *verismo* in his depiction of dirty houses, public dormitories, almshouses, hospitals, prisons, and the underworld of thieves, murderers, and prostitutes. But Di Giacomo's descriptions are compassionate outcries on behalf of human dignity.

Realism assumed new psychological dimensions in the work of Luigi Pirandello, Italo Svevo, and Federigo Tozzi (qq.v.). Pirandello's representative characters are haunted by their quicksilver powers of reasoning, which at times change them into grotesque clowns in search of a self, in search of a life to be lived, or in search of a demiurge to create for them a play—as the internationally famous *Sei personaggi in cerca d'autore* (1921; *Six Characters in Search of an Author*, 1922)—that would summon their essence into existence. The Pirandellian self is always on the brink of dissolving into a hundred thousand different entities in a world without secure coordinates; his characters have difficulty differentiating between reality and fiction, between dream and what "perhaps is not" dream. Pirandello is the most important Italian playwright of the century.

Like Pirandello, Svevo rejected a pure *verismo* for a new analysis of interior reality, as in *La coscienza di Zeno* (1923; *The Confessions of Zeno*, 1930). His intent is to scrutinize the unconscious—by using, for example, the technique of the interior monologue (q.v.)—investigating the psyches of his characters and their conflicts in an interplay of past and present. In a kind of psychoanalytic vivisection, Svevo reveals the ineptitude and emptiness of his antiheroes. Although he has been criticized for grammatical and syntactical incertitude, it is precisely his simple, ordinary language, often arid and imperfect, that makes him so modern and fascinating.

In his youth, Tozzi was influenced by D'Annunzio, by the Christian mystics of his native Siena, and then by Verga, although his "defeated ones" are not characterized by "impersonality." In *Tre croci* (1920; *Three Crosses,* 1921) and *Il podere* (1921; the farm), for instance, the critic Gianfranco Contini (b. 1912) observes that there is a "psychopathological analysis" of the solitude of man without any possibility of redemption. Tozzi penetrates his subject with an anguished intuition, his characters (and he himself) oscillating between reason and hallucination. His work is the autobiography of a tormented writer, utopian and inept, wild and doomed, mystical and sinning.

Another writer influenced by Verga was the Sicilian Vitaliano Brancati (q.v.), an accomplished artist who was able to enter the soul of his people, to analyze their suffering and frustrations. He was particularly successful in satirizing the Sicilian *gallismo,* the erotic obsession of the male that makes him a bragging dominator and seducer of women, even when he is impotent and his sexual bravado is entirely faked. Although his subject matter was often crude and gloomy, Brancati, in a brilliant fusion of pessimism and wit, realism and comedy, portrayed his characters forcefully and vividly. Moreover, the satire of male chauvinism is a metaphor of a Fascist regime built on empty words, not on facts.

Francesco Jovine (q.v.), a southern writer of fiction, one of the most important later followers of *verismo,* like Ignazio Silone or Corrado Alvaro (qq.v.), is concerned with the humiliating conditions of the peasants of his Abruzzi province. Their poverty is due not only to the bareness of their land but also to the exploitation by the rich people with whom they try, unsuccessfully, to deal. In his masterpiece, *Le terre del Sacramento* (1950; *The Estate in Abruzzi,* 1952), a novel about the origins of Fascism, he depicts the defeat of the farmers in their struggle with the feudal landlords, the police, and the Fascist soldiers.

Mario Soldati (q.v.) is also a committed yet popular novelist. His stylistic simplicity and his study of the human psyche are strictly connected with his concern for the moral welfare of his characters as they wrestle with the deceptions of their society.

At the beginning of the 20th c. creative Italian literature was closely tied to the activity of a new generation of critics, the most important and influential member of which was Benedetto Croce (q.v.), whose notions of lyrical intuition and the identification of intuition with expression are argued in many of his books, and in *La critica,* the journal of history, literature, and philosophy he edited (1903–44), and its supplements, *Quaderni della critica,* which played an important role in the intellectual and cultural life of Italy. Croce's criticism of Verga, Pascoli, Pirandello, and other modern writers no longer seems appropriate, but his vision of poetry is as apt as ever: "This is the enchantment of poetry: the unity of tumult and calm, of the passionate impulse of the mind that contains it while contemplating it." Croce must also be praised for his daring anti-Fascist manifesto of 1925.

Giuseppe Prezzolini (b. 1882) founded *La voce* in 1908 with the intention of inspiring a new consciousness in the psychological and moral attitude of the young in regard to contemporary life. Until 1912 *La voce* was primarily a journal of social concern. Afterward it became more literary, and from 1914 to its demise in 1916 it was edited by Giuseppe de Robertis (1888–1963), who gave it real literary merit, welcoming a host of writers who would soon become important, such as Vincenzo Cardarelli, Umberto Saba, Riccardo Bacchelli, Clemente Rebora, Camillo Sbarbaro, Aldo Palazzeschi, Dino Campana, Giuseppe Ungaretti (qq.v.), and Salvatore Di Giacomo.

The first important movement in 20th-c. Italian poetry is called *Crepuscolarismo,* or "twilight poetry," so called by the critic Giuseppe Antonio Borgese (1882–1952), who thought the great 19th-c. sun of Italian poetry had set. The *Crepuscolari* specialized in existential anxiety: the world is empty, the city is made of stones, Sundays are boring. Montale's poem "Non chiederci la parola" (1925; do not ask us for the word) is perhaps the best description of the movement's consciousness: "Do not ask us for the word . . . /Do not ask us for the formula that might open worlds . . ./Today we can tell you only this/what we are *not,* what we *do not* want."

The existential predicament is also visible in Guido Gozzano (q.v.), Sergio Corazzini (1886–1907)—especially in his famous poem "Desolazione del povero poeta sentimentale" (1906; "Desolation of the Poor Sentimental

Poet," 1962)—Corrado Govoni (1884–1965), Aldo Palazzeschi, Dino Campana, Camillo Sbarbaro, Umberto Saba, and Clemente Rebora. Since they opened a new direction (after Pascoli) in Italian poetry, perhaps they should be called the "sunrise poets."

Futurism (q.v.), on the other hand, was devoted not only to poetry, but to painting, sculpture, and theater, as well as to political and social action. The movement was started by Filippo Tommaso Marinetti (q.v.), whose first manifesto, which appeared in French in *Le Figaro* in 1909, exalted speed, danger, rebellion, and war. Marinetti was the herald of Fascism and associated his own movement with it in *Futurismo e Fascismo* (1924; futurism and Fascism). In *Lacerba,* a journal founded by Giovanni Papini (1881–1956) and Ardengo Soffici (1879–1965), Marinetti published such essays as "Parole in libertà" (1913; words set free), which in their grammatical and syntactical license and their typographical oddity sought to violate the logical and sequential representations of literature.

Two journals that took implicit and explicit issue with Fascism were *La ronda* (1919–23) and *Solaria* (1926–36). *La ronda* was edited by Cardarelli, Bacchelli, Emilio Cecchi (1884–1960), and Antonio Baldini (1889–1966); it sought a "pure poetry," cited the virtues of Giacomo Leopardi (1798–1837) and Alessandro Manzoni (1785–1873), and rejected Fascism as an expression of barbarism. *Solaria* affirmed not only such modern European masters as Proust and Joyce (qq.v.) but such younger Italians as Elio Vittorini, Cesare Pavese, Vasco Pratolini, Carlo Emilio Gadda, Guido Piovene (qq.v.), Saba, and those who would become the exponents of neorealism (q.v.).

The important school of 20th-c. Italian poetry is doubtless hermeticism (q.v.), a term coined in 1936 by the Crocean critic Francesco Flora (1891–1962) as an expression of polemical disdain. And, in truth, hermeticism is a poetry for the initiated. Silvio Ramat (b. 1939) describes it as an "ideology of the word," which had to be obscure not only in the face of Fascist censorship but in the endless significations of language. "The poet is a partisan of freedom," Ungaretti said of Apollinaire (q.v.); "he nourishes the dream that one day all persons will be free."

Eugenio Montale, a Nobel Prize winner, claimed that nobody writes verses "to be understood." The problem is to make readers "understand that *quid* which words cannot express." In Montale the simple and modest facts of life and poetry assume a symbolic and emblematic function. Against the "laureate poets" in their ivory towers, he creates a literature of pessimism. Gianfranco Contini calls him a "negative" poet, like Leopardi, but one who has made the highest contribution to a new European poetry. Nor has Montale been unaware of his contribution: "I believe that my poetry has been the most musical poetry of my time. . . ."

Salvatore Quasimodo (q.v.), honored with the Nobel Prize in 1959, is a critic and translator who also started writing poetry in the hermetic climate. But he transcended it for a mythicization of Sicily. There is in him a sense of isolation and a mystery of symbols that pervades his solitude. Diametrically opposed is Carlo Betocchi (q.v.), a poet of humble things, forever faithful to his Christian aspiration, learned in a life that did not spare him long suffering. Betocchi, the holy patriarch of Italian letters, attracts everyone who meets him with a magnetism of peace and light.

The second phase of hermeticism flourished in Florence from about 1930 to 1945. Piero Bigongiari (q.v.), a poet and critic, was and still is the soul of the movement, at once reminiscent of such older poets as Ungaretti and Montale, and prophetic of a new avant-garde. Mario Luzi (q.v.), moving from his hermetic origins, has investigated the precarious condition of man in our time with the *piety* of a religious sensibility. Alfonso Gatto (q.v.) gravitated toward a poetry of lyrical—yet heartfelt—impact with his poems on World War II and the Resistance. Vittorio Sereni (b. 1913), also once hermetic, moved toward a poetry of private sorrow and passivity, of empathy with people exploited by a capitalist society. The early work of a younger poet, Andrea Zanzotto (q.v.), was a continuation of hermeticism. In fact, his masters included Montale, Ungaretti, and Luzi. Later he created a personal and distinctive poetry based on the most daring linguistic innovations, aimed at a "verbalization of the world." Praised by great poets and critics, such as Montale and Contini, Zanzotto, like his hermetic predecessors, has opened the doors to new and audacious trends in poetry.

It was during the twenty years of Fascism and in response to the apparent splendor of that regime that the forerunners of neorealism began to gather force. Among these, Corrado Alvaro, in *Gente in Aspromonte* (1930; *Revolt in Aspromonte,* 1962) dramatized the injustices perpetrated in the south against the poor; Carlo Bernari (q.v.), in *Tre operai* (1934; three workers), expressed the fears, discouragement, and suffering of the proletariat; Elio Vittorini, in *Conversazione in Sicilia* (1941; *In Sicily,* 1947); described the misery of Sicilians as the misery of the world; Cesare Pavese, in *Paesi tuoi* (1941; *The Harvesters,* 1961), exposed the countryside as a place of superstitious and savage archaism; Alberto Moravia (q.v.), with the novel *Gli indifferenti* (1929; *The Indifferent Ones,* 1932), portrayed with a crude realism the false values of the bourgeoisie. Later, in *La mascherata* (1941; *The Fancy Dress Party,* 1952), Moravia presented a sarcastic and grotesque depiction of Fascist dictatorship.

Ignazio Silone must be included among the forerunners of neorealism, although his novel *Fontamara* was published in Italy only after the war, in 1947. Written in Italian in 1930 (during Silone's exile in Switzerland), *Fontamara* was first published in German translation in 1933, and in English (as *Fontamara*) in 1934. It achieved an immediate and astounding international success and was translated into twenty-seven languages. Set in Fontamara, an imaginary town in the Abruzzi, the novel is a poignant, realistic picture of the tragic and debased life of the poor, ignorant peasants (*cafoni*) during the Fascist period.

In the aftermath of World War II it was natural, as Italo Calvino (q.v.) said, that the passion for literature should have become a passion for the fate of the world. Writers sought in the spheres of words and forms something to equal the force and tragedy of their time; the Resistance became the new myth. It was the first time in Italian history that Catholics and Communists, intellectuals and the poor, women and children fought for the freedom of their country, and mythicizing the Resistance provided the richest ingredient in the new Italian fiction called neorealist.

Neorealism is not a school, but, as Calvino has said, "an epoch, a climate." "The Resistance made us believe in the possibility of an epic literature, charged with an energy at the same time rational and vital, social and existential, collective and autobiographical; *a literature of tension.*" Other critics speak of a literature that, perhaps for the first time in centuries, could have changed the course of the history and civilization of a people.

Such writers as Vittorini, Calvino, Pratolini, Giuseppe Berto, and Carlo Levi (qq.v.) portrayed the horrors of war as an insult to human dignity, although even as they condemned the past, they looked toward a better future. "I am sure that a better time will come," an old man tells some adolescents in Berto's novel *Il cielo è rosso* (1947; *The Sky Is Red,* 1948). "I don't know when, but it will come. You have a mission to accomplish in the world, so that men may become better and forget violence and hatred."

The best novel of the Resistance was *Il partigiano Johnny* (1968; Johnny the partisan) by Beppe Fenoglio (q.v.), published posthumously. It dramatizes the life of the partisan in the field, his anguish at the death of his comrades, his solitude, and the desperate conditions of his people. Speaking of Fenoglio, Calvino said: "We now have the book our generation wanted to write; Fenoglio succeeded in writing the novel we all dreamed of writing."

Another important novel of the Resistance is Elio Vittorini's *Uomini e no* (1945; men and not-men), with its background of Nazi-Fascist cruelties. Among other novelists who wrote important works about the Resistance are Carlo Cassola, Giorgio Bassani (qq.v.), Calvino, Pavese, and Moravia, although two of the most instructive anti-Fascist narratives of the Fascist period are Carlo Levi's *Cristo si è fermato a Eboli* (1945; *Christ Stopped at Eboli,* 1947), which relates the author's experience in exile in the primitive town of Gagliano in Lucania, the encounter of a northerner with the immemorial problems of the south; and Vasco Pratolini's *Cronache di poveri amanti* (1947; *A Tale of Poor Lovers,* 1949), in which people are abused and mistreated in the formative days of Fascism. To the many works of fiction describing the horrors of the war must be added the verse of such famous writers as Saba, Govoni, Palazzeschi, Ungaretti, Montale, Quasimodo, Pavese, Gatto, Rebora, and Pasolini, who in their outstanding poems condemned the Nazi-Fascist brutalities.

One of the greatest novelists of the century, another Rabelais or Joyce in his linguistic vitality is Carlo Emilio Gadda, an engineer by profession. His subject is the disorder of modern man in "the forms and cubes of life" in the cement cities no less than in the emergence of Fascism. His best novel is *Quer pasticciaccio brutto de via Merulana* (1959; *That Awful Mess on Via Merulana,* 1965), set in Rome in 1927, with a plot concerning a jewel theft and a murder mystery. But this plot is only a pretext for Gadda, who wants to represent the psychological depth of unrestrained passions during Mussolini's time. Gadda condemns the society of the "Duce" and his regime in this ferocious anti-Fascist novel. Writing, he says, "is often a means of taking revenge, sometimes the only means." Or as Pasolini said of him: "Gadda belongs to a historical time when it was impossible to see the world—this magma of disorder, corruption, hypocrisy, stupidity, and injustice —in a perspective of hope."

Representing a different kind of Roman novel are Pasolini's *Ragazzi di vita* (1955; *The Ragazzi*, 1968) and *Una vita violenta* (1959; *A Violent Life*, 1968). The protagonists are poor boys with an instinct for survival in a world they never made. Pasolini's language of slang, dialect, and vulgarisms grants an immediacy to the instinctual lives of his protagonists. The novels are a document of desperation in the Roman subproletariat. Another sort of desperation animates the workers in Berto's *Il brigante* (1951; *The Brigand*, 1951), a novel of social protest set in the south, in Calabria— which Gramsci called a colony of northern Italy—about feudally exploited and degraded farmers.

There are several other writers of note who are part of the neorealism movement or its aftermath. Michele Prisco (q.v.), a Neapolitan, moved from an analysis of "the bourgeois world of my province" to the larger world and the largest questions—the problem of evil and human violence. Domenico Rea (q.v.), another Neapolitan, is at once violent and humorous, cynical and glamorous, "verista" and expressionist. Anna Maria Ortese (q.v.), who has been called a Neapolitan writer (although she does not identify herself with Naples) because of her famous book of stories, *Il mare non bagna Napoli* (1953; *The Bay Is Not Naples*, 1955), describes the brutal conditions of that city; her novel *Il porto di Toledo* (1975; the port of Toledo)—Toledo is a metaphor for Naples—is a mythopoeic inquiry into the social, moral, and psychical chaos of our time. Leonardo Sciascia's (q.v.) novels concentrate on Sicilian issues, poverty, ignorance, suffering, and the Mafia, but he has lately become active in legislative politics in the hope of bringing some "light" into the crisis of our time. Guido Piovene, an observer of the secret heart, and a severe moralist, momentarily revived the 19th-c. tradition of the epistolary novel with *Lettere di una novizia* (1941; *Confessions of a Novice*, 1950); his posthumously published *Inverno d'un uomo felice* (1977; winter of a happy

man), a collection of stories originally published between 1938 and 1959, revealed a genuine interest in the daily life of his subjects. Mario Tobino's (q.v.) books document the atrocities of the Nazi-Fascist dictatorship, psychological as well as physical. Elsa Morante's (q.v.) *La storia* (1974; *History: A Novel*, 1977), a powerful indictment of World War II, takes its tone (and its epigraph) from a survivor of Hiroshima: "There is no word in any language that may console the guinea pigs who do not know the reason for their death."

Lucio Piccolo (q.v.), the baroque poet whose work is rooted in the southern realism in the manner of Verga, wrote his "past memories" of "baroque churches and old convents, and of souls suited to these places who lived here without leaving a trace." He is able to translate the most complicated subjects into a pure poetry, for he is a poet of extreme musicality. Tommaso Landolfi (q.v.) is a writer of marked singularity, comparable only to Gadda, Antonio Pizzuto (1893–1976), and the Florentine hermetics. A writer given as easily to surrealism as modes of verisimilitude, Landolfi is a translator of such diverse writers as Novalis, Gogol, and Tolstoy. Pizzuto is another iconoclast who, as Contini observes, "eliminates the present and perfect tense for the imperfect . . . of a vague temporal duration . . . and ends by using mainly the infinitive." Pizzuto de-creates the representation of reality and re-creates a new and original language in Italian literature.

The novels of Lucio Mastronardi (q.v.), which deal principally with the people of Vigevano, are remarkable for their linguistic innovations in the manner of Gadda. His writings are in the Italo-Pavesian dialect and are major examples of the modern use of vernacular language.

The end of neorealism can be dated to the publication of Pratolini's *Metello* (1955; *Metello*, 1968), a social and historical novel set in Florence at the end of the 19th c. that suggests that a neorealistic literature of "document, memorial, and testimony" is finished. Another modern novel that is also set largely in the 19th c. and that leads us to the same conclusion is Giuseppe Tomasi di Lampedusa's (q.v.) *Il gattopardo* (1958; *The Leopard*, 1960), which chronicles the political and economic decline of a noble family and the leveling of social classes in a manner reminiscent of Stendhal. And Pasolini, who had been a very active neorealist, proclaimed its death in a poem with that very name, "In morte del realismo" (1960; death of realism).

After the war and throughout the 1950s and early 1960s Italy experienced the so-called "economic miracle." The country was industrialized as never before, and creature comforts became available as never before—but at what price? In his novel *Teorema* (1968; theorem) Pasolini scored the materialism of a big industrial city and the loneliness, emptiness, and boredom of capitalist society. But even worse than the loneliness and boredom of the rich is the alienation of the urban worker in the newly industrialized cities—the man who leaves his home town and works in a factory that does not belong to him, who is regimented in repetitious activity, who barely communicates with his fellows.

The alienation of modern man, his unintegrated relation to the world, is the subject of the novels of Ottiero Ottieri (q.v.), who condemns the factory as an instrument of depersonalization. So, too, does Paolo Volponi (q.v.), as in the novel *Memoriale* (1962; *My Troubles Began*, 1964). "The strongest feeling I felt," says the protagonist, "was that I had become factory property." All loneliness and frustration, however, are not associated with socioeconomic conditions. *Il male oscuro* (1964; *Incubus*, 1966), by Giuseppe Berto, is the story of a man who finds in his own conscious and subconscious an explanation of his physical and mental suffering. *Il paradiso* (1970; *Bought and Sold*, 1973) by Alberto Moravia is a collection of short stories in which wealthy women narrate their extramarital affairs and describe their abnormal lives.

Quasimodo wrote of writers in general, young writers in particular: "There does not exist a work of art which is not a protest against the establishment . . . . The contemporary work of art, in order to survive, must be a work of protest." Or as Silvio Ramat wrote: "Every authentic writer is authentically experimental." These statements help explain the origins of a new avant-garde literature of dissent. The forerunners are Luciano Anceschi (b. 1911), who in 1956 founded the journal *Il Verri*, which is a mine of experimental writing, and Alfredo Giuliani (b. 1924), who in 1961 published the anthology *I novissimi* (the newest), which contains poetry by himself, Elio Pagliarani (b. 1927), Edoardo Sanguineti (q.v.), Nanni Balestrini (b. 1935), and Antonio Porta (b. 1935). In his introduction, Giuliani remarks: "To understand contemporary poets one must refer not to the memory of past poems but to the physiognomy of today's world." In 1963 a group of writers—among them Anceschi, Luigi Malerba (b. 1927), Sanguineti, Umberto Eco (b. 1932), and Bale-

strini—held a glamorous meeting in Palermo, whence issued the volume *Gruppo* 63 (group 63), the official document of neo-avant-gardism in Italy. In quest of a language appropriate to a technological society, Sanguineti emphasized the "consciousness of the relation between the intellectual and bourgeois society . . . . Any literary work is the expression of an ideology."

From a rather different angle of vision, another member of Group 63, Angelo Guglielmi (b. 1924), wrote: "Up to now language has tried to reflect reality as in a mirror. Henceforth, language must take its place at the very heart of reality." The result is that some experimentalists express their ideas through complicated and often frustrating verbal and typographical approaches: concrete poetry, audiovisual texts, and so forth.

There is, to be sure, a certain amount of social and political rebelliousness among these writers. Lamberto Pignotti (b. 1926), for instance, deplored the "anonymity of mass production in technological civilization." In the journal *Quindici*, Umberto Eco argued that the modern writer "must not make an intellectual, but a practical, discourse," and that he must participate in any "political discourse" protest allows. Walter Pedullà (b. 1930) spoke of the work of art as a "consumer's object" and emphasizes the "social function of poetry." Elio Pagliarani proclaimed an "attitude of protest" against the establishment, while Nanni Balestrini said that language must become a "concrete method of transforming the world." The poet Nelo Risi (b. 1930) wrote that the artist is "up to his neck in history, with his ounce of aspiration for the eternal. . . . As long as the artist is conscious of the evils of society, he has to operate beyond personal engagement in the search for a common conscience."

The debasement of language has been examined by Sanguineti in *Il giuoco dell'oca* (1967; the goose game), a game played by casting dice and moving wooden geese from place to place. Sanguineti has made up his own squares—one hundred and eleven vignettes, each with its own illustration: mermaids, monsters, advertisements, the legs of Marilyn Monroe, paintings by Dalí, and so on. This is an example of "open work," a work opened to all meanings, although the goose game is certainly symbolic of life and death. *Super-Eliogabalo* (1969; super-Heliogabalus) by Alberto Arbasino (b. 1930) is an endless play with words with obscure allusions; it is a satire and a farce involving hundreds of historical characters and institutions, all of which circle about the superstar, super-Heliogabulus. *Non libro* (1970; not a book) by Cesare Zavattini (b. 1902) is a book which says it is not a book and which comes with a record and is written in a phantasmagoric language, using typography that immediately suggests the destruction of reality.

Dino Buzzati (1906–1972), whose early novels established his reputation, may be said to have experimented with the idea of the book in yet another way in *Poema a fumetti* (1969; poem in cartoons), which he amusingly asserts is a "work a little inferior to *The Divine Comedy* but much superior to *Faust*." Told in large part through comic strips—drawn by him—it is a modern version of the legend of Orpheus and Eurydice—of Orfi, a young rock musician, and Eura. Buzzati recounts the destruction of myth: "And the last kings of the fables started walking toward exile." On the other hand, Italo Calvino returns to myth with his novel *Il castello dei destini incrociati* (1969; *The Castle of Crossed Destinies*, 1977), first published in the elegant book *Tarocchi* (tarot cards), which contains a superb reproduction of the 15th-c. Viscontean tarot cards. The novel is about mute knights, who take refuge in a castle, where each one is able to narrate his prodigious adventures with different combinations of the cards. Thus, Calvino finds a support against alienation in the return to myth, legend, and fable. The tarot cards may be endlessly combined; they are a machine for generating meanings and stories. Using the same structural-semiotic approach, Calvino's *Le città invisibili* (1972; *Invisible Cities*, 1974) deals with an imaginary Marco Polo who, not knowing the language of his lord, Kublai Khan, describes to him the fabulous cities he has visited with objects and other signs.

After Pirandello, whose narrative and dramatic works are so closely related, the Italian drama gradually asserted itself as an autonomous genre. In this sense, Ugo Betti (q.v.) is perhaps the most important Italian playwright of the century. His theater focuses on the plight of the individual who discovers that he is at variance with what he thought he was. Bewildered by his own feelings, thoughts, and acts, he hopes to find wholeness in the hands of a higher being—perhaps the Christian God. Betti's plays usually take the form of a trial or inquest, the purpose of which is not to investigate a person's guilt (which is a given) but its unavoidability. In some of his plays Diego Fabbri (1911–1980) used Pirandellian conventions like the contrast between theatrical fiction and life, although he also worked in a Christian context, sometimes in the manner of Betti. Fabbri believed that every man, confronted with

the choice between good and evil, will become aware of his spiritual restlessness and choose the good. Eduardo De Filippo (q.v.) is Italy's most popular playwright, and perhaps the most talented comic actor since the death of Totò. His plays are an inventive fusion of standard Italian and Neapolitan dialect. They concentrate on the tragicomic struggle of the lower- and lower-middle-class man to survive economically and emotionally. Luigi Squarzina (b. 1922) is able to seduce an audience with his re-creation of historical settings in which the conflicted fate of an individual emerges; what results is a painful insight into the stupidity and banality of evil. Dario Fo's (q.v.) intention is to change the stage into a tribunal and to make of the playwright a social gadfly. His irony at the expense of his native land sparkles with delight and originality, since Fo is a great clown-actor and he performs in his own pieces.

The number of authors who wrote poetry, plays, and even narrative works in the native dialect of their region is very great indeed, and the literary use of dialects such as Milanese, Neapolitan, Piedmontese, Sicilian, and Venetian goes back at least several centuries. Nevertheless, only a relatively small minority of the writers who chose a dialect rather than standard Italian as their medium of expression may be objectively regarded as worthy of a permanent place in the history of Italian letters.

Until a few decades ago the main thrust of Italian culture was centripetal: dialect authors represented a deviation from a linguistic norm, that of the common national language, and this deviation was generally regarded with at least a degree of intolerance by literary historians and critics. Thus, even very great dialect poets, such as the Milanese Carlo Porta (1775–1821) and the Roman Giuseppe Gioacchino Belli (1791–1863), were often excluded from anthologies and rarely—if ever—studied in schools or universities. It would be too complex to examine here in depth the reasons for this kind of neglect. Suffice it to say that the aspirations toward national unity of the Risorgimento and the centralizing tendencies of the Fascist regime had much to do with it.

A turning point of decisive importance, however, came not too long after World War II with the rise of neorealism in fiction and cinema, partly as a reaction to the Fascist myth of a country that was supposed to be in every way united and uniform. In reality, linguistic diversity in Italy is of such magnitude that foreigners may have difficulty in comprehending it. Dialects of different regions are generally not even mutually intelligible.

Pier Paolo Pasolini was perhaps the first important author to turn to his mother's native language, Friulian, with his first collection of verse, entitled *Poesie a Casarsa* (1942; Casarsa poems). The case of Friulian is a special one: spoken in the extreme northeastern region of Italy, it has no official status, but is regarded by many scholars—especially non-Italians—as differing so profoundly in matters of phonology, morphology, and lexicon from standard Italian as to constitute a separate language, akin to the Rhaeto-Romance dialects of Switzerland. The question is not an easily settled one, since the difference between a "language" and a "dialect" can rest more on sociological and political grounds than on linguistic ones. In fact, it is enough to consider that any "dialect" could achieve the status of a "language" overnight if, due to political upheavals, it were to be recognized officially by a newly established state.

The postwar decades saw not only the flowering of several important dialect poets, but also a growing scholarly interest in the study and reevaluation of dialect writers from earlier centuries and especially from the first half of the 20th c. Thus, Carlo Porta, Giuseppe Gioacchino Belli, and the Neapolitan Salvatore Di Giacomo, to mention only a few, were reprinted in modern editions by important publishers and made the object of extensive critical work by leading scholars. At the same time, the works of a number of poets who had appeared in the first half of the century and had been generally ignored in spite of their obvious merit were rediscovered. Among these were the Milanese Delio Tessa (1886–1939), the Abruzzian Cesare de Titta (1862–1933), the Veronese Berto Barbarani (1872–1945), the Neapolitan Ferdinando Russo (1866–1927), the Piedmontese Nino Costa (1886–1945), and the Genoese Edoardo Firpo (1899–1957). A great deal of attention went also to the Roman poets Cesare Pascarella (1858–1940) and Trilussa (pseud. of Carlo Alberto Salustri, 1871–1950), whose easily intelligible dialect made them popular outside of Rome as well.

In 1952 Pasolini and Mario Dell'Arco (b. 1905), himself a poet in the Roman dialect, published an important anthology entitled *Poesia dialettale del Novecento* (dialect poetry of the 20th c.), which did much to call to the attention of both scholars and readers the significance of the contribution made by dialect poets. Pasolini's extensive introduction, which runs to 119 pages, constitutes to this day an essay of fundamental importance for a critical understanding of dialect literature in Italy.

In recent years, the number of publications dealing with dialect works has continued to increase as scholars rediscover, for instance, the wealth of dramatic works in dialects such as Piedmontese, Milanese, Venetian, and Neapolitan, and as dialect authors from earlier centuries are found worthy of critical editions and of a place in both anthologies and histories of Italian literature.

Among the living dialect poets, one of the most highly regarded is undoubtedly Albino Pierro (b. 1916), who started writing in the dialect of his native Tursi, a town in the region of Basilicata, around 1960, when he published his first collection of verse entitled *A terra d'u ricorde* (the land of memories), and whose later works have had the honor of publication by Laterza, one of Italy's most prestigious publishing houses.

BIBLIOGRAPHY: Arrighi, P., *Le vérisme dans la prose narrative italienne* (1937); Brandon-Albini, M., *La culture italienne* (1950); Livingston, A., *Essays on Modern Italian Literature* (1950); Fernandez, D., *Le roman italien et la crise de la conscience moderne* (1958); Vittorini, D., *High Points in the History of Italian Literature* (1958); De Sanctis, F., *History of Italian Literature* (1959); Calvino, I., "Main Currents in Italian Fiction Today," *IQ*, 4, 13–14 (1960), 3–14; Pacifici, S., *A Guide to Contemporary Italian Literature* (1962); Brandon-Albini, M., *Midi vivant* (1963); Heiney, D., *America in Modern Italian Literature* (1964); Donadoni, E., *A History of Italian Literature,* updated by E. Mazzali and R. J. Clements (1969); Pacifici, S., ed., *From "Verismo" to Experimentalism: Essays on the Modern Italian Novel* (1969); Ballerini, L., ed., *Italian Visual Poetry, 1912–1972* (1973); Molinaro, J. A., ed., *Petrarch to Pirandello* (1973); Wilkins, E. W., *A History of Italian Literature,* updated by T. G. Bergin (1974); Biasin, G. P., *Literary Diseases: Theme and Metaphor in the Italian Novel* (1975); Ragusa, O., *Narrative and Drama: Essays in Modern Italian Literature from Verga to Pasolini* (1976); Gatt-Rutter, J., *Writers and Politics in Modern Italy* (1978); Bondanella, P., and Bondanella, J. C., eds., *Dictionary of Italian Literature* (1979); Perella, N. J., *Midday in Italian Literature: Variations on an Archetypal Theme* (1979); Whitfield, J. H., *A Short History of Italian Literature,* updated by J. R. Woodhouse (1980)

M. RICCIARDELLI

IVANOV, Vyacheslav Ivanovich

Russian poet, essayist, and classical scholar, b. 28 Feb. 1866, Moscow; d. 16 July 1949, Rome, Italy

After attending Moscow University and spending almost twenty years abroad in travel and further study, I. settled in St. Petersburg in 1905 and soon became the leading spokesman of Russian symbolism (q.v.). Until 1912 his apartment (popularly known as "The Tower") was the site of frequent gatherings of the Russian literary and artistic avant-garde, where readings by the most prominent poets of the day were typically followed by I.'s refined commentary. I. later moved to Moscow, and his influence waned rapidly as symbolism lost its literary preeminence. I. welcomed the fall of autocracy in Russia but remained hostile to Bolshevism. From 1920 to 1924 he taught classical philology in Baku. In 1924 he was allowed to depart for Italy, where he lived the last twenty-five years of his life, teaching first in Pavia and later in Rome at the Russicum, the Vatican's institute for the study of Russia and the Eastern Church. I. joined the Roman Catholic Church in 1926, although he did not renounce Eastern Orthodoxy.

I.'s first two volumes of verse, *Kormchie zvyozdy* (1903; pilot stars) and *Prozrachnost* (1904; transparency) exhibit the characteristic features of his poetry: a strong metaphysical orientation, a profusion of references to Western (especially ancient Greek) culture, a special affinity for myth, and a penchant for complex, archaic diction. His next collection, the two-volume *Cor ardens* (1911; Latin: burning heart), is an even more lavish display of erudition and technical virtuosity, and is reminiscent of the ornate, allusion-laden poetry of the Baroque age. Much of *Cor ardens* was written after the death of I.'s beloved wife Lydia, and the victory of love over death is a recurring motif, presented as an ecstatic epiphany that takes its cue from the myth of the "ever-suffering and ever-resurrected" god Dionysus.

I.'s poetic output diminished sharply after around 1915—a reflection of his growing loss of faith in the quasi-religious expectations that had been a central part of his message—but his increasingly rare productions were almost all achievements of a high order. The poetic cycles "Zimnie sonety" (1920; winter sonnets) and "Rimskie sonety" (1924; Roman sonnets) are particularly noteworthy. A final burst of poetic inspiration came in 1944, when I. wrote "Rimsky dnevnik" (Roman diary), a superb cycle that marks a distinct evolution of his style toward simplicity of expression. These late works are included in the posthumously published volume *Svet vecherny* (1962; vespertine light).

Between 1928 and his death I. worked sporadically on what he referred to as a "novel," *Povest o Svetomire Tsareviche* (account of the Tsarevich Svetomir), which was to be the ultimate statement of his views. This is an allegorical narrative, in rhythmic and heavily archaized prose, which points to a vision of a world finally cleansed of sin. I. did not live to complete this work, which was first published—with the missing half reconstructed by I.'s close companion O. Deschartes (pseud. of Olga Chor, 1894–1978)—in Volume I of his *Sobranie sochineny* (1971; collected works).

I.'s great influence as a critic and literary theorist is only partially suggested by his published essays. A brilliant conversationalist with an unsurpassed ability to make polished and incisive analyses on first aquaintance with a new work, I. probably affected Russian modernism more through personal contact than by his printed works. Nevertheless, the latter are extremely important: I.'s early essays, collected in *Po zvyozdam* (1909; by the stars) and *Borozdy i mezhi* (1916; furrows and boundaries), present most of his theoretical ideas bearing on symbolism. In these and other essays I. articulates his belief in the religious ("theurgic") nature of true art, where the symbol serves as the medium for the revelation of "higher reality."

I. also wrote a great deal of literary criticism; his seminal essays on Dostoevsky (1916–17; uncollected in Russian but available in English as *Freedom and the Tragic Life*, 1952) are the best-known examples. Other writers discussed by I. range from Pindar and Homer to Petrarch, Goethe, and Pushkin. Of I.'s numerous works outside the narrowly literary sphere, the most influential is his eloquent defense of culture in I.'s polemic with Mikhail Gershenzon (1869–1925), *Perepiska iz dvukh uglov* (1921; *Correspondence between Two Corners*, 1948).

I. played a key role in the cultural ferment in Russia at the beginning of the 20th c. But as a poet, he remained an isolated figure whose early verse evoked admiration but little real sympathy, and whose late, and probably best, poetry remained virtually unknown to his contemporaries. Although a scholarly evaluation of his oeuvre is only beginning, I.'s place in the pantheon of Russian literature seems assured.

FURTHER WORKS: *Ellinskaya religia stradayushchego boga* (1904–5); *Tantal: Tragedia* (1905); *De societatibus vectigalium publico-*

rum populi romani (1910); *Nezhnaya taina*
(1912); *Alkei i Safo: Sobranie pesen i liricheskikh otryvkov* [trans. and introd. by I.]
(1914); *Rodnoe i vselenskoe: Statyi* (1917);
Mladenchestvo (1918); *Prometei: Tragedia*
(1919); *Dionis i pradionisiistvo* (1923); *Chelovek* (1939); *Sobranie sochineny* (1971 ff.)

BIBLIOGRAPHY: Deschartes, O., "V. I.," *OSP*, 5
(1954), 41–58; Poggioli, R., "A Correspondence from Opposite Corners," *The Phoenix
and the Spider* (1957), pp. 208–28; Poggioli,
R., *The Poets of Russia* (1960), pp. 161–70;
Stepun, F., *Mystische Weltschau* (1964), pp.
201–78; Stammler, H. A., "V. I.'s Image of
Man," *WSJ*, 14 (1967–68), 128–42; Tschöpl,
C., *V. I.: Dichtung and Dichtungstheorie*
(1968); West, J., *Russian Symbolism: A
Study of V. I. and the Russian Symbolist Aesthetic* (1970); Rannit, A., "V. I. and His *Vespertine Light*," *RLT*, 4 (1972), 265–68

ALEXIS KLIMOFF

IVORY COAST LITERATURE

The age-old traditional literatures in African
languages of the Ivory Coast, indeed of most of
sub-Saharan Africa, have been primarily oral.
The colonization of this now-independent West
African country by France early in this century
was accompanied by a forceful imposition of
the French language from elementary school
on. This, coupled with the presence of a multiplicity of African languages (making the choice
of any one as a national tongue difficult), has
resulted in a written literature that is overwhelmingly in French.

Generally speaking, criticism of colonial excesses, cultural self-assertion, the conflict between tradition and modernism, and, more recently, disenchantment with independence and
the new leadership have been the major themes.

Perhaps because of the low literacy rate,
it is in the theater—with its roots in traditional spectacle and its ability to reach a broad
audience—that the Ivory Coast has shown the
most vitality. Born in 1932 in a school setting, dramatic activity was brilliantly fostered
through playwriting and the organization of
theater troupes by Ivoirian students of the celebrated William-Ponty School and others. The
theater was early dominated by three graduates
of that school, François-Joseph Amon d'Aby
(b. 1913), Germain Coffi Gadeau (b. 1915),
and Bernard Binlin Dadié (q.v.), the last the
most outstanding, prolific Ivory Coast writer.

Two tendencies dominate this theater: (1)
historical or legendary themes based on the oral
tradition, e.g., Dadié's *Assémien Déhylé*
(1936; Assémien Déhylé), Amon d'Aby's
L'entrevue de Bondoukou (1939; the Bondoukou interview), and Gadeau's *Kondé Yao*
(1939; Kondé Yao) and (2) more modern
preoccupations, to be found in plays dealing
with certain social ills inherited from tribal life,
or in comedies of manners and political criticism reflecting a widespread disaffection with
contemporary abuses, e.g., Amon d'Aby's
Kwao Adjoba (1953; Kwao Adjoba) or Gadeau's *Nos femmes* (1940; our wives). In this
vein, Dadié's very popular *Monsieur Thôgô-gnini* (1970; Mr. Thôgô-gnini) is exemplary.

Many talented younger playwrights have become active, often centering their dramas
around great figures of the past. Thus, for example, Charles Nokan (b. 1936) re-creates
(taking considerable liberties) the Baoule legend of Queen Pokou in his *Abrah Pokou*
(1970; Abrah Pokou), while Bernard Zadi Zaourou (b. 1938) chronicled the career of the
19th-c. Mandingo (Malinké) leader Samori
Touré, whose resistance to the French colonial
armies has become legendary, in *Les Sofas*
(1975; the Sofas [name given to Samori's
soldiers]). Here, as elsewhere among dramatists
of this generation, historical themes are rarely
presented for their own sake, but rather as a
reinterpretation of the past in the search for solutions to the problems of newly independent
African states.

In keeping with their concern for the continuity of the oral tradition, Dadié and Amon
d'Aby have also published collections of legends and tales: *Le pagne noir* (1955; the black
loincloth) and *La mare aux crocodiles* (1973;
the crocodile pond), respectively. Léon Maurice Anoma Kanié's (b. 1920) *Quand les bêtes
parlaient aux hommes* (1974; when animals
spoke to men) is a similar venture with a significant addition: the author has appended several of La Fontaine's fables translated into
Ivory Coast Creole, a blending of French and
local languages.

Although his forte seems clearly to be the
theater, Dadié also stands out as the leading
poet of the Ivory Coast. His three volumes of
poetry reflect his evolving concerns over the
years. Among other poets of note there is
Joseph Miézan Bognini (b. 1936), whose sensitive exaltation of nature and "controlled fervor" in his collection *Ce dur appel de l'espoir*
(1960; this harsh call of hope) make him one
of the better Francophone lyric poets. The unclassifiable ("dramatic poem"?) *Le soleil noir*

point (1962; the black sun dawns) by Charles Nokan, as well as his poetic "novel" *Violent était le vent* (1966; violent was the wind), both passionate pleas for a true liberation in post-independence Africa, are noteworthy in their sincerity and their formal and stylistic innovations.

Ivoirian writers came rather late to the novel. Their themes tend to parallel those of the dramatists: at the outset, we find a preoccupation with the colonial experience, depiction (and occasionally criticism) of traditional life, and the myriad problems—both individual and societal—implied in the conflict of cultures. This last theme has, of course, carried over into the postindependence period. A common characteristic of many of these novels is their autobiographical nature, following (with variations) a more or less set pattern from village to school, to the big city (African or European), and the final return home. Both Dadié's *Climbié* (1956; *Climbié*, 1971) and Aké Loba's (b. 1927) *Kocoumbo, l'étudiant noir* (1961; Kocoumbo, the black student) are important autobiographical works, the first tracing the moral and political itinerary of its hero during the late colonial period, the second vividly depicting the African student milieu in Paris during the same era.

The confrontation of the old and the new within an African village is the subject of Aké Loba's second novel, *Les fils de Kouretcha* (1970; the sons of Kouretcha), while his *Les dépossédés* (1973; the dispossessed) chronicles the life of a simple peasant and that of his adopted city, Abidjan, during sixty years of colonial rule. New political developments have engendered new themes: disaffection in the wake of independence is at the very core of the most interesting and best written Ivoirian novel to date, Ahmadou Kourouma's (b. 1927?) *Les soleils des indépendances* (1968; the suns of independence). The subject has appeared frequently in recent African fiction, but its treatment here results in a highly successful molding of a Western genre to the realities of African thought and speech. With *Wazzi* (1977; Wazzi) by Jean D. Dodo (b. 1919?) and Tidiane Dem's (date n.a.) *Masseni* (1977; Masseni), women for the first time became the chief protagonists of Ivoirian novels.

BIBLIOGRAPHY: Cornevin, R., *Le théâtre en Afrique noire et Madagascar* (1970), pp. 185–200; Jahn, J., and Dressler, P. D., *Bibliography of Creative African Writing* (1971); Bonneau, R., *Écrivains, cinéastes et artistes ivoiriens, aperçu bio-bibliographique* (1973); Herdeck, D. E., *African Authors* (1973); Blair, D., *African Literature in French* (1976); Baratte-Eno Belinga, T., et al., *Bibliographie des auteurs africains de langue française*, 4th ed. (1979), pp. 74–85

FREDRIC MICHELMAN

IWASZKIEWICZ, Jarosław

(pseud.: Eleuter) Polish poet, novelist, dramatist, literary and music critic, and translator, b. 20 Feb. 1894, Kalnik, Ukraine; d. 2 March 1980, Warsaw

I. studied law at Kiev University simultaneously with his studies at the musical Conservatory from which he graduated. His literary debut took place in 1915 in a Kievan monthly publication. Three years later he moved to Warsaw, where he was to become an influential member of Skamander, the leading poetic group of the 1920s. From 1920 to 1923 I. was the editor of the literary section of the important daily *Kurier polski,* and then served as a secretary to the marshal of the Polish parliament from 1923 to 1925. During the period 1927–39 he was in the foreign service, living in Copenhagen and Brussels. During World War II, I. was in Warsaw, where he was involved with underground cultural activities. After the war, in 1945, he assumed the editorship of the weekly *Nowiny literackie,* where he remained until 1954, when he became the editor of the most important Polish literary monthly, *Twórczość,* a post he held until his death. Besides his formal duties as an editor, I. was always involved in various cultural and political activities. He was the president of the Polish P.E.N. Club for over twenty years, a member of parliament, and a participant in the International Peace Movement. He was also the recipient of a great many literary awards.

I.'s contributions are indeed of vast importance. During his long literary career, I. published nearly fifty volumes of poetry, novels, plays, essays, and books of memoirs. In addition, there are at least as many volumes of his literary translations. Of his poetry, three volumes deserve special attention: his youthful *Lato* (1932; summer), his mature *Ciemne ścieżki* (1957; dark paths), and the collection *Liryki* (1959; lyrics), which offers an excellent representative selection of all his poems. The common denominator of his poetry is its humanism. I.'s works of fiction are closely linked with his poetry by their striking authenticity and vividness of feelings and their intuitiveness

479

—characteristics that were his trademark. Novels as early as *Księżyc wschodzi* (1925; the moon rises) or as recent as trilogy *Sława i chwała* (1956–62; fame and glory) are prime examples of these traits. In all of I.'s novels and short stories there are autobiographical elements and a great sense of identification with the characters, whose fates are mostly tragic. In *Sława i chwała* I. paints a picture of Polish life in the period during and between the two world wars. The destinies of the characters are determined by the political, social, economic, and cultural changes that Poland underwent during this period. Yet the historical events that determine the lives of I.'s characters by no means apply to the Poles alone or solely to this specific period. I.'s underlying philosophy is universal: history determines the fate of each of us, and the individual with all his complexities can be at the same time both its victim and its conqueror. Of all I.'s short stories, perhaps the most memorable are those contained in the volume *Panny z Wilka* (1933; maidens from Wilk). They are imbued with a sense of things passing and with eroticism—a poetically expressed sensuality that is another one of his characteristics.

I.'s musical training and interests are also evident in his literary works. His fascination with sounds and rhythms results in an unexpected symphony of images and produces a sense of a magic world that one half remembers from one's dreams or from childhood. I. also wrote about music and produced opera librettos, and one of his plays (which in general do not match the excellence of his poetry or prose) is built around the life of Chopin: *Lato w Nohant* (1936; *Summer in Nohant*, 1942).

Of I.'s translations, the most noted are those of Rimbaud's poetry, of Claudel's and Giraudoux's (qq.v.) plays, and of work by André Gide (q.v.), as well as some of the short stories of Tolstoy and Chekhov (q.v.).

I. was one of the most important Polish writers of the 20th c. His influence on the younger generation of writers and poets has been enormous, but so is his works' impact upon the ordinary reader. The truthfulness of I.'s theme, combined with the authenticity of its expression, accounts for his works' appeal and for his high place in Polish literature.

FURTHER WORKS: *Oktostychy* (1919); *Zenobia Palmura* (1920); *Hilari syn buchaltera* (1923); *Siedem bogatych miast nieśmiertelnego Kościeja* (1924); *Kochankowie z Werony* (1928); *Fryderyk Szopen* (1928; new ed. as *Chopin,* 1966); *Księga dnia i księga nocy* (1929); *Zmowa mężczyzn* (1930); *Powrót do Europy* (1931); *Pasje błędomierskie* (1938); *Maskarada* (1939); *Kongres w Florencji* (1941); *Wiersze wybrane* (1946); *Nowele włoskie* (1947); *Czerwone tarcze* (1949); *Warkocze jesieni* (1955); *Wzlot* (1956); *Proza poetycka* (1958); *Wiersze* (1958); *Dzieła* (4 vols., 1958–64); *Tatarak* (1960); *Wesele Pana Baltaka* (1960); *Jan Sebastian Bach* (1963); *Opowiadania wybrane* (1964); *Heydenreich* (1964); *Poezje wybrane* (1967); *Wiersze zebrane* (1968); *O psach kotach i diabłach* (1968)

BIBLIOGRAPHY: Kridl, M., *A Survey of Polish Literature and Culture* (1956), p. 498; Miłosz, C., *Postwar Polish Poetry* (1965), pp. 23–25; Miłosz, C., *The History of Polish Literature* (1969), pp. 389–93

MALGORZATA PRUSKA-CARROLL

IZUMI Kyōka

(pseud. of Izumi Kyōtarō) Japanese novelist and dramatist, b. 4 Nov. 1873, Kanazawa; d. 7 Sept. 1939, Tokyo

I.'s native city of Kanazawa was one of the great centers for the flourishing arts and crafts of Japan throughout the Edo (1603–1868) period. I.'s family was very much a part of this traditional world; his mother had deep ties with the Nō theater, and his father was a craftsman specializing in metal engraving. This ambience of traditional culture and art proved to be a major source of I.'s literary background. His writing is enriched by the traditions of *gesaku* (popular) fiction, the Kabuki theater, the art of the storytellers, and local legends. Of particular importance were the prose and poetry of the Nō texts.

Like other aspiring writers of the period, he went to Tokyo, where in 1891 he apprenticed himself to Ozaki Kōyō (1867–1903) and began to learn the writer's craft. By 1895 he had achieved a position in the literary establishment, and his first important works began to appear, at the same time as the rise of Japanese romanticism.

Kōya hijiri (1900; *The Kōya Priest,* 1959–60) is I.'s best and most representative work of this period. It displays the full range of his commitment to romanticism, fantasy, and beauty. Central to the story is his depiction of the disturbingly beautiful seductress, a figure who appears in many of his works and whom critics view as a nostalgic evocation of his mother who died when he was nine. The story is replete with the Buddhist notions of sinful passion and salvation by grace, while its style, called *gembun-itchi,* is a mixture of the classical and the colloquial languages, rich with Chinese words, yet supple and musical in its rhythms.

Just as I. reached this peak of literary development, naturalism came to full flower in Japan, and he found himself increasingly isolated within the literary world. He never wavered, however, in his commitment to romantic writing. In an age when other writers were rushing forward to embrace new styles and to use literature as a vehicle for the expression of the "self," I. remained steadfast in his old-fashioned style of writing. At this time he published *Uta andon* (1910; the paper lantern of poetry), one of the masterpieces of his mature period. This work draws significantly on the literary heritage of both the Nō and Kabuki theaters as well as on Edo travel fiction. At one level it can also be seen simply as a celebration of artistic beauty. It is written in the elegant *gembun-itchi* style that immediately sets this story apart from the spare, clinical narratives of the naturalist writers.

I.'s final work, *Rukō shinsō* (1939; a web of crimson thread) appeared a few weeks before his death. This novel combines all the elements for which I.'s work is known: ghosts from the past, the beautiful temptress, the distorting power of passion, and the redeeming power of mercy.

I. has been greatly admired by such modern writers as Kawabata Yasunari and Mishima Yukio (qq.v.). In a literary career of fifty years, I. recognized that the literature of the present is necessarily based on the literature of the past. And so he looked to the old Edo culture and spun his elaborate, dreamlike fantasies, and with this web of dreams he built a link with the past.

FURTHER WORKS: *Yushima mōde* (1899); *Mu-yūju* (1906); *Nanamotozakura* (1906); *Aika* (1906); *Shikibu kōji* (1907); *Kusa meikyū* (1908); *Onna keizu* (1908); *Shinsaku* (1909); *Koinyōbo* (1913); *Nihonbashi* (1914); *Oshidorichō* (1918); *Yukari no onna kushige shū* (1921); *Rindō to nadeshiko* (1924)

STEPHEN W. KOHL

JABÈS, Edmond
French poet, b. 16 April 1912, Cairo, Egypt

J. was part of the French-speaking Jewish community of Egypt. He comes from a banking family and managed the family business until the expulsion of the Jews at the time of the Suez crisis. Since 1957 he has lived in Paris. He received the Critics' Prize in 1970.

J. began with poems in the wake of the surrealists (q. v.) and Max Jacob (q.v.), which have been collected under the title *Je bâtis ma demeure* (1959; I build my dwelling). His main work, *Le livre des questions*, comprises seven volumes: I, *Le livre des questions* (1963; *The Book of Questions*, 1976); II, *Le livre de Yukel* (1964; *The Book of Yukel*, 1977); III, *Le retour au livre* (1965; *Return to the Book*, 1977); IV, *Yaël* (1967; *Yaël*); V, *Elya* (1969; *Elya*, 1973); VI, *Aely* (1972; Aely); VII, *El; ou, Le dernier livre* (1973; El; or, the last book). It is altogether sui generis: an untold story forms both the pretext and the pre-text for a blend of rabbinical commentaries, poems, aphorisms, wordplay with philosophical implications, and reflective and densely metaphorical prose. Shifting voices and constant breaks let silence have its share and allow a fuller meditative field than linear narrative or analysis would. The seven volumes combine into a profound look at the "law of the book," which is also the law of man who questions and defines himself through the word. J. challenges the unifying tendency of our thinking not only by his method of fragmentation and discontinuity, but also by his concentration on man's singularity as exemplified by the otherness of the Jew and in confrontation with the

irreducible otherness of the infinite, death, God, silence, the void. The images of the desert, with its inevitable wide dispersion of people, and, on the other hand, the concentration camp, grotesque historical parody of an unreachable ontological center, are perhaps the two focal points of J.'s elliptical thought.

Le livre des ressemblances, with its three volumes—*Le livre des ressemblances* (1976; the book of resemblances), *Le soupçon le desert* (1978; suspicion desert), and *L'ineffaçable, l'inaperçu* (1980; the indelible, the unnoticed) —marks a further turn of involution by using *Le livre des questions* as the basis for its meditations. This "book that resembles a book" probes the nature of analogy, which is at the root of our thought and language yet is a tenuous support for man, who was created in the image of a God who does not exist.

J.'s importance lies in his extraordinary fusion of innovation and tradition. He draws on current linguistic theory as well as on the Cabala for work that defies all classification yet treats the most basic human questions with the greatest intellectual and emotional power. His influence was summed up by Jacques Derrida (b. 1930) in 1973: "Nothing of interest has been written in France in the last ten years that does not have its precedent somewhere in the texts of J."

FURTHER WORK: *Ça suit son cours* (1975)

BIBLIOGRAPHY: Blanchot, M., "L'interruption," *NRF*, May 1964, 869–81; Bounoure, G., "E. J.; ou, La guérison par le livre," *Lettres nouvelles*, July–Sept. 1966, 98–115; Derrida, J., "E. J. et la question du livre," *L'écriture et la différence* (1967), pp. 99–116; Waldrop, R., "E. J. and the Impossible Circle," *Sub-stance*, Nos. 5–6 (1973), 183–95; special E. J. issue, *Change*, No. 22 (1975); Guglielmi, J., *La ressemblance impossible* (1978); Zoila, A. F., *Le livre, recherche autre d'E. J.* (1978)

ROSMARIE WALDROP

JACOB, Max
French poet, prose writer, and art critic, b. 12 July 1876, Quimper; d. 5 March 1944, Drancy concentration camp

J. was at the heart of the intensely creative period in which modern French art and poetry came into being. A Breton of Jewish origin, he arrived in Paris in 1894, met Picasso and Apollinaire (q.v.) several years later, and from 1904 onward immersed himself in the experiments that led to the creation of cubism and surrealism (qq.v.). As early as 1909, J., drawn both to religion and the bohemian life, experienced a vision of Christ. This mystic encounter led to his conversion to Catholicism (1915) and left an imprint upon his writing, lending it depth, power, introspection. A forceful but elusive personality, to many of his contemporaries a clown or a mystic, J. did not attain the fame of Picasso or Apollinaire. But he exercised a major influence upon younger writers, serving as their mentor even after his retirement to the semimonastic seclusion of Saint-Benoît-sur-Loire, first from 1921 to 1927 and again in 1936. J. lived there until World War II; in February 1944 he was arrested by the Germans together with other Jews and interned in the concentration camp at Drancy, where he died of pneumonia.

J. united in his work literary and painterly concerns, poetic practice and theory, and he emerged as an important catalyst figure. He helped redefine poetry as a nonmimetic art, expanded lyricism to include humor, parody, wordplay and other devices previously associated with prose, and thought of poetry in terms of means of expression, not message.

The brilliant collection *Le cornet à dés* (1917; the dice cup) expresses best J.'s bent for innovation and remains his most influential work. It contains prose poems built around dream sequences, puns, hallucinations, satirical sketches, images that modulate one into another and convey an oblique vision of the world in the manner of cubist paintings, sometimes no more than a sense of style or the author's attempt to break down literary conventions. J. brings together prose and poetry, strives for effects of flatness in rhythm and diction, and relies on irony, parody, and pastiche to set off his work against the romantic and symbolist (q.v.) schools. In *Le cornet à dés* a puzzling but fascinating universe that has no easily definable meaning seems to emerge.

In his subsequent collections, the innovative *Le laboratoire central* (1921; the central laboratory) or the simpler, more introspective *Les pénitents en maillots roses* (1925; the penitents in pink tights), J. continued to use unorthodox techniques, juxtaposing disparate elements, fragmenting images, disrupting anecdotal and melodic lines. He achieved unity through movement—not linear structures but the sustained verbal play and aggressive rhythms that mirror the poet's creativity and carry value without reference to reality. Autonomy, attentiveness to expression and to linguistic effects, and the desire to divorce the poem from the real form the

core of J.'s aesthetic, developed in the preface to *Le cornet à dés* and two longer works, *Art poétique* (1922; the art of poetry) and the posthumously published *Conseils à un jeune poète, suivis de Conseils à un étudiant* (1945; advice to a young poet, followed by advice to a student; first part tr. as *Advice to a Young Poet*, 1976). These treatises equate art and inventiveness and see the poem as a force that solicits, absorbs, and disturbs the reader.

Primarily a poet, J. experimented with biography, art criticism, tales, drama—a bewildering variety of genres and multiform texts characterized by tension between outward-going observation and introspection, fantasy, and spirituality. *Saint Matorel* (1909; Saint Matorel), an unstructured narrative, recounts with ironic compassion the droll and also serious adventures of a Parisian turned abbot. *La défense de Tartufe* (1919; the defense of Tartufe), an anguished record of J.'s conversion to Catholicism, modulates from speculative inquiry, to self-analysis, to humor and the notation of realistic details. J.'s novels, notably *Le roi de Béotie* (1921; the king of Boeotia) and *Le terrain Bouchaballe* (1923; the land of Bouchaballe) paint a vast verbal fresco of Parisian and Breton society. They reveal a sardonic observer, a mime who delights in recording men's words and gestures, a writer with a rich visual memory and the talent to fix in an image settings, objects, faces, and also a fervent but tormented believer who writes in order to surmount inner conflict.

In J.'s last works the pendulum swings toward spirituality. The posthumously published *Derniers poèmes en vers et en prose* (1945; last poems in verse and in prose) and *L'homme de cristal* (1946; the crystal man) express J.'s mystical side and hint at the final reconciliation of extremes that marked his personality, a personality that gave rise to the iconoclastic texts that rank among the most innovative in modern French letters.

FURTHER WORKS: *La côte* (1911); *Les œuvres burlesques et mystiques de Frère Matorel mort au couvent* (1912); *Le siège de Jérusalem: Grande tentation céleste de Saint Matorel* (1914); *Dos d'Harlequin* (1921); *Ne coupez pas, mademoiselle; ou, Les erreurs des P.T.T.* (1921); *Le cabinet noir* (1922); *Filibuth; ou, La montre en or* (1923); *Visions infernales* (1924); *L'homme de chair et l'homme de reflet* (1924); *Fond de l'eau* (1927); *Sacrifice impérial* (1929); *Tableau de la bourgeoisie* (1930); *Rivage* (1931); *Le bal masqué*

(1932); *Ballades* (1938); *Méditations reli-gieuses* (1945); *Poèmes de Morven le Gaëlique* (1953); *Correspondance* (2 vols., 1953–55). FURTHER VOLUME IN ENGLISH: *The Dice Cup: Selected Prose Poems* (1980)

BIBLIOGRAPHY: Billy, A., *M. J.* (1945); Bela-val, Y., *La rencontre avec M. J.* (1946); An-dreu, P., *M. J.* (1962); Kamber, G., *M. J. and the Poetics of Cubism* (1971); Plantier, R., *L'univers poétique de M. J.* (1976); Brown-stein, M., Introduction to *The Dice Cup: Se-lected Prose Poems* (1980), pp. i–v

VIKTORIA SKRUPSKELIS

JÆGER, Frank

Danish poet, novelist, and short-story writer, b. 19 June 1926, Frederiksberg; d. 4 July 1977, Elsinore

Trained as a librarian, J. was able to earn a liv-ing from his writings alone from 1950 on. His critically acclaimed debut as a poet, *Dydige digte* (1948; virtuous poems), is engagingly ac-cessible even on a casual first reading. Its tone ranges from the idyllic, through the humorous and ironic, to the frustrated and the melan-choly.

The poems of *Morgenens trompet* (1949; the trumpet of morning) differ both in tone and style from *Dydige digte*. Underlying many of them is a despair occasioned by physical or emotional suffering.

In *De 5 årstider* (1950; the 5 seasons) the poet's earlier optimism and predilection for the idyllic once again predominate. The four sea-sons are depicted from a variety of standpoints, most of which are life-affirming. The poems of the "fifth" season, however, transcend the limi-tations of the calendar cycle. In *Tyren* (1953; the bull) J. further restricted his poetic style by rhyme and meter. Increasingly J. is drawn to-ward such questions as death and rebirth, man's isolation, and the irreconcilability of illu-sion and reality.

Many of the poems in *Havkarlens sange* (1956; songs of the merman) and *Cinna, og andre digte* (1959; Cinna, and other poems) are more brooding and sensual than is most of J.'s earlier poetry. This inquietude is, however, offset by the mood of the majority of the poems, which stress the idyllic, the romantic, the lighthearted and whimsical, affirming art's place in life. *Idylia* (1967; Greek: collection of small pictures) is, as its title suggests, a volume of essentially idyllic poetry, although in several

of the poems J. enters the realm of the surreal.

At first glance J.'s novel *Iners* (1950; Iners) would seem to reflect the same idyllic bent as most of his poetry. The protagonist, Iners, at first seems to be just a guileless good-for-no-thing. But he is soon shown to be possessed of malevolent subconscious drives that leave mis-ery and suffering in their wake. *Iners* is a dis-quieting study of a man's demonic nature.

In *Hverdagshistorier* (1951; everyday sto-ries) J. imposes a fairy-tale framework on eighteen loosely connected short stories. Rang-ing from an allegory about the renewal of na-ture to a parable of the triumph of death, the stories in *Hverdagshistorier* probe the surreal and the chimerical with irony, humor, and human sympathy.

J.'s autobiographical fantasy *Den unge Jæ-gers lidelser* (1953; the sufferings of young Jæger) consists of nine prose sketches about signal events in J.'s childhood and youth. Writ-ten in a realistic style, they are nonetheless re-plete with frequent excursions into the realm of illusion.

The protagonist of the psychologically realis-tic novel *Døden i skoven* (1970; death in the forest) is suddenly banished to an isolated for-est house. Unable to adapt to his seclusion, he withdraws inwardly and slowly disintegrates as a human being. J. makes clear that, although the middle-aged Cornelius bears the immediate responsibility for his own downfall, there are forces beyond his control ultimately determin-ing his destiny.

Although J. began his career as an idyllic poet, he ended it as primarily an author of real-istic fiction. He was frequently absorbed with the problems of art's relation to reality and man's isolation. Never the social critic and only rarely the conscious purveyor of metaphysical thought, J. nevertheless made his characters, for better or for worse, conform to conven-tional morality. The fact that much of his fic-tion ends abruptly and equivocally, often be-fore the work's problem can be resolved, should not be viewed as a flaw; for in forcing readers to draw their own conclusions, J. has made them active rather than merely passive participants in the creative process.

FURTHER WORKS: *Tune* (1951); *19 Jægerviser* (1953); *Didrik* (1955); *Jomfruen fra Orléans, Jeanne d'Arc* (1955); *Til en følsom veninde* (1957); *Kapellanen, og andre fortællinger* (1957); *Velkommen, vinter* (1958); *Hvilket postbud—en Due* (1959); *Pastorale* (1963); *Pelsen* (1964); *Drømmen om en sommerdag* (1965); *Danskere: Tre fortællinger af fædrelandets historie* (1966); *Naive rejser* (1968); *Der er en verden også i Verona* (1969); *Alvilda* (1969); *Den som ingen holder tilbage* (1970); *Essays gennem ti år* (1970); *Provinser* (1972); *J. A. P.* (1973); *S* (1973); *Hvor er Ulla-Katrine?* (1974); *Udsigt til Kronborg* (1976)

BIBLIOGRAPHY: Hugus, F., "The Dilemma of the Artist in Selected Prose Works of F. J.," *SS*, 47 (1975), 52–65; Maelsaeke, D. van, *The Strange Essence of Things* (1977), pp. 142–65, 168–74, 192–201

FRANK HUGUS

JAHNN, Hans Henny

German novelist and dramatist, b. 17 Dec. 1894, Hamburg-Stellingen; d. 29 Nov. 1959, Hamburg-Blankenese

Son of a shipbuilder, J. divided his interests among writing, musical theory and composition, and organ building. Opposed to war, he spent the years 1915–18 in Norway. After 1933 he emigrated to Denmark, where he lived with his family, working as a farmer and biologist. He returned to Hamburg in 1950.

Like his literary next-of-kin Alfred Döblin and Hans Erich Nossack (qq.v.), J. was a novelist to the extent to which a novel can be regarded as an allegory of human life. Maintaining in his works the precarious utopian balance between art and propaganda so characteristic of expressionism (q.v.), metaphysical anxiety shaped his message to man fixed in a system with the coordinates *poverty, wealth, man,* and *beast*. The same four concepts emerged as the title of J.'s most significant drama written after his return to postwar Germany, *Armut, Reichtum, Mensch und Tier* (1948; poverty, wealth, man, and beast). In its reduction of the fateful rural existence of a Norwegian farmer to those elemental motives, the play restates J.'s earlier convictions tempered by the harsh events in his own life yet is far removed from any specific intellectual or social cause. Its starkly simple message has the power of early Greek drama, urging mankind to seek salvation in compassionate love—the river unbound uniting all disparate life in deep sympathy (in biological and spiritual symbiosis)—to recapture the lost mythic state of nature.

The earliest examples of this concern are found together with faint narcissistic overtones

in the play *Der Arzt, sein Weib, sein Sohn* (1922; the physician, his wife, his son) and the long novel *Perrudja* (1929; Perrudja). *Perrudja* is a work of cascading images and words that articulate the cosmic pathos of an exile from the conventions of society, who is searching, in the Norwegian wilderness, for complete harmony of existence. This cannot be achieved without its measure of evil, as shown in J.'s magnum opus, *Fluß ohne Ufer* (river without banks), a trilogy consisting of *Das Holzschiff* (1949; *The Ship*, 1961), *Die Niederschrift des Gustav Anias Horn* (2 vols., 1949, 1950; Gustav Anias Horn's written narrative), *Epilog* (1961; epilogue). This novel of suspense, at first seemingly concerned with murder and mutiny during a mysterious voyage ending in shipwreck, develops into a retrospective account that analyzes motives and meaning in the lives of two central characters. The novel is finally expanded to proportions of universal principle through the technique of cyclic repetition—another murder is committed, another murderer assumes his share of guilt, which is but transmuted love.

Reflecting the expressionist urge for direct communication, J.'s plays are, for the most part, built on the thesis that man's despair, that is, the curse of evanescent youth, results from his loss of animal innocence, and that this sanctuary of innocence can be recovered only partially through an archetypal love of which the goddess in *Medea* (1926, Medea) becomes a symbol. This theme, first expressed in *Der Arzt, sein Weib, sein Sohn*, persists through the posthumously published *Die Trümmer des Gewissens* (1961; the ruins of conscience), which tries to assess the consequences of man's fall from innocence in a vision of atomic holocaust as proof of scientific and political vanity. Becoming more and more convinced in his last years that the "league of the weak"—men of good faith—had to take political action, and possibly to sacrifice themselves to save mankind from pointless destruction, J. was working on another drama of protest entitled *Die andere Seite greift ein* (the other side intervenes) on the eve of his death.

His creed he had stated long ago, in his essay "Aufgabe des Dichters in dieser Zeit" (1932; the writer's task in these times): "We have witnessed too much; ignorance no longer becomes us. It is not our misfortune but our hope that man's soul has been found inconstant. Let us rebuild it and strengthen it against the tide of rational catastrophes, to reunite it to the harmonious structure of being."

485

FURTHER WORKS: *Pastor Ephraim Magnus* (1919); *Die Krönung Richards III* (1921); *Hans Heinrich* (1922); *Der gestohlene Gott* (1924); *Neuer Lübecker Totentanz* (1931); *Straßenecke: Ein Ort, eine Handlung* (1931); *Spur des dunklen Engels* (1952); *Thomas Chatterton* (1955); *Die Nacht aus Blei* (1956); *Aufzeichnungen eines Einzelgängers* (1959); *Dramen* (1963); *13 nicht geheure Geschichten* (1963) *Über den Anlaß, und andere Essays* (1964); *Werke und Tagebücher* (7 vols., 1974); *H. H. J.–Peter Huchel: Ein Briefwechsel 1951–1959* (1974)

BIBLIOGRAPHY: Nossack, H. E., "Nachruf auf H. H. J.," *Jahrbuch 1960 der Akademie der Wissenschaften und der Literatur* (1960), pp. 43–48; Muschg, W., *Von Trakl zu Brecht: Dichter des Expressionismus* (1961), pp. 264–334; Marr, W. M., "Compassion and the Outsider: H. H. J.'s *Die Nacht aus Blei*," *GR*, 39 (1964), 201–10; Meyer, J., *Verzeichnis der Schriften von und über H. H. J.* (1967); Jenkinson, D. E., "The Role of Vitalism in the Novels of H. H. J.," *GL&L*, 25 (1972), 359–67; Kobbe, P., *Mythos und Modernität: Eine poetologische und methodenkritische Studie zum Werk H. H. J.s* (1973); Detsch, R., "The Theme of the Black Race in the Works of H. H. J.," *Mosaic* 7, 2 (1973–74), 165–87

KURT OPITZ

JAMAICAN LITERATURE
See English-Caribbean Literature

JAMES, Henry
American novelist, short-story writer, dramatist, critic, and essayist, b. 15 April 1843, New York, N.Y.; d. 28 Feb. 1916, London, England

J. is, next to Faulkner (q.v.), America's most distinguished prolific novelist. His reputation has waxed and waned since his first story ("A Tragedy of Error") appeared in 1864, but it seems safe to include him among a handful of classic American writers of fiction. During his own last years, and between the 1940s and the mid-1960s, his standing as *the* self-conscious craftsman of prose, the writer's writer, was supreme. Whatever the fluctuations of his reputation, his experiments with limited point of view and unreliable narration provided a generation of modernists with a useful model for breaking

out of Victorian conventions of plot, character, and narrative voice. Himself a 19th-c. man in his insistence on the social values of wit, self-possession, and civility, he nevertheless served as a touchstone for several of the more jagged and unsettling voices of the 20th c., notably those of T. S. Eliot and Ezra Pound (qq.v.)

J. was born into an oppressively distinguished American family. His father, Henry James, Sr., was a Swedenborgian philosopher of note, and a good friend of Emerson and other New England transcendentalists. J.'s older brother William became a professor at Harvard and eventually one of America's foremost philosophers. The three youngest siblings, by contrast, led markedly ineffectual lives, while Henry, in between, perfected the techniques of second sonship: since William was the aggressive doer, preempting the space of active pursuit, Henry became the reflector, requiring only the space of imaginative musing. "There was the difference and the opposition, as I really believe I was already aware," he wrote in *A Small Boy and Others* (1913), "that one way of taking life was to go in for everything and everyone, which kept you abundantly occupied; and the other was to be occupied, quite as occupied, just with the sense and image of it all, and on only a fifth of the actual immersion; a circumstance extremely strange." It is a short step from this autobiographical reflection to the privileged role of consciousness over action that underlies J.'s fictional innovations in plot, character, and narrative technique.

Seeking for his sons "a sensuous education" they were unlikely to obtain in America, Henry James, Sr., took them abroad between 1855 and 1860, arranging tutors and boarding schools in several European countries. They visited myriad churches, but prayed in none. J. developed during these years his "pewless" state, his dislike of ideology, his passion for diverse points of view, and his love for European art and culture. In 1860 he returned to America, where he sat out the Civil War, trying Harvard Law School for a year and champing to return to Europe. After two brief trips abroad in 1869 and 1872 he finally left America for good in 1875, settling first in Paris, and then a year later in London.

The hold of European culture on J.'s imagination cannot be overestimated. His earliest successful story, "A Passionate Pilgrim" (1871), centers on the obsessive yet sinister appeal of the Old World, and in one form or another this theme roused J.'s finest powers, from *Roderick Hudson* (1875) to *The Golden*

Bowl (1904). Although *Watch and Ward* (1871) is technically his first novel, *Roderick Hudson* is legitimately viewed as J.'s first characteristic performance. There—in the fable of the talented young American who journeys to Italy to realize his artistic promise and who then comes to ruin in the enterprise—J. sounded his abiding note. Undone by his recklessness and his innocence, Roderick squanders himself, wasting his genius on works he cannot terminate, wasting his feelings on a woman who will betray him. Waste itself emerges as J.'s theme, the waste incurred by an innocent, Emersonian spirit unable to husband its resources or to recognize the tangle of motives lurking both in the self and in others. Already in 1875 the idealistic, journeying spirit has been seen in its American colors; and the cluster of beckoning opportunities, temptations, and traps emerges as experienced, immemorial Europe.

Roderick Hudson metamorphoses into Christopher Newman in J.'s next successful novel, *The American* (1877); this figure achieves its purest form, however, as a woman, Isabel Archer, in J.'s finest early novel, *The Portrait of a Lady* (1881). Even those who dislike J.'s later development agree that *The Portrait of a Lady* is a masterpiece. Isabel's journey from New York to England to Paris and finally to Rome enacts a beautifully modulated passage from youth to maturity, innocence to experience, the illusion of freedom to the awareness of necessity. It is not a bitter novel, however, because the necessity that Isabel discovers is no outward imposition, but rather her own deepest proclivities, as these emerge in the course of her experience. The cast of supporting characters—her charming English cousin Ralph Touchett and his parents, her suitors both American (Caspar Goodwood) and English (Lord Warburton), the accomplished pair who eventually "seduce" her (Madame Merle and Gilbert Osmond)— is fleshed out and nuanced with an authority J. was never to surpass. Capping a group of novels and a host of stories (the well-known "Daisy Miller" [1878] among them) on the "international theme," *The Portrait of a Lady* marks J.'s greatest achievement in the form of the realistic novel. It marks as well the acme of his popularity.

Dickens, Balzac, and Hawthorne were continuous models in J.'s mind; he never ceased to reckon with them. His aesthetic aims, however, may best be described as a midposition between the extremes of George Eliot and Gustave Flaubert. Eliot he saw as the first English novelist to probe moral issues seriously. She alone, in the English tradition, met his standard of *inclusive* treatment of difficult issues. "The essence of moral energy," he wrote in "The Art of Fiction" (1884), "is to survey the whole field." But the problem with Eliot, he later claimed, was her didacticism. Beneath her surfaces he found the limiting insistence on ideology; if you scratched one of her characters you found not flesh and blood but an idea. To free himself from Eliot (more broadly: to free himself from the blinkered innocence of Anglo-American idealism), he turned to Flaubert. During 1875 and 1876 he attended Flaubert's literary Sunday afternoon salons, where he not only met Daudet, Maupassant, and Zola, but also drank in the heady air of free aesthetic inquiry: "It would have been late in the day to propose among them . . . any question as to the degree in which a novel might or might not concern itself with the teaching of a lesson. They had settled these preliminaries long ago" (Leon Edel, *The Life of H. J.*, Vol. II [1962], p. 221).

Yet J. found Flaubert's insistent amorality ultimately as limiting as George Eliot's piety; he began to chafe at Flaubert's rendering "only the visible . . . he [Flaubert] had no faith in the power of the moral to offer a surface . . ." ("Flaubert," 1893). *The power of the moral to offer a surface*: this phrase best captures J.'s own enterprise, his attempt to make visible the drama of the spirit, to follow its movement through the tangle of material objects and obstacles in which it actually, day by day, finds itself. Flaubert's Emma Bovary, J. decided, "is really too small an affair. . . . Why did Flaubert choose, as special conduits of the life he proposed to depict, such inferior . . . human specimens?" (a later essay, also titled "Flaubert," 1902). What was missing was not an optimistic ending, but a consciousness capable of extracting the full moral value of the defeat Emma had endured. When J. rewrote Flaubert's novel so as to find the moral in its surface, the novel he achieved was *The Portrait of a Lady*.

During the 1880s J. wrote what his father would have called "interesting failures": three ambitious novels that, drawing on the naturalist vogue of Zola, sought the larger canvas to illuminate social concerns of the day. *The Bostonians* (1885) surveys with knife-edged detachment the struggles and internal contradictions of the feminist movement in Boston. *The Princess Casamassima* (1886), resurrecting two characters from *Roderick Hudson*, centers on violent political disturbances in England. *The Tragic Muse* (1890) explores more blandly some of the inevitable conflicts between political and aesthetic aspirations in the English scene. Of these three novels, the first was attacked in America and praised in England, the second was attacked in England and praised in America, the third elicited neither praise nor blame anywhere. James as a realistic novelist had reached a sort of dead end.

His way out of this dilemma was extraordinary. He began a last-ditch attempt for the large audience, seeking to capture the London stage. The dramas he wrote, however, were based on outdated models of the "well-made play"; and failure, when it came, in 1895, in the form of *Guy Domville*'s opening night fiasco in a London theater, was spectacular. His career as a playwright thus ended, he finally accepted the lyrical inwardness of his imaginative bent, and entered his major phase, writing in the next eight years five remarkable short novels and three full-length masterpieces.

The Spoils of Poynton (1896), *The Other House* (1896), *What Maisie Knew* (1897), *The Awkward Age* (1899), and *The Sacred Fount* (1901) resemble nothing in J.'s oeuvre so much as each other. Drawing creatively on the theater fiasco by fashioning dialogue so self-sufficient that, as on stage, it requires no further explanation, J. structures these novels scenically. In them he moves back and forth between the subjective perceptions of a character and the objective (though mystifying) conversations of a group. No omniscient narrator explains anything. The more limited the center of consciousness—Maisie, Nanda in *The Awkward Age*, the narrator in *The Sacred Fount*—the more interesting the tensions that are generated. He had now created structures that could make the most of the subjective drama of the journeying spirit.

In *The Ambassadors* (1903) J. returned triumphantly to the "international theme." Lambert Strether, middle-aged, well-behaved, and yet secretly hungering for new experiences, is sent by the straitlaced Mrs. Newsome as her special ambassador to France. There he is to retrieve her errant son Chad, who, it is feared, has lost his Puritan bearings while enjoying the pleasures of Parisian society. The ensuing comedy centers irresistibly on Strether's expanding consciousness, as he reluctantly discovers that Chad has, despite his mother's concern, changed for the better. The prose in this novel, as in the two that follow, is of a metaphoric richness and syntactic complexity rarely equaled elsewhere.

The Ambassadors is a comedy, *The Wings of the Dove* (1902) is a tragedy, and *The Golden Bowl* (1904) is something for which we have no adequate categories. In this last completed novel Maggie Verver, the mythically wealthy princess, discovers that her charming Italian husband, Prince Amerigo, has resumed an affair (hitherto unknown) with her closest friend, Charlotte. Since Charlotte has in the meantime, at Maggie's instigation, become married to Maggie's widowed father, Adam Verver, the psychological complications multiply. Moving discreetly among the points of view of the prince, Charlotte, Adam, and their friends the Assinghams, J. focuses the last half of his novel on Maggie's burgeoning consciousness. As she moves from unthinking complicity to full awareness, she enacts the trajectory from innocence to experience that has been J.'s abiding theme ever since *Roderick Hudson*. Recapturing her husband, mending the marriage between Adam and Charlotte (or apparently doing so: this novel insists on supplying nothing beyond the appearances), managing both of these tasks while outwardly acknowledging neither, Maggie represents J.'s final synthesis of American idealism and European knowingness. The combination is as chilling as it is compelling.

Although J. is primarily a novelist, he also wrote over one hundred impressive short stories. They divide roughly into four categories: stories of the "international theme," of which "Daisy Miller" is the best known; stories of artists and writers—all of these are interesting: perhaps "The Aspern Papers" (1888) and "The Real Thing" (1892) are the finest; ghost stories, of which "The Turn of the Screw" (1898) is the masterpiece, virtually transforming the genre; and stories of "the unlived life," a category all J.'s own, of which "The Beast in the Jungle" (1903) and "The Jolly Corner" (1908) are the most memorable.

J. began his career as a critic, and he maintained that function throughout his life, producing four volumes of essays and numerous uncollected articles. His 1884 piece on "The Art of Fiction" has become a classic statement of the writer's freedom to choose his own form and subject matter: the responsibility of the critic is only to assess what the writer has *done* with his choices. In the same essay J. reveals his own creative principles, defining experience as "an immense sensibility, a kind of huge spider-web of the finest silken threads suspended in the chamber of consciousness, and catching every air-borne particle in its tissue. It is the very atmosphere of the mind. . . ." Experience emerges as a function not of objective actions, but of subjective impressions—not the raw materials but what the mind and heart succeed in making of them.

Throughout his life J. was a literary figure among literary figures—meeting Turgenev and the Flaubert circle in the 1870s, becoming a friend and supporter of Ford Madox Ford, Joseph Conrad, Edith Wharton (qq.v.), and Stephen Crane in his later years. By the turn of the century he was held in high repute by cognoscenti: they called him—half playfully, half seriously—The Master. After World War I broke out, J. became horrified by the tardiness of America's entry into the war. As a gesture of devotion to his adopted country he renounced his American citizenship and in 1915 became a naturalized British subject. Two months before his death he was awarded the prestigious Order of Merit.

In perhaps the most suggestive statement yet made about J., T. S. Eliot said that "he had mind so fine that no idea could violate it." The statement means not that J. repudiated ideas, but that his fiction revealed them never as abstractions, but as the property of thinking, feeling people. Free of overt ideology, "pewless," J.'s fiction served as an exemplary late-Victorian attempt to escape the emphatic moralizing of his Victorian forebears. It was welcomed on those terms by modernists like Conrad, Ford, and Virginia Woolf (q.v.), all of whom found moral issues matters to whisper rather than shout about. In addition, J.'s ceaseless effort to remove himself from his fiction—to let his imaginative world speak in its own voice, not his—acted as a point of reference for the modernist urge away from confession and toward impersonality. To this end J.'s fiction—and perhaps more importantly his prefaces to the New York Edition (1907–17) of his works—meshed smoothly with the nascent New Critical emphasis on showing rather than telling, on responsible craft rather than oracular utterance.

In the last sixty years J. has been subject to a wide range of critical postures: tellingly attacked by E. M. Forster (q.v.) in *Aspects of the Novel* (1927) and by Van Wyck Brooks in *The Pilgrimage of H. J.* (1925); neutrally interrogated by Edmund Wilson (q.v.) in *The Triple Thinkers* (1948) and by F. W. Dupee in *H. J.* (1951); and lavishly praised by Percy Lubbock in *The Art of Fiction* (1921), Laurence Holland in *The Expense of Vision* (1964) and Leon Edel, most extensively in *The Life of H. J.* (5 vols., 1953–72). Since the Vietnam War J.'s reputation has, it seems, been somewhat in eclipse; readers attuned to violence, apocalypse, and the grotesque turn the pages of his novels in bewilderment. But he will endure because, as he wrote to Henry Adams (q.v.) on the eve of World War I, he remained, despite all, "that queer monster, the artist, an obstinate finality, an inexhaustible sensibility."

FURTHER WORKS: *A Passionate Pilgrim, and Other Tales* (1875); *Transatlantic Sketches* (1875); *French Poets and Novelists* (1878); *The Europeans* (1878); *The Madonna of the Future, and Other Tales* (1879); *Confidence* (1879); *Hawthorne* (1879); *Washington Square* (1880); *Portraits of Places* (1883); *The Siege of London* (1883); *Tales of Three Cities* (1884); *A Little Tour in France* (1884); *The Author of Beltraffio* (1885); *Stories Revived* (1885); *Partial Portraits* (1888); *The Reverberator* (1888); *The Aspern Papers* (1888); *A London Life* (1889); *The Lesson of the Master* (1892); *The Real Thing, and Other Tales* (1893); *The Private Life* (1893); *Essays in London and Elsewhere* (1893); *The Wheel of Time* (1893); *Theatricals* (1894–95); *Terminations* (1895); *Embarrassments* (1896); *In the Cage* (1898); *The Two Magics* (1898); *The Soft Side* (1900); *The Better Sort* (1903); *William Wetmore Story and His Friends* (1903); *English Hours* (1905); *The Question of Our Speech, and the Lesson of Balzac* (1905); *The American Scene* (1907); *Italian Hours* (1909); *The Finer Grain* (1910); *The Outcry* (1911); *A Small Boy and Others* (1913); *Notes of a Son and Brother* (1914); *Notes on Novelists* (1914); *England at War: An Essay* (1915); *The Question of Mind* (1915); *The Middle Years* (1917); *The Ivory Tower* (1917); *The Sense of the Past* (1917); *Within the Rim, and Other Essays* (1919); *The Letters of H. J.* (2 vols., 1920); *Notes and Reviews* (1921); *The Novels and Stories of H. J.* (35 vols., 1921–23); *The Art of the Novel: Critical Prefaces* (1934); *The Notebooks of H. J.* (1947); *The Scenic Art* (1948); *The Complete Plays of H. J.* (1949); *The Selected Letters of H. J.* (1955); *H. J.: Autobiography* (1956); *The Painter's Eye* (1956); *Parisian Sketches* (1957); *Literary Reviews and Essays* (1957); *The Complete Tales of H. J.* (12 vols., 1962–64); *Letters* (3 vols., 1974–80)

BIBLIOGRAPHY: Beach, J. W., *The Method of H. J.* (1918); Lubbock, P., *The Craft of Fiction* (1921), pp. 142–202; Brooks, V. W., *The Pilgrimage of H. J.* (1925); Matthiessen, F. O.,

H. J.: The Major Phase (1944); Matthiessen, F. O., ed., *The James Family* (1947); Wilson, E., *The Triple Thinkers*, rev. ed. (1948), pp. 88–132; Leavis, F. R., *The Great Tradition* (1948); Dupee, F. W., *H. J.* (1951); Bewley, M., *The Complex Fate* (1952); Edel, L., *The Life of H. J.* (5 vols., 1953–72); Anderson, Q., *The American H. J.* (1957); Wegelin, C., *The Image of Europe in H. J.* (1958); Poirier, R., *The Comic Sense of H. J.* (1960); Cargill, O., *The Novels of H. J.* (1961); Edel, L., and Laurence, D. H., *A Bibliography of H. J.*, 2nd ed. (1961); Krook D., *The Ordeal of Consciousness in H. J.* (1962); Holland, L., *The Expense of Vision: Essays on the Craft of H. J.* (1964); Lebowitz, N., *The Imagination of Loving: H. J.'s Legacy to the Novel* (1965); Tanner, T., *The Reign of Wonder: Naïveté and Reality in American Literature* (1965), pp. 259–335; Sears, S., *The Negative Imagination: Form and Perception in the Novels of H. J.* (1970); Weinstein, P., *H. J. and the Requirements of the Imagination* (1971); Chatman, S., *The Later Style of H. J.* (1972); Yeazell, R., *Language and Knowledge in the Late Novels of H. J.* (1976); Anderson, C. R., *Person, Place, and Thing in H. J.'s Novels* (1977)

PHILIP M. WEINSTEIN

J.'s critical genius comes out most tellingly in his mastery over, his baffling escape from, Ideas; a mastery and an escape which are perhaps the last test of a superior intelligence. He had a mind so fine that no idea could violate it. . . . J. in his novels is like the best French critics in maintaining a point of view, a viewpoint untouched by the parasite idea. He is the most intelligent man of his generation. [1918]

T. S. Eliot, "On H. J.," in F. W. Dupee, ed., *The Question of H. J.* (1945), pp. 110–11

He has, in the first place, a very short list of characters. . . . In the second place, the characters, beside being few in number, are constructed on very stingy lines. They are incapable of fun, of rapid motion, of carnality, and of nine-tenths of heroism. Their clothes will not take off, the diseases that ravage them are anonymous, like the sources of their income, their servants are noiseless or resemble themselves, no social explanation of the world we know is possible for them, for there are no stupid people in their world, no barriers of language, and no poor. Even their sensations are limited. They can land in Europe and look at works of art and at each other but that is all. Maimed creatures can alone breathe in H. J.'s pages—maimed yet specialized. They remind one of the exquisite deformities who haunted Egyptian art in the reign of Akhenaton—huge heads and tiny legs,

but nevertheless charming. In the following reign they disappear.

E. M. Forster, *Aspects of the Novel* (1927, rpt. 1954), pp. 160–61

Since other novelists have used and misused the J. novel and since by contagion it has modified the actual practice of many novelists who never read J. at all, we had better try to say what the J. novel is. It is consistent to its established variety of skeleton forms; it is faithful to its established method of reporting; and it insists on its chosen center of attraction. To do these things it first of all gets rid of the omniscient author; the author is never allowed to intrude directly or in his own person; the story is always some created person's sense of it, or that of some group of persons, so that we see or feel the coercive restriction of someone's conscious experience of the story as the medium through which we ourselves feel it. Secondly, the J. novel uses device after device, not merely to invite the reader's ordinary attention, but to command his extraordinary attention. . . . The scenes between persons are dramatized as substance, not as ornament; true action is in speech and gesture; and thus the dialogue creates a new form of attention, in which we always sail close-hauled or trembling on the tack. As the the command to attend is obeyed, the reader learns a new game which, as it seems to partake of actual experience, he can take for truth; and which, as it shows a texture of sustained awareness never experienced in life, he knows to be art. To gain that effect, to make art truth, is the whole object of J.'s addiction to the forms of fiction. . . . [1947]

R. P. Blackmur, "H. J.," in Robert E. Spiller, et al., eds., *Literary History of the United States*, 3rd ed. rev. (1963), p. 1062

In many of his books—in *The Ambassadors*, for instance—the characters remind one a little of Proust's. But unlike Proust, he wipes the shadows of damnation from under their eyes, and for their sakes he averts his gaze at embarrassing moments. Little Bilham cries out for the Faubourg St. Germain as Proust presented it; but he is safer with J., because J. will never bring age and ruins toppling on his head. . . . The terrorist explosions toward which his tremendous insights would, in any other writer, move, he must at all events avoid, for the fine high windows of the Jamesian villa are no less breakable than they are valuable. He knows that the material conditions for his values are too deeply embedded in the lives of their opposites to destroy the one without endangering the other. Unlike Proust, he will not play Samson and pull the temple down on our guilty heads. In the end he is a kind of Edwardian Atlas holding up the old cracked heavens.

Marius Bewley, *The Complex Fate* (1952), p. 76

HENRY JAMES

JUAN RAMÓN JIMÉNEZ

UWE JOHNSON

The father's desire to surround his boys with "an atmosphere of freedom" was itself surrounded by contradictions. . . . The senior Henry gave him, he felt, no sense of values save to realize the value of *all* life and *all* experience. At one point the novelist likens his brother and himself to Romulus and Remus, disowned by the parent, thrown into the Tiber of Life, left to flounder as best they could and called upon to build Rome—that is to have the right answers to the Divine Truth which the father affirmed was all around them. The novelist reasoned that this free-and-easy mode of education—or absence thereof—was the best thing that could have happened to him: it made him "convert"—everything had to be translated into his own terms and rendered in the light of his own inner resources which in the end helped him to bring order into his world. He had a terrible need for order, for design, for apprehending—and later communicating—the world around him in an elaborately organized fashion. It stemmed undoubtedly from the disordered fashion in which, as a boy, he was asked to cope with it.

Leon Edel, *The Life of H. J.,* Vol. I (1953), pp. 115–16

It is not simply in the organization of character, dialogue, and action that H. J. reveals The Moral Passion, nor is it reflected further only in his treatment of surroundings, but it represents itself and its ideal in the increasing scrupulosity of the style: precision of definition, respect for nuance, tone, the multiplying presence of enveloping metaphors, the winding around the tender center of ritual lines, like the approach of the devout and worshipful to the altar, these circumlocutions at once protecting the subject and slowing the advance so that the mere utility of the core is despaired of and it is valued solely in the contemplative sight. The value of life lies ultimately in the experienced quality of it, in the integrity of the given not in the usefulness of the taken. . . . He does not find in today only what is needful for tomorrow. His aim is rather to appreciate and to respect the things of his experience and to set them, finally, free.

William Gass, "The High Brutality of Good Intentions," *Accent,* 18 (1958), 71

Art or aesthetic reality was not for J. an order of value to be ranked in relation to others but a process of creation to be engaged in, with a product—the union of form and vision which in the late Prefaces he came to call a *marriage*—to be fashioned and enjoyed. And the process of making his novels is what joined him to the world he knew and rendered in his art and kept him from sorting his characters into categories of good and evil with serenely Olympian assurance and detachment. Neither his criticism nor his fiction makes paramount the rigor of moral judgment. . . . We

critics have tended to make J. guilty of the " 'flagrant' morality" which his father taught him to disdain. The moral implications of J.'s fiction are to be found not only and not principally in the judgments he passes on his characters but in the fully creative function of J.'s form, whether comic or otherwise. His form often creates the follies it mocks, and on occasion he celebrates them rather than simply evaluating or correcting them. Like gods and other parents, authors not only confront moral problems but create them, and J. constantly confessed this fact in his fiction. One of his chief contributions to the lyric dimension of English fiction is his distinctive fusion of moral and technical concerns, which has the effect of founding his moral vision on the act and form of intimate confession.

Laurence Holland, *The Expense of Vision: Essays on the Craft of H. J.* (1964), pp. ix–x

The human mind is, for J., by definition a haunted mind. The haunting, furthermore, was implicit for him in the nature of consciousness, as the mode by which we both encounter life and are detached from it. For J., "experience" had two meanings, which themselves stand in an analogical relation to this opposition in the make-up of consciousness. On the one hand, experience meant action: the effective imposition of one's will upon the external world, participation, mastery; on the other, it meant *re*action, a response of the mind, "a mark made on the intelligence," contemplation, passivity.

The first was something J. could not imagine for himself. . . . By a feat of intelligence . . .he transformed the latter definition into the one delineating the superior mode of being. Finally, experience wasn't experience unless it stirred that "vibration," and anything that did so—a mere act of seeing—qualified. But the other notion lingered in his imagination. . . .

His characters repeat the process their author engages in: they construct imaginary worlds with their "visiting" minds, worlds that are the objectification of their desires but that are also unreal and doomed to collapse when brought into conjunction with the "facts." The facts are always that things are different from what a given character had wanted. The basic pattern of J.'s work is the creation and collapse of the fiction, its failure.

Sallie Sears, *The Negative Imagination: Form and Perception in the Novels of H. J.* (1970), pp. 126–27

JAMMES, Francis

French poet and novelist, b. 2 Dec. 1868, Tournay; d. 1 Nov. 1938, Hasparren

J., educated in Pau and Bordeaux, worked for a while in a law office before deciding to live by his pen. He spent most of his life in his native southwestern part of France, first in Orthez, later in Hasparren, in the Basque country.

J. began to write while still in high school. His literary breakthrough came with the publication of his collection of poetry *De l'angélus de l'aube à l'angélus du soir* (1898; from the morning prayer to the evening prayer), which is among the poet's most important works. It already contained all the themes that J. was to develop further in later volumes, the principal one being that of nature. With a naïveté that at times appears somewhat studied, J. writes about the various aspects of rustic life. He is a keen observer of nature who expresses, with disarming simplicity and sincerity, a love of fields and flowers, of mountains and rivers, a childlike affection for all animals, and a great compassion for the poor and suffering. His very romantic sensibility is conveyed through sometimes strikingly sensuous images.

J. did not pretend to be a profound thinker. His aim was "to tell his truth," that is, his feelings, emotions, and dreams. Such a refreshingly unpretentious look at himself and nature was greeted as a welcome change from the elitist hermeticism of symbolism (q.v.). J. did, however, inherit from symbolism the form he used, a kind of free verse consisting of irregular lines of varied length.

In 1905, under the influence of Paul Claudel (q.v.), and prompted by his own experience of Lourdes as well as his admiration for Saint Francis of Assisi, J. returned to the Catholic faith he had abandoned in his youth. Thereafter, strong religious overtones became characteristic of his writing. In *Les géorgiques chrétiennes* (1912; Christian georgics) he describes the life of a peasant family who, whether they cultivate their fields or feed the animals, or do any other chore, unceasingly praise God's greatness. In keeping with poetic conventions, J. employed the classical alexandrine line.

J. is also well known as a writer of fiction. His early narratives possess great charm; they are natural, romantic, and delightfully old-fashioned. J.'s masterpiece of lyrical prose is perhaps *Le roman du lièvre* (1903; *Romance of the Rabbit*, 1920), the tale of a hare who, having followed Saint Francis to heaven, yearns to escape from the eternal blissfulness of heavenly animal existence to the dangers and excitements of the terrestrial life he had left behind. If most of these fictional works seem to be somewhat too didactic, they are nevertheless remarkable for the wonderful descriptions of nature they contain. J.'s conversion is also noticeable in his fiction; the later works are often colored with overly religious sentimentalism. Although the stories are well told, there is no complicated psychology in J.'s novels. Frequently the characters are too idealized, and they rarely assume a convincing personality of their own, remaining largely types.

J., who has been referred to as a symbolist, neosymbolist, or *naturiste,* never belonged to any systematic school of poetry. He always was only himself, in the process creating *Jammisme,* which embraces but one guiding principle, "the truth that is the praise of God." It is innocence, simplicity, and humility; it extols the beauty of the native soil and the virtues of family life; it is adoration of God and love of all He created. This attitude finds its perfect expression in the poet's totally unpretentious style. His vocabulary is surprisingly simple, at times even childlike, but always very effective when combined with his exceptional gift of observation.

SELECTED FURTHER WORKS: *Clara d'Ellébeuse* (1899); *Le deuil des primevères* (1901); *Almaïde d'Etremont* (1901); *Le triomphe de la vie* (1902); *Pomme d'Anis* (1904); *Tristesses* (1905); *L'église habillée de feuilles* (1906); *Clairières dans le ciel* (1906); *Ma fille Bernadette* (1910; *My Daughter Bernadette,* 1933); *Cinq prières pour le temps de la guerre* (1916); *Monsieur le curé d'Ozeron* (1918); *La vierge et les sonnets* (1919); *Le poète rustique* (1920); *Cloches pour deux mariages* (1924); *Les Robinsons basques* (1925); *Ma France poétique* (1926); *Basses-Pyrénées: Histoires naturelles et poétiques* (1926); *Le rêve franciscain* (1927); *Champêtreries et méditations* (1930); *L'arc-en-ciel des amours* (1931); *L'école buissonnière; ou, Cours libre de proses choisies* (1930); *L'Antigyde; ou, Élie de Nacre* (1932); *Le crucifix du poète* (1935); *Alouette* (1935); *De tout temps à jamais* (1935); *Le pèlerin de Lourdes* (1936); *Sources* (1936); *Sources et feux* (1944); *Solitude peuplée* (1945); *Le patriarche et son troupeau* (1949). FURTHER VOLUMES IN ENGLISH: *Homer Had a Dog* (1946); *The Early White Narcissi* (1953); *Selected Poems of F. J.* (1976, bilingual)

BIBLIOGRAPHY: Lowell, A., *Six French Poets* (1916); pp. 213–68; Drake, W. A., *Contemporary European Writers* (1928), pp. 243–51; Flory, A., *F. J.* (1941); Soulairol, J., *F. J.* (1941); Inda, J.-P., *Du faune au patriarche*

(1952); Mallet, R., *Le Jammisme* (1961); Mallet, R., *F. J., sa vie, son œuvre* (1961); Van der Burght, R. and L., *F. J., le jeune Chrétien* (1961)

BLANDINE M. RICKERT

JANSSON, Tove

Finnish children's book author, short-story writer, and novelist (writing in Swedish), b. 9 Aug. 1914, Helsinki

The daughter of the Finnish sculptor Viktor Jansson (1886–1958), J., too, first began in the field of art. It was the least serious of her artistic endeavors, as an illustrator of children's books, that led her to writing. Today, she is the most widely read of Finland's authors because of her "Moomintrolls." In fact, for a time she reached beyond the world of books, drawing a cartoon series about the trolls that was carried in newspapers around the world (1952–59).

Her debut as a writer came in 1945, with *Småtrollen och den stora översvämningen* (the little trolls and the great flood); out of this rather simple beginning, there developed the realm of the Moomintrolls, with their generosity and tolerance, their inventiveness and powers of imagination (which reflect salient qualities of their creator), their dislike of sternness and pedantic order, and their close if somewhat haphazard family life. As a rule, the Moomintrolls have none of the malice attributed to the trolls of Nordic myth; instead, they resemble cheerful miniature hippopotami who walk, or waddle, upright. They are inveterate if nervous adventurers, but prefer not to wander far from Moominvalley. The canon of the Moomin books consists of *Kometjakten* (1946; *Comet in Moominland,* 1950), *Trollkarlens hatt* (1948; *Finn Family Moomintroll,* 1950); *Muminpappans bravader* (1950; *The Happy Moomin,* 1950), *Farlig midsommar* (1954; *Moominsummer Madness,* 1955), *Trollvinter* (1957; *Moominland Midwinter,* 1958), *Det osynliga barnet och andra berättelser* (1962; *Tales from Moominvalley,* 1963), *Pappan och havet* (1965; *Moominpappa at Sea,* 1966), and *Sent i November* (1970; *Moominvalley in November,* 1971). There are also two shorter tales with extensive illustrations: *Hur gick det sen? Boken om Mymlan, Mumintrollet och lilla My* (1952; *Moomin, Mymble and Little My,* 1953) and *Vem skall trösta Knyttet?* (1960; *Who Will Comfort Toffle?,* 1960). (Several of the books have been given new titles in subsequent editions.) A darkening is perceptible in the later volumes; the inhabitants' growing fear of natural catastrophe becomes more and more apparent, and an atmosphere of loneliness seems gradually to get the upper hand over the happy spirit of community that had prevailed at the start.

With the Moomin books J. offers an equivalent to the "moral messages" of her distant predecessor in Finland's literature for children, Zachris Topelius (1818–1898), whose tales preached patriotism, a sense of duty, and industry. J., however, inculcates a set of softer virtues, among them kindness, the ability to laugh at one's self, and a love of life's small pleasures.

As the Moomin series was drawing to its close, J. began to write directly for a mature public. She has produced three books of short stories—*Bildhuggarens dotter* (1968; *The Sculptor's Daughter,* 1976), the very title of which gives the collection an air of autobiography; *Lyssnerskan* (1971; the woman who hearkens); and *Dockskåpet, och andra berättelser* (1978; the doll's house, and other stories)—and two novels—*Sommarboken* (1972; *The Summer Book,* 1977), composed of views, happy and sad, of a child and its grandmother in the Finnish skerries, and *Solstaden* (1974; *Sun City,* 1977), an unsentimental description of an old-people's home in St. Petersburg, Florida. In the children's books, the idyll, often threatened, is never destroyed; in the narratives for adults, the idyll is frequently artificial, or it undergoes a terrifying metamorphosis, as in "Ekorren" (the squirrel), the finale of *Lyssnerskan.*

BIBLIOGRAPHY: Fleisher, F. and B., "T. J. and the Moomin Family," *ASR,* 51 (1963), 47–54; Jones, W. G., *T. J.: Pappan och havet, Studies in Swedish Literature,* No. 11 (1979); Jones, W. G., "Studies in Obsession: The New Art of T. J.," *BF,* 14 (1981), 60–62

GEORGE C. SCHOOLFIELD

JAPANESE LITERATURE

As the 20th c. began, the chief impetus in Japanese literature involved a concerted effort to break with older Japanese traditions, an impetus that has had both its positive and negative side. On the positive side, Japanese writers embraced Western literary movements and theories and tried to model some works on particular European or American examples. Although the result in many cases was imitative, the impulse to reach out and to adapt Western literature to native needs was basically constructive, with Western modes of literature imparting fresh vitality. On the negative side, writers pointedly rejected traditional Japanese myths, archetypes, and literary conventions, turning away from their own heritage.

But tradition dies hard in Japan, where the conservative impulse is strong. Older forms of prose, poetry, and drama have survived in 20th-c. Japan, albeit undergoing transformation. Even today traditional forms of lyric poetry, such as the thirty-one-syllable *tanka* (or *waka*) and the seventeen-syllable *haiku* (a 20th-c. term for an independent short poem that emerged from the *haikai*) remain popular along with a modern style of free verse inspired by contact with the West. Traditional modes of drama—Nō, Kabuki, and the Bunraku (the Japanese puppet theater)—flourish together with Western-style realistic plays and postmodernist theater.

Likewise, modern fiction, which has emerged as the principal literary genre, after having overshadowed earlier lyrical and dramatic forms, also remains indebted to an indigenous lineage of narrative prose that goes back to chronicles compiled largely in the Chinese language in the 8th c. and to purely fictional narratives written in Japanese that date from the 10th c. This earlier tradition of narrative prose, often interspersed with thirty-one-syllable lyric poems, culminated in *Genji monogatari* (c. early 11th c.; *The Tale of Genji,* 6 vols., 1925–33; new tr., 1976).

During the first three decades of the 20th c. the modern counterpart of older forms of narrative prose proved particularly amenable to expressing the most significant theme in 20th-c. Japanese literature, namely awareness of the self, and Japanese writers began espousing the ideology of individualism. Thus, a characteristically Japanese version of the novel, the *shishōsetsu* (also called *watakushi-shōsetsu*), literally, "I-novel," came into being. Concurrently, Japanese authors capitalized on newly found freedom to deal with topics that suggested social and political awareness. An exemplar of the early 20th-c. *shishōsetsu* is *An'ya kōro* (serial pub., 1921–28; 2 vols., 1938; *A Dark Night's Passing,* 1976), by Shiga Naoya (q.v.). An example of an early-20th-c. novel that deals with social and political awareness is *Hakai* (1906; *The Broken Commandment,* 1974), by Shimazaki Tōson (q.v.). In the words of Natsume Sōseki (q.v.), a critic as well as an outstanding and widely translated novelist, *Hakai* was "the first [genuine] novel of the Meiji era [1867–1912]."

At the same time that the *shishōsetsu* deserves to be seen as a manifestation of a newfound sense of individual identity, reflecting the process of Westernization, this species of modern Japanese novel also evinces connections with earlier Japanese literary genres such as the *nikki* ("diary") and the *zuihitsu* ("miscellaneous essay"), two forms that involved a conception of self, as distinct from that of group or corporate self. Certain situations in *An'ya kōro,* moreover, call to mind close parallels with *Genji monogatari,* the outstanding achievement of all ages in Japanese literature. Likewise, the idea of a socially committed literature predates *Hakai,* being found, for instance, in late-18th- and early-19th-c. tales and romances by Ueda Akinari (1734–1809) and Takizawa Bakin (1767–1848), both of whose great moral concern betrays an indebtedness to Chinese literature.

Besides the dichotomies of old and new, native and Western, self and other, which permeate 20th-c. Japanese literature, certain other dualities may also be perceived. One of these is the split between the so-called *jun-bungaku* ("pure literature") and *taishū bungaku* (literally, "mass literature," or by extension, "popular literature"). Unavoidably, these terms imply class differences of high and low, just as in earlier times there existed similar distinctions, such as *gabun* ("elegant writings") and *zokubun* ("common writings"). Likewise, *tanka* on the one hand had its aristocratic origin in salons of court poets, and *haiku* on the other hand derived from plebeian groups of ordinary citizens. Despite the modernization of these forms by Masaoka Shiki (q.v.) and the composition of thirty-one-syllable *tanka* on everyday topics in a new, modern idiom by poets such as Ishikawa Takuboku (q.v.), the old associations with a particular social class linger. The earlier dramatic forms of Nō and Kabuki also continue to have overtones of social class, the former being thought to belong to an elite level of society, the latter to the ordinary people. One of the 20th-c. authors most adept at creating both "pure" and "popular" literature was Mishima Yukio (q.v.); his *Shiosai* (1954; *The Sound of Waves,* 1956) is representative of the latter category, and *Kinkakuji* (1956; *The Temple of the Golden Pavilion,* 1959) of the former.

Among other general points that deserve attention, several may be singled out. Centralization of Japanese literary activity in the capital city of Tokyo, for instance, has its earlier counterpart in literary history. The names of literary periods (Nara, Heian, Kamakura, Muromachi, Edo) identify literary activity with centers of political administration. In this sense the 20th c. may well be thought of as the Tokyo period. One of the first 20th-c. Japanese authors to exploit the sense of Tokyo as a distinctive place and of its people as being worthy of literary attention was Nagai Kafū (q.v.), himself a native of the city and heir to the older traditions of Edo. To an unprecedented degree modern novelists, poets, dramatists, and critics live and work in the city of Tokyo and depend on a system of communications centered in the modern capital of Japan.

Closely related to the concentration of literary activity in Tokyo, newspapers and serials in 20th-c. Japan serve as the primary medium of literary publication, having also absorbed the function of promulgating ephemeral forms of literature such as the *kusazōshi* ("chapbooks") of Japan, popular in the late 18th and early 19th cs. (The importance of seasonal celebrations and the seasonal element in traditional Japanese aesthetics also deserves consideration in any analysis of the function of newspaper and serial literature in Japan.) The book version of a novel, for instance, even today often follows its appearance in the daily, weekly, or monthly press. Moreover, literary men and women are public personalities to a greater degree than in English-speaking countries, a fact that gives authors added reason for living and working in the Tokyo area. Izumi Kyōka (q.v.) best exemplifies an early-20th-c. Japanese author who began his career and sustained it by writing popular fiction that appeared serially, that exploited traditional aesthetic sensibilities, and that brought him public acclaim.

One other noteworthy characteristic of 20th-c. Japanese literature is the form of language of most literary works. The modern colloquial Japanese language has become established as the preeminent medium for literary expression. Previously, there existed a much larger gap than now between the linguistic forms used in literary texts and ordinary discourse. Although this change has taken place gradually, two stages may be singled out. The first came late in the 19th c., when efforts to find a suitable idiom for translating Western literature into Japanese began in earnest. Most of all, Futabatei Shimei (q.v.) deserves to be remembered for his efforts to bring literary composition more closely into line with the idiom of everyday speech. The second stage dates from the period following World War II, when from 1948 to 1952 a number of reforms in language

and education took place. All the while there has been a decline in the use of Chinese, the earliest literary language in Japan. Natsume Sōseki, for example, is sometimes called the last important 20th-c. author to have left a body of poetry in Chinese. Meantime, literature in translation has flourished. In the late 1970s, for instance, a specialized monthly journal, *Hon'yaku no sekai,* devoted to the theory and practice of translation, appeared.

Fiction

A new era in Japanese literature following the Russo-Japanese war (1904–5) brought fame and popularity to many young writers, and 20th-c. world literature, with all its complexity, took root in Japan. Writers, several of whom remained active into the 1940s and 1950s, felt a surge of inspiration and confidence after Japan forced Russia to sue for peace.

By 1906 Japanese naturalism began supplanting romanticism. Innovations by an intense group of young writers in their thirties hastened the break with tradition. The naturalistic novel was established by Kunikida Doppo (q.v.), Shimazaki Tōson, and Tayama Katai (1871–1930), along with Iwano Hōmei (1873–1919) and Tokuda Shūsei (1871–1943), whose common goal was to depict life as it is, not glossing over its seamier side. Chiefly out of their work arose the *shishōsetsu,* oftentimes a type of autobiographical confessional in which a semifictional hero and an actual writer tend to be identified.

In their efforts to oppose naturalism, Natsume Sōseki and Mori Ōgai (q.v.), both several years older than the above-mentioned writers, rose to prominence. Mori and Natsume still hold a firm place in the Japanese reader's affections. Natsume's crisp conversational style has influenced young writers particularly. In *Kusamakura* (1906; *Unhuman Tour,* 1927; new tr., *Three-Cornered World,* 1965), he taught that the leisure moments one devotes to art and letters offer the sole relief from the unavoidable suffering of existence, an uplifting belief contrary to the naturalists' creed. Natsume's philosophy and theory of literature, in spite of his period of study in England, show an affinity for those of the earlier *haikai* master, Matsuo Bashō (1644–1694). In *Kokoro* (1914; *Kokoro,* 1941; new tr., 1957), written toward the end of his life, he granted man only three equally dreary choices: death, madness, or religion. Natsume's thought therefore combined "art for art's sake" and pronounced Buddhist tenets.

Mori, who began as a romantic, turned to historical fiction and to belief in stoic self-discipline. A prodigious worker, he combined a medical and military career with authorship in the novel, drama, poetry, criticism, translation, scholarship, and philosophy. One edition of his complete works fills fifty-three volumes. During the last decade of his life he devoted his talent to a series of historical stories for which he is best remembered. Many 20th-c. Japanese writers, late in their careers, have similarly immersed themselves in their own national tradition.

Near the end of the Meiji era and into the Taishō era (1912–26), a group of writers who shared their disapproval of the excess of the naturalists published a periodical called *Shirakaba* (1910–23). Humanitarian in outlook and aristocratic in background and temperament, the group's members included Shiga Naoya, Arishima Takeo (1878–1923), Mushakoji Saneatsu (1885-1976), and Satomi Ton (b. 1888). Although the boundary between naturalist and antinaturalist now seems vague, such distinctions at least show how modern writers in Japan have tended to band together into small independent groups. One of the leading writers who first published prior to 1912 is Tanizaki Jun'ichirō (q.v.), who explored human life with daring, sensitivity, and psychological acumen. His writing appeals readily to Western readers, and he rates as one of the eminent literary figures of the 20th c.

Taishō literature usually includes several years of Meiji and the early part of the Shōwa era (1926 to the present). Until recently Japanese commentators have criticized Taishō authors for failing to transcend traditional, feudal, or nationalistic concepts. Nevertheless, the authors of the 1910s and 1920s produced delicately wrought detail and displayed acute perception. Some writers, to be sure, shirked social responsibility and feigned moral decadence, but Western readers may readily discover untranslated literary works that are at once original and part of the 20th-c. *Zeitgeist*. Reevaluation of the contribution of Taishō authors to the creation of a distinctly modern sensibility is just getting under way. In the 1910s Dostoevsky, Tolstoy, the German Nobel Prize winner Rudolf C. Eucken (1846–1926), Henri Bergson, Rabindranath Tagore, and Maurice Maeterlinck (qq.v.) became known in Japan. The art of Cézanne, Van Gogh, and Rodin attracted attention; the aestheticism of Poe, Wilde, and Baudelaire found numerous emulators.

During and after World War I, Romain Rolland, Henri Barbusse, and Vicente Blasco Ibáñez (qq.v.) became widely read in Japan. Satō Haruo (1892–1964) and Kikuchi Kan (1888–1948) emerged as part of an avant-garde group that declared that only in society can man achieve individuality. Although the group traced their intellectual origins to Europe, the members never completely abandoned traditional style and sensibility. Kikuchi Kan worked as the iron-handed editor of *Bungei shunjū* (founded 1923), making it a leading Japanese literary monthly.

Other writers, such as Akutagawa Ryūnosuke (q.v.), Yamamoto Yūzō (1887–1974), and Kume Masao (1891–1952), made their debuts in private periodicals. One of these periodicals, *Shin shichō,* founded in 1907, was associated with Tokyo Imperial University students who had literary aspirations. In 1923 Kawabata Yasunari (q.v.) revived this periodical. Together with Yokomitsu Riichi (q.v.) and their followers, in 1924 he was involved in yet another periodical, *Bungei jidai,* which advanced such European causes as futurism, expressionism, and Dadaism (qq.v.). Kawabata's short-lived group, however intuitive, subjective, sensual, and faintly decadent, owed as much to medieval Japanese drama as to modern European "isms." Kawabata was the first Japanese writer to win the Nobel Prize for literature.

For a time in the 1920s it appeared that leftist literature might overshadow the efforts of these avant-garde writers and modernists. Government authorities, however, repressed the proletarian movement, despite the support of many established writers. Two noteworthy leftist authors who failed to survive beyond World War II are Hayama Yoshiki (1894–1945) and Kobayashi Takiji (1903–1933). Leftist writers who lived through government repression and the hardships of war resumed literary activity after Japan's defeat. The most notable of them are Nakano Shigeharu (b. 1902), author of *Muragimo* (1954; nerve), Miyamoto Yuriko (1899–1951), Hirabayashi Taiko (1905–1972), Miyamoto Kenji (b. 1908), and Hayashi Fumiko (q.v.). Miyazawa Kenji's (q.v.) selfless altruism and his active participation in agricultural reform movements suggest a devotion to humanitarian ends similar to that of the proletarians.

Nonleftist writers active during the 1930s included Ibuse Masuji (q.v.) and Hori Tatsuo (1904–1953). Dazai Osamu (q.v.) best typified the immediate postwar period, a time of excruciating self-examination and extreme nihilism. His autobiographical narratives in some respects anticipated "beat" literature. Many other writers emerged after World War II, the most notable being Mishima Yukio. His spectacular suicide in the conventional manner of the Edo-period samurai in 1970, followed by Kawabata's self-asphyxiation in 1971, startled the world. Other writers representative of the immediate post-World War II years include Inoue Yashushi (b. 1907)—author of *Ryojū* (1949; *The Hunting Gun*, 1961), *Tempyō no iraka* (1957; *The Roof Tile of Tempyō*, 1976), *Tonkō* (1959; *Tun-huang: A Novel*, 1978)—Takeda Taijun (1912–1976), and Noma Hiroshi (b. 1915), who wrote *Shinkū chitai* (1952; *Zone of Emptiness*, 1956).

In the 1960s new writers continued to appear, and certain established authors extended their reputation. The work of Abe Kōbō (q.v.), for example, which has been widely translated, combines a scrupulous attention to the individual's emotional state (a characteristic of much of the best traditional literature) with a deft appreciation of the present human predicament. Ōe Kenzaburō (q.v.), active as author, editor, and critic, has probed into modern youth's confrontation with sex and society. Among older authors, Ibuse Masuji has published *Kuroi ame* (1966; *Black Rain*, 1969), the best novel about the prolonged suffering and the lingering side effects that the atomic bomb can cause.

During the 1970s yet other fresh authors contributed to the vibrant state of Japanese literature. For instance, a fantasy of sex, drugs, and violence by Murakami Ryū (b. 1952), *Kagirinaku tōmei ni chikai burū* (1976; *Almost Transparent Blue*, 1977), won a coveted literary prize and became a spectacular, albeit controversial, best seller. By means of rich imagery and crude bluntness, a repellent and filthy world in an advanced state of disintegration, decay, and corruption is projected. Such works fairly represent one facet of the Japanese literary scene today. Meanwhile, among established authors, Enchi Fumiko (q.v.) published a well-received and highly praised new translation into modern Japanese of *Genji monogatari* in ten volumes. And Endō Shūsaku (b. 1923), a Catholic novelist, has had several of his works translated into English: *Umi to dokuyaku* (1958; *The Sea and Poison*, 1980), *Chimmoku* (1966; *Silence*, 1969), and *Kuchibue o fuku toki* (1975; *When I Whistle*, 1979).

Poetry

Developments in poetry in Japan during the 20th c. have roughly corresponded to the pattern set by narrative prose. Shimazaki Tōson expressed the exuberent recognition of a fresh age in poetry when he wrote, in 1904, "All seemed intoxicated with light, with new tongues, with new imaginings. . . ." An incipient romantic movement soon gave way to symbolism (q.v.) in the early 1900s with the appearance of Ueda Bin's (1874–1916) collection of translations, especially from French poetry, *Miotsukushi* (1905; sound of the tide). The sensuous language of Kitahara Hakushū (1885–1942) in, for example, *Jashūmon* (1909; heretical religion), and the taut yet colloquial idiom of Hagiwara Sakutarō (q.v.), in *Tsuki ni hoeru* (1917; *Howling at the Moon*, 1978) and his subsequent collections, mark the establishment of modern free verse in 20th-c. Japan. Hagiwara, however, who is probably the most widely translated 20th-c. Japanese poet, went on to write in "Nihon e no kaiki" (1938; return to Japan) of abandoning "the mirage of the West across the sea" and of returning "to our ancient country, with its more than two thousand years of history."

Although older lyrical forms have survived, the charge that they are hardly poetry has persisted. The dynamic young nationalistic *haiku* and *tanka* poet Masaoka Shiki led a revolution in *haikai* by insisting that the seventeen-syllable *haiku* must stand as an independent verse. Hitherto all *haiku* were theoretically written for linked verse (*renku*, or *renga*). Masaoka's followers, Takahama Kyoshi (1874–1959) and Kawahigashi Hekigodō (1873–1937), continued the *haiku* revolution begun by Masaoka. Takahama, remaining narrowly loyal to Masaoka's objectives, helped to institute a new orthodoxy in terms of form and technique. Irrepressibly innovative by temperament, Kawahigashi, however, instituted a free style of *haiku*, in which the traditional syllable count, season word, and seasonal topic were no longer held to be essential. Kawahigashi's idea of *haiku* as a form of lyrical expression of an individual sensibility brought this traditional kind of verse closer to modern European-style poetry. A follower of Kawahigashi, Nakatsukasa Ippekiro (1887–1946), on the one hand, carried the free-meter *haiku* to a creative pinnacle, rejuvenating it as a poetic tool to embody the modern experience. On the other hand, Ogiwara Seisensui (1884–1976), another of Kawahigashi's disciples, argued that even the seasonal element, however much it preserved continuity with the past, might be sacrificed for the sake of self-expression. Taneda Santōka (q.v.), who began writing *haiku* as a disciple of Seisensui, also extended the possibilities of free-verse *haiku*. His restless quest for spiritual enlightenment and his search for release from worldly anxiety mark him as kinsman to earlier Japanese poet-monks and followers of Zen Buddhism.

Lest it be thought that the traditionalists were left clinging only to worn-out concepts of an increasingly forgotten past, Takahama Kyoshi's many followers, especially in the periodical *Hototogisu* (founded 1897), argued cogently for an orthodoxy that might be consistent both with modern theories and with the function of literature. A proletarian school of *haiku* also thrived from the 1920s until 1942, when government repression and internal dissension brought the movement to an end. Today, with around one thousand magazines appearing regularly and with a thriving national organization, modern Japanese *haiku* evinces amazing resilience, and a lively international *haiku* movement flourishes outside Japan. No other non-Western literary form has proven as widely influential as the Japanese *haiku*.

Similarly, the thirty-one-syllable *tanka*, prevalent for over twelve hundred years, has retained its supporters and won a growing number of practitioners in the West. During World War II certain extremists urged the exclusion of "decadent" Western poetry in favor of *tanka*. Inspired by the earlier example of Yosano Akiko (1878–1942), Wakayama Bokusui (1885–1928), and Saitō Mokichi (1882–1953), postwar *tanka* poets of various schools have sustained this lyric art. Ishikawa Takuboku, one of the first modern voices in Japanese poetry, is best remembered for his *tanka*.

Drama

Although in fiction new and old have merged to replace premodern forms, in poetry, perhaps because of its closeness to religion, traditional modes persist alongside modern verse. The same holds true in the drama. Some theatergoers prefer modern plays to the Nō, Kabuki, or Bunraku, but not so much that they completely withhold patronage from the traditional forms. Meantime, well-organized groups and associations preserve the traditional theater, its continuity since the Middle Ages unbroken. Because the conventions of these traditional forms of theater are increasingly remote from modern experience, from time to time new productions of a similar sort are offered to the public, including adaptations from the Western drama and opera. For example, a Japanese version of

Yeats's (q.v.) poetic drama *At the Hawk's Well*, at first entitled *Taka no izumi* (perf. 1949; hawk's well) and later revised and called *Takahime* (1969; hawk princess), adapted by Yokomichi Mario (b. 1916) and Nomura Man'nojō (b. 1930), has been presented on Nō stages in Tokyo and Kyoto. Among modern playwrights and theater critics, Kishida Kunio (q.v.) worked assiduously to establish a form of theater that projects the conditions of actual life with originality and psychological acumen. Yashiro Seiichi (b. 1927) is the most recent example of a modern playwright whose work has been performed in English translation. His play *Hokusai manga* (1973; *Hokusai Sketchbooks*, 1979) was staged in Hollywood early in 1981, demonstrating his uninhibited ribaldry drawn straight from Edo culture and portraying the triumphant free expression of a famous creative artist, Hokusai (1760–1849), whose zest for life overcame seemingly insurmountable human adversities.

Abe Kōbō, better known for his surrealistic novels, is also one of the most productive playwrights and imaginative theater directors in Japan. And two of the plays of the prolific Yamazaki Masakazu (b. 1934) have appeared in English translation: *Zeami* (1969; *Zeami*, 1980) and *Sanetomo shuppan* (1973; *Sanetomo*, 1980). Both plays, very much rooted in Japanese culture, deal with the Middle Ages.

Despite the fame of certain modern poets and playwrights, narrative prose writers have probably made Japan's greatest contribution to world literature in the 20th c. Yet, poetry and drama, as well as modern Japanese fiction, command increasing attention from Western readers, not because of their supposedly exotic qualities but because of their literary artistry and attention to problems common to modern life. If some readers may complain of lack of power, others will surely find meaningful comment on human life, death, and love. Nowhere on earth does one encounter a more world-minded literary atmosphere.

The theme that dominates much of modern Japanese literature is the search for the self in society. Toward the end of the Edo era (1603–1867) and in the early Meiji, traditional society collapsed. Old morals, religion, and loyalties proved inadequate. Modern authors, by using all the resources of a rich language with a long literary tradition, have continually groped for solutions to the human predicament. At times some have accepted without question Western ideology, religion, or literary forms, but the best writers have sought original answers to the questions of life, literature, and art. In recent years the search for identity of the self in society continues unabated. Young authors still seek a place for the individual in mass society. They search, so far without success, to find a substitute for the accepted system of duties and obligations that gave structure to traditional society.

Japanese literature reflects the continuing vitality of a prosperous nation of more than a hundred million people. For successful writers the rewards are enormous, both in terms of wealth and public acclaim. Nevertheless, the current educational system places low emphasis on creative writing, which as an occupation is discouraged, making it all the more of a marvel that so much energy and attention is devoted to this particular human activity.

BIBLIOGRAPHY: Kokusai Bunka Shinkōkai, ed., *Introduction to Contemporary Japanese Literature* (3 vols., 1939, 1959, 1972); Keene, D., *Modern Japanese Novels and the West* (1961); Shea, G. T., *Leftwing Literature in Japan: A Brief History of the Proletarian Literary Movement* (1964); Arima, T., *The Failure of Freedom: A Portrait of Modern Japanese Intellectuals* (1969); Keene, D., *Landscapes and Portraits: Appreciations of Japanese Culture* (1971); Japan PEN Club, *Studies on Japanese Culture* (1973), Vol. I, pp. 157–557; Kimball, A.G., *Crisis in Identity and Contemporary Japanese Novels* (1973); Harper, J., et al., eds., *An Invitation to Japan's Literature* (1974), pp. 5–9, 33–40, 96–154; Kijima, H., and Miller, R. A., introductory essays in Kijima, H., ed., *The Poetry of Postwar Japan* (1975), pp. xi–xlix; Tsuruta, K., and Swann, T. E., eds., *Approaches to the Modern Japanese Novel* (1976); Ueda, M., *Modern Japanese Writers and the Nature of Literature* (1976); Ueda, M., Introduction to *Modern Japanese Haiku: An Anthology* (1976), pp. 3–25; Takeda, K., ed., *Essays on Japanese Literature* (1977); Rimer, J. T., *Modern Japanese Fiction and Its Traditions: An Introduction* (1978); Yamanouchi, H., *The Search for Authenticity in Modern Japanese Literature* (1978); Bowring, R. J., *Mori Ōgai and the Modernization of Japanese Culture* (1979); Peterson, G.B., *The Moon in the Water: Understanding Tanizaki, Kawabata, and Mishima* (1979); Takaya, T., ed., Introduction to *Modern Japanese Drama: An Anthology* (1979), pp. ix–xxxvii; Walker, J. A., *The Japanese Novel of the Meiji Period and the Idea of Individualism* (1979); Keene, D., tr., Introduction to *The Modern Japanese Prose Poem: An Anthology of Six Poets* (1980), pp. 3–57; Lippit, N. M., *Reality and Fiction in Modern Japanese Literature* (1980)

LEON M. ZOLBROD

JARNÉS, Benjamín

Spanish novelist and critic, b. 7 Oct. 1888, Codo; d. 11 Aug. 1949, Madrid

The leading writer of fiction and the stylistic virtuoso of the Spanish vanguard of the 1920s and 1930s, J. belonged to the cosmopolitan group gathered around Ortega y Gasset's (q.v.) *Revista de Occidente.* His provincial upbringing and his seminary education contrast with the experimental artistic values he embraced later in his search for new forms and his hyperintellectualized treatment of reality. Although he shied away from social or political commitment in writing, he sided with the Republicans and went into exile after the civil war, living in Mexico from 1939 to 1948. He opposed the idea of literary schools and doctrines, although his works typified contemporary movements in their formalism and stylization. His techniques, however, were not aesthetic ends in themselves but vehicles for resolving the problem of commitment to reality even when the artist's work represents an evasion of this reality.

Thus, J.'s novels are a forum for speculating on questions about human destiny, the relationship between realism and myth, and the nature of art and beauty. In his early novels, such as *El profesor inútil* (1926; the useless professor), *El convidado de papel* (1928; the paper guest), and *Paula y Paulita* (1929; Paula and Paulita), innumerable scenes and character studies appear without much narrative action. J. explores the distinction between eroticism and sexuality, studies women as embodying the eternal feminine, and initiates those practices for which he is most famous: mirrored and doubled characters, shifting points of view, a highly imagistic lyricism, irony, wit, and abstraction.

At the same time, J. carried forward his career as a critic of film and literature for various journals. The articles collected in *Ejercicios* (1927; exercises), *Rubricas: Nuevos ejercicios* (1931; flourishes: new exercises), *Feria del libro* (1935; book fair), and *Cita de ensueños: Figuras del cinema* (1936; appointment with dreams: film personalities) attest to his perceptiveness: he called public attention to the rising stock of Huxley, Giraudoux, Gide, Joyce (qq.v.), and Charlie Chaplin while assimilating their innovations for his own literary gain.

In J.'s greatest novels he invents a new reality whose tension between the conceptual and the concrete remolds the traditional genre. In *Locura y muerte de nadie* (1929; madness and death of nobody) the dominant theme is the search for identity in a depersonalized world. The surrealist (q.v.) *Teoría del zumbel* (1930; theory of the string for spinning a top) inaugurates a fairy-tale atmosphere that, in conjunction with dream sequences here, and fable or allegory in works like *Escenas junto a la muerte* (1931; scenes near death), *Viviana y Merlín* (1930; "Vivien and Merlin," 1962), and *Venus dinámica* (1943; dynamic Venus), seek out the mythic eternalness that is immanent in the vital human condition. Both *Locura y muerte de nadie* and *Teoría del zumbel* celebrate beauty as intellectual voluptuousness. They extend J.'s favorite theme of art as being the supreme experience: art blends reason, the senses, and passion into a horizon of truth, and its equilibrium and harmony rest on grace, joy, and plenitude.

Stylistically, however, J.'s mathematical objectivism, cubist (q.v.) metaphors, abstract dialogues, and self-referential narrative details make his works seem self-conscious and dehumanized. Yet despite their static quality, the novels are interesting milestones in the genre's history. The way in which the surface properties of reality are defined by sensory and conceptual imagery is a major contribution to Spanish avant-garde creativity.

FURTHER WORKS: *Vida de San Alejo* (1928; "Saint Alexis," 1932); *Salón de estío* (1929); *Sor Patrocinio: La monja de las llagas* (1929); *Zumalacárregui, el caudillo romántico* (1931); *Las siete virtudes* (1931); *Lo rojo y lo azul: Homenaje a Stendhal* (1932); *Fauna contemporánea: Ensayos breves* (1933); *Castelar: Hombre del Sinaí* (1935); *Libro de Esther* (1935); *Doble agonía de Bécquer* (1936); *Don Alvaro; o, La fuerza del tino* (1936); *Cartas al Ebro* (1940); *La novia del viento* (1940); *Manuel Acuña: Poeta de su siglo* (1942); *Orlando el pacífico* (1942); *Don Vasco de Quiroga, obispo de Utopía* (1942); *Escuela de libertad: Siete maestros* (1942); *Stefan Zweig: Cumbre apagada, retrato* (1942); *Españoles en América* (1943); *Cervantes: Bosquejo biográfico* (1944); *Ariel disperso* (1946); *Eufrosina; o, La gracia* (1948)

BIBLIOGRAPHY Putnam, S., "B. J. y la deshumanización del arte," *RHM*, 2 (1935), 17–21; Ilie, P., "B. J.: Aspects of the Dehumanized Novel," *PMLA*, 76 (1961), 247–53; O'Neill, M. W., "The Role of the Sensual in the Art of B. J.," *MLN* 85, (1970), 262–68; Bernstein, J. S., *B. J.* (1972); Zuleta, E., *Arte y vida en la obra de B. J.* (1977)

PAUL ILIE

JARRELL, Randall

American poet and critic, b. 6 May 1914, Nashville, Tenn.; d. 14 Oct. 1965, Greensboro, N.C.

Educated at Vanderbilt University, where his teachers Allen Tate and John Crowe Ransom (qq.v.) were formative influences on his craft, J. nevertheless did not align himself with the Fugitive group. An excellent teacher, J. began his career at Kenyon College (1937–39). He held several other positions; as an instructor in the U.S. Army Air Force (1942–46), J. learned much that appeared in his subsequent verse. From 1947 onward, Woman's College of the University of North Carolina (now University of North Carolina at Greensboro) was J.'s home institution. He was consultant in poetry to the Library of Congress from 1956 to 1958.

From *Blood for a Stranger* (1942); to *The Lost World* (1965), J.'s poetry focused in various ways on a sense of loss that he felt in himself and in others, and his favorite mode is the dramatic monologue, frequently in the voice of a child. *Blood for a Stranger* represents the early phase of his development and includes poems about the self and others, who confront a sense of entrapment and reach out futilely to an unresponding world for comfort. J.'s military service, however, provided him a vivid sense and concrete images of the nightmare of the experience of war and of the loss of human value in an inhuman world. *Little Friend, Little Friend* (1945) and *Losses* (1948) contain sharply focused poems founded on these war experiences.

Increasingly for J. in his poetry, dreams or other fictions became the poet's response to the problems of bearing life, meeting adversity, and suffering losses. His child narrators facilitated the development of these poetic constructs, and unsurprisingly J. derived much of his matter from tales of the Brothers Grimm. He turned to the *Märchen,* with its generic emphasis on metamorphosis, in an attempt to recover the principle of change that is natural for a child and inaccessible, he believed, to an adult. Thus the *Märchen* poems frequently gave voice to the profound disillusionment that informs J.'s poetry generally, beginning in *Losses* and continued in *The Seven League Crutches* (1951) and *The Women at the Washington Zoo* (1960). Although perhaps irrepressibly witty in detail, the main body of J.'s poetry is somberly serious.

J.'s translations of Rilke (q.v.) remind us of the affinity for the sensibilities of children and women that the two poets shared, and for some readers the translations have suggested that J. turned to Rilke for philosophical inspiration, which is progressively evident in *The Seven League Crutches* and *The Lost World*. For J., the world had always been the lost world, which he approached with various poetic stratagems but could not change. In *The Lost World*, however, he shed these fictions, and expressed his vision in deeply personal terms, finally in a profound commitment claiming the lost world as his own.

A Sad Heart at the Supermarket (1962)— essays and fables—continued his complaint against a tawdry, valueless world, especially against the demeaning media-inculcated consumer culture of America. Conversational and idiomatic in style, this volume reveals (as J. does elsewhere) a great range and depth of familiarity with music, art, and other literatures. In *Pictures from an Institution* (1954), his most lighthearted work, J. carved his initials exquisitely on some venerable trunks in the grove of academe.

As acting literary editor of *The Nation*, poetry critic for *Partisan Review* and *The Yale Review*, member of the editorial board of *The American Scholar*, and contributor to *Kenyon Review, The New Republic, The New York Times Book Review,* and other publications, J. was a prolific and exacting critic. His *Poetry and the Age* (1953) is a selection of his critical articles; others are gathered in *The Third Book of Criticism* (1969). The former volume stands as a minor classic in American criticism and argues that contemporary poetry can only be judged fairly if we do not insist on imposing on it or other contemporary art any single standard or opinion: one simple aspect cannot be made the test of a complicated whole. As a critic, too, J. had severe—some say cruel— standards of excellence. John Crowe Ransom regarded *Poetry and the Age* as "almost epoch-making in establishing for the first time securely the position which Robert Frost and Walt Whitman occupy in American poetry."

Whether cruel judge or king-maker, J. is an eminently readable critic.

In assessing J.'s contributions to literature, one would be negligent to ignore his extraordinary performance as a teacher, an achievement that could all too readily be overshadowed by his own publications and other literary activities. As a poet, J. received mixed reviews, although certainly more favorable than otherwise. While some of his critics applaud his technical virtuosity, others fault him for what they perceive as carelessness and for promising more than he succeeded in delivering. Critics who, for whatever reasons, are more confident than J. himself in their view of the world, find J.'s quest for the lost world unnecessarily prolonged and anxiety-ridden. His poetry, however, and the facts of his life validate the authenticity of his anxiety. Perhaps his vigorous and seminal critical essays will ultimately emerge as J.'s literary monument. Finally, J. is representative of his age, for like many of his contemporaries he was frustrated by a world reality that resists change. Like many of them, J. altered his medium to produce adaptive fictions, but these ultimately proved to be for him inadequate. Shortly after claiming the lost world as irrevocably and inescapably his, J. suffered a nervous breakdown and was subsequently killed by an automobile in an event that is now acknowledged to have been suicide.

FURTHER WORKS: *Selected Poems* (1955); *Uncollected Poems* (1958); *The Gingerbread Rabbit* (1964); *The Bat Poet* (1964); *The Animal Family* (1965); *Complete Poems* (1968); *Kipling, Auden & Co.: Essays and Reviews, 1935–1964* (1981)

BIBLIOGRAPHY: Rideout, W. B., " 'To Change, To Change!': The Poetry of R. J." in Hungerford, E., ed., *Poets in Progress: Critical Prefaces to Ten Contemporary Americans* (1962), pp.156–78; Lowell, R., et al., eds., *R. J., 1914–1965* (1967); Ferguson, S., *The Poetry of R. J.* (1971); Donoghue, D., "The Lost World of R. J.," in Owen, G., ed., *Modern American Poetry: Essays in Criticism* (1972), pp. 205–15; Mazzaro, J., "Between Two Worlds: The Post-Modernism of R. J.," in Boyers, R., ed., *Contemporary Poetry in America* (1974), pp. 78–90; Rosenthal, M. L., "R. J.," in Donoghue, D., ed., *Seven American Poets: From MacLeish to Nemerov—An Introduction* (1975), pp. 132–70; Quinn, M. B., *R. J.* (1981)

ARTHUR B. COFFIN

JARRY, Alfred

French dramatist, novelist, and essayist, b. 8 Sept. 1873, Laval; d. 1 Nov. 1907, Paris

One of the most celebrated dates in the history of the French theater is 10 December 1896, when *Ubu Roi* (1896; *Ubu Roi*, 1951) was staged by Lugné-Poë at his experimental Théâtre de l'Œuvre. From the first word—a slightly modified obscenity—the battle lines were drawn between the traditionalists and those who saw one of the functions of avant-garde drama as an assault upon the audience.

The protype of *Ubu Roi* was originally composed by J.'s future classmates at the Rennes lycée even before he arrived at the school in 1888, but he immediately entered into the spirit of the play and helped his classmates stage it, using his own marionettes. Although the extent of J.'s revisions is unclear, what began as a collective enterprise had become J.'s own by the time his definitive version of the schoolboy farce was staged in Paris. The principal character, who was originally intended to ridicule an incompetent physics teacher at the school, had become an archetype of all that is basest in mankind: egotism tempered only by cowardice, and unlimited appetite symbolized by his enormous belly. The influence of the play, which in 1896 ran for only two performances, can scarcely be exaggerated: it inspired Apollinaire (q.v.) and through him the surrealists (q.v.); it inspired Cocteau (q.v.) and through him Anouilh (q.v.); it inspired Artaud (q.v.), who in 1927 named his own company the Théâtre Alfred Jarry, and through Artaud much of what is most characteristic in modern French drama. *Ubu Roi's* power to shock has faded considerably over the years, but several recent productions have demonstrated that the crude vitality and savage humor of the play survive undiminished.

In *Ubu Roi* Father Ubu becomes king of Poland and butchers everyone in his path until a Russian invasion sends him packing, along with Mother Ubu, to France. The complementary play *Ubu enchaîné* (1900; *King Turd Enslaved*, 1953) shows how in France, the country of "free men," Ubu chooses to become a slave in chains. In contrast to the conventions of classical drama, in which a character holds fast to the same identity through all the changes inflicted upon him by destiny, Ubu's values undergo a complete metamorphosis from one play to the next, even though his appearance and idiosyncratic language remain the same. The idea seems to be that modern man has no "essence" at all, an idea also expressed by Ibsen in *Peer Gynt,* another play staged by Lugné-Poë in 1896, and in which J. himself played a minor role. As if to further illustrate this idea, Ubu spilled out into other works by J., both dramatic and fictional, and to a degree that is highly controversial also became part of J.'s own identity.

As many anecdotes demonstrate, J. adopted the staccato speech of his character and was known to fire his revolver with an Ubu-like disdain for proprieties. After one such incident, according to Apollinaire, J. told him in Ubu's voice, "Isn't this as lovely as literature?" André Gide (q.v.) put J. into an episode of his novel *The Counterfeiters* without even changing his name, presumably because J. was so much a work of fiction in "real life" that there was no need to transform him any further. J.'s more recent critics protest that this emphasis on the way J. abolished the distinction between life and art serves only to denigrate J.'s many fine novels and other works, which have never received as much attention as the Ubu plays. Yet despite the invigorating misogyny of such episodic novels as *L'amour en visites* (1898; love goes visiting), at the center of which Lucien breaks his engagement by biting his fiancée on the lip, and despite the philosophy of Pataphysics (the science of imaginary solutions) elaborated in a famous chapter of *Gestes et opinions du docteur Faustroll, pataphysicien* (1911; *Exploits and Opinions of Doctor Faustroll, Pataphysician,* 1965), Jarry seems destined to remain indissolubly linked to the monstrous yet all too human Ubu.

FURTHER WORKS: *Les minutes de sable mémorial* (1894); *César-Antéchrist* (1895); *Les jours et les nuits* (1897); *L'amour absolu* (1899); *Almanach du Père Ubu* (1899); *Messaline* (1901; *The Garden of Priapus,* 1936); *Almanach illustré du Père Ubu* (1901); *Le surmâle* (1902; *The Supermale,* 1968); *Par la taille* (1906); *Albert Samain* (1907); *Le moutardier du pape* (1907); *Pantagruel* (1911, with Eugène Demolder); *Gestes* (1921); *La dragonne* (1943); *Ubu cocu* (1944; *Turd Cuckolded,* 1953); *L'autre Alceste* (1947); *La revanche de la nuit* (1949); *L'objet aimé* (1953); *La chandelle verte* (1969); *Le manoir enchanté* (1974). FURTHER VOLUME IN ENGLISH: *Selected Works* (1965)

BIBLIOGRAPHY Shattuck, R., *The Banquet Years* (1958), pp. 146–94; Wellwarth, G. E.,

The Theater of Protest and Paradox (1964), pp. 1–14; Arnaud, N., *A. J.* (1974); Bierman, J. H., "The Antichrist Ubu," *CompD,* 9 (1975), 226–47; LaBelle, M. M., *A. J.: Nihilism and the Theater of the Absurd* (1980)

MICHAEL POPKIN

JASTRUN, Mieczysław

(pseud. of Mieczysław Agatstein) Polish poet, novelist, literary critic, and translator, b. 29 Oct. 1903, Korolówka

J. received his doctorate from the Cracow Jagielonian University. His literary debut occurred in 1923 while he was close to Skamander, the important poetic group of the 1920s. His first volume of poetry, *Spotkanie w czasie* (meeting in time) appeared in 1929. From 1928 to 1939, J. was a high school teacher in Cracow. During World War II he lived in Lvov, where he was involved in underground cultural and educational activities. After the war he came to Warsaw and became a coeditor of the journal weekly *Kuźnica.* From 1950 on J. devoted his entire time to literary work, only occasionally serving in official capacities in the Polish P.E.N. Club.

J.'s chief contribution to Polish literature is his poetry, although his work in his favorite genre, the biographical novel, is fascinating and widely read. J.'s poetry demonstrates his rich artistic individuality. He is concerned as much with individual destinies as in the destiny of all mankind, and his preoccupation with eternity adds a definite mystical element to his poetry. J., however, avoids abstract symbolism by identifying individual experiences with those of mankind in general. His symbolism is derived from personal experiences: in a poem to his little son he negates the cruelty of the passage of time and celebrates the continuous process of rebirth. Seen from the historical perspective, this coming to terms with the passage of time and with eternity becomes something more than the resolution of his personal soul searching, and instead becomes a symbol of the spiritual rebirth of an entire generation whose youth was spent during the horrors of World War II.

J.'s poetry is not facile: its formal complexities match the weight of its themes and philosophy. J. is not a "popular" poet; he forces his readers to think and expects from them a certain degree of literary and intellectual sophistication. His subject matter is serious and often topical. *Sezon w Alpach* (1948; a season in the Alps) and *Rok urodzaju* (1950; the year of

the harvest) are collections of lyrics that render the Polish and Jewish tragedies during World War II. The volume *Poezja i prawda* (1955; poetry and truth), depicting the everyday heroism of the postwar period, demonstrates J.'s faith in the indestructibility of man.

J.'s biographical novels, *Mickiewicz* (1949; Mickiewicz) and *Poeta i dworzanin: Rzecz o Janie Kochanowskim* (1954; the poet and the courtier: the case of Jan Kochanowski), show J. the humanist looking at the great Polish poets from a contemporary point of view.

J.'s translations of Russian poets such as Pushkin and Bagritsky (q.v.) and of French poets such as Apollinaire, Éluard (qq.v.), and Rimbaud are important. Especially well known is his anthology of French poetry, *Symboliści francuscy: Od Baudelaire'a do Valéry'ego* (1965; French symbolists: from Baudelaire to Valéry). He is also a noted literary critic and has written numerous essays about Polish, Russian, German, and French poets and writers.

J.'s role in Polish literature today is that of the guardian of the best of European traditions in Polish poetry, and his poems are examples and inspirations for the younger generation of poets.

FURTHER WORKS: *Godzina strzeżona* (1945); *Rzecz ludzka* (1946); *Poezje wybrane* (1948); *Poezje 1944–1954* (1954); *Genezy* (1959); *Większe od życia* (1960); *Między słowem a milczeniem* (1960); *Piękna choroba* (1961); *Intonacje* (1962); *Mit Sródziemnomorski* (1962); *Strefa owoców* (1964); *Poezje i rzeczywistość* (1965); *W biały dzień: Poezje* (1967); *Poezje wybrane* (1969); *Eseje* (1973)

BIBLIOGRAPHY: Herman, M., *Histoire de la littérature polonaise* (1963), p. 280; Gillon, A., and Krzyżanowski, L., *Introduction to Modern Polish Literature: An Anthology of Fiction and Poetry* (1964), p. 438; Miłosz, C., *Postwar Polish Poetry* (1965), pp. 47–50; Miłosz, C., *The History of Polish Literature* (1969), p. 408

MALGORZATA PRUSKA-CARROLL

JAVANESE LITERATURE
See Indonesian Literature

JEFFERS, Robinson
American poet and dramatist, b. 10 Jan. 1887, Pittsburgh, Pa.; d. 20 Jan. 1962, Carmel, Cal.

J. was once ranked with T. S. Eliot (q.v.) as a major poet. But his pessimism and unorthodox views are apparently responsible for the decline in his reputation until recently. His work, however, is being read again in this country and in Europe, where his poems have been translated into several Slavic languages. J., whose father was a Presbyterian minister and professor of Old Testament literature, attended European and American schools and studied widely in classical and modern languages, literature, medicine, and forestry. His first two volumes of poems contained traditional lyrics, but the publication of *Tamar, and Other Poems* (1924) marked the beginning of his major work, for which he won international recognition.

J. believed that "poetry is bound to concern itself chiefly with permanent aspects of life." His several long, highly charged narrative poems are explorations of this belief, and his many, often delightful, lyrics are celebrations of permanent things, usually the beauty of nature. Together the narratives form a poetry of ideas that moved toward defining what J. called "inhumanism." J. explains it as a "shifting of emphasis and significance from man to not-man; the rejection of human solipsism and recognition of the transhuman magnificence. . . . It offers a reasonable detachment as rule of conduct, instead of love, hate, and envy." To develop "inhumanism," J. took what he could use from Nietzsche's philosophy, followed classical themes and archetypal myths, drew from the historicism of Vico (1668–1744) and Oswald Spengler (1880–1936) and from the theories of the English Egyptologist Flinders Petrie (1853–1942) about the periodicity of civilizations, and adapted a modified materialism from Lucretius' *De rerum natura*.

Most of J.'s narratives are tales of violence, adultery, and incest, with settings in the Carmel-Big Sur region of California. Characteristically, they describe the conflict of a young rebellious figure, usually a female who cunningly uses sex to win her way, and an older patriarchal figure, who is sternly orthodox or hypocritical or both. With few exceptions, these conflicts move from the individualistic and abortive rebellion in "Tamar" (1924) to those of "Cawdor" (1928), "Thurso's Landing" (1932), and "Give Your Heart to the Hawks" (1933), in which, progressively, the individual's rebellion is compared to the values of society.

Like "Margrave" (1932), "Such Counsels You Gave Me" (1937) introduces into the theme of rebellion a hero modeled after Dos-toevsky's Raskolnikov, and in "Hungerfield" (1954) the hero discovers the gross impropriety of his fantastic struggle with death. In many of these poems, J. apparently tested various principles of Nietzsche's philosophy and rejected those that proved untenable. Because of his explorations of Nietzscheanism, and his restatements of the lesson from Greek tragedy that to learn is to suffer, critics have erroneously charged J. with nihilism.

These critics believe that J.'s "Roan Stallion" (1925), *The Women at Point Sur* (1927), "Dear Judas" (1929), and "The Double Axe" (1948) support their opinions, but in these poems the Nietzschean principles of revaluation of values and of the anti-Christ operate to clear the way for J.'s "inhumanism," which challenges institutionalized Christianity but affirms God the creator. It also holds that "man is no measure of anything," that "the beauty of things is . . . absolute," and that "old violence is not too old to beget new values."

In 1947 J.'s very successful *Medea* (1946), a free adaptation from Euripides, was produced in New York; "Solstice" (1935) was a modernized, nondramatic version of *Medea*. *The Cretan Woman* (1954), a verse drama, was modeled after Euripides' *Hippolytus*, which also provided a theme in "Cawdor." *The Tower beyond Tragedy* (1925), a verse play adaptation of the *Oresteia* of Aeschylus, has also been staged several times. In each instance J. reshaped the classical source to conform to his own ideology.

J.'s troublesome and inferior "political" poems approve of World War II and the Korean War as methods of eliminating undeserving human beings, whose "civilizations" have violated the holy beauty of things. He regarded Hitler, Mussolini, Stalin, and Franklin Roosevelt as helpless but necessary victims of circumstances. Accordingly, metropolitan life is seen as vicious and corrupting, life in the mountains as desirable, clean, and lonely. Borrowing from Lucretius, J. believed that the truly worthy and passionate individual might transcend the "flaming world walls" of his being to attain direct access to the "transhuman magnificence" of things, and that, best of all, he might be comforted by the thought that in death his atoms would mingle again with those of nature.

FURTHER WORKS: *Flagons and Apples* (1912); *Californians* (1916); *Roan Stallion, Tamar, and Other Poems* (1925); *Cawdor, and Other Poems* (1928); *Dear Judas, and Other Poems*

(1929); *Descent to the Dead* (1931); *Thurso's Landing, and Other Poems* (1932); *Give Your Heart to the Hawks, and Other Poems* (1933); *Solstice, and Other Poems* (1935); *Such Counsels You Gave to Me, and Other Poems* (1937); *The Selected Poetry of R. J.* (1938); *Be Angry at the Sun* (1941); *The Double Axe, and Other Poems* (1948); *Poetry, Gongorism and a Thousand Years* (1949); *Hungerfield, and Other Poems* (1954); *The Beginning and the End, and Other Poems* (1963); *Not Man Apart* (1965); *Selected Poems* (1965); *Selected Letters of R. J., 1897–1962* (1968); *Cawdor and Medea* (1970); *The Alpine Christ, and Other Poems* (1973); *In This Wild Water: The Suppressed Poems of R. J.* (1976); *The Women at Point Sur* (1977); *Dear Judas* (1977); *The Double Axe* (new enl. ed., 1977)

BIBLIOGRAPHY: Powell, L. C., *R. J.: The Man and His Work* (1940); Squires, L. C., *The Loyalties of R. J.* (1956); Carpenter, F. I., *R. J.* (1962); Coffin, A. B., *R. J.: Poet of Inhumanism* (1971); Vardamis, A. A., *The Critical Reputation of R. J.* (1972); Brophy, R. J., *R. J.: Myth, Ritual, and Symbol in His Narrative* (1973); Nolte, W. H., *Rock and Hawk: R. J. and the Romantic Agony* (1978)

ARTHUR B. COFFIN

JENNINGS, Elizabeth

English poet, b. 18 July 1926, Boston, Lincolnshire

The daughter of a doctor, J. attended Oxford High School and St. Anne's College, Oxford University, where she read English language and literature. She worked as an assistant in the Oxford City Library (1950–58), and at present lives in Oxford. From 1958 to 1960 she was a reader for the publisher Chatto & Windus, and since then she has earned a living as a writer, composing poems (including two volumes for children), editing anthologies, writing books on poetry and religion, and doing reviews and articles for a variety of newspapers and periodicals.

J. started writing poetry when she was thirteen. She describes this juvenilia as "doggerel, but it had a sense of form." This "sense of form" characterizes all her work. Her first collection, *Poems* (1953), won an Arts Council Prize (1953), and her second, *A Way of Looking* (1955), won the Somerset Maugham Award (1956) and helped her to find the courage to become a freelance. There followed four more books of poetry, of which the fourth, *The Mind Has Mountains* (1966), won the Richard Hillary Prize (1966). She also wrote a number of critical works, including a study of the relationship between poetry and religious experience entitled *Every Changing Shape* (1961) and *Christianity and Poetry* (1965). She was sufficiently established by this time that she was able to publish her *Collected Poems* (1967), a volume that includes almost all the poems in her previous books and twelve new poems. Here her major preoccupations can be clearly seen: man's essential loneliness, the fear that this loneliness can generate, and the psychological pain of human relations, as well as her devout Catholicism and love of Italy. Beginning with *Recoveries* (1964) there are many very personal poems about mental illness, based on the experience of her own breakdown.

The work of J. exhibits a remarkable consistency of tone and style; there is not very much development, the early poems resembling the recent ones. There is, however, a deepening and a maturing. Although J. has experimented with prose poems and free verse, most of her poems are in more or less regular forms. They are short, usually less than five stanzas, and the vocabulary is simple. She resists strange and unusual words and proper nouns, and she works for smoothness, evenness, and clarity. Her poems rarely have very detailed settings, even those that are observations of hospital life or descriptions of individual paintings. The attention is always on the inner world, and the purpose is to distinguish nuances of emotion. J.'s tone is one of detached, sober reasonableness, of understatement more often than not. Her effort is always for control.

In a period in which so far there are apparently no major British poets, J., with her honest craftsmanship, works diligently to make accurate, harmonious, and simple statements about friendship, belief, ineffable pain, and beauty.

FURTHER WORKS: *A Sense of the World* (1958); *Let's Have Some Poetry* (1960); *Song for a Birth or a Death* (1961); *The Sonnets of Michelangelo* (1961); *Poetry Today 1957–1960* (1961); *Robert Frost* (1964); *The Secret Brother* (1966); *The Animals Arrive* (1969); *Lucidities* (1970); *Relationships* (1972); *Growing Points* (1975); *Seven Men of Vision* (1976); *Consequently I Rejoice* (1977); *After the Ark* (1978)

BIBLIOGRAPHY: Thwaite, A., *Contemporary Poets of the English Language* (1970), pp. 559–61; Byers, M., "Cautious Vision: Recent British Poetry by Women," in Schmidt, M., and Lindop, G., eds., *British Poetry since 1960* (1972), pp. 74–84; Hamilton, I., "E. J., *Collected Poems*," *A Poetry Chronicle* (1973), pp. 170–71; Morrison, B., *The Movement: English Poetry and Fiction of the 1950's* (1980), passim; Oram, C., "A Life in the Day of E. J.," *Sunday Times Magazine* [London], 27 July 1980, 62

ROBERT M. REHDER

JENSEN, Johannes Vilhelm

Danish novelist, short-story writer, essayist, and poet, b. 20 Jan. 1873, Farsø; d. 25 Nov. 1950, Copenhagen

J. studied medicine at the University of Copenhagen from 1893 to 1898. He traveled to the United States in 1896, around the world in 1902–3, to the Far East in 1912–13, and to Egypt and Palestine in 1925–26. In 1944 J. was awarded the Nobel Prize for literature.

The life and nature of J.'s home region, Himmerland, in North Jutland, remained a focal point in his writing as a longing for a lost paradise, which could only be recaptured through an expansion of the mind in time and space. Through this process he aimed at conquering the modern technological world, the fullest expression of which he found in the pragmatic American way of life. This longing for a reconciliation of the introvert and extrovert, guided by a Darwinist view of man as part of an evolutionary trend, forms the basic theme of J.'s works.

In this first novels, *Danskere* (1896; Danes) and *Einar Elkær* (1898; Einar Elkær), the main characters, obsessed by a paralyzing introspection, which is a dominant feature of Danish literature of the 1890s, are unable to accept an entirely practical, materialistic view of life. The preoccupation with the self is, however, strongly rejected in *Den gotiske Renaissance* (1901; the Gothic renaissance), a collection of travel letters from Spain and the World Exhibition in Paris in 1900, previously published in a newspaper, which glorify the technological, expansive spirit of the Gothic, that is, Anglo-Saxon, race, whose roots J. found in Himmerland.

Its people are portrayed in the realistic short stories in *Himmerlandsfolk* (1898; Himmerland people), and in the two volumes of *Himmerlandshistorier* (1904, 1910; Himmerland stories). The early stories are marked by a preoccupation with the tragic meaninglessness of life and its inevitable end; the later ones are masterful character studies rendered with humor and irony deriving from J.'s awareness of human frailties, as well as from his deep respect for the old peasant traditions. On the other hand, the double novel, comprising *Madame D'Ora* (1904; Madame D'Ora) and *Hjulet* (1905; the wheel), set in the splendidly depicted milieus of New York and Chicago respectively, advocate modern scientific viewpoints. They are, however, marred by lengthy diatribes against metaphysical speculation, by stereotyped suspense effects, and by grotesque character delineation based on J.'s wish to portray not individuals but progressive stages in man's evolution.

J.'s mythical works represent a supreme artistic achievement, in which extrovert and introvert elements are finally brought together. *Kongens fald* (3 vols., 1900–1; *The Fall of the King*, 1933), regarded as the most significant historical novel in Danish literature, attacks the inability to act perceived by the author as the major component of Danish mentality. It is exemplified by the Renaissance king, Christian II, and his companion, the mercenary Mikkel Thøgersen. Breaking with the realistic novel, J. blends dream passages of exquisite lyrical beauty with explosive, ruthlessly naturalistic scenes. The result is a magnificent, deeply pessimistic vision of man's inability to reach happiness.

The expansion beyond time and reality is also present in J.'s smaller works, *Myter* (myths), which were published in eleven volumes between 1907 and 1944. In essays and prose sketches describing nature, animals, and journeys J. symbolically presents his basic ideas: a total acceptance of present reality as the final goal of all longing, and a belief in the cyclical eternity of revitalizing nature.

Several of these myths laid the foundation for the six-volume novel *Den lange rejse* (1908–22; *The Long Journey*, 1922–24), which forms an evolutionary history of mankind and a scientific counterpart to the biblical legends set in the primeval rain forests of Jutland. The challenges of nature are seen as the driving force of the progress that brings about the transition from animal to man. According to J., a basic trait of the Nordic people—the "Gothic race"—is the longing for distant places, for warmth and sun. The Viking migrations, he says, were a result of this longing, as was the first voyage of the "Goth" Columbus, which resulted in the discovery of America, of reality.

The contrast between longing and a stubborn belief in the bliss of the present moment also forms the major theme in J.'s first poetry collection, *Digte* (1906; poems; later enlarged eds. 1917, 1921, 1943, 1948), a milestone in the development of Danish lyric poetry. The collection features a number of prose poems modeled after Goethe's, Heine's, and Whitman's free verse but containing the imagery of modern technology and the metropolis. J.'s subsequent poetry volumes are dominated by verse in traditional meter or alliterative poems in the Old Norse style. They are not self-analyzing; rather they praise woman as wife and mother, children, and Danish nature, sometimes in a most grandiose manner, sometimes with the deepest intimacy, melting together observation, vision, and reflection into a perfect artistic whole.

Eventually rejecting poetry and fiction as a means of communication, J. turned to essays, which he wrote in a terse, matter-of-fact style. In them he set out to popularize the Darwinist, evolutionary view of life, although his ideas were often based on dubious anthropological and scientific theories and deductions. Stylistically, however, these prose works are often of high quality.

Although of little significance as a scientist, J. was one of the greatest innovative spirits in Danish cultural life and the writer who has had the greatest impact on Danish literature of the 20th c.: through his vigorous yet often lyrical style, through his extremely precise powers of observation as well as his visionary perspective, through his intense love for the microcosm in nature and his dynamic international orientation, and finally through his ability to connect the present with eternity, reality with dream.

FURTHER WORKS: *Intermezzo* (1899); *Skovene* (1904); *Myter og jagter* (1907); *Den ny verden* (1907); *Singaporenoveller* (1907); *Nye myter* (1908); *Lille Ahasverus* (1909); *Myter* (1910); *Nordisk ånd* (1911); *Myter* (1912); *Rudyard Kipling* (1912); *Olivia Marianne* (1915); *Introduktion til vor tidsalder* (1915); *Årbog* (1916, 1917); *Johannes Larsen og hans billeder* (1920); *Sangerinden* (1921); *Æstetik og udvikling* (1923); *Årstiderne* (1923); *Myter* (1924); *Hamlet* (1924); *Evolution og moral* (1925); *Årets højtider* (1925); *Thorvaldsens portrætbuster* (1926); *Verdens lys* (1926); *Jørgine* (1926); *Dyrenes forvandling* (1927); *Ved livets bred*

(1928); *Åndens stadier* (1928); *Retninger i tiden* (1930); *Den jydske blæst* (1931); *Form og sjæl* (1931); *På danske veje* (1931); *Pisangen* (1932); *Kornmarken* (1932); *Sælernes ø* (1934); *Det blivende* (1934); *Dr. Renaults fristelser* (1935); *Gudrun* (1936); *Darduse* (1937); *Påskebadet* (1937); *Jydske folkelivsmalere* (1937); *Thorvaldsen* (1938); *Nordvejen* (1939); *Fra fristaterne* (1939); *Gutenberg* (1939); *Mariehønen* (1940); *Mindets tavle* (1941); *Vor oprindelse* (1941); *Om sproget og undervisningen* (1942); *Kvinden i sagatiden* (1942); *Folkeslagene i østen* (1943); *Møllen* (1944); *Afrika* (1949); *Swift og Oehlenschläger* (1950); *Tilblivelsen* (1951)

BIBLIOGRAPHY: Marcus, A., "J. V. J.," *ASR*, 20 (1932), 340–47; Toksvig, S., "J. V. J.," *ASR*, 31 (1943), 343–46; Nyholm, J., "The Nobel Prize Goes Nordic," *BA*, 19 (1945), 131–35; Nielsen, M. L., *Denmark's J. V. J.* (1955); Friis, O., "J. V. J.," *Scan*, 1 (1962), 114–23; Ingwersen, N., "America as Setting and Symbol in J. V. J.'s Early Work," *Americana-Norvegica*, 3 (1971), 272–93

SVEN H. ROSSEL

JERSILD, P(er) C(hristian)

Swedish novelist and dramatist, b. 14 March 1935, Katrineholm

J. grew up in a middle-class suburb of Stockholm and attended medical school. He specializes in social medicine and has also been an administrator. His professional experiences are reflected in his fiction, which often satirizes modern man's helplessness against the structures of society.

Notable among J.'s satirical novels about bureaucratic hierarchies are *Grisjakten* (1968; the pig hunt), which portrays the lack of humanity in administrative thinking; and *Djurdoktorn* (1973; *The Animal Doctor*, 1975), which demonstrates how inconvenient humanitarian concerns are nullified in the name of corporate democracy. The protagonist in *Vi ses i Song My* (1970; see you in Song My) believes he can change the system but is instead manipulated by it. In *Babels hus* (1978; the house of Babel) J. explores the impact of huge financial interests on health services in a hospital.

J. does not confine his satires to Sweden. In *Calvinols resa genom världen* (1965; Calvinol's journey through the world) both the

Soviet Union and the United States are targets of his wit, while *Drömpojken: En paranoid historia* (1970; the dream boy: a paranoid story) takes place in an America marked by intrigues and conspicuous consumption.

Individual destiny is particularly well portrayed in *Stumpen* (1973; the stump), about an alcoholic bum who thinks he is worthless and should be eliminated by society; and in *Barnens ö* (1976; the children's island), about an eleven-year-old boy who learns about life and evil when he is left alone one summer in Stockholm. In J.'s autobiographical sketches about suburban Stockholm, *Uppror bland marsvinen* (1972; revolt among the guinea pigs) we find the prototype for his heroes in the protagonist who masks his bewilderment with humor and comedy.

J. has also written a few plays, among them a play for television, *Sammanträde pågår* (1967; meeting in session), about man's vulnerability in an impersonal bureaucratic society.

J.'s works are full of grotesque, bizarre, and absurd episodes, an aspect of his interest in the manipulative possibilities of the language. His vivid and dynamic style, combined with his professional insights, through which he often achieves a documentary effect in his social satire, have made him one of the most popular contemporary writers in Sweden.

FURTHER WORKS: *Räknelära* (1960); *Till varmare länder* (1967); *Prins Valiant och Konsum* (1966); *Den elektriska kaninen* (1974); *En levande själ* (1980); *Professionella bekännelser* (1981)

TORBORG LUNDELL

JHABVALA, Ruth Prawer

Anglo-Indian novelist and short-story writer, b. 7 May 1927, Cologne, Germany

Born to Polish-Jewish parents who went as refugees to England in 1939, J. became a British citizen in 1948 and earned an M.A. in English literature from the University of London in 1951. She married a Parsee architect and lived in India from 1951 to 1975. She has lived much of the time since 1975 in New York City, collaborating on screenplays and television scripts as well as continuing her writing of fiction.

Soon after settling in Delhi, J. began drawing upon the rich resources of her European literary heritage to create an impressive series of novels and short stories reflecting her experience of India. Her first novel, *To Whom She Will* (1955; Am.: *Amrita*), which deals with the comic maneuverings within two Indian families, recalls the matrimonial minuets choreographed by Jane Austen. The comic strain continues in *The Nature of Passion* (1956) and in *Esmond in India* (1957), but in the latter the irony deepens in its portrait of an unpleasant Englishman and the Indian wife he subjugates.

The Householder (1960) is a delightfully droll story commenting on the irrelevance of ancient customs and the contradictions of new ways. This book and the next, *Get Ready for Battle* (1962), present the funny, sad ironies of failure in human communication, particularly between husbands and wives. In her rendering of individuality based not so much on distinctiveness of personality as on mutual inaccessibility, J. recalls the manner of Chekhov.

A Backward Place (1965) is in many ways J.'s best work. Into India, regarded by many Europeans and some Indians as a "backward" nation, she brings three European women, Etta and Clarissa suggesting sterile elements of Western culture in the Indo-European synthesis, and Judy, who symbolizes the fruitful blending of Europe and the East, the feminine durability and resiliency of India and the resourcefulness and adaptability of the West. Always J.'s keen vision records telling details of Indian locale.

Both in *A New Dominion* (1973; Am.: *Travelers*) and in *Heat and Dust* (1975) are to be found evidences of J.'s affinity with E. M. Forster (q.v.). The "travelers" who experience J.'s India include characters who resemble those who took the earlier passage to India. In *Heat and Dust*, anchored half in the 1970s and half in the 1920s, J. employs wit and precision worthy of Forster to show the futility of attempts at understanding, not merely between Westerners and Indians, but between men and women of one time and another.

J.'s graceful and economical prose proceeds from an intelligence well served by ear and eye. Her people are contradictory of themselves and of each other, but everything they say is true because all things are true of India—as of mankind generally.

FURTHER WORKS: *Like Birds, Like Fishes* (1963); *The Householder* (screenplay, 1965); *A Stronger Climate* (1968); *An Experience of India* (1972); *Shakespeare Wallah* (screenplay, 1973, with James Ivory); *Autobiography of a Princess* (screenplay, 1975); *How I Became a Holy Mother, and Other Stories* (1976)

BIBLIOGRAPHY: Pritchett, V. S., "Snares and Delusions," *New Yorker*, 16 June 1973, 106–9; Williams, H. M., *The Fiction of R. P. J.* (1973); Bell, P. K., on *Heat and Dust*, *NYTBR*, 4 April 1976, 7–8; Annan, G., "The Acceptance World," *TLS*, 25 June 1976, 757; Shahane, V. A., *R. P. J.* (1976); Singh, R. S., *The Indian Novel in English: A Critical Study* (1977), pp. 149–63; Souza, E. de, "The Expatriate Experience," in Narasimhaiah, C. D., ed., *Awakened Conscience: Studies in Commonwealth Literature* (1978), pp. 339–45

CARL D. BENNETT

JILEMNICKÝ, Peter

Czechoslovak essayist, journalist, short-story writer, and novelist (writing in Slovak), b. 18 March 1901, Kyšperk (now Letohrad); d. 19 May 1949, Moscow, U.S.S.R.

Although Czech by birth, J. adopted the Slovak language as the medium of his literary work. Having graduated from an agricultural college, he came to Slovakia as a teacher in 1921, did his two years of military service there, and then returned to his teaching profession. The experience of living in and observing some of the poorest and most backward areas of the country had a profound influence both on his political views (he joined the Communist Party in 1922) and on his writing. Equally important was his two-year stay (beginning in 1926) in the Soviet Union, where he was first a teacher and then journalism student in Moscow. After his return, he worked for a short time for the Slovak Communist press, but soon returned to teaching.

Following the dismemberment of Czechoslovakia at Munich, J. was expelled from Slovakia at the beginning of 1939 by the pro-Nazi Slovak authorities, and he settled again in his native eastern Bohemia. In October 1942 he was arrested by the Gestapo and for his association with the underground Communist Party and sentenced to eight years' hard labor by a Nazi court. When he returned after the war from a labor camp in Germany, he at once became very actively engaged in public life; he died while serving as cultural attaché at the Czechoslovak embassy in Moscow.

J.'s first novel, *Víťazný pád* (1929; glorious fall), completed early in 1926, mainly shows the impact on the author of the beauty of mountainous northwest Slovakia. Social problems, although not entirely omitted, were not yet the focus of his interest, and the struggle that he described was rather that of man against nature. Equally strong, but influencing him in a different direction, was the impression made on J. by what he witnessed in the Soviet Union. His novel *Zuniaci krok* (1930; thundering step), which, two years before Sholokhov's (q.v.) *Virgin Soil Upturned*, described the changes in the life of the Soviet village at the beginning of the collectivization, is often considered to be the founding work of Socialist Realism (q.v.) in Slovak fiction.

Pole neorané (1932; the untilled field) is again set in the mountainous Kysuce region of the first novel, but this time J. concentrated on the chronic poverty, backwardness, economic emigration, and alcoholism with which it was plagued. The realization that such social evils cannot be cured by mere charity and individual effort but only by a removal of the exploiting class through a radical change of the political system, is hastened in the awareness of the main character by his contact with Communist workers in the nearby industrial town of Ostrava.

A similar process takes place in *Kus cukru* (1934; a piece of sugar), whose story is based on the paradox that workers in the sugar refineries were unable to afford sugar and replaced it with saccharine smuggled from abroad. The urban working class here seeks an alliance with the impoverished farmers. In this novel J. wanted to express his belief that "we are all entitled to a piece of sugar, a piece of the sweetness, glory, and fullness of life." Its construction, however, became too obviously subordinated to his political design.

In *Kompas v nás* (1937; the compass within us), a cycle of long stories set alternately in the Soviet Union and Czechoslovakia, J. explored the question of human happiness. He concluded that it could not be found where greed and egoism reigned. True happiness and security could be achieved only within the collective struggle for social justice and a better life for all. Almost as an afterthought appears the idea that people also need to be rooted in a place they could call their home.

After the war J. wrote about the Slovak National Uprising of August 1944, in which he himself could not take part. In *Kronika* (1947; chronicle), life in a Slovak village during this crucial period is being described by a gamekeeper to the local teacher who wants to make a record of it. By presenting a personalized view of momentous historical events, J. avoided the danger of producing a pompous heroic epic. In fact, the novel does not have any individual hero, his place being taken by the village collective, although Communists are portrayed as leaders in the anti-Nazi fight.

Most of J.'s works are marked by his compassion for the poor and oppressed, by his enchantment with the simple and natural life as well as by his commitment to the ideals of socialism and communism. He himself characterized his work as "fight and song," the former representing the political, the latter the balladic element in it. J., who worked hard to achieve formal and stylistic perfection, was conscious of the risk associated with this approach. Indeed, he managed to blend the two invisibly only on few occasions; very often the seam shows, and this is considered to be a shortcoming of his work.

FURTHER WORKS: *Devadesát devět koní bílých* (1921); *Dva roky v krajine sovietov* (1929); *Návrat* (1930, 1938)

BIBLIOGRAPHY: Mihailovich, V., et al., eds., *Modern Slavic Literatures* (1976), Vol. II, pp. 124–27; Součková, M., *A Literary Satellite: Czechoslovak-Russian Literary Relations* (1970), pp. 78–81

IGOR HÁJEK

JIMÉNEZ, Juan Ramón
Spanish poet, essayist, and critic, b. 23 Dec. 1881, Moguer; d. 29 May 1958, San Juan, Puerto Rico

J. left Moguer, where he spent his childhood and adolescence, and which he had so often celebrated in his verse, to study law at the University of Seville. There he also showed an interest in painting, but he abandoned law studies and also stopped painting to devote himself entirely to writing poetry and reading the French and German romantics and the French symbolists (q.v.). He also read with great pleasure the 19th-c. Spanish poets Rosalía de Castro (1837–1885) and Gustavo Bécquer (1836–1870).

In April 1900, J. was invited to Madrid by the modernist (q.v.) poets Francisco Villaespesa (1877–1936) and Rubén Darío (q.v.), who were attracted to his verses published in *Vida nueva*, a Madrid review. J. soon became an active member of the modernist literary circles and helped to found two important reviews, *Helios* in 1902 and *Renacimiento* in 1906.

J. returned to Moguer in the summer of 1900. Deeply depressed by his father's sudden death, he was sent to a sanatorium in France to recover from his first bout with mental illness. His depressions, neurasthenia, morbid fear of dying, and penchant for withdrawing from people would remain with him throughout his life, but at no time did his condition diminish his creativity. In fact, it seemed to drive him on.

In 1916, after a decade of intense productivity, J. traveled to New York to marry Zenobia Camprubí, whom he had met while living in Madrid. He collaborated with her on the Spanish translations of the Indian poet Rabindranath Tagore (q.v.).

At the outbreak of the civil war in 1936, J. and Zenobia left Spain and returned to America. He lectured and taught at many American universities. In 1951 J. and his wife moved to Puerto Rico, where he lectured and gave classes at the university. In 1956, a few days before his wife's death, J. was awarded the Nobel Prize for literature.

It is difficult to imagine a poet more dedicated to his craft than was J., who considered poetry a religion, a path to salvation, a mode of preserving values from the ravages of time. A Platonist, he believed in a universal consciousness that existed apart from individual consciousness and felt it was the poet's task to express this concept through symbolism.

J.'s poetic development is emblematic of his struggle to attain full consciousness. He started by capturing fleeting impressions of nature and the sadness inherent in a universe that is transitory. At a later stage he wished to commune with the universe, until at the end of his life he believed he had mystically encountered absolute beauty and eternity on the deepest level of consciousness permitted to him.

J. himself described these three stages of development: he called his first period, up until 1909, an "ecstasy of love"; he called the second stage, from 1910 to 1921, an "avidity for eternity"; after 1921, he said his poetry was marked by the "necessity for inner consciousness."

J.'s earliest books of poems, *Ninfeas* (1900; water lilies) and *Almas de violeta* (1900; violet souls), although derivative and studied in their melancholy tone and sentimentality, show the poet to have had a facility with a variety of meters, especially the eight-syllable line, and an ability to capture lyric beauty and subtle emotions.

His next books—*Rimas* (1902; rhymes), *Arias tristes* (1903; sad airs), *Jardines lejanos* (1904; distant gardens), and *Pastorales* (1905; pastorals)—were still imbued with a fascination for modernism, but they have a stronger, more mature and original voice. They are delightfully lyrical and at times elegantly simple impressionistic studies of nature, filled with musicality and mystery. Also present is a heartsick, fin-de-siècle malaise.

In *Elegías puras* (1908; pure elegies), *Baladas de primavera* (1910; ballads of spring), and *La soledad sonora* (1911; the sonorous solitude), J. continued to experiment with different meters, especially the alexandrine, and his style became more ornate and baroque. In these works he leaves the parks and gardens to contemplate the countryside with vague nostalgia, heightened sensuality, and chromatic richness, communing with the world in graceful tranquillity, but he is still burdened with a recurring anxiety about death.

His trip to New York in 1916 to be married led to the publication of *Diario de un poeta reciéncasado* (1918; diary of a newlywed poet), which represents a major change in J.'s poetic development and in all poetry in Spain. This work, the first important one in Spain in free verse, clearly reveals that J. had moved beyond the confines of modernism into a new creative sphere. Freed from rhyme and meter, J. explores the metaphysical concerns that would interest him for the rest of his life. He uses the newly found rhythms of the sea to contemplate the delicate but precarious balance between the poet's own consciousness and the frightening immensity of the sea, which personifies solitude. At times he feels engulfed by the sea, and at other times it is he who engulfs it—a standoff of two equals.

In *Eternidades* (1918; eternities), J. established a new norm for his poetry, denouncing all of his past verse. In a famous (untitled) poem that begins "Vino, primero pura" (1918; "Poetry," 1942), in which he compares poetry to a woman, he decides to return to the simplicity of his earlier poetry, for he sees his verse as having become overdressed, laden with jewels —and he now rejects this approach. Not unlike Paul Valéry (q.v.), he seeks "naked poetry," that is, pure poetry purged of everything that is extraneous to its essence. As a result, *Eternidades* is filled with slender, epigrammatic poems that are highly conceptual.

In *Belleza* (1923; beauty) and *Poesía (en verso)* (1923; poetry [in verse]) J. continued to ponder the nature of poetry and the meaning of his own "Work," to which he had begun referring to as *Obra*, with a capital *O*. He is also concerned with poetry's relationship to beauty and death: it is through poetry that J. hopes he will be saved.

In the eloquent *La estación total con canciones de nueva luz* (1936; the total season with songs of new light) a full awareness of the beauty and harmony of the world is revealed by the poet. The very title suggests a paradox with which J. has always grappled: "season" implies impermanence and change, while "total" connotes a synthesis, a hard-won eternity. Within the flux, there is the eternal moment where everything fuses.

The height of J.'s deepened consciousness and full integration with the cosmos can be seen in his brilliant last book, *Animal de fondo* (1949; animal of depth). In it J. created a god, who is fully attuned to the beauty of the universe. It is a song of joy, of mystical union, of the creation of a pantheistic god for all people of all faiths for all ages. It is the testament of his struggle toward perfect consciousness.

It should not be forgotten that J. was also a fine prose writer. Besides having written many essays on the ethics and aesthetics of poetry, he wrote two very important books of prose. One is *Platero y yo* (1914; *Platero and I*, 1956), which consists of short lyrical sketches of the poet and his donkey, set in Moguer. It is J.'s most popular work, and deservedly so, for it portrays in a captivating manner the great theme of death and rebirth. The other is *Españoles de tres mundos* (1942; Spaniards of three worlds), a series of lyrical caricatures written over a period of many years about important literary figures.

Although periodically unbalanced by depression and anxiety, a semirecluse for most of his life and totally self-absorbed, J. gave Spain a body of lyric poetry from which all other 20th-c. Spanish poetry originated. He was a poet's poet, who, in almost complete solitude, portrayed the unending crises of the inner world, passing over the tumult of the outer world; for this he has been criticized. His goal was nothing less than the creation of a system of salvation within the framework of poetry. His work was his life, and his life a search for authentic poetry and metaphysical consciousness.

FURTHER WORKS: *Elegías intermedias* (1909); *Olvidanzas: Las hojas verdes* (1909); *Poemas mágicos y dolientes* (1911); *Melancolía* (1912); *Laberinto* (1913); *Estío* (1915); *Poesías escogidas (1899–1917)* (1917); *Sonet-*

os espirituales (1917); *Piedra y cielo* (1919); *Segunda antología poética (1899–1918)* (1922); *Unidad* (1925); *Obra en marcha* (1929); *Sucesión* (1932); *Presente* (1934); *I (Hojas nuevas, prosa y verso)* (1935); *Canción* (1936); *Política poética* (1936); *Verso y prosa para niños* (1937); *Ciego ante ciegos* (1938); *Antología poética* (1944); *Voces de mi copla* (1945); *Diario de poeta y mar* (1948; new version of *Diario de un poeta reciéncasado*); *Romances de Coral Gables (1939–1942)* (1948); *Tercera antología poética* (1957); *El zaratán* (1957); *La corriente infinita 1903–1954* (1961); *Por el cristal amarillo 1902–1954* (1961); *El trabajo gustoso 1948–1954* (1961); *El Modernismo: Notas de un curso* (1962); *Cartas 1898–1958* (1962); *Primeras prosas 1890–1954* (1962); *La colina de los chopos 1913–1928* (1965); FURTHER VOLUMES IN ENGLISH: *Fifty Spanish Poems* (1950); *Selected Writings* (1957); *Three Hundred Poems 1903–1953* (1962); *Forty Poems* (1967); *Lorca and J.: Selected Poems* (1973)

BIBLIOGRAPHY: Gullón, R., *Estudios sobre J. R. J.* (1960); Schonberg, J.-L., *J. R. J.; ou, Le chant d'Orphée* (1961); Zardoya, C., *Poesía española contemporánea* (1961), pp. 219–40; Young, H. T., *The Victorious Expression: A Study of Four Contemporary Spanish Poets* (1964), pp. 77–137; Predmore, M.P., *La obra en prosa de J.R.J.* (1966); Olson, P., *Circle of Time: Time and Essence in the Poetry of J. R. J.* (1967); Cole, L. R., *The Religious Instinct in the Poetry of J.R.J.* (1967); Palau de Nemes, G., *Vida y obra de J. R. J.* (2 vols., 1974); Cobb, C. W., *Contemporary Spanish Poetry (1898–1963)* (1976), pp. 49–64; Fogelquist, D.F., *J.R.J.* (1976)

MARSHALL J. SCHNEIDER

J.'s work is a sort of *comédie mystique*. Singly, the poems have variety of notes. Yet there is a cryptic quality in them, and a subtle allusiveness to something not explicit, which must repugn the shallow sense, even as it entrances the mind hungry for great vistas. His poems have prosodic value. Yet their chiefest value is that they *create aesthetically* a sense of incompleteness. Aesthetically, they are whole because they contain this *lack*—this positive surge toward an apocalyptic sense which lives in them only by the imprint of its absence. Each of his poems is at once a sensory form, and a spiritual inchoation. . . . One might say that a poem of J. is like an instant in a human life: full-limned, full-equipped with thought, emotion, will; and yet this fullness is but the passing function of an implicit unity which transcends and subscends it.

Waldo Frank, *Virgin Spain* (1926), p. 291

J. R. J. is sometimes described as an apostle of *vers libre*; but if so, he is an apostle who hides his vocation under his mantle. His verse is not printed to look like *vers libre*; and the proportion of lines which will fit into no recognized scheme is not large. The traditions of Castilian verse, which have always permitted assonance as well as rhyme, accentual as well as syllabic metre, give possibilities of which so accomplished a technician is not slow to avail himself. Indeed, it might be said of the Spanish poet, as was said of a French contemporary of his, that he, too, has written free verse, but by some magic his verses always end by being regular. They have, at any rate, the certainty of rhythm and sense of repose which make them convincing as real lines of poetry. . . .

[J. R. J.] found that the poems which he held to be the most simple and spontaneous always proved to be those of the most clean and deliberate workmanship. He cannot share the view that failure and lack of discipline in art is an attitude of any interest, and he does not believe in the existence of finished, popular poetry which is at the same time simple and spontaneous.

John B. Trend, "J. R. J.," *Alfonso the Sage, and Other Spanish Essays* (1926), p. 150

Platero and I is one of those felicitous works in which the author's most brilliant and solid qualities are responsive to the spirit of the times. Seldom has an Andalusian backdrop been shown with such poetic truth; its expressiveness is the most evocative and perfect that any author of that generation [1898] has been able to realize; the warm, solitary, and human simplicity that makes these pages tremble is the best guarantee that such a book will not diminish in the interest that was present from the very moment of its initial appearance. Its theme is nature, nature that is reflected in the eyes of the poet, and the beauty of this theme has no equal except in the crystalline transparency with which the poet's eyes reflect it, so that as soon as the vision is obscured by some veil, we do not know if it is of mist or of tears.

Luis Cernuda, "J. R. J.," *BSpS*, 19 (1942), p. 174

Belleza and *Poesía* (1917–1923), twins one might say, were published in 1923 and both accentuate the essential part of the poet's work, that becomes more and more subjective and intimate with light accents of intellectualism and a constant meditation on those very words: poetry and beauty. Together, the two offer the key to J.'s preoccupation. It is not a question of deciding in his works the relationship between poetry and truth, as in Goethe's case; between beauty and truth as in Keats or Emily Dickinson but between beauty and poetry which with love, woman and death form the abiding themes of his life. Death, for example, is constantly present in the poet of Moguer. . . . At times the *death* of Rilke is recalled by J.'s figure of death. This theme becomes almost an obsession, and it can be seen that this preoccupation with the death of others is nothing other than the mirror of his own imaged death, almost a dialogue with it. Now, too, we can appreciate how the total work of the poet of Moguer could be—and in fact is—a triumph, not over the D'Annunzio style of death, but over death itself; the triumph of beauty and of poetry; the ultimate triumph of the permanent over the temporal and perishable.

Eugenio Florit, Preface to J. R. J., *Selected Writings* (1957), pp. xxii–xxiii

J. reconciles, besides, restraint and intensity: tirelessly sincere, but never given to prattling or gesticulation, he will express moments of plenitude or of rapture while preserving a muted tone, a singular poise and weightlessness. This is especially evident in his folkloric pieces, where colorful effects are shunned. Restraint is also compatible in J. R. J. with the boldness of the experimenter. Here his role as an innovator must be recalled once more, for he never ceased to invent, to search for that straightest line between the emotion and the reader which would be the purest form. He has been, like Gide, always a young poet, for whom every book was a beginning. Hence his considerable variety and—to mention a final wedding of opposition—the fusion of it with a remarkable singleness of intent and style. J. concentrates in each poem on almost a single device, plays but one of the many strings on his instrument at a time. If one virtue or one method may be considered characteristic of his poetry, it is that of concentration above all on the single word, on the force and the magic of which language is capable.

Claudio Guillen, "The Problem of J. R. J.," *New Republic*, 16 Dec. 1957, 17–18

[J.'s] dialogue with nature, enriching the constant spinning of the creative imagination, was crystalized in that admirable work [*Platero y yo,* 1914], lyrical biography, collection of etchings, Andalusian elegy . . . Yes, Andalusian and universal, as the author wanted it, striving to achieve universality by reaching into his own depth until he could touch the most particular and local, the essential human. He concentrated on the simple incidents of living, in the bare instant, to the point of not dividing his life into days, but his day into lives: "each day, each hour, an entire life." Such concentration gave his poetry density and intensity: in

each line we feel him complete, gravitating above it with all the weight of his soul and of his dream —lucid dream of deep realities, penetration into the other face of reality, to the point of converting the temporal into substance of the eternal and the limited into expression of the infinite. To give himself up to poetry was to give himself up to life, to life each day different and the same, like daybreak; to life at its deepest level, with the bird and the rose, the child and the cloud.

Ricardo Gullón, Introduction to J. R. J., *Three Hundred Poems* (1962), p. xxi

In his completness J. is almost unrivaled in Spanish poetry. He began as an Adamic poet in a fresh world of inexhaustible beauty, determined to express every nuance, every emotion. He mastered all the forms of Spanish poetry: the song, the ballad, the sonorous Alexandrine, the sonnet form, free verse, and the concentrated free verse of "pure poetry." He developed extensively most of the essential symbols of Western poetry with his own emphasis: the sea, the rose, the sun, the tree, the flower, the bird, the cloud, the diamond, the glowing coal, the circle. Admittedly he failed to exploit the ugly: as a man he suffered the ugly and the confused; as a poet, discipline in the quest for beauty was paramount. J. is an outstanding example of the modern poet: since the time of Poe and Baudelaire, given the disintegration of the Christian world view, the poet has been cast adrift to create his own metaphysical system of salvation. J. creates such a system, grounded in a fusion of natural religion and aesthetics and employing the modern preoccupation with the extension of time through heightened consciousness. Moreover, his metaphysical system is properly created in a convincing poetic structure. Surely J., a deserving recipient of the Nobel Prize, can be meaningfully compared with major European poets such as Yeats and Rilke. Take him for all in all, J. R. J. may well be the greatest lyric poet in Spanish literature.

Carl W. Cobb, *Contemporary Spanish Poetry (1898–1963)* (1976), pp. 63–64

JIRÁSEK, Alois

Czechoslovak novelist, short-story writer, and dramatist (writing in Czech), b. 23 Aug. 1851, Hronov; d. 12 March 1930, Prague

As a high-school history teacher and researcher in ethnography, J. led an uneventful life, interrupted only by travels during which he studied the locale of his future writings. It was not until World War I that he assumed the role of a spokesman for the Czech people in their efforts to gain national independence; the Manifesto of the Czech Writers of 1917 was connected primarily with his name. From 1918 through 1925, he served in the Czechoslovak parliament as member of the conservative National Democratic Party.

Like the majority of his countrymen, J. considered the 15th-c. Hussite movement as the most glorious epoch in the nation's history and devoted several important works to it. His trilogy *Mezi proudy* (1886–91; between the currents) depicts the events leading to the Hussite revolt. The zenith of the upheaval is the subject of a three-part cycle, *Proti všem* (1894; against the whole world). Another trilogy, *Bratrstvo* (1899–1908; brotherhood), artistically J.'s most mature work, deals with the disintegration of the movement, when the Hussite units transferred to Slovakia. The reign of the "national king" of Bohemia, George of Poděbrady, and the activities of the Czech Brethren are the subjects of J.'s novel *Husitský král* (2 vols., 1921, 1930; the Hussite king), which remained unfinished.

The second most significant period in Czech history for J. was the time of the National Revival, from the 1770s to the mid-19th c. To this era he devoted a monumental five-part chronicle, *F. L. Věk* (1888–1905; F. L. Věk), portraying the national and linguistic reawakening in Prague and in a provincial town; and a four-part cycle, *U nás* (1896–1903; in our country), set in his native eastern Bohemia. The novella *Filosofská historie* (1878; *Gaudeamus Igitur*, 1961) is a charming picture of student life in the pre-1848 decade.

Another period that attracted J.'s interest was the aftermath of the Thirty Years' War, a time of national decline. He described it in somber colors in such books as *Skaláci* (1875; the Skalák family) and *Psohlavci* (1886; the dog-heads), both concerned with uprisings of Czech peasants against their overlords; and *Temno* (1913; the darkness), dealing with the Counter-Reformation. The title of the last-named novel, probably his most popular book, became a household word, designating any dark time in Czech national life. In *Staré pověsti české* (1894; *Stories and Legends of Old Prague*, 1931; new trans., *Legends of Old Bohemia*, 1963) he collected legends and stories from the country's early history.

Especially important among J.'s extensive dramatic works are *Vojnarka* (1891; Vojnarka) and *Otec* (1895; the father), tragic pictures from the life of country people; a Hussite triptych, *Jan Žižka* (1903; Jan Žižka), *Jan*

Hus (1911; Jan Hus), and *Jan Roháč* (1914; Jan Roháč); and the fairy-tale allegories with national and social undertones, *Lucerna* (1905; *The Lantern,* 1925) and *Pan Johanes* (1909; Mr. Johanes). Most of these plays achieved great success on the Czech stage.

J. was one of the most effective writers for his nation's struggle against foreign domination and for the independence of his people. In his writings (which are of uneven quality, to be sure), the Czech reader found a source of patriotic inspiration, and the impact of his work, particularly during World War I and again during the German occupation in 1939–45, is undeniable. In world literature he is considered on a par with Henryk Sienkiewicz (q.v.).

FURTHER WORKS: *Slavný den* (1879); *Na dvoře vévodském* (1881); *Ze zlatého věku v Čechách* (1882); *Konec a počátek* (1882); *Obětovaný* (1883); *Ráj světa* (1883); *Sousedé* (1884); *Poklad* (1885); *Pandurek* (1886); *V cizích službách* (1886); *Maryla* (1887); *Zemanka* (1887); *Skály* (1887); *Nevolnice* (1888); *Na ostrově* (1888); *Maloměstské historie* (1890); *Z Čech až na konec světa* (1890); *Sebrané spisy* (45 vols., 1890–1930); *Kolébka* (1892); *Emigrant* (1898); *M. D. Rettigová* (1891; *Dobromila Rettig,* 1920); *Gero* (1894); *Samota* (1908); *Z mých pamětí* (1911–13); *Sebrané spisy* (47 vols., 1927–34); *Básně A. J.* (1930); *Obnovit paměť minulých dnů* (1954); *Odkaz národu: Soubor díla* (32 vols., 1954–58)

BIBLIOGRAPHY: Nejedlý, Z., *A. J.* (1952); Novák, A., *Czech Literature* (1976), pp. 198–200

                                    RUDOLF STURM

JOAQUIN, Nick

Philippine novelist, poet, short-story writer, dramatist, and essayist (writing in English), b. 3 May 1917, Manila

In 1947 J.'s essay on what was believed to be the miraculous defeat of a Dutch fleet by the Spaniards off the Philippines in 1646 led the Dominicans to offer him a scholarship to study in Hong Kong. But in 1950 he left Hong Kong to write for the *Philippines Free Press,* under the pseudonym "Quijano de Manila" (an anagram of his name). In 1970 he became coeditor of the *Asian-Philippines Leader,* subsequently suspended for its political views when martial law was declared in 1972.

Because of his seminarian training and his antiquarian expertise in Spanish influences on Philippine culture, J. used to be accused of pious nostalgia. More recent critics, however, impressed by J.'s decades of reportage on contemporary issues, both knowledgeable and passionate, have come to understand his sense of the interplay between all periods of history. The struggle for individuality within contesting cultural contexts not only is his recurrent theme but finds expression through the nonchronological structures of such stories as "Guardia de Honor," "May Day Eve," and "The Mass of St. Sylvestre," as well as through fusion of legend, myth, and history in "The Summer Solstice" (all four first published in *Prose and Poems*, 1952) and "The Order of Melkizedek" (first published in *Tropical Gothic*, 1972). Figures representing the voice of conscience and the pressures of the past upon the present dominate his key works: Marasigan, the offstage father in his play *Portrait of the Artist as Filipino* (1952); the elder Monzon in the novel *The Woman Who Had Two Navels* (1961).

His sometimes gemlike style has often been imitated, but rarely with an understanding of its function in his work, which is to suggest with crystalline brilliance the various planes and prismatic angles in human affairs. J. reminds his countrymen of the uneasy coexistence of "primitive" and "civilized" dimensions in all men; the difficulty the moral intelligence has in distinguishing sinner from saint; and the special problem that Filipinos have of reconciling their mixed Asian and Western heritages, and then of shaping the best of these traditions into a continuing, compassionate national identity.

His short stories about these cultural ambiguities having already made him the most anthologized of all Philippine authors, he was declared a National Artist in 1976.

FURTHER WORKS: *Selected Stories* (1962); *A Question of Heroes: Essays in Criticism on Ten Key Figures in Philippine History* (1977); *Reportage on Crime* (1977); *Reportage on Lovers* (1977); *Nora Aunor, and Other Profiles* (1977); *Ronnie Poe, and Other Silhouettes* (1977)

BIBLIOGRAPHY: Furay, H., "The Stories of N. J.," *PSM*, 1 (1953), 144–53; Busuego-Pablo, L., "The Spanish Tradition in N. J.," *PSM, 3* (1955), 187–207; Constantino, J., *"The Woman Who Had Two Navels,"* *PSM*, 9 (1961), 639–50; Casper, L., ed., *Modern Philippine Short Stories* (1962), pp. 21–56; Casper, L., *New Writing from the Philippines* (1966), pp. 137–45; Manuud, A., ed., *Brown Heritage* (1967), pp. 765–92

LEONARD CASPER

JÓHANNES úr Kötlum (Jónasson)

Icelandic poet and novelist, b. 4 Nov. 1899, Goddastaðir, Dalasýsla; d. 27 April 1972, Reykjavík

J., who for most of his life worked as a teacher and who was widely known for his radical political activity, made his debut as a poet in 1926 under the influence of national romanticism, which dominated Icelandic poetry during the first three decades of the 20th c. It was not until 1932, in his third volume of poetry, *Ég læt sem ég sofi* (I pretend to sleep), that he emerged as a powerful revolutionary poet. In *Hrímhvíta móðir* (1937; frost-white mother) J. interpreted Icelandic history from a Marxist point of view, and a great many of his poems of the 1930s and 1940s are directly rhetorical, political appeals to the working class. But in spite of its obvious political urgency, J.'s poetry is always full of glittering beauty, and his love of nature is often expressed in the most tender and delicate ways.

During World War II J. became more cosmopolitan in his poetry, and in *Sól tér sortna* (1945; the sun turns black) he dealt, among other things, with recent events in Spain, Czechoslovakia, and the Soviet Union. In *Sóleyjarkvæði* (1952; poem of Sóley [Sóley being a symbolic name for Iceland]) J.'s political poetry took a new direction, one that soon became a common theme among leftist Icelandic writers. In 1951, only seven years after Iceland became an independent republic, an American military base was established at Keflavík. In *Sóleyjarkvæði* J. blended citations from old folk poetry with verse expressing his own bitterness, and combined patriotism, love of Icelandic nature, political conviction, and sarcasm in a poetic appeal to his nation.

Sjödægra (1955; book of seven days) was a turning point in J.'s poetic development. Gone were his former rhetorical verses in traditional form. Instead, he now expressed himself through a more modernistic imagery, often laden with metaphor and personification. His former revolutionary optimism had turned into a more somber struggle against what he called the "disgusting resignation" of his own generation, which, he says, has forgotten its ideals in the banality of the so-called welfare society.

This tone continued to typify J.'s poetry. In his last volume, *Ný og nið* (1970; waxing moon and waning moon), he finally switched his hopes from his own generation to the youth of Iceland, who he believed would take up the struggle again.

Although J. wrote five novels, the quality of his prose works never equaled that of his poetry, although the themes of his fiction are more or less the same as those of his verse. But in J.'s poetry one can see the development of Icelandic poetry in general during this century: he begins with neoromanticism, goes through the optimistic radical commitment of the 1930s, and adopts modernism after World War II. Throughout his career he was regarded as one of the most important leaders of radical socialism in Iceland, while the quality and the power of his poetry continued to grow to the end of his life.

FURTHER WORKS: *Bí bí og blaka* (1926); *Álftirnar kvaka* (1929); *Og björgin klofnuðu* (1934); *Samt mun ég vaka* (1935); *Hart er í heimi* (1939); *Eilífðar smáblóm* (1940); *Verndarenglarnir* (1943); *Dauðsmannsey* (1949); *Siglingin mikla* (1950); *Frelsisálfan* (1951); *Hlið hins himneska friðar* (1953); *Óljóð* (1962); *Tregaslagur* (1964); *Mannssonurinn* (1966)

NJÖRÐUR P. NJARÐVÍK

JOHNSON, Eyvind

Swedish novelist, b. 29 July, 1900, Överluleå; d. 26 Aug. 1976, Stockholm

The events of J.'s own time and the fact that he grew up in an isolated rural area stimulated his exploration of the history and culture of a wider European context. Except for a short return to Sweden in 1924, J. spent the 1920s in Berlin and Paris amid the turmoil of postwar depression and the upsurge of strong intellectual and political currents. In Sweden during the 1930s J. worked actively against the onslaught of Nazism. As editor of the magazine *Håndslag* he helped establish a link between Resistance workers in Norway and Sweden. Following World War II J. traveled extensively in Switzerland. Its culture and landscape provided the setting for several of his novels, and its political structure became central in J.'s utopian vision of a federation of European states. Among other literary distinctions, J.

was elected a member of the Swedish Academy in 1957, and in 1974 he shared the Nobel Prize with Harry Martinson (q.v.).

J.'s early novels are sociocritical, directed against the complacency and narrow scope of bourgeois society. Among them, *Minnas* (1928; remembering) and *Kommentar till ett stjärnfall* (1929; commentary to a falling star) make use of the interior monologue (q.v.), which J. is credited with having introduced into Swedish fiction. A dominant theme in these early works is the protagonist's inability to deal effectively with oppressive forces. This Hamlet-like conflict was overtly solved in *Avsked till Hamlet* (1930; farewell to Hamlet), but the question of an individual's right to take aggressive action remains an intermittent theme in later novels.

The 1930s were a time of experimentation with primitivist ideas, as in *Regn i gryningen* (1933; rain at dawn), and with autobiography. J.'s tetralogy about the adolescent Olof—*Nu var det 1914* (1934; *1914*, 1970), *Här har du ditt liv!* (1935; here is your life), *Se dig inte om!* (1936; don't look back), and *Slutspel i ungdomen* (1937; postlude to youth)—was the first work to win immediate recognition; the four parts were later published in one volume as *Romanen om Olof* (1945; the novel about Olof).

J.'s production during World War II may be labeled his military service in words. Most remarkable is the voluminous Krilon trilogy—*Grupp Krilon* (1941; group Krilon), *Krilons resa* (1942; Krilon's journey), and *Krilon själv* (1943; Krilon himself). The work condemns Nazi oppression and explores the controversial policy of Swedish neutrality during the war. On an allegorical level the real-estate agent Krilon and his friends represent European states struggling for humanist ideals against the forces of evil. Abundant digressions suspend narrative action to make room for reflections, dreams, and flashbacks. Fictional, allegorical, and symbolic levels are woven together with an obvious delight in storytelling and a firm belief in the power of words to relieve suffering and to sustain an individual's right to dignity and freedom.

The majority of J.'s later novels are built around mythical and historical subjects, and nearly all centuries from ancient Greece to our own are represented. Foremost among them are *Strändernas svall* (1946; *Return to Ithaca*, 1952), based on the story of Ulysses; *Drömmar om rosor och eld* (1949; dreams of roses and fire), revolving around the power struggle between Catholics and Huguenots in 17th-c. France; *Hans nådes tid* (1960; *The Days of His Grace,* 1968), set in the days of Charlemagne's rise to power; and *Livsdagen lång* (1964; life's long day), an eight-episode chronicle spanning the 9th to 16th cs. The historian and the narrator in these novels—both personae of J. himself—are interrelated for a particular purpose: to make the literary work reflect the interaction of times past and present. J.'s increasingly subtle fusion of time levels emphasizes his cyclical concept of history, the illusion of chronological time and the similarity of man's condition under varying circumstances.

Only a few of J.'s novels have reached widespread popularity. One reason may be that J.'s readers are seldom left alone with the story. The fictional world is continually tested and questioned by the many roles of the storyteller. But this characteristic also constitutes the essence of J.'s greatness as a writer, making him the pioneer of 20th-c. Swedish fiction. As a guide and companion, as a masterful artisan in the literary workshop, J. invites his readers to probe and expand the possibilities of the verbal medium and to experience innumerable facets of fictional reality.

FURTHER WORKS: *De fyra främlingarna* (1924); *Timans och rättfärdigheten* (1925); *Stad i mörker* (1927); *Stad i ljus* (1928); *Bobinack* (1932); *Natten är här* (1932); *Än en gång, Kapten!* (1934); *Nattövning* (1938); *Den trygga världen* (1940); *Soldatens återkomst* (1940); *Pan mot Sparta* (1946); *Strändernas svall: Ett drama* (1948); *Dagbok från Schweiz* (1949); *Valda skrifter* (1950); *Ett vårtal* (1951); *Lägg undan solen* (1951); *Romantisk berättelse* (1953); *Vinterresa i Norrbotten* (1955); *Tidens gång* (1955); *Molnen över Metapontion* (1957); *Vägar över Metaponto: En resedagbok* (1959); *Spår förbi Kolonos* (1961); *Stunder vågor* (1965); *Favel ensam* (1968); *Några steg mot tystnaden* (1973)

BIBLIOGRAPHY: Sjöberg, L., "E. J.," *ASR*, 56 (1968), 369–78; Orton, G., *E. J.* (1972); Stenström, T., "Summary in English," *Romantikern E. J.* (1978), pp. 277–83; Schwartz, N., "Summary in English," *Hamlet i klasskampen* (1979), pp. 252–58

MONICA SETTERWALL

JOHNSON, James Weldon

American poet, novelist, and essayist, b. 17 June 1871, Jacksonville, Fla.; d. 26 June 1938, Wiscasset, Maine

J.'s mother, a teacher, was a native of Nassau, Bahamas, his father a black freeman born in Richmond, Virginia. Since there was no high school available to black students in Jacksonville, where J. grew up, he received preparatory and college training at Atlanta University, from which he graduated in 1894. At twenty-three he returned to Jacksonville to become principal of the elementary school he had attended. After instituting a high school and a daily paper, and after studying for and being admitted to the Florida bar, J. left Jacksonville for New York in 1902, to engage in popular songwriting with his brother, J. Rosamond Johnson, and Robert Cole. Republican political activities led him in 1906 and 1908 to appointments as U.S. consul in Venezuela and Nicaragua. In 1916 he became field secretary of the National Association for the Advancement of Colored People, and in 1920 the first black secretary of that interracial activist organization. In 1931 he was appointed to a chair in creative literature at Fisk University in Nashville, Tennessee, a post he held until his death in a car accident in 1938.

J.'s only novel, *The Autobiography of an Ex-Colored Man,* was published anonymously in 1912 and reissued under his name in 1927. J.'s narrator is a black man who can "pass" for white, and who travels through the U.S. and Europe in alternating white and black identities. A consummate musician interested in collecting and transforming black folk music, the narrator is finally dissuaded from his black identity by the sight of a lynching. In his "shame at being identified with a people that could with impunity be treated worse than animals," he takes on white identity permanently, although wondering if he perhaps chose the less worthy option.

In 1917 J.'s poems, dialect verses, and songs were collected as *Fifty Years, and Other Poems.* These works of protest, love, and humor include J.'s well-known poem in praise of the slave creators of the spirituals, "O Black and Unknown Bards." (His prefaces to the two collections of spirituals done with his brother in 1925–26 give an excellent historical analysis of the Negro spirituals.) Many of the poems from the 1917 volume also appear in *Saint Peter Relates an Incident: Selected Poems* (1935). In the latter volume, J. includes "Lift Every Voice and Sing," written in 1900. Set to music by his brother, this song became the "Negro national anthem."

The most famous and noteworthy of J.'s poems are those collected in *God's Trombones: Seven Negro Sermons* (1927). Based on folk sermons of the "old-time Negro preacher," the collection includes an introductory prayer and seven biblical narrations, such as "The Creation" and "Judgement Day." In these folk poems J. succeeds in creating the kind of black poetry he recommends in his lengthy and thorough preface to *The Book of American Negro Poetry* (1922; rev. ed., 1931). There J. writes that traditional dialect verse must be replaced by symbols that "express the racial spirit . . . from within."

J.'s nonfiction prose works include a history of the Negro in New York City, *Black Manhattan* (1930); his autobiography, *Along This Way* (1933); and a long essay, *Negro Americans, What Now?* (1938). *Black Manhattan* concentrates on black Americans' emergence in sports, music, theater, and literature. In *Negro Americans, What Now?* J. defended the integrationist program of the NAACP as the best solution for America's racial problems.

J.'s contribution to American literature lies in the knowledge and discussion of black literature he promoted through his articles and prefaces, and in the few models of excellence he left in his novel and poems. His learning and artistry, coupled with an active and effective political and civil rights career, made of J. a powerful literary and social model for Americans, black and white.

FURTHER WORKS: *The Changing Status of Negro Labor* (1918); *Africa in the World Democracy* (1919, with Horace Katlen); *The Race Problem and Peace* (1924); *Native African Races and Culture* (1927); *The Shining Life: An Appreciation of Julius Rosenwald* (1932); *John Hope: President, Morehouse College, 1906–1931; President, Atlanta University, 1929–1936* (1936)

BIBLIOGRAPHY: special J. issue, *Phylon*, 32, 4 (1971); Levy, E., *J. W. J.: Black Leader, Black Voice* (1973); Wagner, J., *Black Poets of the United States* (1973), pp. 351–84; Baker, H., "Forgotten Prototype: *The Autobiography of an Ex-Colored Man* and *Invisible Man*," *VQR*, 49 (1973), 433–49; Davis, A., *From the Dark Tower: Afro-American Writers 1900–1960* (1974), pp. 25–32; Fleming, R., *J. W. J. and Arna Bontemps: A Reference*

Guide (1978), pp. 3–70; O'Sullivan, M., "Of Souls and Pottage: J. W. J.'s *The Autobiography of an Ex-Coloured Man*," *CLAJ*, 23, 1 (1979), 60–70

CAROLYN WEDIN SYLVANDER

JOHNSON, Uwe
West German novelist, b. 20 July 1934, Cammin

J.'s own biography reflects the tumultuous period of German history in which he came to maturity and which finds expression in his novels. Having spent his childhood in the once-German territory of Pomerania, now part of Poland, J. fled with his family to Mecklenburg, a mostly agrarian area in what is now East Germany, in 1945. From 1952 to 1954 he studied at the University of Leipzig. In 1959 he moved to West Berlin so that his first novel, unacceptable in the East, could be published in the West. From 1966 to 1968 he lived on Riverside Drive in New York City like the heroine of his last novel. He won the Berlin Fontane Prize in 1960, the International Publishers' Prize in 1962, and the Büchner Prize in 1971.

J.'s first novel, *Mutmaßungen über Jakob* (1959; *Speculations about Jakob,* 1963), established his reputation as a major postwar German writer and also set forth what were to be the central formal and thematic concerns of J.'s subsequent writing. All of J.'s novels revolve around a major political crisis with which his characters must come to terms but for which they find no easy ethical answer. "Where is the moral Switzerland to which we could emigrate?" asks a character in his latest novel. The structure and language of J.'s works also indicate to readers the difficulty of finding a standpoint from which it is possible for human beings to assess a situation accurately and truthfully. Drawing upon modernist techniques, particularly those of Faulkner (q.v.), J.'s complex novels make his readers speculate about how to understand the novel as his characters must speculate about how to understand their world.

Mutmaßungen über Jakob is an avant-garde detective story structured around the attempt of the acquaintances of Jakob Abs, an East German railway worker, to understand why he had been run down by a train: an accident? suicide? Their dialogues, interior monologues, and recollections allow the complicated events leading up to Jakob's death to be told. Jakob had been a dedicated worker for East German socialism until he had to help dispatch troop trains to suppress the Hungarian uprising of 1956. But the West is not any better: the British and French are about to occupy the Suez Canal, to the indignation of Jakob and his childhood friend and present lover, Gesine Cresspahl, who works for NATO in West Germany. Gesine will not go back to the East, and Jakob will not move to the West; in the real world of work and politics, there is no place where lovers can live happily together. The novel's intricate plot, involving an attempt to recruit Gesine as a spy for East Germany and her flight from the secret police when she returns for a clandestine visit to the East, remains shadowy and unclear to readers, like the options available to J.'s characters.

J.'s later works continue his examination of the conflict between East and West and his characters' difficulty in finding an adequate epistemological position between the two. *Das dritte Buch über Achim* (1961; *The Third Book about Achim*, 1967) is subtitled "description of a description." Karsch, a West German journalist, tries to write a biography about Achim, an East German bicycle racer and national hero. The novel takes the form of a long telephone conversation in which Karsch explains why he could not write his book. Like any biographer, Karsch finds it difficult to select appropriate biographical details that pin down Achim's character, and he also discovers that East and West German conceptions of what a biography should contain are not easily united. But when Karsch learns that Achim, the socialist hero, had participated in the East German workers' uprising against the regime in June 1953, the biography becomes impossible, for this image of Achim cannot be reconciled with that of the two earlier East German biographies. To remain the new socialist man, Achim has to deny his own history. Karsch breaks off his book and returns to the West.

J.'s first two novels are formally his most interesting, for in them he pursues seriously his attempt to find a way of seeing that would correspond to the official ideologies of neither East nor West and that would meet human needs more adequately than either system does. As J. seems increasingly to have given up hope for that solution, his works have grown more conventional. In *Zwei Ansichten* (1965; *Two Views*, 1966) J. juxtaposes the perspectives of two lovers separated by the building of the Berlin Wall. Both characters conform to certain stereotypes about their countries: D. , the East

German, is a self-sacrificing nurse, while B., from the West, is a self-indulgent commercial photographer with a sports car. D. undertakes the risk of a complicated and dangerous escape from the East to rejoin B., but the love affair does not work out; their "two views" can't be reconciled.

J.'s mammoth and uncompleted *Jahrestage* (Vol. I, 1970; II, 1971; III, 1973; *Anniversaries*, 1975) confronts the most difficult dilemmas yet. Gesine Cresspahl of J.'s first novel and her daughter Marie (conceived during Jakob's visit to the West in *Mutmaßungen*) have moved to New York City, where they live through the difficult days from August 21, 1967, to August 20, 1968. Told day-by-day, Gesine's life is framed by excerpts from *The New York Times,* which recount the brutal events of daily life in the city, racial unrest, political assassinations, the Vietnam War, and the protests against it. Counterposed to the present and narrated with 19th-c. omniscience are Gesine's tales from her childhood in Nazi Germany. Although politically tainted, her life then in a small village in Mecklenburg was more comfortable and compatible with human needs than the present allows. Gesine places her hopes for a human future in the liberalization of Czechoslovak socialism, but it seems likely that the final volume of the novel will end on the day of the Russian invasion of Czechoslovakia, which crushed that possibility. The final volume of *Jahrestage*, often announced by J.'s publisher, has not yet appeared. One suspects J. can find no aesthetic solution to the problems of *Jahrestage* because there is no real solution to them.

In *Jahrestage* all the characters from J.'s previous works reappear, and the childhood landscape Gesine recalls was also the setting of *Mutmaßungen*. In this respect J.'s latest novel is a summary of and conclusion to his previous work. Although *Jahrestage* is an impressive achievement, it nonetheless does not fulfill the promise that J.'s earlier works embodied. In form and content, his first two novels struggled for new solutions; *Jahrestage*, looking to a flawed past for its vision of happiness, resigns itself in the present to its disappointment at what now exists.

FURTHER WORKS: *Karsch, und andere Prosa* (1964); *Eine Reise nach Klagenfurt* (1974); *Berliner Sachen* (1975)

BIBLIOGRAPHY: Popp, H., *Einführung in U. J.s Roman "Mutmaßungen über Jakob"* (1967);

Baumgart, R., ed., *Über U. J.* (1970); Migner, K., *U. J.: "Das dritte Buch über Achim"* (1970); Schwarz, W. J., *Der Erzähler U. J.* (1970); Durzak, M., *Der deutsche Roman der Gegenwart* (1971), pp. 174–249; Boulby, M., *U. J.* (1974); Post-Adams, R., *U. J.* (1977); Hye, R., *U. J.s "Jahrestage"* (1978); Neumann, B., *Utopie und Mimesis: Zum Verhältnis von Ästhetik, Gesellschaftsphilosophie und Politik in den Romanen U. J.s* (1978); Riedel, N., *U. J. Bibliographie* (2 vols., 1976, 1978)

SARA LENNOX

JOHNSTON, Denis

Irish dramatist, scriptwriter, and biographer, b. 18 June 1901, Dublin

After attending St. Andrew's College, Dublin (1908–15), and Merchiston Castle School, Edinburgh (1915–17), J. received his law degree from Cambridge in 1923. He practiced law in Dublin until 1936, at the same time pursuing activities in the theater under the pseudonym of "E. W. Tocher." J. directed, acted, and wrote for the Abbey and Gate theaters in Dublin throughout the 1920s and 1930s, earning a reputation as a major new force in Irish drama. He was also a scriptwriter for the BBC (1936–38); drama critic for *The Bell* (1941–42); war correspondent for the BBC (1942–45); drama critic for Radio Eireann (1947); and scriptwriter for the NBC Theatre Guild of the Air (1947–49). J. was awarded the Order of the British Empire in 1946, and from 1949 to 1973 he served as visiting professor in various American colleges and universities.

J.'s early plays, highly experimental in form, were influenced by the European avant-garde, especially the expressionists (q.v.). His first play, *The Old Lady Says "No!"* (1929), shocked Dublin audiences with its expressionistic theatricality, its frank language, and its satiric thrust. The play is suggestive of Strindberg's (q.v.) *A Dream Play* (1902) in tone and structure, although J. acknowledged George S. Kaufman (1889–1961) and Marc Connelly's (1890–1980) *Beggar on Horseback* (1924) as his model. J.'s play satirizes the failure of the Irish Republic to achieve the goals upon which it was founded. J. criticizes contemporary attitudes and institutions by bringing the Irish patriot Robert Emmet (1778–1803) into 20th-c. Dublin, showing Emmet's despair and frustration at the dismal situation he

finds there. In many of his plays, J. similarly debunks the sentimental idealism he feels impedes progress in Irish culture and politics.

J.'s first Abbey play, *The Moon in the Yellow River* (1931), was a popular success, securing him an international reputation. Another of his popular early works was *Blind Man's Buff* (perf. 1936, pub. 1938), based on Ernst Toller's (q.v.) *The Blind Goddess* (1933). This courtroom "whodunit" explores the weaknesses of the jury system in a conventional well-made-play format, signaling J.'s shift to the more traditional, realistic style of playwriting that is characteristic of his mature work.

Two plays of interest from J.'s middle period are *The Golden Cuckoo* (perf. 1939, pub. 1954) and *The Dreaming Dust* (perf. 1940, pub. 1959). The former is perhaps J.'s funniest and most tender play. Based upon a real event, it chronicles the fate of a singularly unheroic chap who follows his conscience, rebels against authority, and commits an act of civil disobedience. *The Dreaming Dust*, although unsuccessful, is the best of several plays by various dramatists on the subject of Jonathan Swift. J. was fascinated with the enigmatic Swift and wrote as well a fictionalized biography of the writer, *In Search of Swift* (1959). He also published another biography on Synge (q.v.), *John Millington Synge* (1965).

J.'s finest play is his most recent one, *The Scythe and the Sunset* (1958), a drama of the Easter Week rising of 1916. The title parodies Sean O'Casey's (q.v.) *The Plough and the Stars* (1926), and his avowed purpose was to deromanticize the ugly events that O'Casey had somewhat melodramatically treated in the earlier work. J. calls his play an "antimelodrama." Set in a Dublin cafe during Easter Week, it concerns a dozen characters whose lives are reshaped—in some cases ended—by the bloody battle raging in the street below. The drama is rich in characterization and bitter humor—poetic in the vein of Synge and as volatile as the work of Brendan Behan (q.v.). *The Scythe and the Sunset* is one of the finest Irish history plays.

J.'s nine full-length plays, written over a thirty-year period, display considerable diversity in style and structure, although there is unity in their thematic content. J. was concerned with the nature of evil, and he advocated the responsibility of the individual to recognize it and deal with it. All of the plays attest to the writer's comic sense and his sharp wit, which he frequently employed in the cause of satire. In all his works, J. exhibited a passionate devotion to his homeland, coupled with the desire to force the Irish people to confront themselves honestly, without illusions and romantic ideals.

FURTHER WORKS: *A Bride for the Unicorn* (perf. 1933, pub. 1935); *Storm Song* (perf. 1934, pub. 1935); *A Fourth for Bridge* (1947); *Nine Rivers from Jordan* (1953); *Strange Occurrence on Ireland's Eye* (1956); *Siege at Killyfaddy* (1960); *The Brazen Horn* (1976); *The Dramatic Works of D. J.* (2 vols, 1977–78); *The Tain: A Pageant* (1979)

BIBLIOGRAPHY: Canfield, C., ed., "A Note on the Nature of Expressionism and D. J.'s Plays," *Plays of Changing Ireland* (1936), pp. 25–36; Edwards, H., "D. J.," *The Bell*, 13, 1 (1946), 7–18; Hogan, R., "The Adult Theatre of D. J.," *After the Irish Renaissance* (1967), pp. 133–46; Ferrar, H., *D. J.'s Irish Theatre* (1973); Barnett, G. A., *D. J.* (1978)

JACK A. VAUGHN

JONES, David

Anglo-Welsh poet and essayist, b. 1 Nov. 1895, Brockley, England; d. 28 Oct. 1974, London

J. whose father was a printer by profession, was introduced early to words as a visual experience. Visits to his grandfather, John Jones, confronted him with his Welsh heritage and the rich sounds of the Welsh language. J.'s Cockney mother had had an early aptitude for drawing and properly encouraged her son's preoccupation with that art. From 1909 to 1914, J. studied at Camberwell Art School, where he discovered modern French painting, the Pre-Raphaelites, and 19th-c. English illustrators. When World War I broke into his life, J. enlisted in the Royal Welsh Fusiliers, with whom he served as a private on the Western front from December 1915 until he was invalided home in March 1918. The brutality of trench warfare and the loyalty of his soldier comrades are evoked in J.'s 20th-c. epic, *In Parenthesis* (1937), awarded the Hawthornden Prize in 1938.

In 1919 he went on a government grant to the Westminster School of Art, where he encountered the work of William Blake and other English watercolorists, whom he greatly admired. In 1921 he was received into the Catholic Church, rooted in symbol and ritual as modes of experiencing human thought and history, as are J.'s art and writing. J.'s close friendship with Eric Gill (1882–1940), sculptor and

engraver, led in 1922 to his joining the Guild of St. Joseph and St. Dominic, a religious fraternity at Ditchling for those involved in hand-crafted arts. There he learned engraving on wood and copper, which resulted in some of his finest illustrations for St. Dominic's and the Golden Cockerel Press.

The period from 1926 to 1933 was the most prolific in J.'s life: he produced numerous engravings, as well as watercolors and drawings, and began writing *In Parenthesis*, a creative labor that was to take seven years. A striking fusion of Welsh myth, Christian sacrament, and the shattering personal experience of a soldier confronted with modern warfare, J.'s narrative of the Somme offensive of 1916 is a work of great verbal intensity. Utilizing *anamnesis*, a kind of remembrance in which the individual's private stock of data is linked with the common stock of human memory, J. draws upon ancient and medieval heroic myth to strengthen the ultimate meaning of Private John Ball's experience in battle. Thus through many allusions, this Anglo-Welsh soldier is simultaneously a hero of the *Mabinogion*, the *Chanson de Roland*, and Aneirin's medieval Welsh epic *Y Gododdin*.

The 1940s saw J.'s increasing preoccupation with themes from myth and legend, particularly the Matter of Britain. Two of his Arthurian paintings, the culmination of his visual art, hang in the Tate Gallery. J.'s concern for tradition, and particularly with the concept of sacrament as sign, led him to create *Anathemata* (1952). A monumental vision of Britain as the islands appear through the deposits of many cultural epochs, this long poem is a *universum*, a poetic totality including the whole of British history as an ever-accumulating collage or palimpsest. Calligraphy is an important art form in this work, for it unites J. the painter with J. the poet in celebration of a life-giving mystery.

After *Anathemata* appeared, J. continued work on another book of poetry based on themes evolving from the experience of Roman soldiers in the Near East at the time of Christ. Only fragments, in the form of shorter poems, compact and episodic, have appeared. From 1941 onward, over a period of fifteen years, J. also wrote a number of essays, collected as *Epoch and Artist* (1959). Representing a poet-artist's struggle to express in prose the background and theory of his artistic work, the essays are exploratory in mood and reflect the influence of the Catholic philosopher Jacques Maritain (1883–1972). J.'s most significant essay, "Art and Sacrament" (1955), deals with the gratuitous nature of art, the idea of *sign* and its relation to *sacrament*, and the role of the latter in religion and culture. For J., the whole of life and experience is sacramental, an attitude epitomized in the Christian rite of the Eucharist. Significant for J.'s notions of sign and sacrament was an English *résumé* (1934) of *Mysterium fidei* (written 1915; pub. in 2 vols., 1941, 1950 [in Latin] by a Jesuit scholar, Maurice de Taille).

J. remains a somewhat inaccessible poet, for only intrepid lovers of symbolism and densely worded poetry dare enter the labyrinth of his lines. He speaks a language that has been forgotten in modern times. Questers, however, are richly rewarded in sign and song and rite.

FURTHER WORKS: *The Wall* (1955); *The Tribune's Visitation* (1958); *The Tutelar of the Place* (1961); *The Dream of Private Clitus* (1964); *The Hunt* (1965); *The Fatigue* (1965); *The Sleeping Lord* (1967); *Fragments of an Attempted Autobiographical Writing* (1975)

BIBLIOGRAPHY: Johnston, J. H., *English Poetry of the First World War* (1964), pp. 284–340; special J. issue, *Agenda*, 5, 1–3 (1967); Blamires, D., *D. J.: Artist and Writer* (1971); Hooker, J., *D. J.: An Exploratory Study of His Writings* (1975); Mathias, R., ed., *D. J.: Eight Essays on His Work as Writer and Artist* (1976); Hague, R., *A Commentary on the "Anathemata"* (1977)

                                    JANET POWERS GEMMILL

JONES, James

American novelist, b. 6 Nov. 1921, Robinson, Ill.; d. 9 May 1977, Southampton, N.Y.

Because of the Depression, J.'s education ended with high school. He joined the army and was at Pearl Harbor when the Japanese attacked; he was injured in combat on Guadalcanal, and discharged in 1944. He moved to Paris in 1958, then to Sagaponack, Long Island, 1974. He taught at Florida International University 1974–75.

J. was preeminently a novelist of war and military life. His major work is a trilogy based on his World War II experiences: *From Here to Eternity* (1951), *The Thin Red Line* (1962), and *Whistle* (1978)), the last published posthumously. The final three chapters of *Whistle* were completed by a friend, the writer Willie Morris (b. 1934), with the aid of J.'s notes and taped conversations.

From Here to Eternity won the National Book Award and became an immediate best seller. It has been described as the "definitive novel of the American peacetime army" by Maxwell Geismar, and, with J.'s other works, has been translated into a number of languages. It is a detailed account of the life of an enlisted man in the pre-World War II army. In the tradition of naturalism (second only to Dreiser's [q.v.] *An American Tragedy* as a 20th-c. American naturalistic novel, according to F. L. Gwynn), the book set new limits in realistic description of soldiers' language and sexual behavior. As Richard P. Adams showed, with its presentation of the self-reliant individual struggling against dehumanizing institutions, it is in the Thoreau-Whitman tradition. The novel taps the emotional power of the archetypal American folk hero to give the enlisted man tragic stature.

The Thin Red Line, an account of an infantry company on Guadalcanal, demonstrates J.'s narrative power, his ability to create many individualized characters and dramatic episodes, such as the one of the decaying corpse of the Japanese soldier, dragged out of a mass grave.

Whistle is less successful, perhaps because J. waited so long after his war experiences to write it. The novel describes the hospital experiences of four wounded soldiers. The four characters that appear in this novel are the same personae that appear in *From Here to Eternity* and *The Thin Red Line*; in each novel the men are given different names, but they are used to illustrate the various kinds of tragedy that come to the soldier.

Leonard Kriegel has argued persuasively that American masculinity is J.'s most basic subject, as illustrated both by the war novels and by other novels that critics have generally regarded as of less value. These include *Go to the Widow-Maker* (1967), in which a successful playwright asserts his masculinity by learning scuba diving and by his relationship with various women; *In the Merry Month of May* (1971), based on the student protest movement in Paris, May, 1968, in which J. criticizes student protest movements for their disorderliness, self-indulgence, and hypocrisy; and *A Touch of Danger* (1973), a good example of the American private-detective story.

J. implies that the pressures of this society coerce men to demonstrate their masculinity by the use of violence, by sexual athleticism, by skill in sports, and by the ability to drink heavily and to withstand pain courageously. This bleak view is modified by an Emersonian emphasis on the inner, enduring self. Nevertheless, both in the novels and in his private life, J. valued gentleness highly. In all the novels the male characters seem most fully developed; his women seem wooden and one-dimensional.

J.'s attitude toward war is paradoxical. He wrote that his works are antiwar, that an accurate report of war must show the "regimentation of souls, the systematized reduction of men to animal level, the horror of pointless death, the exhaustion of living in constant fear." A true antiwar work must show that "modern war destroys human character." Moreover, J. intimates in his fiction that the dehumanizing institutions of war symbolize the tendency of all contemporary institutions. However, some later works are less critical of war.

Although J. was not a graceful stylist, his intuitive mastery of the traditional novel form, as John W. Aldridge has observed, gave his best works lasting value. His World War II trilogy seems likely to remain among the four or five most valuable fictional treatments in English of the war.

FURTHER WORKS: *Some Came Running* (1958); *The Pistol* (1959); *The Ice-Cream Headache, and Other Stories* (1968); *Viet Journal* (1974); *World War II* (1975)

BIBLIOGRAPHY: Fielder, L., "J. J.: Dead-End Young Werther: The Bum as American Culture Hero," *Commentary*, Sept. 1951, 252–55; Adams, R. P., "A Second Look at *From Here to Eternity*, *CE*, 18 (1956), 205–10; Griffith, B. W., "Rear Rank Robin Hood: J. J.'s Folk Hero," *GaR*, 10 (1956), 41–46; Geismar, M., *American Moderns*, (1958), pp. 225–38; Geismar, M., on *The Thin Red Line*, *NYTBR*, 9 Sept. 1962, 1 ff.; Kriegel, L., on *Whistle*, *Nation*, 8 April 1978, 406–7; Aldridge, J., on *Whistle*, *NYTBR*, 5 March 1978, 1ff.; Giles, J. R., *J. J.* (1981)

LEE A. BURRESS

JOUHANDEAU, Marcel

French novelist, essayist, and short-story writer, b. 26 July 1888, La Clayette; d. 7 April 1979, Rueil-Malmaison

The son of a butcher in Guéret, J. always felt much closer to his mother, a very pious woman; he first planned to become a priest, but after completing his studies in Paris, he worked as a schoolteacher there from 1912 until 1949, devoting most of his time to literature. The eccentric woman he married in 1929, the former

dancer Caryathis, became one of the main characters in his fiction, under the name of Élise: *Élise* (1933; Élise); *Chroniques maritales* (2 vols., 1935, 1938; chronicles of married life); *Nouvelles chroniques maritales* (1943; new chronicles of married life). Their adopted daughter, Céline, appears also in his novels *L'école des filles* (1961; the education of girls) and *Une adolescence* (1971; an adolescence).

J., who in 1914 had destroyed his first literary writings, was a very prolific writer until the very end of his life: he published more than 150 books. Their three main centers of interest are the people he knew, himself (under various fictitious names: Théophile, Juste Binche, Mr. Godeau), and God. The persons who surrounded him in his childhood and youth became the characters of a series of chronicles, which are a transposition of provincial life in the small town of Guéret, in central France (Chaminadour in J.'s fiction), with its satanic or angelic sides.

J.'s first book, *La jeunesse de Théophile* (1921; Théophile's youth), is the ironic and mystic tale of a young man aspiring to an ideal of beauty and the absolute, but too sensual to be a priest. J. then re-created unforgettable faces and figures from his own youth in *Les Pincengrain* (1924; the Pincengrains), *Prudence Hautechaume* (1927; Prudence Hautechaume), *Chaminadour* (3 vols., 1934, 1936, 1941; Chaminadour), *Les miens* (1942; my people), and *L'oncle Henri* (1943; Uncle Henry), while evoking his own struggle between good and evil in *Monsieur Godeau intime* (1926; Mr. Godeau in his intimacy), *Monsieur Godeau marié* (1933; Mr. Godeau married). A series of realistic portraits and cruel or tender anecdotes resurrect the past in the six volumes of *Mémorial* (recorded memories) published between 1948 and 1958. They are completed and brought to the present by acute observation of daily reality noted in a nervous but elegant style in the twenty-six volumes of the monumental *Journaliers* (1961–78; day-to-day happenings).

In a series of moral essays J. pursued a dialogue with God, even from the depths of sin and often beyond good and evil: *L'algèbre des valeurs morales* (1935; algebra of moral values), *De l'abjection* (1939; on abasement), *L'éloge de la volupté* (1951; in praise of voluptuous pleasure), *Les carnets de l'écrivain* (1957; the writer's notebooks). His scandalous confessions are not a sign of complacency about vice but rather an attempt to transcend it. They reveal a rich inner life, an unshakable optimism, and they affirm the omnipotent freedom of man in his confrontation with God.

The diabolic and visionary aspect of J.'s talent appears at its best in fantastic tales such as *Astaroth* (1929; Ashtaroth) and *Contes d'enfer* (1955; tales from hell).

J. is recognized as one of the greatest writers of fiction in 20th-c. French literature. He has managed to create in his novels and stories a universe of his own through the magic of his style, the acuteness of his observation, and a unique vision in which cynical irony is mixed with an almost sacrilegious belief in the absolute value of man.

FURTHER WORKS: *Les Térébinte* (1926); *Ximénès Malinjoude* (1927); *Opales* (1928); *Le parricide imaginaire* (1930); *Le journal du coiffeur* (1931); *L'amateur d'imprudence* (1932); *Tite-le-Long* (1932); *Veronicana* (1933); *Binche-ana* (1933); *Le saladier* (1936); *Petit bestiaire* (1944); *Essai sur moi-même* (1946); *Carnets de Don Juan* (1947); *Ma classe de sixième* (1949); *Un monde* (1950); *L'imposteur* (1950); *De la grandeur* (1952); *Ana de Madame d'Apremont* (1954); *Nouvelles images de Paris* (1956); *Réflexions sur la vieillesse et la mort* (1956); *Saint Philippe Neri* (1957; St. Philip Neri, 1960); *Réflexions sur la vie et le bonheur* (1958); *Trois crimes rituels* (1962); *Chronique d'une passion* (1964); *Que la vie est une fête* (1966); *Et nunc dimittis* (1978). FURTHER VOLUME IN ENGLISH: *Marcel and Élise* (1953)

BIBLIOGRAPHY: Mauriac, C., *Introduction à une mystique de l'enfer* (1938); Turnell, M., Introduction to *Marcel and Élise* (1953), pp. 7–25; Cabanis, J., *J.* (1959); Gaulmier, J., *L'univers de M. J.* (1959); Heppenstall, R., *The Fourfold Tradition* (1961), pp. 170–77; Rode, H., *J.* (1972)

FREDERIC J. GROVER

JOUVE, Pierre Jean

French poet, novelist, and music critic, b. 11 Oct. 1887, Arras; d. 8 Jan. 1976, Paris

By his own account, J.'s childhood was not a happy one, marred as it was by a serious operation followed by years of depression and emotional instability. During these years he developed a taste for music, which thereafter always held a special attraction for him and to which he would devote some of his most probing critical writings. He spent both world wars in Switzerland. After returning to France in 1945, J. settled in Paris, where he remained until his death, save for occasional short trips abroad.

J.'s early career was marked by false starts, ambiguous alliances—with the Abbaye group of poets and with Jules Romains and Romain Rolland (qq.v.)—and unevenness in the quality of his work.

J.'s mature phase as a writer was the product of a period of intense reading and reflection, spanning the years 1922–25. As a result of this crisis, J. boldly repudiated, in his preface to the volume of poetry *Noces* (1928; nuptials), all of his writings prior to 1925. During this period he experienced a "religious conversion" in the broadest sense of the term, to spiritual values inherent in poetry, as J. was careful to point out in the autobiographical essay *En miroir* (1954; in the mirror), and not specifically to Catholicism or any other particular faith or dogma, as some critics have claimed. Almost concurrently, J. became interested in Freudian psychoanalysis. The preface to another poetry collection, *Sueur de sang* (1933; sweat of blood), was misinterpreted in some circles as J.'s espousal of a kind of "poeticized psychoanalysis," and not as the poet intended it, namely, of psychoanalysis as a point of departure for artistic creation.

J.'s dramatic gesture of rejection, his repudiation of his early work, announced a new beginning, to which he alluded by choosing the phrase "vita nuova" (new life), the title of Dante's collection of poems, as the epigraph to *Noces*. This was by no means a cry of victory, but rather a statement of hope. For J.'s poetic development was characterized by a relentless search for a singular voice and language, a search that was remarkable in its unity of composition and imagery. His poetry posits a world of seemingly irreconcilable contraries, which the poet seeks to harmonize. These gravitate around two main figures representing two divergent paths of poetic creation: Christ-Apollo, the "Christ of poetry"; and Mnemosyne, goddess of memory and mother of the Muses. While the former embodies an inaccessible artistic originality, pure creation, the Logos, as it were, the latter functions as the only mediating presence available to the poet, the vast but outworn resources of poetic myths, themes, and language that have inspired the writings of artistic precursors. The struggle between these two opposing forces becomes the focal point of

J.'s poetics, and the desire for resolution provides the dialectical nature of the poetry as a whole.

This drama is played out in successive stages. *Noces* and *Sueur de sang* constitute the preliminary "dark phase" of gradual awakening to the reality of opposites in which the female (as memory's surrogate) is the object of mistrust. *Matière céleste* (1937; celestial matter) and *Kyrie* (1938; Kyrie) contain the poet's slow and patient refinement of the feminine figure in its most erotic manifestations; her death makes possible her emergence under the guise of Eurydice, the lost lover. A mystical stage is subsequently inaugurated in *La vierge de Paris* (1944; the virgin of Paris) and *Hymne* (1947; hymn) centering on the higher, sublimated figure of the "vierge noire" (black virgin). Although the general tenor of J.'s poetry is heavily pessimistic and tormented by a pervasive intuition of failure, his later poetry, particularly *Mélodrame* (1957; melodrama) and *Moires* (1962; moirés), gives evidence of a gradual sense of serenity and resignation.

J.'s language is inextricably linked to the development of his poetry. Violence and rebellion prevail in *Noces* and *Sueur de sang*, and the style of these early collections is dry, almost antilyrical, while the thematics rely heavily on the love/death duality. J.'s mystical phase shows a certain release of tension, but his vocabulary is further restricted, displaying skillful variations on key concepts and images, such as death and darkness, silence, emptiness, and nothingness. In his last collections J. wrote with an exalted tone and frequent use of repetition.

J. experimented for some years (1925–35) with the novel and short narratives, which echo many of the themes and preoccupations of his poetry. But his prose remains "poetic" by virtue of its elliptical style and his shunning of conventional techniques of plot and characterization. *Paulina 1880* (1925; *Paulina 1880*, 1973), *Le monde désert* (1927; deserted world), and *Hécate* (1928; Hecate) explore the conflict between human and divine love, purity and guilt.

A "poet-seer" in the tradition of Baudelaire and Rimbaud, J. translated the quest for pure art into the search for an artistic creation that would be free from historical influences and cross-cultural currents by focusing on an "interior continent" revealed by the unconscious. Yet his manifold, and often disguised, references to other poets and artists constitute a dialogue with a revisionist attitude, which seeks to assert the originality of the modern poet vis-à-vis his forerunners. It is in this sense that J.'s poetry transcends the narrow labels that one may be tempted to ascribe to it to reveal the poetic conscience of a tormented age.

FURTHER WORKS: *Le paradis perdu* (1929); *Vagadu* (1931); *Histoires sanglantes* (1932); *La scène capitale* (1935); *Le Don Juan de Mozart* (1942; *Mozart's Don Juan,* 1957); *Tombeau de Baudelaire* (1942); *Aventure de Catherine Crachat* (1947; contains *Hécate* and *Vagadu*); *Diadème* (1949); *Commentaires* (1950); *Ode* (1950); *Langue* (1952); *Wozzeck; ou, Le nouvel opéra* (1953, with M. Fano); *Lyrique* (1956); *Inventions* (1958); *Proses* (1960); *Ténèbres* (1965). FURTHER VOLUME IN ENGLISH: *An Idiom of Night* (1968)

BIBLIOGRAPHY: Starobinski, J., Alexandre, P., and Eigeldinger, M., *P. J. J.: Poète et romancier* (1946); Callander, M., *The Poetry of P. J. J.* (1965); special J. issue, *NRF*, 183 (1968); special J. issue, *L'Herne*, 19 (1972); Sanzenbach, S., *Les romans de P. J. J.: Le romancier en son miroir* (1972); Brosman, C. S., "J.'s Spatial Dialectics in *Les noces* and *Sueur de sang,*" *AJFS*, 2 (1973), 164–74; Rivas, D. E., "J.'s *Mnémosyne*: An Alchemical View," *ECr*, 18 (1978), 51–61

DANIEL E. RIVAS

JOVINE, Francesco

Italian novelist, short-story writer, and journalist, b. 9 Oct. 1902, Guardialfiera; d. 30 April 1950, Rome

From a poor family in the Molise region, J. studied in provincial towns and in 1925 moved to Rome, where he graduated from the university with a degree in philosophy. A teacher by profession, he also became an active anti-Fascist and took part in the Resistance during World War II. After the war J. wrote for several leftist newspapers and periodicals and in 1948 joined the Communist Party. Although he began his literary career in the late 1920s, his finest creative achievements are concentrated in the ten years before his untimely death.

Un uomo provvisorio (1934; a temporary man), J.'s first and most autobiographical novel, is a psychological study of the alienation and moral uncertainty of a young, introspective doctor who tries to break away from his backward and stifling Molise in the 1920s. J.'s second novel, *Signora Ava* (1942; *Seeds in the Wind,* 1946), derives its title from a mythical folk figure and is set in his native town at the beginnings of the unification of Italy. Written during the war, the novel reveals a less private, more ethically and historically inspired narrative manner. Its dominant theme is the author's rediscovery of the Molise region, with overtones of social indignation becoming prominent in the second half of the book.

J.'s posthumously published and stylistically finest novel, *Le terre del Sacramento* (1950; *The Estate in Abruzzi,* 1952), marks a further shift of his narrative in the direction of a more vigorous social protest and greater political commitment. The novel's setting is again the Molise region, and the action unfolds at the time of the rise of Fascism. It is the story of a group of disenfranchised peasants who are persuaded by rich landowners to work on lands confiscated from the Church. Later, when the peasants have occupied these lands, they are driven off by force by the police and the Fascists. Their young leader, Luca Marano, killed in the final confrontation with the Fascist authorities, emerges as the hero who not only represents new social forces but also attempts to bring about historic changes. Generally considered J.'s masterpiece, *Le terre del Sacramento* made his reputation as one of the most original interpreters of postwar Italian neorealism (q.v.).

In the 1940s, J. also published four collections of short fiction. The settings and themes of these stories, which are often uneven and less satisfactory than longer works, are similar to those of the novels: the probing psychological study of the uprooted provincial intellectual; the careful depiction of southern life; the strong interest in social justice and political issues.

J.'s links with the Italian narrative tradition of the 19th c. and, more precisely, with southern realism, are both evident and natural. His fiction springs from events, usually political ones, yet it always goes beyond them to seek a universal human meaning; it springs from his public interests, yet it is at the same time highly lyric in quality. His basic mode of expression is an intensely personal blend of historical, autobiographical, and ideological elements.

FURTHER WORKS: *Il burattinaio metafisico* (1928); *Berluè* (1929); *Ragazza sola*
(1936–37); *Ladro di galline* (1940); *L'impero in provincia* (1945); *Il pastore sepolto* (1945); *Tutti i miei peccati* (1948); *Giorni che rinasceranno* (1948); *Racconti* (1960); *Viaggio nel Molise* (1967)

BIBLIOGRAPHY: Della Terza, D., "The Neorealists and the Form of the Novel," *IQ,* 10 (1966), 3–20; Moloney, B., "The Novels of F. J.," *IS,* 23 (1968), 138–55; Procaccini, A., "Neorealism: Description/Prescription," *YItS,* 2 (1977), 39–57; Pacifici, S., *The Modern Italian Novel: From Pea to Moravia* (1979), pp. 1–17

ALBERT N. MANCINI

JOYCE, James

Irish novelist, short-story writer, dramatist, poet, and essayist, b. 2 Feb. 1882, Dublin; d. 13 Jan. 1941, Zurich, Switzerland

Born on Candlemas Day, 1882, in Dublin, J. was the first-born of a solidly Catholic family. His father was a Cork gentleman, but suffered severe economic decline into genteel poverty, a condition of J.'s childhood he recorded graphically in *A Portrait of the Artist as a Young Man* (1916), as he turned every aspect of his life, his country's history, and his city's topography into literary art. His Ireland was a Catholic nation that had been under centuries of British rule, and J. is distinct in being one of the few Irish artists of his age who did not come from the ruling Anglo-Irish Protestant Ascendancy.

J.'s education was almost exclusively at the colleges of the Jesuits. He began as a boarding student at the prestigious Clongowes Wood College, but financial factors changed him into a day student at Belvedere. His university days at the Catholic University were relatively undistinguished, probably because he already considered himself intellectually superior to and in revolt against his Jesuit mentors. Their pedagogical methods exposed him to selected statements by great writers, a limitation he turned into effect: in formulating asethetic theories based on Aristotle and Aquinas; in writing short lyric poems; in collecting "epiphanies," overheard snippets of conversation or recorded dreams. His early efforts (none published in his lifetime) were multidirectional, and included an autobiographical essay, "A Portrait of the Artist" (written 1904); a contemptuous broadside, "The Holy Office" (also written 1904); vignettes for journalistic publication; book reviews; a long (but never completed) novel, *Stephen Hero* (posthumously published in 1944); and presumably two plays influenced by Henrik Ibsen.

Although J. was to abandon drama for fiction, his dedication to Ibsen, as to Aristotle, Aquinas, and Dante, was formative. At seventeen he learned Dano-Norwegian to read Ibsen; he wrote to the master and published an essay on his work, "Ibsen's New Drama," in the *Fortnightly Review* in 1900. Ibsen was both a cause and a *cause célèbre* whom he championed in a paper before the Literary and Historical Society at his university and made the subject of a virulent essay, "The Day of the Rabblement" (privately printed, as a pamphlet, 1901), in which he portrayed him as the leading spirit of European modernism, along with Gerhart Hauptmann (q.v.), and a mysterious "third" waiting in the wings. He translated at least one of Hauptmann's plays and sent his own to Ibsen's English translator for approval, yet the only extant J. drama, *Exiles* (written 1915, published 1918) was more in homage to than imitation of Ibsen.

In dedication to the lonely integrity of the artist, J. renounced both his Catholicism and Irish nationalism, and although a mild socialist generally, he abjured politics in general. In *A Portrait of the Artist as a Young Man* Stephen Dedalus denounces "nationality, language, religion," nets flung at his soul to keep it down, and chooses as his weapons "silence, exile, and cunning." J.'s apostasies were in opposition to all demands that his society made upon him: the parochial character of the Irish Literary Renaissance, the Gaelic language revival, and nationalist politics. Yet he opposed British rule and conceded the efficacy of Sinn Fein. For himself he chose exile on the Continent.

Tentative stays in Paris in 1902–3, ostensibly to study medicine, developed into permanent residence on the Continent. In 1904 he left Dublin with Nora Barnacle, his lifelong companion whom he married in 1931, returning sporadically during the early years but remaining on the Continent from 1912 until his death. His stay in Trieste, employed by Berlitz as an English teacher, came to an end with World War I, and after refuge in Zurich he lived in Paris until World War II returned him to neutral Switzerland. In Europe he felt comfortable with a literary tradition rooted in Homer and Dante, a vestige of medieval Catholicism devoid of the 19th-c. pragmatic, and

a modern spirit conducive to his own innovations. He viewed the Ireland he left as "an afterthought of Europe," a "backwash," preferring the "mainstream" of European culture.

In Trieste he gathered together his thirty-six poems as *Chamber Music*, and when they were published in 1907 in London he already had misgivings about their worth. Fragile and somewhat insubstantial (in *Ulysses* [1922] Stephen is teased about his "capful of light odes"), they are redolent of the Pre-Raphaelite tempered with a pseudo-Elizabethan precision, and probably replete with double entendres. J. later claimed that the title came from hearing the urinary tinkle in a prostitute's chamber pot, an anecdote that points to the dual character of much of J.'s work: the blending of the sacred and profane, the exalted and the mundane. At the same time he augmented his handful of vignettes, from a grouping of ten "epicleti" to the final structure of fifteen stories as *Dubliners* (1914); frustrating delays caused by publishers gave him time to add "The Dead."

Dubliners reveals J.'s ear for naturalistic detail, his sense of short fiction devoid of artificial climaxes and resolutions, his deceptively simple style of "scrupulous meanness," and his contention that in writing a "chapter in the moral history" of Ireland he views Dublin as the "centre of paralysis." The book is carefully structured: the first three stories deal with children, the next four with young adults; then there are four on mature adults and three on "public life," and the book culminates with "The Dead." The milieu is the Dublin of British Ireland; the time, at the turn of the 20th c. The characters are almost exclusively middle-class Catholics, ranging from shopgirls and unemployed ne'er-do-wells to the scion of a wealthy butcher and the survivors of a starch-mill owner, a cross-section of the bourgeoisie who populated J.'s city as he was growing up.

The Trieste years were chaotic, frustrating, intemperate, poverty-stricken, and productive. Several of J.'s siblings joined them, and two children, Giorgio and Lucia, were born. A short stint in Rome as a bank clerk ended in illness, and J. returned to Trieste, at which time he scrapped *Stephen Hero* and rewrote his quasi-autobiographical novel as the concise and modernistically lean *A Portrait of the Artist as a Young Man*. Unconnected segments of Stephen Dedalus's life, from infant impressions to his flight to Paris after leaving the university, are stitched together by a structuring principle: only those factors that contribute to his eventual choice of a vocation as "the priest of eternal imagination" are included. The technique is portraiture; the focus is on the artistic potential; the distancing perspective is on the sensitive but arrogant youth. The five-chapter structure establishes the governing rhythm of the novel as each chapter ends on a note of triumph (Stephen vindicated after an unfair caning, ecstatic in the arms of a prostitute, exalted in a cleansed state of grace, transported at the sight of his muse, determined as he prepares to depart for France), but each chapter begins again with the commonplace, the mundane, and the depressed.

The narrative stance of *A Portrait of the Artist as a Young Man* employs Stephen as the exclusive source of awareness, yet the third-person narration, although it tracks his consciousness from baby talk to intellectual articulation, remains outside Stephen's mind, an indirection of style that allowed for a degree of irony as well as empathy. The child sees himself as victim; the university student as a "hawklike man"; but the narrative never loses sight of the limitations of youth. Stephen is the total center of *A Portrait of the Artist as a Young Man*, all other characters (parents, teachers, fellow students, his beloved) exist only in relation to him as Stephen moves through the formative events of his early life. And a series of symbolic systems, consisting of birds, eyes, colors, rats, water, provide the texture of the novel, replacing the traditional fleshing out of narrated sequences that J. abandoned. From Gustave Flaubert primarily J. fashioned a style through which the artist remains "within or behind or beyond or above his handiwork," expounding in *A Portrait of the Artist as a Young Man* the credo of the artist rivaling God in creativity.

As *A Portrait of the Artist as a Young Man* established J.'s reputation, *Ulysses* brought him international acclaim and notoriety. Begun in Trieste, continued in Zurich, completed in Paris, *Ulysses* was published in that *annus mirabilis* of modernist literature, 1922, contemporary with T. S. Eliot's (q.v.) *The Waste Land*. As *A Portrait of the Artist as a Young Man* took its mythic departure from Daedalus and Icarus, *Ulysses* deployed Odysseus, Telemachus, and Penelope, in a complex assortment of parallels, parodies, and pastiches highlighting the events of a single day in Dublin on 16 June 1904. The detailed documentation of an ordinary day was considered the heights and depths of naturalism by early critics, obscene by the authorities of almost every English-speaking country, cloacal by British critics, a libel on Ireland by Irish. For over a half-century *Ulysses* has proven itself to be like the elephant for the blind men in Aesop's fable: Eliot assumed that J., like himself, was comparing the present age unfavorably with classical antiquity. Ezra Pound (q.v.), J.'s significant early champion, lost interest when he realized that Stephen was being replaced in *Ulysses* by an ordinary citizen, *un homme moyen sensuel,* a Dubliner of Hungarian Jewish ancestry.

Although *Ulysses* finds Stephen back in Ireland, disgruntled, guilt-ridden, haunted by his dead mother, teaching ineffectively in a boy's school, at loose ends trying to write a bit of poetry, formulating theories on Shakespeare, holding forth with arcane anecdotes, drinking excessively, and by the end ready to fly once again into exile, the central focus is on Leopold Bloom, whom J. specifically referred to as a "good man." An outsider in an obliquely hostile environment, disappointed at the loss of his infant son and aware of the impending infidelity of his wife, Bloom is nonetheless prudent, sober, cautious, considerate, a man of unusual equilibrium and equanimity, steering an even course through the obstacles and pitfalls of Dublin. Much has been made of the theme of surrogate fathers and sons groping toward each other, but some have discerned that J. handles it with a light and even comic touch. And at the resolution of the novel there is Molly Bloom, whose unpunctuated night thoughts reveal a complex and contradictory wellspring of womanhood, a faithful/faithless Penelope, a sacred/profane Madonna, a patient/impatient Griselda.

J. constructed his *Ulysses* as a self-generating narrative composed of eighteen chapters, each with a style of its own, the stylistic variations graduating into extremely distinctive entities during the latter portions. Variant interior monologues (q.v.) for each of the major characters (with one chapter featuring interior monologues for several minor ones as well) supplement the narrative, which is augmented by verbal intrusions, polyphonic variations, epic cataloguing, parodies of literary styles, disembodied catechisms, a temporary extrinsic narrator, and other devices that distinguish *Ulysses* as generically unclassifiable. Yet the sum of its parts indicates a tightly controlled narrative, highly mosaic and involuted, a comic, ironic, poetic masterpiece that is multifoliate and kaleidoscopic, revealing new dimensions and proportions with each rereading.

The work on *Finnegans Wake* (1939) occupied J.'s time for the next sixteen years, during difficult periods of eye operations and his daughter's mental illness, and segments of this "Work in Progress" appeared regularly in avant-garde periodicals, particularly in Eugene Jolas's *transition*. Exposing isolated fragments in this manner was essential, as was J.'s willingness to comment and explicate and his marshaling of disciples who published exegeses long before the book was published. For *Finnegans Wake* J. invented a "night language" consisting of the dozens of languages he knew overlaid on an English already embellished by Irish brogues and other dialects. Multiple voices carry the narration, overlapping with each other and running headlong through various simultaneous bits of narrative, and produce what at one instance is called a "continuous present tense integument slowly unfolded all marryvoising moodmoulded cyclewheeling history." Whereas Stephen in *Ulysses* feared history as a "nightmare from which you will never awake," *Finnegans Wake* is a multifaceted dramatization of numerous nightmares of history, wildly comic and confusing and constantly replaying itself into endless variations. One pedestrian point of departure is a music-hall ballad of a drunken hodcarrier, Tim Finnegan, killed when he fell from his ladder but revived by splashing whiskey during a brawl at his wake. A more exalted origin is in the Irish hero Finn MacCool, the buried giant in the Dublin landscape, whose resurrection would revive the Irish nation. And with all mankind postulated in numerous Finnegans, hero and hodcarrier, insect and giant, *Finnegans Wake* records universal history in a Möbius strip of past, present, and future.

Five archetypal characters suggest themself in *Finnegans Wake*: a husband/father dubbed H. C. Earwicker; a wife/mother, Anna Livia Plurabelle; twin sons, Shem/Jerry and Shaun/Kevin; and a daughter Issy. In the drama of life and the nightmare of history they play all the parts, committing sins and indiscretions, writing letters and testaments, fighting battles and healing wounds, marrying and dying, falling and rearising, living "life unlivable, transaccidentated through the slow fires of consciousness into a dividual chaos, perilous, potent, common to allflesh, human only, mortal." In contradistinction to *Ulysses*, *Finnegans Wake* is timeless, located in space in the Dublin suburb of Chapelizod that is every city and town, and its adjacent Phoenix Park that is every battlefield and every paradise garden.

Finnegans Wake was published just before World War II began, and the J. family once again prepared to take refuge in neutral exile. J. mentioned several new projects but started nothing, perhaps already aware that he was a very sick man. After only a few weeks back in Zurich, he died after an operation three weeks before his fifty-ninth birthday, having established himself in his lifetime as perhaps the most important literary innovator of the 20th c.

FURTHER WORKS: *Collected Poems* (1936); *Letters* (3 vols., 1957, 1966); *Critical Writings* (1959); *Workshop of Daedalus* (1965); *Giacomo Joyce* (1968); *J. J. Archives* (64 vols., 1979)

BIBLIOGRAPHY: Beckett, S., et al., *Our Exagmination Round His Factifaction for Incamination of Work in Progress* (1929); Gilbert, S., *J. J.'s "Ulysses"* (1930); Budgen, F., *J. J. and The Making of "Ulysses"* (1934); Levin, H., *J. J.* (1941); Campbell, J., and Robinson, H. M., *Skeleton Key to "Finnegans Wake"* (1944); Kain, R. M., *Fabulous Voyager: J. J.'s "Ulysses"* (1947); Tindall, W. Y., *J. J.* (1950); Kenner, H., *Dublin's J.* (1955); Magalaner, M., and Kain, R. M., *J.: The Man, the Work, the Reputation* (1956); Noon, W. T., *J. and Aquinas* (1957); Schutte, W. M., *J. and Shakespeare* (1957); Ellmann, R., *J. J.* (1959); Atherton, J. S., *The Books at the Wake* (1959); Litz, A. W., *The Art of J. J.* (1961); *A Wake Newslitter* (1961–); Adams, R. M., *Surface and Symbol: The Consistency of J. J.'s "Ulysses"* (1962); Hart, C., *Structure and Motif in "Finnegans Wake"* (1963); *J. J. Quarterly* (1963–); Goldberg, S. L., *Classical Temper: A Study of J. J.'s "Ulysses"* (1963); Benstock, B. J., *J.-again's Wake* (1965); Goldman, A., *The J. Paradox* (1966); Cixous, H., *L'exil de J. J.* (1968); O'Brien, D., *The Conscience of J. J.* (1968); Solomon, M., *Eternal Geomater: The Sexual Universe of "Finnegans Wake"* (1969); Hart, C., ed., *J. J.'s "Dubliners": Critical Essays* (1969); Hayman, D., *"Ulysses": The Mechanics of Meaning* (1970); Epstein, E., *The Ordeal of Stephen Dedalus* (1971); Brandabur, E., *A Scrupulous Meanness: A Study of J.'s Early Work* (1971); Ellmann, R., *Ulysses on the Liffey* (1972); Hart, C., and Hayman, D., eds., *J. J.'s "Ulysses"* (1974); Shechner, M., *J. in Nighttown* (1974); Begnal, M., and Senn, F., eds., *A Conceptual Guide to "Finnegans Wake"* (1976); McHugh, R., *The Sigla of "Finnegans Wake"* (1976); Peake, C. H., *J.*

J.: The Citizen and the Artist (1977); Benstock, B., *J. J.: The Undiscover'd Country* (1977); Kenner, H., *J.'s Voices* (1978); Boyle, R. B., *J. J.'s Pauline Vision* (1978)
BERNARD BENSTOCK

I have read several fragments of *Ulysses* in its serial form. It is a revolting record of a disgusting phase of civilisation; but it is a truthful one; and I should like to put a cordon round Dublin; round up every male person in it between the ages of 15 and 30; force them to read it; and ask them whether on reflection they could see anything amusing in all that foul mouthed, foul minded derision and obscenity. To you, possibly, it may appeal as art . . . but to me it is all hideously real: I have walked those streets and know those shops and have heard and taken part in those conversations. I escaped from them to England at the age of twenty; and forty years later have learnt from the books of Mr. J. that Dublin is still what it is, and young men are still driveling in slackjawed black-guardism just as they were in 1870. It is, however, some consolation to find that at last somebody has felt deeply enough about it to face the horror of writing it all down and using his literary genius to force people to face it. In Ireland they try to make a cat cleanly by rubbing its nose in its own filth. Mr. J. has tried the same treatment on the human subject. [1921]

George Bernard Shaw, in Sylvia Beach, *Shakespeare and Company* (1959), p. 52

The *Portrait of the Artist as a Young Man* is a book of such beauty of writing, such clarity of perception, such a serene love of and interest in life, and such charity that, being the ungenerous creature man is, one was inclined to say: "This surely must be a peak! It is unlikely that this man will climb higher!" But even now that Mr. J. has published *Ulysses*, it is too early to decide upon that. One can't arrive at one's valuation of a volume so loaded as *Ulysses* after a week of reading and two or three weeks of thought about it. Next year, or in twenty years, one may. For it is as if a new continent with new traditions had appeared, and demanded to be run through in a month. *Ulysses* contains the undiscovered mind of man; it is human consciousness analyzed as it has never before been analyzed. Certain books change the world. This, success or failure, *Ulysses* does: for no novelist with serious aims can henceforth set out upon a task of writing before he has at least formed his own private estimate as to the rightness or wrongness of the methods of the author of *Ulysses*. If it does not make an epoch—and it well may!—it will at least mark the ending of a period.

Ford Madox Ford, "A Haughty and Proud Generation," *YR*, 9 (1922), 717

To my knowledge, no writer has ever subordinated his life to his work more completely than did J. At the cost of real suffering, which I witnessed, he accepted a condition of permanent slavery, a slavery of both mind and body, that was complete. I can still see him, during one of the days that I spent with him, tortured by a word, constructing, almost rebelliously, a sort of framework; questioning his characters, turning to music for a more fictitious dream, a more vivid hallucination; and finally dropping exhausted onto a sofa, the better to hear the word about to spring shining into being. Then for an hour or more, there would be a long silence, broken only by laughter (his childlike laughter). . . .

Indeed, the reader is obliged to take this life into account. It requires genuine effort on that part of all who would approach J.'s work. But it also restores to reading the meaning and dignity which are lost when one reads most contemporary novels.

The value of this nearly forty-year-long experiment to the victorious completion of a work which constitutes one of the highest achievements in all literature cannot be sufficiently stressed. [1943]

Philippe Soupault, "Autour de J. J.," *J. J. Yearbook* (1959), 127–28

[*Finnegans Wake*] is controlled by a sharp intellect which filters every detail with great discrimination through the meshes of a Machiavellian alertness. One senses its fullness, the reverberations of the psyche as well as of history and culture even if it is impossible to follow all their implications without sharing J.'s polyhistoric and multilingual knowledge. At the frontier between a passing and a new epoch his language is composed of all languages and all the contemporary slangs in order to make understandable the present, past and future travail of the world in its variegated yet eternal recurrence. J. is the vessel of very old knowledge and very new hunches. One feels behind his work a universal wisdom from which the conscious and subconscious receive their impetus. This two-edged intelligence of J. creates the atmosphere in which the subconscious releases the poetic quality: the bleeding from a thousand wounds followed by a Homeric laughter. . . . He stood for a totality of existence, of sex and spirit, man and woman; for the universal against the specialized; for the union of intellect and emotion; for blending history with forecast, fairytale with science. . . . J. contained multitudes. And with these "multitudes" he paved the way to a related, space-time thinking on a larger scale than any writer had done before.

Laszlo Moholy-Nagy, *Vision in Motion* (1947), pp. 345–46

JAMES JOYCE

CARL GUSTAV JUNG

ERNST JÜNGER

J.'s development as a writer is characterized by a continuous and rapid movement away from paradigmatic art—the selection and recreation of a typical and powerfully symbolic unit of experience which illuminates things far beyond the bounds of its own context (that is, the technique which he called the "epiphany")—towards the all-inclusive art of *Finnegans Wake* where, instead of choosing the most typical and illuminating example of a theme, he attempted to present every conceivable trope. In his later years J. seems to have adopted as his motto Voltaire's paradox that the superfluous is a very necessary thing. Caution and literary asceticism were abandoned and the utmost richness was allowed to replace the most "scrupulous meanness." If *Finnegans Wake* can be contained within any one artistic mode, it must be the baroque; the great themes of death and resurrection, sin and redemption, are moulded into firm cyclic outlines, while masses of ornate particulars—a closely woven network of motifs and symbols—define, develop and embellish these thematic abstractions.

Clive Hart, *Structure and Motif in "Finnegans Wake"* (1962), p. 24

. . . what J. tried to do: to declare war against the national language. He said he would fight this war until the end. That is, in a way he based his work on a language that had disappeared—Gaelic. He wanted to destroy an official, imposed language—English. Doing that, he wanted to reach all language. Why did he want to achieve his own revolution by using the maximum possible number of languages? To show that the end of nationalities had been decided. And this is a political act which has a very strong impact.

Another aspect is that he wanted to reach the unconscious. So if you remain attached to one national language, in that way you remain in the preconscious. That is why great numbers of people who only speak one language are enclosed and refuse on the one side the unconscious and on the other side internationalism. J. wants to destroy nationalism, but he wants to go further than internationalism. What he is building with his book is trans-nationalism. Because the language spoken by internationalism is also that of dead languages.

What is his real political action? He is going to dismember, analyze, go through, re-articulate, annihilate, the maximum culture, ideological, historical, mythological, linguistic, and religious residues. His most important political act is the way he obstinately tried to analyze religion. If we take religion as, according to Freud, the most important neurotic phenomenon of our civilization, we have to consider that apart from J., nobody has been able to get out of the religious state. Why did he manage to do that? The reason would be that through his writing he managed to achieve sexual knowledge of our species. J. has the same am-

bition as Freud: he wants to analyze 2000 years of humanity. . . . *Finnegans Wake* is the most important anti-Fascist book written between the two World Wars, at a time when Fascism was gaining throughout Europe. What a Fascist leader does is destroyed by such writing, because it destroys all ideologies. So this book is the strongest action that has been taken against political paranoia. That's why it's both a very amusing and a very serious book.

Philippe Sollers, in Maria Jolas and Jacques Aubert, eds., *J. & Paris*, Papers from the Fifth International J. J. Symposium (1975), Vol. II, pp. 111–12

JÓZSEF, Attila

Hungarian poet and translator, b. 11 April 1905, Budapest; d. 3 Dec. 1937, Balatonszárszó

Son of a soapmaker—who abandoned his family when J. was three—and a laundress in poor health, J. spent some of his formative years with foster parents. Even when his mother was able to work, the boy helped out by doing odd jobs. In 1919 his mother died of cancer. Although J. was an excellent student, his nerves were already overstrained, and he attempted suicide. By age seventeen he was a published poet, his work appearing in the prestigious *Nyugat*.

A tragic combination of circumstances kept him from ever achieving financial or emotional stability. A clash of ideologies with a professor at the university in Szeged prevented him from attaining a degree; his poetry was published but did not put enough bread on his table; his talents and hard work did not secure him steady employment; his idealism, which made him for a while a member of the underground, illegal Communist Party, brought him nothing but trouble. When he was in love, he was unable to marry, in the beginning for financial reasons, at the end because of his deteriorating mental health. Finally, only his sisters remained; fearful of being a burden to them, he threw himself under a passing freight train. Now statues of him stand in public squares in Hungary, and streets are named after him.

His first volume, *Szépség koldusa* (1922; beauty's beggar), published with the help of Gyula Juhász (q.v.), is surprising in its maturity. J. mastered the lessons of his elders and assimilated them, but he did not imitate anyone. There are echoes of Endre Ady's (q.v.) revolutionary vision and symbolist (q.v.) techniques; but the voice is that of the young worker, using the first-person plural. The volume also shows that J. had learned from Dezső Kosztolányi's (q.v.) finely wrought, delicate wedding of substance and form.

Three years elapsed before J.'s second volume, *Nem én kiáltok* (1925; it is not I who shouts), appeared. Those years spanned the promising opening and dispirited ending of his academic career. The young man continued to study, often literally starving, at the University of Vienna, at the Sorbonne, and at the University of Budapest, but did not have the financial means to finish the preparation for a degree. While in Vienna and Paris, he formed friendships with avant-garde poets and left-wing radicals, and met his great benefactor, the patron of the arts and man of letters Lajos Hatvany (1880–1961).

J.'s most ambitious poetic undertaking dates from this time: "A kozmosz éneke" (1923; song of the cosmos) is a "sonnet ring," or *sonetti a corona*, a cycle of fourteen sonnets and a "master sonnet" composed of the first lines of the other fourteen. This virtuoso performance, written when he was just eighteen years old, is a testimony to his ability to think out and execute a complex and challenging project. The mood of the poems of this period ranges from the spirituality of "Imádság megfáradtaknak" (1924; prayer for those who are tired) to the revolutionary muscle-flexing of "És keressük az igazságot" (1924; and we are searching for justice). The title poem of *Nem én kialtok* expresses an idea that remained central to his world view: that his destiny is to become one with the whole world, but—should this prove impossible—he would fight the world's antihuman forces and try to conquer them. The contradictory instincts of self-preservation and yearning to be dissolved in a greater entity were responsible for much of the tension in his poetry. There are similar contradictions in his technique. He is simultaneously a preserver and a destroyer of poetic traditions.

The university years gave him opportunities to experiment with widely differing poetic styles. "Anyám meghalt" (1925; my mother died) and "Beteg vagyok" (1925; I am ill) are expressionistic (q.v.), "Egy átlátszó oroszlán" (1926; a transparent lion) surrealistic (q.v.). The years 1927–29 were critical for J. His health, his marriage plans, his education, his financial situation all failed; even his future as a poet seemed doubtful. After a brief flirtation with the Socialist Workers' Party in 1929 he fell in love with a Communist girl and threw himself into the cause with naïve enthusiasm.

He published a revolutionary volume with a punning title, *Döntsd a tőkét, ne siránkozz* (1931; remove the tree stump, don't whine, *or* knock down capital[ism], don't whine).

In a 1937 curriculum vitae he wrote for a job application he summed up the years 1929–37 in the single sentence:"I have supported myself with my pen ever since." Actually, the "support" was never much above starvation level, although his greatest poems were written in these final years. The volumes *Külvárosi éj* (1932; night in the outskirts), *Medvetánc* (1934; bear dance), and *Nagyon fáj* (1936; it hurts very much) show the tragic dilemma of his life: even as his poetic powers were increasing, his isolation as a man and a poet also increased. His schizophrenia is documented with clinical exactness in "Ki-be ugrál" (1936; it keeps jumping in and out) and "Kirakják a fát" (1936; they are unloading the firewood). "Thomas Mann üdvözlése" (1937; greeting Thomas Mann) may be taken as his poetic testament. There was one last, desperate attempt at happiness, immortalized in the Flóra poems, written for his last love, but when that also failed, he wrote the final tragic poems of despair and resignation.

FURTHER WORKS: *Nincsen apám, sem anyám* (1929); *J. A. összes művei* (4 vols., 1952–67); *Összes versei* (1972). FURTHER VOLUMES IN ENGLISH: *Poems* (1966); *Selected Poems and Texts* (1973); *Poems of A. J.* (1973)

BIBLIOGRAPHY: Rousselot, J., *A. J. (1905–1937)* (1958); Pődör, L., "A Portrait of A.J. the Poet," *NHQ*, No. 1 (1961), 32–44; Reményi, J., *Hungarian Writers and Literature* (1964), pp. 371–77; Klaniczay, T., et al., *History of Hungarian Literature* (1964), pp. 286–94; Lotz, J., *The Structure of the Sonetti a Corona of A. J.* (1965); Nyerges, A., Introduction to *Poems of A. J.* (1973), pp. 9–12; special J. section, *NHQ*, No. 80 (1980), pp. 46–74; Brunauer, D. H., "Parallel Lives: Edgar Allan Poe and A. J.," *Journal of Evolutionary Psychology*, 3, 1 (1982), 1–8

DALMA H. BRUNAUER

JUHÁSZ, Gyula

Hungarian poet, critic, and journalist, b. 3 April 1883, Szeged; d. 3 April 1937, Szeged

J., descended from shepherds of the Hungarian lowland, served a novitiate with the Piarists but left the teaching order before he was ordained. For some years he taught literature in secondary schools in various provincial cities. Literary critics first took notice of him when his poems appeared in 1908 in an anthology published by the Holnap Literary Society. He was also associated with the writers of the literary review *Nyugat,* a monthly publication that became the nucleus of modern Hungarian literature.

As a young teacher and poet, J. had taken little interest in domestic politics or international affairs. But the inhumanity of World War I aroused him to activism, and he became one of the leaders of the radical party (in Szeged), which called for an early end to the bloodshed. After the collapse of the Austro-Hungarian monarchy in the fall of 1918, J. became the dramatic consultant to the municipal theater of Szeged. Later, during Béla Kun's short-lived Communist regime in 1919, he worked as director of Szeged's National Theater. With the establishment of Horthy's regime, J. lost this position and could not regain a job as a teacher. He withdrew more and more from the world, lived in poverty, and on his fifty-fourth birthday committed suicide.

J. was one of the most erudite of Hungarian poets. In his early years he was strongly under the influence of the Greek and Latin classics, the French poets of the Parnassian and symbolist (q.v.) schools, and Endre Ady (q.v.), modern Hungary's preeminent poet. But he soon freed himself from all literary masters. His poetry reflects the burning conflicts in his heart and mind, the deeply felt struggles between his Christian beliefs and his pagan impulses. A critic of political Catholicism, J. extols true Christianity, which means for him unselfish and untiring efforts to obliterate social ills. In a different vein, his poems written to a woman he idolized in his youth and others addressed to a beloved patroness are deeply moving for their expression of unfulfilled cravings.

Noted literary critics contend that his best love poems are the most beautiful, moving poems of their kind in the Hungarian language. Two of his volumes, *Testamentum* (1925; testament) and *Hárfa* (1929; harp) have been particularly singled out as manifestations of J.'s sensitivity and inner need for continual probing for beauty and truth. *Hárfa* reprints some of the best poems he wrote in his youth together with poems he wrote later in life.

Underlying all of his poetry is a tone of pessimism that results from identifying his personal frustrations with the tragedies of his country.

His best poems are those in which the voice of the persona becomes that of his ancestors, singing the beauty of the Hungarian lowland and of the banks of the Tisza River with its poplars and acacia trees. J.'s identification with his cultural inheritance is expressed not only in his seven volumes of poetry, but also in his essays, short stories, and three one-act plays.

J., a major modern Hungarian poet, was a master versifier. Whether he worked within traditional prosody or in free verse, his cadences and rhymes always blended with his topics. Yet, his creative spirit, despite his broad cultural background, was limited by a rather narrow horizon. This may account for the fact that his work has not been as widely translated as it deserves to be. Only a few of his poems have been translated into English.

FURTHER WORKS: *Versek* (1907); *Szép csendesen* (1909); *Uj versek* (1914); *Késö szüret* (1918); *Ez as én vérem* (1919); *Nefelejts* (1921); *Szögedi Szinház* (1926); *Holmi* (1929); *Fiatalok, még itt vagyok!* (1935); *Örökség* (2 vols., 1958); *Összes művei* (3 vols., 1961); *J. G. összes művei* (2 vols., 1980)

BIBLIOGRAPHY: Reményi, J., *Hungarian Writers and Literature* (1964), pp. 279–83; Klaniczay, T., et al., *History of Hungarian Literature* (1964), pp. 208–9

PAUL NADANYI

JUNG, Carl Gustav

Swiss psychiatrist and psychologist, b. 26 July 1875, Kesswyl; d. 6 June 1961, Küsnacht, Zurich canton

J. was born the third child of a clergyman of the Swiss Reformed Church. The paternal grandfather after whom J. was named had been a highly successful medical doctor in Basel, a rector of the university there, and grand master of the Swiss Freemasons. As a youth this grandfather had been acquainted with German romantic poets; in the course of a full life he wrote scientific treatises, as well as plays, and he founded a home for retarded children. J.'s maternal grandfather was also a remarkable man, a theologian and Hebraist, and president of the company of pastors of the Basel church; he is said to have had visions and to have communed with spirits. J.'s father, Paul, also learned in Hebrew as well as the classical languages, married the daughter of his professor of

Hebrew and pursued the life of a modest country parson, also serving as Protestant chaplain of the Friedmatt Mental Hospital in Basel. J. grew up in the parsonage at Klein-Hüningen, then a village of peasants and fishermen, outside Basel, on the bank of the Rhine.

J. studied medicine, specializing in psychiatry, at the University of Basel and completed his studies with a dissertation, *On the Psychology and Pathology of So-Called Occult Phenomena* (*CW*, Vol. 1; *Zur Psychologie und Pathologie sogenannter okkulter Phänomene,* 1902),* based on communications of a medium. In 1900 he joined the staff of the Burghölzli Psychiatric Hospital, Zurich, and in time became assistant to its distinguished director, Eugen Bleuler. There J. engaged in extensive research with the word-association experiment (see *CW*, Vol. 2, *Experimental Researches*) and made the first thorough psychological analysis of the psychic products of schizophrenia, then called dementia praecox (see *CW*, Vol. 3, *Psychogenesis of Mental Disease*).

In 1907 J. came into contact with Sigmund Freud (q.v.), nineteen years his senior, and collaborated with him until about 1913. With *Symbols of Transformation* (*CW*, Vol. 5; *Wandlungen und Symbole der Libido,* 1912; rev. ed., *Symbole der Wandlung,* 1952), J. established an independent path; this work is crucial to the entire further development of his thought.

In 1913 J. resigned both from his associations with the psychoanalytic movement and from his position at the University of Zurich. Continuing his work with patients but publishing little for the next few years, he devoted himself to an exploration of his own psychic processes, an enterprise comparable to Freud's self-analysis. This self-exploration presents the remarkable phenomenon of a thinker steeped in the values and methods of empirical science adopting the means of the poet and the artist —he drew and painted and gave poetic expression to his fantasies—in his quest for knowl-

edge of the psyche. An important product of the same period of reflection was *Psychological Types* (*CW,* Vol. 6; *Psychologische Typen,* 1921).

J.'s psychological concerns led him to remarkably wide-ranging studies of non-European cultures, both past and present. In the early 1920s he became acquainted with such ancient Chinese texts as the *I Ching;* he traveled in Africa, visited the Pueblo Indians, and (in 1938) made a trip to India. His ethnological interests were related to his study of alchemy (the quasi-chemical, quasi-mystical quest that engaged so many fine minds in the Middle Ages), which he regarded as a matter of psychic processes. His research into alchemy is contained mainly in *Psychology and Alchemy* (*CW,* Vol. 12; *Psychologie und Alchemie,* 1944) and in *CW*, Vol. 13, *Alchemical Studies.*

In 1933 J. became president of the International Medical Society for Psychotherapy, an organization consisting of national organizations and individual members. This arrangement, created in response to Nazi pressures on the German Society for Psychotherapy, of which J. had been vice-president, served the purpose of allowing Jewish psychotherapists expelled from the German society to remain in the international organization. Later, in protest to the same pressures, J. resigned the presidency and the editorship of the society's journal.†

The writings of J.'s later years were concerned less with personal psychology than with broader issues of civilization, especially as expressed in symbols. *Aion* (*CW,* Vol. 9, Pt. 1; *Aion,* 1951), for example, is largely devoted to the symbolism of the fish in Christianity, gnosticism, and alchemy, and *Mysterium Coniunctionis* (*CW,* Vol. 14; *Mysterium Coniunctionis,* 1955–56) is "an inquiry into the separation and synthesis of psychic opposites in alchemy." But in his later years J. also effected important theoretical refinements and elaborations of earlier ideas. In his later years, too, he wrote, along with his most difficult works, the three

---

*The primary orientation of the data in this article is J.'s work in English translation. When a work is contained in the *Collected Works,* the sequence of data is as follows: title in English translation; the abbreviation *CW;* volume number of *CW;* German title; date of first publication. When a work is not contained in the *Collected Works,* the sequence of data is as follows: title in English translation; date of publication of English translation; German title; date of first publication. *The Collected Works of C. G. J.* (20 vols., 1953 ff.) is the translation of the definitive *Die gesammelten Werke von C. G. J.* (1958 ff.).

† At the close of World War II J. was criticized in some quarters for what were alleged to have been his Nazi sympathies. Indeed such criticism of J. entered literary discussion during the confused controversy concerning the award of the Bollingen Prize in Poetry to Ezra Pound (q.v.) in 1948. About this controversy and the above-mentioned allegations. see J.'s *Letters, Vol. I: 1906–1950* (1973) and A. Jaffé's *From the Life and Work of C. G. J.* (1971).

books that have been most widely read: *Answer to Job* (in *CW*, Vol. 11; *Antwort auf Hiob*, 1952); an inner biography, *Memories, Dreams, Reflections* (1961; *Erinnerungen, Träume, Gedanken von C. G. J.*, 1961); and a work of popularization, *Man and His Symbols* (1964), written with three collaborators.

In his later life J. was awarded official honors of various kinds in many parts of the world. Indeed by the beginning of the 1930s, he was secure in the fame that caused distinguished figures from all over the world to visit him as "the wise old man of Küsnacht," the town near Zurich where he lived in a magnificent house from 1906 until his death. His influence has grown steadily with the publication of his *Collected Works*.

J.'s early psychiatric work centered upon a careful description of "feeling-toned complexes," which could interfere with such conscious psychic processes as directed memory and thought; his analysis of these complexes provided empirical, and statistically verifiable, evidence for the existence of unconscious psychic processes.

Because of the towering stature of both Freud and J., the relationship between them, and their final parting, has taken on mythological dimensions in the imaginations of many readers. And, indeed, their relationship did in part conform to mythical motifs: the royal father's yearning for a crown prince, the son's rebellion against the father whom he regards as a tyrant. The history of that relationship is recorded in an extraordinary human and historical document, *The Freud-J. Letters* (1974; *Sigmund Freud und C. G. J.: Briefwechsel* 1974), which may be read as a gripping epistolary novel, and which conveys a vivid sense of the intellectual and social setting in which 20th-c. depth psychology developed. (It should be noted, however, that at the time of these letters (1906–13) Freud had already formulated his fundamental ideas, whereas J. was for the most part yet to formulate his.)

The scientific reasons for J.'s divergence from psychoanalysis were first stated in *Symbols of Transformation*, in which he moved toward a conception of libido not as sexual but as qualitatively neutral in the way that the energy of physics is neutral. In this work he developed a new conception of symbols—for example, the events of a hero's life—as transformations of that energy. While being a landmark in the development of psychological theory, the book is also passionate and personal. In his review of the version in the *Collected Works*, R. D. Scott wrote that it is "a most natural expression of life and the life force not surpassed in any other psychological work known to me. This may seem somewhat strange in view of the extreme difficulty the material often presents to . . . intellectual comprehension. . . . It was as J. says . . . 'a landslide that cannot be stopped . . . the explosion of all those psychic contents which could find no room, no breathing space, in the constricting atmosphere of Freudian psychology and its narrow outlook.' It was a landslide which launched him upon the course of his own development into 'the second half of life,' and which led to his own unique contribution to the understanding of the psyche. . . . It contains the emotional force of this eruption. . . . What gives shape and expression to this force is above all poetry, of which the book is full, in the form both of quotations and of the author's expression in the text. The poetic vehicle of feeling is not just a decoration, it is absolutely essential to the finding of one's way among these images. The work is also an intellectual *tour de force* of a very considerable caliber, as witnessed by the extraordinary amount of mythological material put into it, and the extensive research this must have required." (*The Journal of Analytical Psychology*, 2, 2).

Indeed, *Symbols of Transformation* contains a lengthy discussion of Longfellow's *Hiawatha*, which is regarded as a poetic compilation of mythical motifs, including those of the dual mother and dual birth, and of death and rebirth in the form of the sun-hero's battle with a sea monster. Some of J.'s other literary examples in the same work have the effect of suddenly opening vistas. Thus, one discovers Hölderlin and Goethe, for example, thinking in accordance with highly archaic thought forms, such as that in which the sound of speech is associated with the fire of the sun.

Such forms, which J. first called primordial images, or dominants, and later archetypes, express inherited psychic dispositions (as distinct from inherited ideas) to experience the world in certain ways. These forms find their clearest expression in mythology and religion, but they also arise spontaneously in the dreams and fantasies of individuals, and they provide basic themes of art and literature. The archetypes are the structural forms of the collective unconscious, which J. distinguished from the personal unconscious, largely made up of repressed and forgotten psychic material. The more important archetypes include those of the shadow, consisting of contents of the personal unconscious and their personifications, of the anima and animus, or the contrasexual psychic components of the masculine and feminine personalities. They also include the self, which is at the same time the deepest center of the personality, its totality (including consciousness and the unconscious), and its ultimate ordering principle. The self is thus supraordinate to the ego, which is the center of the field of consciousness. The realization of the self—that is, compliance with its demands and the establishment of a harmony between it and the ego—is the chief goal of the process of individuation, which became one of the main subjects of J.'s psychological interest.

By individuation J. meant, negatively, the dissolution of one's identification with internalized parental images and with social roles; he meant, positively, the differentiation and development of the individual personality in its uniqueness but also in its relation to the collective psychic facts of the archetypes. Since the urge to individuation makes itself felt most strongly in the second half of life, J.'s concern with it complements the emphasis of most other forms of depth psychology upon the first half of life and especially on psychic development in infancy and adolescence. These basic ideas of J. are most clearly and succinctly presented in *Two Essays on Analytical Psychology* (*CW*, Vol. 7; *Über die Psychologie des Unbewußten*, 1917; rev. eds., 1926, 1943, and *Die Beziehungen zwischen dem Ich und dem Unbewußten*, 1928).

In later years J. effected important theoretical refinements and elaborations of ideas first adumbrated in *Symbols of Transformation*, for example, establishing an analogy between the archetype and the biological pattern of behavior; coming to see the archetype as "psychoid," occupying an indeterminate status between spirit and matter, and supplementing the customary notions of causality with that of synchronicity, or the meaningful coincidence of causally unrelated events (see *CW*, Vol. 8, *Structure and Dynamics of the Psyche*, and Vol. 9, Pt. 1, *Archetypes and the Collective Unconscious*). And two works of J.'s last years, *Answer to Job*, and *Memories, Dreams, Reflections*, mark an essentially confessional return to the concerns of his self-exploration.

In *Psychological Types* there is an extensive discussion of Schiller's *On the Aesthetic Education of Man*, which J. regarded as a forerunner of his own attempt to create a psychological typology. (J.'s typology describes two main psychological attitudes, those of extroversion, a positive relation to objects, and introversion, a positive relation to inner psychic processes. These terms have entered everyday speech, and

the concepts named by them have been used in literary criticism, as, more rarely, have J.'s concepts of the four main functions of consciousness, thinking, feeling, sensation, and intuition.)

In the same work J. also treated the Swiss author Carl Spitteler (1845–1924); Nietzsche, Dante, Hölderlin, and other writers also figure in his description of attitudes and functions, of the progression and regression of libido, and of symbol formation. He also used their works to illustrate his conception of psychic life as being rooted in history, and of history as having an important psychic aspect, which is illuminated by his psychological concepts. Historical periods, for example, display the principles of compensation, of symbol formation, of the differentiation of psychic functions, that he has examined in individual writers. Hence, he regards Schiller's views on poetry, for example, in light of the remnant of archaic man in the modern European, and of psychic trends at the time of the French Revolution.

J. was fascinated by Nietzsche, and J.'s most searching study of a work of literature was presented in a series of seminars (in English) on the "Psychological Analysis of Nietzsche's *Zarathustra*," in the years 1934 through 1939. In these seminars J. analyzed Nietzsche's book as though it were a vision describing a process of initiation, the characters representing part-personalities, based on archetypes, principally those of the wise old man and the self. J. "amplified" every symbolic detail in the text, bringing it into relation with parallel material from myth, legend, folklore, and literature. Showing his astonishing erudition and his imaginative grasp of great sweeps of history, J. viewed *Thus Spake Zarathustra* in the context of late 19th-c. rationalism, positivism, and materialism, and in the larger context of the Christian era, which he in turn regarded as a historical movement formed in compensation to cultural currents that had preceded it. He also viewed *Thus Spake Zarathustra* in light of the development of other cultures. And since it recorded a countermovement to dominant philosophical trends of Nietzsche's time, J. also regarded Nietzsche's book as an attempt to supply the collective consciousness of Nietzsche's time with psychic contents that would balance its one-sidedness.

Apart from the works already mentioned, J.'s writings about literature are confined to three essays (in *CW*, Vol. 15). The volume in which they appear is entitled *The Spirit in Man, Art, and Literature*, which suggests its highly miscellaneous character; and it is, significantly, the slenderest volume in the series. That is to say, J. was in no sense a literary critic, and he only rarely dealt with literature except in connection with larger and basically nonliterary issues. One of these essays, "*Ulysses*: A Monologue" ("*Ulysses*," 1934), is an attempt to come to terms with Joyce's (q.v.) *Ulysses* by seeing it as symptomatic of the spiritual condition of modern man, especially the brutalization of his feeling. Admirers of Joyce's book must feel that J. partly missed an important point, which is that it records a descent into the depths of the unconscious of a kind to which J. elsewhere gave much sympathetic attention. (J., incidentally, had been consulted concerning Joyce's psychotic daughter, Lucia, and had given Joyce unwelcome advice concerning the closeness of his relationship with her).

In another of these essays, "On the Relation of Analytical Psychology to Poetry" ("Über die Beziehungen der analytischen Psychologie zum dichterischen Kuntswerk," 1922), J. insists that a work of art must not be analyzed reductively, since "it is a creative reorganization of those very conditions to which a causalistic psychology must always reduce it." In the same essay he makes a distinction between literary works, on the one hand, that accord with the conscious intentions of their authors and that draw upon materials of the personal unconscious, and those "visionary" works, on the other hand, that are direct outpourings of the collective unconscious. As to the much-debated question of the relation of art to neurosis, J. claimed that "the artists's relative lack of adaptation . . . enables him to follow his own yearnings far from the beaten path, and to discover what it is that would meet the unconscious needs of his age. Thus, just as the one-sidedness of the individual's conscious attitude is corrected by reactions from the unconscious, so art represents a process of self regulation in the life of nations and epochs." He further explores the relationship of psychology and literature in "Psychology and Literature" ("Psychologie und Dichtung," 1950). As J.'s emphasis on the visionary suggests, his utterances about art and literature are often very much in the spirit of German romanticism, although such statements often express a very different attitude, one preoccupied with a fear of "aestheticism."

Despite the paucity of J.'s writings about literature as literature, his psychology as a whole does imply an attitude toward literature that can be summarized by means of a few characterizing attributes.

First, J. called attention to the archaic elements in literature, elements also to be found in mythology. These are ultimately psychic, in that they originate in dreams, fantasies, visions, and delusional ideas.

Second, in keeping with J.'s emphasis on the value of introversion, works of literature, like dreams and fantasy, are to be interpreted not only with reference to outer reality but also on the "subjective level," on which the persons and situations represented "refer to subjective factors entirely belonging to the subject's own psyche." "Interpretation on the subjective level allows us to take a broader psychological view not only of dreams but also of literary works, in which the individual figures then appear as representatives of relatively autonomous functional complexes in the psyche of the author (*CW*, Vol. 6, *Psychological Types*, pp. 472–73).

Moreover, the subjective level can also apply to literary response, since the work touches complexes and archetypes in the reader. Thus, such common literary motifs as birth, the fight with the dragon, incest, and marriage, may be conceived as representing intrapsychic processes rather than, or in addition to, events between the subject and the object. In this view, birth may, for example, represent the separation of subject and object, the birth of the ego as the center of the field of consciousness. Incest may represent the reunion of the subject with its own unconscious ground, a retrogression of libido, activating unconscious contents, which may then be brought to consciousness. And marriage may be seen under the aspect of the *hieros gamos*, the sacred marriage, symbolic of the unification of isolated parts of the personality and the resolution of what J. called the problem of the opposites, including, for example, those of the ego and the shadow. Equally, literary works are often concerned with the process of individuation, which they present in projected form.

Third, literature is to be viewed in the context of history, which reflects the vicissitudinous development of consciousness, both collective and individual. The role of the literary work in this development is compensatory, reviving contact with those unconscious forces that are needed for a balanced conscious viewpoint. Literature, like dreams, can be regarded prospectively as well as reductively, that is, with respect to antecedent causes.

To these points a fourth must be added: literary works are often merely "aesthetic." This deserves separate mention because there was in J.'s attitude toward literature an odd ambivalence—it sometimes seems a deliberate, even blustering philistinism—that is important to understand. For J., aestheticism "is not fitted to solve the serious and exceedingly difficult task of educating man, for it always presupposes the very thing that it should create—the capacity to love beauty. It actually hinders a deeper investigation . . . because it always averts its face from anything evil, ugly, and difficult, and aims at pleasure, even though it be of an edifying kind" (*CW*, Vol. 6, p. 121).

One might then expect J. to have been sympathetic toward 20th-c. art and literature, much of which is not aesthetic in this sense, but when he talked about such works, he almost always did so in a way that expresses scorn toward them—precisely for being evil, ugly, and difficult. Visionary literature is safely above the accusation of aestheticism, and naïve and trivial literature is safely beneath it. Thus, he often talked at length about H. Rider Haggard's (1856–1925) *She* as an embodiment of the anima, and he admitted: "Indeed, literary products of highly dubious merit are often of the greatest interest to the psychologist" (*CW*, Vol. 15, pp. 87–88).

J.'s distrust of aestheticism and admiration for the visionary colored his judgment of literary works when he did try to judge them. Thus, for example, he claimed that Spitteler's *Prometheus and Epimetheus* has greater truth than Goethe's *Faust* and Nietzsche's *Thus Spake Zarathustra*, although the latter are more satisfying aesthetically. Indeed, in *Psychological Types* he speaks of Nietzsche's "aesthetic defenses" against the true content of his vision.

This ambivalence is illuminated by a passage in a letter (of 28 February 1932) in which, reversing the judgment of *Faust* just given, J. says that it "is the most recent pillar in that bridge of the spirit which spans the morass of world history, beginning with the Gilgamesh epic, the *I Ching*, the Upanishads, the Tao-te-Ching, the fragments of Heraclitus, and continuing in the Gospel of St. John, the letters of St. Paul, in Meister Eckhart and in Dante." In other words, for J. truth was scientific, and it was religious; and despite his own artistic works in drawing, painting, poetry, and sculpture, with part of himself he belonged to the ancient tradition that regarded art as idolatrous, an "aesthetic defense" against the primacy of a certain kind of religious experience.

J.'s views have inspired some notable works of literary criticism, written from a specifically Jungian viewpoint, including Maud Bodkin's *Archetypal Patterns in Poetry* (1934) and Christine Gallant's *Blake and the Assimilation of Chaos* (1978). His influence is indirectly present in a great many works that can be brought under the headings of "myth criticism" and "archetypal criticism." Indeed, J. is the single source of "archetype" as a critical term important to various recent critics, especially Northrop Frye (q.v.), although such critics often do not accept unreservedly J.'s concept of the collective unconscious. Hermann Hesse's (q.v.) stories and novels reflect his experience in Jungian analysis—see the letters between J. and Hesse in J.'s *Letters, Vol. 1: 1906–1950* (1973). (*Vol. 2: 1951–1961* was published in 1975.) Such experience is also directly the subject of a novel, *The Manticore* (1972), by the Canadian writer Robertson Davies (b. 1913).

J.'s influence on literature and on the *Zeitgeist*, including the climate of literary opinion, is more indirect than direct, and that influence is, for various reasons, difficult to isolate, label, and measure. The first is the extreme difficulty of many of J.'s works owing to the complexity of his thought and to the fact that he dealt with such little-known subjects as gnosticism and alchemy. Thus, people may be moved and intellectually stimulated by J.'s writings, without being certain that they have understood them. The second is the currently modest position of J.'s analytical psychology among competing scientific paradigms. The third is that J. was in many ways genuinely prophetic, so that some of his ideas came to have their impact fifty or more years after he first published them, thus obscuring the question of whether late variants of those ideas derive directly from J. or are independent attempts to answer needs that he had foreseen. Thus, many current psychologists, without crediting J. as their source, are concerned with "self-realization," which is essentially J.'s "individuation," fully described several decades earlier. And fourth, J. created his psychology at a time when writers of literature shared some of his interests, and often the similarities between him and them are based on indirect causes rather than being the result of direct influence. Thus, the similarities between the concerns and even the specific ideas of J. and William Butler Yeats (q.v.) are astonishing, yet neither directly influenced the development of the other's thought. And J. was engaging in his mythological researches at a period when a great many writers, including Thomas Mann, Hermann Broch, and T. S. Eliot (qq.v.), were concerned with mythological themes. But Eliot, for example, claimed during the Bollingen Prize controversy never to have read J., and J., in a letter at about the same time (1948), admitted that he had never heard of Eliot.

J. has a remarkably wide readership among people whose interest is more in literature than in psychology, and ironically, they read him in part for precisely the reasons that put him so on guard against the dangers of "aestheticism" in literature. The title of a collection of J.'s essays in translation, *Modern Man in Search of a Soul* (1933), helps to explain this.

Modern man lacks a soul in a real and definite sense. Earlier, people assumed that they had souls, souls that were subject to various perils. For most of us, "soul" is a word signifying something we would like to have but fear we lack, or an intellectual hypothetical entity; or a poetic image. For J., on the other hand, the existence of the soul was an absolute, unshakable certainty, not the creation of an act of faith. At the same time he maintained an unswerving allegiance, which he proclaimed again and again, to the values of empirical science. Thus, one of the dilemmas afflicting writers and readers of literature for far more than a century —the dilemma created by the split between the objective world and our less substantial, subjective selves, which make themselves known murkily in our anxieties and neuroses—was for J. resolved from the very outset of his mature work. For him the psyche was objective; and a psychic fact, such as that of a fantasy, was as real as any fact concerning, say, a piece of wood or steel. Moreover, for J. the psyche was of enormous richness, betraying a complex history and marvelous subtleties of organization. In recreating a sense of wonder concerning the psyche, in elaborating a phenomenology of its imaginative forms, in showing the complex life of those forms in the great currents of history, J. has helped modern man to know that he has a soul and to find nourishment for it.

BIBLIOGRAPHY: Martin, P. W., *Experiment in Depth: A Study of the Work of J., Eliot, and Toynbee* (1955); Neumann, E., *Amor and Psyche* (1956); Jacobi, J., *Complex, Archetype, Symbol in the Psychology of C. G. J.* (1957); Neumann, E., *The Archetypal World of Henry Moore* (1959); Neumann, E., *Art and the Creative Unconscious* (1959); Bennett, E. A., *C. G. J.* (1961); Fordham, M., ed., *Contact with J.: Essays on the Influence of His Work and Personality* (1964); Jaffé, A., *The Myth of Meaning in the Work of C. G. J.* (1967); Jaffé, A., *From the Life and Work of C. G. J.* (1968); Serrano, N., *C. G. J. and Hermann Hesse: A Record of Two Friendships* (1968); Ellenberger, H. F., *The Discovery of the Unconscious* (1970); Neumann, E., *The Great Mother: An Analysis of the Archetype* (1972); Storr, A., *C. G. J.* (1973); McGuire, W., and Hull, R. F., eds., *C. G. J. Speaking: Interviews and Encounters* (1977); Vincie, J. F. and M., *C. G. J. and Analytical Psychology: A Comprehensive Bibliography* (1977); Brome, V., *J.: Man and Myth* (1978); Edinger, E. F., *Melville's "Moby-Dick": A Jungian Commentary* (1978); Gallant, C., *Blake and the Assimilation of Chaos* (1978); Brivic, S. R., *Joyce between Freud and J.* (1979); Homans, P., *J. in Context: Modernity and the Making of a Psychology* (1979); Jaffé, A., ed., *C. G. J.: Word and Image* (1979); O'Neill, T. R., *The Individuated Hobbit: J., Tolkien, and the Archetypes of Middle-Earth* (1979); Olney, J., *The Rhizome and the Flower: The Perennial Philosophy of Yeats and J.* (1980)

                                    WILLIAM WILLEFORD

See also Psychology and Literature

JÜNGER, Ernst

German novelist and essayist, b. 29 March 1895, Heidelberg

Even as a boy, J. was at odds with middle-class life and, generally, with the age into which he was born. He joined the rebellious youth movement, than ran away to serve briefly in the French Foreign Legion—see his *Afrikanische Spiele* (1936; *African Diversions,* 1956). In 1914 he enlisted in the army and distinguished himself at the western front. From 1919 to 1923 he served in the army of the Weimar Republic.

J. began his career as a writer by setting down his unusual war experiences. *In Stahlgewittern* (1920; *Storm of Steel,* 1929) recounts the heroic exploits of an infantry soldier and a leader of assault troops; it is also a statement of J.'s conviction that World War I was but the first encounter in a planetary conflict of ever-increasing violence. J. further expounded and explored his war experiences in *Der Kampf als inneres Erlebnis* (1922; fighting as an inner experience), *Das Wäldchen 125* (1925; *Copse 125,* 1930), and *Feuer und Blut* (1925; fire and blood).

From 1923 to 1925 J. studied philosophy and zoology at the University of Leipzig. Although he did not finish his studies, he developed an abiding and productive interest in entomology, as is seen in *Subtile Jagden* (1967;

delicate pursuits). After moving to Berlin in 1927, J. became active in radically nationalistic organizations, serving their journals as contributor and editor. During that time he developed his political philosophy, which he designated as *heroischer Realismus* and which may be characterized as "militant nihilism" or "aggressive totalitarianism." Convinced that the world was engulfed in a fundamental crisis, the ideas and ideals of democratic humanism having lost their cohesive force and motivating power, and that the ultimate struggle for power and world domination was imminent, he called for "total mobilization" in *Die totale Mobilmachung* (1930; total mobilization). In *Der Arbeiter* (1932; the worker) J. describes the emergence of a new type of man who, by virtue of his technical skill and military prowess, is destined to conquer and reorganize a chaotic, strife-torn world. *Der Arbeiter* is J.'s most significant political treatise; it is the only radical, honest, and comprehensive exposition of totalitarianism written in Germany.

Yet J. disdained the Hitler regime; its policies, he felt, could only lead to ultimate disaster. He expressed his misgivings in the novel *Auf den Marmorklippen* (1939; *On the Marble Cliffs,* 1947), a thinly veiled allegory of the heinous practices of totalitarianism (although veiled enough to get by the censor); the book also reaffirms the ideals and values of the humanistic tradition. It thus exemplifies the work of the "inner emigration," of those who were opposed to the Hitler regime but did not go into exile.

At the outbreak of World War II J. was called back into the army. This time around he saw no action, serving with the forces of occupation and as staff officer with the commander-in-chief of occupied France. *Strahlungen* (1942 ff.; radiations) is his diary of the war and the occupation years in Germany until 1948. J. keenly observed the course of the war, never in doubt about its outcome. He had close contact with some of those officers who militantly opposed the regime. *Der Friede* (written 1943, pub. 1947; *The Peace,* 1948), while recognizing Germany's responsibility and guilt, is a plea for a constructive and enduring peace. This pamphlet marks the end of J.'s involvement in politics. He withdrew to the countryside; since 1950 he has lived in Wilflingen, a small village in southern West Germany.

After the war, J. was for a time forbidden to publish in Germany because of his erstwhile identification with the Nazi regime (he could and did publish in the Netherlands and Switzer-

land, however). *Heliopolis* (1949; Heliopolis) is an antiutopian novel dealing with the unresolved conflict between liberty and tyranny, between the humanistic tradition and nihilism. *Heliopolis* is also significant as a comprehensive recapitulation of the author's ideas as they had evolved in the course of thirty years.

Although J. continued to write novels—among them *Gläserne Bienen* (1957; *The Glass Bees,* 1961), science fiction with strong political overtones; *Die Zwille* (1973; the slingshot), primarily an account of the author's boyhood); and *Eumeswil* (1977; Eumeswil), a fantasy of the future—he preferred the genres of the essay and the travel book.

J.'s essays are significant for two reasons: they exhibit wide-ranging concerns, and their style is exemplary. An early but outstanding attempt at nonfiction prose was *Das abenteuerliche Herz* (1929; rev. ed., 1936; the adventurous heart), concise accounts of adventures of the mind and the imagination. *Sgraffiti* (1960; sgraffiti) is its companion volume. The essays of the early 1950s probe issues of nihilism and existentialism (q.v.): *Über die Linie* (1950; crossing the line), *Der Waldgang* (1951; withdrawing to the woods), and *Der gordische Knoten* (1953; the Gordian knot). *Das Sanduhrbuch* (1954; the book about the hourglass) ponders the problem of time; it is one of J.'s most engaging and convincing accomplishments.

Some of J.'s essays are highly speculative. In *An der Zeitmauer* (1959; at the wall of time) he tries to show that mankind, and, indeed, the cosmos are about to enter upon a new age. Political prospects are the theme of *Der Weltstaat* (1960; the world state). Opposing the widely held belief that the conflict between East and West is irreconcilable, J. holds that the adversaries are the unwitting agents of historical forces aiming at the ultimately constructive reorganization of the planet. This essay complements *Der Arbeiter* as well as *Der Friede.*

Annäherungen (1970; approaches) is J.'s longest and, in many ways, most provocative essay. Actually, it is a collection of essays dealing with drugs—his own experiments supplemented by literary references (De Quincey, Baudelaire, Aldous Huxley [q.v.], and others). In the early 1920s J. used ether, cocaine, and hashish; thirty years later he turned to mescaline, ololuqui, and LSD. His reasons were threefold: to indulge his propensity for adventure, to gain new and deeper metaphysical insights, and to open vistas into what he felt to be a new cosmic age. No book deals as comprehensively and probingly with drugs and drug-taking as does *Annäherungen*.

J. traveled widely and made good use of his experiences. His observations are keen, his perceptions clear. He disdained what he calls "psychological digestive processes"; instead, he recorded what the senses perceive and the mind suggests. J.'s travel books are also stylistically of a high order. They include *Dalmatinischer Aufenthalt* (1934; sojourn in Dalmatia); *Myrdun* (1943; Myrdun), about Norway; *Atlantische Fahrt* (1947; Atlantic voyage), about Brazil and Morocco; *Am Sarazenenturm* (1955; at the Saracen tower), about Sardinia; and *Zwei Inseln: Ceylon und Formosa* (1968; two islands: Ceylon and Formosa).

FURTHER WORKS: *Blätter und Steine* (1934); *Sprache und Körperbau* (1947); *Ein Inselfrühling* (1948); *Besuch auf Godenholm* (1952); *Rivarol* (1956); *Serpentara* (1957); *San Pietro* (1957); *Jahre der Okkupation* (1958); *Ein Vormittag in Antibes* (1960); *Werke* (10 vols., 1961–65;); *Das spanische Mondhorn* (1963); *Typus, Name und Gestalt* (1963); *Sturm* (1963); *Geheimnisse der Sprache* (1963); *Grenzgänge* (1966); *Im Granit* (1967); *Lettern und Ideogramme* (1970); *Ad hoc* (1970); *Zahlen und Götter* (1974); *Sämtliche Werke* (18 vols., 1979 ff.); *Paul Léautaud in memoriam* (1980); *Siebzig Verweht* (1980)

BIBLIOGRAPHY: Brock, E., *Das Weltbild E. J.s* (1945); Martin, A. von, *Der heroische Nihilismus und seine Überwindung: E. J.s Weg durch die Krise* (1948); Stern, J. P., *E. J.: A Writer of Our Times* (1953); Mohler, A., ed., *Die Schleife: Dokumente zu . . . E. J.* (1955); Loose, G., *E. J.: Gestalt und Werk* (1957); Paetel, K. O., *E. J. in Selbstzeugnissen und Bilddokumenten* (1962); Schwarz, H. P., *Der konservative Anarchist: Politik and Zeitkritik E. J.s* (1962); Kranz, G., *E. J.s symbolische Weltschau* (1968); Des Coudres, H. P., *Bibliographie der Werke E. J.s* (1970); Loose, G., *E. J.* (1974); Katzmann, V., *E. J.s magischer Realismus* (1975)

GERHARD LOOSE

KABARDIAN LITERATURE
See North Caucasian Literatures

KADEN-BANDROWSKI, Juliusz
Polish novelist and short-story writer, b. 24 Feb. 1885, Rzeszów; d. 8 Aug. 1944, Warsaw

Born to a family of artists and intellectuals, K.-B. initially intended to become a musician; however, because his arm was broken twice in his early childhood, he abandoned these plans and instead turned his attention to literature. Shortly after graduating from secondary school, K.-B. was on his way to the Caucasus, from where he went to Germany and Belgium to study music history and theory. From abroad K.-B. sent accounts of cultural life in the West to Polish newspapers. He returned to Poland in 1913, and when World War I broke out he fought against Russia with the Polish Legion organized by Józef Piłsudski, the leader of the Polish independence movement. Thenceforth, both the literary and the political careers of K.-B. were closely tied to the ideology of Piłsudski.

K.-B.'s first novel, *Niezguła* (1911; dull-witted person) rejected revolutionary ideology as a means of solving social conflicts and questioned the validity of the symbolist (q.v.) movement, which dominated the Polish literary scene before World War I. Although his early fiction reveals some stylistic affinities to symbolism, K.-B. broke with its essential aesthetic premises: the cult of individual "I," and the belief in the existence of an ideal world of beauty. In his early fiction K.-B. tried to show plain reality, without any embellishment, ugly and devoid of idealism.

During World War I K.-B.'s writings were almost entirely devoted to the struggle of the Polish Legion. One of the most interesting accounts of this period is the novel *Łuk* (1917; the bow), in which he describes the disintegration of traditional social and moral values, psychological perversion, and the decline of human integrity caused by the war. After the war K.-B. participated in numerous cultural and political activities and was one of the founders of the Polish Academy of Literature.

Still, writing remained his greatest passion. In the early 1920s he published a number of prose works devoted to his childhood, but fame came only with the publication of the political trilogy consisting of *Generał Barcz* (1923; General Barcz), *Czarne skrzydła* (2 vols., 1928–29; black wings), and *Mateusz Bigda* (1933; Mateusz Bigda), written in an expressionistic (q.v.) style. K.-B. was often called the official writer of the new, independent Poland, but his relationship with the state was complex and far from unequivocal. On the one hand, he mocked revolutionary rhetoric and held the parliamentary system in contempt; on the other, he did expose and criticize the weaknesses of the political system established in Poland after Piłsudski's coup d'état of 1926. The trilogy contains a clear message: if you want to save the country, rid yourself of corruption, political dishonesty, and demoralization.

Compelled to go into hiding during World War II, K.-B. continued to write. Unfortunately, almost all his manuscripts from this period have been lost. He died of a wound inflicted by a German shell during the Warsaw uprising.

FURTHER WORKS: *Zawody* (1911); *Proch* (1913); *Zbytki* (1914); *Bitwa pod Konarami* (1915); *Iskry* (1915); *Piłsudczycy* (1915); *Mogiły* (1916); *Spotkanie* (1916); *Wyprawa wileńska* (1919); *Wiosna* (1920); *Podpułkownik Lis-Kula* (1920); *Rubikon* (1921); *Przymierze serc* (1924); *Wakacje moich dzieci* (1924); *Miasto mojej matki* (1925); *W cieniu zapomnianej olszyny* (1926; *Call to the Cuckoo*, 1948); *Europa zbiera siano* (1927); *Nad brzegiem wielkiej rzeki* (1927); *Rzymianie wschodu* (1928); *Na progu* (1928); *Stefan Żeromski, prorok niepodległości* (1930); *Pióro, miłość i kobieta* (1931); *Za stołem i na rynku* (1932); *Aciaki z 1A* (1932); *Pod Belwederem* (1936); *Droga wolności* (1936); *Wspomnienia i nadzieje* (1938); *Życie Chopina* (1938)

BIBLIOGRAPHY: Kridl, M., *A Survey of Polish Literature and Culture* (1956), p. 501; Krejči, K., *Geschichte der polnischen Literatur* (1958), pp. 489–91; Miłosz, C., *The History of Polish Literature* (1969), pp. 425–26; Krzyżanowski, J., *A History of Polish Literature* (1978), pp. 615–20

EDWARD MOŻEJKO

KAFFKA, Margit

Hungarian novelist, short-story writer, and poet, b. 10 June 1880, Nagykároly; d. 1 Dec. 1918, Budapest

On her mother's side, K. was descended from generations of by then impoverished Hungarian gentry. Her father, a lawyer, died when she was six. She completed her schooling and obtained a teaching certificate, and then earned a higher degree in 1902. For fifteen years she taught school in Miskolc and Budapest. Her poems began to appear in *Magyar géniusz* in 1901, and she began to publish fiction in 1905. She was a contributor to the avant-garde journal *Nyugat* from its founding in 1908. She was married twice. In 1915 K. gave up teaching to devote all her time to writing. Both she and her only son died in the influenza epidemic just as World War I ended.

K., the most outstanding Hungarian woman novelist of the early 20th c., first attracted notice with a spirited essay and some traditional verse. She soon broke with traditional subjects and modes of expression, however. Her contributions to *Nyugat*—daring experiments in free verse and short fiction—outraged conventional sensibilities. She wrote memorable poems about the war, about social injustice, about her own struggles to juggle the duties of a teacher and a mother with those of a writer; she also wrote some of the finest love poems in Hungarian literature (to her second husband).

Her first short-story collection, *A gondolkodók, és egyéb elbeszélések* (1906; the thinkers, and other short stories), is skeptical and disillusioned. The "thinkers" of the title story await their own inevitable disillusionment with cynical detachment. Her other notable collections are *Csendes válságok* (1910; quiet crises), *Csonka regény és novellák* (1911; unfinished novel and short stories), *Süppedő talajon* (1912; on sinking ground), and *Szent Ildefonso bálja* ((1914; the ball of St. Ildefonso). With few exceptions, these are stories of two types of women: those who are re-

pressed and those who manage to break out of their bondage. Eventually most of her stories about women were republished in two volumes with the revealing title *Lázadó asszonyok* (1958; women in rebellion).

In longer fiction, she and Zsigmond Móricz (q.v.) represented the breaking-away from 19th-c. models. Móricz received K.'s epoch-making novel *Szinek és évek* (1912; colors and years) with the enthusiasm of a brother and comrade-in-arms. He declared, "A critic of society can draw many more conclusions from it about the workings of society than from life itself." It combines acute insights into the country's changing social structure with authentic psychological portrayals; its daringly innovative, impressionistic style is ideally suited to the topic. The heroine, Madga Pórtelky (modeled after K.'s mother), develops from a callow provincial girl to an enlightened, disillusioned, tough, yet serene woman. Twice widowed, the mother of four, Magda looks with satisfaction at the promise of a new life that is opening for her daughters. K.'s technique involves daring leaps in the plot, which force the reader to assess the nature of each new situation instantly. Magda's development is seen against the backdrop of her class, the provincial gentry, which sinks into oblivion as she rises spiritually.

K.'s next novel, *Mária évei* (1913; Maria's years), is in a sense the antithesis of *Szinek és évek*: Maria, a first-generation career woman, is unable to make a satisfactory adjustment to modern life and is destroyed. By contrast, Éva Rosztoky, in *Állomások* (1917; stations), the novel that followed, succeeds and becomes her own person.

During World War I, K. wrote two pacifist works: the long story "Lírai jegyzetek egy évről" (1915; lyric notes about one year) and the novel *Két nyár* (1917; two summers).

Hangyaboly (1917; ant colony), her last novel, plumbs the depths of myth and archetype in showing the maturing process of a few young women during their senior year in a convent school. At the time of its publication it attracted attention—both favorable and unfavorable—because of its strident anticlerical overtones; today it can be admired for its ripe imagery and its skillful portrayal of the kinds of career choices confronting young women in the early years of the century.

K. is the most significant woman writer of Hungary. Other women of the period either reveled in their dainty femininity or denied it. K.

was able to raise the problems confronting women to the level of the universally human, combining the stories of individual women with the history of the disintegrating Hungarian gentry.

FURTHER WORKS: *Versek* (1903); *Levelek a zárdából* (1904); *Nyár* (1905); *Könyve* (1906); *Képzelet-királyfiak* (1909); *Tallózó évek* (1911); *Utólszor a lyrán* (1913); *Az élet útján* (1917); *Kis emberek, barátocskáim* (1918); *A révnél* (1918); *K. M. összes versei* (1961); *K. M. regényei* (1968)

BIBLIOGRAPHY: Reményi, J., *Hungarian Writers and Literature* (1965), pp. 284–91; Brunauer, D. H., "A Woman's Self-Liberation: The Story of M. K. (1880–1918)," *CARHS*, 5, 2 (1978), 31–42; Brunauer, D. H., "The Woman Writer in a Changing Society," *Center for Women's Studies Lectures and Seminars*, Tokyo Women's Christian University (1978), pp. 40–44

DALMA H. BRUNAUER

KAFKA, Franz

Austrian novelist and short-story writer, b. 3 July 1883, Prague, Austro-Hungarian Empire; d. 3 June 1924, Kierling

K. was the son of a self-made merchant; his mother belonged to one of the leading families in the German-speaking, German-cultured Jewish circles of Prague. He was regarded as a competent student despite his habit of self-disparagement. In 1901 he began studying at the German Karl-Ferdinand University in Prague. Here he met Max Brod (q.v.), who became his lifelong friend and eventually his literary executor. Acceding to parental pressure, as well as to his own desire to separate completely his inner life from his public life, K. settled on the study of law, and received his degree in 1906. The next year he began work in the office of an insurance company. The atmosphere, reminiscent of that associated with his father at home, was authoritarian. K. established the pattern of enduring the office by day and writing stories by night. In 1908 he moved to the semigovernmental Workers' Accident Insurance Institute, where a more agreeable atmosphere prevailed. Still, he was tormented not only by the disharmony between his civil-service career and his literary endeavors, but also by poor health and indecisiveness about marriage. Tuberculosis manifested itself in 1917. Despite K.'s initial re-

luctance, he agreed to undergo treatment. By 1922 he was obliged to relinquish his civil-service position completely. In his mature years K. was engaged several times to be married, but all the engagements were broken. He had frequent stays in sanatoriums, and otherwise lived in Prague, Berlin, and Vienna. From 1912 on, K. strengthened his originally very tenuous ties with Judaism. His tuberculosis having run its fatal course, he died after almost seven years of struggle in a sanatorium in Kierling, not far from Vienna.

K. was invariably dissatisfied with his literary efforts. He instructed Brod to destroy after his death his considerable amount of unpublished writing. Instead, Brod edited and published the material. He has been taken to task by critics for presumed errors and arbitrariness in arranging and editing K.'s manuscripts—essentially to accord with Brod's own religious, eschatological propensity. Against this charge, the imputation of willfulness, Brod has defended himself rather convincingly.

K.'s fear and mistrust of his father, his complete incompatibility with his father's domineering nature—the latter manifested in mental abuse, threats, and savage sarcasm directed against his son—found written expression in 1919 in the lengthy, unsent *Brief an den Vater* (1952; *Letter to His Father,* 1953). K.'s unresolved hatred and love for his father, presented here in a way that reveals at once a measure of infantilism as well as a great deal of self-knowledge and psychological awareness, is regarded as an important basis of K.'s literary works. K., acccording to his own word, wrote to escape his father's heritage, that is, the striving, middle-class world that K. was obliged to labor in. Writing was necessary to his survival. And marriage would threaten his writing and so destroy him.

K.'s first published story of greater than sketch-length was "Das Urteil" (1913; "The Judgment," 1945). It gives an indication of the intensely autobiographical orientation that would characterize K.'s subsequent works, whether their symbolism is to be understood as psychological, religious, metaphysical, or existential—or indeed as all four at once. The judgment in question is the death sentence of the father on the son Georg, who thereupon commits suicide, not perhaps primarily to carry out his father's judgment, but because his father, by exploiting a common bond with Georg's friend, by driving away Georg's bride, by thus expanding his primacy in Georg's life and suffocating all else, has left Georg with nothing but a vision of his father—and that is destroyed by the judgment. In addition to the obvious Freudian relevance of the narrative facts, one may also suggest that Georg's father is the symbol of an Old Testament God, or, alternatively, a God produced by man's inner division.

In "Die Verwandlung" (1915; "The Metamorphosis," 1936) the son Gregor Samsa—the family name is clearly an analogue of the name Kafka—a rising young businessman, awakens one morning to find himself changed into a monstrous bug. The paradoxically realistic and restrained narrative relates the ever more intense suffering of the bug from the progressive alienation of the family for whom he had been the chief support. The nexus of the alienation is the father, whose influence, as in "Das Urteil," expands until he becomes the agent of the bug's willing death. From a short epilogue we gather that with the timely disposal of the bug that was Gregor, the family's respectability and inner harmony, under the father's dominance, may be regained.

Ein Landarzt (1919; *The Country Doctor*, 1940) is a collection of fourteen tales. The theme of the title story is the disruption—finally turned into chaos—of the country doctor's orderly but unperceptive existence by an irrational and oblivious world. Like Parzival before the Grail King, the country doctor fails the test of human sympathy before the boy with a mysterious and repulsive wound. At least at the primary narrative level, K. here departs from his preoccupation with sons and fathers. On the other hand, if we wish to see the country doctor as an unwilling father figure in relation to his young, doomed patient, the broad outlines of the earlier K. topos reemerge.

"In der Strafkolonie" (1919; "In the Penal Colony," 1941) again presents a father figure, or certainly an authority figure, the old commandant of the penal colony. Or rather, it does not present him, for he has died before the story begins; but his cruel heritage, though waning, has not yet been eliminated by his successor. Still devoted to the use of the old commandant's exquisite and horrible execution machine is the officer in whose charge the machine has been put and who is demonstrating it to a visiting explorer, finally indeed placing himself in its bed. While it is easy and tempting to credit K. with a visionary perception of the future horrors of concentration camps and World War II—and particularly the horrors perpetrated on the Jews—probably a critically sounder approach, relating "In der Strafkolonie" more integrally to the body of K.'s writings,

would be to regard this tale as a symbolic amplification of K.'s perception of himself as a victim not undeserving of punishment—although for no clear reason—at the hands of the preceding generation, which is naturally equated with authority.

K.'s last four story-length narratives were collected in a group published shortly after his death under the title *Ein Hungerkünstler* (1924; *The Hunger Artist,* 1938). The hero of the title story has chosen his unusual profession because he cannot adapt to the world about him. To be sure, this profession makes its own special demands on him: extreme resignation and passivity, while still not exempting him from the abuse and suspicion of the world. This artist, moreover, confined in a cage while he scorns earthly food, has nothing substantial—at any rate nothing recognized as substantial—to offer his audience. The circus crowds eventually become indifferent to his striving for accomplishments beyond the compass of their own narrow orbits. Desiring admiration, he earns incomprehension, and is left to die unwatched. The crowds gravitate to the cage of a healthy, hungry black panther, who even in his captivity is admirably adapted to the expectations of the world.

The theme of incommensurability between an artist of questionable talent and a world of limited horizon is also developed in another story in the same collection, "Josefine, die Sängerin; oder, Das Volk der Mäuse" (1924; "Josephine the Songstress; or, The Mouse Folk," 1942). The creatures designated in the subtitle, perhaps ironically symbolic of the Jews, seem also to be parallels of the uncomprehending crowds who at first throng to, then ultimately desert the hunger artist. Josefine, too, is a mouse. Although she makes much to-do about her supposed talent for singing, and prevails upon her reluctant fellow mice to attend whenever she feels impelled to give a concert, in fact, she is only squeaking, much as any mouse does. But then, K. suggests, developing the paradox with characteristic irony, no harm is done and perhaps there is even some benefit in the mouse folk's subscribing to the delusion foisted on them by Josefine. On the other hand, after Josefine dies, she is in the long run doomed to oblivion, for the mouse folk have no truck with history.

K.'s first novel, *Amerika* (1927; *America,* 1938), was written between 1912 and 1914. The first chapter, called "Der Heizer" (1913; the stoker) had been published separately soon after its completion. K.'s other two novels, which, like the first, were never completed, are *Der Prozeß,* begun in 1914 (1925; *The Trial,* 1937) and *Das Schloß,* begun in 1921 (1926; *The Castle,* 1930). For each of the novels it may well be that K. had in mind a sequence of chapters different from the one that emerged from Brod's hands.

Amerika is exceptional among the novels in that the environment, however strange and inscrutable, is at least not consistently hostile to the hero Karl Rossmann. And, if we take the novel as it stands, it ends atypically on something like a happy note—but also conceivably an ironic note. Karl is neither very intelligent nor very forceful. Or, when forceful, he is misguidedly so, as K. makes clear in the opening chapter; Karl's intercession on behalf of his new friend, the stoker, reflects the naïve idealism that will precipitate him from one scrape to another, as he is subjected to the unpredictabilities of life in the United States.

Karl repeatedly fails to comprehend the gap between myth and reality in America. How can there be such an enormous gulf between the rich and the poor? How can his benign Uncle Jakob condemn him, on account of disobedience, to leave his splendid house and take to the road? (*Amerika* is a road novel as well as, at least to some extent, a *Bildungsroman.*) How much abuse must Karl take before he realizes that his road companion Delamarche (K. appreciated puns), is less than a friend? In the light of Karl's misapprehensions, one is justified in wondering if the "Nature Theater of Oklahoma" in the (presumed) final chapter is going to prove quite as happy as Karl is led to believe: something for everybody, and freedom from bureaucracy.

In *Der Prozeß* the unpredictable counterforce—here more distinctly antagonistic—is a court of dubious legality, the ambiguous minions of which persistently and illogically bedevil the hero Josef K. Hardly less a bumbler than Karl Rossmann, Josef K. does not enlist our sympathy as a victim to the extent the latter does in *Amerika,* for Josef K., though self-confident, is otherwise largely without emotion. The court retains ultimate jurisdiction over his case, but it gives him a certain leeway, which perhaps vitiates any inchoate impulse on Josef K.'s part toward confrontation. In the end, he is executed by strangling and knifing, having refused, with unwonted courage, the opportunity to commit suicide.

The structural center and climax of *Der Prozeß* is a parable, representative of a genre that K. esteemed and cultivated. This particular parable, "Vor dem Gesetz" ("Before the Law"), concerns a man from the country, that is, a simpleton, prevented by a doorkeeper from entering an opening in the wall before him. His timorousness before the threats of the doorkeeper and his desire nonetheless to enter are in enervating balance, the result of which is a lifelong torment of inertia before the opening in the wall. As the man from the country is dying, the doorkeeper tells him that the entrance, now to be closed, had been meant for him all along.

To a degree the situation of the man from the country is like that of K.'s country doctor and, again, like that of Parzival. Except that in *Der Prozeß* it is not the suffering of someone else—the young patient, the Grail King—before which the hero falls silent. It is his own suffering, perhaps his own salvation that is at stake. And like Josef K. he lacks the impulse, quite possibly even the requisite sympathy with himself, to take a chance, to break out of his angst and ask what is going on.

In *Das Schloß,* K.'s longest but evidently least complete novel, the adversary consists in a mysterious officialdom in an equally mysterious castle. The castle and its officialdom at once attract, repel, and bemuse the hero, here known simply by the letter K., the ultimate reduction of the author's significantly autobiographical nomenclature. The goal of the fictional K., ostensibly a surveyor summoned to a job by the castle—but this and most other "facts" are ambiguous—is to enter the castle to ascertain the details of his commission so that he may get on with the work. His original purpose, however, suffers a loss of focus in the course of his long and futile, and often indirect, efforts to enter the castle from the dependent village to which he is relegated.

But *Das Schloß* is much more than the mere satire on bureaucracy it might appear to be at first glance. As the inhabitants of the castle are enigmatic and not to be counted on, so the castle itself is an uncertain entity, never seeming to K. to be quite the same thing as it was earlier. Metaphysically as well as physically it is not to be comprehended. Ultimately K., certainly a more forceful quester than Karl Rossmann or Josef K., but maladroit for all that, abets his own failure even when he appears to be on the verge of success. The inaccessible, to state the inevitable conclusion parabolically, remains inaccessible.

The authorial K.'s range of theme is not great, and his world view, intensely autobiographical as it is, is essentially cheerless. Potential danger or catastrophe lie everywhere, apt to descend on the helpless but not guiltless human victim quite unpredictably and illogically. What the victim is guilty of is usually unclear—perhaps simply of existence. And yet K.'s virtuoso development and modulation of his own thematic range—let us grant, moreover, its perfect timeliness—in addition to his uniquely wrought prose style, clear, precise, and to the point, have made him a leading figure, and a leading influence, in 20th-c. literature. Owing but little to his own literary and philosophical models, chiefly Goethe, Dostoevsky, Kleist, Flaubert, Dickens, and Kierkegaard, hardly known beyond a rather narrow circle of friends and enthusiasts during his lifetime, thereafter to be suppressed as a consequence of the racist nonsense of Nazism, K. since World War II has exerted a pervasive and continuing effect not only on the narrative literature but as well on the drama and film of Western Europe and the Americas.

FURTHER WORKS: *Betrachtung* (1913; *Meditation*, 1940); *Beim Bau der chinesischen Mauer: Ungedruckte Prose aus dem Nachlaß* (1931; *The Great Wall of China*, 1933); *Gesammelte Schriften* (6 vols., 1935–37); *Beschreibung eines Kampfes* (1936; *Description of a Struggle*, 1958); *Gesammelte Werke* (11 vols., 1950–74); *Tagebücher 1910–23* (1951; *The Diaries of F. K.*, 2 vols., 1948–49); *Briefe an Milena* (1952; *Letters to Milena*, 1953); *Briefe an Felice Bauer* (1967; *Letters to Felice*, 1973). FURTHER VOLUMES IN ENGLISH: *The Penal Colony: Stories and Short Pieces* (1961); *The Complete Stories* (1971); *I Am a Memory Come Alive: Autobiographical Writings* (1976); *Letters to Friends, Family, and Editors* (1977); *Letters to Ottla and the Family* (1982)

BIBLIOGRAPHY: Brod, M., *F. K.: A Biography* (1947); Wagenbach, K., *F. K.: Eine Biographie seiner Jugend* (1958); Brod, M., *Verzweiflung und Erlösung im Werk F. K.s* (1959); Sokel, W. H., *F. K.: Tragik und Ironie* (1964); Politzer, H., *F. K.: Parable and Paradox* (1966); Foulkes, A. P., *The Reluctant Pessimist: A Study of F. K.* (1967); Emrich, W., *F. K.: A Critical Study of His Writings* (1968); Greenberg, M., *The Terror of Art: K. and Modern Literature* (1968); Urzidil, J., *There Goes K.* (1968); Janouch, G., *Conversations with K.* (1971); Thorlby, A., *K.: A Study* (1972); Gray, R., *F. K.* (1973); Beicken, P. U., *F. K.: Eine kritische Einführung in die Forschung* (1974); Kuna, F., *F. K.: Literature as Corrective Punishment* (1974); Nagel, B., *F. K.: Aspekte zur Interpretation und Wertung* (1974); Rolleston, J., *K.'s Narrative Theater* (1974); Hibberd, J., *K. in Context* (1975); Binder, H., *K. in neuer Sicht* (1976); Flores, A., ed., *The K. Debate* (1977); Robert, M., *Seul, comme F. K.* (1979); Stern, J. P., *The World of F. K.* (1980)

RICHARD H. LAWSON

While I lay special worth on the hopeful side of K.'s work, which rejoices in activity, that is to say in the fundamental recognition of the fact that man, with his spark of reason, will, and ethical perception is not altogether the plaything of super-mighty powers, who judge according to other laws than his, which he does not understand and never can understand, faced with which he is lost, and only thrown unconditionally on God's mercy —the old problem of Job—while underlining then the position of human freedom in the case of K., I do not of course wish to forget that this attitude of K.'s is only an occasional flash, and that passages which describe man as powerless, crowd in on the reader in an overwhelming majority. But the propositions of freedom and hope *are there, too!*

Max Brod, *F.K.: A. Biography* (1947), p. 171

Any individual work by K. may baffle the reader when considered in isolation. If examined within the context of K.'s other works and personal documents, the nature and meaning of his images become clear. The individual work will then appear as a variation of a single theme—the inner autobiography of the author—and a step in its development. Each work is aesthetically self-sufficient and, if completed and published by K. himself, a complete and satisfying statement of one approach to the master theme.

There is, nevertheless, a difference in the degree of transparency K.'s images possess in different works. The central images of his long narratives —Gregor Samsa's bug form, the Court in *The Trial*, the Castle in the late novel of that name— are more opaque and denser than the symbols of his shorter pieces. The reason is that the central images of the long works have a variety of functions and meanings. Indeed, they unite mutually contradictory meanings and functions.

Walter H. Sokel, *F.K.* (1966), p. 8

There is not one self-explanatory word in a typical K. narrative. His mature prose shows nothing but a surface spread over happenings that remain profoundly impenetrable. Paradoxically this enables K., the visionary, to furnish his stories amply with realistic detail. Since even the inanimate objects he describes point to an undefined and mysterious background, they no longer relate to one another according to the customs and conventions of reality. Clefts, cracks, and crevices open, revealing the depth behind the realistic detail. The same is true of the figures acting on a stage thus prepared. Ostensibly most of them are well grounded in reality, even in the reality of K.'s own life.

Heinz Politzer, *F. K.: Parable and Paradox* (1966), p. 17

The crucial element . . . in this story ["Der Jäger Gracchus"] as well as in all of K.'s stories—the element, too, that characteristically distinguishes K. from his contemporaries—is the fact that the hunter who moves in this earthly world is a "dead" person who does not belong to this earthly world at all, whom no one understands, and who, by the same token, does not understand any living person.

This "dead" person who is "in a certain sense alive, too," embraces in the midst of the earthly world the duality of death and life. Only now can one understand why this story represents the universal in its universal significance, the totality of all that is, the All-encompassing that has crossed the borders between life and death, that is found both *above* and *within* all that is. In him the mystery of all that is has awakened: everything that all human beings, mountains, and stars, from the beginning of time to the present, have told one another and continue to call out to one another.

A twofold aspect results from this: on the one hand, this dead and, at the same time, living man possesses total perspective, universal knowledge of all that has been and is . . . . On the other hand, by reason of this intermediate position of his between life and death, he no longer fits into any fixed earthly or spiritual classification; he sails "without a rudder," completely disoriented upon the earthly waters, and is, therefore, able to reach and comprehend neither the limited world of ideas of the much-occupied living, nor the "gate" of the Hereafter that "shines on high."

Wilhelm Emrich, *F. K.: A Critical Study of His Writings* (1968), p. 10

K. is an extreme instance of a writer who abandoned himself to all the forces that could destroy a man, without trying to put in their way any of the conscious blocks that most of us use . . . to separate ourselves from unacceptable insights. We are likely to go wrong, though, if we try to rule K. out of court because of any objection we have to the defeats his characters suffer. If the comparisons with William Sansom and Poe show nothing else, they show that K. was too scrupulous an artist to be challenged on any grounds except that of the art of novel-writing and story-writing which

was his deliberate choice of activity. His lasting quality will be found in a work that grows out of this basic integrity. But to see the work as a whole means taking into account much more than individual passages. The patterns of whole stories and novels go towards making the full picture, and then too the pattern of K.'s whole life as a writer has to be sought.

Ronald Gray, *F. K.* (1973), p. 28

What first impresses itself on the reader of K.'s work is a vision of an incomprehensible world, a mood of total impotence in the face of the unintelligible power of circumstances, as a consequence of which "the inner world of the subject is transformed into a sinister, inexplicable flux" (Georg Lukács) requiring exorcism by the harshest punitive measures. Yet it is equally true that beneath the nightmare a more positive assessment of reality can be detected. Though for the most of the time it was impossible for K. to make such an assessment an integral part of his poetics, he could on occasion intimate that, as he explained to [Gustav] Janouch, reality is also "the strongest force shaping the world and human beings. . . . Dreams are only a way round, at the end of which one always returns to the world of most immediate reality." The final chapter of *The Castle*, for example, describes such a return. One must also understand the therapeutic and utopian quality of K.'s nihilism. If he could not bring himself unambiguously to celebrate the positive aspects of human existence, then he at least indirectly pointed the way, by pushing the nihilistic view of it to its limits.

Franz Kuna, *K.: Literature as Corrective Punishment* (1974), pp. 10–11

Accustomed to an ever-decreasing gap between fiction and "reality," the reader of K.'s time had developed an analytic sense, an insistence on verisimilitude that continually questioned the synthesizing process whereby fictional characters had come into being. K.'s response was to incorporate both reactions of the reader, the synthetic and the analytic, the constructive and the destructive, into an entirely new approach to the notion of character. Virtually all his stories are focused on a single hero: yet nothing is harder than to evolve an image of the "character" of a K. hero, even though he is usually placed very close to the reader's perspective, makes constant appeals to common sense, and seemingly has nothing to hide.

James Rolleston, *K.'s Narrative Theater* (1974), p. 140

F. K.'s life was a private tragedy mingled with farce, almost as strange and terrible as that of any of his fictional heroes. His biography is a story of mental conflict and torment which he himself recorded in his diaries and letters with the genius of a great writer and the scrupulous accuracy of a hypochondriac and introvert. He paints a compelling self-portrait of a man unfit for life who failed miserably in all his endeavours. The knowledge that his problems arose from his mentality as much as from external circumstances did not help him solve them, for his mind was to him more real than anything else in the world. His searching vision was turned inwards. From the city of Prague he observed, yet apparently all but ignored, the historic events of his time, the Great War, the collapse of the Austro-Hungarian Empire, the birth of Czechoslovakia. He believed that his pronounced individuality, his vocation as a writer and his Jewishness made him an outsider. From a position of isolation he created stories of estrangement for which he has become famous.

John Hibberd, *K. in Context* (1975), p. 7

KAISER, Georg

German dramatist and novelist, b. 25 Nov. 1878, Magdeburg; d. 4 June 1945, Ascona, Switzerland

K. quit school at the age of sixteen and, after a short stint in the book trade, served an apprenticeship in an import-export firm. In 1898 he set out for Argentina, earning his passage as a coal trimmer on a freighter. A severe case of malaria forced him to return to Germany in 1901. His great breakthrough as a writer came in 1917, with the spectacularly successful premiere of *Die Bürger von Calais* (pub. 1914; the burghers of Calais). He quickly became the leading playwright of expressionism (q.v.) and the most performed dramatist in Germany after Gerhart Hauptmann (q.v.). When the Nazis came to power, they wasted no time in silencing K., whose antimilitarism and pacifism they loathed. They accused him of "cultural Bolshevism" and "Jewish tendencies," and prohibited the publication and performance of his plays in Germany. He continued to live near Berlin until 1938, when he fled into exile, first to Amsterdam, then to Switzerland. Attempts by Albert Einstein and Thomas Mann (q.v.) to obtain a U.S. visa for K. failed. Feeling more isolated than ever, K. continued to write until his death from an embolism.

By the time K. made a name for himself, a good third of his total dramatic production had already been written, although not much of it was published. His approximately twenty-five pre-expressionist plays explore the possibilities of tragedy and comedy as well as tragicomedy.

They show K. to have been very much under the sway of contemporary literary trends; they also show the effect of an intensive study of Nietzsche and Schopenhauer, whose ideas were to exert a powerful and lasting influence on K. The dilemma posed by the conflict between instinct and intellect, body and mind, the problematic nature of love, the dehumanizing effect of a society clinging to ossified norms and values, man's inhumanity to man, themes that become ever more significant for K.'s later work, are already very much in evidence.

The need for a regeneration of man and the blindness of the masses form the background of one of K.'s earliest plays, the "bloody grotesque" *Schellenkönig* (written 1896, pub. 1966; king of diamonds), a one-act play in verse in a neoromantic vein. It unmasks the hollowness and inhumanity of a society living by the grotesquely distorted norms and values of mere form as the measure of all things.

An inquiry into the nature of love is made in *Claudius* (written 1911, pub. 1918; Claudius) and *Friedrich und Anna* (written 1911, pub. 1918; Friedrich and Anna), presenting two diametrically opposed human responses to the meaning of love. In Claudius, a knight in black armor married to a fair maiden, K. shows us a crass example of love that is utterly confined to the frenzy of blind passion and a murderous drive for the exclusive possession of a prized object. Friedrich's love, on the other hand, is based not selfishly on any property rights but on the unconditional recognition and acceptance of the other, Anna, as a human individual in her own right. K.'s later work would seem to support the idea expressed in these early plays that the problem of love is primarily a question of man's regeneration so that he may transcend the egoistic desire to treat others as manipulable objects of self-gratification.

The antithetical opposition of body and mind is the focus of interest in *Rektor Kleist* (written 1903, pub. 1918; principal Kleist), a "tragedy of illness and yearning." Kleist, a sickly hunchback, while strongly believing in the authority of the intellect, nevertheless longs for the vitality of life, from which he feels excluded. He would like to think that his intellectual abilities make up for his physical handicaps, but he becomes responsible for a schoolboy's suicide, thus exemplifying the "uncanny wisdom" of the gym teacher's saying: "In a sick body a sick spirit." Yet the vitalistic gym teacher is shown to be equally guilty. Both the fanatic adherence to vitalistic principles and the self-righteous proclamation of the supremacy of the intellect are proven wrong and dangerous in their one-sidedness.

The revolutionary poetic vision and concomitant new form of expressionism, as well as its messianic call for a spiritual regeneration of mankind, provided a perfect mode for K. In his view, a drama presents not so much a story or a plot as an idea—hence, the necessity of form to establish the inner coherence of the *Denkspiel* (thought-play). The idea not only determines the structural principles of K.'s plays: it also makes the characters into typical exponents of ideas, that is, abstractions, who no longer speak a personal idiom. Language, silence accentuated by gestures and pantomime, symbolism (especially color symbolism), stage setting, decoration, and lighting—all derive their functional meaning from the idea they serve to develop.

In *Von morgens bis mitternachts* (written 1912, pub. 1916; *From Morn to Midnight,* 1919), the Cashier awakens from the deadly monotony of his trivial existence and, with embezzled money, sets out in search of passionate life. But he fails in his quest, a victim of his illusion to be able to *buy* a new life. Genuine human values are not to be had for money. The Cashier, himself a prisoner of a perverted value system based on purchasing power, never achieves a spiritual regeneration.

Die Bürger von Calais, a powerful drama of pacifism, celebrates the birth of the "New Man." The destructiveness of traditional heroic patriotism, based on martial ideals only, is overcome by a nonviolent heroism born of humanitarian idealism. K. turns a historical incident into a timeless parable of the true hero who lays down his life for the common good.

The exalted vision of one shepherd (the New Man) and one flock (mankind regenerated) reaches its high point in *Hölle Weg Erde* (1919; hell way earth), K.'s only play depicting the realization of utopia on earth. The optimism of this ecstatic vision, however, amounts to no more than a short-lived flicker of hope. The *Gas* trilogy, written about the same time, projects an utterly pessimistic view for the future of mankind. In the three plays, *Die Koralle* (1917; *The Coral*, 1929), *Gas I* (1918; *Gas I,* 1924), *Gas II* (1919; *Gas II,* 1924), each a complete drama in its own right, K. explores the implications of a technological society in an age of capitalism whose exploitational character reduces human beings to mere exponents of mechanical functions.

The Billionaire, in *Die Koralle*, has tried in vain to rid himself of the haunting memory of an unhappy childhood in abject poverty by a ruthless pursuit of power through wealth. When his children turn against him and espouse the cause of the downtrodden and exploited, he has to face the haunting specter again, but now sees no other salvation than that of self-extinction. In *Gas I* the Billionaire's Son has put his social theories into practice. But it quickly becomes obvious that even revolutionary social measures cannot restore man's dignity and human potential as long as purely materialistic values are the decisive factors determining the lives of the workers. In *Gas II,* the possibility of a totally mechanized world has become reality. Once more the call for regeneration is sounded and goes unheard, resulting in the apocalyptic annihilation of mankind.

In *Der gerettete Alkibiades* (1919; *Alkibiades Saved*, 1963), a masterpiece of dramatic form, K. again turns to the conflict of life and spirit. Because of the excruciating pain caused by a thorn in his foot, Socrates disdains public honor, devises a new theory of art, and invents platonic love. The new spiritual values he promotes all owe their existence to the secret wound of the thorn in the flesh. Yet if the thorn in the flesh gives rise to revolutionary spiritual values, it demonstrates at the same time the ultimate mastery of the body. Only death constitutes a synthesis of sorts.

The plays written in the post-expressionist years, until K.'s flight into exile, range from exclusive "worlds of the mind" to comedies, in a more realistic vein, and musicals that appear to be a concession to the general public's taste for lighter fare. But K. was also very much aware of the growing danger of nationalistic and militaristic sentiment and the threat posed by the rising tide of Nazism.

Die Lederköpfe (1928; the leatherheads) represents K.'s first direct dramatic reaction to the contemporary political scene. An impassioned indictment of war, the play illustrates the degradation of man to an anonymous puppet in the hands of a belligerent dictator. K.'s intent was "to denounce the facelessness of the SA and to encourage antifascist resistance." *Die Ächtung des Kriegers* (1929; outlawing the warrior), a short but brilliant Platonic dialogue, voices K.'s critique of the Kellogg Pact (1928). The fatal flaw, as he points out with Socratic irony, resides in the paradox that "the warrior remains a man of honor—but war is a crime." Direct allusions to the political and social situation of the early 1930s are also to be found in *Der Silbersee* (1932; the silver lake), a "winter's tale in three acts,"

K.'s last play to be performed on a German stage before his works were proscribed by the Nazis.

In exile K. continued to write against the evils and horrors of war. *Der Soldat Tanaka* (1940; *Private Tanaka*, n.d.) and *Napoleon in New Orleans* (1941; *Napoleon in New Orleans*, n.d.) are eloquent protests against the destructive curse of war. His pacifist ideals were voiced, for the last time, in *Zweimal Amphitryon* (1943; twice Amphitryon), the first of three "Greek" dramas in blank verse, in which K. reverted to the classic five-act form. It combines the denunciation of war with the expressionist's vision of a New Man to be born from the union of the divine with the human. Love, the redeeming power, will lead to the salvation of the world.

The remaining two "Greek" dramas, *Pygmalion* (1944; Pygmalion) and *Bellerophon* (1944; Bellerophon), can be viewed as the testament of K. the artist. They deal with the fate of the artist in this world, once more exposing the irreconcilable antagonism between life and art, between a society in need of salvation, in which the spiritual values of the artist count only in so far as they represent a promising investment fund, and the divinely inspired artist and misunderstood savior, scorned and rejected by those for whom he guards the divine spark.

Although K.'s work also comprises two novels, several short stories and essays, as well as poetry, he is first and foremost a playwright. His dramas of ideas combine a strong intellectual impulse with a consummate instinct for theatrical effect. His work, uneven as it may be at times, occupies an important place in the history of German drama and has left its mark on modern theater in general, influencing not only Max Frisch and Friedrich Dürrenmatt (qq.v.) but also, among others, American playwrights like Eugene O'Neill and Elmer Rice (qq.v.). Brecht (q.v.), expressing his indebtedness to K., perhaps sums it up best: "In fact, K. already gave a new purpose to theater by making it an intellectual affair. . . . He has made possible the entirely new attitude of the audience of the scientific age."

FURTHER WORKS: *Der Fall des Schülers Vehgesack* (written 1902, pub. 1914) *Die jüdische Witwe* (written 1904, rev. 1909 ff., pub. 1911); *Der Geist der Antike* (other title: *Die Falle;* written 1905, pub. 1923); *Der Präsident* (other titles: *Der Kongreß, Der echte Blanchonnet;* written 1906, pub. 1927); *Margarine* (other titles: *Der Zentaur, Konstantin Strobel;* written 1906, rev. 1913 ff., pub. 1925); *David und Goliath* (other title: *Großbürger Möller;* written 1906, rev. 1914 ff., pub. 1920); *Die Sorina* (1909); *Die Versuchung* (other title: *Die Muttergottes;* written 1910, pub. 1917); *König Hahnrei* (written 1910, pub. 1913); *Ballade vom schönen Mädchen* (written 1910, pub. 1911); *Der mutige Seefahrer* (written 1910, rev. 1911, 1925, pub. 1926); *Hyperion* (1911); *Europa* (1915); *Das Frauenopfer* (written 1916, pub. 1918); *Juana* (1918); *Der Brand im Opernhaus* (1919; *The Fire in the Opera House*, 1927); *Der Protagonist* (1921; *The Protagonist*, 1960); *Noli me tangere* (1922); *Kanzlist Krehler* (1922); *Gilles und Jeanne* (1923); *Die Flucht nach Venedig* (1923; *The Flight to Venice*, 1923); *Nebeneinander* (1923); *Kolportage* (1924; *Literary Trash*, n.d.); *Gats* (1925); *Zweimal Oliver* (1926; *Two Olivers*, 1927); *Der Zar läßt sich photographieren* (1927); *Papiermühle* (1927); *Oktobertag* (1927; *The Phantom Lover*, 1928); *Hellseherei* (1929); *Mississippi* (1929); *Zwei Krawatten* (1929); *Es ist genug* (1931); *Das Los des Ossian Balvesen* (written 1934, pub. 1972); *Agnete* (written 1935, pub. 1972); *Adrienne Ambrossart* (1935; *Adrienne Ambrossart*, 1935); *Rosamunde Floris* (1937); *Alain und Elise* (written 1937, rev. 1938, pub. 1940); *Vincent verkauft ein Bild* (written 1938, pub. 1972); *Pferdewechsel* (written 1938, pub. 1972); *Der Gärtner von Toulouse* (1938); *Der Schuß in der Öffentlichkeit* (1939); *Villa Aurea* (1939; *Vera*, 1939); *Klawitter* (written 1939–40, pub. 1952); *Der englische Sender* (written 1942, pub. 1972); *Die Spieldose* (1943; *The Musical Box*, n.d.); *Das Floß der Medusa* (1943; *Medusa's Raft*, 1951); *Stücke, Erzählungen, Aufsätze, Gedichte* (1966); *Werke* (6 vols., 1971–72)

BIBLIOGRAPHY: Kenworthy, B. J., *G. K.* (1957); Paulsen, W., *G. K.* (1960); Shaw, L. R., "G. K.: A Bio-Bibliographical Report," *TSLL*, 3 (1961), 399–408; Kauf, R., "G.K.'s Social Tetralogy and the Social Ideas of Walter Rathenau," *PMLA*, 77 (1962), 311–17; Garten, H.F., "G.K.," in Natan, A., ed., *German Men of Letters* (1964), Vol. II, pp. 157–72; Jones, R. A., "German Drama on the American Stage: The Case of G. K.," *GQ*, 37 (1964), 17–25; Reichert, H., "Nietzsche and G. K.," *SP*, 61 (1964), 85–108; Last, R.W., "Symbol and Struggle in G. K.'s *Die Bürger von Calais*," *GL&L*, 19 (1966), 201–9; Schürer, E., *G. K.* (1971); Garten, H. F., "G.

K. Re-examined," in Robson-Scott, W. D.,
ed., *Essays in German and Dutch Literature*
(1973), pp. 132–55; Weimar, K. S., "G. K.—
At Last!!!(?)," in Weimar, K. S., ed., *Views
and Reviews of Modern German Literature*
(1974), pp. 213–30; Turnstall, G. C., "Light
Symbolism in G. K.'s *Die Bürger von Calais*,"
JEGP, 78 (1979), 178–92

FRIEDHELM RICKERT

G. K. is probably the greatest dramatic artist of
our time writing in the German language. His arrangement of scenes, his dialogue, his skill in construction and development will be a pattern for
many others, long after the idea-content of his
plays has been exhausted. In almost two score dramas K. has acquired a technique that functions as
effortlessly as effectively, and often derives the
highest measure of the dramatic from a minor
motive. This procedure is, dramatically, highly instructive. . . .

And yet, it is never mere technique that sets
K.'s subjects in motion . . . ; undoubtedly, G. K. is
born of the spirit—he is not only spirited but also
spiritual. His words are always striking (so are his
titles), sparks sputter at the poles where sentence
and sentence meet in dialogue, yet it is not only
words' wit that makes his plays dramatic, but the
antithesis of character, the wittiness of situation.
And who, after *The Burghers of Calais*, after
From Morn to Midnight, after *The Sacrifice of a
Woman* and *The Fire in the Opera House* would
doubt that G. K. is a poet with vision? Only, this
poet is never lyric, but always dramatic.

Victor Wittner, "G. K., Playwright," *Theatre Arts*,
Oct. 1931, 813–14

K. is considered one of the chief exponents of Expressionism . . . the best known example of which,
in his repertoire, is *From Morn to Midnight*, the
story of man's futile attempt at realizing his ideals,
compressed into the events of a single day. The
drama depicts such typical scenes of modern life
as a sport palace, a cabaret, a bank, all symbolizing various human activities. Most of the characters are nameless abstractions or types—a bank
cashier, a lady, a stout gentleman, a mask. No attempt is made to have us know his characters;
their features "are apprehended in the same vivid,
perfunctory way that a man in a desperate hurry
at a crowded railway station, looking for somebody or something, takes in the faces of other
travellers."

K.'s language is factual, concise, at times even
brutal, his style laconic, staccato, emphasizing
with telegraphic brevity the haste and tempo of
the action. As in all his plays, he evinces a deep
understanding of theatrical contrasts, stage effects,
and dramatic tension. Always an eager student of
the scenic and staging techniques of modern stage

designers—particularly the stylists and construc-
tionists—he makes extensive use of such striking
technical devices as the revolving stage, cyclo-
rama, platforms, and masks.

Horst Frenz, "G. K.," *Poet Lore*, 52 (1946),
363–64

G. K.'s production, viewed as a whole, shows an
astounding compass and variety: it ranges from
romantic—occasionally even lyrical—plays to carefully contrived dialectical pieces; from the satirical to the ecstatic; from comedy and revue to
tragedy. Its material is drawn from such diverse
sources as Greek legend, the Platonic Dialogues,
the events of history, the problems of the modern
industrial world and K.'s own fertile imagination.
In the form of his drama there is such variety as
to suggest that a resourceful talent was for ever
experimenting with new methods of expression,
while the language, though it always retains its
own distinctive note, catches the raciness of colloquial speech, argues and reasons with cool detachment or explodes in outbursts of emotion.
Work follows upon work in a bewildering stream,
and with a prolificness that can have few parallels;
differing and often contradictory solutions are offered to the same problem, as the approach to it
shifts. There appears to be no order, no underlying unity.

B. J. Kenworthy, *G. K.* (1957), p. 198

The kinship between Wedekind, Sternheim, and
K. lies in their tendency to unmask "the essence"
of social reality not by naturalistic imitation,
which would still lull us in illusions, but by crass
and shocking formulations. Their drama seeks to
demonstrate in pure and, therefore, abstract and
distorted conditions (in the experimental laboratory, as it were) the true nature of existential or
social problems. . . . In his *Burghers of Calais*,
probably his greatest work, K. demonstrates by
two highly dramatic surprise effects the true nature of heroism as pacifism and self-sacrifice. In
his *Alkibiades Saved* he demonstrates by a highly
ironic tour de force the true nature of the intellect
as both a wound and a heroic fraud. Here the
trick, K.'s basic dramatic form, merges with the
dramatic content and idea. . . .

Nietzsche saw the historical Socrates as the initiator of Greek decadence and the pioneer of the
Christian "slave revolt"; K. sees in Socrates the
fateful innovator who ends the age of naive self-
assurance and ushers in a self-conscious, i.e.,
guilt-ridden, civilization. The mind replaces the
muscles. Reflection drives out spontaneity. The
cripple wins out over the athlete. But Socrates'
revolutionary philosophy does not result from the
cripple's resentment of the strong and healthy; it
results from his compassion for them.

Walter H. Sokel, *The Writer in Extremis* (1959),
pp. 108–9

This central idea, the "renewal of man" . . . links his work closely to the expressionist movement, from which it received its most vital impetus. It gives his writings the moral impulse which is the hallmark of literary Expressionism. But while with most of the other Expressionists the force of this impetus shattered form and reduced language to an inarticulate stammer, K. harnessed it to a rigid, almost classical form. These two principles—the driving force of expressionist zeal, on the one hand, and the rationally constructed, "cubist" form, on the other—actually merge in his plays. This antinomy is reflected in the very language of K.—in the juxtaposition of impassioned, rhetorical outpourings and terse, clipped dialogue. This unique language of K.'s, which he also uses in his narrative writings . . . , is an essential ingredient of his work; it is as far removed from colloquial speech as is verse (to which it finally rose). With its repetitions, its symmetries and climaxes, its precisely calculated dashes and exclamation marks, it has an intensely musical quality. However, it is not a music of halftones and subtle shades but of glaring, white-hot passion and the violent clash of ideas. K. admits of no distinction between "feeling" and "thinking." For him both are one—merely different degrees of intensity.

H. F. Garten, "G. K.," in Alex Natan, ed., *German Men of Letters* (1963), Vol. II, p. 158

Twice Amphitryon is the first of his three so-called Greek dramas, the other two being *Pygmalion* and *Bellerophon*. In these plays, K. not only reverted to classical themes, but also to the traditional five-act structure and to the blank-verse form. Stylistically, the retreat of the Expressionist had ended in the safe haven of traditional forms, but K.'s message remains the same: the play, inspire by Molière and Kleist, is his final protest against militarism. . . .

In *Twice Amphitryon*, some of K.'s main themes are intertwined: first, his protest against war; second, the salvation of the world by a pure woman; and third, the promised birth of a child as the future redeemer. The curse of war destroys all that is good in man; it can only be overcome if love, as exemplified by Alkmene, rules the world. And a new world can only be created by individuals; therefore it must be started by a single man, the child.

Ernst Schürer, *G. K.* (1971), pp. 170–71

KALLAS, Aino

Finnish short-story writer, dramatist, and poet, b. 2 Aug. 1878, Viipuri; d. 9 Nov. 1956, Helsinki

K. was born into the culturally prominent Krohn family, known for contributions in the arts and sciences. After she married Oskar Kallas, an Estonian folklore scholar, she lived in Tartu, Estonia, until 1918, when that country became independent and her husband joined the diplomatic corps of the young nation. From 1922 to 1934 the couple lived in London. K.'s last years were spent in exile in Sweden and Finland.

K. found an inexhaustible source of literary motifs in the grim history and rich folklore of her new homeland, Estonia. In the two volumes of *Meren takaa* (1904–5; beyond the sea) and the short novel *Ants Raudjalg* (1907; Ants Raudjalg) she vents, in a vein of stark realism, her indignation at the vestiges of the centuries-old serfdom in Estonia under the ethnically German aristocracy and the new threat of Russian nationalism, which was hindering the ascending forces of national identity.

K.'s contact with the intellectually progressive Young Estonia circle and with the aesthetics of impressionism and of symbolism (q.v.) left its mark on the short stories in *Lähtevien laivojen kaupunki* (1913; the town of departing ships) and *Seitsemän* (1914; seven). Her focus shifted from Estonian social issues to problems of a more universal nature and to the individual psyche. Her full artistic mastery over subject and style, however, came in the 1920s. In *Barbara von Tisenhusen* (1923; *Barbara von Tisenhusen*, 1927), *Reigin pappi* (1926; *The Rector of Reigi*, 1927), and *Sudenmorsian* (1926; *The Wolf's Bride*, 1930) K. delves, in a strange and archaic language, deep into the mysteries of human emotions. Outwardly faithful to historical facts and folk legends, all three tales recount the awesome power of love. An intriguing tension prevails between the seemingly calm and neutral narrative voice and the explosive and gruesome narrative content. While utilizing unusual linguistic idiom and depicting alien social customs, K. sings the praises of the irrational and celebrates the high mass of love.

K.'s dramatic works, mostly adaptations of earlier short stories, were written mainly in the 1930s, while all of her poetry was produced during periods of crisis and transition in the author's personal and artistic development. K.'s five volumes of diaries are also artistically meritorious and are of permanent documentary value as well.

K. belongs to the classics of Finnish literature. The best of her tales, the meticulously chiseled stories of the 1920s, testify to an unparalled craftsmanship and can stand comparison with those of any European short-story writer. Their setting in this obscure corner of Europe, their timeless themes, and their agelessly antique language guarantee a growing interest in their author.

FURTHER WORKS: *Lauluja ja ballaadeja* (1897); *Kuloa ja kevättä* (1899); *Kirsti* (1902); *Suljettu puutarha* (1915); *Tähdenlento* (1915); *Nuori Viro* (1918); *Musta raita* (1919); *Katinka Rabe* (1920); *Vieras veri* (1921); *Langatonta sähköä* (1928); *Novelleja* (1928); *Pyhän Joen kosto* (1930); *Marokon lumoissa* (1931); *Bathseba Saarenmaalla* (1932); *Mare ja hänen poikansa* (1935); *Talonpojan kunnia* (1936); *Sudenmorsian* (1937); *Valitut teokset* (3 vols., 1938); *Kuoleman joutsen* (1942); *Kuun silta* (1943); *Löytöretkillä Lontoossa* (1944); *Polttoroviolla* (1945); *Mallen tunnustukset* (1945); *Kanssavaeltajia ja ohikulkijoita* (1945); *Uusia kanssavaeltajia ja ohikulkijoita* (1946); *Kolmas saattue* (1947); *Seitsemän neitsyttä* (1948); *Virvatulia* (1949); *Rakkauden vangit* (1951); *Päiväkirja vuosilta 1897–1906* (1952); *Päiväkirja vuosilta 1907–1915* (1953); *Päiväkirja vuosilta 1916–1921* (1954); *Päiväkirja vuosilta 1922–1926* (1955); *Päiväkirja vuosilta 1927–1931* (1956); *Vaeltava vieraskirja vuosilta 1946–1956* (1956); *Elämäntoveri* (1959); *A. K. kauneimmat runot* (1959). FURTHER VOLUME IN ENGLISH: *The White Ship: Estonian Tales* (1924)

BIBLIOGRAPHY: Ahokas, J., *A History of Finnish Literature* (1973), pp. 238–42

VIRPI ZUCK

KAMBA LITERATURE
See Kenyan Literature

KAMBANELLIS, Iakovos
Greek dramatist and screenwriter, b. 12 Dec. 1922, Naxos

K. studied to be a draftsman in Athens. During 1943–45 he was a prisoner of the SS at Mauthausen concentration camp. He had never considered a career in playwriting until he saw productions of Karolos Koun's Art Theater during the winter of 1945–46. Impressed by Koun's innovative staging of foreign and Greek drama, he began to write for the theater.

K. has been a major force in modern Greek drama since his first play was produced in 1950. Making his reputation with dramas that reflect a strong sense of Greek social reality much in the tradition of American realist drama of the 1930s through the 1950s (Elmer Rice, Arthur Miller [qq.v.], and others), he has more recently fused the fragmentation of epic theater to produce a form of impressionistic celebration (*panayeri*) of Greek folk traditions and spirit. At the same time these works satirize contemporary social and political life.

Three of his early plays form a loose trilogy: *Choros pano sta stahna* (1950; dance on the wheat), *Evdomi mera tis dimiourgias* (1955; the seventh day of creation), and *E avli ton thavmation* (1957; the courtyard of miracles) all concern lower-middle-class/working-class protagonists who end by committing suicide because they are unable to reconcile personal and social realities.

The best of the three, and perhaps K.'s greatest work, is *E avli ton thavmation*. Believing that Greeks express themselves through *groups* rather than as isolated individuals, K. depicts a working-class apartment-house courtyard of Athens during the 1950s. He presents eleven characters, each with his own "miracle" or dream that is expressed but ultimately shattered before the end of the play. In the end the courtyard itself will be torn down to make way for a modern apartment building. Stelios, a gambler and a cuckold, and extremely sensitive, finally commits suicide. The other characters will learn, with deep bitterness, to survive in the new Athens.

K.'s more recent play, *To megalo mas tsirko* (1973; our great circus), suggests a broader thematic and impressionistic approach to drama. Playing off the traditional Greek satirical review (*epitheorisis*), K. uses scenes, songs, and signs to display Greek history as a cycle of alternating tyranny and revolution, a cycle that moves toward idealism and then back again through betrayal and selfishness. The characters and situations are archetypal rather than realistic—hence both Greek and universal. Produced during the dictatorship of 1967–74, this play helped give rise to a group of new plays that were both entertainment and strong satire of the political reality.

K.'s talent lies in his rich demotic language, which captures the life and spirit of the Greek people. He is also able to create dramatic moments that reflect both group life and a vividness of character for each individual. His recent works tend toward impressionism but are not abstract. He rejects psychological development, seeing it as an Aristotelian plot mechanism, and instead favors thematic and chronological "jump cuts."

As a screenwriter, K. helped form the new Greek cinema of the 1950s by writing films such as *Stella* (1955; Stella), and *Drakos* (1956; fiend).

FURTHER WORKS: *E Ilikia tis nichtas* (1958); *O gorillas ka e ortansia* (1959); *Paramithi horis onama* (1959); *Yeitonia ton angelon* (1963); *Viva Aspasia* (1966); *Odissea yirise spiti* (1966); *Apoikia ton timorimenon* (1970); *Aspasia* (1971); *To kouki kai to revithi* (1974); *O echtrhros laos* (1975); *Prosopa yia violi kai orchestra* (1976); *Ta tessera podia tou trapeziou* (1978); *Paterino polemo* (1980)

BIBLIOGRAPHY: Karampetsos, E. D., "Tyranny and Myth in the Plays of Four Contemporary Greek Dramatists," *WLT,* 53 (1979), 210–14

ANDREW HORTON

KAMPMANN, Christian

Danish novelist and short-story writer, b. 24 July 1939, Gentofte

After finishing secondary school K. passed his university exams, but he decided not to attend the university. He worked as a journalist in Jutland and in New York, where he also attended the Columbia Graduate School of Journalism.

K. is a representative of the so-called neorealistic school in Denmark, which carried on the tradition of the psychological novel of the 1930s. Making his debut with the short-story collection *Blandt venner* (1962; among friends) K. set out to analyze critically middleclass milieus and values. His novels and short stories show the characters to be prisoners of an environment that determines and limits everyday life. Sexual frustrations, dominant themes in K.'s books, are the result of these social conditions and conventions, which pervert man's desire for security and tenderness.

In his second collection of short stories, *Ly* (1965; shelter), K. revealed the hollowness and hypocrisy that lie beneath the surface of an apparently pleasant and unproblematic reality, and in the novel *Sammen* (1967; together) he continued the unmasking of the bourgeoisie.

While K. up to this point had striven for complete objectivity, he began to experiment with the narrative structure in *Nærved og næsten* (1969; near and nearly), which deals with man's loneliness and inability to establish meaningful relationships. This work, together with the novels *"Vi elsker mere"* (1970; "we

love more") and *Nok til hele ugen* (1971; enough for the whole week), both of which accuse popular magazines of acting as social tranquilizers, and *En tid alene* (1972; a time alone), a scathing indictment of an uncaring and unfeeling society, can be read as preliminary studies to K.'s major accomplishment, a four-volume series about the greatness and fall of an upper-middle-class family. K. used a classical genre, the traditional family novel, but although the private sphere has a major role, the period background is given a most significant function and reflects the cold war of the 1950s, the prosperity of the 1960s, and the economic crisis of the 1970s. *Visse hensyn* (1973; certain considerations) describes the life of the Gregersen family during the years 1954 to 1957; political, social, and economic consciousness is lacking, and problems are never allowed to be acknowledged. *Faste forhold* (1974; firm relationships) shows the family fifteen years later, when a changing pattern of life emerges, and insecurity and restlessness become increasingly evident. In *Rene linjer* (1975; pure lines) the old life style has definitely broken down, but experiments with new ways of living create complications. In *Andre måder* (1975; other ways) the characters search for alternative life styles such as collective living, liberation from stifling sex roles, and, possibly, another economic system.

Although composed as novels, K.'s two latest books, *Fornemmelser* (1977; feelings) and *Videre trods alt* (1979; continue despite everything), are autobiographical in content. They constitute an attempt by K. to break through fiction in order to tell the truth about himself: his bisexual experiences and the bigotry of a society that places the homosexual in a subjugated position.

K.'s superb character delineations, his faithful rendering of place, and his vivid narrative style have gained him a prominent place among the contemporary realistic authors of Scandinavia.

FURTHER WORKS: *Al den snak om lykke* (1963); *Uden navn* (1969); *Pinde til en til en skønskrivers ligkiste* (1971)

MARIANNE FORSSBLAD

KANNADA LITERATURE
See Indian Literature

KARAKALPAK LITERATURE
See Uzbek Literature

KARANTH, Kota Shivaram
Indian novelist, dramatist, and essayist (writing in Kannada), b. 1 Oct. 1902, Kota, Karnataka

From his birthplace in a village in the South Canara district in southern India, K. took his first name. Although he has traveled widely, he writes mainly of the rural folk of his native region. Existence is harsh in this rainy land, and K. evokes the life of these simple but rugged people as they pit themselves against a hostile nature to eke out a living. His novel *Bettada jiva* (1947; mountain people) is an excellent example of such a portrait. In his most famous novel, *Marali mannige* (1940; *Back to the Soil* 1950; repub. as *The Whispering Earth,* 1974), K. minutely analyzes the complex relationships of three generations of a rural family and the clash between modern ideas and traditional values.

Chomana dudi (1949; *Choma's Drum,* 1978), which typifies K.'s keen social observation, depicts the struggles and sorrows of an untouchable who tries to free himself from bonded labor and become a farmer. In the novel *Kudiyara kusu* (1951; *The Headman of the Little Hill,* 1979) K. draws on his knowledge of ethnography to portray the Kudibi, a tribal hill people. A more recent novel, *Mukajjiya kanasugalu* (1968; *Mookajji's Visions,* 1979), for which he received India's highest literary award, the Seat of Learning Prize, deals with a woman who, having been widowed at the age of eight, has to live celibate until her death at eighty-five.

K. has written several plays, works of social protest against injustices to the poor and downtrodden. They are reminiscent of the dramas of John Galsworthy (q.v.) in their compassionate sociological analysis.

K. also wrote the first Kannada encyclopedia for children and the first Kannada dictionary. He is currently promoting the folk-oriented rural Kannada dance-drama called Yakshagana, directing and touring with groups throughout India and overseas. He has written a study of this folk theater, *Yakshagana bayalata* (1957; *Yaksagana,* 1975).

FURTHER WORKS: *Karnarjuna* (1929); *Hasivu* (1931); *Bharatiya chitrakale* (1930); *Bauddha yatre* (1933); *Chitramaya dakshina kannada* (1934); *Bala prapancha* (1937); *Hegadarenu* (1937); *Sarasammana samadhi* (1937); *Sirigannada arthakosha* (1940); *Cikka doddavaru* (1941); *Halliya hattu samastaru* (1944); *Balveya belaku* (1945); *Gita natakagalu* (1946); *Navina natakagalu* (1946); *Audaryada urulalli* (1947); *Gajaraja* (1947); *Jnana* (1947); *Aidu natakagalu* (1948); *Dehajyotagalu mattu praniprabandhuagalu* (1948); *Mangana maduve* (1948); *Moga padeda mana* (1948); *Sanyasiya baduku* (1948); *Karulina kare* (1949); *Prajaprabhutvannu kuritu* (1949); *Abuvinda baramakke* (1950); *Kaleya darshana* (1950); *Bittida bele* (1951); *Cigurida kanasu* (1951); *Devadutaru* (1952); *Jaruva dariyalli* (1952); *Panjeyavara nenapigagi* (1952); *Apurva pashcima* (1953); *Battada tore* (1953); *Samikshe* (1956); *Vijnana prapancha* (1959); *Jagadoddhara ... na* (1960); *Maigallana dinacariyinda* (1960); *Ala nirala* (1962); *Huccumanassina hattu mukhagalu* (1965); *Janapada gitegalu* (1966); *Mailikallinodane matukategalu* (1966); *Onti dani* (1966); *Svapnada hole* (1966); *Oda huttidavaru* (1967); *Innonde dari* (1968); *Vicar sahitya nirmana* (1968); *Alida mele* (1969); *Calukya vastu, shilpa* (1969); *Karanta prapancha* (1969); *Mugida yuddha* (1969); *Shanishvarana neralalli* (1969); *Mai mangala sulyalli* (1970); *Ukkide nore* (1970); *Hiriya kiriya hakkigalu* (1971); *Karnatakadalli chitrakale* (1971); *Kevala manushyaru* (1971); *Nambidavara naka, naraka* (1971); *Bidi barahagalu* (1972); *Dharmarayana samsara* (1972); *Hettala tayi* (1973); *Patalakke payana* (1973); *Gondaranya* (1974); *Kanyabali* (1974); *Mujanma* (1974); *Celuvina kannada nadu* (1975); *Ileyemba* (1975); *Karnatakadalli nrtyakala* (1975); *Karnatakadalli shilpa* (1975); *Manodehiyada manava* (1975); *Muktadvara* (1975); *Ade urur, ade mar* (1977)

BIBLIOGRAPHY: Sitaramiah, V., "K. S. K.," *IndL,* 3, 3 (1960), 107–11; Moorthy Rao, A. N., "S. K.'s *Marali mannige,"* *IndL,* 5, 2 (1962), 28–30; Mugali, R. S., *A History of Kannada Literature* (1975), pp. 122–24; Aithal, S. K., "S. K.'s *Ade urur, ade mar,"* *IndL,* 22, 4 (1979), 12–20; Sitaramiah, V., "S. K.: A Multi-faceted Personality," *I&FR,* 16, 4 (1979), 19–20

K. BHASKARA RAO

KARAOSMANOĞLU, Yakup Kadri
Turkish novelist, short-story writer, essayist, and translator, b. 27 March 1889, Cairo, Egypt; d. 13 Dec. 1974, Ankara

Moving to Istanbul in 1908, K. attended law school at the University of Istanbul. For two years he taught philosophy and literature.

K. joined the nationalist forces in the Turkish war of independence (1919–22), and when the Turkish Republic was inaugurated (1923), he became a member of the Turkish legislature. In the early 1930s, he belonged to the Kadro group, which advocated Marxist ideas in an influential periodical of the same name. From 1934 to 1954 he served as Turkey's ambassador to Albania, Czechoslovakia, the Netherlands, Iran, and Switzerland. From 1961 to 1965, he returned to the Turkish legislature.

Although his fame rests on his novels, K.'s literary career has embraced many other genres —essays, plays, short stories, memoirs, monographs, and prose poems. With the publication of his first book, *Bir serercam* (1913); a happening), a collection of short stories, K. emerged as a masterful stylist and a passionate nonconformist. *Rahmet* (1923; mercy), his second collection of short stories, marks the beginning of his commitment to the literature of social *engagement*.

Erenlerin bağından (1922; from the garden of the sages) is a cycle of twelve prose poems expressing the joys and agonies of the mystic spirit. This manual for a blessed life ranks as one of the best achievements in the genre in Turkish.

In 1922 K. published the outstanding novels *Kiralık konak* (mansion for rent) and *Nur Baba* (Father Light). *Kiralık konak* tells the tale of the downfall of the imperial Ottoman society as exemplified by the disintegration of one aristocratic family. *Nur Baba* exposes the sybaritic life among the followers of an antiorthodox Islamic sect; spiritual communion with God and brotherly love—once the highest principles of Islamic mysticism—have been reduced in this sect to mere physical love.

Hüküm gecesi (1927; night of the verdict) is a scathing *roman à clef* about the Young Turks and the convulsive politics of the twilight years of the Ottoman Empire. It is a compelling study of ambition and avarice, a tour de force of political fiction. *Sodom ve Gomore* (1928; Sodom and Gomorrah) is a panoramic and poignant study of Istanbul under occupation after World War I. K. painted a powerful picture of the intellectual and spiritual crisis of the East confronted with the West.

K.'s best-known novel is the prize-winning *Yaban* (1932; stranger), which is set in central Anatolia at the time of the war of independence. It is a study of the emergence of the new Anatolian man, torn between nationalism and religion, between the claims of east and west, oppressed by poverty, yet imbued with hope.

This novel, which depicts Turkey as an unmerciful wasteland, was the first to expose the wretched conditions of the peasant villagers in republican Turkey. Dominated by the superstitious, fanatically reactionary sheiks and imams, who exploit the ignorance of the people, the peasants, K. believed, had been abandoned by the urban intellectuals, who had turned a cold shoulder to their misery.

K.'s last major novel was *Panorama* (2 vols., 1953–54; panorama), a wide-ranging canvas of Turkish society. K. demonstrated in *Panorama* that the Turkish revolution of the 1920s, like other national revolutions, deteriorated and fell prey to reactionary forces.

Few novelists in the 20th c. have portrayed the Turkish upheavals with the craftsmanship and psychological insight that characterize the novelistic art of K.

FURTHER WORKS: *Ergenekon* (1929); *Ankara* (1934); *Bir sürgün* (1937); *Okun ucundan* (1940); *Alp dağlarından ve miss chalfrin'in albümünden* (1942); *Atatürk* (1946); *Millî savaş hikâveleri* (1947); *Atatürk'ün gerçek siması* (1955); *Zoraki diplomat* (1955); *Hep o sarkı* (1956); *Anamın kitabı* (1957); *Vatan yolunda* (1958); *Politikada 45 yıl* (1968); *Gençlik ve edebiyat hatıraları* (1969)

TALAT SAIT HALMAN

KARELIAN LITERATURE
See Finno-Ugric Literatures of the Soviet Union

KARINTHY, Frigyes
Hungarian humorist, novelist, dramatist, and poet, b. 24 June 1887, Budapest; d. 29 Aug. 1938, Siófok

The liberal atmosphere of K.'s childhood home, as well as his mother's early death and his experiences as a schoolboy, had a profound effect on his creative life. The young K. was a medical student for a short time, but then he switched to journalism, contributing short, humorous pieces and skits to a number of Budapest newspapers before World War I. He married an actress who fell victim to the influenza epidemic of 1918. His stormy second marriage to Aranka Bőhm is well documented in recent Hungarian literary memoirs. K. had a son from each of his two marriages: Gábor

(1914–1974), a reclusive poet, and Ferenc (b. 1921), a well-known contemporary Hungarian writer.

K. was Hungary's first truly urban, cosmopolitan writer. Although his life and work were closely associated with his native Budapest, he, unlike most of his contemporaries, was never attracted to specifically Hungarian issues and problems. His themes were universal, and he approached them with the enlightened rationalism of an 18th-c. *philosophe*. He was also a satirist in the Swiftian manner, and his writings reveal a 19th-c. humanist's faith in—and a 20th-c. man's fear of—modern science.

K. achieved his first major success with a series of literary parodies, *Így írtok ti* (1912; that's how *you* write). In these delightful and trenchant caricatures K. satirized the pet themes and characteristic mannerisms of the popular and influential writers—both Hungarian and foreign—of his time. But K. had always been more than just a humorist; his humor, with its speculative undercurrents, went beyond the conventions of his day and often veered toward the grotesque and the tragic.

K.'s stories and sketches contain a curious mixture of adolescent optimism and jeering pessimism. His evocation, in some of his darkest tales, of a dislocated, nightmarish world is strongly reminiscent of Kafka (q.v.)—although there is no evidence that he was directly influenced by Kafka. His world view was, however, affected by Freud's (q.v.) psychoanalytic theories and by August Strindberg's (q.v.) paradoxical views on male-female relationships. K. also combined his interest in science fiction (one of his early loves was Jules Verne) with his predilection for satire. His *Utazás Faremidóba* (1916; *Voyage to Faremido*, 1965) and *Capillária* (1921; *Capillaria*, 1965) are modern-day sequels to *Gulliver's Travels*. In both novels he depicts a world in which flesh and spirit, instinct and rationality, are hopelessly disjoined.

One of K.'s most popular works, the semi-autobiographical *Tanár úr kérem* (1916; *Please Sir!*, 1968) presents a gallery of portraits of boys growing up in a very Victorian turn-of-the-century Budapest. Their timidity and repressed grandiosity are revealed in a series of bittersweet sketches that deal with such things as the rigors of school life, the dreadful prospect of failure, and the mystery of awakening sex. His celebrated *Utazás a koponyám körül* (1937; *A Journey round My Skull*, 1939) is also autobiographical; it is an engrossing account of the author's struggle with a developing brain tumor, and of his journey to Stockholm, where he was operated on by a famous Swedish surgeon. In his serious prose as well as in his contemplative dramas and rough-hewn, expressionistic poetry, K. often returned to the same themes he treated lightly in his humorous pieces and comic one-acters. As a journalist he was also keenly aware of the absurdities of public and private life.

Some critics feel that K.'s undisciplined life style, as well as the grimly exploitative world in which he lived, prevented him from realizing his creative potential. The author himself often expressed these sentiments. Actually, K.'s intellectual brilliance came mostly in flashes; his wit and satire, in some of the longer works, tends to become repetitive and mechanical. His masterpieces are to be found among the brief sketches and essays that he considered mere trivia.

FURTHER WORKS: *Kötéltánc* (1923); *Mennyei riport* (1937); *A lélek arca* (2 vols., 1957); *Hőköm szinház* (3 vols., 1957); *Számadás a tálentomról* (1957); *Az egész város beszéli* (4 vols., 1958); *Hátrálva a világ körül* (1964); *Naplóm, életem* (1964); *Miniatűrök* (1966); *Összegyűjtött művei* (1975 ff.). FURTHER VOLUME IN ENGLISH: *Grave and Gay: Selections from His Work* (1973)

BIBLIOGRAPHY: Vajda, M., "F. K.: Humorist and Thinker," *NHQ*, 2 (1961), 84–99; Reményi, J., *Hungarian Writers and Literature* (1964), pp. 298–305; Tabori, P., Introduction to F. K., *Voyage to Faremido; Capillaria* (1965), pp. vii–xxi; Szalay, K., "F. K.," in F. K., *Grave and Gay: Selections from His Work* (1973), pp. 239–46

IVAN SANDERS

KARVAŠ, Peter

Czechoslovak dramatist, novelist, and short-story writer (writing in Slovak), b. 25 April 1922, Banská Bystrica

K. completed high school in Slovakia and studied at the universities of Prague and Bratislava. During World War II he worked in radio and took part in the uprising against the Germans of 1944. After 1945 he was dramaturge of the National Theater in Bratislava, cultural attaché in Bucharest, Romania (1949–50), staff member of the Ministry of Culture, and editor of the journal *Kultúrny život*, among other positions. An active member of the Communist Party of

Slovakia and of its Central Committee, he received important awards from the state. After the invasion of Czechoslovakia by Warsaw Pact armies in 1968 K. lost his membership in the Communist Party for favoring liberalization and opposing the invasion.

K. is a very prolific writer, and his talent has found expression in short stories, plays, satires, and novels, all written with a keen sentivity for tragic as well as comic social situations and containing rational analyses of people and historical events.

Although K. was acclaimed for some of his existentialist (q.v.) short stories, he established himself as principally an imaginative and influential playwright. The highly praised drama *Meteor* (1945; meteor) analyzed the state of mind of people on the threshold of World War II. Some of K.'s plays have been performed in other European countries, four of them in East Germany, where they are valued for their modern technique, humor, and sober social criticism and concern. He has brought Slovak satire to a high level.

In the 1950s, when Socialist Realism (q.v.) became the official literary dogma, K. wrote a number of works characterized by staunch loyalty to the prevailing political postulates. In all his works K. dealt with social problems, the horrors and barbarities of war, and the revolt against oppression. He ridiculed human frailties, especially those weaknesses seen in the enemies of progress, lampooning them from a Marxist point of view. His successful, politically motivated collection of stories *S nami a proti nám* (1950; with us and against us), depicts the anti-German uprising in Slovakia with all its horrors, inhumanity, and sacrifices; German soldiers, Slovak and Soviet partisans, village people, heroes and traitors are portrayed in a variety of tragic and tragicomic situations.

His attempts at writing novels were less successful. Of a planned trilogy, in which K. intended to describe the social and political life in Slovakia from 1918 to 1945, with its social and ideological clashes, he completed only the first two volumes: *Toto pokolenie* (1949; this generation) and *Toto pokolenie v útoku* (1952; this generation on attack)

In 1963 K. was among those Slovak literati who exhorted writers to be mindful of their duty to be the "conscience of the nation," and bitterly criticized the period of the cult of personality. He was silenced by the government but was recently "forgiven" his "deviations." Although he is now allowed to work, he has not published anything in the last few years. Never-

theless, he continues to influence younger writers in his yearning for a more humane and just society.

FURTHER WORKS: *Most* (1946); *Niet prístavu* (1946); *Spolok piatich P* (1946); *Hannibal pred bránami* (1946); *Polohlasom* (1947); *Bašta* (1948); *L'udia z našej ulice* (1951); *Čert nespí* (1954); *Srdce plné radosti* (1954); *Diet'a a meč* (1954); *Čertovo kopýtko* (1957); *Zločin Dariny Piovňovej* (1958); *Diplomati* (1958); *Zmŕtvychstanie deduška Kolomana* (1960); *Polnočná omša* (1960); *Antigona a tí druhí* (1962); *Jazva* (1963)

BIBLIOGRAPHY: Noge, J., *An Outline of Slovokian Literature* (1968), pp. 100–101; Richter, L., *Slowakische Literatur* (1979), pp. 177, 192

JOSEPH M. KIRSCHBAUM

KARYOTAKIS, Kostas
Greek poet, b. 30 Oct. 1896, Tripolis; d. 21 July 1928, Preveza

The greater part of K.'s youth was spent in Hania, Crete, although his father's profession of civil engineer kept the family on the move. After graduating from the law school at the University of Athens in 1917, K. registered at the School of Philology to escape military service, only to be inducted in 1919, the year he was admitted to the bar; he was discharged in 1920. The remainder of K.'s short life was spent in public service. For three years he was a member of the parliament, successively representing a number of different cities. Transferred to the Ministry of Welfare, he traveled extensively, visiting Italy, Germany, Romania, and France. Ultimately, he was assigned to a disappointing post in Patras. Depressed and tired with his life, K. committed suicide at the age of thirty-two.

K. published only three collections of poetry during his lifetime, *O ponos tou anthropou ke ton praghmaton* (1919; the pain of men and things), *Nepenthe* (1921; nepenthe [the name of a pain killer]), and *Eleghia ke satires* (1927; elegies and satires). A few of his early poems and essays were published posthumously. A melancholy young man who considered himself one of life's rejects and relied increasingly on medicine to maintain his health, K. wrote poems that expressed his own sense of disillusionment and futility. His first collection is clearly the effort of a young man; his second shows a growing sureness of hand as it begins to display his tendency to the morbid. The last, a mature expression of the dark themes that haunted his life, is permeated with the spirit of defeat and pessimism for which he became famous. It is in the bitter and mocking phrases of his last poem, "Preveza" (Preveza) that K.'s pessimism finds its strongest expression. In its imagery all is deathlike: Having by now decided to end his own life, he expresses indifference to death, mocking its pretensions.

K. was the most worthy representative in his own country of that French-influenced generation of the 1920s that manifested the anguish of the period between the wars. With language rich in irony and sarcasm, he unashamedly broaches the subject of his suicidal despair in a manner that, while conservative both in its meter and its rhyme, manages to suggest a mind whose occasional lapses into sentimentality could not overshadow its originality and strength.

FURTHER WORKS: *Apanta* (2 vols., 1965–66)

BIBLIOGRAPHY: Myrsiades, K., "K. K.," *Charioteer,* 14 (1972), 20–25; Friar, K., Introduction to *Modern Greek Poetry* (1973), pp. 44–46

KOSTAS MYRSIADES

KASCHNITZ, Marie Luise

German poet, essayist, novelist, short-story writer, and radio dramatist, b. 31 Jan. 1901, Karlsruhe; d. 10 Oct. 1974, Rome, Italy

An officer's daughter from an aristocratic family, K. grew up in Potsdam and Berlin. After finishing school, she learned the book trade, whereupon she established herself as a book dealer in Rome. During the 1930s and 1940s K. lived in a number of German cities where her husband, an archaeologist, held university posts. After World War II she returned to Rome. K. accompanied her husband on numerous trips around the Mediterranean, visiting historical sites that greatly influenced her work. By the end of her career she had received many literary prizes for her work and was one of the most respected writers in contemporary German literature.

Although K. published two novels in the 1930s, *Liebe beginnt* (1933; love begins) and *Elissa* (1937; Elissa), it was not until after 1945 that she began to write extensively. Shocked by the war and its effect on humanity,

she expressed in poetic works such as *Totentanz, und Gedichte zur Zeit* (1947; dance of death, and poems of the times) and *Zukunftsmusik* (1950; music of the future) an anguish that is nevertheless tempered by hope and guarded optimism. Her combining of traditional and modern forms, along with her highly original diction, resulted in a distinctive style.

When her husband died in 1958, K.'s world collapsed. In the poetry collection *Dein Schweigen—meine Stimme* (1962; your silence—my voice) she reflects on life and death, living together and living alone, but in her sorrow and despair and her inability to grasp the meaning of existence, she eventually comes to terms with life and learns to deal with her loneliness.

Although K. excelled in poetry, she was a master of prose as well. One of her most interesting novels, *Das Haus der Kindheit* (1956; house of childhood), takes place in a kind of museum where the visitor is confronted with childhood memories through visual images of the past. At first, everything seems remote and unreal to the visitor. Not until the end does the meaning of the visit become clear. In *Wohin denn ich* (1963; whither then I) and *Tage, Tage, Jahre* (1968; days, days, years), written in diary form, K. is able to transform her personal experiences into something that transcends the merely autobiographical. This may also be said of *Beschreibung eines Dorfes* (1966; description of a village), an impressionistic description of the village of Bollschweil K. knew well.

K. characterized her own narrative style as belonging somewhere between poetry and prose. This is especially true of her short stories, which contain many lyrical passages. Man's existential loneliness and sorrow as well as his insistent hopes and ambitions are observed and recorded with poetic sensitivity and insight. Of all her short stories, K. considered "Das dicke Kind" (1951; the fat child) her best work. Through the technique of distancing, she heightens the suspense and resolves it.

The content of K.'s essays ranges from philosophical meditation on everyday occurrences to a deep concern about important scientific issues. *Griechische Mythen* (1946; Greek myths) are very personal interpretations of eternally relevant myths. Her Roman essays, *Engelsbrücke* (1955; bridge of angels), are reflections on literature, art, life, and death. And the collection *Zwischen Immer und Nie* (1971; between always and never) is a perceptive analysis of literary characters and themes.

As a dramatist, K. preferred writing for the

radio to writing for the stage, since radio allowed her to use a greater variety of artistic devices. Here again she turned to both mythical and contemporary subjects. Among the latter, two have been especially popular: *Die Kinder der Elisa Rocca* (1962; the children of Elisa Rocca) and *Die Fahrradklingel* (1965; the bicycle bell). Both of these deal with man's inhumanity to man and have a moral tone that is akin to the fable.

K. treated many of the same subjects that occupied other writers of the period, but what made her stand apart was her compassionate point of view and her positive attitude toward life.

FURTHER WORKS: *Menschen und Dinge* (1945); *Gedichte* (1947); *Gustave Courbet: Roman eines Malerlebens* (1949); *Ewige Stadt* (1952); *Neue Gedichte* (1957); *Lange Schatten* (1960; *Long Shadows*, 1966); *Hörspiele* (1962); *Ein Wort weiter* (1965); *Überallnie* (1965); *Ferngespräche* (1966); *Die Wahrheit, nicht der Traum* (1967); *Vogel Rock* (1969); *Steht noch dahin: Neue Prosa* (1970); *Nicht nur von hier und heute* (1971). FURTHER VOLUME IN ENGLISH: *Selected Later Poems of M. L. K.* (1980)

BIBLIOGRAPHY: Plant, R., "The Strange Poetic World of M. L. K.," *AGR,* 32 (1966), 15–16; Linpinsel, E., *K.-Bibliographie* (1971); Elliott, J. C., "The Child as Protagonist in Short Stories of M. L. K.," *Faculty Journal,* Tennessee State University (1973–74), 11–16; Baus, A., *Standortbestimmung als Prozeß: Eine Untersuchung zur Prosa von M. L. K.* (1974); Walter, D. E., "Grundhaltungen in Gedichten der M. L. K.," *DU,* 27 (1976), 108–14

ANNI WHISSEN

KASHUBIAN LITERATURE
See section under Polish Literature

KASSÁK, Lajos
Hungarian poet, novelist, and editor, b. 21 March 1887, Érsekújvár; d. 22 July 1967, Budapest

K., both as a writer and as a literary organizer, was responsible for creating, in the early decades of the 20th c., a Hungarian avant-garde movement that was at once plebeian and elitist. K.'s own political radicalism and his proletarian background—his father was a pharmacist's assistant; his mother, a washerwoman—did not prevent him from labeling most forms of popular art as kitsch. He was a natural enemy of bourgeois culture, but his unrelenting insistence on his own brand of revolutionary art and his refusal to relinquish his leadership also alienated many sympathetic friends and protégés. In his later years, K. became increasingly isolated and embittered, and during the repressive early 1950s, when his "formalism" was officially condemned, he disappeared completely from the literary scene. It was only toward the end of his life that the historical importance of his work began to be appreciated both at home and abroad.

K. was among the first poets in Hungary to reject traditional poetic forms in favor of free verse. His first collection, *Éposz Wagner maszkjában* (1915; epic in the masque of Wagner), reveals the influence of his early idol, Walt Whitman. Although he was philosophically opposed to artists joining political parties, and had great disdain for writers who did become involved in practical politics, K. was a lifelong socialist, and many of his works deal with the problems and promises of working-class life. However, he could be doctrinaire even without subscribing to official doctrines, and many of his writings are tractlike in their didacticism. His discriminating aesthetic sensibility is in evidence in relatively few works, but these have a sinewy eloquence and stateliness that is quite impressive. For example, his most famous early poem, "Mesteremberek" (1915; "Craftsmen," 1977), is a soaring tribute to the proletariat.

To a large extent K.'s fame rests on his role as an editor and mentor of young modernist poets. During his long career he published a number of periodicals; the most important of these were *Tett* (1915–16), *Ma* (1916–19; 1920–22), and *Munka* (1928–39). *Ma,* which he edited first in Budapest and later in Vienna, was especially significant, since it introduced the latest avant-garde "isms" to Hungarian readers. After the fall of the 1919 Hungarian Commune K. spent six years in exile in Vienna, where he met, and collaborated with, the editors and leading contributors of other influential avant-garde journals.

The 1920s proved to be K.'s most creative period. Inspired by the aesthetics of surrealism, futurism, even Dadaism (qq.v.), he produced many of his most important poems; *Világanyám* (1921; my world-mother) contains his most daringly experimental work. It was also during the 1920s that K. began to paint, using the purely abstract idiom of the constructivists.

While most of K.'s poetry bears the stamp of the various avant-garde trends of his time, as a prose writer he remained a down-to-earth realist. His most important prose work is a voluminous autobiographical narrative, *Egy ember élete* (8 vols., 1928–39; the life of a man); he describes with dispassionate candor his youthful wanderings, his days as a factory worker, his struggles as a budding artist, and his uneasy relationship with fellow writers and public figures. K. was a crusader for avant-garde art all his life. Nevertheless, critics nowadays seem to agree that his most lasting achievements were his realistic autobiographical writings.

FURTHER WORKS: *Misilló királysága* (1918); *Máglyák énekelnek* (1920); *Tisztaság könyve* (1926); *Megnőttek és elindulnak* (1932); *A telep* (1933); *Az utak ismeretlenek* (1934); *Fújjad csak furulyádat* (1939); *Mélyáram* (1962); *Összes versei* (2 vols., 1970); *Az izmusok története* (1972)

BIBLIOGRAPHY: Reményi, J., *Hungarian Writers and Literature* (1964), pp. 388–93

IVAN SANDERS

KÄSTNER, Erich

West German poet, novelist, journalist, and dramatist, b. 23 Feb. 1899, Dresden; d. 29 July 1974, Munich

After interrupting his education for a year of military service during World War I, K. studied German literature in Rostock, Berlin, and Leipzig. In 1925 he received a doctorate for a dissertation on Frederick II and German literature. When he lost an editorial position in 1927 he went to Berlin and became a free-lance writer. Although the Nazis burned his books in 1933, he remained in Germany during Hitler's rule. At the end of the war he became active as a journalist in Munich, editing *Die neue Zeitung* and the children's periodical *Pinguin* until 1948. During the postwar years he was also an active participant in the Munich cabaret Die Schaubude (after 1951, Die kleine Freiheit). In 1957 K. was awarded the Büchner Prize for literature, and from 1952 to 1962 he was president of the West German chapter of the PEN Club, an international writers' organization.

K. is most widely known for his children's books and popular light novels. Two of them,

the famous children's story *Emil und die Detektive* (1928; *Emil and the Detectives*, 1930) and *Drei Männer im Schnee* (1934; *Three Men in the Snow*, 1935), written for adults, were successfully filmed in the 1930s. In his works written especially for young people, K. successfully combined a lively, warm humor with moralizing didacticism to expose human frailty and folly while attacking social ills. K.'s juvenile novels are particularly significant for their reflection of the author's social optimism, an optimism based upon his deep belief in the regenerative power of the race that is most visible in each new generation of youth.

Of far greater literary moment, however, are K.'s lyric poems. K. is the most important, and perhaps also the only truly successful, poet of the primarily prose-oriented "new factualism" movement that began in Germany in the 1920s. His first four collections of verse—*Herz auf Taille* (1928; heart on the waist), *Lärm im Spiegel* (1928; noise in the mirror), *Ein Mann gibt Auskunft* (1930; a man gives information), and *Gesang zwischen den Stühlen* (1932; singing between the chairs)—established the new approach to poetry that continued to characterize all of his lyric creations. Combining stylistic elements of expressionism (q.v.) with conservative verse forms and his own social philosophy, K. produced a light yet serious poetry, in tone reminiscent of the politically critical works of Heinrich Heine (1797–1856) and similar to the early didactic lyrics of Bertolt Brecht (q.v.).

In those first groups of poems, the pedagogue-moralist K. attempted to reach two closely related goals: to lay bare the festering social and political malaise of pre-Hitler Germany; and to use the devices of irony, criticism, mockery, accusation, and laughter to warn of the consequences of social indifference, militarism, and perverted nationalism. The powerful accuracy of K.'s perception of the prewar German situation is well exemplified in the prophetic satirical poem "Kennst du das Land, wo die Kanonen blühen?" (1928; "Knowst Thou the Land Where Only Cannons Grow?" 1963), a parody of a poem by Goethe, in which K. predicted with terrible precision the rise of the Nazis.

The most visible postwar development in K.'s poetry is a strong preference for concise, yet sensitive aphorisms and epigrams. The collection *Kurz und bündig* (1948; short and to the point) remains the best document of his efforts in that direction.

The tragic novel *Fabian* (1931; *Fabian: The*

Story of a Moralist, 1932), a mainstream literary work of the "new factualism," is K.'s only major work of fiction that examines prewar moral and social decay and the predicament of Germany's "lost generation." Although it has been criticized as lacking a convincing world view, *Fabian* is witty and clever in its conception. Characterized by precision of language and expression, and resembling many of the early poems in its thrust, the novel successfully penetrates and exposes inhumanity, while justifying morality through its portrayal of immorality.

K.'s dramas are less successful than his fiction and poetry. *Die Schule der Diktatoren* (1949; the school of the dictators), a comedy that unmasks inhumanity once more in a grim portrayal of the human fall foretold by K.'s poetry, is his most significant play, yet its characters lack sufficient graphic power to make the work effective.

The major strength of K.'s writings lies in their universality and timelessness. Although K. wrote of specific problems pertaining to his own society and time, his works still force the reader toward constructive introspection. Therein lies the measure of their absolute worth.

FURTHER WORKS: *Leben in dieser Zeit* (1930); *Pünktchen und Anton* (1931; *Annaluise and Anton*, 1932); *Der 35. Mai; oder, Konrad reitet in die Südsee* (1931; *The 35th of May; or, Conrad's Ride to the South Seas*, 1933); *Arthur mit dem langen Arm* (1932); *Das verhexte Telefon* (1932); *Das fliegende Klassenzimmer* (1933; *The Flying Classroom*, 1934); *Emil und die drei Zwillinge* (1933; *Emil and the Three Twins*, 1961); *Die verschwundene Miniatur; oder auch, Die Abenteuer eines empfindsamen Fleischermeisters* (1935; *The Missing Miniature; or, The Adventures of a Sensitive Butcher*, 1937); *Doktor E. K.s lyrische Hausapotheke* (1936); *Georg und die Zwischenfälle* (1938; repub. as *Der kleine Grenzverkehr*, 1949; *A Salzburg Comedy*, 1957); *Streiche des Till Eulenspiegel* (1938; *Till Eulenspiegel, the Clown*, 1957); *Bei Durchsicht meiner Bücher* (1946); *Tucholsky* (1946); *Zu treuen Händen* (1948); *Der tägliche Kram* (1949); *Die Konferenz der Tiere* (1949; *The Animals' Conference*, 1949); *Das doppelte Lottchen* (1949; *Lottie and Lisa*, 1950); *Der gestiefelte Kater* (1950; *Puss in Boots*, 1967); *Des Freiherrn von Münchhausen wunderbare Reisen und Abenteuer zu Wasser und zu Lande* (1952); *Die kleine Freiheit* (1952); *Die Schildbürger*

(1954); *Die 13 Monate* (1955); *Der Gegenwart ins Gästebuch* (1955); *Eine Auswahl* (1956); *Don Quichotte* (1956; *Don Quixote*, 1957); *Als ich ein kleiner Junge war* (1957; *When I Was a Little Boy*, 1959); *Über das Nichtlesen von Büchern* (1958, with Paul Flora); *Heiterkeit in Dur und Moll* (1959); *Heiterkeit kennt keine Grenzen* (1960); *Notabene 45* (1961); *Gullivers Reisen* (1961); *Heiterkeit braucht keine Worte* (1962); *Das Schwein beim Friseur* (1962); *K. in Probepackung* (1962); *Liebe will gelernt sein* (1962); *Wieso, warum!* (1962); *Von Damen und anderen Weibern* (1963); *Der kleine Mann* (1963; *The Little Man*, 1966); *Der kleine Mann und die kleine Miss* (1967; *The Little Man and the Little Miss*, 1969); *Kennst du das Land, wo die Kanonen blühen?* (1967); *Unter der Zeitlupe* (1967); *Was nicht in euren Lesebüchern steht* (1968); *Da samma wieda* (1969); *Friedrich der Große und die deutsche Literatur* (1972); *Wer nicht hören will, muß lesen* (1972); *Ein Mann, der Ideale hat* (1973); *Der Zauberlehrling* (1974); *Die Zeit fährt Auto* (1974). FURTHER VOLUME IN ENGLISH: *Let's Face It: Selected Poems* (1963)

BIBLIOGRAPHY: Winkelman, J., *Social Criticism in the Early Works of E. K.* (1953); Winkelman, J., *The Poetic Style of E. K.* (1957); Enderle, L., *E. K. in Selbstzeugnissen und Bilddokumenten* (1966); Beutler, K., *E. K.* (1967); Benson, R., *E. K.: Studien zu seinem Werk* (1973); Wagener, H., *E. K.* (1973); Last, R. W., *E. K.* (1974)

LOWELL A. BANGERTER

KATAEV, Valentin Petrovich

Russian novelist, dramatist, short-story writer, essayist, and poet, b. 28 Jan. 1897, Odessa

K.'s literary career spans seventy years, beginning in 1910 with the publication of his first poem. K. was born and educated in Odessa; his younger brother Yevgeny was also a writer (see Ilf and Petrov). K. belongs to the southern school of Soviet writers, also known as the Odessa school, whose members were noted for their gift of humor and a certain romantic flavor in their work. By his own admission and as evidenced in his early works, K. greatly admired Ivan Bunin (q.v.). Although not one of the Petrograd literary group called the Serapion Brothers himself, K. clearly came under their influence during the 1920s.

K.'s first postrevolutionary work of any consequence was the short story "Otets" (1925; the father), which was followed by his most successful satirical novel, *Rastratchiki* (1926; *The Embezzlers*, 1929). Mixing farce, satire, and realism, *Rastratchiki* is best understood against the background of the NEP (New Economic Policy), that brief period of Soviet history when a certain amount of free enterprise was permitted and in which the heroes of the novel—two drunken officials of a Moscow trust—abscond with a sum of money and go on a merry, if short-lived, adventure.

During the 1930s and 1940s, K.'s writing took a more serious turn and followed the typical pattern of the period: the integration of all aspects of technology into fiction. In *Vremya, vperyod!* (1932; *Time, Forward!*, 1933), a novel about the first Five-Year Plan (1928–32), the satirical element appears deliberately blunted. What sets this work apart from other "industrial" novels is that it is more genuine, concerning itself with the production process itself in the real setting of the huge metallurgical plant at Magnitogorsk. The novel is vivid and dynamic in its depiction of the workers bent on breaking a world record for concrete pouring, and captures some of the genuine excitement of that period. Written in cinematic style, with people and objects shown in constant motion, rapidly changing scenes, flashbacks, and terse dialogue, this novel is stylistically closer to expressionism (q.v.) than to psychological realism.

Beleet parus odinoky (1936; *Lonely White Sail; or, Peace Is Where the Tempests Blow*, 1937) is K.'s most engaging and lyrical work. This semiautobiographical story set in Odessa during the eventful year of 1905 has as its main characters two nine-year-old boys from different backgrounds. Humor, warmth, and spontaneity permeate this novel, in which K. displays a deep insight into child psychology. While *Beleet parus odinoky* was warmly acclaimed as the first part of a tetralogy—the second part was *Khutor v stepi* (1956; *The Cottage in the Steppe*, 1957), the third *Zimny veter* (1960; winter wind)—the book that was destined to become the fourth part, *Za vlast Sovetov* (1949; for the power of the Soviets), a novel describing the wartime underground activities in German-occupied Odessa, came under severe criticism for its failure to portray "correctly" the role of the Communist Party in the resistance movement. K. was obliged to publish a revised version in 1951.

In the post-Stalin years K. has turned to a modified genre of memoirs, in which he combines biography and autobiography, fact, fiction, semifiction, and contemplation. The two best examples of this genre are *Svyatoi kolodets* (1966; *The Holy Well*, 1967), an unusually complex story for Soviet literature, almost surrealistic in style and admittedly cinematic in technique, and *Trava zabvenia* (1967; *Grass of Oblivion*, 1969), a moving, unchronological narrative in which K. attempts to arrest the passage of time and cleverly juxtaposes portraits of Mayakovsky (q.v.) and Bunin, the two mentors of his early literary years.

K. is also well known as a playwright. His remarkable dramatic talent, laced with humor and a penchant for satire, produced a series of farcical plays, of which *Kvadratura kruga* (1928; *Squaring the Circle*, 1934) is the most famous. The problems of everyday Soviet life are the subject of these comedies. K. also successfully adapted several of his novels for the theater.

Throughout his long career K. has exhibited a remarkable power of adaptability in the face of official pressure yet has managed to retain a certain degree of freshness and independence of style. From 1955 to 1961 K. was the editor-in-chief of the literary magazine *Yunost,* in which were published works by younger, less orthodox Soviet writers. K. still lives in Moscow.

FURTHER WORKS: *Ostrov Ehrendorf* (1924); *Avangard* (1929); *Doroga tsvetov* (1934; *The Path of Flower,* 1935); *Ya syn trudovogo naroda* (1937); *Zhena* (1943; *The Wife,* 1946) *Syn polka* (1945); *Pochti dnevnik* (1962); *Malenkaya zheleznaya dver v stene* (1964); *Kubik* (1968); *Sobranie sochineny* (9 vols., 1968–72); *Razbitaya zhizn; ili, Volshebny rog Oberona* (1972; *A Mosaic of Life; or, The Magic Horn of Oberon: Memoirs of a Russian Childhood,* 1976)

BIBLIOGRAPHY: Borland, H., *Soviet Literary Theory and Practice during the First Five-Year Plan, 1928–1932* (1950), passim; Brown, E. J., Introduction to *Time, Forward!* (1961); Hayward, M., and Shukman, H., Introduction to *The Holy Well* (1967), pp. 9–16; Struve, G., *Russian Literature under Lenin and Stalin, 1917–1953* (1971), passim; Slonim, M., *Soviet Russian Literature: Writers and Problems, 1917–1967* (1973), pp. 237–39, 259, 287; Brown, D., *Soviet Russian Literature since Stalin* (1978), p. 256; Russell, R., *V. K.* (1981)

NADJA JERNAKOFF

FRANZ KAFKA

GEORG KAISER

KAWABATA YASUNARI

KATEB Yacine

Algerian novelist, poet, and dramatist (writing in French and Arabic), b. 6 Aug. 1929, Constantine

The son of Islamic parents, K. was raised on tales of Arab achievement as well as on the legends of the Algerian heroes who had resisted the French invaders from the beginning.

After attending Koranic school (the elementary school of the traditional Arabic world), K. entered the French-language school system. When he was only sixteen years old, he took part in the demonstration in Setif on May 8, 1945, which resulted in the massacre of thousands of demonstrators by the police and the army. K. was jailed and reflected later that this period was crucial in his development, for during his imprisonment he discovered the two things closest to his heart. One was the Algerian struggle for independence from France, which was a struggle by those who had neither rights nor possessions against those who had both. The other was poetry; one of K.'s best-known poems, "La rose de Blida" (1963; the rose of Blida) was written about his mother, who, believing him to have been killed during the demonstration, suffered a mental breakdown. After K.'s release from prison, he embarked on what has since been basically an itinerant life.

The same themes and symbols, the same vision, are the subject of all of K.'s writings before 1970: poems, novels, plays, and criticism. As he himself has said, all of his works "are a single work written in one long breath and still in gestation." The first expression of his lifelong work was the powerful poem "Nedjma; ou, Le poème ou le couteau" (1948; Nedjma; or, the poem or the knife). The reader is introduced to the figure of Nedjma—the girl-spirit who will move hauntingly through K.'s work—and to the palm trees, the primeval desert, the archetypal ancestor who even in incestuous, moronic decadence contains a certain glory derived from the magnificence of accumulated victories and defiant inviolability.

The publication of the novel *Nedjma* (1956; *Nedjma*, 1961) was to assure K. his place in modern literature. So unusual is the form and structure of *Nedjma* that only an impression of it can be offered. The story involves Nedjma, the four men bonded by friendship and revolutionary ardor who love her, and a gallery of secondary characters of varying importance. The vitality of the work lies not in its narrative content, although it is a highly readable novel, but in the novel's structure, which is best described as radial. The action is not chronological. It moves out from a central point, returning time and again to that point only to move out on another radius. Universality is implied in the center and in the circumference and an infinite variety of shapes and repetitions are suggested by analogy to the arabesques and geometric forms of Islamic art.

Nedjma, the daughter of a French woman and an Arab from the Keblouti clan, becomes mythic through being portrayed in an ethereal way. As the star (*nedjma* in Arabic) she symbolizes the nationalism of the new nation, the importance of the desert in Algerian life, the quest of the unattainable. As a member of the Keblouti clan, she embodies the attachment of traditional Algerians to their clan, the strong emotional ties of those who can trace their kinship back to a legendary ancestor. *Nedjma,* widely considered a masterpiece, is the greatest French-language work to come out of North Africa. In it, the French language and the Arab soul have joined to achieve a new dimension in literature.

The impulsive flow of inspiration that produced *Nedjma* seems to have yielded to a more contrived and facile idiom akin to that of guerrilla street theater and the political cartoon. Representative of this later style is *L'homme aux sandales de caoutchouc* (1970; the man with the rubber sandals), a series of vignettes highlighting the military history of Vietnam and the plight of the transient Algerian labor force in Europe.

Since 1972 K. has lived in Algiers and has renounced French to devote his talents to the production of plays in the local Arabic dialect. Structurally these plays resemble *L'homme aux sandales de caoutchouc.*

K.'s works have been criticized as regressive by some Algerian critics who wish to see their country reject the heritage of the past in order to concentrate on becoming a modern technological nation. Most critics, however, both French and African, agree that K.'s major works masterfully blend past and present and successfully interweave personal vision—even hallucination—and cultural tradition.

FURTHER WORKS: *Soliloques* (1946); *Abdelkader et l'indépendance algérienne* (1948); *Le cercle des représailles* (1959); *La femme sauvage* (perf. 1963); *Le polygone étoilé* (1966); *Les ancêtres redoublent de férocité* (perf. 1967)

BIBLIOGRAPHY: Sellin, E., "Algerian Poetry: Poetic Values, Mohammed Dib, and K. Y.," *JNALA*, Nos. 9–10 (1971), pp. 45–68; Mortimer, M. P., "K. Y. in Search of Algeria: A Study of *Nedjma* and *Le polygone étoilé*," *ECr*, 12 (1972), 274–88; Déjeux, J., *Littérature maghrébine de langue française* (1973), pp. 143–79; Déjeux, J., "Les structures de l'imaginaire dans l'œuvre de K. Y.," *ROMM*, Nos. 13–14 (1973), pp. 267–92; Déjeux, J., "K. Y., romancier, poète et dramaturge algérien," *PFr*, No. 15 (1977), pp. 127–47; Aresu, B., "Polygonal and Arithmosophical Motifs, Their Significance in the Fiction of K. Y.," *RAL*, 9 (1978), 143–75

ERIC SELLIN

KAVANAGH, Patrick

Irish poet, journalist, and novelist, b. 21 Oct. 1904, Inniskeen; d. 30 Nov. 1967, Dublin

K. dropped out of Kednaminsha Grammar School at age twelve and began, despite the limitations of his rural life, to read and write poetry. At twenty-two he had become, like his father, a farmer and cobbler. Keenly aware that his poetic aspirations alienated him from country people, he nevertheless sent poetry to local newspapers and to the *Irish Statesman*, whose editor, AE (George Russell, q.v.), published some early verse and encouraged the peasant poet. The reception of his first volume, *Ploughman, and Other Poems* (1936), encouraged K. to go to England, where his autobiography *The Green Fool* (1938) was published but withdrawn because Oliver St. John Gogarty (1878–1957)—Joyce's (q.v.) Buck Mulligan —threatened to sue for libel.

By 1939 K. had moved to Dublin, where his sense of isolation was intensified by his reception by other writers who dismissed him as an uneven, uneducated country poet. In spite of the publication of his tour de force *The Great Hunger* (1942) and of *A Soul for Sale* (1947), which mirrors his frustration and fear of failure, poverty drove him to journalism.

In spring 1955 he survived an operation for lung cancer. Late that summer on the banks of Dublin's Grand Canal he had an epiphany; feeling reborn, he began to write some of his best pastoral poetry. In New York, his brother Peter printed on a hand press what became *Recent Poems* (1958). *Come Dance with Kitty Strobling, and Other Poems* (1960) was a Poetry Book Society's selection. Although in the

1960s his health continued to deteriorate, K. wrote *Self-Portrait* (1962), a corrective of his two earlier portraits of the artist, *The Green Fool* and the autobiographical novel *Tarry Flynn* (1948). Heavy drinking hastened his death.

For K., poetry was the struggle "with the crude ungainly crust of earth and spirit"—himself in and as the clay of County Monaghan and the flowering rubble of Dublin. The ploughman writer bent reality to fit his vision of ordinary life in rural Ireland. At first influenced by English romantics and AE, he discovered *Poetry* magazine and fell under the influence of imagism (q.v.), learning the value of showing instead of telling. Frank O'Connor (q.v.) influenced him to temper romantic subjectivity with new perspectives on rural people and scenes. In K.'s poems nature is almost sacramental: nature is a teacher, the poet both recorder and seer.

The Great Hunger, perhaps his greatest poem, epitomizes K.'s artistic subject and stance. Experiencing the deprivations of Irish life, the farmer Maguire is starved for satisfactions denied him by the land, family, and religion. Skillfully blending flashbacks and dramatic presentation with dialogue, interior monologue (q.v.), and organic rhythms, K. examines the effect of environment—psychological and physical—upon the Irish Catholic peasant for whom tilling fields does not bring a harvest for spirit or flesh. Body and soul are stunted by the requirements of the agrarian economy, its mores and morality.

Whereas rural Ireland was the stony gray inspiration for the compelling "Great Hunger," Dublin was the "pig-sty" where some literary pigs were more equal than others; when "Paddies" patronized the farmer poet, he struck back with satire. Frustrated in his desire for recognition, irate at what seemed to be Dublin's hypocritical, provincial smugness, K. became the poet-critic exposing cultural and literary fraud. As a journalist he damned whatever and whoever offended him, declaring war on his contemporaries with crusading zeal, disparaging poets who came after Yeats (q.v.) and avowing an almost religious commitment to poetry. During the 1940s he lashed out at the Irish Literary Renaissance, laughed at Anglo-Irish portraits of peasants (by Yeats, Lady Gregory [1852–1932] and Synge [q.v.]), and decreed politics an unfit poetic subject. Mocking writers like Austin Clarke (q.v.) for their interest in the Celtic Twilight, K. attacked the Irish literary and artistic establishment. In his role as bellicose critic and poet-prophet, he became a pariah to his Irish critics.

The late poems, however, witness a change of mood. From the passionate Swiftian denunciations of his middle-period writing, he returned to the simple, common vocabulary of praise and the solaces of the banal beauty of canal water, grass, and passersby. After his "rebirth" he reaffirmed his dedication to poetry as the direct, lyric treatment of nature and ordinary life. His best poems celebrate the homely clay; plain, blunt, conversational, they reject the mythopoeic and symbolic frameworks of Yeats and Joyce, although his spare lyrics owe something to late Yeats, and his ability to document authentic details of country life owes something to Joyce's re-creation of Dublin. Unadorned with complex allusions, unencumbered by a sense of history, his poetry and prose are about the poet's relation to his parochial environment. His poetic assertions of self and soil became a testing ground for younger Irish poets such as Seamus Heaney (q.v.). The confessional qualities of his writing—autobiography, *roman à clef*, "pruse" (sic), or poems—mark him as a voice of the new personalism in literature.

FURTHER WORKS: *Collected Poems* (1964); *Collected Pruse* (1967); *Lapped Furrows* (1969); *November Haggard* (1971); *Complete Poems* (1972); *By Night Unstarred* (1978); *Lough Derg* (1978)

BIBLIOGRAPHY: Payne, B., "The Poetry of P. K.," *Studies*, 49 (1960), 279–94; Freyer, G., "P. K.," *Éire*, 3, 4 (1968), 17–23; Kennelly, B., "P. K.," *ArielE*, 1, 3 (1970), 7–28; Kavanagh, P., *The Garden of the Golden Apples* (1972); Warner, A., *Clay Is the Word: P. K., 1904–1967* (1973); O'Brien, D., *P. K.* (1975); special K. issue, *JIL*, 6, 1 (1977); Nemo, J., *P. K.* (1979); Kavanagh, P., *Sacred Keeper* (1979)

MARTHA FODASKI-BLACK

KAVERIN, Veniamin

(pseud. of Veniamin Zilberg) Russian novelist, short-story writer, and memoirist, b. 19 April 1902, Pskov

Born into a family of musicians, K. studied the violin until he was fifteen. He attended the University of Petrograd (now Leningrad) and received degrees in Oriental languages (1923) and Russian literature (1924). While at the university he studied under the leading Russian formalist (q.v.) critics, Boris Eikhenbaum (1886–1959) and Yury Tynyanov (1894–1943; later his brother-in-law).

K. began writing fiction in 1920, and in 1921 he joined the Serapion Brotherhood, a group of talented young writers dedicated to defending the autonomy of art. With his close friend Lev Lunts (1902–1924), K. represented the group's Western wing, which sought inspiration from Western writers of fantasy and adventure—Robert Louis Stevenson, Edgar Allan Poe, and E. T. A. Hoffmann. His early stories reveal their influence and also that of the formalists. In them K. plays with literary conventions à la Laurence Sterne (recommended as a model by formalist and fellow Serapion Brother, Viktor Shklovsky [b. 1893]), experiments with plot construction and narrative techniques, refuses to philosophize or to describe reality, and shows little concern for political or social problems.

By 1928, however, K. had become drawn to the problem of the intelligentsia and the revolution: the most famous work of his early period, *Khudozhnik neizvesten* (1931; *The Unknown Artist*, 1947), deals with the dilemma of the artist in a Communist society. The novel, which purports to be a documentary, depicts the struggle between the eccentric painter Arkhimedov, portrayed as a modern Don Quixote, and his engineer friend Shpektorov, the new technocrat who is contemptuous of ethical values and art. In the end Arkhimedov is destroyed, but his art triumphs, for he leaves behind an unsigned painting of exceptional beauty portraying the suicide of his wife.

K. returned to the theme of the artist and his struggle to remain true to his vision in his fine recent novel *Pered zerkalom* (1972; before the mirror). This time his protagonist is a woman painter, Lisa Turaevna. Like the Soviet bacteriologist Tatyana Vlasenkova, heroine of his postwar trilogy *Otkrytaya kniga* (1956; *The Open Book*, 1957), Turaevna struggles against everyday and political pressures and endures to triumph. Both novels cover a wide span of time and chronicle the development of the heroine from girlhood to middle age. *Otkrytaya kniga* is written in the form of a diary and memoirs; *Pered zerkalom* in the form of letters between Turaevna and her lifelong friend Karnovsky. While *Otkrytaya kniga* deals with the period between the revolution and World War II, *Pered zerkalom* focuses on the period 1910–30, with special emphasis on the artistic experience of the 1920s. A desire to preserve the memory of that period for the present generation is also evident in K.'s own recent memoirs, *Sobesednik* (1973; interlocutor) and *Osveshchennye okna* (1978; illuminated windows).

K. has played a part in all of the many and varied phases of Soviet literature from 1922 to the present. In the 1930s he adapted to the demands of Socialist Realism (q.v.), but he did not capitulate to it. His novels never ceased to engage and interest readers. In the postwar period he has been outspoken both in his own works and in his defense of the works of other authors. For this he has been censured by the regime more than once.

FURTHER WORKS: *Mastera i podmasterya* (1923); *Konets khazy* (1925); *Devyat desyatykh sudby* (1925); *Bolshaya igra* (1926); *Vorobinaya noch* (1927); *Bubnovaya mast* (1927); *Skandalist; ili, Vechera na Vasilevskom Ostrove* (1928); *Prolog* (1931); *Chernovnik cheloveka* (1931); *Ukroshchenie Robinzona; ili, Poteryanny ray* (1934); *Ispolnenie zhelany* (1937; *The Larger View*, 1938); *Rasskazy* (1942); *Dva kapitana* (1945; *Two Captains*, 1957); *Sem par nechistykh* (1962); *Kosoy dozhd* (1962); *Zdravstvy, brat, pisat ochen trudno* (1965); *Dvoynoy portret* (1966); *Shkolny spektakl* (1968); *Dvukhchasovaya progulka* (1978)

BIBLIOGRAPHY: Piper, D. G., *V. A. K.* (1970); Oulanoff, H., *The Prose Fiction of V. A. K.* (1976); Beaujour, E., "K.'s *Before the Mirror*," *SEEJ*, 24 (1980), 233–44

SONA STEPHAN HOISINGTON

KAWABATA Yasunari

Japanese novelist, b. 11 June 1899, Osaka; d. 16 April, 1972, Kamakura

K. lost all his closest relatives by the age of fourteen. His diary, virtually his first literary product, published only in 1925 as *Jūrokusai no nikki* (the diary of a sixteen-year-old-boy), records the boy's observation of his dying grandfather (the "sixteen" in the title refers to the old style of reckoning age). As a middle-school student well versed in the Japanese classics, K. chose to become a writer and soon began to contribute short stories to a local paper. In 1924 he became a leading member of the "New Perceptionist" group of young writers interested in the literary and art trends from the West. During this experimental period K.'s works revealed the modernist influence. Soon after his reaffirmation of his inheritance of Japan's literary tradition K. began to publish in serial form the celebrated *Yukiguni* (1935–48; *Snow Country*, 1956); this work was succeeded by numerous serialized novels that appeared after the defeat of Japan. K. was also noted as an acute critic and discoverer of new talents. He won the Nobel Prize for literature in 1968. Four years later he took his own life.

Izu no odoriko (1926; *The Izu Dancer*, 1955) established K.'s reputation. On a journey a young student encounters a fourteen-year-old dancer, a member of a family of traveling entertainers. The youth appreciates their kindness and feels a genuine innocent love for the girl. The autobiographical hero, a receptive observer, foreshadows his fictional successors. This simple story ends with a separation, as in most of K.'s novels.

K. generates a pervasive sadness not with the depiction of catastrophic conflicts, but with great subtlety, as best exemplified in *Yukiguni*, a story about a country geisha, Komako, who falls in love with Shimamura, a dilettante from Tokyo. This novel demonstrates K.'s remarkable style, uniquely his own, and characterized by refined simplicity and evocative images. Lyric descriptions of nature are central to the narrative progression in K.'s novels. Their basically episodic form emerges through the allusive links of successive scenes, not according to a well-defined plot structure. As is often pointed out, this form echoes the Japanese poetic tradition, especially that of *renga*, linked verse.

The traditional Japanese sensibility discerns the quality of evanescence in beautiful objects. The search for and admiration of beauty are dominant Kawabata themes. Beauty in K. is not unattainable absolute beauty; it is manifested in the innocence and purity of a girl or in the warmth of a woman's love, or in a kind of devotion exemplified by the hero in *Meijin* (1954; *The Master of Go*, 1972). Pursuit of such beauty cannot be isolated from an awareness of deprivation or from the encroachment of fatigue, degeneration, and death.

Sembazuru (1952; *Thousand Cranes*, 1959) and *Mizuumi* (1954; *The Lake*, 1974) explore the degradation and guilt into which man is liable to be led through the attraction of beauty. *Sembazuru*, centering on the tea ceremony, recalls the karmic, incestuous relationships in the famous 11th-c. Japanese novel *The Tale of Genji. Mizuumi*, with few references to the tradition, is perhaps the most experimental among K.'s postwar novels. Hallucinations, stream-of-consciousness, and free associations in the complex shifts of time are used to portray an ex-teacher's impelling desire to follow beautiful women. In spite of the character's grotesquely ugly degeneration, this exploration into the dark subconscious is again permeated with lyrical pathos.

Direct human relationships are avoided in *Kinjū* (1933; *Of Birds and Beasts*, 1969), whose hero, rejecting human affection, raises birds and dogs, and in *Nemureru bijo* (1961; *House of Sleeping Beauties*, 1969), a bizarre, but nonetheless masterfully controlled story of an old man who visits an establishment to sleep for a night with drugged girls. This evasion is carried to an extreme in a strange story, *Kataude* (1964; *One Arm*, 1969), in which a human relationship exists only through a severed arm. These works might be read as satires on dehumanizing alienation, but again the lyrical and often reflective note implicitly calls for the recovery of a wholesome communion.

K.'s most important work, *Yama no oto* (1954; *The Sound of the Mountain*, 1970), subtly embodies his profound understanding of human nature and suggests the possible achievement of such a communion. This difficult task is undertaken in the spiritual chaos following Japan's defeat. The aging protagonist, Shingo, is deeply concerned about the marital crises of his two children and tries, as much as he can, to assist. The novel attempts to redeem and reaffirm that traditional Japanese sensibility that enjoys communion with nature and caring human relationships. Stylistically as well, this novel is K.'s finest achievement. The dialogue, which exhibits his accomplished ease in creating scenes from daily life, is skillfully interwoven with the hero's dreams, recollections, and reflections. The poetic descriptions of nature, often consisting of extremely evocative one-sentence paragraphs, are suggestive of the psychological state of the protagonist. At the same time these passages also allow the reader's participation in the hero's communion with nature.

K.'s works represent a rare combination of tradition and modernity. The quiet realism, the seeming formlessness, and above all the poetic intensity in K., while testifying to the tenacious literary legacy of Japan, suggest to the West many innovative possibilities.

FURTHER WORKS: *Kanjō sōshoku* (1926); *Asakusa kurenaidan* (1930); *Hana no warutsu* (1940); *Maihime* (1951); *Hi mo tsuki mo* (1953); *Tokyo no hito* (1955); *Niji ikutabi* (1955); *Onna de aru koto* (1957); *Kaze no aru michi* (1959); *Koto* (1962); *Kawa no aru shitamachi no hanashi* (1962); *Utsukushisa to kanashimi to* (1965; *Beauty and Sadness*, 1975); *Rakka ryūsui* (1966); *Gekka no mon* (1967); *Utsukushii Nihon no watakushi* (1969; *Japan the Beautiful and Myself*, 1969); *Bi no sonzai to hakken* (1969; *The Existence and Discovery of Beauty*, 1969)

BIBLIOGRAPHY: Tsukimura, R., "A Thematic Study of the Works of K. Y.," *JATJ*, 5 (1968), 22–31; Seidensticker, E. G., "K.," *HudR*, 22 (1969), 6–10; Tsukimura, R., "Theme and Technique in *Mizuumi*," in Japan P.E.N. Club, ed., *Studies on Japanese Culture* (1973), Vol. I, pp. 433–39; Miyoshi, M., *Accomplices of Silence: The Modern Japanese Novel* (1974), pp. 95–121; Ueda, M., "The Virgin, the Wife, and the Nun: K.'s *Snow Country*," in Tsuruta, K., and Swann, T. E., eds., *Approaches to the Modern Japanese Novel* (1976), pp. 73–88; Tsuruta, K., "Two Journeys in *The Sound of the Mountain*," in Tsuruta, K., and Swann, T. E., eds., *Approaches to the Modern Japanese Novel* (1976), pp. 89–103; Ueda, M., *Modern Japanese Writers and the Nature of Literature* (1976), pp. 173–218; Tsuruta, K., "The Colour Scheme in *House of the Sleeping Beauties*," in Tsukimura, R., ed., *Life, Death and Age in Modern Japanese Fiction* (1978), pp. 21–34; Tsukimura, R., "The Symbolic Significance of the Old Man in *The Sound of the Mountain*," in Tsukimura, R., ed., *Life, Death and Age in Modern Japanese Fiction* (1978), pp. 45–54

REIKO TSUKIMURA

KAZAKH LITERATURE

During the first decade of the 20th c., Kazakh literature departed decisively from a long heritage by shifting abruptly from the famed verbal poetic art of its past while adding imaginative prose and modern drama to its genres. Lyric verse, written very late in the 1880s, still circulated mainly in recitations from memory. Few of the compositions by the popular Ibrahim (Abay) Qŭnanbay-ŭlï (1845–1904), for example, had yet been printed. His first volume, *Qazaq aqïnï Ibrahim*

Qŭnanbayŭlïnïng ölengderï (1909; poems by the Kazakh poet Ibrahim Qŭnanbay-ŭlï), significantly, came out in St. Petersburg rather than a Kazakh town.

Longer works of written prose in Kazakh were closely linked with Tatar influence in centers of upper Kazakhstan, like Orenburg and Troitsk. The first edition of a Kazakh novelette, Mir Jaqib Duwlat-ŭlï's (q.v.) 94-page *Baqïtsïz Jamal* (1910; unlucky Jamal), typically appeared in Kazan, the Tatar capital. This story was characteristic of a school of sentimental tragedy, which viewed Kazakh girls as miserable in arranged marriage and polygamy. Duwlat-ulï also composed fiery anti-Russian poetry and cooperated with the prominent Kazakh poet and translator Aqmet Baytursin-ŭlï (1873–1937) in editing the early newspapers *Qazaqstan* (1911 and 1913) and *Qazaq* (1913–18, intermittent).

The first published Kazakh drama, *Nadandïq qurbandarï* (1914; victims of ignorance), by Kölbey Toghïs-ŭlï (dates n.a.), was the creation of a reformist author and modernizer. Drama and theater rapidly developed as indoctrination media in the 1920s for the largely illiterate (over 93 percent in 1926) Kazakh population. Controversial plays were offered by Säken Seyfullin (1894–1938): his *Qïzïl sŭngqarlar* (1920, pub. 1922; red falcons); by Mŭkhtar O. Auez-ŭlï (Auezov, q.v.): the tragedy *Änglik–Kebek* (1917, pub. 1922; Änglik and Kebek); and by Duwlat-ŭlï: his *Balqiya* (1922; Balqiya). The three new playwrights underwent scathing ideological criticism after 1917 for these and other writings. Of the three, only Auez-ŭlï survived, by careful accommodation, the Soviet political purges of the 1930s. Many Kazakh writers, including prolific Communist versifiers and prose writers such as Beyimbet Maylin (1894–1938), known widely in Kazakhstan for his novel *Azamat Azamatovich* (1935; Azamat Azamatovich), about nationalism, perished during the purge years. That stifling ideological control over Kazakh letters intensified noticeably from the date the state-run Writers' Union of Kazakhstan was established for supervisory purposes in 1934.

Curiously, the tone of writing in recent decades often resembles the didactic spirit of pre-1917 novelettes such as the short *Qalïng mal* (1914; the bride price), by Ispandiyar Köbey-ŭlï (1878–1956), which also condemned the custom of obligatory dowry and arranged marriage. A series of tendentious novels illustrating Soviet slogans came out, for example, under the

signature of Writers' Union chief Ghabiden Mŭstafin (b. 1902), starting with his *Ömir ne ölim* (1938; life or death), about mining and industrialization in Kazakhstan. His most widely circulated and translated novel, *Millioner* (1948; millionaire farm), dealing with collectivization of Kazakh agriculture, was followed by the autobiographical *Qaraghandï* (1952; Karaganda), an ideological recasting of his earlier *Ömir ne ölim*.

Communist spokesmen describe the short story as a "militant genre," but the greatest literary success in the new Kazakh prose fell to a long historical novel, *Abay* (2 vols., 1945, 1947; *Abai: A Novel,* n.d.), by Auez-ulï, depicts the life and times of the pre-Soviet poet Ibrahim Qŭnanbay-ŭlï, known as Abay. It won the Stalin Prize in 1949 and was translated into many languages, including English.

A new, possibly minor, phase in Kazakh development arrived with a few works from bilingual Kazakh authors writing in Russian (very early in the 20th c., Kazakhs had sometimes composed in Chaghatay or Tatar). Increasingly known for such literature, among others, is Olzhas Omar-ŭlï Suleymanov (b. 1936), educated in Moscow and Alma-Ata, and author of a powerful literary polemic, *Az-i-ia* (1975; Asia) arguing for Asia's cultural influence over Europe/Russia. He earlier published short volumes of verse in his own Russian, including *Solnechnye nochi* (1962; sunny nights) and *Glinianaya kniga* (1969; the clay book). An interesting interethnic language experiment is the two-act play entitled, in the Russian-language version, *Voskhozhdenie na Fudziamu* (1973; *The Ascent of Mount Fuji,* 1975), by the Kazakh writer Qaltay Mŭkhamedzhanov (b. 1928) and the Kirgiz writer Chïngïz Aytmatov (q.v.), which explores guilt and responsibility among creative writers under Stalin's repression.

Drama in Kazakh moved, after the controversies of the early 1920s, into Soviet stylistic and thematic grooves, with establishment playwrights like Ghabit Makhmud-ŭlï Müsrepov (b. 1902). His *Amankeldï* (1936, rev. version 1958; Amankeldï) is considered by Marxists a perfect specimen of Socialist Realism (q.v.) in its use of stock characters involved in class warfare in Kazakhstan against implacable enemies during the Russian civil war of 1918–21.

Notwithstanding public encouragement given different genres, poetry has continued as before to be the most popular among readers. Kazakh poets incessantly receive exhortations to produce socially and politically useful verse. Nevertheless, a great deal of universal lyric, as well as narrative, poetry appears in print. Younger poets in the 1960s and 1970s also revealed a fascination with the history and significance of their native land for ethnic-group identity and for deep Kazakh attachments. Erkesh Ibrahim (Ebekenov, b. 1930) published five books of poetry before 1969, starting with *Qarlïghash* (1958; the swallow) and including two about Kokchetau, his native locality in northern Kazakhstan. Others, like Sagi Zhienbayev (b. 1934), Qayrat Zhŭmaghaliev (b. 1937), and Dukenbay Doszhanov (b. 1942), took more interest in humanity and nature than in the prescribed topicality reflected so much in the writings of older poets, such as Tayïr Zharokov (1908–1965). Zharokov's many volumes of verse, beginning with *Zhŭldiz zharïghï* (1932; radiance of the star), through *Stalin sŭngqarларï* (1941; Stalin's falcons), to the several editions of *Qïrda tughan qŭrïsh* (1954 ff.; steel born in the prairie), and others, responded directly to the persistent call for metrical elucidation of the Communist Party outlook.

BIBLIOGRAPHY: Winner, T. G., *The Oral Art and Literature of the Kazakhs of Russian Central Asia* (1958); "La littérature kazakh," *Philologiae Turcicae Fundamenta* (1964), pp. 154–55; Allworth, E., "The Changing Intellectual and Literary Community" and "The Focus of Literature," in Allworth, E., ed., *Central Asia: A Century of Russian Rule* (1967), pp. 349–96, 397–433

EDWARD ALLWORTH

KAZAKOV, Yury

Russian short-story writer, b. 8 Aug. 1927, Moscow

Having begun a career as a jazz musician, K. began to publish short stories in 1952 and then entered the Gorky Institute of World Literature, graduating in 1958. In the 1950s and 1960s K. traveled extensively in northern Russia. These travels generated, among other works, his *Severny dnevnik* (1961; northern diary).

Appearing after twenty years of Stalinist fiction glorifying agricultural and industrial production, K.'s early short stories had a special impact. His return to the lyricism, open-endedness, and the "eternal questions" of pre-Soviet authors, especially Chekhov, Bunin (qq.v.), and the Turgenev of *A Sportsman's Sketches*,

seemed a radical step during the period of the so-called first thaw (1953–57). K.'s use of character, plot, setting, and language is antithetical to traditional Socialist Realism (q.v.). His characters are seldom heroic. Some are irredeemably negative: the hypocritical mendicant who tries to seduce his hostess's daughter in "Strannik" (1956; "The Mendicant," 1963); peasants grossly insensitive to the women close to them in "V gorod" (1961; "Going to Town," 1963) and "Na polustanke" (1954; "At the Station," 1963); the egotistical artist embittered by professional rejection in "Adam i Eva" (1962; "Adam and Eve," 1963). Other characters are presented ambiguously: Egor in "Trali-vali" (1959; "Silly Billy," 1963) may be lazy but he has moments of inspiration when he sings; a son leaving the village is unduly brusque with his tearful mother because he is afraid of his own emotions. Positive characters are shown not for their personal qualities but as people in the throes of a poignant experience—closeness to a loved one in the wilds in "Osen v dubovykh lesakh" (1963; "Autumn in the Oak Woods," 1963), the passing of first love in "Goluboe i zelyonoe" (1963; "The Blue and the Green," 1963). Plot is reduced to a minimum so that the quality of subtle and complex emotional shifts may dominate.

Central to K.'s work—and this is his most important, if least remarked, departure from Socialist Realism—is the view of man as an integral part of nature, subject to its eternal cycles. Men, women, children, and animals are manifestations of nature, rather than its subjugators, and ultimately must be part of it. The circus bear in "Teddi" (1961; "Teddy," 1963) detaches himself from his unnatural life and returns to the woods; city life distorts the love of man and woman in "Osen v dubovykh lesakh." People divorced from nature are out of touch with their inmost selves: the woman who returns from the city to her village in "Zapakh khleba" (1962; "The Smell of Bread," 1963); the sailors on vacation in "Proklyaty sever" (1964; "The Accursed North," 1963). In "Nikishkiny tayny" (1951; "Nikishka's Secrets," 1970), an eight-year-old boy mutely and vividly communes with the woods in his imagination. The nonverbal nature of his experience is conveyed by a spare narrative that approximates the boy's simple language.

K. was attacked for his atypical stories by some Soviet critics, who found his work pessimistic, overly literary, and not clear enough in its moral position. Similar criticism was later

made of the work of many of the new generation of writers. This conflict of views was
openly acknowledged in the early 1960s and
may be understood as a result of the transition
of post-Stalinist society into a more settled and
prosperous state after the deprivations of forty
years of social upheaval. By the end of the
1950s the model shock-worker (Stakhanovite)
hero of earlier Soviet literature was no longer
appropriate to the complex life of literate urban
readers. K.'s work heralds and reflects this
change.

K. was one of the first to write in a fresh,
sincere voice about questions of conscience in
contemporary life. By setting his stories in the
wilderness of northern Russia, K. could present
universal moral issues in isolation from their
sociopolitical context. This method made him
an influential forerunner of the two major types
of short story to emerge in the 1960s: Young
Prose, which examines the problems faced by
the new generation of urban youth—especially
the works of Anatoly Gladilin (b. 1935), Vasily Aksyonov (q.v.), and Andrey Bitov (b.
1937); and Village Prose, in which personal
moral values are restored by a return to the
simple, eternal life of country folk—for example, works by Vasily Belov (b. 1933) and Valentin Rasputin (b. 1937). While K.'s stories
are not of the literary quality of the 19th-c.
masters he draws upon, they contain some
moving vignettes of universal appeal and embody the characteristic artistic and moral integrity of the Russian literary tradition.

FURTHER WORKS: *Pervoe svidanie* (1955);
Manka (1958); *Na polustanke* (1959); *Po
doroge* (1961); *Rasskazy* (1962); *Tropiki na
pechke* (1962); *Lyogkaya zhizn* (1963); *Selected Short Stories* [in Russian] (1963);
Dvoe v dekabre (1966); *Vo sne ty gorko
plakal* (1977). FURTHER VOLUMES IN EN-
GLISH: *Going to Town, and Other Stories*
(1963); *Autumn in the Oak Woods* (1970)

BIBLIOGRAPHY: Gibian, G., Foreword to *Selected Short Stories* (1963), pp. ix–xxv; Whit-
ney, T. P., ed., *The New Writing in Russia*
(1964), pp. 97–102; Kramer, K. D., "Jurij
K.: The Pleasures of Isolation," *SEEJ*, 10
(1966), 22–31; Collins, C., "Nature and Self
in K.," *SEEJ*, 12 (1968), 397–406; Brown,
D., *Soviet Russian Literature since Stalin*
(1978), pp. 157–61, 218–19

PRISCILLA MEYER

KAZANTZAKIS, Nikos

Greek novelist, poet, dramatist, essayist, and
travel writer, b. 18 Feb. 1883, Heraklion,
Crete; d. 26 Oct. 1957, Freiburg, West Germany

The central fact in the life of K. is that it began
on Crete in the last generation of that island's
centuries-long resistance to foreign domination.
Its central symbol is an event that occurred
when he was a child, in 1889, during one of the
final rebellions against Turkish rule. "My
mother, my sister, and I sat glued to one another, barricaded within our house. We heard
the frenzied Turks in the street outside, cursing,
threatening, breaking down doors, and slaugh-
tering Christians. . . . My father stood in wait
behind the door, his musket loaded. In his
hand, I remember, he held an oblong stone
which he called a whetstone. He was sharpen-
ing a long black-handled knife on it. We
waited. 'If the Turks break down the door and
enter,' he had told us, 'I plan to slaughter you
myself before you fall into their hands.' My
mother, sister, and I had all agreed. Now we
were waiting." The story is recounted in K.'s
posthumously published "spiritual autobiography," *Anafora ston Greko* (1961; *Report to
Greco*, 1965), which is not always reliable as
literal history. But K. tells it again in the most
factual of his novels, *O Kapetan Mihalis*
(1953; *Freedom or Death,* 1956)—a likely
indication of its historicity and a certain sign of
its symbolic significance for the man who would
become the greatest and most controversial of
modern Greek writers. From so insular a beginning, K., who lost the Nobel Prize by a single
vote in 1957, became one of the most universal
of writers, at once Greek and more broadly European. That he left Crete as a young man and
spent most of his life in the West merely reaffirms his homeland's attraction, for he returns
constantly to it in his art, raising such local incidents to the level of universal metaphor.
Drawn both to the intellectual constructs of the
West (he wrote his dissertation at the University of Athens on Nietzsche and studied with
Henri Bergson [q.v.] at the Collège de France)
and to the unique heritage of his native Crete,
K. created a literature expressive of Greek and
of modernist culture alike.

One theme that unifies his career—from the
early translations, textbooks, verse dramas, and
travel books through the fourteen-year enterprise of his *Odyssia* (1938; *The Odyssey: A
Modern Sequel*, 1958), to the novels of his
final phase—is the fight for linguistic reform. It

is difficult for outsiders to comprehend the significance of the language issue in modern Greek culture. There are two separate Greek languages: one, the *demotiki*, the spoken tongue, grafting naturally to ancient Greek the results of centuries of interpenetration with foreigners; the other, the *katharevousa*, an invented language, designed after Greek independence to bypass foreign influence and restore the pristine glories of classical Greek. The latter is an artificial and inflated language, well suited to scholars and bureaucrats; the former is wonderfully adaptable, the language not just of the people but of the poets as well. Yet, for nearly a century, the scholars and bureaucrats (particularly under right-wing regimes) endeavored to impose their language upon the poets.

K. devoted much of his life to this battle; it served to brand him as a radical and affected the reception of even his greatest works within Greece. *Odyssia* has repeatedly been accused of being too revolutionary in vocabulary and diction, and the radicalism of K.'s language has inevitably become associated with the independence of his thought. There was an early move to excommunicate him from the Orthodox Church; *O telefteos pirasmos* (1955; *The Last Temptation of Christ*, 1960) was attacked as heretical (in one case by a critic since proven not to have read the novel); the Archbishop of Athens refused to allow K.'s burial from the cathedral. It is hardly coincidental that K. lived most of his life as an artist outside Greece—except for the years of World War II, which he felt he had to share with his suffering countrymen—or that his reputation for a long time was greater beyond Greece's borders (he has been translated into some forty languages), or even that his grave in his native Heraklion has become something of a shrine.

For his work is inevitably and unmistakably Greek, or, more specifically, Cretan. A second unifying theme of K.'s canon is the metaphor which he labels the "Cretan Glance" and which he defines as that attitude with which man, "without hope yet without fear," acknowledges the limitations and dangers inherent in human life and despite them—because of them even—persists in living fully at the edge of the abyss. "This glance which confronts life and death so bravely, I call Cretan." The metaphor is obviously drawn from the heroic yet futile Cretan resistance to Venetian and then Turkish oppression, and it is at the heart of each of his works of fiction: not merely in *O Kapetan Mihalis*, which is based on the Cretan revolt of 1889, or in *Vios kai politia toy Alexi Zorba*

(1946; *Zorba the Greek*, 1953), whose action similarly takes place on Crete; but also in those novels set on the mainland—*I adherfofadhes* (1963; *The Fratricides*, 1964), based on the civil war of 1946–49; or in the Greek lands of Asia Minor—*O Hristos xanastavronete* (1954; *The Greek Passion*, 1953), concerned with the exodus that followed the defeat by Turkey in 1922; or in lands beyond Greece—*O telefteos pirasmos*, set in biblical Galilee and Judea. It informs each of the movements of K.'s Odysseus as he progresses beyond Ithaca to the Mycenaean mainland to Minoan Crete to Egypt and the African interior and finally to the Antarctic seas, a movement as much philosophical as it is historical and geographical. Each of K.'s heroes—he calls each one a "colossus"—is a development from the Cretan *pallikari*, the heroes of the long resistance whose portraits are found even today throughout the island.

But the Kazantzakian colossus has Western roots as well: here his source is the Nietzschean *Übermensch*, that philosophical hero who extends his grasp beyond the normal but who does no more than all men could, as K. views it, were they willing to bear the cost. This union of disparate forces (made still more disparate by a dash of the Bergsonian *élan vital*) is characteristic of K.'s thought; characteristic, too, is the unresolved tension that emerges from such a union. For Kosmas, the artist figure of *O Kapetan Mihalis*, a character derived and extended from K.'s self-image, the tension is between his Western education and a Cretan tradition to which he is impelled but which he knows is archaic; for Jesus in *O telefteos pirasmos* it is between his desire for a simple human life and the impulse toward godhead; for Odysseus, who encapsulates them all, it is between the just and joyful needs of the body and the more imperative demands of the spirit. When Odysseus at the end of his long and challenging journey dissolves, quite literally, into pure spirit, we may assume that his creator has chosen one supreme good over the other; but then we note the vital, even sensuous verse in which this final progression is recorded, and we realize that the conflict has simply been moved to some higher level. In the end, it is the tension itself for which K. strives. The only novel of his in which a full thematic resolution is reached, *O ftohoylis toy Theoy* (1956; *Saint Francis*, 1962), is also, not coincidentally, the least successful of his mature fictions.

The continuity of K.'s imagery and thought is apparent throughout his work, from the early poetic essay called *Salvatores Dei: Asketiki*

(1927; *The Saviors of God: Spiritual Exercises,* 1960), where he first elaborated his complex dialectic, to the late novels for which he is best known outside Greece. But it is *Odyssia* which he considered his masterwork and for which he believed he would be remembered. (Had he lived one more year after its appearance in English he would surely have won the Nobel Prize.) K.'s epic poem is a quite conscious challenge to Homer, encompassing all the knowledge of our world as Homer's does of Bronze Age Greece: the poet called it simply *Odyssia;* it was Kimon Friar, with whom he collaborated on the superb English translation, who suggested the subtitle, *A Modern Sequel.* Here we find functioning in concert all those concerns that dominate individual novels: the themes of Cretan and Greek history (*O Kapetan Mihalis*), of radical politics and the need for renewal (*O Hristos xanastavronete*), of spirituality and myth (*O telefteos pirasmos*), of an evolving philosophy of art and humanity (*Vios kai politia toy Alexi Zorba*). *Odyssia* manifests as well a profound sensitivity to ancient civilizations and mythopoesis, a deep knowledge of and insight into modern archaeological and anthropological discoveries, and a moving and convincing statement of humanistic concern.

It is *Odyssia* that leads us to inevitable comparisons to K.'s modernist contemporaries: to the moral sense of Thomas Mann (q.v.); to the vision of ascendant man, the spirit of place, and the personal travel essay of D. H. Lawrence (q.v.); to the the encyclopedic structure and mythic perspective of James Joyce (q.v.). But it is the differences between K. and the Western modernists that are most revealing: the conviction and intensity at the heart of the metaphor of the Cretan Glance make Mann's pervasive irony seem out of place; its humane center makes the mystical Lawrence of, say, *The Plumed Serpent,* seem rather jejune; its inherent feeling for the workings of myth makes the Homeric analogue of Joyce's *Ulysses* appear somewhat formal and even superficial. The particular humanistic involvement of K.'s art—Western in its intellectuality, Cretan at its core—distinguishes the artist from all his contemporaries. The strengths and flaws alike of K.'s art are derived from this mixture of Cretan and Western influence. He is representative of the modernist literary experience and, because of this mix, uniquely beyond it.

FURTHER WORKS: *Ti ida sti Rousia* (1928); *Toda-Raba* (1934; *Toda-Raba,* 1964); *Is-*

pania (1937; *Spain,* 1963); *Iaponia-Kina* (1938; *Japan/China,* 1963); *Anghlia* (1941; *England,* 1965); *Omirou Iliada* (1955); *Theatro* (1955); *Boudhas* (1956); *Epistoles apo ti Galatia* (1958; partial tr. in *The Suffering God: Selected Letters to Galatea and to Papastephanou,* 1979); *Le jardin des rochers* (1959; *The Rock Garden,* 1963); *Tertsines* (1960); *Taxidevontas* (1961; *Journeying: Travels in Italy, Egypt, Sinai, Jerusalem, and Cyprus,* 1975); *O Morias* (1961; *Journey to the Morea,* 1965); *Tetrakosia Grammata toy K. ston Prevelaki* (1965); *Symposion* (1971; *Symposium,* 1975). FURTHER VOLUMES IN ENGLISH: *Three Plays* (1969); *Alexander the Great* (1981)

BIBLIOGRAPHY: Stanford, W. B., *The Ulysses Theme* (1954), pp. 211–40; Prevelakis, P., *N. K. and His Odyssey* (1961); Izzet, A., *N. K.: Biographie* (1965); Kazantzakis, H., *N. K.: A Biography Based on His Letters* (1968); Janiaud-Lust, C., *N. K.: La vie, son œuvre* (1970); special K. issue, *JML,* 2, 2 (1971–82); Bien, P., *K. and the Linguistic Revolution in Greek Literature* (1972); Bien, P., *N. K.* (1972); special K. bibliographical issue, *Mantatoforos,* No. 5 (1974); McDonough, B. T., *Nietzsche and K.* (1978); Friar, K., ed., *The Spiritual Odyssey of N. K.* (1979); Lea, J. F., *The Politics of Salvation* (1979); Levitt, M. P., *The Cretan Glance: The World and Art of N. K.* (1980)

                                MORTON P. LEVITT

K. has found many new ways of understanding Ulysses in terms of modern thought. He has devised many new and significant adventures for him. He has presented a fully integrated portrait of the hero—as wanderer and politician, as destroyer and preserver, as sensualist and ascetic, as soldier and philosopher, as pragmatist and mystic, as legislator and humorist. He has combined many scattered elements in the ancient and modern tradition. But the earnestness with which he urges his Cretan view of life must not make us accept his Odysseus as an entirely new conception of the hero. On the contrary this neo-Greek hero is something much more like a "synthesis" of the whole post-Homeric myth. And the prevailing mood is fundamentally that of the Stoics. As one studies K.'s philosophic writings in general one constantly recalls the *Meditations* of Marcus Aurelius.

W. B. Stanford, *The Ulysses Theme* (1954), p. 239

According to K. something of the nature of the divinity is expressed in poetic creation. Amid the general corruption, certain privileged beings are endowed with the capacity to carry on the work of "God." Generally speaking, the action of all rational creatures participates in this mystery. But poetic creation is the God-bearing activity par excellence. The poet's longing for immortality is not only a desire to triumph over the common lot of man. It is the manifestation of a supernatural reality, of the primordial impulse "penetrating plants, beasts and men." But "God," if He is ever present, is not almighty. Man's dedication to creative activity alone "saves God" (*The Saviors of God*). Beneath this pretense of submission to the spirit of creation smoldered a tyrannical ambition and a haughty faith in the power of man such as had not been seen since the Renaissance. [1958]

Pandhelis Prevelakis, *N. K. and His Odyssey* (1961), p. 27

The Cretan Glance for K., therefore, was an attempted synthesis of those contraries which he believed underlie all human and natural endeavor, but a synthesis not so much of permanent as of momentary harmony, which in turn builds into a greater tension and explodes toward a higher and more inclusive synthesis in an ever upward and spiraling onrush, leaving behind it the blood-stained path of man's and nature's endeavors. This may explain much that, from a more restricted point of view, seems contradictory in his life and thought, but which takes on another value when seen as the ever-shifting sections of larger and, in themselves, ever-changing unities. . . . It is a double vision between whose dual tensions rises the third inner eye that soars on the balancing wings of good and evil, that no sooner creates a new law than it begins immediately to conceive of an opposed and contrary law with which to knock it down.

Kimon Friar, Introduction to *The Odyssey: A Modern Sequel* (1958), p. xx

K.'s great cohorts, the "bodyguards of the Odyssey" as he called them [Homer, Bergson, Nietzsche, and Zorba], along with a host of secondary, though by no means inferior figures, Christ, Lenin, Dante, Buddha, Greco, Psycharis and others, whom he enshrined in a series of *terza rima* cantos, helped enrich him with the formal means, the discipline, the example . . . for the technical consummation of his creation. But from his dreams and travels he drew the raw material of his work. . . .

Each of K.'s works should be viewed as the repetition, elaboration or elucidation of a concept or image from the *Odyssey*. The novels . . . all embody one of the many germs of the Odyssean conception; the travel books to a lesser extent, without the same concentration. Here it is essential to clarify the often overlooked fact that K. was a writer (and a man) of one single, all-encompassing vision: Within the *Odyssey* can be found the points of departure for all his later novels. Through the novels K. sought a level from which he might successfully address himself to a much broader readership than his poetry would have ever permitted. . . . The travel books are of a different category: They do not elaborate, they prefigure.

F. A. Reed, "Translator's Note," in N. K., *Journey to the Morea* (1965), pp. 178, 183

I have always nurtured much admiration and . . . a sort of affection for [K.'s] work. I had the pleasure of being able to give public testimony of my admiration in Athens, at a period when official Greece was frowning upon her greatest writer. The welcome given my testimony by my student audience constituted the finest homage [K.'s] work and acts could have been granted. I also do not forget that the very day when I was regretfully receiving a distinction that K. deserved a hundred times more, I got the most generous of telegrams from him. Later on, I discovered with consternation that this message had been drafted a few days before his death. With him, one of our last great artists vanished. I am one of those who feel and will go on feeling the void that he has left. [1959]

Albert Camus, quoted in Helen Kazantzakis, *N. K.: A Biography Based on His Letters* (1968), p. 560

If we study K. apart from demoticism we severely limit our understanding not only of him but of the general conditions of Greek literary life. Linguistic problems have been intimately connected with literary ones in Greece, and with political life as well. . . . It is vital for us to realize that the problem of language obsessed K. from the very start and that this obsession was one of the few constants stretching unchanged throughout all the other permutations of his career. . . . The totality of K.'s work seems to have as its common denominator—perhaps even more than the search for God, even more than political or humanitarian zeal—a determination to mobilize the twenty-four recalcitrant letters of the Greek alphabet and make them express his complicated soul.

Peter Bien, *K. and the Linguistic Revolution in Greek Literature* (1972), pp. 4–5

When one looks back over K.'s *Odyssey* and recalls its thousands of vivid details as well as its irresistibly forceful major passages . . . one sees that one has had part in what is likely the most remarkable sustained accomplishment in verse that the modern imagination has been privileged to record. When one notes, too, that this huge, questing hymn to daring and fecundity has been written, not at all in a Miltonic striving for "greatness," but in the most intense and personal creative joy, one is but the more impressed, and the more indebted to both poet and translator. . . .

The final good of the new *Odyssey*, I suspect, will not be to glorify the Nietzschean hero, or make aesthetically viable the ideas of Bergson, Nietzsche, or Spengler, or even "man's dauntless mind," but to restore the sense of the heedless delight in living to a jaded populace. To poets it is, and it will be a living demonstration of the profound vitality that words may be made to carry by a poet who is himself profoundly vital, and of the human power that makes the best poetry nearly as valuable as life. . . . It is this power which appropriates the forms of writing and uses them to create and explore new realms of the imagination, and ultimately to establish them, so that they may become the most enduring ground of the spirit. In this connection, Odysseus is likely to prove a hero to us in more ways than even his chronicler has envisioned, and K. himself in all ways.

James Dickey, in Kimon Friar, ed., *The Spiritual Odyssey of N. K.* (1979), p. 49

KEMAL, Yaşar

(Anglicized as Yashar Kemal, born Yasar Kemal Gökçeli) Turkish novelist, short-story writer, and essayist, b. 1922, Adana

K., Turkey's most famous novelist, frequently mentioned in the Western press as a leading contender for the Nobel Prize for literature, was born in southern Turkey, where he was exposed to the squalor, brutality, and injustices of village life. At five, he saw his father killed while praying at the mosque. During the same incident, K. lost one eye. At nine, he started going to school, walking to a remote village. He never went beyond eighth grade.

In the ensuing years, K. worked at a variety of jobs—cotton-picker, construction foreman, farmhand, clerk, cobbler's helper, petition writer, and substitute teacher—and these youthful experiences brought him closer to both the deprivations and the dauntless spirit of the laboring classes. During this same period he also developed an interest in and acquired a strong knowledge of Turkish folklore.

Among K.'s first publications were some poems and several surveys of Anatolian folklore. His first book, *Ağıtlar* (1943; laments), was a compilation of folk elegies. In 1950 he was arrested on charges of disseminating Communist propaganda but was acquitted. Moving to Istanbul in 1951, K. joined the staff of the leading Istanbul daily, *Cumhuriyet,* as a roving reporter, later becoming a columnist and special-feature writer. He also wrote screenplays for several successful Turkish films based on Anatolian legends and themes.

K.'s journalistic writing, utilizing a colloquial and lyrical style, set a new trend in reporting. His travelogues, interviews, and feature stories have been collected in a number of volumes. In 1963 K. left *Cumhuriyet* to devote himself to creative writing and to campaign for the leftist Turkish Labor Party. He also published a political weekly, *Ant*.

K. first attracted literary attention with *Sarı sıcak* (1952; yellow heat), a collection of short stories, and *Teneke* (1955; tin can), a novella, but it was not until the publication of *Ince Memed* (1955; *Memed, My Hawk*, 1960) that he was catapulted to national literary fame. This action-filled novel presents as a folk hero a bandit who—somewhat like Robin Hood—takes up arms against the exploiters of the poor. *Ince Memed*, which has been translated into twenty-five languages, set K. on the road to international renown and remains his all-time popular work.

Ince Memed was followed by *Ortadirek* (1960; *The Wind from the Plain*, 1964), a moving saga of destitute peasants traveling in search of work. This novel, compared by some critics to Steinbeck's (q.v.) *The Grapes of Wrath*, further enhanced K.'s literary reputation as a master of the "village novel," which became a major mode of Turkish fiction from the mid-1950s onward. With two subsequent major novels, *Yer demir gök bakır* (1963; *Iron Earth, Copper Sky,* 1979) and *Ölmez otu* (1968;*The Undying Grass*, 1978), it forms a trilogy about the tragic life of the Anatolian peasant as well as his indomitable spirit in the face of natural disasters and the injustice perpetrated by privileged landowners. The final book of the trilogy is also an interesting novelistic study of myth and fantasy.

Ince Memed II (1969; *They Burn the Thistles*, 1977) is the sequel to his best-known work. Although it continues the story of his original protagonist, it can be read as an independent novel. His huge two-volume novel *Akçasazın ağaları* (the lords of Akchasaz), consisting of *Demirciler çarşısı cinayeti* (1974; *The Lords of Akchasaz: Murder in the Ironsmiths Market,* 1979) and *Yusufcuk Yusuf* (1975; turtledove Yusuf), explores the human drama and the traditional strifes of southern Turkey.

In his fiction, K. delineates the suffering of the underprivileged in the countryside, mainly in and around the Chukurova region. His style is both lyrical and dramatic. Most of his characters are vivid. The narration combines the directness of social realism with techniques reminiscent of stream of consciousness (q.v.). His ear perfectly attuned to the vernacular of the peasant, K. excels in dialogue.

K. has made a deliberate attempt to create a modern mythology out of the tales and legends of southern Turkey. His abiding interest in folklore has led him to write new versions of some of Turkey's best-known folk tales: *Üç anadolu efsanesi* (1967; three Anatolian legends); *Ağrıdağı efsanesi* (1970; *The Legend of Ararat*, 1975), a simple and moving story about starcrossed loves in eastern Turkey; *Binboğalar efsanesi* (1971; *The Legend of the Thousand Bulls*, 1976), based on the stories of the Yürük nomadic tribes; and others. In addition to his retelling of this traditional material, K. seems to be striving toward the creation of a mythic world of his own in a manner similar to Faulkner's (q.v.) Yoknapatawpha.

In the 1970s K. began to explore the city of Istanbul and the coastal towns in his fiction. *Al gözüm seyreyle Salih* (1976; *Seagull*, 1981) is an evocation of a Black Sea fishing town written in a lilting, almost poetic style. *Kuşlar da gitti* (1978; the birds too are gone) is a novella of corruption and pollution in Istanbul. In *Deniz küstü* (1979; the sea is angry) K. paints a gripping panorama of human drama against the backdrop of the sea.

K.'s short stories have been collected in *Bütün hikâyeler* (1967; enlarged ed., 1975; complete stories). His novella *Teneke* was successfully adapted for the stage in 1965. In 1967 the dramatization of his *Yer demir gök bakır* shared first prize at the Nancy (France) International Theater Festival. K. has won numerous awards in Turkey and abroad, the first being the Varlık Prize of 1955 for *İnce Memed*.

K.'s popularity and stature stem from his dynamic plots, a narrative style that blends stark reality with lyricism, a skillful use of myths and local color, and vivid peasant characters of universal interest.

FURTHER WORKS: *Yanan ormanlarda elli gün* (1955); *Çukurova yana yana* (1955); *Peri bacaları* (1957); *Taş çatlasa* (1961); *Bu diyar baştan başa* (1971); *Çakırcalı efe* (1972); *Bir bulut kaynıyor* (1974); *Baldaki tuz* (1974); *Yılanı öldürseler* (1977). FURTHER VOLUME IN ENGLISH: *Anatolian Tales* (1968)

BIBLIOGRAPHY: Tube, H., on *Anatolian Tales, Spectator,* 9 Aug. 1968, 198; Blythe, R., on *Iron Earth, Copper Sky, Listener,* 13 June 1974, 777; Jones, D.A.N., on *The Legend of Ararat, TLS,* 5 Sept. 1975, 998; Theroux, P., on *They Burn the Thistles, NYTBR,* 10 July 1977, 11; Pollitt, K., on *The Undying Grass, NYTBR,* 18 June 1978, 14; special K. issue, *Edebiyat,* 5, 1–2 (1980)

TALAT SAIT HALMAN

KENYAN LITERATURE

Kenya has produced written literature in five languages—English, Swahili, Kamba, Kikuyu, and Luo—but most Kenyan authors writing today express themselves in either English or Swahili.

In English

The earliest literary works in English were ethnographies and autobiographical narratives, the prototype being Jomo Kenyatta's (1893–1978) *Facing Mount Kenya* (1938), an anthropological account of traditional Kikuyu life and culture. Muga Gicaru (b. 1920) in *Land of Sunshine: Scenes of Life in Kenya before Mau Mau* (1958) and R. Mugo Gatheru (b. 1925) in *Child of Two Worlds* (1964) described growing up in a Kikuyu village during the interwar years, when educational opportunities were scarce and nationalistic feelings were beginning to spread throughout the country. The struggle for political independence, which precipitated a Kikuyu civil war in the 1950s known as Mau Mau, was recorded in autobiographical works by Josiah Kariuki (b. 1929), Karari Njama (b. 1926), and Waruhiu Itote (b. 1922). In all these life histories the experiences of the narrator were treated as if typical of the Kikuyu people as a whole; the individual was a representative of his community, his ethnic group, and, in a larger sense, his nation.

The emergence of James Ngugi, now known as Ngugi wa Thiong'o (q.v.), as Kenya's first novelist may have been the consequence of the same ethnic autobiographical impulse, for he too was a Kikuyu writing about the impact of Western education and colonial political unrest on the lives of his people, ordinary rural citizens who had been deprived of their land by white settlers. In *The River Between* (1965) he tells of the rise of Kikuyu independent schools under the leadership of a "man of two worlds" who tries to unite his community through mass education. In *Weep Not, Child* (1964) he portrays a Kikuyu family split apart by the pressures of Mau Mau; the hero, a young boy, is nearly driven to suicide when he loses his opportunity for further education. In both works Ngugi stresses the importance of fusing old and new, traditional and Western, so that Africans could progress politically without losing their cultural identity.

Ngugi's later novels, *A Grain of Wheat* (1967) and *Petals of Blood* (1977), deal with postcolonial social problems in Kenya that have their roots in the past. Like Chinua Achebe (q.v.) of Nigeria, Ngugi attempts to understand present realities in his country by searching for their origins in earlier times. He has written fictional chronicles of his nation's history.

A number of Kenyan authors have followed in Ngugi's footsteps by writing nationalistic novels about Mau Mau and its aftermath. Of these, the most talented is Meja Mwangi (b. 1948), whose *Carcase for Hounds* (1974) and *Taste of Death* (1975) elevated the armed struggle to legendary status by focusing on the exploits of heroic freedom fighters. More recently Mwangi has turned his attention to urban problems in Nairobi, examining the human consequences of economic exploitation in the postcolonial era by detailing the lives of laborers, vagabonds, and slum dwellers, who face their daily battle for survival with ingenuity and resilient humor.

Mwangi's latest novels have less in common with Ngugi's sober historical reappraisals than they do with the humorous literature that emerged in Kenya in the 1970s. The book that started the trend toward lighter fiction was Charles Mangua's (b. 1939) *Son of Woman* (1971), a picaresque novel that pokes fun at every stratum of Kenyan society by viewing it from the gutter through the eyes of an opportunistic trickster. In *A Tail in the Mouth* (1972) Mangua went a step further in irreverence and satirized even the Mau Mau freedom fighters. Mangua's refreshingly flippant novels broke sales records in Kenya and encouraged the development of an indigenous popular literature.

The most successful popular writer to emerge in Kenya in recent years has been David Maillu (b. 1939), who built a publishing house, Comb Books, on earnings from his first "mini-novels," *Unfit for Human Consumption* (1973) and *Troubles* (1974), and his best-selling narrative poems, *My Dear Bottle* (1973) and *After 4:30* (1974). Although Maillu has been criticized

for writing mildly pornographic works, he has maintained that he is a serious moralist who chooses to clothe his social messages in frank, sexually explicit humor. He has tended to concentrate on urban characters—civil servants, politicians, secretaries, prostitutes—who suffer misfortunes because they cannot purge themselves of bad habits and insatiable appetites. He is truly a writer for the masses.

Other writers of fiction worthy of mention are Grace Ogot (b. 1930), whose tales of traditional Luo life skillfully evoke the past; the half-brothers Leonard Kibera (b. 1942) and Samuel Kahiga (b. 1946), whose short stories and novelettes deal with psychological aspects of social change; and Mwangi Ruheni (b. 1934), who specializes in domestic comedies and crime fiction. Such writers have contributed thematic diversity to Kenyan fiction.

Kenya has not produced as many dramatists or poets as it has novelists, but the plays of Francis Imbuga (b. 1947) and the poetry of Jared Angira (b. 1947) have earned a measure of public recognition. Imbuga has explored poignant human dimensions of social and political turmoil in modern Africa, sometimes tracing the roots of a personal tragedy to profound changes in the cultural values of contemporary society. Angira has brooded on the predicament of modern man in the Third World; his verse has remained simple, direct yet quite resourceful in projecting sharp images in which the new generation of Africans can see themselves and their experience reflected.

In Swahili

Kenya is not as rich in Swahili-language literature as Tanzania (*see* Tanzanian Literature), but a significant number of plays, poems, and novelettes are available. The oldest and possibly most famous work is James Juma Mbotela's (dates n.a.) *Uhuru wa watumwa* (1934; *The Freeing of the Slaves in East Africa*, 1956), a narrative based on reminiscences about the slave trade. More recent examples include Ahmad Nassir bin Juma Bhali's (b. 1936) *Poems from Kenya: Gnomic Verses in Swahili* (1966), short enigmatic poems published in a bilingual edition, and J. N. Somba's (b. 1930) novel, *Kuishi kwingi ni kuona mengi* (1968; to live long is to see much), a story about the life of an average man in modern society. Kenyan publishers have also been active in bringing out Swahili translations of literary works written by African authors in English.

In Kikuyu

Although the production of literature in other Kenyan languages has been negligible, a start has been made in Kikuyu with the publication of two new works by Ngugi wa Thiong'o: a play co-authored by Ngugi wa Mirii (b. 1951) about the exploitation of peasants and workers in independent Kenya, *Ngaahika ndeenda* (1980; I will marry when I want), the public performance of which in 1977 led to Ngugi wa Thiong'o's arrest and detention for nearly a year; and a protest novel about neocolonialism, *Caitaani mūtharaba-Inī* (1980; the Devil on the Cross), which was the first piece of full-length fiction to appear in Kikuyu. Because he now seeks to address himself primarily to a local audience, Ngugi has declared his intention to continue writing in his mother tongue rather than in English. If other writers follow suit, there may be a surge in the production of African-language literature in Kenya in the years to come.

BIBLIOGRAPHY: Liyong, T. lo, *The Last Word: Cultural Synthesism* (1969); Ngugi wa Thiong'o, *Homecoming: Essays on African and Caribbean Literature, Culture and Politics* (1972); p'Bitek, O., *Africa's Cultural Revolution* (1973); Gurr, A., and Calder, A., eds., *Writers in East Africa* (1974); Cook, D., ed., *In Black and White: Writings from East Africa with Broadcast Discussion and Commentary* (1976); Roscoe, A., *Uhuru's Fire: African Literature East to South* (1977); Wanjala, C., *The Season of Harvest: Some Notes on East African Literature* (1978); Wanjala, C., *For Home and Freedom* (1980); Lindfors, B., ed., *Mazungumzo: Interviews with East African Writers, Publishers, Editors and Scholars* (1980); Ngugi wa Thiong'o, *Writers in Politics* (1981)

BERNTH LINDFORS

KEROUAC, Jack

American novelist, essayist, short-story writer, and poet, b. 12 March 1922, Lowell, Mass.; d. 21 Oct. 1969; St. Petersburg, Fla.

Born Jean Louis Lebris de Kerouac, K. grew up in Pawtucketville, a French-Canadian community in Lowell, Massachusetts. A star athlete in high school, he attended Columbia University on a football scholarship. There his predilection for spontaneous, unconventional behavior began to emerge. After breaking his leg in a freshman football game, K. dropped out of Columbia to work at a series of odd jobs that included shipping out on a Merchant Marine vessel to Greenland. Back at Columbia the following fall, he abruptly quit the football team after the season's first game. K. then enlisted in the Navy, only to be discharged on psychiatric grounds after six months. In 1944 he met Allen Ginsberg and William Burroughs (qq.v.) in New York City, and the alliances that resulted in the beat movement began to be formed.

K.'s first novel, *The Town and the City* (1950), is an autobiographical account of the decline of his own family. Despite its generally positive critical reception, K. judged the novel a failure because he felt he had not yet discovered his authentic voice. With the development of his theory of "spontaneous composition" in 1951, that voice emerged. K. attempted to abandon altogether conscious control of language so that the very "sound of the mind" could flow unfettered by traditional notions of craft. In marathon sessions that frequently lasted days, he attempted to write swiftly, "excitedly," in a semi-trance that resembled Yeats's (q.v.) later "automatic writing."

The result of K.'s new aesthetic was *On the Road* (1957). Because of its formal singularity, it was slow in finding a publisher. Finally, Malcolm Cowley (q.v.) persuaded Viking Press to publish the novel, but only after Cowley himself heavily revised K.'s original manuscript. It was an overnight sensation, catapulting K. into sudden fame after years of obscurity; yet, ironically, it is largely not the novel K. wrote. Remaining is K.'s vigorous chronicling of his travels across America and Mexico with his fellow beats, particularly Neal Cassady (1926–1968), the prototype for Dean Moriarty in the novel. Remaining also is the celebration of alcohol, drugs, jazz, and unbridled sex that gained the work its early notoriety. But except for a certain looseness of structure, the novel as published is relatively conventional in form, its stylistic wildness subdued by the editors.

The Dharma Bums (1958), K.'s next published novel, contains an excellent portrait of the poet Gary Snyder (b. 1930), K.'s friend, on whom Jaffe Ryder, the novel's protagonist, is based, and is informed throughout by K.'s interest in Zen Buddhism. But perhaps because it was written at Viking's request for a sequel to *On the Road* it too lacks the stylistic spontaneity of K.'s more essential works, which are the twelve novels he wrote between 1951, when he developed his theory of spontaneous prose, and 1957, when *On the Road* at last appeared. Each of these novels is informed by K.'s new aesthetic; none was published until after the success of *On the Road.* Possibly the most important of these is the posthumously published *Visions of Cody* (1973), which grew out of the 1951 manuscript of *On the Road* and at one point even bore that title. The novel's shifting points of view, its occasional parody and imitation of other works of literature, and its digressive nature and rambling style lend it the improvisational quality of jazz and make it the most representative example of K.'s spontaneous writing. Other successful novels of this period include *Dr. Sax* (1959), an expressionistic meditation on death; *The Subterraneans* (1958), an autobiographical account of K.'s affair with a mulatto woman that was written in only three days; and *Maggie Cassidy* (1959), K.'s nostalgic evocation of the provincial roots from which he never fully escaped.

With the passing of the 1950s, K.'s significance came increasingly to be regarded as less literary than sociological. Alcoholic and largely forgotten, he died at the age of forty-seven, only a few months after Neal Cassady's nude corpse was discovered in Mexico. It now appears certain that his place in modern letters will be determined less by his role as a leader of the beat movement than by how the degree of success of his literary experiments is perceived.

FURTHER WORKS: *Mexico City Blues* (1959); *The Scripture of the Golden Eternity* (1960); *Tristessa* (1960); *Lonesome Traveler* (1960); *Book of Dreams* (1961); *Big Sur* (1962); *Visions of Gerard* (1963); *Desolation Angels* (1965); *Satori in Paris* (1966); *Vanity of Duluoz* (1968); *Scattered Poems* (1971); *Pic* (1971)

BIBLIOGRAPHY: Duffey, B., "The Three Worlds of J. K.," in Waldmeir, J. J., ed., *Recent American Fiction* (1963), pp. 175–84; Webb, H. M., Jr., "The Singular Worlds of J. K.," in Moore, H. T., ed., *Contemporary American Novelists* (1964), pp. 120–33; Charters, A., *K.* (1972); Dardess, G., "The Logic of Spontaneity: A Reconsideration of K.'s 'Spontaneous Prose Method,' " *Boundary 2, 2* (1975) 719–43; Hipkiss, R. A., *J. K.: Prophet of a New Romanticism* (1976); Tytell, J., *Naked Angels: The Lives and Literature of the Beat Generation* (1976), pp. 52–78, 140–211; Donaldson, S., ed., *"On the Road": Text and Criticism* (1979), pp. 311–605

CHARLES B. HARRIS

KESEY, Ken

American novelist, b. 17 Sept. 1935, La Junta, Col.

K. attended the University of Oregon and Stanford University. In 1966 he was found guilty of possession of marijuana, and in 1967 he spent five months in jail in California.

K. quickly became one of the most exciting American novelists of the 1960s, not only because of his writing but also because of his life style. Tom Wolfe's (b. 1931) *The Electric Kool-Aid Acid Test* (1968) chronicles the activities of K. and his followers, who live the counterculture life style. Roaming the country in their Day-Glo-painted bus and tripping on hallucinogenic drugs, the Merry Pranksters, the name K. gave to his communal group, seemed to many to be vigorously challenging American mores.

K.'s protagonists are good men. Harder than ever to find in the age of the antihero, K.'s good man proves to be as distressing to the society around him as have some good men in the past. The story of a K. novel becomes the story of one man's sensitizing those who know him to the point that they not only realize their own flaws but also simultaneously admire and hate the protagonist who has shown them the truth.

K.'s first novel, *One Flew over the Cuckoo's Nest* (1962), implicitly questions the ability of society to diagnose its own insanity. The setting is the ward of a mental hospital, a ward filled mainly with voluntarily admitted patients who in fact are reasonably normal but who do not feel themselves strong enough to make it in the world outside. The representative of social authority in this microcosm is the Big Nurse, Miss Ratched, a coldly efficient despot, whose goal is the coercion of the men under her domination into a condition of sterile, automated tidiness. To Chief Bromden, the hulking Columbia River Indian who acts as the tale's narrator, she is an agent of the "Combine." Chief Bromden's paranoid delusion has assumed the metaphor of an omnipotent, omniscient, force—the Combine—that manipulates him through the wiring system that he imagines is being systematically installed in each of the inmates.

Into this hospital comes Randal Patrick McMurphy, ex-marine, brawler, card shark, and odds-watching gambler. Having claimed insanity to escape from the rigors of a prison work farm, McMurphy at first views his stay in the hospital as merely a long poker game, just one more ploy in the life of a confirmed hedonist. In a modern fable that alternates between light comedy and Black Humor (q.v.), McMurphy wins all his rounds with the Big Nurse but the last. She fashions an eventual triumph of sorts by getting the doctors to perform a lobotomy on McMurphy. Before then, however, he has pulled his fellow inmates, sometimes against their will, back to a condition of self-respect.

McMurphy is reincarnated in K.'s second novel, *Sometimes a Great Notion* (1964), in the person of Hank Stamper, raw and aggressive scion of an Oregon lumber empire. The struggle is again with a society unwilling to accommodate a strong individualist, but the issues are deepened and complicated by the fact that Hank's principal antagonist turns out to be his cerebral, introspective half-brother, Lee, and by K.'s development of Lee as an equally appealing character. K. manipulates the clash of fraternal egos to a powerful climax, before reconciling the brothers to a tragic understanding of their own vulnerability to an indifferent fate and to a group of townspeople who have been made intolerably uncomfortable by the sight of the Stampers' strength.

Lingering lovingly over the Oregon land and the people it nurtures and assaults, K. is occasionally guilty of marring *Sometimes a Great Notion* with stretches of prolixity. But such lapses are few, and the novel is remarkable for the skill with which K. manages the narrative.

Since 1964, K. has published very little. *Kesey's Garage Sale* (1973) is a collection of fugitive pieces by K. and by his friends. If, as he sometimes indicated, he has decided to move beyond the novel, it is a decision that his audience can only regret, for K.'s voice and themes have been a special kind of stimulus reminding his age of the evil as well as of the good, of which it is capable.

BIBLIOGRAPHY: Malin, I., "K. K.: *One Flew over the Cuckoo's Nest*," *Crit*, 5, 2 (1962), 81–84; Fiedler, L., *The Return of the Vanishing American* (1968), pp. 177–87; Barsness, J. A., "K. K.: The Hero in Modern Dress," *BRMMLA*, 22, 1 (1969), 27–33; Olderman, R. M., *Beyond the Waste Land: A Study of the American Novel in the Nineteen-Sixties* (1972), pp. 35–51; special K. issue, *Lex et Scientia*, 13, 1–2 (1977); Pratt, J. C., ed., *"One Flew over the Cuckoo's Nest": Text and Criticism* (1977); Strelow, M., ed., *K.* (1977)
                                    CHARLES LARSON

KHANDEKAR, Vishnu Sakharam

Indian novelist, short-story writer, essayist, and critic (writing in Marathi), b. 11 Jan. 1898, Sangli; d. 2 Sept. 1976, Miraj

After finishing secondary school in Sangli, K. spent some time at college in Poona, but had to abandon his studies because of financial presures. An idealistic commitment to uplifting the rural populace led him to become a schoolteacher in the small coastal village of Shiroda in 1920. From 1938 until his death he lived in the upcountry town of Kolhapur, where for some time he wrote film scripts, but later devoted himself wholly to his literary writing, becoming one of the few Marathi writers to have lived by their pen.

The spirit of the idealistic teacher pervades K.'s vast output, which includes fifteen novels. His early novels, such as *Don dhruva* (1934; the two poles) and *Pandhare dhag* (1940; white clouds), recommend the Marxist path for the abolition of the "two poles" of poverty and wealth. K. was also attracted to the teachings of Gandhi but found his philosophy of nonviolent change, symbolized by the "white clouds" of Gandhian homespun clothes, inadequate for effecting a revolution. After 1942, disheartened to see Marxist as well as Gandhian ideals corrupted, K. did not write a novel for several years; he produced only three in the later period. In *Yayati* (1959; *Yayati*, 1978), he devotes himself to castigating the hedonistic materialism of modern times, seeing in Yayati, the mythic king who "borrowed" his son's youth to satisfy his own lust, the symbol of modern man.

While few Marathi writers have become as dear to middle-class readers as K., several critics have passed severe judgments on him. Written according to a thesis, his fiction generally lacks a dynamic, living quality. The thesis itself being a "teachable" simplification, the portrayal of life seldom achieves any depth or complexity. K.'s genuine feeling for the downtrodden does not result in a palpable depiction of their life, the author being circumscribed by his own middle-class background. His extremely ornate style, studded with epigrammatic sentences, similes, metaphors, and allegorical constructions, appears contrived. But with all his faults, K. remains a writer with an exemplary commitment to humanistic values.

FURTHER WORKS: *Rankache rajya* (1928); *Navamallika* (1929); *Dhundhurmas* (1929); *Hridayachi hak* (1930); *Kanchan-mrig* (1931); *Gadkari: Vyakti ani vangmaya*

(1932); *Ulka* (1934); *Jivankala* (1934); *Dattak* (1934); *Vayulahari*(1936); *Vidyutprakash* (1937); *Davabindu* (1937); *Navachandrika* (1937); *Don mane* (1938); *Poojan* (1938); *Chandanyat* (1938); *Hirava chapha* (1939); *Rikama devhara* (1939); *Sukhacha shodh* (1939); *Pakalya* (1939); *Samadhivaril phule* (1939); *Hastacha paus* (1939); *Pahile prem* (1940); *Jalalela mohor* (1941); *Surya-kamale* (1941); *Kalika* (1941); *Avinash* (1941); *Krauncha-vadha* (1942); *Oonpaus* (1942; *Cultured moti* (1942); *Mandakini* (1942); *Gharatyabaher* (1944); *Nava pratakkal* (1944); *Pahilya-vahilya* (1944); *Pahili lat* (1944); *Phule ani dagad* (1944); *Stri ani purush* (1944); *Mrigajalatalya kalya* (1944); *Sayankal* (1944); *Surya-kamal* (1944); *Gokarnichi phule* (1944); *Jivanakala* (1944); *Vanabhojana* (1944); *Kalpalata* (1945); *Manjirya* (1945); *Marathicha natya-sansar* (1945); *Nave kiran* (1946); *Tisara prahar* (1946); *Goph ani gophan* (1946); *Phule ani kate* (1946); *Teen sammelane* (1947); *Sanjawat* (1948); *Soneri savalya* (1948); *Jhim-jhim* (1948); *V. M. Joshi: Vyakti ani vichar* (1948); *Ashru ani hasya* (1949); *Agarkar: Vyakti ani vichar* (1949); *Preeticha shodh* (1952); *Ashru* (1953); *Prasad* (1957); *Abhishek* (1958); *Manjhadhar* (1959); *Keshavasut: Kavya ani kala* (1959); *Murali* (1960); *Vanadevata* (1960); *Usshap* (1961); *Rimjhim* (1961); *Te divas, tee manase* (1961); *Rang ani gandh* (1961); *Resha ani rang* (1961); *Amritavel* (1967); *Dhagaädache chandane* (1972); *Dhwaj phadakat thevuya* (1975)

BIBLIOGRAPHY: Sardesai, G., "V. S. K.: A Social Humanist," *IndL*, 11 (1968), 92–97; Bhagwat, A. K., "V. S. K.," in Bhagwat, A. K., ed., *Maharashtra—A Profile: V. S. K. Felicitation Volume* (1977), pp. 1–18

VILAS SARANG

KHANTY LITERATURE
See Finno-Ugric Literatures of the Soviet Union

KHLEBNIKOV, Velemir Vladimirovich
(pseud. of Viktor K.) Russian poet, dramatist, short-story writer, and essayist, b. 9 Nov. 1885, Tundutovo; d. 28 June 1922, Novgorod

K. was born in the Astrakhan district, the son of an ornithologist father and historian mother; his early associations with science were to have lasting effects on his work. K. studied mathematics and biology at Kazan University, and his first published work was a scientific article. In 1906, K. was imprisoned for one month for his involvement in student revolutionary activities. In 1909 he studied Sanskrit and Slavic historical philology at St. Petersburg University.

His literary associations began in 1908, when he became acquainted with Vyacheslav Ivanov and Mikhail Kuzmin (qq.v.), and soon became the center of a group that represented the beginnings of Russian futurism (q.v.).

K. spent much of his adult life a penniless wanderer, living for a time in various Russian and Ukrainian cities and obsessively computing mathematical formulas to derive the cyclical laws of history. In 1921 he traveled to Tehran with the Red Army as an adjutant to the general staff. His Persian experiences are recorded in the long poem "Truba Gul Mully" (written 1921, pub. 1928; Gul Mullah's pipe). He died after a month's illness aggravated by malnutrition.

K. is the modern Russian poet of the epic. Pagan Slavic mythology and the folk epic—as in "I i E" (1913; I and E), "Deti Vydry" (1913; the children of Vydra), and the play *Devy bog* (1912; a maiden's god)—and fantastic utopian dreams—as in the "super tale" *Ladomir* (1920; partial tr., *Goodworld*, 1976)—are the basis of much of his work. K.'s cosmogony is a unique poetic world whose meaning only gradually becomes clear to the reader after he learns K.'s system of myths and pagan view of the world. K.'s attraction to the epic was part of his preoccupation with the nature of time, and such long poems as "Gibel Atlantidy" (1912; the destruction of Atlantis), "Deti Vydry," and "Sinie okovy" (written 1922, pub. 1928; blue chains); the "super tale" *Zangezi* (1922; partial tr., *Zangezi*, 1976), a mixture of prose and poetry arranged in twenty sections called "planes"; and the play *Mirskontsa* (1913; *World from the End*, 1976) are all organized by his theory of historical repetition and are in part explained by it. By juxtaposing numbers connected with various historical events, K. tried to discern an underlying, rationally deducible periodicity. In this he shared a basic futurist-utopian vision of man freed by the discovery of the laws of existence to realize his creative potential.

At the heart of all K.'s poetry is his philosophy of language. Russian futurism was oriented toward the word in its material uniqueness— the physical aspect of the word on the page. Instrumentation—the manipulation of rhyme, alliteration, vowel harmonies—became a vehicle to transform meaning, to revitalize long-forgotten relationships among words themselves. On the one hand, associative freedom, even accident (for example, typographical errors) played an important role in the creative process in order to expose as arbitrary the encrustations of conventional meanings so that the real, "interior" meanings of words might be more perceptible. The result is the apparent disconnectedness, randomness of associations, and unmotivated semantic shifts that so often occur in K.'s writings. On the other hand, K. viewed his task to be a scientific distillation of language aimed at the determination of original meanings. "Nasha osnova" (1920; our base), K.'s most important theoretical essay, deals with neologisms formed by the manipulation of existing roots. Ultimately, *zaum* ("transrational language") was an attempt to achieve a language of universal comprehensibility that would lead to world peace. His poem "Zaklyatie smekhom" (1910; "Incantation by Laughter," 1976) was based on the rich variety of Russian prefixes and suffixes used with the root word for laughter. *Zangezi* is a kind of poetic testament and compendium of *zaum* forms.

K.'s fiction is characterized by this same concentration on language and time. His most important prose piece, the autobiographical story "Ka" (1916; "Ka," 1976), contains violent, unmotivated shifts in time and the simultaneous interpenetration of historical periods.

K. would have liked to think of himself as the N. I. Lobachevsky (1792–1856)—a great mathematician—of the poetic word, suggesting new ways to view poetic time and space. He remains a difficult and eccentric master whose writing is fundamental to Russian modernism.

FURTHER WORKS: *Bitvy 1915–1917: Novoe uchenie o voyne* (1915); *Noch v okope* (1921); *Sobranie proizvedeny* (5 vols., 1928–33); *Sobranie sochineny* (4 vols., 1968–72). FURTHER VOLUME IN ENGLISH: *Snake Train: Poetry and Prose* (1976)

BIBLIOGRAPHY: Markov, V., *The Longer Poems of K.* (1962); Markov, V., *Russian Futurism* (1968), passim; Baran, H., "K.'s Poem 'Bekh,'" *RusL*, No. 6 (1974), 5–19; special K. issue, *RusL*, 9, 1 (1981)

GERALD PIROG

KHODASEVICH, Vladislav Felitsianovich

Russian poet and essayist, b. 16 May 1886, Moscow; d. 14 June 1939, Paris, France

K., one of the leading figures of Russian émigré literature in the 1920s and 1930s, was a descendant of the symbolists (q.v.) who longed for a return to Pushkin. The last of six children of a Polish father and a Jewish mother—he had a lifelong fascination with Jewish culture—he described himself in his fanciful autobiographical sketch "Mladenchestvo" (1933, repub. 1965; infancy) as physically weak but mentally sharp. Brought up in the atmosphere of literary "Decadence," he was dissatisfied with what he felt was the 20th c.'s blindness to the great "classical" tradition of Russian harmony and versification. Never very political, he grew unhappy with the tendentiousness of the new Soviet age, and emigrated to western Europe in 1922, becoming ever more pessimistic in his life of poverty. His jaundiced outlook and miserable circumstances are poignantly described by his widow, Nina Berberova (b. 1900) in her chronicle of émigré literary life, *The Italics Are Mine* (1969). His death in 1939 marked the end of the European phase of Russian émigré culture in this century: World War II either killed or further scattered its representatives.

K. was not a prolific writer. His entire collected verse amounts to five small volumes of mostly short poems: *Molodost* (1908; youth); *Shchastlivy domik* (1914; the happy little house); *Putem zerna* (1920; the way of the grain); *Tyazhelaya lira* (1921; the heavy lyre); and *Evropeyskaya noch* (1927; European night). The last three constitute his mature verse, and were collected by K. himself in 1927 and republished with notes and additions by his widow in 1961. They show an unrelenting progression toward gloom and hopelessness, which the great critic D. S. Mirsky (1890–1939?) characterized as some of the most pessimistic verse in the history of Russian literature.

K.'s poetry is built on mystical solitude: the poet is always turning inward. Torn between his real physical needs and hatred of all the putrefaction he sees around him, K. seeks to deny his own physical self and to enter a completely solipsistic universe in which he exists alone with his verse, his soul, and his mental inventions. In his great "Ballada" (1921; ballad), as he sits in a chair rocking back and forth in meager surroundings in a St. Petersburg rooming house, he becomes Orpheus, transcending the real world to move into a world of pure creation, like Cincinnatus in *Invitation to a Beheading* by Vladimir Nabokov (q.v.), whose work K. was among the first to discover and champion.

K. emigrated first to Berlin (he was to spend

the last fifteen years of his life in Paris), where with fellow émigrés Andrey Bely and Maxim Gorky (qq.v.) he undertook the publication of a journal to appear simultaneously in Europe and the U.S.S.R. It failed, and K. felt increasingly isolated and hopeless. His verse assumed a cruel sharpness in its presentation of the ugly, prosaic, even gruesome detail. In "Pered zerkalom" (1924; before the mirror) the truth speaks to him and it speaks constant torment. The poet looks at himself and sees the deformity of pain. Indeed, deformity is everywhere, as he writes in "Dachnoe" (1923; suburbia). The world is full of grotesque shapes. Nothing makes sense anymore, and K. cannot bear what his poetic eye perceives.

So pervasive did this discordance become that K. literally silenced himself. After 1927, for all intents and purposes, he ceased writing poetry, devoting himself instead to the composition of several hundred critical essays of a general cultural and specifically literary nature, as a columnist for a Paris émigré daily, *Renaissance*. These essays sparkle with wit and intelligence and give a very sad picture of the émigré literary scene. Unlike his rival critics in emigration, Georgy Adamovich (1894–1972) and Marc Slonim (1894–1976), K. maintained that a Russian émigré literature was possible, but what it needed was a new method, a way not to follow the past or, as he put it, the same old tracks. Even here, however, K. was torn. Full of belief in this literary future, he was as full of doubt about its realization, for as he once put it, in the essay "Krovavaya pishcha" (1932; a food of blood), "to a very great degree, one can call the history of Russian literature the history of the destruction of Russian writers." So long as the emigration realized, as he wrote in "Podvig" (1932; the exploit), that "culture does not live either in refrigerators or in idle recollections . . . [and that it is preserved not by] those who think of the past, but by those who work for the present and future," it had hope.

Curiously, and without realizing the contradiction, K. placed this hope in a renewal of the past, a reconstruction of the Pushkin tradition. He wrote much about Pushkin, although he never produced a complete, full-length book on him. His love of Pushkinian metrics, moreover, was so overwhelming that he passed over too hurriedly much of the experimentation that was going on all around him. As a result, much of his imposing reasoning and classically honed verse was ignored by younger poets; he had but little influence, unlike his contemporary,

Georgy Ivanov (1894–1958). But there is today a great renewed interest in his work, both in the West and the U.S.S.R., as Nadezhda Mandelshtam (1899–1980) has pointed out in her memoirs.

K. combines a symbolist mystical yearning for a kingdom of beauty that lies beyond the ugliness of the real with a classical sense of form derived from Pushkin. The tension produced by this unusual mixture makes of him an original, while his grotesque perception of the physical allies him to his Western contemporaries, who were portraying the very same decay that would culminate in World War II.

FURTHER WORKS: *Derzhavin* (1931); *O Pushkine* (1937); *Nekropol* (1939); *Literaturnye stati i vospominania* (1954)

BIBLIOGRAPHY: Nabokov, V., "On Hodasevich" (1939), *Strong Opinions* (1973), pp. 223–27; Hughes, R., "K.: Irony and Dislocation: A Poet in Exile," *TriQ,* 28 (1973), 52–66; Smith, G. S., "Stanza Rhythm and Stress Load in the Iambic Tetrameter of V. F. K.," *SEEJ,* 24 (1980), 25–36

PHILIPPE RADLEY

KHOWAR LITERATURE
See Pakistani Literature

KIKINGO LITERATURE
See Zairian Literature

KIKUYU LITERATURE
See Kenyan Literature

KILPI, Volter
Finnish novelist and essayist, b. 12 Dec. 1874, Kustavi; d. 13 June 1939, Turku

K.'s father was a merchant-ship captain based at Kustavi, on the coast north of Turku; he maintained his connection with the Kustavi district throughout his life. His family name was really Ericsson, but he and two brothers adopted the Finnish name he is known by. Following a university education, K. became a librarian and was eventually appointed director of the Turku University Library. He began to lose his hearing at a rather early age and became progressively deafer throughout his life.

He married the playwright Helga Vanhakartano in 1907.

K.'s first creative writings were neoromantic. *Bathseba* (1900; Bathsheba) is a sentimental poetic narrative in which a leading theme is the difficulty of human communication. His essays in *Ihmisestä ja elämästä* (1902; on man and life) voice the aestheticism common at the time and show the influence of Goethe, Schopenhauer, and Nietzsche. During the 1918 civil war and its aftermath, he published right-wing political pamphlets advocating a monarchy for Finland.

K. found his most original vein much later in the novel *Alastalon salissa* (1933; in the hall of Alastalo), the product of long labor. In it his aestheticism was left behind, although his preoccupation with the inner life only deepens. The prologue is a prolonged meditation on death inspired by the sight of an old churchyard and recalling a church service attended as a child. All the older people who were then present are now buried there. Memories of a wedding, of men, women, and girls, of an autumn Sunday morning press into the narrator's consciousness. This long, nostalgic book has been compared to the works of Proust and Joyce (qq.v.), and the rendering of the thought processes of the characters anticipates the "subconversations" of Nathalie Sarraute (q.v.). Nevertheless, the characters and setting are entirely K.'s own. The time is around 1860. A group of merchant seamen and farmers come to Captain Mattsson's house to discuss a new shipbuilding venture. One of the men in attendance is Pukkila, his resentful rival. Another memorable character is Härkäniemi, a philosophical bachelor. Primarily through interior monologue (q.v.) the varied life of the community is unveiled. Much humor enlivens the novel, and a long sailor's yarn narrated by Härkäniemi lends variety.

K.'s book of short stories *Pitäjän pienempiä* (1934; humbler folk of the parish) parallels on a humbler level the depiction of the more prosperous class in *Alastalon salissa*. One especially effective story is "Merimiehenleski" (a seaman's widow), written in the form of a sequence of meditations of an old woman. She had lost her husband at sea many years before. There are no children to break the long silences left in her hut by his repeated departures and his final permanent absence. She is consoled by memories of her husband and by religious piety, but her prayers finally turn into imprecations against an unlistening God.

There is an autobiographical aspect to the novel *Kirkolle* (1937; on the way to church). A boat takes a large group of islanders to church. The gathering, the journey, and the arrival provide the action, but the main purpose of the book is the analysis of the churchgoers' feelings and the description of the midsummer Sunday setting. If the physical destination is a Christian church, the spiritual destination is agnostic in nature. Only the present existence is real, in all its paradoxical richness. The title of a book of meditations, *Suljetuilla porteilla* (1938; at closed gates), is perhaps unintentionally significant, for the author's difficult style has become almost hermetic. But an unfinished, posthumously published work shows a renewed clarity of expression: *Gulliverin matka Fantomimian mantereelle* (1944; Gulliver's journey to Fantomimia) is an interesting attempt to transport Gulliver into the modern world, where time-travel seems a familiar possibility.

K. is never likely to be popular. Even for Finnish readers, there is an obstacle in his handling of the language, his penchant for coinages and compounds of his own creation. Nonetheless, K. was a highly individual writer whose experiments in novelistic technique may justify comparison with the much better-known vanguard of the major currents of world literature.

FURTHER WORKS: *Parsifal* (1902); *Antinous* (1903); *Nykyaikaisista taidepyrinnöistä* (1905); *Kansallista itsetutkistelua* (1917); *Tulevaisuuden edessä* (1918)

BIBLIOGRAPHY: Ahokas, J., *A History of Finnish Literature* (1973), pp. 209–17

REINO VIRTANEN

KIMBUNDU LITERATURE
See Angolan Literature

KINNELL, Galway
American poet and translator, b. 1 Feb. 1927, Providence, R.I.

A Princeton graduate, K. has taught at many universities in the U.S. and abroad; he spent three years at the University of Hawaii, but then returned to the east coast. Clearly K. teaches more out of necessity than a fully developed sense of vocation; he seldom writes reviews or essays, although his novel *Black Light*

(1966) is very powerful. For K., poetry is the first and last concern.

K.'s early poetry was filled with a miraculous sense of the commonplace. His long poem, "The Avenue Bearing the Initial of Christ into the New World," in *What a Kingdom It Was* (1960), celebrated the diversity of urban life, turning the welter of sensations into a Whitmanesque embrace of change and transformation. Allied in sensibility to the poetry of Robert Bly (q.v.) and James Wright (1927–1980), K. avoided irony in favor of an intensity created out of an imagery of incandescent attentiveness. Thematically his early poetry revolved around questions of suffering and death, using an essentially religious consciousness to question the human condition. Yet the religious fervor of the poetry never inhibited a full acceptance of the secular notions of pleasure and joy.

In *Body Rags* (1967) and *The Book of Nightmares* (1971) K. brought to fullest expression his sense of what he calls the "poetics of the physical world" by dealing with the courage, pain, and rage of "torn love." The main influences on this poetry, besides the obvious presence of Whitman, are the flower and animal poems of D. H. Lawrence (q.v.) and the natural-ecstatic sequences of Theodore Roethke (q.v.). K.'s attention is often drawn to ways of registering both long-term and intense awareness of suffering and loss: the lines of the human face, the consuming power of fire, and the manifold forms of music and song, all appear often in his poems, and in many guises. His subjects can as readily be drawn from scenes of urban alienation as from the natural landscape of New England.

K. has also translated the poems of Villon— *The Poems of François Villon* (1965; rev. version, 1977)—and Yves Bonnefoy (q.v.)—*On the Motion and Immobility of Douve* (1968). These translations reflect the same qualities that animate his poems: states of extreme desire and moments of great subjective power are presented in a language dense with human urgency.

FURTHER WORKS: *First Poems, 1946–1954* (1954); *Flower Herding on Mount Monadnock* (1964); *The Avenue Bearing the Initial of Christ into the New World: Poems 1946– 64* (1974); *Mortal Acts, Mortal Words* (1980)

BIBLIOGRAPHY: Howard, R., *Alone with America* (1969), pp. 258–71; Davie, D., "Slogging for the Absolute," *Parnassus*, 3, 1 (1974), 9–22; McKenzie, J., "To the Roots: An Interview with K.," in Boyers, R., ed., *Contemporary Poetry in America* (1974), pp. 240–55; Lieberman, L., *Unassigned Frequencies: American Poetry in Review* (1977), pp. 212–14; Molesworth, C., *The Fierce Embrace: A Study in Contemporary American Poetry* (1979), pp. 98–111

CHARLES MOLESWORTH

KIPLING, Rudyard

English short-story writer, novelist, and poet, b. 30 Dec. 1865, Bombay, India; d. 18 Jan. 1936, London

K. was born into a family of artists and politicians in British-ruled India. His childhood in India and his schooling in England, when he was separated from his parents, provided much material for his early work, such as the story "Baa Baa Black Sheep" (1888). He worked as a journalist in India from 1882 to 1889 and at the same time began writing poetry and stories. He returned to England, then came to America (in 1892), where he lived for four years. Eventually, he settled permanently in Sussex, England. The death of his only son in World War I darkened his later life and work, as can be seen in books such as *The Irish Guards in the Great War* (1923), written as a memorial to his son.

K. is readily acknowledged as a good second-rank poet and versifier; in T. S. Eliot's (q.v.) words, K. as a poet seems to be a "laureate without laurels." The poems in a very early work, *Departmental Ditties* (1886) show both K.'s romantic and his satirical tendencies. They are marked by acute observation, effective scenic presentation, and a sharp, racy style, which are in refreshing contrast to the then popular gushing style and Victorian verbosity. Wordplay and jollity are characteristic of K.'s early verse.

K.'s adoration of the British Empire produced some fine poems depicting the average British soldier's (Tommy's) life—his sense of community, his sufferings and joys. *Barrack-Room Ballads* (1892) contains some of the best known of these poems, including "Danny Deever," a deeply moving poem that became very popular among British servicemen. In these poems and other writings K. developed his idea—to him, a moral concept—of the "white man's burden," a mystique of the Empire, basing his ideas on what he called the "call to duty" and fulfillment of "the Law," which he believed British institutions embodied.

K. dealt with many other themes in his verse. "The Sons of Martha" (1907) expresses his faith in activism. In "The Gods of the Copybook Headings" (1919) he satirized man's slavishness to the gods of the marketplace. A notable late poem is "The Waster" (1930), about a man who "suffers unspeakable things, in body and soul and mind."

K.'s masterpiece, and his supreme achievement in fiction, is *Kim* (1901). It is so sprawling and discursive that at first the reader might overlook the continuity of its theme. It portrays the young orphan Kim on the Grand Trunk Road, his association with Mahbub Ali, the man of many parts, and his deep attachment to the Tibetan lama, and traces the various stages of the boy's spiritual growth. *Kim* is episodic and kaleidoscopic; it encompasses the wonderful spectacle, the vision that reveals the mysteries of the Wheel of Life and of Buddhism. It is no conventional English novel, nor is it a modern psychological novel; it has a form of its own molded by its picaresque façade and its visionary and prophetic quality.

The novels *The Light That Failed* (1891) and *Captains Courageous* (1897) are also distinctive both in structure and meaning. *Captains Courageous* is the story of Harvey Cheyne, the spoiled child of an American millionaire, who falls into the sea, is rescued by the fisherman Manuel, and learns the art of roughing it. Cheyne's experience is part of America's great pioneering tradition. Transformed by the fishermen's rugged life, he develops a faith in activism and acquires moral values. *The Light That Failed* unfolds the complexities of the relationships between the painter Dick Heldar, two contrasting women, Maisie and Bessie, and Dick's friend Torpenhow. Dick's eyesight fails (hence the title), he bids goodbye to Bessie, goes to Port Said, and is killed by enemy fire. The novel presents the themes of love, war, and death in the context of Dick's personal predicament.

Realism, acute observation of men and landscapes, creation of atmosphere, exploration of myth, the animal world, fantasy, and the abnormal and paranormal are the significant qualities of K. as a writer of short stories, a great many of which were written for children. The sweep of his imagination is very wide and covers many continents. Stories such as "The Phantom 'Rickshaw" (1888) vividly demonstrate how K. explores the supernatural world. "The Miracle of Puran Bhagat" in *The Second Jungle Book* (1895) is an extraordinary tale of the transfor-

mation of Sir Puran Dass into a saffron-robed Buddhist *sanyasi*, who has renounced worldly life. The theme of "The Bridge-Builders" (1898) is the bridge between the human and divine worlds—the characters Findlayson and Peroo both see the vision of Hindu gods in the Ganges—and the story sings the gospel of work.

During the last two decades of his life K. suffered from ill health and a steep decline in popularity. The later K. seems pessimistic and inclined to explore in greater depth the darker elements of human experience, as can be observed in such stories as "Mary Postgate" (1915), "The Gardener" (1926), and particularly "Dayspring Mishandled" (1928). These later tales, full of pathos and tragedy, and his later poems, too, reveal a sense of bitterness and a belief in the powerlessness of man in an uncertain world.

An artistic reporter for posterity of imperial England, an unusually skillful short-story writer, a novelist with an individualistic sense of the form of fiction, and a poet of haunting rhythms—K. achieved a reputation not equaled in his early years by any other Englishman except Thomas Hardy (q.v.). His work also aroused controversies, and he became an object of severely adverse criticism. Nonetheless, he was the first Englishman to receive the Nobel Prize for literature (1907), at the age of forty-two. His popularity was phenomenal; so was the reaction against him in the 1940s. A K. revival is now under way, however, and the stage is set for a more balanced appraisal of his achievement.

FURTHER WORKS: *Schoolboy Lyrics* (1881); *The Phantom 'Rickshaw* (1888); *Plain Tales from the Hills* (1888); *Wee Willie Winkie* (1888); *Soldiers Three* (1888); *Life's Handicap* (1891); *The Naulahka* (1892, with Charles Wolcott Balestier); *Many Inventions* (1893); *The Jungle Book* (1894); *The Seven Seas* (1896); *Soldier Tales* (1896); *Recessional* (1897); *The Day's Work* (1898); *Ballad of East and West* (1899); *Stalky & Co.* (1899); *The White Man's Burden* (1899); *The K. Reader* (1900); *Just So Stories* (1902); *Traffics and Discoveries* (1904); *Puck of Pook's Hill* (1906); *Collected Verse* (1907); *Actions and Reactions* (1909); *Rewards and Fairies* (1910); *For All We Have and Are* (1914); *A Diversity of Creatures* (1917); *The Graves of the Fallen* (1919); *The Years Between* (1919); *Letters of Travel 1892–1913* (1920); *A Choice of the*

Songs from the Verse of R. K. (1925); *Sea and Sussex* (1926); *Debits and Credits* (1926); *R. K.'s Verse 1885–1926* (1927); *The One-Volume K., Authorized* (1928); *A Book of Words: Selections from Speeches and Addresses Delivered between 1906 and 1927* (1928); *Limits and Renewals* (1932); *R. K.'s Verse 1885–1932* (1933); *All the Mowgli Stories* (1933); *Something of Myself* (1937); *Uncollected Prose I and II* (1938); *Complete Works* (35 vols., 1937–39); *R. K.'s Verse* (1940); *A Choice of K.'s Verse* (1941); *R. K. to Rider Haggard: The Record of a Friendship* (1965); *American Notes: R. K.'s West* (1981)

BIBLIOGRAPHY: Carrington, C., *R. K.: His Life and Work* (1955); Tompkins, J. M. S., *The Art of R. K.* (1959); Bodelsen, C. A., *Aspects of R. K.'s Art* (1964); Rutherford, A., ed., *K.'s Mind and Art* (1964); Connell, L., *K. in India* (1966); Dobrée, B., *R. K.: Realist and Fabulist* (1967); Rao, K. B., *R. K.'s India* (1967); Shahane, V. A., *R. K.: Activist and Artist* (1973); Amis, K., *R. K. and His World* (1975); Wilson, A., *The Strange Ride of R. K.* (1977)

V. A. SHAHANE

KIRGIZ LITERATURE

The Origins: 1924–34

The appearance of written Kirgiz literature in 1924 coincided with the establishment of the Kirgiz, a Turkic and Muslim people, as a nation within the framework of the Soviet Union. The first printed work by a professional writer, Aalï Tokombaev's (b. 1904) poem "Oktiabr'din kelgen kezi" (when October came) was published in the premiere issue (7 November 1924) of the first Kirgiz language newspaper, *Erkin-too* (continued as *Sovettik Kïrgïzstan*). The Kirgiz used the Arabic alphabet until 1927, when a change was made to the Latin alphabet; the present-day Cyrillic alphabet was adopted in 1940. *Erkin-too*, the monthly *Jangï madaniyat jolunda* (now called *Ala-too*), and the Komsomol organ *Leninchil jash* have played an important role in the genesis and development of written Kirgiz literature. An editor of the first two, Kasïm Tïnïstanov (b. 1900?; disappeared in mid-1930s), is considered the initiator of important national trends

in Kirgiz literature. His *Kasïm ïrlarïnïng jïynagï* (1925; collection of Kasïm's poems) describes the beauty of the Kirgiz homeland and extols the Kirgiz cultural heritage. The earliest significant work of fiction was the novella *Ajar* (1927; Ajar) by Kasïmalï Bayalinov (b. 1902), which deals with woman's plight in prerevolutionary society and with the tragic consequences of the uprising of central Asian Muslims against Russian rule in 1916. The theme of the position and role of women was also treated in the plays *Kaygïlu Kakey* (1927; unfortunate Kakey) by Moldogazi Tokobaev (b. 1905) and *Töraga Zeynep* (1929; Zeynep, the head of the village soviet) by Sïdïk Karashev (dates n.a.).

Restructuring and Consolidation: 1934–53

During the 1930s a campaign directed from Moscow against national communism and against all manifestations of independent national character came to weigh heavily on Kirgiz literature. Between 1930 and 1934 preparations were made for the definitive structuring of literary activity in the U.S.S.R. Writers' associations—in this case the Association of Writers of Kirgizia—were one product of these plans, and they assumed a fundamental role monitoring all literary activity. In 1934 Socialist Realism (q.v.) was proclaimed as the guiding principle in Soviet literature; in addition, non-Russian writers were expected to take Russian culture and literature as their models. This pressure, which intensified until Stalin's death in 1953, created a virtual flood of panegyrics about Lenin and Stalin; a prominent example is the ode to Stalin published in 1936 by Aalï Tokombaev and Joomart Bokombaev (1910–1944); the poem "Rossiya" (1945; Russia) by Alïkul Osmonov (1915–1950) extols Russia as a kind of super-fatherland of the Kirgiz.

Despite the pressure for conformity this second period did witness the broadening and strengthening of the base of Kirgiz literature. The most honored novelist of this period, Tügelbay Sïdïkbekov (b. 1912) devoted his works *Keng-Suu* (1937–38; Keng-Suu) and *Temir* (1939–40; Temir) to an approved theme, the collectivization of land; *Keng-Suu* is modeled on Sholokhov's (q.v.) *Podnyataya tselina*. Works dealing with collectivization and the emancipation of women fell within accepted boundaries, but another theme of this period, the 1916 revolt of central Asian Muslims, was at first a source of friction. This revolt and its suppression by the tsarist government had affected the Kirgiz in particular. When a play dealing with this issue, *Onaltïnjï jïl* (1929; year 16 [i.e., 1916]) by Naamatov (dates n.a.) was staged in Frunze, it was denounced as a nationalist falsification of history and suppressed. A verse epic on this theme, *Kanduu jïdar* (1937; bloody years) by Aalï Tokombaev was likewise censured and was eventually rewritten under the title *Tang aldïnda* (1961; before dawn). In contrast, the musical play *Ajal orduna* (1935; instead of death) by Joomart Turusbekov (1910–1943) was applauded for presenting the uprising as a conflict between social classes rather than between the Kirgiz and Russians.

Thus, between the 1930s and 1950s Kirgiz literature was forced to concentrate on the efforts of the Soviet state to build a new society under the leadership of the Communist Party. The Kirgiz, however, also had an oral literature, the history of which can be traced back several centuries and the roots of which probably extend into the distant past. This tradition was alive into the Soviet period. Folk poets and esteem, and Kirgiz, Russian, and other scholars were able to record much of this oral literature and publish both texts and studies about it. This oral literature has been a source of inspiration and a symbol of Kirgiz ethnic identity in literature, opera, and ballet. However, its most important component, the epic, also fell into disgrace in the final years of Stalin's rule, when all epics of the Turkic peoples were banned as nationalistic and harmful (unlike the Russian epics). *Manas* (Manas), the Kirgiz folk epic of the 16th–17th cs., named after its principal hero, was denounced in 1952, a move that met with unexpected resistance from the Kirgiz public, including Kirgiz members of the Communist Party. The defenders of this national heritage were eventually forced to surrender; after Stalin's death in 1953, however, *Manas* was rehabilitated along with the other central Asian epics.

The Coming of Age: 1953 to the Present

The rehabilitation of *Manas* inaugurated the gradual liberalization of the later 1950s and 1960s, when a new generation of writers who sought greater flexibility of form and individuality in the choice and treatment of themes came to the fore. Novels and short stories by writers such as Chïngïz Aytmatov (q.v.),

Shükürbek Beyshenaliev (b. 1928), Sagïndïk Omurbaev (b. 1930), Shabdanday Abdïramanov (b. 1930), Tolegen Kasïmbekov (b. 1931) and others were well received not only in Kirgizia but through translations into Russian in the wider framework of the USSR. Poets of note include Sooronbay Jusuev (b. 1925), Jalil Sadïkov (b. 1932), and Bayïlda Sarnogoev (b. 1932). Süyünbay Eraliev (b. 1921) introduced blank verse with his poem "Jïldïzlarga sayakat" (1966; journey to the stars), a work admired by many but criticized by some for its innovative and cosmopolitan character.

A particular feature of contemporary Kirgiz literature is the appearance of bilingual Kirgiz-Russian authors. This group, led by Aytmatov, includes promising newcomers like Cholponbay Nusupov (b. 1957). These writers display a perfect command of both languages, an admiration and affection for Russian culture, and loyalty to the Soviet political and social system. At the same time their works contain a resounding affirmation of Kirgiz ethnic identity and show an attachment to national values that could not have been expressed by writers of the earlier generation.

Today Kirgiz literature is vigorous, sophisticated, and many-sided. Its genesis, evolution, and future are interwoven with those of the multinational Soviet state of which Kirgizia is a part. This integration has both positive and negative aspects. The rate of literacy, a mere two percent of the population in the early 1920s, has now reached ninety-nine percent. Works written by Kirgiz authors enjoy a wide audience through translations into Russian and other languages of the Soviet Union, and they play a special role in strengthening ethnic and cultural ties between the Kirgiz and their central Asian kinsmen, such as the Uzbeks and Kazakhs. At the same time, Kirgiz literature is subject to forces beyond the control of the Kirgiz themselves. Nevertheless, it has shown a reassuring resiliency, and some of its works deserve a place of honor among the literary creations of any period or nation.

BIBLIOGRAPHY: "La littérature kirghiz," *Philologiae turcicae fundamenta* (1963), Vol. II, pp. 760–61; Allworth, E., "The Changing Intellectual and Literary Community," and "The Focus of Literature," in Allworth, E., ed., *Central Asia: A Century of Russian Rule* (1967), pp. 349–96, 397–433; Kydyrbaeva, R. Z., "[Kirgiz] Literature," *Great Soviet En-*

cyclopedia, 3rd ed. [Eng. tr.], Vol. 12 (1976 [i.e., 1973]), pp. 500–502

SVAT SOUCEK

KIRK, Hans Rudolf
Danish novelist, b. 11 Jan. 1889, Hadsund; d. 16 June 1962, Copenhagen

Although K. grew up in a conservative middle-class milieu as the son of a doctor, he never lost sight of the fact that his family came from a long line of impoverished fisherfolk from western Jutland. He studied law at the University of Copenhagen, receiving a degree in 1922. Between 1923 and 1925 he held a position as a local government official. Thereafter he became a journalist and devoted himself entirely to writing. During the German occupation K. was interned in a concentration camp, from 1941 to 1943. After the war he became a major contributor to the communist newspaper *Land og folk.*

Since his early youth K. had been a convinced Marxist. In his writing he analyzes the relationship between the distribution of capital and people's outlook on life, illustrating how economic and social conditions determine the beliefs and habits of groups within society. His first and finest work, *Fiskerne* (1928; *The Fishermen,* 1951), is a novel that tells of the move by a whole community of fishermen from desperately poor homes on the west coast of Jutland to a fertile island. Belonging to a stern, pietistic movement within the Danish Lutheran church called "Indre Mission," whose religious fellowship gave the poor and oppressed the strength to face their harsh existence, the fishermen and their families form a sharp contrast to the well-to-do farmers of the island, whose faith is based on more traditional Christianity. The dramatic confrontation between the two groups and the gradual takeover of the entire parish by the newcomers is the theme of the book. Their radical and zealous religiosity is regarded by K. as a deflection of the energy that should have been used in the class struggle.

This view is further elaborated by K. in his next two novels, *Daglejerne* (1936; the laborers) and *De nye tider* (1939; new times), in which he sets out to expose the exploitation of the poor by those in power, and to show the development of a new, classless society by way of its liberation from religious and capitalist ties. With *Borgmesteren går af* (1941; the mayor resigns), a biting satire on government bureaucracy, K.'s writing changed character. The

setting is no longer the old rural society, and the tendentiousness of his presentation becomes obvious. In *Slaven* (1948; the slave), a historical novel set in the 17th c., he formulates his ideas about the evils of capitalist society. The book describes the events on board a ship sailing from South America to Spain on which all social and economic classes are present. *Vredens søn* (1950; the son of wrath) presents Jesus as a purely historical figure. As a leader of the oppressed he could have liberated the Jewish people, in K.'s opinion, if he had embraced a social revolution rather than a religious one.

K. introduced the novel with a collective protagonist to Denmark and was also the first to signal the beginning of a new social and political awareness in the literature of the 1930s. His early novels, in particular *Fiskerne,* are distinguished by the author's intimate knowledge of the people about whom he writes and by the objectivity of his narration. In his later works, however, K.'s analysis of society became increasingly one-sided and dogmatic, and his characters turned into lifeless mouthpieces for his political ideas.

FURTHER WORKS: *Djævelens penge* (1952); *Klitgaard & sønner* (1952); *Skyggespil* (1953); *Borgerlige noveller* (1958); *Danmarksrejsen* (1966); *Breve fra Horserød* (1967)

BIBLIOGRAPHY: Mawby, J., *Writers and Politics in Modern Scandinavia* (1978), pp. 14–21

MARIANNE FORSSBLAD

KISHIDA Kunio
Japanese dramatist and critic, b. 2 Nov. 1890, Tokyo; d. 5 March 1954, Tokyo

Born into a samurai family, K. went through military school and received a commission. He disappointed his father, a military officer, however, by resigning in order to take up the study of French literature at Tokyo University in 1916 instead of carrying on the family tradition. He left the university before graduation and went to France in 1920, determined to learn the craft of playwriting. In Paris he studied with the famous director Jacques Copeau at the Théâtre du Vieux Colombier.

K. returned to Japan in 1922 to try to create a truly modern Japanese drama based on the creation of poetic and psychologically accurate dialogue he found in the European works he discovered while living in Paris. K.'s efforts to replace a Japanese drama still heavily dependent on more traditional means of expression also led him into drama criticism, theater management, and stage direction, but all these activities shared the same purpose: to create a contemporary drama responsive to the psychological realities that he felt were crucial to portray if the Japanese theater were to become a viable form of modern literary expression.

K.'s early one-act plays are marked by a highly effective fusion of realistic dialogue and elegant fantasy. *Chiroru no aki* (1924; autumn in the Tyrol) places a Japanese protagonist in a European setting, in which he develops an affection for a European woman staying in the same small Austrian hotel. *Buranko* (1925; the swing) shows a young Tokyo couple coming to grips with the shifting roles of sense and sensibility in a marriage. The most successful of his early plays, *Kamifūsen* (1925; paper balloon), is a more lyrical examination of the same predicament.

By the late 1920s K.'s reputation had grown to the point that he was asked to write full-length plays for production in Tokyo, and much of his best work dates from this period. *Ochiba nikki* (1927; diary of fallen leaves) remains one of K.'s most poignant statements about the meaning of his French experience. The protagonist of the play is an elderly Japanese woman, of great wit and charm, whose son had married a French woman some years before; her granddaughter, Henriette, now stays with her. K.'s grasp of the nuances of the differences in cultures and his genuine ability to create effective stage personality makes the old lady, whose death scene concludes the play, one of his most moving creations. France figures again in *Ushiyama hoteru* (1929; Ushiyama Hotel), which chronicles in a sardonic, almost nihilistic fashion, the lives of a group of Japanese living in a dingy hotel in Vietnam, then a French colony.

After a long series of experiments, K. reached the final phase of his development in *Sawa shi no futari musume* (1935; Mr. Sawa's two daughters), which combines evocative dialogue with trenchant commentary on the social and psychological climate of the time. Like the characters in the earlier plays of K., those presented here are sophisticated and worldly (Mr. Sawa himself has lived in Europe), but their attempts at self-understanding are altogether Japanese.

By the beginning of World War II, K. had stopped writing, although he continued certain theatrical and cultural activities until 1944. After the end of the war he wrote a few short pieces but was hampered by ill health and heavy duties with the Bungakuza, an important acting troupe. He died while directing a play for the Bungakuza.

K.'s plays remain among the most respected modern classics of the Japanese stage and are still admired for their subtle dialogue, vivid atmosphere, and an emphasis on the centrality for the drama of individual psychology, a concept at variance with the Marxist dramaturgy popular in influential theater circles in Tokyo before the government suppression in the late 1930s. The Kishida Prize, the most important drama award in Japan, indicates the esteem in which K.'s work is still held. K.'s plays provide the best theatrical record of the Japanese in search of their own spiritual identity during the difficult decades between the two world wars.

FURTHER WORKS: *Furui omocha* (1924); *Hazakura* (1925); *Mura de ichi ban kuri no ki* (1926); *Mama sensei to sono otto* (1930); *Asamayama* (1931); *Shokugyō* (1935); *Saigetsu* (1935); *Fūzoku jihyō* (1936); *Zenshū* (10 vols., 1955)

BIBLIOGRAPHY: Japan UNESCO Commission, ed., *Theatre in Japan* (1963), pp. 213–41; Ortolani, B., "Shingeki: The Maturing New Drama of Japan," in Roggendorf, J., ed., *Studies in Japanese Culture* (1963), pp. 163–85; Rimer, J. T., *Toward a Modern Japanese Theatre: K. K.* (1974)

J. THOMAS RIMER

KLEIN, A(braham) M(oses)

Canadian poet and novelist, b. 14 Feb. 1909, Montreal, Que.; d. 20 Aug. 1972, Montreal, Que.

After attending McGill University, K. studied law at the University of Montreal. After 1933 he practiced law in Montreal, was involved in Zionist organizations, and, from 1939 to 1955, edited the *Canadian Jewish Chronicle*. In the late 1940s he made many speeches for the Canadian Jewish Congress and, in 1949, ran unsuccessfully for parliament as the CCF (socialist) candidate. After two nervous breakdowns in the 1950s, K. became ever more reclusive, rarely seeing anyone outside his immediate family, until his death.

K.'s first collection of poems, *Hath Not a Jew . . .* (1940), contained poems written in the late 1920s and early 1930s. These deal with the situation of the Jews throughout history and are written in a language that is deliberately archaic, in the manner of Edmund Spenser, Shakespeare, and Christopher Marlowe. Much of this hybrid verse is surprisingly fresh, colorful, and scintillating, especially in the poems for children, based on Jewish folklore and Hasidic tales from Poland, the land from which K.'s family had emigrated. There is almost no reference to Canada or identifiable mention of Montreal.

In the early 1930s, however, K. turned away from his exclusively Jewish concerns and wrote biting satires about the relations between urban rich and poor. These poems (in *Collected Poems,* 1974) were not included in the four collections published during his lifetime, but they foreshadowed his fusion of private vision and public observation in *The Rocking Chair* (1948).

This collection, which explores the French-Canadian community and sensibility, is a landmark in the history of Canadian poetry. Stylistically K. benefited from acquaintance with the work of Gerard Manley Hopkins (1844–1889), Yeats, Auden, and Dylan Thomas (qq.v.), while remaining distinctively original (probably because of his mastery of a variety of languages). In a rich, sometimes even ornate language, he applies his very considerable insight into the nature of minority groups to the French-Canadians, Canadians in general, and Canadian Indians, and even to the scattered Canadian poets. He expresses the collective Canadian consciousness, a tapestry of minority groups, each in its own cultural garrison (or ghetto) and surrounded by a vast and forbidding landscape. He also articulates the attempt of each cultural or regional community to achieve some harmony with the land and, perhaps through the land, with a larger order of things in the universe. "Portrait of the Poet as Landscape" is a key poem that has provided direction for later poets such as Irving Layton, Leonard Cohen, and Margaret Atwood (qq.v.).

K.'s novella, *The Second Scroll* (1951), is a Zionist version of the quest romance. Influenced by Joyce (q.v.), about whom he hoped to write a book, and perhaps by Dante, K. developed another version of the personal odyssey that holds spiritual significance for mankind at large. The messianic redemption in store for man appears to be foreshadowed in the reunion of the Jews with their holy land. The utopian Israel of this book may bear little resemblance to the reality of today, but the vision and some of the language, particularly in a brilliant recreation of Michelangelo's Sistine Chapel paintings as prophecy of Israel's tragedy and triumph, remain compelling and, by analogy, relevant to the Canadian attempt to achieve community.

There remains much unpublished work, including poems, a novel, and several versions of a folk play. K.'s was essentially a religious sensibility, and his great theme was the transcendence of evil through imaginative sympathy. While he was intensely concerned about the fate of Jewry, he was also able to interpret Canadians to themselves, and to affirm the value of cultural coexistence in the world at large.

FURTHER WORKS: *Poems* (1944); *The Hitleriad* (1944)

BIBLIOGRAPHY: Pacey, D., *Ten Canadian Poets* (1958), pp. 254–92; Marshall, T., ed., *A. M. K.* (1970); Waddington, M., *A. M. K.* (1970); Rosenblatt, J., ed., special K. issue, *Jewish Dialog,* Passover, 1973; Fischer, G., *In Search of Jerusalem: Religion and Ethics in the Writings of A. M. K.* (1975); Mayne, S., ed., *The A. M. K. Symposium* (1975)

TOM MARSHALL

KLYUEV, Nikolay Alexeevich

Russian poet, b. 1887, Vytegra; d. Aug. 1937?, Siberia

Born to peasant parents, K. was steeped from childhood in northern Russian folk traditions. His family was associated with the illegal religious sectarians, God's People (*Khlysty*), for whom K. was chosen to be a composer of ritual songs. It is likely that in 1906 or 1907 he went to Iran, India, and central Asia on secret sectarian business.

Although K. had no formal education, he was well read in religious and mystical literature. K. began a correspondence with Alexandr Blok (q.v.) in 1907 and participated in Vyacheslav Ivanov's (q.v.) "Tower", as this literary salon was called, in St. Petersburg. K. met Sergey Yesenin (q.v.) in 1915 and began a stormy literary and intimate relationship lasting until Yesenin's suicide, which inspired one of K.'s greatest poems, "Plach o Yesenine" (1927; "Lament for Esenin," 1977).

After 1924 K. wandered about Russia visiting monasteries and shrines. He was arrested in 1933 on charges of "*kulak* [well-to-do

peasant] agitation" manifested by his dissemination of his powerful epic poem about village
life under Soviet rule, "Pogorelshchina" (written 1926–28?, pub. 1954; "The Burned
Ruins," 1977). Little is known about K.'s last
years, after he was exiled to Siberia.

One of the first representatives of the so-
called "peasant poets," K. wrote poetry that is
characterized by vivid local color, an abundance of archaic and peasant language, daring
and sometimes sexual imagery, and a deep
understanding of Russian nature and art, especially icon painting and folk songs, as can be
seen in works such as *Lesnye byli* (1913; true
forest stories), *Mirskie dumy* (1916; secular
thoughts), and "Pesni zaonezhya" (1916;
songs of the Onega region). K. successfully
combined folk mannerisms with the sensibilities
and poetic techniques of Russian symbolism
(q.v.). Much of his poetry—for example, *Brat-
skie pesni* (1912; brotherly songs)—is influenced by the ecstatic sectarian traditions.
Deeply embedded in his work is an apocalyptic
eschatology based on a mystic faith in the Russian peasantry and a profound opposition to the
technical civilization of the West. The island of
Kizhi in Lake Onega in his native region is connected in K.'s poetry with an ancient utopian
peasant culture. His *Izbyanye pesni* (1920;
songs of the peasant hut), however, written on
the death of his mother, contains some of K.'s
best and most accessible lyrics. They are written with a touching directness, unburdened by
metaphysical and mystical import.

K.'s most accomplished works are his long
poems: *Chetvyorty Rim* (1922; "The Fourth
Rome," 1977), *Mat Subbota* (1922; "Mother
Sabbath," 1977), "Zaozere" (1927; beyond
the lake), "Plach o Yesenine," "Derevnya"
(1927; the village), and "Pogorelshchina."
They all express K.'s vision of a mysticism of
Mother Earth and his grief over the destruction
of what he believed to be the deepest wellsprings of the Russian spirit.

K. has been called by some one of the most
decadent of the Russian symbolists "an Oscar
Wilde or Paul Verlaine in bast shoes," and by
others a truly national poet sprung from the soil
of ancient Rus. In the U.S.S.R. he is condemned as a *kulak* poet, although a small
volume of his poetry has recently been published there. He is unquestionably a major
figure in modern Russian poetry and awaits
deep and comprehensive study.

FURTHER WORKS: *Sosen perezvon* (1912);
Lviny khleb (1922); *Lenin* (1924); *Izba i*

pole (1928); *Polnoe sobranie sochineny* (2
vols., 1954); *Sochinenia* (2 vols., 1969);
Stikhotvorenia i poemy (1977). FURTHER
VOLUME IN ENGLISH: *Poems* (1977)

BIBLIOGRAPHY: Trostky, L., *Literature and
Revolution* [first pub. 1923] (1971), pp.
59–66; Zavalashin, V., *Early Soviet Writers*
(1958), pp. 91–100; Stammler, H., "N. K."
(in German), in N. K., *Sochinenia* (1969),
Vol. II, pp. 7–50; McVay, G., "Yesenin's Posthumous Fame and the Fate of His Friends,"
MLR, 67 (1972), 595–97; McVay, G.,
Esenin: A Life (1976), pp. 58–71, 169–71,
284–87; Ivask, G., "Russian Modernist Poets
and the Mystic Sectarians," in Gibian, G., and
Tjalsma, H. W., eds., *Russian Modernism*
(1976), pp. 85–106; Glad, J., Introduction to
N. A. K., *Poems* (1977), pp. ix–xx

GERALD PIROG

KOEPPEN, Wolfgang

West German novelist and essayist, b. 23 June
1906, Greifswald

The impoverished descendant of Pomeranian
country squires, K. was raised as an only child
by his mother. He studied philosophy, literature, and theater arts at the universities of
Hamburg, Greifswald, Berlin, and Würzburg,
worked as a seaman, actor, assistant theater
director, and free-lance journalist, and traveled
widely in Germany, France, Italy, and the
Netherlands. His eventual job as a journalist
and critic for the *Börsen-Courier* in Berlin
lasted only until Hitler's rise to power. Still, K.
managed to publish his first novel, *Eine
unglückliche Liebe* (1934; an unhappy love)
in Germany, then spent considerable time in
Holland while writing his next novel, *Die
Mauer schwankt* (1934; the wall sways),
which, in spite of its disguised criticism of the
Nazi regime, was reissued in 1939 in Germany
under the title *Die Pflicht* (duty). Generally,
however, K. kept a low profile throughout the
period of the Third Reich, trying to be neither
used nor persecuted by the people in power.
Since the end of World War II K. has lived predominantly in Munich as an independent
writer, journalist, and critic and has traveled
extensively throughout Europe, America, and
the Soviet Union.

K.'s most important literary contribution has
been a series of three novels that present a critical assessment of the psychological, social, and

political situation in West Germany during the 1950s. In contrast to the two prewar novels, which concentrate on one person's alienation from his bourgeois environment, without much overt reference to current events, this postwar trilogy depicts revealing cross sections of West German society by following a diverse cast of characters for a day or two at quite clearly defined points in historical time and space.

In *Tauben im Gras* (1951; pigeons in the grass) it is obviously Munich in the spring of 1951, still under American military government but on the way toward physical recovery. The emotional recovery of the individuals from the shock and disruption of the war is less certain. A once hopeful writer is unable to produce, while his immature wife gradually pawns her crumbling inheritance. The collapse of the old order has left the people uprooted and confused but has also given them a chance for change and new beginnings, as in the case of a young war widow who has fallen in love with a black GI and dreams of life in a U.S. paradise. Whether such liberated attitudes will withstand the mounting pressures of the return of authoritarianism and of bigotry in Germany is left open to question.

Restoration of the old authoritarian law and order appears to be in full swing in *Das Treibhaus* (1953; *The Bonn Parliament*, 1953) as we follow Keetenheuve, a former emigrant and now member of the Bonn parliament, in his attempt to defeat proposals to reinstitute the German army and military conscription. His idealistic hopes for a liberal and truly democratic Germany have been eroded in this atmosphere of intrigue, opportunism, and pragmatic wheeling and dealing. He fails both socially and politically and ends in suicide.

Der Tod in Rom (1954; *Death in Rome*, 1961), the most pessimistic of the three novels, centers on the reemergence of Nazism in various forms. Judejahn, a former SS general and thus the embodiment of death and destruction, is in Rome to discuss his possible return to Germany with his former fellow Nazi, Pfaffrath, now a big-city mayor in West Germany. These and other figures in the novel typify certain tendencies in postwar Germany: opportunism, religious revival, hedonism, aesthetic nihilism, and, behind it all, the specter of a neo-Nazi movement.

K.'s style, in its rhetorical, learned, and provocative brilliance, is the dominant feature of his works. Huge cumulative sentences, long, evocative stream-of-consciousness passages overflowing with cleverly chosen details (including news headlines, slogans, and popular hit songs), and montages of quickly shifting scenes and moods create an overall poetic effect in a manner reminiscent of Joyce, Faulkner, and Döblin (qq.v.), with moments of lyrical beauty, biting satire, loneliness, and despair.

K.'s trilogy had a highly controversial reception. But public interest soon waned, and K. turned to writing sophisticated literary travelogues, such as *Nach Rußland und anderswohin: Empfindsame Reisen* (1958; to Russia and other places: sentimental journeys), which, being less provocative in tone and content, received widespread acclaim among critics and the general public and led to various literary awards, beginning with the Büchner Prize in 1962. More recently K. has moved toward a blend of the psychological novel and social criticism in his semifictional autobiography *Jugend* (1976; youth). There is a special youthfulness in K.'s relentless stylistic and topical nonconformism even as he reaches old age, and it may continue to irritate potential readers, but K.'s work clearly deserves more attention than it has received so far.

FURTHER WORKS: *Amerikafahrt* (1959); *New York* (1961); *Reisen nach Frankreich* (1961); *Romanisches Café: Erzählende Prosa* (1972)

BIBLIOGRAPHY: Bance, C. F., "*Der Tod in Rom* and *Die Rote*: Two Italian Episodes," *FMLS*, 3 (1967), 126–34; Demetz, P., "W. K.," *Postwar German Literature* (1972), 168–72; Erlach, D., *W. K. als zeitkritischer Erzähler* (1973); Craven, S., "W. K. and the Human Condition," *GL&L*, 29 (1976), 201–15; Greiner, U., ed., *Über W. K.* (1976)

EBERHARD FREY

KOESTLER, Arthur

English novelist, essayist, and science writer, b. 5 Sept. 1905, Budapest, Hungary

As a child, K. saw his family and native land disintegrate as a result of World War I. Much of his early manhood was spent in the Weimar Republic, and he watched his first career (as a journalist) and German society destroyed by the Third Reich. While wandering across Europe in the 1930s (with a brief sojourn in Palestine during the British Mandate), he experienced the famines and chaos of the Soviet Union, the Stalinist purges and doublethink in the Communist Party (he joined in

1931 and resigned in 1938), the horror of the Spanish Civil War (during which he was captured by Franco's troops and sentenced to death), and the political corruption, paralysis, and fall of the French Third Republic. Escape to and settlement in Britain in 1940 marked his seventh country and sixth language since birth. He later became a British citizen, and except for travels to America and the Continent, he has remained in that country. He was made a Commander of the Order of the British Empire in 1972 and a Companion of Literature in 1974.

K.'s early life explains the apocalyptic element in his work. In everything that he has written he has viewed the world and himself as moving toward destruction, only to be saved by rebirth in a new form. K. and his heroes tend to be embattled and persecuted: K. in prison in Spain in his memoir *Spanish Testament* (1937), rewritten as *Dialogue with Death* (1942); K. fleeing occupied France in his memoir *Scum of the Earth* (1941); Rubashov, the old Bolshevik, caught in Stalin's purges in the novel *Darkness at Noon* (1941); and even Spartacus, the slave leader, hunted by the Romans and attacked by his own followers in *The Gladiators* (1939). Of K.'s over thirty books, these remain his most vividly written.

At the beginning of his literary career, readers and critics hailed K.'s works because his apocalyptic mood confirmed and explained their sense of the times. In 1941 *Darkness at Noon* was welcomed as much for its apparent answer to "The Riddle of Moscow's Trials" (the title of the front-page *New York Times Book Review* piece) as for its psychological intensity. The novel is autobiographical in many ways, a testament to its author's Communist Party experiences and an announcement of his rebirth in a post-Communist phase. All of this lies beneath the political and intellectual drama of Rubashov's downfall and the decay of the Russian Revolution. The novel is considered one of the most powerful political fictions of the century.

When K. turned his talent full force to anti-Communism, many readers were willing to follow and others to join. In his book of essays *The Yogi and the Commissar* (1945), one of the first Cold War tracts, he articulated widely held fears about Stalinism and Communism. When, a few years later, hundreds of thousands of readers felt enlightened by his memoir of his Communist Party experiences in the collection of essays edited by Richard Crossman called *The God That Failed* (1949), and enthusiastic

audiences greeted his speaking tours of Europe and America, he was at the height of his popularity.

K.'s next works, however, especially his two volumes of memoirs *Arrow in the Blue* (1951) and *The Invisible Writing* (1954), were less orthodox in their anti-Communism and more penetrating in their psychological analysis of the true-believer syndrome—they received a very mixed reception. K. was attacked by the same public who had earlier championed his works. There is an analogy between the public's response to K.'s writings on Communism and his version of his affair with Communism: in the beginning, the embrace was too passionate and when disillusion came, the split was rancorous.

Then, in the preface to his book of essays *Trial of the Dinosaur* (1955), K. declared his literary-political career over. He was finished with "these questions" and he wanted "a vocational change." Since that time, K.'s subjects have included science and mysticism, capital punishment (he opposes it), and extrasensory perception. He has baffled many of his former followers with his postpolitical writings. But the premises and themes of his recent work resemble those of his political writing. His central scientific theory—bisociation, that is, the collision of opposites, synthesis, and new form—is analogous to his political-literary structure of dialectic and apocalyptic transformation. He continues, at a distance and in muted tones, his autobiography: his topic may be science or mysticism, but his subject is his lifelong narrative of the self.

Throughout his long career, K.'s influence has been felt on many fronts. From 1937 to 1955, he was a committed writer, one of the main representatives of a whole generation of politically active European authors. Since 1956 he has been immersed mainly in questions of science and mysticism, and a large public, including many young persons, has followed his explorations. K. and his work live on and his reputation as one of the most diverse and often protean writers of our century continues.

FURTHER WORKS: *Arrival and Departure* (1943); *Twilight Bar: An Escapade in Four Acts* (1945); *Thieves in the Night: Chronicle of an Experiment* (1946); *Promise and Fulfillment: Palestine, 1917–1949* (1949); *Insight and Outlook: An Inquiry into the Common Foundations of Science, Art, and Social Ethics* (1949); *The Age of Longing* (1951); *Reflections on Hanging* (1957); *The*

Sleepwalkers: A History of Man's Changing Vision of the Universe (1959); *The Lotus and the Robot* (1961); *The Act of Creation* (1964); *The Ghost in the Machine* (1968); *Drinkers of Infinity: Essays, 1955–1967* (1969); *The Case of the Mid-Wife Toad* (1972); *The Roots of Coincidence* (1972); *The Call Girls* (1973); *The Heel of Achilles: Essays, 1968–1973* (1975); *The Thirteenth Tribe* (1976); *Janus: A Summing Up* (1978); *Bricks to Babel* (1981)

BIBLIOGRAPHY: Orwell, G., "A. K." *Dickens, Dali, and Others* (1946), pp. 31–45; Pritchett, V. S., "K.: A Guilty Figure," *Harper's*, Jan. 1948, 84–92; Deutscher, I., "The Ex-Communist's Conscience," *Heretics and Renegades* (1957), pp. 112–131; Aiken, H. D., "The Metaphysics of A. K.," *NYRB*, 17 Dec., 1964, 22–25; Calder, J., *Chronicles of Conscience: A Study of A. K. and George Orwell* (1968); Toulmin, S., "The Book of Arthur," *NYRB*, 11 April 1968, 16–21; Harris, H., ed., *Astride the Two Cultures: A. K. at Seventy* (1975); Sperber, M., "Looking Back on K.'s Spanish War," *DR*, 57 (1977), 152–63; Sperber, M., ed., *A. K.: A Collection of Critical Essays* (1977)

MURRAY A. SPERBER

KOLB, Annette

German novelist, and essayist, b. 3 Feb. 1870, Munich; d. 3. Dec. 1967, Munich

Reference works traditionally cite K.'s date of birth incorrectly as 1875, an error she encouraged by consciously misrepresenting her age. K.'s mother was a celebrated French pianist, her father a Bavarian landscape architect (rumored to have been an illegitimate son of the noble Wittelsbach family). Although raised in Bavaria, K. grew up bilingual (in German and French) and bicultural, and her mother's cosmopolitan salon encouraged her to pursue her political ideals as well as music and literature.

The Bavarian locale, an aristocratic milieu, music, and Franco-German politics and cultural relations are constant elements in her work. During World War I she won notoriety with her pacifist essays *Dreizehn Briefe einer Deutsch-Französin* (1916; thirteen letters of a Franco-German woman), condemning both French and German chauvinism. Denounced in both countries, she fled to Switzerland for safety, returning to Berlin and thence to Badenweiler near the Alsatian border only after the war. During this period she devoted herself to German-French rapprochement.

With *Das Beschwerdebuch* (1932; the register of grievances) she began to warn against totalitarianism, indeed to predict Hitler's ascent to power. In 1933, a persona non grata to the Nazi regime in Germany, K. emigrated, finally arriving in the U.S., where she spent four and a half difficult years. She had contact with the émigré circle around Thomas Mann (q.v.), whose wife Katja had been her childhood friend. Mann incorporated K. into his novel *Doctor Faustus* (1947) as Jeanette Scheurl. K. eventually returned to Munich, still promulgating German-French understanding and championing both Adenauer and De Gaulle. In her later years, she won acclaim as a humanitarian and a grande dame of European letters.

K.'s three novels draw on her family background for settings and incorporate her political ideals. The romantic tale *Das Exemplar* (1913; the paragon) is written in informal, flowing language that captures the melancholy tone of love and renunciation. There is a sociopolitical component in K.'s satirical portrayal of the English aristocracy; the most convincing element of the narrative is the psychological (although perhaps overly sentimentalized) portrait of the heroine Mariclée, whose lofty, romantic obsession for her "paragon" strengthens her when she renounces him to gain her own independence.

Daphne Herbst (1928; Daphne Herbst) depicts in a mature, disciplined style a young woman too delicate for the harshness of modern life. A gentle lament for Munich court society, the novel is nonetheless critical of the attitudes that hastened its demise. The death of Daphne, whose heightened emotions enervate and alienate her, symbolizes the decline of old values.

Overt autobiographical detail forms the backbone of K.'s last novel, *Die Schaukel* (1934; the swing). It is a mosaic of impressionistic flashbacks and foreshadowings that distance the reader from the narrative and underscore the insecurity of the stately serene Munich of K.'s youth. It is a nostalgic picture where "the swing stands still" in a time and place seemingly untouched by world events.

K.'s Franco-German allegiance and her political role as mediator of both cultures place her above convenient national categories. Her German revels in Gallic conceits, using foreign words, frequent rhetorical questions, and exclamation points for emphasis. Her diction, although sometimes archaic, is musical and elegant and a fitting medium for the values of tolerance, humanity, and grace—tempered with a dash of pessimism—with which she tried to inspire the 20th c.

FURTHER WORKS: *Kurze Aufsätze* (1899); *L'Âme aux deux Patries: Sieben Studien* (1906); *Wege und Umwege* (1914); *Die Last* (1918); *Zarastro: Westliche Tage* (1921); *Were Njedin: Erzählungen und Skizzen* (1924); *Spitzbögen* (1925); *Veder Napoli e partire* (1925); *Versuch über Briand* (1929); *Kleine Fanfare* (1930); *Festspieltage in Salzburg* (1937); *Mozart: Sein Leben* (1937); *Glückliche Reise* (1940); *Franz Schubert: Sein Leben* (1941); *König Ludwig II. von Bayern und Richard Wagner* (1947); *Blätter in den Wind* (1954); *Memento* (1960); *1907–1964: Zeitbilder* (1964)

BIBLIOGRAPHY: Rinser, L., *Der Schwerpunkt* (1960), pp. 9–22; Soergel, A., and Hohoff, C., *Dichtung und Dichter der Zeit* (1961), Vol. I, pp. 677–82; Rauenhorst, D., *A. K.: Ihr Leben und Werk* (1969); Lemp, R., *A. K.: Leben und Werk einer Europäerin* (1970); Benyoetz, E., *A. K. und Israel* (1970)

THOMAS SVEND HANSEN

KOMI LITERATURE

See Finno-Ugric Literatures of the Soviet Union

KOLMAR, Gertrud

(pseud. of Gertrud Chodziesner) German poet, b. 10 Dec. 1894, Berlin; d. 1943, Auschwitz, Poland?

K.'s father was a well-to-do Jewish lawyer. The introverted child's home environment fostered in her a love of nature, gardening, and the animal world. She was interested in history as well, particularly in the French Revolution (in 1933 she made Robespierre the subject of a scholarly essay and a poetic cycle). Fluent in French, English, and Russian, she became a translator and interpreter, working as a postal censor and with prisoners of war during World War I. Having experienced an unhappy love affair at that time, she never married. In the postwar period K. worked as a teacher and private tutor, specializing in the education of deafmute, sick, and otherwise handicapped children. After the death of her mother in 1930 the

poet devoted herself to the care of her aged father; thus she chose not to emigrate after the Nazis' accession to power. The letters she wrote between 1938 and 1943 to her younger sister, who had escaped to Switzerland, were published posthumously and reflect the quiet, heroic courage, the dignity, and the resigned wisdom of a sensitive soul. Some of her poetry from those years is on Jewish themes. From 1941 on K. had to do forced labor in two Berlin factories. Her father was sent to Theresienstadt concentration camp in September 1942, and K. was deported in late February of the following year. The date and place of her death are uncertain, but she is presumed to have perished at Auschwitz.

K.'s first publication was *Gedichte* (poems), a book of forty poems issued in 1917, which caused no great stir. She did not publish again until 1930, when two of her poems appeared in the prestigious *Insel-Almanach*. The poet had no use for "modernity," kept aloof from the literary marketplace, and cultivated a low-pressure timelessness, creating quietly and self-effacingly in the manner of Emily Dickinson and developing a poetic idiom all her own, which combined visionary fervor with formal discipline. She excelled as a nature poet but also produced powerful, sensual, often lengthy poems on love, sexuality, motherhood, and children. Her explorations of female sexuality were quite novel and daring for someone of her generation and background. "Weibliches Bildnis" (partial trans., "Image of Woman," 1975), a cycle of seventy-five poems on which she worked for a decade, presents a typology of womanhood. That she favored the cyclical form is evidenced also by "Kind" (child), "Tierträume" (partial trans., "Animal Dreams," 1975), "Das Wort der Stummen" (words of the silent), and *Die Frau und die Tiere* (1938; woman and animals; pub. under the name Chodziesner). Except for the last-mentioned, these cycles were not published in her lifetime; they are included in *Das lyrische Werk* (1955; enl. ed., 1960; the poetic work).

The poetic sequence "Alte Stadtwappen" (old city coats of arms) came into being in 1927–28; eighteen of these fifty-three poems were issued in 1934 as *Preußische Wappen* (partial trans., "Prussian Coats of Arms," 1975). These poems are fanciful and symbolic depictions of the human situation generally, as well as poignant attempts to distill from various emblems the essence and the genius of the poet's now misguided land. The cycle "Bild der Rose" (partial trans., "Rose Sonnets," 1975) contains mostly sonnets, and in the late sequence "Welten" (1947; partial trans., "Worlds," 1975), K. abandons her customary conservative form, strict meters, and regular rhyme schemes in favor of free-flowing unrhymed verse.

K.'s two plays were never published, but her works of fiction *Susanne* (Susanne) and *Eine Mutter* (a mother) did appear in 1959 and 1965 respectively. The latter, a short novel writttten in 1930–31, is a strange mixture of soap-opera melodrama, detective story, and symbolic fairy tale, presenting its Jewish protagonist as the archetypal woman.

FURTHER WORKS: *Tag- und Tierträume* (1963); *Das Bildnis Robespierres* (1965); *Die Kerze von Arras* (1968); *Briefe an die Schwester Hilde* (1970). FURTHER VOLUME IN ENGLISH: *Dark Soliloquy: The Selected Poems of G. K.* (1975)

BIBLIOGRAPHY: Kayser, R., "Das lyrische Werk von G. K.," *GQ*, 33 (1960), 1–3; Picard, J., "G. K.: Reminiscences," *Jewish Frontier*, March 1960, 12–17; Wallmann, J. P., "Deutsche Lyrik unter jüdischem Dreigestirn," *Merkur,* 20 (1966), 1119–94; Blumenthal, B. G., "G. K.: Love's Service to the Earth," *GQ*, 42 (1969), 485–88; Hamburger, M., "The Poetry of G. K.," *BUJ,* 24, 2 (1976), 65–67; Langer, L. L., "Survival through Art: The Career of G. K.," *Leo Baeck Institute Yearbook,* 23 (1978), 247–58

HARRY ZOHN

KONWICKI, Tadeusz

Polish novelist and film director, b. 22 June 1926, Nowa Wilejka

Born in Poland's northeastern region, K. spent World War II in that territory occupied first by the Soviets, then the Germans, and then by the Soviets again. In 1944 he joined the Polish underground Home Army and fought against the Soviet occupiers. In 1945 he moved to central Poland, entered the Jagiellonian University in Cracow, and soon emerged as a journalist and novelist whose fiction gained full recognition after 1956. In 1950 and 1954 he was awarded State Prizes in literature; his movie *Ostatni dzień lata* (shown in the U.S. under the title *Last Day of Summer*) won the Grand Prize at the Venice Film Festival in 1960, and his novel *Nic albo nic* (1971; nothing or nothing) was selected in a readers' poll as the novel of the year.

K.'s early short stories in *Przy budowie* (1950; at the building site) and an unfinished novel, *Władza* (Vol. 1, 1954; power) followed the rigid dictates of Socialist Realism (q.v.) prevailing in Poland in the early 1950s. As soon as some artistic freedom was reestablished in 1956, K. published his semiautobiographical novel *Rojsty* (1956; marshes), which he had completed as early as 1948. The novel contained some of the central motifs that were expanded in his subsequent fiction and in the films he began to direct and produce in 1954: a guilt complex stemming from a killing, sexual frustrations, a fear of being persecuted by the authorities, and an all-embracing nostalgia for the lost land of his youth. These themes were given a coherent artistic form in the dreamlike plot of his novel *Sennik współczesny* (1963; *A Dreambook for Our Time,* 1969) and were further explored in other novels.

Another important theme in K.'s fiction is a highly critical attitude toward certain social problems in contemporary Poland, which is often juxtaposed with the previous ones. K. blends the present and the past into a nightmarish vision of life constantly threatened with destruction and death. When his criticism of political conditions in Poland became too vocal in 1976, the authorities banned reprints of all his already published work as well as publication of any works he might write in the future. K. responded with a novel, *Kompleks polski* (1977; *The Polish Complex,* 1981), published in a literary quarterly, *Zapis*, issued illegally, that is, without official censorship. Another major novel, *Mala apokalipsa* (1979; small apocalypse), was also published in *Zapis*. Together with a number of major Polish writers he has become a member of the literary opposition. K.'s films, released between 1956 and 1976, explored similar problems and themes.

K., an accomplished literary artist, has cast a sharp, critical, and often satirical eye on modern Poland. In his mature works he has become more and more preoccupied with philosophical and moral dilemmas beyond the borders of his own country and thus has become more universal.

FURTHER WORKS: *Powrót* (1954); *Z oblężonego miasta* (1956); *Dziura w niebie* (1959); *Ostatni dzień lata* (1966); *Wniebowstąpienie* (1967); *Zwierzoczłowiekoupiór* (1969; *Anthropos-Specter-Beast,* 1977); *Jak daleko stąd, jak blisko* (1972); *Kronika wypadków miłosnych* (1974); *Kalendarz i klepsydra* (1976)

BIBLIOGRAPHY: Miłosz, C., *The History of Polish Literature* (1969) pp. 499–501; Krzyżanowski, J. R., "The Haunted World of of T. K.," *BA*, 48 (1974), 485–90; Krzyżanowski, J. R., "The Polish Complex," *PolR*, 25 (1980), 98–110

JERZY R. KRZYŻANOWSKI

KOREAN LITERATURE

The appearance of the first truly modern literature in Korea was preceded by the transitional dominance of a "new literature" of enlightenment. The modern literary movement was launched by Ch'oe Nam-sŏn (1890–1957) and Yi Kwang-su (1892–?). The "new poetry" movement dates back to the publication of "Hae esŏ pada ege" (1908; "From the Sea to the Children," 1964), by Ch'oe Nam-sŏn in *Sonyŏn*, the first literary journal aimed at producing cultural reform by introducing Western civilization to the masses. Inspired by Byron's *Childe Harold's Pilgrimage*, Ch'oe celebrates, in clean masculine diction, the strength of the young people who will carry out the necessary social and literary revolution. However, neither Ch'oe nor his contemporaries succeeded in going beyond the bounds of traditional prosody, with its set alternation of four and three syllables, or in modernizing traditional forms of speech and allusion. In his stories, Yi Kwang-su adopted a prose style that approximated the everyday speech of the common people. Yet his stories, which dealt with the enlightened pioneers who championed Western science and civilization, still followed the conventional theme of the "reproval of vice and promotion of virtue."

In 1919, shortly before the unsuccessful movement for independence from Japan, translations from such Western poets as Paul Verlaine (1844–1896), Remy de Gourmont (1858–1915), and Fyodor Sologub (q.v.) began to exert a powerful influence on Korean poetry. The indirection and suggestiveness of French symbolism (q.v.) were introduced by Kim Ŏk (1895–?), the principal translator. Against the didacticism of the age Kim set Mallarmé (1842–1898); against its rhetoric and sentimentality he set Verlaine, concluding in the process that free verse was the supreme creation of the symbolists. Kim's fascination with symbolism culminated, in March 1921, in the publication of *Onoe ŭi mudo* (dance of anguish), the first Korean collection of translations from Western poetry. Kim's translations from English, French, Esperanto, as well as from Japanese, were written in a mellifluous, dreamy style. The exotic and melancholy beauty of autumn, as well as expressions of ennui and anguish, all appealed to poets who sought to express their frustration and despair at the collapse of the independence movement of 1919.

The movement for literary naturalism was launched in the 1920s by a group of young writers who rallied around a new definition of universal reality in hopes of rectifying defects of form and content in fiction. Yŏm Sang-sŏp (1897–1963), the first to introduce psychological analysis and scientific documentation into his stories, defined naturalism as an expression of awakened individuality. Naturalism's purpose, Yŏm asserted, was to expose the sordid aspects of reality, especially the sorrow and disillusionment occurring as authority figures are debased and one's idols are shattered. Many works of naturalist fiction were first-person narratives. A desire to portray reality led writers to touch upon certain problems, but only those encountered by the writers, members of the intelligentsia, who were offering themselves as the subjects of case studies. Most stories written in this vein dealt with the miseries of the urban poor, or with the characters' attempts to cope with socioeconomic pressures. The disharmony between the writer and his society often induced the writer to turn to nature; and the land and the simple folk furnished themes and motifs for some of the better Korean stories in the Zolaesque tradition, among them "Pul" (1925; "Fire," 1974) by Hyŏn Chin-gŏn (1900–1943) and "Kamja" (1925; "Potato," 1974) by Kim Tong-in (1900–1951). But the most persistent theme in these stories is the assault on orthodox moral codes.

Naturalism in Korea was never a unified literary movement. Naturalist writers were productive over a span of several decades and wrote works that diverged widely in their treatment of basic themes. "Nalgae" (1936; "Wings," 1974) by Yi Sang (1910–1937), which traces the ceaseless activity of the hero's mind, is a stream-of-consciousness story. Others wrote panoramic novels, case studies of emancipated women, or historical novels.

The 1920s produced several major poets. Han Yong-un (1879–1944), revolutionary, reformer, monk, poet, and prophet, published *Nim ŭi ch'immuk* (1926; the silence of love) comprising eighty-eight meditative poems. Han and succeeding poets of resistance against the Japanese were constantly aware of their country's plight. Han sought insights into the terrible fate he and his country faced, and he found Buddhist contemplative poetry the lyric genre most congenial to this pursuit. Kim So-wŏl (1902–1934), a nature and folk poet, used simplicity, directness, and terse phrasing to good effect, as in his "Ch'ohon" (1925; "Summons of the Soul," 1964), an impassioned plea to his love that she return to him. Many of his poems in *Chindallaekkot* (1925; *Azaleas*, 1980) were set to music.

The Manchurian incident of 1931 and the Japanese invasion of China in 1937 induced the military authorities to impose wartime restrictions. The grinding poverty of the lower classes at home and abroad, especially in the Korean settlements in southern Manchuria, was the chief concern of the writers of the "new tendency" movement, a movement in opposition to the romantic and decadent writers of the day, which later became proletarian in spirit. Writers of the class-conscious Korean Artist Proletariat Federation (KAPF), organized in 1925, asserted the importance of propaganda and regarded literature as a means to the political ends of socialism. The movement also attracted fellow travelers, who emerged from the shadows with the Russian slogan *V narod* ("To the people") on their lips.

Modern Korean literature attained its maturity in the 1930s through the efforts of a group of extraordinarily talented writers. They drew freely upon European examples to enrich their art. Translation of Western literature continued, and works by I. A. Richards, T. S. Eliot (qq.v.), and T. E. Hulme (1883–1917) were introduced. This artistic and critical activity was a protest against the reduction of literature to journalism by influential magazines of the day, and to its use as propaganda by leftist writers.

The first truly successful poet of modern Korea was Chŏng Chi-yong (b. 1903), a master of his medium and a continuing presence. A student of Blake and Whitman, Chŏng rendered details with imagistic (q.v.) precision. His first published collection of poems, *Chŏng Chi-yong sijip* (1935; the poems of Chŏng Chi-yong), was followed by *Paengnoktam* (1941; White Deer Lake), which marks the high point of his career. The collection symbolically represents the progress of the spirit to lucidity, the fusion of man and nature.

A poetry of resistance, voicing a sorrow for the ruined nation with defiance but without vio-

lence or hatred, is the legacy of Yi Yuksa (1904–1944) and Yun Tong-ju (1917–1945). In such poems as the posthumously published "Kwangya" (1946; "The Wide Plain," 1980) and "Ch'ŏngp'odo" (1939; "Deep-Purple Grapes," 1980) Yi Yuksa sang of his winter of discontent and trial, and of his hopes for Korea's future. The poetry of Yun Tong-ju, an unimpassioned witness to Korea's national humiliation, expresses sorrow in response to relentless tyranny.

Korean fiction of the 1930s took shape in the void created by the compulsory dissolution of KAPF in 1935. Barred from all involvement with social or political issues, writers became preoccupied with technical perfection and the pursuit of pure art. Some, such as Yi Hyo-sŏk (1907–1942), returned to nature and sex; others retreated to the labryinth of primitive mysticism, superstition, and shamanism, for example Kim Tong-ni (b. 1913); still others sympathetically portrayed characters born out of their time, defeated and lonely. Narrative sophistication and subtlety were achieved through a denial of the writer's commitment to his art or to himself. A notable exception was Yŏm Sang-sŏp (1897–1963), who produced a document of the time in his novel *Samdae* (1932; three generations), a dialogue between liberalism and socialism and a study in the disintegration of traditional values and social classes.

The early 1940s brought disaster to all branches of Korean literature, as the Japanese suppressed all writings in Korean. The Sino-Japanese war extended into the Pacific in 1941. Censorship, which had begun with the Japanese annexation of Korea in 1910, was intensified. Korea was liberated on August 14, 1945, and the Republic of Korea (South Korea) was born on August 15, 1948. On the literary scene the controversy between left and right that had raged in the late 1920s and early 1930s was revived. There were frantic groupings and regroupings, and most of the hardcore leftist writers, such as Yi Ki-yŏng (b. 1896) and Han Sŏr-ya (b. 1900), had gone to North Korea by 1948.

Some poets who came of age in the 1940s also went north, while others gave up writing entirely. In general, though, the liberation of 1945 produced a flowering of poetry of all kinds. Some poets, like Pak Tu-jin (q.v.), Shin Tong-yŏp (1930–1969), and Hwang Tong-gyu (b. 1938), were determined to bear witness to the events of their age. Some, like Sŏ Chong-ju (q.v.), Pak Mogwŏl (1916–1978), and Shin Kyŏng-nim (b. 1936), sought to further assimilate traditional Korean values. Still others, like Kim Su-yŏng (1921–1968), Kim Ch'un-su (b. 1922), Hwang Tong-gyu, and Chŏng Hyŏn-jong (b. 1939), have drawn variously on Western traditions to enrich their work. All have sought to voice their own authentic testimony regarding the moments of crisis their culture has known.

The single overwhelming reality in Korean fiction since the Korean War has been the division of the country. As a symbol not only of Korea's trials but of the division of mankind and his alienation from himself and his world, the thirty-eighth parallel torments the conscience of every protagonist in modern Korean fiction in search of his destiny. Among South Korean writers, Hwan Sun-wŏn (b. 1915) and O Yŏng-su (b. 1914) have attempted to capture the images of the people in lyrical prose. Sŏnu Hwi (b. 1922) shows historical consciousness in his works, while Chŏn Kwang-yong (b. 1919) depicts a hapless human type all too common during Korea's years of servitude. Son Ch'ang-sŏp (b. 1946) has delved relentlessly into the conscience of the lost generation of the Korean War, Kim Sŭng-ok (b. 1941) into the inaction, self-deception, and boredom of the alienated generation of the 1960s. Yi Pŏm-sŏn (b. 1920) has studied the defeat and disintegration of good people; Sŏ Chŏng-in (b. 1938), the frustration of the educated; Yi Ho-ch'ŏl (b. 1932), the ways in which modern society negates man's freedom and individuality. Noteworthy writers of the roman-fleuve include Hwang Sun-wŏn, An Su-gil (b. 1911), and Pak Kyŏng-ni (b. 1927), the mother-in-law of the poet Kim Chi-ha (b. 1941). Pak's multivolume T'oji (1969 ff.; land) has been acclaimed for its commanding style and narrative techniques. In general, these works explore complex contemporary realities and universal human types.

The "new" drama movement, which began in 1908, saw the rise and fall of small theater groups, such as the T'owŏrhoe, organized in 1923 by a group of Korean students studying in Tokyo, and finally the Kŭk yesel yŏn'guhoe (Theatrical Arts Research Society), organized in 1931 (dissolved by the Japanese in 1938) by members of a Western literature research society. Through their experimental theater, the members of the society staged contemporary Western plays and encouraged the writing of original plays, such as Yu Ch'i-jin's (b. 1905) T'omak (1933; clay hut). The paucity of first-rate playwrights and actors, the dearth of plays that satisfy dramatic possibilities, and the general living standards of the audience have caused the relative inactivity in the field. Domestic plays and historical pieces continue to be written and staged, but the future of the dramatic arts in contemporary Korea is uncertain.

In the 20th c. a number of Koreans have written in Western languages or in Japanese. Li Mirok (1899–1950), who wrote in German, and Younghill Kang (1903–1972) and Richard E. Kim (b. 1932), writing in English, have produced autobiographical accounts of their formative years. The Diving Gourd (1962), a novel, and Love in Winter (1969), a collection of short stories, by Yong Ik Kim (b. 1920) combine traditional subjects and modern techniques in portrayals of the farmers and fisherfolk of the south. Among Korean writers born or residing in Japan, Yi Hoe-sŏng (b. 1935; known in Japan as Li Kaisei) is outstanding. His story "Kinuta o utsu onna" (1970; "A Woman Who Ironed Clothes," 1977), a kind of short Bildungsroman, won the coveted Akutagawa Prize in 1972.

Modern South Korean writers are constantly occupied with the complex realities of modern urban life, and with the lives and emotions of a people enduring continuous uncertainty and repression. That lively literary activity continues in such a setting attests to the resilience, strength, and tenacity of 20th-c. Korean writers.

BIBLIOGRAPHY: Lee, P. H., Korean Literature: Topics and Themes (1965), pp. 101–19; Lee, P. H., Introduction to Flowers of Fire: Twentieth-Century Korean Stories (1974), pp. xiii–xxv; Pihl, M. R., "Engineers of the Human Soul: North Korean Literature Today," Korean Studies, 1 (1977), 63–110; Kim, C., "Images of Man in Postwar Korean Fiction," Korean Studies, 2 (1978), 1–27; Lee, P. H., Introduction to The Silence of Love: Twentieth-Century Korean Poetry (1980), pp. xi–xix; Lee, P. H., "Literature and Folklore," in Kim, H., ed., Studies on Korea: A Scholar's Guide (1980), pp. 165–75

PETER H. LEE

KOSINSKI, Jerzy

American novelist, essayist, and critic, b. 14 June 1933, Łódź, Poland

K., who is very reticent about his past, admits that he was a mute for a time during his childhood in war-torn Poland. He earned degrees in history and political science in Łódź and taught at the Polish Academy of Sciences in Warsaw from 1955 to 1957. Disillusioned by the collectivist Communist state, K. created dossiers for people he invented in the Communist bureaucracy, who then "recommended" his traveling to the U.S. After arriving in America in 1957 K. continued his graduate studies in history and political science. He has been professor of English at Wesleyan, Princeton, and Yale universities, and since 1973 he has served as president of the American Center of PEN.

The Painted Bird (1965), K.'s first novel, depicts a brutally violent peasant world of eastern Europe during World War II and a lost boy's struggle for survival. The novel traces the boy's growing acceptance of violence and revenge as the only way to contend with his environment. But he does not stop at this point. Instead he develops a spirit of retaliation against everyone he encounters. The surrealistic, gothic setting suggests a Bosch painting. K.'s descriptions of this world and the horrors of Nazism are presented in a powerful, stunning language.

K.'s work illuminates the quest for identity, which is constantly threatened by the encroachments of modern society. His fictional characters find themselves trapped in an external world that is beyond their comprehension and control. They struggle against the constant danger of dissolution for a glimpse of self-recognition. Such ideas place the works of K. in the direct line of those of Kafka, Beckett, and Robbe-Grillet (qq.v.).

Steps (1968) records, in a cinematic series of disjointed fragments, the sensitive protagonist's inability to come to grips with the world and society. The novel both suggests and denies the possibility of regaining individual selfhood in a world that accepts only collective forms of behavior. This collectivism, against which an individualistic ethic is struggling to reassert itself, provides the background of all of K.'s novels.

K.'s third novel, *Being There* (1971), is a spare allegory and comic story of a man of limited mind, named Chance, who is propelled into positions of great power by his accidental appearance on television. K. explores the pervasive power of television over the modern consciousness and its ability to manipulate our emotional responses. Television becomes the source of all Chance's values and actions, creating him in its own image.

In *The Devil Tree* (1973) K. continued his experiments with fragmented form. Events are presented starkly and simplistically like scenes in a documentary film, although a significantly revised and expanded version was published in 1981. In this novel K. uses a flat, contemporary language that reflects the despair of his wealthy and aimless protagonist. An exemplar of the rootlessness of modern man, the protagonist wanders from Bangkok to Africa, and slides unintentionally from sexual exploits to murder.

Cockpit (1975) is K.'s longest and structurally most complex novel and carries to the extreme the tradition of the picaresque fictional mode. Its protagonist, Tarden, is a former agent of the powerful security agency of the American government. Now a fugitive, Tarden has successfully erased his presence from the world of dossiers and transcripts, and projecting into alternative identities, he continues to move freely across the contemporary landscape, testing his independence from the world and attempting to control its effects. Celebrating the private self as an institution of the highest order, *Cockpit* is an inventive extension of the novel of incident, which has become K.'s trademark.

Blind Date (1977) is the most obviously philosophical of K.'s novels. The main character, George Levanter, a businessman, lives by his wits. As a survivor of World War II and a defector from eastern Europe, he gets involved in several violent and sexual adventures. K. discusses the ideas of Jacques Monod, the French biologist and philosopher who views life as a series of random chances, the blind dates of the title. Such a philosophic perspective, however, weakens the narrative strength of the novel.

In *Passion Play* (1979) K. harnesses his usual obsessions about the fragmentation of contemporary existence to the oldest recorded ballgame, polo, and produces a kind of toughened code of individual responsibility and control somewhat akin to Hemingway's (q.v.). Fabian, the champion polo player, leads an itinerant life of sport and sex but acknowledges a degree of self-discipline and celebration unusual in a K. hero. K.'s descriptions of polo matches and sexual encounters in the novel match his finest writing.

K. wrote two volumes of social psychology under the pen name Joseph Novak. *The Future Is Ours, Comrade* (1960) analyzes the individual and collective behavior of Soviet citizens in their daily interactions. In *No Third Path* (1961), in which the psychology of the Soviet citizen is examined, K. scrutinized wider questions about the makeup of Homo sovieticus.

K.'s fiction depicts in precise and graphic prose the awful "thereness," the brute factuality of the modern world. The wasteland of *The*

Painted Bird and *Steps* pictures this world as effectively in its time as Eliot's (q.v.) *The Waste Land* communicated the spiritual milieu of the 1920s.

K.'s genius lies in his ability to re-create a sense of primitive and dark reality by means of violent and sexual images. The charge of self-indulgence is often mitigated by the taut, objective qualities of his prose. In his ability to reveal the springs of modern life, he is one of the most skillful novelists of our time.

FURTHER WORKS: *Notes of the Author* (1965); *The Art of the Self* (1968); *Pinball* (1982)

BIBLIOGRAPHY: Cahill, D., "J. K.: Retreat from Violence," *TCL*, 18 (1972), 121–32; Plimpton, G., and Landesman, R., Interview with K., *Paris Review*, No. 54 (1972), 183–207; Cahill, D. J., Interview with K., *NAR*, 258, 1 (1973), 56–66; Klinkowitz, J., Interview with K., *Fiction International*, No. 1 (1973), 31–48; Coale, S., "The Quest for the Elusive Self: The Fiction of J. K.," *Crit*, 14, 3 (1973), 25–37; Sanders, I., "The Gifts of Strangeness: Alienation and Creation in J. K.'s Fiction," *PolR*, 19, 3–4 (1974), 171–89; Coale, S., "The Cinematic Self of J. K.," *MFS*, 20 (1974), 359–70; Klinkowitz, J., "J. K.," *Literary Disruptions: The Making of a Post-Contemporary American Fiction* (1975), pp. 82–101; Cunningham, L., "The Moral Universe of J. K.," *America*, 139 (1978), 327–29
SAMUEL C. COALE

KOSSAK, Zofia

Polish novelist and short-story writer, b. 8 Aug. 1890, Kośmin; d. 9 April 1968, Górki Wielkie

K. studied art in Warsaw and Geneva, but she never pursued it professionally. Instead, in 1922, she began a literary career with a volume of World War I memoirs titled *Pożoga* (*The Blaze,* 1927). During World War II K. was active in the Polish Underground, and in 1943–44 she was a prisoner in Auschwitz. She left Poland after the war and resided in England until 1956. After a few months in France she returned to Poland at the beginning of 1957 and lived there until her death.

In 1928 K. was acclaimed as the "new Sienkiewicz" (q.v.). The work that caused such acclaim, *Złota wolność* (golden freedom), a his-

torical novel about politics, patriotism, and religious conflict in 18th-c. Poland, was soon followed by three others: *Krzyżowcy* (1935; *Angels in the Dust*, 1947), *Król trędowaty* (1937; *The Leper King,* 1945), and *Bez oręża* (2 vols., 1937; *Blessed Are the Meek*, 1944; *The Meek Shall Inherit*, 1948). These were historical novels dealing with the Crusades. As early as the publication of these three books, critics cooled in their opinion of K.'s works, but the public received them enthusiastically. The numerous novels that followed all reflected K.'s preoccupation and fascination with religion and history. Her shorter works of narrower scope, such as *Beatum scelus* (1930; Latin: the blessed guilt), a tale of a miraculous painting of the Madonna, or *Szaleńcy boży* (1932; God's madmen), a colorful collection of the lives of the saints, also give evidence of her abiding interest in these two subjects.

While living in England, K. wrote her memoirs about Auschwitz, *Z otchłani: Wspomnienia z lagru* (1946; from the abyss: memoirs from the camp). This book, so different in subject and character from her other works, has a stark and piercing vividness. While her historical novels could be compared to panoramic oil paintings, full of color and large in scale, her memoirs from the camp resemble black and white, brutally direct sketches. Their narrative is halting, unlike the flowing narrative of her historical novels; and a great sense of pain and of probing into the limits of human endurance is evident.

During the final eleven years of K.'s life, after her return to Poland in 1957, she wrote a number of short stories for young people and still more historical novels, most notable of which is the three-volume novel *Dziedzictwo* (1961–67; heredity). As always, K.'s chief focus is religion and history.

The steady and consistent decline in critics' favorable response to K.'s novels and tales was caused by what they uniformly regarded as K.'s shallow knowledge of history and her limited familiarity with philosophy and theology. K.'s knowledge of Catholic doctrine was considered minimal and her treatment of history often more fantastic than factual. Nevertheless, no critic ever found her wanting in narrative talent or in vivid imagination. K. demonstrated considerable literary skills, and her knowledge and love of the visual arts is evident in all of her writings. The panoramic quality of her historical novels, the appeal of colors, the richness of detail, and the likability of her characters account for her considerable popularity among readers. The wealth of factual material assembled by K. in her historical novels and the faithful rendition of the language of a given historical period she described balance the shortcomings in K.'s interpretation of history and in her understanding of philosophy and theology. K. is neither a critic's nor a scholar's writer, but her works fare extremely well with her readers, and the passing of time does not diminish their popularity.

FURTHER WORKS: *Kłopoty Kacperka góreckiego skrzata* (1926; rev. version, 1946; *The Troubles of a Gnome*, 1928); *Wielcy i mali* (1927); *Legnickie pole* (1930; expanded 1946; final version 1962); *Nieznany kraj* (1932); *Trembowla* (1939); *Przymierze* (1946; *The Covenant*, 1951); *Puszkarz Orbano* (1947); *Gród nad jeziorem* (1947); *Suknia Dejaniry* (1948); *Z miłości* (1958); *Bursztyny* (1958); *Warna* (1958); *Pątniczym szlakiem* (1959); *Topsy i Lupus* (1959); *Troja północy* (1960)

BIBLIOGRAPHY: Kridl, M., *A Survey of Polish Literature and Culture* (1956), p. 499; Gillon, A., and Krzyżankowski, L., *Modern Polish Literature* (1964), p. 170

MALGORZATA PRUSKA-CARROLL

KOSZTOLÁNYI, Dezső

Hungarian poet, novelist, short-story writer, essayist, critic, and translator, b. 29 March 1885, Szabadka (now Subotica, Yugoslavia); d. 3 Nov. 1936, Budapest

K. was born to educated middle-class parents; his father was the principal of a secondary school. He studied at the universities of Budapest and Vienna from 1903 to 1906. Having already published extensively, K. became a staff member of *Budapesti napló* in 1906 and a regular contributor to the literary journal *Nyugat* from its founding in 1908. A prolific writer, he supported himself entirely by his pen. In addition to numerous volumes of poetry and short stories, five novels, and nine short plays, he published some forty volumes of translations and enough essays and journalism to fill thirty volumes. In 1913 he married the actress and author Ilona Harmos, who later wrote his biography. In his later years he worked zealously in the cause of Hungarian linguistic purity. K. received many honors both at home and abroad; he was a Chevalier of the French Legion of Honor and the first president of the

Hungarian PEN Club. After years of suffering, he died of throat cancer.

In his first volume of poems, *Négy fal között* (1907; between four walls), his chief themes emerged: childhood memories, love of family, awareness of the fleeting nature of things, death, and a tug-of-war between God and the "Nihil" (nothingness). There is also an interesting juxtaposition between the idyllic but melancholy spirit of the Hungarian countryside and the exciting intellectual ferment of the metropolis, Budapest.

If his first volume made his name known, the second made him famous. *A szegény kis gyermek panaszai* (1910; the complaints of the poor little child) combines novelty of subject matter with a virtuosity of poetic form. The poet of twenty-five looks back on himself as a child, speaks in the voice of that child, and in a series of poems of great insight and charm, recreates a whole submerged world. It remains his most universally loved volume. But if he never surpassed this collection, he nevertheless maintained a very high level throughout his career. *Őszi koncert; Kártya* (1911; fall concert; cards)—two books in one volume—contains his longest poem, celebrating his love for his wife. *Mágia* (1912; magic), *Lánc, lánc, eszterlánc . . .* (1914; ring around the rosy), and *Mák* (1916; poppy) are full of magic and enchantment; they close his early period, which was noted for its strongly Parnassian, symbolist (q.v.) and impressionist elements.

In *Kenyér és bor* (1920; bread and wine) a change is evident. The difficulties of the war years, and the collapse and chaos that followed, caused K. to lose the bittersweet melancholy of the basically happy person he had been, and it was replaced by true despair. The title of his next volume expressed this shift best: *A bús férfi panaszai* (1924; the complaints of the sad man) is an eloquent statement of the human predicament. His next volume, *Meztelenül* (1928; naked), contained free-verse poems. Although K. was as great a master of free verse as of rhyme and the traditional verse forms, this volume never achieved the acclaim or popularity it deserved.

In 1935, on the occasion of his fiftieth birthday, *Összegyűjtött költeményei* (collected poems) was published. This book contained a whole new volume of poetry, *Számadás* (the summing-up), which some critics consider his greatest poetic achievement. A posthumous volume, *Szeptemberi áhitat* (1939; September devotion), brought out his previously uncollected poems, including the last poem published (1935) in his lifetime, the beautiful title poem.

K., one of the two or three greatest Hungarian poets of his age, and one of the perhaps half a dozen greatest Hungarian poets of all time, was almost as important as a writer of fiction. In his early volumes of short stories he moved from realism in the manner of Maupassant to a sometimes fantastic romanticism and then back to realism. In 1921 he published a short novel, *A rossz orvos* (the bad doctor), an in-depth psychological study of the disintegration of a family. A divorced couple's only child dies because of the incompetence of a "society doctor." Although the mother remarries, the memory of the dead child links the parents by indestructible ties of mutual reproach.

K.'s first full-length novel was *A véres költő* (1922; later retitled *Nero, a véres költő*; *The Bloody Poet*, 1927), which examines the character of Nero from youthful promise to utter depravity. K. perceives Nero primarily as a dilettante poet who cannot accept the fact that he lacks the artistic genius he admires in others. The novel was enthusiastically read—in German translation—by Thomas Mann (q.v.), and subsequent editions carried his Prefatory Letter.

A visit to his native Szabadka filled him with pity for his now destitute family and provided the inspriation for two compassionate novels, *Pacsirta* (1924; Lark) and *Aranysárkány* (1925; the golden kite). "Pacsirta" is the affectionate nickname of an ugly spinster pitied and doted upon by her parents. In no other work did K.'s deep Christian compassion emerge as movingly as in this family portrait. At the same time he gives a delightful picture of life in a small country town at the turn of the century. In *Aranysárkány* a golden kite flown by a group of schoolboys symbolizes a way of life that has forever vanished. But K.'s palette soon darkens: the hero, an upright teacher, is destroyed by forces he cannot control. K.'s last novel, *Édes Anna* (1926; *Wonder Maid*, 1947), the story of a "perfect servant" who murders her masters, is a fascinating sociological study in aberrant behavior.

He concluded his fiction-writing career with two triumphant volumes of short fiction. *Esti Kornél* (1933; Kornél Esti) is sometimes called an episodic novel, but it is best considered a short-story cycle, told by or about a delightful ne'er-do-well, the author's naughty alter ego. K. immortalized this charming creature not only in *Esti Kornél* but also in a famous poem, "Esti Kornél éneke" (1935; song of Kornél Esti) and in seventeen more short stories in his next—and last—collection, the gigantic *Tengerszem* (1936; tarn). The majority of Hungarian critics considers *Tengerszem* K.'s crowning achievement in fiction.

As a translator, K. was best noted for his 1914 volume *Modern költők* (modern poets); with this he helped to create the taste with which he expected himself and his contemporaries to be judged. The posthumously published *Idegen költők* (1942; foreign poets) further consolidated his reputation as a supreme interpreter of lyric and narrative poetry of many lands and tongues. His translations of four of Shakespeare's plays have also been justly praised; they are faithful, brilliant, and eminently actable.

As a journalist and essayist, K. was known for his wit, originality, beautiful style, and breadth of interests, and he invented several new journalistic genres. Indeed, there are critics in present-day Hungary who maintain that K.'s true significance is just now emerging, and that it lies in his activities as an essayist.

SELECTED FURTHER WORKS: *Boszorkányos esték* (1908); *Lótoszevők* (1910); *A vonat megáll* (1911); *Bolondok* (1911)); *Beteg lelkek* (1912); *Mécs* (1913); *Öcsém* (1915); *Tinta* (1916); *Bűbájosok* (1916); *Káin* (1918); *Katona-arcok* (1918); *Páva* (1919); *Béla, a buta* (1920); *Tintaleves papirgaluskával* (1917); *Alakok* (1929); *Szent Imre himnuszok* (1930); *Zsivalygó természet* (1930); *Kínai és japán versek* (1931); *Bölcsőtől a koporsóig* (1934); *A bábjátékos* (1940); *Hátrahagyott művei* (11 vols., 1940–48); *Novellái* (3 vols., 1943); *Írók, festők, tudósok* (2 vols., 1958); *Babits-Juhász-K. levelezése* (1950); *Összegyűjtött versei* (2 vols., 1962); *Elbeszélései* (1965); *Mostoha és egyéb kiadatlan művek* (1965); *Álom és ólom* (1969); *Füst* (1970); *Nyelv és lélek* (1971); *Hattyú* (1972); *Én, te, ő* (1973); *Sötét bújócska* (1974); *Ércnél maradóbb* (1975); *Patália* (1976); *Egy ég alatt* (1976); *Látjátok, feleim* (1977); *Színházi esték* (2 vols., 1978)

BIBLIOGRAPHY: Klaniczay, T., et al., *History of Hungarian Literature* (1964), pp. 212–14; Reményi, J., *Hungarian Writers and Literature* (1964), pp. 252–65; Sőtér, I., "The Place of Hungarian Poetry in Europe," *NHQ*, 25 (1967), 34–43; Brunauer, D. H., and Brunauer, S., *D. K.* (1982)

DALMA H. BRUNAUER

KÖTLUM, Jóhannes úr
See Jóhannes úr Kötlum

KRAMER, Theodor

Austrian poet, b. 1 Jan. 1897, Niederholla-
brunn; d. 3 April 1958, Vienna

K., the son of a Jewish country doctor, was educated in Vienna. From October 1915 to the
end of World War I he served in the army, and
after being seriously wounded in Volhynia he
was stationed in Italy as an officer. Following a
brief period at the University of Vienna, K.
worked in the book trade and contributed poetry to a number of periodicals and newspapers,
winning various prizes. Illness forced him to
become a free-lance writer in 1931, and two
years later he married the actress Inge Halber-
stam. In July 1939 K. emigrated to England,
and from January 1943 on he was employed as
a librarian at the County Technical College in
Guildford (Surrey). His wife having left him
and his mother having perished at Auschwitz,
the poet became increasingly lonely and depressed. He was afflicted with a variety of ail-
ments but continued to create prolifically. K.
died six months after his return to Vienna.

K. wrote poetry exclusively. Playing, as he
put it, the accordion rather than the harp and
making music on an "organ of dust," this powerful social realist strove to be the voice of the
underprivileged and inarticulate. His sociopsy-
chologically observed typology of rural and
urban outsiders and outcasts of society includes
peasants and prostitutes, ditch diggers and
drunkards, hired hands and hunchbacks. It
was the poet's aim to give an unvarnished and
unsentimental picture of their world and to
express in his poetic "landscapes" and "cityscapes" even complex and abstruse situations,
relationships, and feelings with directness and
folk-song simplicity. His bittersweet poems are
written in a variety of forms, including the cyclical, but most of them are short, have simple
rhymes, and abound in colloquialisms. Despite
the naturalistic bleakness and elegiac tone of
these poems, K.'s great sensitivity and empathy
make much of his poetry poignant and hauntingly beautiful. A childlike faith and tenderness
often shine through the decay, the dissolution,
and the despair.

K.'s first collection, *Die Gaunerzinke* (1929;
the tramp's mark—the title refers to the marks
made on certain houses by vagrants to serve as
a guide for other tramps and thieves), was
widely noticed and praised, but in exile the poet
had to endure a decade of disappointment
trying to find a publisher for what he regarded
as his best and most mature work, the collection *Lob der Verzweiflung* (1972; in praise of
despair). To this day only one tenth of K.'s

output of about ten thousand poems has appeared in print. A Theodor Kramer Society was
founded in Vienna in 1980 in an effort to remedy this situation.

FURTHER WORKS: *Kalendarium* (1930); *Wir
lagen in Wolhynien im Morast* (1931); *Mit
der Ziehharmonika* (1936); *Verbannt aus
Österreich* (1943); *Die untere Schenke*
(1946); *Wien 1938: Die grünen Kader*
(1946); *Vom schwarzen Wein* (1956); *Einer
bezeugt es . . .* (1960)

BIBLIOGRAPHY: Zohn, H., "T. K., Neglected
Austrian Poet," *GL&L*, 9, 2 (1956), 11–24;
Schmied, W., "T. K.," *WZ*, 3, 1 (1957), 1–16;
Chvojka, E., "T. K.," *Akzente*, 9 (1962),
143–57; Zohn, H., "T. K.s letzte Jahre," *Wie-
ner Juden in der deutschen Literatur* (1964),
pp. 73–82; Zohn, H., "Lob der Verzweiflung,"
MAL, 6 (1973), 211–16; Klinger, K.,
"Lebenslängliche Isolation: T. K.," in Spiel,
H., ed., *Die zeitgenössische Literatur
Österreichs* (1976), 352–57

HARRY ZOHN

KRASKO, Ivan

(pseud. of Ján Botto; other pseuds.: Janko
Cigáň and Bohdan J. Potokinov) Czechoslovak
poet (writing in Slovak), b. 12 July 1876,
Lukovištia; d. 3 March 1958, Bratislava

After attending high school in Slovakia and
Romania, K. studied engineering in Prague,
worked in the chemical industry in Bohemia,
and served as a soldier in Poland and Russia
during World War I. Between 1918 and 1938
he was a civil servant and politician: he was a
member of Parliament (1920–29) and a senator of the Agrarian Party (1929–39).

K. turned to literature during his university
years and soon was hailed by leading poets and
critics as an important new talent. He introduced modernism and symbolism (qq.v.) into
Slovak poetry. He was a gifted representative of
the tragic view of life, common in European
poetry at the turn of the century. His poems
show an affinity to those of Verlaine, Baudelaire, Rimbaud, and Mallarmé in their self-centered lyricism and despair. His rhythms, structure, and diction differed from the poetic style
of the two leading Slovak poets, Hviezdoslav
(pseud. of Pavel Országh, 1849–1921) and
Svetozár Hurban Vajanský (1847–1916).
Their traditional attitude toward national strug-

gles and their introspective lyricism found some echo in K.'s poetry, but K.'s verse generally lacks the spark of hope and the faith in his nation's future and resurrection that were present in the work of the older poets.

K.'s two slender collections of poems, *Nox et solitudo* (1909; Latin: night and solitude) and *Verše* (1912; poems), reflect his pessimism, the unfortunate situation of the Slovak people at the turn of the century, and the spiritual crisis of modern man. An example of his despairing mood is the poem "Jehovah" (1909; "Jehovah," 1924), in which K. curses his people and invokes Jehovah's vengeance on the Slovak nation for its idleness. Other poems in the 1909 volume reflect similar attitudes. K.'s feeling of belonging to his enslaved nation is expressed in "Otrok" ("The Slave," 1924), in which he returns to his roots with a protest against enslavement and a dim hope that resurrection of his people is still possible. There is, however, none of the visionary quality of the previous generation of Slovak poets. K. rarely moves from a defeatist attitude to a call for action and struggle. His deep attachment to his homeland, from which he was separated in his youth, is also expressed in the poems "Otcova rol'a" (father's field), "Baníci" (miners), and "Vesper dominicae" (Latin: Sunday evening). In "Vesper dominicae" K. writes in gentle terms of his return home, where his mother, in tears, remembers him while she is praying. Poems that express K.'s compassion for the sad fate of his nation and his protest against its enslavement are not, however, dominant in his poetry. Most characteristic of his work are personal lyrics, imbued with a tragic and pessimistic view of life, replete with dark metaphors, and only rarely turning from despair to a hope of overcoming destiny.

Although K. did not resume writing after World War I, his poetry strongly influenced the generation of Slovak poets between the wars. Moreover, many Slovak poets of today echo his introspective lyricism, his sympathy for humanity, and his concise clarity.

BIBLIOGRAPHY: Krčméry, Š., "A Survey of Modern Slovak Literature," *SEER*, 7 (1928–29), 160–70; Selver, P., "The Literature of the Slovaks," *Slavonic Review*, 12 (1934), 691–703; Mráz, A., *Die Literatur der Slowaken* (1943), p. 152; Noge, J., *An Outline of Slovakian Literature* (1968), pp. 49–51; Richter, L., *Slowakische Literatur* (1979), pp. 51–56

JOSEPH M. KIRSCHBAUM

KRAUS, Karl

Austrian satirist, cultural critic, aphorist, and poet, b. 28 April 1874, Gitschin, Moravia, Austro-Hungarian Empire (now Jičín, Czechoslovakia); d. 21 June 1936, Vienna

When K. was three years old, his father, who was a wealthy manufacturer, moved with his family to Vienna. K.'s school and university years coincided with the heyday of the Viennese Burgtheater and the lively literary activity so characteristic of the Austro-Hungarian capital. From both K. received decisive impressions. Although he matriculated in the law school at the university, he attended only philosophical and literary lectures without ever working toward a degree. He resisted his strong inclinations toward the stage; his dramatic gifts, however, subsequently evolved into his uncommon accomplishments as a reader of his own works and those of others.

K.'s bent for polemics and satire is manifest in his early pamphlets, *Die demolierte Literatur* (1896; the demolished literature) and *Eine Krone für Zion* (1898; a crown for Zion). An event of decisive importance for his literary career was his founding of *Die Fackel* in 1899. The early contributors to this periodical included August Strindberg, Frank Wedekind, Georg Trakl, Otto Stoessl (qq.v.), Detlev von Liliencron (1844–1909), Peter Altenberg (1859–1919), Richard Dehmel (1863–1920), Else Lasker-Schüler (1876–1945), and Berthold Viertel (1885–1953), but from 1911 to the time of K.'s death in 1936, *Die Fackel* was written exclusively by K. himself. It was, in a sense, a spiritual diary, but it was also a militantly ethical periodical that began before long to play a unique role in the world of German letters. As conceived by K., the concern of his fighting mission, although pursued in *Die Fackel* by purely literary means, was less with literary matters than with generally spiritual and ethical matters. His writing posed a constant challenge to the prevailing corruption of the spirit in all domains of public life—in politics, law and justice, literature, and art. K. came to be the accuser of everything that was rotten in the state of Austria. His most embittered hatred had its target in the press, which he attacked with a persistence that might suggest that he considered such activity the purpose of his life. Indeed, to unmask the press as the embodiment of intellectual prostitution, as the instrument par excellence of the trivialization and mechanization of life, as a menace to the already sorely imperiled state of peace, was to him a fate-imposed obligation.

That K. saw the press and the dangers of its enormous power as he did—the Vienna press of his age showed journalism in its ugliest form —followed inevitably from the ethical imperative that was the supreme law of his life and his every endeavor. Because he measured everything by absolute standards, condoning no compromise however trivial, he was bound to regard the journalist who works under the aegis of day-to-day contingencies rather than of ultimate principles as the embodiment of everything evil. The slightest deviation from absolute integrity signified to him man's dehumanization, which, undermining society, must finally lead to its general collapse.

K.'s polemical essays, in which he fought against the enslavement of man's natural drives by state and church, appeared in book form in the volumes *Sittlichkeit und Kriminalität* (1908; morality and criminality) and *Die chinesische Mauer* (1910; the great wall of China). Like all his writing, these essays were first published in *Die Fackel*.

K.'s conception of language was of central importance to him and is of similar importance in any evaluation of his work. The word and the thing, he held, were one. In language he saw the magic passkey to unlock all doors. Indeed, his feared and fearful attacks—the purpose of which was to unmask the hypocrisy and the corruption of his age by making them, through the instrumentality of his mordant wit, a laughingstock for his readers—used language as a means to destroy the adversary. Purity of language was to him the measure of the writer's integrity.

K. was thus not only the merciless and incorruptible critic of his age but also the teacher of a new and wakeful awareness of language. There are many whose ears he trained to discern the hollow ring of vacuous phrases, of puff and lie, of shamelessness and perfidy that assaulted them from the columns of the daily press, particularly in that time of war. And there are many whom he strengthened in the integrity of their conduct.

The drama *Die letzten Tage der Menschheit* (abridged tr., *The Last Days of Mankind*, 1974) was written during World War I, first appeared as a special issue of *Die Fackel,* and was published in book form in 1922. It bursts all conventional dimensions and was a climax in K.'s creative career. In K.'s words, "by earthly measurements" a performance would require some ten nights on the stage. It is actually intended to be read rather than performed; the imagination of the reader has to provide the stage. K. never doubted that Austria's declaration of war in 1914 marked the beginning of the end of that state. This satirical tragedy evolves through the prophetic power of its creator into an apocalyptic warning of an impending world-engulfing disaster. It represents a vast fresco of events at the front as well as behind the lines and back home. A more powerful denunciation of war has never been written. The work has no single hero, although each scene, in this immense concert of scenes, has a hero of its own. There is no unity of time, place, or action, but the unity of the idea is for that very reason all the more compelling. On the basis of *Die letzten Tage der Menschheit,* professors at the Sorbonne in Paris repeatedly proposed K. for the Nobel Peace Prize.

K. was one of the very few who never succumbed even for a moment to the chauvinistic poison that filled the air in those years. The only writer of rank to stand firmly against the Austrians who were embracing the war en masse, he challenged with absolute courage the powers that be. In Berlin, where the tide of enthusiasm for war was running high, he read in public his sketch "Kant und ein Kantianer" (1917; "A Kantian and Kant," 1977), in which he contrasted the philosopher with Emperor Wilhelm II, who liked to fancy himself as fashioned in the mold of Kant and as one who embodied Kant's categorical imperative, but who was here referred to as a "second-class stage hero." The hope that the war would end in a German victory was to K. absolute treason, high treason against the spirit.

In his satirical sketches, epigrams, and dramas, K. waged a relentless war of cultural criticism against which the press, his favorite target, had no defense but that of trying to ignore the attacker. His other victims, hopelessly discredited and held up as laughingstocks, also preferred on the whole to limit themselves to reproaching him with the negative character of his criticism, which they claimed "could only destroy but not build up." To be sure, the great satirist must have a clear conception of absolute values. His endeavor to remove the worthless must be inspired by the desire to make room for the worthwhile; and a profound faith in positive values and affirmative truths is actually the basic prerequisite for his creativity.

K. was always ready to praise excellence where he saw it. He admired the great satirists of the past like Georg Christoph Lichtenberg (1742–1799) and Johann Nestroy (1801–1862) and contemporary writers as well: Strindberg, Wedekind, Altenberg, Trakl, Lasker-Schüler, and others. He revived interest in the great poets of the German baroque, and through his public readings of Shakespeare's plays he successfully opposed the trend of abandoning Shakespeare's works to the commercialized theater of the big city, with its optical illusions and sound effects. In his "Theater der Dichtung" (literary theater), what he called his public readings, standing alone at the lectern, he revealed the true power of the works of Goethe, Hauptmann (q.v.), and many other writers.

In matters of form K. was no innovator. He said of himself that he was one who continued in the tradition of Shakespeare (in the Schlegel-Tieck translation) and the "lambent flame of language" of the older Goethe, both of whom exerted the strongest influence on him. In matters of content, however, his work is far removed from the poetry of the neoclassicists and neoromanticists. It bears the imprint of his age, having its roots in the past and at the same time pointing the way to the future.

Many of K.'s poems are cerebral, their content frequently identical with his militant prose. Yet among his poems there are pieces of great lyrical power in which beauty of language and emotional content merge in perfect harmony. They are to be found in K.'s nine volumes of *Worte in Versen* (1916–30; words in verse). A collection of penetrating essays on questions of language, which K. was preparing for publication during the years 1933 and 1934, appeared only after his death under the title of *Die Sprache* (1937; language). The collected volumes *Sprüche und Widersprüche* (1909; aphorisms and contradictions), *Pro domo et mundo* (1912; Latin: for home and world), and *Nachts* (1918; at night) prove K. to be one of the greatest masters of the aphorism.

K. died when Austria was facing the menace of Nazism at its western borders—this was two years before the forced Anschluss. The outbreak of barbarism in neighboring Germany may have precipitated his death. His last work, written during this time, was not published until 1952: through an analysis of language and speech, *Die dritte Walpurgisnacht* (the third Walpurgis Night) portrays the horror of the Hitler era—the dictatorship of the Führer and his literary henchmen. In this work K. provides a perceptive analysis of the diabolical nature of the Third Reich.

During his lifetime the impact of K.'s work was essentially restricted to Vienna. Since the end of World War II wider circles in the realm of German letters have begun to bear witness to his importance and have acknowledged his influence, although not as yet in full proportion to his extraordinary contribution to the artistic and intellectual life of his age. Although K.'s works condemned his time and although he foresaw prophetically the dangers inherent in modern civilization, leading to an ultimate apocalypse, his work in its totality is nevertheless a profession of faith in man and in the worth of life. He was deeply confident that his work would endure and that through it he would live on when he was gone. In this, too, he has proved to be prophetic.

FURTHER WORKS: *Heine und die Folgen* (1910); *Nestroy und die Nachwelt* (1912); *Weltgericht* (1919); *Ausgewählte Gedichte* (1920); *Literatur; oder, Man wird doch da sehn* (1921); *Untergang der Welt durch schwarze Magie* (1922); *Traumstück* (1923); *Wolkenkuckucksheim* (1923); *Traumtheater* (1924); *Epigramme* (1927); *Die Unüberwindlichen* (1928)*; *Literatur und Lüge* (1929); *Zeitstrophen* (1931); *Shakespeares Sonette* [translations] (1933); *Shakespeares Dramen* [translations] (2 vols., 1934–35). FURTHER VOLUMES IN ENGLISH: *Poems* (1930); *In These Great Times* (1976); *Half Truths and One- and One-Half Truths: Selected Aphorisms* (1976); *No Compromise: Selected Writings* (1977)

BIBLIOGRAPHY: Liegler, L., *K. K. und sein Werk* (1920); Heller, E., *The Disinherited Mind* (1952; new ed., 1971) pp. 235–56; Muschg, W., *Von Trakl zu Brecht* (1961), pp. 174–97; Daviau, D., "The Heritage of K. K.," *BA*, 38 (1964), 248–56; Schick, P., *K. K. in Selbstzeugnissen und Bilddokumenten* (1965); Field, F., *The Last Days of Mankind: K. K. and His Vienna* (1967); Iggers, W. A., *K. K.: A Viennese Critic of the Twentieth Century* (1967); Weigel, H., *K. K.; oder, Die Macht der Ohnmacht* (1968); Zohn, H., *K. K.* (1971); Janik, A., and Toulmin, S., *Wittgenstein's Vienna* (1973), pp. 67–91; Williams, C. E., *The Broken Eagle: The Politics of Austrian Literature from Empire to Anschluss* (1974), pp. 187–235; Stern, J. P., "K. K. and the Idea of Literature," *Encounter*, Aug. 1975, 37–48; Grimstad, K., *Masks of the Prophet: The Theatrical World of K. K.* (1981)

FREDERICK UNGAR

At the beginning of April 1899 the first issue of his [K.'s] *Fackel* appeared, and the most bitter and persistent attacks ever launched against the press dated from that time. The warning voice of conscience had awakened, and it spoke to a deluded time; that voice wanted to prove how deeply that time had sunk into bondage and how dangerous was the enemy, who was on the point of destroying an old culture. It was unavoidable that against the assault of such an enlightener the solid resistance of all those who considered the tendencies of the new epoch the expression of their own nature was marshaled. And nobody will find it surprising that the lowest, most underhanded and perfidious means ever used by a tyranny over the mind were brought into action against K. K., to force him into silence or at least to make the motives of his fight suspect. But for many . . . he was a spiritual liberator. One listened to these unaccustomed harangues, one felt joy at this young, self-intoxicating power; and not a few have to thank this daring fighter for the fact that they would remain true to themselves and were not pulled down into a God-estranged time.

Leopold Liegler, *K. K. und sein Werk* (1920), p. 51

K.'s work, as that of few other writers, stands totally devoted to one basic idea that language is of crucial importance to human existence. Every aspect of his endeavors, his public readings, his adaptations of Shakespeare and Offenbach, his poems, dramas, essays, and aphorisms serve the one purpose of revitalizing the word. This cannot be otherwise, for any contradictions or discrepancies in K.'s work (and life) would render him guilty of the same hypocrisy with which he charged his contemporaries. However, this cohesiveness demands that any judgment of K.'s writings involve them as a unit. If his central idea concerning language possesses continued validity, as the increasing attention today to the role of language would indicate, then so do all of his works which exemplify only this idea.

Despite the outward lack of success of his life-long crusade on behalf of language, K.'s dedication to his principles continued with undiminished vigor to the end of his life. . . .

Donald Daviau, "The Heritage of K. K.," *BA*, 38 (1964), 255

. . . Like Wittgenstein and Schoenberg, both of whom admired his work greatly, the satirist was obsessed with problems of language. To K. language is not merely the medium of thought: thought and language are related in a complex and semi-mystical dialectic which he, as a poet, was never concerned to analyse in any philosophical way. Thought, he asserts, does not possess an independent existence in this world, but through the prism of the material circumstances of life is dispersed and scattered among the elements of language. Or, to vary the metaphor, the world is sifted through the sieve of language. Above all, the function of words is not decorative: this is the burden of the satirist's attack on the Impressionists in Austria, an attack exemplified by K.'s description of Hofmannsthal in his attempt to revivify the baroque drama as "living among golden goblets in which there is no wine."

K. practised what he preached. With a style of extraordinary concentration, allusiveness and wit, with a moral fanaticism that bordered on the pathological, the satirist elevated language to apocalyptic significance and intensity. Since he was convinced that words are possessed of an innate magical potency by which they can revenge themselves on societies and individuals who pervert them or use them idly, K. would agonise for hours over the revision of his work and claimed in one of his epigrams that he worked longer on a single word than other men on a novel.

Frank Field, *The Last Days of Mankind: K. K. and His Vienna* (1967), pp. 12–13

K. K.'s satire is more deeply rooted in its own medium than the work of any other recent writer of German prose. "The German language," he said, "is the profoundest of all languages, but German speech is the shallowest." The genius of K. K. could not have arisen from the ground of another language; for the inspiration of his satirical work is the contrast between his faith in words and the speech of the faithless: and it is German that offers the biggest scope for this faith as well as its blasphemers.

His thinking was a voyage of exploration in a landscape of words. No other western language allows adventures on such a scale, for every other language has been more thoroughly explored, surveyed and ordered. What in modern English may be a wrestle with words, is a vast conflagration in German, with victories more glorious and defeats more devastating; and what, in the workaday life of words, is a relaxed walk through an English park, is in German a venture into exposed territory. While the English writer or speaker, over long stretches of his verbal enterprise, is protected by the tact and wisdom of the linguistic convention itself, his German counterpart risks revealing himself as an idiot or a scoundrel through the ring and rhythm of his first sentence. Had Hitler's speeches been accessible to the West in their unspeakable original, we might have been spared a war. For this war was partly caused by Hitler's innocent translators, unavoidably missing in smooth and diplomatic French or English the resonance of the infernal sphere. Only German, in all its notorious long-windedness, offers such shortcuts to the termini of mankind. It was K. K. who knew them all.

Erich Heller, *The Disinherited Mind*, new 3rd ed. (1971), pp. 236–37

NIKOS KAZANTZAKIS

YAŞAR KEMAL

KARL KRAUS

MIROSLAV KRLEŽA

K. appeared to his contemporaries, by turns, as a prophetic thinker, a passionate Jewish prophet in the Old Testament sense, a pacifist in the spirit of Christianity, a well-intentioned educator, a benign sponsor of young or neglected poets, a social revolutionary, a conservative guardian of the German and Austrian tradition, an exalted model, a sadistic slanderer, and a cynical mocker of all values. To some he was a breathtaking incarnation of the absolute, an infallible oracle, a prophet desperately trying to show mankind the right way of pointing it back to the "origin" which, to him, was forever the goal; to others, he was an embittered, monomaniacal misanthrope, a man who directed his cannon fire at sparrows, an object of fear, vituperation, and blind hatred. This ambivalence is seen in K.'s relationship to some of his contemporaries, for in a number of instances apostles turned apostates, disciples became defectors, friends changed to foes, and those once championed were later chastised. Only relatively few disciples had the strength of character and the absolute integrity that K. demanded of them. More often than not, such falls from grace took place under unedifying circumstances and had both personal and literary repercussions, sometimes leading to acrimonious polemics and public pillorying.

Harry Zohn, *K. K.* (1971), pp. 88–89

K.'s response to the political developments of his time is more sustained, more perceptive, more urgent and more direct than that of any contemporary Austrian writer. He descends into the political arena in a way completely alien to his fellow writers. It is possible to quote many instances of K.'s contempt for and condemnation of "politics" as a degrading and immoral human activity, and he frequently takes pride in declaring his indifference to political issues. He warns that his concern lies with the form of his satirical statements rather than with their content. Charges of "aestheticism" were levelled against him during his lifetime. . . .

One way and another, K. dominates any study of the politics of Austrian literature during this period [1914–1938]. For all his involvement in the Viennese environment, there is something profoundly un-Viennese about his sheer intransigence and the absoluteness of his ethical and cultural values; he manifests none of that fickleness, inconsistency, arbitrariness, easy-going complaisance and mental slovenliness for which . . . he castigated his fellow citizens. . . .

C. E. Williams, *The Broken Eagle: The Politics of Austrian Literature from Empire to Anschluss* (1974), pp. 232, 235

Literature, K. believes, must take issue with the world of which it is a part. In the event, it is committed to being a critique of the press and all aspects of life that appear to be dominated and determined by the language of the press. Thus stylis-

tic form—the linguistic intensity which derives from the verbal exploits and the self-conscious and language-conscious turns I have mentioned—spills over into content, the meta-language of quotation and critique is mode of writing and theme at once. Quotation is to K. what slices of social life were to the naturalists—what the interrelation of institution and individual was to the European realists—what nature was to the poetry of Weimar. Quotation is major source of literary inspiration. Its function in K.'s work anticipated the "documentary theatre," but went far beyond its present-day users.

J. P. Stern, "K. K. and the Idea of Literature," *Encounter*, Aug. 1975, 42–43

KRĖVĖ, Vincas

(formerly Vincas Krėvė-Mickevičius) Lithuanian prose writer and dramatist, b. 19 Oct. 1882, Subartonys; d. 7 July 1954, Marple Township (near Philadelphia), Pa., U.S.A.

In his youth K. attended the theological seminary at Vilnius (1898–1900), then studied philology at the universities of Kiev and Lvov. After earning his doctorate at Lvov in 1908 he taught in Baku until 1920, and served there briefly (1919–20) as the Lithuanian consul to the then independent republic of Azerbaijan.

After his return to Lithuania in 1920 K. played a major role in political, cultural, and academic life. He was professor of Slavic literatures at the University of Lithuania (1922–43), dean of the Faculty of Humanities there (1925–37), the first president of the Lithuanian Academy of Arts and Sciences (1941), and editor of numerous literary journals and academic publications. In 1940, during the first weeks of the Soviet occupation, K. served as Foreign Minister and Acting Prime Minister of Lithuania. However, after having realized what the Soviet plans for the country were, he resigned from the two posts and, shortly before the second Soviet occupation of 1944, went into exile. After a sojourn in Austria, K. emigrated in 1947 to the U.S. to join the faculty of the University of Pennsylvania, where he taught Slavic and Lithuanian literatures until his retirement in 1953.

Essentially a late romanticist with touches of realism, K. first drew inspiration and material for his works from Lithuanian folklore and from the distant past of Lithuania. These sources found their best expression in *Dainavos šalies senų žmonių padavimai* (1912; the old folktales of Dainava) and two plays, *Šarūnas* (1911; Šarūnas) and *Skirgaila* (1925; Skirgaila). In the folktale book he created, in a highly stylized rhythmic prose akin to folk literature, legends of ages long gone by, while in the two plays he revived, in a heroic style, both the legendary and historical past. For these dramas K. chose some of the most crucial and problematic periods of Lithuanian history and evolved his own interpretation of them. Moreover, these momentous periods of history are not introduced just for their own sake. They serve more as background and influencing factors on the leading characters, who are not helpless puppets controlled by the forces of history but conscious architects of the present and future. Men of flesh and blood, of manifold and complicated egos, with deep-rooted personal problems, the legendary prince Šarūnas and the historical Skirgaila are tragic figures struggling valiantly with their own times. While *Šarūnas* is a closet drama of epic design and proportions, *Skirgaila* is a tragedy of masterfully knit, compact composition and Shakespearean overtones, a masterpiece of its genre.

K. also explored with a keen eye and deep psychological insight the rustic life of Lithuania as it existed at the turn of the century. To this category belong the collection of short stories *Šiaudinėj pastogėj* (2 vols., 1921–22; under the thatched roof); its sequel, *Raganius* (1939; the sorcerer); and the play *Žentas* (1921; the son-in-law), all more realistic than romantic in approach and treatment of the subject. *Šiaudinėj pastogėj* contains some of the best examples of the Lithuanian short story. Their characters, in contrast to the heroic figures of Šarūnas and Skirgaila, are simple country folk almost untouched by modern civilization and its inhibitions, although they have their own peculiar beliefs and philosophies.

A writer of diverse interests and wide erudition, K. was particularly well acquainted with Oriental thought and literature, as well as with the history of early Christianity. Two works were the creative outgrowth of these interests: the collection *Rytų pasakos* (1930; tales of the Orient), which introduced the Oriental style to Lithuanian literature, and a biblical epic in prose, *Dangaus ir žemės sūnūs* (2 vols., 1949, 1963; the sons of heaven and earth). K. worked on this epic on and off throughout his entire literary life. In this work, employing a quasi-biblical style, K. paints a wide and vivid panorama of the world of the Jews in the time of Christ and gives a rather unorthodox interpretation of the wellsprings of Christianity. Of particular interest is the tragedy of Herod, woven into the epic in the form of playlike dialogues. As conceived by K., Herod's tragedy lies primarily in the collision of the two widely different worlds—the Jewish and the Hellenistic—within himself and his milieu. This interpretation of Herod's doom adds a new dimension and contributes substantially to the treatment of the Herod theme in world literature.

One of the pathfinders of modern Lithuanian literature and its foremost representative, K. attained the stature of a classic in his own lifetime.

FURTHER WORKS: *Sutemose* (1921); *Likimo keliais* (2 vols., 1926, 1929); *Mindaugo mirtis* (1935); *Miglose* (1944); *Pagunda* (1950; *The Temptation*, 1965); *Raštai* (6 vols., 1956–63); *Likimo žaismas* (1965). FURTHER VOLUME IN ENGLISH: *The Herdsman and the Linden Tree* (1964)

BIBLIOGRAPHY: Senn, A., "On the Sources of a Lithuanian Tale ['Gilšė'])," in Schirokauer, A., and Paulsen, W., eds., *Corona* (1941), pp. 8–22; Maciūnas, V., "V. K.'s Place in Lithuanian Literature," *Studi baltici*, 9 (1952), 11–23; Senn, A., "V. K.: Lithuania's Creator of Heroes," in *World Literatures* (1956), pp. 170–84; Senn, A., "V. K. and Lithuanian Folklore," in Halle, M., et al., comps., *For Roman Jakobson* (1956), pp. 444–48; Ostrauskas, K., "V. K.: A Lithuanian Classic," *BA*, 38 (1964), 265–67; special K. issue, *Lituanus*, 11, 3 (1965); Senn, A. E., "V. K.'s Journey to America," *JBalS*, 7 (1976), 255–63

KOSTAS OSTRAUSKAS

KRISTENSEN, Tom

Danish poet, novelist, and critic, b. 4 Aug. 1893, London, England; d. 2 June 1974, Svendborg

K.'s father was a craftsman who hoped for success in America, but who never got any farther than London. In 1896 the family returned to Copenhagen, where life for some years proved to be financially quite insecure. The family moved from lodging to lodging (an experience reflected in the novel *En anden* (1923; another), and the young K. gained a detailed knowledge of the various neighborhoods of the fast-growing capital of Denmark. He entered the university and eventually received a degree in Danish, English, and German literature and languages, but instead of pursuing a teaching career, he began to test his talent as a poet and a critic.

K.'s debut was with the striking collection of poems *Fribytterdrømme* (1920; dreams of a freebooter), in which chaotic inner and outer worlds are charted with an exquisite sense of form and rhythm. These poems have been seen as a major contribution to Danish expressionism (q.v.), but K.'s use of expressionistic techniques is actually quite moderate, and he records his obsession with colors and contours and his fascination with action and violence with a strict adherence to traditional meter. Some of these poems reveal an aesthetic intoxication with a many-splendored outer reality, be it the streets of Copenhagen, the grubby life in sleazy taverns, or the exotic settings of the Far East. Other poems show that K.'s ebullient enthusiasm for chaos and color exists together with a deep-seated anguish, an inner emptiness that cannot be filled by any philosophy, religion, or political conviction. Thus, K.'s aestheticism borders on nihilism.

K.'s later collections of poetry, *Mirakler* (1922; miracles) and *Påfuglefjeren* (1922; the peacock feather), expressed the same duality; but gradually the intensity of the early poetry gave way to a more classical diction, as in *Den sidste lygte* (1954; the last streetlight). From the beginning to the end, these texts suggest, however, that it is only through the creative act that K. can find that moment of rest for which he yearns. These poignant, well-wrought poems, with their mixture of sensuousness, humor, and intellectualism, place K. as one of the best Danish poets of the 20th c.

K.'s first novel, *Livets arabesk* (1921; the arabesque of life), is one of the few expressionistic novels written in Denmark; it depicts an illusory revolution that, through the degeneration of the protagonist, shows how the hollow bourgeois tradition is crumbling. The revolution is, however, rendered from an aesthetic viewpoint rather than from a political one, and the text becomes at places a veritable orgy in the forms and colors of physical and psychic violence. Much more subdued is *En anden,* in which one of K's quite nihilistic characters subjects himself to a Freudian investigation of his childhood and later life in the Far East.

Hærværk (1930; *Havoc,* 1968) is a superior, intricately composed roman à clef, which brilliantly captures the mood of the newspaper rooms and bars of Copenhagen. Its protagonist is a gifted journalist who very determinedly ruins his marriage and career in an attempt to find meaning through debauchery. This haunting odyssey through low life does not, however, lead to self-destruction, and the protagonist emerges as a quite undaunted survivor. Perhaps the novel testifies to the strength of the nihilist.

After this tour de force K. mainly produced nonfiction: travel books; collections of an autobiographical nature, which recall, with a good portion of self-irony, the milieu of the young poet and his compatriots; and collections of his literary criticism written for the newspaper *Politiken.* In these articles K. shows himself once again to be a masterful stylist and also a keen and sympathetic observer of the literary scene. Among his major interests were American and English literature, and his writings on the so-called "lost generation" testify to a close identification with authors who, like himself, vainly sought a foothold in a world without redeeming values. As a critic he may remind his readers of Edmund Wilson (q.v.), another searcher for ideological positions, for like Wilson, K.'s writings are eminently pedagogical: without ever becoming popular in a vulgar fashion, he writes with both an admirable clarity and an elegant turn of phrase that raise his journalism to the level of superior literary criticism.

FURTHER WORKS: *Bokserdrengen* (1925); *En kavaler i Spanien* (1926); *Verdslige sange* (1927); *Vindrosen* (1934); *Mod den yderste rand* (1936); *Digte i døgnet* (1940); *Mellem Scylla og Charybdis* (1943); *Hvad er Heta* (1946; rev. ed., 1959); *Mellem krigene* (1946); *En omvej til Andorra* (1947); *Rejse i Italien* (1951); *Til dags dato* (1953); *Det skabende øje* (1956); *Oplevelser med lyrik* (1957); *Den evige uro* (1958); *Mord i pantomimeteatret* (1962); *I min Tid* (1963); *Åbenhjertige fortielser* (1966); *Fra Holger Drachmann til Benny Andersen* (1967); *Hvad var mit ærinde* (1968); *Blandt københavnere* (1973); *Med disse øjne* (1973)

BIBLIOGRAPHY: Byram, M.A., "The Reality of T. K.'s *Hærværk*," *Scan*, 15 (1976), 29–37

NIELS INGWERSEN

KRLEŽA, Miroslav

Yugoslav novelist, short-story writer, dramatist, poet, essayist, travel writer, and memoirist (writing in Croatian), b. 7 July 1893, Zagreb

Upon finishing the lower grades of secondary school in Zagreb, K. was sent to a preparatory military school in Peczuj (1908) and later to the Military Academy in Budapest. His attempt to join the Serbian army as a volunteer in the Balkan Wars (1912) proved disastrous. Suspected by the Serbs of being an Austrian spy

(Croatia was at the time part of the Austro-Hungarian Empire), K. was forced to return to Austria-Hungary, where he was treated as a deserter, thrown out of the academy, and in 1914 sent to the front as a common soldier.

After World War I K. returned to Zagreb, where he lived as a professional writer in open and extremely vocal opposition to the monarchist regime of Yugoslavia. During World War II he chose to live in seclusion and to remain silent, although he could not escape occasional harassment by the pro-Nazi Croatian government. K. greeted the postwar Communist regime with enthusiasm, immediately resuming his prominent role in Yugoslav political, cultural, and literary life, only this time on the side of the establishment. K. was vice-president of the Yugoslav Academy of Arts and Sciences from 1947 to 1957 and president of the Union of Yugoslav Writers from 1958 to 1961; since 1951 he has served as director of the Yugoslav Lexicographic Institute in Zagreb and the editor-in-chief of the *Encyclopedia Yugoslavica.*

K.'s literary career, which spans a period of almost seventy years, began just before World War I with lyrical poetry and plays of expressionist (q.v.) orientation. During the war K. changed from an idealistic lyricist with a pagan enchantment with youth, life, and nature to an embittered and pessimistic individual whose poetry and prose—from 1914 to around 1922—reflected his strong antiwar feelings, particularly his profound disgust with senseless deaths of his countrymen sent to fight for the sake of a doomed empire that had oppressed them for centuries. In the early 1920s, deeply impressed by the outcome of the Soviet revolution and by its ideology, K. became an eloquent spokesman for revolution, and consequently became more and more concerned with the social ills plaguing Croatia and the rest of Europe after World War I.

In the late 1920s and early 1930s, K.'s literary activities reached their peak, and it was in that period that he produced most of his best works in poetry, fiction, and drama. After World War II K. stayed predominantly in the realm of prose and drama, although a fine group of philosophical poems, written mainly during the war, is found integrated in his memoirs and diaries.

K.'s most praised poetic work, *Balade Petrice Kerempuha* (1936; the ballads of Petritsa Kerempuh), is a collection of poems that represents the synthesis of K.'s entire poetic oeuvre. Written in the Croatian *kajkavski* dialect, the "ballads" are, in K.'s own words, "a free variation on the old theme of *jacqueries* [peasants' revolts]." Through them, K. masterfully summarizes some thousand years of his unfortunate nation's history. At the same time, he expresses his impatience with his nation's lack of rebellious spirit and its slavish acceptance of the oppressive conditions of life imposed upon it by its various masters.

Another masterpiece, the Glembaj saga, is a complex work consisting of eleven prose fragments and three of K.'s most outstanding plays, *Gospoda Glembajevi* (1928; the patrician Glembajs), *U agoniji* (1928; revised second-act ending and a third act added 1959; in agony), and *Leda* (1930; Leda). The plays and six narratives were published together in *Glembajevi* (1932; the Glembajs), the remaining five narratives as part of *Novele* (1937; novellas). By focusing on individual members of the Glembaj family from various generations and on their ruthless cimb to the top of the Austro-Hungarian socioeconomic elite, the short stories trace a century and a half of the family history filled with gruesome murders, greed, lust, alcoholism, and venereal diseases that eventually manifest themselves in madness, suicidal mania, and vices of all kinds. The short stories provide the necessary background for the morbid and grotesque drama of the last degenerate Glembaj offspring, a drama that coincides with the fall of Austria-Hungary and is portrayed in the three plays, which are set in Zagreb between 1913 and 1924.

Of K.'s four novels, his first, *Povratak Filipa Latinovicza* (1932; *The Return of Philip Latinovicz*, 1959), is the most popular and the most widely acclaimed. Its protagonist, Filip, is a typical K. hero, a deeply disturbed and disillusioned intellectual who cannot seem to find his place in life. In search of inner peace, Filip, a painter, returns home after twenty-three years of living abroad. He hopes that contact with his native soil will inspire him to create a painting of ultimate beauty and perfection and give his life a meaning and a direction it has never had. At home, Filip is haunted by traumatic childhood experiences and is unable to become reconciled with his mother, a former prostitute, whom he cannot forgive for her lack of love and affection. Ironically, he comforts himself with Bobočka, a newcomer in the town who has the same notorious reputation his mother once had. In Bobočka's circle Filip experiences a sort of a catharsis, as he realizes that his problems are not unique and that the world is full of unfortunate loners and drifters of his kind. The fact that Filip survives, while some other characters die a violent death, gives an optimistic touch to this otherwise gloomy novel in which, under heavy clouds, everything, including human beings, seems to rot in muddy soil drenched with human blood.

The satirical and allegorical novel *Banket u Blitvi* (3 vols., 1938, 1939, 1962; a banquet in Blitvia) treats the deplorable political situation in Europe in the interwar period through the conflict of the Blitvian (a play on words on *Litva*, Serbo-Croatian for Lithuania) dictator Barutanski (*barut* means "gunpowder") and an idealistic intellectual, Niels Nielsen, who believes that a man must fight for a better world even at the risk of his life. K. does not fail, however, to underline one of the classic Communist theses that individual efforts "in the struggle against crimes and lies end up as romantic adventures."

It has been pointed out many times that throughout his life K. stood in the forefront of the struggle against human stupidity, mediocrity, petit-bourgeois mentality, and backwardness in general. He has believed that the world we live in can and must be reformed until the new man emerges, free from all the prejudices and ready to live in harmony with himself and his fellow men. Like many outspoken men, K. has been a very controversial figure, especially in the interwar period, when he was attacked from many sides. Many may not like his baroque style or the dark colors of his moods; others may resent his arrogance and intellectual snobbery, or disagree with his political views, but few could deny that K. always stood firmly behind his ideas and defended them fiercely and fearlessly no matter how dangerous and how powerful were his opponents. Furthermore, it is hard not to admire K.'s enormous creative energy, reflected in over forty volumes of an extremely diversified oeuvre and in his extensive participation in many aspects of his nation's cultural and political life. Today, K. is the most impressive literary figure in Yugoslavia and a true giant of Croatian literature.

FURTHER WORKS: *Legenda* (1914); *Maskerata* (1914); *Zaratustra i mladić* (1914); *Podnevna simfonija* (1916); *Pan* (1917); *Tri simfonije* (1917); *Saloma* (1918; enl. with rev. end, 1963); *Hrvatska rapsodija* (1918; includes *Kraljevo* and *Cristoval Colon*); *Pjesme* (3 vols., 1918–19); *Lirika* (1919); *Michelangelo Buonarroti* (1919); *Eppur si muove* (1919); *Tri kavalira gospodjice Melanije* (1920); *Hrvatska rapsodija* (1921; includes *Smrt Franje Kadavera* and *Veliki meštar sviju hulja*); *Magyar kiŕalyi honvéd novela— Kraljevsko-ugarska domobranska novela*

(1921); *Hrvatski bog Mars* (1922); *Galicija* (1922); *Adam i Eva* (1922); *Golgota* (1922); *Vučjak* (1923); *Vražji otok* (1923); *Novele* (1924); *Izlet u Rusiju* (1926); *Knjiga pjesama* (1931); *Moj obračun s njima* (1932); *Eseji I* (1932); *Sabrana djela* (9 vols., 1932–34); *Hiljadu i jedna smrt* (1933); *Simfonije* (1933); *Legende* (1933); *U logoru* (1934; includes *Vučjak*); *Evropa danas* (1935); *Pjesme u tmini* (1937); *Deset krvavih godina* (1937); *Djela* (12 vols., 1937–39); *Eppur si muove* (1938); *Knjiga proze* (1938); *Na rubu pameti* (1938; *On the Edge of Reason*, 1976); *Knjiga studija i putopisa* (1939); *Dijalektički antibarbarus* (1939); *Francisco José Goya y Lucientes* (1948); *Djetinjstvo u Agramu godine 1902–1903* (1952); *O Erazmu Rotterdamskom* (1953); *Kalendar jedne parlamentarne komedije* (1953); *Sabrana djela* (1953 ff.); *Davni dani* (1956); *Aretej* (1959); *Eseji* (6 vols., 1961–67); *Poezija* (1967); *Izabrana dela* (1969 ff.); *99 varijacija* (1972); *Djetinjstvo i drugi spisi* (1972); *Put u raj* (1973); *M. K.: Jubilarno izdanje* (1973 ff.); *Pet stoljeća hravtske književnosti*, Vols. 91–94 (1973); *Dnevnik* (5 vols., 1977). FURTHER VOLUME IN ENGLISH: *The Cricket beneath the Waterfall, and Other Stories* (1972)

BIBLIOGRAPHY: Šinko, E., "M. K. and His Work: The Outline of a Study," *Yugoslavia*, 15 (1959), 59–64; Kadić, A., "M. K.," *BA*, 37 (1963), 396–400; Matković, M., "M. K.," *The Bridge*, No. 1 (1966), 15–23; Vaupotić, M., *Contemporary Croatian Literature* (1966), 34–35, 92–99, 158–61, 184–85; Kadić, A. "K.'s Tormented Visionaries," *SEER*, 45 (1967), 46–64; Pawel, E., "Three Generations," *PR*, 34 (1967), 606–13; Schneider, S., *Studien zur Romantechnik M. K.s* (1969); Suvin, D., "Voyage to the Stars and Pannonian Mire: M. K.'s Expressionist Vision and the Croatian Plebeian Consciousness in the Epoch of World War One," *Mosaic*, 6 (1973), 169–83; Ferguson, A., "A Critical Literary Approach to M. K.'s *The Return of Philip Latinovicz*," *JCS*, Nos. 14–15 (1973–74), 134–44; Eekman, T., *Yugoslav Literature 1945–1975* (1978), pp. 42–49

BILJANA ŠLJIVIĆ-ŠIMŠIĆ

KROETZ, Franz Xaver

West German dramatist, b. 25 Feb. 1946, Munich

K. spent his childhood in Simbach on the Inn in Lower Bavaria and attended acting school in Munich. In 1972 K. joined the West German Communist Party, and his work took on an overtly political orientation.

K.'s plays deal primarily with the inarticulate working classes, and his dialogue is written in a terse, seemingly disconnected manner often in a Lower Bavarian dialect full of mundane aphorisms and clichés. The subject matter of his work usually includes shocking incidents of violence and overt sexual acts. These events, however, are couched in the same banal, heavy, unspectacular mood as his dialogue.

In his best-known work, *Stallerhof* (1971; *Farmyard,* 1976), Sepp, a middle-aged hired hand, seduces Beppi, the farmer Staller's mentally retarded daughter. Staller apparently kills Sepp's dog and orders Sepp off the farm. Beppi is discovered to be pregnant. Staller's wife prepares to abort the child but relents, and at the end of the play the labor pains begin. Typically, the play is heavily punctuated with pauses and progresses by short stichomythic scenes, most set in different locales. The tone is fatalistic, and the characters do not achieve any perception; nor does the environment impinge upon them, as in strictly naturalistic plays.

After K. joined the Communist Party, his work moved from this rather abstract, universalized portrait of lower-class life to an attempt to draw conclusions about it. His monodrama *Wunschkonzert* (1972; *Request Concert,* 1975) depicts the loneliness of a middle-aged woman who performs the meticulous ritual of an evening at home and then just as meticulously commits suicide. The solo character does not speak. The only sound is the radio airing a request concert. In his notes K. assigns the cause for the character's resignation and muteness to "exploitation and repression," which, if not self-directed, would have led to a "revolutionary situation."

K.'s work is strongly influenced by the *Volksstück* (literally, "folk play," but characterized by a lower-middle-class or proletarian milieu and the use of dialect) as exemplified in the plays of Ödön von Horváth and Marieluise Fleisser (qq.v.), and he is perhaps indebted directly to Georg Büchner's (1813–1837) *Woyzeck.*

Nevertheless K.'s contribution to the drama and his style are distinctive. He eschews exposition, letting the event speak for itself without comment or sentiment. He sees the use of language in the theater as an artificial convention, asserting that "the most important action of my

characters is their silence. . . . Their problems lie so far back and are so advanced that they are no longer able to express them in words."

K. is part of a vanguard of new dramatists including the playwright-filmmaker Rainer Werner Fassbinder (b. 1946), who directed a film version of K.'s *Wildwechsel* (1973; wild-game path) for German television. Their intention is to move the German drama away from self-congratulatory bourgeois attitudes and its traditionally heavy reliance upon language and toward a sparer, more elemental concern with the deeper recesses of the human being as an inchoate social animal.

FURTHER WORKS: *Heimarbeit* (1971); *Hartnäckig* (1971); *Männersache* (1971; *Men's Business,* 1976); *Michi's Blut* (1971; *Michi's Blood,* 1976); *Geisterbahn* (1972); *Lieber Fritz* (1972); *Oberösterreich* (1972); *Dolomitenstadt Lienz* (1972); *Ein Mann, ein Wörterbuch* (1973; *A Man, A Dictionary,* 1976); *Maria Magdalena* (1973); *Agnes Bernauer* (1975); *Das Nest* (1976); *Mensch Meier* (1978); *Der Stramme Max* (1979); *Nicht Fisch nicht Fleisch* (1981)

BIBLIOGRAPHY: Gilman, R., Introduction to F. X. K., *Farmyard, and Four Plays* (1976), pp. 7–23; Klaic, D., "The Theatre of F. X. K.," *Y/T,* 6, 1 (1974), 94–97

PETER SANDER

KROLOW, Karl

West German poet and essayist, b. 11 March 1915, Hanover

After studying Germanic and Romance philology, art history, and philosophy in Göttingen and Breslau (now Wrocław, Poland), K. began his literary career in Göttingen in 1942. He subsequently moved to Hannover, then in 1956 to Darmstadt. In 1966 he became vice-president of the German Academy for Language and Literature, of which he had been a member since 1954. Among the awards that K. has received for his writings are the Büchner Prize (1956) and the Rainer Maria Rilke Poetry Prize (1977).

Influenced in his early writing by Annette von Droste-Hülshoff (1797–1848), Oskar Loerke (1884–1938), and Wilhelm Lehmann (1882–1968), K. created nature and landscape poems that combine graphic precision with visual sensitivity, keen images and metaphors with simplicity and clarity of diction and expression.

The poems of *Hochgelobtes, gutes Leben* (1943; highly lauded, good life) and *Gedichte* (1948; poems) feature a profusion of natural detail captured in simple, conventional forms. Four-line stanzas with traditional rhyme schemes abound. To the extent that man is visible in the poetry of the 1940s, he appears as a Robinson Crusoe type, coping with the everyday problems of the postwar world. Political or social commentary is either absent or presented very indirectly through the isolated symbolic human figures.

During the early 1950s K. began to experiment with new techniques, forms, and themes. *Die Zeichen der Welt* (1952; the signs of the world) contains songlike long forms, hymns and odes that document K.'s movement from rhymed lyrics to unrhymed free rhythms. Unlike the earlier nature poems, the creations of this second period place heavy emphasis on the artificial components of human existence. Civilization, culture, and technology are the substance of poems dealing specifically with war, politics, literature, art, and music. In *Wind und Zeit* (1954; wind and time), K. employed short free forms, abstractions, and the precise language and perceptual mode of mathematics to intensify his focus on the rigid artificiality of modern civilization.

The appearance of *Tage und Nächte* (1956; days and nights) marked the beginning of a third phase in K.'s poetic development. Under the influence of modern French and Spanish poetry, Dadaism (q.v.), and especially the writings of Hans Arp (1887–1966), K. wrote surrealistic poems that incline toward the absurd. He began to view poetry as a grotesque play of words. As a result, in the collections of the late 1950s and the 1960s, the thematic emphasis on culture reached a peak and then receded. The poems of this period are noteworthy for their laconic, dry language and a tendency toward anecdotal narration.

K.'s more recent poems, those contained, for example, in *Zeitvergehen* (1972; the passing of time) and *Der Einfachheit halber* (1977; for simplicity's sake), reflect a tempered synthesis of important aspects of earlier creative directions. They reveal a decline in the surrealistic element, coupled with a refinement of the mathematical precision of the early 1950s and a perfecting of the short, hasty, terse poetic miniature form that characterizes K.'s works of the late 1960s.

Marked above all by an air of resignation and melancholy, K.'s lyric creations are eminently representative of the mainstream of postwar German poetry. As such, they are poems that are powerful for their innate humanity and their precise penetration of modern existence.

FURTHER WORKS: *Heimsuchung* (1948); *Auf Erden* (1949); *Von nahen und fernen Dingen* (1953); *Verzauberung* (1956); *Fremde Körper* (1959; *Foreign Bodies,* 1969); *Tessin* (1959); *Schatten eines Mannes* (1959); *Aspekte zeitgenössischer deutscher Lyrik* (1961); *Ausgewählte Gedichte* (1962); *Die Rolle des Autors im experimentalen Gedicht* (1962); *Unsichtbare Hände* (1962; *Invisible Hands,* 1969); *Schattengefecht* (1964); *Corrida de toros* (1964); *Reise durch die Nacht* (1964); *Gesammelte Gedichte* (1965); *Landschaften für mich* (1966); *Poetisches Tagebuch* (1966); *Das Problem des langen und kurzen Gedichts heute* (1966); *Unter uns Lesern* (1967); *Minuten Aufzeichnungen* (1968); *Alltägliche Gedichte* (1969); *Bürgerliche Gedichte* (1970)*; Nichts weiter als Leben* (1970); *Deutschland deine Niedersachsen: ein Land, das es nicht gibt* (1972); *Zu des Rheins gestreckten Hügeln: Goethereise 1972* (1972); *Ein Gedicht entsteht* (1973); *Miteinander* (1974); *Gesammelte Gedichte* (1975); *Ein Lesebuch* (1975); *Bremen Color* (1976, with Jochen Mönch); *Das andere Leben* (1979). FURTHER VOLUMES IN ENGLISH: *Leave Taking, and Other Poems* (1968); *Poems against Death* (1969)

BIBLIOGRAPHY: Domandi, A. K., ed., *A Library of Literary Criticism: Modern German Literature* (1972), Vol. II, pp. 71–76; Fritz, W. H., ed., *Über K. K.* (1972); Rümmler, A., *Die Entwicklung der Metaphorik in der Lyrik K. K.s* (1972); Paulus, R., *K. K. Bibliographie* (1972); Anderle, M., "Die Entwicklung der Lyrik K. K.s unter französischem und spanischem Einfluß," *Seminar,* 13 (1977), 172–88; Kolter, G., *Die Rezeption westdeutscher Nachkriegslyrik am Beispiel K. K.s* (1977)

LOWELL A. BANGERTER

KRUCZKOWSKI, Leon

Polish novelist, dramatist, and journalist, b. 28 June 1900, Cracow, d. 1 Aug. 1962, Warsaw

K. grew up in modest surroundings, but his father, a bookbinder, managed to provide his seven children with education. K. finished a technical college in Cracow in 1918, and after two years of military service earned his living by teaching, while being actively engaged in cultural and educational socialist organizations. He began his writing career in 1918 with a volume of verse, but it was only after the success of his first novel, *Kordian i cham* (1932; Kordian and the boor) that he was able to dedicate himself fully to writing. As an officer in the Polish army, he was captured by the Germans during the 1939 campaign and spent the war in a prison camp, returning to Poland in 1945. Consistent and outspoken in his Marxist convictions as novelist before and as playwright after World War II, K. also remained a journalist throughout his career.

K. was an outstanding representative of the trend known as the "literature of the fact" in the 1920s in Russia; in Poland the phrase was the trademark of a group of progressive writers known as "The Suburbs," who believed in literature's duty to create "social documents." *Kordian i cham,* a historical novel, was meant as such a social documentation of the Polish insurrection of 1830–31. Moreover, it was based on an actual document, the diary of a village teacher, Deczyński, which K. fictionalized, changing certain facts to emphasize his thesis: that the nobility and the peasant masses fought for different concepts of a free Poland. This new approach to Poland's history, permeated with Marxist spirit, was K.'s answer to Stefan Żeromski's (q.v.) famous historical novel *Popioły* (1904; *Ashes,* 1928), set in the time of the Napoleonic wars. It also refuted the heroic image of Kordian, the hero of the 1830 insurrection, as portrayed in Juliusz Słowacki's (1809–1849) play by that name (1834). K.'s Kordian, a young officer, is puny compared to the valiant "boor" Deczyński.

K.'s second novel, *Pawie pióra* (1935; peacock feathers), is also conceived in terms of the class struggle, this time between the village poor and the kulaks (wealthy farmers). Set on the eve of World War I, the novel portrays the awakening class consciousness of the Polish peasantry, presented as a collective hero. It echoes Stanisław Wyspiański's (q.v.) *Wesele* (1901; the wedding) in its satire on the intelligentsia's fraternization with the village, and polemicizes against the program of the Peasant Party in interwar Poland.

K.'s third novel, *Sidła* (1937; the trap), is his least successful. It deals with the psychological effects of unemployment undermining the middle-class hero's self-respect and ruining his marriage, and shows the emerging struggle between the revolutionary elements and the forces of Nazism in the Poland of the 1930s. Psycho-

logical analysis and creative imagination are not K.'s strong points, and these weaknesses could account for his preference for social and historical documents. His works also reflect a journalist's passion for participation in current events.

K. turned to the drama after 1945. His plays deal with philosophical and ethical problems, especially those created by the war and its aftermath. He believed that great theater, from its beginnings to today, has been, in his words, "a tribunal or a tribune," that is, a kind of court or a platform from which to express one's views. His own plays, particularly *Odwety* (1948; retributions) and *Niemcy* (1949; the Germans) are meant to be both. *Odwety,* which introduces the first Communist hero in Polish literature, portrays the moral tragedy of the postwar "lost generation"; *Niemcy* shows the impossibility of remaining neutral in a world of evil, the fallacy of an individual's claim to freedom from responsibility for the Nazi crimes. The characters, as is usual with K., are sharply divided into heroes and villains. *Śmierć gubernatora* (1961; death of the governor), whose plot is borrowed from a Russian short story by Leonid Andreev (q.v.) is less dependent than other of K.'s works on the dictates of Socialist Realism (q.v.), of which K. was a convinced advocate and an acclaimed master. The message of this play is that power —any power—subjugating individual free will is evil; and this idea does not fit well in the Marxist conception of man and the world.

At the source of K.'s successful career—literary and, in the postwar period, political—lies his unswerving adherence to socialist beliefs as much as a humanitarian concern for suffering and social injustice.

FURTHER WORKS: *Bohater naszych czasów* (1935); *Przygoda z Vaterlandem* (1938); *Spotkania i konfrontacje* (1950); *Śród swoich i obcych* (1954); *Odwiedziny* (1955); *Pierwszy dzień wolności* (1960)

BIBLIOGRAPHY: Krzyżanowski, J., *A History of Polish Literature* (1978), pp. 644–45; Miłosz, C., *The History of Polish Literature* (1969), pp. 427–28, 512

XENIA GASIOROWSKA

KRÚDY, Gyula

Hungarian novelist, b. 21 Oct. 1878, Nyíregyháza; d. 12 May, 1933, Budapest

K. was one of the great loners of modern Hungarian literature. An amazingly prolific writer who produced over sixty novels and three thousand short stories, he nevertheless remained an unaffiliated and curiously anachronistic figure all his life. He was married twice (his first wife, a writer, was seven years his senior, his second, twenty-one years his junior), but domestic life did not seem to suit his temperament. His bohemian habits also took their toll. His health rapidly declined in the 1920s, and he died in great poverty at the age of fifty-five.

K.'s early work reveals the influence of Kálmán Mikszáth's (1847–1910) anecdotal realism, as well as the social consciousness of the Russian realist masters; but he was among the first to abandon an essentially 19th-c. narrative mode, which was to dominate Hungarian fiction for many more years, in favor of a more diffuse, impressionistic, and lyrical prose style. K.'s family belonged to the provincial nobility, but by the turn of the century, this class was past its prime.Unlike Mikszáth, K. had no more stories to tell about it. Instead, he tried to hold onto a fast-vanishing, decadent world by fantasizing about the lives of its heroes. The accent in his fiction was no longer on the narrative but on mood, language, and a subjective authorial point of view.

As an adventurous, robust young writer, K. took turn-of-the-century Budapest by storm. He had the air and habits of an aristocrat and lived the life of a bohemian artist. His drinking, gambling, and womanizing became the stuff from which his fiction was made. K.'s treatment of high life and low life in the big city differed greatly, however, from that of other urban writers who dealt with this subject. He romanticized the present by inventing a kind of instant past. In his pages the Hungarian countryside became a quaintly seductive place; his Budapest was filled with inns, music halls, and brothels that really existed only in K.'s mind.

In his first literary success, *A vörös postakocsi* (1914; *The Crimson Coach,* 1967), which has remained his best-loved and most frequently republished novel, K. presented the amorous adventures of Szindbád, who in different disguises appears in much of his fiction and who is the fictionalized and idealized alter ego of K. himself. Szindbád is a great seducer of woman, but he is also a chivalrous and gentle man, a rake with a heart, a somber hedonist.

There are autobiographical elements in almost all K.'s writings—the novel *N. N.* (1922; N. N.) is perhaps the most poignant evocation of his childhood—but autobiography becomes fable and legend as the author imaginatively re-creates the past. Because his tone is always nostalgic and elegiac, the past thus evoked becomes dreamlike, other-worldly; and in novels such as *Asszonyságok díja* (1920; women's prize), *Hét bagoly* (1922; seven owls), and *Boldogult úrfikoromban* (1930; in my late lamented youth) it is invariably contrasted with a present that is harsh and prosaic. The inability to adjust to a changed world lends tragic dignity to many of K.'s characters. For example his best short story, "Utolsó szivar az Arabs szürkében" (1928; "The Last Cigar at the Grey Arab," 1966) is a masterful study of a melancholy aristocrat, about to fight a senseless duel with a young journalist.

As stylized and deliberately archaizing as his writings may appear, K. was a natural writer. In scores of novels he wrote about the same people and described similar settings; but the profusion of images and impressions enliven even his weaker writings—his many sketchy short stories or his stilted historical fiction. K.'s wistful, decadent sensibility and ironic sentimentality still evoke admiration; and his sophisticated mingling of reality and myth, past and present, lend an air of modernity to his fiction that few readers were aware of when the works first appeared.

SELECTED FURTHER WORKS: *A podolini kísértet* (1906); *A bűvös erszény* (1908); *Szindbád ifjúsága* (1911); *Szindbád naplója* (1912); *Napraforgó* (1918); *Az útitárs* (1919); *Kleofásné kakasa* (1920); *Őszi versenyek* (1922); *Pesti nőrabló* (1922); *Jockey Club* (1925); *Valakit elvisz az ördög* (1928); *Az élet álom* (1931); *A tiszaeszlári Solymosi Eszter* (1931)

BIBLIOGRAPHY: Reményi, J., *Hungarian Writers and Literature* (1964), pp. 229–38

IVAN SANDERS

KUKRIT Pramoj

Thai novelist, philosopher, historian, and journalist, b. 20 April 1911, Sing Buri

K., the youngest son of Prince Khamop, received his early education in Thailand. At the age of fifteen he was sent to England to complete his secondary schooling; he then went to Oxford, from which he graduated in 1933. Returning to Thailand, he worked in the ministry of finance and later in banking; he also taught at two Thai universities. K. entered politics in

1946, serving as a cabinet minister for a time. His experiences as a politician, as well as his several months as a Buddhist monk, have colored his literary works. He has also been active in Thai theater, acting and directing.

K. did not reach prominence as a literary figure until the early 1950s. His major works were written between 1950, when he left active politics, and 1973, when he returned to it (he was prime minister, 1975–76). In 1950 he founded the now greatly respected newspaper *Siam Rath,* in which all of his major works were to appear first. Because of this newspaper serialization, it is almost impossible to set exact dates to his works.

Sam kok chabab nai thun (c. 1949–51; three kingdoms: a capitalist's version) was K.'s first major novel. It retells the story of the Chinese classic of the 14th through 17th cs., *Three Kingdoms,* but from the point of view of the traditional villain, Tsao Tsao, rather than that of the hero, Liu Pei, to prove that the concept of heroism or villainy depends on the narrator's political point of view.

K.'s greatest novel, *Si phaendin* (1953; *Four Reigns,* 1981), tells the life story of a Thai upper-class woman, Ploy, from 1892, when she goes to live in the Grand Palace as a servant of a royal princess at the age of ten, until her death in 1946 as a married woman outside the palace, with children and grandchildren. But the story of Ploy is a pretext for analyzing and commenting on the times and ever-shifting fashions. The book is, indeed, a detailed social record.

Another novel, *Phai daeng* (1953; *Red Bamboo,* 1961), tells of a Buddhist monk's conflicts with a local communist agitator in a fictitious town in central Thailand.

Huang maharnob (early 1950s; the deep ocean) is K.'s most important nonfiction work. In it he shows the truth of Buddhist doctrine as proved by biology, and vice versa. The book has been criticized because K. assumes the truth of Buddhist teachings *a priori.* This is one of the strangest books of philosophy in Thai, and a puzzling work to many readers.

K.'s writings are always didactic, but his style is so fluent and humorous that he has an enormous readership in Thailand.

FURTHER WORKS: *Thok khmer* (early 1950s); *Lai chivit* (1950s); *Phuen non* (3 vols., 1950s–60s); *Tsu hsi t'ai hao* (1950s); *Lok suan tua khong phom* (c. 1961–62); *Yiu* (1968); *Khrong kraduk nai tu* (1971); *Tueng khong khon rak ma* (1978); *K. pho krua hua pa* (1979); *Tob panha hua jai* (1980)

BIBLIOGRAPHY: Wyatt, D. K., "K. P. and *Red Bamboo,*" *Solidarity,* 5, 6·(1970), 68–73
                                    AYUMONGOL SONAKUL

KUKUČÍN, Martin

(pseud. of Matej Bencúr) Czechoslovak novelist and short-story writer (writing in Slovak), b. 17 May 1860, Jasenová; d. 21 May 1928, Zagreb, Yugoslavia

K. spent his early years in Slovakia, where he taught school briefly, and studied medicine in Prague. Because of his disappointment with social and political developments in Slovakia, he spent his adult life as an émigré, first in Dalmatia and later in Chile. He made two short visits to Slovakia, and died in self-imposed exile in Yugoslavia.

Early in his career K. enriched Slovak literature with a number of well-written short stories about the village people he knew from his youth. He describes their philosophy of life, their sorrows and joys, their humor and misery with perfection of detail and a deep knowledge of their psychology. His "village heroes" are portrayed with profound humanism and humor, even if their fates are tragic, and K.'s deeply ethical view of life transcends the descriptive realism of his characters. In his stories he reflected the moral and religious concepts of his people and their spiritual heritage. The gentry and the middle class in Slovakia had lost a sense of Slovak identity by the end of the 19th c., and K. portrayed the patient heroism of the village people as a means of arousing a sense of nationhood. An example of K.'s masterful narrative technique is his short story "Neprebudený" (1886; unawakened, *or* the village idiot), in which the tragic end of a village idiot, who falls in love with the village belle, is presented by contrasting innocence and cruelty in the semifeudal world of a poor village.

While living in Dalmatia, K. produced his great novel *Dom v stráni* (2 vols., 1903–4; house on a hillside). With warm realism, K. depicts a conflict between two social classes—a landowning family and the patriarchal family of a simple farmer—against the background of the beautiful Dalmatian countryside. The great love of two young people, the children respectively of a proud peasant and of a no less proud landowner, fails to change the existing human relations and social order, which are stronger than human feelings. The structure, style, and psychological analysis of this novel make it one of the best examples of Slovak realism. It has been translated into several languages.

During his years in South America K. prepared material for a five-volume novel, *Mať volá* (1926-27; motherland calls). This sad saga of Croatian immigrants in South America, with its central theme of the struggle for a livelihood and for human dignity, is different in style and structure from his previous works. K. evolved in this work from depicting the life of individuals or communities to the description of universal concepts of a new social order based on Christian principles.

K. also wrote historical novels and three plays. He was mainly attracted by the stormy events in Slovakia in the 19th c., and he portrayed the events and historical figures realistically. In several nonfiction books he described his travels and life in Chile, Argentina, France, and Yugoslavia.

In K.'s short stories, which influenced a number of writers, Slovak realism reached its purest literary form. K. is deservedly credited with helping to replace romanticism, which anachronistically prevailed in Slovak literature, with a moderate realism tempered by humanism, humor, and sympathy for simple people.

FURTHER WORKS: *Dedinský jarmok* (1883); *Obecné trampoty* (1884); *Z teplého hniezda* (1885); *Ryšavá jalovica* (1885); *Na obecnom salaši* (1887); *Zápisky zo smutného domu* (1888); *Na podkonickom bále* (1891); *Dies irae* (1892); *Keď báčik z Chocholova umrie* (1894); *Veľkou lyžicou* (1895); *Svadba* (1895); *Mladé letá* (1899); *Komasácia* (1899); *Bacuchovie dvor* (1923); *Obeť* (1924); *Lukáš Blahosej Krasoň* (1929); *Bohumil Valizlosť Zábor* (1930); FURTHER VOLUME IN ENGLISH: *Seven Slovak Stories by M. K.* (1979)

BIBLIOGRAPHY: Krčméry, S., "A Survey of Modern Slovak Literature," *SEER*, 7 (1928–29), 160–70; Selver, P., "The Literature of the Slovaks," *SlavonicR*, 12 (1934), 691–703; Mráz, A., *Die Literatur der Slowaken* (1943), pp. 140–44; Potoček, C. J., *M. K.: A Link between Two Worlds* (1943); Noge, J., *An Outline of Slovakian Literature* (1968), pp. 35–38; Rudinsky, N. L., "M. K., 1860–1923" and "Preliminary Notes on M. K.'s Criticism of Americanized Slovaks and His Opposition to the Slovak Gentry," *Slovak Studies*, 18 (1978), 7–64, 153–65

JOSEPH M. KIRSCHBAUM

KUNDERA, Milan

Czechoslovak novelist, short-story writer, dramatist, and poet (writing in Czech) b. 1 April 1929, Brno

K. comes from a highly cultured middle-class background. His father was a famous pianist and musicologist, an expert on the composer Leoš Janáček. As a result of the Nazi occupation, political consciousness came early for K. When he joined the Communist Party at the age of eighteen, he had no doubts about the course history had to take in order to fulfill the promise of the Liberation. This was in 1947, one year before the Communist seizure of power in Czechoslovakia. K.'s relationship with the Party, however, was to be problematic and unsteady; in 1950 he was dropped from membership, but was reinstated in 1956, after the "thaw," only to be dropped once more in 1970, as a result of his participation in the Prague Spring of 1968. Since 1969 his writings have not been allowed to be published in his homeland, and he has lived and published abroad since 1975, having received an extended travel visa from the Czechoslovak government. He has taught at the University of Rennes in France and now lives in Paris.

K.'s first publications, three books of verse, were in tune with the spirit of the times and won him the approbation of the official cultural establishment. The most publicized of his poetic cycles, *Poslední máj* (1955; the last May), celebrates the wartime martyrdom of the young Communist militant and writer Julius Fučík (1903–1943).

In the 1960s K. shifted to prose, having discovered the ambiguities of history and the uses of the language of irony. His three series of short stories under the title *Směšné lásky* (1963, 1965, 1968; *Laughable Loves*, 1974) established him as a modern master of the black comedy of the bedroom. In the setting of a people's democracy, the pursuit by K.'s Don Juan-like character of the "golden apple of eternal desire" can never break with the literary convention of farce. But his metaphysical anguish makes him a spiritual descendant of Mozart's Don Giovanni, although cloaked in darker meanings by overtones of Kierkegaard's interpretation of the Don Juan figure in his *Diary of a Seducer*.

Under the influence of the Kraus-Krejča actors' workshop, K. tried his hand at drama. His first play, *Majitelé klíčů* (1962; the owners of the keys), was an immediate if much debated success. The action, set in the period of the Nazi occupation, confronts the values of personal heroism in the name of a public cause with the attitudes of cowardly privatism, stemming from the necessary but questionable instinct for survival. During the ensuing controversy, K. protested in the essay "Slovo má autor" (1962; the word belongs to the author), published as an afterword to the play, that his heart was firmly on the side of heroism, but the implications of his play were considerably more ambivalent.

In his first novel, *Žert* (1967; *The Joke*, 1974), K.'s obsessive master theme of the ironic interplay between erotic and political potencies and their mutual interchangeability emerged. Since its plot describes the wrecking of the career of a young Czech Party intellectual during the Stalinist purges, the novel was immediately read as a manifestation of the new political thaw. K. was allowed to transform his novel into a script for a film, which he directed himself and which played successfully to international audiences.

In June 1967 K. delivered a major address at the Fourth Congress of Czechoslovak Writers. He reminded his colleagues of their extraordinary historical burden. Czech culture and even the Czech nation itself, he warned, existed not by the force of historical necessity but rather by the grace of its literature.

K.'s second novel was first published in France as *La vie est ailleurs* (1973; *Life Is Elsewhere*, 1974), where it was honored with the Médicis Prize for the best foreign novel. The original Czech text, under the title *Život je jinde*, even though completed in 1970, saw light only in 1979, when it was published by the émigré press run by Josef Škvorecký (q.v.). It is a chronicle of the early fame and premature demise of Jaromil, a Communist poet of distinctly bourgeois origins. In the career of this character K. examines the peculiar modern relation between poetry and revolutionary power. He diagnoses both forces as unclean, born of resentment and fear of impotence.

Valčík na rozloučenou (1979; *The Farewell Party*, 1976) has had a similar publishing history. This novel is another sexual comedy with a philosophical thrust. In a Bohemian spa that claims to cure infertility, men and women perform their mating dances with grim single-mindedness, as practiced gladiators of a society out of joint with nature and indifferent to history.

The novel *Kniha smíchu a zapomnění* was first published in France as *Le livre du rire et de l'oubli* (1979; *The Book of Laughter and Forgetting*, 1980). It is a polyphonic treatment of the theme of loss of memory and also seems to be an act of exorcism directed at the author's homeland, which he sees as petrified in a sleep resembling death. K. dubs Gustav Husák, the Czechoslovak president installed by the Russians, as the "president of forgetting."

K.'s significance as a writer cannot be divorced from the meaning of his people's recent historical experiences. His message of disillusionment falls on ready ears in the most sophisticated Western circles precisely because it is thoroughly existential, rather than ideological. It has to do with life's everyday texture and taste. The message is all the more effective because it comes from a true insider, a man whose social sensibility was bred in the international left's best hopes for humanity. For his countrymen, K.'s skepticism has the sting of a particularly Czech anxiety, a submerged deathwish, perhaps, in a culture perpetually in danger of being again overrun and delivered into oblivion.

FURTHER WORKS: *Člověk zahrada širá* (1953); *Monology* (1957); *Umění románu: Cesta Vladislava Vančury za velkou epikou* (1960); *Sestřičko mych sestřiček* (1963); *Dvě uši dvě svatby* (1968); *Ptákovina* (1969)

BIBLIOGRAPHY: Roth, P., "Introducing M. K.," in M. K., *Laughable Loves* (1974), pp. 1–16; Doležel, L., "A Scheme of Narrative Times" [on *The Joke*], in Matejka, L., and Titunik, I. R. eds., *Semiotics of Art: Prague School Contributions* (1976), pp. 209–17; Harkins, W. E., Supplement to Novák, A., *Czech Literature* (1976), pp. 349–55; Trensky, P. I., *Czech Drama since World War II* (1978), pp. 73–84; Banerjee, M. N., on *Život je jinde* and *Le livre du rire et de l'oubli*, WLT, 54 (1980), 131–32; Updike, J., on *The Book of Laughter and Forgetting*, NYTBR, 30 Nov. 1980, 7, 74–78; Adams, R. M., "The Cold Comedian," NYRB, 5 Feb. 1981, 22–23

MARIA NĚMCOVÁ BANERJEE

KUNERT, Günter

German poet, short-story writer, and novelist, b. 6 March 1929, Berlin

During his youth in Berlin, then the capital of Nazi Germany, K. experienced racial discrimination and other hardships because of his Jewish mother. After the war he briefly attended the Berlin Academy for Applied Arts before turning to writing. His first poems, published in the magazine *Ulenspiegel* in 1948, won him the praise and support of Johannes R. Becher (1891–1958), the expressionist (q.v.) poet who had become Minister of Culture in the newly founded German Democratic Republic. Initially promoted by the East Berlin cultural establishment, K. enjoyed considerable literary success, received various prizes, and was able to travel extensively in Europe and the U.S., even spending a semester (Fall 1972) as writer-in-residence at the University of Texas, Austin. Because of his stubbornly independent political attitudes, however, he gradually fell out of favor with the East German regime. In 1979 he was permitted to emigrate to West Germany.

K.'s early writings were much indebted to Bertolt Brecht (q.v.) and the Americans Carl Sandburg and Edgar Lee Masters (qq.v.); his later works show the increasing influence of Franz Kafka (q.v.). Quite unlike the lofty, rhetorical sentiments and extreme pathos of Becher, from the outset K.'s poetic stance has been cool and distanced, devoid of any shrill emotionality, and his diction is laconic, matter-of-fact, even colloquial. In his early poems, published in the volumes *Wegschilder und Mauerinschriften* (1950; road signs and wall inscriptions), *Unter diesem Himmel* (1955; under this sky), *Tagwerke* (1960; daily chores), and *Das kreuzbrave Liederbuch* (1961; the well-behaved songbook)—selections from these volumes were later included in *Erinnerung an einen Planeten* (1963; memories of a planet—he favored the traditional genres of song, ballad, and sonnet, but he also began to experiment with two newer forms, familiar from the poetry of Brecht: the dialectical minimal poem (a sparse poem of only five to ten lines characterized by extreme reduction of language and a dialectical logical structure) and the longer poem with epic qualities, employing a "gestic" style, fragmented sentences, and unrhymed verses with irregular rhythms. These two forms are dominant in his later poetry, collected in *Der ungebetene Gast* (1965; the uninvited guest), *Verkündigung des Wetters* (1966; weather announcement), *Warnung vor Spiegeln* (1970; beware of mirrors), *Unterwegs nach Utopia* (1977; on the way to utopia), *Verlangen nach Bomarzo: Reisegedichte* (1978; longing for Bomarzo: travel poems), and *Abtötungsverfahren* (1980; procedures for mortification).

Although primarily known as a poet, K. has also written masterful, Kafkaesque short stories and miniature prose sketches reminiscent of Brecht's Keuner stories, published in the collections *Tagträume* (1964; daydreams), *Die Beerdigung findet in aller Stille statt* (1968; a private funeral will be held), and *Tagträume in Berlin und andernorts* (1972; daydreams in Berlin and elsewhere). His attempts at longer forms such as radio and television plays—for example, *Der Kaiser von Hondu* (1959; the emperor of Hondu) and *Ehrenhändel* (1972; affairs of honor)—and the novel *Im Namen der Hüte* (1967; in the name of hats) have been less successful. Recent experiments, however, with forms such as the short, Kafkaesque detective novel—*Gast aus England* (1973; guest from England)—and the satirical travel diary—*Der andere Planet: Ansichten von Amerika* (1974; the other planet: views of America)—reveal promising new dimensions to his talents.

Because of his avowed desire to provoke his reader into self-awareness, K. has attempted to avoid any clearly defined ideological stance and has thus been able to appeal to audiences in both East and West. His major concerns—the conflict between individual self-realization and collective social goals, the threat of stagnation and persistent inhumanity undermining genuine efforts for positive social change, the dehumanizing effects of necessary technological advances—find poetic statement in moods ranging from unreserved confidence in the future, sardonic humor about human frailties, acerbic satire of present conditions, and dark despair about the ultimate futility of human endeavor. Recurrent themes and images—the pilot, for example, as a symbol for man's cosmic aspirations, as opposed to the buccaneer who perishes in his search for El Dorado—emerge in ever new variations to express a dialectical tension between the ideal and the real, between hope and disillusionment. Not surprisingly, in both his poetry and prose K. shows a marked preference for the parable, a form that can lend concrete expression to an abstract idea without becoming politically too explicit.

While K.'s early works proclaim an optimistic faith in social progress and collective human regeneration, his stance since the early 1960s has become increasingly skeptical, even bitter, often verging on profound melancholy. His struggle to achieve a balance between social preoccupations and the needs of the individual is in many respects paradigmatic for life in East Germany. It will therefore be interesting to see to what extent living in the West will now affect his poetic production.

FURTHER WORKS: *Der ewige Detektiv* (1954); *Vom König Midas* (1958); *Die Weltreise im Zimmer* (1961); *Unschuld der Natur* (1966); *Kramen in Fächern* (1968); *Betonformen Ortsangaben* (1969); *Ortsangaben* (1971); *Notizen in Kreide* (1970); *Offener Ausgang* (1972); *Die geheime Bibliothek* (1973); *Im weiteren Fortgang* (1974); *Der Mittelpunkt der Erde* (1975); *Das kleine Aber* (1976); *Warum schreiben? Notizen zur Literatur* (1976); *Jeder Wunsch ein Treffer* (1976); *Keine Affäre* (1976); *Ein anderer K.: Hörspiel* (1977; *A Different K.: A Radio Play*, 1977); *Camera obscura* (1978); *Unruhiger Schlaf* (1978); *Die Schreie der Fledermäuse: Geschichten, Gedichte, Aufsätze* (1979); *Ein englisches Tagebuch* (1980); *Ziellose Umtriebe: Nachrichten vom Reisen und vom Daheimsein* (1981)

BIBLIOGRAPHY: Demetz, P., *Postwar German Literature* (1970), pp. 89–92; Flores, J., *Poetry in East Germany* (1971), pp. 280–92; Hofacker, E. P., "G. K. and the East German Image of Man," *Monatshefte,* 66 (1974), 366–80; Hilton, I., "G. K.: The Way Ahead," *BA,* 50 (1976), 46–54; Kahn, L., "Orpheus in the East: G. K.'s Orpheus Cycle," *MLQ,* 38 (1977), 78–96; Jonsson, D., *Widersprüche—Hoffnungen: Literatur und Kulturpolitik: Die Prosa G. K.s* (1978); Krüger, M., ed., *K. lesen* (1979)

HELENE SCHER

KUNIKIDA Doppo

(pseud. of Kunikida Tetsuo; known as Doppo) Japanese short-story writer, b. 15 July 1871, Chōshi; d. 23 June 1908, Chigasaki

K. grew up with a sense of pride in his samurai heritage mingled with an awareness that samurai ideals were ill suited to the competitive modern age; due in part to his father's financial insecurity, he was unable to finish college, and he supported himself as a teacher and then as a war correspondent.

K. is remembered for his literary works (including some marginally successful experiments in modern verse), but in fact he spent the greater part of his brief professional life as a journalist, distinguishing himself initially with lively accounts of his shipboard experiences during the Sino-Japanese War of 1894–95. He met his first wife, a willful "modern" woman who shared his Christian faith, at a reception

for newly returned war correspondents, and when she deserted him after six months of marriage, both his religious faith and the romanticized view of love he had absorbed from his reading in the English romantics were destroyed. Perhaps as a result of this early disillusionment, he became the first writer of his generation to break away from puerile sentimentalism.

From his earliest attempt at fiction, the prose-poem "Takibi" (1896; "The Bonfire," 1970), to his last important story, "Take no kido" (1908; "The Bamboo Gate," 1972), there is a remarkable consistency of theme and imagery in K.'s writing. Lonely wanderers or figures in the distance symbolize the endless stream of humanity drifting into and out of the world, but individually leaving no mark upon it. Early stories, such as "Gen oji" (1897; "Old Gen," 1955) and "Wasureenu hitobito" (1898; "Unforgettable People," 1972), and the lyrical essay "Musashino" (1898; Musashino) express this theme in a voice close to song, while later stories, such as "Shōjikimono" (1903; "An Honest Man," 1972) and "Take no kido," attempt to invest the symbolic characters with individual personalities and place them in a dramatic context.

Turgenev's *Sportsman's Sketches* first provided K. with a Western model of poetic fiction, while the example of Maupassant brought to his later work a greater command of detached narration. In contrast to the so-called naturalists, with whom he is usually grouped, however, K. never relinquished the view of the moral nature of man he learned from his reading of Wordsworth. He was being praised as a pioneer naturalist near the end of his life (he died young of tuberculosis), but he firmly rejected the label.

As much as K. owed to his Western models, he left an entirely original and coherent body of works that draw from his own experience and imaginative power. Written in a period of Japanese literature that was primarily transitional and derivative, his stories not only served as models for such later masters as Shiga Naoya and Akutagawa Ryūnosuke (qq.v.) but they continue to be read and enjoyed in their own right.

FURTHER WORKS: *Musashino* (1901); *D.-shū* (1905); *Unmei* (1906); *Tōsei* (1907); *Byōshōroku* (1908); *D.-shū dai-ni* (1908); *Azamukazaru no ki* (2 vols., 1908–9); *Aitei tsūshin* (1908); *Nagisa* (1908); *K. D. zenshū* (10 vols., 1964–67)

BIBLIOGRAPHY: McClellan, E., "The Impressionistic Technique in Some Modern Japanese Novelists," *ChiR*, 57 (1965), 48–60; Rubin, J., "Five Stories by K. D.," *MN*, 27 (1972), 273–341

JAY RUBIN

KUNZE, Reiner

German poet and prose writer, b. 16 Aug. 1933, Oelsnitz

The son of a miner, K. studied philosophy and journalism in Leipzig from 1951 to 1955 and then became a teacher. He turned to professional writing soon after the East German government forced him to abandon his academic career in 1959. Although he repeatedly affirmed his support of the principles of Marxism, he continued to come under political attack because of his criticism of the policies of the regime. Most of his books were published in the West; only occasionally, during times of cultural thaw, did his works appear in the GDR. After years of increasingly severe harassment he was forced to emigrate to West Germany in 1977. Among his literary awards is the prestigious Büchner Prize (1977).

K. established his reputation with the poetry collection *Sensible Wege* (1969; sensitive paths). These poems show an increased maturity and stylistic control, compared with his earlier works. Some are directly political or topical, and many contain indirect or veiled criticism of the repressive atmosphere in the GDR. Irony and understatement are typical characteristics. Communication is a favorite theme, both in its general human aspects and in contexts specifically applicable to the poet, who lived in virtual isolation in a small East German town. The poems of *Zimmerlautstärke* (1972; with volume turned down) are similar in style and theme. The irony is sharper, however, and references to politics—for example Solzhenitsyn (q.v.), the Russian invasion of Czechoslovakia —more pointed.

K.'s most successful work is *Die wunderbaren Jahre* (1976; *The Wonderful Years*, 1977), a collection of short prose sketches. Written in a laconic style reminiscent of the poetry, these texts paint a devastating picture of life in East Germany—of the Communist Party and its policies, of the difficulty of maintaining a sense of human dignity—as well as in post-1968 Czechoslovakia. On a deeper level, these specific issues reflect K.'s concern with the delicate balance between individual freedom and

responsibility to others. K. directed a film version of this book, for which he also wrote the screenplay, published as *Der Film "Die wunderbaren Jahre"* (1979; the film *The Wonderful Years*).

Like many writers who were pressured into leaving the GDR in the late 1970s, K. remains dedicated to the principles of socialism, and he is less than happy in his role as a symbol of resistance to political oppression. His considerable literary talent should ensure his continued success, whatever the themes of his future works may be.

FURTHER WORKS: *Vögel über dem Tau* (1959); *Wesen und Bedeutung der Reportage* (1960); *Aber die Nachtigall jubelt* (1962); *Widmungen* (1963); *Poesiealbum 11* (1968); *Der Löwe Leopold* (1970); *Brief mit blauem Siegel* (1973); *Das Kätzchen* (1979); *Auf eigene Hoffnung* (1981). FURTHER VOLUME IN ENGLISH: *With Volume Turned Down* (1973)

BIBLIOGRAPHY: Piontek, H., *Männer die Gedichte machen* (1970), pp. 203–20; Wallmann, J., "Der Fall R. K.," *NDH*, No. 136 (1972), 93–115; Mytze, A., ed., *Über R. K.* (1976); Wallmann, J., ed., *R. K.: Materialien und Dokumente* (1977); Linn, M., "R. K.'s *Die Wunderbaren Jahre*," *DU*, 30, 6 (1978), 70–81

JERRY GLENN

KUO Mo-jo

Chinese poet, dramatist, and essayist, b. 16 Nov. 1892, Tung-he, Ssu-ch'uan Province; d. 12 June 1978, Peking

K. was trained in medicine in Japan but never practiced it. Instead, he became interested in literature and cofounded the Creation Society, which advocated the concept of "art for art's sake" during the height of the new literature movement in the early 1920s. Soon thereafter K. fled to Japan, where he stayed for ten years to escape the purge of Communists. When he returned to China in 1937, he became a prominent scholar of ancient Chinese social history and was a key figure in the national defense literature movement of the 1930s. After 1949 he was active in the upper echelons of the government of the People's Republic and became president of the Chinese Academy of Science.

K.'s prominence in literature came after the publication of *Nü-shen* (1921; partial tr., *Selected Poems from the Goddesses*, 1958), a poetry collection full of impulsive outbursts echoing the feelings of reform-minded intellectuals in search of a new China. The language was uninhibited, and K. was particularly criticized for his frequent use of foreign words. He continued with his poetry writing, collected in *Hsing k'ung* (1923; starry sky), *P'ing* (1927; vase), *Hui-fu* (1928; recovery), *Chan sheng chi* (1938; battle cries), and other volumes, but none received the same acclaim as *Nü-shen*. Nevertheless, he remained consistent in his sloganlike outcries, especially on nationalism. After 1949 K. published more poems in collections such as *Hsin-hua chung* (1953; in praise of new China), *Ch'ang ch'un chi* (1959; forever spring), and *Tung feng chi* (1963; east wind). In most of these, K. glorified political causes. His poems of the 1970s were written in a more formal, classical style.

K.'s most celebrated dramatic work is *Ch'ü Yüan* (1942; *Ch'ü Yüan*, 1955). It is a creative reconstruction of the political defeat of China's first known poet-statesman, Ch'ü Yüan (c. 343–290 B.C.), whose loyalty led to his despair and self-destruction. K. utilized this historical play as propaganda for nationalism during the war with Japan. In *Ts'ai Wen-chi* (1956; Ts'ai Wen-chi), K. dramatized the return from the Huns to the Chinese kingdom of Ts'ai Yen (c. A.D. 162–239), a famous Han poetess. By using Ts'ai's return to vindicate the villainous image of statesman Ts'ao Ts'ao (A.D. 155–220), K. was in line with the current political issue of redefining Ts'ao's role in Chinese history.

K. also wrote a few essays of literary criticism and some short stories, none of which were outstanding. He often wrote stories with a very strong tendency toward autobiography, and he sometimes just retold historical anecdotes.

A prolific writer, K. was the only one to survive the numerous political purges against writers because his versatility and flexibility enabled him to adapt easily to every new political tide. K.'s early poetry shows a lack of discipline, and his later poems lost the impulsive energy that was his earlier trademark. His plays and later poetry reveal how he followed the Maoist doctrine that creative writing should support political and revolutionary activities.

FURTHER WORKS: *M. shih chi* (1935); *M. hsüan chi* (1936); *K. M. wen chi* (1949); *M. wen chi* (1957); *M. shih tz'u hsüan* (1977)

BIBLIOGRAPHY: Moy, C., "K. M. and the Creation Society," *Papers on China* (Harvard), 4 (1950), 131–59; Schultz, W., "K. M. and the Romantic Aesthetic: 1918–1925," *JOL* 6, 2 (1955), 49–81; Průšek, J., *Three Sketches of Chinese Literature* (1969), pp. 99–140; Gálik, M., "Studies in Modern Chinese Literary Criticism: IV. The Proletarian Criticism of K. M.," *AAS*, 6 (1970), 145–60; Roy, D. T., *K. M.: The Early Years* (1971); Lee, L. O., "K. M.," *The Romantic Generation of Modern Chinese Writers* (1973), pp. 177–200

MARLON K. HOM

KUPRIN, Alexandr Ivanovich

Russian short-story writer, novelist, and essayist, b. 8 Sept. 1870, Narovchat; d. 25 Aug. 1938, Leningrad

K.'s father, a minor official, died when Alexandr was only one year old. His mother had to work hard in order to survive, and K.'s childhood and youth were thorny. He graduated from a Moscow Cadet Corps School in 1887, finished officer school, and became a lieutenant in the army. In 1894 he left the military and became a "free man," but with no means of support. He then worked as a land surveyor, carpenter, tutor, actor, estate manager, and newspaper reporter. He traveled extensively in Russia, mixing thoroughly with the people and learning about all walks of life. He has often been called the "poet of life" and the *bytovik* (realist). In 1889 he published his first short story. Opposed to the 1917 Bolshevik revolution, he emigrated to France. But he returned in 1937 to the U.S.S.R., where he died a year later.

K.'s rich life experience is reflected in his stories, which have lively plots and little philosophy and didacticism, and which are realistic, with some romantic coloration. Fame throughout Russia came to K. with his *Poedinok* (1905; *The Duel*, 1916), published during the Russo-Japanese War. In this novel K. depicts officers negatively, seeing their life as senseless and brutal, and their conduct as unscrupulous. The hero, an idealistic lieutenant, loses his struggle against the traditional routine and dies in a duel. *Poedinok*, along with the shorter works "Shtabs-Kapitan Rybnikov" (1906; "Captain Rybnikov," 1916) and "Gambrinus" (1907; "Gambrinus," 1925), appealed to the radical and antimilitaristic intelligentsia; the social and political aspects of these works should not, however, obscure their aesthetic merit.

A sizable number of K.'s stories deal with

love. An early novelette, *Olesya* (1898; *Olessia*, 1909), is a delightful tale about a girl living in the wilderness and her genuine love for a man who tries to escape from the conventions and hypocrisies of civilized society. This romantic episode develops against the background of a primeval forest. Realistic details are interwoven with witchcraft, and beautiful descriptions of nature are mingled with depictions of base human traits. *Sulamif* (1908; *Sulamith: A Prose Poem of Antiquity,* 1923), a stylized Biblical narrative, and "Granatovy braslet" (1911; "The Bracelet of Garnets," 1917), sweet and melodramatic, are real hymns of boundless, passionate love, while the novel *Yama* (1912; *Yama: The Pit,* 1922) is a moralistic, somewhat sentimental story about the life of prostitutes, dedicated to "young people and mothers." K. emphasizes the evil of prostitution, but does not attempt to solve this age-old social problem.

The diversity of subjects in K.'s novels and stories can easily be traced through all of his writing. Among the best-known works are "Molokh" (1896; Moloch), a story about factory workers, their managers, and engineers; "Allez!" (1897; "Allez!," 1920) and "V tsirke" (1902; at the circus), dealing with circus life; "Kak ya byl aktyorom" (1908; "How I Became an Actor," 1920); "Listrigony" (1908–11; "The Laestrygonians," 1917), a charming series of sketches about Balaklava Greek fishermen in the Crimea; and "Izumrud" (1907; "Emerald," 1920), about a race horse, a story reminiscent of Tolstoy's "Yardstick."

K.'s literary output in exile was insignificant. He published an autobiographical novel, *Yunkera* (1928–30; the cadets) and a novelette, *Zhaneta* (1934; Zhaneta). In *Yunkera* the older K. paints a sunny picture of the young Moscow cadets—a picture completely different from that given in *Poedinok,* while in *Zhaneta* K. shows the reader the hopeless existence of an aging Russian émigré professor—helpless, degraded, and crushed by the burden of life.

K. admired strong, healthy, enterprising, adventurous people. He loved children and animals; he felt deeply about nature. In some respects K.'s writing could be compared to that of Jack London, Kipling (qq.v.), and Bret Harte. In K.'s works one will find neither sophisticated psychological analysis of the protagonists, nor stylistic innovations, nor social "messages" à la Gorky (q.v.). In K.'s stories, however, the reader always feels humaneness, compassion, sincerity, and truthfulness. His narration flows easily, his sentences are unconstrained, and his syntax lacks the pretentiousness so much in vogue with his contemporaries, the symbolists (q.v.). All these qualities have secured him a firm and respectable place in Russian literature.

FURTHER WORKS: *Izbrannoe* (1937); *Izbrannye sochinenia* (1947); *Sobranie sochineny v shesti tomakh* (1957–58); *Sobranie sochineny v devyati tomakh* (1964). FURTHER VOLUMES IN ENGLISH: *A Slav Soul, and Other Stories* (1916); *The River of Life, and Other Stories* (1916); *The Bracelet of Garnets, and Other Stories* (1917); *Sasha, and Other Stories* (1920); *Gambrinus, and Other Stories* (1925); *The Garnet Bracelet, and Other Stories* (n.d., 195?)

BIBLIOGRAPHY: Phelps, W. L., "K.'s Picture of Garrison Life," *Essays on Russian Novelists* (1911), pp. 278–84; Jackson, R. L., "A. I. K.'s 'River of Life,'" *Dostoevsky's Underground Man in Russian Literature* (1958), pp. 108–12; Slonim, M., "A. I. K.," *From Chekhov to the Revolution* (1962), pp. 173–77; Williams, G., "Romashov and Nazanskij; Enemies of the People," *CSP,* 9 (1967), 194–200; Luker, N. J. I., *A. K.* (1978)

SERGE KRYZYTSKI

KURDISH LITERATURE

Kurdish literature in the 20th c. has been profoundly influenced by conditions over which Kurdish writers themselves have had little control. Lack of political unity and of national independence, together with social and economic underdevelopment, have impeded the growth of a modern literature. The partitioning of Kurdistan, as the area inhabited by the Kurds was commonly known, among Turkey, Syria, Iraq, and Iran after World War I frustrated attempts to create a single literary language, while literary manifestations of Kurdish national sentiment often brought severe repression. The condition of Kurdish letters has been most bleak in Turkey. In Iraq, however, the southern Kurdish dialect, Sorani, has been recognized as an official language. Newspapers and books have appeared in relative abundance, and a cohesive body of intellectuals has formed who have been the principal animators of modern Kurdish literature.

Kurdish literature is a young literature still in the process of formation. Its development has received little systematic attention, even from

Kurdish intellectuals. The first anthology, a slender volume of poetry, was published only in 1938, and the two volumes of the first serious history of Kurdish literature, *Shi'r u edebiyatî kurdî* (Kurdish poetry and literature), by Refik Hilmi (dates n.a.) did not appear until 1941 and 1956 respectively. Western scholars have virtually ignored the subject.

Kurdish newspapers and journals have played an important role in literary development; they have served as gathering places for intellectuals and have offered an outlet for their work. The most important periodicals have been *Jin* (1920–63), *Gelawêj* (1939–49), and *Dengi gêtî taze* (1943–47), all Iraqi, which published classical and contemporary poetry and short fiction, and in which questions of modern language and literary development were debated.

In the first two decades of the century poetry was the preferred means of literary expression. Although classical meters and traditional subjects still predominated, innovation was apparent in the work of leading poets. Reza Talabani (1842–1910) was famous for his satirical, often obscene, verse. Because of his attachment to Sufism, his work abounds in religious subjects and adheres to classical norms, but in his later years he turned to contemporary social conditions for themes and to the vernacular for new forms of expression. Adab (1859–1916) was also a transitional figure. He sang of beauty, love, and the joy of life in traditional Eastern fashion, but in his *Divan* (1936; collection) many poems portray genuine human emotions in realistic surroundings.

Two main tendencies were apparent in poetry between the two world wars: civic verse, inspired by the struggles for political independence and cultural revival, and romanticism, which perpetuated the themes of the past. There was much innovation in form and content. Ahmad Muhtar (1897–1935) preserved the classical techniques, and his love poetry remained abstract and melancholy, but, increasingly, he focused his attention on the hard life of the common people and, implicitly, called for social reform. Other poets, such as Dildar Yunus (1918–1948), altered the centuries-old poetical canons. Alongside the *aruz* (the quantitative Arabic meter), a seven- and nine-syllable verse came into use. Rhyme became freer and the poems more conceptual, and the Kurdish vocabulary and syntax were strengthened at the expense of foreign models.

Prose writers, more rapidly than poets, embraced the new political and social themes and sought new techniques to express them. In the process the Kurdish short story was born. It was a distinctive literary form with little plot and character development but great emphasis on the author's message.

All the stages through which Kurdish literature passed in the first half of the 20th c. are reflected in the work of Tawfik Piramerd (1867–1950), perhaps the outstanding figure in modern Kurdish literature. He possessed a superb knowledge of Kurdish classical poetry, which he skillfully adapted to the new tendencies of the post-World War I era. He favored simple meters that resembled the rhythms of the Kurdish oral tradition, as in *Pend y pêshînan* (1936; proverbs), his own reworking of folk poetry in nearly 6500 *beyts* (couplets). Piramerd was also a master of the short story. He found inspiration in the Kurdish past, and his adaptation of the national legend, *Duwanze suwar y Meriwan* (1935; the twelve horsemen of Meriwan), has become a classic.

Since World War II patriotic and social themes have dominated both poetry and prose, with realism emerging as a distinct literary current. The outstanding poet of the early postwar period was Abdulla Goran (1904–1962). His youthful poems were romantic songs of love and nature written in traditional *gazels* (short lyrical poems often of a mystical-religious content), *qasidas* (longer poems of a meditative or didactic character), and quatrains. Later he abandoned the *aruz* completely and used a variety of rhythms and rhymes in such works as *Behesht u yadgar* (1950; paradise and memories), in which affection for the homeland sets the tone. Goran also helped to create a new genre in Kurdish literature—the verse drama. His *Gul y xönawi* (1950; the bloody rose), which describes the plight of two lovers separated by social class, has enjoyed enormous popularity. The leading prose writer of the postwar period has been Shakir Fattah (b. 1910), many of whose short stories, such as *Shebengeberoj* (1947; sunflower), attacked the patriarchal and religious structure of Kurdish society.

Kurdish poetry and short fiction have achieved high artistic levels, but the novel and a modern theater have yet to make their appearance. Subjects for both abound and only await authors capable of transforming legend and new social situations into sustained works of art.

Kurdish literature in the Soviet Union stands apart from the main currents described. Only in the 1930s were the first genuine literary works produced, and since then Kurdish literature has reflected the general vicissitudes of Soviet literature. The outstanding writer is Arabe Shamo (Arab Shamilov, b. 1897), whose novels have described his own life and that of Kurdish refugees from Turkey.

BIBLIOGRAPHY: Edmonds, C. J., "A Kurdish Newspaper: 'Rozh-i-Kurdistan,' " *Journal of the Central Asian Society,* 12 (1925), 83–90; Edmonds, C. J., "A Kurdish Lampoonist: Shaikh Riza Talabani," *Journal of the Royal Central Asian Society,* 22 (1935), 111–23; Bois, T., *Connaissance des Kurdes* (1965), pp. 128–40

KEITH HITCHINS

KUZMIN, Mikhail Alexeevich

Russian poet, novelist, dramatist, translator, and critic, b. 6 Oct. 1872, Yaroslavl; d. 1 March 1936, Leningrad

K.'s family was of the minor nobility. His interests in European culture, classical antiquity, and philosophy lasted throughout his life and influenced his art. K.'s life and work were characterized by a peasant/dandy dichotomy. At one time traveling with a group of Old Believers, at another owning 365 waistcoats, he exhibited a wide range of interests and knowledge. From 1891 to 1894 K. studied musical composition with Rimsky-Korsakov in the St. Petersburg conservatory. After the revolution, while taking an active part in the development of cultural affairs for the Bolshevik government, he nevertheless came under increasing attack. After 1929 K. was no longer permitted to publish. He died on the eve of the Stalinist purges, in which he probably would have been included. His work is still not published in the Soviet Union.

K.'s writings are typified by a calm acceptance of life and an awareness of its perpetual change. His art is also strongly autobiographical; his first novel, *Krilya* (1906; *Wings,* 1972), caused a scandal because of its homosexual theme. Love, homosexual or heterosexual, is an important theme in much of K.'s work. Influenced by the philosophy of Plotinus, he saw love as the means through which man improves himself. Religion is also an important aspect of much of his work.

His first collection of poetry, *Seti* (1908; nets), evidences many characteristics of his early work, for example, clarity of form and use of prosaic detail, in striking contrast to the then current symbolist (q.v.) style. There is also an emphasis on the concrete over the abstract, and a celebration of the present. K.'s later verse differs in many respects from his early work. The poetry, while maintaining the earlier clear form, became increasingly elliptical and metaphorical. The sharp juxtaposition of images in the poems of the 1920s reflects his growing interest in German expressionism (q.v.) and the cinema of the period.

K.'s drama was also innovative. Breaking with Stanislavskian realism, he gave his early plays rococo settings. His later plays are more abstract than his earlier ones. His dramatic works revolve around love and personal relationships, including homosexual ones, a fact that caused some difficulties with the censors.

K. was a central figure in the literary and artistic world of his period. The time has come for a serious and objective appraisal of this multifaceted man about whom so little has been heard for the last fifty years.

FURTHER WORKS: *O Alexee, cheloveke Bozhem* (1907); *Priklyuchenia Eme-Lebyofa* (1907); *Tri pesy: Opasnaya predostorozhnost, Dva pastukakh, Vybor nevesty* (1907); *Komedia o Evdoky iz Gelopolia* (1907); *Alexandryskie pesni* (1908; *Alexandrine Songs,* 1980); *Komedia o Martiniane* (1908); *Nezhny Iosif* (1909); *Podvigi velikovo Alexandra* (1909); *O prekrasnoy yastnosti* (1910); *Puteshestvie sera Dzhona Firfaxa po Turtsy i drugim zamechatelnim stranam* (1910); *Gollandka Liza* (1911); *Osennie ozera* (1912); *Glinyanie golubki* (1914); *Plavayushchie puteshestvuyushchie* (1914); *Tikhy strazh* (1915); *Venetsianskie bezumtsy* (1915; "Venetian Madcaps," 1973); *Voennie rasskazy* (1915); *Chudeshnaya zhizn Iosifa Balzamo, grafa Kaliostro* (1916); *Vozhaty* (1918); *Dvum* (1918); *Zanaveshennye kartinki* (1920); *Ekho* (1921); *Nezdeshnie vechera* (1921); *Vtornik Meri* (1921); *Lesok* (1922); *Paraboly* (1923); *Uslovnosti* (1923); *Novy gul* (1924); *Sobranie stikhov* (3 vols., 1977); *Forel razbyvaet lyod* (1929; *The Trout Breaks the Ice,* 1980). FURTHER VOLUMES IN ENGLISH: *Wings: Poetry and Prose of M.K.* (1972); *Selected Prose and Poetry* (1980)

BIBLIOGRAPHY: Field, A., "M. K.: Notes on a Decadent's Prose," *RusR,* 22 (1963), 289–300; Green, M., "M. K. and the Theater," *RLT,* 7 (1973), 243–66; Malmstad, J. E., "The Mystery of Iniquity: M. K.'s Dark Streets Lead to Dark Thoughts," *SlavR,* 34 (1975), 44–64; Granoien, N., "*Wings* and the World of Art," *RLT*, 11 (1975), 393–405; Karlinsky, S., "Russia's Gay Literature and History: 11th–20th Centuries," *Gay Sunshine*, No. 29/30 (1976), 9–11; Malmstad, J. E., and Shmakov, G., "M. K.'s 'The Trout Breaks through the Ice,'" in Gibian, G., and Tjalsma, H. W., eds., *Russian Modernism* (1976), pp. 132–64; Malmstad, J. E., "M. K.: A Chronicle of His Life and Times," in M. K., *Sobranie stikhov* (1977), Vol. 3, pp. 17–313

JOHN R. RANCK